# THE
# HISTORY
# OF THE

# BRITISH SOUTH AFRICA POLICE
## 1889 – 1980

This book is dedicated to the men and women who
made a new and raw country their home, giving
service to it, many with their lives.

Theirs comprises the tale of a singular, and
outstanding Police Force.

It is a tale that needed to be told.

The History of the British South Africa Police

Published by Something of Value Pty Ltd (Australia) ABN 34 054 688 701
P.O. Box 27, 182 Warrandyte Road, North Ringwood, VIC 3134, Australia

Volume One "The First Line of Defence" (1972) and Volume Two "The Right of The Line"
(1974) first published under the authority of the Commissioner of the BSA Police, Salisbury,
Rhodesia.  Copyright BSAP Regimental Association Board of Trustees 2000

Volume Three "The End of The Line" Copyright Hugh Phillips 2000

"The History of the British South Africa Police" incorporating all three volumes first
published by Something of Value Pty Ltd (Australia), 2000

Design and desktop publishing by Adcraft Publishing, Melbourne

Origination and printing by Jenkin Buxton Printers, Melbourne

ISBN: 0 646 40119 X

# THE
# HISTORY
# OF THE

# BRITISH SOUTH AFRICA POLICE
## 1889 – 1980

by Peter Gibbs

**Volume One**
"The First Line of Defence" 1889 - 1903

**Volume Two**
"The Right of The Line" 1903 - 1939

⁓

by Hugh Phillips
**Volume Three**
"The End of The Line" 1939 - 1980

# CONTENTS

# CONTENTS

# FOREWORD

By former Senior Assistant Commissioner Mr. George 'Bill' W.F. Ellway, PMM.
President
BSA Police Regimental Association.

At the end of July 1980, the British South Africa Police ceased to exist and was replaced by the Zimbabwe Republic Police. The newly independent State of Zimbabwe had been born just over three months earlier and the new force was entrusted with the traditions and qualities that had been nurtured over the years since 1889.

Peter Gibbs, in two admirable volumes, here abridged, has encompassed the period from 1889 to 1939. Hugh Phillips, who served in the Force for 29 years, takes up the story and follows the fortunes of Rhodesia's 'First Line of Defence' until it reaches its own 'End of the Line' in 1980.

This is a detailed history of a police force that, through circumstances not of its choosing, found itself cast in a very different role to that traditionally followed by other police forces. The book covers 41 years, of which the last eight saw the police moving along two very different paths.

It is a story of the men and women, African and European, who followed those two paths.

It is the story of a police force that grew from small beginnings to become one of the most admired, professional and respected in the world.

It is a story with which many ex-policemen and women, many ex-Rhodesians and many Zimbabweans — and others too — will be able to identify, and with pride.

I am deeply honoured to have been asked to write this Foreword, not only in the hope that all who read 'End of the Line' will enjoy and feel a part of the memories that are evoked through its pages, but also because it will be published in the auspicious year during which our Honorary Commissioner, Queen Elizabeth the Queen Mother celebrates her 100th Birthday.

Lastly, all former members of the Force will no doubt be pleased to learn that the publisher and Hugh Phillips plan an edition concentrating largely on the history of the tens of thousands of Africans who served. We wish them well in this complex and worthy task.

Harare, Zimbabwe
October, 2000

# VOLUME ONE

The First Line of Defence

**1889 – 1903**

by Peter Gibbs

## PREFACE

WHEN I WAS asked a couple of years ago by the then Deputy Commissioner, Mr. R. J. V. Bailey, to write the history of the British South Africa Police, I told him I thought a suitable length for such a book would be up to 100,000 words. I started writing and by the time I had written 30,000 I was still in 1891. There seemed so much to be put on record; and as I believed this was the first time a continuous history of the force had been undertaken I felt it should not be unduly compressed. So, as long books can be unwieldy and militate against reading in bed we decided to divide the story into two.

This is the first volume, covering the period from the formation in 1889 of the original force known as the British South Africa Company's Police to a convenient point for a break in the story when the BSAP itself was reorganised in 1903. In fact the history of the force divides itself clearly into two distinct periods: before and after the reorganisation in 1903. The first was a period of quasi and actual military service—the blood and thunder as I have called it—and the second, apart from participation outside the country in the two world wars, has been a period of service as a civil force. Both periods have their own interest and excitements; but they make two entirely different types of story.

For this first volume my research has been principally among the historical sources. I make no claim for the book to be a work of scholarship; indeed, the purpose has been to present what is, hopefully, a readable story. Consequently I have not encumbered the text with reference notes but I have appended to the book a representative list of sources which I have consulted. It is impossible for this list to be complete because I have picked up information in all sorts of odd corners.

But there is one source to which I must make special, and grateful, acknowledgement and that is the incomparable research recorded by Colonel Selwyn Hickman, MBE, the Commissioner of the BSAP from 1954 to 1955. Apart from numerous contributions by him to Rhodesiana (the authoritative journal of the Rhodesiana Society) from which I have drawn a great deal of information (provided by others as well as Colonel Hickman), his two books, *Men Who Made Rhodesia* and *Rhodesia Served the Queen*, are packed from cover to cover with invaluable—and not elsewhere obtainable—material. He has performed a signal service to the historiography of Rhodesia as a whole and the BSAP in particular. I make no denial that I have used many of his facts; in fitting them into the story I have given them my own interpretations for which he cannot be held responsible.

My thanks are due to various members of the force who have "helped me in my enquiries". In the next volume, when the period comes nearer to the present, I shall be relying on their always willing help to a much larger extent. The National Archives have been, of course, an ever present source of comfort and inspiration; Alan Stock, editor of *The Outpost*, his staff and files have played their helpful part. My thanks go also to Deputy Commissioner Digby Allen who has taken such a lively interest in the book's publication; to Eric Crabbe (former Chief Inspector, BSAP, and one time editor of *The Outpost*) for his meticulous editing of the text; to Peter Scales and Charles Paxton of the Police Reserve Air Wing who have flown me to outlandish places with their usual professional competence; to Mrs. Connie Minchin who guided me through the Siege of Mafeking with infectious enthusiasm; and finally to Mrs. Eleanor Pitt (mother of a member of the force) who has typed and retyped the manuscript with unremitting patience.

PETER GIBBS
Bulawayo,
February 1972

# INTRODUCTION

IT IS UNUSUAL for the police force of a country to be created before that country actually exists. But although Cecil Rhodes's pioneers only entered the land that lies between the Limpopo and Zambezi rivers in July 1890 and only formally occupied Mashonaland by raising the Union Jack at Fort Salisbury in September — the first troops of what were to become the British South Africa Company's Police had been established and recruiting had been started, outside the country, as early as November the previous year. Before long the force was to play a formidable part in what has been called "the scramble for Africa".

The history of southern Africa, after the advent of Europeans in 1652, has been written many times and has been given as many interpretations. Especially where the British are concerned, the interpretations range from the heroic to the iconoclastic — from a blind reverence for honourable intentions to accusations of utter treachery. The men who played their parts in the history have been similarly treated: they have been applauded, condemned, sometimes even derided but whatever their attributes, their real motive was unmistakable: to extend their national influence and to acquire for themselves what Africa has had to offer.

In the late 19th century there were two dominating personalities in southern Africa, representing the acquisitive urge of their respective peoples. Paul Kruger was the President of the South African Republic (the Transvaal) and Cecil Rhodes was the Prime Minister of the Cape Colony. South Africa, as now, was divided into four provinces: the Transvaal and Orange Free State, then independent and separate Boer republics; Natal and the Cape of Good Hope, both British colonies.

Kruger personified Afrikaner's aspirations to independence and conservatism, while Rhodes represented British expansionism. Though their characters and situations were more complex than that, it has often been said that the only desire of the Boers was to be left in peace in the republics they had set up in the heart of the continent, away from British interference. It was also true however that Kruger had harboured ideas to expand the Transvaal eastward to Delagoa Bay (Maputo) and west to Lake Ngami in current day Botswana.

Rhodes, although dedicated in his peculiar way to increasing British influence throughout the world, as he grandly conceived it, was by no means an imperialist in the sense of striving to extend the direct authority of the British Government. To him "colonialism" meant, paradoxically, independence from Britain and full control of their own affairs by those people and their descendants who had had the spirit to leave the motherland and settle in its various colonies. Not that he rejected altogether the benefits of wealth and influence which the Imperial connection could bring him.

Rhodes was a strange mixture of idealism and self-interest. By sheer chance he had come to South Africa just at the time when diamonds in fabulous quantities had been discovered in West Griqualand; and by an equally unlikely chance he had joined his brother in Kimberley where he found he could use his acquisitive genius to make a fortune on a scale almost unprecedented in those days. It is often said in his favour that he never used his fortune for his own personal ends. But what are a man's ends? No one can tell. The man may not even know them himself. In Rhodes's case he may have seen, in the power his money brought him, simply a means to achieve his ideals; on the other hand he may have seen, in the opportunity to pursue his ideals which the money gave him, a means to increase his power. Not one of us can judge him; we can only know for certain what he did, not why he did it.

In the First War of Independence, as the Boers called it, in 1880, the British had suffered a humiliating defeat by the Transvaal burghers on Majuba Hill, leaving Kruger to bask in the assured independence of his Republic. But his western flank was still exposed and there was still habitable country between his borders and the Kalahari, and if this were to be occupied by a European power it would renew the threat to his independence. The country was known as Bechuanaland and, although so far it had not actually been annexed by the British Government, some British police (forerunners of the Bechuanaland Border Police, the BBP) had already been sent into the territory. But they were not enough to deter Kruger and in 1884 he sent two groups of burghers to stake the claims of the Transvaal, one in the Vryburg district and another at Rooi Grond, near where Mafeking is today. They simply occupied any land that appealed to them, without any consideration of the tribesmen already living on it. The Boers had always delighted in setting up republics wherever they settled, thereby emphasising their exclusive independence, and following their established tradition they founded the Republic of Stellaland, round Vryburg, and the Republic of Goshen at Rooi Grond.

This was before Rhodes was actually Prime Minister of the Cape, but he was already a member of the Cape Parliament, representing Barkly West near Kimberley. (The Cape Colony at that time had taken in West Griqualand and extended to the Bechuanaland border.) He was already trying to persuade the Cape Colony to think in terms of expansion to the north as a "colonial", as opposed to "imperial", project. He said, "I look upon this Bechuanaland territory as the Suez Canal of the trade of this country, the key to the road to its interior." He was thinking of the Cape Colony's trade, not Britain's. But his colleagues in the Cape Parliament lacked his vision and they would have been content to leave the unattractive Bechuanaland country to the Boers.

But suddenly, in 1884, Germany announced that she had annexed Angra Pequena (Luderitz Bay) on the South West African coast, and all the hinterland round Walvis Bay. This development was of as much concern to the British Government as its obvious threat was to Kruger; and Britain hurriedly sent out John MacKenzie, a missionary, as "special commissioner". MacKenzie, who had been in this part of the world before and nursed a pathological hatred for the Boers, had the temerity to raise the Union Jack at Rooi Grond and was surprised at the near-riot he caused. Even the British Government thought he had been a little tactless and they recalled him. Kruger thereupon proclaimed the territories of Stellaland and Goshen to be under the protection and control of the South African Republic — which was obliging of him, but must have tended to confuse their own republican status.

This was more than Rhodes could swallow. He managed to convince the Cape Government to send him to Vryburg with the surprising title of Deputy Commissioner; and, what was equally surprising, he came to an agreement with the Stellalanders by which they all kept their land titles — to land which they had openly filched from the local tribesmen — on the understanding that the whole of Bechuanaland would ultimately become a British Protectorate. It was a deal in the true Rhodes tradition. As he often said, "Every man has his price."

But the Goshenites at Rooi Grond were not so pliable and refused to talk to him. Rhodes decided that there was only one answer: to appeal to Britain for help. Even the Cape Government was worried by the German annexation in South West Africa. "Decisive measures," they told Britain, at Rhodes's instigation, "should be taken for the maintenance of British authority in South Africa."

The British Government sent Sir Charles Warren — who was a soldier but seemed to have spent most of his time dabbling in archaeology — to Bechuanaland with instructions "to remove the filibusters, to restore order in the territory, to reinstate the natives on their lands, to take such measures as may be necessary to prevent further depredation, and finally to hold the country until its further destination is known". To help him with this task, they gave him 4000 of some of the finest troops in the British Army and made him a Major-General. As the Boer "filibusters" numbered only about 300, it was hardly surprising that the Republics of Stellaland and Goshen surrendered without a shot being fired. Shortly after that, the whole of Bechuanaland (which is now Botswana) was proclaimed a British Protectorate. In the less jingoistic atmosphere of Cape Town, Rhodes seems to have found it wise to attempt to justify the appeal to Britain which had resulted in dispossessing the Boers of Bechuanaland. "Do you think," he asked the Cape Parliament, "that if the Transvaal had Bechuanaland it would be allowed to keep it? Would not Bismarck have some trouble with the Transvaal? And without resources, without men, what could they do? Germany would come across from her settlement in Angra Pequena. There would be some excuse to pick a quarrel — some question of brandy or guns or something — and then Germany would stretch from Angra Pequena to Delagoa Bay."

Soon after this, in 1888, Rhodes achieved the amalgamation of the diamond mines in Kimberley. He was convinced this was the only way to control the industry and ensure that the price of diamonds could be kept at the maximum, by regulating the supply so that it was always just short of the demand. For some time he and his partner, Alfred Beit, had been buying up claims in the Kimberley mines and they were finally left with only one rival, Barney Barnato. Rhodes made his final deal with Barnato, after bargaining with him all night in a little iron shanty of a house in Kimberley, by writing out his personal cheque for £5,338,650 as the dawn was breaking, and thereby securing all the remaining claims on the Kimberley diamond fields. And so the de Beers Consolidated Company was born and Rhodes was able to set himself on the path of empire-building by inserting a somewhat unusual article in the Company's trust deed, permitting it in effect to use its money "to acquire a country and form an empire", as he himself described it. Rhodes at last had the instrument he needed — the instrument by which he could use his wealth to achieve political power, or to fulfil his ideals, whichever may have been his true ambition.

Meanwhile gold had been discovered on the Witwatersrand, in the heart of the Transvaal, on as lavish a scale as the diamonds. But, for Rhodes, the discovery had not brought him the success he had enjoyed in Kimberley.

Mining gold was very different from washing diamonds out of the sand. It needed technical competence and, above all, patience — which was not one of his attributes. Indeed, the goldfields on the Rand were attracting more successful men, in their own sphere, than Rhodes. The company which he did launch, Gold Fields of South Africa, was one of the relatively smaller fry. But prospectors, always pursuing the fortune on the other side of the hill, were forging north into the country between the Limpopo and Zambezi and reports were coming through of new, promising discoveries in, this time, virgin country. Here was the chance for de Beers, or its offshoot, to "acquire a country", with exclusive rights to profitable investment. Here, wealth could generate power and power could generate more wealth.

The idea of obtaining a Royal Charter for his newly proposed company, the British South Africa Company, to occupy, and operate in, the new territory, has often been credited to Rhodes. The belief that it was Rhodes's original notion has more recently been challenged. But whether or not it was his own idea, it appealed to him immensely. If his new company (which would, of course, be controlled principally by his own de Beers) were to be granted a Charter by Queen Victoria he could have the best of both worlds: the venture would be "colonial" in that in practice it would be undertaken and controlled by the people on the spot; it would be "imperial" only so far as it would receive from the British Government political backing and, if the worst happened, military protection. But before petitioning the Crown for a Charter it would clearly be necessary to obtain from the people at present in the territory at least some semblance of the right to operate there — some claim to preference over anybody else who might be after the same thing.

The way in which Charles Rudd, on behalf of Rhodes, obtained from Lobengula, the Matabele chief in Bulawayo, a concession to "win and procure" all the "metals and minerals situated and contained in my Kingdoms, principalities and dominions" is a long and involved story. Rudd and his colleagues had numerous rivals for the chief's favours and only after much coming and going, after months of negotiations in the chief's malodorous kraal — to say nothing of a series of machinations of doubtful moral validity — did they succeed. But it was on the strength of possessing this "Rudd Concession", signed by Lobengula with a cross — in exchange for which they had promised to pay him £100 a month and make him a present of 1000 rifles, 100,000 rounds of ammunition and a gunboat on the Zambezi — that the new British South Africa Company successfully petitioned the Queen for a Royal Charter. The Charter acknowledged, in appropriate legalese, "That the existence of a powerful British Company, controlled by those of Our subjects in whom We have confidence, and having its principal field of operations in that region of South Africa lying to the north of Bechuanaland and to the west of Portuguese East Africa, would be advantageous to the commercial interests of Our subjects in the United Kingdom and in Our Colonies," and empowered the Company to promote "trade, commerce and good government (including the regulation of liquor traffic with the Natives)", to suppress "the slave trade" — of which there was no evidence at all — and open up the territories "to the immigration of Europeans". The Company would also "to the best of its ability preserve peace and order" and for this purpose was authorised to "establish and maintain a force of police".

These preliminaries having been settled after months of involved negotiations and intense bargaining in South Africa and England, Rhodes was now left with the task — relatively straightforward by comparison — of occupying the territory and carrying out his plans to create a new country in the African wilderness. For this task he had some active colleagues and equally formidable antagonists. Of the latter, Lobengula and the Matabele tribesmen were the most intractable. The "kingdoms, principalities and dominions" over which Lobengula ruled included Mashonaland as well as Matabeleland, although his authority over the Mashonas was exercised solely by terrorism. The Mashonas were known to be a submissive people not organised or motivated like the warlike Matabele. There is evidence that at one stage Rhodes and his colleagues toyed with the notion of carrying "by sudden assaults all the principal strongholds of the Matabele nation ... to enable the prospecting, mining and commercial staff of the BSA Company to conduct their operations in Matabeleland in peace and safety". However, as the Matabele warriors, numbering at least 12,000, had already been alerted to the threat of invasion by the comings and goings at Bulawayo for the last couple of years, wisdom and caution prevailed and it was finally decided to avoid Matabeleland as far as possible by entering the territory farther to the east and making straight for the heart of the Mashona country. (The assault on the stronghold of the Matabele nation, to enable the BSA Company to conduct its operations in Matabeleland, was certainly to come, but not for another three years.)

Rhodes's principal, active colleagues in the occupation of Mashonaland were Frank Johnson, Maurice Heany and Dr. Leander Starr Jameson. Johnson had joined the BBP in 1884, at 17, and had risen to quartermaster-sergeant. He has been described as having "more than his fair share of African bluster and lungs like a bull of Basan". Leaving the Bechuanaland police after a brief career, he had gone prospecting on his own in Matabeleland and had achieved the distinction of being hauled before Lobengula himself, charged with an assortment of crimes, including witchcraft, for which he had been fined and expelled from the country.

Heany had also been in the BBP — a trooper. He was an American and had come to South Africa 10 years earlier. Rumour had it that he had deserted from West Point. He had joined Johnson and two other young men (Borrow, one of Sir Charles Warren's anti-filibusters, and Corporal Jack Spreckley, also of the BBP) and they had formed the grandly named Great Northern Trade and Gold Exploration Company. In time, these four were to play boisterous parts in the British South Africa Company's ventures in the new territory.

Dr. Jameson's position was a little more sedate. He was slightly older, a contemporary of Rhodes, with the security of a profession behind him. He had first met Rhodes in Kimberley, where he had set up in practice, and had been infected with the bug of empire-building by contact with Rhodes's fantasies rather than by the craving for profitable adventure which had incited the younger men. He was a townsman by circumstance although he was to become a man of the veld by experience. His first participation in the affairs of the new territory was to travel 700 miles from Kimberley to Bulawayo by oxwagon simply to oblige Rhodes, for whom the negotiations with Lobengula were not going fast enough. He made two more journeys in the same context, one virtually on horseback, at Rhodes's instigation — all these within a few months; but he was becoming enmeshed in Rhodes's adventures to the north, so that by the time the decision had been made to occupy Mashonaland he was a dedicated participant in the enterprise.

The time came at last when detailed plans for the physical occupation of the country had to be made and Rhodes, who was determined to avoid committing himself to a military expedition organised by the Imperial or any other authorities, made the characteristic decision to appoint Johnson as a contractor to the BSA Company. The occupation would be a commercial undertaking; the whole business of founding a new country would be put out to contract. Johnson was asked to quote a price for recruiting, provisioning, equipping and paying a pioneer force of nearly 200 men, who would become the first white settlers in the new country; also for making "a good wagon road" from Palapye, in Bechuanaland, to Mount Hampden, which was to be the destination in Mashonaland; and for "holding and occupying" the new territory until 30 September 1890, after which the Company would relieve him of his responsibilities. Johnson's tender was £87,500 and, as nobody else had been asked to quote, he was awarded the contract for which he wrote out an agreement himself and Rhodes signed it. The profits, which he estimated at over £25,000, were to be shared equally between him, Heany and Borrow. It was never clear who would have been responsible if the contractor incurred a loss.

Rhodes believed at first that this was all it would cost him to occupy the country. He certainly promised Johnson and his partners — and, indeed, all the pioneers — free land and free mining claims when they reached Mashonaland, but as these were costing him nothing he could afford to be generous. But there was one factor he had overlooked or had probably chosen to disregard: the danger of sending a body of men into a wilderness inhabited by warlike savages without some protection against attack. The British Government — as represented by Sir Henry Loch, the High Commissioner in Cape Town — was adamant that the pioneer force must be provided with an adequate military escort. Naturally Loch was not prepared to recommend to his Government that it should assist in financing Rhodes's commercial enterprise by supplying troops at the expense of the

British taxpayer. He made it clear to Rhodes that he would have to arrange the escort at his own expense. Rhodes demurred; but when Sir Henry Loch threatened to recommend to Britain that the Charter should be cancelled if he refused to comply, Rhodes realised he had no option.

At first, Rhodes proposed raising a police force of only 100 men. The Imperial authorities, having assured themselves that he was willing to pay for them, agreed that these could be provided simply by raising an additional troop of the BBP; by that means, there would be no need to set up another recruiting and training organisation. In the event, these first 100 men were almost all former members of the BBP. At this stage the whole conception of the pioneer column was still in embryo and it wasn't expected that the police force would actually have to cross into Mashonaland. It would stay in Bechuanaland, close to the border, and be available to deal with the Matabele if they staged any dangerous demonstrations. But as the later idea developed of 200 pioneers — who would really only be civilians, although it was agreed to attest them for the duration of the march — making their perilous way to Mount Hampden, 450 miles inside the Matabele-dominated country, even less cautious characters than Sir Henry Loch were beginning to feel that a force of only 100 men would be a far from adequate escort. Frederick Selous himself, who had been appointed to act as guide to the pioneer column and knew the territory as well as anyone, persuaded Rhodes that he needed at least 250. This disturbed Sir Henry Loch even more; indeed, the High Commissioner was by no means the only person in high places who was growing nervous — and Rhodes and his co-directors in London were eventually persuaded to raise a force of 500 — all to be paid for by the BSA Company.

It was becoming a formidable force in its own right, needing a separate organisation and a distinctive identity, and it would march with the pioneer column into Mashonaland, to become a permanent feature of the establishment.

And so it was that the British South Africa Company's Police came into existence — before anyone had set foot as a settler in the new country.

## Chapter One

## FORT MATLAPUTLA

FORT MATLAPUTLA, IN Bechuanaland, the first officially established camp of the British South Africa Company's Police — still blatantly outside the territory which the force had been formed to serve — looked across to the north from the rising ground on which it was pitched, over flat, unrelieved savannah country, to the dark line of Lipokole Hills some 15 miles away. Beyond the hills lay Matabeleland — and Lobengula with his 12,000 warriors.

Fort Matlaputla stood three miles south of the Macloutsie River — and was named after a small stream that ran into the river — 25 miles from Camp Cecil where Frank Johnson was assembling his force of pioneers who, in terms of his contract with Cecil Rhodes, were to be the first settlers in the new country. It has been said that the two camps were kept apart during the initial training period, to avoid dissension, because the pioneers were being paid more than double that of the police. The camps stood in the country that is called Botswana today, although it was known at the time as "the disputed territory" because Lobengula, chief of the Matabele, and Khama, chief of the Bamangwato, each claimed it as his own. The disputed territory, although unidentified in exact extent, was nearly 50 miles wide at its western end, and it tapered towards the east for about the same distance, between the converging Shashi and Limpopo rivers. The Macloutsie ran through the middle of the territory, and joined the Limpopo shortly before it met the Shashi. Like most of Botswana the country was arid,   featureless bushveld, with little more vegetation than its ubiquitous, stunted thorn trees.

The BSAC Police camp boasted the designation of a fort because it was dominated by one of those elementary earthworks which were so unashamedly given that label in those days. These so-called forts were usually constructed by simply digging four ditches along the sides of a square and piling up the earth and rubble from the ditches to form the walls, which were never more than about five feet high. But Fort Matlaputla, by all accounts, was a much better construction; pentagonal in shape, which showed imagination, and its earthen walls were braced internally by heavy baulks of timber. Ramps built within the walls led up to internal bastions on which heavy weapons could be mounted — formidable pieces of artillery such as seven-pounders or Maxim guns. The fort was built to hold 200 men if called on to put up a desperate defence. Captain Leonard of the BSAC Police, who later commanded it, said, "Against artillery or effective rifle fire, such as the Boers' , it would be useless as it is commanded from the north and east by higher ground. But it is strong enough to keep out a rush of natives." How long it could have withstood a determined siege was fortunately never put to the test.

The pioneer force, and the police force which was to provide its escort, had been formally established some time early in 1890 by "Regulations for the British South Africa Company's Forces", printed in impressive format on the instructions of Frank Johnson. The exact date of printing is unrecorded. But recruiting had actually begun the previous year. Frank Johnson was responsible for recruiting the pioneers, but the first man engaged in October 1889 by Rhodes himself, to start recruiting for the BSAC Police, was William Bodle — who, if only for this reason, can be regarded as the father of the force.

Bodle was a Sussex man from Alfreston and is reputed to have enlisted in the Sherwood Foresters in 1872, when he was 17 — although his BSAP Record of Service states "6th Inniskilling Dragoons, 17th Lancers, 1873-1879". However, it is known that he was keen to find some active service and for this reason he exchanged into the 6th Inniskilling Dragoons (a regiment from which more than one of the early officers and warrant officers of the BSACP were to come), but at what stage he was in the Lancers is not clear. One record states that he joined the Inniskilling Dragoons in South Africa "to fight the Zulus" but that he was to be robbed of this, his first chance of active service, because he only arrived in South Africa "when the last Zulu War was over". However, the BSAP record gives him the Basuto War Medal, and in any case he marched later to Bechuanaland with General Warren's expedition, although this time he was certainly denied the chance of an actual fight. But the dry, dusty country must have appealed to him for some reason, for he next joined the newly-formed Bechuanaland Border Police and became its regimental sergeant-major. While he was still in the BBP he actually travelled up to Bulawayo, in Matabeleland, accompanying the Deputy Commissioner of

Bechuanaland, Sir Sydney Shippard, on a visit to Lobengula in 1888 — when, to oblige Rhodes, who was lobbying Lobengula for permission to enter his country, Shippard had made a formal call on the Chief, impressively attired in a frock coat and sola topi. So Bodle was no stranger to the country and well able, as recruiting officer, to judge his candidates' fitness to serve there.

The first actual attestations in the BSAC Police appear to have been Corporals G.W. Davis and C. Swarton, with Troopers H.J. Hellet and C. Stadlar, on 2 November 1889. Even allowing for officialese, it is difficult to understand why these very first recruits were given Nos. 20, 68, 33 and 67 respectively — perhaps alphabetical influence played a part in the attestation sequence? Three more were attested on 10 November and one on the 11th. They received numbers 23, 30, 31 and 69. Between 18 and 24 November, 23 more were attested, making 31 in all during that month. The last batch, on the 24th, included F.K.W. Lyons-Montgomery and J.H. Hillier. Lyons-Montgomery was allotted No. 1, perhaps for reasons of prestige, because he was made the first troop sergeant major — presumably on the strength of his having been a lieutenant and adjutant of the volunteer regiment in Kimberley known as the Diamond Fields Horse. Hillier, who was made Quartermaster Sergeant, was given No. 34. He had actually ridden with either the 8th Hussars or 12th Lancers (the record is uncertain) in the Charge of the Light Brigade at Balaclava, 35 years before. He was well into middle age and provides a fascinating link between BSAP and the Crimean War.

Seventeen more members were attested in December 1889. Among these was Trooper H.A. Arnold (No. 10) who attested on 12 December. Writing many years later, Arnold confirmed rumours of mutterings among the police recruits about their pay, saying, "There was some trouble at first about our pay. We had been promised an extra two shillings a day; as this promise was not fulfilled it nearly led to a mutiny." History is silent about what actually transpired.

Attestations continued through the early months of 1890, and by July of that year, when the pioneer column moved into Matabeleland, the strength of the BSAC Police was 24 officers, a Regimental Sergeant-Major (Bodle), five troop sergeant-majors (Lyons-Montgomery, J.C. Stewart, W.J. Cunningham, G. Stanley and W. Hole), 20 sergeants, one orderly-room sergeant, one lance-sergeant, 74 corporals, seven lance-corporals, two farriers and 442 troopers — 577 in all, not allowing for any discharges or deaths that might have occurred up to that time.

The first officer to be directly appointed as such to the BSACP, Captain Patrick William Forbes, had joined on 16 November 1889. Forbes, also of the Inniskilling Dragoons, had fought in the Zulu War and he too had marched with Warren's expedition.

The printed regulations for the BSA Company's Forces placed the pioneer corps (as distinct from the police) "under the immediate command of Major F. Johnson" — he who had contracted with Rhodes to deliver the pioneers to Mashonaland — who was given a temporary military rank for the duration of the expedition and was to be "solely responsible for the interior economy and supply of his corps". But although Johnson — who had no military experience, except as a quartermaster in the BBP — nominally commanded the pioneer corps, the regulations put him firmly under the orders of the OC, Company's Police, for any "movements, employment in camp, on line of march or in action". In other words, his duties were still little more than those of a quartermaster. He resented this very much. At the time when he had contracted with Rhodes to take the pioneers to their destination he had believed he would be in complete charge. It had only been later, when Rhodes was prevailed upon to provide the column with a police escort, that the authorities also insisted that the senior police officer, who was to be a colonel of the regular army, should take overall command. This insistence certainly made for conflicts of interest: Johnson's financial interests, requiring that the journey be completed with the least possible delay, might well clash with a regular colonel's military considerations. As Johnson said in a letter to Rhodes, " ... it will be quite competent for the OC of the Company's Police to delay the Pioneer Expedition for a month or more if he thinks fit". And in the event, although no circumstances arose to create serious differences, there was no love lost between the two.

The nominal establishment of the pioneer corps (as distinct from the police force) was to be three troops of 50 men each and an artillery detachment of 36 men — about 200 in all, with the supernumeraries. Each troop would have a captain, subaltern, troop sergeant-major, two sergeants and a bugler — all given temporary rank and attested for the duration of the march. Each troop was to be a complete unit, with its own transport, ammunition and entrenching tools. The drill and the care of horses was to be the same as laid down for the police.

When it came to the police force itself, the regulations set out the establishment in considerably more detail. There were to be five troops, each with a captain, two subalterns, a troop sergeant-major, four sergeants, eight corporals, one farrier, one bugler and 70 troopers — a total of 88 men in each troop. Again, each troop was to be a complete unit with its own ammunition and transport, the latter consisting of four ox-wagons. The officer commanding a troop "will require from his two subalterns a thorough knowledge of the men and horses of their half-troop". The subalterns were to pay particular attention to "the manner of their NCOs towards the men, checking any undue familiarity or favouritism".

Eight "smart, well-educated men" were to be chosen from each troop to be trained as signallers — signalling was by semaphore flags and heliograph — and as many as possible from each troop to serve the seven-pounder and Maxim guns. "Whilst not expecting from volunteers the precision and smartness of regular regiments, the CO requires officers, NCOs and troopers of the Company's Police to be implicit in their obedience of all orders, and trusts that they will avoid falling into the fatal error (of believing) that slovenly drill and appearance are workmanlike." NCOs and men "will be careful to salute all BSAP officers, whether in uniform or not, and all officers of Imperial and Colonial corps when in uniform, whenever they meet them". The reference to "BSAP" instead of "BSACP" was obviously an unintentional piece of inspired prophecy.

It was laid down that when the force advanced into Matabeleland no officer or man would be allowed to shoot game, either round the camp or on the line of march, unless permission was given. NCOs and troopers would not be allowed more than 300 yards from camp without permission. OCs of posts and standing camps were urged to provide accommodation for their men "before the rainy season commences"; grass huts would never be permitted. If only grass or thatch were obtainable for roofs, the thatch was to be covered with hides put on wet and securely fastened down; water barrels were to be provided and kept full in case of fire. "OC troops and detachments will make every effort to provide amusements suitable for the troopers ... whenever it is possible to do so gardens will be cultivated for the supply of fresh vegetables for the troops."

On the march, "the transport officer will be responsible to OC Column that the wagons do not straggle". When forming laager, the tents of each troop were to be pitched as close as possible to the wagons of that troop and to each other. All ranks would "invariably sleep in their clothes, with arms by their sides". On an alarm sounding, each man would hurry into the laager with arms and ammunition, each troop falling in by its own wagons. The man in charge of each tent would be the last to leave, when he would "seize the pole by its foot, pull it out of the tent door, leaving the tent fiat".

Each OC troop would inspect his troop's arms and ammunition daily, saddles and horse kit weekly, personal kit and equipment monthly. "All officers are to attend stables at whatever hour they are so ordered. The subaltern of the day will attend all stables ... OC troops or detachment will be allowed to inflict minor punishment for minor offences." And both the pioneers and the police would be subject to the discipline of the Cape Mounted Riflemen Act, 1878, of the Cape Colony — the High Commissioner in Cape Town having declared by Proclamation "that the Regulations framed under the Act shall be applicable to all members of the British South Africa Company's Police in the territories comprised within the limits of the Queen's Order in Council (i.e. the Chartered Company's territories)"; and, a little ominously, "that it shall be lawful to carry out in Bechuanaland any duly confirmed sentences of imprisonment (of the members of the force)". Thus were sown the seeds of an established military discipline.

Finally, the Regulations set out "rules for the guidance of officers and others in dealing with natives". Every effort was to be made "to establish friendly relations with natives in the Kraals". NCOs and troopers were forbidden to visit kraals without permission of the OC, "except in urgent necessity". At each camp, an area would be marked off "for natives bringing products for sale ... to be supervised by a trustworthy sergeant or NCO, assisted if necessary by one or two steady men".

"Any person belonging to the Expedition, whether European or Native," the Regulations admonished, "who interferes with native women or ill-treats any native in any way, will be most severely dealt with." The authority of native chiefs and headmen was to be recognised and their confidence gained "by absolute fairness". Any offence by a native was to be referred to his chief; "no punishment (was to be inflicted — by the police themselves, one assumes) without the order of the OC".

Such were the terms of service under which men clamoured to join the British South Africa

Company's Police. One, Victor Morier — son of the British Ambassador in St. Petersburg (Leningrad) and a friend of one of the BSA Company's directors — who joined as a trooper in June 1890 (No. 540) said a little patronisingly, "neither the Police nor the Pioneers are quite all we heard from the enthusiasts in London. The Pioneers are exactly the same class of men as our troopers, chiefly miners thrown out of employment by the smash of the Johannesburg gold fields." This was the time when the mines on the Witwatersrand had exhausted the ore at the shallow levels and the new methods of treating the remaining sulphides left in the deeper shafts had not yet been discovered. Consequently, the Rand was experiencing a considerable slump. "A sprinkling of army and navy deserters," Morier goes on in the same vein, "clerks, etc., who have come out from home, and men drafted from the Cape Mounted Rifles and the Bechuanaland Border Police." Not the gentility, apparently, with whom he had expected to be associated. Captain Leonard — who will be introduced shortly — wrote in the same vein, "Such a mixed lot I never saw in my life from the aristocrat down to the street Arab. Peers and waifs of humanity mingling together like the ingredients of a hotch-potch." Another early member, Corporal Divine, subsequently wrote, "We had an unfrocked clergy-man in the regiment, a doctor who had lost his diploma but who performed an amazing amputation with a razor and a tenon-saw on a man who had been seized by a crocodile. We had lawyers, artists (both landscape and theatrical), one had been a ring-master in a big circus another artist, a quiet unassuming German, whose pictures occasionally appeared in the London Graphic, was cook of the Corporals' mess."

The police, attracted from various parts of South Africa and overseas, were formally recruited at Kimberley, where they were issued with uniform and equipment by Quartermaster Sergeant Hillier — the Crimean veteran. A trooper subsequently said, "The dear old gentleman did his job very well. A bit peppery, but all 'quarter' blokes are." From Kimberley they were sent by mail cart — which Morier describes as "an overgrown kind of dog-cart ... seven of us perched on top of the mail bags" — to Palapye, more than 500 miles away and a fortnight's journey travelling day and night, with only one break at Mafeking. It certainly gave the new men a taste of conditions to come. Leonard's description of the mail cart was that it had "room enough for two to travel in with tolerable comfort, and four with a certain amount of discomfort; but nine of us, two being considerably above the average (in weight, besides 2500 lbs. of correspondence, were a trifle too much for it". Presumably most of these first drafts travelled after the 1889-90 rainy season because there is no record of any trouble from the rains at this period, unlike those that cause widespread havoc the following year. From Mafeking they went on to Palapye in the more spacious accommodation of an ox-wagon — through more miles of seemingly interminable bush, growing thicker here — and at Palapye those able to ride were given horses on which they rode the last 150 miles to the Macloutsie. "We shot guinea-fowl and partridges on the way up for food," says Morier, "and I was lucky enough to get a springbok." Altogether, they had come nearly 700 miles through dry, stony, featureless bushveld.

At Fort Matlaputla, Morier described one of his days in camp. "At 6.30 an hour's drill. Breakfast and then stables until 10 o'clock. Then a mile tramp with three horses down to the water, then half an hour's mealie chopping. Fatigues of one kind or another till dinner-time (lunch) then another drill till 3 o'clock. Till 5 cleaning stables, clothes and accoutrements. At 5, either picket or guard-mounting. 7 o'clock, feeding and cleaning horses again, ditto at 9. Lights out at 9.30. Every third night we sleep booted and spurred on guard with 10 hours sentry go out of the 24 ... weather, one degree below freezing at night, 95 degrees of heat in the sun at mid-day." He was writing in July 1890. "Our little tent is so crowded, however, that we don't feel the cold much at night." If Morier had suffered some class consciousness when he joined, it appears to have soon rubbed off, for only on one later occasion were his letters and diaries to contain patronising references to his companions.

In addition to the five troops of BSAC Police assembling at Fort Matlaputla, there were three troops of the Bechuanaland Border Police, about 200 men, in a separate camp close by, commanded by Major Raleigh Grey — also from the Inniskilling Dragoons. Five years later, this officer was to be even more actively associated with the Company's police when Dr. Jameson launched his raid into the Transvaal. Now, he and his men waited by the Macloutsie simply to support the Company's pioneers and police while they were organising. While they waited, there was only one other troop of BBP, stationed at Mafeking, to serve the whole of Bechuanaland. Indeed, apart from the concentra-tion of forces on the Macloutsie — which were fully preoccupied with Rhodes's northern adventure

— the fourth troop at Mafeking was the only body of armed men north of Kimberley. The BBP on the Macloutsie were not intended to take any part in the expedition to Mashonaland, but they remained where they were until the pioneer column had left and was safely clear of any likely clash with the Matabele.

The five BSAC police troops at Fort Matlaputla were first given designations — 'B', 'C', 'D', 'H' and 'I' — which were currently unused by the BBP. The four BBP troops at the time were, apparently, 'A', 'E', 'F' and 'G'. That is to say, the original conception was that the new troops were merely to be additional to the existing BBP force. But when it was agreed at last that the Company's Police was to become a force in its own right, quite separate from the BBP, its five troops were redesignated 'A', 'B', 'C', 'D' and 'E', under the command respectively of Captains H.M. Heyman (Cape Mounted Rifles), P.W. Forbes (Inniskilling Dragoons), C. Keith-Falconer (an aide de-camp to Lady Loch, wife of the High Commissioner in Cape Town), E.C. Chamley-Turner (Royal Scots, but for the last two years in the BBP) and A.G. Leonard (East Lancashire). It is assumed at the early officers were seconded to the Company's force by their respective regiments. Leonard was preceded for a short while by a Captain Tompkins, of whom there appears no further record. Leonard himself had come from England by cabled invitation from Colonel Sir Frederick Carrington, commanding the BBP. He had left Southampton on 4 April 1890, arrived in Cape Town on the 23rd, left Kimberley 4 May, Palapye 13 May and arrived at Macloutsie on the 18th. Of the troop sergeant-majors, Lyons-Montgomery, No. 1, came from the Diamond Fields Horse in Kimberley; two came from the Inniskilling Dragoons and one from the Life Guards. Leonard says, "they were inclined to be rather independent and gentlemen at large". At a later stage, an artillery section, 'F' Troop, was formed under the command of Captain C. F. Lendy (Royal Artillery), with men drawn from other troops.

On 1 March 1890, Major S.G. Pennefather, of the 6th Inniskilling Dragoons, was promoted to Lieutenant-Colonel and appointed to command the BSAC Police and, to Frank Johnson's horror to overall command of the whole pioneer column. In a clear sign of his resentment at the situation, Johnson ceased signing his correspondence "OC Pioneer Corps" and substituted "Contractor for the construction of the road from Bamangwato to Mt. Hampden". He telegraphed to Rhodes, "You may assure Pennefather ... that I will work most cordially with (him) and obey all instructions," adding caustically, "provided that I am relieved of responsibility for the Matabele War which will be most probable if the Pioneers are accompanied by a force of police."

Like Captain Forbes, also of the 6th Inniskilling Dragoons, Pennefather had seen service in the Zulu War. He had also served as a Captain with the Warren Expedition to Bechuanaland, so he at least knew something about the country. But Pennefather didn't endear himself to the other members of the expedition. Captain Leonard wrote later that he "is noisy, discourteous and loses the little head he has on every possible occasion and when he has lost it, it takes him all his time to find it again ... his most noticeable features are an entire absence of tact and a furious temper". There is no doubt that Pennefather was far from popular with the pioneers and he lasted less than two years as commanding officer of the police before being recalled to regimental duty. But Leonard's bitterness toward his CO was possibly exaggerated by a professional lack of regard held by the East Lancashire Regiment for the Inniskilling Dragoons. He later described Forbes, from the same regiment, as "the typical British bull-dog, with as much brains".

'B' Troop ranked the senior troop from the start because Captain Forbes and most of its members were the earliest attestations. It had been labelled 'B' Troop right at the beginning, adopting the first unused BBP symbol. 'C' and 'D' Troops had also been 'C' and 'D' originally — thus following 'B' in order of attestation — and these three troops continued with the same labels when they became the BSACP. But the new 'A' Troop had previously been 'H' and the new 'E' Troop had been 'I', so they were both well down the seniority list.

'B' Troop, the senior, provided the Headquarters Staff, attached to which was Captain Sir John Willoughby, Bart., as Chief Staff Officer. Willoughby was an officer of the Royal Horse Guards, "the Blues", with whom he had fought in the Egyptian campaign of 1885. It was suggested that his outstanding attribute was a particularly irritating manner. In fact, Rhodes later chose him to conduct negotiations with the Portuguese because this was just the attribute needed for the particular business on hand. Leonard, who seems to have been particularly critical of officers from the more fashionable regiments, wrote, "Willoughby's turn-out is too funny for words. A gaudy red field cap, a khaki jacket, a pair of baggy blue trousers with broad red stripes, and brown leather buttonboots, while his seat on a horse is ugly in the extreme." Nor was Leonard impressed by the capability of the higher command as a whole. "The orders that fly about the camp at times," he wrote, "might well be classified under the headings 'confusing', 'contradictory', 'curious' or 'amusing'. Whether the mighty brain of the Colonel or Staff Officer is responsible for such orders I cannot say."

But Leonard was not always so uncharitable about his colleagues. Of Captain Chamley-Turner, commanding 'D' Troop, he wrote, "He is tall and well-made and about as charming a companion as one could wish to meet." Leonard was also complimentary about Surgeon-Captain R.F. Rand who had been appointed by Rhodes as senior medical officer of the BSAC Police. He was an FRCS, England, and an MD, Edinburgh, and had practised in Jamaica where he had had considerable experience of tropical diseases. Rhodes had met him in Kimberley and was so impressed with him that although Rand had gone to Johannesburg to run a successful practise, Rhodes managed to persuade him to join in the adventure to Mashonaland. Unlike Rhodes's other medical friend, Dr. Jameson, who was more interested in political intrigue, Rand confined himself to his medicine. Leonard wrote, "I have met scores of medical men in my time, but never one so completely wrapped up, so devoted to his profession ... his devotion is so great that it amounts to positive slavery." Not that Leonard could suppress his feelings about his fellow-officers for long. "The officers, socially speaking, are not a bad lot, but there is no *esprit de corps* among them."

The headquarters staff was completed by Lieutenant M.D. Graham, Pennefather's adjutant, who was the only South African-born senior officer in the police at the time.

His grandfather had founded Grahamstown in 1812 and his father had been Lieutenant-Governor of Kaffraria. Graham had gone to school in England and had been commissioned in the Northampton Regiment. And not least of the establishment at Macloutsie were Canon Balfour, the Protestant Chaplain of the BSACP, and young Mother Patrick and her half a dozen Catholic Sisters from the convent at Grahamstown. "They go about their work quietly," said Leonard, "and with a manner so unassuming as if they were doing nothing out of the way. They do the work of menials — washing and cooking — and not allowing the natives to do anything but fetch and carry."

## Chapter Two

## THE OCCUPATION OF MASHONALAND

TOWARDS THE END of June 1890, General Methuen, Adjutant-General of the British forces in South Africa, inspected both the police and the pioneers at their camps on the Macloutsie. The General was clearly determined to conduct a thorough inspection. Pennefather, at Fort Matlaputla, wrote to Johnson, at Camp Cecil, on 18 June.

"The General thinks it advisable that I should see your Corps at drill a couple of days before the inspection which will begin on Monday next at your Camp. I am therefore going down on Thursday afternoon and shall want to see them at mounted drill, advance and rear guards, skirmishing, drill in close order and formation of square. The General will also see the Manual of Firing exercises and judging distance; also some firing at objects of unknown distances; revolver practice also, probably. You seem to have a lot of officers detached. I have been giving no leave except on Saturday afternoons and Sundays, but I must leave that to your own discretion. Only I shall expect to see every officer, except Mandy, on parade. The General requires each officer, Captain or Subaltern, to drill his own troop. The General has been at us all day and is well satisfied with the result. He will be at us again each day until Saturday. If your inspection is satisfactory you will be allowed to go on to the Tuli at once, I believe, and start making your base there. We can talk over the details of that when I see you."

According to Leonard, the General's inspection of the police included "a big field day with blank ammunition, the BBP defending the east face of the camp and we taking the offensive." History is silent on the outcome of the battle. However, both inspections seem to have satisfied the General. There is a story, probably apocryphal, that before leaving the pioneers he called the officers together and, having politely asked them to produce their maps, said, "You first go to a point marked Siboutsi. I do not know whether Siboutsi is a man or a mountain. Mr. Selous, I understand, is of the opinion that it is a man, but we will pass that by. Then you get to Mount Hampden. Mr. Selous is of the opinion that Mount Hampden is placed 10 miles too far to the west. You'd better correct that. Perhaps on second thoughts better not. Because you might possibly be placing it 10 miles too far to the east. Good morning, gentlemen."

The inspection of the two forces having satisfied such high military authority, the police and the pioneers were brought together for the first time on 27 June 1890, when the pioneers moved off from Camp Cecil and 'A' Troop of the police from Fort Matlaputla, under Captain Heyman, joined them on the first combined march of the expedition. Their destination was a point some 60 miles to the east, on the south bank of the Shashi River — still in "the disputed territory" — which had been chosen as the base camp from which the expedition was to be launched into the dangerous Matabele country. An advance party under Frederick Selous, the official guide to the expedition, had already chosen a site for another fort. This fort, when it was built, was first named Fort Selous, but for some uninspired reason — or perhaps because Johnson took a strong dislike to Selous — the name was changed to Fort Tuli, under the impression that the river it overlooked was the Tuli River. Actually, the Tuli is a tributary of the Shashi, into which it runs from the north about 20 miles upstream from the site of the fort. But the name Tuli, which means the River of Dust, survives today for the point on the Shashi River where the second camp and fort were built.

The route from Macloutsie to Fort Tuli was the first part of the road which had to be cut as the column proceeded, through virgin bush. Fortunately for the police they were not actually involved in making the road — which task consisted, of course, of cutting down the bush and hacking it away, avoiding the outcrops of rock and, where possible, the bigger trees. The pioneers cut the road — each of their troops alternating on this duty for a few days at a time, working some miles ahead of the main column — while the police attended to their own escort duties, forming the advanced and rear guards, and providing scouts on the flanks. Not that there was any great expectation of attack by the Matabele while the column was still south of the Shashi River.

The general geography of Matabeleland and Mashonaland was known well enough to people like Selous, Johnson, and Heany — who was commanding one of the pioneer troops. They had been in these parts on numerous hunting and prospecting expeditions. So the route chosen for the pioneers to follow had been well defined before they set off, although they naturally had no knowledge of the detailed terrain in which they would find themselves. But a point had been chosen on the Shashi River where they would actually cross into Matabeleland; thence they would follow a course skirting the eastward side of the Matabele country, in an almost straight line to Mount Hampden which was nearly 400 miles to the north, leaving Lobengula's Bulawayo at least 150 miles to the west from the nearest point on the line of march. Lobengula had given Rhodes' permission to enter the country, but it was never certain that his warriors would allow the white intruders an undisputed passage.

Seen from the air today, the Shashi is one of those rivers that twist like bright snakes across the brown and green face of Africa, their beds gleaming with white sand under the sun in the dry season — which is most of the year — and flashing silver on those few occasions when they are in flood. The Shashi, like many of them, is a considerable river; 800 yards, or almost half a mile wide, at the point where Selous chose to take the column across. When dry, the sparkling white bed of sand looks innocent enough, but the sand is coarse and heavy and a vehicle of any weight will soon sink down to its axles. Walking across it is heavy going; not the ideal choice for a rugby football ground, as it was used at a very early stage of the expedition for a match between the pioneers and the police — played in heavy military boots.

However, while the pioneers cut the road, it fell to the police to lay out and construct the fort and camp. The site of the original Fort Tuli — a second fort was built 10 years later on the outbreak of the Boer War, as will be related — was later preserved as a national monument. The fort was built on a kopje, rising from a hollow basin partly surrounded by hills, but with an open view to the north across the Shashi into Matabeleland. In the mid 1970s a flagstaff still dominated the kopje on which it was built, and on appropriate occasions a patrol officer of the BSAP would raise the flag for the benefit of any animals in the district who might happen to be looking that way. The camp was pitched round the base of the kopje and, in time, a considerable township was to grow up. The site of the fort was often criticised by knowing visitors because the central kopje on which it stood was almost surrounded by the semi-circle of outer kopjes, from which it could well have been dominated by long-range guns, or even rifles. And the perimeter of the outer kopjes would have been far too extensive to be adequately defended, except by a very large force.

However, Johnson, in his planning had had a brilliant idea in two senses of the word. He had obtained from the Royal Navy at Simonstown a 10,000 candle-power searchlight and mounted this on a wagon on top of a pile of ammunition boxes. Another wagon carried a steam engine and dynamo. Every two hours, at night, the engine was started and the searchlight switched on, sweeping the surrounding bush from its elevated position for a whole minute. Its effect was probably wasted at Fort Tuli, which was on the south side of the river and unlikely to be attacked by Matabele impis, but there is no doubt that later, as the column moved on through Matabeleland and Mashonaland, the piercing eye which penetrated the darkness of night suggested to the Matabele a formidable display of witchcraft against which they would be ill-advised to contend. The fact that it was only switched on at two-hours' intervals, and then only for a minute — a policy probably dictated by considerations of economy of effort — added no doubt to its unnerving effect. Moreover, if the rotating eye could pierce the darkness of night, how easily could it not spot an enemy trying to hide in the bush, even in the light of day? Although this can is conjecture, the searchlight probably contributed more to the safe passage of the column than any other factor.

Although it fell to the police to lay out Fort Tuli and the surrounding camp, it appears that Major Johnson, as OC pioneers, had some hand in the construction, because on 4 July Pennefather, who must have visited Tuli during the previous week, sent Johnson a highly critical letter from Fort Matlaputla. In his previous letter to Johnson, prior to General Methuen's inspection, he had addressed him as "Dear Johnson", and signed himself "Yours sincerely". But the breach between the two, which was later to become formidable, had in all probability already opened, for Pennefather now addressed him as "The Officer Commanding, Pioneer Force, Tuli", beginning, "Sir, I must point out to you that you have not carried out what was the essential part of my plan for the formation of the Camp, which is plainly shown on the rough sketch with which I furnished you, namely, that the laager should afford flank defence from the Eastern and South-Eastern faces of the Kopje." Pennefather went on to complain that in the written orders which he had given Johnson he had distinctly stated that the pioneers would camp on the north and north-west faces of the laager and the police on the south and south-east faces. Although Pennefather did not say so, Johnson had apparently made other dispositions. "I cannot agree with you," said Pennefather, "in thinking that the force at your disposal, which I think amounts to 180 effective men with two seven-pounder guns and two machine guns, is insufficient to man such a very strong position as the one which you now hold," adding, "more especially if the laager had been placed as I intended."

The letter went on in detail about accurately laying off positions by compass. "I am inclined to think they have not been so laid off, as I took carefully myself the compass bearings of the face of the laager which I marked out and the bearing of the centre of the Kopje from the Southeastern point ... As a permanent post will be established on the Kopje I am anxious not to have the ground fouled in any way, therefore I do not wish any camp to be pitched there." Early photographs of Tuli distinctly show lines of tents on the top of the kopje, and report has it that these were the officers' lines. Perhaps it was believed that they would not be so likely to "foul" the ground. The fort, he said, would be occupied by some of the police who would be left behind when the advance was made, so "you had better employ the Police on the construction of the Fort ... You have placed the Police horse lines in a much worse position than that indicated on my sketch." After more critical comment on Johnson's dispositions, the letter ended, "Be good enough to inform me as soon as possible when you will have on the Tuli all the stores and mealies which you propose to take in with you, and when you expect the road to be completed to the (Mtshabetsi). I also send a sketch of the manner in which the timber breastwork on the Kopje should be constructed. I do not think you will find it necessary to move much of the ammunition to the top of the Kopje and to do so would be unnecessary. I am, Sir," he concluded, with pointed formality, "Your obedient servant, Edward G. Pennefather, Lt.-Col., Commanding B.S.A. Co's Forces."

On 6 July, 'B' and 'C' Troops of the police moved up from the Macloutsie to join 'A' Troop at Tuli, leaving 'D' and 'E' at Fort Matlaputla. Concentrated now at the new camp was the entire pioneer force and three troops of police: nearly 500 men, with their horses, wagons, oxen and native drivers. Horses, trek oxen and slaughter cattle amounted to anything up to 1000 animals. Even so, the population of Tuli — human and animal — was to grow much larger in the months to come.

While these forces were assembling, half a dozen of Lobengula's men appeared at the camp. Although they carried assegais and sticks, and some had ox-hide shields, their appearance hardly posed a formidable threat to a body of armed men. Some were in loincloths, others in ragged shirts and shorts — one even had a waistcoat. They brought a message from the Chief asking if the white men had lost anything, for by coming into his country the invaders were obviously looking for something. Whatever answer was given to this cynical enquiry, the Chief's messengers went off peaceably enough.

The column crossed the Shashi on 11 July — the whole pioneer force with 'A' and 'B' Troops of the police, leaving 'C' Troop at Fort Tuli as a garrison to maintain the line of communication. The new country had been entered at last. But despite these careful plans, if Lobengula's impis attacked the column, it would have to fight its own way through, because back-up from the troops at Tuli and Matlaputla would be slow in arriving.

Credit for the success of the march from Tuli to Fort Salisbury, as planned and without loss of a single life, must principally go to Frank Johnson and his pioneers, for it was they who cut the road and found their way through virtually uncharted bush, and manhandled their wagons and supplies over boulder-strewn tracks, across sand and rocky drifts, and up and down sheer-sided river banks. It was no mean undertaking for those days, with no mechanical aids to transport and no communication with the rest of the world. But in everything the pioneers accomplished they were supported and assisted by the police, who carried also the particular responsibility of protecting them from the ever likely menace of attack by Matabele impis.

If they had been attacked — and it was no thanks to any special planning that they were not — the pioneers would have had to fight as grimly as the police. They too had been attested as soldiers for the duration of the march and put through an equally rigorous training. The expedition was a joint effort, every privation and every hazard shared, but while the police were executing a military duty, for the pioneers the march was only the first stage in their adventure, after which they would be faced with the task of settling themselves in a new, still untamed country. Not that there was anything altruistic or heroic in their purpose; they were there certainly for the adventure, but they were encouraged just as surely by the prospect of the glittering prizes they would find.

For the first 200 miles after crossing the Shashi the route lay through the lowveld of south-eastern Matabeleland, with four principal river crossings, the Umzingwani, Bubye, Nuanetsi and Lundi. Here the country is very different from Botswana's bushveld. The trees are taller, the undergrowth is thicker and the horizon is continually broken by massive granite kopjes. This was the most dangerous part of the journey, with many opportunities for the Matabele to conduct ambushes. Shortly after the column had crossed the Lundi, Johan Colenbrander, the Company's representative at Lobengula's Kraal at Bulawayo, rode into camp with a message from the Chief threatening that if the column continued any further he would send his impis to stop it. Pennefather is credited with a reply which said, "I take my orders from the Queen." Another version says "from Mr. Rhodes" — "My orders are to go to Mashonaland and go I will." Nevertheless, for all Pennefather's brave words, there was distinct alarm in the laager that night and the searchlight worked overtime.

The police scouts, checking to left and right of the column's line of march, had to take particular care not to ride too far into the bush where they could become easily and irretrievably lost. Later, Johnson was to describe to Leonard what he called "the absurdity of the formation (that had been used) on the line of march ... All the men," he said, "were frittered away in small flanking and advance parties, the former only 200 yards from the road and never going away from it. Evidently because Pennefather was afraid they would lose their way and there was no touch kept between any of the parties. In reality they were no protection to the column and as there were no supports, no reserve and no main body, you can imagine what would have happened had we been attacked." However, Johnson's opinions can be somewhat discounted by his bitterness at being relegated to a subordinate position in the command.

At last, after nearly five weeks' marching, forming laager every night and standing-to in the first light of every dawn — the time when it was the usual practice of the Matabele to make their attacks — the column reached the foot of a range of granite hills which seemed to bar their progress any farther north. Selous was sure, from his knowledge of the country, that once past this barrier they would find themselves on the highveld, which stretched as a more open plain for the last 200 miles to their destination. He went forward with some scouts and found a relatively easy path he named Providential Pass. On 13 August the column mounted the pass and reached the summit, where, although still well timbered, the plain stretched out ahead to lines of blue-grey hills on the horizon. After the oppressive heat of the lowveld, the air was fresh and bracing, and the sun shone benignly on a land which seemed to confirm the prospect of all the riches the pioneers had been promised.

When the column reached the summit of Providential Pass it moved forward into the more open country and pitched camp four miles south of where the town of Fort Victoria (Masvingo) stands today, on the land which was to become Clipsham Farm — where Sir Raymond Stockil, Leader of the Opposition in the Southern Rhodesian Parliament many years later, farmed for a long time. The outline of a pentagonal earthwork — shades of Major MacAdam and Matlaputla — is still just visible today, but even so it is believed that this is not the remains of the original fort, which probably stood near by but is said to have crumbled into disrepair after about 12 months. Even the second fort only stood for another year, after which, owing to lack of water in the vicinity, the town of Fort Victoria was moved to its present position — and a more substantial fort was built in 1892.

The column rested here for a few days while the outline of the fort was being marked out, and was joined by 'C' Troop of the police, under Captain Keith-Falconer, which had moved up from Tuli to become the garrison at Fort Victoria. And here the first permanent police station in the country was set up — established as an outstation even before anybody knew where police headquarters were likely to be. For the present, headquarters were still on the move, attached to 'B' Troop and accommodated in tents which were struck every morning on the march.

The first orders ever given to a Member in Charge were issued to Captain Keith-Falconer on 18 August 1890 by Colonel Pennefather before the latter moved on from Fort Victoria. Unlike his many successors, Keith-Falconer was not given a station to take over; his first order was to "put the Fort, which has been traced out, in a defensible condition without delay". He was to place "an abattis obstacle", six feet high and made up of thorn trees, round the fort at a distance of 50 yards from the crest of the parapet. "Inside this abattis you will construct an entanglement of barbed wire when you have sufficient material ... you will keep all the wagons in laager until you consider that the Fort is defensible; you will then send wagons down to Tuli with the best spans, retaining two wagons and spans at your station."

Cattle and horse kraals were to be constructed, the slaughter cattle being kraaled separately from the trek oxen. Distances up to 500 yards were to be marked out all round the fort, for ranging purposes, and up to 1000 yards on the face where the Maxim gun was to be mounted. Native labour could be obtained at the expense of the Company, for erecting huts for the men and stables for the horses, and digging gardens. Huts were to be of wattle and daub, thatched with grass, and the roofs covered with wet hides; stables of dry stone or wattle and daub, with the same roof. A stone store was to be built in the centre of the fort and iron roofing for this had been sent for. "In the case of any (native) labourers absconding, stealing or misconducting themselves in any way, you should send them to the chief and demand the punishment of the offenders. Even with registered natives you must be careful that they do not have access to the arms, ammunition or equipment of your detachment."

Some "trading goods" — sheets of calico, brass beads, packets of salt — would be left with the Member in Charge to buy mealies, sweet potatoes and other supplies, and to pay for labour. "A monthly return of supplies bought or natives employed must be sent to S.O." (presumably, the Staff Officer.)

"You must obtain all information as to the names of chief living in your vicinity, and the numbers of their tribes. You should inform these chiefs that the English (sic) have come to settle in their country, point out to them the advantages they will gain by this in the way of security, as well as their being able to sell produce and work for wages near to their own homes, and arrange with them to let you know when parties of white men come into their country to settle and prospect."

Patrols were to be organised within a radius of 15 miles from the fort, and the names of all parties prospecting in the vicinity were to be sent to headquarters. Private traders would be allowed to trade with the natives, provided no liquor trade was carried on. "Should you find that any trader is supplying liquor to natives you are authorised to detain him and his wagons at your Fort ... Any person attempting to obtain concessions from chiefs on this side of the Sabi River will also be detained by you, reference being made to Headquarters." One is inclined to wonder what Act or Regulation the arresting officer relied on, if any such arrests were made.

Prospectors and others were to be prevented, "as far as possible", from digging in or injuring the ancient ruins at Zimbabwe. Patrols of two men, "starting early one morning and returning on the evening of the next day", were to be sent to examine the country on the Matabele side. "One man of each of these patrols should be able to speak Zulu well." Any information "of a considerable movement on the part of the Matabele" was to be sent forward without delay to headquarters — wherever that might be. "In getting information from the natives, the latter should be closely examined as to numbers, about which they are generally very inaccurate.

"You must do your best to prevent the destruction of big game in the country; you would probably do well to prohibit shooting large game within six or seven miles of the Fort. No traders or hunters should be allowed to shoot game merely for the skins. When the horses of your detachment are in good condition, you may permit men of the detachment to ride them out shooting. Each man will be allowed 10 rounds a month for sporting purposes. If you find that game is wantonly killed, or the meat not used, permission to shoot will be withdrawn."

There was to be one mounted and one dismounted parade every week, and frequent rifle practice when the supply of ammunition permitted, "particular attention being given to shooting at unknown distances between 200 and 400 yards ... The men should be encouraged to get up sweepstakes amongst themselves at target practices."

Leaving Captain Keith-Falconer and 'C' Troop to settle themselves into the routine of the first BSAC Police station at Fort Victoria, the column moved on over the relatively easy terrain of the highveld. But there were still rivers to cross, which were no less obstacles to the progress of the wagons simply because they ran through relatively open country. By the end of August the column had reached a point, close to the headwaters of the Sabi River, where it was decided to build yet another fort and leave another police troop as the last link in the line of communication with the projected destination at Mount Hampden, now less than 100 miles ahead. The fort was named Fort Charter, and the process of detaching a garrison, this time 'A' Troop under Captain Heyman, with

Lieutenants H.V. Brackenbury and the Hon. Eustace Fiennes, was repeated. Heyman (later Colonel Sir Melville Heyman) was the son of a General in the Royal Artillery and had been born at Gibraltar. He had come to South Africa in 1877 and served in the Cape Mounted Rifles for twelve years. He had served in numerous campaigns of the Kaffir Wars and was probably the least flamboyant and most able of the early officers of the BSAC Police. Even Leonard relaxes his usual critical manner and describes him as "a good officer with plenty of experience in South Africa".

The rest of the column, escorted now only by 'B' Troop under Captain Forbes and the Headquarters Staff, left Fort Charter on 3 September, and nine days later, on 12 September, reached the banks of the Makabusi River. Here they decided to halt and the site of the future capital of Rhodesia was chosen almost by impulse. It has been said that the kopje overlooking the vlei through which the Makabusi runs (which is the Kopje now overlooking the city), was mistaken for Mount Hampden, the acknowledged destination of the column; and that the mistake was probably caused by Mount Hampden having been marked on their maps ten miles too far to the east or west, whichever it was, as General Methuen had warned them. This is a pretty enough little story, but hardly likely to be true. Admittedly, Frank Johnson — who was difficult to get on with, to put it mildly — had had a row with Selous during the last stages of the march, and had struck him summarily off the roll of Company employees, so one assumes that Selous was no longer acting as the official guide. But there were others, such as Heany and Borrow — and even Johnson himself — who had been in the district before and they were unlikely to have made a mistake about which of the kopjes was Mount Hampden, the landmark which they themselves had established and marked on their maps.

So Johnson's order for the day, on 12 September 1890, formally stated, "It is notified for general information that the column, having arrived at its destination, will halt." Next day, the pioneers and police were paraded on a stony patch of open veld, which is now Cecil (Africa Unity) Square; the Union Jack was hoisted on a hurriedly rigged flagstaff cut from a msasa tree; prayers were led by Canon Francis Balfour, Chaplain of the BSAC Police; the site of yet another hastily constructed fort was named Fort Salisbury, after the Prime Minister of Great Britain; and Mashonaland had been formally and effectively occupied as a promising commercial enterprise by the British South Africa Company.

Within the next two weeks the pioneers were disbanded, to fan out over the surrounding countryside in search of the farms and mining claims they had been promised as part of their contracts, while 'B' Troop and the staff of the police established themselves in their first fixed headquarters, in wattle and daub huts, roofed with thatch and covered by hides "put on wet and securely fastened down" as the Regulations prescribed. A hundred miles back along the road, 'A' Troop had settled in at Fort Charter; another 100 miles away was 'C' Troop at Fort Victoria; and a further 200 miles, 'D' Troop at Fort Tuli still outside the country the force had been formed to serve; while, yet another 60 miles along the tenuous link with civilisation, 'E' Troop waited at Fort Matlaputla with ever-mounting impatience.

## Chapter Three

## UMTASA'S KRAAL

VICTOR MORIER, THE ambassador's son — six feet four and nearly 280 pounds — had arrived at Fort Matlaputla as a new recruit for 'E' Troop on 8 July, three days before the column had crossed the Shashi at Tuli on the start of its journey to Mashonaland. A colleague described him as "a very heavy man who considered that none of the troop horses, which were of the light South African type, were up to his weight, so he had been allowed to bring up with him from Kimberley two chargers which were really almost miniature Clydesdales". Morier was disappointed to find that, despite being a friend of one of the directors of the Company, he was not immediately sent to Tuli to be welcomed as an indispensable member of either 'A' or 'B' Troop, to join them on the push into Matabeleland. Nor did the conditions he found at Matlaputla fill him with much cheer. The authorities must have taken from him and sent on to Tuli the horses he had brought up with him, because he wrote to his mother, "'E' and 'D' Troops are left behind here as we have not a single horse yet. We depend absolutely on supplies sent up in ox-wagons from Kimberley, a road over 700 miles long. There is not a single experienced transport officer — everything at the mercy of tuppeny-ha'penny wagon drivers. Supplies are most erratic — not a glass, knife or fork to be got for love or money. Ten American cigarettes fetch as much as five shillings and you are lucky if you get a filthy pint of beer for two-and-sixpence." He had only been in camp one day when he wrote this, so he had lost no time in discovering the worst. "The whole route from Kimberley," he continued — admittedly with more personal experience of what he was saying but even so, one suspects, with a little exaggeration — "is strewn with dead and dying horses for want of food, water and (because of) the hurry with which they are being sent up to the front."

They were sleeping seven to a tent. "The men complain of the fearful amount of fatigue duty now that the other three troops have left ... I have done a drill at 6.30 this morning and am told off to a fatigue party for making new latrines this afternoon."

With no horses to ride themselves, they were nonetheless continually burdened with stables, as they were left with "all the sick horses of the Troops which have gone on". Fatigues included duty at Mother Patrick's hospital. "There are five Roman Catholic Sisters of Mercy in charge of it ... one gave me some milk and an egg, the first I've seen since Kimberley." His class-consciousness was still worrying him a little. "For a mercy there is hardly any alcohol of any kind served out, so things are quiet. But with the rough lot of men here, it would be dreadful if there was any drinking." A little later he was to write, "I think the Police an excellent body of men but a large percentage of them have never been on a horse in their lives and scores have never held a rifle."

To add insult to injury: "'D' Troop left on Saturday. It was heartbreaking for us to see them march off and we were left to strike their tents and clear up their lines." But 'D' Troop, of course, was going no farther than Tuli. "I see no prospect of getting into Matabeleland unless I can exchange into another Troop."

On 25 July he was still complaining that "the work since 'D' Troop left is simply appalling — I have had four 24-hour guards in the last week which means two nights in bed in the week". In an attempt to relieve the burden he volunteered as a signaller and was actually put under instruction. The telegraph line from the south stopped at Palapye; thence the BBP operated a heliograph system to Macloutsie and in August 1890 the BSACP established three posts, at 20 mile intervals, between Macloutsie and Tuli. The system was relatively reliable, although any thick morning mists naturally put it out of action. And later, when the weather was overcast, the service was sometimes suspended for days at a time. "A signaller," Morier wrote, "is sent off for a month at a time to a heliograph post where one is more or less one's own master and gets plenty of shooting ... Last night while on sentry go I heard a lion roaring quite close to camp. This," he admitted, "is rather an unusual occurrence. The big game has been frightened away from the immediate vicinity, though within 20 or 25 miles one can get plenty of wildebeeste, springbok and zebra."

The only alarm raised at Fort Matlaputla was when a prisoner, a BBP deserter, escaped from the guard tent in the middle of the night — "Grant, a very desperate character", Morier described him.

Leonard wrote in his diary, "it is evident he (Grant) has a screw loose, though I cannot agree with those who call him a lunatic". Sir John Willoughby had remained behind at Fort Matlaputla when the column moved on, to deal with Company's business, which appears to have been of more pressing urgency than his duties as Chief Staff Officer. Grant burst into his tent and held a loaded revolver — Willoughby's own — at his head and the Captain of the Blues was forced to hand over some of his property. However, when Grant tried to make him put on some clothes so that he could drag him outside as a hostage, Willoughby somehow raised the alarm and the guard turned out with loaded rifles and surrounded the tent. Grant managed to escape in the confusion and was only caught some days later after a long chase through the bush. "We have him bound hand and foot now," Morier reported; although in a later letter he said, "We have (him) in our guardroom as a close prisoner ... We know he means to break out again but dare not handcuff him till he uses violence which he is too cute to do."

Morier at last achieved his ambition of becoming a signaller. "I am up here in the fort," he wrote on 5 August, "8 hours a day telegraphing furiously." Some of the furious telegraphing must have been a little imaginative, for he said, "We hear this morning on good authority that all the Matabele regiments are leaving Bulawayo and moving south" — an item of intelligence that had little substance in fact. However, he was obviously in touch with the progress of the column. "Pennefather, with two Troops — 'A' and 'B' of the Police and the Pioneers, are about 150 miles across the Shashi River. 'C' Troop is following him, trying to catch him up. 'D' Troop is strongly fortifying itself at Tuli." It says a great deal for the heliograph system that such ready communication was maintained across the wilderness of Matabeleland. "As soon as we get our horses and stores," he went on hopefully, "we, 'E' Troop, are to move straight through to Mount Hampden. If there is a row we move on at once, horses or no ... P.S. I have been promoted to Lance Corporal and have reverted to regimental duty." Leonard writes that "the best man out and away that I have among the home-born is young Morier", and that he promoted him "because he has lots of influence with the men yet is a great favourite as he has such an excellent way with them". However, the promotion didn't get Morier completely off some hard work. "Yesterday afternoon," he wrote on 12 August, "I and another man branded 92 horses. We had some nasty vicious brutes among them. We are now fully provided with horses, such as they are." Then came another bitter blow. 28 August: "We had orders to leave this camp a fortnight ago but were only packed and ready yesterday. Half an hour before leaving a dispatch came ordering the Troop to stay here and send on the horses — we had 108 — to the Column as they had lost half theirs ... The whole Troop feels down on its luck, a sulkier, more grumbling and cursing lot of men you could not imagine." Indeed, it was during this month that Leonard, the officer commanding at Macloutsie, discharged three NCOs for insubordination and an attempt to stage a mutiny.

Morier moved on from the Macloutsie at last, on 19 September. Although the record isn't clear, it seems that the artillery, 'F' Troop, had now been set up, because he wrote on 21 September, "We arrived here (Fort Tuli) two nights ago and start again at 2 a.m. to-morrow en route for Fort Victoria ... we hear the Pioneers are to be disbanded on the 1st of next month and turned adrift in the country, and the Police to be reduced to a small standing army of which *my Artillery Troop* will be the nucleus." (Author's italics.) What the artillery consisted of is unknown, but from reports of later incidents it probably included one or more seven-pounder guns, which must have been carried by ox-wagon, as it would have been impracticable to drag them on their own carriages 400 miles through the bush.

The pioneers were certainly about to be disbanded and the scramble for gold claims in the new country would soon begin. Even the police had been promised a share in the booty; 100 claims to be shared among the officers and 50 claims for the NCOs and men in each troop. "Each Troop," wrote Morier, "is sending up five Troop-elected gold prospectors who are to make our fortunes in no time." "D Troop Mine", still working 60 years later near the Angwa River, in the Sinoia district, was pegged in the name of five troopers of 'D' Troop: W.C. Ingram (No. 253), F.T. Taylor (No. 466), G. Hughes (No. 457), F.J. Powrie (No. 460) and W.M. Taylor (No. 471), who all attested in February, March and April 1890.) Not that Morier had any urge to be one of the prospectors. "I am very thankful I am not a Pioneer. To be set adrift now, when Lobengula's death or overthrow would let loose all his amiable nation on us in a minute, does not seem inviting. The disbanding (of the pioneers), if true, seems very premature."

It appears that Morier left Fort Tuli with only a small party under Captain Lendy. Another large party of police did move up from Tuli later in the year, leaving on 12 December at the height of the rainy season, and the terrible conditions they experienced will be related later. However, the rains would not have started in earnest when Morier left in September, but even so he went down with fever shortly after leaving Tuli and had to be left at one of the post stations which had been established every 50 miles. "I was pretty bad for five days with a temperature of 104° to 106° but was restored by Warburg's tincture. This is the great remedy nowadays out here and its effects are certainly wonderful." After recovering, he caught up again with the party, whose speed was limited by its ox-wagons, and Captain Lendy allowed him to ride on ahead to Fort Victoria in case he had a relapse. Writing from the Lundi River, the accepted boundary between Matabeleland and Mashonaland, he said, "From Tuli to here is the most deadly stretch, both for man and horse. Victoria, being on the high veld, is considered much healthier." The road cut by the pioneers was still in reasonable condition, before the rains had come, but it was not particularly easy to follow at night because it was hardly worn at all and plenty of tree stumps had been left. At one of the post stations, a wagon brought in the body of a young member of the police who was a "post rider" carrying the mail from one station to the next. Morier had seen him earlier on the road. "The poor fellow was very bad with fever when I passed him (at Setoutse) three days ago." With moving simplicity Morier describes his death. "(When I was at Setoutse) I gave him all the quinine I had left. (After I had moved on) he was put by his companions into a passing wagon, hoping to get to Victoria, but he died just as he got here. We have just buried him. We made as deep a grave as we could by the roadside. I read the funeral service; there were only three of us and five niggers. The poor fellow's name was Bigg." (No. 121, attested 4 January 1900). "He belonged to 'C' Troop. I have carved a cross on a tree over the grave and put up a little fence. It looks very decent and the spot is very pretty."

Up to half a dozen police troopers operated as riders from each of the post stations, spread at 50-mile intervals all the way from Tuli to Fort Salisbury. The mail travelled each way weekly. When the pioneer column had arrived at Fort Salisbury on 12 September, Pennefather had sent off an official report to Rhodes the next morning and this arrived at Macloutsie, 490 miles away, at 10.30 a.m. on the 18th, only five days later. But as time went on the mail's reliability was handicapped by the dreadful toll of horse-sickness. Morier said, "The horses die suddenly half-way (between stations) and the men have to walk 20 or 30 miles, carrying the bags or abandoning them, according to their various constitutions." He said he had passed two post-stations on his way up "where the men were absolutely barefoot and not a boot to be got. There are thousands somewhere. I am riding bare-behinded, the seats of both my regulation breeches being through, and no stuff — needles or thread — to mend." Morier, for all his sense of superiority, was developing the truest attribute of a policeman: the ability to apportion the blame for everything on the ineptitude of higher authority. "All this could be easily avoided," he writes, "but there is mismanagement in many of these things." Rations, he reported, were scarce and he foresaw great hardship when the rains came and the post-stations would be cut off, with only a few days' food in stock. "The horses here are literally starving, there being no food except what they can pick up on the veld." No wonder there was dreadful mortality among the horses. Leonard subsequently wrote that during the 1890-91 rainy season 97% of the horses died. "I have seen some hundreds die," he said, "sometimes at the rate of 11 a week."

One of the enigmatic figures who had accompanied the pioneer column to Mashonaland was Rhodes's friend, Dr. Leander Starr Jameson. Jameson was a contemporary of Rhodes in age and had come to Kimberley 10 years before to practise as a doctor. He had been caught up in Rhodes's enthusiasms for the adventure to the north and had played a considerable, if dubious, part in the negotiations with Lobengula. He was a town-bred man and had never been on a horse until he arrived in Kimberley, but by the time he rode with the column into Mashonaland he had already spent literally weeks in the saddle. The main enigma about him was his position with the column. The official chain of command was clear enough: Major Frank Johnson, by virtue of his signed contract with Rhodes, was responsible for the expedition, but militarily under the overall command of Colonel Pennefather. Although this was a situation which had its anomalies, and caused a great deal of bitterness on Johnson's part, the division of responsibilities between them was nevertheless quite clear.

Jameson's position, on the other hand, was totally undefined. He held Rhodes's Power of Attorney, which meant in effect that he carried the authority of the Company to which Johnson was under contract, and he was presumably in a position to negotiate with Johnson any variations in the terms of contract that might seem desirable. He represented the financial control of the expedition and, as later events were to show, he was not above using his arbitrary powers to involve the Company in all sorts of embarrassing commitments. However, he never actually interfered with the pioneer expedition itself , perhaps only because neither the need or temptation to interfere happened to present itself.

But Jameson had unquestionable control of any political considerations that might arise. He was more or less a politician accompanying an army — with all the dangerous possibilities this implies. Later — probably when he had gained more confidence — he was in the habit of taking military command of any expedition he accompanied, assuming unto himself the right to outrank even senior officers and relegating them to the status of mere military advisers.

When the column reached Fort Charter he had decided to embark on a purely political foray. No doubt he had worked out the whole scheme with Rhodes before he left, but it seems unlikely that the idea, with its dangerous international implications, had had the blessing of the Imperial authorities. One of the civilians with the column was Mr. Archibald Colquhoun, who was destined to become the Administrator, or chief executive, of the Company's new territory as soon as it was occupied. Colquhoun had been an official of the Indian Civil Service, but he had been suspended from duty after putting a letter, which severely criticised his superiors in the service, in the wrong envelope. Consequently the letter had found its way to the India Office in London, to be read by the very people it criticised. Luckily for him, this appealed to Rhodes's strange sense of values and he gave Colquhoun the new job in Mashonaland.

From Fort Charter, Jameson had taken Colquhoun and Selous, whose services Frank Johnson had abruptly terminated, with two other civilian officials and a small police escort, on a little expedition of his own. When Jameson asked Johnson if he could spare Selous, Johnson sat down without a word and wrote out a peremptory order saying, "Captain Selous, having resigned his commission this day, is struck off the strength of the regiment accordingly".

Their destination was the kraal of Umtasa, paramount chief of Manicaland — the territory lying between Mashonaland and Portuguese-occupied Moçambique — with whom Jameson intended to negotiate a so-called treaty of friendship which would, incidentally, make over the whole of Manicaland to the BSA Company. The site of Umtasa's kraal was later to become the original Umtali (Mutare) — that is to say, today's Old Umtali, west of the foot of Christmas Pass, close to where the road to Inyanga branches off the Salisbury road. Jameson himself never reached the kraal, for he broke a couple of ribs in a riding accident on the way and had to be carried painfully back to Fort Charter on an improvised stretcher. He left Colquhoun to carry out the negotiation with Umtasa on the Company's behalf.

Umtasa's kraal was some 150 miles from Fort Charter, across easy riding country. When the party reached it, Colquhoun concluded a treaty with the chief which ceded all the mineral and agricultural rights in Manicaland to the Company. In exchange for these not inconsiderable rights the Company generously undertook to provide Umtasa with protection from the Portuguese and an annual payment in gold of 100 pounds.

The Portuguese equivalent to the BSA Company, the Moçambique Company, operated some mines in the Revue River valley and their local headquarters were at Macequece, some 20 miles eastward over the Penhalonga Mountains. The Portuguese had been in Moçambique for 300 years; and having penetrated Manicaland from time to time, although they had never made any effective settlement so far inland, they regarded the area very much as their own preserve. Umtasa had been living amicably with them all his life. In fact, it was only thanks to Colquhoun's activities that the need for any protection was likely to arise. And the task of providing that protection now fell on Trooper Trevor of the BSAC Police, left by himself at Umtasa's kraal. (There were two Troopers Trevor in 'B' Troop, R. Trevor (No. 69) and J. Trevor (No. 70), presumably brothers. The record does not make it clear which this was.)

Colquhoun and the rest of the party had returned to Fort Charter and Trevor was officially named the Intelligence Representative of the British South Africa Company, which was a remarkable role for a young trooper in the police. Jonas, a Cape boy, was left with him and fortunately they were both good Zulu linguists. Trevor seems to have carried out his intelligence duties remarkably effectively because he managed to send a message, which was received by Colquhoun in Fort Salisbury on 22 October, that the Portuguese were up to no good, and the particulars of his message subsequently proved to be quite correct.

Colquhoun was now in Salisbury, formally installed as the Administrator, bearing on his somewhat inadequate shoulders all the responsibility for the Company's affairs in the new territory. Leonard's description of Colquhoun was that he was "clever, but weak".

(Almost immediately after the column had halted, and the pioneers had been disbanded, Jameson and Frank Johnson had left on a short expedition of their own, eastward through Portuguese territory to Beira, ostensibly to survey a more convenient route to Salisbury from the sea than the 2000 miles from Cape Town. It was an epic journey, even though it accomplished nothing more than to prove that the Indian Ocean was right where it was supposed to be. Within a few months Jameson turned up again in Mashonaland with new ideas for negotiations with African chiefs in Portuguese territory, which will be covered later. But meanwhile Colquhoun was on his own.)

Trevor's message from Umtasa's kraal reported that Portuguese forces, under a provocative Goanese named Manuel Antonio de Suza — aka Gouveia — were concentrating at Macequece; and that, accompanied by the Moçambique Company's principal agent, Baron de Rezende, and the military commandant, Colonel d'Andrade, Gouveia intended to move to Umtasa's kraal and force the chief to repudiate the rights he had given to the BSA Company.

Colquhoun hurriedly sent off Lyons-Montgomery (No. 1), Troop Sergeant-Major of 'B' Troop, with 10 troopers to join Trevor at Umtasa's kraal. The party, accompanied by a scotch-cart carrying supplies, followed the route which the road and railway from Salisbury to Umtali generally follow today. The journey took them only five days and brought them to the chief's kraal on 30 October. One is constantly amazed today at the accuracy and speed with which these early travellers moved across unmapped and unfamiliar country. Trevor had already built himself a hut at the base of the kopje on top of which Umtasa, like all canny African chiefs who lived in constant fear of attack — had established his kraal, and the new party of police pitched their camp nearby. Meanwhile, on 27 October, Lieutenant Graham, the adjutant of the BSAC Police, left Salisbury to catch up the party and take command, on the understanding that he would be followed by Captain (recently promoted to Major) Forbes, who was now acting as Commandant. (Pennefather was in South Africa on leave — he had passed through Macloutsie as early as 30 October and did not return to Salisbury until the following January). Forbes, accompanied by Lieutenant S. Shepstone, arrived at Umtasa's on 1 November. Captain Heyman (also now a Major) was ordered to send Lieutenant E.W. Fiennes, and as many of 'A' Troop as were available at short notice, across to Umtasa's from Fort Charter, and to follow himself with stores and transport, as soon as he could be ready. In the event, Heyman himself does not seem to have gone to Umtasa's kraal on this occasion. His lieutenant, the Hon. Eustace Fiennes, who went off with those men who were available, had not been a regular soldier. He was the son of a lord and had been a member of the London Stock Exchange, although he had served, by some unexplained circumstances, in the Canadian Militia.

A formidable force was gathering — although with four officers, including Forbes, and a troop sergeant major, it appears to have been somewhat top-heavy. But Colquhoun was worried. He believed he had secured Manicaland for the Company and now the prize was in danger of being snatched from him. Thus it came about that the first emergency to be dealt with by the Company's police — in the new territory in which the force had been formed to preserve law and order and carry out the normal duties of a police force — had nothing to do with crime or even internal security, but was concerned solely with Rhodes's political machinations.

Victor Morier, moving on from Fort Victoria with Captain Lendy and two guns, had just arrived at Fort Charter when the orders came for 'A' Troop to go to Umtasa's kraal. His boyhood with his father as a British ambassador at various cities in Europe had made him an accomplished linguist, and his ability to speak Portuguese had apparently been noted at the Company's headquarters, for he says, "At Fort Charter I received a dispatch from Mr. Colquhoun ordering me to go to Umtasa's kraal as fast as I could." One assumes that this mention of "dispatch" referred to the orders sent to Major Heyman, for it was unlikely, even in those days, that the Administrator would send an order directly to a mere police trooper. Morier left immediately and with one other trooper he covered the 150 miles to Umtasa's in five and a half days. "We lived on monkey-nuts and boiled rice, having started with only two days' rations ... I am here (at Umtasa's) with nothing but one horse blanket and a toothbrush, a dirty white shirt, bottomless breeches and sole-less boots and a patrol cap." One suspects that some of his letters home were so written as to make an heroic impression on his parents. He made one pertinent observation, however. "Manica is undoubtedly Portuguese, but the Company on the strength of a treaty made by Mr. Colquhoun with Umtasa have determined to annex the place, make a rush to the coast and gain possession of a seaport." When the events which followed are taken into account, together with Morier's excellent assessment, it is difficult to believe that the purpose of Colquhoun's drastic concentration of police on the Portuguese border was limited to securing Manicaland for the Company.

Forbes and Shepstone had reached Umtasa's kraal from Salisbury on 5 September, a couple of days before Morier's arrival. (With Forbes and Pennefather now both away from Salisbury, acting command of the police force seems to have fallen to Lieutenant C.W.P. Slade of 'B' Troop.) Next morning Forbes sent Graham, Lyons-Montgomery and a trooper to Macequece. With the help of native guides, they crossed the Umtali River, over the Penhalonga range of mountains and along tracks which were all but impassable even for led horses. They carried a letter to Colonel d'Andrade, the military commandant, saying that the BSA Company would oppose, with force if necessary, any move of Portuguese forces towards Umtasa's kraal. It was a blatant threat by representatives of one European power — however indirect their authority — against those of another. However, d'Andrade was away when Graham arrived and Graham was received in the Portuguese Fort at Macequece with surprising hospitality by Baron de Rezende, who gave him lunch and introduced him to Gouveia. The circumstances must have seemed incongruous to Graham, who had joined the BSA Company's forces to serve as a policeman and now found himself as a supposed emissary of Britain taking lunch with a nobleman in a fortress in a foreign country. The Baron graciously sent some food out to Lyons-Montgomery and the trooper, who were bivouaced outside the Fort, down by the river. D'Andrade returned just before sundown. When Graham handed him the letter, d'Andrade opened it and said politely that he would give his answer in writing after dinner, and they all sat down to another lavish meal. But d'Andrade seemed to be in no hurry to reply to the letter and Graham left the Fort to spend the night with his companions, after having been told by d'Andrade that the answer would not be ready until six o'clock next morning.

When Graham was summoned to the Fort at dawn next morning, d'Andrade said he had read the letter but he found its contents so absurd that it merited neither reply nor even consideration. "If I chose," he said provocatively, "with one sweep of my hand I could wipe you all out of Mashonaland."

Graham and his party returned to Umtasa's kraal, where all seemed peaceful enough until the afternoon of 10 November, when Gouveia arrived with 200 armed native troops in the gorge on the far, eastern side of the kraal, from which the police were camped. Umtasa and his people were perched on the kopje between the two forces. Not that there was any comparison between the strengths of the two forces. In addition to Forbes, Graham, Shepstone and Lyons-Montgomery, there were only 14 troopers. Fiennes, with his party, was still on his way from Fort Charter, struggling to drag his wagons across the Odzi River.

At 8pm on the 10th, Forbes sent Graham with a letter to Gouveia and although its contents are not on record the letter presumably ordered him to withdraw his force on the strength of the treaty between Colquhoun and Umtasa. Graham took four hours looking for Gouveia and ultimately found him in a hut at the top of the kraal. Gouveia said, "I have come here in my own right and no Englishman will turn me out." Once more, Graham found himself in an unexpected situation for a policeman and he was forced to return, a little dejectedly, to Forbes.

Next day, Umtasa sent an appeal to Forbes for advice. Gouveia, he said, was threatening him and he reminded Forbes of Colquhoun's promise of protection. Forbes, who was playing for time until Fiennes arrived, advised Umtasa to do the same and to avoid discussion with the Portuguese for as long as he could. Forbes was sure, and he was proved right, that d'Andrade and Rezende would be joining Gouveia to apply pressure on Umtasa.

On the 12th, Fiennes rode into Forbes's camp with 25 troopers, and later that day Forbes received very welcome unofficial reinforcements in the shape of Captain Hoste, a merchant seaman, Lieutenant Tyndale-Biscoe of the Royal Navy and two other footloose pioneers who had come from Salisbury, suitably armed, to enjoy the fun. With 48 officers and other ranks, including the civilians, Forbes — whom Leonard had unkindly described as "the typical British bull-dog, with as much brains" — now felt no hesitation in challenging Gouveia and his men. He sent a message to Umtasa telling him to invite the Portuguese to an indaba in his hut the next day.

Morier was with the party now. He had arrived with his companion on the 11th. It was intended that he would act as interpreter to the Portuguese, but as events turned out there was to be very little talking. In his letters home he described the assault which Forbes launched on the 13th. "The Portuguese were comfortably installed up in Umtasa's kraal holding indabas with him and threatening him with extermination for having made treaties with us. Their band of armed bearers — 200 — were encamped at the bottom of the hill. They had ordered Umtasa to attack us if we made any move against them but we were too smart and sudden for them. Ten of us made a sudden raid up into the kraal, while the remainder disarmed the bearers at the bottom of the hill. We had an awful climb. It was two o'clock with a blazing sun and the kraal about 300 feet up perched on perpendicular rocks. The niggers couldn't make out what we were after and were luckily too surprised to barricade the narrow little gates in the stockade, through which one has to creep on all fours. We seized the Portuguese (d'Andrade, Rezende and Gouveia), pulled down their flag and proceeded to clear out as fast as we could. The niggers had flown to arms the moment they had recovered from their astonishment and were dancing round us shouting furiously and waving their assegais and brandishing their guns. There must have been over 1000. I am convinced, had we not got straight away, in another two minutes we would have been massacred. We were only saved by Doyle who has an extraordinary power over natives. I was considerably relieved," he added, "when I crept through the narrow hole and was outside the kraal." Reference to Doyle was presumably to Dennis Doyle, one of the irregulars who had joined in the escapade from choice. He had served as an interpreter in the pre-pioneer negotiations with Lobengula. Lobengula had once said, "All white men are liars, but Doyle is the father of all liars." Leonard called him "Doyle, the ubiquitous — here one day, somewhere else the next — and God knows where the day after."

Forbes himself placed the Portuguese officials under arrest. Someone present at the time said afterwards, "It was very amusing to see him chasing d'Andrade round the hut, the latter declaring that no Englishman would take him alive." However, they were secured at last and charged with "intriguing and conspiring with natives in a British territory" a crime that would be hard to trace in any statute law. Possibly in appreciation of the hospitality which the Baron had shown to Graham at the Macequece Fort, Forbes released Rezende "on parole" — whatever that meant. He sent d'Andrade and Gouveia under escort to Salisbury, whence they were escorted further south by Sub-Lieutenant M.H.G. Mundell, No. 362, of 'B' Troop. Mundell was an ex-Life Guardsman, six feet four inches tall, noted for his spick-and-span appearance in any circumstances — his Christian names were Marmaduke Howell Gwynne, no less. During the journey south with his prisoners, at the poststation at Semelale which was half-way between Tuli and Macloutsie, Mundell happened to meet Dr. Jameson who was returning to Salisbury after his expedition to the Indian Ocean (whence he had been taken to Cape Town by a steamer which had miraculously picked him and Johnson up when their canoe was struggling with an adverse tide, into which they had been swept, off the mouth of the Pungwe River).

Leonard, then commanding at Macloutsie, happened also to be standing talking to Jameson when Mundell turned up with his prisoners. "D'Andrade," wrote Leonard, "is not unlike a dark-skinned dancing master." D'Andrade refused to speak to Jameson but, working himself up to a pitch of excitement he told Leonard, in good English, that "he knew Mr.Gladstone and that he had great influence in European courts, which he intended to exert to the utmost". Gouveia, who was wearing striped pyjamas, simply burst into tears and pleaded for release. Jameson, exercising his still undefined authority, ordered Mundell to release the prisoners, and, although Mundell continued with them as far as Kimberley, they were allowed to proceed without further duress to Cape Town where the incident had assumed international proportions and they were duly feted as heroes. In fact, the Governor-General's train had been sent up to Kimberley to fetch them.

The only casualty of the raid on Umtasa's kraal was Trooper F.D.A. Payne (No. 57) also of 'B' Troop, who had been deputed to haul down the Portuguese flag which had been raised in front of the chief's hut and to substitute the Company's flag. The top of the flag-pole — which had probably been improvised somewhat hastily when Gouveia had arrived — broke off, falling on Payne's head and knocking him out. (Payne subsequently became a well-known miner in the Gwanda district. Although his number was 57, he had attested as early as 22 November, 1889.)

**Chapter Four**

**UNORTHODOX OPERATIONS**

HAVING HUMILIATED D'ANDRADE, Rezende and Gouveia, Forbes moved his whole force forward to Macequece. Lyons-Montgomery and Morier had been sent ahead to reconnoitre and they marched boldly into Macequece and told the Portuguese corporal and one private, who had remained as the garrison, that they had occupied it. Lyons-Montgomery went back to tell Forbes that the way was clear, leaving Morier, as he says, "for 24 hours as Commandant and army of occupation". Seven Spaniards and several Frenchmen who were employees of the Moçambique Company came to visit him, "all delighted to find somebody who talked their native tongue". Next day, all the English prospectors in the district turned up too, "so we had a great meeting of white men".

A few days later, Forbes, Lyons-Montgomery and Morier, with seven other troopers, left Macequece for the coast, 150 miles away, with the grand intention of occupying Portuguese East Africa — which had been a Portuguese colony for 300 years — and securing a seaport at Beira for the BSA Company. Again, it was a somewhat unusual assignment for a posse of policemen, operating outside the territory they had been attested to serve. It was also a little unorthodox to send 10 men to occupy a country the size of Italy. But there can be little doubt that this buccaneering expedition had been in Colquhoun's mind from the moment he sent Forbes with a considerable concentration of police to Umtasa's kraal; indeed, the whole idea of extending the Company's possessions to the coast must have been behind Jameson's original foray from Fort Charter into Manicaland. Morier's report, already quoted, of Colquhoun's determination "to annex the place, make a rush to the coast and gain possession of a seaport", is sufficient to show that the intention was common knowledge among the pioneers and police. Even Leonard, while still at Macloutsie, had believed that the official policy was to open up an alternative route to the east coast, because he had seen an urgent heliographed message to Pennefather saying, "Rhodes says it is useless to attempt opening via Tete or Zambezi. If you have men, start making road via Pungwe Bay." And The Times correspondent, a Mr. Beauman, must have known about it too, for he attached himself to Forbes's party and even continued beyond Macequece into Moçambique. Sadly, he was killed and eaten by a lion when hanging back modestly behind his companions to answer a call of nature and one, probably hyperbolical, report of his tragic end has it that all that was found of him were his boots with his feet still in them. Nor was he the only victim of lions. Trooper W.S. Mason· (No. 437) is also on record as having been taken, but the actual circumstances are unrecorded.

As usual, Morier's description of his experiences on the journey eastward from Macequece has an heroic twist. "We had an awful forced march, 80 miles on horseback, then 110 miles on foot, 25 to 30 miles a day in the tropical sun, I almost barefoot, my back raw from the sun owing to the holes in my shirt. Nothing to eat most of the way until we got into the game region, but kaffir corn. On the Pungwe River, hippopotami and crocodiles in hundreds. Herds of buffalo, hartebeest, antelope, zebras, etc. positively blocking the road. We saw several lions and unfortunately lost (Trooper) Mason" He makes no mention of Beauman. "When we were within 50 miles of the coast we were stopped by a dispatch from the Administrator and had to tramp back."

Colquhoun, it seems, was growing nervous. If he had ever supported a "rush to the coast" he had now changed his mind. Forbes had written to him on 22 November, just as he was setting off from Macequece. "By carrying out the programme we have decided on we shall secure the north bank of the Pungwe, all the country between the Pungwe and Busi and all the necessary seaboard." But despite his previous keenness for an adventure to the east, the Administrator now realised that Forbes was in danger of overreaching himself, politically and strategically. He gave orders for Forbes to be recalled and Trooper Arnold (No. 10) was sent off after him. "I started off," Arnold wrote later, "with a tin of bully beef, eight biscuits and an indifferent horse ... When I arrived at Umtasa's both I as well as the poor beast were quite knocked up ... I discovered that Major Forbes had left a few hours previously for the coast. Another dispatch rider was immediately sent after him." The new dispatch rider must have travelled fast to catch up Forbes's party in the conditions described by Morier, because a week later Forbes wrote again, from a point where he had struck the Pungwe River, "Your dispatch caught me up here and only just in time to stop me going down the Pungwe. It is a great disappointment to the men being stopped just at the last moment."

For the time being, that was the end of Rhodesia's first bid for a seaport. Forbes, a trifle crestfallen, returned to Salisbury leaving Lieutenant Shepstone, with 10 troopers, literally holding the Fort at Macequece. "I am staying here (too)," said Morier, "as interpreter and clerk." He added, "Baron Rezende (who had been released on some mythical parole after his arrest at Umtasa's kraal) has cleared off to the coast with all his employees. He is going to Lisbon to raise the devil there."

Back at Fort Tuli in the emptiness of the "disputed territory", a considerable settlement, almost a small town, was beginning to grow. 'D' Troop under Captain Chamley Turner was preparing to move on into Mashonaland and on 15 December 'E' Troop under Captain Leonard came up from Fort Matlaputla, leaving the BBP to maintain the line of communication through Bechuanaland. With none of the BSAC Police left on the Macloutsie, Tuli was now the southernmost station of the force, to which new recruits reported from Kimberley and from where those with no inclination to stay any longer were discharged. Leonard, who had once described the early recruits to the force as "peers and waifs of humanity mingling together like the ingredients of a hotch-potch", was beginning to take a less jaundiced view, at any rate of his own Troop. "All hard seasoned men," he describes them, "in the prime of manhood. Most of them are Afrikanders who have lived in the open veld all their lives, who can shoot straight, ride well, and keep their wits about them. Unfortunately, as mounted infantry they are too tall and too heavy and whoever enlisted them as such is much to blame. Many of them are Colonials," he goes on, somewhat contradictorily, "born of English, Scots and Irish parents who came out and settled some 30 or 40 years ago in Natal and the Cape. Some came out as youngsters on their own hook. A goodly number are Dutch and Huguenot descent and the minority are recent arrivals from England and America." It is difficult to decide, from Leonard's summary, who were in the majority.

Tuli was the main point of entry to the Company's territory, and Chief Khama of the Bamangwato tribe in Bechuanaland was persuaded by the Imperial authorities to cede to the Company the land contained within a radius of ten miles from the site of the fort. This area, known-as the Tuli Circle (it is really only a semi-circle, as its central point at the fort is almost on the bank of the Shashi River) was now proclaimed as a cordon sanitaire from which all but the Company's cattle and all native settlement — were excluded to prevent the possible spread of rinderpest. Its cession by Khama also gave to the Company its first formal title to occupy the land in the way it had already been occupying it blatantly for months. The Tuli Circle still remains Zimbabwean territory to this day, intruding provocatively into Botswana. By this arrangement, the police at Fort Tuli at last found themselves legally within the country they were attested to serve.

The first ceremonial parade in the history of the police (as distinct from the parade at Fort Salisbury on 13 September in which the pioneers had participated as well as the police) was held on 18 October 1890, while Fort Tuli was still primarily a police camp and before the township had started to grow. On that earlier occasion the pioneers, impatient to be discharged from their military constraints, had not behaved in a particularly ceremonial manner. Now, important visitors had arrived: the great Rhodes himself; Sir Henry Loch, Governor of the Cape Colony and British High Commissioner in South Africa; Lord Elphinstone, his aide-de-camp; Sir Graham Bower, official secretary; Major Sapte, the military secretary; prominent members of the Afrikaner Bond and of the Cape Legislative Assembly; and the Governor's son with his tutor. It would have been an impressive assembly if there had been anyone besides the local giraffe to witness it. Sir Henry Loch, representing the Queen, inspected the parade which was commanded by Captain Leonard and consisted of three officers, five sergeants and all of 49 rank and file. One assumes the parade was concluded by a march-past — a part of the ceremony that could hardly have been described as prolonged. The dusty, stony ground at the foot of the fort kopje was not particularly conducive to military precision — remember, they had no horses — but the great men seem to have been satisfied and Leonard later described the troops as "beautifully sized ... they looked a splendid lot in their serviceable kit and smasher hats, looped up at one side by a silver badge, which showed marked signs of wear and tear and made them appear all the fitter and more shipshape." Whether, when the formalities were over, Rhodes actually intended to travel on into his new country is not clear, but the report has it that he was dissuaded from doing so owing to the approach of the rainy season.

Leonard's comments on Rhodes are interesting. "My first impression of him is not at all favourable and I must confess to a feeling of genuine disappointment ... A big, heavy looking carelessly dressed man, not unlike a Dutch farmer, with an awkward slouching figure and a dull, rather expressionless face, who talks in a curious dreamy way as if he was half asleep and was taking no interest in what he was saying and was thinking of something totally different." But later: "I am already beginning to alter my mind and to think he is very deep, for under that dull exterior which is but a mask he is continually taking in all around and about him ..."

In the orderly room, Leonard showed Rhodes a letter from Dr. Rutherfoord Harris (Rhodes' secretary in Kimberley) countermanding an order sent from Macloutsie for supplies for the dry canteen. "On my explaining that the order did not include liquor," Leonard says, "he took it from me and glanced at it, deliberated for a minute or two, then wrote in pencil across the margin "Kindly execute order" and signed his name."

Rhodes complained to Leonard that the horses were being ridden too hard by the police on the dispatch service. Leonard said Harris had given him positive orders, in Rhodes's name, to carry urgent dispatches "at the expense of horseflesh and at all risk". Rhodes said angrily, "Harris has no right to give such orders. You must warn the men to ride quietly and cautiously, as I don't want the horses ridden to death." Leonard concluded that there was nothing humane in Rhodes's concern for the horses, but that his anxiety arose "from the sound principle of hard and practical commonsense".

In this context of meeting the senior officials of the Company, Leonard's exchanges with Dr. Jameson a few weeks later (when Jameson was passing up-country, on the occasion when he ordered Sub-Lieutenant Mundell to release d'Andrade and Gouveia) are equally interesting. Jameson told Leonard of grand plans for a service of stern-wheelers run by the Company plying regularly up the Pungwe River from Beira, declaring this would all be happening by next April (this was in December 1890). The river was navigable for 100 miles from its mouth, whereafter an equally regular service of coaches would carry passengers and mail to Salisbury. Jameson clearly expected that the Company would have taken over the Portuguese territory by then, in spite of the disappointing outcome of Forbes's first attempt. Leonard says, "He told me he did not think there would be any (more) fighting with the Portuguese and that the complications about Manica would be settled amicably." Events were to prove Jameson a little over-ambitious.

On the same occasion Jameson told Leonard that Pennefather should not have gone on leave as soon as the column arrived in Salisbury — just when the dispute with the Portuguese had erupted. Rhodes, he admitted, had given the Colonel leave. "That's Rhodes all over. He never can say 'No'."

Not only had the Officer Commanding gone off at this critical time, but the Chief Staff Officer, Willoughby, had also been allowed to go on leave to England. Although Leonard may not have been so directly outspoken to Jameson himself, he nevertheless wrote in his diary at the time, "If Pennefather's absence is immoral, Willoughby's is equally so. Neither of them should have been allowed to leave his duties either on public or private grounds, and as one (Pennefather) went to see his wife and the other (Willoughby) presumably to raise syndicates, they ought to have been obliged to resign their respective positions in the Police." No wonder that Leonard's diaries, when they were published as a book called How we made Rhodesia, had to be withdrawn from circulation under threat of libel actions.

Later, when Pennefather returned to duty, Leonard wrote, "I hear from many sources that Colquhoun and Pennefather do not hit it off. Colquhoun, according to Pennefather, assumes too much power and tries to command the Corps and (Pennefather), naturally, resents it. To a certain extent this is not to be wondered at as Pennefather has been away so long. Whatever Colquhoun's faults, it is excessively bad form of the Commandant of the Force to openly criticise the Administrator, but I am not surprised at this as a man who will speak to his officers as I have heard him and publicly censure them before their own men is not fit to command a regiment, no matter what his other qualifications may be."

Leonard had another visitor at about the same time: Frank Johnson. Reference has already been made about Johnson's criticism, which he poured forth to Leonard, on this same occasion, of the formation adopted by the pioneer column and its escort on the march, and Pennefather's fear that the flanking parties would get lost. And in recording Johnson's further remarks one must again take into account his bitterness at being outranked by Pennefather in command of the column. During the

march, he told Leonard, all the police officers were at loggerheads, "Pennefather varying the performance by pitching into all of them, especially Slade and Heyman. In fact, cliques and squabbles were
quite the order of the day, and the feature of the march; and at Victoria, where we halted for some days
and Pennefather went out shooting, he had to take Willoughby with him because Forbes and Heyman
refused to serve under him." Johnson described Willoughby as "always interfering in everything,
teaching, or rather trying to teach, men who had known how to form laager when he was in the
nursery".

From September and October onwards, Tuli continued to grow. During the winter months in June
and July 1890, when the column had been assembling, the days had been cool, the nights cold, with
light frost in the mornings. There were frequent dust-storms when a strong wind blew from the east.
But when the rains came and the rivers in Matabeleland and Mashonaland started to come down in
flood, making the road impassable, would-be new settlers by the score, with their wagons and
animals, were held up there for weeks at a time. Mr. Cran Cook (Director of the Historical Monuments
Commission in the 1970s and one time member of the BSAP) said, "In one period of three months
over 1000 people are said to have gone through (Tuli); taking even 10 people to the wagon, that would
mean 1600 oxen plus possibly 100 or so horses ... at times there must have been somewhere in the
region of 3000 to 4000 animals being grazed for indefinite periods at Tuli. The area of grazing would
have been limited because of the danger of attack by the Matabele and also because lion were
common there."

As Tuli grew, its amenities — primitive as they were — grew with it. A barber's shop, a baker's
shop, a billiard saloon, a blacksmith, a wheelwright and a soda-water factory, even a newspaper, The
Tuli Times — all these were to come in due course. Leonard acted as the local magistrate, without
any legal authority and no legal training. He describes his first case when the manager of the
Bechuanaland Trading Association laid a charge of assault against one of his white assistants, whom
he had discharged. With Solomonic balance of justice, Leonard ruled that although the accused was
no longer an employee, the manager was still to provide him with board and lodging, but he was not
to enter the BTA store or he would be turned out of the camp. The actual assault, apparently, went
unpunished. Leonard says, "The cream of the whole thing lies in the fact that we are under no law
here and I hold no magisterial power, but law and order must be maintained so I try to administer the
law of commonsense as best I can."

But this is looking a little farther ahead. On 12 December 1890, Captain Chamley-Turner was
ordered to leave Fort Tuli with 'D' Troop, for Fort Charter to reinforce 'A' Troop, which had been
heavily reduced in strength by its contribution to the Portuguese excursion. It seems, also, that the life
of 'F' Troop, the so-called artillery, had been short-lived and, instead of supporting Heyman at Fort
Charter, most of its members had been dispersed between the post stations as dispatch riders.

By the time 'D' Troop was ready to move from Tuli, on 16 December, the rains had started in
earnest. The conditions it faced were said to "make the march of the pioneer column appear like a
picnic". One member of the party, Lieutenant R.P.J. Codrington, wrote, "We left Tuli on December
16th, the men in ragged uniforms and worn-out boots, although it was known that many of them
would have to do the 240 miles to Fort Charter (it was nearer 300) on foot as 50% of the horses had
died. There was no doctor nor any medicine except a few ounces of quinine and only 10 days' food.
We were all put on half rations within the first week."

Even the Shashi was flooded and the wagons had to be manhandled across the river with the water
up to their boards. The road was deep in mud. Owing to the shortage of food, the column had to move
on whenever the rain chanced to stop, day or night. The ground was too soft to hold tent-pegs, so the
men had to sleep in the open. They somehow crossed six flooded rivers and finally came to the Lundi
on 31 December.

The troop reached the Lundi at eleven o'clock one morning. They were running short of food and
were still 30 miles from Fort Victoria. But it was a fine, sunny day and the rains had temporarily
abated, at least in the immediate vicinity. The river was running strongly and, at the drift cut by the
original column, the water was only about three feet deep. However, by three o'clock, when the troop
had completed its preparations for a crossing, the river, fed by heavy rains upstream, had risen to a
rushing torrent, at least seven feet deep.

One of the troop's corporals was C.F.H. Divine (No. 358, later Lieutenant-Colonel Divine, DSO,

VD). Divine has been described as "fiery, impulsive, yet full of initiative", and this last attribute was certainly to be displayed at the Lundi crossing. He happened to be "the champion swimmer of Table Bay" (his own description), whatever that implied. He went some distance upstream along the river-bank, leading his horse on a good length of rope. Then he "took off" into the stream, as he described it, "while the horse was 'persuaded' by my comrades to follow me". Fortunately he had judged the speed of the current well, for he reached the north bank right at the ford. A trooper in charge of the poststation on the north bank was waiting to welcome him and he took Divine's horse while the latter swam back across the river to repeat the process. That afternoon Divine made half a dozen crossings, "the last one nearly finishing me". Other swimmers in the troop followed his example and even some of the non-swimmers braved the torrent, riding on the backs of their horses. By dark, all the mounted men had crossed, not one of them washed downstream, and they spent the night drying themselves and their clothes before a spectacular bonfire.

The river was still running hard the next morning, even though the water level had dropped by some feet. Between them, Divine and Sergeant C.E. Judge (No. 417) improvised an enterprising method of bringing the rest of the men and the ammunition across. They tied together a series of tent ropes and ox reims to make a light line, long enough to span the river. Then one of them, with the line looped over his shoulders, swam across to the other side. A heavy rope was attached to the line and he pulled this over and secured it to a tree. The troops then emptied three 64-gallon barrels of lime-juice — supplied, presumably, as an antidote to scurvy — and lashed the barrels to tent-poles to form a three-cornered raft. They lashed more tent-poles to the barrels to make a floor and fixed thereon a packing case which had contained saddlery, to carry supplies. The raft, as Divine said, "floated beautifully", and it was attached to the heavy rope by a reim. The first load which was pulled across was made up principally of tents, and the improvised ferry operated "at high pressure, from dawn to dusk". Other troopers took the transport oxen upstream and drove them protesting into the water, while the more intrepid swimmers plunged in on the downstream side and splashed about noisily to dissuade the oxen from breaking away and returning to the bank. Finally, the wagons were hauled across by the heavy rope. It is a fitting commentary on the strength of their construction that the heavy wagons of those days stood up, as always, to the buffeting to which they were subjected by the flood of water and the uneven road surface at the bottom of the drift.

Having crossed the Lundi, the troop took two or three days to sort itself out and put the transport in order again. Then they resumed their journey, to be faced with the Tokwe River before they came to Fort Victoria. The Tokwe had two channels, one fairly shallow and one that could be classed as deep. Divine made the first crossing of the deep channel in the dark, with four Cape natives who could swim. The Tokwe already had a bad reputation for crocodiles, but the natives for once showed no fear, explaining consolingly to Divine that they had nothing to be concerned about as a crocodile would always take a white man first.

By the time the troop reached its destination at Fort Charter, 84 of its members were riding on the wagons, down with malaria. Divine said that even when they arrived there, there was "no supper, only army biscuits, and no medicine ... yet I never heard a word of complaint from the fever-stricken men on the wagons".

Captain Chamley-Turner, the OC of 'D' Troop, one time of the Royal Scots, had not at first been popular with his men. The Royal Scots were great disciplinarians and this had not appealed to the colonials in his troop. But they had come to appreciate that it was thanks to this discipline that they had survived the march at all and by the time they reached Fort Charter there was not a man in the troop who would not follow wherever he led.

As was usual at the time in most of the outstations, food was desperately short. However, there seemed to be plenty of nourishment to be found at the native villages. Shortly after the troop arrived, Chamley-Turner sent Divine and three troopers on a foraging expedition, giving them a supply of calico sheets, brass trinkets, beads and salt — the now established currency. No more than 20 miles from Fort Charter, Divine found pumpkins, rice, mealies, monkey nuts, and mealies in encouraging quantities. Enough to load 20 carriers. But when the long drawn-out process of barter had been completed, the baskets to carry the food which had been promised, and the able-bodied men who had offered their services as carriers, were conspicuously missing. "I left one man in charge of the goods," said Divine, "and with the other two drew revolvers and entered every little round hut, and made a prisoner of every man we could find and took possession of what bags and baskets we needed. We took each man we got and handed him over to the guard." Not, however, without some resistance. In one hut two natives attacked a trooper and he fired a shot over their heads. When the column of carriers was sent off at last to Fort Charter, Divine remained at the kraal with one trooper, threatening to set light to the village and burn it to the ground if he heard that any carrier had thrown away his load before reaching the fort. Police work in the new territory was certainly not handicapped by unwarranted restraints.

Four of the members of 'D' Troop, on arrival at Fort Charter, volunteered as post riders. One was Trooper R. ("Jock") Carruthers-Smith (No. 527). Sixty years later, he was one of the last surviving members of the original force. The post riders were sent to Makourie, somewhere near where Felixburg is today. Their beat was either to Fort Victoria, 40 miles away, or to Inutetsi, near Charter.

Whenever a dispatch came through they were expected to be on the road within 10 minutes. Smith wrote, in his Reminiscences of a Dispatch Rider, "I generally started on horseback, later I dismounted, fixed my overcoat and rifle on the saddle and jogged along, bare-footed behind the old crock". He seldom met anyone along the route. On the way to Fort Victoria he had to cross two rivers, one of which was "full of crocs, and I had some nasty experiences". He said that the BSA Company must have had over 1000 horses at the beginning of the expedition, but by March 1891 "I don't think they have more than 50 left amongst the different troops." By May, he said, "we have lost a great many men during the last three months through fever. There must have been quite 50 casualties in the different troops." All the casualties were certainly not fatal. Indeed, the actual number of deaths in the force during the first two years, from any cause, numbered only 29.

But, for all the privations, the outlook for a humble police trooper was not without encouraging hope of reward. "The Company has given us two lots of 50 (gold) claims to be divided between the troop. This comes to half a claim each as there are 84 men in our troop who are entitled to a share. They have also allowed us 10 claims each for our services; 10 of us have formed our claims into a syndicate named The Good Hope Gold Mining Syndicate. I am in two other syndicates and we each hold one share in 50 and I am obliged to pay out an average of £3 or £4 a month towards expenses, so I have to take pretty good care of my money these days. I could leave the police after the first year if I liked and take a civil billet, but it would pay me better in every way to complete my two years as I get five shillings per day clear as soon as I start on my second year." Carruthers-Smith, after he did leave the force, established himself as a prosperous settler. But according to his reminiscences, he had little cause to thank the early syndicates for setting him on the path to success.

By the beginning of the new year, 1891, Dr. Jameson had returned to Salisbury. It will be remembered that as soon as the pioneer column had arrived there, he and Frank Johnson had made an exploratory journey to Beira, had been picked up by a steamer and taken to Cape Town, and Jameson, on his return journey up-country to Salisbury, had met Sub Lieutenant Mundell with the two Portuguese prisoners. Jameson — who, more than any other of his contemporaries, was determined to alter the map of Africa by his own buccaneering efforts — now embarked on another concession hunting expedition to a native chief, this time with the spice of gun-running thrown in.

Gungunyana, the paramount chief of Gazaland, had his kraal not far from the north bank of the Limpopo River, down in the south-eastern corner of Moçambique. Gazaland was as big as Matabeleland and Mashonaland put together and would be a tremendous acquisition to add to the BSA Company's territory. The price of the concession for Matabeleland and Mashonaland, when Rhodes had obtained it from Lobengula, had been 1000 rifles, 100,000 rounds of ammunition, a gunboat on the Zambezi and £100 a month. This time, Gungunyana was to be offered 1000 rifles, a mere 20,000 rounds of ammunition and £500 a year.

The distance to Gungunyana's kraal from Salisbury was some 500 miles, through appalling country even in the dry season. Jameson took two companions with him: Moodie, a miner and Doyle, the interpreter. They started off with two horses and a mule and 20 carriers. The carriers deserted and the mule with most of their provisions was carried away by a flooded spruit at an early stage of the journey. They took 47 days to reach Gungunyana's kraal, while the rain beat down on them incessantly, and Moodie and Doyle went down with fever, Doyle in an almost desperate state. Jameson ran a high temperature too, but he knew that if once they stopped they would never move on again. By the time they arrived at the kraal they were all in a dreadful condition, fever-stricken and emaciated.

Captain Leonard at Tuli had been ordered to send 25 of "the biggest and finest men" from 'E' Troop to report to Dr. Jameson "up-country". Their build was important as they were to be used to impress Gungunyana. With three wagons carrying supplies and ammunition, they left Tuli on 27 January under Sergeant C.W. Cronly-Dillon (No. 395) but the conditions were so appalling that they did not reach Fort Victoria until the end of March, suffering two deaths on the way. One of the casualties was Sergeant G. Kirkman of 'E' Troop (No. 360). The other was Trooper J.H. Clarke (No. 618). The party was too late for Jameson's purpose, so their impressive stature was never put to use, but at least they were spared another unpleasant journey of more than 300 miles to Gungunyana's kraal.

But the BSAC Police were not to be left out entirely from what was developing as a piratical expedition. The Company, with commendable foresight, had included in the objects set out in its Royal Charter the power to "acquire, hold, charter and otherwise deal with" steam vessels — a provision that might have seemed somewhat redundant in Mashonaland. However, a little steamer had been bought in Port Elizabeth named the Countess of Carnarvon. This steamer was now sent up the coast with the rifles and ammunition promised to Gungunyana, and carrying Captain Pawley and an armed detachment (number not recorded) of the BSAC Police.

However, none of this detachment appears to have been drawn from the existing Troops, and it is assumed that the men were specially recruited in South Africa. The only reference in police records is to one T.C. Blundell who, "while in the Company's employ was on special service, Gazaland, 6 February to May, 1891". Nevertheless, the BSAC Police can add gun-running to their early activities, for the Countess of Carnarvon sailed up the Limpopo to a landing stage at Chai-Chai, 20 miles upstream, having flagrantly ignored the signals to stop waved by the Portuguese customs house at the mouth of the river. Pawley and the police disembarked and the cases of rifles and ammunition were off-loaded. The steamer then discreetly withdrew, to return to pick them up in a week's time. The Portuguese from the customs house soon arrived at the landing stage and Pawley, as a good police-man, refrained from argument and accepted on behalf of the Company the imposition of a fine of £2000 for illegal importation. The customs men decided the cases were too heavy to confiscate and that as all the rifles were old and rusty they were not worth removing and, taking Pawley's word that the fine would be paid in due course, they withdrew. As soon as they had gone, Pawley compounded the felony for which he had been fined by collecting some native carriers, and he and his men deliv-ered the contraband to Gungunyana's kraal. When they returned to the river with Jameson and his two companions they found the Countess of Carnarvon under arrest by a Portuguese gunboat. They were all taken aboard the gunboat as prisoners and carried to Port Elizabeth, where the police details were presumably discharged, as nothing more seems to have been heard of them. But, as in the case of d'Andrade and Gouveia, the principal prisoners — Jameson, Moodie and Doyle — became the heroes, and the captors were labelled as the guilty parties.

There is a story, which seems unlikely to be true, that on the landing stage at Chai-Chai, before being taken prisoner by the Portuguese, Jameson handed the paper confirming the concession he had bought from Gungunyana to one of the police troopers, and gave him the two horses — which would have been an embarrassment on the steamer anyway — telling him to ride off and meet him in Port Elizabeth, 800 miles away. The story goes that the trooper arrived there before the Doctor. This stretches credence a little far. In any case, like the gun-running policemen, nothing was ever heard of the concession again.

## Chapter Five

## TWO THREATENED INVASIONS

AS MORIER HAD remarked, Baron Rezende had gone to Lisbon, after the arrests at Umtasa's kraal, "to raise the devil there". In effect, he raised an army — if it could be called one. The treatment of their officials in Moçambique had stirred a wave of righteous indignation in Portugal and a volunteer force of 500 inexperienced young men, with no conception of the frightful conditions they would encounter in Africa, sailed from Lisbon early n 1891. They landed at Beira at the end of February, at the height of the rainy season. Two months later, less than 100 survivors of this pathetic little force struggled into the Fort at Macequece.

The party of BSAC Police, which had withdrawn to Umtali after Forbes's abortive march towards the coast, was now under the command of Major Heyman, with Lieutenant Eustace Fiennes as his second in command. (Forbes had returned to Salisbury, where he was appointed Resident Magistrate. Lyons-Montgomery said of him, "He is liked by everyone. I hope he never returns to the (Inniskilling Dragoons) as we would all miss him very much.") The force now numbered 70, but as Morier characteristically described it, "We are 70 wretched, fever-stricken men of whom only 38 are fit for duty owing to the others having no boots." When the news came that the Portuguese were advancing from Beira, Colonel Pennefather — recently returned from leave — had actually travelled down to Umtali, but news soon followed of yet another threatened invasion of the Company's territory — this time by a body of Boers from the Transvaal — and the Officer Commanding hurried back to Salisbury, leaving Heyman on his own. Before he left, Pennefather ordered Heyman to take all the men available that is, the 38 who had boots — to occupy the hills overlooking Macequece and await events.

Heyman first sent forward six men with a seven-pounder gun, under Sergeant R. Hickey (No. 456), drawn by a span of 10 oxen. There was no need this time to take the party over the Penhalonga mountains as a wagon road had now been cut to Macequece, although this naturally had to follow a wide detour and it was still rough going for the seven-pounder, which had to be dragged along on its own carriage. On 5 April this advance party sent back a report that 70 white Portuguese — the only survivors of the new army from Lisbon — had occupied Macequece and that they had with them some 700 black troops (described by Morier as "Regulars, i.e. uniformed West Coast natives and East Coast bearers") and several machine-guns. They had raised the Portuguese flag and were "fortifying themselves strongly".

Heyman left Umtali on the 6th with the remaining 32 men of 'A' Troop who had boots, a doctor (presumably Surgeon-Captain Rand), 10 armed Pioneers (the irregulars, still hankering for a fight) and Morier, who had been promoted to Sub-Lieutenant, as interpreter. They had only six horses between them. When they caught up the advanced party, Heyman and Morier went forward at daybreak to approach the Fort with a flag of truce. They encountered a picket of Angolan soldiers, who disrespectfully blindfolded them and led them into the Fort. They were taken into the presence of Major Carlos Xavier, the new Portuguese commander, who told Heyman, through Morier as the interpreter, that martial law had been proclaimed in Moçambique and he had every intention of driving out the BSA Company's forces. With a simulated show of confidence, Heyman warned him that he had a large force at Chua, west of Macequece, and if the Portuguese advanced there would be a fight and this would probably result in war between Portugal and Britain. Once again, a mere policeman was finding himself embroiled in an international incident, and having to indulge in a game of bluff at the same time. Xavier replied curtly that he was well aware of what might happen. Heyman and Morier were dismissed and, blindfolded again, were led out of the Fort, to be released by the Portuguese soldiers while still at a safe distance from Heyman's reputed army at Chua.

Heyman waited until Sunday, 10 April, when at three o'clock in the morning he took his men to the top of the kopje above Chua, looking down on the open ground stretching to Macequece. They dug in and set up the seven-pounder, standing to an hour before daylight. When the dawn came, they were intrigued by the sight of a native impi, 300 strong ,in full warpaint, climbing to the top of another kopje on their left. Umtasa had sent one of his subordinate chiefs, Chief Matika, to watch the battle which everybody in the vicinity knew was coming — so that, when the issue was decided, he would know which was the most promising side to support.

That afternoon, a Portuguese officer also carrying a flag of truce climbed the Chua Kopje, apparently to return Heyman's call. He brought a summons from Major Xavier ordering Heyman out of Portuguese territory, but, as the Portuguese Commander had already made himself quite clear, the message seemed redundant and Heyman suspected that the officer — whom they had not had the chance to blindfold before he arrived — had merely come to spy out the police position. He must have been able to satisfy Xavier that Heyman had been bluffing about the size of his force, for as soon as he returned to the Fort a decent number of Portuguese came out and established themselves on a nearby kopje, actually overlooking Macequece — thereby forestalling Heyman who had intended to seize it that night, and from which he had hoped to shell Macequece next morning. The two forces now faced each other on neighbouring kopjes, half a mile apart, with Chief Matika and his impi watching expectantly from the wings. The ground between them sloped down to a deep, well-wooded ravine, whose opposite bank was about 400 yards from the police positions on the top of the kopje. There was nothing more that Heyman could do that day.

At midday next day, Monday, the rest of the Portuguese army moved out of the Fort in two groups and advanced along each side of their kopje about half-way down. At half past one the whole force deployed into skirmishing order, extending their front to almost half a mile. At two o'clock precisely they fired a volley at Heyman's advanced picket, which he had sent forward to the Macequece side of the ravine. After returning the fire, the picket prudently fell back. Heyman fired a warning shot from the seven-pounder and the Portuguese replied with a hail of Snider bullets that whistled across the crest of the kopje. The police answered with shrapnel from the seven-pounder and concentrated fire from their Martini-Henrys. A real battle had opened, however puny the opposing armies. But the Portuguese found good cover in the ravine, and Morier said that "the repeating rifles of their European troops made us think at one time that they had brought a machine-gun into action".

Miraculously, the police suffered no casualties. In what may perhaps have been a vain attempt to fool the Portuguese, Heyman sent a trooper on to a boulder on top of the hill — wisely out of range of the Portuguese fire to make a show of semaphoring messages to imaginary reinforcements in the western distance. It is possible, of course, that the ruse did discourage the Portuguese from attempting a flanking movement, for they never attempted anything but a direct assault. A few of Heyman's men moved forward down the slope of the hill to take advantage of the cover on their side of the ravine and to engage the Portuguese more closely. The exchange of firing went on for over two hours, after which the Portuguese retreated, although the police seven-pounder had been put out of action by a Portuguese shell. However, the last round it fired had chanced to hit the Macequece Fort and it is probable that the Portuguese, believing that the critical range had been found, then decided to abandon the fight. About half their white troops had been killed or wounded. Most of the natives had fled as the battle progressed. But so had all the police servants and bearers, who had been waiting on the reverse side of the kopje with the horses. "The only one remaining behind," says Morier, "was my Manica boy, Barufo, who drove our horses and cattle to a place of safety under heavy fire."

Next morning Heyman sent a patrol into Macequece and they returned to report that the town was deserted and had obviously been abandoned in a hurry. The Portuguese had left a considerable stock of stores, nine machine-guns, seven Hotchkiss, two Nordenfeldts and thousands of rounds of ammunition. The police moved in to the Fort on the hill and were somewhat disappointed to find the abandoned guns had been disabled, but they retrieved the ammunition. They then spent a happy hour or two dynamiting the buildings in the town, but were first careful to remove some fine pieces of furniture that had been made in Portugal, which subsequently found a new home in the police mess at Umtali.

Heyman's force was, of course, quite inadequate to undertake any effective pursuit of the routed enemy, but under the pretext of checking their movements he sent Lieutenant Fiennes with six mounted troopers eastward into the Portuguese territory. Heyman was far less impulsive a character than Forbes and it is doubtful whether he would have sanctioned, however tacitly, another swashbuckling attempt to acquire a route to the sea, and a seaport for the BSA Company. Even so, the purpose of Fiennes's journey was difficult to distinguish from that on which Forbes had embarked a few months before, and the journey met a very similar fate. When Fiennes and his party reached Chimoio — a long way before they ever got to the Pungwe-- they met a party travelling the other way which included Bishop Knight Bruce and Major Sapte, military secretary to the High Commissioner in Cape Town. These formidable gentlemen were making a pioneering journey from Cape Town to Salisbury via the east coast route. They were so shocked to find an armed British force, however minute, invading a foreign territory, that Sapte summarily ordered it back. Later, when Rhodes heard what had happened, and that the swashbuckling attempt to add Portuguese East Africa to his territories had again been abandoned, he said, "Why didn't Fiennes say Sapte was drunk and put him in irons?"

Shortly before the Macequece action, at a detached post between Umtali and Macequece, Troopers T. W. Glover (No. 451) and T. Matthews (No. 448), both of 'A' Troop from Fort Charter, had gone down with malaria. They were alone, and their Mashona servant, who believed the disease was catching, deserted. Matthews died on 17 March, and for a whole week Glover lay helpless beside the corpse. When no news came of them, Lieutenant Fiennes (the onetime stockbroker), Sergeant T. Paxton (No. 205) and Trooper B. o'Hara (No. 506), all also of 'A' Troop, set out from Umtali in torrential rain. The Revue River was in flood and Fiennes first attempted to cross it alone, but was carried downstream half a mile and had to be rescued when he became entangled in the reeds. Finally they all managed to make the crossing and when they reached the post they buried Matthews. Glover was almost at his last gasp, and the only medicine they had with them was a small bottle of powdered quinine and some brandy. By some miracle Surgeon-Captain Rand, with a party of two troopers and two prospectors, joined them. They carried Glover back to Umtali, improvising a raft to tale him across the river. One man carried a rope, while the others swam beside the raft to steady it. Glover recovered and left the force in 1892 at the age of 32. He lived another 60 years.

Fort Tuli was still virtually the principal depot and base of the BSAC Police although the head-quarters staff was 400 miles away. It was not a state of affairs that inspired Leonard's confidence. "The corps," he wrote, "is more like a commercial and filibustery body of volunteers than a regiment of mounted infantry or police". In January 1891 Pennefather, returning from leave, was held up at Tuli by the rains, and later by an attack of dysentery, to add to Leonard's discomfort. "At the present time," said Leonard, "orders are being issued at Salisbury by Forbes as Acting Commandant and at this end by Pennefather as actual CO; while a month or two ago, when the latter was in Natal and Forbes and Heyman were in Manica, Slade (Lieutenant C. W. P. Slade of 'B' Troop), a very good fellow but a militiaman without any experience, commanded the corps although many in it were senior to him." The story has it, told by ex-Trooper HA Arnold, that on the original march from Macloutsie to Tuli in June 1890, Slade had upset Pennefather by a breach of etiquette halting a Troop and not ordering the troopers to dismount. The Colonel had thereupon ordered Slade, "who was very stout" says Arnold, to take charge of the unmounted men and legend has it that he had to walk the 400 miles to Salisbury.

Leonard goes on, "With Harris (Rutherfoord Harris, Rhodes's secretary in Kimberley) at one end and Pennefather at the other, I am, as Commandant of the Advance Base, between two stools." Pennefather told Leonard on no account to take orders from Harris; "he openly calls Harris an utter fool and tells us to ignore him," said Leonard. "But, on principle, Harris's orders should be obeyed even by Pennefather himself as he is the mouthpiece of Rhodes and therefore of the Company."

In February 1891, when Pennefather had returned to Salisbury at last and resumed formal command, he was so alarmed by the number of horses that were dying, and the ever decreasing number available to the force, that he banned their use from post-stations and instead ordered mail to be carried by scotch-carts drawn by oxen. Leonard had no option but to comply with Pennefather's order and he withdrew the post-riders from the stations in his district. When Rhodes heard about this he was furious and told Harris to instruct Leonard to re-establish the post stations between Tuli and Fort Victoria. Leonard received these instructions on 14 March, and following his principle that Rhodes's orders should have preference over those of his commanding officer, he hurriedly sent out eight    troopers from Tuli, with eight precious horses, to man the stations again. Two days later a telegram arrived from Harris cancelling the previous order. A week later, on 22 March, another telegram from Harris said, "I re-affirm orders to reestablish post stations with salted horses only" (that is, horses which had survived an attack of horse-sickness) "to be used for specific dispatches when so marked," adding consolingly, "this is final instruction."

Pennefather, now back in Salisbury, rode down to Umtali to join Heyman when the Portuguese troops from Lisbon advanced to Macequece with the intention of driving the BSA Company's forces out of Manicaland. But while he was there, and before Heyman moved forward to Macequece, news came of another threatened invasion of the Company's territory, this time by a force of Boers from the Transvaal, so Pennefather hurriedly returned to headquarters in Salisbury.

During the previous year, 1890, a Boer farmer named Adendorff had slipped across the Transvaal border — while the BSA Company's authorities and police were preoccupied with launching the pioneer column on its adventure into Mashonaland — and had obtained from Chibi, a Banyai chief in the south-eastern area of Matabeleland, a concession permitting him to bring a group of farmers into the country. Chibi had been persuaded to believe, a little misguidedly, that if these people settled in his district they help to protect him from his Matabele neighbours. Armed with the concession, Adendorff had sought out Rhodes when the latter was on his way back from Tuli after the ceremonial parade, and he had tried to persuade Rhodes to buy it from him. Rhodes — who was not always so legalistic when it suited his purpose to be otherwise — refused on the grounds that Chibi, being subject to Lobengula had no power to grant a concession. It was not the sort of obstacle to doing business that usually deterred him. Adendorff, hoping to put pressure on Rhodes, went back to the Transvaal and enlisted the support of several hundreds farmers, and even went so far as to draw up a constitution, in the familiar Boer tradition, for "The Republic of the North". The prospect of a new, independent Republic always excited the Boers, and it was said at one stage that 1500 farmers were preparing to go north with Adendorff.

For a time there was much talk of the projected Adendorff Trek, but by 1891 most of it seemed to have died down and the man himself appears to have faded from the scene. Now rumour had it that a Colonel Ignatius Ferreira — who had been decorated by Queen Victoria for bravery in the Zulu War (she gave him a CMG) — was organising a trek and intended to cross the Limpopo into Matabeleland.

Leonard, at Tuli, had first been alerted on 11 March to believe that something was going on, by a cable from Harris saying, "By Mr. Rhodes's orders hold 25 men in readiness to start and permanently occupy good position in Chibi's country probably near the Nuanetsi. Final instructions will come in a day or two." Here was another blatant example of short-circuiting the higher command of the force. To Leonard, the message seemed to confirm rumours that had recently been circulating of new preparations for a Boer invasion. Following the usual pattern, the order must have been amended a few days later, because Leonard wrote "The post in Chibi's country is not to be held, but instead we are to watch the principal drifts on the Crocodile (the Limpopo) that lead into our possessions." This made more sense, because the Nuanetsi flowed from Matabeleland and through a fair slice of Portuguese territory before it reached the Limpopo, and was nearly 150 miles east of Tuli anyway; and although there was good local precedent for sending a handful of policemen into foreign parts, to exercise a flagrantly irregular authority, Leonard's 25 men would have been completely out of touch, and in an unenviable situation if faced with a determined force. It is probable that Harris, when talking of the Nuanetsi, had been ignorant of the local geography.

The principal drifts that led into Matabeleland from the south were Massabi's Ford, which crossed the Limpopo some 30 miles from Tuli and about 15 miles downstream from the junction of the Limpopo with the Shashi; Main Drift, also across the Limpopo, 40 miles farther east, and about 10 miles downstream from the present Beit Bridge; and Middle Drift, half-way between the other two. Leonard wrote, "What amuses me about the telegram is the number 25 again, but this time, no giants need apply! Why always 25? Is it pure coincidence, or does Harris's military mind consider that I can spare this number exactly, whereas 30 might cripple me?" However, for some reason not explained (he is unlikely to have deliberately disobeyed orders, even from Harris) he sent only 20 men, under Lieutenant W. Hicks-Beach, to another drift altogether — Rhodes Drift, 20 miles due south of Tuli in the "disputed territory", which crossed the Limpopo before it met the Shashi. He probably chose it because it was the nearest drift over the Limpopo to Fort Tuli although for that reason it was probably the least likely one that any serious invaders would use. Hicks-Beach's orders were to make a small earthwork, examine everyone crossing the river and, if necessary, stop them. By what legal authority he would be acting he can certainly have had no idea at the time.

Just at this time Sub-Lieutenant Mundell, returning from Kimberley after his journey south with d'Andrade and Gouveia, arrived back at Tuli with a batch of 37 new recruits — "not a moment too soon," said Leonard, "as we are very short-handed, Jameson's Giants having made a great hole in our total, while fever has incapacitated a large percentage". Taking advantage of his increased strength,

Leonard sent off 30 more men, this time to Massabi's Ford under Sub-Lieutenant A.E. Grey, with the same unconstitutional orders. The police force was certainly beginning to earn its later description as the country's "first line of defence".

The threat of a Boer invasion was clearly being taken seriously even by the Imperial authorities — who were prodded, no doubt, by Rhodes. On Sir Henry Loch's orders, the officer commanding the BBP, Sir Frederick Carrington, was given overall command from Mafeking, along the course of the Limpopo as far as the Indian Ocean; and Willoughby was appointed his lieutenant, to command at Tuli and the Limpopo drifts. How Pennefather fitted into this chain of command was anybody's guess. Willoughby was subsequently replaced by Major Goold-Adams of the BBP, principally because he had recently taken it upon himself to visit Pretoria and be rude to President Kruger. When Kruger had protested to the Imperial authorities, the High Commissioner had cabled the British Agent in Pretoria, "Disown Willoughby and say Her Majesty's Government disown him altogether." Of Goold-Adams, Leonard wrote, "This makes the ninth commanding officer I have lately had, still, however, leaving me six to go on with, namely, Rhodes, Harris, Carrington, Goold-Adams, Willoughby and Pennefather ... It is the magnificence and magnitude of Sir Frederick's command that staggers me," he went on, "covering a front of over 1000 miles and running across more than half the breadth of the Continent." Not that Leonard was ever formally notified of the arrangement, knowledge of which came to him through what he described as "the usual circumbendibus method in force here". His first official intimation was a cabled order from Carrington to send 50 men and a Maxim gun to Sterkstroom Drift, asking at the same time how many mounted men he would have left, after guarding the drifts, to form a flying column. Actually, he had no suitable men for a flying column, or for defending the Sterkstroom Drift. The new recruits he had received were still remarkably raw.

In a brave attempt to give an appearance of legality to the action being taken — or even likely to be taken — by the Company's forces, Sir Henry Loch issued a Proclamation to the effect that any attempt by the Boers to invade British territory would be construed as a hostile act against the British Government. President Kruger, on whom pressure was also put by the Imperial authorities, took the hint and warned his subjects that any such action would be illegal and offenders would even be prosecuted by his own Government. But this had no effect on Colonel Ferreira and his farmers, who had never had much regard for governmental authority, and while there was no actual intelligence, north of the Limpopo, of the Boer movements, rumour continued to suggest that something was planned.

With his forces bolstered by some BBP troopers, Leonard was eventually able to deploy around 140 men, with two Maxim guns between them, at the various drifts. At Massabi's, Grey had constructed a small open earthwork — dignified as usual by the label of a fort — 1000 yards from the river on the north bank, facing the distant Zoutpansberg Mountains, 30 miles away in the Transvaal. Leonard wrote, "the men here seem comfortable enough in their rough reed huts" — surely a contravention of the printed Regulations — "and are lucky in having such luxury as fresh milk and eggs in plenty". At Middle Drift the valley was hardly wider than a gorge, with rugged kopjes on each bank falling almost to the edge of the river. But at Main Drift a so-called fort was built on a rocky hill 400 feet high, dominating a mass of rugged peaks and ridges, liberally sprinkled with baobab trees, grotesque in their leaflessness at that time of the year.

Leonard sent Captain W.A. Barnett with a party to Middle Drift, Lieutenant R.H. Ord-Capper (who had originally marched to Fort Salisbury with 'A' Troop) to Main Drift, and Lieutenant S. Flower to reinforce Grey at Massabi's. He was obliged to do this by superior orders — from whomever they might have come — much against his own judgement. "If our 140 men and two guns," he wrote, "were concentrated in a central and well-chosen position, being obliged to patrol and watch the remaining drifts, we might make a stand against 500 Boers." As it was, the small parties he sent to each of the three crossings would be virtually impotent. The shortage of horses handicapped him as usual. "We have 16 horses only among a total of 140 men, while it is certain that every Boer will be well mounted." During May a report reached Tuli of a party of eight Boers, "said to be on their way to Bulawayo to stir up Lobengula against the Company", who had appeared at Rhodes Drift, and Leonard rode down with Sergeant Fitzgerald (presumably E.W. Fitzgerald, No. 4, of 'B' Troop, who was unaccountably at Tuli). The party waiting at Rhodes Drift, which included three Englishmen, said they wanted to enter the country to engage in transport riding to Fort Salisbury. Leonard saw no reason to doubt their intentions and let them through. "The fact is," he said, "we have Boers on the brain."

A new coach service to Tuli, from Pietersburg in the northern Transvaal, had recently been inaugu-rated by Mr. C.H. Zeederberg, whose name and coaches were to become household words in the Mashona and Matabele territories — and subsequently in the combined territory when it became Rhodesia. The coaches crossed the Limpopo at Rhodes Drift. Dr. Jameson, on yet another return trip from the south, after his abortive bid for a concession from Gungunyana, arrived at Tuli by coach on 3 June. The rumours of a Boer invasion presented just the sort of situation that appealed to his instincts of political intrigue and he hurried off in a scotch-cart to visit the drifts, and no doubt to confuse the men guarding them with his own peremptory orders.

On 24 June he had visited Main Drift, 10 miles east of the present Beit Bridge and that morning he left to return towards Massabi's. Ord-Capper, who was in command at Main Drift, had been down with fever and was still recuperating in camp a few hundred yards down river. Surgeon-Lieutenant E. Goody, the assistant medical officer of the corps (who had also marched north with the Headquarters) happened to be at Main Drift that morning. He had probably travelled from Tuli to attend to Or Capper, although judging by an incident in the story that follows there did not seem to be much still wrong with him.

Goody was actually at the drift when a party of more than 100 Boers, with their oxwagons and retinue of native servants, started to assemble on the far, Transvaal bank of the river. Their appearance in such numbers must have suggested a determined invasion. As had been expected, Colonel Ignatius Ferreira, CMG was leading the trekkers and he and four of his companions rode calmly across the river with nothing but apparently peaceful intention. On reaching the north bank, they were immedi-ately placed under arrest by the Surgeon-Lieutenant, as the senior police officer present, whose duties did not normally offer this type of excitement. Later historical comment on Goody's action is divided between expressions of admiration for his courage and initiative; and a less flattering report that a sergeant, who was actually waiting at the drift when the intruders came across, turned to a mere trooper beside him (H.W. Chawner, No. 615) to ask his advice on how to handle the situation; Chawner — whose job incidentally, was simply to look after the commissariat — said, according to his own version, "Disarm them and make them prisoners and send for the Doctor." He meant Dr. Jameson, of course but Goody was thereby handed his moment of triumph.

Not surprisingly, Goody was at a complete loss about how to act next and he had no alternative but to take the advice Chawner had actually intended. A man was sent off to recall Jameson, who was overtaken on the road eight miles away. When Jameson returned to the drift he characteristically overrode Goody's authority by ordering the prisoners to be released and rode across with them to the far bank to address the assembled Boers. He pointed back across the river to a Maxim gun on a kopje, its line of fire commanding the drift, and promised the Boers, with confident arrogance, that no man, if he came armed, would reach the other side alive. Fortunately for him, his outrageous threat was not put to the test. He then invited them to enter the Company's territory, to settle peaceably in the new land, provided they swore allegiance to the Queen and obeyed the laws Colquhoun was busily drawing up in Fort Salisbury.

Leaving Ferreira and his colleagues to think matters over, Jameson returned to the north bank and waited until the next morning, when a deputation of three Boers came over to talk to him. It was either at this moment, or just when the deputation was returning, that Ord-Capper, his health and exuberance recovered, decided to put in some practice with the second Maxim at the camp a little way down the river, and his shots started to fall alarmingly close to the drift. The firing soon ceased but the incident, with its obvious implications, took some explaining away.

Boer delegates came and went across the river for the next two days — during which time Main Drift was reinforced by a party sent hurriedly across from Massabi's — and although Ferreira and one other, Jerome, agreed to enter the Company's territory on Jameson's terms, the remainder withdrew reluctantly and returned to their farms in the Transvaal. Not that Ferreira and Jerome were accepted immediately as free citizens of the new country. Leonard, at Tuli, wrote, "They were sent in as prisoners on parole on 29th and are here living at Pilgrims' Rest, the hut we keep for travellers, while they have their meals with us in the mess tent." The prisoners "on parole" certainly made good use of their opportunities, for by the time they were released and allowed to proceed up-country they had succeeded in launching no less than the "Mashonaland Agricultural and Supply Syndicate", with Leonard and three other police officers as sleeping partners and Colonel Ferreira, CMG, as managing director. Shares of £50 were promptly issued, half of which were bought by Leonard and his colleagues on the spot, and Jerome was appointed secretary at £10 a month. "Now that I have been weak enough to commit myself," wrote Leonard, "my heart misgives me."

While the Boer invasion had still been threatening, 'D' Troop under Chamley-Turner at Fort Charter and what remained of Lendy's 'F', artillery troop, was ordered to take up a position at Narka Pass, some way south of Fort Victoria and north of Chibi's country, to cover the tracks normally used by the early Boer hunters when they had travelled to Mashonaland from time to time. Any man in the Troop whose conscience did not allow him to fight the Boers was allowed to remain behind and a few (the number is not on record) took advantage of this concession. Leonard's men, guarding the drifts, had apparently not been given this option, although since the issue was not brought positively to their notice it is doubtful if any of them had worried about it.

Neither the police nor the pioneers had been in that part of the country north of Chibi's before and at one point the natives, to mark their disapproval, stole some of 'D' Troop's cattle. The kraal in which it was believed they were harbouring the stolen animals was located, and Chamley-Turner took 15 men — including Carruthers-Smith — to attack the kopje on top of which, as usual, the kraal was perched. This intrepid party charged to the top with bayonets fixed to find, not unnaturally, that the kraal was deserted.

Carruthers-Smith writes of the incident with an unbecoming relish. "We broke down the barricades," he says, "and went inside. All the huts were empty of natives, most of them contained a few goats and sheep. We got all the animals out and then set fire to the huts which was great fun for us though not for the natives. That afternoon we saw some natives up amongst the rocks and charged up at them. They fired a few shots and threw down stones but we managed to escape all injury. We gave them a volley and a few extra shots but I don't think we did any damage. The next day no natives were to be seen anywhere and we stayed at the kraal for three days, killing all the fowls, goats and sheep. We all had a fine time because up here it is not every day that we can get fowls for dinner. We sent into camp for a wagon to carry away grain. I think this will teach the natives a good lesson as they have been stealing a lot of cattle and everything else they can get hold of."

Remembering the orders given to the first Member-in-Charge at Fort Victoria, on the subject of relations with the natives, one wonders how this incident helped the local inhabitants to appreciate "the advantages they will gain in the way of security now that the English have come to settle in their country".

## Chapter Six

## THE MASHONALAND MOUNTED POLICE

ON 15 JUNE 1891, a few days before the Boers under Colonel Ferreira had appeared at Main Drift, a new officer of the BSACP had arrived at Tuli with a batch of recruits. As it happened, these were almost the last to be attested in the original force. There appears to have been only one later attestation in January 1892, of a man taken on for special dudes as a telegraphist who somewhat ungraciously deserted within six months.

The officer, Lieutenant the Hon. Charles White, was the first to arrive in Rhodesia of three brothers, all of whom were destined to play interesting roles in the country's early history. Although they all rejoiced in the title of Honourable, they were not so aristocratically connected as this might have suggested. Their grandfather, a bookseller's assistant in Dublin, had acquired an Irish peerage — as Lord Annaly — after he won £20,000 in a lottery, and being gratuitously accepted by the Establishment. Their father had then become a Member of the House of Commons. Charles had been commissioned in the 7th Royal Fusiliers in 1881 and was subsequently promoted to captain. It puzzled Leonard, when White arrived at Tuli, to understand why, having reached this relative eminence in rank, he should have accepted from Rhodes a mere lieutenancy in the Company's police.

These arbitrary appointments by Rhodes of commissioned officers in the corps, whatever their rank, had been causing a fair amount of dissension. It had been readily accepted, when the force was first formed, that experienced military officers should be appointed to the commissioned ranks. It was the only foundation on which such a force could be created. In most cases they had merely been seconded from their regiments and were likely to be returned in due course — although, as events will show, quite a few chose to resign their commissions and take up appointments, or settle, in the new country. But in any case, following pressure by the younger officers and NCOs, Rhodes had promised that future appointments would only be made by internal promotion. But he had not kept his promise. A Captain W.A. Barnett had been directly appointed from the North Staffordshire Regiment on 10 April 1891; Lieutenant S. Flower, a Scots Guardsman, had arrived a week later; and Captain T. Jones, described as "Jones of the Artillery", had turned up on 15 May. The arrival of Lieutenant the Hon. Charles White, exactly a month after this, hardly served to settle the ill-feeling that had arisen.

The truth was that Rhodes, in his own way, was a snob. It was not the snobbery of a man indulging in his wealth or position; he was fabulously well-off and too dominating a personality for that. But he moved in circles which flattered his vanity, and as long as the people he met did not ask him for money he could not resist displaying his powers of patronage. As Jameson would have said, "That's Rhodes all over. He can never say no."

Nevertheless, Charles White seems by his personality to have overcome any handicap which his situation might have engendered. Even Leonard, although remarking critically on bringing in new officers "over the heads of all the subalterns", was generous in his comment about White. "He is an exceedingly nice fellow," Leonard wrote, "very smart, and useful into the bargain, so he is a decided acquisition to us." But Leonard never missed an opportunity to be caustic. "I cannot altogether say the same for the recruits," he added, "although individually they are all nice young fellows and smart enough, because they are all with one exception, out from England." This was at slight variance from his previous praise for his "Afrikanders". "Most of them," he added, "are gentlemen at large and never had a profession of any kind."

White seems to have remained at Tuli with Leonard after his arrival, and on 1 July he was appointed to command the Tuli Depot, leaving Leonard as OC 'E' Troop. The Tuli Depot, in fact, was now becoming the most active base in the force although from this time onwards it was concerned with discharges rather than engagements. Leonard makes no outraged comment about this arrangement, which certainly reduced his own standing at Tuli, probably because he had already sent in his papers preparatory to resigning from the force.

There doesn't appear to be any particular reason why he decided to leave the force. Even in his long, windy book, in which he indulges in plenty of introspection, he makes no direct reference as to why he left the police and the country. He certainly never ceases to criticise the Company and the police organisation — particularly the senior officers — but he clearly relishes the opportunities to do so. If anything, he appears to have thoroughly enjoyed his service and, for all his caustic references to his former commanders, he seems to have done very much as he liked. He left Tuli on his way to leave and retirement, accompanied by a Trooper and a pack-horse, on 21 September 1891, arriving in Salisbury on 3 October. He met a number of wagons travelling in the opposite direction for Tuli, carrying, in his characteristic words, "parties of discharged and dissatisfied policemen who had little to say in favour of the country". Of Fort Victoria, which he had not previously visited, he said, "A miserable lot of huts and a wretched earthwork. To call it a fort is irony of the deepest description. All falling to pieces, with one or two shanty stores standing in a large sandy plain. While a second fort — a new set of huts in process of construction — is all there is of this half-way house to Salisbury."

His description of Salisbury, when he reached it, is interesting as a contemporary impression of a man who, however critical, was always realistic. "The town, which as far as population is concerned is not large, is fairly so in extent considering it is only a year old, but it straggles all over the place, as the few hundred huts comprising it are frightfully scattered about. Stores and auctioneers seem to predominate and the hotels and bars are driving a fine trade, with whiskies-and-sodas at half a guinea, and whiskey, or to be more correct Portuguese potato spirit made on the coast and put into whiskey bottles, at £3 a bottle. Many people here are disappointed with things in general and dissatisfied by the scarcity and dearness of provisions, and the poorness of mining prospects in particular." He said that Bodle, "our late Regimental Sergeant Major", was running a general store near the fort. "On Sunday I walked over to the hospital," he wrote, "to pay my respects to Mother Patrick and the sisters, whom I found in the best of health and spirits and as usual employed in good works."

He was fortunate, too, in running across Colonel Ferreira and Jerome, the managing director and secretary of the Mashonaland Agricultural and Supply Syndicate, whose dubious venture he was able to bring "to an abrupt termination and a summary winding-up ... I was just in time to prevent them collaring the proceeds and clearing out via Beira without any settlement." Exercising his official influence, he procured a warrant and forced them to refund his shares. It is doubtful if his colleagues at Tuli who had taken shares in the Syndicate at the same time were as lucky. Incidentally, these included White, who could only have been in the force a few days before he had succumbed to the smooth talk of the two prisoners on parole.

From Salisbury, Leonard set out on foot for Beira, with a companion and a scotch-cart. The last stage of the journey was made by a small craft down the Pungwe River. What he did when he reached England, and his leave-pending-retirement had expired, is not on record. But he had certainly played a conspicuously active part in the foundation of the BSAC Police, and for all his acid comments and endless fault-finding, he left behind in his book How We Made Rhodesia one of the most valuable contributions to the early history of the force.

It was all very well for the BSA Company to indulge in the luxury of Dr. Jameson's politico-buccaneering adventures so long as it could afford to do so. And there is some irony in the fact that the Imperial authorities, by insisting on the raising of a police force in the form of a military unit, had given Rhodes and Jameson — against their will — the very instrument that had enabled them to embark on adventures which put those same authorities in such invidious diplomatic situations.

Not that the role of the BSA Company's Police, during the first two years, had been entirely military. The police had certainly been launched on more than one purely military adventure. And in an untamed country in the depth of the wilderness, police work was necessarily concerned with creating a state of law and order, rather than having to maintain it, and consequently it was often obliged to act in a provocatively military way. But, taking the particular circumstances into consideration — circumstances that had no parallel in established communities — the BSACP were providing a service which a purely military unit might not have been ready to offer. From the beginning, the force was the only official public service in the country, and until specialists in particular fields of government administration came along, it was saddled with all sorts of administrative chores — of which running the mail service and providing communication with the outside world were only a couple. Troopers were frquently told to help surveyors marking out the farms and townships, or to act as clerks in the magistrates' offices.

But a cost of £150,000 a year to keep up the force was more than the Company, and the handful of settlers, could bear. The capital Rhodes had raised for the Mashonaland venture was almost exhausted and the prospects of profitable revenue were slow in materialising. For the time being, Dr. Jameson also seemed to have exhausted his territorial ambitions although time was to prove that his days of buccaneering enterprise were by no means over. And although the number of settlers was growing rapidly, and a few of the newcomers had but a token respect for the niceties of legalistic behaviour, the population was still too small and sparsely spread through the Mashonaland territory to create any need for a law-enforcing agency on any scale among the settlers themselves. It had naturally been feared, at the beginning, that the settlers would need protection from the savagery of the natives. If they had settled among the Matabele this may well have proved a justified fear. But the Mashonas had turned out to be surprisingly submissive and harmless; and the Matabele, although prone to murderous attacks on the Mashonas themselves, showed no open hostility to the white men. By the middle of 1891 — after the Imperial authorities had warned off the Company from any further incursions into Portuguese territory, and the threat of Boer invasion had receded — the days of carefree adventure were over; and as only a nucleus of the 650-strong BSAC Police force was engaged at any one time in post-riding and routine patrols, the remainder — in addition to the miscellaneous chores for which they were told off — were pestered by their officers with endless drills and parades, and training to keep them in a high state of military efficiency — like a peace-time army with no real prospect of a war. It was not a situation that encouraged an *esprit de corps*. Nor was it a situation that lent itself to Rhodes's sense of profitable enterprise, however much it may have helped to satisfy his thirst for power.

After Jameson had returned from his Gazaland adventure early in 1891 he had virtually taken over the running of the country in his characteristically domineering way, although Colquhoun was still nominally the Administrator. Jameson's attitude was more than Colquhoun, a relatively weak man, could bear, and in September he asked Rhodes for six months' leave, "with permission to resign my appointment at the termination of that period". Rhodes promptly accepted the request for leave, and the resignation. On 1 October 1891, Jameson became Administrator of Mashonaland in his place, and at last assumed a recognised official authority.

Jameson had already made up his mind to cut down the police force. In truth, he had no option. There was no money to pay for it. Neither was he convinced that it served any useful purpose. He once said to Pennefather, "When your men are doing nothing you show them in your returns as 'available for duty' but the moment I ask a man to do something, I am told he must get extra duty pay." He told Rhodes he would reduce the force from 650 to 150 of all ranks before the end of 1891, and this he did. He raised in its place a volunteer unit, and by Christmas that year the Mashonaland Horse had come into being with Major P.W. Forbes as its commanding officer — presumably in a voluntary capacity. Forbes had already taken over duties as a magistrate, first at Hartley and then at Salisbury, so it can be assumed that he had already left the force. Similarly, Heyman had become the magistrate at Umtali, and Lendy, the artilleryman, at Fort Victoria.

When the 500 redundant policemen were discharged, over a period of some months, some left the country — probably the majority — others became absorbed in the growing settler population; they were offered farms for which they had only to pay a small rent, provided they developed the land. How many left, how many stayed, how many became farmers, it is impossible to say. But in Rhodesia's subsequent history, names of original members of the BSAC Police continue to crop up, particularly in the next few years when the volunteer forces were engaged in the First Matabele War and the subsequent Matabele and Mashona rebellions.

As previously mentioned, the Matabele had shown no overt intention of making direct attacks on the white settlers in Mashonaland, who were spread out so thinly over the country. But the Mashonas were the Matabele's traditional prey and Lobengula's impis were constantly harassing them. Consequently there had been periodic calls on the police in attempts to restore the peace and to hand out some summary justice. The Matabele launched a large-scale raid in August 1891 on the kraal of Chief Lomagundi, north-west of Salisbury. The pretext for the raid was that the chief had failed to acknowledge his subservience to Lobengula by visiting him in Bulawayo and paying his annual tribute. Major Forbes seems to have relaxed his magisterial duties for a few days and led a force of police as far as the Angwa River (just west of Sinoia), but he was too late to make contact with the impi which, having indulged in a systematic massacre of the chief, his family and retinue, had returned triumphantly to the south carrying with them a promising selection of young women and girls.

Other recorded incidents of police activity in 1891 include the dispatch of a force to the Mazoe district where a French prospector had been murdered by natives. There was no such thing as painstaking criminal investigation at that stage, and when the suspects showed some belligerent resistance to the police, a few of them were shot and rough justice was done. On another occasion, at a kraal to the south-east of Salisbury, the police sought, again by a raid in force, to arrest an actual suspect, a headman charged with stealing from and assaulting a white farmer. Another pitched battle left 25 natives killed.

Even so, both Jameson and Rhodes were determined to relieve themselves of the financial burden of a professional military force and believed that the settlers themselves could, and should, provide for their own protection if any actual fighting was needed. A civil police force consisting of no more than 150 men would be retained, and they could "call in the military," — the volunteer Mashonaland Horse — if any fighting was to be done. So, early in 1892, the name of the police force was changed to "The Mashonaland Mounted Police", Colonel Pennefather returned to the Inniskilling Dragoons, and Captain the Hon. C. White was brought up from Tuli to become the new chief of police. Every one of the other original officers seems to have gone back to his regiment or resigned. There would appear to be no official records of how these organisational changes were made, but it is believed that the town branch of the police in Salisbury was known as the Mashonaland Constabulary — also under White's command — and that the new MMP operated from stations at Hartley, Mazoe, Marandellas, Lomagundi, Melsetter and Umtali, with the three original outstations at Charter, Fort Victoria and Tuli maintaining the link with the outside world. As the establishment of 150 included the constabulary in Salisbury, the numbers at each of the other stations could not have been more than a handful.

In 1892 Victor Morier died, aged 25. With his intimate experience of the border country between Manicaland and Moçambique, and his fluency in Portuguese, he had been appointed late in 1891 to the Boundary Commission to determine the border and to put an end to the perennial squabbles. It was a well-merited appointment for so young a man. Before taking up the appointment he went to England on leave early in 1892. The malarial bug which had first attacked him on the road from Tuli to Fort Victoria had been irremovably implanted in his system. On his return voyage to South Africa in May he died at sea of cerebral malaria — one more of the tens of thousands of promising young men throughout the world who succumbed to the scourge before Dr. Ronald Ross had been able to convince people, against their dogmatic beliefs, that the malarial germ was transmitted only by the bite of a mosquito.

## Chapter Seven

## THE OCCUPATION OF MATABELELAND

IT WAS ALWAYS admitted by the early settlers in Mashonaland that any harassment by the Matabele during the first two or three years following the occupation was directed primarily against the Mashona tribesmen and that the settlers themselves were not actually molested. Even so, trouble of this sort seems to have been rare during the 18 months following the raid on Lomagundi's kraal in August 1891. But in 1892 there had been a sizeable raid on the Mashonaland Agency Company's camp near Fort Victoria, where a large number of Mashonas working for the Company fled and only with difficulty were they induced to return to work. What casualties they suffered are unrecorded. There was another occasion, in the same district in March 1893, when Captain Lendy, the one-time commander of the BSACP artillery troop, became embroiled with, this time, a Mashona chief. He settled the trouble, whatever it was, by bombarding the chief's kraal with artillery and blowing it up — a somewhat drastic solution from which he was later to suffer some painful repercussions.

But the African Review of 15 April 1893, in implicit confirmation of the good relations between Lobengula and the BSA Company in Mashonaland, reported that the Chief had given every possible assistance to the capture within his territory of two white men who had robbed a wagon near Palapye, on the pioneer road south of Palapye. Lendy had actually gone to Bulawayo to take over the prisoners from Lobengula and escort them, via Tati, to Fort Matlaputla. Lobengula, the African Review said, "expressed his desire to (help) again, in similar cases, should they occur ... This is noteworthy as showing the cordiality existing between the King and the BSA Co., and as showing that the administration of justice is being actively carried out in the country."

This may have been an isolated incident — it may also have been a degree of wishful thinking on the part of the editor of the African Review but it tends to support the thought that the invasion and occupation of Matabeleland by the Company's forces, which was launched six months later in October, was not really so much for the safety of the settlers in Mashonaland as those with eyes on the reputed wealth of Matabeleland claimed it to be.

During the four years which followed the transformation of the surviving nucleus of the BSA Company's Police into the Mashonaland Mounted Police, the police force as a unit played only a secondary role. Although these four years saw some of the most momentous events in Rhodesian history — the Matabele War, the Jameson Raid, the Matabele and Mashona Rebellions — except in the case of the Jameson Raid, when virtually the whole force was involved, the parts played by the police, significant as they were, were played principally by individuals, or by groups of police acting as part of other military units. In fact, the numbers to which their strength had been reduced allowed for little else. And sometimes it is difficult, from the records of events, to distinguish who were police and who belonged to the various volunteer units, because so many mixed forces were sent out on individual operations and they all used the same designations of rank. It would be beyond the scope of this history of the police force to recount these events in full detail, but they must be outlined, and the part played in them by the police must be set on record.

There is no doubt there was a strong element among Lobengula's young warriors which resented the alien intrusion in their territory and, from the day the column had crossed the Shashi, Lobengula had been hard pressed to keep them in check. Probably he was just as resentful himself, but he recognised the age-old truth that decisive action is merely the art of the possible. Although Rhodes had made him a gratuitous contribution of 1000 rifles in exchange for the Rudd Concession, Lobengula was sensible enough to realise that in a direct confrontation his impis would have little chance against the white men. He could not restrain his young warriors altogether, nor probably did he want to try. But the situation of the settlers in Mashonaland was by no means dangerous; and Jameson must have believed this, otherwise why had he dispensed with his "first line of defence"?

Indeed, his readiness to disband his professional armed force might not unreasonably be construed as a belief, on his part, that any further military adventures were unlikely. His newly adopted policy might well suggest that the Company had now accepted the inevitable and that Mashonaland would henceforth be the limit of its sphere of operations. The settlers would now shake down into a peaceful, self contained community, with no more predatory ambitions for territorial conquest across the borders.

However, whatever Jameson's own views may have been, some provocative incidents certainly occurred during the middle months of 1893, and the settlers started to become restive. This was not the first or the last time in history when "border incidents" were to be used as convenient justification for pursuing an aggressive policy. Nevertheless there has always been, and there still remains, controversy as to whether or not these "border incidents" at Fort Victoria were deliberately provoked by the Company, and particularly by Jameson with his acknowledged tendency towards political intrigue.

Lobengula certainly sent another strong impi to the Fort Victoria district in July 1893. It was alleged in some circles at the time — principally by the anti-imperialists in Britain led by Henry Labouchere, the editor of Truth — that he had sent his warriors at Jameson's express invitation, with the object of punishing certain Mashona tribesmen in the district who had stolen some lengths of the Company's telegraph wire — surely rather a remarkable suggestion: that the Company should call in the Matabele to discipline the Mashonas on its behalf. When the impi appeared, so the allegation went on, Jameson turned against Lobengula and accused him of sending a predatory force to invade the Company's territory — thereby justifying strong counteraction. Labouchere wrote in Truth: "The Mashonaland 'bubble' having burst" — implying that the occupation had been a commercial failure — "a war was forced on Lobengula in order to get hold of Matabeleland. All the circumstances show that the coup had been carefully prepared long beforehand. When the train had been laid, a quarrel was picked with the Matabele, who had entered Mashonaland at the Company's request, and they were attacked and shot down by this same Jameson while doing their best to retire in obedience to his orders."

This is less than fair to Jameson, for all his buccaneering instincts. He would hardly have sought to provoke a major confrontation with the Matabele just after he had discharged three-quarters of his only regular military force; nor were any of his new volunteer units mobilised or equipped for a campaign. In fact, when he did at last decide to invade Matabeleland it took him 11 weeks to make preparations. One must assume that Jameson, up to July 1893, believed that the development of Mashonaland could continue peacefully, without fear of trouble from the Matabele, and that he had no intention at that time of occupying Matabeleland and defeating Lobengula, no matter how keen he may have been to do so.

But when the Matabele impi threatened Fort Victoria by its presence in the district in July, Jameson, who was nothing if not impulsive, abruptly changed his policy. The impi actually raided part of the town, carrying away and in some cases murdering the Mashonas working for the white inhabitants. Although the residents were able to muster a force of some 400 armed men — police and volunteers — they were in an unquestionably dangerous situation. While they assembled with their womenfolk in the fort — at the same time setting up Maxim gun emplacements and barbed-wire entanglements — they sent off an urgent message to Jameson in Salisbury to bring reinforcements to their rescue.

It is more than probable that when Jameson hurried down to Fort Victoria on the post-cart on 17 July he was determined to avoid an armed clash with the Matabele, believing that his uncanny power of persuasion — which he had exercised so successfully on numerous occasions with Lobengula — would suffice to send the impi back to Bulawayo. It is equally probable that when he faced the impi in an indaba held outside the fort on the morning of the 18th, and the younger indunas showed outright belligerence to his demand that they should withdraw from the district, he changed his mind and decided to invade Matabeleland.

Whatever may have been the sequence of Jameson's impulses and intentions — and we shall never know more than the bare facts of what he actually did, no matter how much we may try to impute his motives — it is certain that, directly after the incidents of 18 July, he made a positive decision to invade Matabeleland. He had given the Matabele until sundown that day to withdraw across the Shashe River (not to be confused.with the Shashi in the south) which had been tacitly accepted at the time as marking the boundary between Mashonaland and Matabeleland, some 30 miles east of Fort Victoria. During the afternoon, Lendy — then the magistrate at Fort Victoria, but exercising for the time being an undefined command over the scratch force of police and volunteers — decided that Jameson's orders were not being obeyed to the letter, and he led a charge of mounted men against a party who, he alleged, had refused to withdraw. A dozen or so of Lobengula's warriors were killed before the remainder retreated across the Shashe.

This action by Lendy was the basis of Labouchere's charge that the Matabele were shot down while doing their best to retire in obedience to Jameson's orders. And in addition to this, a direct accusation against Lendy of deceit had been made in the House of Commons, following the incident when he had shelled the kraal of the Mashona chief. By chance, Lendy was to die six months later, while engaged in the innocent pastime of "throwing the shot". He ruptured an intestine and died of peritonitis. In a spirit of outraged indignation, the Rhodesia Herald said, "although the sudden rupture which killed him could not have been caused by depression of spirits, nor his death consequently be charged to the irresponsible venom of his parliamentary traducers, still one could wish that the accusers had been struck dumb before they had spoken". Earl Grey, a director of the BSA Company, attending a memorial service to Lendy in England, publicly announced that "the Directors of the Company associate themselves unreservedly with all that Captain Lendy did ... his conduct received the approval of Dr. Jameson and Mr. Rhodes, for in shelling the stronghold of the Mashona chief who had defied British authority and whose defiance, as long as it remained unpunished, established a grave and serious danger to the future peace of the country, had faithfully carried into effect the orders he had received". For not the last time in history, the verdict on a policeman's conduct varied between the opposing extremes of condemnation and commendation expressed respectively by such as Henry Labouchere and Albert, the fourth Earl Grey.

Lendy's pursuit of the impi from Fort Victoria, and the skirmish near the Shashe River, are usually construed as the first shots in the Matabele War, although no more fighting occurred for the next three months. They will certainly be interpreted as such by those who wish to regard the war as forced on the settlers by the Matabele, implying that what followed was inevitable. Jameson, who had undoubtedly made up his mind now what he was going to do, told Rhodes that the Company would have to conquer Matabeleland or leave Mashonaland. In an exchange of terse telegrams (Rhodes to Jameson: "Read Luke XIV 31." Jameson to Rhodes: "All right. Have read Luke XIV 31.") Rhodes warned Jameson of the disparity between the number of men he, Jameson, could put in the field and the number of Lobengula's warriors, and Jameson in reply declared his determination to take the implied risk. He was already busy raising a volunteer force in Fort Victoria, and another in Salisbury. Even the British Government, actuated by another convenient "border incident" in Bechuanaland when a BBP patrol was allegedly fired on by the Matabele, felt constrained to intervene. Encouraged by Sir Henry Loch, the High Commissioner, Commandant Pieter Raaff, an early arrival in Mashonaland and by now the resident magistrate at Fort Tuli — another Afrikander recipient of one of Queen Victoria's CMGs during the Zulu War — hurried off to Pretoria to raise a volunteer force in the Transvaal. (There was a certain incongruity about a force of Afrikanders joining the British Government's BBP in an operation ostensibly to come to the rescue of the acquisitive BSA Company.)

It took Jameson 11 weeks to raise and equip the two columns which were to invade Matabeleland — the Salisbury Horse of 265 men and the Victoria Rangers of 388 men. Major Patrick John Forbes — now Resident Magistrate in Salisbury and, one assumes, no longer on the strength of the Police — was in command of the Salisbury Horse, which moved from Salisbury to Fort Charter on 5 September; a Major Allan Wilson — who had served in the Cape Mounted Rifles and the Basutoland Police, but had no previous record with the BSA Company's forces — commanded the Victoria Rangers. They joined forces on 16 October at Iron Mine Hill, between Umvuma and Gwelo — where the Salisbury Horse had had a brush with the Matabele two days earlier — and Forbes took overall command. That is to say, he was theoretically the military commander. But Jameson was with the column; so was Willoughby, as Jameson's "military adviser". Even with these handicaps to his leadership, Forbes had little difficulty in defeating the Matabele, who contested the invaders' advance with superb, if misplaced courage.

Forbes, Jameson and Willoughby, with their victorious army, marched into Bulawayo — which the retreating Lobengula had left in flames the day before — on 4 November. Meanwhile, as early as 3 October, 230 "Raaff's Rangers" from Pretoria and Johannesburg had marched into Fort Tuli, where they were attested as members of the British South Africa Company's Police — which force had been virtually disbanded — and what survivors there were had become the Mashonaland Mounted Police anyway. They had then moved across to Macloutsie where they joined 225 officers and men of the BBP under Major Goold-Adams, and they had all marched north into Matabeleland, in the direction of Bulawayo, on 18 October. They were attacked but not seriously impeded by a Matabele impi on the Ingwezi River (near Mphoengs on the Bechuanaland Border) on 2 November and Goold-Adams did not arrive in Bulawayo until 15 November, 11 days after Jameson. Jameson had already hoisted the Company's flag on a tree in the old white men's camp near the burnt-out remains of Lobengula's Kraal. He had been just in time. If he had arrived a week or two later the southern column, which derived its orders from the British High Commissioner in Cape Town, would probably have secured Matabeleland for the Imperial Government as an extension of the Bechuanaland Protectorate, in which case the territory would never have become part of the BSA Company's domain — and might have finished up as part of Botswana and not of Rhodesia.

The Mashonaland Mounted Police, as the force had then been renamed, took no part at all in this campaign (for the conquest of Lobengula's territory) known as the Matabele War. Forbes was the nominal commanding officer of the invading army, but although still in the Company's service as a magistrate he had virtually retired from the force; Lendy, also a Company's magistrate and retired from the Police, was in command of the artillery — a couple of seven-pounders, a Nordenfeldt, a Gardner and a couple of Hotchkiss. But Captain the Hon. Charles White was still the officer in command of the Mashonaland Mounted Police, although he somehow seems to have found his way into the Salisbury column in charge of the scouts. There must have been many of the old BSACP who had taken their discharge and settled in Mashonaland, and who joined one or other of the columns, but until Bulawayo was entered none of the old names appear in the records of events.

But after Bulawayo had been occupied Jameson decided to send Forbes out with a force to pursue Lobengula who had withdrawn with his surviving warriors into the bush towards the north. This force came to be known as the ill-fated Shangani Patrol, from which a party of 33 men led by Allan Wilson was detached, surrounded and ultimately wiped out by the Matabele. "Allan Wilson's last stand" on the Shangani has a bibliography of its own; responsibility for the disaster, and apportionment of credit for the heroism of the episode, are a continuing source of controversy. Suffice it to say that Forbes, the one-time victor of the assault on Umtasa's Kraal, displayed fatal indecision and carried a considerable share of the responsibility. Among the victims who stood fighting to the end until they were all finally overwhelmed by the Matabele were Captain Frederick Fitzgerald, No. 391 of the BSAC Police, who had attested on 1 March 1890, had been a corporal in 'E' Troop, a sub-inspector of the Mashonaland Mounted Police at Fort Victoria, and had commanded No 1 Troop of the Victoria Rangers; and Trooper Frank Leon Vogel, a New Zealander, who appears to have joined the force in 1891, had been serving as a trooper in the Mashonaland Mounted Police in Salisbury and had at one stage been acting as Assistant Secretary to Jameson.

That seems to have been the extent of the personal involvement of members of the police force in the Matabele War of 1893.

Two notices in the British South Africa Company's Gazette (the official Gazette of the government authority), issued after the Matabele War, are of passing interest in that they might well have affected members or ex-members of the police. The first, on 5 October 1894, read ...

*Loot Committee*

Notice is hereby given that all those entitled to participate in the distribution of the loot taken during the late war, or in the proceeds thereof, who have not already registered their right with the Loot Committee, are hereby required to do so on or before 31st October, and that on and after that date the Committee will decline to recognise any right not then registered.

And, a month later ...

*Matabeleland Expedition*

Notice is hereby given to members of the above Force that the final dividend will be paid on 1st December to each member of the expedition who is entitled to a proportion of the proceeds of the sale of cattle captured during the late war, or the Registered Holder of such right.

More directly pertinent to the police was a notice on 29 January 1896, which read ...

*E. Troop BSAC Police Syndicate*

All interested in the above syndicate of 50 claims granted to E Troop in 1890 are requested to forward full names and addresses ... The original grant (of mining claims) having been obtained this day, the Syndicate will now be re-formed, and Prospectors sent out, to defray the expense of which a first call is now made of £5 per share, which must be paid ... failing which the unpaid shares will fall to the remaining members. Signed: R.Y. Fletcher , P. Holland, W.H. de Smidt

## Chapter Eight

## PITSANI

ONCE THE MATABELE had been apparently subdued, the newly consolidated territory of Matabeleland and Mashonaland enjoyed relative peace and tranquility for the next couple of years. The volunteer forces, the proud conquerors of Matabeleland, were disbanded and some 400 either took up the grants of land which the Company had offered in recompense for their services, or found other activities in the development of the newly occupied territory. The land had cost the Company nothing, beyond the cost of the campaign to capture it, so they could afford to be generous. Bulawayo grew rapidly from a primitive settlement to an ambitiously planned township, with wide streets and avenues marked out in square blocks. Here and there a cluster of solid brick buildings with corrugated iron roofs started to rise, until by the end of 1894 — within a year of Lobengula's defeat — the white population had grown to 1500, of whom at least 200 were women. And out into the surrounding districts went the prospectors, determined to prove that the real prizes had been waiting for them all along, on the other side of the hill.

A new division of the police was formed, the Matabeleland Mounted Police, commanded by Inspector William Bodle, the father and first RSM of the BSACP, who had apparently given up his job running a general store to join the Salisbury Horse for the invasion of Matabeleland. During 1894 the strength of the Matabeleland division rose to 250. The fact that both the Mashonaland and Matabeleland divisions were usually known as the MMP results in some confusion when trying to sort out the records; and there is still more confusion as to whether or not the combined Mashonaland and Matabeleland divisions were formally known, at that time, as the Rhodesia Mounted Police. Captain the Hon. Charles White — who was still the Chief Commissioner, even though he had descended from his Olympian heights and gone scouting in the Matabele war — referred to his command as the Rhodesia Mounted Police on one occasion in 1894 in an official memorandum setting out its new organisation. But the name "Rhodesia" was not officially adopted until May 1895. Nevertheless, it was already gaining popular currency. So, for the sake of convenience, the combined divisions can be referred to as the RMP.

The Mashonaland division was under the command of Inspector H. Hopper (No. 596) who had joined the BSACP in September 1890. He had only 150 men, compared with Matabeleland's 250 — a fair indication of the current belief that the Mashonas were more docile than the Matabele.

Back in 1889, when preparations had been going on for the original occupation of Mashonaland, recruiting for the BSACP had been substantially assisted by the difficulties being experienced at the time on the gold mines in the Transvaal; difficulties which were due to the apparent impossibility of extracting the gold from the sulphide ores now being found at the lower levels of the mine shafts. It appeared that the oxide ores, from which the gold had been readily extracted, were only to be found relatively near the surface, at depths no lower than 500 or 600 feet, and these were now running out. In consequence, the mining industry on the Rand had suffered a damaging slump and this had a major influence on Rhodes and his colleagues when they had decided to transfer their attention to the promised El Dorado in Mashonaland — and at the same time it had provided a significant source of recruits for the BSACP.

Mashonaland had turned out to be something of a disappointment, in terms of promisingly rich mining prospects on the scale of the Rand, even at the upper levels. However, Matabeleland was now at the disposal of the Company and its settlers, and perhaps this would turn out to be more rewarding.

But meanwhile, on the Rand, a new process had at last been discovered for successfully treating the sulphide ores. This was known as the cyanide process; and from 1891 onwards the mine shafts in the Transvaal — and 50 years later in the Orange Free State — sank deeper and deeper into the earth, until the time would come when they would be extracting rich, tractable ores at depths of more than 10,000 feet.

All this may sound irrelevant to the history of the police force in Rhodesia, but the discovery of the cyanide process on the Rand was nevertheless the first link a chain of events culminating in an incredible incident in which members of the force were to be the principal players. And the significance of the incident is all the more important in that the ultimately reconstituted force, which was to be known as the British South Africa Police, was a direct result of its outcome.

Rhodes and Jameson were both adventurers — Rhodes as a financier and Jameson as an amateur soldier. Their adventures in Mashonaland and Matabeleland, richly promising as they were intitially, turned out to be disappointments. Rhodes was unsatisfied, financially, with his new territories and the Rand was now beginning to look more promising; Jameson was now the Administrator of Mashonaland and Matabeleland combined, but he was also far from satisfied, emotionally. His restless spirit was not the sort to be placated by a regular job, however high-sounding its title. Even he was beginning to be attracted by the Rand, as a promising new outlet for his buccaneering urge.

By 1895 the white population of Johannesburg — attracted from all over the world by the new boom on the gold-fields, thanks to the discovery of the cyanide process — had grown to more than 100,000. These people, whom the Boers called "Uitlanders", considerably outnumbered the burghers of the Transvaal themselves. But President Kruger and his Volksraad, happy enough that their Republic should profit from the proceeds of the industry of these ungodly intruders, were determined not to allow them any unnecessary benefits. They denied them citizenship of the Republic and any consequent voice in government. Not, as one of the Uitlanders' leaders put it, "that they (the Uitlanders) cared a fig for the franchise". The Britishers, in particular, had no wish to give up their British citizenship to become burghers of the South African Republic. But what they wanted, not unnaturally, was to have a say in government and the consequential power to reduce taxes — which, in reality, were far from an unreasonable burden — considering the enormous fortunes that were already a cumulating on the Rand. They had a long list of other grievances: Dutch as the only official language; suppression of numerous popular liberties; and, most aggravating of all, blatant corruption on the part of the Boer politicians and officials, outwardly encouraged by the Government. As Kruger put it so engagingly: "in a country where there are no pensions, officials should not be debarred from making a little profit".

It is still debated whether Rhodes and Jameson acted in concert in a deliberate conspiracy to take over the Transvaal and add it to the British South Africa Company's territorial acquisitions, under the pretext of rescuing the Uitlanders from the tyranny of Kruger and his Government. There is no doubt that Rhodes fanned a spirit of revolt among the financial leaders in Johannesburg. But the international situation was far too complex for a man of his political sophistication to believe that the balance of power, even in an obscure Republic in Africa, could be upset by a puny application of force. Jameson, on the other hand, had no such doubts. He had conquered Matabeleland with a few hundred volunteers and was convinced he could repeat his triumph in the Transvaal.

However, he did realise that this time he would have to move more circumspectly. He wrote to Rhodes, in the middle of 1895: "The Company's police and volunteers should be made as efficient as possible in order to be prepared for eventualities, so that if a revolt does occur in Johannesburg and help is required, I shall be in a position to use my discretion as to how, when and where, if at all, Police and volunteers should be utilised." What worried him was that Bulawayo was a long way from Johannesburg and if there was an uprising it might all be over before he could get there. He needed a base in Bechuanaland, close to the Transvaal frontier, as near as possible to Johannesburg. His choice was the little post-station in southern Bechuanaland, Pitsani Botluko — 30 miles north of Mafeking, only three and a half miles from the Transvaal border and 170 miles from Johannesburg.

For some reason which probably had hidden political implications, Captain the Hon. Charles White was replaced as Chief Commissioner of Police in Rhodesia by his elder brother, Major the Hon. Henry Frederick White, of the Grenadier Guards, who arrived in the country early in 1895. Another White brother, the youngest, arrived as well — Captain the Hon. Robert White, of the Royal Welsh Regiment. Their grandfather's lucky lottery win certainly had a strange influence on the early history of Rhodesia. Charles seems to have quickly dropped from the scene, at any rate for the time being; H. F. White was now the Commissioner and Robert, or "Bobby", became his Chief Staff Officer. These senior appointments were all conceived and arranged in the boardroom of the British South Africa Company and Rhodes's implied promise to the original force that promotions would be made from within was blatantly sacrificed to political expediency.

Rhodes, under the pretext that he needed police protection for the construction of the railway he intended to build from Mafeking to Bulawayo — although he had not yet started it — persuaded the

Imperial Government to proclaim a strip of land within the Bechuanaland Protectorate along the border with the Transvaal as Company territory. The proclamation was made on 18 October 1895 by the new High Commissioner in Cape Town, Sir Hercules Robinson — who had just been reappointed after a long interval at the age of 70 and was unquestionably a tool of Rhodes. The proclamation was accompanied by a notice appointing Dr. Jameson as Resident Commissioner of the ceded territory and Major the Hon. Robert White (Bobby) as Magistrate. How effectively Jameson would be "resident" in the new territory only events would show. The official instructions to the Company, originating from the Colonial Office in London, urged the Company and its police "to bear in mind that the whole strip forms a frontier with an independent state and the Chartered Company now becomes charged with the responsibility of maintaining the integrity of that frontier and performing all police and other similar duties in connection with it". The obligation and trust imposed on the police force to respect the integrity of the Transvaal's boundary, even to serve in upholding it, was specific. It is not hard to believe that the author of such pointed instructions must have had justifiable suspicions of Rhodes's intentions.

Jameson's duties as Administrator of Mashonaland and Matabeleland — to which was now added the Resident Commissionership in southern Bechuanaland — did not prevent him commuting almost continuously between Bulawayo, Johannesburg, Cape Town and Pitsani. By some clever trickery he had persuaded some of the Reformers, as the leaders of the prospective revolt in Johannesburg were known, to sign an undated letter — which he drafted himself — addressed to him and pleading with him to come to the rescue of "thousands of men, women and children of our race who will be at the mercy of well-armed Boers ... property of enormous value will be in the greatest peril".

The idea was that he would take the letter with him to Pitsani now — this was in October, still a couple of months before the proposed date of the revolution — fill in the date when the rising actually materialised and pass the letter on to The Times in London for publication. Then there would be no doubt in anyone's mind of the genuine, urgent call for help to which he would be responding. His men would be the gallant rescuers of embattled women and children in dire peril and the world would applaud them for their courage in tackling the unscrupulous and vicious Boers.

The actual organisation of the rising in Johannesburg never reached any serious dimensions. Amateur efforts were made to smuggle arms into the town, but although the original target was 5000 rifles, only a handful ever arrived. There were plans to seize the state arsenal in Pretoria and one of the Reformers had shocked his colleagues by proposing "that the armed forces of the Committee should take possession of the Robinson Mine, fortify it and fight to a finish", but no one else offered any constructive military plans. Most of them were making too much money to want to risk any really revolutionary action.

However, this was not the sort of situation to deter Jameson. On the day following the High Commissioner's convenient proclamation of BSA Company territory in southern Bechuanaland, and with the ostensible purpose of protecting workers on railway construction which had not been started, from dangers of which there was no evidence, Jameson began to move almost the whole of his police force out of Mashonaland and Matabeleland, down the old pioneer road south, to Pitsani. The strength of the RMP at the beginning of the year had been approximately 400. Major Bobby White, the Chief of Staff, had been to Cape Town in April and had succeeded in recruiting a number of men of the Duke of Edinburgh's Own Volunteer Rifles ("the Dukes"), whose Colonel complained that, while he regretted that his best men had been filched, what really hurt him was that they had not handed in their kit. (In the event, these men never entered Rhodesia but were drafted straight to Pitsani. But they were attested nonetheless in the RMP.) Several dozen others of the Rhodesia Horse, the volunteer force in Mashonaland, were drafted into the RMP ranks, so that by October the total strength exceeded 450. Naturally, this increase in the police, together with some local mobilisation of volunteer forces, gave rise to rumours about why all this was going on, and the favourite was that Rhodes was planning an assault on Barotseland, north of the Zambezi. But before the end of the year, Jameson was to send 356 NCOs and men to Pitsani, to join the "Dukes" already there, leaving less than 100 to look after the 150 square miles of Mashonaland and Matabeleland.

One of the members of the first detachment ordered south from Salisbury was A.J. Tomlinson, who had joined the Mashonaland Mounted Police as a trooper in 1893, was now a corporal and was to retire over 30 years later as Lieutenant-Colonel and Acting Commissioner of the BSAP. He has written that he started off from Salisbury in September 1895, in a party of 26, under Sub-Inspector Charles Southey, also of the MMP (No. 810). If he is right in saying that they moved to Bulawayo in September, then Jameson was clearly anticipating the High Commissioner's proclamation, which was not made until 18 October. But it is very likely that Jameson did so, because he sent the first troop of the RMP south into Bechuanaland from Bulawayo the very next day, 19 October. He was obviously determined not to waste any time.

Tomlinson says that on the march from Salisbury to Bulawayo they had no wheeled transport and their blankets and kit were carried on pack-horses. The only food they had on the journey was what they could requisition from wayside stores. When they arrived in Bulawayo, Tomlinson was promoted to Sub-Inspector, which was a commissioned rank. There were three officers to a troop, an inspector in command and a sub-inspector to each half-troop.

In all, four troops and an artillery troop — 14 officers and 356 other ranks — moved progressively down the old pioneer road from Bulawayo, through the Mangwe Pass, through Tati and Palapye to Pitsani, more than 400 miles away. They took about six weeks for the journey, the first troop arriving on 30 November. The four troops, which moved south in alphabetical order at intervals of a few days, were designated 'A', 'B', 'C', and 'D' The "Dukes" were split up between them when they arrived. 'A' Troop was under Captain (Inspector, MMP, No. 824) Martin Straker who, although he had not joined the BSACP in time for the pioneer expedition, had been a sergeant-major in the force since 1890. He was to serve with the BSAP until 1910. His junior officers were Lieutenants R. Cashel and H.J. Scott, both Sub-Inspectors, MMP.

Captain (Inspector, MMP) Lawson Leigh Ballantyne-Dykes (one cannot resist quoting such a plethora of names) commanded 'B' Troop. Lieutenant A.J. Tomlinson, the future Acting Commissioner of the BSAP, became one of his Sub-Inspectors. The other was Lieutenant (Sub-Inspector, MMP) H. Chawner (BSACP No. 615), the corporal in charge of the commissariat — when the Boer expedition had threatened Main Drift on the Limpopo in 1891 — who had advised his sergeant to "send for the doctor". 'C' Troop was under Captain W.J. Barry, an Inspector in the MMP, who was to die of wounds received in the forthcoming operations; he had Lieutenant (Sub-Inspector, MMP) A.P.L. Cazalet as one of his junior officers. Cazalet had joined the BSACP as a trooper in 1893. He, too, was to be wounded in the same engagement, but was to survive and serve in the BSAP until 1909. The second junior officer in 'C' Troop was Lieutenant G.H.P. Williams (Sub-Inspector, MMP).

'D' Troop's commander was Captain Gordon Vallancy Drury of the BBP, one of the members of that force who transferred to the RMP at that time (as will be related shortly). He had served in the Royal Marines and 11th Hussars and later, in 1902, was to act as Chief Staff Officer of the BSAP. Drury's junior officers were Lieutenants W.E. Murray and H. Constable, both Sub-Inspectors, MMP. The Artillery Troop was commanded by Captain (Inspector, MMP) Frank Bowden, with Lieutenant L.S. Spain as his Sub-Inspector; Bowden served subsequently in the BSAP. (The artillery consisted of a 12-pounder gun and six Maxims.) In overall command was Lieutenant-Colonel the Hon. H.F. White, Chief Commissioner of the RMP (later to become Brigadier-General the Hon. H.F. White, CB, CMG, DSO), with Major (Chief Inspector) William Bodle as second in command.

Having handed over a large slice of the Bechuanaland Protectorate to the BSA Company, the Imperial Government, with apparent relief at having shed its responsibilities, decided to disband the BBP — the force which had been originally created with a few men sent out from Britain in 1884 and more fully established by recruitment, principally of members of the Royal Engineers, from Sir Charles Warren's expedition to subdue the Republics of Stellaland and Goshen in 1885. A considerable number had transferred to the BSACP in 1889. (A fitting memorial to the Bechuanaland Border Police is preserved today in a fine, shining copper plaque in the Church of St. John the Evangelist, at Mafeking, listing all the members of the force who died, either in its own service or in the service of associated units to which they had transferred, including the BSACP.)

Although Jameson had been satisfied to leave less than 100 police in Rhodesia — thus indicating he had no qualms over security in the Mashonaland and Matabeleland territories — and was now collecting a force nearly four times as strong to guard a non-existent railway in Bechuanaland from the depredations of demonstrably peaceful tribesmen, who wanted nothing more than to be left alone, he was nevertheless determined even to increase this force by persuading the BBP men to join him before they dispersed altogether. The officer commanding the BBP was Lieutenant-Colonel Raleigh Grey, who had been in close contact with the Company's police at the time when the pioneer column had been assembling prior to the occupation of Mashonaland. He came from a distinguished family and was one of the officers of the Inniskilling Dragoons — like Pennefather and Forbes — who had come to Africa to serve in the Zulu Wars. He has been described as "a cool, practical soldier, with rigid ideas of military discipline, who was not the sort of man to be attracted towards any such adventure as Jameson had in mind, unless assured that it had official backing". Jameson, very wisely, told him nothing of his intentions. It is incredible how Jameson seemed to be able to conceal what he was planning to do — it would have been difficult to keep the intentions secret. But besides the White brothers, who were undoubtedly Jameson's principal co-conspirators and it is obvious that this is why they were given their appointments — the only person in the know appears to have been Sir John Willoughby (now a Lieutenant-Colonel) who was to take over military command of the expedition when it was ready to be launched. In reading the records of what occurred, particularly after the Raid was over, one is constantly suspicious of the protestations of ignorance, before the event, made by so many of the participants; but the protestations are so consistent and sound so convincing that you tend to believe them.

Nine officers and 113 other ranks of the BBP transferred to the Company's forces. They formed two troops, 'G' and 'K'. Major the Hon. C.J. Coventry, originally from the 3rd Worcestershire Regiment and later Colonel Coventry, CB, became Raleigh's second in command. 'G' Troop was commanded by Captain A.V. Gosling (who served later in the BSAP), with Lieutenants A.H.J. Hoare and E.A. Wood (later to become Brigadier-General Wood, CMG, DSO and three bars); 'K' Troop was under Captain C.L.D. Monroe (one time of the Seaforth Highlanders) and Lieutenant W.J. McQueen (who also served later in the BSAP). From the BBP also came a medical officer, Surgeon-Captain E.G.F. Garraway (later Lieutenant-Colonel Sir E.G.F. Garraway, KCMG, Resident Commissioner of Basutoland) and a Veterinary Officer, Lieutenant W. Lakie. While the RMP were assembling in camp at Pitsani, the two ex-BBP troops remained for the time being in their old barracks at Mafeking — an arrangement which probably helped to allay suspicion among their members of any unusual goings-on.

In addition to this formidable military force assembling on the Transvaal border, Jameson collected an impressive array of military brass to form his staff. While he himself was the acknowledged leader, although in civilian clothes, Willoughby was destined to take military command. Comparing Jameson and Willoughby, Marshall Hole says, "Willoughby is of a more calculating nature without any outstanding brain capacity, but with one eye always open for a chance of profit. Both, however, were endowed with a sort of piratical craving for adventure, and in both the gambling instinct was a powerful motive." It was the first time Willoughby had actually been in command of an active force and his experience as "military adviser" to Jameson during the invasion of Matabeleland was hardly an outstanding qualification for leadership. He had apparently withdrawn from the BSACP after the occupation of Mashonaland, for he had set up a prosperous business, involved in mining ventures and property transactions, known as Willoughby's Consolidated Investments. What his position was in relation to his commission in the Royal Horse Guards — by whom he had been seconded for service with the Company's Police — is not altogether clear. He had joined Jameson in the Matabele adventure and somehow or other, during this confused period of his military career, he had been promoted from Major to Lieutenant-Colonel.

Bobby White was the Chief Staff Officer; Major C.H. Villiers of the Royal Horse Guards was his deputy; Captain K.G. Kincaid-Smith of the Royal Artillery (later Colonel Kincaid-Smith, CB, CMG, DSO) was the Artillery Staff Officer; Captain J.H. Kennedy of the BSA Company's civil service, was the Quartermaster, with Captain E. Holden of the Derbyshire Yeomanry, his assistant. There were two Surgeon-Captains on the staff, W. Farmer of the Company's civil service and Seaton Hamilton of the 1st Life Guards. Lieutenant H.M. Grenfell, also of the 1st Life Guards, was the Remount Officer; Lieutenant J.C. Jessor Coope, a Mashonaland pioneer, was the Transport Officer, and Lieutenant A.H.C. Masters was the Staff Veterinary Officer. As if these were not enough, four more officers were loosely attached: Major J.B. Stracey of the Scots Guards, Captain C. Foley of the 3rd Royal Scots, Lieutenant H.R. Holden of the Grenadier Guards and Major Maurice Heany, one of the original leaders of the pioneer column. A Major Crosse, of the 5th Dragoons, also came along as an interested  spectator. It would have been difficult to conclude that all this brass was needed to control a little quiet police work among the Bechuanaland natives.

The RMP camp, pitched about a mile to the east of a native kraal known as Pitsani Botluko, some three and a half miles from the Transvaal border, was hardly an ideal spot at which to keep contented a force of nearly 400 lusty men. The two troops of the ex-BBP in Mafeking still had their barracks and the amenities of the town, such as they were. They even had some refuge from the eternal sun under the weeping willows along the banks of the Molopo River. But the RMP camp at Pitsani was pitched on arid, open veld, from which every tree of any size had been removed over the preceding 10 years by enterprising contractors supplying timber, first to the diamond mines at Kimberley and later to the gold mines on the Rand. Today, most of the larger trees have grown up again and the district has reverted to the relatively wooded bushveld which is the general feature of eastern Botswana. But as the temperature rose into the 90s in the summer months of late 1895 the general aspect of the district had little to distinguish it from that of a desert.

However, Pitsani did have a reasonable water supply from springs and wells, and mainly because of this it had a redeeming source of interest as a post-station where the coaches running between Mafeking and Bulawayo changed mule teams — and there was even a little hotel where the coach passengers were given a meal. But the presence of the coach station had one unremitting disadvantage, in that hordes of flies of particularly vicious temperaments congregated in the vicinity of the mule stables and commuted regularly between the stables and the camp, where the police horses served as an additional attraction.

Jameson and his colleagues, for all their inexperience in military planning, could never have expected to be able to keep such a large force of troops for any length of time as a static garrison in such poor conditions. How they were able to persuade the troop commanders and NCOs that the conditions would soon be relieved by moving on somewhere else, without giving away the true plans, remains an mystery. When the force did move on after about two months, the principal sufferers were a firm of general suppliers in Mafeking who had spent a lot of money building a store at Pitsani and stocking it with wagon-loads of provisions, including beer, for the troops, whom they confidently expected to be stationed in those parts for the next three or four years while the railway was being built.

Jameson did have the sense to keep Willoughby away from Pitsani as long as he could. The commanding officer elect was told by Jameson to keep himself busy in his investment company's office in Bulawayo, to allay suspicion. Nevertheless, Willoughby arrived from Bulawayo in the middle of December. According to plans in Johannesburg, such as they were, the rising was to take place on 26 December and during that month Jameson could hardly restrain his impatience to get moving. The first frustration had come on 9 December in a telegram from Colonel Frank Rhodes (Cecil's brother) in Johannesburg, saying "the polo tournament here is postponed for one week or it would clash with race week". The reference to "polo tournament" was, of course, a childish code for the rising, but "race week" meant what it said, and no reasonable person would allow a revolution to interfere with that. Concerned by the delay, Jameson sent two of his staff officers — Heany, the Mashonaland pioneer, and Holden, of the Derbyshire Yeomanry — to Johannesburg. Out of uniform, they had no difficulty in travelling through the Transvaal. Their instructions were to encourage the Reformers to speed up the rising. When they arrived, Frank Rhodes sent another telegram: "Inform Jameson do not send any more heroes before January. No room for them." This sounded ominously like a further postponement. Jameson, always impatient, replied: "Grave suspicion has been aroused. Surely in your estimation do you consider that races is of the utmost importance compared to immense risks of discovery daily expected." This is revealing. The danger of "discovery" had become the pressing consideration — not the allegedly shocking plight of the women and children in Johannesburg.

A plethora of telegrams passed between Jameson at Pitsani; Frank Rhodes; Jameson's brother, Sam, also in Johannesburg; Rutherfoord Harris, Cecil Rhodes's secretary, now in Cape Town; and a man named Woolf in Johannesburg, who had undertaken to stock a number of supply points on the road from Pitsani with provisions and remounts for the use of Jameson's force on the march. On 18 December Woolf wired, "There is not likely to be any postponement." On 23 December, Rutherfoord Harris telegraphed Jameson: "Company will be floated" — another puerile code "next Saturday (28 December) 12 o'clock at night. They are anxious you must not start before eight o'clock and secure telegraph silence." In other words, he must cut all the telegraph lines. "We suspect Transvaal is getting aware slightly." Jameson replied next day saying he suspected the Boer burghers in Zeerust and Lichtenburg — which lay north and south close to his route to Johannesburg — were hearing rumours and had already held meetings, and he believed they would concentrate and block his road. "Will endeavour delay till Saturday," he said to Harris. "If you can by cable do all you can to hasten it. Every day is of the utmost importance. Colonel Rhodes," whose messages were frustrating Jameson, "intolerable." Harris replied, "You must not move before Saturday night."

In Johannesburg, Jameson's impatience was beginning to frighten the Reformers. They were still not sure if they wanted him to come at all, but if he came too early it would be disastrous. On the 27th (Friday) they received a telegram from him saying, "I stand to lose 50 good BSA Company Police. Time expires next week and can tell them nothing." This was not strictly true. Jameson was obviously referring to some 50 men in the BBP who had refused transfer to the BSA Company's forces, but who Jameson still hoped would change their minds when he could produce his emotional letter from Johannesburg, pleading for help for helpless women and children. That was why the revolution must start this month. These 50 men would all be taking their discharge on 31 December. Johannesburg replied, "It is all right if only you will wait. Heany comes to you from Colonel Rhodes by special train today." Indeed they sent both Heany and Holden back to him with a message telling him on no account to move without direct instructions from Johannesburg — and, to make doubly sure that he got the message, they sent their two messengers by different routes.

Holden was the first to arrive at Pitsani, on Saturday evening, having ridden 170 miles from Johannesburg in 70 hours. By the time he arrived Jameson had already cabled to Rutherfoord Harris, "I shall start without fail tomorrow (Sunday) night," and he was not the sort of man to be persuaded to change his mind. When Holden delivered his message, Jameson received it with no comment at all. A special train from Johannesburg to Mafeking had been chartered by Colonel Rhodes for the other messenger, Heany. In those days there was no direct railway line from Johannesburg to Mafeking and the train had to go south through Bloemfontein and Colesberg to De Aar, and then north through Kimberley to Mafeking — nearly 1000 miles. No wonder Holden's horses reached Jameson first. A special train must have been a formidable expense, but this was not the sort of detail to worry the Rhodes brothers. Heany arrived at Mafeking at half-past four on Sunday morning, knocked up an unfortunate storekeeper, bought a pair of field boots and a kitbag (he was still out of uniform) and somehow acquired a horse. He covered the 26 miles to Pitsani by eight o'clock and found Jameson in his tent.

Heany, who had led No. 1 troop of the pioneers in the occupation of Mashonaland, was much closer to Jameson than Holden and could be expected to have some influence on him. History has it — although, of course, there is no formal record — that having read Heany's message, Jameson merely said, "I'm going in. What are you going to do?" and Heany replied "I'm coming with you." Jameson sent off a telegram to Rhodes himself in Cape Town: "Shall leave for the Transvaal tonight ... I want to start immediately to prevent loss of lives as letter states ... We are simply going to protect everybody while they change the present dishonest Government and take vote from whole country as to form of government required by the whole." The telegram may have been intended to justify to Rhodes Jameson's apparent impatience. On the other hand, it may have been part of the plot to enable Rhodes to produce evidence of the purity of motive of the invasion. Being Sunday, the telegraph office in Cape Town closed at 10 o'clock in the morning, and by the time Rhodes received the message, after a series of domestic delays, it was too late for him to reply, even if he had wanted to.

Willoughby, who had been keeping himself in the background, now took up his command in earnest. He called an unmounted parade of all ranks at three o'clock that Sunday afternoon, when, the four troops having been formed into a square (and the artillery, presumably, wedged in somewhere), Jameson read to them suitable extracts from the notorious letter from the Reformers in Johannesburg. He called on the men to march with him into the Transvaal to come to the rescue of their fellow countrymen who were in such peril. The specific responsibility imposed on the force by the Imperial authorities, for "maintaining the integrity of the frontier", although not mentioned, was apparently to be disregarded — just as the primary duty of the force to police Mashonaland and Matabeleland had virtually been ignored altogether. The two troops of ex-BBP in Mafeking, Jameson said, would march simultaneously and join them at Malmani, a little dorp inside the Transvaal border. Remounts, rations and forage were waiting for them along the route (to be provided by the obliging Mr. Woolf) and troops from Johannesburg would come out to meet and support them. He had no intention, he assured them, of interfering with "the persons or properties of the Boers"; their sole object was to help their fellow men in their hour of need. There would be no fighting — in his own words, "no red blood spilt" — although if they were attacked they would naturally defend themselves. None of the men would be compelled to come with him, "but I am confident you will all respond to the call". It was a pretty safe assumption. The troops cheered; Heany said they sang "God save the Queen" and, having been ordered to reassemble at sundown, mounted and in full marching order, the parade was dismissed.

Naturally, in spite of all the vaunted secrecy, the camp had been full of rumours for some time that something was brewing. Nobody really believed that their only purpose was to guard a non- existent railway. Now that the truth was known the rank and file accepted the prospect as an attractive, almost boisterous, adventure — far preferable to hanging around Pitsani any longer. And Jameson's oratory skills had worked them up to a state of great enthusiasm. The same could probably be said of the junior officers. But the senior officers, many of whom had Imperial commissions, now aware that Jameson was inciting them unashamedly to invade a country with which they were not at war, showed under-standable concern — not so much about the morality of the ended expedition, but about their own positions should anything go wrong. They sought out Willoughby, their commanding officer, and told him of their anxieties. Willoughby, who had no vestige of authority to do so, assured them that their commissions would be safe, whatever happened. His statement to them is not on record and when many of them subsequently faced criminal charges they decided, in an exaggerated sense of service loyalty, not to incriminate him by revealing what he actually had said — but he must have given them some plausible guarantee. In any case it satisfied them at the time. The whole force     paraded again at six o'clock — each man with one day's rations, 120 rounds of ammunition and 50 lb. grain for his horse — and half an hour later they had moved off in the direction of the Transvaal border.

In Mafeking, that afternoon, the ex-BBP men were similarly paraded by Lieutenant-Colonel Raleigh Grey. Major Bobby White, the Chief Staff Officer — who was in the town, it is assumed to ensure that everything went according to Jameson's plan — attended the parade. One hundred and thirteen ex-BBP had transferred to the Company's force, while there were still those 50-odd men of the now defunct force awaiting discharge in a few days. These formed a temporary troop, 'F' Troop, which paraded at the rear. Raleigh Grey's conscience had apparently been fully satisfied by Jameson and Bobby White that any operation on which they were to embark had the official backing of the Imperial Government, because he told his men pretty much the same as Jameson had told his, although with much less emotion. Whether he was able to read to them the plaintive letter from Johannesburg is not clear from the records. But he probably knew nothing of its existence — which Jameson had most likely kept to himself, lest the compromising circumstances in which it had been written should leak out prematurely.

Raleigh Grey and his second-in-command, Major Coventry, spent most of the time on that parade trying to persuade the members of 'F' Troop to change their minds about taking their discharge, and to join the expedition. One of the men asked whether, if they did come along, they would be marching under the orders of the Queen or the BSA Company. Perhaps, after all, Grey was not so convinced of full Imperial sanction, for he dodged a direct answer by replying that "we are going to fight for the supremacy of the British flag in South Africa". Whatever the moral justification for such an announcement — inferring British supremacy in an acknowledged foreign country — it neverthe-less had its desired effect on a few of the troopers; and nine members of 'F' Troop, who signified their readiness to join the expedition, were called out of the parade, formed into a new squad and marched off, to the cheers of the assembled troops, to be formally attested in the BSA Company's service. The cheers were heard in the middle of the town in Mafeking, where they caused considerable surprise that any troops should be in a cheerful mood after having been made to parade on a Sunday afternoon. Indeed they aroused the suspicions of an inspector of the Cape Police. (Mafeking, of course, was in the Cape Colony and therefore under the jurisdiction of the Cape Mounted Police. The BBP, when they existed, had only operated inside the Bechuanaland Protectorate — whose border was a few miles to the north — although they were actually housed in Mafeking for convenience, in the "Imperial Reserve", an area which had been left in the possession of the British Government and excluded from the land annexed to the Cape Colony. But they had no police authority in the town. The same circumstances still applied, even though they were now ostensibly operating for the BSA Company.)

The Cape Police inspector became even more concerned when he heard that the parade was to assemble again later that evening and when Raleigh Grey's column finally moved off at 10 p.m. he sent a sub-inspector and a sergeant to tail them. The column started off innocently enough along the road to the north — it might well be moving into the Protectorate for some perfectly legitimate duty. A couple of miles out it wheeled to the right and the troops trotted across the veld in the direction of Malmani, across the Transvaal border, assumedly under the impression that now it was dark no one in Mafeking would have any idea in which direction they were actually going.

With the column, on one of the ammunition wagons, went Major Bobby White's dispatch box. He had been careful to lock up in the box his diary and all the letters and telegrams which he had exchanged during the last few months with Jameson and others involved in the conspiratorial arrangements for the expedition. Most of the telegrams had wisely been sent in an agreed code — something a little less amateurish than the exchanges between Pitsani and the Reformers. But most obligingly, he had packed the code books in the dispatch box too.

"Die trommel van Bobby White", captured later by the Boers, was to become an interesting exhibit in the criminal proceedings subsequently brought by the Transvaal authorities against the Reformers.

## Chapter Nine

## THE JAMESON RAID

THE TWO DIVISIONS of Jameson's force converged at five o'clock the next morning, Monday, at Malmani, 35 miles inside the sovereign territory of the Republic of South Africa. The little army was an impressive array of military force, even if somewhat top heavy, with more than one commissioned officer to every 12 other ranks. There were 16 officers on the staff, including the Officer Commanding; also 16 officers of the RMP and nine of the BBP — 41 in all; to whom must be added Major Crosse, the privileged spectator, and Jameson himself who, although not in uniform and not overtly armed, could not fail to be identified as part of the expeditionary force. There were 356 other ranks of the RMP, and 122 of the BBP – 478 in all. They started off with 640 horses. The combined artillery consisted of eight Maxim guns, two seven-pounders and one 121/2-pounder.

How many wagons or carts accompanied them does not appear to be on record, but they had 158 mules and about 150 native drivers and leaders, so the wagon train was not inconsiderable. It was a provocative force and must have been the cause of some concern to any peaceful citizen of the South African Republic coming face to face with it unexpectedly. The RMP wore dark grey Bedford cord tunics and breeches copied from the uniform of the Cape Mounted Rifles, with grey felt "smasher" hats — as they were known — the broad brim pinned up on the left side and the crown of the hat wrapped round with a blue puggaree with white spots. In their photographs the RMP troopers have the appearance of wearing the feathers of some exotic bird — indeed, the style was known at the time as "guineafowl" or "bird's eye" pattern. The BBP hat was relatively sober by contrast: brown felt, the right side of the brim pinned up and a plain white puggaree. The BBP tunics and breeches were of plain khaki twill, set off by dark blue puttees. There was nothing of the freebooter about their appearance, whatever their purpose.

Malmani was no more than a little dorp but it boasted a telegraph post. Before the two forces moved on together at about half-past six somebody on Jameson's staff, with more diligence than common sense, knocked up the still sleeping telegraphist to find out if he had received any alarming messages. He had heard nothing, but when he looked out into the village street and saw a formidable column of armed men, obviously foreign to the country, moving off in the direction of the interior, he made an immediate telegraphic report to Pretoria. Orders had been given by Willoughby to cut the telegraph line. There is a story, which is patently unlikely, that the troopers to whom the job was assigned cut a wire fence, in the belief that this was the telegraph. Probably the telegraph line was cut, but equally probably it was cut too late. A report from the Cape police inspector in Mafeking had also reached the authorities at Kimberley as soon as the telegraph to the south had opened that morning though this report was, of course, addressed to the Cape authorities and not the Transvaal. Nevertheless, however the news travelled, the invasion was known to the Commandant General of the South African Republic in Pretoria by eight o'clock that morning. Prior rumours that something of this nature was developing had reached President Kruger some days before. He had said, "Wait until the time comes. Take a tortoise: if you want to kill it you must wait until it puts out its head, and then you cut it off." Now, all the commandos in the western Transvaal were alerted to prepare for the execution.

The road eastward towards Johannesburg — in those days it was really no more than a track — ran generally through open country. Very little of the farmland on each side of the road was even fenced and the column would have had no difficulty in deploying in an emergency. But 30 miles from Malmani the road entered a relatively narrow pass between two kopjes, close to a lead mine, and Bobby White — who had been over the route some weeks before — had advised Willoughby to make sure that the column passed through before nightfall. Indeed, it subsequently transpired that a Boer commando from Lichtenburg, some miles south of the road, had been sent out during the day to set up an ambush in the defile and intercept the invaders, but on this occasion Willoughby outmarched the Boers and he was through the pass about three hours before they arrived. Nevertheless, the pace at which the column was being pressed was strenuous and after a forced march of almost 24 hours the troops as well as the animals were beginning to tire.

SOUTHERN AFRICA 1890

The Pioneer Column and men of the British South Africa Company Police enter Matabeleland; July 1890

**Above:** A fort in the laager established in the Mangwe Pass during the Matabele War of 1893.

**Right:** Cecil John Rhodes and partner Alfred Beit, 1888

**Below:** The Pioneer Column and BSACP force laagered at Fort Tuli, 1890

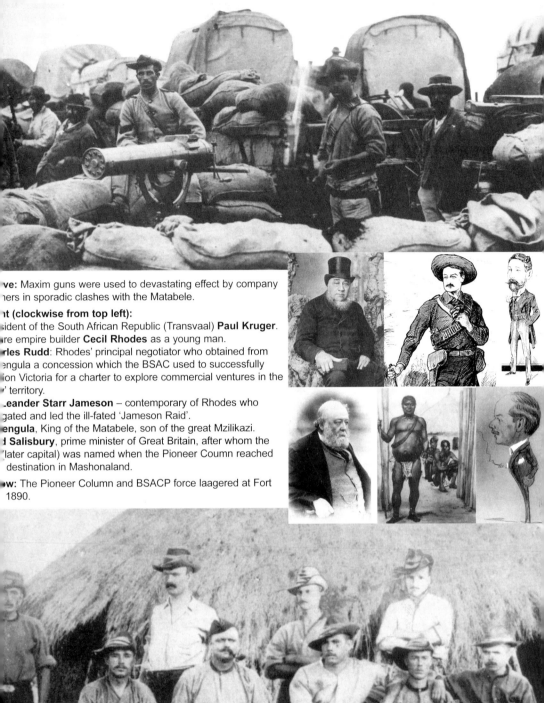

**...ve:** Maxim guns were used to devastating effect by company
...ers in sporadic clashes with the Matabele.

**...t (clockwise from top left):**
...sident of the South African Republic (Transvaal) **Paul Kruger**.
...re empire builder **Cecil Rhodes** as a young man.
**...rles Rudd**: Rhodes' principal negotiator who obtained from
...engula a concession which the BSAC used to successfully
...ion Victoria for a charter to explore commercial ventures in the
...' territory.
**...eander Starr Jameson** – contemporary of Rhodes who
...gated and led the ill-fated 'Jameson Raid'.
**...engula**, King of the Matabele, son of the great Mzilikazi.
**...d Salisbury**, prime minister of Great Britain, after whom the
...(later capital) was named when the Pioneer Coumn reached
...destination in Mashonaland.

**...w:** The Pioneer Column and BSACP force laagered at Fort
...1890.

**Above left:** The spirit of early Rhodesia; women in laager

**Above Right:** Matabele *impi* captured after skirmish, 1893.

**Left:** Cecil Rhodes holds 'Indaba' with Matabele *indunas*

**Below:** Wounded BSACP trooper receives medical attention

**Opposite page (top):** Dramatised illustration of attack on wagon laager

**Opposite (bottom):** 'A gallant deed': BSACP patrol encounters stiff resistence from Matabele *impi*.

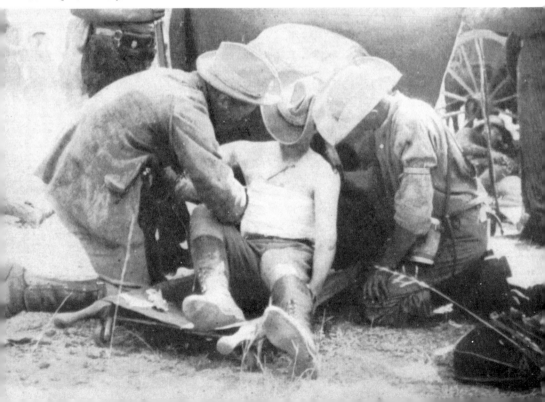

**Above left:** The flag is raised at Fort Salisbury, 12 Septe
1890. The site was later named Cecil Square.

**Above Right:** Harare, Zimbabwe, 2000. Cecil Square is
known as Africa Unity Square.

**Left:** Heroes of the Mazoe Patrol. Inspector R.C. Nesbitt
at centre.

**Below:** Survivors of the Mazoe Patrol. Inspector R.C. N
VC at centre.

**Opposite page (left):** British South Africa Company troo
1890. From "The Regiment" – A History and the Uniform
the British South Africa Police by Richard Hamley. Publi
in 2000 by Covos-Day Books (SA). Website www.mazo

**Opposite page (right):** Matabele warrior, circa 1890.

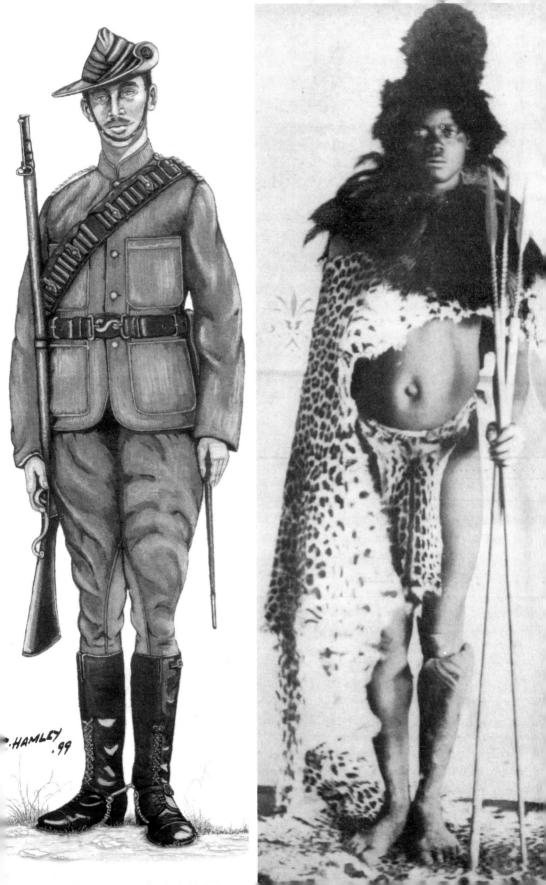

.HAMLEY .99

**Left:** Spirit mediums Nehanda and Kaguvi (Kagubi) put to execution in 1897 for instigating Mashona rebellion.

**Below (left):** Major R.C. Nesbitt VC.

**Below (right):** Major F.C. Booth VC.

**Bottom of page:** BSAP officers and men, Inyanga, 1903.

At midday on that first day, Monday, a burgher from Zeerust — which was north of their route had caught them up, bringing a message from the Commandant-General of the Republic, relayed through the Commandant of the Marico District. The message had plainly warned Jameson, in surprisingly polite terms, that he was breaking the law. Jameson had replied, "I intend proceeding with my original plans which have no hostile intention against the people of the Transvaal, but we are here in reply to an invitation from the principal residents of the Rand to assist them in their demand for justice and the ordinary rights of every citizen of a civilised state."

The column halted for an all too brief rest late in the evening and pressed on during the night to cover another 20 miles to Doornpoort still west of Krugersdorp, where Jameson had hoped to meet a supporting force sent from Johannesburg to join him. Here at Doornpoort — which they reached early on Tuesday morning, 31 December — was the first of Mr. Woolf's supply of stores and horses which he had assembled under the guise of "the Land Transport and Trading Syndicate", on the unlikely pretext of setting up a new coach service to Mafeking. But the horses were a disappointing lot and most of the men preferred to keep their own, tired as they were.

The supplies were equally discouraging: a shortage of forage for the horses, and insufficient food for a decent meal for the men who had started off with rations for only 24 hours. They moved on again, soon to be caught up by a Sergeant White, one of the remaining BBP in Mafeking awaiting discharge. White had been sent out early on Monday morning by the local Resident Commissioner — an official, of course, of the Cape Government — and had ridden more than 100 miles in some 50 hours. He carried an official-looking package from the Commissioner, which he handed first to Raleigh Grey. But Grey's conscience must have been beginning to prick him and he declined to open the package. He sent Sergeant White to Willoughby, who was equally reticent and passed him on to Jameson. Jameson also refused to have anything to do with it and finally Willoughby had no option but to open it himself. As commanding officer, he could hardly have sent the sergeant back to the Resident Commissioner without at least an acknowledgement. The package contained letters individually addressed to himself, Jameson and Grey; also to Major Coventry and Captain Monroe, both ex-BBP. All the letters were in identical terms, conveying direct orders from the High Commissioner in Cape Town to return immediately to Mafeking with the invading force. The telegraph between Mafeking and Cape Town had certainly been busy early on the Monday morning.

The High Commissioner also instructed Willoughby to circulate these orders among all the subordinate officers. It is doubtful if Willoughby did so. The seniors, to whom the letters had been addressed, spent half an hour discussing the situation, during which they must have suffered painful misgivings about their positions. Finally Willoughby sent the wretched Sergeant White all the way back to Mafeking with merely a curt message that the Resident Commissioner's dispatch was being attended to.

Willoughby subsequently wrote an official report, which he painstakingly titled, "The official report of the Expedition that left the Protectorate at the urgent request of the leading citizens of Johannesburg with the object of standing by them and maintaining law and order whilst they were demanding justice from the Transvaal authorities" — a naive attempt to deny any intention of a military invasion, with its implied threat of taking over the country. Their sole purpose, he was saying, had been merely to oblige everybody by helping to keep the peace. Referring, in this report, to the orders from the High Commissioner brought by Sergeant White, Willoughby blandly commented, "It appeared impossible to turn back in view of the fact that we had been urgently called to avert a massacre."

Again, the column moved on and late on Tuesday afternoon they encountered a detachment of police from Krugersdorp who had been sent out to report on their movements. The leader, Lieutenant Kruger — a grandson of the President — came too close and was captured by one of Willoughby's advanced patrols. Willoughby had him disarmed, but after giving an undertaking not to move from where he was for three hours, the policeman was released and the column proceeded. Just after midnight some scouts were fired on by a party of Boers, lying in wait behind cover. The advanced guard drove them back, but one RMP man was wounded. The first red blood had been spilt.

The messenger from Zeerust with the Commandant General's warning, and subsequently Sergeant White, had merely been the forerunners of a persistent series of emissaries who were to be sent out at frequent intervals in attempts to deflect Jameson from his crazy purpose. Whether, had any of the them been successful and turned him back, his own and his officers' situations would have been less hazardous within the jurisdiction of their own people is doubtful. But a number of lives could certainly have been saved and the harsh treatment later meted out by the Republic to the Reformers in Johannesburg would probably have been avoided. Nevertheless, Jameson's obstinately persisted.

Next morning was New Year's Day and the column had halted at a farm where Woolf's next depot of provisions had been established. The supplies here proved to be a little more adequate. Here they were now confronted by two mounted Boers, with a formally sealed letter from the British Agent in Pretoria. The letter was addressed to Jameson himself this time, and he had no excuse to pass it on to somebody else. Again it emanated from the High Commissioner in Cape Town. "Her Majesty's Government," it said, "entirely disapprove your conduct in invading the Transvaal with an armed force. Your action has been repudiated. You are ordered to retire at once from the Country and will be held personally responsible for the consequences of your unauthorised and most improper proceeding."

This must have faintly pricked, if it did not altogether penetrate, Jameson's conscience, for he replied, submissively for him, "I should of course desire to obey His Excellency's instructions but as I have a very large force of both men and horses to feed, having finished all my supplies in the rear, I must perforce proceed to Krugersdorp or Johannesburg this morning for this purpose." But he was not the sort to carry submissiveness too far. "At the same time," he went on, "I must acknowledge that I am anxious to fulfil my promise on the petition of the principal residents on the Rand to come to the aid of my fellow men in their extremity." He had repeated this so often that he probably now believed it himself. "I have molested no one and have explained it to all Dutchmen met that the above is my sole object and that I shall desire at once to return to the Protectorate."

During that days' march, the column was followed by a party of Boers who kept about a mile to their rear. Willoughby strengthened his rearguard with an additional Maxim gun. But there was no actual engagement. The Boers, well knowing what was waiting for the invaders ahead, had no need to risk action at this stage. Two more messengers had appeared, early that morning, this time on bicycles. They were neither Boers, nor emissaries of the British authorities. In fact, they had been sent out by the Reform Committee, the presumed leaders of the revolution. The actual content of the letters they brought was never known. One letter disappeared altogether and the other only survived in a mutilated condition, picked up in fragments two months later from the veld, where it had been torn up after Jameson had shown it to Willoughby. The letter, apparently signed by Frank Rhodes and Lionel Phillips, as far as it could subsequently be reconstructed, indicated that "the rumour of massacre" in Johannesburg which had prompted Jameson to come to the relief of the town "was not true". Some reference was made to having "armed a lot of men" but not being "in possession (of the) town". The letter said "shall be very glad ... to see you". It ended, "men to ... follow" — words which were construed by Jameson and Willoughby as a promise that assistance for the column was being sent out from Johannesburg. Jameson replied "As you may imagine, we are well pleased with your letter. We have had some    fighting and hope to reach Johannesburg by tonight, but of course it will depend on the amount of fighting we have. Of course we shall be pleased to have 200 men meet us at Krugersdorp as it will greatly encourage the men who are in great heart, although a bit tired." This message never reached Johannesburg. The messenger set off back to the town confidently enough, hiding Jameson's reply in the open-ended tube under the saddle of his bicycle. Not unexpectedly, he was captured by the Boers and the bicycle was abandoned in the veld. Months later, the piece of paper was found by a mechanic in a cycle shop.

As the column approached Krugersdorp, in the heat of the New Year afternoon, Willoughby — so he said later in his report — wished to avoid a march through the town "on the military grounds of the possibility of there being opposition" a strange reason for a military decision. But Jameson, the amateur general with no inhibitions or hesitancy, overruled him. The truth was that he still expected to find reinforcements from Johannesburg waiting for him in the town. Willoughby therefore sent an arrogant note to General Cronje, the Boer commandant, threatening that if his march was resisted he would shell the town. Jameson's foresight in bringing a proper army with field-guns was to be vindicated — in spite of the protestations he had made to the parade at Pitsani that he had no intention of interfering with "the persons or properties of the Boers". In his message Willoughby added considerately that the women and children should be moved out of danger. Cronje ignored the threat and posted his commando in a defensive position three miles west of Krugersdorp.

Meanwhile the column had reached Hind's store, seven miles from Krugersdorp, where Mr. Woolf had let them down again and there were hardly any provisions for men or horses. A detachment of Boers was seen to be retiring, this time ahead of the column. Willoughby sent the seven-pounders forward and a few ineffectual shots were fired. Moving on again, the column came over the crest of a steep rise at about four o'clock in the afternoon, to find that the road to Krugersdorp ran straight across a shallow valley and up another hill on the far side. There were some mine dumps, buildings and prospecting trenches on the face of the furthest hill. This was the Queen's Mine and it was here that Cronje had posted his commando. At the bottom of the intervening valley was a broad river, which would have to be negotiated in any attack on the Boer positions.

The 12-pounder was brought up and trained on the mine buildings, at a range of 1900 yards, but the shrapnel bursting over the Boers' line had little or no effect on their protected positions. Willoughby sent Raleigh Grey with his two ex-BBP troops to make a flanking movement towards the Boers' left, and Colonel H.F. White took two troops of RMP (not identified in the records) forward in skirmishing order. This frontal attack only got as far as the watercourse, without attempting to cross it, where it was driven back by heavy fire from all parts of the enemy line.

The RMP suffered about 30 casualties that afternoon. Again, the casualties in this first engagement are not identified. The Boers had opened fire from behind their cover in the mine buildings and when most of White's men withdrew the Boers came out and took prisoner some 30 of Grey's troopers who had found what shelter they could on the enemy's left. There is a story in the subsequent accounts that one of the wounded troopers ungratefully shot dead a Boer who came to help him.

Realising that it was hopeless to continue along the direct road through Krugersdorp, Willoughby decided to take the column southward across the veld towards Randfontein. Someone told him that if he could find it, there was a track by which he could cross the swampy stream known as Luipard's Vlei. Bobby White, in his earlier reconnaissance, had kept to the road and none of them had any maps of the surrounding country. The result was that in no time the column lost itself in the bush. It was now late in the afternoon and the light was failing. They soon found themselves back on the outskirts of Krugersdorp. They heard firing on their left and could just make out a large body of men moving towards the Queen's Mine buildings. Willoughby, who was nothing if not an optimist, was sure these were the reinforcements which Colonel Rhodes had promised to send from Johannesburg, and the firing he could hear indicated they had engaged the Boers. He immediately left his transport where it stood, with one troop to guard it, and led the remainder of his force at a canter across the veld in the direction of the firing. This was going to be a dramatic meeting with the revolutionaries. He and his men rode for a full mile before they realised with dismay that the shots were directed at them and that the shadowy figures they had seen were Boers and not revolutionaries from Johannesburg. They wheeled about, and by the time they returned to the halted transport they heard reports of another body of Boers gathering close to them to the south, which was the direction Willoughby had been trying to take towards Luipard's Vlei. It was now too dark to engage this new Boer force. Even if Willoughby had felt inclined to do so, it was clearly impossible to attempt an escape eastward into the unmapped bush in the dark.

The column camped for the night where they stood. There was no possibility of looking around for a more favourable site. They had some protection from sloping ground to the east, in which direction they set the guns, and they drew up the ammunition wagons to form the other three sides of a square. The Boers kept up a fusillade directed into the centre of the column's position, but Willoughby's field-guns had some actual success, in that they silenced most of the Boers with shrapnel bursting in the direction from which the shots seemed to be coming. However, the Boer's occasional fire denied the men of the column any rest that night. They had now been on the move for three nights and three days; they had only had one proper meal during the whole journey, which was breakfast that morning, and apart from the fatigue of the march, they had been involved that day in two gruelling engagements. There were already 30 casualties in the ambulance wagon. In more creditable circumstances, their situation would have been heroic.

The future Colonel Tomlinson wrote later, "Just before we moved off in the coming daylight I remember seeing Corporals Still and Beard had met their end and a man named Brown who had been transferred from the Town Police at Bulawayo, whom I turned over because I thought he was still asleep, was also dead."

The early patrols which Willoughby sent out next morning established that the Boers were waiting behind a railway embankment, at the top of the rising ground to the east; but the way to the south appeared, surprisingly enough, to be open. Without any breakfast, the column moved out at 5 a.m. in successive troops and in remarkably good order, considering their condition — but still, owing to the lack of maps — without any positive plan. Moreover, the innocent looking situation to the south was deceptive and the Boers were leading them into a trap. Parties of Boers started to harass them from the rear and on the flanks. At this point a wire fence ran along each side of the road and some delay, and consequent danger, occurred while the wire was being cut to allow the flanking parties to move to their defensive positions. Raleigh Grey received a bullet in his foot. They bandaged him up and he remounted. Lieutenant Cazalet received two wounds and was carried to the already crowded ambulance wagon. It was here also that Captain Barry received the wound from which he was later to die. One wagon carrying some wounded men, which was tending to lag behind the column, was captured by the Boers.

For all their difficulties, Jameson and Willoughby were still unrealistically optimistic that they would reach Johannesburg, which was now only about 12 miles away. They were beginning to recognise the landmarks now. Early that morning, before they had broken camp, Jameson had sent one of his men on to Johannesburg — it is doubtful if he got there — with a verbal message, "I am getting on all right but you must send out to meet me." One wonders if he still had visions of a triumphant entry into the town as the champion of oppressed humanity. Nevertheless, his visions of publicly acclaimed heroism suffered a severe jolt at about half-past eight when a dispatch rider, with Boer escort, arrived with another message from the British Agent in Pretoria. The High Commissioner had made a formal Proclamation.

"Whereas it has come to my knowledge that certain British subjects, said to be under the leadership of Dr. Jameson, have violated the territory of the South African Republic and have cut telegraph wires and done various illegal acts, and whereas the South African Republic is a friendly state in amity with Her Majesty's Government, and whereas it is my desire to respect the independence of the said state, now therefore I do hereby command the said Dr. Jameson and all persons accompanying him to immediately retire from the territory of the South African Republic on pain of the penalties attached to their illegal proceedings, and I do hereby call upon all British subjects in the South African Republic to abstain from giving the said Dr. Jameson any countenance or assistance in his armed violation of the territory of a friendly state."

Jameson and every member of his force had been proclaimed outlaws, cast off by their own people, deprived of any protection of the law.

Despite its harassment, the column had continued to move forward. Tomlinson writes, "We passed Randfontein where the British miners came out and cheered us." It was here that Trooper Bletsoe of the RMP was killed. The miners subsequently buried him and subscribed for a headstone for his grave. At one stage a concentration of Boers developing on one of the flanks had been broken up by a daring charge by two troops of the RMP led by Major Bodle. The column even managed to occupy a farm-house named Vlakfontein, and a breathing space enabled the artillery to be drawn up to shell the kopjes ahead on which the main Boer forces were gathering. They cleared one ridge and the troops advanced to its summit under heavy enemy fire from the flanks. It was during this assault that Major Coventry was severely wounded. But the hapless tactical situation at Krugersdorp was to be repeated almost in its entirety; and when they reached the crest of the ridge they faced an intervening valley and, on the farther side, another broken, stony kopje, known as Doornkop, which commanded the track along which they were advancing and a small spruit which lay directly ahead.

The column was halted and the guns drawn up again. For half an hour Willoughby's tired men kept up an obstinate defence against the Boer attacks which were now being launched virtually all round. The ground in front was exposed to the enemy's direct fire, their own and their gun's ammunition was being depleted, while the Maxims were becoming so heated from lack of water that soon they were all jammed. Willoughby, still the optimist in spite of his new-found outlaw status, sent out scouts to see if any way could be found out of the impasse.

Now the Staats Artillerie — the Republic's only professional armed force, for whom Kruger had imported Krupp guns from Germany — made its appearance and opened fire at less than a mile's range. Jameson's force had already been reduced by casualties to only some 400 fighting troops. The survivors suffered gnawing hunger and were almost dead on their feet for want of rest. Someone — it was never established who — raised a white flag at about 9.15 a.m. Tomlinson says, "A trumpeter was seen to go forward with someone else holding a pole on which was a piece of white cloth. The cease-fire was sounded faintly at first, which became more pronounced as firing began to die down. Then followed a stillness which was remarkable. Batches of us gradually stood up and all wondered what would take place next."

In another personal narrative, Sub-Inspector Chawner wrote, "I had been sent back by Lieut.-Col. Harry White with a message concerning some wounded men and was riding along alone looking for my Troop when I came to a stone wall enclosing an orchard. There I saw Dr. Jameson and Sir John Willoughby sitting alone against the wall with tears of emotion streaming down their faces. I afterwards saw a mounted man riding along with a white puggaree tied to a lance. The rain of bullets, which had been falling incessantly upon us from the time it started beyond Krugersdorp early in the morning, stopped, and the Boers streamed out of Doornkop Ridge. One of the leaders, a big stout man, rode up to the wall and I heard him use the identical words the Doctor had used to Ferreira in 1891, "I told you so, Jameson." Chawner had miraculously escaped death, with a bullet hole through the collar of his tunic at the back of his neck.

The Boers started coming out, cautiously at first, from behind their cover and Willoughby, accepting at last that the game was up, scribbled a note saying, "We surrender, providing you guarantee safe conduct out of the country for every member of the force." He went forward himself and handed the note to one of the Boers to take to the Commandant. It must have been a bitter moment for an officer of the Blues. Commandant Cronje replied, "I acknowledge your letter. The answer is that if you will undertake to pay the expense that you have caused the South African Republic and if you will surrender with your arms, then I shall spare the lives of you and yours." Willoughby says in his report that he accepted the terms in writing and asked the Commandant to bear in mind that his men had been without food for 24 hours. The Boers started handing out bread and biltong to the troopers. Commandant Malan of Rustenberg told Jameson that Cronje had had no authority to guarantee to spare his, or anybody else's life. He assured Jameson that the decision would be speedily reversed.

Tomlinson writes, "Word was passed along to instruct the troop to assemble opposite the burghers. Gradually we all drifted in with the poor, tired-out horses and arms were laid on the ground. Officers assembled where there was a stone wall," as Chawner had also noted, "some lying wounded, our artillery and machine guns nearby. Some hour or so elapsed and our men were moved away under escort with their horses. Officers were bundled into ox-wagons and eventually Krugersdorp was reached and we were placed at the foot of the Paardeberg monument. The men and horses were camped a little distance off."

Next morning, the officers were taken before the Magistrate at Krugersdorp. The proceedings were limited to taking their names, with a brief interrogation to which Willoughby replied for them all. Then a procession was formed led by the rank and file, mounted on their horses; Jameson followed in the dubious luxury of a Cape cart and the officers were herded once again into the ox-wagons. The column was flanked for its whole length by files of jubilant, mounted burghers, like the outriders of a circus. As Tomlinson describes it, "Salvoes of rifle fire were indulged in by our captors as the procession neared villages on the route and all inhabitants turned out to see the unusual sight."

Surgeon-Captain Garraway, the BBP medical officer, remained at Krugersdorp with 10 men to assist him, under a Boer guard, to attend the wounded and bury the dead. He wrote later — in touching contrast to Tomlinson's report of the Boers' behaviour on the road to Pretoria — "Nothing could exceed the kindness of the people, both Dutch and English, who came up afterwards. Milk, brandy, meat and bread were sent for the wounded and ambulance carts came out from Krugersdorp. I was worked pretty hard all day and only got to the burying later in the afternoon. To my surprise there were only six to bury, 2 BBP and 4 BSA men. One of ours (BBP) was a youngster not very long out from home. All the BSA were youngsters. The men from Roodepoort Mine which was close by came over and helped me to bury the dead which I did in one long trench. It was dark when I got back to the farm house where our men were. I found that an escort had arrived to take us to Krugersdorp. The men were put on a wagon and I on a horse and we started off quietly. I had got most of the severely wounded in during the afternoon. After a long, cold ride we arrived at Krugersdorp at 1 a.m. and I was left at the temporary hospital while the men were taken down to the Court House."

When the main column of prisoners reached Pretoria, the rank and file were accommodated in a camp on the racecourse, still under guard. The officers were crammed into small cells in the forbidding Pretoria "tronk". Only Jameson was given the doubtful privilege of a separate cell. The Boer authorities were now busy rounding up the Reform Committee in Johannesburg. Sixty-four of Johannesburg's leading citizens were arrested, 20 of them within the hallowed precincts of the Rand Club. To make room for these more important prisoners in Pretoria jail, the officers were now moved to the grandstand on the racecourse — with the exception of Jameson, Willoughby, the two Whites, Stracey and Grey — who retained their status of criminal importance and were kept in the cells.

On the morning of 11 January 1896 the less important survivors of Jameson's force, numbering 26 officers and 399 other ranks — some still recovering from their wounds — were marched to Pretoria station and put in two special trains for Natal. Surgeon-Captain Garraway, who had now been brought from Krugersdorp to join them, wrote, "We officers were put into First Class carriages and well supplied with fruit and liquor. We were cheered as we left the station and at every station passed." At six o'clock next morning they were detrained at Volksrust, on the border of Natal, where they were to be handed over to the British authorities. True to type, the authorities were not ready for them and they were all locked up in the wool sheds at the railway station. They were allowed out in batches to wash in a nearby stream. Three days later a British general, in civvies, arrived with his staff, all similarly dressed. Perhaps the idea was to play down any suggestion of military glamour, for Garraway says, "They were not over-civil at first and made us feel more like felons than prisoners of war." Another tedious week passed and then a train arrived from Pretoria with the six important prisoners who had been left behind — Jameson, Willoughby, the Whites, Stracey and Grey (Coventry was still in hospital.) The other Imperial officers, who had already come to Volksrust with the main body — Villiers, Kincaid-Smith, Foley, Monroe, Hamilton, the two Holdens, Gosling and Grenfell — were now put in the train to join Jameson and the leading conspirators. They were all taken to Durban, embarked on the British troopship Victoria and shipped back to England where, on arrival, they were to be arrested and criminally charged.

After two weeks in the wool sheds at Volksrust, the remainder were also moved on to Durban by train — this time under an escort of 7th Hussars — and embarked in the specially chartered Harlech Castle. "Here," said Tomlinson, "we were outfitted to a certain extent, tailors visiting the officers, but it was not divulged who paid expenses." One is inclined to suspect an application of conscience money on the part of the BSA Company. Those members of the force with homes in South Africa were allowed to land at Cape ports and the rest were taken to England. Twenty wounded men had been left behind in Pretoria, from where they were subsequently sent back to England — except Captain Barry, the only fatal casualty among the officers, who died of his wounds. Lieutenant Spain of the RMP, sub-inspector of the Artillery Troop, contracted typhoid. Garraway says Spain caught the disease at Volksrust "due to the utter absence of sanitary precautions (in the wool sheds) where there was typhoid in the village at the same time". As far as it is known, Spain survived; but a Trooper Spurrier of the RMP, another typhoid case, died during the voyage in the Harlech Castle.

Thirty-nine members of Jameson's force were never accounted for — neither taken prisoner, killed nor wounded. Probably, they disappeared into the bush when the cease-fire sounded. The Boer casualties were four killed — of whom one had been accidentally shot by his own side and one, presumably, shot by the wounded BBP trooper outside Krugersdorp. Three were wounded.

It is not within the limits of a history of the Rhodesian police to dwell on the consequences of what has gone down in history as the Jameson Raid; nor is it the place to make moral or political judgements.

For the record, Jameson and all the officers repatriated on the Victoria were arrested by officials from Scotland Yard immediately on arrival at Gravesend near London and taken to Bow Street police court. There they were charged in terms of the Foreign Enlistment Act of 1870 that "within Her Majesty's dominions, and without licence of Her Majesty, they did unlawfully prepare and fit out a military expedition to proceed against the dominions of a certain friendly state to wit, the South African Republic." After a long trial at the Old Bailey, which was to become one of London's social events of the season, Jameson was sentenced to 15 months' imprisonment without hard labour; Willoughby to 10; Bobby White to seven; H.F. White, Grey and Coventry (who was brought to London when he had recovered from his wounds) to five months each. They were locked up in

Holloway Gaol, before it was to become London's prison for women. The rest were acquitted. Willoughby, Grey, Coventry and both the Whites were compulsorily retired from the British Army, but their commissions were later restored in recognition of subsequent meritorious service.

The subsequent careers of some of those who were convicted are worth noting: Jameson became Prime Minister of the Cape Colony, also President of the BSA Company, and was created a Baronet and Privy Councillor; H.F. White became a Brigadier-General, CB, CMG, DSO; Grey became Sir Raleigh Grey, KBE, CVO, CMG; Coventry became Colonel Coventry, CB. There is no record on the subsequent career of Bobby White. (Charles, the first of the Whites to be commissioned in the BSACP, who had been fortunate enough to relinquish the Commissionership of the RMP in favour of his older brother before the Jameson Raid, was to distinguish himself with the volunteer forces during the Matabele and Mashona Rebellions).

The 64 reluctant revolutionaries arrested in Johannesburg were charged with high treason before the High Court of the South African Republic. The evidence of "die Trommel van Bobby White" did nothing to assist in their defence. Four of the defendants, including Colonel Frank Rhodes, were sentenced to death. All the others were sentenced to two years' imprisonment, a fine of £2000 and banishment from the Republic for three years. The death sentences caused such an outcry in Britain that Kruger commuted them to life imprisonment the next day.

When one of the less important prisoners committed suicide early in May 1896, he took further fright and reduced the sentences on the four leaders to 15 years each; the others were released on paying their fines (two refused to pay and were held in prison for another year). At the end of May the four leaders were released on payment of £25,000 each — another charge, no doubt, on the BSA Company's finances — and a welcome windfall to the Republic's coffers.

Mr. Woolf had wisely departed for Cape Town, where he avoided the inconvenience of prosecution for his profitable participation in the conspiracy.

## Chapter Ten

## REBELLION

THE JAMESON RAID came to its inglorious end on 2 January 1896 and nearly 90% of the Rhodesian police, with almost all the officers and NCOs, were effectively removed from the strength of the force which had been specifically created to keep law and order in its own country. Instead of 150 men to police Mashonaland and 250 for the virtually untamed territory of Matabeleland — which were meagre enough numbers anyway — there were now not more than 80 left for the whole country.

Inspector Southey, OC Matabeleland, had a total of 48 (officers, NCOs and other ranks); Hopper had even less in Mashonaland. Of Southey's men, 22 were stationed in Bulawayo and the remainder were distributed in twos and threes at Gwelo, Iron Mine Hill (between Gwelo and Umvuma), Selukwe, Belingwe, Inyati, Mangwe, Tuli and Matopos. Admittedly, in the event of emergency, help could be expected from the volunteer forces, now formed into one unit known as the Rhodesia Horse Volunteers. But these would first have to be mobilised — many of them were also scattered about the country — and in any case they were unavailable for the continuing day-to-day duties of crime prevention and detection, and the usual calls on the services of a police force. In fact — and in spite of the conscientious efforts by lonely, individual members to carry out their duties — there was no effective police force in the country at all.

This was the situation in March 1896 when the Matabele rose in violent rebellion against their white conquerors.

Some historians have suggested the Matabele would have risen anyway and their knowledge that the police had been removed from the country (that the white men were not invincible), served only to encourage the rebels to rise when they did and did not actually cause them to do it. This was the opinion of Frederick Selous, the scout and hunter with long experience in Africa, who had been the guide for the pioneer column. He had settled with his wife on a farm at Essexvale near the site of the present Falcon College at the time when the Matabele rebellion broke out, and he was intimately concerned with the ensuing campaign to suppress it. He wrote in the preface to his book, Sunshine and Storm in Rhodesia (published in August 1896), "Dr. Jameson ... when he left Matabeleland never dreamt that the removal of the police force would have any more effect upon the Matabele than the disbandment of the police in Mashunaland (sic) in 1891 had had upon the natives in that country. This opinion," he went on, "must have been shared by the great majority of the inhabitants of Matabeleland, since no remonstrance was made by any public man at the time that the police left Bulawayo. We know now that the removal of the white police force was a mistake; but it is easy to criticise after the event, and as at the time the mistake was made no one in Rhodesia was wise or prescient enough to foresee the possible effect it might have on the natives of Matabeleland, it would be the height of meanness and injustice to hold Dr. Jameson morally responsible for the present insurrection." Some historians subsequently echoed his sentiments.

But Selous — who was a close friend and supporter of Jameson — and might excusably have been influenced by some prejudice in his favour — entirely misses the point; perhaps not deliberately, but certainly with a jaundiced eye. No-one would ever "hold Dr. Jameson morally responsible" for the rebellion. The rebellion had its own causes, the moral responsibility for which was widely spread. His particular moral responsibility lay in his own decision to sacrifice the safety of the white inhabitants of the country for the sake of a reckless adventure for his own self-promotion. In Matabeleland alone, 130 white men, women and children were murdered within a week of the outbreak of the rising.

It is sheer speculation to suggest that many of these would have been saved if there had been 250 police in the territory instead of 48. But the measure of the responsibility of Jameson, Willoughby and the White brothers is that they deliberately removed the possibility of the police being available to save any of them. Their action was positive — not simply a sin of omission. When they were brought to trial they were charged only with invading a friendly state — a charge with as much political as criminal content. But up to that time nobody had been murdered except the unlucky casualties of the raid. The murderers, when they struck in Matabeleland, were positively aided and abetted by the absence of those men whose prime duty was to be there as the public's first line of defence.

Selous himself tends to contradict his own defence of Jameson when he wrote, later in his book, "I have strong reason for believing that (Umlugulu, one of the chief instigators of the rebellion) only made up his mind that the time had come for the attempt to be made to drive the white men out of the country when he learnt that the whole of the police force of Matabeleland, together with the artillery, munitions of war, etc., which had been taken to the Transvaal by Dr. Jameson, had been captured by the Boers."

It is also difficult to completely exonerate Bodle and the other officers of the RMP who participated in the raid. For sure, they were kept in the dark for a long time about Jameson's real intentions and, until the euphoria of the final moment at Pitsani, they had believed that they were acting under legitimate orders within the territory in which, however unwarranted, their force had been given police authority. However, with the benefit of hindsight, one can't help feeling, however unworthy the thought perhaps — that, without any thought of protest — they set out lightheartedly from Bulawayo on an exciting adventure into Bechuanaland and abdicated their primary responsibilities. Nobody in a public service — particularly in a military force — is thanked by his superiors for questioning their decisions. But it would not have been outside the legitimate duties of the OC Matabeleland Mounted Police — Inspector William Bodle to point out, if the thought ever crossed his mind — that to take all but 10% of his force away was robbing it of its usefulness and leaving a dangerous vacuum.

He was, in fact, removing its first line of defence from the territory in which he held the principal responsibility "for the safety of persons and property" and putting nothing in its place.

Half the white population of Matabeleland, which now totalled nearly 2000, was in Bulawayo and the rest were spread thinly over the vast wilderness of the country. Spread with them were some 10,000 survivors of Lobengula's impis, whose lives and training had been devoted to the art of fighting and who had already been presented with a convenient supply of rifles and ammunition by Rhodes in exchange for the Rudd concession. After the invasion of Matabeleland, Jameson had ordered that all the arms in the hands of the Matabele were to be surrendered. This was virtually an impossible undertaking to fulfil in practice; and in any case the Imperial authorities who had never been convinced of the settlers' need to attack the Matabele in the first place — decreed that the order was to be construed "in a liberal spirit".

The Mashonas, who were not a fighting people, had to all appearances accepted the white man's presence and his imposed discipline grudgingly but passively. The Matabele would never have done so. And to compound the ills which the white settlers had brought on them by taking their land, a plague of rinderpest now swept through the country and started to decimate their cattle. The white conquerors had already filched most of their cattle from the Matabele, on the pretext of punishing them for resisting their well-intentioned invasion. Now, to stop the spread of rinderpest, they went out and shot nearly all the cattle the Matabele had left — many, of course, had already died of the disease and in the end, designedly or not, almost all the surviving animals turned out to be those in the hands of the whites.

The rinderpest epidemic was only one of a number of factors which hastened the inevitable revolt. Matabeleland suffered one of its devastating droughts in the summer of 1895-96 and was at the same time visited by swarms of locusts, which the tribesmen attributed to white men's witchcraft, deliberately imposed for their discomfiture. Another factor was the arrogant attitude towards their own people of most of the native constables who had been recruited by the police and actually armed with Martini Henry rifles and bayonets. These men had been recruited from the survivors of Lobengula's crack regiments, on the assumption that they would thereby carry a high measure of respect among their own people. They operated primarily under the orders of the Native Commissioners and the departure of most of the white police force had left them with the notion that they were now the elite representatives of legal authority. In these circumstances it is quite possible that they became more arrogant than ever. Indeed, in the Company's official report for 1894-95, it was stated, "The reports of the different Native Commissioners in connection with this force are most satisfactory. Native labour is much more plentiful" (author's italics) "and the police have been useful in branding cattle and also assisting indunas and natives generally in procuring evidence and settling native disputes." One wonders what methods were used for securing plentiful labour. Whatever the reason, the native tribesmen grew to abominate them as tools of the white oppressors.

The spark which lit the fuse of the rebellion was struck on the night of 20 March 1896 when eight native constables, with their own native carriers, camped outside the kraal of Umgorshlwini in the Essexvale district, among the hills near the Umsingwane River. While the constables were sitting quietly round a camp fire a number of tribesmen approached in an extended line and started a provocative war dance.

One of the dancers, armed with an assegai, worked round to the other side of the fire. There was no doubt of his intention and two constables jumped up to catch him. They disarmed him and struggled to handcuff him. At that moment, someone fired a shot from the nearby kraal. Intended no doubt for a policeman; the bullet struck the prisoner in the back, killing him instantly, the handcuffs still on one wrist. With surprising intrepidity, all the constables rushed the kraal but whoever had fired the shot escaped, dropping his rifle in his hurry to get away.

The dancers promptly dispersed and the constables returned to the light of the fire where they waited uncertainly. Another shot came, this time from the surrounding bush, and one of their native carriers fell, a bullet through his head. Not unwisely, as Selous relates the incident in his book, "the representatives of the law then thought it advisable to beat a retreat". Another of their carriers, a young boy, was found next day under the kraal fence where he had been beaten to death with knobkerries. Later that night, another native constable, asleep in a hut in a neighbouring kraal, was attacked and stabbed to death.

The fuse was lit. Two days later, on 22 March, the deadly charge exploded and murderous attacks on the white settlers began. In the first attack, in the Essexvale district, seven white men, two native servants and an Indian cook were slaughtered. A native commissioner was killed in his office. Two miners were murdered and their bodies mutilated. The same evening, a group of natives who had presented themselves to a mine manager for employment turned on him and killed him.

In the Insiza district, north of Bulawayo, two doctors were killed in early attacks. The wife of one — a recent bride from England — escaped into the bush, but she was found and stoned her to death. The entire Cunningham family, at a farm-house close to the Insiza River, were battered to death by knobkerries and axes — Mr. Cunningham and Mrs. Cunningham, their two daughters, only son and three of their grandchildren. A native commissioner with two policemen (Sub-Inspector Mark Handley and Trooper George Case) and two storekeepers (George Hurford and L.H. Corke who had both recently retired from the MMP) held out in the NC's office for three days while their ammunition lasted; then they were beaten to death with knobkerries. Before the first rush of the rising was over, 190 Europeans had been killed in Matabeleland.

Sadly enough, the suppression of the Matabele Rebellion does not figure as a battle honour in the annals of the Rhodesian police because, by leaving the country on an adventure into the Transvaal, the force had opted out of any corporate participation. The few attested policemen left in the country played predictably gallant parts; but, as previously in the Matabele War, they operated necessarily as individuals — sometimes on their own and and at other times in mixed forces with the volunteer units which were hurriedly raised in Bulawayo to deal with the desperate situation.

There was one early rescue of a party of besieged whites in which a number of the Matabeleland police, under Inspector Southey, took part as a unit. The manager of a mine only a few miles from the Cunningham farm, Thomas Maddocks, was attacked and killed on 23 March by a gang of 15 Matabele armed with knobkerries and axes. It is possible that this was the same gang which had attacked the Cunninghams a few hours earlier. Two of Maddocks' miners were wounded but they managed to escape and bring news of the attack to a store owned by Harry Cumming, close to the Regina Ruins and not far from what was later to become Fort Rixon. A large party of local settlers — 34 men, a woman and one child — had already gathered at the store for mutual protection and Cumming had ridden off on his own to Bulawayo, 45 miles away, for help. He found some difficulty in securing the help he wanted because similar requests were coming from all round Bulawayo and the organisation of relief was still in its early stages. However, Lieutenant-Colonel the Hon. Maurice Gifford, who had served as a scout in the Salisbury Column in 1893, was at last persuaded by Cumming to collect a party of 30 volunteers, to whom Southey and 14 of the MMP were attached.

Gifford's party left Bulawayo at 8 p.m. on Tuesday, 24 March, and reached Cumming's store at 9 o'clock on Thursday morning. The store, not larger than a small single storey house, was a rectangular brick building with a thatched roof. It stood in open grassland, but a wooded kopje rose to dominate it about 500 yards away. The refugees, who were virtually unarmed, had removed the thatch from the store building and its veranda as an obvious precaution against its being fired by the Matabele. They had knocked holes in the walls and placed bags of earth to protect the door and windows.

The rescue party's horses needed rest before setting off on the 45-mile journey back to Bulawayo and the remainder of the day was spent improvising such defensive measures as were practicable. Although the Matabele were in evidence on the surrounding kopjes, they left the whites alone until half-past four the next morning. It was still a dark, moonless night and out of the darkness they poured rifle fire into the store. Sergeant O'Leary, of the MMP, who had moved forward from the store veranda, was shot dead. Southey went out under fire to bring in his body. The Matabele came storming up to the veranda and another policeman, Corporal Strutt, was jabbed in the arm by an assegai. (One account says that Strutt subsequently died.) But the holes, enabling the defenders to fire from behind cover, proved their worth; and although the Matabele even started clawing at the bags of earth, the fire from the defenders beat them off and they retreated up the kopje. When daylight came they still kept at a safe distance. Rescuers and rescued (36 men, one woman and a child) were able to move off at 6.30 a.m. on Friday, reaching Bulawayo at noon on Sunday.

Six men had been wounded and, according to Selous, "an educated American negro, a servant of Mr. Wrey's" had been killed at the same time as Sergeant O'Leary. O'Leary was subsequently buried in a little graveyard on the Cunningham farm, where a memorial to the murdered family was subsequently erected, simply marked "Sgt. John O'Leary. MMP. 27 March 1896." Two troopers of the Bulawayo Field Force lie with him.

This was virtually the only occasion during the Matabele rebellion when a force of police, as a unit under one of their own officers, was involved in an engagement with the rebels. And it is an indication of the situation at the time that the party consisted of the commanding officer of the whole Matabeleland force and no more than 14 men. Even so, they formed only a small section of Gifford's rescue party.

Nevertheless there were other casualties among the MMP. When the news of the outbreak reached Gwelo, Trooper Bowker was sent out to warn the people in the Lower Gwelo district and was murdered by the rebels. Thirteen more members were killed, or died of wounds, while operating with the composite forces which were engaged in suppressing the rebellion in the Bulawayo district and the Matopo Hills: Sub-Inspector F.C. Norton, Battery Sergeant-Major A. Ainslie, Sergeants M. Eadio and F.C. Warringham, Corporal J.K. Porter, Troopers P. Bennett, W.H. Bush, G.O.A. Morgan, L. Cheves, W. Bern, R. Heathfield, J. Bell and F. Millar.

Of the native police during the rebellion Selous says, "It is but fair to say almost all the police who had been first enrolled, and who had done more than a year's service, held themselves aloof from the rebels, the great majority of defections occurring amongst those who had been but lately enrolled." There were 330 native constables in Matabeleland at the outbreak of the rebellion. About 150 remained "loyal" — as they were labelled in the jargon of the day. The remainder responded to more predictable demands on their loyalty. Selous tells of one police station at Makupikupeni, in the Essexvale district on the road from Bulawayo to Filabusi where, on the approach of a patrol under Colonel Spreckley (an 1890 pioneer commanding the volunteer Bulawayo Field Force) the seven native policemen and a sergeant at the station hastily fled with their arms and ammunition and went over to the rebels in the hills. On another occasion a native commissioner in the same district, who had 90 native police under his control — each armed with a Martini-Henry rifle and 70 rounds — heard a disconcerting rumour that they were plotting to murder him. Rather than wait for the inevitable, he decided to march them into Bulawayo. Nothing untoward occurred on the march, which must have been a nervewracking experience for the NC.

It was not until they all arrived in Bulawayo that he discovered that his police had not even known that a rebellion had started. Nevertheless, now they had heard about it, he took the precaution of having them all disarmed. At about the same time, in the Bulalima district, 30 native police, hearing that a Matabele induna had ordered the murder of an assistant native commissioner, warned the intended victim and escorted him to safety.

One of these policemen was murdered by the rebels. The remainder marched into Bulawayo of their own volition and dutifully reported to the Chief Native Commissioner. He promptly disarmed them — which was perhaps a little ungracious — but he did have the decency to find other jobs for them in Government service.

A number of defensive forts, such as they were, were set up in the district round Bulawayo. They were the usual earth and stone works thrown up to enclose a rectangle, if possible on a crest of rising ground commanding the surrounding veld. Their garrisons camped close by, ready to retire into the questionable protection of the fort if attacked by the Matabele. In the event, none of these forts ever saw any action. A fort at Bembesi was garrisoned by members of the Afrikander Corps — one of the volunteer units raised at the time — and was put under the command of a Captain L.C. Geyser. The authorities sanctioned the taking of any grain found in native kraals; such were the legitimate spoils of war. But Captain Geyser was even more enterprising and he started to sell the grain in Bulawayo. This, in the authorities' opinion, was carrying things a bit too far. He was replaced at Fort Bembesi by Sub-Inspector Barrett of the MMP, who took an unpopularly tough line which resulted in eight Afrikanders — who still persisted in their profitable grain-marketing practice and were less than amenable to Barrett's discipline — being court-martialled, fined and discharged.

Meanwhile there had been an attack on a Mr. Rixon's farm some 25 miles to the east and Inspector J.A. Warrick, who had been sent to the farm with a detachment of MMP, reported, "With the assistance of surrendered natives I have erected a fort in what I think the most suitable position commanding a view of Rixon's valley and the open country along the Insiza River. The fort consists of a stone wall substantially built with a row of sandbags on which the top is not complete owing to the scarcity of sandbags. It is about 40 ft. square. I am building a good substantial hut at each corner which will be finished within a few days. My instructions were to establish a fort in a suitable position, which may mean anything — a temporary or a permanent one." The fort at Bembesi was then abandoned and the garrison moved across to Inspector Warrick's new fort on Mr. Rixon's farm. And so the police came to Fort Rixon where Warrick's fort was subsequently preserved as a national monument. At the foot of the hillock on which the fort was built, a little fenced-in cemetery contained police graves, one with the standard iron memorial cross at its head bearing the inscription "J. Babbs, B.S.A.P. — .11.96", and another simply "Clarke BSAP — ".

During the first three months of the rebellion in Matabeleland the whole burden of defending Bulawayo, providing rescue parties and containing the rebel forces fell on the volunteer units — with, as has been indicated, individual members of the Matabeleland Mounted Police contributing such service as they could given their reduced power. Cecil Rhodes happened to arrive in Salisbury, via Beira, just at the time when the rebellion started and he accompanied a relief column of volunteers which left Salisbury for Bulawayo on 6 April. Characteristically, what worried him most was the expense the BSA Company was incurring in its operations against the rebels. He had no desire to add to the expense by calling on the Imperial authorities to send him regular troops, for whom the Company would be expected to pay. But once again, as on the occasion when he had planned to send his pioneer column to Mashonaland without the expense of a military escort, the British Government overruled him. They were determined to exercise control over police and military affairs in Rhodesia to make sure there would be no more embarrassing events such as the Jameson Raid.

On 21 May, two months after the first rising in the Essexvale district, Colonel Sir Richard Martin, of the 6th Dragoons, arrived in Rhodesia. A formal notice issued by the High Commissioner in Cape Town on 3 June proclaimed that "Colonel Sir Richard Edward Rowley Martin, RCG, is appointed Commandant-General of the Police Forces in the Bechuanaland Protectorate, Matabeleland and Mashonaland, to have general control over all forces, including Municipal and Native police." His full title was to be Commandant-General of the Police Forces and Inspector General of the Volunteer Forces. For the time being, the designation "Commandant-General" was to replace "Commissioner". Major-General Sir Frederick Carrington — who had commanded the BBP and of whom Leonard, at the time of the threatened Boer invasion in 1891, had written, "it is the magnificence and magnitude of Sir Frederick's command that staggers me" — arrived two weeks later to take command of all the forces engaged in the active military campaign against the rebels — forces which were to include Imperial troops now arriving from the Cape. (Incidentally, one of General Carrington's staff was a Lieutenant-Colonel R.S.S. Baden-Powell.) The relation between Carrington's and Martin's respective authorities seems in retrospect to have carried the seeds of confusion, but one assumes that Sir Frederick outranked Sir Richard only in any matter involving use of the police in military operations.

Another officer sent out by the Imperial authorities to serve under Martin — again expressly for the purpose of imposing Imperial discipline on the RMP — was Captain J.S. Nicholson of the 7th Hussars, who was to take over command of the Matabeleland Mounted Police.

The Regimental Orders of the Matabeleland Mounted Police, signed by Captain Nicholson from July 1896 onwards, set out in daily detail the guards to be posted in Bulawayo, where the rebels were still uncomfortably active. Four men guarded the main entrance to the laager (today's City Hall square); four more at the commissariat (presumably at the Police Camp). Four provided a look-out on the roof of Williams's Building (on the corner of Selborne Avenue and Fort Street, now demolished, opposite where Tredgold Building stands today). Four guarded the ammunition (presumably at the magazine), four guarded the hospital (in Jameson Street, now the Income Tax building) and four more "Brand's cottages". (It is believed that this was the name given to some buildings on the corner of Main Street and 9th Avenue, whose formal name was "Critic Buildings". This belonged to the impressively styled Bulawayo Town Stands Syndicate, of which a Claude Brand was a member.) There were also two mounted patrols: one from 6 a.m., through the day, with four troopers; the other from 5 p.m., through the night, consisting of an officer and six troopers.

It is difficult to know the number of men Nicholson now had in his Matabeleland force. Regimental orders throughout 1896 record numerous discharges but contain no reference to enrolments. One assumes that the strength of the force was being built up. It is clear, however, that men were attached from time to time from other units, just as the policemen themselves were drafted to many of the patrols. One order read, "1 corporal and 8 men (MRF) attached to B Troop." MRF was the Matabeleland Relief Force brought from the Cape under a Major Plumer. Many of the participants in the Jameson Raid, who had been shipped back to England, had returned almost immediately to Africa and joined Plumer's force in Kimberley. Moreover, there are numerous entries in Nicholson's orders such as, "Sub-Inspector Carney and 24 NCOs and men (25 horses) leave Bulawayo for Fig Tree (sic) on detachment duty today and are struck off the strength of the station." This was in July 1896, so the strength of the force as a whole must have increased considerably in the previous few months. And also in July, "Party, under command Lieutenant (crossed out, altered to Inspector) Reid, 1 1st class sgt, 2 corps, 12 men to Usher's Farm, 7 days rations, to join HQ column." The HQ column would have been Carrington's headquarters, operating in the Matopos. The garrisons at the forts, too, were constantly being relieved. "Sub-Inspector Carney, 1 corporal and 8 troopers to Solusi Fort"; "1 Sgt and 9 men to Inyati Fort". "O.C.s Forts will send in pay lists ... all men coming in to Bulawayo from forts to report to Regimental Orderly Room, MMP." (These were in August) Nicholson's orders are liberally enlivened, almost every day, with "absent from guard, fined 3/6"; "disobeying an order, returning to barracks drunk and resisting NCO, fined 10/-"; and sentences of 7 days IHL (imprisonment with hard labour) and £1 fine, 14 days IHL and £2 fine – crimes mercifully unspecified. Trooper Campbell is sent out to superintend the heliograph; and Sergeant Harris is ordered to take charge of the .45 Maxim with belts and ammunition "for use at the hospital" — surely not on the patients — with two troopers detailed to serve it. By December that year, Nicholson saw fit to issue an order to the effect that "there are numbers of natives and others seen wearing police uniform". Consequently, any losses of uniform by serving members would constitute "a breach of discipline and will be dealt with as a military offence".

The relief column of Rhodesia Horse Volunteers, which Rhodes accompanied from Salisbury, was made up of 150 men. It left Salisbury on 6 April. Two months later violence erupted in Mashonaland — a rising which ultimately claimed the lives of 119 European men, women and children. That the authorities at the time, and indeed all the settlers, should once again have acquiesced in the removal from the territory of a considerable portion of white manpower, is a measure of their entrenched belief that, unlike the Matabele, the Mashonas had gladly accepted the white man's intrusion and were too supine and unaggressive to constitute a threat to peace. In this case, one cannot impute deliberate bad faith; the move was made with the very best intentions. Even if one is uncharitable enough to suggest that Rhodes himself might have been influenced by a consideration that volunteers brought to Matabeleland from Mashonaland would be 'cheaper' than Imperial forces brought in from the south, one has to admit that saving in time was a vital factor. And in the event, the column from Salisbury arrived in Bulawayo two months before any Imperial troops.

The only criticism that can be made in hindsight is that the move was remarkably stupid. Even the Acting Administrator in Salisbury, Judge Vintcent, had issued a notice in the Gazette in April saying there was "no reason to believe that there is any probability of a similar rising of natives in Mashonaland". However, his notice continued with an ill-expressed warning that "should the natives of Mashonaland take advantage of the present crisis and attack isolated stores, mining camps and farms, it is important to impress upon such persons as are in outlying and isolated positions the necessity for vigilance". One feels that if the natives attacked it would then be a little late for "vigilance". The Rhodesia Herald reported that after the police had been withdrawn from the Mazoe district their camp had been ransacked. This suggests that although the column sent to Bulawayo had been made up of volunteers, the lack of manpower in the territory had caused whole districts to be left unprotected. Dr. Jameson and the White brothers had a lot to answer for.

The first murder in the Mashona rebellion was of a Native Commissioner at a kraal near Hartley on 15 June. The same day, two prospectors who happened to arrive at the same kraal were seized, bound hand and foot and thrown mercilessly into the Umfuli River. Their bodies were never found and it is assumed they were taken by crocodiles. Next morning, some young Mashonas came into the Police Camp in Salisbury to report that two white traders had been murdered near the Hunyani River. The news was ominous, but the murders near Hartley had not yet been reported and there was no real cause to suspect that the trouble on the Hunyani presaged a general rising. Trooper A.L. Swemmer of the Mashonaland Mounted Police (BSACP No. 420) was sent to investigate the Mashonas' report and on the way later that evening, when it was getting dark, he met a young white man named Talbot riding on his bicycle in the opposite direction, bound for Salisbury. Talbot was a pupil working with a Mr. Norton who owned Porta Farm in the Hunyani district. He had cycled the 20 miles in and out of Salisbury already that day on an errand for his employer and had arrived back at the Norton homestead at six o'clock in the evening. The cattle were grazing peacefully in the lands but no human was to be seen. He entered the house and found chaos: furniture broken up, pictures wrenched from the walls, blood on the floor and empty cartridge cases below one window. The blood trail led out through the back door of the house and in the long grass 300 yards away he found the bodies of Mrs. Norton, her baby, the baby's white nurse and a white farm assistant.

It transpired later that Mr. Norton had gone to a neighbouring Mashona kraal early that morning to recover his farm labourers, all of whom had deserted the previous night. He had been attacked and killed and his body was later found among the neighbouring kopjes. His attackers had then moved over to the homestead and wiped out the rest of the family. When Swemmer met Talbot and heard the gruesome story they both returned to Salisbury and later that night Inspector R.C. Nesbitt and seven MMP rode out to the Norton homestead where they buried the victims of the attack.

The story of the bloody rising in Matabeleland was to be tragically repeated in Mashonaland. Defensive laagers were formed in Salisbury, Victoria, Charter, Melsetter and Umtali. From the districts round the towns came the same calls for rescue as Bulawayo had heard three months earlier, and owing to its similarly denuded strength the Mashonaland Mounted Police — during the early period of the Mashona rebellion — suffered the same frustrations as the force in Matabeleland, playing their parts as best they could but operating generally with the mixed forces drawn from volunteer units.

During these early days of the Mashona rebellion there was one incident in which individual members of the MMP played a conspicuous part, and which therefore qualifies for a positive place in the history of the force. The heroic story of what came to be known as the Mazoe Patrol has been written many times, but it cannot be better told than by repeating the terse, official report made after the event by Inspector R.C. Nesbitt — who was subsequently awarded the Victoria Cross for the part he played in it.

Randolph Cosby Nesbitt, born in Queenstown in the eastern Cape in 1867, had been a trooper in the Cape Mounted Rifles. He joined the BSACP at Macloutsie in January 1890 (No. 129) and was posted as a sergeant to 'C' Troop, the troop which had followed immediately behind the pioneer column and had established the first permanent police station at Fort Victoria under Captain Keith Falconer. He had taken his discharge from the BSACP as a sub-inspector in 1891, when Jameson had drastically cut back the original force. He had gone back to the Cape, where he had been Chief Constable at Fort Peddie for a year and he had rejoined the Mashonaland Mounted Police in 1894, after the invasion of Matabeleland, when it had been reestablished with a strength of about 150. He now held the commissioned rank of Inspector and was the senior officer in Salisbury. It was he who had ridden out to the Hunyani with a party to bury the Norton family.

On the afternoon of 17 June, a Mr. Salthouse, manager of the Alice Mine in the Mazoe Valley, some 30 miles from Salisbury, heard there had been trouble on the Hunyani. His young wife had only recently arrived from England, and believing it would be wise to move into Salisbury he called together his 12 neighbours, two of whom also had wives. They prepared for the journey and set off on the 18th in a tented wagon and a donkey-cart. One of the men was down with fever and rode in the wagon with the three women. Five miles out they were attacked by rebels; three men were killed and the party were forced to return to the mine.

There they made a makeshift laager and two of their number, Blakiston and Routledge both of the telegraph department — rode over to the telegraph office and sent a message through to Salisbury. The telegraph office was nothing more than a pole and grass hut with a heavily thatched roof, standing alone among the trees. It is surprising that the rebels had not set it on fire. It seems that the two men rode to the office both on one horse. On their return, Blakiston rode and Routledge ran beside him. Blakiston was shot dead, 400 yards from the laager. Routledge was chased by rebels into the bush, where he too was shot. Had they not sent the message which cost them their lives the plight of the party would not have been known in Salisbury and they would all have been inevitably wiped out.

A small party of four volunteers, under Lieutenant Dan Judson, was sent out from Salisbury that evening. Judson later reported, "Due to hazards on the road I deemed it necessary to send for reinforcements and six men arrived from Salisbury the following morning (19th). During the day I had to return several men to Salisbury as their horses were flagging ... That afternoon, after encountering heavy fire from the natives, we arrived at the Mine safely, to find the rebels attacking in force ... We decided to maintain our position until further men arrived ..."

When Judson and his men failed to return to Salisbury, Inspector Nesbitt was sent off with a party of MMP. This is his report.

"According to instructions I proceeded to Mazoe at 10.30 p.m. on the 19th June with a patrol of 12 men to the relief of Mr. Salthouse and his party and Lt. Judson's patrol. No natives encountered until reaching Mazoe Valley, half a mile from Salvation Army Farm at about 4.20 a.m.

Met Native Constable Hendrick making for Sby. with urgent despatch from Lt. Judson who was surrounded by about 1000 natives and whose ammunition was running short. Took Hendrick back with me.

Exercising great caution, I managed to evade attack until within half a mile of Mr. Salthouse's party. Passing through gorge the enemy opened fire from dense cover on my left flank. Firing into darkness, pushed through, but Sgt. Nesbitt's horse wounded. (This was A. Nesbitt, a brother of the Inspector, who had come up with the pioneer column.)

Reached Mr. Salthouse's laager at about 5 a.m. on 20th, and was advised that the six mules sent with Mr. Zimmermann had been lost. Held a council consisting of myself, Capt. Brown, Lt. Judson and Mr. Salthouse, when it was decided to return forthwith. After bullet-proofing coach with iron sheets and dismounting six men in order to use their horses for the coach, we left the laager at about noon with my party consisting of 12 mounted men, 18 dismounted men and three women. Sent advance guard of four mounted men and a rear guard of four mounted men, the remaining four mounted and the dismounted men being with the coach.

After about a mile the whole party attacked but managed to silence enemy fire sufficiently to enable coach to pass through very dangerous "donga". From here on kept under heavy fire from right flank until, at Vesuvius camp, the enemy were reinforced. The firing became hotter and McGeer, Jacobs (a lieutenant and trooper respectively in the Salisbury Field Force) and two horses were killed. Constantly harassed, so pushed advance guard further forward to cover our advance.

Proceeded in disorder until some 21 miles from Salvation Army Farm where it became necessary to rush a gorge where extremely heavy fire was sustained owing to the dense nature of the long grass and reeds, with enemy within 10 yards of us. Here Tpr. van Staaden (Salisbury Field Force) and four horses were killed, Mr. Burton and Tpr. Hendricks were dangerously wounded and Ogilvie, Berry and two horses slightly wounded. Mr. Arnott and Tpr. Hendricks, who were part of my advance guard, had pushed through this trap and, thinking all was over, rode for Sby. The enemy followed another four miles keeping up a harassing fire and wounding another horse, this making a total of about 14 miles' (three and a half hours') constant fighting.

On nearing Mount Hampden and open country, the enemy retired and I proceeded without further delay, reaching Sby. about 9.30 p.m.

I estimated the enemy's strength to be at least 1500, many of them being armed with Lee-Metford, Martini and Winchester rifles, and appearing to be well supplied with ammunition. I have every reason to believe that Cape Boys and Matabeles were the leaders of this attacking party. I compute that the enemy's loss must be about 100. The men of the patrol behaved splendidly all through; many of them had never been under fire before. I would especially mention the good services rendered by Messrs. Ogilvie, Pascoe and Harbord."

That, in the unemotional words of Nesbitt's report, is the story of the Mazoe Patrol. He makes no mention that during the journey to Salisbury the man suffering from fever — who was in poor shape — gave up his place in the wagonette to the wounded and somehow fought with the others. Nor that the women, two of whom had seen their husbands killed before their eyes, spent the time calmly handing ammunition to the men and attending to the wounded. When they reached the outskirts of Salisbury, there were only three horses left out of 18 to drag the battle-scarred wagonette. All the survivors of the party were either lying wounded in the wagonette or trudging along on foot. Since the first attack when the party had left the Alice Mine on the 18th, eight men's lives had been lost but 11 of the original party were brought to safety.

The Mazoe district, which was the focus of the early stages of the insurrection in Mashonaland, had now been virtually abandoned to the rebels. It was not until the middle of August that a force of 170 volunteers — a considerable proportion of the total military strength in Salisbury at the time was sent out to establish Fort Mazoe and commence a long drawn out operation which finally overcame the rebels in that district.

There is little relevance in this operation to a history of the police, except that Lyons-Montgomery, BSACP No. 1, attested November 1889 — Troop Sergeant-Major of the original 'B' Troop, now a Captain in the RHV — was the first casualty in the fighting which ensued, being severely wounded in the head. He was actually operated on, by Surgeon-Lieutenant R. J. Wyllie, within the unhygienic confines of the Mazoe fort and then taken into hospital in Salisbury. He suffered, for a time, paralysis of the legs and his friends in Salisbury subscribed to send him to England for treatment. He returned to South Africa during the Boer War and had recovered sufficiently to serve as recruiting officer in the Cape Colony.

He lived for 45 years after being wounded and died in Jersey during the German occupation, in 1941, at the age of 82. His original cap badge used to hang in a frame in the ante-room of the Officers' Mess in Salisbury: a blue disc with the old-gold badge of the lion holding the elephant's tusk, encircled with the words, also in old-gold, THE BRITISH SOUTH AFRICA COMPANY's POLICE.

## Chapter Eleven

## BSAP

MEANWHILE, THE CAMPAIGN against the rebels in Matabeleland had been dragging on inconclusively. The volunteer forces, and the units under Carrington, had managed to remove the Matabele threat to Bulawayo and the districts, but the rebels had retired to their strongholds in the Matopo Hills, from where it seemed they might carry out an indefinite guerrilla campaign. Carrington told Rhodes that he would need 5000 men to defeat them altogether. He had already suffered 200 casualties among 1000 men. Perhaps Rhodes was as much appalled by the wastage in human life as by the expense to the Company. But he had never had much time for professional soldiers; he suspected they were interested in military campaigns simply as ends themselves, with the promotions and medas to be gained from them. He believed that every man had his price and if you could negotiate with him you could find out what his price was for whatever you wanted from him. He was convinced from experience that this principle applied as surely to a Matabele chief as to anyone else. He decided, therefore, to negotiate directly with the rebel leaders. It has often been implied that he set about making contact with the Matabele behind the backs of the military authorities. This is not true. Carrington grudgingly gave his consent, which was essential to Rhodes from every practical aspect. Nevertheless, the story of the indabas Rhodes held with the Matabele in the depths of the Matopo Hills, and their successful outcome which brought peace to Matabeleland in August 1896, is a story of one man's supreme courage and statesmanship. It is no detraction from his good faith to assume that he was well aware that, had he left the job to Carrington and the Imperial authorities instead of fixing it himself, the BSA Company — who were footing the bill — would very soon have been broke.

However, in Mashonaland, the Company had been compelled by force majeure to accept British troops — by the pressure of the dangerous situation as well as the determination of the Imperial authorities to take a hand. Four companies of Mounted Infantry had arrived in Cape Town from England on 19 May, at that time destined for Matabeleland. They were never sent there and remained in camp at Wynberg. On 25 June, two of these Mounted Infantry companies, with headquarters, artillery and medical detachments, were sent up the coast to Beira under Lieutenant Colonel E.A.H. Alderson of the Royal West Kent Regiment (the Queen's Own). When Alderson arrived in Mashonaland towards the end of July he took command of the entire Mashonaland Field Force which comprised his own 380 Mounted Infantry, a troop of 70 mounted volunteers known as the Natal Troop who had already come up from Durban — their original intention had been to go to the assistance of Matabeleland — with all the volunteer forces and the few odd policemen operating in the territory. His campaign against the Mashona rebels continued for five months. His was a highly mobile campaign which ranged widely over the territory, and it is a measure of the pugnacity of the despised Mashonas — and Alderson's ineffectiveness — that by November the rebel leaders were still at large and the situation was as dangerous as ever. Earl Grey, the new Administrator, wrote, "Alderson and his mounted infantry made so rapid a promenade militaire through the country that in many places the result is nil and the natives are (still) in a state of mutiny." By December Alderson and the survivors of his Mounted Infantry were on their way back to Beira from where they had come.

Again, as in Matabeleland, individual members of the MMP had participated — sometimes singly, sometimes in groups — in the Field Force operations. But the police, up to that time, had never acted as a unit. It is not possible from the records to determine the casualties suffered by members of the MMP during this period, as the list of casualties described as members of the Mashonaland Field Force might well contain some of the police. However, right at the outbreak of the Mashona rebellion, Trooper C. Cartright — who had been sent our to Gwebi to investigate a reported murder — had been wounded on 15 June; and two others involved in the same incident, Corporal F.G.K Jackson and Trooper F. Wills, were murdered by rebels three days later.

In his book, With the Mounted Infantry and the MFF (everybody in those days wrote books about their private little campaigns, successful or not) Alderson says he found only five policemen in the town when he first came to Salisbury. Before he left he made an estimate of what he considered the strength of the white police force in Mashonaland should be. He listed the number he believed should be stationed in each town and district — Salisbury 150, Hartley 75, Fort Victoria 50, Marandellas and Mazoe 40 each, Umtali 30 and so on — to a total of 580. "Taken generally," he wrote, "this distribution was approved of, though the Company still thought it excessive, especially in the case of the 150 men in Salisbury."

Alderson's estimates were of more than just academic interest to the authorities, cesause a decision had already been taken to re-establish an integrated police force in Rhodesia. Properly set up, as a professional military unit, it would become Rhodesia's first line of defence, as well as the guardian of law and order, and would be charged with the task of settling the rebellion once and for all. As early as 30 September a notice had appeared in the British South Africa Company Government Gazette — the official gazette, "Published by Authority" and grandly claiming below its title, "Justice, Commerce, Freedom", in that order. Government Notice No. 111 proclaimed, "A Police Force to be styled the 'Rhodesia Mounted Police' is being enrolled for service in Rhodesia." This suggests that the name Rhodesia Mounted Police had not previously been formally accepted." However, as already mentioned, Charles White had used it two years before and it has already been used a number of times for convenience in this story. Now it was official. There was a reference in a later Government Notice, No. 120 issued on 28 October, to the effect that the new force would revert to the title of BSA Company's Police, but no use seems to have been made of that archaic name at this stage."

The intitial period of service for NCOs and troopers was to be one year — as it had been in all cases previously — with the option of signing on for successive years. A Regimental Sergeant-Major was to be paid 9s. a day, a 1st Class Sergeant 8s., 2nd Class Sergeant 7s., 3rd Class Sergeant 6s., Corporal 5s. 6d., Trumpeter 6s. and the unfortunate Trooper only 5s. However, this was a marked improvement on the 4s. for the original BSACP troopers. Everybody would get an extra 6d. a day on re-engagement after the first year; 1s. after two years. The pay for a trooper on enlistment remained at five bob a day for the next 20 years, until after the First World War.

The force was still to be under the discipline of the Cape Mounted Riflemen Act, with its power to imprison defaulters. Recruits from England had to be between 20 and 35 years of age; if born in South Africa, 18 to 35 — a noteworthy distinction. Men from England had to pay their own fare to Cape Town — in those days it was a matter of £20 or less — but the Company would pay £15 for the train fare to Bulawayo — a lavish sum which must have included food or provisions for the four days' journey. "All applicants will be required to produce certificates of good character and to pass a medical examination, and will be tested in riding and shooting before being enrolled." Recruits took an oath, "to serve the British South Africa Company within the limits of the Matabeleland Order in Council, 1894" — which Order somewhat breathlessly defined the Company's territory as "Parts of South Africa bounded by the Portuguese Possessions, the South African Republic to a point opposite the mouth of the River Shashi, by the River Shashi and the territories of the Chief Khama of the Bamangwato to the River Zambezi, and by that River to the Portuguese Boundary, including an area of 10 miles radius round Fort Tuli and excluding the area known as the Tati districts as defined by the Charter." The Oath concluded summarily, "I further declare I have no share or interest in any South African venture inside or outside the said Company's territories and I promise I will not acquire any such share or interest during my service."

A Proclamation in the Gazette on 16 December 1896 read, "The whole of the Military and Police Forces engaged or established in the Territories shall be and remain under the direct control of the High Commissioner of the United Kingdom in South Africa." The force was to enjoy its autonomy but not its independence.

Carrington, who had earned as little military glory as Alderson, had followed the latter out of the country via Beira during December and Sir Richard Martin, the Commandant-General, was now responsible to the High Commissioner in Cape Town for all military forces in Rhodesia. In his General Orders on 29 December 1896 he laid down the "Fixed Establishment of the Mashonaland and Matabeleland Divisions of the British South Africa Police (sic)." In actual fact the title BSA Police was not formally proclaimed until the following year in the High Commissioner's Notice No. 18/1897 which read, "The White Police Forces serving within the limits of the Bechuanaland Protectorate and the British South Africa Company's territories will, in future, be designated 'The British South Africa Police' and will be composed of four divisions." These would be the Bechuanaland Division (with headquarters still at Mafeking and some genuine railway construction in the Protectorate now to be guarded); the Matabeleland and Mashonaland Divisions; and a new North Zambezi Division, with headquarters at Mount Darwin, in the north-east corner of the territory.

The C-G's Order in December 1896 had set out the fixed establishment of the Mashonaland and Matabeleland Divisions, based on the structure of a cavalry regiment in the British Army. Each division was to comprise a Commandant with local rank of Lieutenant-Colonel, District Staff Officer (Major), Quartermaster (Lieutenant), Paymaster (Lieutenant) and Regimental Sergeant-Major. It was to be divided into six Troops, each Troop with an Inspector (local rank, Captain), two Sub-Inspectors (Lieutenants), one 1st Class Sergeant, two 2nd Class Sergeants, four 3rd Class Sergeants and a Trumpeter. No mention here of corporals. "A troop including rank and file will not exceed 100." An artillery troop was to form part of the depot troop in Salisbury and Matabeleland was to make do with a mule battery in Bulawayo. Other appointments included Quartermaster-, Orderly Room-, Paymaster- and Rough Riding-Sergeants (all 1st Class at 8s. a day) and a Provost Sergeant (2nd Class at 7s. a day).

The mule battery consisted of two "mountain screw guns", 26-inch rifled muzzle-loaders (RML). They had belonged to the Indian Army's 10th Mountain Battery and had been brought to Natal in 1880, where they were captured by the Boers at Majuba and later recaptured by the British. They could be dismantled and transported, each gun requiring five mules: one for the muzzle, one for the breech, one for the carriage, one for the wheels and one for the axle — 774 lb. in all. When offloading from the mules to assemble the gun, the drill required the gunner involved to lean over the hindquarters of the animal — which was a hazardous operation. The record time for limbering up and assembling is said to have been one minute, 47 seconds. The gunners wore red bands round the top of their puggarees and considered themselves the elite of the force.

A later order by the Commandant-General admonished "officers, NCOs and men of the Police to work in a spirit of most amicable co-operation with the Company's Administrator, Magistrates, Mining and District Commissioners, and Native Commissioners, and to comply with their requests and suggestions for the employment of the force in all cases where they see no objection of policy or law to such employment". On the borders of the Bechuanaland Protectorate, the South African Republic and the German Protectorate (the Caprivi Strip today) the force was to act as a border authority "to prevent encroachments and settle border difficulties with the German and Transvaal border authorities". Memories of the old force indulging in "border encroachments" in reverse seem happily to have been forgotten. Any matter involving law or policy was to be referred to the High Commissioner for "advice and instruction".

Bodle, after his unhappy interlude with Jameson in the Transvaal and a sea voyage under escort all the way to England, was now back in Kimberley repeating the duties of recruiting officer for the new Rhodesian police force — duties which he had originally performed seven years earlier for the BSACP. Later, he was to move to Bulawayo and become Nicholson's second-in-command of the Matabeleland Division. One recruit who joined in September 1896, Trooper E.W. Meyer, wrote, "Major Bodle was very particular as to certificates of good character". However, the medical examination must have been somewhat perfunctory, for Meyer had been blinded in his left eye by a cricket ball and nobody spotted that in Kimberley. They put him through the riding and shooting tests on the Kimberley rifle range and he says condescendingly, "It was rather amusing to see some of the recruits trying to mount on the off side."

The recruits were sent on from Kimberley by train to Gaborone — at that time the northern limit of the railway line (which was now actually being pushed on to Bulawayo, where it would arrive only little more than a year later). But from Gaborone, the recruits still had a 400 mile journey by ox-wagon to Bulawayo. Meyer was in a party of 100 recruits and the journey, through country of a type with which most of them were painfully unfamiliar, took 42 days. Meyer writes, "The day following our arrival (in Bulawayo) we were marched down from the Police camp to the ordnance store, a wood and iron building where the post office stands today, and our kit was literally thrown at us. As each man went in a sergeant rattled off a list and two issuers threw the stuff down on the floor from the shelves. You then proceeded to make it up into a bundle in the two large red blankets which were part of the issue. The issue included rifle, bayonet, bandolier, three pairs of boots, jack, field and ammunition. This bundle had to be slung over the shoulder and carried from the post office to the back of the camp where our wagons had outspanned."

Next day they were issued with 50 rounds of ammunition. They were marched to the Chartered Company's office, on the corner of Main Street and 9th Avenue, a wood and iron bungalow — which subsequently won its title to fame as Raaff's Boot and Repairing Depot and was later pulled down and replaced by the South African Mutual building. "Here," says Meyer, "we had a weary wait as each man had to go in and swear to serve Her Majesty Queen Victoria north of Cape Town and south of the Zambezi." Two or three foreigners refused to take the oath. One wonders if they were concerned with the need for allegiance to the Queen or with the prohibition from taking part in any "ventures" in the Company's territories. They were brought before the magistrate and discharged from the force. Theirs had been a brief but itinerant police career. History is silent on how they made their way back to wherever they had come from — if they did.

"The next morning," Meyer wrote, "we set off early towards the Matopos and halted at Colonel Plumer's camp. It was called Mlimo Camp and occupied by some of the Mafeking relief force. After we were lined up, Colonel Plumer addressed us and we proceeded towards Fort Usher. Colonel Plumer's men were setting fire to their huts and leaving on their long trek to Mafeking."

The rebellion in Matabeleland was finished; Rhodes had concluded his peace; the Imperial troops were packing up and leaving; the new police force — every one a raw recruit — was taking over.

The new force took over at the same time, and equally untrained, in Mashonaland. The new establishment, under the overall command of the Commandant-General provided for a Commandant of each Division. Nicholson (John Sanctuary Nicholson was his full name) was the Commandant in Matabeleland; the new Commandant in Mashonaland was to be Captain the Honourable Frederick Rossmore Wauchope Eveleigh de Moleyns (no less), of the 4th Hussars. He assumed the local rank of Lieutenant Colonel — which made the names sound even more impressive — and took over command of the local forces from Alderson on 12 December. The first 180 men of his new force had luckily arrived in Salisbury two days before, more, one suspects, by chance than careful staff work. These men had been recruited in the Cape and Natal and had been taken to Beira in the Durban Castle. One of them wrote later that he had been attested on the ship. They were accommodated on arrival in Salisbury in the Legislative Council building in Cecil Square, which was in course of erection and had no doors and windows.

Inspector Hopper, who had been left in charge in Mashonaland when Jameson took most of his men off into the Transvaal, now became Chief Inspector (local rank, Major) and second-in-command to de Moleyns. His position during the previous 18 months had been painfully ambiguous. From August 1895, when H.F. White had taken over the commissionership from brother Charles and became concerned with more diverting preoccupations than police work in Rhodesia, Hopper had signed Orders of the Mashonaland Mounted Police "pro, Chief Commissioner of Police". When H.F. White left with Jameson in November, Hopper signed more confidently as Acting Chief Commissioner of Police. From April 1896 shortly before the rising in Mashonaland — he seems to have faded temporarily out of the picture. One report is that he was sent to Fort Victoria During his absence, and until de Moleyns's appointment as Commandant, orders for the MMP (such as the force was at the time) were issued first by Regimental Sergeant-Major J.P. Hyland (a trooper in the original 'E' Troop, BSACP (No. 464, attested April 1890) and later by Inspector Nesbitt. Hopper only comes back into the picture in October 1896 when he was appointed second-in-command, and he signed Orders "pro, Officer Commanding, Rhodesia Mounted Police (in Mashonaland)" for the next two months. From the middle of December onwards, when Hopper was sent off on operations, Orders were signed by the new Staff Officer, Mashonaland, Major A.V. Gosling — one of the BBP officers who had thrown in his lot with Jameson, had been tried with the others in London and happily acquitted.

The story of how the new BSA Police in Mashonaland, raw as they were, took up the fight against the recalcitrant rebels, where Alderson and his MFF had left off, began on the very day de Moleyns took over. Colin Harding (of whom more later) wrote in his book Far Bugles: "The majority of this newly raised BSA Police Force came direct out from home and had little or no knowledge of police work. They were strengthened by 50 Mounted Infantrymen who volunteered to serve in the new force and proved a valuable addition, for they could ride as well as shoot." These paragons were from the Natal Troop, not Alderson's MI. A Native Contingent was being raised at the same time. By early 1897 some 300 "Black Watch", as they were popularly known, were attached to the Mashonaland Division.

On 12 December 1896 de Moleyns sent Hopper out to the Hartley district with a force of 80 white

police — probably bolstered with the ex-Natal Troopers. This was the district in which the first victims of the rebellion had been murdered. One of the leading rebels, Chief Matshayongombi, had his
kraal deep in the granite hills south-west of Salisbury, the site of which is on the farm Fort Martin
Extension, later owned by Mr. B.S. Marlborough. The old pioneer road from Hartley to Salisbury, not
used since the turn of the century, was clearly traceable through the farm and at one point passed
within a quarter of a mile of the kraal. It says something for the wild, rugged country of this part of
the farm — a concentration of thickly wooded, steeply contoured kopjes — that although Mr.
Marlborough knew that the kraal site was somewhere on his property, and that it could be identified
by a group of caves whose rocky entrances had been blown up by dynamite, he had been on the farm
for nine years before he found it. Indeed, in the end it was only traced down by a search organised as
a training exercise by the Hartley Police Reserve — of which Mr. Marlborough was a member —
some time in the 1960s.

Earl Grey, the Administrator, when he had criticised Alderson for his promenade militaire, had
added, "Alderson committed two blunders — after his third attack on Matshayongombi he should
have blown up the cave and left a fort behind. He did neither and the result is that Matshayongombi
believes we are afraid and impotent." Grey had at least managed to prevail on Alderson, after some
difficulty, to build a fort at Hartley. "The evidence which this fort gives," he went on, "that we intend
to stay there is puzzling Matshayongombi and is already beginning to make him uncomfortable and
the latest news is that he is quarrelling with the Mondoro, who has taken some of his wives." The
"Mondoro" was the main rebel leader — or, more correctly, the principal witch-doctor; his name was
Kagubi and he made his headquarters at Matshayongombi's kraal. "I have every hope," said Grey,
"we shall be able, without taking any active measures against his kopjes, to reduce him to a state of
submission." It proved to be an unrealistic hope.

Now that Alderson had gone, Grey's policy of establishing forts in the hope that they would intimidate the rebel leaders was actively pursued. Hopper's job, with his force of 80, was to build a fort,
which was later named Fort Martin, on a convenient kopje (also on Mr. Marlborough's farm) no more
than a mile from the Chief's kraal but standing in relatively open country and offering a commanding
view from its summit. The Chief's kraal would be within range of a seven-pounder gun mounted on
the kopje. Inspector Nesbitt, who was to command the fort when it was ready, wrote later, "Fort
Martin is very healthy, being splendidly situated very high ... it is impregnable and the best possible
place." On another smaller kopje, 100 yards to the north,  the Black Watch were encamped.

One member of Hopper's force was Trooper L.S. Glover (BSAP No. 70) who had arrived in
Salisbury with the Durban Castle batch of recruits on 9 November. (On the reorganisation of the force
in 1896, regimental numbers started again from No. 1 — the series which ran until 1980.) Only a
month later, and with negligible training, he was sent out on active duties. But not before he had
acquired the true policeman's inherent capacity to complain. Nor did he endorse Nesbitt's belief in the
healthy situation of Fort Martin. He writes, "the now almost incessant rains, overwork, lack of
sufficient food and quinine, gave the malarial bug every chance to turn men into wrecks ... not that
quinine was properly appreciated when you had to line up while an orderly passed down the rank
dipping the point of his knife into the gun powder and tipping that on the back of your tongue, after
which you were allowed to break and run for water". The food, always a ready target for the practised
complainer, was "a pound tin of bully-beef between four men (for the day) and when the weevily,
grub-infested biscuits gave out we had to take a Boer-meal ration that also carried a lively population".
The men were issued with black waterproof capes. "The natural receptacle for the meal," he says,
"was a pocket of your waterproof and a corner of your cape made a mixing board. When it was raining the sugar ration went straight into your mouth, the tea into another pocket to be chewed at leisure;
for to find twigs, bark or dry wood enough to start a fire was another story and your hat was as
(useless) to fan a smouldering fire to flames as to keep the rain off."

Glover succumbed to fever and was taken to the camp hospital at Hartley, which he describes as "a
rectangular wattle-and-daub shack where there lay about 20 of us, heads to the walls and feet mixed
... the only available food was ground rice three times a day if you could eat, and you lay in the muck
of your own sweat — and hell was your portion until the blessed sweat broke out". It was while he
was in hospital that Glover had what he called "my first introduction to the British South Africa
Police": the arrival of four mule wagons with rations from Salisbury "and an escort of 20 fine young

fellows, just out from England, dressed in blue tunics with brass buttons, cord breeches, puttees and smart hats" — a somewhat incongruous spectacle in the wilds of Mashonaland at the height of the rainy season. One assumes that when Glover had joined the newly constituted force, not more than a couple of months earlier, it had still been known as the Rhodesia Mounted Police and the clothing issue had been more utilitarian than decorative. Now it was clearly the BSAP, officially proclaimed or not. Glover survived his fever. He was fortunate. In the cemetery below the old fort at Hartley Hill lie eight BSAP victims of malaria, seven of whom died in the early months of 1897.

Colin Harding has already been mentioned, as the author of Far Bugles. Much later, in 1938, he was to write another book with reminiscences of his BSAP days which he called Frontier Patrols. By then he was Colonel C. Harding, CMG, DSO, and had been Administrator of Barotseland and a Provincial Commissioner in the Gold Coast Colony. He had arrived in Bulawayo in 1894 with no money and had worked successively as a "sawyer's mate" at £3 a week, a bricklayer and a solicitor's clerk. He had returned to England for family reasons early in 1896, but when he heard of the Matabele rebellion he had hurried back to Africa. At Cape Town he and a friend got a job taking a batch of horses to Mashonaland, by ship to Beira and then walking them to Umtali. Having delivered the horses he joined the Umtali Volunteers and earned the doubtful distinction of commanding a firing party which executed Makoni, one of the rebel chiefs. After that he served as a "galloper" on Alderson's staff and when the BSAP was formed he was offered a commission as Sub Inspector (Lieutenant) in the Mashonaland Division.

Commissioned at the same time were Jack Norton Griffiths, who had been a sergeant in the Natal Troop — and was subsequently to become a member of the House of Commons and to be knighted; W.J. MacQueen, who had been second-in-command of one of the BBP troops which had joined Jameson's raiders (not being an Imperial officer he had avoided prosecution) and was to serve in the BSAP for 18 years, until 1914; and Jack Roach, who had commanded the Artillery Troop of the Pioneer Corps (as distinct from the BSACP) in the occupation of Mashonaland.

Harding's first responsible assignment with the BSAP was to take 10 troopers and 15 "Black Watch" to Chief Simbanoota's kraal near Balihuli, 13 miles from Salisbury on the Ruwa River, to recapture some stolen cattle. Whether or not he was successful is not recorded. From there he moved another 12 miles east where he was joined by a party under Major Gosling and between them they built a fort near the kraal of another of the rebel chiefs, Chief Chikwakwa. At the time, Chikwakwa's kraal was on what is now the Warrendale farm near Goromonzi (which subsequently became the property of the Nesbitts and on which Mrs. Jack, Inspector Nesbitt's niece, still lives today). After the attack on Chikwakwa's kraal, as shall be related, his people moved some 20 miles to the north-east, to what is now the Chikwakwa Tribal Trust Land. The original kraal was on the long, rugged, wooded, granite kopje known as Goromonzi today, about three miles north-east of the present Goromonzi police station. There is another similar rugged kopje north of and adjacent to Goromonzi. The two kopjes are connected by a high spur. Another Mashona chief, named Gondo, had his kraal on the smaller northern kopje. He, too, must have moved away with his people after the attack, because an entirely different kopje known today as "Gondo's" is some miles to the south.

Gosling and Harding built their fort — the usual stone wall 40 feet square, topped by sandbags — on a mound half a mile west of Chikwakwa's kraal. The mound is clearly identifiable today, although the terrain is wooded and uneven. From the mound there is a splendid view to the north over the valley of the Chinyika River, with ranges of blue-grey hills etching the horizon. The Mashonaland country here is more open, with grander sweeps of hills and valleys than in the Hartley district, but the kopjes are just as rugged, and massive rocks and boulders, many resting on or against each other, form warrens of spacious caves, some almost completely closed. Access to the caves is usually precarious.

The fort at the foot of Chikwakwa's kopje was to be the last in the series of forts built in Mashonaland during the period of the rebellion. It was named Fort Harding — no little compliment for a recently commissioned sub-inspector, particularly as a major had also had a hand in its construction. When the fort was finished Gosling withdrew, leaving Harding in command of a garrison of 20 white and 20 black police.

The main purpose of the police presence at Fort Harding was to bring the two chiefs, Chikwakwa and Gondo, to heel. The Native Commissioner from Mtoko, W.L. Armstrong — who had been a member of the BSACP (No. 537) which he joined in July 1890 — was already making hopeful overtures with the chiefs for a peaceful surrender. Some form of truce had been arranged, but it was allegedly broken one night by the rebels crossing the open land between Harding's fort and the kopje, and cutting loose three police horses. On 7 February, de Moleyns, the Commandant himself, arrived with 30 more white police — a provocation which prompted Chikwakwa's people to fire on one of his patrols. Armstrong's negotiations for a truce became patently fruitless and three days later, in response to a call from de Moleyns, Captain Jack Roach brought from Salisbury another 40 policemen and a third seven-pounder gun.

The police decided first to attack Gondo's kopje and then to work along the ridge to Chikwakwa's. The fort which Gosling and Harding had built was too near to the kopjes for effective, plunging shell fire and so the guns were taken back half a mile on to a ridge — where the original Goromonzi police station was subsequently built. The stone gun emplacement, facing towards Chikwakwa's kraal, is still visible today. (The present Goromonzi police station, established in 1902, is about two miles to the south-west.) Gondo's people, on their kopje, enjoyed the protection of some particularly convenient caves, and when Roach commenced his bombardment they retired into their depths, confident in the knowledge that, even if the shelling stopped and troops attacked, nobody would take the risk of following them inside. Still more reinforcements arrived from Salisbury, so that there was a veritable army threatening the two kopjes, but de Moleyns himself apparently withdrew to more pressing demands of his rank in Salisbury for Roach now took overall command of the operation.

On 16 February, Harding led an assault on Gondo's kopje with 29 troopers and 65 of the "Black Watch". The police had brought with them some simple hand-grenades of dynamite, which they now hurled into the caves. It was on this occasion that the "Black Watch" established a somewhat disreputable legend in their history by applauding with resounding cheers every time a grenade burst and drove out a crowd of Gondo's people, to become easy targets for the waiting Maxim. When Gondo's kopje had been "cleaned up" — to use an appropriate military expression — the assault was carried across the connecting spur to Chikwakwa's stronghold and this was also taken without loss, although Chikwakwa himself appears to have escaped. The police seem to have completed this "cleaning up" operation without sustaining any casualties.

There is a little cemetery close to Fort Harding with eight recorded graves of members of the BSAP. One is of Trooper Harry White (No. 174) who died at Chikwakwa's, but not until 23 April, some time after this action. He probably died of fever. Of the others, one is of Trooper J. Close (No. 424) who was killed in an action at Mashonganyika's kraal — not to be confused with Matshayongombi's as shall later be related; the other graves are of Sergeant W.M. Robertson (No. 492); Troopers S.H. Bennison (No. 416) and G. Irwin (No. 519) who died at Kunzwi's kraal; and Trooper J.G Brady (No. 53) who died — probably killed — at Chininyika's kraal. The missing two graves are of Troopers H.B. Standing (No. 891) and J. Turner (No. 1175) both of whom died at Goromonzi in 1901, again probably of fever.

Harding and his colleagues must subsequently have faced some criticism for the less than humanitarian methods they used to clear out Gondo's caves, for he later found it necessary to write in explanation, "What compelled us to use dynamite was the fact that the Mashonas, when attacked, retreated at once into these caves (refusing to come out and surrender, even when their lives were guaranteed) and shot down our officers and men at all times without the slightest risk to themselves" — an allegation which is difficult to reconcile with the casualty list at Chikwakwa's.

"Repeatedly I have sat for a considerable time outside the caves, urging men, women and children to come out to safety. I have helped many a man from a cave which was to be blown up and not until I (was) convinced that only men remained was dynamite inserted in the strongholds.

The great risk to the people who used the dynamite was that, unless it was placed right inside its value was negligible. To do this, one had to go right up to the mouth of the cave, when you would be a sure mark for any hidden armed native inside, whom you could not see or locate."

## Chapter Twelve

## THE END OF THE REBELLION

IN THE EARLY months of 1897 the Mashonaland Division consisted of 200 "undrilled" troopers (as Harding himself called them), 50 ex-Natal Troop mounted infantrymen and 300 "Black Watch". Compared with the situation during the preceding years, the strength was lavish. But although the surviving rebels no longer presented a life and death menace to the white settlers, they still constituted a threat to peace. The subjugation of the Matabele for that in effect was what Rhodes had accomplished, for all his talk of a negotiated peace had removed the principal influence behind the Mashona rebellion; and the Mashona leaders, left alone in the redoubts to which they had retreated, might well have lapsed into the submissive passivity which was, and had long been, their tribal hall-mark. But a thirst for vengeance, in the guise of justice, is a besetting attribute of even the most civilised peoples and the settlers were resolutely determined to dispense justice by meting out to the criminals the punishment they believed they deserved.

Thus the task of finally eradicating the rebels imposed a heavier burden on the police than would normally have fallen on them even in the still undeveloped state of the country. They were faced, in fact, with a task similar to that for which Carrington had asked for 5000 men and which Rhodes had decided could only be concluded by negotiation. Moreover, the rebel guerrillas in Mashonaland were spread over a far wider area than they had been in Matabeleland. To find some help for this extra duty would be a godsend. Consequently the authorities were considerably encouraged when they learnt that a tribe known as the Budjga in the Mtoko district in the north-east, under a chief named Gurupila, were for some good reason of their own markedly unfriendly with the Mashonas. Perhaps this enmity could be exploited to the benefit of the settlers.

Armstrong, the Native Commissioner, was sent off to Mtoko in March accompanied by Harding, 20 white police, 25 Black Watch and a Maxim. The expedition must have ranked as of some importance because the Hon. Hubert Howard, Earl Grey's secretary, was also included in the party. With pack-mules and native carriers they carried provisions for a month. The object of the exercise was to offer Gurupila and his fighting men (if they could be so described) an attractive opportunity to share with the white men the pleasure of routing the Mashonas.

Armstrong and his party left Fort Harding on 4 March and were constantly harassed by rain and Mashonas. The prospects of the expedition seemed far from propitious. Harding says, "the mules were restless, the new police jumpy, the weather wet and the guide unreliable". The site chosen by the guide for the first night's camp was dominated by surrounding kopjes and Harding says they could see the Mashona fires winking in the hills on each flank — a spectacle that is difficult to reconcile with his complaint of continuous rain. They arrived at Gurupila's after three days' march (it was about 70 miles from Fort Harding) and when Armstrong had talked to the chief, streams of what Harding describes as "friendly natives" began to roll in with their assegais, rusty guns, wives and babies — a surprising miscellany to serve as reinforcements for the BSAP. Harding says, "Gurupila had a grudge against one or two Mashona chiefs, a love for Mashona cattle, and still room in his well-filled harems for one or two young Mashona girls."

Harding's force had now been encouragingly increased from 50 to 550. He fixed 6 a.m. the next morning for the time to break camp and move off, but it was not until 6 p.m. that evening that, in his own words, "the last Gurupilite had filled his calabash with water and affectionately wrapped his old flint gun in a calico rag to keep the lock dry". The army's departure was thus unavoidably postponed but next morning it actually moved off, headed for the rebel strongholds in the district east of Salisbury. Harding and Howard led with the police and the Maxim, while Armstrong followed in as dignified a state as he could achieve, "surrounded by numerous native drummers in the midst of the friendlies".

When they made a camp after the first day's march, "the friendlies came dribbling in at all hours of the night singing and dancing. It was useless to have roll call for no one knew to within a hundred or two how many there should be. We were rather like a huge snowball which increased in size as it progressed."

Next day they ran into their first trouble with the Mashonas, who ambushed them in a rocky defile between Mrewa and the Nyadiri River. Harding found that nobody, not even in his own force, knew how to use the Maxim. He chose to hand it over to Trooper Lucas "who admitted he was not an expert but had driven a mowing machine". Not unexpectedly, the gun was soon out of action with a cartridge broken off in the chamber. It was probably just as well, for Lucas had already scored a near miss on Armstrong. The immediate prospect of meeting the Mashonas in battle — or possibly the menace of the Maxim — had unnerved "the friendlies" and more than half of Gurupila's fighting men hurried off back in the direction of Mtoko. Somehow, Harding's regular police and the more intrepid friend-lies who had stayed with him made their way through the defile, and next day he felt bold enough to launch an actual attack on the kraal of a Mashona chief, Shaungwe, at the top of an 850-foot kopje not far from Mrewa. Even so, Harding admits, "I feared more from the erratic fire of my would-be friends than from my avowed enemies." The attack failed to dislodge Shaungwe and Gurupila was mortally wounded. His body was taken away by his own disillusioned people, who now deserted Harding altogether.

"We were now in desperate straits," Harding says. "Our friendlies had proved unreliable, my own men were down with fever, provisions were short, and with only about 20 reliable white troops we were outnumbered 50 to one by the hostile warriors who daily threatened attack." It was now 17 March, nearly two weeks since they had left Fort Harding, and they were still on the Nyagui River, at least 30 miles from Salisbury. Harding sent Howard off to Salisbury — besides Harding himself, Howard was probably the only man with any real experience in the veld. In any case it was a shrewd move because the Administrator's secretary could be expected to command some top-level attention; and when Howard reached Salisbury the Commandant, Colonel de Moleyns, organised a party and led it himself to the relief of Harding on the Nyagui.

Glover had meanwhile been moved from the camp hospital at Hartley to Salisbury. Like many oth-ers there who had been brought in from the veld, he was subject to recurrent bouts of fever. "Doctors," he complained, "were overworked, and untrained orderlies depended overmuch on a thermometer; if your temperature was normal then you were fit and had to go (on patrol); a situation that finally caused a flare-up. Patrols, especially if there was wheeled transport, were always difficult to get started and seldom got more than four or five miles out the first day and then camped down for the night." On one such occasion, when a patrol pitched camp in the veld, a man just out of hospital was warned for guard. He protested that he was too weak, but as his temperature showed normal his protest was over-ruled. He died during the night. Glover says, "There was no strike but a deputation went back to the CO and made it plain that there would be no more of that." So a barrack ward was established in the still windowless and doorless Legislative Council building, to which men released from hospital were sent for a week's observation and rest.

Glover was now a sergeant and he was sent out with eight troopers — all intermittent malarial cases like himself — to guard a maize crop 25 miles out of Salisbury somewhere on the Enterprise Road. "We found a couple of good huts on a kopje overlooking the maize land and expected no trouble till the grain was nearly ripe, so we took things easy, two patrolling by day and all taking turns at night. Weeks went by with no quinine from Salisbury and fever became more and more prevalent." No one was fit enough to walk all the way into Salisbury to fetch some quinine. "We feared, and rightly, a go of the shakes or a spleen attack when one can do nothing to help oneself, and having only a hazy idea of the direction (to a mission about 12 miles away) we failed to make the effort (to reach the mission) and in that low feverish state we felt we were forgotten men." Fortunately, a priest at the mission heard of their plight and brought them some life-saving quinine.

If the authorities had forgotten them and their possible need for quinine, the memory of their existence was restored promptly enough when the call for help for Harding's force was received by de Moleyns. The Commandant's relief party had set out from Salisbury and was passing within a few miles of Glover's camp. An officer was sent over to order Glover and his troopers to join the column. Glover, who was never inclined to be complimentary, described the relief party when he saw it as "a scratch crowd of office-wallahs and staff ... plus cook boys, 'Black Watch' and a goodly number of friendly Mashonas".

Glover's eight troopers were told to bring nothing but their arms and ammunition — not even a blanket. They would only be away for forty-eight hours and they were to travel light and fast. They were away for two months; and they lost all their kit, which had been newly issued to them when they had been sent out to guard the maize.

When the relief party reached Harding on the Nyagui on 24 March — a week after Howard had ridden off for assistance — they found only Harding himself, Armstrong and three troopers with any semblance of health. Twenty men were prostrate with fever. De Moleyns's official report said, "Everyone suffered severely from sickness on this expedition (to Mtoko), the country being low-lying and unhealthy, and in addition a large number of horses died of sickness." The sick men were now sent into Salisbury in the excruciating discomfort of an ox-wagon. A new party of reinforcements arrived from Salisbury, and de Moleyns took the opportunity of attacking a concentration of Mashonas on Domborembudzi, the prominent domed hill north of the present road from Salisbury about 15 miles before it reaches Mrewa. The Mashonas were certainly driven off the kopje with some loss, but little progress was thereby made towards the final objective. The principal rebels were still holed up, defying authority, in their convenient caves deep in the hills.

It would be tedious to recount in detail all the engagements in the campaign waged by the BSAP against the Mashona rebels in May and June of 1897. The force was carrying the full responsibility now: no more operating with Imperial forces or merely supporting the volunteers. (A troop of 7th Hussars appears, unaccountably, to have been left in Mashonaland, almost as if it were one of the forgotten legions. It was the 7th Hussars who had provided the escort for the Jameson Raiders from Volksrust to Durban and they turn up again unexpectedly in the records of July 1897, supporting the BSAP in the final engagements in the Mashonaland campaign. They actually built Fort Lomagundi, seven miles west of Sinoia.) During this period the BSAP established itself incontestably as Rhodesia's first line of defence; and although the growing numbers of its members were still green with inexperience as policemen they suffered no lack of painful indoctrination in the facts of life in the bundu — and with a little tuition in the ordinances they would soon acquire some rough competence as effective representatives of the law.

In Matabeleland, not only had the danger of physical attack by the rebels been removed but the guerrilla situation — which still disturbed Mashonaland — had also been disposed of. The task of the Matabeleland Division was no longer a military operation. The police could go about their legitimate duties, even though at that stage some of the niceties of legal procedure had, by force of circumstances, often to be ignored. And there were still some unusual calls on their services which a police force would hope not normally to have to perform. A regular roster of mounted patrols, each made up of a corporal and three troopers, was sent out from the newly established stations round Bulawayo to search the ruins of the scores of homesteads and mining camps which had been destroyed by the rebels. It was during these patrols that the gruesome remains were discovered of many of the 205 men, women and children murdered during the Matabele rebellion. The police grew used to handling the pitiful remains of mutilated, dismembered bodies, wrapping them in blankets, carrying them into their camps in scotch-carts and burying them in the little cemeteries that are still dotted about the country. Occasionally reports came in of unsurrendered arms still in the hands of tribesmen. But usually, when the reports were followed up, the kraals were found deserted and the arms abandoned. The rebellious spirit of the Matabele had been broken and not one was now prepared to face the penalty of illegal possession of arms.

Under Colonel Nicholson's command, the Matabeleland Division was divided into five troops which were at first designated: 'A' at Gwanda, 'B' at Gwelo, 'C' at Filabusi, 'D' at Bulawayo and 'E' at Fort Usher. 'C' Troop, with its headquarters at Filabusi, established before the close of 1896, had outstations at Balla Balla, Fort Rixon, Belingwe and Mpateni (in the Belingwe district). The stations were still always known as "forts". Fort Filabusi was in the form of a pole and dagga stockade eight feet high, enclosing an area 30 yards by 18 yards, with a surrounding trench eight feet wide and six feet deep, its excavated earth thrown up against the walls of the stockade. The outstations were of the same pattern if slightly smaller. Inside each fort were somehow crowded two pole and dagga buildings, with doors and window-frames knocked up from discarded packing cases, for use as ration store and guardroom. Also, again crowded somehow into the confined space of the fort, a raised walk-way of compacted earth ran round the inside of the stockade to enable sentries to peep over the top. During the first months after the forts were built full guards were mounted daily, but these were later discontinued. Not one of these so-called forts was ever subject to attack. Indeed, the days of rebel onslaught were-over; but British military practice eagerly inherited by the BSAP, ancient and modern — has always tended towards a state of commendable preparation for the last war or emergency.

'C' Troop at Filabusi had its full share of ex-Jameson Raiders. Captain Frank Bowden, who had commanded Jameson's artillery troop, was the first OC. Among his lieutenants were A.J. Tomlinson (the future Acting Commissioner) and H. Constable — both fellow Raiders — and he also boasted two Honourables among his officers, with appropriately hyphenated names: Lieutenants Yarde-Buller and Horsley-Beresford. On one occasion when an alarming report came in that the natives at Mpateni were not surrendering their arms with exemplary promptness, and that guerrilla trouble was brewing again, Bowden was reinforced by the "Police Mounted Battery" — presumably the mule battery with the screw-guns which had been fobbed off on to the Matabeleland Division — under Captain Hoel Llewellyn, accompanied by an imposing array of brass consisting of the Commandant, Nicholson himself; Major Bodle, now his second-in-command; and Captains Chawner, Cashel and Straker. No doubt they had an enjoyable excursion, but by the time they reached their destination the suspects had, as usual, decamped and all they found were a few muzzle loaders. However, the Police meted out the customary retribution by destroying the native crops.

Returning to the Mashonaland campaign, the decisive engagement took place on 24 July at Matshayongombi's kraal. Some three months earlier Matshayongombi had sought to buy immunity from attack by sending an emissary to the Native Commissioner offering five muzzle-loading guns and £15 10s. 6d. in tax. When this handsome bribe was unaccountably refused he had marked his displeasure by attacking Fort Martin with 300 or 400 rebels. This was as far back as 17 March. Inspector Nesbitt was in command at Fort Martin and although he was never in danger of being over-whelmed by the Mashonas — he had said himself that the fort was "impregnable" — his troops took three hours to beat off the attack. Three African police were killed and two wounded. The attackers suffered heavy casualties before they withdrew — too dispirited ever to try again.

On an even earlier occasion, de Moleyns had led out a force of 170 men with the apparent intention of attacking the Matshayongombi stronghold and capturing Kagubi, "the Mondoro". But according to Earl Grey, who was apt to be carping about the senior officers, "de Moleyns again was irresolute — made a night march to within a mile of the enemy and then (turned) right about to build a fort instead of instantly putting the matter to the touch". It is unusual to name a military stronghold after your enemy, but for some strange reason de Moleyns gave the name Fort Mondoro to the fort he constructed close to Matshayongombi's kraal (from which derivation, no doubt, the Mondoro Tribal Trust Land owes its name). In the event, the location of the fort proved even more unhealthy than usual and after a heavy toll on its garrison it was soon abandoned.

Whether de Moleyns was resolute or irresolute, it took him from March to July to prepare with Inspector Nesbitt a definitive plan of attack on Matshayongombi's kraal. However, this was launched at last from Fort Martin at dawn on 24 July. Colin Harding, having returned from his boisterous expedit on to Mtoko, had been given command of the whole African Police contingent and was now an Inspector; and on is occasion he led a force of his "Black Watch" in the van of the attack. He was supported by both mounted and unmounted white troopers and Inspectors Gosling, Nesbitt, Roach and a Sub-Inspector Ellett.

There is nothing precipitous about the series of kopjes on which Matshayongombi located his extensive kraal. The climb to the higher levels is slight and gradual and the area is really a complex of jumbled hills enclosing relatively flat clearings in which numbers of stockades were erected without any formally defensive pattern. Only in the heart of the kraal, reached by devious paths and contours among the labyrinthine hills, is there any semblance of a stronghold. Here there is a ring of massive boulders, 30 and 40 feet high — small kopjes in themselves. The chief's lair could only be found by passing through narrow gaps between the boulders. (This is why it took Mr. Marlborough so many years to find it; he must have walked through those kopjes many times and passed it close by.) Within the area formed by the encircling boulders other massive rocks lie on or against each other, forming deep, spacious caves into which hundreds of people could retreat with complete immunity from attack.

The first stockades were rushed and taken without loss. But opposition stiffened as the troops neared the heart of the position, and although Matshayongombi's people were driven within the circle of rocks and down into the caves, the attackers suffered casualties. Trooper J.C. Lalor-Hull was killed;

Trooper A.S. Simmonds was mortally wounded. Two troopers, D. Dennett and V. Downes were severely wounded and three more (including Captain J.S. Brabant who had attested in the BSACP (No. 111, in January 1890) were slightly wounded. Three of Harding's African police were killed and two wounded. One was shot through the face and the bullet was later extracted by Dr. Alexander Fleming, who had been Principal Medical Officer of the police since 1894.

In this instance, within the surrounding ring of towering boulders — formed by nature into a defensive circle as if specifically for the purpose — the hazard of approaching the mouths of the caves and throwing in the dynamite grenades without being shot by the rebels was considerable. It is probable that this was where most of the police casualties occurred. Today, massive chunks of the overhanging granite lie where they have fallen across the mouths of some of the caves, but these are the results of systematic dynamiting carried out on the morning after the attack, for such an operation could not have been undertaken during the fight. Pickets had been placed around the outside of the circle of boulders and had remained on guard all night to ensure that no Mashonas escaped. But the earlier hand-grenading had had its desired effect and early in the morning Matshayongombi himself appeared wounded at the mouth of one of the caves and was mercilessly shot down. After the dynamiting many of Matshayongombi's people were entombed but 278, including 215 women and children, came out and surrendered during the next four days.

Some reports suggest that the lone troop of 7th Hussars took part in the attack on Matshayongombi. It seems definite that they were in the vicinity but it is probable that they merely waited in support on the far side of the Umfuli River to cut off any of Matshayongombi's people who tried to escape. They were to be very disappointed.

There is a little cemetery close by Fort Martin where Troopers Lalor-Hull and Simmonds were buried. There are also in the cemetery the graves of Sergeant-Major R. Tennant, who fell down the precipitous face of the Fort Martin kopje and fractured his skull; Sergeant S. H. Mauric, who died of malaria in 1898; and Moony, the Native Commissioner, who had been murdered in the district at the outbreak of the Mashona rebellion.

Although the attack on Matshayongombi's kraal can be considered the decisive engagement in the campaign — there was still some mopping up to do. Gosling returned to Fort Harding with 160 white and 100 black police, and three seven-pounders, to attack another chief, Mashonganyika (dangerously confusing) whose kraal was a few miles southwest of Chikwakwa's, still in the Goromonzi district. After six days' fighting the stronghold was destroyed — again by considerable recourse to dynamite — and it is recorded that only one rebel escaped alive from the caves. But Mashonganyika, the chief, had wisely made off before the attack. Gosling then moved on and attacked Chief Kunzwi's kraal, where Sergeant Robertson was killed and Troopers Bennison and Irwin died of wounds. Four African police were killed. Again the rebels were decimated but, like Chikwakwa and Mashonganyika, Kunzwi himself escaped.

While the back of the rebellion was virtually broken, some of the rebel chiefs were still at large, notably Kagubi himself, Chikwakwa, Mashonganyika and Kunzwi, and Chief Mangwendi in the Mrewa district. But the BSAP's punitive net was closing in on them and they began to show signs of suing for peace. Early in September, de Moleyns, Gosling, Harding and two African Commissioners (Armstrong and Campbell) met Mangwendi, Kunzwi and Chikwakwa somewhere in the region of Bogoto, south of Mrewa. It is clear that the chiefs had little support left — so many of their followers were now dead men — otherwise such a meeting with its obvious implication of surrender would never have come about. The chiefs agreed to instruct the surviving rebels to surrender at Fort Harding and hand in their arms. Kagubi, the Mondoro, was then still at large, but he was captured on 27 October (it is difficult to find where this happened). He was tried for murder and executed, as also were Mashonganyika and two of his sons, whom Campbell, the Native Commissioner, had actually seen murder his brother. Gondo went to prison for eight years, Chikwakwa was acquitted and for some reason Kunzwi was never tried.

In the middle of 1898, Fort Harding was abandoned and a new police post was established at Fort Enterprise, near Kahiya, close to the Enterprise gold-field, eleven miles north of the original Chikwakwa's kraal, on the boundary between the present Mashonakop and Neptune farms. Fort Enterprise was as unhealthy as ever and when three policemen had died of fever, and were buried in a cemetery beside the fort, the garrison was removed to the first Goromonzi station.

Fort Martin had also remained the administrative police post in the Hartley district until late in 1898, when the first station was established in Hartley itself. Up to then, Hartley town was looked on as a primitive mining camp, too rough to expect self-respecting policemen to live in it. However, one assumes that it was for that reason itself that it was ultimately decided that the police were needed there and Inspector Nesbitt's "impregnable" Fort Martin was abandoned.

During both the Matabele and Mashona rebellions 32 members of the police were killed — either killed in action, died of wounds, or murdered — and eight were severely wounded in action.

Although, at the outbreak of both rebellions the police units in each territory were but negligible factors in the forces ranged against the rebels, by the time the campaigns ended the BSAP was the sole force left in the field and now carried the full responsibility for maintaining peace and order in Rhodesia.

## Chapter Thirteen

## CANNON KOPJE

ON 10 OCTOBER 1946 an elderly gentleman (who for obvious reasons shall be nameless), who had joined the BSAP in 1896 and whose regimental number in the new series had been a single digit, wrote to the Commissioner of Police, Colonel Ross, a letter of congratulations on the 50th anniversary of the Regiment's birthday. He regretted, he said, "the abolition of the once firmly established custom (in the BSAP) of the eye-opener at dawn, this abolition bringing in its wake the discarding of moustaches". As he explained, "They just won't grow luxuriantly without being fertilised daily at dawn by whiskey and milk ... May the ancient craft," he went on, "of dealing with men singly or in crowds, with or without ruffling their hair as circumstances demand, continue to flourish in the years ahead" — an unexceptionable sentiment. The gentleman's own career in the BSAP had been colourful, influenced perhaps by the "eye-opener". In 1900 he was reprimanded in Salisbury for improper conduct and later the same year fined 5s. at Pitsani for insolence to an NCO. In 1903 at Chisewe (now a corporal) he was reduced to trooper for being short of stores and rendering false returns; in 1904 fined 10s. for assaulting an African constable at Goromonzi; next year admonished for breaking out of camp after setting the guard; and in 1908 fined £2 for "drunk and irregular conduct" on patrol. That same year he was discharged, time expired, with character "All good". The BSAP was clearly growing up.

For two years following the suppression of the Mashona rebellion, Rhodesia enjoyed peace and a good measure of prosperity. The BSAP naturally had their alarms and excursions, but they were at last able to consolidate their position and establish themselves as the accepted agents of law and providers of the multitude of unorthodox services which the public has always expected from its police. In essence and although Rhodesia was still in the early stages of development — the pattern of police work which was established during those years has remained virtually unchanged. New methods, new systems, new techniques have naturally evolved; new circumstances and new demands have constantly changed the emphasis of the work. But fundamentally, the pattern was set in those early days. The first stations were established, the first regular patrols sent out; animals were apprehended, sudden death was investigated; men were dealt with "singly or in crowds, with or without ruffling their hair"; calls of distress — some genuine, some false were answered; "first informations of crime" were received, dockets were opened, prosecutions pursued; members were promoted, punished, discharged, married, transferred, took leave, fell sick, retired, died. An enduring force was created, whose continuity and traditions with the possible exception of the "eye-opener" — persist today.

There was, however, one basic difference between the BSAP of the last years of the 19th century and the force as it was to be reorganised in 1903 after the South African war. The Bechuanaland, Matabeleland and Mashonaland Divisions of the force were still entirely separate units. (The short-lived North Zambezi Division, based on Mount Darwin, was merged into the Mashonaland Division in June 1898. Its members had to apply for transfer and were re-attested.) Each of the three remaining divisions was autonomous; there was no common administration, no transfers between divisions. Each had its own Commandant, answerable only to the Commandant-General, who had no immediate administrative responsibility. Colonel Nicholson became Commandant-General, in succession to Sir Richard Martin, in 1898. Lieutenant-Colonel J.A.H. Walford commanded No. 1 Division, based in Mafeking but operating in the Bechuanaland Protectorate, and was left to his own devices; Lieutenant-Colonel Bodle was now the Commandant of No. 2 Division in Bulawayo and Lieutenant-Colonel de Moleyns of No. 3 in Salisbury. They each had individual authority over their commands. The Commandant-General's orders were issued from "BSAP Headquarters, Salisbury," up to November 1898; thereafter, when Nicholson took over and until the reorganisation in 1903, they were issued from "BSAP Headquarters, Bulawayo".

This peace-time development of the force was to last for no more than two years. The Matabele rebellion was over late in 1896; the last Mashona rebels held out until late in 1897. But before the end of 1899 the BSAP were again on active military service, operating once more as Rhodesia's first line of defence.

If Jameson and his raiders into the Transvaal had accomplished anything, it had been to unite the Boers against the British. For all Kruger's early antagonism to the Uitlanders, there had always been a few burghers of the South African Republic who had accepted that a prosperous and unrestricted mining industry on the Rand, no matter if it were operated by foreigners, was of benefit to the Boers themselves. But the Jameson Raid, with its acknowledged taint of official British connivance, had changed all that. In the Transvaal, antagonism to Britain was now unanimous and President Steyn of the Orange Free State another independent republic — had been persuaded to ally himself with Kruger in the event of war with Britain. Many of the Dutch in the Cape, who had previously supported Rhodes as the champion of South African as distinct from British colonial interests, now turned against him and promised help to the two Boer republics if it was needed. Only Natal remained obstinately jingoistic.

Ever since the Jameson Raid, Kruger had been using a considerable proportion of the revenue which the Uitlanders were providing for him on preparations for war. He spent a quarter of a million pounds on a ring of forts around Pretoria — real forts in stone and concrete — and another £100,000 on the Johannesburg Fort overlooking the town (now the Johannesburg prison). He imported Mauser magazine rifles for all the burghers in the Transvaal — who were compelled by law to buy them from the Government — and more Krupp guns for his Staats Artillerie.

There was now a new British High Commissioner in Cape Town, Sir Alfred Milner, a man of very different calibre from his predecessor. Milner was determined to support the demand for political power which the Uitlanders were still pursuing in the Transvaal in direct opposition to Kruger's hardening policy. Between these two resolute characters a clash was inevitable. They held an abortive "summit meeting", as it would be called today, which dragged on for five days in the unpretentious waiting-room of Bloemfontein railway station, followed by a number of equally abortive exchanges of proposals for a settlement between the State Attorney of the Transvaal, Jan Christiaan Smuts, and Joseph Chamberlain, the British Colonial Secretary. When negotiations reached a deadlock the South African Republic presented Britain with an ultimatum on 9 October 1899, demanding immediate withdrawal of all British forces from the borders of the Republic and removal from South Africa altogether of all troops who had arrived in the British colony of Natal since the first of June

There had been at least 10,000 British troops in Natal for some time. In September, 6000 more had arrived from Bombay and Calcutta. An additional 4000 were now converging on Durban from Malta, Mauritius, Egypt and Crete. And on 7 October news reached the Republic that an army corps 50,000 strong was being mobilised in England and would reach South Africa in December. It was not unreasonable for Smuts to refer in his ultimatum to "an extraordinary strengthening of the troops on the border of the Republic". The Transvaal itself could possibly mobilise no more than 30,000 burghers. The ultimatum concluded, with the usual diplomatic sarcasm reserved for these occasions, "In the event unexpectedly of no satisfactory answer the Republic will be compelled to regard the action of Her Majesty's Government as a formal declaration of war and will not hold itself responsible for the consequences."

Britain was given 48 hours in which to reply. Predictably no reply was forthcoming. Ten thousand Transvaal burghers were gathering at Laings Nek, on the Natal border, which they crossed on 16 October; and four days later, in the early morning, they attacked the nearest British garrison at Dundee, whom they took completely by surprise, many of the soldiers caught literally as well as metaphorically with their pants down. The South African War had started.

It was not until 28 December that the Commandant General of the BSAP issued a formal Order stating, "A state of war existing between Her Majesty's Government and the South African Republic and the Orange Free State, Southern Rhodesia shall be deemed to be included in the sphere of active operations." It must be assumed that up to then the Imperial authorities had had more pressing considerations than the position of Rhodesia on their mind. Nevertheless, a great deal of activity had already been going on. As early as July, Lieutenant-Colonel R.S.S. Baden-Powell — who commanded the 5th Dragoon Guards in India but had been quite fortuitously on leave in London — arrived at the Grand Hotel, Bulawayo, accompanied by his wife and two staff officers — who also brought their wives with them. One of the officers was Major Lord Edward Cecil, son of Lord Salisbury, the British Prime Minister. Baden-Powell and his officers were in mufti and they had travelled up from the Cape under assumed names. (The railway had reached Bulawayo in 1897.) One suspects a touch of the Baden-

Powell theatricality in assuming a disguise which can have fooled nobody. But for all their apparent informality, they had been officially charged by the War Office with raising two white regiments — the Protectorate Regiment to be raised in Bechuanaland and the Rhodesia Regiment (the first use of that name) in Bulawayo. The British authorities seem to have been in no doubt that war was coming and that although the Boers from the two Republics would probably move south-west and south into Natal and the Cape, Rhodesia and Bechuanaland would both need protection.

Another officer to arrive shortly after Baden-Powell was Major Herbert Plumer of the York and Lancaster Regiment. He and Baden-Powell had both been in Matabeleland with the Imperial forces during the Matabele rebellion and Plumer himself had organised in Kimberley the relief column which had come north to Bulawayo and which had included many of the Jameson raiders return- ing from their involuntary trip to England. Plumer has been described as "a rather small, delicate and retiring person, short-sighted and apparently more interested in novels than his companions". Although he was received in Bulawayo popularly enough when he arrived, he was not at first regarded as a commander in whom much confidence could be placed, particularly in the eyes of those Rhodesians who had not been associated with him in the Matopos campaign.

In Bulawayo, August and September were spent raising 500 men — some from outside Rhodesia — for the Rhodesia Regiment and training them on the race-course. On 11 September, a month before war was declared, Bodle marched off with 100 of the BSAP to Tuli. On this occasion, in the context of an emergency, the Matabeleland and Mashonaland divisions acted together. About two-thirds of the force came from Bulawayo, the rest were from Salisbury under the command of Major Nesbitt. An advanced party under Sergeant McGee (BSACP No. 282, who had joined in 1890) with two corpo- rals and 24 men had preceded them. At Tuli they constructed a new so-called fort on the relatively flat top of a longish kopje formed really of two adjoining hills — adjacent to the more conical kopje on which the pioneer fort had been built. They constructed stone fortifications and emplacements for their guns, but they were in no less vulnerable a situation than that of which Leonard had complained in 1890 when he said that the original Fort Tuli, surrounded by a semi-circle of outer kopjes, was dangerously vulnerable to any long-range guns, or even rifles, which might be mounted on their dominating heights. Later in September Plumer followed Bodle to Tuli with some 400 partly trained men of the Rhodesia Regiment and by the time war was actually declared the force of which he now took overall command (as a regular major he outranked Bodle) numbered about.550 men, with a 12- pounder Nordenfeldt, one portable Maxim gun, two 0,45 Maxims on naval carriages and the two old mountain screw-guns. In October a Boer commando from the Zoutpansberg district was operating near the Limpopo River and parties sent by Plumer to Rhodes and Pont Drifts (both due south of Tuli, five miles apart from each other) were engaged in skirmishes with some casualties on both sides. On 21 October a captain in the Rhodesia Regiment was mortally wounded and three troopers were taken prisoner by the Boers. On 2 November the Boers made a determined attack at Rhodes Drift and Plumer's men were forced to retire on Tuli. The Boers crossed the Limpopo into what had once been the Khama-Lobengula "disputed territory", in the angle between the junction of the Limpopo and Shashi rivers. They captured and occupied Bryce's store, some five miles inside the territory — which was now confirmed as part of Bechuanaland, just south of the Tuli Circle and for three weeks they held the two principal drifts across the Limpopo. Their strength is reputed to have been 1000 burghers and Plumer would have been hard pressed if they had made a determined incursion into Matabeleland and attacked the vulnerable fort at Tuli. But for no demonstrable reason they retired across the Limpopo on 20 November; Plumer followed with a reconnaissance force 35 miles into the semi-desert of the Northern Transvaal plain, but made no contact, and decided that the commando had been withdrawn to some other theatre of the war. However the reconnaissance, involving hard riding in arid heat and almost waterless conditions, was no small feat of horsemanship and his men acquired a new respect for this little major with the "delicate and retiring" appearance.

One of the epics of the story at Tuli at that time is the service rendered to the police and soldiers by Mrs. Fenella Redrup (later Deputy-Mayor of Bulawayo) who had trained as a nurse at St. Bartholomew's in London. Only recently married, she volunteered late in October to go to Tuli to nurse the troops. She described the conditions she found as "appalling". She wrote, "Some of the offi- cers had huts but the men slept out in the open in all weathers. Colonel Bodle gave up his hut to me. The hospital was a mud hut and the sick and wounded lay on the floor in their ordinary clothing, which was never changed." There was only one doctor (of the RAMC) and no other woman. She found two medical students among the police, "who helped me a great deal". There were no medical supplies and she had to wash out the old dressings and use them again and again. She appealed to the people in Bulawayo, who collected money and sent down some of the things she needed, but she had to wait three weeks before they arrived. On one occasion a man was accidentally shot through a kidney and the doctor tried to operate on a table made from a packing case. "I would not dare to tell you the details of that terrible operation," she said. Inevitably, the man died. Mrs. Redrup continued her heroic work at Tuli until Plumer moved off to the relief of Mafeking in January 1900.

It was during this period, too, that the troops established the celebrated rubbish dump below the fort, which still lies almost untouched today, spread literally over acres — principally bully-beef tins and broken bottles, now preserved by law against the depredations of souvenir hunters as a lasting monument to Rhodesia's illustrious history. And in November 1899 a tragic comedy occurred at a remote station used as an observation post, 50 miles from Tuli at Gong's Poort. A BSAP trooper, T.C. Fenton, was drinking in his hut with two friends late one evening and because his dog was making a disturbance on the stoep he went outside and kicked it where it appeared to be lying in the dark. The dog turned out to be a lion; and the severely mauled Trooper Fenton died in the wagon in which his friends were carrying him back to Tuli.

Before Baden-Powell left Bulawayo for Bechuanaland he arranged with the Rhodesia Railways workshops to armour two trucks and a locomotive to provide an armoured train with which to keep open the line to Gaborone. The same was to be done at Mafeking with an armoured train operating northwards to complete the link. The work in Bulawayo was speedily carried out and before he left Bulawayo Baden-Powell inspected and commended the job that had been done. A photograph of the inspection shows him still preserving the dubious anonymity of mufti. The armour of the trucks consisted simply of light section steel rails laid on top of each other, flanges downwards, supported by short stanchions to a height of 4 ft. 6 in. above the floor, along the sides of the trucks. Heavy timber baulks fixed to the floor provided mountings for Hotchkiss and Maxim guns. The locomotive was protected by steel plate covering the more vulnerable parts of its anatomy and by closing where practicable the gaps between the engine cab and tender. A train was usually made up of locomotive and tender, with an armoured truck fore and aft. The trucks were roofed with canvas awnings to protect the occupants from rain and sun and these were removed in anticipation of action. Communication with the driver was by speaking-tube, although on more than one occasion under enemy fire the crash of bullets against the armour drowned any orders shouted down the tube and the driver had to rely on his own interpretation of the tactical situation.

The actual number of armoured trains that were made up and operated by the BSAP from Bulawayo — as distinct from those in Mafeking — is not clear from the records. One source says four and another six. Colonel Nicholson himself supervised the trains' activities and the first which left Bulawayo on 11 October, the day war was declared, was operated under the immediate command of Captain Hoel Llewellyn of the BSAP, who earned the DSO for the part he played. Another followed a few days later under H.W.H. Wallis, the Acting District Engineer in Bulawayo, who was also a captain in the Southern Rhodesia Volunteers. Each carried some fourteen NCOs and troopers of the BSAP, a Maxim and a Hotchkiss. The trains were to play an important part in the operations which ensued in Bechuanaland, as shall later be related.

Baden-Powell and Major Lord Cecil left Bulawayo in September for Ramathlabama, on the Bechuanaland border with the Cape Colony, where the new Protectorate Regiment was being recruited and trained. It must be assumed that they put on their uniforms when they arrived there and that their wives continued southwards, probably to Cape Town, because the latter were certainly not with their husbands in Mafeking when it was later besieged. Baden-Powell was at first meticulous in keeping himself and the Protectorate Regiment out of Mafeking, although Ramathlabama is only some 12 miles north. The over-sanguine belief of the British authorities at the time was that the Boers' attention could be diverted from Mafeking itself and that they would regard the purpose of the new regiment to be simply a protection for the railway in Bechuanaland. If they believed that, they would leave the town alone and move south into the Cape Colony. Why, it was argued, should they be interested in Mafeking anyway? It had no strategic value. Indeed, as actually happened, besieging the town would tie up thousands of burghers unnecessarily. But the inhabitants of Mafeking were not so confident and felt themselves dangerously close to the Transvaal border. During September, as the likelihood of war increased, they importuned Baden-Powell to bring the regiment into the town to protect them. Although he had been charged by the War Office primarily to look after Bechuanaland and Rhodesia, he was quite ready to accept the Mafeking people's point of view. He wrote later, "I got permission from the Cape Government to place an armed guard in Mafeking to protect (a supply of stores in the town) but as the strength of that guard was not stipulated I moved the whole Regiment into the place without delay." He had already sent in one of his officers to raise a Town Guard among the local inhabitants; and the settlers in Mafeking district were spontaneously raising a volunteer unit to be known as the Bechuanaland Rifles. Mafeking was already adopting the Baden-Powell philoso-phy — which was one day to become a cult — whose principal creed is to "be prepared".

In addition to these forces now assembling in Mafeking was the No. 1 Bechuanaland Division of the British South Africa Police, consisting of 10 officers and 81 other ranks. As in the case of the BBP before it, the Division was responsible for policing the Bechuanaland Protectorate and was only stationed in Mafeking for convenience. Its depot, whose buildings still stand today, was in the Imperial Reserve — an area of nearly two square miles to the west of the town which was still the property of the British Government and had been excluded from the land annexed to the Cape Colony. It was by virtue of this arrangement that the BBP, and later the BSAP, had occupied barracks outside the actual Bechuanaland Protectorate. The Reserve, and the houses and buildings scattered about it — including a magazine standing out in the open which, when it was used for its original purpose, must have constituted an alarming hazard — have remained virtually unchanged in 85 years.

The Commandant of No. 1 Division of the BSAP in Mafeking was Lieutenant-Colonel J.A.H. Walford. His second-in-command was Major F.W. Panzera, a former BBP officer (not one of those who joined Jameson in the Raid) who had some artillery experience and to whom Baden-Powell was to give command of all the artillery — such as it was — and the locally based armoured trains during the siege. (There is an surviving photograph of an armoured train at Mafeking with 28 officers and men of the BSAP standing alongside it; and another picture showing the train heavily camouflaged by thorn-bush. An observer watching the camouflaged train moving across the treeless veld might well conclude that the railways were busy transporting Birnham Wood to Dunsinane.) After the siege, Baden-Powell was to describe Panzera as a "smart and practical gunner, endowed with the greatest zeal, coupled with personal gallantry in action". His origin is not on record, but after his death he achieved the tribute of a stained glass window in the Anglican church of St. John the Evangelist in Mafeking. Other BSAP officers were Surgeon-Major F.H. Holmden; Captain H. Greener, the Paymaster; Captains the Honourable D.H. Marsham and C.A.K. Pechell who were both to lose their lives during the siege; Captains A.P.W. Williams and J.W.A. Scholefield; and Lieutenant R.M. Daniel, who assisted Major Panzera with the guns. Marsham, third son of the Earl of Romney, had served with the territorials in England before joining the BBP from which he had also transferred to the BSAP (again not joining Jameson on the Raid); Pechell, the son of an Admiral, first commissioned in the King's Royal Rifle Corps, had joined the BSAP in August 1898; and Daniel later became Resident Commissioner of the Bechuanaland Protectorate and subsequently, as Colonel Daniel, farmed in Matabeleland near Figtree. Baden-Powell put Greener, the Paymaster, on his own staff and, accord-ing to B-P's report, Greener "kept account of all Government expenditure and receipts in connection with the defence, feeding population, etc., in addition to ordinary police and administrative accounts". Not unexpectedly, expenditure far exceeded revenue and some remedial steps had to be taken. So one of the more unusual functions to be performed by the police paymaster was to attach his signature to a series of one pound notes, locally printed and issued as currency at a later period of the siege.

The police depot in Mafeking, known as the BSAP Fort, was really a complex of buildings of which the solid stone fort — originally built by Sir Charles Warren in 1885 and still standing somewhat decrepitly today — was simply one of the units. The other old depot buildings, which are now used as government offices and stores, are of a more habitable Victorian style. Indeed, they have an air of prim respectability. The fort itself is really a cluster of primitive stone hovels — they can be described as nothing better surrounded by a high stone wall and have the appearance of abandoned farm out-buildings. Not one of the buildings is more than 20 feet square. The massive perimeter wall and the thick walls of the buildings themselves are constructed simply of loose stones; and any bonding the stone may possibly have boasted has long since been washed or crumbled away. In the central building, which comprises two rooms, two wooden lintels and door posts have miraculously survived — or so it must be surmised, for it is unlikely that anyone would have gone to the pointless trouble of replacing the originals. Through the front wall of the same building are two openings — it would be absurd to call them windows about 18 inches square, with iron bars close enough to each other to prevent at least human passage through them. At one stage during the siege this cluster of primitive buildings was to be the central feature of a lively battle.

When Baden-Powell had moved the Protectorate Regiment into the town, Mafeking could boast a military force of 39 officers and 705 other ranks, made up of 21 officers and 448 other ranks of the Protectorate Regiment; four and 77 of the Bechuanaland Rifles; four and 99 of the Cape Police; and, in a characteristically high proportion of commissioned ranks, 10 and 81 of the BSAP. He also recruited a Railway Detachment and a "Cape Boy" Contingent, which had no pretence of military training but brought his total strength to about 1200. The garrison's artillery, of which Major Panzera proudly took control, consisted of four seven-pounder muzzle-loaders, a one-pounder Hotchkiss and a two-inch Nordenfeldt, with seven .303 Maxims. The total firepower was about the same as Jameson had taken with him into the Transvaal and could hardly be regarded as a formidable defence against a determined siege.

Later during the siege, Panzera — who is on record as having been a martinet — working with the engineers in the railway workshops constructed a 16-pounder muzzle-loader (which now rests on its laurels in the Royal United Services Museum in London). It consisted of a six-inch diameter steel tube "with iron rings shrunk on in two tiers", with cast bronze breech block, trunnions and ring. It achieved a range of 4000 yards — which was twice the range of the muzzle loaders — and they christened it "the Wolf" in honour of Baden-Powell, who was reputed to have emulated that animal's proclivities when scouting in the Matopos. And at some point in the siege somebody discovered an old six-pounder ship's gun in a garden in the Imperial Reserve. Some time about 1852 a German trader had sold it perfidiously to an African chief, promising no doubt that it would protect him from all comers. The chief had used it against the Boer freebooters, who presumably had captured it from him, and it was now playing an undignified role, stuck in the ground as a gate-post. A wooden carriage and wooden wheels, with a disselboom trail and heavy wooden mounting, was built for it in the railway workshops and its cannon balls were melted-down pieces of shells from the Boers' 94-pounder Creusot, which so consistently failed to explode. The besieged population of Mafeking christened the old gun "Lord Nelson" and it still stands today in the town square as a link with some forgotten naval history of perhaps 200 years ago. Close by stands one of the four seven-pounder muzzle-loaders — quite a modern piece of ordnance by comparison.

The guns which the Boers brought up to oppose this artillery during the siege were to be far more formidable. They admittedly included two old muzzle-loading seven-pounders, which had been captured from Jameson; but all the others were breech-loaders: a 12-pounder, a nine-pounder Krupp, a five-pounder Armstrong, and two 14-pounder quick-firing high velocity cannons. And shortly after the siege had started "Creaky" arrived — christened thus by the defenders owing to the ominous noises brought to their vigilant ears whenever the Boers started pushing it around. "Creaky" was a 15cm, 94-pounder, breechloading Creusot, one of Kruger's proudest — and most recent additions to his armoury.

A full account of the siege of Mafeking would be by no means particularly relevant to a history of the BSAP. But the participation in the siege by the No. 1 Bechuanaland Division most certainly is. Consequently the events of the siege must be outlined, even if only briefly, and the part played by the BSAP given due recognition.

On the day their reckless ultimatum to Britain expired, 11 October, 7000 Transvaal burghers crossed the Cape Colony border — where Jameson had crossed it in the other direction four years before — and advanced on the little town. Baden-Powell described Mafeking as "a very ordinary looking place, just a small tin-roofed town, small houses plumped down upon the open veld". Except for the course of the headwaters of the Molopo River — it could hardly be called a river valley — winding from east to west through the southern outskirts of the town, the plain on which Mafeking was plumped down is virtually featureless. Here and there are outcrops of rock and folds in the ground and it was only these that enabled the opposing forces to avoid each other's constant line of sight and carry out any tactical movements at all. The Boers divided into two forces, one of which made for the railway south of Mafeking where they tore up a length of line. On 12 October Captain Williams of the BSAP, with 15 troopers, took one of the armoured trains down the line and met a party of Boers about five miles out, who retired immediately they were fired at from the train. Trooper Hooper is reputed to have fired the first shot in the battle for Mafeking — possibly the first in the South African War. Proceeding further south, Williams found the line already cut and, by necessity, had to return to the town. Baden-Powell had already sent the other of his two armoured trains south to Vryburg, to fetch some armaments which after protracted negotiations he had persuaded the authorities in Cape Town to send to him. On the way back the train was ambushed by the Boers where the line was cut, the crew was forced to surrender and the precious armaments were lost to the enemy. For some reason this train appears not to have had a BSAP escort.

The second Boer force deployed round Mafeking and immediately began to besiege the town. Later, the Boer forces round Mafeking were estimated to rise to 8000. Baden-Powell had disposed his own forces in well chosen positions, with an ambitious system of trenches, dugouts and shelters — and his first defensive perimeter was nearly six miles in length.

On Saturday 14 October, a patrol of the Protectorate Regiment encountered a party of Boers on the open plain north of the town and Baden-Powell sent out the only remaining armoured train to support the patrol, manned again by Captain Williams and this time 50 NCOs and troopers of the BSAP with two Maxims and a Hotchkiss gun. The train was ambushed four and a half miles out and some ineffective fire was at first exchanged with the Boers. The Boers milled about excitedly round the stationary train, brandishing their rifles in the air and firing random shots. One or two were shot down by the marksmen in the train, who were adequately protected by its armour. Williams bawled some orders down the speaking-tube but the noise of firing from the trucks was too loud and he had to order a cease-fire before he could finally prevail on the driver to move forward into a position where the fire-power could be more effectively used. When the train stopped again he was able to bring fire from both trucks to bear on the Boers, who now withdrew to what cover they could find, leaving three of their luckless companions sprawled out on the veld.

Baden-Powell — watching the fight, as became his practice, through a telescope from the roof of his headquarters in the town — feared the train might be cut off in a flanking movement by the Boers, whom he could now see were concentrating in the area some hundreds strong. He sent out another detachment of the Protectorate Regiment; and after a sharp engagement in which two of the Regiment were killed and 16 wounded, the two sides seemed to have had enough and they both withdrew. The BSAP men in the armoured train calmly climbed out of their trucks and picked up the British wounded; the train puffed back into Mafeking, unmolested; then it puffed out again into the veld and they picked up the bodies of the two British dead. The Boers, with their horse-drawn ambulance, were performing the same service for their own casualties. But the BSAP, in their first real action in the siege, had somewhat miraculously survived.

On 16 October the Boers opened their artillery bombardment which was to become the principal feature of the seven months' long siege. Some historians have tended to play down the effect on Mafeking of the bombardment; and this tone was set right at the beginning by Baden-Powell himself who informed the Boers, after the first shelling, that the only casualties had been a hen killed and dog wounded. The effect of the bombardment was by no stretch of the imagination comparable with the holocausts created in later wars; moreover, the inferior bricks used in the buildings were so soft and powdery that they offered no resistance to the Boer shells, which usually passed through the walls without exploding. When the 95-pounder Creusot was first used, one of its shells passed right through the Mafeking Hotel and exploded harmlessly in the veld. Nevertheless some buildings were extensively damaged, notably the convent and the hospital; and there is no doubt that the bombardment was a serious factor. Apart from the considerable casualties it caused, relative to the numbers of people involved, it imposed a severe strain on the nerves of the townspeople and the garrison.

The second action in the siege, on the night of 27 October, was an attack by 53 men and an officer of the Protectorate Regiment on a trench which had been advanced by the Boers to within 2000 yards of the town perimeter. The least said about this attack, which was launched late in the evening, the better. The night was already dark and the burghers resting in the trench were taken completely by surprise. The attackers cut them down mercilessly with bayonets — their rifles had been purposely left unloaded lest they should fire at each other in the anticipated close fighting — and in a few ghastly minutes 60 Boers were killed and wounded where they lay or sat, without any prior attempt to take them as prisoners. For some unfathomable reason — which can only be comprehended in the context of Victorian jingoism — the officer leading this carnage was awarded the Victoria Cross. However, the surviving burghers managed to dispense some rough justice by shooting dead six and wounding nine of his men as they ran back towards their own trenches in the town.

Four days later, 31 October, the Boers launched one of their only two serious attacks on the town, the whole brunt of which was taken by the BSAP. The BSAP's specific responsibility in the defence was the southern sector dominated by what was misleadingly called Cannon Kopje, suggesting an elevated position and the need for a stiff climb before it could be attacked. There is no such thing as a kopje within 10 miles of Mafeking in any direction. The lie of the land simply rises and falls like the ground swell on an oily sea. On a crest of rising ground directly south of the town is the site of another fortified position established by Warren in 1885, and the position is certainly about 100 above the level of the town itself. But it is a mile and a half away and the slope of the general configuration of the ground rising towards it is hardly perceptible. The same applies to the ground falling away from the crest in all the other directions. The site of Cannon Kopje is simply the highest point south of the town of a featureless landscape although it admittedly commands an all-round view of the adjacent country.

It is difficult to tell how the fortifications at Cannon Kopje were really set out at the time of the siege. The so-called fort, as it has been reconstructed today, is exactly as Sir Charles Warren had first set it out in 1885. The elaborate and well defined parapets which have now been reproduced had mostly crumbled away from disuse when Walford and his police took it over in 1899. However, there is a photograph taken in 1899 which shows a system of stone parapet walls topped by sandbags, with a steel windmill, some 40 feet tall and without its fan, set up as a look-out tower; and it is known that the present pattern of trenches at the rear of the fort (that is to say on the townward side) were used by Walford's garrison.

The garrison, commanded by Walford himself and including Captains Marsham and Pechell, consisted of 44 members of the BSAP and half a dozen of the Protectorate Regiment serving the two Maxim guns. There was no heavy armament. Early in the morning on 31 October, at about half-past four, as soon as the outline of the look-out tower had become visible to the Boers against the dawn light in the east, the burghers opened up an artillery bombardment from their western laagers. It was a remarkably accurate fire and at an early stage the look-out tower was hit and damaged. But not before Trooper von Dankberg had taken up his unenviable post at the top. Von Dankberg was a German baron who for some obscure motive had joined the BSAP, giving as his reason a little unaptly, "The British Army is the pleasantest to serve with in the world." There was nothing particularly pleasant about his service during the next half-hour. As the Boers themselves had previously discovered through their telescopes, he looked like a monkey up a tree and they had christened the Cannon Kopje position "Babiaans Fort". But no monkey would have stayed where he was, to experience what von Dankberg went through that morning. Shrapnel clattered against the iron framework of the tower and one of the angle-iron legs was actually severed. One report says that shell-splinters tore his coat and a long range sniper's bullet cut a hole in his tunic. This was probably a little exaggerated, but his shattered telescope was evidence enough that he had had an unhealthy time. Another account says that "he escaped injury by a miracle and continued imperturbably to send down information". Baden-Powell, watching as usual from the roof of his headquarters through his own telescope, actually found time to draw a sketch of the action on the Kopje. It depicts a neat, almost unruffled scene and, although shells are bursting and men are falling, it hardly reflects the sense of crisis of the occasion. It shows the lower part of the tower with the broken angle iron leg but unfortunately the sketch is cut off at the top and omits von Dankberg's monkey-like perch.

The bombardment went on for half an hour, during which the telephone link with Baden-Powell's headquarters was put out of use. Even before the heaviest firing ceased Walford moved his garrison from the trenches at the rear of the position to man the parapets on the crest of the rise. He could see lines of skirmishers advancing towards him from east, south and west. Behind the skirmishers were numbers of riderless, stationary horses standing patiently in the veld. A later Boer report commented that this was a sure indication that the horsemen were lying somewhere in the long grass adding, with heavy humour, "naturally not to dry beans". Baden-Powell brought one of the old seven-pounders in the town to bear upon the attackers and he says in his own report, in characteristic jargon, "The (gun) made excellent practice."

The Boers advanced to within 300 yards of the fort and the BSAP, putting up a stubborn defence, suffered some casualties, including Captain Marsham — who was hit three times, one bullet penetrating his chest and killing him outright and Captain Pechell who was mortally wounded. However, the exemplary steadiness and concentration of the BSAP wore down the burghers and some time about seven o'clock the attackers withdrew, whereupon the Boer ambulances came out to collect their own casualties. A large force of Boers had meanwhile assembled in the Molopo Valley, between Cannon Kopje and the town, but when they saw that the attack had failed they also withdrew to the western laagers. Baden-Powell wrote in his report, "The intention of the enemy had been to storm Cannon Kopje, and thence (from the Kopje) to bombard the south-eastern portion of the town and to carry it with the large forces they had collected in the Molopo valley. Their whole scheme was defeated by the gallant resistance of the (BSAP) garrison and by the telling fire it brought to bear on them ... the enemy's loss was not known, but ambulances were seen about the field picking up for a considerable time, and native spies reported that there was much mourning in the laagers and that several cart-loads of dead had been brought in and buried" — probably a characteristic exaggeration.

A more critical comment comes from a Dutch source, a report entitled "Die Beleg van Mafeking". "Due to lack of stimulation," it says, "from Veld-Kornet Martins and other Potchefstroom officers to fulfil the task they had begun and now almost carried through, the attack was doomed to failure although success was within sight. At seven o'clock the order to retreat resounded through the Boer lines. The burghers, in one thick crescent-shaped line around the hill jumped up from the tall grass, hesitated a moment, and then ran hastily to their horses and the camp, while the English from the fort and the town poured a shower of bullets and shells over them." This comment is endorsed in more succinct phrases by the official British report which said, "The achievement of the BSAP was as noticeable for its good fortune as for its valour, for nothing could have saved them from an enemy but half as resolute as themselves."

Besides the two officers, four other ranks of the BSAP were killed outright: Troop Sergeant-Major W.H. Conniham (No. 2391), Troop Sergeant-Major H.B. Upton (No. 1169), Trooper A.J. Martyn (No. 2566) and Trooper F.S.T. Burroughes (No. 2517); two more died of their wounds: Troopers C.W. Nicholas (No. 2569) and F.R. Lloyd (No. 2435). They are all buried in the Mafeking cemetery and except for those of the two officers, who lie buried side by side under conventional headstones, the graves lie in a regimental rank under highly ornamental crosses of iron with the letters i.h.s. tastefully entwined in grape vines. Wounded were Sergeant-Major E.O. Butler (No. 2544), Sergeant A.J. Cook (No. 2462) and Corporal F.C. Newton (No. 2508). By a tragic chance, Captain Pechell's brother had been killed 11 days earlier on Talana Hill, overlooking Dundee, where the Boers had made their first surprise attack on the British Army in Natal.

Baden-Powell rode out to Cannon Kopje later that day to congratulate Walford and his garrison. One historian says that the mood of the survivors was resentful that they had not been given proper support during the engagement; and the correspondent of the London Times, who was in Mafeking throughout the siege, wrote privately in his diary that the fort and garrison had been insufficiently protected. "It is too late to say much now," he wrote, "but we have paid a heavy price for our neglect and carelessness." Nevertheless, this was an occasion when a small party of the BSAP had stood firmly as Rhodesia's first line of defence; for it is conceivable that if the attack on Cannon Kopje had succeeded the large Boer force, now within the defensive perimeter, might have brought about the fall of Mafeking with dangerous repercussions on the northern territories.

## Chapter Fourteen

## THE RELIEF OF MAFEKING

THE STORY OF the operations in southern Bechuanaland in the closing months of 1899, and of Plumer's move from Tuli to Mafeking in the new year, is once again a record of movement and action by composite forces of which the BSAP were but a part. However, in these campaigns, the BSAP often operated in separate detachments under their own officers; and one gets the impression from reading the long — and usually confused — accounts that they were regarded as a more professional force than the other colonial units. Plumer said of the BSAP after the war, " ... a very fine force. They were thoroughly well trained and were good in many ways which others failed in such as horsemastership, their horses were well looked after." He also said, referring to the British forces as a whole, that "at the end of the war, the Boer, man for man, was the better shot", but added that the BSAP were an exception to this. "I should say perhaps they were better (than the Boers) because they had had a lot of previous training, some of them had had a year or more training in the police, and had had a great deal of shooting and they were certainly better." But Plumer never risked being fulsome in his praise. He added grudgingly, "I do not think they were exceptionally good, but I think they were better." On another occasion he said, "The BSAP were very well mounted, and were very good horsemasters, and their horses were really a pattern of what a horse should be after 12 months' service in the field."

Opening the operations in Bechuanaland, Captain Hoel Llewellyn of the BSAP (Matabeleland Division) had travelled down from Bulawayo to Notwane (which was also known as Crocodile Pools), a few miles south of Gaborone. He had arrived there on 16 October. Although he brought the armoured vehicles with him he must have travelled down in a considerable train, because with 15 members of the BSAP as escort he was also accompanied by 35 railwaymen and he collected 150 more from various stations down the line. In theory, the railwaymen were non-combatants, but many of them saw some fighting even if they did not take an active part in it. Indeed, some were taken prisoners by the Boers. Their first job was to lengthen the "dead-end" siding at Crocodile Pools to prepare for the many railway vehicles which were to come down from Bulawayo. As the story will show, the railway became an important factor in combating the Boers in southern Bechuanaland and in the ultimate relief of Mafeking.

Llewellyn had only just arrived at Crocodile Pools when he heard that the Boers had wrecked Lobatsi station 30 miles south, where they had taken prisoner the pump mechanic and his wife and were moving northward up the line. He took an armoured train to meet them and in an engagement some miles south his riflemen killed three Boers, suffering no casualties themselves. Nevertheless the Boers still pressed on, bringing artillery with them. They occupied some kopjes close to the railway and lay waiting in the bed of a spruit a couple of miles from Crocodile Pools station; and although attacked by Llewellyn and his BSAP in the armoured train, who shelled the kopjes with the Hotchkiss gun, they could not be dislodged. By 21 October Crocodile Pools had become untenable. The 100-foot bridge close to the station over the Metsimanswane River was dominated by the Boer guns and a few days later they blew it up. The railway base was then moved back nearly 150 miles to Mahalapye, although Llewellyn continued to operate south as far as Mochudi (25 miles north of Gaborone) where on 31 October he was able to rebuild a culvert which the Boers had dynamited.

On 4 November, Lieutenant-Colonel G. D. Holdsworth of the 7th Hussars, who was Nicholson's chief of staff, arrived at Mahalapye and took overall command of the operations. From that time onwards the operations involved larger,· composite forces, although the BSAP under Llewellyn continued their lively part and two further detachments from Bulawayo, under Major Straker and Captain Drury (both one-time Jameson raiders), arrived to bring the BSAP complement to over 100. By the end of November the Boers had been pushed back beyond Gaborone, which now became the railway base.

Plumer, on the northern Transvaal border, was formally under the direct command of Baden-Powell, besieged 400 miles away in Mafeking. One officer who served at Tuli wrote, "We who served under (Plumer) suffered from his taciturnity. Sometimes for hours he seemed as if he were struck dumb, incapable of issuing an order. He appeared to be awaiting some revelation or inspiration which never came."

Baden-Powell's orders to him were clear enough: to defend the border as far as this could be carried out from Tuli as a centre; to provide a display of strength which would induce the Boers to keep an equally strong force to protect the northern Transvaal; and to create diversions, if necessary advancing into the Transvaal for the purpose. But a rider was added: "No portion of your force is to cross the frontier until you receive orders."

By the end of December the Shashi and Limpopo were both running strongly. The likelihood of another Boer incursion from the south was remote. Plumer's force, over 500 strong, was kicking its heels and wasting its time. Its taciturn commander, out of touch with his own commanding officer, consulting nobody, disregarded his orders and moved to the relief of Mafeking. Leaving a small detachment at Rhodes Drift, he marched 480 men — including 100 or more of the BSAP under Colonel Bodle westward along the northern bank of the Limpopo and reached Palapye, 175 miles away on the line of rail, in 10 days. By the time they reached Palapye every man of the force, including his numerous detractors, was solidly behind him.

The Times History of the South African War says, "A less bold leader than Plumer might have been afraid to take the responsibility of leaving Tuli where he had been instructed to stay, while there was still a chance that the Boers might return for the invasion of Rhodesia."

From Palapye, Plumer's force was moved by rail to join Holdsworth, who was now operating south of Mahalapye and was in fact patrolling within 90 miles of Mafeking, nearly as far as Crocodile Pools. Plumer took over command of the whole force, now numbering just on 1000 men with four field-guns and two armoured trains. He attacked the Boer position at Crocodile Pools, repaired the bridge and moved on to Lobatsi, only 45 miles from Mafeking, on 1 March. He probed south as far as Ramathlabama, sending Bodle in charge of a mixed force including BSAP — but Bodle was forced to withdraw. Blessed at last with "revelation and inspiration" Plumer struck out westward from the line of rail and established a base at Kanye, 20 miles into the Bangwaketse Reserve, in arid Kalahari desert country. From there he moved his mounted troops south to a small town, Sefetili, 30 miles south of Kanye and 30 miles from Mafeking. They reached Sefetili on 23 March.

In Mafeking there had been little change. On 26 December, Baden-Powell had launched an early morning assault on what was euphemistically known as Game Tree Fort, a couple of miles north of the town, but which was really nothing more than a system of Boer trenches in a fold of the landscape, marked by a small cluster of trees. The attacking force was a combination of the Protectorate Regiment and the Bechuanaland Rifles, with the BSAP armoured train and Panzera's guns in support. The Boers had not unexpectedly cut the railway line and the train was prevented from moving far enough out of the town to provide the flanking fire which had been planned. Another part of the plan was that the driver should blow his whistle as soon as the attacking troops had deployed and started to move forward, and when they heard the whistle Panzera's guns would stop their preliminary bombardment. But as the train's movement was restricted it was unable to make accurate observation; so the whistle was blown too early, before the attacking troops were ready to move, and the Boers, unmolested by artillery, were waiting at their parapets ready to meet them with deadly rapid fire. Two assault waves went forward but the attempt was hopeless, doomed from the start, and 24 British troops were killed and 26 wounded.

When the survivors retired and the firing ceased, the armoured train remained out in the veld to pick up the casualties. On this occasion the Boers came out of their trenches and helped the BSAP to carry the dead and wounded to the train. When the train moved sorrowfully into the town it was met by a large, silent, patently bitter crowd. The 24 victims of the suicidal attack on Game Tree Fort on Boxing day, 1899, lie side by side in another long, regimental rank in Mafeking cemetery.

The only other action of any consequence in Mafeking itself came on 12 May, five days before the town was at last relieved. The old BSAP fort, rather than the members of the police, featured in this episode. An enterprising Boer attack, 300 strong, overran the fort, confining within their own stronghold three officers and sixteen men of the Protectorate Regiment, including their commanding officer, Colonel Hore. (One report says that Captain Williams and three BSAP troopers were among the prisoners, but there appears no confirmation of this.) The prisoners were confined in the restricted area of the two central rooms, described as "an evil-smelling storehouse where, in spite of the heavy patter of bullets, they were tolerably safe". That is to say, they were safe enough if they lay down flat on their faces, for more than one shot from their own side found its way through the iron-barred openings in the front wall. Their captors, who surrounded the prisoners, were themselves surrounded by the town garrison — a situation which posed some delicate tactical problems for both sides. They were hard pressed throughout the day and at six o'clock in the evening the Boer leader — Field Cornet Eloff, grandson of a former President — threw open the door of the rooms where the prisoners were confined and shouted, "Colonel Hore, I surrender to you. If you go out and stop the firing I will give in." It was a risky undertaking for the Colonel to emerge from the confines of the fort and attempt to persuade his own side to desist from shooting at it, but somehow he managed successfully. The British losses during the day were four killed and 10 wounded; the Boer casualties, killed and wounded, were 59, while 108 were taken as prisoners — including Elof. When Baden-Powell met him under escort in the town he said, "Good evening, Eloff, you're just in time for dinner."

The war in Natal, and south of Mafeking in the Cape Colony, had started off disastrously for the British. But after Field Marshal Lord Roberts had taken over as commander-in-chief in January 1900 the tide had begun to turn. Ladysmith in Natal and Kimberley in the Cape Colony had both been surrounded and besieged by the Boers. The siege of Ladysmith had imposed real hardship and distress on the population. Kimberley (where Cecil Rhodes had been trapped and was making a nuisance of himself to the military) was relieved on 15 February; Ladysmith (containing Frank Rhodes and Jameson) on the 28th. Mafeking was still holding out and amazing the world. If the world could have seen the real circumstances of the siege it might not have been so amazed nor might it have lavished such exaggerated emotionalism on the embattled population, supposedly defending themselves heroically against fearful odds. In truth, their principal hardship was boredom. The Boer shelling certainly constituted a danger; occasionally a military engagement came uncomfortably close. But the people had reasonable quantities of food, there was no hazard to health (malaria was endemic in any circumstances) and any danger of the enemy triumphing in a climax of murder and rapine was purely visionary. Indeed Lord Methuen, the commander in the Cape, had discounted the need to organise a relief force. He had believed, rather, that in time the Boers would just give up and go away. However, when Lord Roberts relieved Kimberley and then directed his main thrust eastwards towards Bloemfontein and Pretoria, it was clear that something had to be done about Mafeking and he ordered Methuen to assemble a relief column to march north.

The column which assembled in April 1900 at Barkly West near Kimberley, was over 1000 strong, and commanded by a Colonel Mahon. It consisted principally of South African volunteer forces: the Imperial Light Horse, the Diamond Fields Horse and the Kimberley Light Horse. To these were added a battery of the Royal Artillery and 100 imaginatively styled "Union Fusiliers", made up of 25 each English, Scottish, Irish and Welsh regular infantrymen. No country in the United Kingdom was going to be allowed to crow over another as the gallant rescuer of the heroes of Mafeking.

In command of the Imperial Light Horse was Colonel Edwards (later, Major-General Sir A.H.M. Edwards, KBE, CB, MVO), who had first been commissioned in the Seaforth Highlanders and had transferred to the Dragoon Guards wherein he had risen to Lieutenant-Colonel. After the relief of Mafeking he was to become Assistant Adjutant-General of the British Army; in 1905, Military Secretary to the Viceroy of India; from 1906 to 1912, Chief Constable of the Metropolitan Police; and he was to crown this glittering career with appointment as Commissioner of the BSAP from 1913 to 1923, serving also as Commandant-General of all Rhodesian forces during the 1914-18 war.

On the staff of Colonel Mahon's relief force was the evergreen Sir John Willoughby, back from durance vile in Holloway gaol. Colonel Frank Rhodes, released from Pretoria gaol after his commuted sentence of death, was also on the staff. The column left Barkly West on 4 May, lost 5 killed and 26 wounded in a Boer ambush at Kraaipan, not far from Mafeking, and arrived at Jan Massibi's Farm on the Molopo River a few miles west of Mafeking on 15 May. Plumer and his Rhodesian force had arrived from the other direction only a few hours earlier.

During the previous seven weeks, after setting up his base at Sefetili on 23 March, Plumer had made a number of thrusts towards Mafeking. On 13 March, Bodle with a party of BSAP patrolled south as far as Pitsani and Lieutenant H. Chapman was captured by the Boers. (Somehow or other, presumably during his captivity, Chapman came into possession of a Boer telescope which is now in the

Queen Victoria Museum in Salisbury. He was to serve as a private in the British Army in the 1914-18 war and to be killed in action.) He was not as lucky at the time as Captain Drury, Sergeant R.E. Murray and Troopers Matthews and Rogers. They too found themselves surrounded by Boers who ordered them to put up their hands. Murray is reputed to have refused, saying "damned if I'll do that for an Afrikander". When the Boers threatened to shoot him on the spot Drury sensibly intervened and gave him a direct order to comply. The Boers took away their leggings, boots and some of their clothes and left them in the veld. They finally arrived in Pitsani and rejoined Bodle's party considerably the worse for wear. (Later, as Lieutenant-Colonel, Murray was to command the BSAP Service Column in East Africa in 1914. Matthews was to be, at one time, manager of Meikles Hotel in Salisbury and Rogers became secretary of the Mashonaland Turf Club.)

On 31 March a force under Plumer himself, including a detachment of BSAP, penetrated to within six miles of Mafeking. They approached the laager of one of the Boer commandos engaged in the siege and fire was exchanged at 600 yards. A party of Boers, more intrepid than usual, made a rush on the BSAP but were checked with a Maxim by Captain Frank Bowden (one-time commander of Jameson's artillery troop). For his cool handling of a dangerous situation Bowden was subsequently awarded the DSO. Plumer's force was nevertheless obliged to retire to Ramathlabama, having lost 11 killed, 33 wounded and four taken prisoner — a heavy toll. It was clear that the Boers round Mafeking were not vulnerable to a direct assault on the open plain to the north of the town. The Boers took the bodies of three of the British soldiers into Mafeking for burial. That the precursors of their relief should be three dead men was a discouraging omen for the population.

In April, 50 BSAP under Captain Colin Harding — who had been temporarily seconded "for special duty north of the River Zambezi" but had now returned to Southern Rhodesia — left Bulawayo for Sefetili to join what was now known as No. 2 Squadron, which already consisted of 73 BSAP officers and men commanded by Captain A.J. Tomlinson. Tomlinson's second-in-command was Lieutenant R.S. Godley (whose brother Major A. Godley, of the Royal Dublin Fusiliers, was on Baden-Powell's staff in Mafeking). Lieutenant E.A. Wood (a Jameson raider and later a Brigadier-General) commanded the left troop and the Troop Sergeant-Majors were W. McGee (who had taken the advanced party to Tuli at the outbreak of war) and H. Wilcox. The party from Bulawayo was followed a few days later by Major Nesbitt with Lieutenants Moore and Howes and 100 BSAP from the Mashonaland Division, all dramatically mounted on greys. Nesbitt took over command of the squadron from Tomlinson but, as shall be related, was down with fever during the final advance on Mafeking.

These in their turn were followed by a surprising reinforcement to Plumer's force made up of both Canadians and Australians. 'C' Battery of the Royal Canadian Artillery with six guns had left Canada in February, had arrived at Cape Town on 26 March and gone into camp at Stellenbosch. On 14 April they had marched back into Cape Town; they began embarking in S.S. Columbian at half-past three next morning; they were all aboard with their guns by mid-day and the ship sailed at three o'clock in the afternoon. They arrived in Beira on 21 April where they were joined by 100 Queensland Mounted Infantry, already landed there. No more than two hours after the last RCA man had disembarked, their train — with the guns aboard — left for Rhodesia. They detrained at Marandellas, where Mr. Zeederberg was waiting for them with all his mail coaches. (Delivery of mails throughout Rhodesia had been temporarily suspended.) The coach ride to Bulawayo covered 285 miles. Four of the guns kept up with the coaches, dragged enthusiastically by Mr. Zeederberg's mules. The other two, drawn by horses, followed at a more sedate pace. They left Bulawayo by train on 7 May and were in Sefetili on 14th — a total of 785 miles and 24 days from Beira. Although not directly a part of BSAP history, it is a saga well worth recording.

Plumer now had 800 men, of whom 450 were mounted. He had eight guns, all drawn or carried by mules. Two days before the Canadians and Queenslanders arrived he had received a message from Lord Roberts to say that Mahon, with the southern column, would reach the Molopo River on 15th — in three days' time. Thus when the newcomers arrived there was one day left for a march of 28 miles. It was surprisingly fortuitous that they had arrived just in time for Plumer to set off to reach the Molopo on the same day as the southern column; there must have been an element of luck but the staff work — for which Nicholson in Bulawayo was principally responsible — deserves its measure of credit. Plumer marched to Jan Massibi's during the night; Mahon's vanguard arrived at daybreak. Mahon, the senior officer, now took command of the combined force.

Early in the morning on 16 May 1900 the combined relief force moved towards Mafeking along the shallow banks of the Molopo River. Here, with the advantage of broken ground — relatively superficial as it was — the Boers were in a more vulnerable situation than on the open plain surrounding the rest of the perimeter of the town. A.J. Tomlinson wrote, "Two troops of the BSAP, the Mashonaland troop and mine, were detailed as right flank guard, and as Nesbitt was down with fever at the time command of this flanking party devolved on me. Captain Bowden's (separate) troop formed a portion of the advanced guard. The enemy was encountered 10 miles outside Mafeking." The Boers had spread themselves out in a semi-circle astride the river and at their centre they were occupying a house on a Mr. Israel's farm. A detachment of BSAP under Bodle crossed the river to the other side, where with the help of the Queenslanders they drove out the Boers and captured the farm-house. "Long-distance ranges were opened," Tomlinson goes on, "the right flank came in for a steady fire, advancing as we did by alternate half-troops, dismounted in open order, and it was not long before our casualties began." Godley was shot in the right shoulder: the bullet actually travelled down the side of his body, under the skin, and was miraculously stopped at his waist by his Sam Browne. His batman remained with him and helped him across the river where a supply wagon came up and he was lifted aboard. Tomlinson continues, "Our horses were kept in the rear and suffered but one casualty ... Towards the afternoon the Boers retreated and we were not molested as the columns were re-formed for the march into Mafeking."

Godley's own account said, "I felt a blow, apparently on my ribs and found myself lying on my back. On trying to move, I experienced great pain there, and in my right arm. I must have lost consciousness for a few moments. The next thing I remember is seeing my servant on the ground beside me, and the squadron some way ahead. With the aid of my batman I managed to struggle across the river to the convoy on the other side." The wagon on to which they lifted him carried a load of mealies and he was painfully hoisted on to the top. "I suffered considerably from thirst ... my gratitude was great when Colonel Garraway our PMO" — the Surgeon-Captain of the BBP who had tended the wounded raiders at Krugersdorp — arrived with a succulent orange." When the wagon ultimately reached Mafeking, his brother was waiting for him and took him by ambulance to the Convent, which was being used as an extra hospital.

Mahon's force had first sighted Mafeking — on which the emotionalism of the whole British Empire was now fully concentrated — about midday. Someone described his first view of the town which had achieved world-wide notoriety as "a tiny cluster of white near the eastern horizon, glistening amid the yellowish-brown of the flats". It was after this that the action had followed near Israel's farm, when the Boers had unsuccessfully tried to close their semi-circle on the advancing column and had brought rifle and artillery fire to bear on both of Mahon's flanks. But apart from the diversion caused by the engagement between Bodle and the occupants of the farm-house, the column never hesitated and continued moving forward throughout the day, only halting late in the afternoon when it reached some higher ground and when the Boers harassing them began to melt away in despair.

The thunder of marching in to the relief of Mafeking was stolen by Major "Karri" Davies of the Imperial Light Horse (who had been one of the imprisoned Reform Committee in Johannesburg at the time of the Raid). He was scouting ahead of the column with eight troopers and finding no resistance rode blandly into the town, totally unnoticed at about 7 p.m. It was the hour when the garrison was drawing rations and everybody was a little preoccupied. He spoke to a man passing by and explained he was part of the relief column. The man was far from impressed. He said, "Oh yes, I heard you were knocking about" and hurried on for his rations.

That night the news reached London and half a million people went crazy. Plays at the theatres were interrupted as managers rushed on from the wings shouting "Mafeking has been relieved"; audiences rose, cheered and sang predictably "God Save the Queen"; tens of thousands danced in the streets. The word Mafeking, distorted to "mafficking", thereafter became part of the language, even attaining the accolade of inclusion in the staidest of English dictionaries, to be defined as "celebrating an event uproariously". The cause of the vehemence of the rejoicing, utterly out of proportion to the scale of the event, is not difficult to fathom. The British Empire at the turn of the century was at the zenith of its far-flung power; its military might had been challenged and humiliated by a bunch of uncouth farmers. At last the Boer farmers had been put in their place and Britain's divinely endowed superiority had been restored. Hip-hip-hurrah! Three cheers for the soldiers of the Queen!

At 11 o'clock that night, in bright moonlight, Mahon's force resumed its march and the head of the column reached the town about 3.30 a.m. The air was still and as the morning grew light a rising cloud of dust began to encircle Mafeking and hang suspended over the veld, as the burghers hurriedly decamped and moved eastwards to the Transvaal border. Plumer's force had been living rough in the bush for seven months; for the last five months it had been almost continuously on the move. Mahon's men had just completed what was virtually a forced march of 250 miles. The troops in Mafeking itself had sustained a nerve-wracking ordeal, for all its relative quiescence. No one, not even Baden-Powell, was in a mood to prevent the Boers from making good their escape.

The casualties suffered by the defending forces during the siege and by the relief column during the final assault are recorded on an obelisk in the town hall square. The memorial names as killed two officers and 51 other ranks of the Protectorate Regiment; five other ranks of the Cape Police; two other ranks of the Bechuanaland Rifles; two officers and 18 other ranks of the Town Guard; one officer and five other ranks of the Rhodesia Regiment; seven other ranks of the Imperial Light Horse; two other ranks of the Kimberley Regiment (or Kimberley Light Horse); and two officers and 13 other ranks of the BSAP. Besides those of the BSAP who died on Cannon Kopje, the memorial names Troopers W.D. Knox, D. Francis, W. Francis and S.C. Armstrong of No. 1 (Bechuanaland) Division of the BSAP, killed or died of wounds. (The brothers Francis lie in a grave with one of the best preserved headstones in the cemetery.) Four more BSAP men died during the siege: Corporal J.E. L. Worrall, Troopers E.J. Mathias, B.R. Schenk and M.J. van Heerden. The memorial names two troopers of the No. 2 (Bulawayo) Division killed during the final assault: C. Mann and — Golding (the initial is indecipherable).

The Church of St. John the Evangelist, across the road from the memorial, designed by Sir Herbert Baker — who designed the cathedrals of Cape Town, Pretoria and Salisbury — was built in 1902 "in memory of those who died during the Siege as an act of thanks for the relief of the town". Rhodes presented the pillars of Rhodesian sandstone which stand in the nave and support the roof.

The pulpit, as its carved inscription declares, was "erected by all ranks of the Bechuanaland Protectorate Service in affectionate memory of their comrades of the Protectorate Division of the BSAP who fell in the South African War 1899-1902".

## Chapter Fifteen

## WAR AND PEACE

AFTER THE RELIEF of Mafeking, Mahon's and Plumer's combined forces, including Bodle with the BSAP from Rhodesia, moved into the Transvaal here they became involved on the periphery of Lord Roberts's advance to Pretoria. When Pretoria had been captured they were released and returned to Rhodesia, their active service ostensibly over. From British Army headquarters came the signal, "The BSAP, having returned to their regular duties, the Field Marshal Commander-in-Chief desires to place on record his high appreciation of the admirable work done by the Corps throughout the campaign. Lord Roberts much regrets he was unable to see the BSAP before they left his command and requests that you (Bodle) will accept yourself and convey to officers, NCOs and men how much he valued the gallant service they have rendered during the past year of hard work, hard fighting and often scanty fare."

The sentiments, unexceptionable as they were, were to prove a little premature. The Boer leaders obstinately refused to agree with the British that they had been defeated. They organised half a dozen separate guerrilla campaigns which they pursued for another two years, ranging across the face of the sub-continent from the eastern Transvaal to Namaqualand and tying down more than 200,000 British troops. One of the Boer leaders, Commandant de la Rey, operated in the western Transvaal and, at the end of 1901, after he had been ranging about the country freely for more than twelve months, obtaining most of his supplies by raiding British Army stores, the British decided at last that something positive had to be done and a considerable force under General Lord Methuen was assembled in an attempt to contain him and bring him to heel.

The BSAP were sent for again. Captain Drury, with Lieutenants Chapman and Ingham (the latter had taken part in the Jameson Raid as a trooper), left Bulawayo with 125 other ranks on 27 September 1901, and Lieutenant Agar followed with 25 more at the beginning of 1902. Bodle had already gone south. As soon as Methuen's force was assembled the BSAP squadron became part of it. Methuen's army — it can be called no less — of 16,000 men was one of the most miscellaneous forces assembled during the war. One brigade, known as the Kimberley Column to which the BSAP was attached, totalled 1300 men of 14 different fighting units — an average of less than 100 from each unit. The BSAP, with 150, was one of the larger groups. And even they must have been split up into small sections because The Times History of the South African War mentions, on one occasion, "the British South Africa Police, 25 men", and on another, "the British South Africa Police, 10 men". But it is clear from the force's own Orders that they were often operating in larger units, and it seems that their principal contribution was to provide an escort for a battery of the Royal Artillery as it followed the peripatetic manoeuvrings of the campaign.

It would be unnecessarily tedious, in this history, even to outline this campaign, which swung backwards and forwards for months in the Lichtenburg-Klerksdorp-Wolmaranstad area in the south-western corner of the Transvaal. The fluctuating fortunes of the campaign, beyond their effect on the squadron's movements, had relatively little to do with the BSAP. The squadron was but a small element in a complicated, unwieldy machine, which was enmeshed — sometimes disastrously — in disjointed manoeuvres and actions aimed at mopping up the enemy.

Captain Drury's Orders on 3 December 1901 said, "The G.O.C. thanks his force for the good work performed during the recent trek and has pleasure in notifying the results: 36 prisoners, 27 rifles, 42 wagons, 22 carts, 110 cattle, 13,100 sheep, 102 horses, 56 mules, 106 donkeys, one steam portable mill and 34 ploughs." One assumes that most of this bag was lifted from Boer farms. The Orders continue, "He has recognised with satisfaction the care now taken of the horses by the men, the result being the decreased (crossed out and altered to 'increased deficiency' (sic)) of his column." Four days later the Orders reported "frequent cases of spying by the enemy under a flag of truce on the pretence of asking trivial questions". Ten days later: "The G.O.C. (Lord Methuen) expresses his thanks to the force for the admirable manner in which his orders were carried out today, which resulted in the capture of Potgieter's entire laager." Potgieter was one of the guerrilla commandants.

On Christmas Day, 1901, Bodle's orders at Klerksdorp announced, "On the forthcoming trek the

Division will travel as light as possible, every article of kit that can be dispensed with being left behind. Tents, furniture, etc. will be on the usual mobile scale." Next morning the squadron marched off at 4.30 a.m. The following day it was at Yzer Spruit, on 3 January at Doornbult, on 6th at Vryburg, 8th at Klipfontein, 12th at Lichtenburg. The bag between 27 December and 6 January was "nine prisoners, 360 cattle, 7900 sheep, nine wagons, seven carts, five rifles, 28 horses, 24 donkeys, two mules, destroyed quantity of grain, killed two Boers, four wounded". And to quote just once more, from 12 to 19 January, "23 prisoners, 19 rifles, 1370 cattle, 550 trek oxen, 8400 sheep, 65 wagons, 26 carts, 53 horses, 8 mules, 102 donkeys, four Boers wounded".

On 9 January at Vryburg, RSM Murray, the future Lieutenant-Colonel, was promoted to Sub-Inspector (Lieutenant). Corporal Wheeler was wounded on 1 January, Corporal Stuart and Trooper Ball on 5th. In an action at Drewfontein on 21 January, Troopers Roper and Ledger were killed, Sergeant Hill and Troopers Jones, Thorle and Simpson wounded. Seven horses were killed and six "lost in action".

Drury's Order at Wolmaranstad on 13 February required that "in case of a serious night attack, horse holders (one man to every four horses) will go to the horses and the remainder of the men will fall in armed outside the lines". The British Army was now building lines of blockhouses across the country as cordons to prevent movement of the Boer guerrillas. Some of these massive stone buildings, 30 feet high, can be seen dotted about the South African landscape today. "Until further orders all blockhouses will be occupied day and night. Sentries on blockhouses are to be in the (trenches) outside the blockhouses and facing the enemy ... All the picquets with the exception of sentries are always to stay inside the blockhouses at night." Another precautionary order: "Officers commanding units will take steps to temporarily stop up, with a loose stone or two, those portions of loopholes (in the walls) of blockhouses which bear upon any portion of the town or camp, as these loopholes should only be used in daytime and then only in case of emergency." Somebody seems to have been taking some dangerous potshots in the dark.

"When the column marches in the dark no smoking is allowed until either the OC gives permission or until the sun is above the horizon. Officers and men should understand that lighting up just as it gets light may spoil the whole effect of a night march ... No one is permitted to enter houses or take fowls, pigs, etc., when on march until permission is given." A subsequent Order states, significantly, "all fruit and vegetable gardens are out of bounds". And, with commendable frequency, "A ration of rum is authorised for issue tonight."

On 5 April 1902: "Any person arriving with white flag or other communication from the enemy is to be detained until his presence has been reported and orders received concerning his disposal. No conversation should be held with any such person, except by the Intelligence Officer or his authorised agent, and if ordered to be brought into camp should be blindfolded. Whilst detained pending orders the best arrangements should be made to prevent their observing our camp or any movement therein."

On 26 May a court of enquiry was held at Vryburg "into the circumstances of the capture of Lieutenant Agar and 18 NCOs and men of the BSAP by the enemy at Klip Drift on 7 March". The court found "that the officers and party were taken prisoners by reason of the chances of war and not through any neglect or misdeed on their part".

In April some of the Boer leaders — each of whom had been operating independently of the others for nearly two years — had been making overtures to the British command for peace talks and they were now being assembled at Vereeniging, with the help of the British authorities, to attempt to reconcile their own disparate philosophies. On 31 May Bodle said in his Orders, "From information obtained from a Boer prisoner it is clear that the Boers in the neighbourhood understand that they can attack us notwithstanding the absence of their Commandant with the Boer delegation at Vereeniging. Extra care should be taken therefore by all to prevent the enemy from gaining any advantage or from capturing any animals." And although the leaders who gathered at Vereeniging finally succumbed, and Botha, de la Rey, Smuts and Hertzog signed the British terms of surrender at five minutes past eleven on the night of 31 May 1902, Bodle's Orders on 1 June declared, "Notwithstanding the announcement made today of peace having been signed last night, no precautions are in any way to be relaxed until further orders."

But peace had come at last after two and a half years. On 4 June the squadron, now at Lichtenburg, marched off to Mafeking at 7 a.m. "The camp is to be thoroughly cleaned before leaving. All weak horses to go with the wagons. A spare ration of rum to be issued tonight." And next day, "The Lieutenant-Colonel Commanding (Bodle) desires to thank Captain Drury, the officers, NCOs and men of the BSAP for the very efficient and cheerful manner in which they have performed their duties in the field since they joined Lord Methuen's force in September 1901."

The honours awarded to members of the BSAP during the war were a CMG to Bodle and DSOs to Walford, Holmden, Williams and Greener of the Bechuanaland Division; and to Hoel Llewellyn and Bowden of the Matabeleland Division. Nicholson also received the DSO, but this seems to have been credited to him as an officer of the 7th Hussars, from which he had originally been seconded to the Matabeleland Mounted Police and from which he had never formally transferred. Five men — Lieutenant Myburgh of Mashonaland; Troop Sergeant-Major de Legh, Sergeant Murray and Corporals Howitt and Jearey of Matabeleland — were specially mentioned in Lord Roberts's despatches.

The BSAP's contribution to the defence of Rhodesia — 500 miles outside the borders of the country — had been brought successfully to a close and the force could now attend to its more mundane responsibilities.

On 26 March 1902, two months before peace came to South Africa, Cecil Rhodes died at Muizenberg in the Cape peninsula. His had been an extraordinary career. He had wielded an unusual measure of power for one man, using it sometimes well and sometimes ill. It is a mistake to assume that the influence of a powerful man, whoever he may be, is all-pervading and that without him the ends he pursues would never come about. Rhodesia (obviously with another name) would have come into existence even without Rhodes. The country would probably have been different in character and constitution, but not necessarily to a great degree. It must be remembered that there were others besides Rhodes whose interests and influence played important parts in the creation of Rhodesia. In one way, too, he used his power to bring negative results. He aimed, he said, in uniting southern Africa — federation of all the states south of the Zambezi was later in his life to become his professed ideal. Instead, he divided it. The Jameson Raid, if not proved to have been directly his own responsibility, was beyond historical doubt the offspring of his policy. Whether there would still have been a full-scale war in South Africa if the Raid had never happened is obviously impossible to conjecture. But the sequence of events was positive and it was the Raid that had started them in train. It is the tragedy of Rhodes's life and death that in his last years he witnessed division and strife among the people of his adopted sub-continent rather than the unity and progress which was his proclaimed ideal, and he cannot have failed in his own conscience to recognise the contribution to the schism he had made.

But Rhodesia had always accepted him unquestioningly as her hero. He had had his enemies in the country but they all recognised his calibre. Moreover he himself had chosen to be buried there. So his body was carried north in the private railway coach in which he had so often travelled between Cape Town and Kimberley. The war was still dragging on, mainly in guerrilla skirmishes, and north of Kimberley the funeral train was escorted as far as the Bechuanaland border by one of the armoured trains. The funeral train itself reached Bulawayo on 8 April and after Rhodes's body had lain in state in the Drill Hall his coffin was placed on a gun-carriage and carried 30 miles to the place he had chosen in the Matopos for his grave — his "View of the World". Twelve oxen drew the gun-carriage up the steep climb to the crest of his granite kopje.

After the funeral the Administrator wrote to Colonel Nicholson. "The precision with which the Police duties were carried out," he said, "and the efficiency and fine appearance of the men themselves were the subject of most favourable remark from all visitors attending the ceremonies and were particularly gratifying to Colonel Rhodes and the other relatives." It must have been an emotive occasion for Frank Rhodes — apart from grief at his brother's death — as he watched the police and recalled how he had helped Jameson to seduce them from their duty on the occasion of the Raid; how also the impulsive actions of their own officers had contributed to his own (happily commuted) sentence of death; and how he had shared with some of them, too, the hazards of the final advance to the relief of Mafeking.

"I desire particularly," the Administrator continued, "to refer to the complete and satisfactory arrangements made by Major Straker (who had apparently come back from Bechuanaland and taken command in Matabeleland while Bodle was still engaged on active service) for conveying to and from the Matopos Hills the large body of visitors and official guests, and the admirable manner in which the traffic was controlled by him and those working under him, a most difficult task and one carried out with great patience and tact." One can appreciate the need for patience and tact as the ox-wagons and buggies tangled themselves inextricably in unprecedented traffic jams. "I understand," he went on, "that Lieutenant Griffith was responsible for the catering for the official visitors and this was also managed in a manner which was most commendable." Acting as caterers at a public ceremony was apparently another accepted function of the police.

Queen Victoria had died in 1901 and the coronation of her successor, King Edward VII, was due in London on 26 June 1902. Arrangements for a BSAP contingent to attend the ceremonies had therefore to be made before Bodle's squadron had returned from the Transvaal; and Major Straker, with three sergeants, three corporals and a trooper were detailed from the Matabeleland Division, while Mashonaland was to be represented more modestly by Troop Sergeant-Major Dacomb, with one sergeant only, a corporal and two troopers. In the event, the whole contingent was to enjoy an extended holiday thanks to the King, who obligingly fell ill two days before the date set for his coronation. The ceremony had to be postponed until 9 August. Even so, it appears to have taken another two months before the contingent was able to tear itself away from the attractions of the British capital and return to Rhodesia, for a reference to "the termination of the coronation festivities and the departure of the Colonial Troops (from London)" does not appear in the Commandant-General's Orders until 27 October. Dutifully and predictably, the Orders commend "the smartness, soldierly bearing and good behaviour" of the contingent.

But all the tumult and the shouting died at last and, as had happened 10 years before in 1892, the establishment of the police force fell once again under the merciless axe of economy. The force, when it had been reduced during the war by some 200 to 300 on active service (the number had fluctuated from time to time) had been able to cope adequately on this occasion with its duties at home; and although a number of the returning warriors were only too eager to take their discharge, there were still to be some redundancies. The records are not clear as to the extent to which the establishment was reduced, but the Commandant General's Order of 13 March 1903 says, "Owing to the reduction in establishment of the BSAP no further promotions or appointments are to be made without the sanction of the C-G."

Another incipient economy was revealed by an Order in April requiring that "a number of South African-bred donkeys, broken to saddle work for use by the BSAP" were to be given a fair trial and reports on their usefulness were to be made. The Order continued consolingly, "They are not intended to replace horses, but for saddle and pack work to enable foot patrols to be sent long distances and to remote parts of the country where horses cannot be taken without serious risk of losing them." To the conceivable relief of later generations of the force, there appear to be no embarrassing photographs remaining of members mounted on or leading donkeys on duty. A similar experiment with camels, which was to be duly recorded pictorially, was to follow — but that was to come some time later.

Also in March, the No. 1 (Bechuanaland) Division ceased to exist and a new force with no connection with the BSAP, the Bechuanaland Protectorate Police (the BPP as distinct from the previous BBP), came into being. An anomalous situation which had originated solely to oblige Rhodes and Jameson in their dubious machinations had come to an end at last.

In June that year the military tides of commissioned rank in the BSAP were ordered to be dropped in official communications. "In future all officers will use the tides Commandant, Chief Inspector, Inspector and Sub-Inspector." Nevertheless there seems to have been no abandonment of military titles on unofficial occasions.

And on 23 August 1903 Lieutenant-Colonel Chester-Master succeeded Nicholson as Commandant-General. Nicholson had come to Matabeleland in 1896 on temporary secondment from the 7th Hussars to pick up the pieces after the imbroglio of the Jameson Raid (how that episode keeps bedevilling the early history of the force!) and he had served unremittingly for seven critical years. Now he was to retire to the less exacting demands of a directorship of the family business, which rejoiced in the manufacture of "London Dry" gin.

One of the first Orders issued by the new Commandant General on 18 September laid down that "vacancies in the establishment of officers are to be filled up, as far as possible, by selection from the non-commissioned ranks of the force". A candidate for a commission must have served two years in the force, must be less than 27 years old and recommended by his commandant. There would be a qualifying examination in subjects such as military and police duties "in the field and off". If he passed the examination he would become a probationer and be allowed "to exercise the functions of an officer with certain limitations". The proposals limited the number of probationers in the force to two at a time. A probationer would be a member of the officers' mess but would pay no subscription to it until his commission was confirmed. After six months' probation he faced another examination and if he passed this he became a sub-inspector. In the unvarnished official wording of the Order he would be "allowed two tries". If he failed at the second try he would be given an honourable discharge. It would have been an untenable situation if he had gone back to the ranks. Accepting the chance of becoming a probationer had its element of a serious gamble.

The probationer system was later to fall away, but the principal of promotion from within had at last become enshrined — a principle which Rhodes had promised 14 years before but which had been repeatedly disregarded ever since. Lately, some promotions within the force had certainly been made, but until this order appeared there had been no guarantee that the old system of obtaining commissions by influence would not go on. The first probationer, Quartermaster-Sergeant E. Brudenell-Bruce (not an inappropriate name for consideration for a commission) was appointed on 1 October 1903.

And on that same day a new concept of the British South Africa Police was born. The concept at the time was known as "amalgamation" and although the BSAP force today is a far more complex organisation, it was then that the seeds of the ultimate pattern were sown. No longer were the Matabeleland and Mashonaland Divisions — the only two that remained — to be separate entities, run almost as two disconnected forces. There would be one commandant in overall command (wearing the insignia of a crown and star), two chief inspectors in command of the Divisions (each wearing a crown), an establishment of inspectors (three stars), sub-inspectors (two stars) and acting sub-inspectors (probationers with one star).

The Commandant-General's Orders for 5 October read, "The duties of the BSAP combine those of a military force for the defence (of Southern Rhodesia) and those of a police force for the preservation of peace, prevention of crime and apprehension of offenders. As the latter duties naturally predominate in peace-time, it is necessary for the force to be broken up into detachments for the more effective policing of the Colony."

There would be 11 troops, each "a complete and separate unit" with an inspector in command. One was to be the Depot Troop, to which all recruits would be posted on enlistment. The Depot Troop would be held as a reserve force in case of sudden emergency and would supply all drafts needed to keep up the strength of the district troops. Five district troops would be stationed in Mashonaland and five in Matabeleland. Each troop's district would be arranged to fit in, as far as possible, with a magisterial area. It was to be a patently civil organisation. Nevertheless "the Regiment", as its designation had already been established, was still basically a military force, with military traditions and military procedures. Significantly, all officers were required to buy copies of the "King's Regulations and Orders for the (British) Army" and in framing Orders for the BSAP "reference will be made to these".

"Before being posted to a District Troop every recruit will be put through a thorough course of military training and will at the same time receive instruction in Criminal Law and police duties at the Depot." The course would normally take six months. Although previous recruits had been subjected to arbitrary periods of training some of reasonable length, some short and inadequate, some virtually negligible this was the first time that a predetermined, universally applied course at Depot was instituted. "On being posted to a District Troop he will be further instructed in police duties ... and will be sent out on patrols with an old hand."

In November 'A' Troop was established with headquarters in Salisbury; 'B' at Goromonzi, 'C' at Sinoia, 'D' at Umtali, 'F' at Fort Victoria, 'G' at Gwanda, 'H' at Gwelo, 'J' at Filabusi, 'K' at Bulawayo and "L' at Fort Usher. ('E' was apparently reserved for Depot.)

Lieutenant-Colonel William Bodle, DSO, became first Commandant of the newly amalgamated force. An Order setting out "The Most Important Duties and Responsibilities of Officers", issued in October 1903, declared, "The authority of the Commandant is paramount on all occasions; and all orders, or even the expression of a wish emanating from him, must receive an unhesitating and cheerful obedience." (The same instruction enjoined all officers "to consider their duty first and their amusement afterwards".)

There was no need for an Order to enforce his authority where Bodle was concerned. He was already a tradition in the force; members could not conceive of a force without him. It was exactly 14 years since, at Cecil Rhodes's personal insistence, he had been the first man enlisted in the BSACP, had been appointed Regimental Sergeant-Major, and had recruited the first members of the force in Kimberley. There had been but two short breaks in the continuity of his police service in Rhodesia since then: the first had resulted from Jameson's economies in 1892 when he had resorted to running some sort of store in Salisbury; the second, also caused by Jameson, was his enforced repatriation to England after the Raid. He had returned within six months, to repeat for the new Rhodesian police in 1896 the same service of recruitment and invigoration he had rendered to the BSACP seven years before.

Bodle was a soldier. He had enlisted at 17 in the Sherwood Foresters, 31 years before. For the next 17 years he had been a Regular, a professional soldier. Thereafter, although in name a police-man, he had spent by far the greatest part of his service involved in the military episodes of Rhodesian history — the Occupation, the Matabele War, the Jameson Raid, the Matabele Rebellion, the Relief of Mafeking and the campaign in the western Transvaal — all in 14 years. He had virtually been campaigning all the time with little experience of peace-time police work. He was an inveterate soldier and always behaved like one. His martial instincts at the time of the Raid had preferred a military adventure to the tamer duty of keeping the peace. In the Bulawayo Club, where he was a member during his relatively short service in Matabeleland as officer commanding the police, he was always known even by his intimates as "the RSM". His did not appear the background and experience for administering a force whose primary duty would be to gain the confidence of an undisciplined public.

Yet, for all this, he made a fine peace-time Commandant of the new BSAP. He was to serve for six more years, until 1909, and the force was to enhance its image under his command. Not that he was by any means the only officer of the early generation of members of the police in Rhodesia who contributed to the reputation of the BSAP during the first years of this century; and the contribution by these others still remains to be recorded in the force's history.

But 1903 seems a fitting point in time — with the reorganisation of the force and Bodle's appoint-ment as its Commandant — at which to close the first part of this history of the BSAP.

Bodle's total service spanned two eras: the early era of an active military, and the later era of a primarily civil, force. The BSAP was now entering the second era. From the Occupation to the close of the South African War the force had been repeatedly engaged in military drama, in blood and thunder — even on its internal duties it had usually marched about bristling with arms. Thereafter, from the date of cessation of hostilities in South Africa in 1902 — apart from participation by some of its members outside Rhodesia in the two world wars — the British South Africa Police, although maintaining its status as a Regiment, acted in its primary capacity as a civil force. Its members pursued their duties unarmed; still the first line of defence, they carried arms for training and ceremonial purposes only. And they grew proud to be able to boast, over the next 58 years, that nobody had been killed by police action in the execution of their duties.

# VOLUME TWO

The Right of The Line

**1903 – 1939**

by Peter Gibbs

## PREFACE TO THE SECOND VOLUME

THIS SECOND VOLUME of the history of the British South Africa Police has turned out to be quite different from what I expected. I cannot recall exactly what I did expect before I started to write it, but it was certainly not what follows here. (This, I may add, is not an unusual experience for an author. )

The first volume covered what I described as a period of blood and thunder — a period of almost continuous military glamour. I knew that the next volume would have to cover a period when all that sort of excitement was over. There would be no more swashbuckling adventures, no invasions of foreign territories, no battles with rebels in the hills. Apart from the relatively short interlude of WWI, nothing of great historical moment seemed to have happened in Rhodesia during the first 40 years of this century. The story would have to be confined to sober accounts of a police force carrying on its civil duties. I think I visualised having to write a pedestrian recital of mundane events: when so and so was posted to Mphoengs; what year it was they pulled down the stables in Bulawayo; what the RSM said to the new recruit; and all that sort of thing. But — fortunately, I think — it has not worked out like that.

The BSAP was first created as a regiment and has never since been formally deprived of that status. I fully recognise that the history of a regiment is the history of its members, and the essence of the story rests in who the members were and what they did. But some 9000 European members (apart altogether from the Africans) have enlisted in the BSAP since the force was re-formed in 1896 — not counting their predecessors in the BSACP and RMP. Out of these the vast majority have served as good policemen, while some have even distinguished themselves. Indeed, the number who have distinguished themselves in the service of the BSAP is embarrassing to a historian who wants to do full justice to the annals of the force. It is so embarrassing that he has no option but to bring in individuals by name only when they play a direct part in the story he is unfolding. Otherwise, this history might tend to become a series of potted biographies — which would not, I believe, fulfil the purpose for which it is being written.

Again and again, when reading of men who have played a conspicuous part in the affairs of the BSAP, I have come across fulsome references to their characters — particularly in their obituaries: integrity, popularity, efficiency, devotion to duty and all the attributes which every policeman knows he himself possesses in abundance. Indeed, from what I can gather, every member of the force has been a paragon of virtue — with one or two refreshing exceptions. I have heard some disparaging comments about individuals from time to time, but to repeat most of these would be unfair if the individuals are dead, and actionable if they are still alive. (This does not mean that I have not, on occasion, been compelled to record some member' shortcomings.)

But, as I have said, the story has worked out quite differently from the way I expected it to develop. I have found that there is an important story to be told — which, I believe, has never been pieced together before — of the fortunes and misfortunes of the BSAP as a force, as distinct from the preoccupations of its individual members. The members come into the story for the part they played in it, not just for the sake of mentioning their names. The story of the BSAP as a force is inextricably linked with the social evolution of Rhodesia. In the earliest pioneering days — in the short period of Rhodesian history before the end of the 19th century — it was the military episodes (in which the BSAP played a significant part) which moulded the pattern of society; after the Anglo-Boer war it was the pattern of society which moulded the development of the BSAP. So the history of the force itself, from that time, reflects the mood of the country and how the force became the servant of the people, instead of vice versa. (In the early pioneering days the public never groused about lack of police protection — they never expected to have it; during the first 30 years of the 20th century they never ceased grousing about it.)

As I have said, the story of the BSAP since the Anglo-Boer war does not seem to have been previously pieced together. The same can be said of the story of Rhodesia as a whole. Book after book has been published about the pioneering days and when I wrote the first volume of this history I had a wide range of sources. But of Rhodesian history during the first half of the 20th century very little has been published. Consequently, my sources for this volume have been almost entirely limited to the Press (including the invaluable Outpost) and to the records from original sources preserved in the National Archives. I believe this is the first time most of these latter sources have been used, in any context. Originating, as they do, from the hands of many responsible authorities — and preserving, at the same time, interjections from a number of irresponsible citizens — the records present the factual and revealing story of how the force developed in what I have called its formative years.

It is inevitable, of course, that records such as these should dwell more on frustrations and shortcomings than on successes and virtues. The writers of those letters and reports which remain on record seem forever to be carping, with hardly a murmur of approbation and, least of all, praise. But after all, that is what the responsible authorities are there for, to deal with the problems. And the irresponsible citizens certainly never write unless they have something to complain about. It is the problems and the complaints and the way they are handled which make history — and not the good work efficiently and unobtrusively done. And although the span of time covered by this volume produced little excitement in comparison with the earlier days, it was a tremendously important period in the development of the force. It was during these formative years that the BSAP learned the need to shed the image and trappings of one of Queen Victoria's mounted infantry regiments and — while still preserving its regimental dignity — to establish public respect for its reputation as an efficient police force.

The period of this volume covers 1903 to 1939. I have ended this history before WWII because, at the time I am writing, the records in the Archives for that and any later period are still closed. All public records are positively closed for 30 years after their date of origin and there is no access to them within that time. Some confidential files remain closed for longer. It would, therefore, be valueless to attempt to continue this history, beyond the outbreak of WWII, with no access to original sources. Moreover, anyone who attempted to write it at this stage would be seriously inhibited by deference to the feelings of persons still living, or their immediate descendants; and in any case objective history cannot be written when the writer is too close in time and personal experience to the events.

There is one detail in my narrative on which I feel I should make some comment. Throughout the book I have used the word "natives" when referring to the black people, rather than "Africans" which, for very good reasons, is the accepted usage in Rhodesia today. In any other context I would not think of writing "natives". But people called them "natives" throughout the period of which I am writing, and it would be an anachronism to call them by a term which only came into use later. It would be as anachronistic as if, when writing of a white member of the force in the early days, I insisted on calling him "patrol officer" because the use of "trooper" and "constable" in that context has now been discarded. Admittedly, the latter change was made for different reasons from those affecting the use of the word "native", but that is beside the point. I am writing history and I must record the usages of the period.

The period of this volume spans the 1914-1918 war years when the BSAP raised two Service Companies — which became popularly know as "Murray's Column" — for service in the campaign in German East Africa. Naturally, I have included a brief outline of the activities of Murray's Column in this history — no history of the BSAP would be complete without it. But I have to confess that I have undertaken no research whatever into the subject. Mr. G. A. ("Tony") Tanser has done this comprehensively and has completed the manuscript of a book on Murray's Column which describes the campaign in meticulous detail. He very generously lent me a copy of the manuscript and although I have not quoted directly from it I have used it as the source from which I have written my brief account. I wish to record my sincere thanks to Tony Tanser for his kindness in allowing me to do this and my admiration for his painstaking work in putting this important narrative on record.

Most of the other sources used in this volume have been culled from the National Archives and I owe a tremendous debt to the staff for their ever-willing and helpful co-operation in finding for me the material I have sought. I have received unstinting help from Deputy Commissioner Digby Allen (now retired) and his successor Deputy Commissioner Len Jouning — and many others at Police General Headquarters. Major Don Berry — 16 years in the BSAP and later commissioned in the Permanent Staff Corps — has kindly read the manuscript and given me some valuable advice. So has Captain Jack Seaward who served in the force from 1920 to 1946. Once again Mrs. Eleanor Pitt has typed and retyped the manuscript with exemplary patience after I have repeatedly changed my mind and played havoc with her superbly typed first, second and sometimes even third drafts. I cannot adequately express to her my thanks.

PETER GIBBS March 1974

ABBREVIATIONS

| | |
|---|---|
| BNP | Barotseland Native Police |
| BSACo | British South Africa Company |
| BSACP | British South Africa Company's Police |
| BSAP | British South Africa Police |
| CC | Civil Commissioner |
| C-G | Commandant-General |
| CNC | Chief Native Commissioner |
| CSO | Chief Staff Officer |
| FIC | First Information of Crime |
| MMP | Matabeleland, or Mashonaland Mounted Police |
| NC | Native Commissioner |
| NRP | Northern Rhodesian Police |
| NRR | Northern Rhodesian Regiment |
| OB | Occurrence Book |
| RMP | Rhodesia Mounted Police |
| SAP | South African Police |
| SO | Staff Of ficer |
| SRC | Southern Rhodesia Constabulary |
| SRV | Southern Rhodesian Volunteers |

## THE STORY SO FAR

IN 1889, THE force known as the British South Africa Company's Police was first formed by the Company of that name (sometimes also called the Chartered Company) which had been granted a Royal Charter by Queen Victoria purporting to authorise it to occupy and develop the territory known today as Rhodesia. The territory was occupied at the time by a number of native tribes, principally the Matabele and the Mashona. Queen Victoria had no evident right to give to the Chartered Company territory which she did not own. But Cecil Rhodes, the Company's Managing Director, had deftly wheedled out of Lobengula, the Matabele Chief, a piece of paper on which was written a statement — which Lobengula could not read but had been persuaded to sign with a cross — giving Rhodes permission to come into the territory and take away any gold he could find. This, in fact, was all that Lobengula had conceded, even if the document he signed was really valid. But another impressive document was drawn up, this time in London, which began "Victoria, by the Grace of God ... To all to whom these presents shall come, Greeting", and went on, with lavish and regal generosity, to permit Rhodes and his company to occupy the territory and, among other things, to "promote trade, commerce and good government ... and to establish and maintain a force of police."

A party of 200 prospective white settlers — all male, young and adventurous — was assembled in July 1890 in the wilderness of Bechuanaland (now Botswana) and, forming what came to be known as the Pioneer Column, marched into the country which was later to become Rhodesia. The British South Africa Company's Police force, numbering nearly 500 men, which had been established on the lines of a British mounted infantry regiment and led by officers seconded from the British Army, accompanied the Pioneer Column as a military escort and garrisoned a line of communication with the south through Forts Tuli, Victoria and Charter to Fort Salisbury. The Pioneer Column had carefully avoided Matabeleland, the south-western portion of the territory where Lobengula waited with some 12,000 unfriendly warriors, and made for a destination, marked on the map as Mount Hampden, in Mashonaland — the north-eastern portion of the territory where the natives were inclined to be more tractable. The column halted a few miles short of Mount Hampden at a point they christened Fort Salisbury, and Mashonaland was occupied by the Pioneers in September 1890 without loss of life, in fact without firing a shot.

The newly-occupied territory was operated and governed by the Chartered Company as a commercial proposition, the settlers providing the enterprise and initiative and the Company — which ostensibly provided the money — reaping the profits, if any. In the event, the commercial proposition fell a long way short of expectations, and although numbers of new settlers — now male and female — followed the Pioneers into Mashonaland, the expected El Dorado seemed to be developing into what one pioneer, admittedly overwrought at the time, described to the great Rhodes himself as "a bloody fiasco". In 1892, in the first of the drastic economies forced upon it — to be repeated time and again over the years — the Company cut down the police from a strength of 650 to a mere 150, and the name of the force, for some unrecorded reason, was changed to the Mashonaland Mounted Police.

Next year, in 1893, a series of border incidents with Lobengula's warlike Matabele, coupled with the tempting prospect of fresh woods and pastures new, prompted the settlers to invade and occupy Matabeleland. This time the invasion was disputed by the native tribesmen, but the settlers routed the Matabele in a couple of short, sharp engagements which have since been dignified by the label of the First Matabele War. With Matabeleland now added to the Company's territory, a new division of the police force was formed, known as the Matabeleland Mounted Police, this time with a strength of 250, under the command of Major Bodle — who had been the first man attested in the original Company's police in 1889. In 1895 the combined territories of Mashonaland and Matabeleland became formally known as Rhodesia, and the two divisions of the police, although operated as two separate units, became the Rhodesia Mounted Police under a Chief Commissioner.

Then Dr. Jameson, who had been appointed the Administrator — the Company's chief executive officer in the territory — decided to invade the Transvaal, for no other reason than the urge for a swashbuckling adventure, and he led away — seduced, is probably the better word — nearly 90% of the Rhodesian police force on a buccaneering expedition which came to be known as the Jameson Raid, leaving behind no more than about 80 men to police the whole of Rhodesia. The  members of

Jameson's lunatic expedition were forced to surrender to the burghers of Kruger's South African Republic on New Year's Day 1896 and were shipped off to Britain in disgrace. Some of the senior officers, including the Chief Commissioner, were sentenced to imprisonment, but many of the rank and file, discharged from the force, managed to make their way back to Rhodesia.

With the scattered settler population in Matabeleland left virtually unprotected by police, the natives rose in rebellion in March 1896 and murdered hundreds of white men, women and children. Only a handful of policemen were available to help the volunteer forces which were hurriedly raised to put down the rebellion. In June the natives in Mashonaland followed the example of the Matabele and the same story of massacre of white settlers ensued, while the negligible force of police was able, at first, to give only token help to the volunteers fighting the rebels.

But on 1 October 1896, a new police force was established in Rhodesia, named the British South Africa Police, its nucleus consisting of 50 members of the Rhodesia Mounted Police — some of whom had served continuously since the original formation of the force as the BSA Company's Police — but expanded by recruitment from Britain and South Africa to a white force some 400 or 500 strong, backed by a force of similar strength of locally enlisted native policemen — popularly known as "the Black Watch". The rebellion in Matabeleland ended in August 1896 after negotiations between Rhodes himself and the Matabele chiefs. But the guerrilla campaign in Mashonaland dragged on for another year, and the burden of this campaign — and the success of finally suppressing the rebels — fell on the newly established BSAP.

There were now four divisions of the BSAP — which had been conceived in London and virtually imposed on the Company as a safeguard against a repetition of irresponsible adventures. The Imperial Government in London kept control of the force — it sent three of its senior officers out as Commandant-General and Commandants in Matabeleland and Mashonaland respectively — but nevertheless the Company had to pay for it. The four divisions were the Bechuanaland Division, with headquarters at Mafeking; the Matabeleland Division at Bulawayo; the Mashonaland Division at Salisbury; and the North Zambezi Division at Mount Darwin.

In 1899 war was declared between Britain and the Boer republic of the Transvaal, which bordered Rhodesia. As Rhodesia was a British territory the Boers might well have been inclined to invade it, so a defensive force was established at Fort Tuli, close to the Transvaal border. A large portion of the force consisted of members of both the Mashonaland and Matabeleland divisions of the BSAP. When, after a few months, the threat of Boer incursion into Rhodesia receded, the force moved south through Bechuanaland to take part in the relief of Mafeking, the town on the northern border of the Cape Colony which had been surrounded by the Boers and held in a state of siege for seven months. Meanwhile, the BSAP Bechuanaland Division had been entrapped with other British units in Mafeking and had played a conspicuous part in the defence of the town; and thus it came about that members of the BSAP were part of both the besieged and the relieving forces.

After Mafeking was relieved in May 1900, the BSAP provided troops for service in a long drawn out campaign against the Boers in the western Transvaal, and they were only finally released for return to peace-time duties when the Anglo-Boer war came to an end in May 1902.

Then it was that the Chartered Company was driven once again to economise by reorganising the force. The Bechuanaland Division was disbanded and replaced by a force entirely independent of Rhodesia, the Bechuanaland Protectorate Police. The North Zambezi Division — which operated, incidentally, only south of the Zambezi — had already been combined with the Mashonaland Division. So now there were only two divisions of the BSAP, Matabeleland and Mashonaland, and these were merged for the first time into one homogeneous force under one Commandant only — Bodle, now a Lieutenant-Colonel. Ostensibly the combination was motivated by a striving towards greater efficiency, but in truth the Company's guiding principle — forced upon it by circumstances — was economy. The force was still to be run on the lines of a British mounted infantry regiment, but the emphasis was henceforth to be on its civil, rather than its military, duties.

It was with what was known at the time as the "amalgamation" of the BSAP, in 1903, that the first volume of this history concluded.

## Chapter Sixteen

## THE NEW ROLE

THERE WAS NOTHING particularly remarkable about the state of affairs in Rhodesia during the first decade of the 20th century, after the conclusion of the Anglo-Boer war; except that the country was still ruled by a Chartered Company — a form of government which had been discarded as obsolete in every other part of the world. The British South Africa Company had financed the occupations of Mashonaland and Matabeleland in 1890 and 1893 and had assumed virtually sovereign powers of government in the territories; it had had to meet the cost of suppressing two native rebellions, in 1896 and 1897; it had been put to tremendous expense by its peripheral participation in the South African war from 1899 to 1902; and it was still carrying the financial burden (alleviated, of course, by substantial taxes paid grudgingly by the settlers) of running the country and providing public services — not least of which was a police force. There was no question of the Company looking to the Government to find the money and carry the can, because it, the Company, was the Government.

The concept of a police force in Rhodesia in the early years of the century was something very different from the popular idea of a police force almost anywhere in the world today. Not only was Rhodesia a sparsely inhabited wilderness, with an indigenous population of primitive tribesmen who created their own unorthodox problems, but the times were very different from today and the world was still, on the whole, remarkably backward in the material sense. In the most developed civilised communities life was still almost primitive by modern social standards. Even in sophisticated cities like London, Paris and New York nearly all road traffic was still horse-drawn; the motor car had certainly been invented but in those days it had something of the rarity and mystery which the spacecraft has today. No aeroplane had yet left the ground: flying was unthinkable. Telephones were primitive and their use comical; radio was dreamed of, but considered utterly impractical. Communications, by modern standards of rapidity, simply did not exist. The words broadcasting, television, hire-purchase, air-conditioning, parking, and a host of other household expressions, had not entered the language: they are in constant use today, but they all denote concepts which up to then had never been heard of. That was the state of affairs even at the hub of civilisation; add to this the isolation of Rhodesia in the depths of the African wilderness, and one has some idea of how misleading it is to try to equate the role of an early Rhodesian police force with that of a force almost anywhere in the world today.

Then, as now, there were two distinct divisions of the population in Rhodesia, separated by a yawning gulf. The natives, all of them, were very, very primitive in their customs and their behaviour and were discounted completely by the white settlers in the context of participating in a civilised society. They were useful enough for the labour they provided, inefficient as it was, but the settlers persuaded themselves that the tribesmen — having been delivered from the barbarism they had suffered before they, the settlers, came — should be grateful that their country had been occupied by the white men. So they decided there was no moral impropriety in keeping them in a state of rigid subservience and exploiting their readiness to work for next to nothing — a readiness prompted solely by the need to earn sufficient money to pay the poll-tax which the Company imposed.

It is difficult to be exact, but it would seem that the total native population, spread over the 150,000 square miles of Rhodesia, was no more than 200,000, probably considerably less, at the beginning of the century. However, although the African population of Rhodesia has increased many fold since then, there is one link we have with those days which enables us to picture the primitive state of the indigenous people at that time: deep in the tribal trust lands today there are still some kraals whose huts, and the manner of living therein, are hardly less primitive than they were then. The tribesmen lived — as some still do — in a communal society, scratching away at the soil to produce sparse crops when they felt like it, herding their cattle and goats with disastrous effect on their land, propitiating their family spirits with appropriate witchcraft and lazing in the sun with no thought for the morrow.

But, although these conditions still lurk in the land today, there is little in the modern environment to help us picture the circumstances in which a police force had to operate 70 years ago. Admittedly, the scene as a whole has not changed much — it has changed very much less than in most parts of the western world. The country is too extensive for the still relatively sparse population, white and black, to have made the sort of impact on the environment which has so drastically changed the face of more densely populated lands. Probably the most effective way of describing the scene 70 years ago is simply to say: take away from the countryside the made-up roads, the bridges over the rivers, the irrigated lands, the cultivated forests, the game parks, the lakes and dams, the electric power lines; take away from the towns the tarred streets, the surrounding suburbs, the concrete buildings — in fact any building more than one storey high, and most of the others — the garages, the supermarkets, the street lighting, the water-borne sewerage, the ordered African townships. Then you will have Rhodesia as it was before the first world war. It was 30 or 40 years after the Rhodesian towns were established before almost all their central stands were built on — there are still some gaps today — and in the early days of the century a town consisted of scattered buildings only, while people making their way about it walked across empty spaces as often as they followed the roads — which were always either thick in dust or deep in mud. Indeed, every empty stand had its diagonal footpath from corner to corner, and in many cases it was possible to walk from one end of the town to the other without using the streets at all except when actually crossing them. And the grass grew and the thornbush proliferated, so that even in the centre of the towns there was plenty of opportunity for evil-doers to take effective cover.

The business premises in the towns were simply square brick buildings under iron roofs, each with a verandah that was nothing more than a lean-to. In the streets away from the town centres some of the old houses, with their distinctive colonial style of architecture, still stand today — squat, square, single-storey, with broad verandahs and ornate wooden pillars, the tin roof rising to its apex plumb in the centre of the building so that if nothing else can be said for the design it is at least symmetrical. On occasion, the architect has indulged in fancy gables and turrets — still roofed with corrugated iron — and in their days these were considered particularly avant-garde. In those days too — indeed for many years afterwards — it was believed that nothing but corrugated iron could withstand the pounding of tropical hailstones, so slates and tiles were condemned before ever they were tried. Some of the more affluent residents built their houses, not so much in the ordered avenues of the town's suburbs — which should more appropriately have been called the town's fringes — but farther out, on what would be known today as peri-urban plots with extensive, often wooded grounds, quite out of touch with each other and the rest of the town — a situation which presented a perennial problem of adequate police protection. Indeed, police work in the towns, with no system of communication except the police whistle, no street lights, no transport other than horse or bicycle, presented some distinct problems.

The country districts were even emptier. The first census taken in Rhodesia in 1904 gives the white population as 12,600 of whom about 7000, including most of the women and children, were in the towns. So there were some 5000 settlers spread out over the country districts on isolated farms, or on the mines — most of which were small workings, equally cut off from the world — an average of one white man in 30 square miles. There were no telephones, certainly no all-weather roads; so, outside the towns, the provision of police protection could, of necessity, be little more than token.

This, then, was the situation with which the police authorities in Rhodesia were faced during the first decade of the 20th century, after the war in South Africa was over — this, and the overriding necessity to spend as little money as possible, because the Company had just not got it. And it was always the police on whom the predatory, economising eye of the authorities fell first. In 1900 the High Commissioner in Cape Town had written to the Company's Administrator in Salisbury, "Having regard to the satisfactory state of the country, the improvement in means of communication and the increased fighting strength of the resident European community" — this was when the Rhodesia Regiment had first been formed, on the basis of a territorial unit — "I think a reduction in the strength of the BSAP is now possible." And Rhodes himself had sent a message which showed that he, too, was concerned about expense. "Our whole object," he telegraphed to the Administrator in Salisbury, "is to show that we can manage the country with our present reduced numbers (of the BSAP) and I hope you are not filling up vacancies in the police in Rhodesia."

Up till now, the separate divisions of the BSAP in Matabeleland and Mashonaland had accepted that their role, in each case, was primarily military. After all, when the Anglo-Boer war had broken out in 1899 it was only a couple of years since the native rebels inside the country had been waging vicious guerrilla campaigns, needing large scale military operations to deal with them. So it was not unreasonable for the BSAP to have been preoccupied, in those two years, with the danger of the same sort of thing happening again. Admittedly they had established the patrol system during that time, by which single troopers, with a native constable and a pack-horse, set out on long patrols through the countryside, taking anything up to three or four weeks, calling at the isolated farms and mines in the district and of necessity sampling the bibulous hospitality of the residents, always grateful to see another white face. It was on this system of extensive patrols, introduced in the 1890s, that district policing in Rhodesia was ultimately to be based. But headquarters was concerned with the troop rather than the trooper, and it was the maintenance of the troop as a military unit, ready for defensive or aggressive action, that took preference over considerations of crime prevention or detection. Then the Anglo-Boer war itself had come along and posed a military threat to the country; and although the Rhodesia Regiment was raised as an effective military unit, the only fully trained permanent professional force was the BSAP, which thereby qualified as Rhodesia's first line of defence.

During the war the internal police force, and even the volunteer defence forces, had naturally been depleted by members sent away on active service — at one stage nearly 300 of the BSAP had been away — but there had been no sign of the natives 'taking advantage' of these absences as they had done in 1896. The truth was that the blacks had been well and truly subdued and the spirit of rebellion, if it lurked at all, had been broken. Nor, when the war was finished, was there any likelihood of the country being invaded from outside. So the BSAP, if it felt so disposed, could now concentrate on its prime purpose as a police force, "the preservation of peace, the prevention of crime and the apprehension of offenders."

But Colonel Bodle himself, the new Commandant — in command now, for the first time, of both divisions as one force — had been a soldier all his life, and his fourteen year' service with the Rhodesia police had been spent almost exclusively on military operations. He was still imbued with the Troop system, and the organisation of the force — although admitted frankly in force orders to be concerned with predominantly peace-time duties — was still that of a British mounted infantry regiment on active service, and a highly drilled and disciplined regiment at that.

In 1903, while the reorganisation was still being planned, the Administrator — the Company's chief executive in Rhodesia, then Sir William Milton — wrote to the British High Commissioner in South Africa, Lord Milner, "It is not my intention that the Police Force should be converted to a civil force like the London Metropolitan Police. The character which we wish the force to assume is rather that of the Royal Irish Constabulary ... the analogy of the Cape Police is still more suitable; (that force) having a strong military element in its character, it is entirely under the control of the civil department of the Cape Government, unless called out for military service." It is obvious what the Administrator was hinting at. He wanted the BSAP to have "a strong military element in its character" but at the same time to come directly under the Company's control — after all, the Company was paying for it — while the Imperial authorities were still determined to keep it under theirs. "I appreciate," Milton went on, "your Excellency's reason for maintaining the ultimate control of the Defence Forces in this territory," but, without actually saying so, he hinted that the High Commissioner could not possibly object to transferring to the Company "control of a purely civil force at some future date." In the event, the transfer was actually to be made six years later, in 1909, by which time the force had settled down, with some reservations, to its civil role.

But in 1903 many individual members of the BSAP had certainly not accepted the civil role, reservedly or not. That, at any rate, was the opinion of most of the magistrates. Ever since the earliest days, the police and the magistrates had usually failed to see eye to eye. That was not — and is still not — an unusual phenomenon, even in circumstances very different from those appertaining to the dispensation of justice to primitive native tribesmen. Nice points of law in favour of otherwise patent offenders, such as magistrates are ever apt to pursue, seemed even more inappropriate when applied in favour of people who showed no comprehension of the law, or any inclination to be beholden to it anyway. So, in the opinion of the police, the magistrates were simply thwarting them in their estimable work.

In March 1903, the Secretary of the Law Department, who had been a magistrate himself, wrote to the Attorney-General, Mr. C.H. Tredgold (father of Sir Robert Tredgold, later Chief Justice), "The BSAP in general have shown a languid interest in criminal work generally. The majority of the members of the force appear to regard themselves as a purely military body. They view any invitation to assist the civil authorities in the investigation of criminal matters as beyond the supposed scope of their duties. In fairness," he added, "this lack of enthusiasm appears to be confined to the lower ranks."

The Attorney-General endorsed the Secretary's views. Quoting examples of BSAP failings, he said he knew of a police lock-up which was used as a storeroom for mealies, so the prisoners enjoyed the convenience of being able to escape through the high windows by climbing up the mealie bags. Whenever it was necessary to apprehend a prisoner the handcuffs were always the wrong size, and the police were so perfunctory in searching them that it was becoming an accepted custom for prisoners to take pieces of iron into the cells to knock holes through the walls. He quoted the case of a trooper who had failed to arrest a European charged with a series of assaults, although the man had already been apprehended by a native (presumably a native constable). He refrained from commenting whether he thought this had been deliberate or the result of sheer ineptitude. But he added that when cases were brought before a court there was often "no deposition, no exhibit, an entire absence of anything but sheer carelessness, incompetence and neglect." On one occasion, he said, "although a smart Corporal of the BSAP was placed in charge of an investigation of murder and did good service, he made several grave errors and omissions through the want of the most elementary knowledge of criminal law and evidence." He quoted another occasion, when a mule needed as an exhibit in a theft case had been sent out on transport work that very morning by the member prosecuting the case. "It is a universal complaint by all magistrates that prisoners are brought before them without the necessary evidence, and sometimes no definite charge."

Tredgold also quoted an instance when a magistrate in court had given some peremptory instructions to the police. This horrified the local officer in charge, Captain Chawner — who, having joined the old Company's Police in 1891, and participated in the Jameson Raid, was properly conscious of his own seniority and unappreciative of more recent elevations to authority. "Do you think a magistrate should address an officer of the Police in this manner?" he wrote plaintively to the Commandant. The Commandant's answer is not on record but the Administrator's pencilled comment on Tredgold's report which quoted Chawner's letter, was "This is typical!" Tredgold quoted another case, where a Lieutenant Greenway of the BSAP — who had joined in 1898 — had received a warrant for the arrest of a European who had inconveniently absconded to the Transvaal. Greenway, hearing that the fugitive might be in Krugersdorp, blandly posted the original warrant, which naturally carried no authority outside Rhodesia, to the South African police in Krugersdorp. "There are no apparent measures," said Tredgold, "to instruct the police in the most ordinary of police duties. There is a tendency (on the stations) to place all police work into the hands of one man ...," while the rest, he implied, contented themselves with the less exacting demands of regimental life.

At an early stage, before the South African war, constabularies had been formed by the municipal councils to carry out police duties in the towns, and it was mainly thanks to these units, which were quite independent of the BSAP, that the latter was able to concentrate on its more rumbustious operations. Inevitably the town constables were regarded, both by the public and the members of the BSAP themselves, as inferior beings, in an entirely different class from a trooper in a mounted infantry regiment. So far, in this history, the constabularies have not been mentioned because they had no part in the early chain of events from which the BSAP proper was evolved. Moreover, their early records are disappointingly sparse, but it would appear that a Town Police had been formed in Salisbury as early as 1892 and was brought together with a similar force in Bulawayo in 1903 to form the Southern Rhodesia Constabulary, the SRC. And some links with the BSAP were now clearly being forged; as time went on the two units, which ultimately merged, worked more closely together.

The SRC was placed under the direct control of the Company at an early stage. In the letter from the Administrator to Lord Milner in 1903, already mentioned, when the former hinted at transferring the BSAP itself to the Company's control' he said, "As regards the Constabulary, the transfer to the Administration has (already) been approved," and in 1904 a Proclamation by the High Commissioner regularised — a little belatedly it seems — the operation of a Constabulary by the Company, with the proviso that its activities would be confined to municipalities and areas governed by town management boards — town police, in fact. In 1904 the Commandant-General, Colonel Chester Master, responsible for all police and military forces in Rhodesia, formally inspected the SRC at the Kopje station in Salisbury, and Chief Inspector Drury — BSAP veteran of the Jameson Raid, relief of Mafeking and the campaign in the western Transvaal — was gazetted officer commanding, with the local rank of major. At the same time, in the first of a series of moves in the Box and Co. category — with which members of the force were to become increasingly familiar over the years — Chief Inspector Fuller, who had up to then commanded the SRC, became the Chief Staff Officer of the BSAP and was, in fact, destined to succeed Colonel Bodle as Commandant when the latter retired in 1909; at which later stage Drury was to come back from the SRC to be Chief Staff Officer and was himself to succeed Fuller as Commandant in 1911.

In the event, the SRC was to be amalgamated with the BSAP in 1909, when the latter was at last transferred to Company control. Until then, the two were quite separate forces in spite of the interchange of senior officers. Indeed, it is on record in BSAP General Orders in 1905 that "Sub Inspector Murray BSAP is attached for duty to SRC until further notice, and during such time he will cease to draw pay from the BSAP." (Author's italics.) There could be no more positive distinction than that. However, both forces were policing Rhodesia, so henceforth the part they played will be combined in this history. That each force had a different corporate status accounted a great deal for the disdain for police work exhibited by many members of the BSAP during the next few years, and for their obsessive belief that they were ordained for higher things. If the town and country forces had been one unit from the first reorganisation in 1903, the presumption that the BSAP was a military and not a civil force would not have died so hard, and the disruptive cleavage between Town and District would not have persisted as long as it did after the final amalgamation in 1909.

The urge for economy nearly brought some frightening consequences in 1904, when the authorities were inspired by certain proposals which, if they had been pursued to their full conclusion, would have transfigured the image and character of the British South Africa Police entirely, even perhaps permanently.

Early in September, Lord Milner, the High Commissioner in Cape Town, had sent a letter to Sir William Milton which started off promisingly enough. "Any retrenchment effected during recent years," he wrote, "has been chiefly at the cost of the BSAP and I do not think that the present expenditure on that force is excessive." That, surely, was encouraging. He added, "In order to protect a settled white population a regular force, always equipped and ready, which can be sent anywhere at short notice, is essential, and I think that the bulk at any rate of that force should be white." That was still encouraging. Then came the bombshell. "Having regard to the extreme gravity of the financial position" — Rhodesia had never known anything else — "I am prepared to try the experiment of substituting 100 Basutos for an equal number of whites." (The force had about 470 white members.)

By an incredible exercise of self-restraint the higher ranks of the administration and the force seem to have kept the proposal entirely to themselves. It certainly never reached the Press which — in its contemporary mood of jingoism — would have torn it to shreds. Anything suggestive of endangering the white settlers' interests for the sake of saving expense to the Company — or for the sake of pursuing the Imperial Government's pernicious regard for the black man — was grist to the Press's mill. One can hear the echo of the cry, down the years: "doing a white man out of a job and giving it to an incompetent black, for the sake of saving money" — which, of course, subject to justification or otherwise of "incompetent", was just what the proposal intended.

However, the proposal was not without its supporters. Colonel Fuller, the chief staff officer, told the Administrator, "From my knowledge of a similar force in the Protectorate" (Bechuanaland) "I am of the opinion that Basutos of the right class will prove fully capable of carrying out the duties required of a country police force in this territory." Even Colonel Bodle said he was willing to give the proposal a trial. Indeed, he worked out the costs of employing 200 Europeans as £46,145; 400 Basutos as £36,100, 300 local natives as £11,020 — a total of £93,265 for a year: compared with £150,000 which the Company was then paying for a force of less than 500 Europeans, and some 300 local natives.

A great deal of correspondence on the subject passed between the Company's office in London, the High Commissioner in Cape Town and the Administrator in Salisbury. The financial situation in Rhodesia was so acute that the Company was being forced to raise more capital. The London office told Milner, "The Board is asking shareholders to provide further funds for the work of the Company and it is essential that shareholders be assured that every effort will be made to prevent diversion of the new capital from industrial development to administrative deficits." In other words, the new money was not be squandered on the cost of running a white police force.

One man in Salisbury, Mr. Clarke, the Resident Commissioner, did have the temerity to say to the Administrator that he doubted if the Basutos would be acceptable to the Matabele, owing to the language difficulty. The Basutos, he said, were unable to read: how could they enforce the pass laws? The Administrator, on whom the pressure to reduce expenses must have been weighing considerably — and who always, from the tone of his correspondence, seemed ready enough to disparage the BSAP — replied, "It will be no difference from introducing men from England. It is doubtful if 10% of them (from England) acquire any real knowledge of native language and customs. And colonials," — men from South Africa — "are not attracted."

Milner went so far as to acknowledge that the circumstances in Bechuanaland and Rhodesia were "sufficiently dissimilar to make it uncertain whether the success of employment of Basutos would be reproduced." But his uncertainty was not strong enough to prevail against the pressures for economy to which he, too, was subjected. "The Basutos," he went on, "are the most intelligent and adaptable of the South African native races ... regard must certainly be shown for any pledges given to the Matabele, but I do not think the introduction of a small body of Basuto police would encounter any opposition on their part or lead to difficulty." Milner had not spent any time either in Matabeleland or Mashonaland so the suspicion cannot be resisted that he might have been indulging in wishful thinking. The Resident Commissioner in Basutoland itself told Milner he believed that a promise to make grants of land after completion of service would attract good men. He instanced the land promised by Rhodes to the Fingoes who had gone up to Rhodesia with the pioneer column — the origin of the present Fingo Location near Bulawayo today.

And finally, to clinch the matter once and for all, a cable was sent from Cape Town to Salisbury saying, "High Commissioner consents trial 100 Basutos to replace Europeans. If successful might later be increased though HC does not entirely approve further reduction BSAP" — which was considerate of him. The cable was confirmed by a formal minute forwarded to the Administrator on 21 September.

But, for some undisclosed reason, the proposal was never implemented. In fact, no further reference at all appears in the records. The last item of correspondence to be found is a letter dated 30 September from the Resident Commissioner in Basutoland, already referred to, suggesting grants of land on completion of service. The rest is silence; and the seriously threatened transfiguration of the BSAP never came about. Bodle's next formal report to the Company on 1 December made no mention of it; he merely said "the (European) strength will be 450 in a very short time. Today it is 468, of which 'E' Troop (depot and headquarters) is 120. Twelve months ago the strength exceeded 600." Whether he was reporting the reduction in strength proudly or sadly is a subject for speculation.

In parentheses, it should be recorded that an extraordinary general meeting of the British South Africa Company, held in London on 12 October to authorise the raising of more capital, was, in the words of the Bulawayo Chronicle, "uncontrollably turbulent". But nobody mentioned the subject of police, Basuto or otherwise. The whole trouble was about the calibre of the directors. As a "conspicuous shareholder" proclaimed, "A man is wanted who can again fire the imagination of the British public as Mr. Rhodes did, and thus induce the public to take over Rhodesia ..." However, the resolution to raise the new capital was carried in the end, and Rhodesia remained the property of the Company — as it was to remain for 19 more years.

## Chapter Seventeen

## MUTINY AND ALARM

THE FIRST DECADE of the century, from the point of view of BSAP history, was marked by the influence of a man who, by repute, was one of the most remarkable to have been a member of the force. It is often difficult to determine what qualities make a man more remarkable than others within a particular professional team. Are they simply qualities of character, or have they been moulded by the special, perhaps fortuitous circumstances of his position?

James Blatherwick enjoyed special circumstances in his position in the force, of course. Special circumstances and special privileges — those are the perks of a Regimental Sergeant Major. What is more, the very special authority of an RSM impels a man to develop characteristics which probably would not otherwise have become apparent. There are, of course, many people in the world blessed with the characteristics of a good Regimental Sergeant Major who never become one because their walk in life, fortunately, does not recognise the rank, or any category of activity equivalent to it. Some of these people repress the characteristics as best they can, or have them repressed by their fellow men; others display them freely and make themselves universally unpopular.

But for a professional RSM the characteristics are the tools of his trade; the test of his true character is his ability to make use of them fairly, justly and, above all, effectively. After all, his whole *raison-d'etre* is to extract the utmost from his men in physical effort, mental alacrity and unquestioning obedience. He has no other concern whatsoever. He is not required to plan, or to make policy decisions — the commissioned officers and the staff are there for that. Below the level of executive responsibility, he is the most powerful man in the force, or the regiment, or whatever it is; he is totally responsible, not for what his men are required to do, but for their doing it — and how they do it. Admittedly he is buttressed by an unchallengeable authority, but the effectiveness of that authority depends entirely on how he uses it personally.

Blatherwick joined the BSAP in 1896, as a Troop Sergeant Major. He was 27 at the time and had served for six years with the Bechuanaland Border Police, wherein he had attained that rank. He came up to Rhodesia with what was known as the Matabeleland Relief Force — most of whose members had been in the old Rhodesia Mounted Police and had been sent to England in disgrace after the Jameson Raid. They had made their way back to Mafeking to join the Relief Force, which was also attracting men from the BBP. The force was hurrying north to play its part in suppressing the Matabele rebellion. It arrived in Bulawayo in June that year and Blatherwick was sent out immediately with a squadron of RMP — the BSAP had not yet been formed as such — under Lieutenant Cashel, on what was known as the Gwaai patrol. For the time being he must have remained as a member of the Bechuanaland Border Police because his record of service with the BSAP — which force came into being on 1 October — shows him as joining it on 19 December that year.

He was lucky to return from the Gwaai patrol with his life after a surprise encounter in the bush with a party of Matabele, which developed into a dangerously hand-to-hand engagement. Cashel subsequently wrote, "Sergt.-Major Blatherwick was being engaged single-handed with some of the enemy. Seeing this, I galloped up to him. Blatherwick, covering one of his opponents with his revolver, pulled the trigger, but the cartridge missed fire. The next moment his intended victim hurled his assegai at the Sergt.-Major, striking him in the lower part of the back as he rode past. "One wonders if "the lower part of the back" was a euphemism for the posterior. "The latter was quickly avenged, however" Cashel went on, with commendable nonchalance, "for almost at the same moment I dropped the fellow at close quarters." There appears no further record of how serious Blatherwick's stab in the back really was, but he does not seem — from Cashel's account — to have been removed wounded from the field.

Next year, now in the BSAP, he was promoted to Regimental Sergeant Major. The record is not clear as to who was the RSM when the new BSAP was first formed in October 1896, but Blatherwick was nevertheless one of the earliest incumbents of the rank, which he held for 16 years. He was promoted to Inspector in 1913 — a rank which somehow lacked the colour and unbridled authority of the RSM — and was commissioned in 1917, becoming Commandant, Depot. He died the following year — during the tragic epidemic of influenza in 1918. His wife had died from the same cause two weeks earlier. He had gone south with the BSAP during the Anglo-Boer war, to the relief of Mafeking and the campaign in the western Transvaal. So, like all the senior members of the force after that war, his service before 1903 had been almost entirely military; and without detracting from Jimmy Blatherwick's lustrous image — almost as the father figure of the BSAP — there can be no doubt that he regarded his men as mounted infantrymen rather than policemen, and the BSAP as a regiment rather than a police force.

Paradoxically, his was not a soldierly figure — although his seat on a horse was impeccable. He was a heavy man with a paunch and double chins; he was apt to hunch up his shoulders, and although it was the fashion in those days to wear what was known as the "pouch belt" — in place of the modern Sam Browne — high across the chest, tucked up under the right armpit, Blatherwick always seemed to have exaggerated what might today be called "the uplift"; and this, coupled with his lugubrious drooping moustache, gave him something of a strangled expression. He was, of course, the terror of the recruits. Someone wrote of him, "His eyes were heavy-lidded and stern with an extraordinary expression of latent power. He could make the boldest man quake in his shoes, but many troopers had occasion to remember the generous, kindly nature underlying the hard martial exterior. His wit was caustic but not cruel. His latest saying was invariably the staple topic of conversation among the recruits." A later Commissioner said, after his death, "While the lash of his sarcasms never failed at the time to sting the recipient, they left no permanent scar, and I know of no one who retains any sort of ill-feeling or of malice against him for anything he ever said or did." One is tempted to wonder if every recruit — or even hardened trooper — who felt the lash would readily have echoed the Commissioner. It needs a resilient character to forgive and forget sarcasm, particularly if the sarcasm is deserved, and policemen are no more blessed with forbearance than ordinary mortals. The Commissioner added, "I think his most marked traits and characteristics were his absolute sense of justice, his methods of give and take, i.e., tact and a total absence of vindictiveness. These were all wrapped up in a strikingly rugged personality, which, with his entire lack of ostentatious display of authority, endeared him to all." Allowing for the emotional licence to which references to the dead are invariably subject, the Commissioner's tribute to Jimmy Blatherwick was, from all accounts, well deserved.

In May 1903 the Southern Rhodesia Constabulary in Bulawayo went on strike. This was shortly before the reorganisation of the BSAP that year, when the Mashonaland and Matabeleland divisions were to be combined. Nevertheless, the SRC, operating in the towns, was still a separate force, controlled by the Company; although, as has already been remarked, there was some exchange of senior officers between it and the BSAP. Indeed, although this is not specifically stated in the records, most of the officers in the SRC appear to have been drawn from the BSAP. Chief Inspector Fuller was still in command of the SRC in the first half of 1903 and was stationed in Bulawayo.

A recent arrival in Rhodesia to join the SRC had been a Constable Miller. He had served for seven years in the Essex and Metropolitan Police forces, followed by six years in the British army, with service in South Africa. He was, in fact, something of an old sweat. He probably took his duties in the backwater of Bulawayo with a degree of perfunctoriness. In any case late one afternoon his NCO, a Sergeant Gibson, who does not appear to have been a popular favourite, accused him of failing to patrol his beat in a satisfactory manner and ordered him summarily into No. 1 cell, there to be incarcerated for the night, pending appearance before the commanding officer in the morning.

This was not the sort of treatment Miller had received either in the British police or in the army. Expressing some forceful objections to the Sergeant's proposed arrangements, he turned away from Gibson and made off towards the mess room. According to the report of the affair in the Bulawayo Chronicle next morning, Sergeant Gibson, in the exercise of his authority, "seized the Constable by the throat and then struck him." During the inevitable affray which ensued, "Sergeant Gibson was severely punished."

Although most of the spectators of this little fracas were unquestionably on Miller's side, as subsequent events were to show, some semblance of authority seems to have been mustered and Miller was duly consigned to his appointed cell. However, the support for Sergeant Gibson was far from unanimous, and 42 of the 60 constables on the station marched to Chief Inspector Fuller's quarters, there to demand that either Miller be released or Sergeant Gibson be put in the cells too. This was not the sort of peremptory demand to inspire much sympathy from the commanding officer and, as the Chronicle delicately put it, "Captain Fuller" — a Chief Inspector's courtesy title — "could not see his way to complying with this request."

So the constables declared a strike. It seems that at some time during the evening Fuller invited them to send a deputation of two — one of whom was a Constable McAulay — to discuss the situation with him and that he told the deputation that Miller's release, to which he was prepared to agree, would be nevertheless conditional on the strikers returning to their duties. He added that he would not act on his own prerogative to dismiss the strikers from the force, but he would allow them to resume duty if they agreed to do so. The strikers held a meeting at 11 p.m., by which time they had probably well fortified themselves. A Constable Foster took the chair. In a spirit of collective solidarity, of which a modern trade union would have been proud, the meeting voted to continue refusing duty until Miller had been released. Only five constables paraded for the midnight relief.

Next morning the strikers were addressed by Fuller and Captain Drury — who was still with the BSAP. (Drury was to change places with Fuller the following year, when the latter was to become the BSAP's Chief Staff Officer. As an interesting aside, the two officers now facing the strikers were both future commanding officers of the BSAP.)

Fortified now by the support of a fellow officer, Fuller took a firmer stand and threatened to discharge the lot unless they returned to duty. He was prepared to concede, however, that if they went back he and Captain Drury would listen to their grievances. "Has not Captain Drury always given you a fair hearing?" he asked rhetorically, and they embarrassed the unfortunate Drury by giving him a rousing cheer. This demonstrative response upset Fuller's newly found resolution and he offered them 20 minutes to make up their minds. But Constable Foster, the chairman of the meeting the previous night, was not giving in so readily. He shouted out, "Show we're agreed boys!" and called for a show of hands to support a continuation of the strike. The vote was almost unanimous and, in a surge of noisy bravado, they all trooped off except eight men who agreed to resume duty.

The other 34 were ordered to hand in their kits and depart. Fuller, for reasons which will become apparent, gave instructions that three men — McAulay, Foster and another ringleader Halsey — were not to be paid off. Miller was then released from his cell, but detained in his quarters. Sergeant Gibson, whom Miller now charged with assault, was similarly detained. Captain Drury made a dramatic public announcement that the safety of the town would be amply provided for, as the 26 constables still on the strength had all volunteered to carry out double duty.

Miller was duly brought before the magistrate next morning and charged on three counts — two of neglecting to perform his duties, and one of striking a superior officer. Sergeant Gibson was called as a witness and, according to the Chronicle, "he bore a black eye, but the accused's face did not carry any disfigurement." Five of the now ex-constables declared on oath that the sergeant had been the aggressor. On the strength of their evidence, which nobody made any attempt to refute, Miller was acquitted of the charge of striking his superior officer; he was found guilty on both counts of neglect of duty and fined £10, or one month's imprisonment, on each count. Twenty pounds was a heavy fine in those days.

According to the Chronicle, "After the adjournment of the court a subscription list was opened and a considerable sum gathered in a couple of minutes. Mr. H. Rosenberg volunteered to make up any deficiency in the money collected for the fine, and some of the ex-constables carried him (presumably Miller) shoulder high and the crowd cheered." Miller, in a spirit of exemplary generosity, withdrew his own charge of assault against the Sergeant he had duffed up.

But this was not the end of the affair. Next morning McAulay, Foster and the third man Halsey, appeared at a preliminary examination before the magistrate on a charge of "beginning, inciting or joining in any mutiny or sedition" — a grave and heavily punishable offence. The magistrate, in his summing up, said, "There is no doubt that the force has been guilty of mutiny. I have no sympathy with the men. They could all have been liable to heavy punishment. Had it not been for the particular circumstances I would have had no hesitation in committing all three of the accused for trial." But, fortunately for them, there had been some doubt about whether they had been discharged from the force before the charge of incitement to mutiny had been laid against them.

On the day following the strike they had been ordered to hand in their kits. Their beds and bedding had been taken from them and presumably they had had to find somewhere else to sleep. They had been told to report at the office the next day, and when they did so — in the happy expectation, no doubt, of being paid what was owed to them — they had been arrested. Fuller, giving evidence in court, maintained that by simply ordering them to hand in their kits he had not actually discharged them from the force. In his opinion, they would not be legally discharged until they had received their discharge certificates, duly signed by the proper authority. But, he argued, even if they had been discharged in effect, he still had the power to prosecute them for offences committed while they had been in the force. "Dismissal," he said, "is not the full punishment."

"I cannot hold that," said the magistrate. "I am convinced that if he has been discharged from the force a man cannot be prosecuted under the Act." And in his opinion Fuller had effectively discharged them. "No doubt the police force has been guilty of mutiny. As the Chief Inspector has said, they are not carpenters who can go on strike when they please. They have taken an oath. I have no sympathy with the accused or the other strikers. They have been all liable to heavy punishment. The only point is whether the men were discharged. I do not hold that to constitute legal discharge the men should have had some documents handed to them." Reluctantly, he released them all, saying the papers in the case would be sent to the Attorney-General; but no subsequent action ensued.

The Chronicle, in a leading article which hardly pursued a consistent point of view, said, "In most instances public sympathy is with the strikers, but we do not think the public in this instance is on the side of the strikers ... of course, it might be called a harsher name, but let that pass ... The native population of Bulawayo far outnumber the whites and it is particularly necessary that the police should not be absent from their stations." The fear of a repetition of 1896 still haunted the white population of Bulawayo. "We know there is a latent opposition to the police ... we grumble at this, that and the other crime because it is not discovered and punished. But we lose sight of the number of criminals who are caught and punished and also of the really large number of crimes that would be committed were it not for the police. It is a good sign when a police force has little to do, because it indicates that through their efficiency they have made crime nearly impossible. This has been the case in Bulawayo and we fancy no mining camp or border town can show a better record than this town" — a comment somewhat at variance from the article's earlier grumble of crimes not being discovered and punished.

Indeed, the Bulawayo Chronicle's attitude to the effectiveness of the town police was not, at the time, noticeable for its consistency. In March that year, a couple of months before the strike, someone had broken the plate glass window of the Grand Hotel bottle store in Main Street, early one Saturday morning, and had extracted 34 bottles. "That such a bold robbery could have taken place in this prominent part of the town," the Chronicle commented reproachfully, "and that the noise of the breaking glass did not attract attention, has caused astonishment at the vigilance (sic) of the local constabulary." A month later, the Chronicle reported the case of a prisoner at the police court, who was convicted of a charge under the Police Offences Act and fined £100 — a stiff sentence — or six months imprisonment. On hearing his sentence the prisoner made a long statement to the Court, which must have had a soporific effect on all concerned, for when he had finished he simply left the dock and walked out of the court through the side door. Rumour in the town next day had it that he had fled into the veld and was making for the South African border. "The Police," said the Chronicle, in an unusual burst of approbation, "are exercising their vigilance in this matter. If the prisoner is not caught soon it will not be their fault." As an anti-climax, he was found in a house somewhere in the town. "Accordingly, five stalwart constables visited the premises and quietly took the prisoner into custody."

In Salisbury, at about the same time, Trooper James Gilbert of the BSAP was sent out into the Bindura district to arrest two Europeans. It may be that when he found them he had some difficulty in apprehending them and that he therefore adopted the precept of "if you can't beat 'em, join 'em", for he agreed to escape with them across the Zambezi. However, they were all captured by a BSAP patrol from Mount Darwin before they reached the river. Duly incarcerated in Salisbury prison, Gilbert escaped by the simple method of breaking through the gaol wall, accompanied by one Phineas Orton, described as "the desperado who stuck up Constable Horne on the Goromonzi road." (Horne had been sent out to arrest Orton who held him up "in approved Ned Kelly style", relieving him of his horse and gun. Orton had subsequently been apprehended.) Gilbert and Orton, after breaking out of the prison, were recaptured in due course, but four months later they made another bid for freedom from a working party of 12 white convicts in Salisbury's Cecil Square. Gilbert threw himself on a warder who "pitched his Winchester over his head." This time a third man, Smidt, joined them in their bid to escape. Another warder, still in possession of his Winchester, brought Orton down with a bullet in his left shoulder. Gilbert wisely surrendered. But Smidt got away and was never seen again. The Bulawayo Chronicle said patronisingly, "The townsfolk (in Bulawayo) are laughing at the authorities for sending convicts to a frontier town (Salisbury) and insufficiently guarding them. The BSAP. patrols have as yet met with no signs of Smidt who is 6ft. 1/2 inches. It is concluded he has cleared to Portuguese territory. Orton is doing well. The arm and shoulder were smashed."

But it was not only the criminal classes who found themselves in trouble. In March 1903 four Salisbury constables — MacKenzie, James, Begg and Battison — were brought before the magistrate charged with refusing to pay their mess accounts. Evidence showed that, in accordance with their conditions of service, they were being paid eight shillings a day and provided with rations, which consisted of tea, rice and sugar, pepper, bread, fresh and tinned meat. Mutinously, they had refused to pay for the extras — butter, jam and vegetables — for which the regulations laid down a charge of two guineas a month. Inspector Warr, prosecuting, admitted that the free rations were inadequate and that "the health of the force required that there should be extras." The accused claimed that they had joined the force on the condition that they would receive free rations. They had already been fined 15 shillings each for their first refusal to pay their mess accounts, and now that they persisted in their refusals they had been charged. The magistrate dismissed the charges. "It is to be hoped," said the Chronicle, "that as a corollary the men will be refunded their 15 shillings and that the extra charge of two guineas will be abolished." And so it was.

Another victim of the system was Surgeon Inspector Yeates, who had been a medical officer of the BSAP for two years. Yeates was an Australian who had spent 11 years at sea as a ship's doctor before joining the force. He had served, too, in the leper settlement on Robben Island in 1901 and 1902 when the already unhappy inmates were visited by an epidemic of bubonic plague. Now he was charged with carrying on the profession of a medical practitioner in Rhodesia without a licence. It was evident that he had been indulging in private practice. But, as his attorney argued, his status in the force was the same as that of any other officer. "If his superior officer ordered him to attend a private patient," was the attorney's somewhat specious argument, "he would be compelled to acquiesce, otherwise he would be disobeying a superior officer. He is fully entitled to a fee for his services. The BSAP is under the control of the High Commissioner (in South Africa) and the accused is entitled to come under the special provisions which free such Government servants from the liability of taking out a licence." The magistrate found Yeates guilty, alleviating the reflection on his professional standing by fining him only half a crown.

The early months of 1904 brought one of those recurrent alarms of native unrest, and fears of violent rebellion, such as were apt to arise periodically over the years. Twelve months earlier the rumour had been spread, among the whites, that the Company intended to increase the poll-tax on natives from 10 shillings to two pounds a year. In the event, the tax was merely doubled, to one pound. The reasons for the increase were two-fold: to provide a welcome addition to the Company's revenue; and to keep the natives working more assiduously so that they could acquire the money to pay the tax.

Rumours of possible trouble had started in the Plumtree district and somebody had passed them on to London where the Daily News reported in November 1903, "According to a correspondent Rhodesia is on the eve of another of those sanguinary revolutions which have twice broken out in that still only half-conquered piece of South Africa." The ostensible cause of the outbreak, the paper said, would be the new taxation law "which has just passed the so-called Rhodesian Legislature." By some process of convoluted reasoning it added that a revolt would be welcomed by the promoters of the Rhodesian gold mining companies, whose ventures were "now in a bad way."

The Native Commissioner at Tegwani in the Plumtree district, asked to investigate the rumour, reported that he could find no evidence of an intended rising. The Chief Native Commissioner in Bulawayo decided to call the Matabele chiefs to an indaba at Fort Usher on the 22 January, at which the increased tax would be announced and the chiefs, hopefully, persuaded of its justification. "I do not think it advisable," he wrote, "that they should come into Bulawayo, for various reasons," and he applied for authority to slaughter half a dozen head of cattle to make the occasion a convivial affair.

Although the alarm had been raised in Matabeleland, nobody really became excited there. But the authorities in the eastern districts reacted in a flurry of trepidation. Reports were received of gatherings of natives in the reserves, particularly in the Inyanga district, and Mr. Taberer, the Chief Native Commissioner in the province, reported to the Administrator, "Personally I think the meetings are held for very grave reasons, the natives however excusing themselves by saying they are held for 'rain' ". And Mr. Hulley, the NC in Umtali, said, "I do think we will get difficulty in collecting the increased tax." In a private letter to Taberer, Hulley wrote, "I have arrived at the opinion that the natives in this country intend to rise. I am firmly convinced that we are in for such a row as we have not had up here yet."

Chief Inspector Straker commanded the BSAP in the Umtali district. He was one of the members of the original BSACP and had been promoted to sergeant-major as early as 1890. Almost inevitably, he had served in the Jameson Raid and he had also participated in the relief of Mafeking. He reported to Colonel Bodle on 18 March that he had heard rumours, from a reliable source, that the natives in the district intended storing the current year's crop of grain in the mountains and then coming down and causing trouble among the whites. On the 24th he telegraphed, "From very latest information, matters will start sooner than expected, probably in two or three weeks. Have selected (defensive) position and warned settlers. Of greatest importance that 4000 rounds Metford and 8000 Martini come here at once. Could send small escort for same to Rusape if required but being very short handed can ill spare men."

The Administrator did not take Straker's state of alarm too seriously. "The report," he told Bodle, "is similar to those received last year from Mazoe and Lomagundi, which were set at rest by a patrol and a meeting between the CNC and the chiefs. I propose sending Hulley and Taberer to Inyanga ... It would be as well to send a small patrol of 12 BSAP under Major Straker to push through in one march from Rusape to Inyanga (in order to minimise the risk of horse sickness) to be followed by 15 to 20 native police with a small BSAP escort." This patrol was duly sent out from Salisbury. Straker joined it at Rusape and took it through to Inyanga.

It transpired that Straker's principal fount of intelligence — his "reliable source" — was two whites in the Inyanga district, a farmer and a storekeeper, who each kept a native woman. They certainly could not have had more direct contact with native opinion and they both affirmed, on what they were inclined to accept as unimpeachable authority, that the tribesmen intended to rise after their crops had been reaped. The NC at Inyanga, infected by the atmosphere of alarm, telegraphed on 24 March to the CNC, "Natives already reaping and drying their rapoko. Usually not reaped until end of April. Trouble may be expected any day now." Taberer, despite his own misgivings, replied, "I don't think much notice should be taken ... the natives in the Inyanga district were very short of grain last year and will naturally reap the rapoko crop as soon as it is ripe to eat." However, a week later he was reporting to the Administrator, "There is distinct unrest among the chiefs at present, their demeanour is anything but respectful ... we may expect trouble at any time between the fall of the present moon and the next five weeks." Sub-Inspector Gwynne, commanding BSAP Inyanga, reported, "We have been directly told it will take place very shortly." And on 1 April — appropriately as it turned out — Straker telegraphed Bodle, "Rising to be general and simultaneous throughout Mashonaland. Towns will be attacked after rural districts wiped out. Expected very shortly."

The Administrator, Sir William Milton, in spite of his own doubt about the rumours, felt obliged to cable the Secretary of the Company in London that owing to reports of possible disturbances in Inyanga, he might have to authorise the increase in the strength of the BSAP. Indeed, Bodle fortuitously seized the opportunity to urge the Commandant-General that until the newly imposed poll-tax had been paid, no further reductions in the force should be allowed; rather should it be increased. "My orders at present are not to engage any new recruits until the strength has been reduced to 550 of all ranks, while at present it is 50 in excess. A large number of men will be time-expired during the next six months." He added that he had many applications to join the force from men in South Africa, "and I recommend that in view of the alleged unrest amongst the natives I should be allowed to engage some of these." It was a creditable attempt to make use of the opportunity to increase the strength of his force but the Commandant-General was not impressed. "I am not aware," he replied coldly, "that the present circumstances call for any such extraordinary precautions." Reports from the southern districts, he said, were "uniformly satisfactory. There is no doubt that certain people in the country have made up their minds that there is going to be a rising and every little incident is construed as tending in that direction".

However, by some unusual short-circuiting of rank, Straker had a "conversation by telegraph" with the Commandant-General on 1 April, which consisted of 23 questions and answers — tapped out laboriously, letter by letter, in the Morse code — and held up the telegraph traffic for a couple of hours. Among other suggestions, Straker recommended removal of women and children from the district, saying he did not think it advisable that the police should be split up into small parties for the protection of farms. The Commandant-General was again unimpressed by any such alarmist proposal. "Should any breach of the peace occur," he told Straker admonishingly, "you will be in command of all the loyal people in the district and responsible for the discipline of them all. You should consult the government officials and any local people who can give good advice." Beyond that, Straker's "conversation" accomplished nothing except to bring a complaint from the Administrator's office that ordinary telegraph work had been severely disrupted while the "conversation" had been going on.

By 6 April the state of alarm had almost entirely evaporated. The Administrator cabled London, "Rumours Inyanga not substantiated. Evidence insufficient and not reliable. Attitude natives satisfactory and condition affairs normal. Consider no cause for alarm". There had also been a slight flurry in the Fort Victoria district. But the NC at Fort Victoria had written to the CNC at Salisbury, "The Police have received information from their Commandant that there are rumours of a rebellion and rumours are increasing, but only among white people. I am of the opinion it is pure imagination, but if talk goes on and it reaches the natives it cannot be good for the native mind. Cannot the Police be told they must rely for their intelligence on the Native Department? The officers of the Police are not sufficiently acquainted with natives to form opinions on the subject," — an attitude on the part of the Native Department that was to persist for many years.

Nor was this sentiment, at that time, confined to the NC at Fort Victoria. Even the Chief Staff Officer, on behalf of the Commandant-General, wrote to Bodle, "During the past few months there have been scares amongst the white inhabitants, resulting from reports which have gained currency out of all proportion to their importance, and in some cases the scares have been augmented rather than allayed by the ill-timed precautionary measures of the BSAP ..." He enclosed a "Confidential Circular Memorandum" to be distributed to senior officers. "When an officer takes command of a district Troop," the Memorandum admonished, "one of his first and most important duties is to make himself acquainted with the views of the Commandant as to the steps he is expected to take for the protection of his stations, and of life and property in the district, in the event of any disturbance among the natives ... This should not be left until rumours of unrest are reported ... White residents scattered amongst a large uncivilised native population are always subject to scares."

But the Administrator managed to salvage one saving grace from the whole exaggerated affair. He wrote to the Commandant-General, "The incident has shown how easily somewhat remote points can be reached by reliefs in case of emergency. The advanced party of BSAP (sent out from Salisbury to Inyanga) covered 120 miles by rail and 52 miles by road in 24 hours." A well-conducted troop movement, even though subsequently proved to have been quite unnecessary, has always endowed those responsible for it with a measure of satisfaction.

## Chapter Eighteen

## CRIME AND PUNISHMENT

THE 1904 CENSUS gave the towns a white population of about 7000 — men, women and children, of whom two-thirds were men. It is difficult to guess how many natives there were in the towns, but they were probably about the same number. The natives were, of course, migrants. Their real homes were with their fellow tribesmen in the Reserves. They came into the towns to earn enough money to pay the poll tax and they went back to their kraals every rainy season to make sure their wives ploughed their lands and sowed the mealies.

The white settlers were already a miscellaneous lot. The conventional picture of the early settler in Rhodesia has always been that of a fine physical specimen, toughened by hard living, conscientiously shouldering the burden of building a civilised society in an unpromising wilderness. For some, that was a fair enough description; others were just ordinary human beings doing their limited best. But there was already a surprising proportion of less worthy citizens; and the cases reported in those earlier days in the Bulawayo and Salisbury newspapers, of whites prosecuted for a colourful range of crimes, bid fair to rival in number and variety the reports in the same papers today when the white population is 20 times the size. It is impossible to make direct comparisons but reading the daily reports of cases in the "police courts" (as they were known in those days) and at the periodical criminal sessions of the High Court, one gets the impression that the incidence of crime by whites then was not much lower than it is today in spite of the enormous difference in the size of the population. There were no drug offences, of course, and no traffic offences (although one report in the Chronicle in 1903, headed "Furious Riding" tells of a Mr. P. Cohen who was fined five shillings, or in default 24 hours imprisonment, for "riding a bicycle at a greater speed than 8 mph to the danger of the public in Wilson Street." And Constable Thomas Murphy, "by his vigilance stopped the flight of three cyclists who had ventured out after dark without lamps. All three were apprehended within an hour." One, a small boy, was fined one shilling). But fraud, embezzlement, forgery, murder, robbery, theft, incest, illicit gold dealing, keeping brothels and supplying liquor to natives, were normal occurrences. A fair proportion of the accused were acquitted by the juries on the flimsiest of extenuating circumstances, and acquittals always brought a round of cheers from the spectators in court which, according to the Press reports, was usually "instantly suppressed". The juries occasionally added to their verdicts expressions of sympathy for the accused. There were no juvenile courts. A white boy aged 15, "the author of certain obscene writing on the window of the Post Office," was given eight cuts; one aged 14, found guilty of stealing a bicycle, given 15 cuts. Their trials were held in open court and the boys' names published. "Two young women of colour" were charged on the same day with keeping brothels in Bulawayo. One was fined 30 shillings, or seven days; the other £4, or 14 days. The magistrate felt it as well to explain the difference in the penalties: one of the brothels appeared to have been conducted in an orderly manner, he said; the other had not. "If you carry on this business in future," he advised the second defendant, "you had better endeavour to carry it on in a quiet manner."? The defendant graciously thanked His Worship for the advice. While, as an example of considered justice, Mr. Jacobs was fined £2 or 14 days, being the owner of two dogs which, although properly muzzled in terms of the regulations to prevent rabies, had the temerity to rush out and bark at Corporal Gordon of the BSAP who was riding into camp at Bulawayo from Lower Rangemore Farm.

The same incidence of lawlessness prevailed in the country as in the towns, so in theory it was incumbent on both police forces — the BSAP and the SRC — to deal with it. In practice, the BSAP handled it superficially, as if it were an unreasonable intrusion in their affairs and the SRC muddled on as best they could without much more success. There was no detective branch, no businesslike criminal investigation. Members of both forces merely pursued the cases assigned to them in accordance with their individual stocks of common sense, or lack thereof.

Two of the earliest recorded cases of major crime in Bulawayo bear out this lack of professional competence. In February 1903 the Standard Bank in Bulawayo consigned £1450 by registered mail to the Geelong Mine in the Gwanda district — £650 in bank notes, the rest in gold and silver coins. It was the regular practice for the numerous mines in the country districts to receive the monthly pay rolls in this manner. The money was put on this occasion into various paper bags and three tins, all wrapped up together in one brown paper parcel, sealed with the bank seal. The parcel was delivered to the Post Office to be sent forward in the registered bag.

There was a police post at the Geelong Mine, at which the BSAP operated the postal agency — the usual arrangement in the outside districts at the time. Trooper Newton officiated as the acting post-master, and when Zeederberg's coach arrived with the mail early one morning he and Trooper Lawrence began to sort it out. When, having released the padlock with the appropriate key, they opened the registered bag, an empty paper packet fell out, then an empty tin and a brick, and finally two more tins, both of which had been opened. They called the sergeant, Sergeant Hough; they called the secretary of the mine. They all counted what money was left, which amounted to £99.16s. Somebody had extracted £1350. Lieutenant Murray, stationed at Gwanda, collected the exhibits, placed them in a big bag and took them to Bulawayo.

Meanwhile, as soon as the loss had been reported, the SRC in Bulawayo had smartly arrested two post office officials, Thomas Glanville and Reginald Benfield, and charged them with the theft. They were lodged for the night in Grey Street gaol. As was usual when white men were arrested, the public were indignant — not at the offenders, but at the police. As the Chronicle reported, "The authorities, recognising the feeling of indignation by the public at young men being publicly escorted through the streets in company with native offenders" — this was the gravamen of the complaint — "very wisely had Messrs. Glanville and Benfield removed from the gaol to the court earlier in the morning." Their friends and sympathisers crowded the court house. "The defendants looked very well after their confinement in gaol," the overtly sympathetic Chronicle continued. "The magistrate very considerately allowed seats to be provided for them in the dock."

The police had virtually no evidence against the accused except that they, as well as a number of other post office workers, had handled the packages from the Bank. Lieutenant Murray deposed that the brick found in the bag when it arrived at Geelong was not the sort of brick made at the mine, and he advanced the unsolicited information that he had seen bricks of that sort lying at the back of the Post Office building in Bulawayo. The magistrate — it was a preliminary examination — spent two days listening to a confused jumble of evidence on how the accused, and all sorts of other people at the same time, had come and gone at odd hours of the day and night in the office where the registered bags were stored; how, in the course of their duties and other activities, they had locked and reopened office doors and safes and blithely exchanged custody of keys and seals — all this presented to the court without any lucid thread of evidence specifically connecting the accused with the theft; nor any convincing proof that it had actually been perpetrated in the Post Office itself and not at the bank or on the coach on the way to Geelong.

Nevertheless, the two accused were committed for trial at the High Court, where the whole confused story was repeated; but the jury found them not guilty and embellished their verdict by expressing their sympathy with the defendants, while the spectators in court burst into the customary cheering. No further action in the Geelong case ever ensued and so the police failed to bring to justice the perpetrators of the first major theft in Bulawayo — unless, in truth, they had been right all along in charging Glanville and Benfield and the jurymen had simply allowed their sympathies to override their juridical duty.

The second early recorded case of major crime in Bulawayo which the police bungled, in a far more serious manner, was that of the murder of a Mrs. Ross, described as an "old lady of 57", in her house "at the upper end" — presumably the north end, near 1st Avenue — of Main Street, in November 1905. Mrs. Ross had a granddaughter named Gertrude Milne, who was 18. Gertrude slept with her grandmother in a single bed. A boy aged 14, named Bertram Wood, also lived in the house, sleeping in an adjoining room. He is stated in the report to have been Gertrude's brother, presumably a half-brother. There was a lodger in the house, but he slept in a room with a separate, outside entrance. Disappointingly, perhaps, the lodger does not come into the story, except that he was wakened at two o'clock one morning by Gertrude rattling on his door, telling him that her grandmother had had her throat cut.

The lodger wisely refrained from going into the house and setting eyes on the gruesome sight of Mrs. Ross with her throat cut. He called the neighbours and, in his own words, he scoured the neighbourhood "for upwards of an hour" looking for a policeman, without success. It seemed beyond him to realise that if he had gone straight to the police station he could have been there in 20 minutes.

One of the neighbours cycled to a Dr. Strong's house (wherever that may have been) and Dr. Strong gave him a note to the police station where, miraculously if belatedly, he found a sergeant on duty. There seems to have been a reluctance for anybody to venture to the station on his own initiatve.

The police when they arrived found the old lady on the floor beside the bed, demonstrably with her throat cut. They could find no weapon except a slightly stained kitchen knife, which they produced in court as the murder weapon, although they had not taken the trouble to have it properly examined and the stain proved subsequently not to be blood. Gertrude declared that her grandmother must have rolled off the bed after being attacked while she lay beside her, although what might conceivably have been an alarming disturbance had not, according to her story, wakened her.

The police, for want of a better suspect, arrested young Bertram Wood and charged him with murder, principally on the grounds that he had washed his vest the next morning, although he had been wearing it on the night of the murder and they had not noticed any suspicious stains at the time. Gertrude had a small blood-stain on her nightdress, but she claimed a little unconvincingly that this must have happened while she had been lying asleep beside the victim when the gory deed was committed. There were no other blood stains on the bed; all the mess was on the floor. However, the police decided to arrest Gertrude too and charge her as an accessory to the crime. She turned up in court dressed dramatically from head to foot in the deepest mourning.

The police proffered no motive for the crime, no evidence of how the boy could possibly have done it, nor how or why the girl could have helped him. Nor was there any evidence that the three members of the family had not been on the best of terms. However, Bertram and Gertrude were both committed for trial and held in custody, within the insalubrious precincts of Grey Street prison. But a month later they were brought back before the magistrate, who told them, "The Attorney-General has gone to considerable trouble to review your case" — which, considering the circumstances, was the least he could do. "I have read a letter from him enclosing a warrant for your liberation. At the request of your lawyer I wish to inform you publicly that you are discharged," adding gratuitously, "I have much pleasure in doing this." The Press report said "There was a faint murmur of applause in court. A smile of relief lit up Miss Milne's face. Wood showed apparent indifference."

Twelve months later, the police made some partial and belated amends for their inept conduct of the case. The case had originally been handled by the SRC, but this time it was the BSAP who rose to the occasion and found some suspicious property in a native kraal. A native named Ben was arrested and Gertrude Milne was brought up from Johannesburg, where she had gone to live, and she was able to identify some clothes and crockery, which had been found in Ben's possession, as taken from her grandmother's house. There was no evidence against Ben of anything but theft, but he was nevertheless charged with murder. Indeed, the evidence was so slim that at his first High Court trial the jury failed to agree. Juries — all white of course — were not noted for liberality in trials of natives, particularly if the offence was what was known as "black on white", and so the very fact that there was disagreement about convicting him suggested strong doubt of the validity of the charge. The judge ordered a retrial. Four days later, Ben was tried again with a new jury and less than five hours after the court had assembled he was found guilty and sentenced to death. The docket was thankfully closed.

From its earliest days, Rhodesia as a gold-mining country has offered ready temptation to the bullion thief. It is surprising how few instances there have been of real full-blooded bullion robbery, considering the amount of gold in bars which must have been transported over the years in open, unprotected vehicles, from mines isolated in the depth of the country, along unfrequented roads.

The only bullion robbery on the open highway in the country's history was carried out in daylight as early as 1906, and has left a permanently jarring effect on the annals of the BSAP. In this case the robbery was made on what was, for those days, the well-used main road from Filabusi to Bulawayo. A Mr. Plaistowe, the secretary of the Killarney mine, set off one Saturday morning, armed with a loaded revolver, accompanied by a native driver, George, in a Cape cart drawn by four mules, carrying 1744 ounces of gold in bars — worth, at the time, about £6000 — the current output of the Killarney-Hibernia and Celtic mines.

At about 10 o'clock they were six miles from the Filabusi police camp, on the way towards Balla Balla, where the road, which was bordered by fairly thick bush, dipped into a dry river bed. As the mules strained to pull the cart up the farther slope, three men, so Mr. Plaistowe subsequently alleged, sprang out of the bush brandishing rifles. The men's heads were masked by hoods of dark cloth, with slits cut out for their eyes, and caps pulled down over their foreheads, in true bandit style. "Throw out the gold," one of them shouted, according to Mr. Plaistowe, "hold up your hands or I'll shoot and you'll be a dead man!"

Plaistowe said he put his hand down to grab the revolver which should have been on the seat beside him, but the jolting of the cart had moved it out of his reach. Because he failed to comply with the robber's demand, one of the masked men fired at the leading mules. One mule was killed instantly and another wounded. As the wounded animal struggled, the cart tilted sideways and Plaistowe was pitched out into the road. The robber covered him with his rifle and again threatened to shoot unless he set off back along the road, whence the cart had come. Plaistowe, by his own account, called out, "I know the game is up. You have got the upper hand of me. I can do nothing." He started walking, not daring as he confessed afterwards, to look round to see what the robbers were doing.

Meanwhile, George the driver had prudently departed into the bush. He made his way to a store near the Marvel mine where he found a Zeederberg coach drawn up, whose passengers had heard the shooting but had thought that someone was out hunting. Once the alarm was raised the BSAP at Filabusi sent out a mounted patrol to search the neighbourhood. As the Chronicle proudly announced the next morning, "The news was telegraphed to Bulawayo within three hours of the actual occurrence." Another mounted patrol set out from the BSAP camp in Bulawayo, while a sergeant and a constable from the SRC, presumably regarded as specialists in crime detection, were hopefully sent off to Balla Balla by train.

Under the headline, "Robbery under Arms," the Chronicle declared in a burst of righteous cliche, "The police authorities must strain every nerve, and must leave no stone unturned, until they have hunted these criminals down ... It is not too much to say," the article went on admonishingly, "that, up to the present, the proved capacity of the police has not been such as to inspire unbounded confidence. They have a chance now to show what mettle they are made of."

They showed their mettle, good and bad. They searched the veld round the scene of the crime and came across one gold bar weighing 767 ounces. The robbers had obviously found the swag too heavy to be carried away all at once. With exemplary perspicacity, they deduced that the robbers would return to claim the bar and they set up a guard to watch it. They were not to be disappointed. One of the robbers showed up. He was a BSAP trooper.

Joseph Phelan, an Irishman by name and nature, had joined the force a couple of years before and had served most of his time at Filabusi. The Chronicle described him as "tall, bony, fair, with open countenance, 35 to 40 years old". Some months previously he had surprised a newly-joined recruit, Trooper Page, by scarcely veiled suggestions that working together they might hold up a consignment of gold from one of the neighbouring mines, suggestions which Page had interpreted as being not altogether frivolous. Indeed, Page seems to have listened to his talk with some interest and to have decided against collaborating with him, not from any moral scruples, but because he doubted if Phelan's plans were practicable. In any case, Page never made any report to his superior officer, which would have been the least he would have done had he not had some sympathy for the idea himself.

A few days before the robbery, Phelan had been granted a week's leave, which he spent quite openly with an acquaintance, Jack Friend, who was working the nearby Green Oak Mine on tribute. Someone operating a mine himself and legitimately sending in gold to the bank would be the only possible outlet for stolen bullion. As soon as Phelan had been arrested he had been sent to Bulawayo in leg-irons, and the next day the police arrested Friend as an accomplice. Four days later a third man, MacMurray, was arrested too — hopefully to complete the trio of bandits — but he was released after being held for three weeks. The problem was that nobody could identify the masked men and the police had no circumstantial evidence against MacMurray, such as they had against Phelan and Friend. Plaistowe could not help — he was in a state of nervous collapse; and the evidence of George the driver was confined to, "I saw a man standing by the side of the road with a gun as if he was going to shoot. When he wanted to shoot, I jumped out." After a preliminary examination, at which Plaistowe was the principal, if somewhat incoherent, witness for the prosecution, Phelan and Friend were committed for trial at the High Court in Bulawayo. At the trial, four months later, Trooper Page told the court of Phelan's remarkable interest in the transport of gold bars and his efforts to seduce him, Page, from the rigid path of duty. He came out quite openly in his evidence with the propositions Phelan had made to him, without any apparent belief that they might reflect on him personally. A fellow trooper from Filabusi, named Urquhart, called as a witness by the defence, declared that Page had once said to him, "Don't have anything to do with Phelan, he is no class. The first chance I get I shall send him along" — an admission which had the intended effect of discrediting Page's evidence.

But Phelan was also to have another stroke of undeserved fortune. Mr. Plaistowe, the principal witness in the case, was unable to give evidence at the trial. During the four months which had elapsed, he had been certified insane and was now in Fort England, the mental asylum in Grahamstown, where he was later to die. Whether his experience that morning on the road from Filabusi had contributed to his unfortunate condition is not on record, but it certainly could not have helped a potentially disturbed mind. The evidence he had given at the preliminary examination was read to the court but in the          circumstances it lacked conviction. The jury retired to consider their verdict for less than half an hour, and returned to pronounce both prisoners not guilty. Once again, the Chronicle reported, "The verdict was received with loud cheers, which were instantly suppressed".

The High Court sat in Bulawayo in the court room on the first floor of Agency Chambers, on the corner of Main Street and 6th Avenue, under an impressively pinnacled tower. (The court was to continue there for another 32 years until the new High Court, at the top of 8th Avenue, was opened in 1938. Agency Chambers and the old court room, by then partitioned into tatty offices, were burnt down in 1966.) When the trial finished and Phelan was released, he was congratulated by his numerous sympathisers and he walked jauntily along Main Street to the corner of Selborne Avenue where Page happened to be standing outside the Exchange Bar. According to Phelan, who perforce appeared in the magistrates's court again next day, Page "had a sarcastic smile on his face," so Phelan called him a liar and removed the smile with three telling blows. Someone caught hold of Phelan and Page hit him back. Urquhart was following close behind, so Page went for him too.

Phelan was arrested and taken to the guard room at the Camp, and he and Urquhart were charged next morning with creating a disturbance in a public place. Phelan was still described as a trooper in the BSAP. When a police witness said that Page had given no provocation for the assault, Phelan's attorney asked him, "Don't you think that four months imprisonment, mainly on Page's evidence," — Phelan had been in custody since the preliminary examination — "on a charge of which he is eventually proved innocent, is any provocation?" The Magistrate interrupted and told the witness not to answer the question. "However," said the magistrate, pronouncing Phelan and Urquhart guilty, "there are mitigating circumstances, otherwise I would have sent both the accused to prison for six months." He fined them £10 each.

Phelan was at last dismissed from the BSAP. A week later he sent a long letter to the Chronicle. "As many of your readers will remember," he wrote, "I was a resident of Grey Street gaol for five months. On arrival I was put in leg irons and told to have a bath in a long wooden trough ... " and he went on to describe his prison experiences in sordid detail. Six months later he was in court again, charged with theft from the Pavilion Hotel, where he was now employed as a barman. But the Phelan luck held and once more he was discharged; thereafter, to the relief of the police authorities, he at last passed out of the public eye.

Early in 1904 the headquarters of the BSAP were transferred from Bulawayo to Salisbury. This sounds an improbable statement when the evidence is clear that police headquarters had originally been established in Salisbury — after all, Salisbury was the capital and in any case Bulawayo as a settlement had not even existed at the time — and there is no apparent evidence of a formal move to Bulawayo at any time later. But in 1898, Colonel J.S. Nicholson succeeded Sir Richard Martin as Commandant-General; and although the C-G was the general officer commanding all armed forces (including the Southern Rhodesia Volunteers, admittedly the only military unit besides the BSAP at the time) he was actually the effective commander of the four divisions of the BSAP because each was under an independent commandant and there was no other overall authority.

Colonel Nicholson, who had been sent out to Bulawayo by the Imperial Government to assume command of the Matabeleland Mounted-Police in 1896, had not moved from Bulawayo when he was appointed Commandant-General. Whether his immobility was a personal preference or an official policy is not on record. All BSAP General Orders from 1898 to 1903 were issued from "General Headquarters, Bulawayo." When Colonel Nicholson retired he was succeeded as Commandant-General by Colonel Chester Master, who had not had any direct association with the BSAP and who set up his headquarters in Salisbury. At the same time Colonel Bodle, who had been Commandant of the BSAP Matabeleland Division since 1898, was promoted to be the first Commandant of the amalgamated BSAP. The Commandant-General, therefore, became a more elevated personage, having the Rhodesia Regiment now under his wing as well, and was farther removed from responsibility for the BSAP than his predecessor had been when the divisions were separate units. Bodle had spent a considerable part of his five years as Commandant of the Matabeleland Division on active service in South Africa, but whenever he returned to Rhodesia he made Bulawayo his headquarters. No doubt it was part of the official plan, when the 1903 amalgamation of the force was effected, that headquarters should be moved to the capital, but Bodle had nevertheless assembled his original headquarters establishment in the Police Camp in Bulawayo.

The formal move from Bulawayo to Salisbury was made in February 1904 and a correspondent wrote to the Bulawayo Chronicle, "I am sorry that the Mayor has been unable to fall in with the suggestion of giving the BSAP a public farewell on the occasion of their departure from Bulawayo. But Colonel Bodle must feel very grateful at the reception" (surely, the valediction) "he and his men received on Monday evening on the departure of the Salisbury train. Although no band was present, a good number of the public made up for the loss of music by the heartiness of their cheering".

The seeds of resentment in Bulawayo, at the transfer to Salisbury of activities public and private, had already been sown and were to multiply over many succeeding years. Not that rumours of moves were always well-founded. As the Chronicle said the very next week, "The Attorney-General said that the rumour that the High Court was to be moved to Salisbury came as a surprise to him and was unfounded. This is satisfactory, but it does not affect the main argument that there is a tendency to drag things Salisbury way" — a tendency which was to burgeon during the next 70 years. Commerce in Bulawayo, setting the style for future generations, complained of the town's loss of purchasing power, on a presumed scale which would have surprised most of the impecunious troopers.

But, unreasonably or not, the move implanted the first suspicion among the people of Bulawayo that the Company, economising at the expense of the settlers, had little regard for their protection. It was a theme that was to resound again and again over the years. In July 1905, Major Robert Gordon, who was to become a prominent Rhodesian citizen over the next 40 years — culminating his career as Honorary Colonel of the 2nd Battalion of the Rhodesia Regiment — wrote to the paper, "Economy is being overdone in the sweeping reductions lately made in the Police force. Almost daily we hear accounts of burglary. I understand there are only two white policemen for night duty, one for the town and one for the suburbs. This is quite sufficient to invite the present state of lawlessness and if the inhabitants are not protected from these scoundrels (be they white or black) then I sincerely hope the authorities will show leniency towards anyone who protects his property and perhaps his life by shooting first".

The Mayor referred Colonel Gordon's complaint to the Attorney-General, who replied that there were 32 white and 22 black members of the SRC in Bulawayo — although one of the town councillors begged publicly to doubt the accuracy of his statement. So far as he knew, the councillor said, there were only four. He agreed there were more on the establishment, but most of the men, he declared to the Council, "are engaged in 'mental' work". The Attorney-General had added in his statement that a great deal of unnecessary fuss was being made and that the town had "as many white police as it deserves and is as well off as any town in South Africa". "That reply," said the Chronicle, "both in its tone and the arguments advanced, would have disgraced a sulky school-boy. Bulawayo is one of the worst policed towns in South(ern) Africa."

In October 1905 the paper published another complaint, on a different but already familiar theme. The subject of whether or not the native police should be armed had been contentious, even among the higher authorities, for some time. In May 1903 the Administrator had written to the Commandant-General, "I think that the native police should not at present be armed with rifles. If guns are absolutely necessary they should be shotguns, but I think on most occasions sticks will be sufficient armament." The subject had never been definitively resolved.

"One is compelled," wrote the Chronicle's current correspondent, "against one's will to lose heart with everything connected with Rhodesia. In 1896 it was an open secret that the Rebellion would never have taken place if those responsible for the native police programme had been dismissed from the service of the Chartered Company before their insane thoughts had been allowed to be put into practical form. Then, unfortunately for many lives, and for the country even today, there was a native Matabele police force trained to use the rifle. And, needless to say, how quickly the blackguards used it to kill and murder the whites in a most bloodthirsty manner ... Yesterday, passing the shooting butts, to my dismay and bewilderment, I saw about 12 of these niggers of the same blood as the murderers of '96 taught the art of using the rifle ..."

The letter was a clarion call and on the following Saturday night the citizens of Bulawayo gathered convivially in the Grand Hotel to hold a protest meeting and condemn the Government's action in training native policemen to shoot. "It is plain," somebody said, "that the plan has been to cut down the BSAP to almost vanishing point and to substitute a cheaply paid force of native police trained in the use of the rifle." Behind the scenes at BSAP Headquarters the Chief Staff Officer was anxiously reporting to the Administrator: "This was an isolated case of target practice by district native police and the result of a misunderstanding. A circular has been sent to all district police inspectors reminding them that native constables are not required to undergo any target practice without instructions from headquarters." It was fortunate, perhaps, that the CSO's report never came to the ears of the good people of Bulawayo. Its implication — that although the native constables might be armed, they were to be denied any target practice — might conceivably have been interpreted as making them even more potentially dangerous.

However, a decision was at last made and published in Force Orders on 16 February 1906. "For ordinary duties," the Orders laid down, "district native police raised in 1903 (450 Southern Rhodesian natives) will carry native arms only (knobkerries) and rifles will only be issued for purposes of drill or carrying out armed duties in company with or in charge of a European member. The Reserve Company at Headquarters of 150 Angoni native police are required to be trained as part of the military force which might conceivably be called on to protect white settlers against natives in Southern Rhodesia. This Company, which should always be ready for duty in quelling any minor breach of the peace or disturbance among local native inhabitants, to be issued with Martini-Henrys and five rounds per man for target practice." It was not a decision which would have appealed to the protest meeting at the Grand Hotel.

Early in November the hypothesis of inadequate police protection in Bulawayo was strengthened by a newspaper report that "a dastardly attempt was made last night to hold up and rob three ladies and a boy at 12.30 a.m. by four white men in the Market Square." The ladies and the boy were in an open carriage, driving home from a Presbyterian bazaar. One of the assailants seized the horse's head, while another wrenched the whip from the driver's hand. The horse bolted down the street, pulling up obligingly at the Imperial Hotel. No doubt suitably solaced, the ladies continued their journey towards Hillside and on the road they met by chance two policemen to whom, somewhat unavailingly in the circumstances, they reported the alarming incident. The policemen (one assumes they were SRC) were ungallant enough to allow the ladies to continue their journey unescorted, and when the ladies arrived at their house at Hillside they were ambushed again by two of their former assailants. They wisely threw away the parcels they were carrying — which contained some trinkets left over as unclaimed prizes at the bazaar — and the dastardly robbers picked up the swag and disappeared.

This was manna for the Chronicle. "This report adds emphasis to our repeated assertions that the local police force is incapable of dealing properly and effectively with the criminal classes in Bulawayo. It should not be difficult in a white population of 4 000 to mark down persons of doubtful or suspicious character and either get them removed from amongst us or keep them under close surveillance. The same may be said of occasional obnoxious visitors. In spite of rather contemptuous assertions by the Attorney-General we are firmly convinced that the force is insufficient in number. We need men on the streets at night rather than mounted on fat ponies at street corners in the broad daylight hours ... If it is foolish to rely on the police for protection it will be necessary for people to go armed and rely on themselves."

But it was the "black on white" offence which worked up the settlers to their most incensed mood — particularly, of course, when the victim of an attack was a woman. In 1904 the death sentence, although not mandatory, was introduced even for attempted rape of a white woman by a black man. In one reported case the trial judge himself said, "No violence appears to have been used. It was more of a sneaking attempt to get hold of the woman than anything else." He at least forebore to pass the death sentence in this instance, but he sentenced the culprit to 36 lashes with a sjambok and nine years' imprlsonment.

Another "dastardly" case — to use the newspaper's favourite word — of an attempted rape of a white woman was reported at Selukwe. "It was only natural," said the paper, "For the Mine men to endeavour to secure the culprit and wreak their vengeance upon him." They managed to catch up the train which they believed was taking the prisoner from Selukwe to Gwelo, at the first halt on the way, but the BSAP had forestalled them by taking him across the veld, tied to a horse. When he was finally tried at the High Court, he was found guilty of "assault with intent to commit rape of a white woman" and sentenced to death. But the Chronicle would have had it otherwise. Reporting the police action in frustrating the intending lynchers, the Chronicle said, "It could almost be wished that he had been caught, as a swift end might have been wrought while blood was still hot and a more vivid example given to the other natives of the white men's regard for the security of their womenkind ... there are cases where the slow tedium of a trial and the possible escape of a culprit through a legal technicality are not to be borne by an indignant and maddened populace".

Shortly after this a native was found one afternoon in an unoccupied bedroom of the Palace Hotel in Bulawayo. His intention was to commit a modest burglary. He was caught and held by a member of the staff on the upper floor of the hotel; a policeman arrived and he was handcuffed. In the meantime, the report that a native had been found in a bedroom, with its sinister implications, had been sufficient to attract a crowd, thirsty for blood, which gathered at the entrance to the hotel. The prisoner foolishly broke away from the policeman, vaulted the stair rail and escaped into Abercorn Street, pursued in full cry by the crowd, which overtook him at the corner of 8th Avenue. Fortunately for him the policeman was something of a sprinter and two other constables also appeared on the scene. With some difficulty, the three managed to rescue him from the crowd, which was intent on murder. The paper, reporting the prisoner's subsequent appearance in court said, "He bears traces of the handling he received on Friday. His face is cut in many places, his body shows many bruises, he limped slowly into the dock. Constable Rorke was also badly bruised and unfit for duty for three or four days. He lost his cap and baton during the struggle."

In Force Orders of 23 August 1906 there appeared an interesting sidelight — "It has been brought to the notice of the Commandant-General that there have been some recent instances of European members of the BSAP marrying native women in secret. The existence of such relations between the women of uncivilised native tribes and the members of a European police force is most undesirable from all points of view and cannot be permitted. It is therefore notified that in future any instance of intimate relations between a European member of the force and a native woman which is shown to exist either with or without observance of native marriage laws will be considered as a breach of discipline and the offender will be liable to summary dismissal from the force." This Order was followed shortly afterwards by a Circular from the CSO saying, "I have been informed by the Commandant-General that the practice of European Policemen living with native women, either by marriage or according to native law or otherwise, is not confined to Troopers: this is from information he has received."

It was during this period, before the absorption of the SRC by the BSAP (as shall be related in the next chapter), that camels were introduced into Rhodesia as an experimental form of transport for the police and other mobile services. The instigator of the idea seems to have been Colonel J.T.E. Flint, formerly of the 1st (Kings) Dragoon Guards, who had commanded the Mashonaland Division of the BSAP from 1899 until the separate divisions in Matabeleland and Mashonaland were amalgamated in 1903. There is no record of when Flint actually joined the force but he appears to have retired when Bodle took over and to have taken a farm in the Fort Victoria district. His chief claim to fame during his service was his ability as a swordsman mounted on a horse to cut an apple in half at a gallop. On other occasions, this time dismounted and stationary, he would slice the apple in half with a swift downward stroke of the sword while some intrepid junior held it for him in the palm of his outstretched hand. Considerately, he always checked the downward stroke in time to avoid any injury to the young man's hand. To be accorded the honour of holding the apple was a sign of preference for promotion. On one occasion he promoted a trooper to sergeant as a reward for drinking 10 glasses of beer in succession.

One report has it that in 1903 Flint was given six months' leave to go to India to buy camels. Whether this was before he retired and whether the animals were to be bought specifically for the police is not clear. The report did say, "These ruminants might be employed in the remote parts of Mashonaland to carry mail to such places as Mount Darwin, which is at present carried by native runners." But some camels were imported and the police certainly used them, notably at Gwanda and Tuli (where the camel stable still stands today) although the experiment does not seem to have been very successful. Unfortunately there are no accounts by individual members of their experiences with these animals — which, to say the least, were probably very uncomfortable; the only report that has been found says that when they first appeared in Manica Road in Salisbury, two horses took fright and crashed through a plate glass window. In 1905 a camel riding school was set up at the Transport Camp in Salisbury (presumably not part of the police depot). After two months a man named Matthews was given three camels to take to Sinoia. When they arrived, 30 horses got wind of them and stampeded into the veld. The whole idea was an enterprising experiment but it was probably doomed to failure from the start.

Another sidelight from Force Orders in 1906, addressed to Officers Commanding Troops: "The Police, not always being certain of the legality of actions taken by Europeans under the provision of certain Ordinances, have brought cases against them as 'test cases' in the magistrates' courts. This procedure is entirely wrong. It is unnecessary, vexatious, causes so-called offenders great inconvenience and perhaps pecuniary loss. It also brings the Police into disrepute amongst the European inhabitants who will come to look on the Force as persecutors instead of being for their protection."

In 1907 a Circular issued by the CSO read, "The season is approaching when the BSAP will be asked to escort Hut Tax collectors to various centres, and I wish again to impress on all ranks the necessity of using the utmost vigilance while on this duty. The number of unemployed and undesirables coming in from the other colonies is increasing" — the reference was to white immigrants — "and attempts to hold up the escorts may be anticipated. Escorts should consist of two Europeans and three Native Police. When the escort has to sleep out a regular guard must be posted at night." But events do not appear to have justified the CSO's alarm.

And it was in the same year, in September 1907, that the first fingerprint bureau was opened in Bulawayo.

## Chapter Nineteen

## GROWING PAINS

IN FEBRUARY 1909, control of the BSAP was formally transferred from the High Commissioner in-Cape Town to the Company's Administrator in Salisbury. Both the police forces in Rhodesia were now at last independent of the Imperial Government — with one reservation: the BSAP was debarred from undertaking any military operations unless the High Commissioner had first formally declared the force to be "on active service". In effect, this meant that such a declaration would be made only if Britain herself was at war; and the BSAP was consequently restricted to its civil role, although this made little difference to the force's traditional image and behaviour as a regiment of mounted infantry. As for the SRC, there never had been any suggestion that it was anything but a purely civil force, operating only in the towns.

Although the two forces were not formally amalgamated until 1 December 1909, the process of the BSAP taking over some of the town stations from the SRC had been going on for some time. Early in 1908 the stations at Fort Victoria and Enkeldoorn — neither of which, admittedly, was very urban in its circumstances — were taken over, and by June in that year the BSAP had assumed most of the town police functions in Umtali. The Rhodesia Herald reported that the same thing was likely to happen soon in Gwelo and that it was only a matter of time for Salisbury and Bulawayo to follow suit. "But", declared the Herald, "before amalgamation is effected, one of two things must occur. Either the SRC will be turned into a military force ... or the BSAP will lose its military character and become a civil force. The former will not be tolerated by the townspeople, who would protest to a man at being ruled by the military." Nevertheless, there was another consideration. "Under the existing regime," the Herald said, "members of the BSAP are not entitled to draw s uperannuation allowances" — that is to say, some payment on retirement — "but under the new order of things the men are sure to be granted this right, and an injustice against which they have long protested will be removed." It would be difficult, in the light of these comments, to decide whether the Herald opposed or supported the proposed change.

On 4 September that year the Gwelo Times reported that the Gwelo station had been transferred to the BSAP "Major Drury (commanding officer of the SRC) handed over this portion of his command to Colonel Bodle, Major Straker and Captain Masterman. The BSAP will undertake the duty of patrolling the town from today. The present members of the SRC will be transferred to the BSAP ... the object, of course, is economy, because the SRC are better paid than the BSAP ... The members of the SRC have always been an efficient force and all, from Sub-Inspector Shaw downwards, have earned the gratitude of the townspeople. The amalgamation is not popular with the members" — which, considering the pay situation, was understandable — "but they recognise the force of circumstances.

"In future," added the Gwelo Times, "the BSAP will not rank as a military body." This was, perhaps, not altogether true, but indirectly the implication was correct. "The only military force after amalgamation has been completed will be the SRV (Southern Rhodesian Volunteers) and with the increased responsibility of that force it is to be hoped that the Government will consider the advisability of making the Volunteers a more useful and efficient force." (Certainly all was not well with the SRV. In September 1908, at a meeting in Bulawayo of NCOs and men of the Western Division, all the 80 present at the meeting agreed to resign in a body, in protest against the Government's action in reducing the "capitation fee" — a monthly allowance to any member who provided his own horse — from £2 to £1. The decision of the meeting was reported to have been followed by "a flood of resignations." Five months later, following a report by a hurriedly convened Commission, the allowance was raised to £2 10s and the moral of the SRV was correspondingly reinflated.)

That the amalgamation of the two police forces was widely regarded simply as another scheme on the part of the Company to economise, was emphasised by the Bulawayo Chronicle. "The expressed (intention) of the Government is to reduce the pay of the SRC to bring both the forces into line. Objections have been raised in the Legislative Council, but these were overruled and the Government has persisted in its scheme, sanctioned by the High Commissioner." Indeed, in June 1909 Colonel Raleigh Grey — a former BBP man who had been imprisoned with Jameson after the Raid, had returned to Rhodesia in a private capacity and was now an elected member of the Southern Rhodesia Legislative Council — moved a resolution "that this Council recommends to the Administrator that the Southern Rhodesia Constabulary be maintained as a separate force." The people in the towns, he said, were objecting strongly to the efforts at amalgamation. Already, the experiment in Gwelo and Umtali had "proved an absolute failure." The members of the BSAP were young men recruited in England, mainly from the public schools, and although they were "admirable for the purpose required" he doubted if they were suitable as town policemen. The town police should consist of men with experience in constabulary work "and of a certain age." Young and inexperienced men were no good in the towns. (The incidence of sophisticated crime certainly tended to bear this out.) Most of the SRC had been recruited from the Metropolitan Police and the Royal Irish Constabulary. The strength of the SRC was now 66. (In 1903, it had been exactly double that number.) "Men in the towns," said Grey, "are experts and must be paid higher than the ordinary police."

Another member of Council, Mr. R.A. Fletcher, was generous enough to concede that the young men of the BSAP were "suitable for the work they at present carried out," but he doubted if they would make good town policemen. The present first-class constables in the towns, he said, were being paid 10 shillings a day. A BSAP trooper during his first three years was paid half that amount.) The proposal was to transfer them to the BSAP and reduce their pay to seven shillings. All the good men would leave the force.

The Attorney-General, a servant of the Company and impressed by the need for economy, opposed Grey's motion. He refuted the allegation that the experiments in Gwelo and Umtali had been a failure. "Nothing has occurred in either town," he said, "which might not have occurred with a policeman at every corner." He denied that the SRC had been recruited from men already trained as town policemen. Many of those who had been taken on were "raw to police work". He agreed that there had been a strong leavening of older men, but not so many of these still remained in the force. "There will be little change," he declared. "There will be a certain class of man for town work and another for country work. The amalgamation will lead to greater chances of promotion."

Major Raleigh Grey's motion was carried by the Council against the Attorney-General's opposition. Not that the motion had any effect. The Council was little more than a consultative assembly, created as a sop to counter the settlers' complaints of the Chartered Company's autocracy. All the effective power rested with the Executive Council, which was comprised of Company officials only. When the decision was finally taken by the Executive, in defiance of the Legislative Council's motion, and the intention to complete the amalgamation was announced, the Rhodesian Journal declared in a burst of near-sediton, "We trust that every BSAP trooper will refuse to volunteer to take over any of the constabulary duties, and public opinion will support them in making such a refusal. We are delighted that the Salisbury section of the BSAP are to a man standing out against such a proposal." No doubt there was some agitation in the BSAP ranks, such as the journal hinted, but no evidence can be found that there was any serious militant action. The Company's axe of economy was too sharp a bludgeon to encourage effective resistance.

In the event, amalgamation of the two forces was not completed until 1910, and whether the pay anomalies were resolved, or the force lost a number of good men, is unclear from the records. What is clear is that when the process had been completed, administration — as distinct from command — of the now combined force was placed directly under the Attorney-General. It took the authorities three years to learn the pitfalls of a situation where the same departmental authority controlled both the police and the judiciary, but they saw the light at last and the force was duly restored to the direct rule of the Administrator in 1913.

In June 1909 Bodle retired from the command of the BSAP. He was 53 at the time. He had been the first man to be attested in the BSACP and had served through all the excitements and changes of the force's history. He was the personification of the 19th century soldier who had risen from the ranks and in the process had acquired the dignity of command. He never wholly mastered the intricacies of English grammar: he was often heard to exclaim, "Us wants gentlemen in the Corps, us do." Most of the early officers of the force, seconded from the British Army, had started their army careers with commissions — this was the case with all Bodle's predecessors as Commandants of the previously separate divisions of the BSAP, and also with two of his later successors Major-General Edwards and Colonel Essex Capell. Men such as these with their upper-class backgrounds enjoyed substantial advantages when being considered for promotion, while Bodle's success had resulted solely from the strength of his personality, his character and his ability. His impact on the force, even as its RSM, was very different from Blatherwick's. Had Blatherwick lived, it is unlikely that he would have been promoted to command the force, nor would he have made a successful commander. It was not that, compared with Blatherwick, Bodle's was necessarily a less rugged personality — he had been no doubt as forceful an RSM as Blatherwick: he had had tough characters to control. But Bodle had an intellectual capacity which singled him out as a man competent to command; reinforced by his crowded experience of campaigning in Africa, he led the BSAP during its early years as a civil force — still with "a strong military element in its character" — with distinction, and he commanded a universal respect.

When Bodle retired he left Rhodesia and went back to England, where he married for the first time. Some years later when WWI seemed imminent he applied his military experience to organising the City of London National Reserve — a formation of the territorial army. As shall be related, he acted for some time during 1914 in selecting recruits in England for the BSAP — a fitting reversion to his original role in the force 25 years earlier. He was then given command of the Norfolk and Suffolk Territorial Brigade. He kept on pestering the War Office to send him to the front, but his age was against him. However, they finally succumbed to his importunities and in 1916, now aged 60, he went to France to command a Labour Battalion. But the rigours of the trenches at his time of life were too much even for his indomitable spirit and he retired in 1917 with the rank of Brigadier-General. In 1919, immediately after the end of the war, he was roped in again by the Company to find recruits for the BSAP. He died in 1924. A memorial copper plaque, first placed in the Regimental Institute in the Morris Depot of the BSAP in Salisbury, was unveiled by the Governor of Southern Rhodesia, Sir Cecil Rodwell, in the presence of the then Premier, the Hon. H.U. Moffat, in May 1930. The plaque was moved to the Police Chapel when the latter was built in 1963.

On Bodle's retirement, Major J.H. Fuller — the Chief Staff Officer and one time commanding officer of the SRC — was promoted to Lieutenant-Colonel and appointed Acting Commandant. He was given substantive rank the next year, in 1910, when the commanding officer of the BSAP became known — for a short time only — as Commissioner. (This was when the formal amalgamation of the forces had been completed.) Fuller was a relative newcomer to the BSAP. He had started his career at sea, in merchantmen under sail, but he had served in Africa for 23 years, having first joined the BBP as a trooper in 1886. He had transferred to the Cape Police when British Bechuanaland had been annexed to the Cape Colony and he had joined the Mashonaland Constabulary (the Salisbury town police) in 1899 with the rank of Chief Inspector. He had been appointed the first commanding officer when the SRC had been formed in 1903 and had become the Chief Staff Officer of the BSAP the following year. So, unlike almost every one of his BSAP colleagues, he had taken no part in the boisterous adventures of the force's early history.

Fuller does not seem to have made much mark during his two years in command. Indeed, his performance when the SRC went on strike in Bulawayo in 1903 had hardly augured a forceful commissionership. He was a bulky man with a kindly, benevolent expression, which was in no way impaired by his drooping white moustache; and although he may not have been a memorable commanding officer he was, by all appearances, an upright and warm-hearted person. One of his few claims to fame when commanding the force was to become involved in a civil action taken against him by a Trooper Oldrieve claiming £20 damages for false imprisonment and malicious prosecution. Oldrieve had lost the case but had appealed against the magistrate's judgement. The judge trying the appeal asked Oldrieve's counsel, "Your allegation of false imprisonment rests on the marching of the appellant under escort to the office and marching him away again" "Yes", replied the counsel. "It seems to me," said the Judge, "that the staff sergeants did all the imprisoning." He dismissed the appeal.

On 20 May 1909, while he was still Chief Staff Officer, Fuller had written to the Administrator, "In accordance with your verbal request, I submit names of officers who in my opinion should be superannuated on the amalgamation (of the BSAP and SRC]." This was written very shortly before Bodle retired in June and one is left with the suspicion that the Administrator had been waiting to consider these "superannuations" until Bodle was out of the way — for the names to be considered were all of men who had served with Bodle for a long time and had played their part in much of the force's early adventurous history.

Major Hopper headed Fuller's list. He was 52, and the only reason Fuller gave for including him was "on account of age". Hopper had joined the BSACP in September 1890 (the month of the occupation); he had deputised for Colonel H.F. White, the Commissioner of the RMP, when White had gone off with Jameson on the raid into the Transvaal in 1895; he had been left on his own, on that occasion, to police the whole of Mashonaland with less than 50 men; and he had been in charge of the detachment which built Fort Martin, near the Hartley Hills, during the operations against the Mashona rebels. Next on the list was Major Straker, age 46, also an 1890 recruit. He had gone on the raid with Jameson and had taken part in the relief of Mafeking. Fuller reported him as "unfit for his present rank through want of education and training in regular police work" — which, considering his history, was something of a harsh judgement. Captain Cazalet, now aged 54, who had been wounded during the Jameson Raid, was included "on account of his age for his present rank". Captain Chawner, another 1890 man and a Jameson raider, now 48 — who had distinguished himself as a trooper by giving unsolicited advice to his superior officer when a party of Boers threatened to cross the Limpopo into Matabeleland in 1891, and had more recently complained to the Commandant of the manner in which he, as an officer of the Police, had been addressed by a magistrate — was reported as "unfit for present rank through age, deafness and (lack of) training". Since none of the early members of the force had been given any training other than as recruits, the verdict on this score was perhaps a little severe. Lieutenant Gwynne, age 44 — whose only claim to fame had been as the member in charge at Inyanga in 1904 when everybody in the district, including himself, had predicted a violent native rising — was labelled as "unfit on account of age and weakness of character in command". And finally Lieutenant the Honourable Walter Yarde-Buller, an 1897 recruit now aged 50, was included in the list "on account of age". All Fuller's recommendations were in due course accepted and the officers retired, without any pensions; as also was the aptly named Captain Money, who had been the Paymaster for some years, but whose functions were now to be handed over to the Treasury.

Thus were summarily retired a number of good men who had served the force with their respective degrees of loyalty and ability through periods of exacting service and often under active service conditions. In fact, all these officers had attained their ranks during service in the Anglo-Boer war. There appears no record of when a compulsory retirement age was introduced in the force, but it was possibly soon after this occasion, because there is similarly no record of a repetition of these arbitrary "superannuations".

At about the same time Inspector Nesbitt was informed as tactfully as possible by Fuller that Major Drury, who had been commanding the SRC, was to be promoted to Chief Inspector (the senior officer), Mashonaland District, over Nesbitt's head. Nesbitt, the VC hero of the Mazoe Patrol, had actually held the rank of Major during the Anglo-Boer war, but in Fuller's minute on 1 October 1909 he gives Nesbitt only the honorary title of Captain. Nesbitt had been acting on occasion as a Native Commissioner. "It is considered necessary," Fuller wrote, "that the offices of Inspector, BSAP, and Native Commissioner should not be held by the same officer and separate appointments will be made from 1st October. Captain Nesbitt may elect which office he will hold. If he wishes to be transferred to the Native Department he will be recommended for appointment as a Native Commissioner at a salary of £580 and quarters." Influenced perhaps by having been passed over by Drury for the Chief Inspector's job, Nesbitt chose the Native Department. (He had been one of the early BSACP members enlisted in January 1890, No. 129 on the original roll, and posted as sergeant to 'C' Troop. Drury, on the other hand, had only become a member of the BSAP six years later, when he had transferred from the BBP with a number of others to join Jameson on the raid.) Thus it was, in this case, that the BSAP lost one of its most illustrious members. Nesbitt was then 42. (Drury was 45.) He was to serve as a Native Commissioner for another 18 years.

In 1910, soon after the amalgamation of the two forces, with the responsibility for policing the towns now firmly on the shoulders of the BSAP, the bogey of inadequate policing of Bulawayo once more raised its head. This time the complaint came from no less a person than the magistrate, Mr. Ryk Myburgh, who turned down an application by a Bulawayo citizen for a liquor licence on the grounds, openly expressed by him in court, that although Bulawayo's white population had increased, the police strength had been reduced "and the authorities in Salisbury do not seem to trouble." He added the provocative remark that "until the public in Bulawayo agitate for more police protection I personally am against granting further facilities for the sale of drink."

His remark stung the Attorney-General, who was always apt to be touchy on the subject of police strength in Bulawayo. The Attorney-General wrote testily to the Administrator, "Invitation to the public to agitate is distinctly serious. Mr Myburgh's apparent attempt to shield himself behind his quasi-judicial position must, in my opinion, fail, as even a Judge must confine himself to such evidence as is before him and to such matters as the decision of the case may require." But Myburgh, called to task by the Administrator, was unrepentant. "I enclose a letter from the Officer Commanding 'K' Troop (Inspector R.E. Murray)," he answered. "This shows the force has been decreased since 1904 (from 40 European constables to 17) with an increased population of approximately 2000, with 66 miles of streets. I have personally, and not infrequently, of late seen breaches of the law by both Europeans and natives in the public streets which could not possibly have occurred had the town been properly policed." All this had little effect on the Attorney-General. The magistrate's outburst in court, he told the Administrator, "is not a complaint against a mere arithmetical reduction but a statement of neglect of Bulawayo by the Government and an invitation to the public to seek redress." He added darkly, "Notice should be taken of the matter ... In this position, figures do not help us much but if they ever are of any assistance, I give the following ..." and he proceeded to enumerate the changing strength of the forces over the years, which is not without interest.

In 1904, according to the Attorney-General, the SRC had in all 141 officers and men and 52 natives; of these Bulawayo had five officers, 68 men and 21 natives. In 1908 the whole SRC had been reduced to six officers and 74 men (80 in all) with 64 natives, and still policed Bulawayo, Salisbury, Gwelo and Umtali. In 1910 the amalgamation of the forces had taken effect and the Bulawayo strength was now one officer, 30 men and 28 natives in town; two officers, 18 men and 21 natives in camp. "I mention the men in camp," said the Attorney-General, "because it is a clear understanding that these men can be used in town if required." Even so, it must be remembered that the town and district police were still distinct units, each recruited on a different basis, and the district police were still reluctant to be diverted from the agreeable routine of their rural patrols. In fact, as has already been related, the Attorney-General himself had admitted the clear distinction by telling the Legislative Council, when the subject of amalgamation was debated, "There will be a certain class of man for town work and another for country work." Considering the increase in Bulawayo's population, Mr. Myburgh's complaint seems to have been not altogether without substance, although it was somewhat unorthodox for a magistrate to criticise Government policy in open court and to invite public agitation. Whether he was duly disciplined does not appear to be on record. Nor is there any record of a significant increase in the Bulawayo force.

There was some drain from the strength of the BSAP generally at the time, caused by white members accepting commissions in the Barotse Native Police. The Administrator of North West Rhodesia (the western portion of present Zambia, also administered by the BSA Company) wrote to the Administrator of Southern Rhodesia early in 1911 saying, "The Board (of the Company) are anxious that I should give the commissions as far as possible to men in your police force; but I should like to have men on a certain amount of probation because the older and experienced (white) non-commissioned officers, who will never receive commissions, are inclined to grumble at promotions from outside unless the young officers brought in are both well educated and well qualified. Regarding Corporal Sillitoe," he went on, "I understand he is leaving the force in April in any case, on completion of three years, and is quite willing to take his discharge now and take his chance on probation for a commission in the BNP."

Subsequently to this transfer to Barotseland, Corporal Sillitoe, after service in East Africa during the 1914-18 war, joined the Colonial Service as a political officer in Tanganyika. In 1923 he returned to England to become Chief Constable of a succession of British police forces — and ultimately as Sir Percy Sillitoe, KBE, Director-General of Britain's Security Services. (Not unreasonably, the BSAP likes to believe that his three years' apprenticeship as a policeman in Rhodesia set him firmly on course to a distinguished career.) When Trooper Cussans, another candidate for a commission in the BNP, was released by the BSAP, the Secretary of the Law Department in North West Rhodesia wrote somewhat plaintively, "The Commandant (of the

BNP) will be obliged if Trooper Cussans can be allowed to take his uniform with him, they having nothing in store."

From another sector of Southern Rhodesia's border at about that time, the Attorney-General received from a certain gentleman (who shall be nameless but who was a Justice of the Peace in the Deka district, between Wankie and the Bechuanaland border) a complaint of lack of protection for the 50-odd Europeans who were spread out over a considerable area. The Masarwa — Bushmen from Bechuanaland — were, he said, "constantly dodging to and fro across the border and although murder and other crimes have been committed, the culprits have eluded capture. The white farmers suffer from grass burning and they anticipate that cattle thieving will take place before long." There was a BPP station at Kazungula, 75 miles to the north, whence a patrol was sent only very occasionally down the western, Bechuanaland, side, of the border road; while any BSAP patrols on the eastern side, from Victoria Falls or Wankie, were even rarer. He asked for two native policemen to be attached to him. "I will make myself responsible for them and use them to detect crime and report to the police at Wankie."

The Attorney-General was not averse to the proposal. "He is a very old settler," he wrote to the Administrator. "It might well be worth considering his suggestion as a cheap way of policing the neighbourhood. "The Attorney-General's mania for economy always took the upper hand. But Inspector R.E. Murray, OC 'K' Troop — whose headquarters were in Bulawayo but covered the whole of northern Matabeleland — was not so enthusiastic. "I am not prepared to recommend," he reported, "that (this man) be given two native police. Recently there has been a lot of correspondence in connection with illegal arrests across the border in Bechuanaland. These arrests were made on his instructions to the native police. Some time back some of the natives were flogged by his orders and he was convicted of assault at Wankie. I have to caution every NCO who goes to Wankie to be very careful about this man and take no instructions from him as a Justice of the Peace except when he issues a warrant ... the Government would regret it in a very short time if they granted his request." The Administrator supported Murray and turned down the gentleman's proposal — to the disappointment, no doubt, of the Attorney-General.

At about the same time the Native Commissioner of the Bulalima-Mangwe district — down on the south-west border — reported that one of the Angoni native police (the Reserve Company, actually trained as a military force) engaged on a cattle cordon, had discharged his rifle uncomfortably close to a local native's head and he had been convicted of assault. "Although this is the first prosecution against the Native Police," the Native Commissioner wrote, "there have been previous complaints about their bearing and behaviour. It appears to be a pity they are allowed to carry rifles at all, except when required on some special duty in a remote part of the district where they might chance on a lion." The member in charge of the Tati Concession Border Guard — that is to say, the BSAP unit on the Bechuanaland border — a Lieutenant who boasted the elegant name of Halliday Lidderdale, sprang to the defence of his men. "I have had only one complaint two years ago," he reported. "One of the Chief's men said a native policeman was courting his daughter." But Halliday Lidderdale had been prepared to brook no nonsense. "I put a stop to the affair," he proudly declared. "As regards the bearing and behaviour of the native police, they keep very much to themselves. They certainly carry rifles on patrol and they carry their arms in a soldierly way. The white residents have often commented on their respectful demeanour, sober habits and discipline — so different from the local natives. I naturally feel that the complaint reflects discredit on me and I am anxious, if anything is wrong, to put it right. But as I have kept the native police strictly, perhaps over-strictly, in hand, I do not anticipate finding anything seriously amiss." The Native Commissioners were still, so it seems, ready to be over-critical of the police.

There were others prepared to be critical, not so much perhaps of the members themselves but of the system. In May 1912 the editor of the Rhodesia Journal took it on himself to draw to the personal attention of the High Commissioner in Cape Town an article by a contributor to his paper. "We are certain," the article had declaimed, without too close an adherence to syntax, "that the public of Rhodesia are not aware that the members of the BSAP are subjected to treatment that is absolutely (sic) worse than that inflicted upon any soldier, however bad his offence, so long as the 'crime' is merely a crime against disciplinary rules. Do they realise that constables, for not very heinous misdemeanours, can be and are constantly being tried by the superior officer who is invested with the power of a magistrate and can inflict sentences of fines or imprisonment or both, and the policemen in question have to serve out their sentences in the common jail, treated as ordinary criminals. Found guilty of some irregularity in connection with patrolling his beat, dressed in convict's clothes, put in with convicts to share their labour, food and conversation; not because he, like them, had been guilty of a serious crime but because he had, it was alleged, broken a disciplinary police rule."

The instigator of the cause of this publicity had been a Constable Douglas, who had made a habit of diverting his night beat in Bulawayo, so that he could find some convenient bench on which to rest himself from his arduous duties. In four months' service with the force he had already earned two entries on his defaulter sheet and had finally been reported as "absent from outside Lennon's store at the required time and from outside the Royal Hotel at 4 a.m." On that occasion he had been run to earth in Rhodes Street near the Masonic Hotel at 4.45 a.m. without his lamp — which some conscientious colleague had found under a seat outside the Park Hotel. (One is tempted to infer that both the Masonic and Park Hotels offered the amenities Constable Douglas was looking for while the Royal — where he should have been at 4 a.m. — was not so obliging.)

He was tried by Chief Inspector McQueen (one of the longest enduring of the BSAP officers who had survived the Jameson Raid) on two counts of failing to work his beat in a proper manner. The previous convictions on his defaulter sheet included one for the heinous offence of having an untidy shelf at inspection time and one occasion of absence from his station without leave. McQueen, who later reported that he had "not the slightest hesitation in finding Constable Douglas guilty," fined him £2 on one count and gave him 14 days' hard labour on the other. McQueen was noted for the severity of his punishments. As one of the troopers in Bulawayo when McQueen was OC subsequently wrote, "he was very conscious of his rank and standing ... he was more feared than popular."

As was the custom, Douglas served his sentence within the penal confines of Grey Street prison. That was the burden of the Rhodesia Journal's complaint. Although merely an offender against police discipline he had been made a convict. (It so happened that the editor of the Rhodesian Journal and Constable Douglas were fellow members of the Royal and Ancient Order of Buffaloes — a circumstance which doubtless fortified the editor's sympathy.)

Douglas was discharged from the force after serving his sentence. However, he may have derived some satisfaction from the knowledge that as a result of his experience the Olympian Executive Council — prompted no doubt by the High Commissioner in Cape Town, to whom the report had been sent but who was no longer responsible for the force — resolved on 29 June 1912 "that members of the BSAP sentenced to imprisonment not exceeding 14 days for minor offences shall be confined in the Guard Room either at Salisbury or Bulawayo. "It was at about this time, too, that the terminology "prisoner at large" for a member confined to his station pending a trial, was replaced by the less offending phrase "on report" — another slight relaxation of personal indignity.

In June 1912 Lieutenant Pitt-Schenkel — who had joined the BSAP in 1897 and was now in command of 'G' Troop at Gwanda — travelling to Tuli by buckboard, outspanned one evening at an isolated water-hole in thick bush and uninhabited country. He walked away from his camp with his shot-gun, looking for guinea-fowl, and lost himself. It was two days before Tuli and Gwanda realised he was missing, and another two before one of the search patrols found him, alive but very weak after four days without food or water. The trooper and native tracker who found him (whose names, unfortunately, are unrecorded) had followed his spoor for two days and two nights.

Unkind legend has it that, true to character, Pitt-Schenkel put the trooper "on report" for being unshaven when he found him.

**Chapter Twenty**

**THE OLD ORDER CHANGES**

FROM 1910 TO 1911 Fuller, as the Officer Commanding the BSAP, had been designated Commissioner — the first time the title had been used since the days of the old Mashonaland Mounted Police. In 1911 the Imperial Government appointed an Inspector-General of Overseas Forces. Although the BSAP was nominally under the direct control of the Rhodesian administration, it was still subject nevertheless to Imperial surveillance, and the Inspector-General was now required to include it in his report. For the time being the Officer Commanding BSAP became known again as the Commandant although, confusingly enough, there are some references to him as "Acting Commissioner". Fuller retired in 1911 and Drury took his place. Drury's tenure of command was to be no more remarkable than Fuller's. Indeed, the organisation and morale of the force were seriously to deteriorate during that time. Much of the blame for this rested on the personal antipathy to Drury shown by Sir William Milton, the Administrator, but Drury does not seem to have been a robust enough character to have been able to overcome Milton's lack of confidence and to show his own mettle.

Drury had first served in the Royal Marines and the 11th Hussars, after which he had joined the BBP and had transferred to the BSAP in 1895 to accompany Dr. Jameson on the Raid. He had subsequently served with the BSAP in the relief of Mafeking and throughout the campaign in the Western Transvaal. In fact, he had contributed invaluable service to the BSAP's military adventures; and his soldiering had been well balanced by experience of civil police work when he commanded the SRC for a number of years. Later, he had been the Chief Staff Officer of the BSAP. Nominally, he was well qualified by service and experience to command the recently amalgamated force. He was 47 years old with nearly 30 years of well-conducted service life behind him. Unfortunately, for all his dapper, military appearance — the antithesis of the amiable Fuller — and his proven capacity as a regimental officer, he was not born for higher command.

The Imperial Government's Inspector-General of Overseas Forces reported in 1913 that the state of these forces, including the BSAP, was generally unsatisfactory This was hardly surprising considering the makeshift way in which most of them had been established. And so, although the last three appointments of commanding officers, covering 10 years, had been made from serving members of the BSAP, the Company — at the instance of the Imperial authorities — reverted for the time being to the practice of bringing in a senior officer from outside In this case they brought in a man who was destined, a year later, to become the Commandant-General — an office which had fallen away when control of the BSAP had been transferred to the Company in 1909 — and they prevailed on the Company to accept him as one of their officials and to pay his salary. (The previous Commandants-General had been Imperial officers.)

There was a purpose in this capricious departure from the declared policy of establishing the BSAP as a self-contained Rhodesian unit. It was generally accepted by the Imperial military authorities that war in Europe was imminent, in which case the colonial units, particularly in Africa, would be needed for action against possible aggression by Germany's own colonial possessions. Until the BSAP should be declared by the High Commissioner to be "on active service" the force was under the control of the Company. After any such declaration, the Imperial authorities would take over. Only by making the officer who would command it in the event of war an official of the Company could he legally be responsible for its command and training before it was declared to be on active service.

So they appointed the new man as Commissioner of the BSAP, with the understanding that in the event of war he would become the Commandant-General and assume command of all the military forces in Rhodesia, including the SRV and the Rhodesia Regiment — and the forces in Northern Rhodesia.

Major-General Sir A.H.M. Edwards, KBE, CB, (later also to be awarded the MVO) had already had a passing connection with the BSAP when, as Colonel Edwards, he had commanded the Imperial Light Horse in Mahon's Column, which had been joined by the BSAP contingent in its advance to the relief of Mafeking. Edwards, although he happened to be born in India, was a Scot by ancestry and he spent his youth principally in Scotland. He was commissioned in the Seaforth Highlanders when he was 21, and after transfer to the Dragoon Guards — one of the aristocratic regiments of the British Army — he had risen to the rank of Lieutenant-Colonel. After the relief of Mafeking he became the British Army's Assistant Adjutant General and had subsequently served as Military Secretary to the Viceroy of India. Retiring from the Army in 1906 with the rank of Major-General he had then served for six years as Chief Constable of the Metropolitan Police. So the new Commissioner of the BSAP was a man of immense experience in both military and police affairs, and he played probably the most important part in the force's history in moulding it into the pattern and tradition it was subsequently to follow. His calibre as a commanding officer was far above that of any of the previous officers, of any rank, since the force had first been created.

It so happened that, shortly after he had arrived, he was asked to preside at the first meeting of the BSAP Old Comrades' Association, held in the Court House at Bulawayo on Empire Day, in May 1913. He was elected President and Major R.C. Nesbitt, VC, Vice-President. At the inaugural dinner the same evening, Edwards admitted he was a stranger among the members, but he hoped that "time will have the effect of fostering nothing but a spirit of goodwill between me and those I have the honour to command. Whatever changes I am going to make," he went on, "I have no doubt they will be interpreted in the right spirit." Little did his listeners realise how profound the changes were going to be.

Only a week later, less than four months after he had taken up his Commissionership, Edwards reported to the directors of the Company, "The force has suffered in the past from dual control," implying that the Administrator had been interfering with the senior command. "The Administrator has had no confidence in the Acting Commissioner (Drury). Consequently, the Acting Commissioner had lost heart and had no confidence in himself and the force had no acknowledged head to whom it could appeal for support or instruction. When I took over, the state of affairs appeared chaotic. I could approach no subject without detecting ignorance and want of supervision. Those who had their heart in the Corps were in the last stages of despondency while many, I fear, had, owing to lack of support, lapsed into a state bordering on degeneracy.

"It says much for the personnel of the force that notwithstanding the difficulties they had to contend with, discipline was maintained. I have spent the short time I have been here trying to inaugurate a system and to reorganise the force on a more satisfactory basis. I have in each case met with warm-hearted support and co-operation. "

He had already told the Administrator that the existing conditions of service and method of recruiting made it impossible for the force to operate efficiently. With a fixed establishment of only 516 white members, the average wastage had been 135 a year for the last three years, almost all from the rank and file. "The majority of recruits," he said, "except those enlisted for town duty, are ex-public school boys." He had been a public school boy himself, but he knew their limitations. "They openly make a convenience of the force" he complained, "as a stepping-stone to obtaining other employment". Referring to the town police, for whose recruitment preference had all along been given to men with experience in city forces in Britain, he said, "Men who have already served in towns in England do not transplant well because conditions in Rhodesia are so different. What is wanted is the same class of men" — by that he meant other than public school boys — "but who have not been in any force in England." He pointed out that a number of men in Britain "of excellent character and physique" applied from time to time to join the local police forces but were rejected solely because they were not tall enough. He believed these were the men who should be sought, for both town and district in Rhodesia. But he was against bringing men out to join the police without knowing if they would be suitable. He therefore suggested that some arrangements should be made for men such as these to be given a course of drill and first aid, and the rudiments of police work, in their home towns in Britain. Then, if they turned out to be any good, they could be sent out to Rhodesia. It was a sensible suggestion, but not one that could be practicably applied. He made another suggestion, which was later to be adopted, that Colonel Bodle might be appointed recruiting officer in England.

But his most radical proposal for reorganisation of the BSAP — which he advanced as early as April 1913, only three months after assuming command — was the abolition of the Troop and the introduction of what he called the district system of policing Rhodesia. The term "district" in the context of the structure and operation of the force had been used loosely for a long time, but it had never meant anything specific in the organisation. The force's unit was the Troop — the unit of a regiment of mounted infantry — of which there were eleven, each "a complete and separate unit" with an Inspector in command. Admittedly 10 of the Troops were known as "District Troops" and five of these were in Mashonaland — Salisbury (A), Goromonzi (B), Sinoia (C), Umtali (D) and Fort Victoria (F); and five in Matabeleland — Gwanda (G), Gwelo (H), Filabusi (J), Bulawayo (K) and Fort Usher (L). But their "District" appellation was no more than a means of distinguishing them from the Depot Troop (E). The District Troops were certainly each allocated roughly specified areas for their operations but these had no relation to the legally demarcated magisterial districts of which there were eight in the whole country: Salisbury, Umtali, Hartley, Charter, Victoria, Gwelo, Bulawayo and Gwanda.

It might be inferred that the change from 10 Troop headquarters to eight District headquarters of the BSAP was nothing very radical. But in actual practice the change had the effect of breaking down the concept of the Troop system which had for so long dominated the force, perpetuating the military tradition and keeping the police and the magistracy at arms' length. The new Commissioner's proposals were to give each magisterial district a responsible superintendent of police, stationed at the district headquarters, with whom the magistrate would be in constant contact. The district superintendent would have assistant district superintendents in charge of sub-districts corresponding to assistant magisterial areas. Sub-districts would be divided into sections, sections into patrol areas and beats, each with a responsible sub-inspector, NCO or trooper in charge.

There would be eight districts, 25 sub-districts and 42 posts and detachments. The policeman — even though for traditional reasons he might still be called a trooper — would be the representative of police authority on the spot, responsible for whatever action had to be taken, as opposed to a mere link in the chain of a military structure. The Chief Inspector, originally the senior officer under the Commandant, would become the Assistant Commissioner; Inspectors would become District Superintendents, of whom there would be eight; sub-Inspectors would become Assistant District Superintendents, of whom there would be 16; Warrant Officers would become Inspectors; and the Troop Sergeant Majors and 1st Sergeants would become Sub-Inspectors. On mobilisation for active service, an Assistant Commissioner would rank as a major, a District Superintendent as a captain and an Assistant District Superintendent as a lieutenant.

The Commissioner's new organisation was approved in toto, on 26 May 1913, only four months after he had taken command. The effect on the morale of the force was immediate. But Edwards was not finished with his crusade for reform. In his report to the directors of the Company on 31 May, he had said that the strength of the force was inadequate, either as civil police or a military body. He needed 60 more men at once — 10 for the towns and 50 for the districts. "Protection by the police cannot be ensured," he said. "Some patrol areas take three weeks to a month to cover. It is impossible to form a mobile column without dislocating civil police work and protection." The concept of the "mobile column", as a demonstration of armed force parading its strength through a native reserve, had always appealed to the authorities. At a later stage a number of such columns were to be sent out through the districts.

Edwards was concerned, too, about the BSAP artillery, of which he said there was "a remarkable variety of guns of different calibres. They are, as a matter of fact, obsolete. I could allot them to defence of towns and posts, and possibly on armoured trains." For all his reforming zeal, his mind was still running on the force as a military unit. Indeed, outside the towns, a military presence was still the official concept of protection for the settlers, whatever might be said about the force's civil role. Animal drawn artillery, he said, was useless in Rhodesia. The only guns that would be of any use would be 10-pounder mounted battery guns carried on mules led by natives, with an establishment of white police as gunners. Four guns, he thought, would be ample. "But", he complained, "there is no one available to train in gunnery."

The men in the force, he reported, were inadequately and badly housed. "I have visited stations where buildings are tumble-down, leaking, without roof, some with no mess room, kitchen or washing accommodation. Native police lines are in ruins, unfit for human habitation. Unless I had seen them I would never have credited that such a deplorable state of affairs could exist." Some years earlier three residents of Gatooma had sent a letter to Fuller complaining of "a filthy collection of huts, termed by courtesy 'a Black Watch camp' which seriously depreciates the value of our property". The collection of huts was still standing, in the same condition, when Edwards arrived.

The horses, he complained, were of "a very bad class. The prices paid for them could never produce satisfactory animals". He wanted 50 more horses immediately. And he was appalled that so few members of the force could speak even a colloquial native language. "At present only 11 officers and three NCO's have passed the Government native language tests and earned the annuity. The test is unnecessarily severe for rank and file and cannot be attempted without special tuition. Unless members of the force can speak, not write, the native tongue — three-quarters of their value is wasted. A small bonus should be paid to anyone passing a colloquial test."

He even tackled the vexed question of arming the native police. He did not believe that the ordinary native constable needed anything more than a knobkerrie. But he complained that the Angonis, who had been enrolled "to protect the white settlers and to be always ready to quell disturbances among the native inhabitants," were not permitted to take a course in musketry and were consequently untrained for any such duties should they arise. "The Government is not getting value for the money expended," he wrote. "As these men are Angonis and unable to speak (the local language) they would be useless to act as native police, otherwise I would have suggested their transfer to the district." The Administrator, still sensitive to public reaction whenever the subject of arming natives arose, approved a patently unsatisfactory compromise that they should be trained "to shoot at short distances with Martini-Henry rifles sighted only to point-blank range, i.e. 300 yards".

The town police — whose pay, it will be remembered, was reduced when the SRC was absorbed by the BSAP — were still complaining about pay and rations. For once the Administrator seemed to be on their side, and his Secretary had written a memorandum saying "The town police are recruited from a different class of men to the country police. The country trooper is not going to be a trooper always, nor is he very highly trained in the technique of his work. He will in many cases make a good settler and it is quite right that he should have a little nest-egg of deferred pay to help him start life when he leaves the police after three or four years" — a policy, in fact, that encouraged the young recruit in the country police to "make a convenience of the force", which was precisely what Edwards was complaining of. "On the other hand", the Secretary went on, "the Government should attempt to keep the town policeman. He is highly trained and the longer he stays in the force the more useful and efficient he becomes. It is bad policy to dangle in front of him any attraction in the shape of a lump sum of money which will be an inducement for him to leave at the end of his term and perhaps quit the country."

The new Commissioner's reaction to this memorandum was simply to pencil a comment in the margin, "Difficulty in using two methods of payment in the force". Perhaps he recognised that it was a deliberate policy of the Company to encourage new settlers through recruitment for the country police. His own solution to the problem of reducing the wastages, both in town and country, was to extend the period of first engagement. Pursuing his ideas, he proposed new conditions of service on 28 June 1913: original engagement, five years; re-engagement, successive periods of two years each. One shilling per day deferred pay for town police only, payable after five years (about £90) — in direct contradiction to the Administrator's ideas.

It was Edwards who first proposed the use of motor cycles by the BSAP "with a view to economising in horse flesh". In August 1913 he asked for three to be bought that year: "One at Bulawayo for the District Superintendent who has a very large district, one at Gatooma for the Assistant District Superintendent and one at Gwanda for the District Superintendents for work on the Gwanda-Belingwe and Gwanda-Tuli roads." He recommended the purchase of 2 1/2 h.p. FN motor cycles (a French make) at £60 each, "to be charged against remounts". With characteristic caution, the Administrator endorsed the request "Two only approved. Why not an English make?" (Even so, there are no records extant today that any motor-cycles were introduced into the force at that time.) And it was about this time that Edwards introduced the OB (Occurrence Book) to be kept by every station: "Every occurrence, no matter how trivial, is to be entered in detail." This was followed by the FIC (First Information of Crime) form — of which tens of thousands must subsequently have been filled in. Edwards's wrath was stirred on the occasion of one of his own visits to a station, where he found a number of FICs lying about the charge office because, as he noted in his report, "the member in charge did not think they would lead to anything!!!"

But the new Commissioner's energy and drive were not enough to overcome the inertia of the Company's executives. By October — that is to say five months after his report to the directors — the Administrator was still writing to the Secretary of the BSA Company in London, "I am not prepared to endorse the Commissioner's views entirely (on the need to increase the force]. Possibly some increase may be found necessary to some urban and more thickly populated districts. But I would lay stress on the fact that the great mass of the population, both white and black, is law-abiding". This was probably true, in spite of the sensational press reports. "There is practically no resident criminal class in the country. Much can be achieved by a gradual and discriminating policy of redistribution of the force." On the subject of horses, he added, "Neither of our last two Commandants were either good judges (of horse flesh) or good horse-masters. Police requirements do not call for the best and biggest horses procurable especially for mere out-station work, for which purpose hardy cobs of the 'sand pony' type are just as serviceable and much cheaper than large animals of the troop horse type for which the Imperial Government has been accustomed to pay at a high rate. Much has been and can still be saved by using inoculated mules, motor bicycles and bicycles. I doubt if 50 remounts will be required." And so, from the point of view of increasing the strength of the force in both men and horses, the matter rested.

While he was spending the first few months of his Commissionership concentrating on pulling the force together, out of its state of disorganisation and despondency, Edwards was not to be spared the eternal indictments by the public of police inefficiency and turpitude. Typical was the complaint made to the Administrator in March 1913 by a farmer in the Plumtree district that the police had branded him as a thief without any investigation at all. "Through their high-handed action", he complained, "I have lost two days when they could least be spared, attending court at Fort Usher, to be brought in 'Not Guilty'. If the local farmers are to be harassed in this manner I suggest that the station be withdrawn or more suitable people put in charge." The case concerned possession by the farmer of a greyhound bitch which was claimed by a native to belong to him. The magistrate acquitted the farmer, but this did not deter him, with Solomonian justice, from ordering the dog to be given back to the native. "I demand a written apology from the Police," the farmer wrote angrily, "in order that I may vindicate myself from this despicable charge." Edwards wisely advised the Administrator merely to acknowledge the farmer's letter.

A situation needing more deliberate attention revealed itself in a letter to the Administrator from the High Commissioner in Cape Town on 26 March. "I have seen newspaper reports on two outrages alleged to have been attempted by natives on white women in Salisbury on the same night recently ... I would be glad to obtain detailed information as to the amount and efficiency of police protection afforded to the inhabitants of that town by day and night."

The report which Edwards wrote in reply is worth quoting at some length for the picture it gives of the circumstances in which a town police force in Rhodesia had to operate at that time. In Salisbury, the town police — as distinct from the district force — consisted of one officer, three NCO's, 18 European and 14 native constables. They worked on four "reliefs" — the day shift from 9 a.m. to 5 p.m.; a four-hour relief from 5 p.m. to 9 p.m.; the night shift from 9 p.m. to 5 a.m.; and another four-hour relief from 5 a.m. to 9 a.m. There was an additional mounted patrol covering the residential areas from 4 p.m. to 7 p.m. and four native police posts, at convenient points in the town, with three constables at each post, available from 6 p.m. to 6 a.m. As there were, of course, no telephones, anybody who wanted one of these constables had to go and fetch him. The "so-called streets, avenues and thoroughfares" as Edwards called them, extended for some 50 miles.

"To provide European police to cover all this ground," he wrote, "in addition to the sanitary lanes and tracks, would be impossible without large and uncalled for expenditure. The beats are therefore confined to localities in which buildings are more or less concentrated and streets laid out in preconcerted plan. These cover 21 miles. The remaining portion in which residences are erected at irregular and often great intervals is visited by periodical patrols." He was satisfied with the efficiency of his men but they were handicapped by unlighted streets and unmetalled roads. "Progress on foot or by bicycle is impossible in the rainy season." The areas of the town without any buildings were covered by undergrowth up to eight feet high, which "renders detection of those wishing to evade the eye impossible". These were the days — which were to continue for another 30 years — when a curfew operated in the towns and no native was allowed abroad after 9 p.m. unless he had a "brief", written hurriedly by his employer usually on an odd scrap of paper, authorising him to be away from his quarters. "Passes given by masters to their servants to be out at night are granted much too freely" Edwards complained. "They should be restricted to cases of emergency when the natives should be made to carry a lantern." He blamed much of the trouble on "apathy and neglect by the inhabitants to take most ordinary precautions to guard themselves against molestation or attack by natives".

Out in the districts, the principal concern of the District Superintendents in October that year seems to have been an influx of Dutch families from the Transvaal, looking for land. "Whether they will make satisfactory settlers or not," reported the OC, Victoria District "I cannot say. Their general cry is 'Poverty'. They seem to have nothing but their animals, wagons, carts and some food. Some have gone Melsetter way, some to Lalapanzi, and others to Umvuma." From Umtali, the Superintendent reported, "Several Dutch families have trekked into Rusape and Melsetter sub-districts. Generally they have not taken up land, neither do they possess the means to do so. They are under police supervision." The OC in Bulawayo wrote "On my way between West Nicholson and Tuli I passed 15 wagons and 84 Dutch immigrants, practically paupers except for their wagons and to my mind most undesirable". While the Superintendent at Gwanda said, "A large party of Dutch immigrants came into the territory from the Transvaal during the month, with 15 wagons and are en route to Enkeldoorn via Belingwe". Generally, these people seem to have left the police guessing about where, or how, they intended to settle. The Administrator's comment on the reports was, "I doubt if we can keep these people out or eject those already in, but they will not come in now in greater numbers before the rains. The matter should be dealt with before next winter". What happened to these particular people is not on record. Most likely, they found what they were looking for and established themselves as industrious settlers, part of the Afrikaner community which has since established itself as an intrinsic part of Rhodesian society.

It was about this time, in mid-1913, that pleuro-pneumonia broke out among the cattle in Barotseland, while a famine was raging at the same time in Bechuanaland. The north-west corner of Rhodesia lay uncomfortably between these two hazards. The BSAP set up a cordon along the west bank of the Zambezi from Victoria Falls as far as Kazungula, nearly 50 miles upstream, to prevent any movement of cattle or hides. The patrol was made up of Troopers Tait, Wilson and Armstrong, each with three local tribesmen recruited as special constables. The patrol's duties were not particularly exacting. Trooper A.J. Tait wrote later, "We hunted and fished but we never saw any cattle or hides. When things got dull we made a dash on our mules to the Falls to report progress. This, of course, took a weekend to do and we foregathered at the old Falls Hotel. On the Monday we were all glad to get back to our camps ..."

Tait sent a dutiful report every month to the Corporal in charge, Victoria Falls, but never received any acknowledgement. Knowing the police, this did not necessarily surprise him. After some time, Wilson and Armstrong were recalled to their stations and Tait was left on his own. He moved his camp to Kazungula and settled down in some degree of comfort. Once a month he sent one of his special police to Victoria Falls for supplies. As nobody seemed to be taking any notice of his reports he stopped sending them, mainly to see what happened. Nothing happened. His pay cheque was deposited regularly into his bank and he settled down to an undisturbed life of hunting and fishing.

He did not hear about the outbreak of war in August 1914 until some weeks after it happened. By that time he had been engaged on his agreeable duties for over a year. When the news reached him he sent in an application for discharge from the force so that he could join the army. An indignant letter from the Corporal at the Falls demanded to know what he was doing, as the cordon had been closed down for months. He replied that he had never been recalled and asked for half a crown a day extra duty pay, back-dated to the time when he had been left alone, to compensate for the hardships he had suffered. Someone's conscience must have been pricked when the failure to recall him came to light, for he was given a shilling a day extra pay for the last 12 months. When he returned to Salisbury he found he had been posted to the Rhodesian Native Regiment.

In January 1914 the authorities acted on the proposal Edwards made that Colonel Bodle should be appointed the BSAP's recruiting officer in England. The Secretary of the BSA Company in London wrote to Bodle inviting him to "assist in the work of selecting recruits for the BSAP for the year ending 31 December 1914". He would interview candidates at the Company's office and those he found suitable would be given a test in riding and shooting at Hyde Park Barracks, home of the 1st

Life Guards. Arrangements had been made for the Guards to give these tests for the princely fee of three shillings a head, plus the cost of any ammunition used. As the Guards Adjutant said, "Ammunition will only be a small item, as five rounds ought to be sufficient to see if a man can shoot at all." Bodle was to be paid £1 for every recruit enlisted, to a maximum of £100 for the year, and his travelling expenses. There is no record of the outcome of Bodle's activities, which were in any case soon to be interrupted by the war. But the suggestion which Edwards had previously made that candidates for the town police in Rhodesia should be given a course of drill and rudiments in police work, to see if they had any promise, was turned down by the Metropolitan Police as impracticable, and the BSAP still had to take its chance with the men it brought out to Rhodesia to join the force.

In May 1914 Edwards applied for an increase in pay of a shilling a day for 60 sub-inspectors and sergeants, and sixpence a day for 54 corporals. The total European strength at the time was 550, so only 20% of the force would be recipients of this new beneficence. Edwards said he was making the request to forestall any criticism by members of the Legislative Council that the force was in danger of losing these men because they were being underpaid.

"We can ill afford £1600 per year increase in pay," complained the Financial Secretary, in a pencilled note on the Commissioner's memorandum, "The reason adduced by the Commissioner, to anticipate the wishes of the politicians, is a pernicious one. Is it the fact that senior NCOs leave our service on account of inadequacy of pay? I think they mostly leave when they have saved a competence and then they make good settlers. And do we want to encourage elderly policemen? The fact is that our troopers get too high a rate of pay to start with." The Administrator added his own predictable comment, "These papers may be put aside," he wrote. "The returns show that the existing rates and allowances compare not unfavourably with those in the Union (of South Africa]. I have informed the Commissioner that I am unable to authorise any increase."

The years just prior to the first world war saw the birth of an enterprise which in time was to play a significant part in the life of the BSAP: the launching of a regimental magazine. With uncharacteristic lack of originality — uncharacteristic, that is, of the man who conceived the project — it was christened The Police Review and its first number of 14 pages (six of them advertisements), in a drab green cover, appeared in March 1911. The enterprise was the brain-child of one Wilfrid Bussy, who first conceived the idea in 1909 when he was a trooper in Gwanda ("G" Troop). One of his colleagues at the time was Trooper E.A. Banning.

Bussy had been a professional journalist before joining the force. He had served for two years in the Press gallery in the House of Commons and had contributed as a freelance to more than one London paper. Why he had made such a drastic change in his career does not appear on record. He was half English, half French and bilingual; and a talented artist. He spent a couple of years in the wilderness of Gwanda germinating his idea before he was finally able to persuade the authorities to transfer him to 'K' Troop in Bulawayo, where at least he could find what was unheard of in Gwanda, a printer to produce the paper. Banning, according to his own account, had meanwhile left the police to become a professional elephant hunter, but he was so impressed by Bussy's enthusiasm that he took a temporary job in Bulawayo so that he could help by canvassing advertisements for the first issue, as a voluntary contribution. He wrote later, "The manner in which I collected advertisements could hardly be described as strictly orthodox, but these methods were applied only to firms or individuals whose success in business was not entirely due to strictly orthodox methods either. 'Half a page from you, brother, or else ...' usually did the trick". (Another version of the history of the magazine omits any reference to Banning and says that Bussy and the 'K' Troop cook collected all the advertisements in a week, but Banning's account seems more colourful.)

Sergeant-Major Hough — who has previously featured in this history on the occasion of the Geelong pay roll robbery — now of 'K' Troop, was elected Chairman of the magazine committee. Corporal E.B. Law became the business manager. A certain Trooper Liversedge took a leading interest in the enterprise in the early stages, but he was soon to be moved to other fields of endeavour after a series of contraventions of the Game Ordinance and Police Regulations. Philpott & Collins — who are still selling books and magazines in Bulawayo today, but no longer operate a press — printed and produced the first issue of 200 copies on 5 March 1911. The first issue was soon sold out and by the end of 1911 the circulation had reached 600.

The credit for early official support for the magazine goes to Inspector R.E. Murray, OC of 'K' Troop, who became President of the venture and took final responsibility for what was or was not allowed to appear in print. Fuller, the Commissioner at the time it was launched, insisted that it should be clearly labelled 'K' Troop Police Review, lest anyone should be so misled as to believe that the authorities in Salisbury had anything to do with it. However, by the time Drury succeeded Fuller the magazine had been accepted as being respectable and the restriction on the imprint was relaxed. On 7 July 1911 a Circular issued to all stations by the CSO read, "I am directed by the Commanding Officer to bring to your notice the commendable manner in which the Police Review has been undertaken and the great support it has received from the public. The Commanding Officer desires this Review to be recognised as a Regimental paper and trusts that members will do their best to increase the circulation and support the Editor with contributions from their respective Troops" — a blighted hope that has bedevilled successive editors ever since.

The success of the enterprise from the start — for all its lack of sophistication — was due entirely to Bussy who was a talented and versatile writer. Like all editors of fledgling publications he had to write most of the copy himself, using a variety of styles under various pseudonyms. He was, perhaps, apt to be a trifle gushing and emotional, and his writings were often riddled with sentimentality, but that was the journalistic manner of those days. At one stage he wrote a "History of the British South Africa Police" up to the end of the century, wherein he related the early saga of the force, incident by incident and shot by shot — derived from almost non-existent sources of research — and published it in 25 lengthy instalments in successive numbers of The Police Review. All the time he was editing the magazine he was performing his duties as a trooper, including early morning stables. However, it must be assumed that he was not actually sent out on long patrols.

In June 1912 Bussy went down with enteric fever and was laid low for five months. To preserve the continuity of publication, another man, Trooper Moore Ritchie, was appointed. It says much for the official esteem which the magazine had now succeeded in earning, that Moore Ritchie was brought to the editorial chair in Bulawayo all the way from Mtoko, where he had been stationed as a fledgling trooper. (Moore Ritchie relates how, as part of his move to his new post, he was given the job of escorting a lunatic from Salisbury to Bulawayo.) Uncharacteristically for a service such as a police force, the authorities actually appointed a man who was qualified for the job. Moore Ritchie had been a journalist in Ulster. One of the reasons he himself gave, for what he called "a total change of life" by joining the BSAP, was his "over-zeal as an apprentice pressman in my home". The Police Review was now established as the official organ of the force and the editor was relieved of all police duties and given a salary which rose and fell with the monthly profits.

Although Bussy recovered from his illness he was nevertheless discharged from the BSAP as medically unfit. He must have been a restless character for he went back to London, then returned to Rhodesia to edit the Rhodesia Journal, and took over The Police Review again for a few months when Moore Ritchie resigned in August 1913. Except at a much later period in the mid-1930s — and then only for a month or two — this was the only occasion when the magazine, as the organ of the BSAP, was edited by someone not actually in the force. In the end Bussy was to die, still relatively young, editing a newspaper in Rangoon. When Moore Ritchie left he moved first to the South African Police (recently formed after Union in 1910) to become a sergeant and the sub-editor of Nongqai, the magazine which the SAP inherited from the former Natal Police. In due course he moved on to a successful career in Fleet Street. He wrote a number of books and made a name for himself as a radio broadcaster and commentator. He died in 1972.

In 1914 The Police Review became, for the duration of the war, The Rhodesian Defence Force Journal (as unimaginative a title as ever) embracing all the Rhodesian military forces. It was edited for two years by Trooper Gerald Grove (later Sir Gerald Grove, Bart). In 1923 it was to become once again the regimental magazine of the BSAP and somebody was to be inspired enough to re-christen it *The Outpost*.

## Chapter Twenty-One

## SCHUCKMANNSBURG AND MURRAY'S COLUMN

WHEN BRITAIN DECLARED war on Germany on 4 August 1914 the BSAP was still looked on as Rhodesia's first line of defence. Immediately, the force was formally declared by the High Commissioner in Cape Town to be "on active service" and Major-General Edwards assumed the office of Commandant-General, in command of all military forces in both Southern and Northern Rhodesia. Command of the BSAP itself fell on Major Algernon Essex Capell, who had been sent out from England the previous year as second-in-command. For the time being, under the threat of grave military commitments, the force was to be denied the privilege it had been promised — originally by Rhodes himself — that all promotions would be made from its own ranks. Not that this caused any resentment among the members at the time; Edwards had been welcomed for the way he had restored the force's morale, and Capell for the contribution he could make at a time of acknowledged stress.

Although a proverbial English public school boy from Felsted, Capell had had considerable experience in Africa, having joined the Cape Mounted Rifles in 1889 — the same year as that in which the BSA Company's Police had first been formed. He had served with the British forces through the Anglo-Boer war and had won the DSO; after that he had spent some years in the higher ranks of the South African Constabulary (precursors of the South African Police) and before coming to Rhodesia had served three years as Chief of Police in the British West Indian colony of Grenada. Like Edwards, he brought a wealth of much-needed experience to the service of the BSAP. In both cases, their preferment over even long-serving members of the force was in a very different category from those arbitrary appointments in the early days, which Rhodes had handed out indiscriminately to his influential friends.

Even before war was declared in August 1914, "Mobile Troops" had been organised, ready for emergencies, made up of selected members of the Depot and District Troops. As early as 31 July, Edwards, in a secret minute addressed to the Administrator setting out "precautionary measures in anticipation of war with Germany", had included an order to increase the strength of the BSAP post at the Victoria Falls to one officer, 10 other ranks, a machine gun detachment and 25 armed native police (Angonis from the Reserve Company stationed at Depot), and to send Major Capell himself to command it. Diminutive as the garrison was to be, Capell's inclusion suggests an acceptance of the strategic importance of the post in the context of the BSAP as Rhodesia's first line of defence. A detachment of the Northern Rhodesia Police (successors to the BNP) of similar strength was to be posted at the other end of the Falls Bridge; and an NRP mobile column (similar to a BSAP mobile troop) was to be assembled at Livingstone, "if necessary withdrawing men from police posts in the vicinity and on the line of rail".

On August 8, four days after war was declared, orders were issued for No. 1 Mobile Troop of the BSAP — about 100 strong — to assemble in Salisbury, and the troop was ready to move out of Depot as a self-contained military unit, within 24 hours. The officer in command was Assistant Superintendent Francis Trant Stephens — now ranking as Lieutenant — who was 32 and had joined the BSAP in 1903. He was to finish the war with an MC and OBE. In Bulawayo, No. 4 Mobile Troop was mobilised, under Lieutenant George Parson (a future Lieutenant-Colonel and recipient of a DSO and bar), and Depot provided a machine gun section under Lieutenant Alder Lewis Tribe, with 40 Angonis of the Reserve Company.

To the authorities in Rhodesia the threat of possible enemy aggression on the north-west border seemed very real. When Bismarck — Germany's "Iron Chancellor" — had been sacked by the Kaiser in 1890, he had been succeeded by Count Georg Leo von Caprivi, who concluded a number of profitable deals with the British Government involving exchanges of territory-in Europe and Africa. One of these deals had been the surrender by Britain of its island in the North Sea, Heligoland, in exchange for Zanzibar in the Indian Ocean. A subsidiary item in the transaction had been the surrender of a      narrow corridor of land, nearly 300 miles long, running across the northern border of Bechuanaland Protectorate, to give the German colony of South West Africa (Damaraland) access to the Zambezi River. The corridor was known at the time as the "Caprivi Zipfel" — the Caprivi "fragment" or, as it was known in Britain, the Caprivi Finger, because on the map it pointed ominously at the vulnerable conjunction of Barotseland, Bechuanaland and Rhodesia, and the even more strategically vulnerable Victoria Falls Bridge. In later years, after Germany had been defeated and South West Africa had become a British mandated territory, the "finger" became known less provocatively as the Caprivi Strip. Early in the century the colonists had established an administrative township for the Caprivi area at Schuckmannsburg, on the south bank of the Zambezi almost directly opposite Shesheke on the north bank — the native town which was the residence of the son of Lewanika, Paramount Chief of Barotseland. In his precautionary plans Edwards had increased the strength of the NRP post at Shesheke to all of 20 men, with an officer in command. Its prime task was now "to obtain and transmit information to Headquarters," and strictly to censor "all communications passing through Livingstone to the Commander of the German forces in Schuckmannsburg" .

In the context of hostilities between the two European powers, this direct confrontation between their colonial dependencies, across the Zambezi, had its explosive element. Mr. Wallace, the Administrator of Northern Rhodesia, wrote to Edwards on 28 August, "... for the sake of native anxiety and for our prestige it would be a good thing for us to occupy Schuckmannsburg and the district. We should possess the place after the war in preference to the Union (of South Africa) as it has always belonged to Lewanika and was in fact the winter grazing of many of his cattle". But the Imperial authorities were not in the mood to be too hasty. The High Commissioner had telegraphed from Pretoria on 25 August to the Resident Commissioner in Salisbury, "Not intention of HMG to assume offensive against Caprivi Zipfel. German post at Schuckmannsburg should only be occupied if in opinion of local civil and military authorities it is essential to do so in order to protect British interests in the neighbourhood".

On 1 September Edwards was still telling Wallace, "The question of a force to enter the Caprivi Appendix (sic) is still outstanding". By the 11th, Wallace was growing impatient. "I wish something could be done about Schuckmannsburg," he wrote, "It seems so stupid to wait on doing nothing whilst everything is in favour of our acting at once. If reinforcements did come to the Germans we should look fools ... there is talk of some of the settlers taking action on their own." Probably it was this threat of local buccaneering that decided the authorities to act at last, for the High Commissioner cabled on the 13th, "Measures may now be taken to occupy Schuckmannsburg. The force employed should consist entirely of police." And he added, significantly, "Any territory occupied will be disposed of by the Imperial Government for purposes of effecting settlement at end of war". There was no apparent doubt of what the outcome of the war would be.

But while the Imperial authorities had been reluctant to commit themselves to a campaign, the scale of which would be difficult to predict — and for which the forces available from the Rhodesias might well be dangerously sparse — Edwards had already made the first moves. A month earlier, on 10 August, indeed only six days after the declaration of war in Europe, No. 1 Mobile Troop, with the Angonis and the machine-gun section — over 100 NCOs and men with their horses — entrained at Salisbury at midday. No. 4 Troop, some 80 NCOs, men and horses, joined them next morning at Bulawayo and the combined force detrained at Palm Grove Siding at Victoria Falls early on the morning of the 13th. This rapid concentration at the Falls proved that, whatever may have been its shortcomings as a civil police force, the BSAP still possessed "a strong military element in its character," and was more than eager to spring to the defence of the country as a fighting unit. Major Capell, already at the Falls, assumed command; and two days later Headquarters, in the familiar exercise of ambivalence so often practised by military officialdom, ordered No. 4 Troop to return to Bulawayo and its disgruntled members to be sent back to their stations. No. 1 Troop, apparently, was regarded as fully capable of dealing with the business on the north-west border — a belief which was to prove amply justified — and someone in authority had probably raised the old bogey of a native uprising inside the country if the strength of the BSAP in the districts were too drastically reduced

Lieutenant Stephens took a party from No. 1 Troop — consisting of a sergeant, three corporals and 25 troopers — to build a fort at Kazungula on the south bank, 50 miles upriver from the Victoria Falls, where the Chobe runs into the Zambezi at the point of conjunction of the three territories. When the fort was completed Stephens and most of his party returned to the Falls, leaving as a garrison the sergeant, a corporal and eight troopers, with eight Angonis, two months' supplies and 500 rounds per rifle.

On 15 September, two days after the High Commissioner's cabled consent, No. 1 Troop — here-inafter referred to, as the lawyers say, as the column — set out from its camp at the Falls en route to Shesheke, bound at last to assault the enemy at Schuckmannsburg. The column now consisted of four officers, 41 white ORs, 37 Angonis and three Maxim guns. They crossed the river by the Victoria Falls bridge, after which the next camp was made on the north bank of the Zambezi seven miles upstream. Some delay ensued while the column waited for three wagons which were being sent by the NRP with supplies from Livingstone. The wagons when they arrived were found to be grossly overloaded. They would never have stood up to the lamentable condition of the road to Shesheke, had not two more been sent out hurriedly from Livingstone so that their individual loads could be lightened. When the column moved on at last and drew abreast of Kazungula, now on the other side of the river, the garrison was brought across by canoe and the fort which had been so laboriously constructed was left unoccupied.

Five days out from the Falls, the column bivouacked on the banks of the Kasia River, where it runs into the Zambezi, and the horses and mules were let loose to graze under the less than watchful eyes of Troopers Currie and Bailey. At half past two in the afternoon one of these gentlemen felt obliged to report that, in his belief, half the animals were missing. Those remaining in sight were rounded up and the count revealed a shortage of 13 horses and three mules. Continuing searches in the veld throughout the afternoon recovered 11 horses and the three mules, but horses Nos. 028 and 982 were irretrievably lost. One report says that when the column moved on, Sergeant Duncombe (no relation to a much later Senior Assistant Commissioner) and three men were left behind with the unenviable task of trying to find them. A happier outcome ensued, however, when at some stage in the column's march a horse became entangled in the reeds when crossing a river. Trooper F.C. Booth — who shall be mentioned later — dived into the water, at the risk of displeasure on the part of the crocodiles, and freed the horse — an action which brought him a deserved commendation.

The column reached Shesheke at daybreak on 21 September — after a six days' journey covering 95 miles — where a small force of native NRP was waiting with a number of boats in readiness, under Lieutenants Hornsby and Castle, both of whom incidentally had served previously in the BSAP.

The ultimate purpose of the expedition was, of course, to reduce the threat of a German attack on the British colonies by capturing Schuckmannsburg — which was now three miles upstream on the opposite side of the river. But before attacking the town Capell decided to save a lot of trouble by calling on the Germans to surrender. The BSAP officers drew lots for the privilege of delivering the summons to the German commander and it fell to Lieutenant Stephens to act as "parlementaire" — to use the accepted expression of the time. He was to be accompanied by Corporal Vaughan as flag-bearer and Native Corporal Bugler Kapambue. The affair was to be carried out in style.

The last time a member of the BSAP had acted as the bearer of a demand on the commander of an enemy garrison to surrender had been in 1891, when Captain Heyman had attacked the Portuguese fort at Macequece. On that occasion, he and Sub-Lieutenant Morier, who had accompanied him as the interpreter, had been blindfolded before being taken to the fort. Heyman's demand had been rejected and he had been sent back empty-handed; but he had won the ensuing battle, such as it was, more by luck than military judgment, for his own force was considerably inferior to the Portuguese. He had then taken possession of the fort — which almost immediately thereafter he had been ordered to hand back to the Portuguese, as the whole operation by the BSAP on that occasion had been highly illegal.

Now, at Schuckmannsburg, the opposing parties were formally at war and the investing force was considerably stronger than the garrison. The only real parallel with Heyman's earlier exploit was that a member of the BSAP, recruited to preserve law and order in Rhodesia, was acting on foreign soil in a capacity very different from that of a policeman. Stephens and his party, carrying a flag of truce, were rowed across the river to the south bank at 9 a.m on 21 September. They were met on landing by two armed native sentries and escorted to the presence of Herr von Frankenberg, the German Resident. Unlike Heyman and his companion, they were not subjected to being blindfolded, nor were they the emissaries of a puny force whose only weapon was pure bluff. Stephens discussed the situa-tion with the Resident — presumably through an interpreter — for over an hour, but the presence of Mobile Troop No. 1, with its machine guns, on the opposite bank of the river, must have been suffi-ciently persuasive, for von Frankenberg finally agreed to hand over the town without any resistance. Stephens and his companions were back across the river to report to Capell by 2 p.m. At that stage neither the standard-bearer nor bugler appears to have played any dramatic part in the proceedings.

At 3 p.m. the whole column, except a section left behind to look after the horses, was taken across the river in the boats which the NRP had thoughtfully assembled for this purpose. The first German sentry they encountered refused to surrender his rifle and had to be forcibly disarmed although, apparently, no shots were fired. Having landed, the column paraded in good order and marched some two miles along a sandy path to the German police camp, where it then formed up in the camp square. Von Frankenberg was waiting dutifully and Major Capell formally called on him to surrender. He complied with becoming readiness and the German flag was hauled down from the flagstaff. (The flag is in the regimental museum in the Morris Depot at Salisbury today.) The senior German NCO, Sergeant Fischer, refused to surrender — there appears to have been no commissioned officer in the town — and Sergeant Onyett of the BSAP, with a section of troopers, arrested him and his 28 native police. In the gentlemanly manner in which these affairs were conducted in those days, von Frankenberg and Sergeant Fischer were released on parole, within the camp, as soon as the police had been disarmed. The natives were prudently kept under guard.

By the time all this was over the sun was going down, so it was too late to stage the formal ceremony of taking over the enemy stronghold. The column remained in the German camp for the night and at eight o'clock next morning, 22 September, it was formally paraded facing the camp flagstaff — the BSAP Maxim section under Lieutenant Tribe on the right (presumably regarded as the senior unit because of its permanent role), No. 1 Troop under Lieutenant Stephens in the centre, and the NRP with their one Maxim gun, under Lieutenant Hornsby, on the left. To witness the ceremony and ensure the whole thing was done decently and in order, Mr. Venning, the magistrate at Shesheke, was brought over the river with several other prominent residents (presumably at that stage in colonial history, all white, even though Shesheke was a native town). The local dignitaries stood with bared heads behind the flagstaff facing the parade, and at 8 a.m. Lieutenant Castle of the NRP was granted the privilege of breaking the Union Jack.

With due punctilio, fit for such an occasion as this when an enemy stronghold had been captured by British arms, Major Capell called for three cheers for His Majesty King George V, after which the troops were ceremoniously dismissed. Their tents and equipment had now been brought across the river and they were to remain in Schuckmannsburg camp for the next six weeks — almost a forgotten outpost of the Empire. The only recorded incident during their period of occupation was a Board of Enquiry, on 28 October, on the loss of horses 028 and 982. The Board's report was sent to the Commissioner in Salisbury and the two horses were duly struck off the strength, "lost on service". Von Frankenberg and Fischer were sent under the escort of Corporal Gardiner and Trooper Davey for internment in Bulawayo, and in reversal of the previous discriminatory treatment, the native police were sent back to their kraals. By 3 November a relief garrison of NRP from Mongu and Broken Hill had happily arrived, and the column returned to the Victoria Falls (it took only five days this time) whence it left by special train for Salisbury on the 8th.

Thus had the BSAP struck all but the first blow in the war against Germany's colonial empire in Africa. (Troops from the Union of South Africa had landed unopposed at Luderitz Bay on the Namaqualand coast four days earlier, on 18 September.) The long-suffering Sergeant Duncombe and half dozen troopers were sent back to Kazungula to garrison the fort, where for some months they emulated Trooper Tait as carefree huntsmen and fishermen.

While the threat of possible enemy aggression from the north-west had been so comfortably disposed of, the German presence in the north-east was more disturbing. The whole of Tanganyika (Tanzania) was a German colony, directly confronting the British colonies of Northern Rhodesia and Nyasaland (Zambia and Malawi) along a 200 mile frontier which ran from the southern tip of Lake Tanganyika to the northern end of Lake Nyasa. If the Germans should break south across the border into Northern Rhodesia or Nyasaland, Southern Rhodesia itself would also be threatened.

As early as 24 August a report reached Salisbury that the telegraph between Abercorn and Fife, within Northern Rhodesia, had been cut. This was followed by successive reports of attacks and counter-attacks by the opposing forces; of warlike naval engagements between vessels of the rival powers on both the lakes; of towns besieged, invaders repulsed, posts gallantly defended. These were the opening shots in a campaign that was to continue for four years and in which the BSAP were in time to become intimately involved.

But some months — and considerable fighting — were to follow before the Southern Rhodesians were engaged in this campaign at all. During the first 12 months the whole brunt was carried by the Northern Rhodesian forces — the NRP and the NRR (the Northern Rhodesian Regiment, a newly-raised native regiment). As time went on, resentment by people in Southern Rhodesia at the failure by the Company — which was still their Government — to make any move in support of their northern neighbours started to grow. The mood was particularly strong in the BSAP — due more to frustrated belligerency than any high moral purpose. Most of the civilians of similar persuasion had been able to make their way to Britain to join the Imperial forces; but the police — except in a few favoured instances — had been kept at their stations under pain of prosecution for desertion.

In July 1915 the NRP and NRR were heavily attacked by the Germans at Saisai, a fort they had built and had been holding on the border. Although the Northern Rhodesians finally repulsed the enemy after sustained attacks that lasted seven days, reports of the seriousness of the fighting began to disturb the public in Southern Rhodesia. In Salisbury it happened that a meeting had been called on the afternoon of 4 August — the first anniversary of the outbreak of war — by a vociferously jingo-istic section of the population. The ostensible purpose of the meeting was to launch a new appeal for the "Overseas Contingent Fund", which paid fares for men wanting to go to England to join up.

In the event, £500 was raised at the meeting. But that morning the Rhodesia Herald had carried a stirring report of how the Germans had been driven back from Saisai the previous day, and the mood of the meeting veered towards applying its charity nearer home. The Mayor, Colonel Raleigh Grey, declared, "Our first duty is to defend our country, and Northern Rhodesia is as much our country as Southern Rhodesia". He urged that the money should preferably be used to send help to the Tanganyikan border. With almost unseemly haste, the authorities reacted to the public hysteria, and that same evening Major Masterman, Chief Staff Officer of the BSAP, made an impressively dramatic announcement during the interval at the Palace Theatre that a contingent of BSAP would be leaving for the border at once. It is safe to assume that the audience thereupon rose and sang God Save the King.

On 12 August the C-G's orders confirmed that the High Commissioner had approved the principle of sending BSAP infantry companies for service in the north-east. The companies, which were to be 125 strong, would be wholly independent units, with their own artillery and medical services. An advertisement had already appeared in the Herald on 9 August, signed by Major Masterman as acting CSO, provocatively headed IMMEDIATE ACTIVE SERVICE — PROSPECT OF FIGHTING. The latter was, of course, the main draw. The notice proclaimed that 120 men were needed to form an "infantry Company for active service on the North-eastern border of Northern Rhodesia". They would be enlisted under the Police Ordinance for the duration of hostilities and paid five shillings a day.

Within a week, 137 serving members of the force had volunteered to join the first Company, but their enthusiasm was summarily dampened by an order limiting transfers to two from each Troop. The rest were still needed to police Rhodesia. So, apart from certain officers, 'A' Company started with only 16 serving members of the BSAP. The remainder were recruited directly to the new force, prin-cipally from ex-members of the 1st Rhodesia Regiment, which the authorities had disbanded — for some unfathomable reason — after service in the campaign against German South West Africa (which Generals Botha and Smuts had successfully concluded within the year). Now they became members of the BSAP, as did a number of men who transferred from the SRV.

The new Companies were given no distinguishing badges, no plumes to wear in their bush-hats — those coveted appendages of all colonial forces. Their only insignia were BSAP shoulder-flashes in blue cotton. The equipment issued to them — governed, of course, by considerations of availability — included cavalry water-bottles, mess tins, haversacks and cloaks, and two bandoliers each, one of which had to be used as a belt. Any already serving member of the BSAP who transferred to a Company was obliged to surrender his riding breeches in exchange for two pairs of shorts. If the BSAP was a regiment of mounted infantry, a more appropriate description of the new Companies could be dismounted cavalrymen.

The first of the new BSAP Companies — 'A' Company — left Salisbury on 17 August by train for the north. As is still the case today, the railway to the north from Salisbury ran first south-west to Bulawayo, and then swung north to the Victoria Falls and Livingstone. At Bulawayo, the Company in transit was formally greeted by Major Murray, the local BSAP commanding officer. It is reasonably certain that Murray had no idea at the time that he would soon be intimately involved with the men who were now merely passing through his district.

The Company was under the command of Captain J.S. Ingham who, although still a relatively young man at 43, had already served for 19 years with the BSAP. Indeed, he was a veteran of the Jameson Raid and had been captured by the Boers at Doornkop. (Once again, how the Raid keeps echoing through the annals of the force!) He had been commissioned in 1900 and had served in the campaign in the western Transvaal in the closing stages of the South African war. His Company, with all the supernumeraries, was now 142 strong — with 20 donkeys. (This was an infantry unit, so there were no horses.) From Bulawayo they travelled on to the Victoria Falls where they were joined by Lieutenants Stephens and Parson — the one-time commanders of the Mobile Columns at the outbreak of war — with 21 other ranks, to make a total force of 165.

Half the Company detrained at Broken Hill under Ingham. Parson took the other half on by train to Ndola. Each half then marched step by dusty step to Kasama — which is 350 miles from Broken Hill as the crow flies, and 250 from Ndola. From Kasama they marched together another 100 miles to Abercorn. It was a fitting start to a campaign that was to consist of marching and counter-marching through semi-tropical bush for months, even years, on end. Altogether, they took nearly six weeks to march to Abercorn, where they arrived early in October.

While 'A' Company was foot-slogging its way, mile after interminable mile, across the rolling forest country of north-eastern Rhodesia (today's Zambia), 'B' Company was being hurriedly recruited and preparing to depart from Salisbury. Although all its members were formally attested in the BSAP — and became subject to the Police Ordinance of 1903 (which had been promulgated when the force was "amalgamated" in that year) — the new Company started off with few serving members. Virtually all those who could be spared from internal police duties had been absorbed in 'A' Company. One report says that 'B' Company's ranks were merely "stiffened by the inclusion of some BSAP specialists and three intelligence officers." On the whole, although both the BSAP Companies were made up principally of men with volunteer or, in some cases, previous police experience, they were far from trained or homogeneous forces. They were put through a crash course at Depot on the parade ground but, for all RSM Blatherwick's stentorian efforts, they were still relatively raw when they were hurriedly whisked away.

Command of 'B' Company was given to a man who, although now attested in the BSAP, had previously been an officer in the SRV. Major Walter Baxendale was a prominent citizen of Bulawayo, where he had been Mayor in 1912. To facilitate his acceptance by the BSAP he had dropped in rank to Lieutenant, but his majority was restored when given command of the Company. Two other officers from the SRV in Bulawayo were also attested in the BSAP and included in the Company: the brothers Captain A.G. and Lieutenant J.B. Hendrie. The Hendries were to fight throughout the campaign and survive; Baxendale was to be killed in 1917 at Iringa. J.B. Hendrie's formal commission declared him "an Officer in our Land Forces ... in the rank of Lieutenant" signed by "George R.I." (George V), but although it was post-dated to 19 August 1915 it was not issued until 1920. Presumably the King had more pressing considerations during the war than signing commissions for colonial officers. Both the Hendries were later mentioned in despatches: "Lt. St.J.B. Hendrie, B.S.A. Police" and signed by Winston S. Churchill as Secretary of State for War on 1 March 1919. (The "St.J.", which occurs more than once in the records, was simply a flight of fancy on the part of someone in the War Office. Hendrie's names were John Bryce.)

Edwards, the Commandant-General, had been in two minds about whom he should appoint to the command of 'B' Company. He was keen to keep the command within the BSAP but there was no one he could, in good conscience, appoint over the head of Baxendale. Nevertheless, although Baxendale nominally commanded the Company when it left for the north, Edwards also sent with it Major R.E. Murray — the District Superintendent in Bulawayo — to be engaged, as the Rhodesian Defence Journal reported, "on special service on the Border". This created a situation with obvious anomalies. The formal Commander-in-Chief in north-eastern Rhodesia was Colonel Hodson of the NRP. With Ingham in command of the BSAP's 'A' Company and Baxendale in command of 'B', where was Murray to fit in?

'B' Company left Salisbury early in September for the same final destination as 'A' Company, but started off in precisely the opposite direction. The 130-odd men travelled by rail due east to Beira, whence they sailed by the proverbial cattle-boat, S.S. Ipee, up the coast to Chinde at the mouth of the Zambezi, then up the Zambezi to Chindio at its confluence with the Shire, and finally up the Shire to Port Herald. They then set off on a relatively easy march of less than 200 miles to Fort Johnstone, at the southern tip of Lake Nyasa; followed by another voyage by steamer to Karonga, near the northern end of the lake, and a final 100 mile march due west to Fife. The total marching distance was considerably less than that of 'A' Company and in any case the foot-slogging had been relieved by the balm of a cruise on the lake. Fortunately, 12 months earlier, immediately after the outbreak of war, the British steamer "Guendolen" had cleared the lake of all German vessels.

The Rhodesian Defence Journal, when it reported that Edwards had sent Murray with 'B' Company for "special service on the Border," had of course no idea that Murray carried a letter from Edwards to Colonel Hodson, containing secret orders appointing Murray his Chief Staff Officer. There seems to have been some delay in Murray's presentation of the letter to his new Commander-in-Chief — if he ever did so — for it is on record that almost immediately after 'B' Company's arrival at Fife, he went off with a combined force of NRP and NRR, and 50 BSAP from 'B' Company, to pursue a strong German patrol in the neighbourhood. Murray himself took command of this force. The Germans apparently withdrew and nothing developed from the incident.

It is possible that this force had been hurriedly collected in a situation of emergency and that Murray was prevented by events from presenting Edwards's letter to Hodson when he arrived at the border. Nevertheless, one is tempted to wonder if that really was the case, or whether Murray was playing a subtle game of military politics. He had an abrasive character, as events were to prove. He seems not to have given Hodson the letter with Edwards's orders, for he certainly never became CSO — a position which continued to be held by Lieutenant-Colonel Fair of the NRP. Hodson wrote to him on 30 September from Headquarters at Abercorn in an estimably friendly vein, signing himself "Hoddy", which was not a characteristic way for a Commanding-Officer to address his Chief-of-Staff. He suggested that Murray should remain at Fife with 'B' Company, as he had more experience with European than native soldiers. With Baxendale in command of 'B' Company, this would leave Murray virtually as a supernumerary and he replied that the two BSAP Companies should be combined and placed under his command. (At the time, 'A' Company was operating from Abercorn and 'B' from Fife, and they were patrolling the border between them.) The correspondence between Murray and Hodson became openly quarrelsome and Hodson wrote to Edwards on 19 October complaining of Murray's "dictatorial manner". He had told Murray he was determined the two Companies should not be combined as a unit, "unless the C-G says so".

On 18 February 1916, the C-G said so. A new Commander-in-Chief, Brigadier-General E. Northey, was appointed to the Nyasaland-Rhodesia border; the unfortunate Hodson was relegated to "OC, lines of communication"; Murray was promoted to Lieutenant-Colonel; both BSAP Companies were put under his command; and thus came into being a force which was to wage a far-ranging campaign with the Germans in Tanganyika for the next 18 months, and to go down in Rhodesian history as "Murray's Column".

Although "Murray's Column" was intrinsically a formation of the BSAP, and not a few of its members had served — or were to serve after the war — in the force, the full story of its participation in the German East African campaign is not essentially a part of BSAP history. There were too many other units than the BSAP involved in the campaign for a detailed account to fall properly within the scope of this book. Nevertheless, some brief outline of what transpired in German East Africa is owed to those members of the BSAP Companies who served with Murray.

Mention has already been made of how the German colony of Tanganyika confronted the British colonies of Northern Rhodesia and Nyasaland along the line of frontier which connected Lakes Tanganyika and Nyasa. Away on its northern border, Tanganyika also confronted Kenya Colony, then known as British East Africa. And it was on this border that the main clash occurred between the German and British colonial forces existing at the outbreak of war. By comparison, the early operations on the Nyasaland-Northern Rhodesian border were little more than minor skirmishes.

The German commander was General Paul von Lettow Vorbeck (usually known as von Lettow), a soldier who had already learnt something about warfare in Africa when the Hereros had risen against the German colonists in Damaraland. For the first 18 months following the outbreak of war in 1914, although they never advanced far into Kenya, von Lettow and his troops displayed overwhelming superiority to the British forces on the border, and inflicted a series of crushing defeats.

In February 1916, General Smuts — who, with Botha, had by then dealt successfully with German South West Africa — took over the Allied command in East Africa, stepping into the shoes of the series of unsuccessful British generals who had preceded him. He commanded a mixed force numbering some 30,000 in all, of British and Indian troops, South Africans and Rhodesians (in this case, the 2nd Rhodesia Regiment, under the command of Colonel Essex Capell, and the 1st Rhodesia Native Regiment, under Colonel A.J. Tomlinson — both seconded by the BSAP). He set up his head-quarters in Nairobi. His command also covered the force on the Nyasaland-Northern Rhodesian border under Brigadier-General Northey, separated from him by 500 miles of enemy territory. Northey's force was not unreasonably known as "Norforce" and comprised some 3000 troops, of whom Murray's two BSAP Companies — less than 300 men — formed a relatively small detach-ment. In the ensuing campaign, which was to continue for two and a half years, "Norforce" became what has been described as "the anvil of Smuts's hammer descending from the north". It was almost continuously in contact with enemy formations driven south and west by the main body.

The detailed story of the German East African campaign is lamentably complicated, as the separate Allied forces operating from the northern and south-western borders pursued von Lettow's elusive formations and were repeatedly roughly-handled in the process. But the overall strategy of von Lettow's campaign was simple enough. He started in 1914 with some 8000 troops, European and native. He knew that so long as the war continued he could receive no reinforcements and no mater-ial from outside. Nevertheless, in a spirit of admirable dedication to the German cause, he determined to divert from other theatres of war as many Allied troops as he could, and to keep them diverted as long as he could. In this he was altogether successful. When the Armistice was signed in Europe in 1918 he still had 4000 men in the field, undefeated, who were still keeping five times as many Allied troops occupied in pursuing them.

The pattern of the campaign was complex because both sides continually broke up and re-formed their forces into various combinations, pursuing each other up and down the country, turning to fight, breaking away, and meeting to fight again another day, on new ground and as often as not in new formations. By September 1916 Smuts's forces in the north had captured Dar es Salaam, also the railway which ran across the territory from the coast to Lake Tanganyika, and were in posses-sion of virtually the whole coastline. But they had failed to defeat von Lettow, whose admittedly diminishing forces were still at large and prepared to go on fighting. "Norforce", with its 3000 men, had penetrated deeply into Tanganyikan territory and was extended over a front of 200 miles. Smuts's army was even more dispersed. It was a campaign of continual movement — of marches and counter-marches, and sharp, fierce engagements, von Lettow constantly avoiding commitment to a major battle but continually harassing the Allied forces.

By January 1917 the rains had brought troop movements on both sides almost to a standstill. Smuts — whose reputation was at risk by his inability to bring the campaign to a successful conclusion — was fortuitously called to London to represent South Africa at the Imperial Defence Conference. After a short interlude under a British general the command fell, in May, on another South African, van Deventer. The campaign dragged on, but von Lettow's troops were driven at last into a corner in the south-east of Tanganyika. However, he was still far from defeated and in November 1917 he crossed the boundary — the River Rovuma — into Portuguese East Africa.

Van Deventer's troops, including "Norforce", pursued him 500 miles down the inhospitable wilder-ness of Portuguese East Africa. The Allies were pursuing the Germans and the Germans themselves were driving the thoroughly alarmed Portuguese garrisons before them. But when he came to the Zambezi von Lettow was forced to turn right about and strike north again, still pursued by, but dodging and avoiding — and sometimes harassing — van Deventer's forces, including "Norforce,". Almost 12 months after he had entered Portuguese East Africa, he passed round the northern tip of Lake Nyasa, crossed the border into Northern Rhodesia, broke through the Abercorn-Fife line which the BSAP Companies had been responsible for patrolling three years before, and captured Kasama. Four years after the outbreak of war, the Germans were occupying a Northern Rhodesian town.

When the news of the Armistice was received on 13 November 1918, von Lettow was still moving southwards, 200 miles inside Northern Rhodesia, to Chambeshi. The news was conveyed to him by a detachment from "Norforce", carrying a flag of truce. By the terms of the Armistice, von Lettow was forced to cease fighting and hand over his forces to the Allied command. He marched the remnants of his force (155 Europeans, 4168 Africans) to Abercorn where he formally surrendered. In the more gentlemanly manner in which war was conducted in those days, van Deventer allowed von Lettow's officers and white other-ranks to retain their arms, as a mark of respect for the stout way in which they had fought the campaign and in recognition of the undeniable fact that they had not actually been defeated in the field. No doubt he removed their ammunition as a reasonable precaution.

That is the outline of the campaign in which "Murray's Column" played its due part. Murray himself was a forceful leader, if something of an irascible character. From the day he was drafted for "special service on the border" he was determined to secure unfettered authority over the BSAP Companies and to get rid of the two commanders who had originally been appointed by the C-G. When the two companies were combined and Murray was given overall command, Ingham and Baxendale both found themselves in anomalous situations. Murray called on Ingham, at Abercorn, to send some of his stores to 'B' Company at Fife. Ingham, before complying, was rash enough to ask what his own position was. Murray answered, "None," and suggested Ingham should make plans to return to Salisbury. When, a little later, 'B' Company under Baxendale took part in a successful attack on a German post at Bismarcksburg, on the south-eastern shore of Lake Tanganyika, Murray put Baxendale in charge of the party left to garrison the post and withdrew his Company for other operations under his own control. Thus, the two original commanding officers of 'A' and 'B' Companies were summarily disposed of. Apparently the C-G had full confidence in Murray and interfered not at all with his arbitrary decisions. (Baxendale was later killed in an operation in which "Murray's Column", as such, was not directly involved.)

At an early stage in the campaign Murray earned himself a reputation for unreasonable bitterness by an incident almost parallel with that which was to bring notoriety to the American, General Patton, 30 years later during the second world war. Visiting a field hospital Murray roundly abused certain of the patients, accusing them of malingering — "scrimshankers" was the epithet he used. On a later occasion a high-ranking medical officer, visiting the column in the field in an official capacity, warned Murray that the health of some of his men was in a dangerous condition and that he should give them recuperative leave. Murray was furious and railed at the doctor for interfering with his command. Three months later, in October 1917, he had to send 55 of his men back to Salisbury for this very reason. His numbers were so reduced that Northey decided that the BSAP Companies were no longer strong enough to continue as separate entities and they were absorbed into the machine-gun and depot units of "Norforce". So that was the end of "Murray's Column" as such, which for 18 months had played such an invaluable fighting part in "Norforce's" campaign.

Although the strength of the two BSAP Companies at any one time had been in the neighbourhood of 300, a total of just under 500 men had served at one time or another during that period. In August 1917 a new BSAP Mechanical Transport Section was formed in Salisbury, but it only managed at first to raise 25 qualified motor mechanics, although its total recruitment, including drivers, amounted in the end to 179, and it brought 90 much needed motor vehicles to the weary troops on the border. It lost one of its recruits, Trooper Davis, on the way north. He rashly went for a swim in the Zambezi and was taken by a crocodile.

By then Murray was in bad health himself. Like so many of his men he had suffered repeated bouts of malaria, but he had consistently refused to be taken to hospital. In January 1918 he became so ill that he was obliged to relinquish his command, and he left for Salisbury in an atmosphere of mixed emotions at his headquarters. While he had always been held in respect and awe by his subordinates — if only for his military achievements — the troops had never felt for him any affection and, somewhat aptly, when he was seen off from his field headquarters someone had painted on his car the epitaph, "Goodbye, scrimshanker".

His was a sad end to an honourable career. He had served the BSAP well. He had joined in 1899, at 25. He had won the DCM during the Anglo-Boer war; he had been commissioned in 1901, in the field; and he had made his name as an efficient and respected Superintendent, particularly in command of 'K' Troop covering the district from Bulawayo to the Victoria Falls. Indeed, it was for his standing in the force that the C-G had chosen him to accompany the BSAP

Companies to the Nyasaland-Northern Rhodesian border as Chief Staff Officer — the appointment he never took up.

When he returned to Salisbury he was sent south on sick leave and he bought a small farm at Bellville on the Cape Flats, north of Cape Town. But what was left of his health deteriorated. In June 1920 he was sent to London for a medical board and he died at Hayling Island, off the Hampshire coast, while still a member of the force. He was given a military funeral, and the War Graves Commission set up a tomb-stone carrying the BSAP crest.

During the campaign he was awarded the DSO. Parson, the young lieutenant who had commanded the No. 4 Mobile Troop (from Bulawayo) at the outbreak of war, and had joined Ingham's 'A' Company on its journey north, also won a DSO. Stephens, the erstwhile commander of No. 1 Mobile Troop (from Salisbury) with Captains Onyett and A.G. Hendrie won MCs; Sergeant-Major McGee, Sergeant Barton and Corporal Trevelyan DCMs; 55 members of the BSAP Companies, including five Africans, were mentioned in dispatches by Northey in April 1917, when he wrote, "I cannot speak too highly of the work done by Colonels Hawthorn (NRP) and Murray, whose columns have been marching and fighting the whole time, even throughout the last few months of constant heavy rain".

It is difficult to estimate either the number of members of the BSAP during the 1914-18 war who saw active service with some fighting force in Europe or Africa, or the actual strength of the force left from time to time during the war period to police Rhodesia. There is no collective record of who went away, who stayed, who joined or who left. It is only possible to garner information from fragmentary records. Some members managed to get away to Europe and join the Imperial forces; some served with Murray's Column; others joined the Rhodesia Native Regiment and served with the South African forces in Kenya. One of the latter was Trooper Frederick Charles Booth who, almost immediately after joining the force in 1914, had ridden with No. 1 Mobile Column on the expedition to capture Schuckmannsburg, and on that occasion had earned a commendation for freeing a horse from an under-water entanglement. He transferred to the RNR, as a sergeant, as soon as the new regiment was formed in 1916. In May 1917 he was awarded the DCM, "for conspicuous gallantry on many occasions". Then, the next month, he won a Victoria Cross. "During an attack in thick bush on the enemy's position, under very heavy fire, Sergeant Booth went forward alone and brought in a man who had been dangerously wounded."

Although not directly on BSAP duty at the time of winning the Victoria Cross, Booth was a fully-fledged member of the force, seconded for war-time duties. He was 27 at the time. Later that year he was wounded and sent back to Salisbury where the BSAP and the townspeople gave him what was inevitably described in the Press as a "tumultuous reception". He was sent back to England, where he was transferred to an Imperial regiment and he finished the war as a Captain.

## Chapter Twenty-Two

## ALARMS AND EXCURSIONS

THERE WERE ONE or two occasions when the BSAP left behind in Rhodesia were not restricted entirely to normal police duties. The first of these occasions, after the unopposed expedition to Schuckmannsburg, was in late 1914 when a strong force had been sent to the southern border, near where Beit Bridge was later (in 1929) to be built across the Limpopo.

When Britain declared war on Germany the antagonism between Briton and Boer in the Union of South Africa inevitably manifested itself again. After all, they had been fighting each other only 12 years before. But Botha, the Prime Minister of the Union, and Smuts, the Minister of Justice, for all their Afrikaner descent, recognised that South Africa's active support of Britain was imperative: strategically, Britain could not afford to allow South Africa to remain neutral, and Germany would certainly not have respected her neutrality if it had been attempted. Nevertheless, there was a strong Afrikaner element opposed to supporting Britain; and when Botha responded to a request by the British Government to capture the German radio installations at Luderitzbucht and Swakopmund, in German South West Africa — and the Germans openly promised to restore the independence of the old Boer republics in the Transvaal and Free State if they supported her against Britain — a number of the Boer leaders rose in revolt against Botha's Government and some 12,000 rebels joined them in the field.

Botha moved 40,000 men of the South African defence forces against the rebels, who were easily defeated at Mushroom Valley in the Free State and Rustenburg in the Transvaal. In fact, Rustenburg — which is 300 miles away — was the nearest the rebel forces ever came to the Rhodesian border. But the threat that they might invade or be driven north into Rhodesia was within the bounds of possibility, and the BSAP sent 100 mounted men south from Salisbury hopefully to resist them.

Trooper Seymour-Hall (as he was at the time) wrote 57 years later that in 1914 he was stationed at Gwanda with 'G' Troop. The district superintendent at Gwanda was Inspector de Legh, one of the original members of the BSAP, who had joined in 1896. He had taken part, with Plumer's force, in the relief of Mafeking. When the news came through of a rising in the Union and the possibility of the rebels moving north to Rhodesia became apparent, de Legh took a patrol of a dozen men to the Main Drift on the Limpopo (a few miles east of the present site of Beit Bridge) to reinforce the three unfortunate troopers who formed the only barrier to invasion at this vital point in the country's defences. The main force of 100 under Major Capell himself, with two Maxim guns, travelled from Salisbury by train to West Nicholson and rode south to Mazunga, where it encamped, still 40 miles north of the river at Main Drift. There was, one assumes, some good reason why these 100 mounted men remained shyly in the background and ventured no closer to the border, but the 15 men now at Main Drift would have been sadly embarrassed if 1000 or so Dutch rebels had suddenly put in an appearance. However, the revolt in South Africa collapsed before the end of 1914 and the first Mazunga patrol (there was to be another in 1918, as shall be related) returned undramatically to Salisbury.

Excursions like these to Schuckmannsburg and Mazunga, with the prospect that more such demands were probable as the war proceeded — although, in fact, they never arose — naturally led to some concern as to how the force could cope with its normal police duties. That the natives would take any opportunity to rise which might be presented to them was the constant fear of the authorities.

The Commandant-General wrote to the Administrator soon after war had been declared, "In the event of the Police ever being mobilised for active service it may be necessary to enrol residents to act as special constables". He suggested 10 shillings a day to cover "pay, horse allowance, forage and rations". The Administrator replied eagerly, "If we get a whole-time special constable for 10/- per day who will find his own horse and forage for that, we shall do well". He promptly endorsed the proposal. A hundred men were enrolled.

But the established strength of the force was still worrying the Commandant-General. In June 1914 the strength was 550 — the same as it had been 10 years earlier. On 6 August he had written, "The difficulty in obtaining recruits from England and elsewhere will be increased now that war has been declared. The Corps is at present 16 under strength and the immediate recall to regiments of 26 army reservists, at a time when their services are most urgently required, will make us 42 short of establishment". He suggested, and the Administrator approved, that 50 ex-members of the force, "of good character and resident in Rhodesia" should be engaged for three months with option of extension to six "to suit the emergency". In the event, some of these men remained in service for the duration of the war.

But after the two infantry companies had been raised to form "Murray's Column," and the army reservists had escaped thankfully to rejoin their regiments in Britain, there were still plenty of men in the force hankering to get away and join the fighting services. The Secretary of the BSA Company in London wrote to the War Office in April 1915, "The BSAP being on active service members are not allowed to take discharge, and as many are desirous of doing so to take up commissions in Europe the Commandant-General has had to rule that no discharge may be granted unless the member's services are applied for by the Imperial authorities. The Commandant-General has reason to believe that certain members of the force have been in direct communication with the War Office and wishes to point out that it cannot be safely assumed that these particular men are the most suitable candidates in the force for commissions. The force is at present under strength, but the Commandant-General is prepared to consider any application received directly from the War Office". The War Office replied that it would not consider any applications unless recommended in the first instance by the Commandant-General and so a state of virtual deadlock ensued.

The problem of policing the scattered peri-urban areas round Salisbury was, naturally, not alleviated by the situation, and the authorities still faced complaints of inadequate police coverage. A petition presented to the Administrator on 6 May 1916, signed by 28 residents on the Hatfield Estate, asked for one native constable to be stationed on the estate. It was a modest enough demand. Of the 70 people living on the estate, nearly all the men went to work daily in Salisbury. As the petition reported in some alarm, "Recently a vacant house has been burnt down and the thatched roof of another house set on fire, both acts of natives. Natives on the main road shout and create disturbance" — the perennial complaint. "They are believed, in many instances, to be drunk and dangerous."

Two days later, not to be outdone, the residents of Parktown and Ardbennie followed with their own more emotive petition "for protection of women and children who are left unprotected during the absence in the day time of their natural protectors who are employed in Salisbury". The Secretary of the Treasury, to whom the petitions found their way for obvious reasons, was characteristically unsympathetic. "Is there any greater call for this now," he asked, "than there has been during the past 10 years during which people have lived at these places? If necessary here, are there not many other places round Salisbury and possibly other towns in which similar demands might be expected? I am not sure it is the business of the Government," he added reproachfully, "to follow up every settlement on the outskirts or beyond the boundaries of townships with a police station. "Faced with Treasury intractability, the Commissioner attempted to assuage the petitioners by arranging for European constables from the stations at Hillside and Parktown to visit Hatfield once a week, "making a total," as he proudly explained, "of five visits every seven days". In addition, a married European constable would be stationed at Hillside and another at Parktown: one assumes that the married state was expected to ensure a more continuous presence in the area.

Some months later the Bromley Farmers' Association wrote to the Commandant-General complaining, "We are practically surrounded by native reserves teeming with natives, over whose comings and goings there is no control. Visits of the Police are few and far between and in any case do not check the evil in any way". The Association followed its letter by individual reports from residents confirming the state of lawlessness. Mr. J. reported: "The compound has been robbed four times, and mealies stolen from lands three times in a month". Mr. S. actually saw three natives carrying mealies from his lands. He had sent an employee to the police at Goromonzi to charge him with "disobedience" but as he himself could not go to the court to give evidence, "the boy," he complained, "was discharged". Mr. D. said, "There have been at least 20 robberies in the past month. I found a native on my farm without a pass. I detained him for three days, waiting for an opportunity to hand him over to the police. No police came and I had to release him". Mr. P., on the other hand, had taken a prisoner to Goromonzi, leaving his farm before daybreak, but when he reached the court he was too late. He had also had two pigs stolen during the night — and a grass fire. And, worse still, "native women are being brought on to my farm for prostitution".

This catalogue of "the evil" — as the first letter had described it — seems to have left the Commissioner relatively unmoved. "Every endeavour will be made," he replied simply "to patrol the area." He did add that as it had been decided not to hold a periodical court in the Bromley district, "the provision of a police station would be of no real benefit to the residents".

On 3 September 1918, two months before the Armistice, the member-in-charge at Gwanda had sent an alarming report to Headquarters in Salisbury. The natives in the Nuanetsi district had risen, he said, and 10 white men had been killed. A native working "at the Lundi end of the Nuanetsi and Limpopo rivers" — whatever that meant — had brought the news to the BSA Company's Nuanetsi Ranch. He claimed to have been caught and bound by the rebels and to have been told that all the English had been killed by the Germans, and that the Shangaans were about to finish off the whites. They had been ordered by their leaders to rise with the new moon. An impi was on the way to Messina and another was marching on Gwanda. No wonder the member-in-charge was alarmed.

The alarm spread to Bulawayo, whence the District Superintendent telegraphed Salisbury on the same day. "Following from Gwanda. District full of rumours. Shangaans rising. Everybody very uneasy asking what steps Police taking for their safety." On the following day a native named Klass made a long statement at Chibi to Captain Pitt-Schenkel, the Superintendent of the Victoria District. He had been with a party of white men to the Northern Transvaal, he deposed, and one night in camp a number of Shangaans had attacked them, tied all the white men together and cut their throats. He, too, had been tied up but had managed to work himself loose. "I saw with my own eyes the Shangaans tying up the white men. I saw the Shangaans cut their throats and disembowel them." The Shangaans had told him that natives had come from East Africa saying the Germans were very strong and the English were running away. Now was the time for the Shangaans to strike.

Headquarters treated the report with commendable gravity. The Commandant-General issued a Special Garrison Order on 6 September. "Lieutenant-Colonel A. E. Capell will proceed in command of the following details by special train." His destination was not specified but one must assume it was Fort Victoria. The details were to comprise "15 BSAP mounted. Three BSAP and Lewis gun. One .303 machine gun. Two platoons Rhodesia Native Regiment, with three officers, eight European NCOs and 100 askaris. 25 recruit askaris as machine gun bearers. Two wagons, one ambulance. NCO (medical) with necessary medical stores. One month's rations, with camping equipment for light travel. 10,000 rounds of .303 ammunition". This formidable party clearly meant business. Actually, it left Salisbury with only 15 days' rations for men and animals, but it was followed by another train carrying supplies for 14 more days — supplies which included eight gallons of 'dop' and 160 tins of jam.

The expedition came to be known as the Mazunga Patrol. Mazunga is nearly 130 miles southeast of Fort Victoria as the crow flies (on the main road from West Nicholson to Beit Bridge) and as the patrol is known also to have reached both West Nicholson and the Limpopo River, it must have covered a tremendous area. In spite of the alarmist reports, it never came across any evidence of native unrest. Indeed, on 11 September, Capell telegraphed Headquarters to say that Klass, who had been made to accompany the column, had absconded. "This fact," said Capell, "and the rambling nature of his statement, seems to point to the conclusion that the whole business is a gigantic hoax." Three days later, the Native Commissioner at Nuanetsi reported, "Everything quiet. A native was caught with a stolen shot-gun. He had been tied up and later ran away. Possibly this was Klass." While a message from the NC at Belingwe, dated 16 September, suggested even another source of the alarmist rumour. "Three weeks ago," the NC reported, "one of Liebig's Europeans, who was burning a fire line through the bush in the Chibi district, approached an assembly of Shangaans who were holding a ritual dance. No strangers were allowed near. The European approached, was badly assaulted and his clothes torn. He managed to get on his horse and rode some distance but the horse fell dead." History is silent on how he had extricated himself from this dilemma. The NC concluded that the white man had come upon a circumcision dance. Whatever the source of the original report, it had set in motion an extensive military operation.

Lieutenant J.S. Bridger, who was in command of the advance party, wrote in a subsequent report that he was "engaged on special patrol duties in these areas" from 6th to 26th September. Bridger, at the time, was Assistant District Superintendent at Bulawayo and must have moved down to the patrol area as soon as the Commandant-General issued his Special Order. "The patrol," said Bridger, "proceeded under 'mobilisation' conditions and traversed most difficult and rocky country, thickly covered by dense thorn bush." He was not complaining about the conditions, as such. He had a more substantial motive for his report. His purpose was to claim a special "field allowance" to make good the damage to his uniform and kit. "The distance I covered on horseback," he complained, "by road and footpath in the 21 days was 430 miles, the result being that I suffered much damage to clothing, far above the normal rate of wear and tear. As I drew rations I am unable to claim travelling or out-of-pocket expenses."

Bridger's claim for a field allowance caused a flutter in the official dove-cots at the highest level. Lieutenant-Colonel Masterman — now Controller of the Defence Force — and even the Commandant-General himself, spent valuable time considering it. But as Masterman wrote in philosophical vein to the C-G, "One has to take the rough with the smooth as far as one's work is concerned, and our duties combine both the easy life of the towns and the real active work of a police force. To admit that on mobilisation we are to allow for the extra wear and tear of clothes is introducing a principle one cannot recommend". So Bridger was duly informed, "that this claim cannot be admitted. Mobilisation work of this nature is one of the duties inherent for police officers in this country".

The only other report on record about the Mazunga Patrol is from Major G. Stops, Superintendent at Bulawayo at the time. (Next year he was to be Commandant, Depot.) He seems to have joined the patrol to take charge of supplies. He proudly reported when the exercise was over that all the supplies had been accounted for except 1lb. 5oz. of sugar and 2lb. 14oz. of rice. "As some of the supplies were delivered at the last minute at the train by the contractors wrapped up in brown paper, and no spring balance was obtainable to weigh out the rations, I consider this is very satisfactory and that the deficiency be struck off charge." The harness for the vehicles had not been equal to the demands made on it and new traces had had to be improvised from chains at Mazunga. "The cost of these chains was considerable and I suggest they be placed on charge at Bulawayo for use in Scotch Cart ... At West Nicholson I was compelled to hire ox transport from W.H. Rogers to carry the heavy supplies. At Mehato Halt I had to reship on to another wagon, the property of Lemco (Liebig's Extract of Meat Company) ... this was imperative owing to the attitude of Lemco Ltd., who would not allow outside transport to cross their ranch." To add to Lemco's record of unhelpfulness, when one of the troopers from West Nicholson borrowed a mule from them to send a native constable with an urgent despatch, "he was under the impression that the loan was free but Lemco have rendered an account for £2". Stops concluded his report with the information that 222 rounds of .303 ammunition had been used for field practice, and 230 rounds of .450 in target practice for the native police. Now that the Rhodesian native had been to war and fought for the Empire, public clamour against arming him — and even giving him target practice — was relatively rare.

Reports revealed one more legacy of the Mazunga Patrol which remained to be cleared up. The Beira and Mashonaland Railways reported plaintively that 2nd class saloon coach No. 89027, which had been occupied by the BSAP en route from Salisbury to Fort Victoria, had arrived at Gwelo with a broken ornamental glass door pane. Captain Lockwood, who had been in charge of the detachment, was asked to make an investigation, and he duly reported — predictably, one feels — "It was broken by accident when taking kits and saddlery into the train. I do not think anyone is to blame".

Some of the Native Commissioners, when it came to expressing their opinions about the native police, were still showing themselves hard to please. In his annual report for 1918 the NC at Belingwe complained, "The class of native police recruited outside the district has proved highly objectionable". One of the men in his district, he said, had been convicted of assault; another had been committed for trial for an offence under the "adultery ordinance"; a native sergeant was appearing at a preliminary examination accused of rape; and another man had abused the hospitality of his "entertainer" when on patrol and had been found in bed with "one of the entertainer's wives. But," the NC added bitterly, "as the entertainer's marriage has not been registered, apparently no offence lies". The report reached Capell, the Assistant Commissioner, who dismissed it with the sardonic comment, "If the native police were recruited in Paradise I fear they would not satisfy Mr. Campbell".

Public complaints of inadequate police protection still persisted. They all followed the same general pattern. In February 1919 Hatfield again took up the cry and its "General Purposes Committee", however that was constituted, pressed for a police station in the area — which, they said, now had a population of over 100 men, women and children — declaring that "The weekly daylight round of a policeman from Parktown is ... more or less useless. It is very questionable if it even has a moral effect on the native population. There are complaints on all sides of the way the Kaffirs are getting out of hand. The noise by day and night is sometimes hideous." One aggrieved resident had complained that "tom-toms are being beaten, which alone I think is disgraceful within hearing of a white man's abode".

The CSO called for reports. Constable Munson from Parktown wrote, "I patrol Hatfield Estate mounted once a week. Rarely do I get a complaint; when I do it is of a trifling nature". Constable Sheppard said, "A large number of natives pass through Hatfield when travelling between Salisbury and Hunyani. They travel in a very orderly manner. I have never seen one under the influence of drink or in any way creating a disturbance". He sometimes sent his native constable to patrol the Estate on his bicycle. "His book is signed by plot-holders and no complaints have been received." Lieutenant Raison — Assistant Superintendent, Salisbury town — instructed to make a personal investigation wrote, "Four or five residents are anxious to get a police station in Hatfield. This would give the place a more important bearing, with beneficial results to the land owners". He suggested that a certain lady living on the estate had possibly given away the reason for the agitation. "I have heard some singing in the direction of Brown's place" was the only complaint she could think of when asked to make a formal statement to the police. Asked if she had been annoyed by the many natives who passed her house she said she had not. But she had added, quite gratuitously, "We want to be like Avondale. "The last sentence in the statement was underlined, presumably by Lieutenant Raison.

The Commissioner was conspicuously unmoved. His only comment on the situation which was passed on to the Hatfield General Purposes Committee was "The special constable living in the locality is considered to be sufficient protection". The Committee reacted with predictable indignation. "Do we understand," they demanded in a letter on 12 June, "that we must wait until a woman or child has been raped, murdered or otherwise maltreated before we can show sufficient cause for policemen to be stationed at Hatfield?" They had not been impressed by Lieutenant Raison's investigation of their complaint. "It is suggested," they wrote, "that he should come out and interview the men, and not crawl around for half the day to half the people when he knows there are only women at home." The correspondence had now been going on for four months. "I do not think the case for more police protection has been strengthened by this letter," the Commissioner noted in its margin. However, some action was presumably taken for on the 21 August the General Purposes Committee wrote another letter — still requesting "a night patrol once a week" which, in the light of earlier demands, was surprisingly modest — but continuing, "The Committee thanks the Commissioner for what has already been done. There is a marked difference in the behaviour of natives living in and passing through Hatfield. But," they could not resist adding, "a much greater improvement is hoped for".

## Chapter Twenty-Three

## DESERTION AND DISSENSION

THE AFFAIRS OF the force in the years immediately following WWI were naturally concerned principally with the problems of recruiting and the need for readjustment to a peace-time footing. On 14 January 1919 — two months after the Armistice — the Executive Council in Salisbury (still the autocratic instrument of Chartered Company rule) cabled the Secretary of the BSA Company in London with instructions to recruit 150 replacements for members of the force due for discharge. During the war, of course, men had been retained even though their contracts had expired.

Bodle, now retired as a Brigadier-General, was once again given the job of interviewing recruits in London. (It was now 30 years since he had chosen the first recruits for the Company's Police in Kimberley.) He was told to select the new men "from ex-soldiers and yeomen" under 30 years of age who had served in the war. One suspects that the term "yeoman" — implying, as the dictionary defines it, "not ranking as one of the gentry" — was intended to exclude men who had been to public schools, as subsequent controversy on the merits and demerits of the English public schoolboy will reveal. Out of the 150 men required all but 30 were to be chosen from those who had served in "a mounted corps". The 30, assumedly, were for the town police and the remainder for the district. They were to be sent out to Rhodesia in batches of 50 every month, but they would have to pay for their passage by ship to Cape Town themselves and also for the railway fare from Cape Town to Salisbury. This last imposition was to cause perennial dissension. And as it transpired the flow of recruits never came anywhere near the numbers suggested.

In February Edwards recommended to the Board of the Company that they should grant pardons to seven members of the force who had been convicted of desertion in absentia when they had slipped away from Rhodesia during the war to join the forces overseas. A pardon, he said, should be granted "provided the individual concerned had enlisted 'at home' or elsewhere" and that he could produce a certificate signed by his Commanding Officer that he had rendered good service. "However," Edwards added, "I am not at all anxious that any of these individuals, who failed us at a time when the services of every man who could be spared were required on our own border and in East Africa, should be permitted to re-enlist in the BSAP." The Board — with the unique power of criminal conviction and pardon which, as a mere commercial concern, it incongruously wielded — duly agreed to Edwards's recommendation. The Directors told him reassuringly, "If only seven deserted during the whole period of the war, this is itself satisfactory proof of the steadiness of the force and the sense of loyalty of the men."

One would-be deserter had got no farther than the railway station at Bulawayo before he was arrested, charged with desertion and sentenced to imprisonment. His name was James Fife Douglas, who some years later was to serve for 13 years as the force's Olympian and respected RSM. Because "Jock" Douglas subsequently played such a prominent and colourful part in the history of the BSAP — second only in reputation and regimental renown to the incomparable James Blatherwick — his story must be told in full: not merely for the sake of recalling the misdemeanours and misfortunes in the early part of his career, but to give full credit to a man who reinstated himself after such inauspicious beginnings. It was unlikely enough, in the context of a highly disciplined force such as the BSAP, that a man would even be considered for promotion to RSM if he had any defaulter's record at all. Douglas's record was formidable: it included convictions for "neglecting to obey an order", "drunk while off duty", "misconduct while on investigating duty", "absence without leave" — and, as a crowning felony, "desertion".

His official record of service states that he enlisted in the Royal Scots Greys at Perth, in Scotland, in 1894. In an application for a transfer which he made many years later when he was in the BSAP, he claimed to have served for three years and four months as an NCO in the Gordon Highlanders before he joined the Scots Greys. Some unkind official noted on the occasion of that application that if he had actually served for so long in the British Army before he joined the BSAP he must first have enlisted when he was 14, which was unlikely. Whatever the truth may have been, he certainly served with the Scots Greys during the Anglo-Boer war and was discharged at Pretoria in 1902 with the rank of corporal, character "very good". He had been on active service for three years, was mentioned in dispatches during the relief of Kimberley and received both the Queen's and King's medals. He then joined the Cape Police, serving at De Aar, and bought himself out in 1904, character again "satisfactory". Then he seems to have spent some years prospecting for gold in the Zambezi valley. As so many other fortune hunters of that era were to find, the riches they expected to pick up so readily were perennially elusive. So he finally made his way to Salisbury and enlisted as a trooper in the BSAP, in April 1910. Accompanying his application for enlistment was a letter from Major-General Scobell, written from Government House, Cape Town, saying "Douglas was a first-rate soldier, a good signaller" — which meant that he was proficient in waving semaphore flags — "and an NCO of excellent character and influence. I am sure he would make a very good mounted policeman."

But he was soon to find himself in conflict with authority. Those were the days when police defaulters were dealt with by the courts. Only three months after he enlisted he was convicted by the Salisbury magistrate on two counts: fined £4 (or one month's imprisonment with hard labour) for neglecting to obey an order and £2 (or 14 days) for being drunk "when off duty". However, he managed to keep his record clean for the next five years. He was transferred to the detective branch of the town police in Bulawayo in 1914. When his six months' probation in the branch was over the Officer Commanding CID, Major Brundell, reported, "Detective Douglas has given satisfaction. I have found him to be absolutely reliable, energetic and capable ... he has passed the exam in the Finger Print System. I recommend his (permanent) appointment." He was promoted to 3rd class detective sergeant.

A year later, in 1915, he was sent to the Filabusi district to investigate an allegation of illegal possession of gold amalgam by certain white mine employees. In his own words he had been instructed to "rush the place of the Austrian manager of the Blue Reef Mine early in the morning and ascertain if the information is correct." In the event, he accomplished nothing at all; indeed, he seems to have caused a great deal of trouble and embarrassment. The official records of what actually transpired on this lively occasion contain a number of reports by civilians as well as members of the police at Filabusi, but probably Douglas's own version of events, in a report he was ordered to make to the District Superintendent in Gwelo, is the most illuminating.

"Prior to retiring for the night," he wrote, "Mr. Hawkin and myself had a whisky and soda split, and I swear as there is a God above me that no other liquor of any description passed my lips that day." Then followed a long and confused dissertation on his fruitless attempts next morning to pursue his investigations. He continued, "(the next) evening I adjourned to the Mess hut at the Slope Mine. A bottle of whisky was produced after dinner, all partook of this and then we lapsed (sic) into conversation. The conversation as is usual on the outlying mines consisted of the subject of women. One miner related how his home had been broken up by a Policeman in Bulawayo. The Policeman, while on night duty, was found by the miner in bed with his wife. The Policeman was charged, fined and transferred to Salisbury, the miner's wife accompanying him."

But it was not only at Filabusi that Douglas had been indulging in indiscretions. Some weeks earlier he had been sent to Gwelo to attend the High Court. Brundell, whose first opinion of Douglas had now been sadly modified, had reported to the Staff Officer, "It is proved beyond doubt that Detective Sergeant Douglas cohabited with Mollie Schultz at Gwelo on 18 October. (He has also) disclosed official and confidential information to civilians." The allegation was that Douglas himself had regaled his drinking companions with details of the case of the wife-stealing policeman. "I am of the opinion that the services of Detective Sergeant Douglas should no longer be retained and accordingly recommend his discharge." In another report Brundell said, "Mollie Schultz is an ex-barmaid from the Savoy Hotel, of doubtful repute. They were recently living at the Palmerston Hotel (Bulawayo) in different rooms but connected, and are now occupying rooms at Earp's Chambers."

Lieutenant Hough, in Gwelo, reported "There is no doubt Detective Sergeant Douglas did stay at the Gwelo Hotel with the woman Mollie Schultz as husband and wife. There was a good deal of singing going on by the woman and she also played the piano at the hotel ...  but beyond this I could not find any evidence of bad behaviour." While a Constable Smith stated, "The songs were sentimental ones and everyone present commented on the lady's accomplishments." But one Stanley Perry (rank unclear) said in an affidavit, "I saw the names of Mr. & Mrs. Douglas on the hotel board and they were occupying one bedroom. I spoke to Douglas about it and he informed me that he got married in Bulawayo by special licence last week ... I was instructed by the Superintendent CID to examine the marriage register and could find no trace of a special licence issued to James Douglas."

The Commissioner, to whom the reports were sent, was not inclined to deal with Douglas as drastically as Brundell had recommended. But he decided to take stern action. He wrote to the Secretary of the Department of the Administrator, "I am satisfied that Detective Sergeant Douglas has been guilty of grave irregularities and indiscretions. He has in my opinion proved himself to be totally unfitted to be entrusted with Police enquiries or work of a confidential nature and I have therefore ordered him to revert to uniformed District Police Duty and in doing so he automatically reverts to the ranks." (One can only conclude that duty in the districts was still regarded more as a military presence than as police work involving enquiries "of a confidential nature".) So, on 15 November 1915, Constable Douglas took the night train from Bulawayo and reported for duty in Gwelo next morning. On 11 December he was sent to Que Que. His orders read, "You will leave Que Que this afternoon with Trooper Bacon for Gokwe on transfer. Remain properly dressed en route and report to NCO at Gokwe ... mule 45 having strayed will be sent to Gokwe at first opportunity."

A gentleman named George Gull ran a taxi service and garage in Bulawayo (later well known as Gull and Kimpton's). On the morning of 13 December a rickshaw carrier brought him a note signed by "Charlie Anderson" asking for a taxi to take the writer to Plumtree. Gull knew no one named Charlie Anderson but he took a car to the railway station where he saw Douglas, whom he knew, in plain clothes. Douglas told Gull he had written the note and signed it "Charlie Anderson" because, as he was later to explain rather lamely at his trial, "I was afraid the native might have handed it to someone else." Gull also knew of Douglas's recent brushes with authority. He felt suspicious and said he would have to go back to the garage for enough petrol for the journey. He would then come back and pick up Douglas. At the garage, Gull consulted his partner and they decided to report their suspicions to Brundell. Brundell sent Lieutenant J.S. Morris (the future Commissioner) and a detective back to the railway station with Gull. At the station Morris asked Douglas to show his pass permitting him to be absent from Gwelo, and when Douglas was unable to produce any such thing he was placed under arrest and taken to the cells at the police station. He was carrying a bag of clothing. He was not charged that day, but his name was entered in the Occurrence Book as "detained". Searched by Sergeant J.E. Salt, he was found to have 21 £5 notes, one gold sovereign (there was no £1 note in those days), and eight shillings in silver.

A Board of Officers was convened by order of the Commissioner. The Board consisted of Major A.J. Tomlinson, Captain C.E. Pitt-Schenkel (who always wore a monocle) and Lieutenant A. Raison (who, on an earlier occasion, had upset the Hatfield residents by only calling on their wives). Sub-Inspector J. Skillen was the prosecutor. The charge against Douglas was that he did "wrongfully and unlawfully desert from the British South Africa Police at Gwelo on 12 December 1915." Douglas pleaded not guilty.

The evidence which was led of his absence from duty and subsequent arrest at Bulawayo was indisputable. In his own sworn statement Douglas, referring to his recent demotion, said, "Owing to certain complaints against me I was reduced to Constable. I had no trial. This hurt me somewhat. I was ordered to go to the Gokwe district in the Zambezi valley. I decided that (rather than go there) I would see the Commissioner at any cost. On my arrival at Bulawayo I made enquiries and heard that the Commissioner had left for Livingstone. I knew if I was seen in town that I would be arrested and I decided to remain just outside Bulawayo at the Terminus Hotel (Matopos]. I mentioned Plumtree on the note to Gull to make him bring plenty of petrol to get to the Terminus Hotel. I used the name 'Charlie Anderson' because I was afraid the native might hand the note to someone else for enquiry. I had no intention of deserting. I wanted to get to see the Commissioner and if I had got to Gokwe I would not have seen him for a long period. I am sure I would have got fever again and with the rains now on it would be impossible to get from Gokwe for several months. I admit absence without leave. My intention was to come back from the Terminus Hotel immediately the Commissioner returned. I came to Bulawayo in a goods train from Gwelo. I travelled from Que Que by motor-car. I intended forwarding my money home. I drew it about two months ago in Bulawayo."

Douglas's statement is quoted here at length so that it may be weighed in support or in contradiction of the legend — which has since persisted — that his clumsy attempt to desert from the force was prompted solely by patriotism, by a burning desire to "join up" and fight in the war. If that was his desire it was certainly shared by many members of the BSAP and, as has been shown, seven others had fulfilled it by deserting. But he never advanced it in his own defence. Perhaps he thought that to admit any intention to desert, even for the purpose of "joining up", would be fatal, particularly as it had been made abundantly clear to the whole force that a deserter, no matter how patriotic his purpose, would be heavily punished. And yet one cannot help feeling that a plea of patriotic motives would have found more sympathy with the Board of Officers than the patently untrue story he asked them to accept. That he intended to cross the border at the nearest accessible point, Plumtree, is obvious; that having succeeded he would have somehow found his way to England to join the fighting forces is probable. But one suspects that, whatever his motive, it was not uninfluenced by a wish to run away from the unpleasant situation in the force which he had brought upon himself.

The Board found him guilty of desertion and sentenced him to four month's imprisonment with hard labour. In accordance with the law, the verdict and sentence were reviewed by a High Court judge, the Hon. Mr. Justice Russell. Russell said in his judgement that "Trooper (sic) Douglas was charged with desertion. In his defence the accused said he had come to Bulawayo to see Colonel Edwards and had not tried to escape from the Force. The facts against the accused are that he had a considerable sum of money in his possession when he came to Bulawayo. In his note to the taxi-driver he had indicated Plumtree as his destination. His intention was to desert. The decision of the Board of Officers is confirmed." One point made by Douglas in his appeal was that the Commissioner was not competent to convene a Board of Officers because the actual wording of the Police Regulations required such a board to be set up by "the Superintendent". The constitution of the Board, he claimed, had therefore been ultra vires. Russell readily dismissed this piece of pedantry.

Douglas served his sentence in Depot, incarcerated in a cell in the little square wood and iron build-ing which still serves as the guard-room today. He spent his time working in the grounds, tending the flower-beds and planting trees, in the domain over which at a later, happier period he was to rule the roost as the RSM.

When he had finished his sentence he was posted to Fort Victoria, still a constable. But he had not altogether mended his ways. In June 1916, Major Masterson, the District Superintendent, wrote to the Commissioner, "I am transferring Constable Douglas to Salisbury in order to keep him out of mischief. If he stays here any longer I am positive there will be trouble over the woman Miss Correcci, or Correlli, or whatever her name is." The Commissioner asked for more details and Masterson reported, "One evening a certain resident of Victoria went for a walk with the woman with whom Douglas has got mixed up. They returned to the person's house and Douglas followed them. He was on duty at the time. He pretended to be very surprised to find a third party present. He started a cock and bull story of a murder having been committed near the Gaol and said he was turning out 'boys' to hunt the murderer. He wanted to know how many 'boys' the owner of the house had ... There is no doubt," Masterson added, "he is trying to get his discharge."

Douglas was duly transferred to Salisbury and a few months later he put in a formal application for immediate discharge. He said, "I have not been doing my duty towards my Parents, my Country, or my full duty as a Policeman. I am an old soldier and have in previous years had the honour of serving my Country when she was in difficulties and I then helped to add glories to the Regimental Colours. I should like to be given the opportunity of doing so again ... I have tried very hard to go to the Front and for same have suffered a long term of imprisonment. All my attempts have been frustrated. My heart, my thoughts and my mind are for ever at the Front at Flanders." (It was on this occasion that he claimed the hitherto unrecorded service in the Gordon Highlanders.)

But once again his motive was hardly one of unmixed patriotism. He had not been wasting his time in Salisbury. He was engagingly frank on the subject. "My reason for this application," he wrote in a covering letter, "is that intimate relations exist between me and (a certain lady) of Salisbury, and as she is persistent in her intentions I wish to leave Rhodesia as soon as possible. She tells me that she is in a state of pregnancy, but I am satisfied in my own mind that I am not responsible for this. Under the circumstances I am anxious to leave Rhodesia before further trouble ensues." It was as good a reason as any for wanting to fight for his country.

For once someone in authority took his side. The Assistant District Superintendent, Salisbury Town, endorsed his application, "I recommend he be sent on active service to East Africa on account of his relations with (the lady), together with the fact that he is undoubtedly a good stamp of fighting man."

And so, at last, Douglas was granted his wish and in February 1917 he was seconded to the Rhodesia Native Regiment for service in German East Africa.

While the Mazunga Patrol in 1918 had been initiated in response to a presumably dangerous situation — no matter how unjustified the presumption turned out to be — it served as a pattern of police routine which was to be repeated a number of times during the immediate post-war years. The next such exercise was known as the Makoni Patrol which left Depot in Salisbury on 8 October 1919. Whether there had been any reports of unrest is not explicit in the records. More probably the patrol was conceived as a show of force to discourage any lurking tendencies among the natives to display discontent. But the Order establishing the patrol did say, "A garrison is required at Rusape for about eight days" although it made no mention of what the garrison might be needed for; and it laid down that a mounted patrol, with 33 horses and 20 mules, would arrive at Rusape "about 20th October". When Stops, now the Depot Commandant who led the patrol, made his subsequent report, he stated the object to have been, "to patrol the Makoni and Wedza Reserves and to train recruits, 23 of whom accompanied the patrol." Indeed on this occasion, recruits appear to have made up the whole patrol, apart from the supernumeraries. The first march was to Rusape, which it reached as planned on the 20th, and it moved next day into the Makoni Reserve, accompanied by the Native Commissioner. "We patrolled rugged country," wrote Stops, "at times only possible for dismounted men — deep valleys, large precipitous dongas." There were many small kraals, suggesting a large native population, but "we saw no more than 12 able-bodied natives during the day ... I saw a type entirely new to me. One can't say they were insolent, but they certainly appeared to be wanting in respect. It is usual for the chiefs and headmen to visit our camp, or assemble at spots on the line of march, but this was not done. The few natives we saw were of poor physique, but wiry, typical hillmen."

He said that owing to the nature of the country, which was made up of mountain ranges and broken kopjes, it would be impossible to move anywhere out of rifle range of any hidden antagonists. "Should trouble occur," he reported, "operations would have to be carried out by either European or Native infantry — the latter for preference, as Europeans would experience considerable difficulty in climbing the hills, many of which are almost impossible for men wearing boots. To move any transport other than packs would be impossible." The natives in the Wedza Reserve, he found, were "a better off, more civilised type."

As for the effect of the patrol on training the recruits, "this did not come up to my expectations." When they had set out from Salisbury, "the majority of the men could not ride, and they took too much out of the horses in the first few days." Only after leaving the Wedza Reserve had they become even fair riders, able to partake in skirmishing and attacking exercises. "If it can be avoided," wrote Stops, "no recruits should be sent out on patrol until they have completed training in Depot." The discipline as a whole had been good, but Corporal R. (obviously not a recruit) had been an offender, "whose example has unhappily been reflected in some of the others. As a saddler his services were valuable. I had also placed him in charge of the stores. This was at the bottom of his trouble ... The horses as a whole could not be considered as good serviceable animals. A month's active service would have dismounted at least two thirds of the men." In general, Stops's report does not suggest the 1919 Makoni Patrol had been a conspicuous success, but hopefully the authorities learnt something from it.

The first batch of Bodle's recruits did not arrive in Salisbury until the middle of 1919 and they were soon showing signs of discontent. They were all men who had seen active service during the war — seasoned campaigners, very different from the younger recruits, virtually straight from school, who had preceded them during the pre-war days and were to follow in the next few years. Naturally, there were some barrack-room lawyers among them. They claimed to have been misled by Bodle in London to believe that at the end of their three year' engagement they would be given free passages back to England. They now found this was not part of their contracts. Their conditions of pay and the issue of free kit, they declared, had also been misrepresented to them. Nor had they received free dental treatment, as they claimed to have expected. And, no doubt looking for as many grounds for complaint as possible, they protested that they had not been given "acceptable third class passages" on the ship to Cape Town.

There was clearly some justification for this last complaint, as one of the Company's directors revealed in a private letter to the Secretary. On 24 August, Mr. Malcolm (later Sir Dougal Malcolm) who happened to be travelling to Cape Town on the same ship as a second batch of recruits, wrote

"Those 50 odd boys going out to join the BSAP, whom we saw in Bodle's office on Tuesday, and who are on board, came to me through a spokesman about their messing accommodation which is that of the Tommies (serving soldiers in transit) and pretty rough. They are not Tommies but demobilised men: i.e., civilians going out under civil contract with us to be attested as policemen in Rhodesia — and not, at the moment, under military discipline at all. I have managed for them to have their meals in the 3rd class saloon" The previous, first batch — who were complaining in Salisbury — had not been so fortunate.

It is popularly believed — as numerous references in subsequent writings suggest — that the police in Salisbury went on strike in 1919 as a result of the discontent. However, there is nothing on record which confirms any such positive action. The Rhodesia Herald reported on 21 July that members of the BSAP had been holding meetings demanding more pay to counter that perennial bogey "the high cost of living". The sergeants had held a meeting on Monday night — the corporals and troopers on Tuesday. "Meetings of the Town police are to be held to support their comrades in the Camp." The Herald, in a leader, displayed open sympathy for the men's demands.

Rumours were insistent in the town that the newcomers intended to strike. But the Company seems to have propagated equally insistent reports that the men had known full well to what they were committing themselves when they signed their contracts in London, and to have added gratuitously that, in any case, the conditions in the BSAP were better than those of any metropolitan force. (It so happened that in that same month, July 1919, British police in Liverpool went on strike. The city was taken over by looters and army units had to be called in to restore order.) The Company's propaganda seems to have been more effective than the men's, for public feeling ran high in Salisbury against the police who, it was asserted, intended to strike and abandon the inhabitants to the savagery of the natives. The Association of the Comrades of the Great War called a meeting at the Drill Hall in August to declare dramatically to the populace that they would police the town themselves if necessary.

One of the prominent speakers at the meeting was Mr. G.M. Huggins, the surgeon (later Sir Godfrey Huggins and, later still, Lord Malvern) who had just returned from the war himself. He had served in France as a Captain in the Royal Army Medical Corps. He declared, in the unambiguous manner for which he was to become famous, that the public would not tolerate a police strike. But nevertheless it was Huggins himself who quelled the noisy protests when two members of the self-appointed Police Committee stood up and asked to be allowed to put their case before the meeting. Huggins insisted that in the spirit of fair play they should be given a chance to speak. The chastened audience listened quietly to the two men who both, in all prudence, gave their word that they and their colleagues would not leave the town unprotected but were nevertheless determined to fight for redress of their grievances. When they had finished Huggins, with characteristic generosity, undertook to check the facts as they presented them and, if these were deserving of consideration, to make representations on their behalf to the authorities. (This was the first occasion on which the man who was later to become the longest serving Prime Minister in the British Commonwealth took any open part in public affairs.)

Huggins's representations bore immediate fruit. On 2 September Drummond Chaplin, the Administrator, cabled the Board of the Chartered Company in London. "After full investigation of police demands it appears necessary to make concessions of which most important are permanent increase of sixpence per day to troopers and constables after they have passed recruit stage and temporary increase of ninepence in ration allowance. Total cost this financial year about £10,000. Concessions proposed are considerably smaller than demands but if granted now will I think provide solution." The Board, possibly impressed by events in Liverpool and even nearer home (the police in London were now also threatening to strike), immediately cabled agreement and the extra one and threepence a day seems to have silenced the dissenters.

But the need for more recruits was still acute. Almost every station was under establishment. On 27 October the Assistant Superintendent, Bulawayo Town, reported to the CSO, "The strength of the station is less than half the authorised. People are noticing there are very few policemen about and they are beginning to comment. Fortunately things are very quiet and there have been no crimes of a serious nature, but if we were unfortunate enough to have a serious black peril case it would set the people clamouring against the Government." Force Orders in December revealed, however, the Commissioner's principal concern. "In wishing them the compliments of the season General Edwards would like to impress on all ranks that the advent of Peace must not be interpreted to mean that Police work is to be of a humdrum nature, performed without interest or in a perfunctory manner, and that now more than ever will it be necessary for the BSAP, not only to prove themselves reliable Policemen, but thoroughly efficient soldiers." (Author's italics.)

The Commissioner's concern was echoed — although in a very different context — by a public meeting called in February 1920 in a small town in Matabeleland. (This account deliberately refrains from naming the town to avoid identification of the principal character in the incidents which ensued.) The purpose of the meeting, as advertised, was to discuss "the undefended state of the country" which was blamed primarily on "the lack of police protection". The sponsor and chairman of the meeting, whom we shall call Mr. A. (which was not his initial), warned the audience of the need to be prepared for "attacks by askaris (native police) led by Europeans and versed in the art of indirect machine gun fire" — a practice, which, one feels, would constitute more of a conjuring trick than an art. Inevitably, he reminded the meeting of the 1896 rising. Reporting the meeting to the CSO, the District Superintendent said, "Mr. A., who was once in the BSAP, has always made a hobby of agitating for white police, holding that the local natives in the police would be a source of danger." The CSO's only response was to express his hope that the force would be up to full strength (i.e. pre-war establishment) by June.

Nothing more was heard from Mr. A. for some months, until he wrote, in pencil, to his local Civil Commissioner, "Kindly forward the enclosed statements to His Honour the Administrator of Rhodesia, to His Majestys the Kings of South Africa, as a grievances from some of His Majesty's loyal subjects." There was only one statement enclosed, also in pencil, signed by a Mr. S., but clearly in Mr. A.'s handwriting — which showed the distinct effect of some spirituous influence. "Having been staying on Mr. A.'s farm for the last three days I have seen what he has to put up with over insolence from the natives, in neglecting their duty and also no protection from the Police." Mr. S. signed himself, "as an old Pioneer who has known Mr. A. for the last 23 years." Mr. A. followed this with another letter to His Honour the Administrator asking to be given 200 rounds of Lee Metford ammunition, "sealed, which the Police can inspect on their monthly patrol, that is, if you have any police in the country. Owing to the loss of cattle and other thiefs, also destruction of animals, as loyal subject of the King we are asking his support, not being anxious to take the law in our own hands." One is inclined to wonder for what other purpose than to take the law into his own hands he had asked for the Lee Metford ammunition. He concluded, "As a farmer I am asking for police protection."

Asked by the CSO for his comments, the District Superintendent replied, "Although he is an old hand in the country, Mr. A. has yet to learn how to deal with natives, I knew Mr. A. 11 years ago and he was then, as now, of perpetually intemperate habits. I visited his farm and he said there should be not less than 50 European police in (the local) camp. All three letters are in Mr. A.'s handwriting, though one is signed by Mr. S. The style and phraseology adopted by the writer is, I suggest, sufficient explanation of his condition at the time he wrote them." The Administrator replied to Mr. A. that "reports show that police protection is not lacking." He reminded him that European police had visited his farm 10 times in five months and that a trooper in charge of a small-pox cordon had been stationed within two miles of his house for over a month. Mr. A. replied, on one of the days the trooper actually visited him, "There are no police in the district to deal with small pox or other poxes." (A few years later The Outpost reported, in what was manifestly an actionable statement, "Troopers engaged in small-pox cordons received a penny a head for vaccinating natives. It is alleged than many of them, when they ran out of serum, used condensed milk for which the natives gratefully paid a penny a time." In actual fact, of course, it was not the natives who paid, but the Government.)

It appears from the records that the authorities refused to be drawn into further correspondence, so Mr. A. wrote again to the Civil Commissioner saying the police force was inefficient; the men were dissatisfied with conditions of service and therefore not to be trusted; the demeanour of the natives was due to Bolshevik propaganda; and the arrangements for the defence of the country were hopelessly inadequate. The CC passed the letter to the Commissioner with a note saying, "This comes from a man who is a leading resident and spokesman in this community and who appears to take himself very seriously. My opinion is that he is obsessed with a not quite normal fear of the danger of possible native unrest. "The Commissioner patiently commented, "His obsession of native unrest renders it quite impossible to deal with him in a rational manner".

## Chapter Twenty-Four

## TRAPS AND PATROLS

"JOCK" DOUGLAS'S SECONDMENT to the Rhodesia Native Regiment in 1917 had been his salvation. Constrained by conditions of life on active service, his qualities as a soldier reasserted themselves and he soon made his mark in the regiment. Within two months he was appointed Acting Sergeant-Major and a year later he was promoted to RSM. In January 1919 he was mentioned in dispatches, described as "a strict disciplinarian, keen and energetic". The adjutant of the RNR wrote, "Much of the credit for the good name obtained by the Regiment in the field during the time this Warrant Officer held the position of RSM, is due to him." But the war and the campaign in East Africa were over and in March that year he was transferred back to the BSAP where he was obliged, at first, to resume his rank as a constable. True to form, immediately on his arrival in Salisbury, he wrote to the CSO, "I have the honour to report for your information that whilst on leave in Johannesburg I married a lady named Dorothy Myra Curtis (certificate and photo attached) and I now beg to request that permission to be married may be granted me." Nothing is on record of how the CSO reacted to this characteristic request to be granted permission for a fait accompli. By all accounts, the marriage was surprisingly successful.

He also applied for reinstatement as a second sergeant in the CID. But he was understandably doubtful of his chances. "Should this application not be favourably considered," he wrote, "I would ask that I may be appointed as Drill Instructor with the rank of Warrant Officer. In support of this I would point out that I have had a long experience in both cavalry and infantry work."

Brundell, commanding the CID, was not enthusiastic to have him back. "On review of all the circumstances" he wrote to the Commissioner, "and notwithstanding the subsequent conduct of this man whilst on Active Service (which, I understand, has been good) it would, in my opinion, be a dangerous precedent to follow" — he meant, of course, "to create" — "by reinstating a man in the manner indicated (second class detective sergeant). It is of primary importance that the character and integrity of all members of this Department should be above the slightest reproach and I am therefore not prepared to recommend his application."

No one had been confirmed as RSM since Blatherwick had been commissioned in 1917. In June 1919 Douglas was promoted to Temporary 1st Sergeant, to perform the duties of depot instructor. He was told that he was only filling a temporary position in Depot to deal with the unusual influx of recruits. In August Capell, then acting as Commissioner, reported him "a fine policeman and a good soldier". But the need for the temporary instructor seems soon to have fallen away and next month he reverted to duty in Salisbury town as a 2nd sergeant. However, in March 1920, he was back in Depot as Acting RSM and Major Stops, the Commandant Depot, reported in May, "He has given entire satisfaction during the period he has been acting as RSM. He sets a fine example to juniors whose respect he commands. He is a good disciplinarian. I recommend he be confirmed in his rank and appointed RSM." And so, after an initiation in his career which can only be described as unusual, "Jock" Douglas took his providentially ordained place in the annals of the BSAP.

In August 1920 an entirely new item was added to the responsibilities of the police — an item which has for ever grown more onerous over the ensuing years and has probably caused more animosity between the police and the public than any other of their mandatory activities. A speed limit of 15 miles per hour was introduced for motor traffic. Faced with the duty of enforcing it, the CSO wrote to the Controller of the Defence Force (who, presumably, was responsible for the supply of equipment), "15 mph is a ridiculously slow pace for a motor-car travelling along an unfrequented road with visible cross roads. Not one per cent of the drivers take the slightest notice of it. Prosecutions necessitate the use of three European constables with two stop-watches. The only reliable watch," he added, "that is the slightest use for this work is that used by the Metropolitan Police in London and they should be obtained by the Company's representative in London from the Commissioner of Police, New Scotland Yard."

Precise instructions for the manner in which "speed trapping" was to be operated were issued in a circular from the CSO. A portion of the street was to be marked off as a measured furlong. Three constables were to be employed: "Number One at the entrance to the control, Number Two concealed at the far end and Number Three concealed 100 yards on." Numbers One and Two would be in plain clothes, each with a stop-watch; Number Three would be in uniform. There followed a lively description of how Number One "considering (an approaching motor-car) to be exceeding the speed limit, i.e. over 15 mph" would signal to Number Two to be on the alert. Then, as the car passed him he would signal again and set going his stop-watch. Number Three, if he had properly interpreted the signals — which were not too readily visible through the dust raised by the car — would do the same. "If Number Two is satisfied the car is exceeding the speed limit (when it passes him) he will signal to Number Three who will step out into the road and stop the car." At motor-car speeds in those days, even exceeding 15 miles an hour, the procedure could be relatively leisurely. Numbers One and Two (the former having laboriously covered the furlong on foot in the wake of the car) would then approach the victim. "Stop-watches will be compared in the presence of the driver of the car, who will be allowed to see them — also the Table written out to show at what rate per hour the car had been driven within the furlong." This part of the procedure, too, could be leisurely. There was so little motor traffic that it was unlikely that another car would come along before the first had been dealt with and the constables had returned to their strategic positions

The CSO's circular promised that some members would be specially trained for this exacting work.

And in the same year the CSO referred to the Assistant Superintendent, Salisbury Town, a complaint by the Rev. J.W Stanlake about the propriety of some pictures exhibited in certain shop windows. "I have seen the pictures," the Assistant Superintendent replied, "and am not prepared to state that the possession or exhibition of them constitutes a contravention of Ordinance 14 of 1911. "He listed the works of art with some apparent relish "Thorwaldesen's Venus", a nude female, "I believe a copy of an original painting"; a nude female looking into a stream, "there is nothing indecent about it"; two pictures of women "with shoulders and breasts exposed"; a picture of a nude female "showing back and one breast"; two pictures of nude women, titled for some unfathomable reason "The Scourge" — "they are shown sitting on a rock catching water in a bowl, legs crossed and breasts exposed; a nude woman and child, "Youth and Cupid" — the woman is in a reclining posture, with the child leaning on her thigh"; and finally a nude female "in a sitting posture, breasts showing, hand to ear, listening— 'The Echo'."

The CSO ruled, "While it may be held that the exposure of these pictures to the public is undesirable, it cannot be held in any way to be a contravention of Ordinance 14 of 1911. The Commissioner will be glad if you will interview the proprietors of the firms concerned and inform them that this complaint has been made and point out the undesirability, in view of our large native population, of exhibiting such pictures in shop windows."

In July 1921, at a farm near Gwelo, the white woman who occupied it on her own had sent for the police because one of her native labourers had refused to work. It was a routine situation, with which the BSAP have ever been familiar. A trooper and native constable duly visited the farm and warned and cautioned the native that he would be charged under the Masters and Servants Act. The woman appeared quite satisfied with what the police had done, but unfortunately soon after they withdrew the native proceeded to murder her. Subsequent evidence suggested she had given him a great deal of provocation, but he was nevertheless convicted and hanged. Inevitably, before the case came to court, the police were heavily criticised for having left the woman alone with a potential murderer. The District Superintendent at Gwelo naturally came in for most of the opprobrium and, harassed from all sides, he suggested to the CSO that a statement, giving the real facts, should be made to the Press. The Commissioner replied, "It is tacitly acknowledged throughout all British Police Forces that a certain amount of mud will be thrown, and experience has shown that it seldom serves any good purpose to take any notice of it."

The next rural patrol in strength had been sent out in 1921. On this occasion, it was a fully professional affair and the recruits were left behind. Major Stops was in command again — this time in his substantive rank and not as Depot Commandant — and Captain Onyett was his adjutant. Unfortunately, nobody gave this patrol a distinctive name by which it could go down in history, but its itinerary included Enkeldoorn, Wedza, Macheke, and the Mangwendi and Chikwakwa Reserves. There was a small problem to be faced at the outset. The Chief Staff Officer wrote, "As the Dutch are celebrating Nachtmaal on 3rd and 4th September, it will be inadvisable for the patrol to camp at

Enkeldoorn." However, the difficulty seems to have been resolved by making Brigadier-General du Toit, a local resident, an "honorary sub-district commandant" in the local defence scheme. As the CSO explained, "Having been a soldier all his life, commanding one of the Dutch columns during the (Anglo) Boer War and holding his present rank under General Botha during the German South West Africa campaign, he is anxious to continue some military duties. He is calling a meeting of section commanders at Enkeldoorn, where he is going to arrange manoeuvres. The Staff should travel to Enkeldoorn a few days before." Presumably the "section commanders" belonged to the local volunteers. The Brigadier-General obviously took his military duties seriously, as he wrote to the CSO from "Versailles," P.O. Enkeldoorn — a felicitous address — "Please send me some Fulscap paper ... "

The Nachtmaal difficulty was further assuaged by a letter from H.S. Coetzee — who signed himself as "Section Commander, P.B. Riversdale, Enkeldoorn" — addressed to "Honourable General Edward, Commanding General, Salisbury." Confirming that "Holy Communion would take effect (sic) at Enkeldoorn on Sunday, 4th September, 1921," he added, "if you still have an intention to honour us with your presence which will be highly esteemed and appreciated, I beg that you will kindly instruct me accordingly." The C-G replied that he hoped to be in Enkeldoorn for the occasion and it must be assumed that he honoured his undertaking.

The object of the patrol, on this occasion, was "to carry out military training only". It consisted of 60 mounted men with 40 armed native police, accompanied by three 10-mule wagons and one eight-mule "trolley". A subsequent report (assumedly by the Adjutant, Captain Onyett) said, "Wagons are not suitable as first line transport with mounted troops in war time, when motor transport or pack animals, or hired light carts would have to be used, according to the country (in which they were operating) or the vehicles available. Taking into consideration the ease with which suitable vehicles (scotch carts, trolleys, motor-cars, etc.) could be purchased in case of emergency, the wisdom of purchasing any more Limbered Wagons is questionable, as they could not replace our wagons for normal duties."

The need for economy was still a pressing consideration. Early in 1922, District Superintendents were invited to prepare "Confidential Economy. Reports" suggesting savings that could be made in the operation of their stations. The suggestion from Gwelo was typical of opinion throughout the supervisory ranks. "If a reduction in lower ranks is contemplated, the clerical work should be completely reorganised, and a simpler and less expensive set of books issued." The Commissioner was not so ready to accept this opinion. "No two officers appear to have the same ideas," he wrote, "and others, after recommending that some form or other should be adopted later on, then turn round — after their suggestion has been adopted — and say it s totally unnecessary and the cause of much extra labour!

"My own view is that recommendations (that certain books should be abolished) are made more on account of the way the books are kept than because they are expensive. Nothing but tuition can overcome this, and if an officer finds his subordinates unable to keep the official books he should (1) remain at his post until he is satisfied that the subordinate has mastered the subject or (2) arrange for sending someone to instruct him or (3) remove the subordinate if he cannot learn. There are hundreds of men in the force who can do this work with ease and I am not prepared to make any change on account of the few that fail." So that was that; and the books and forms, as first introduced mainly in 1904 (except the OB and the FIC, which came in 1913) remained virtually the same for years to come.

In 1922 what came to be known as the Rand Rebellion broke out among the white miners on the Witwatersrand in the Union of South Africa. The rebellion had started as a strike but a communist-inspired group had taken control. A formidable headquarters staff was established by the strikers, commandos were drilled, and recruits were systematically instructed in how to deal with the police. For a week the rebels virtually took control of Johannesburg. General Smuts, the then Prime Minister, proclaimed martial law and thereupon suppressed the rebellion with ruthless military action, at a cost of 230 white lives.

At the instance of the Commissioner the superintendent at Gwanda, Lieutenant Bridger, issued a circular to all stations in the district. "In view of the trouble on the Witwatersrand where Whites have been fighting and killing one another and a large number of natives have been repatriated, it may be taken for granted that all sorts of rumours get about among the Natives. If it comes to your notice, or to the notice of patrols in the ordinary course of duty, that rumours are about and that the Natives are anxious, you will be good enough to draw the attention of the Native Commissioner in your district without delay. It is to be clearly understood that patrols are not to be despatched with a view to ascertaining whether there is or is not anxiety in the minds of the natives.

"A sharp look-out," the circular continued, "is to be kept for Europeans entering the Territory by means other than the Railways — especially in districts adjoining the Transvaal. It is quite possible that rebels fleeing from the Arm of the Law may attempt to enter Rhodesia — in bodies or moving individually." Once again the alarm proved unfounded and there appear to be no reports of refugees from "the Arm of the Law".

Another year elapsed before the exercise of a Mobile Patrol was repeated, this time in the winter of 1923. Meanwhile the CSO had issued a circular instructing all members to make themselves acquainted with "the scheme of Internal Defence" in their area, which the defence authorities had been busily planning. "All members," the circular admonished, "should be able to reply to questions from residents about rallying points, Sub-District Laagers, Section and District Commandants, etc."

Once again, the patrol's first move was to the Charter district and the column camped at The Range, 10 miles east of Enkeldoorn. Lieutenant Bugler wrote appreciatively in a pencilled report on 7 July, "Most of the day was devoted to the hospitality of Enkeldoorn." However, the column marched off next day at 6.30 a.m., harassed by "a good deal of motor traffic". One assumes from this that they met more than one motor-car. "The mounted transport under Sergeant Searson," said Bugler, "was thrown well about ... the mules strayed into a garden and the occupant was rather annoyed. I managed to make peace before I left."

Again, the patrol was a professional affair, without recruits, consisting of 25 mounted troopers and 40 armed native police. Leaving Depot, the mounted troopers took the main Salisbury-Enkeldoorn road, while the native police marched (on foot, of course) down the old Charter Road, via Seki. The two detachments met at Marshbrook. The Orders for the exercise required the patrol to be joined en route by "as many mobilisable men as possible" — implying, one assumes, any men who could be spared from local duty. The District Superintendents were enjoined to accompany the patrol through their own areas in the capacity of "Intelligence Officers".

From The Range, the column marched "over rolling country that brought to mind the Sussex downs," as Bugler described it, to Buhera and Gutu. "Intelligence" reported in advance that, disturbed by the prospect of an armed incursion into the Reserve, the natives in the western part of Buhera district, under Chief Nyika, would probably retire to the Mashaba and Manese hills. However, the report continued, "there are no particular strongholds in either, or caves of any note. Both the ranges are easy of access on the east and west slopes. The gap formed by the Manese spruit, known as Sikapakapa, used to be a place of refuge (for local tribesmen) from the Matabele."

It is clear from these surviving reports that the concept of the patrols was based on a still lurking fear of risings in the native reserves, and a continuing belief — fathered perhaps by a subconscious wish — that even though the war was over the BSAP's role was as military as it was civil. Headquarters had already set a belligerent tone, by listing the information which was to be collected by the patrol: the position of native strongholds and best way to reach them; suitable positions for advanced bases; plans of attack. "Intelligence", in the shape of the District Superintendent, reported, "The Chigarra Hills have some extensive caves. The terrain is difficult in parts and would afford good refuge for large numbers of natives and cattle ... the kopjes are easily surrounded. The Makankwe Hills, their old stronghold, are heavily wooded and water is scarce ... but they are a noted place of refuge and were a safe retreat against the Matabele ... Marabgwe Hill has a very commanding position and (the surrounding country) could be shelled from it." 'Intelligence' clearly anticipated military action as part of his police duties, not — apparently — without some relish.

The patrol ranged as far south as Chibi, followed a wide westward sweep through Belingwe and Selukwe, and back to Chilimanzi, then struck north again through the Mondoro Reserve to Salisbury. In straight lines from point to point, the route exceeded 500 miles, and there must have been many deviations. No use was made of the railway this time. The troopers rode, and the native police marched, every step of the distance. It was a formidable exercise, carried out, as far as one can gather from the records, with a high degree of military efficiency, and it imposed a severe test of endurance on men and horses. The authorities had no doubt learnt a lot since the Makoni Patrol four years earlier, when Stops had complained that "a month's active service would have dismounted at least two-thirds of the men."

## Chapter Twenty-Five

## UNDER "RESPONSIBLE GOVERNMENT"

EVEN BEFORE THE war the white population of Rhodesia had grown openly antagonistic to the Chartered Company's oligarchic rule. As soon as the war was over they determined to be rid of the Company. In truth the Company, which had never made any profits directly from its occupation of the territory, was only too pleased, on its part, to rid itself of an economic and administrative burden. Two alternatives were proposed: either the settlers would assume government of the country themselves, or Rhodesia would join the Transvaal, the Orange Free State, the Cape Colony and Natal to become a fifth province of the Union of South Africa. After a lively political campaign between the respective champions of the two proposals the all-white electorate chose, by a referendum held in 1922, what they called "responsible government". The voting, by three-quarters of an electorate of 19,000, was 8774 for "responsible government" and 5089 for "Union". On 12 September 1923 Southern Rhodesia became officially a British "self-governing Colony" — a unique constitutional entity. The formal transfer of governmental control from the British South Africa Company to the newly elected Legislative Assembly — under Sir Charles Coghlan as the first Premier — took place at noon on 1 October and the first Governor, Sir John Chancellor, who had arrived in Salisbury the previous day, was sworn in as the representative of King George V.

At sunset on the previous evening, when Retreat was sounded by the native trumpeters at the BSAP Depot, the Chartered Company's flag was hauled down for the last time by RSM Douglas, assisted — according to Sergeant Hughes-Halls — by himself and Sergeant Harmer. Next morning, the Union Jack was raised in its place.

The change from rule by the Chartered Company to self-government by the people of Rhodesia made no essential difference to the role or functions of the BSAP, but the status of the force was profoundly affected. Although control of the force had been transferred, in 1909, from the British High Commissioner in Cape Town to the Company's Administrator in Salisbury, some traces of the old colonial apron-strings had been retained, and in certain circumstances — such as on declaration of war — the High Commissioner still had the power to issue Proclamations affecting the force. The BSAP, too, had fallen within the ambit of the Inspector-General of Overseas Forces of the Imperial Government, and it was his report in 1913 which had led primarily to the appointment of Major-General Edwards as commanding officer. The same external influence had brought in Major Essex Capell in 1914 as second-in-command.

Now all this was changed. Apart from certain constitutional reservations — limited, virtually, to the passage of racially discriminating laws by her new Parliament — Southern Rhodesia was now independent and in unfettered control of her own internal affairs. The police force was answerable to, and subject to the direction of, the Southern Rhodesian Government and nobody else. The old Police Ordinance of 1903, which had for so long controlled the hopes, frustrations and destinies of the members of the BSAP, was replaced by a Police Act. The Police Ordinance had been imposed, and had been subject to arbitrary amendment, by the tycoons of the Company. The Police Act was now, at least in theory, subject to the democratic processes of Parliament.

Edwards retired from the office of Commandant-General on 31 January 1923, aged 61. (When he retired the rank was discontinued and the senior officer in the BSAP was once again the Commissioner.) His had been a colourful career. He had first seen active service, as a lieutenant in the Seaforth Highlanders, 35 years earlier on the north-west frontier of India, in one of the many punitive expeditions by British India against the Pathan tribes. On that occasion he had been mentioned in dispatches and promoted to Captain. In 1896, as a Major, he had been transferred to the 5th Dragoon Guards. In the Anglo-Boer War he had commanded the Imperial Light Horse. In those days commanding officers led their troops physically into battle and it is recorded of Colonel Edwards that he was the first to leap into the enemy-held emplacement to capture "Long Tom", the Boer heavy gun which had dominated Ladysmith for many weeks during the siege of that town. He rode into Ladysmith with the first squadron to effect its relief, as he was to ride into Mafeking — with the relief force which included the BSAP — three months later. For his services during the South African War he received the Queen's Medal with four clasps and subsequently — when Queen Victoria died and Edward VII succeeded her — the King's Medal with two; and the CB. Near the end of the war he commanded 'A' Division of the new South African Constabulary; in 1903 he had commanded the Transvaal Volunteers; in 1905 he returned to the 5th Dragoon Guards as Colonel of the Regiment. Then he became successively Assistant Adjutant-General of the British Army; Military Secretary to the Viceroy of India; Chief Constable of the Metropolitan Police; and finally, as a worthy climax, Commissioner of the BSAP and Commandant-General of the Rhodesian forces. Actually his spell with the BSAP and Rhodesian forces from 1913 to 1923 was the longest assignment in his career. It was as if he had for ever been moving up step by step and finally reached the pinnacle.

The value of his services to Rhodesia was immeasurable. As this history has disclosed, his arrival in 1913 and the immediate impact of his personality and dynamism — buttressed by his far-reaching experience — rejuvenated an ailing force and set it on the exemplary course from which it has never since deviated. He had his frustrations — caused principally by the dead hand of Company rule, which was conditioned all the time by consideration of the interests of its shareholders. Fortunately he had had time before war broke out to reconstruct the foundations of the BSAP as a firm base on which future developments could be built. And when war came he brought to the beleaguered British interests in central Africa a wealth of wisdom and experience which no one else in the Colonial establishment of the day could have hoped to match. At the end of the war he was awarded the MVO, this time by King George V. Thus his services had been recognised by three reigning sovereigns.

Essex Capell, now Colonel, acted as Commissioner from the date of Edwards's retirement and was confirmed in the rank on 1 April 1923. Beyond the official records of his services and periodical references in official reports to his activities there is relatively little to be learned about Capell from published sources — except from his own book on the East African campaign which will be mentioned later. There is no doubt that he was a supremely efficient commanding officer. For some reason all the reports on the stations which he visited in 1921, while he was still Assistant Commissioner — reports which are subject in ordinary circumstances to destruction after a prescribed period — have been preserved, and in reading them one is constantly impressed by their superb attention to detail and the unstinting fairness of his comments even when he found cause for criticism. If reprimand was deserved it was meted out in full; but he was just as liberal with his praise.

During the first few years of "responsible government" recruiting for the BSAP was a matter of major importance.

It was natural for the Government of a newly independent country to be tempted to recruit its police force from amongst its own people. In December 1923 the local papers carried advertisements inviting applications from unmarried men, "medically and dentally fit". Recruits would be attested in Salisbury and "Rhodesians may be accepted at 19 for the Mounted branch, and men from 20 to 25 may be accepted for Town duty". (The wording suggested that Rhodesians only would be accepted for the district police but others might possibly be taken for the town.)

At the same time, however, the strangely titled "Police Review and Parade Gossip". in London carried an advertisement announcing "vacancies for NCOs in the Colonial Police" — in the Straits Settlements, Federated Malay States, Ceylon, Uganda and Hong Kong (for all of which applications were to be made to the Crown Agents for the Colonies) — and also in the British South Africa Police, the Southern Rhodesia Constabulary (which had been defunct for 14 years) and the Northern Rhodesia Police — applications for these to be made to the BSA Company in London. (Although it was no longer the governing authority the Company still retained extensive interests in both the Rhodesias, and until a High Commissioner for Southern Rhodesia was appointed on 1 October 1924 it continued as the agent in London for the new Government. The Company offices were in No. 2, London Wall Buildings, which was then known as Rhodesia House. The High Commissioner, when he came to be appointed, occupied a suite in Crown House in Aldwych.)

Now that there was no longer a Commandant-General in Rhodesia there was likewise no Chief Staff Officer. Major George Parson (the commander of No. 4 Mobile Troop in 1914 who had subsequently been awarded the DSO) was now the Staff Officer, BSAP. In December 1923 he wrote to Mr. Candler of the BSA Company in London, "We have applied to be allowed to recruit 30 men in England. We cannot get the class of men we require out here. At least, not in sufficient numbers. Many Dutch apply but they are so illiterate we cannot possibly take them on." Following receipt of this letter the Company circulated an internal memorandum saying, "The Staff Officer, BSAP, is accepting from England a few specially selected men from 20 to 25, of good Public School type who are prepared to pay their own fare to Rhodesia and pass a stiff medical examination in Rhodesia at their own expense."* That is to say, they had to pay for their own passage to Rhodesia, pay for a medical examination when they got there, and make the best of a bad job if they failed. "Maximum height, 5ft. 10ins., maximum weight, 11st. 7lbs. (161 pounds.) Tall and heavy men are not required as the Police horses will not carry them." Answering a question by Candler about the cost of his food to a policeman in Rhodesia, Parson wrote, "In Depot the rate of messing is fixed by contract at three shillings a day. On outstations it depends entirely on the luxuries consumed. The highest I have heard of is three and ninepence. The average can be taken as three and threepence. "

But for the time being the quest for recruits in England had to be abandoned. Parson wrote to Candler on 15 February 1924, "The Government won't at present authorise the recruitment of 30 men in England, so our little scheme is hung up." The truth was that there was considerable unemployment in the Colony and the Government was loath to court unpopularity by bringing in new men. Not that this was of much help to the police authorities. "We cannot get the type of man we want in South Africa or Rhodesia," Parson continued. "A sprinkling of the Colonial is a very good thing but the public school boy is what we require now. We have to be careful about height because men put on weight in course of time and our animals cannot carry them."

(Acknowledging Parson's letter, Candler mentioned as an aside that Lieutenant Surgey — who was one day to become a Deputy Commissioner — had called at the Company's London office, in uniform, after the unveiling of the Cavalry War Memorial. "He looked particularly smart and is a great credit to you. He tells me that (the ceremony) was quite a good show and that the BSAP representatives looked as well as anyone. In fact from what I can judge I don't think there were any Colonial contingents to touch them.")

A formal letter dated 7 July from the SO in Salisbury, now Lieutenant A.V. Adams, addressed to the Assistant Secretary of the BSA Company in London, reported that "There is still great difficulty in accepting overseas applicants whilst bound by the present policy of recruiting." Preference was being given to Rhodesian youths; then, if these were not sufficient, to South Africans, from whom there were many applications.

"I have been able," Adams continued, "to take a few from overseas but these have usually been recommended by ex-officers of the BSAP or other old Rhodesians, or else are of outstanding public school type and with excellent athletic records." He apologised for not complying with a request by the London office to cable when there were any vacancies. "The Government," he explained, "will not authorise cables in connection with recruiting which is officially confined to the Colony."

But in Rhodesia, in the higher ranks of the force, the policy was far from popular. On 31 July Capell reported to the Attorney-General, R.J. Hudson (Later Chief Justice Sir Robert Hudson) — who was also the Minister of Defence, to whom the BSAP were now responsible — "of 754 applications from the Union of South Africa considered last year, only 63 were attested, the remainder being totally unfit either medically, educationally, or on account of criminal records." He said all the efforts to find recruits locally had been unsuccessful. The present establishment of the force was 354 district police and 133 town police, which included the CID. The wastage was at least 60 every year. "I strongly recommend authority for (immediate) recruitment of 30 men by the London office," adding, "recruits should be required to pay their own passages to Salisbury by boat and rail." Capell was still keen on the public school boys. After all he had been one himself. "The most suitable type," he told Hudson, "is found in the ranks of ex-public school boys ...  Good sportsmen may usually be expected to prove good policemen." (In the very early days of the BSAP, Rhodes used to send out men from England with a note to the Administrator saying, "He is a good cricketer and ought to make a good policeman.")

The Attorney-General seems to have accepted some of Capell's representations because on 8 August a cable was sent to London — in direct conflict with the previous hard-and-fast policy — "Men are required for the Town (Dismounted) Police. Successful candidates to pay own fare to Cape

*There appear to have been some exceptions to this. One 1920 recruit has told the author that his fare was paid. But the records clearly show that this was not the rule.*

Town and take medical examination at own expense. "Nothing was said in the cable about the train fare to Salisbury. And yet a pencilled note on the file copy of the cable says "3rd class passages and rail, about £40." The cable continued, "Class desired: Ex-army NCOs from rural districts." No mention of public school boys; indeed by specifying NCOs the contrary was implied. "Good education. Unmarried. Will be required to undergo one month's training at the Depot in Rhodesia without Extra Duty pay. "The need for the men was clearly urgent, for this was followed 10 days later by another cable saying "Please recruit and send forward draft 12 men for town police." Candler passed on the cabled message to the Rhodesian section of the South African pavilion at the British Empire Exhibition at Wembley, with an accompanying letter saying, "No men are being recruited (here) for the Mounted Branch at present. There is a certain amount of unemployment in Southern Rhodesia."

It was in July 1923 that The Rhodesian Defence Force Journal ceased publication and Volume 1, No. 1, of The Outpost appeared in its place. (Many years later the title was changed to Outpost, a subtle but effective difference.) The cover picture was a drawing set in a square frame of a trooper on a horse, with a wreath at each corner of the frame encircling the regimental battle honours: Mashonaland, 1897; Boer War 1889-1902; German West Africa 1914; German East Africa 1915-1918.

For his first number the editor had a stroke of fortune, for he was able to publish a gratifyingly sensational story of police activity which had been unfolding during the previous months of that year. The particular incident became known as the "Rain Goddess Case" and its story throws a revealing light on the type of work in which the BSAP was routinely engaged.

In the Mount Darwin district on the north-eastern border of Rhodesia a white-haired old native named Chisiweti — who had been a grown man when the white men first came to the country — was the Paramount Chief of the Mtawara tribe. One of his subordinate chiefs — an equally white-haired, wrinkled old man — carried the traditional name of Chigango, the High Priest of the cult of the Rain God. The Rain God controlled the skies and released the rain when it was needed — or, if he was in an obstinate mood, withheld it. As one of his functions, Chigango was responsible for looking after the Nechiskwa, the second wife of the Rain God, who was chosen by the tribe when she was a young girl and was optimistically expected to remain a virgin all her life.

The rainy season before the last one, in the summer of 1921-1922, had been poor and the native crops had suffered disastrously. Popular opinion held that this could only have happened because someone had seduced the Nechiskwa, who was 12 years old at the time. Suspicion fell on Chigango's eldest son, Manduza. Manduza wisely retreated across the border into Portuguese territory, which was less than half a mile from his kraal. When, later in February 1922, the Rain God relaxed the intensity of his displeasure at the seduction of his wife and permitted a few belated showers and storms, Manduza felt safe to return to his people. Unfortunately for him the rains next year, the summer of 1922-1923, were late again. A few showers had fallen early in the season, just enough to start the crops growing. But then they ceased altogether and the crops became scorched and withered.

Chigango's position became difficult. Over the many long years of his life he had built up an enviable reputation as a rainmaker. On four previous occasions when drought had been troubling his people he had nicely surmised that rain would come in the next 24 hours and had hurriedly offered up a human sacrifice to the Rain God; so that each time, when the storm which he had confidently — and privately — foreseen had burst, his infallibility as the High Priest had been indisputably confirmed.

On this occasion he found himself in an awkward situation because the obvious choice for a sacrifice must be his own son, whose conduct had been the cause of the evil. He had already tried ritual offerings to the Rain God of limbo and beer but these had proved unavailing, so he was left with no option but to do his duty. Having once again made sure of his timing, and having secured the willing assistance of two of his headmen, he offered up Manduza as sacrifice by burning on 4 January 1923 and on 5 January heavy rains fell and continued unabated for 39 days. The sacrifice of one had demonstrably saved hundreds of others from death by starvation.

The next day, 6 January, a native Tizora arrived at the police camp at Mount Darwin to report a murder. Tizora's action was not prompted by any manifestation of public spirit; rather, as the late lamented Manduza's brother — and Chigango's second son — he realised his own vulnerability if the rain stopped and another sacrifice became necessary. He admitted that the victim, his brother, had been sacrificed to the Rain God because he had seduced one of the God's wives. With exemplary filial consideration he said nothing of his father's part in the crime but named Bandimba and Chiriseri, his father's two headmen, as the murderers. He obligingly handed to the police his dead brother's registration certificate.

The member in charge at Mount Darwin was Corporal A.W. (Sandy) Fraser. When he heard the report he suspected it to be another of the not uncommon rumours of this sort of happening. However although he anticipated no real trouble he decided to send a strong patrol to Chigango's kraal. Some show of strength was needed because the natives were apt to grow excited if they suspected that the routine of their sacred tribal customs was being interfered with. Troopers Batezat and Grimmett, with four native police, set off that morning for Chigango's kraal 43 miles away, taking the informant Tizora with them.

Tizora led them to Nyamakangwa, "Meat of the Crows", the tribe's traditional sacrificial site under a mopani tree in the foothills of the Mavuradonha Mountains. In the ashes of a recent fire, and even in spite of the incessant rain, the charred remains of a human body were unmistakable. As Grimmett reported, "I saw the remains of a big fire and in it the remains of a human being, which were smelling badly. There was no flesh on the bones." Nevertheless it does not appear that the patrol felt any oblig-ation to take the human remains out from the ashes so that they could be presented as evidence at Mount Darwin.

The patrol did not return to Mount Darwin for a week. It had a lot of investigations to complete. On 13 January it marched into the police camp escorting a whole phalanx of 82 natives, men and women, all formally detained "on suspicion". Among them were Chisiweti, the Paramount Chief, Chigango the High Priest, Chiriseri, one of Chigango's headmen and the Nechiskwa. (There is no further reference in the reports to Bandimba, the other headman named by Tizora.) After the usual frustrating process of interrogation Fraser decided that — with the exception of one woman and eight men "who professed total ignorance of the whole thing in true native style" — all the rest had taken some part in the murder. He said he "sifted the remaining 73 into different degrees of guilt" and decided to charge seven of the principal culprits — all men — with murder "using the evidence I had obtained from the lesser offenders. I proved Chigango was the producer of the act, Chiriseri was the stage manager, Chisiweti was the agent and the other four, as it were, took leads. The remainder comprised a big chorus."

The High Court was due to sit in Salisbury on 29 January, in a couple of weeks. Mail from Mount Darwin had first to be taken 40 miles by carriers to Bindura, and Fraser could not hope for a reply, and formal instructions, for at least 10 days. Then it would be too late to hold a preliminary examina-tion and send the prisoners to Salisbury before the session of the High Court. So he decided to open a preliminary examination before the local magistrate on his own authority. "I thought," he wrote later, "that my procedure might have been severely criticised by the Law Department, but the necessity for prompt action, the absence of any real material evidence and the fact that all these natives" — 73 of them — "were being detained (and might be for another three months and so cause trouble) influenced me in the action I took." Fortunately for him, the Attorney-General approved his decision. The seven accused were committed for trial on 18 January, indicted by the High Court by telegram, and duly delivered to the Court by the time the session opened.

However when they appeared before the Judge charged with murder, he remanded them for three months to the next session of the Court. The defending counsel of one of the accused had asked for time to gather expert evidence on tribal customs. He hoped to be able to show, he said, that human sacrifice was an accepted tradition in the tribe and that this should weigh in favour of the accused. The Judge was not so sanguine. He said he would agree to the request for a remand, but added pointedly, "Nevertheless, I shall instruct the jury not to be influenced in any way by tribal custom in arriving at their verdict. That has nothing to do with the act itself but may subsequently be urged in the accused's favour for mitigation of sentence."

When the trial was resumed on 23 May a photograph appeared in the Rhodesia Herald of three old men with deeply lined faces, white hair and beards, in white prison smocks, manacled together. Three of the seven accused, finally brought to trial, faced the camera with expressions of dignity and benevolence. Each one had grown up before the country had been occupied by whites, and they belonged to a world in which ritual murder and human sacrifice were held in reverence rather than shame. The counsel for the defence, helped unstintingly by Corporal Fraser, had spent frustrating weeks trying to find an expert witness on tribal customs who would be willing to give evidence; and only at the last moment had he been able to persuade a Mr. Edwards of the Native Department at Mrewa to do so. On the strength of what Edwards described to the Court, Advocate Lewis, who had been briefed to defend Chigango only, argued that his client had acted in conformity with his religious beliefs and that respect must be paid to the religions and customs of the natives. He even suggested that the white man's religious beliefs were not altogether averse to human sacrifice, in evidence of which he handed in as an exhibit a Bible printed in Shona with a convincing picture of Abraham preparing to offer up his son Isaac. Advocate Bertin (later, Minister of Justice), acting for all the other six accused, was less inclined to expect the Court to be impressed by these religious customs and asked that his clients should be found "guilty but insane". To which the Judge retorted, "Two more inconsistent pleas could not possibly be set up in one and the same case."

The jury were absent from court, considering their verdict, for only 10 minutes. They acquitted Chisiweti, the Paramount Chief, and found the other six guilty of murder. They made a strong recommendation for mercy. When formally sentencing the six to death, the Judge added that he endorsed the recommendation and that it was "practically certain they would not suffer the extreme penalty of the law." Nor did they. Although held "at His Majesty's pleasure" they were shortly released on parole, and on the day they returned to their people the skies opened in torrential downpour, which did little to shake the popular faith in the cult of the Rain God.

It would be tedious to recount the progress of all the Mobile Patrols if they had followed the same pattern and had had no individual characteristics. But each was different from the one before. Another of these relatively major operations was mounted in 1924, this time to the south-west area of Matabeleland. The patrol, with Captain Onyett in command on this occasion, left Salisbury by train for Gwelo on 14 September. The records show that three first-class tickets were bought, obviously for the officers; 38 second-class for the other ranks; and 24 third-class for the native police. Six trucks were booked for 44 horses, and the whole journey cost £92.7s. Six weeks later the same bookings were made for the return journey from Bembesi to Salisbury at a cost of £220 1s 9d.

From Gwelo the patrol marched west and was met at the junction of the Vungu and Shangani Rivers (near Nkai) by Major Ingham, now the District Superintendent at Bulawayo. Ingham had already written to the CSO that water was scarce. "I believe," he wrote, "that a new pump is on the market which is handy for obtaining water from sand rivers consisting of a pointed steel tube which can be driven into the sand and a small hand pump attached. Perhaps the patrol can be supplied with one of these." History is silent as to whether this revolutionary piece of equipment was made available. The patrol followed the Shangani River to Allan Wilson's crossing, close to the patch of bush where Wilson and his patrol of 32 white men had been wiped out by the Matabele in 1893; thence via Lake Alice (characteristically dry) southward to Shiloh and Nyamandhlovu, through the Nata Reserve to Plumtree and Mphoengs; east to Kezi; north up the Antelope Road to Fort Usher; and finally via Umzingwane and Heany Junction to Bembesi — almost a complete circle round Bulawayo at a radius varying from 30 to 100 miles. The march covered anything up to 500 miles in all, through native reserves for virtually the whole distance. Sub-Inspector McGee at Plumtree warned, "There will be great difficulty about water. In nearly every instance the column will have to dig for it." The SO told Onyett, "Ask Mr. Carlisle of Strathmore Farm, Essexvale, to grant permission for the patrol to make use of the road through his ranch and to water the animals en route ... I understand that Mr. Carlisle is inclined to be aggressive if use is made of his road without permission." History is also silent about how the gentleman reacted on this occasion.

Mules and wagons had also been sent from Salisbury to Gwelo by train. Lieutenant Warnock-Fielden, the transport and supply officer, reported, "The mules on arrival at Gwelo were very exhausted and in this sandy and almost waterless country it has only been possible to continue moving by dividing the transport into two lines" — the light wagon and the ambulance, with kits and two day' rations, moving with the column; and the heavy wagons with the main supplies and stores moving only at night by the "best watered routes," timed to meet the column at prearranged points. The staff at headquarters, in their wisdom, decided to recall Warnock-Fielden when the column reached Plumtree. Onyett protested. "If I had to do what Fielden is doing now, I would have little or no time for training and the efficiency of the patrol would be seriously impaired." But staff officers are notoriously impervious to protests by their subordinates; and although the reply is not on record it must be assumed that Fielden's recall was repeated, for Onyett next wrote, "I do consider it really essential that Lieutenant Fielden should remain with the patrol," adding submissively, "but the purport of the Controller's letter is quite clear — that he does not. In deference to his wishes Lieutenant Fielden will return to Salisbury from here (Plumtree) ... Though I cannot move with the transport, I shall do my best to carry out some of the duties hitherto performed by Lieutenant Fielden, but I must ask that no responsibility be placed on me in the event of anything untoward occurring through the absence of an officer who can deal solely with transport and supplies, difficulties which are evidently much more real than the Controller imagines."

The Commissioner was unmoved by Onyett's protests. "This is satisfactory," he endorsed Onyett's letter. "Lieutenant Fielden has gained the actual experience that I desired. Now," he added unfeelingly, "Captain Onyett will experience the difficulties often met with by officers on active service who have to control larger bodies of men and more transport than he has, without the assistance of any transport officer, and at the same time to shoulder grave responsibilities." So, through the second half of its wide arc round Bulawayo — through Mphoengs, Kezi and Fort Usher to Bembesi — the patrol struggled on without a transport officer, with no apparent ill effects, and — if the number of tickets purchased from the railway is anything to go by — returned by rail from Bembesi to Salisbury in full strength.

The records show that a month later, in November 1924, Lieutenant J.M.W. Parr was at Tuli with a special BSAP detachment. It is doubtful whether this had any connection with Onyett's patrol. A Bechuana chief, Mabirwa, had apparently brought some of his cattle over the border, presumably for grazing within the Tuli circle — that appendix to Rhodesian territory that still protrudes into Botswana today. Parr telegraphed headquarters on the 10th, "Mabirwa and cattle removed over our border to Bechuanaland on 8th. Mabirwa adopted attitude of passive resistance and at first force was necessary. The movement later became routine (sic) and was completed 8th to 9th no casualties ... do not consider presence of patrol at Tuli essential after 12th when Mabirwa will be well under control of Bechuanaland authorities." Headquarters replied, "When Bechuanaland authorities have effective control of situation you will return to Salisbury with all details. Entrain via Gwanda."

The conditions of service published in 1924 stated the rate of pay for troopers (district) and constables (town) to be £185 per annum on enlistment. Many men enlisted in London in the belief that this was what they would receive. When they arrived in Salisbury they found the rate for district troopers during the recruits' course had been reduced to £120, rising to £150 for the rest of the first year. They only reached the advertised £185 after three years. (The recruiting office in London had not been told of the reduction and continued issuing forms showing the old rate of pay.) The Town constables were luckier; they received the £185 on attestation and attained the dizzy affluence of £240 per annum after 10 years in that rank. So the pay for a recruit for the district branch was £10 a month; from this £4.10s. was deducted for messing; he had to pay £1.5s. for a servant; he was allowed to spend £3 at the canteen for deduction from his pay; he was allowed up to £5 additional credit at the canteen which was invariably used and often exceeded; so he was left with less than nothing from his £10. Many a recruit was presented with a pay slip showing £-,s,-d, for receipt of which he had to sign, and to which he had to affix a penny stamp provided at his own expense.

Corporals (district) and 3rd class sergeants (town) received £260, rising to £280; sergeants (district) and 2nd class sergeants (town) £300 to £320; sergeant-majors (district) and 1st class sergeants (town) £335 to £350; sub-inspectors (district and town) £360 to £375; and inspectors £385 on appointment and £400 after three years in the rank. The distinctions in the titles of the ranks below sub-inspector still emphasised the cleavage between the district and town branches of the force, implying that members of the former were still mounted infantrymen while the latter were merely policemen. The conditions of service undertook to provide "free quarters, arms and equipment, saddlery, horses, forage, bedding, medical and dental services" — the last being clearly a concession following the agitation in 1919. They also provided "a liberal issue of clothing free on attestation", with an allowance of 10 shillings a month for replacements after the first year's service. "No member," they admonished, "may have a share in an undertaking of a commercial or speculative nature in Rhodesia during his ervice without permission." Five month' leave would be granted after the first (three years') engagement, provided that the member was then re-engaged for further service. Further leave would be granted every three years. A member would receive a bonus on passing the Native Language Examination and also the Civil Service Lower Law Examination.

At one time the application form to be filled in by prospective recruits declared, "Must be able to ride and shoot" and "Must be able to read and write" — in that order. The Secretary of the BSA Company in London wrote, "The clause saying the applicants must be able to read and write has the effect of turning away some of the well educated enquirers who think it suggests a low standard of education in the Corps." He politely suggested that the statement seemed unnecessary anyway, because the men had to apply in their own handwriting. It was sensibly deleted from the forms. On the subject of riding and shooting, the Secretary said, "In this age of petrol the type of young man (without much means) who has had the opportunity of learning to ride is rare, even in the country districts (in England]. The maximum age being 25, men with war service are now practically excluded. This reacts against the likelihood of applicants being used to firearms." To which Adams, the SO, replied, "The ability to ride and shoot is not essential" — he ignored the fact that the application form said it was — "the inclination, rather than the ability, is what is required. The question in the form (Are you accustomed to travel on horseback and to use firearms?) is included to give an opportunity for, say, an accomplished horseman, or an expert shot, to record the fact." And to the Secretary's plaint that "the greatest hindrance is the cost of reaching Salisbury, which we estimate at about £50," Adams was equally unhelpful. "The type of man we seek," he replied, "will be willing and able to pay his fare and expenses if really desirous of being accepted for service in Rhodesia."

An article in the London Daily Mail published some time in 1924 could possibly have frightened off many likely recruits. Not that it criticised the force or disparaged life in Rhodesia. On the contrary. The article was written, no doubt, in the fervent hope that it would help to attract as recruits to the BSAP young men of the type popularly believed by the British public to people the Colonies. The writer had probably made a short visit to Rhodesia and had returned starry-eyed to England. One can confidently assume that he had never been a member of the BSAP. Of course it has to be remembered that even as relatively recently as the 1920s people were still susceptible to sentiments which would be dismissed as utterly corny today. But it is difficult to believe that the extravagant heroics of the article could have made any appeal to young men who, although they might not have actually fought in it, had certainly grown up during a war which had shattered most illusions of romantic adventure. However the Company must have thought it was first class stuff, for they distributed a lavish number of reprints. The article is worth quoting in full, if only to record the image of the BSAP that was sometimes doled out in those days.

*Policing the Matabele* "Shorn of the fighting and the adventure that marked the 90's, life in the mounted police of Rhodesia still holds enough romance amply to satisfy the need of the average man. The days when Lobengula ruled the warlike Matabele, and the unrolling of the map of Africa was a task attended by constant danger and calling for ceaseless vigilance, have gone for ever. But the free life of the open air amid the waste spaces of Britain's youngest colony is still one to stir the blood of any healthy Englishman. The British South Africa Police, to whom is entrusted the task of carrying justice over a territory four times the size of the British Isles, numbers only 600 men split up in tiny detachments of two or three, living isolated lives in the heart of the bush. It is practically the only remaining corps of colonial police forces that attracted so many young Britons abroad three decades ago, and now, as then, its ranks are mainly filled from the public schools. The lure of sunlight days in the saddle and of nights under the stars, of big game and small, of carefree existence in the young country, are still irresistible to adventurous youth. To each man on a sub-station is assigned an area for which he is responsible. It may be anything up to 2,000 square miles in extent but once in every month he has to patrol it and to visit every isolated European farm and every native kraal. It may take him a fortnight or three weeks but off he goes with his rifle, his horse and his pack donkeys — a modern knight seeking adventure — down lonely veld tracks, across great open spaces, up the hills and down the plains he rides camping by the streams when dark comes down to dream over his fire. The grey of dawn finds him in the saddle, the midday blaze of the  tropic sun sends him to the shelter of the trees."

Nevertheless, behind the fulsome sentimentality there lurked a considerable smattering of truth. There was no doubt that, shorn of romantic exaggeration, the life of a trooper in the BSAP held considerable attraction for a young man.

Following the threatened strike in 1919 — and probably emanating from Huggins' efforts at mediation — an Annual Police Conference had been established. The Conference consisted of delegates appointed by stations and districts, and on each occasion it was opened with great reluctance by the Commissioner. The Conference hopefully adopted resolutions proposing improvements in conditions of service, which were then submitted to the Commissioner — who would think up all the compelling reasons for turning them down. The Conferences were held every year, but the earliest meeting of which records remain was in 1924 when Capell opened the proceedings with the comment, "You will notice that anything I say to a Police Conference has first to be reduced to writing for the reason that words are so prone to misconstruction that it would not surprise me in the least to see it reported in The Outpost that I had promised an all-round rise in pay. For the life of me I don't know what you have come here to discuss, unless it is the vexed question of the alteration of the Police blazers." Then he left the delegates to their deliberations. Their agenda hopefully included such items as pensions, gratuities, leave and clothing allowances.

The next issue of The Outpost carried a trenchant article by an anonymous contributor. "Police Conferences," the writer declared, "are of little value and they tend to discredit the reputation of the Corps. Constituted under an oath of allegiance to His Majesty the King, to serve as our motto says, 'The King, the Law and the People' "— the writer's translation of "patria" — "we are under a contract different from any other form of service." With a fulsome pen that would have done credit to the Daily Mail, the writer described the profession of a policeman as "that of an exalted spirit of magnanimity, regulated by principles of honour, integrity, obedience and self-denial. We have been selected to serve in the Force because we are physically fit for privations and hardships, and spirited enough to defend and protect the State, not only for mercenary consideration but from a sense of loyalty, patriotism and adventure... At Conferences, discussions are liable to take place and comparisons drawn which are subversive to discipline. A study of military history leads one to the conclusion that any Corps is better off without discussions."

Predictably this drew a lively reply in the next issue of The Outpost. The sentiments about "spiritedly defending the State, not for mercenary reasons but from loyalty, patriotism and adventure, seem to me," said a new correspondent, "somewhat far-fetched, to put it mildly. Otherwise," he asked, "why is it necessary to recruit annually approximately 100 men for a Corps with an effective European strength of only 500, of whom about 300 are constables and troopers?" He was not against the principle of holding conferences; indeed, they served an essential purpose. But the fault of the BSAP meetings, he believed, was that there was no continuity of policy. "New members are elected each year; anyone is eligible regardless of his length of service; too many representatives are elected; discussions are not confined strictly to the subjects brought up and resolutions are often passed which, on mature consideration, might be shown to have no hope of being sympathetically received by the Government." He might have been describing what happens at conferences the world over.

The controversy was manna for the Editor. Next month, inevitably, another correspondent entered the fray. "Conferences," said the latest protagonist, "savour of the Russian workmen and soldiers' councils. One cannot compare the police forces in England with this Corps. We are a military police force, the regular army of Southern Rhodesia, under a disciplinary and not a conference system. Does the writer of the letter know that in one district a dozen men refused to vote for anyone to attend the last conference? Has he ever read any military history? In France, in 1792, the system of conferences began to spread in the army. Discipline gave way everywhere, soldiers held conferences and got so familiar with their superior officers that one regiment, the Royal Champagne Regiment, mutinied because their officers did not ask them to dinner! Right through the military history of any period or nation where latitude of discussions or conferences had been allowed, there followed decay of discipline. Conferences have never been allowed in the British Army."

And when, at the next conference in 1925, Capell came back to give his replies to the delegate's resolutions, he said uncompromisingly, "Re: the absence of certain delegates due to apathy on the part of elected members, I cannot find fault with that apathy. These conferences were born in the womb of mutiny. The promise that these conferences should be held — a promise I should never have made — was made to mutineers. I consider that a collective expression of opinion by soldiers cannot be conducive to discipline. That it does no harm in this case is due to the fine class of men recruited in the BSAP and the fine character of the rank and file of the BSAP. That is the only reason it does no harm."

Most of the resolutions on this occasion were concerned with the usual routine subjects: married allowance, the issue of a second pair of leggings instead of puttees, and so on — the two subjects of pay and promotion, which had for ever been uppermost in the mind of any self-respecting policeman, were taboo. There was a proposal on the agenda to discuss examinations. The minute reads, "The subject was not discussed on the order of the President (Capell]." But he did reply to the proposal that "proper hot water be laid on in the Depot." A generation of men, he said, had been trained in these barracks — good hard men. Post-war man had a tendency to become soft. It was hard men that were wanted. "I recommend cold baths in the morning and shaving in cold water — which I do myself. I will not sanction hot water installation. I would as soon think of recommending an issue of Lanolin or face powder."

In March 1926 The Outpost reported that the Conference for that year had been postponed indefinitely. "We cannot help thinking that this confirms the suggestion that there is little discontent in the Corps."

In June 1925 the British Government, after years of prodding by Edwards and Capell, had agreed to issue medals to members of the BSAP who had served in the East African campaign during the war. The decision, welcome enough as it was to the recipients, engendered the usual resentment among those who had been unlucky enough — as they regarded it — to be denied the chance to go. The Outpost, welcoming a cause to sponsor, complained in an editorial "The position of a man (in that situation) who attends regimental functions and is obviously of an age to have served in the Great War is by no means enviable. His tunic, if he happens to be in uniform, is destitute of medals, except perhaps the Long Service ... During the war they experienced some of the rewards and some of the disadvantages of men on active service. They received a small war gratuity and they were allowed to make themselves useful in training others to go. They lost their leave, or had it curtailed; in spite of soaring prices they struggled along without increase of pay; they were liable to sentences for infringement of regulations that could never be dealt out to men in peace time. And yet no medal of any sort is their portion." Nor was it to be forthcoming.

Less miserably, in the next issue in July, The Outpost was able to report the visit to Rhodesia by the Prince of Wales (later, King Edward VIII). Of the BSAP mounted escort which attended him, he was reported as saying — one feels predictably — "The finest cavalry I've met since leaving England. The celebrations for the visit included a parade at the Salisbury Drill Hall. Six hundred servicemen were at the right of the line and 100 BSAP, with colours uncased, came next. At a show held for the occasion the police dog, Caesar, a doberman, took seven first prizes."

The dog section had been established early that year under Sergeant W.J. Collins, an acknowledged expert on bull terriers. He was already one of the leading judges of bulldogs and bull terriers in Rhodesia, and had also made a name as a judge in South Africa. Four dogs had been bought for the section and although the record does not state their breed it is assumed — from the reference to Caesar — that they were dobermans. One had died of distemper. Sadly, Sergeant Collins was himself to die at "Parktown Dog Camp" the next year, in February 1926. When the BSAP dog section had been formed he had been sent to Quaggapoort to study the training methods used by the South African Police. An obituary in The Outpost said, "With infinite patience and care he had trained the BSAP dogs to a high state of perfection."

In May 1925 a member of the Legislative Assembly, Major Boggie (not a policeman) proposed a motion "that the name of the BSAP be abolished and a more appropriate name substituted." He was not inspired to suggest any suitable alternative. His unconvincing reasoning was that since the Colony had assumed its own government it was generally recognised by the public that the letters "SA" referred to the Union of South Africa and not to Rhodesia. "Confusion," he complained, "exists between BSAP and SAP. Potential recruits overseas are unable to distinguish between the two."

The argument made little impression on the Assembly and although the motion found a seconder it enlisted no other support. Lieutenant-Colonel Munro (also not a policeman) said, "The BSAP is not a police force, but a half-military force." (What the other half was, if it was not a police force, the member neglected to explain.) "They look upon themselves as a Regiment with great traditions." Another member named Robinson, who had been in the BSAP for seven years and had resigned as a Lieutenant in 1914, asked that if any change was to be made the opinion of serving members should first be sought.

"The only reason for changing the name," said Mr. G.M. Huggins, "would be at the practically unanimous request of the members. The BSAP has excellent traditions. So far as I know," he added characteristically, "it has only one blot on its record and that was caused by a lot of irresponsible recruits." Sir Robert Hudson, the Minister responsible for the BSAP said, "It is the only police force in the world to have a King's Colour ... I have made enquiries and it is the wish of all ranks that the name of British South Africa Police should be retained." Major Boggie graciously withdrew his motion.

A confidential circular to officers issued by the SO at about the same time declared, "It is the duty of all officers to (make a social) call at Government House. Officers from outside districts, when passing through Salisbury or Bulawayo, will call at Government House if His Excellency is in residence. Dress: serge tunic and trousers, belt, medal ribbons, cap."

## Chapter Twenty-Six

## COMMISSIONERS AND RECRUITS

CAPELL FORMALLY RETIRED in February 1926. He had served Rhodesia with distinction, not only in the BSAP, but as Commanding Officer of the 2nd Rhodesia Regiment during the East African campaign. He wrote a book about the campaign, a book which he called *The 2nd Rhodesia Regiment in East Africa*. The book has its interest for the BSAP because so many members of the force — like Capell himself — were seconded to the regiment. But the campaign is not strictly part of the force's history. However, Capell made in his book one felicitous reference to the BSAP — of which, after all, he was still the nominal second-in-command. The reference is painfully fulsome — written in a style which, if used today, would invite a good deal of derision. But it is worth repeating here for the sake of the sincere sentiments lurking behind his extravagant phraseology.

"How was it that Rhodesia could raise the (2nd Rhodesia) Regiment? that any able-bodied Rhodesian could leave his interests, his farm, his fortune and family in a land thickly peopled with savages? (Because) a handful of men, trained for war, ready and keen, fit for any front, any fight, remained behind to do their duty — a duty that hurt, as bitter as gall and wormwood, and today, because of them, Rhodesia can proudly boast that no colony or territory of the Empire sent so large a proportion of its manhood to answer the mute call of an anxious-eyed motherland in need of her sons.

This handful of men was collectively styled the B.S.A.P. Called out 'on active service' they stand undecorated, for no medal came their way: but an unstinted need of honour is their due, for they permitted, sanctioned and guaranteed the exodus, and fully redeemed an unspoken pledge.

Cede ye to them the right of the line, as a tribute to worth, for value received."

It was principally in answer to this plea by Capell that on future ceremonial occasions the BSAP contingents were always granted the privilege of "the right of the line".

Capell had gone on leave pending retirement in the previous September and Lieutenant-Colonel A.J. Tomlinson had become Acting Commissioner of the BSAP. Tomlinson was 55 when he took over command of the force and was to serve as Acting Commissioner for only eight months before he too retired. He was never confirmed in the full rank of Commissioner.

Tomlinson was by now the longest serving member in the force, by a long way. He had served in the police in Rhodesia for 32 years. Born in India in 1870, he had first joined the Malabar Volunteer Rifles when he was 22 and, attracted for some reason by the wider horizons in Africa, had attested the following year in the old Bechuanaland Border Police as a trooper. In 1894 he had come to Rhodesia and transferred to the Mashonaland Mounted Police, again as a trooper. A year later, now a Corporal, he was ordered south with a party of MMP from Salisbury when Dr. Jameson was collecting his little army at Pitsani. Passing through Bulawayo on the way south he was commissioned as Sub-Inspector (Lieutenant) and when he arrived at Pitsani, having ridden 700 miles from Salisbury, he was placed second in command of 'B' Troop on the ill-fated expedition into the Transvaal. During this, the notorious Jameson Raid, he was in the thick of the one-sided fighting until Jameson's men were forced, by overwhelming opposition, to surrender to the Boers. (A number of extracts from his graphically written account of the Raid were quoted in Volume 1 of this history.) Like so many of the members of the MMP who were taken prisoner at that time and shipped to England in nominal disgrace, he made his way back to Rhodesia as soon as he heard the news of the Matabele rising. He was one of the founder members of the new force, the BSAP, when it was formed on 1 October 1896 and when the Anglo-Boer war came he marched to the relief of Mafeking with Plumer's column. As a Captain on that occasion he rode into the beleaguered town at the head of No. 2 Squadron of the BSAP.

In 1911 he commanded the BSAP contingent sent to London for the coronation of King George V. When the war came he was given command of the 1st Rhodesia Native Regiment — to which a number of other members of the BSAP were also seconded — and he served in the East African campaign until he was badly wounded. He spent four months in hospital before he returned to Rhodesia to take up his career again in the police.

No particular crisis seems to have disturbed the force during the short span of Tomlinson's term as Acting Commissioner, nor does there appear anything of historical importance on record during that period. One feels that after his protracted and energetic career in the BSAP — nearly a third on active military service — he had deserved a quiet spell of office, short as it was, and that is what the fates seem to have allowed him to enjoy. He retired on 5 May 1926 and as The Outpost commented — very truly, no matter how tritely — "The personality of a man who can join such a Force as the BSAP as a trooper and rise to Commanding Officer is one that would make itself felt in any walk of life". In fact he held the distinction of being the first of the commanding officers of the BSAP to have joined the force as a trooper; and although in future the policy of promoting men through the full succession of ranks was to be the rule, which has never subsequently been broken, as the first of that breed he fully deserved the credit accorded him by The Outpost. After he retired he lived in Rhodesia for another 35 years and died at the age of 91. The Tomlinson Depot, at which the African police are trained today, was named after him. Incidentally, when he retired he removed the force's last link with that recurring bogey, the Jameson Raid, which had plagued the Regiment for 30 years.

He was succeeded as Commissioner by Colonel George Stops who also rose through the ranks. Stops had joined the BSAP as a trooper in October 1896, 27 days after the new force had been established. Thereafter, for the next five years — regularly, year after year like the seasons — he rose to another rank: corporal, 3rd sergeant, 2nd sergeant, 1st sergeant, sub-inspector. After that it took him 10 years to go any farther, until he was commissioned in 1911. But as a sub-inspector he had been posted seven times, from one Troop to another, in as many years — an almost unheard-of progression through the force. (This was when there were 10 separate Troops, each a self-contained military unit, before Edwards re-formed the force into Districts.) In those days movement from one Troop to another was the exception. Stops started in 'K' Troop, Bulawayo; moved to 'G', Gwanda (1903); to 'E', Depot (1907); to 'F', Fort Victoria (1907); to 'C', Sinoia (1909), where he assumed command; back to 'G', Gwanda (1909); to 'L', Fort Usher (1910), again in command, where he was commissioned; and finally to 'B', Goromonzi (1913). Then, when Edwards introduced the Districts, he went to Hartley as District Superintendent (1915) and back to his original stamping ground in Bulawayo as DS in 1916. Later, after the war, he was to command in both Umtali and Salisbury. Although it is not an established fact, one is tempted to believe that Stops's career covered more widely dispersed postings than those of any of his contemporaries in the force.

Unlike many of the other members with the same rank and length of service, he remained in Rhodesia throughout the war. Dr. Eaton, the Surgeon Major in Bulawayo classed him as unfit for active service, which was surprising for a man who had had such an energetic career. In 1917 he was appointed recruiting officer for the Southern Rhodesian forces, with the rank of Temporary Major; and "owing to the dearth of senior Police Officers", as the Commandant-General described the situation — due to Capell, the Assistant Commissioner, and Tomlinson, an Acting Assistant Commissioner, being away on active service — Stops and Major W. S. Spain (the only survivor of the old BSACP still in the force) were each given a grant of £50 a year "to carry out the necessary Police inspection work", normally performed by Assistant Commissioners.

For some months in 1918 Stops reached the dizzy heights of Acting Commissioner while Edwards was out of the Colony. But when Tomlinson returned in 1919 he was back at Bulawayo as District Superintendent. As Edwards explained, "Tomlinson's return to duty will render it impossible for you to remain Temporary Assistant Commissioner and you will therefore lose the £50 per annum. Tomlinson must not be blamed for the situation. 1) he is senior to you. 2) he was acting as Assistant Commissioner before he went away. 3) I find that on his return I cannot reappoint him as Assistant Commissioner as there is barely sufficient work for the one I have — Capell. I will do my best to get you a bonus of £50 per annum for the work you did for the Imperial Government in connection with movements of troops through Bulawayo in 1917. I trust this will soften the blow caused by the loss of the Assistant Commissioner's £50." The blow was probably caused more by loss of rank and prestige.

But it was a temporary setback. In 1920, now permanently confirmed as Major, he became Commandant, Depot; he took command of Umtali District in 1922 and Salisbury in 1925. In 1926 he at last became the Commissioner, with the rank of Lieutenant Colonel. (In those days the Commissioner was paid £1100 a year, with quarters.) He was promoted to Colonel in 1930, with no increase in salary. One thing could be said of Stops as a Commissioner and that was that he knew every district in the country from personal experience.

During Stops's commissionership recruiting was still the paramount problem. In those days two principal reasons undermined the permanence of young members' service with the force. Troopers in the district branch, for all the attractions of "sunlit days in the saddle and nights under the stars", were readily seduced by prospects of making money by growing tobacco, whether or not they had any capital. On a relatively small scale, compared with later heydays, it was a boom period for tobacco; if a young man had some capital he bought land and became a prosperous grower; if not, he took a job as a farm assistant and collected a bonus for a bumper crop. As for the town police, the reason they left the force was not so felicitous: they simply disliked their work — which was, as the SO conceded in a letter to London, "both exacting and, at first, somewhat tedious". Indeed, the situation in the town police must have been acute for, with an optimism that was almost touching, a circular to District Superintendents in January 1926 informed them that "applications will be considered from suitable men in the District Police for posting to Town duty on three months probation, pending permanent transfer". The records are silent on how effective the appeal had been, but taking all the circumstances and prejudices into consideration it is unlikely that it earned much response. A mounted man who spent his service looking down on the footsloggers in the town was hardly likely to choose to become one of them.

Writing later in 1926 Adams, the SO, said, "The prosperity of the Colony is in some measure reflected in the number of men who are now applying for their discharge to take up civil employment. These have now reached such a proportion that it is no longer feasible to grant discharge by purchase except in the most urgent circumstances". (Discharges could be purchased, by men recruited in England, for £50 during the first year, £40 in the second and £30 in the third. South Africans paid £25, £15 and £10; and men recruited in Rhodesia, £20, £10 and £5. In December he cabled to London, "What is position recruiting? Shortage acute." London asked, "May we extend height for district to six feet?" Adams replied, "Yes, provided not too heavy".

The senior ranks in Salisbury were still pressing for ex-public school boys. A new Staff Officer, Lieutenant J.E. Ross (a future Commissioner) wrote in February 1927, "A special effort should be made to attract them in view of their extreme suitability as Policemen and" — he added surprisingly — "as potential settlers". This was just what most of the police authorities were complaining of. (Even before the war Edwards had said, "The ex-public school boy openly makes a convenience of the force as a stepping-stone to obtain other employment".) Referring to recruits for the district branch who had recently arrived, Ross made the classic remark that "the last batch are on the young side but that is a fault which quickly disappears". He added, "They are also slightly stocky," and he confirmed what had been agreed by cable: "There would be no objection to Mounted Recruits being a little over the maximum height. Weight rather than height should bar a prospective recruit."

That same month a batch of recruits who had travelled to Cape Town in the Walmer Castle and had, as usual, paid their own fares all the way to Salisbury, refused to attest when they arrived. The record — which is contained merely in a copy of a cable to London — does not make it clear how many were involved. When called on to attest and to confirm that they accepted the conditions of service, they had voiced two complaints. They said that in London they had been promised free food and now they found that three shillings a day for messing was to be deducted from their salaries. Also they had been told they could marry at any time the fancy prompted them. Now they found they were not allowed to marry during the first five years of their service, and after that only if there were vacancies in the married establishment. (The subject of permission to marry had long been contentious in the force. In the early days married men had been rare, for obvious reasons. If a man did possess a legal wife he was allowed to draw double rations. When cash allowances were introduced in lieu of rations, married men became expensive. So a limit was placed on the number of married men entitled to draw the double ration allowance. But this caused all sorts of complications and the authorities decided to limit the number of members allowed to marry at all.) History is silent on what happened to those men who refused to attest but it can be assumed that they established themselves as reputable Rhodesian settlers. Nevertheless, they were lost to the BSAP.

Lanigan O'Keeffe was now the High Commissioner for Rhodesia in London. Bodle had died in 1924 and the onus for recruiting had been taken over by the High Commissioner's staff. It was not a duty they were finding too rewarding. Writing from Crown House, Aldwych, in March 1927, O'Keeffe attempted to describe their difficulties. The most usual reasons for rejecting applicants, he said, were "defective or deficient teeth, varicose veins, inadequate chest measurement or slightly defective sight". The shortcomings in teeth accounted for more than all the other causes of rejection put together. Apart from those who made definite applications to be accepted, "numerous well-educated young men, or their parents, make enquiries. They say they will 'consider the matter' and are not heard of again". Among ex-public school boys the objections usually came from the parents, who showed an engaging concern about what their sons were letting themselves in for. They called at the office, "asked questions, examined the Book of Regulations, Standing Orders, Instructions, etc." — and even the Commissioner's annual reports. When they were not satisfied they seldom gave away what it was that had finally put them off. But there was possibly one item which influenced them more than others. "The number of men," said O'Keeffe, "who yearly leave the Corps at their own request appears to be looked on as a suspicious circumstance." (In truth it was, of course, a reflection of the rival attractions of the country.) The perennial complaint, of having to pay the rail fare from Cape Town to Salisbury, was "a serious difficulty." O'Keeffe pointed out that the Crown Agents for the Colonies, who acted for the authorities in all the Colonial territories — everywhere in the British Empire, in fact, except the self-governing Dominions and Rhodesia — paid railway fares and expenses even to candidates travelling to London to be interviewed. And as soon as a recruit had been accepted they gave him an allowance to outfit himself, they paid his fare in full to wherever he was going, and they paid his salary from the day he left England. He had been medically examined free of charge. The BSAP paid none of these. A recruit for the force had to pay for his medical examination — whether he passed it or not — pay for his passage to Cape Town, pay his rail fare to Salisbury, and he only started to draw his salary from the day he attested in Rhodesia. "We have the reputation, "O'Keeffe complained mildly, "of being rather mean".

Stung presumably by O'Keeffe's comment, the Rhodesian Government actually agreed to pay the train fare to Salisbury in future and, in a burst of unprecedented generosity, to give each recruit a book of meal tickets for the journey.

However, as in so many human affairs, the pendulum began to swing the other way and the situation of demand for recruits exceeding the supply was soon reversed. In his report for 1927 the High Commissioner recorded that he had received more than 2000 "definite applications" to join the BSAP and that many other enquiries had also been made. The number actually accepted during that year was no more than 72. And then in April 1928 Ross cabled London "Cease recruiting mounted and foot until further notice. Corps wastage below normal and a number of suitable local applicants offering".

In a private letter to a member of the High Commissioner's staff, Ross explained the situation in Salisbury. Tobacco prices had fallen heavily, so men were not leaving the force; and because of the depressed conditions in the Colony the increase in establishment — which had been growing cautiously but steadily since attainment of self-government in 1923 — was now to be halted. "We have worked up a system," he wrote plaintively, "by which we were assured of a regular supply of very excellent recruits ... The stamp of man you are sending us is splendid, and far beyond those offering in the Union (South Africa) and this country".

However the pendulum swung back again later in the year, even if a little indecisively. Seven recruits for the district branch sailed from Southampton in the Walmer Castle on 14 December. Three more for the district, and two for the town, followed in the Windsor Castle two weeks later. In January 1929, with a further request for 20 recruits for the district, and eight for the town, Ross told London, "Our casualty list seems to fluctuate with the finances of the country ... things do seem to be looking up a little again" — he meant the finances, not the casualty list — "hope we shall be able to go back to the old system which was so successful."

But Stops, the Commissioner, was not too happy. He wrote to O'Keeffe, in March 1929. "I have today signed the discharge of seven Town police. With one exception, they have less than two year' service. None of them have any real fault to find with the conditions of service. They simply do not like the job of Town Policemen. (Macdonald left to become a Wesleyan parson so perhaps he may be forgiven. )

"Would it be possible," Stops asked, "to get a few men for the Town Police from Scotland? Not the big cities, where they appear to have Communist tendencies, but the country districts." And in contradiction of what had become almost holy writ, he added, "Rather than have the Public School boy or the young man who thinks too much of himself, I would go short."

O'Keeffe still had reservations about possible success in keeping members of the town police from leaving. "If a man is any good he will soon be offered a better job and this makes him discontented," he wrote. "No decent Salisbury girl would be seen out with a man who stands about street corners in uniform."

An article in the Police Review and Parade Gossip appearing at about that time quoted the European strength of the force at 500 — comprising 360 district men, 100 town police and 40 CID. There were 1000 native constables "who do not carry arms". Aimed, presumably, at encouraging hesitant mothers to allow their sons to join the BSAP, the article declared, "Without cost to himself and under the protective influence of discipline — a real safeguard for young men on first contact with colonial conditions — a Police trooper has exceptional facilities for acquiring the experience essential to his future success as a permanent settler". With that sort of propaganda being disseminated, the police authorities in Rhodesia could hardly complain if their new members tended to make "a convenience of the force".

Also at about this time the ranks of the town police in Salisbury were up in arms about a comment said to have been made by RSM Douglas. A general election was taking place at the time and the recruits in Depot were being sent out for duty at the polling stations. Before sending them from Depot, Douglas was alleged to have told them, "I want you to act as gentlemen and members of the BSAP and not like bloody town police". Accusations and denials that the dreadful words had been spoken were freely bandied between the detractors and champions of the RSM. Finally, the Staff Officer instructed the District Superintendent in Salisbury to hold a general parade and to announce to his town members "that the Troopers (recruits) concerned deny that when they were paraded for duty the RSM made any derogatory remarks in regard to the town police". They were hardly likely, under Douglas's close vigilance, to have failed to deny it. "The RSM also denies making the remarks attributed to him and states that as an old Town Policeman himself he has always held the kindest feelings to that branch of the Force." (Fortunately for Douglas at the time, very few members knew the true details of his history.) The Commissioner added his own message, "that he desires all members of the Town Police to accept his assurance that no comparison, unfavourable or otherwise, to one or other branches of the Force will be tolerated, and that as members of the BSA Police we all possess an equal status, and we are all liable for the same duties, either in Town or District; and he trusts they will disabuse their minds of any other impression". The general belief, outside the towns, was that Douglas had said it — and with every justification.

Back in 1913 the BSAP Old Comrades Association had been inaugurated under the presidency of Major-General Edwards. The Association had never really flourished, due probably to the distractions of the war years. A new organisation, the BSAP Regimental Association, was formed to take its place in 1926 and the inaugural reunion was held in the grounds of Charter House in Salisbury on 14 November. The Commissioner, Lieutenant-Colonel Stops, presided. The Association would be open to members and ex-members of the BSACP, the MMP (which stood for both the Mashonaland and Matabeleland Mounted Police), the BSAP and the BSAP Service (Murray's) Column. A constitution was agreed, providing for a committee consisting of three ex-members of the force, two serving members, an honorary secretary and an honorary treasurer. "The latter," commented The Outpost, "is to be ex-officio the Paymaster of the BSAP. This will ensure stability and permanence of funds" — surely an unwarranted slur on the integrity of ex-policemen. It was reported to the meeting that there was £43 3s 1d left over from the Old Comrades Association and this was promptly appropriated by the new. The first ex-members elected to the Committee were Captain Blagrove, Mr. S. Weeks and Mr. E.B. Law; the serving representatives were RSM Douglas of the district police and Sergeant Gillson of the town branch. Sergeant Coni was elected secretary. At the banquet which followed at the Grand Hotel that night Hudson proposed the first toast to the Association — the forerunner of hundreds of similar toasts to follow in the years to come at reunions all over the world. He put down the failure of the original association to the unfortunate choice of its name — "Old Comrades". Evidently people were at last beginning to shake off some of the corny sentimentality of the

Edwardian days. Thus was inaugurated an organisation which was to become one of the farthest-flung and most staunchly supported of such associations of men who have served together and have there-after sought to perpetuate the *esprit de corps*. The truth is that members of the force have always retired at relatively early ages — even if they have served their "twenty-one" or more — and they have moved on to other fields of interest in all parts of the world. Even at the first banquet RSM Douglas, responding to the toast, had been able to say, "The Regiment is only a small one but the men who have served in it are to be found all over the world".

In 1927, while the recruiting drive was still in full swing, the first steps were taken to equip the force with motor-cycles on an organised basis. Since the time when Edwards had suggested buying some machines before the war, "with a view to economising in horse flesh", no positive steps seem to have been taken and now, more than 10 years later, it came to be recognised that the use of motor-cycles by a police force could offer much more than merely something to replace its horses. The motor-cycle as a means of transport was by now well-developed, but the BSAP was still entirely dependent on horses for its mobility. In February that year District Superintendents were informed by circular, "Should funds permit, it is proposed during the coming financial year, to issue a Government motor-cycle at certain District headquarters". Even now this was only a pious hope. But, "if you have any-one willing to do so," the circular continued, "one man in your district will be allowed to use his own private motor-cycle for outside duties". He would be classed as a motor-cyclist and would not be called on for mounted patrols except in an emergency. He would receive threepence a mile — fourpence "if a sidecar is used for the conveyance of Government passengers".

But in September The Outpost was able to publish a picture on its cover of what it called "The New Arm of the Law" — eight members astride motor-cycles, resplendent in white pith helmets, khaki tunics and breeches, puttees (not leggings), bandoliers and — true to the regimental tradition — spurs. The machines were BSAs, that is to say they were manufactured — as every proper young enthusi-ast knew — by the Birmingham Small Arms Company. (How widespread in the future was the comment, by uninformed Colonials of course, that they "didn't know the British South Africa Company made motor-bikes".) The Outpost, in a burst of editorial enthusiasm, said, "The familiar pic-turesque figure on horseback will still be found on patrols, but with the advent of good roads" — a purely relative conception — "and the necessity for a man to be on the scene of a crime with the utmost dispatch, the up-to-date motor-cycle will undoubtedly be a boon to the policeman and a thorn in the side of the criminal. A man on a motor-cycle could cover a distance of some 60 miles in about two hours without undue exertion" — another relative conception — "and commence his investiga-tion. With forced riding he would need two days to cover the same distance on horseback and would need another horse to follow up the malcontent (sic) at a forced rate of speed. A motor-cycle consumes no food unless in use and requires no grooming and, in the hands of a competent rider, should need no vetting for quite a considerable time other than minor road repairs". It would have been interest-ing to hear the writer's frank comments after he had used a motor-cycle for some time under the existing road conditions. Although the BSA machines were to become in time the standard equipment of the force, they were not exclusively used at first, and a photograph of the Bulawayo Traffic Section taken a couple of years later in 1929 shows a motley collection of an Ariel, an AJS and an Indian.

In March 1927 Stops issued a sharp circular to District Superintendents. "Despite increased activity," he complained, "District Police duties as a whole by no means reach that standard of effi-ciency required of a modern Force. Generally there is a distinct lack of vision as to what does or does not constitute efficient Police work." Many members, he said, believed that all that was necessary was to be up-to-date in the office, to carry out routine patrols and to investigate charges "brought to the office table". Much more was being made of office work than was necessary. Every member, except the NCO in charge, "on completion of clerical duties should immediately vacate the office". Patrols, as such, seemed rarely to be serving any more useful purpose than "showing the uniform". The troopers, he knew, were accepting hospitality from the farmers they visited, "not confined to a meal, but from 4 p.m. to after breakfast next morning". The native police accompanying the patrols often covered more mileage on foot than the troopers on their horses. At the same time they were acting as grooms and servants to the troopers. "This is entirely wrong. Should such practices continue," he warned, "the native police will be given definite instructions as to (the limit) of their duties".

He laid down that patrols were to average at least 20 miles a day. If a patrol was to be less than 50

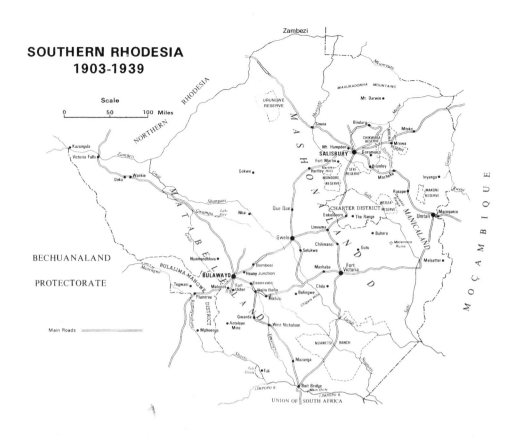

# SOUTHERN RHODESIA
# 1903-1939

Scale

0    50    100  Miles

1912: An early experiment with patrol camels – it wasn't to last.

Clockwise from top left: **Salisbury town Constable**, 1909.
**Corporal on motorcycle patrol** in Mobilization Order, 1923.
A legend of the Force, **Ron Trangmar** in training prior to the 1950 Empire Games in New Zealand.
**RSM "Jock" Douglas** (left) after retirement and in temporary service with the Rhodesian army with **RSM "Tiny" Tantum**, 1941.
Members of the **Sergeant's Mess**, Salisbury, 1909; RSM "Jimmy" Blatherwick bottom row, centre;
A rare occasion; RSM Douglas drinking tea, mobile patrol, 1929.

**Above:** Salisbury C.I.D., 1943; Det. Sgt Frank Barfoot (—ure Commissioner) 4th left, 2nd row.

**—ht:** Bulawayo motorcycle section, 1935.

**—tom:** The BSAP Coronation Contingent (King —orge VI, 1937) marching on to London's —stminster Bridge led by Major J.S. Bridger, with —M "Tiny" Tantum on the flank.

**Above:** A stellar cast; Commissioner J.S. Morris (bottom row, centre) and senior officers, Salisbury, 1939 including future commissioners B.G. Spurling (top row, extreme right) and A.S. Hickman, bottom row extreme right.

**Below:** Police 'A' team, Salisbury, 1960. Commissioner B.G. Spurling (bottom row, centre); Assistant Commissioner (future head of C.I.O.) K. Flower (bottom row, extreme left).

**Opposite page**, clockwise from top left:
**Commissioner Spurling** with Police forensic scientist John Thompson, 1963
Her Majesty **Queen Elizabeth the Queen Mother** reviewing the BSAP at Depot's Newcastle Ground, May, 1960.
BSAP receive the **"Freedom of the city"**; Salisbury, September, 1960.
**The Outpost**; 1953. **Riot Squad** prepare for action; Harare Township, 1960.
**Commissioner Spurling** (centre) and senior officers; 1961. Assistant Commissioner K. Flower, extreme right.

the OUTPOST

MAGAZINE OF THE BRITISH SOUTH AFRICA POLICE — SOUTHERN RHODESIA

# MEN OF THE MOMENT

*The Governor of Rhodesia, Sir Humphrey Gibbs.*    *The Commissioner of Police, Mr. F. E. Barfoot.*    *The Chief Justice, the Hon. T. H. W. Beadle.*

## AFTER POLITICIANS' U.D.I.

# Queen's men would be in a dilemma

**The Star's Africa News Service**

Salisbury, Wednesday.

AS THE RHODESIAN DRAMA UNFOLDS, five men who play key roles are waiting quietly in the wings. Once the politicians have taken their decision, these are the men who would be most directly concerned. They are faced with a stupendous decision, for each has taken an oath of allegiance to the Queen.

RHODESIA

PRIME MINISTER
SALISBURY

7th December, 1965.

I am particularly happy to send this Christmas message to the Regular and Reserve Officers and Men of the British South Africa Police, because it gives me the opportunity of letting you know how grateful the Government and the people of Rhodesia are to all members of the Force for the devotion and dedication to their duties which they have demonstrated during the past year.

Despite what may be said overseas, we all know that Rhodesia is a tranquil and peaceful country, and I believe that this tranquillity is due in no small measure to all members of the Police who, under the most exacting of conditions, carry out their duties with tact, diplomacy and a cheerfulness which is wholly in keeping with the finest traditions of the Force.

At this moment it is fitting that we should recall the birth of Our Lord, and remember the significance of this event for all mankind. I hope that each and every one of you will have the opportunity, even if momentarily, to take time from the daily round of your duties, to think of what Christmas means in the peace and comfort of your homes.

I send you my best wishes for health and prosperity in the New Year, and a Happy Christmas to you all.

**Top left:** Grist to the mill: press reaction to prospect of Rhodesia's Declaration of Unilateral Independence

**Above:** Ian and Janet Smith toast UDI; Salisbury, 11 November, 1965

**Left:** The Prime Minister's personal message to the Force following the government's declaration of UDI. *(Previously unpublished; courtesy John and Simon Lovett, ex-BSAP)*

**Below:** SNAFU: the Force carries on with its daily duties – BSAP foot patrol making the rounds.

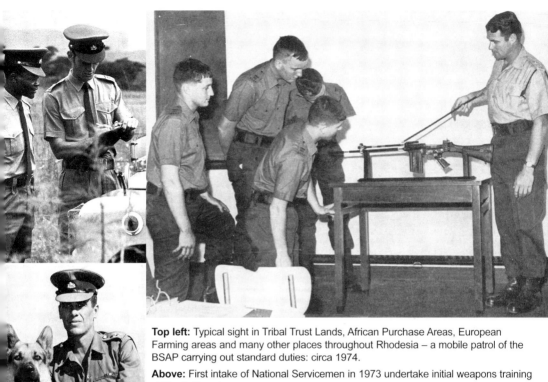

**Top left:** Typical sight in Tribal Trust Lands, African Purchase Areas, European Farming areas and many other places throughout Rhodesia – a mobile patrol of the BSAP carrying out standard duties: circa 1974.

**Above:** First intake of National Servicemen in 1973 undertake initial weapons training at Morris Depot.

**Left:** Inspector Gareth Tudor-Jones and Police Dog Bandit – 1975 winners of the "Best Trained police Dog" competition.

**Below:** "Tough and rugged" – BSAP Field Reservists take time out to pose for the camera in the north-east operational area.

**Top, from left:** More legends of the Force
Champion shot **"Don" Hollingworth**
Weapons expert **Dave Perkins**
The inspirational **Douglas Chingoka**
Farrier **Bill Coetzer**

**Middle left:** One of the first Police "Landie[s]
to detonate a landmine; in the Mount Dar[win]
area, 1972.

**Middle right:** Soon all vehicles, including
Police Land-rover, were mine-protected (fr[om]
"Wheels" by Colin Eyre, 1980.

**Left:** PRAW pilots Mike Browning and Do[n]
Howard prepare for dawn flight over
Manicaland, 1975.

**Below:** Reservist 'blues'.

miles for the return journey, and the trooper was away for only one night, he would not be expected to take a pack animal with him. In that case he would be allowed to accept hospitality, "if asked", but only to afford necessary rest for himself and his horse. He must leave again at sunrise. On longer patrols he would take a pack animal, in which case "acceptance of any hospitality will be treated as an offence". It would also be an offence if he ordered any native, "a member of the force or not," to groom, feed or saddle his horse. And whatever the circumstances, he would be expected to be in the saddle by sunrise.

Stops complained that, for many members, investigation rather than prevention of crime seemed to be their "chief object in life". Prosecutions handled by the force, during the past year, had increased by 7500. "It has been claimed that this has been due to police vigilance. It has also been claimed, in another police force, that a large decrease in prosecutions has been due to the same thing. Which is right? In my opinion, the latter. Our primary object is, by constant patrolling and display of real energy to prevent offences rather than permit them, and then subsequently to attempt a cure by prosecution." This was conventional stuff, no doubt expected of a Commissioner, but Stops was clearly determined to apply the pressure and keep the men on the move. He concluded his circular, "When not required for other duties, members will carry out road patrols up to six miles from the station, early morning and afternoon ... Night patrols by Europeans and Natives will be instituted as part of the routine duties of every station between 6 p.m. and 9 p.m.".

Shortly after this — but in a different context altogether — the Cape Town Argus reported that 30 young men had arrived by the mail steamer to join the BSAP "which is again striving to build the reputation it had before the war as a force of gentlemen". This stung Capell, now retired, to reply "We in Rhodesia do not even know if it had the reputation referred to. What we do know is that the personnel of the Regiment" (author's italics) — a nicely discriminating touch — "has not deteriorated during or since the war ... We know that we can pick and choose between hundreds of youngsters of South Africa and England, all offering their services; and rest assured that we do pick and choose ... Snobs do manage to get in now and then, and I can only imagine that (your reporter) gathered his information from one of them".

The year 1928 was a milestone in the history of the BSAP for it saw the introduction of the full-dress gabardine uniform for all European ranks, the basis of the "greens", or winter uniform of the force today. It consisted, at the time of its introduction, of a tunic buttoned up to a high-neck collar — only officers, RSMs and sergeant-majors wore collars and ties — with a pair of matching gabardine trousers for the town branch and Bedford Cord riding breeches for the district. For the time being khaki puttees were worn with the breeches; leather leggings were not introduced until 1930. The outfit was crowned by a white pith helmet, shining brass spike and brass chain chin-strap. The Outpost remarked, with an unbecoming lack of enthusiasm, "One cannot deny that the new uniform is serviceable. Serviceability must be considered before beauty".

The new uniform was first revealed at an inspection at Depot by the Governor. Up to then the town police had worn a blue serge tunic and trousers, with a blue and white striped armlet when actually on duty, in faithful imitation of the London bobby — except that the helmet was white, with a puggaree. Again, according to The Outpost, "A dusty day on point duty at the Show does not improve the appearance of blue. Blue does not suit everyone; worn by a tall slim man it shows to advantage but to the short and fat, especially the latter, it accentuates the streamlines". There had been a fear among members that they would have to buy the new "greens" themselves. But the old parsimony of Company rule seemed to have melted away, at any rate for the time being, and for once the Treasury displayed an unfamiliar burst of generosity by providing the new uniform for all serving members.

That year, 1928, saw two Mobile Patrols leave Depot. There appears nothing on record about the first but the second consisting of mounted troops marched off early in the morning of 28 October to Kilmuir Farm, 20 miles along the Mrewa road. Two more days on the march brought it to the Shavanhohwe River. The object of this patrol was said to be training, but the authorities were never averse to a show of strength in the Reserves. Fortunately the natives can have had no idea of what was happening, because the official report records that when field exercises were carried out on the march "the initial stages of these manoeuvres were an undeniable failure, as the various sections failed to keep touch, with the result that when the order for action was given one section was off in the blue and was not located until after the whole affair was over". No one could complain, on that account, that the exercise lacked realism; after all, it was not an unusual military situation. A camp was pitched on the banks of the Shavanhohwe River and next day the troops, with two days' rations, were sent out "under active service conditions, and the day was spent in mock action in intense heat". A week later they were back in Depot.

Two more Mobile Patrols set out in 1929. The first in June, under Lieutenant Surgey — consisting of a sergeant, two corporals, six troopers, a native sergeant and 19 askaris — was the first motorised patrol the BSAP had undertaken. The object, as officially stated, was "to give demonstrations of mobility and to impress on certain sections of the semi-enlightened (sic) native community that, contrary to their alleged belief, the European must be regarded as a good veldsman, a good walker and able to move as a fighting unit without the assistance of carriers and local guides". To demonstrate these marching proclivities the patrol set off in a convoy of Thorneycroft six-wheeler lorries.

However they did prove that they were "good walkers" in the end, and from a point about 50 miles north of Sinoia the men dismounted from the lorries and continued on foot. They made for Chanetsa's country in the Urungwe Reserve — deep in the tsetse fly belt. They caused some consternation on arrival because the natives in the area had hopefully believed that the presence of tsetse fly would prevent the white police on their horses ever reaching them. (Not that there was much need for police activity in the area. As the report said, "The kraals were mostly miserable affairs, inhabited mainly by old men and crowds of women. There were no cattle, sheep or goats ... Some colossal baboons were shot and it was evident that large mobs of these animals found a happy hunting ground in the native lands.") By the time the patrol returned to Salisbury after nearly a month on the operation, each lorry had covered 700 miles and the men had marched over 400 miles on foot. "The Thorneycroft lorries behaved splendidly," said the report, "and did not give the slightest trouble. We found the infantry equipment comfortable to wear and easy to slip on and off whenever halting for five minute rests every hour during long marches. Generally speaking the shooting was not good owing to the length of the grass, but in spite of this we found no difficulty in the supply of fresh meat once we had left the fly fence area". In the long run this patrol, carried out mainly on foot, was probably the most gruelling of all these exercises in the years between the wars.

The second patrol in 1929 was led once again by Onyett, now a Major. There were two troops, under Lieutenants A.S. Hickman (another future Commissioner) and E.H. Rowley, the latter commissioned the year before. They had with them two sergeant-majors, three sergeants, a corporal in charge of the Lewis gun section, one farrier corporal and 40 troopers — that is to say, it was again an all-white patrol. A Thorneycroft six-wheeler followed with supplies. Gone were the days of limbered wagons and improvised harness for the mules. This cavalcade of horsemen must have made an impressive show. The object, so the record states, was to "remind the natives that we had an army" — an interesting distinction from a police force — "and to impress on them their responsibilities regarding hut tax, dog tax, etc.". It was certainly an effective way of doing just that. Hickman and Rowley took their troops independently through the Sabi Reserve. Hickman visited the Matendere Ruins and Rowley the Mtshotsho. Hickman climbed the Ndevendzo Range on horseback — the first rider to do so.

## Chapter Twenty-Seven

## A NEW GENERATION

LIFE IN RHODESIA in the 1930s had reached the half-way stage between the pioneering days at the beginning of the century and the relative sophistication — relative, that is to say, to western standards — which was to follow the second world war. In the mid-thirties the total white population of the Colony was still less than 80,000 — 30 years later it was to be three times as many. It is very difficult to say what the indigenous population was at the time, but with the constant influx of migrant labour from Northern Rhodesia and Nyasaland it must have been in excess of a million. The black people were still known as "natives" — what had already become a pejorative label was not to be discarded, popularly or officially, for another 20 years. By the early 30s, they were being grudgingly allowed on to the pavements in the towns and not made to walk out in the streets to make way for their white betters, as tradition had previously insisted. The relaxation probably owed more to the new demands of motor traffic, sparse as it was, than to any misplaced liberality on the part of the white inhabitants.

In fact, the problems of race relations in Africa had not yet impinged on the consciousness of the ordinary Colonial — who was still basically a "settler". Except in the families of a few early pioneers, the first Rhodesian-born generation was only now starting to grow up. Race relations were simple: the whites ran the country; the blacks either worked for them, or existed as they had existed for centuries in the primitive limbo of what were now called "native reserves". In the new white settler society the native was still the hewer of wood and drawer of water, nor was there any belief that he would ever be anything else. As an alternative to the loin-cloth he wore his master's discarded clothes. A native wearing a suit was unheard of; very occasionally he possessed a pair of boots or shoes — also discarded by a white man. That a native would ever drive a motor vehicle, or even become a clerk, was unthinkable.

Nevertheless, for the whites, life had changed beyond recognition from the early day of the century. The towns were now enjoying the normal amenities of the period: electric light, water-borne sewerage, tarred streets, telephones, up-to-date cinemas (or "bioscopes" as they were universally known in Rhodesia and South Africa). And while the main roads connecting the towns were apt to be cut by flooding rivers during the rains, they were otherwise passable in all weathers thanks to Rhodesia's unique solution to the problem of the alternating menaces of mud and sand — a solution achieved by laying a single pair of parallel tarred strips down the centre of the road, along which cars hurtled head-on towards each other from opposite directions, and only pulled off to their left to pass each other at full speed at the last possible moment. The farmers and the miners in the country districts probably felt that they had not gained much in comfort or amenities since the early days, except for motor vehicles in place of ox-wagons and the advantage of the stripped roads where these were useful to them. But while electric power was beginning to find its way across the veld — only slowly at first — most farmers still had to rely on their own power plants chugging away in the outhouse — plants which, nevertheless, had improved considerably on the primitive installations of 30 years earlier.

While the small towns were still very small, Bulawayo and Salisbury were growing steadily but not spectacularly. By the mid-thirties the white population of each was about 10,000. (The migrant natives housed in the locations and in the kayas at the bottom of the garden were probably two or three times that number.) In the last few years before the second world war the white population in each of these towns increased by about 1000 every year, Salisbury leading by a few hundred one year and Bulawayo the next, so that they perennially competed for the peculiar honour of being the biggest town in Rhodesia. It was not until after the war that Salisbury took a pronounced lead which was to quadruple its population during the next 25 years, while Bulawayo started to lag behind.

One of the reasons why Bulawayo kept up with Salisbury in the years before the second world war was the long established presence of the headquarters of the railways. The railways were still run by a private concern, Rhodesia Railways Ltd., owned by the BSA Company — part of Cecil Rhodes's unfulfilled dream of a rail link from Cape Town to Cairo. The railway Company was by far the largest single employer of labour — white and black — in the country at the time.

In 1929 the white workers on the railways came out on strike for more pay. It was a wholly effective stoppage which lasted just short of three weeks and, with no other means of public transport available whatever, brought the country to a virtual standstill.

It is not for this history to comment on the issues which prompted the strike, or the merits or demerits of the parties involved in the dispute. In the end it was settled by a compromise, as these affairs invariably are. But it provided a series of enjoyable field-days for a number of policemen — who are never averse to an entertaining break in their normal routine. A number of NCOs and troopers were brought down to Bulawayo from Salisbury and Gwelo to reinforce the local police, but the whole affair was conducted on a gentlemanly and friendly basis. There was no violence, in fact no incidents of any sort. The authorities, reacting to type, hurriedly enrolled 600 European special constables in Bulawayo and gave them truncheons, police whistles and arm bands. One report says they were split up into 'A', 'B', 'C' and 'D' Companies, "each with civilian commanders and NCOs of the Police in charge of platoons ... on 26th February the Bulawayo railway station was successfully "carried". In other words, any unfortunate natives found hanging about were sent packing.

In the following year, 1930, the first organised recovery of a body from the Zambezi River, at the Victoria Falls, was undertaken. This was not, on this first occasion, an entirely BSAP operation although the police played their full part. In July that year two women visitors to the Falls Hotel, Miss Allison and Mrs. Kirby, were attacked by a native in the Rain Forest — which runs along the top of the main gorge directly opposite the crest of the falls themselves. The attacker sprang on Mrs. Kirby and forced her down on to the ground. Miss Allison was powerless to do anything but run for help. When she returned, both Mrs. Kirby and her attacker were not unexpectedly missing. The wet, slippery grass where Mrs. Kirby had been held down had been flattened, and it was all too evident that the native must have pushed her over the edge into the gorge. The drop at this point is some 400 feet, down into the seething cauldron of waters at the foot of the Devil's Cataract.

Later that evening a native was stopped on suspicion by the BSAP guard at the Southern Rhodesian end of the Victoria Falls bridge. He broke away, ran across the bridge and, faced with a European member of the NRP (Constable Jordan) at the Northern Rhodesian end, he tried to climb over the parapet of the bridge and fell down the cliff. The cliff was not actually vertical at this point and somehow his precipitate fall was arrested before he reached very far. Jordan could hear him groaning down below in the darkness. Carrying only a lantern, Jordan was lowered down the face of the cliff at the end of a rope held by eight native constables. He reported afterwards, "At 30 to 40 feet down I found no trace of the native. About 10 feet lower I came upon a jagged piece of rock which showed a bloodstain, and immediately below a pool of fresh blood on a rock". He was lowered farther down the face of the cliff until, he said, "at 50 to 70 feet I found the native lying in a horizontal position on a slope, alive and breathing. His nose was broken, his eyes swollen, blood was streaming from his head and he had cuts on his shoulders".

Native Constable Nyambe (NRP) followed down on the end of another rope. They tied up the fugitive — whose name was later found to be Koni — and hauled him to the surface, still alive. He died on the way to the hospital. At the inquest which followed the magistrate returned a verdict of death by misadventure, adding "I am definitely of the opinion that the deceased was the native who assaulted Mrs. Kirby".

A few days later a body was seen wedged between some rocks on the edge of Cataract Island, at the bottom of the gorge. Viewed through binoculars, there could be no doubt that it was Mrs. Kirby's. Discussions were held between the NRP and BSAP on the spot about whether it could be recovered but the Commissioner of the NRP telegraphed Stops, "No useful purpose would be served by descent. Considerable risk attached thereto. Gorge approximately 400 feet deep".

The Southern Rhodesia Attorney-General endorsed the Northern Rhodesian Commissioner's opinion. He instructed Stops, "There is to be no attempt to descend the cliff. I will not be party to a project which may, and probably will, entail loss of life, and which would serve no useful purpose".

But the late Mrs. Kirby had some relatives at the Wankie Colliery who were concerned enough on her behalf to work out a plan to erect a crane on the cliff and lower someone to recover her body. A telegraphed message from Stops to BSAP Victoria Falls said, "Yulelogs (code for Attorney-General) has instructed manager Wankie that railways and colliery may be permitted to co-operate in attempt to recover body. Corporal West (BSAP) as married man will not be permitted to participate in attempt to descend gorge". So the doubtful honour was accorded to Trooper Huggins, with two more volunteers, Mr. Crittall and Mr. Evans, riggers from the Colliery.

A steel cable was strung across the gorge from the Rain Forest to Cataract Island, with a travelling pulley over which ran another cable attached to a crane erected at the top of the cliff. From the end of the second cable dangled a specially made steel box, four feet square, which was steadied by a rope attached to a winch on Cataract Island. The box, carrying the three intrepid volunteers, had to be lowered 250 feet and took half an hour to descend. They spent a quarter of an hour on the island recovering the body — which was now clear of the water as the level of the river was subsiding — and it took 40 minutes to wind them up. Thus was completed the first of a number of recoveries — in some cases rescues of people still alive — carried out at the Victoria Falls by the joint efforts of the NRP and BSAP over the ensuing years.

Although Jordan of the NRP had claimed to have descended 70 feet to rescue the fugitive Koni, official comment later doubted if he had had to go down half that distance, and also pointed out that he could have saved himself a lot of trouble by taking a path which happened to zigzag down the face of the cliff at that point. If he had known of the path, he would certainly have taken it in preference to hanging on to a rope over an apparent precipice in the dark — and the length of his climb down the cliff and up again must have seemed almost interminable, so he can be forgiven a little exaggeration. Nevertheless the authorities conceded that the existence of a path of which he knew nothing in no way detracted from the bravery of his conduct and he was awarded the King's Medal. Trooper Huggins was not so fortunate. When it was suggested that he and the two men from the mine should be recommended for a similar award, Stops wrote, "I do not consider in view of the systematic and extensive arrangements for the descent of the Gorge, that the enterprise was, though admittedly an unpleasant one, accompanied by any great danger, and I consider the Minister's acknowledgement of their public-spirited action a suitable and sufficient award. In regard to the award of the King's Medal to Constable Jordan of NRP, it can be admitted that his prompt action in arranging to be lowered at night over the cliff in search of a supposedly guilty native merited some further recognition".

RSM "Jock" Douglas retired in 1932. He had been awarded the King's Police Medal and Long Service and Good Conduct medal early that year. There had been some delay since he had first applied for the latter, because of his defaulter's record. But in July 1931, the Commissioner had written, in support of a recommendation for the King's Police Medal, "Douglas has been largely instrumental in the reorganisation of Depot and the formation of a valuable instructional staff ... he has been responsible for training of all recruits, European and native, and for conducting refresher courses for other members of the Force. In carrying out these duties he has displayed exceptional ability and merit ... a fine example has been set by him on and off duty ... his reduction to constable for a disciplinary offence on 15 November 1915 has hitherto debarred him from the grant of the Long Service and Good Conduct Medal, for which he does not become eligible, until 19 December 1931 (16 years from the date of conviction). In consequence I am unable to submit a recommendation for the grant of the Meritorious Conduct Medal, which would otherwise have been done". But he got his KPM and LSGCM, and retired on a pension of £197 11s 0d a year.

Colonel J. S. Morris replaced Stops as Commissioner on the latter's retirement in February 1933. (In the New Year Honours Stops had been awarded the CBE.) Morris was the first Commissioner to have been a member of the CID. In those days members were not transferred to the CID at an early stage of their career as they are today. Today a member becomes a detective when still a young policeman and remains in the CID for the rest of his service. It was not so in Morris's time. Indeed, when he joined in 1909 there was no CID at all. Those were still the days when the BSAP was made up of 11 self-contained Troops and was behaving like a regiment of mounted infantry. Morris, aged 19, was posted as a trooper to 'C' Troop at Sinoia. He became a corporal in 1911 and transferred to the CID in 1913 as a 3rd Detective Sergeant.

He was a Lancastrian from Didsbury and had been educated at Manchester Grammar School. From the beginning of his service he was marked out as a young man of unusual intelligence and character, and within four years of joining the force he passed "with merit" the promotion examination for a commission. He was actually commissioned in April 1914, when he returned to the uniformed branch and was appointed Assistant District Superintendent, stationed first at Inyati and next year at Gatooma. His elevation to that rank within five years is probably something of a record in the history of the force.

Like many other officers of the BSAP he was seconded on military service during the first war and in 1917 was sent to India. Here he met and married a nursing sister in Queen Alexandra's Military Nursing Service. She had been on active service since 1914 and had served throughout the tribulations of the Gallipoli campaign with the 29th Division of the Mediterranean Expeditionary Force, before being posted to India. She had been in the thick of actual warfare — which was more than could be claimed by her husband who was later to command all Rhodesia's military forces. On his return from India Morris became officer in charge of the CID in Salisbury (the CID was still commanded from Bulawayo). In 1926 he was promoted to Superintendent and in 1928 he took acting command of the CID during absence on leave of the commanding officer, Major J.C. Brundell.

Then he left the CID to put on uniform again filling a succession of staff appointments at headquarters before he became, late in 1929, the Assistant Commissioner (there was only one incumbent of that rank in those days and he was the Commissioner's actual deputy). During his period on the staff at headquarters he re-drafted the Police Act, which up to then had followed the general lines of the old 1903 Police Ordinance. In 1930 he spent some time in the Union of South Africa, first with the Active Citizen's Force at their camps at Potchefstroom and Ladysmith; and then with the South African Police at headquarters in Pretoria followed by a Senior Officer' Course at Roberts Heights. The emphasis was certainly on military subjects, with courses in tactics, map reading, air cooperation, military law, artillery and musketry. He was away from Rhodesia for three months altogether, and the SAP generously provided him with a horse and batman.

He had acted as Commissioner on more than one occasion in the absence of Stops, before the latter's retirement. Morris's rise to the top was almost meteoric, but this was a fair reflection of his ability as an officer; and his preferment was a godsend to the force in the testing years which were to come, as the threat of war loomed up once again. It might be said of Morris that he was a perfectionist — but this is to some extent true of every Commissioner. Perfectionism is an attribute that grows spontaneously from supreme command.

Morris was appointed Commissioner in February 1933 at a salary of £1000 a year. The amount was quite arbitrary, determined by the whim of the Government. In November that year he wrote to the Minister of Defence "On my appointment as Commissioner of Police my pay at the rate of £1000 per annum was approved, but no provision was made for any incremental increase. The late Commissioner's (Stops) salary was £1200". Stops's pension was £1008. "I respectfully submit that the scale of pay for a Commissioner should be definitely laid down and should provide for increments. I hesitate to make any recommendation," he added with due humility, "of what the maximum should be, but suggest it should not be less than £1100 with annual increments of £25 up to that amount" Considering what Stops had been getting, the suggestion was modest enough. "I should like to point out that a Commissioner paid at the rate of £1000 is in receipt of only £40 per annum more than a Chief Superintendent of the CID on the maximum scale." The authorities were unmoved. Morris had to wait six years before he was given a rise — other than an acting allowance when he was put in command of all the Rhodesian forces.

A month after Morris's appointment Sergeant Major George Acland Tantum (who stood 6 feet 4 inches, weighed 238 lb., and was predictably known as "Tiny" Tantum) was promoted to RSM to fill the vacancy caused by "Jock" Douglas's retirement. Tantum was quite a young man, at 35, and had served for eight years, from 1914 to 1922, in the 2nd Life Guards before attesting as a constable in the BSAP in 1927. (What he had done between 1922 and 1927 is not on record.) When, almost immediately after his attestation, he applied for promotion to sergeant, Assistant Superintendent Adams wrote, "he is inclined somewhat to take life easily, but it is considered that with responsibility he would make a good disciplinarian and be able to handle men". That, in fact, was what he was destined to be — a good disciplinarian. "Perhaps," the report went on, "he is more gifted with 'brawn' than 'brains', but he is suited to the rank of sergeant".

He had proved himself a trifle prone to injury. As a 238 lb. constable in 1927 he had fallen seven feet into an inspection pit in a garage in the dark, "when not on duty". Result, broken ribs and 16 days in hospital. Exactly a year later, "when not on duty", he had fallen from a moving car. The car had been full, so he had jumped on to the "running board" holding on to the door. Someone had inconveniently opened the door and pushed him off. Result, broken wrist. (For the benefit of the modern motorist, the "running board" was a flat step along each side of the car.) A few years later, this time "in execution of duty", he had hit a native who was assaulting a native constable and broken his little finger. The native was convicted of assault. A year after his promotion to RSM he was thrown by his horse, which had stepped into an ant-bear hole. Result, sprained ankle, dislocated shoulder, "while on duty".

The first concern of the new Commissioner in 1933, apart from his own salary, was the old problem of recruiting. Rhodesia was beginning to recover from the effects of the world-wide depression — from the traumatic period when white men had been employed by the Government in manual labour at relief work on the roads. Cautiously at first, Morris sought to find more men from Britain but with better education than that of the few who had recently been sent out. Even O'Keeffe wrote from London in May 1933, "I was not enamoured with one or two we have sent out recently. One, I believe, was a kitchen hand in the Merchant Service. He filled the bill very well in every other respect, but personally I should have thought he would hardly be the type really wanted for the BSAP". Men were still applying locally but Morris insisted, in a circular issued in November, "Unless an applicant (in Rhodesia) can produce evidence that he has matriculated or passed an examination such as Oxford or Cambridge Seniors, he will be set an educational test in arithmetic, dictation and general knowledge". He cabled to O'Keeffe in January 1934, "Six men may be required for the foot branch. They must pass an education test. Ex-policemen from England have not been satisfactory". It was at this stage that he introduced the first scheme for Police Cadets, whereby youngsters from school — still living at home — acted as minions at the local police station before formally enlisting when they were old enough — and provided they had not been disenchanted with the prospect of a career as a policeman. One of the original Cadets was J.L. (Jackie) Wordsworth who retired from the force 35 years later, in 1969, with the rank of Senior Assistant Commissioner — believed to be an all-time record in length of service, even longer than that of A.J. Tomlinson.

But Morris was not altogether averse to engaging for town police work in Rhodesia men of the same type as those enlisted in the Metropolitan Police. What concerned him was that a man who had already been a policeman in England was usually no good for the BSAP. As Edwards had said 30 years earlier, "Men who have already served in towns in England do not transplant well because conditions in Rhodesia are so different". This was still true in spite of the fact that the Rhodesian towns had since had 30 years in which to mature. O'Keeffe wrote to Morris in September 1935 telling him of a new system that had been introduced in the Metropolitan Police. Commissions in that force, he said, could now be obtained only by entry through the Metropolitan Police College at Hendon — and admission to that exclusive institution, except in the case of 30 selected serving members every year, was limited to young men from universities or public schools. (In those days "universities" in England still meant either Oxford or Cambridge.) The effect had been to dampen their hopes of promotion to commissioned rank among the majority of members of that force. For that reason, O'Keeffe argued, many of them would be anxious to enlist in the BSAP.

Morris replied that from long experience the BSAP had found that enlisting ex-members of other forces, including the Metropolitan Police, had never been satisfactory. "I have always regretted taking these men," he said. "The better men usually remain in their own force and seek advancement there." Nevertheless in view of the new situation, whereby good men were possibly being frustrated, he was prepared to try again, with men aged from 20 to 22 years and six months; their maximum service in the Metropolitan Police to be two years and six months; their probationary periods in that force to have been completed and their appointments confirmed. The number of such men sent out to Rhodesia in each squad was to be limited to four. (A squad consisted of 10 recruits.) A month later he relented so far as to allow the proportion to be increased to seven out of a squad of 10. The concession showed a considerable change of heart on his part.

A couple of weeks later O'Keeffe had to cable, "Unable to obtain sufficient ex-MP candidates without reference to Commissioner MP". Morris replied, "No objection approach Commissioner". The Commissioner of the Metropolitan Police said surprisingly that he was happy to assist and he sent forward 23 applications; O'Keeffe selected seven.

That same year, in 1935, the native mine workers on the copper belt in Northern Rhodesia came out on strike. In the context of race relations in the colonial environment of the 1930s, the strike was more of a social protest than an industrial dispute. The first sign of violence manifested itself at Nkana when a number of European gentlemen on their convivial way home from the golf-club, driving through the Nkana mine location in the lordly way that was their wont, were assailed by a barrage of stones. This was the incident which started the trouble, and it was followed by the inevitable confrontation of a native mob by a body of armed police (in this case the NRP). The police opened fire and six natives were killed.

It so happened that on that date, 28 May 1935, celebrations were being held in Lusaka to mark its elevation to the status of the new capital of Northern Rhodesia. (Up to then, Livingstone had been the capital.) A flight of four Vickers Victoria troop-carrying aircraft of the Royal Air Force was visiting Lusaka for the occasion. When the news of the trouble on the copper belt was received, 60 askaris of the NRP in Lusaka were hurriedly embarked on the aircraft. It must have been a terrifying experience for most of these young natives who had probably never seen an aeroplane before. Departure of the flight was first delayed by bad weather; then, when they arrived at Ndola, there was not enough petrol to fly on to Nkana. History is silent on how these askaris did finally reach the scene of action.

Two days later, on 30 May, a party of BSAP were entrained at Bulawayo. Their journey to Ndola by special train would take at least 36 hours. Meanwhile the trouble on the copper belt had spread to Luanshya — which was described in the Press as "like an armed camp" — and the compound at the Roan Antelope mine had been "wrecked by the mob". All the Europeans at Bwana-Makubwa 10 miles south of Ndola — which was more isolated than the other mines — had been brought into the town. Some of the aggrieved Nkana golfers were said to have brought out their own guns and fired on the strikers in revenge for their rough treatment in the location, and the police had also moved these gentlemen to Ndola "for their own safety".

By the next day, the 31st, the Press was able to report that the situation on the copper belt was generally quieter. It was on this morning that three of the RAF troop carriers arrived in Salisbury from Lusaka. (The fourth arrived later that day.) Their purpose was to fetch a contingent of BSAP and fly them first to Broken Hill, then on to Ndola. The Vickers Victoria was a twin-engined wood and canvas biplane, with the engines attached to the vertical struts between the upper and lower wings. Compared with modern aircraft, and considering its totally unstreamlined appearance, it could justifiably be described as a "flying crate". Its cruising speed was 90 knots. Sixteen men with their arms and equipment could be loaded — not necessarily comfortably — in each aircraft. On this occasion, two of the aircraft took 16 men and the other two, 13 each — a total of 58. Captain J. E. Ross (a future Commissioner) was in command of the detachment; Lieutenant B. G. Spurling (another future Commissioner) was Troop Leader; Inspector Hampton was acting RSM and Sergeant Cordell was the clerk. Sergeants Gaylard and Fachie were the section sergeants. There were two sections of troopers and two mixed sections of troopers, corporals and constables. There was also a Lewis gun section under Sergeant Graham.

The dress was "Fighting Order" — leggings, shorts, web equipment, helmet, haversack, water bottle, field dressing, rifle, bayonet and 10 rounds. (No pack or blankets.) NCOs carried revolvers in place of rifles and bayonets. The Lewis gun section, of course, took its gun and ammunition. It was a heavily equipped force to pack into four relatively primitive aircraft.

After they had sat in the stationary aircraft in uncomfortably cramped circumstances for more than an hour, the troops were all ordered to disembark. Some, no doubt, felt disappointed; others considerably relieved. The pilot in command had decided they had left their departure too late and would not be able to land in daylight at Broken Hill, where there were no landing lights on the airfield. However, they were packed into the aircraft again next morning and took off at five past six; they arrived at Lusaka two and a half hours later, at 8.35; they left Lusaka at five past nine, landing at Broken Hill in three quarters of an hour, at 9.50. After an hour and 10 minutes on the ground they took off for Ndola at 11 o'clock. Thereafter, the record seems a trifle unreliable — for it gives the arrival at Ndola as 2.55 p.m. — nearly three hours later. Even the Vickers Victorias would manage a flight of 150 miles in a better time than that. When they arrived, of course, the trouble was over and the strikers had gone back to work (The special train from Bulawayo had arrived early that morning at Luanshya, also when the excitement was over.) Nevertheless the airlift was an interesting exercise, and presumably served as a pattern and a lesson on which later contingency planning could be based.

For Morris this episode was only an interlude in his perennial search for the right recruits. The flow from the ranks of the Metropolitan Police, restricted as it was, soon dried up. In 1936 the Secretary of the force at New Scotland Yard wrote to O'Keeffe saying, "In recent months we have found it increasingly difficult to secure the requisite number of suitable recruits to maintain the strength of the Metropolitan Police force. Consequently the Commissioner requests you not to press your request to bring vacancies in the British South Africa Police to the notice of suitable candidates". So that was that. O'Keeffe himself wrote to Morris, "owing to much improved trade conditions in this country British lads are finding it easier to obtain employment here". Morris had suggested, in an earlier letter, that O'Keeffe's staff should "go out into the country to find recruits. Those from counties away from London are usually pretty good". O'Keeffe retorted that in the last batch sent out to Rhodesia there had been one from London, and one each from Bedfordshire, Hertfordshire, Scotland, Yorkshire, Belfast, Surrey, Oxfordshire, Cornwall, Essex, Somerset and Hampshire. Where else, he asked Morris, ought he to start looking?

Hickman, who was the Staff Officer in 1937, wrote to the High Commissioner, "A superintendent has noted (in his annual report) that he has not been favourably impressed with recruits who were previously officers in the Mercantile Marine. Whether it is the nautical atmosphere of 'one man, one job' I cannot say, but as a class they lack initiative and are born 'swingers' — a characteristic foreign to the Police Force. The Commissioner is generally in agreement with these sentiments". (The epithet "swinger" had a very different meaning from its connotation today. It derived from the nautical term, "swinging the lead" and denoted avoiding as much hard work as possible.)

Nor was Morris himself too easy to please. On one occasion he wrote to O'Keeffe, "I am not too well satisfied with the last batch of District recruits. On the whole they are by no means as good as those sent out during the past two years. They are not what I would describe as good British lads of the type and stamp we want for the Police". On another occasion he wrote, "Some ex-Metropolitan Police have turned out all right. But I prefer a policy of not taking men from other forces".

However, in terms of a recent Anglo-Egyptian Treaty in 1937 a number of British members had been discharged from the Egyptian police and the Colonial Office had asked the High Commissioner if the BSAP would take some of them on. "I am prepared," wrote Morris, "to consider a few ex-Egyptian Police Constables — no more than two in any 10 recruits. I feel that in agreeing to this number we are doing something to assist. It is not as though they are resigning of their own accord ... I should like to take this opportunity to say the men you sent out in April (he was writing in May) appear to be a first class lot."

This was certainly a change. But his approbation was not to last for long. In November he reported to O'Keeffe that one of the recruits attested in April had since been sentenced to imprisonment. "The cast-off public school type is no use to the Police ...  I do not wish to take the matter up through other channels," he added darkly, "but I shall have no option if men continue to arrive whom we cannot accept and are obviously unsuited to Police work." Moreover, he complained, many of the new men sought to leave the force within the first three years.

O'Keeffe passed this letter to Mr. Baggott, of the High Commissioner's Office, who now handled police recruitment. Baggott understandably took some umbrage at Morris's remarks and pointed out to O'Keeffe how the Commissioner in his May letter had said the April batch had been a first class lot. "I do not like the 'threat' in paragraph 5," said Baggott. "I think the Commissioner should at least give me a chance as I have so far sent out only one batch of men." O'Keeffe mounted his high horse and wrote to Morris, "My Official Secretary has shown me your letter to which I have taken the strongest exception. When you say, 'it is essential that men remain and complete their term of engagement' it is necessary for me to point out that there is no clairvoyant on the staff." He added with some pungency, "If I may offer a suggestion, it would be that an independent investigation as to the treatment meted out to recruits after their arrival in Salisbury may have a beneficient effect on the Corps generally .... I pass without comment your reference to 'cast-off public school types' .... but I must inform you that neither myself nor any member of my staff is prepared to remain under threats from you and therefore I am sending a copy of your letter and my reply to the Hon. Minister of Defence". Uncharacteristically chastened, Morris mildly replied, "No threat was intended in my letter. I am sure Mr. Baggott will do his best to select suitable men".

Unhappily, in official correspondence on subjects such as these, it is only the shortcomings and complaints that come to light. Men like Commissioners and their staff are too busy dealing with the problem cases and the contretemps that arise from day to day to waste time handing out bouquets for everything that goes right. After all, that is primarily what they are there for — to deal with the problems. Faults always stand out and claim the attention of authority. Good work is taken for granted and attracts no approbation from above. If there were no human failings in an organisation like a police force it could almost be left to run on its own. Once the policy was determined there would be little left for the staff to do. So the records always seem to be full of the shortcomings and tell us little about the successes.

In truth, despite all the carping, recruiting for the BSAP during those years was a story of resounding success. It brought to Rhodesia a whole generation of members of the force who were to serve it with distinction for the next 30 years — to serve through another world war, again either seconded to Imperial forces or held reluctantly to police the Colony; and, after the war was over, to lead the force to a new pitch of efficiency. Walmer Castle, Arundel Castle, Windsor Castle, Armadale Castle, Kenilworth Castle, Dunnottar Castle, Garth Castle, Warwick Castle, Balmoral Castle, Winchester Castle, Edinburgh Castle, Dunvegan Castle, Grantully Castle: they each brought from Southampton, or London, their drafts of expectant young men. (The author must apologise for any omissions from this list. These are the ships with their batches of recruits recorded in the files of the national archives; possibly the records of some others are missing. A number of men also came out singly in other ships.)

The nominal rolls of these drafts reveal a glittering catalogue of names. It would be invidious to mention a single one of them. They include future Commissioners, Deputy Commissioners, top brass, men of all ranks; men who have distinguished themselves not only by their careers in the force but also by their characters and personalities displayed both as serving members and Rhodesian citizens. Men, too, who without particular distinction made good policemen and served the force loyally. At the time of writing this history almost every one of them has retired. Some have died, many are still alive. They represent an important generation of members who joined during that period and who in their time contributed lustre and repute to the traditions of the force.

## Chapter Twenty-Eight

## THE FORMATIVE YEARS

BY THE LATE 1930s the clouds of war had begun to gather again. As early as 1933 the British Colonial Secretary had sent a circular memorandum to, among others, the Governor of Southern Rhodesia suggesting that Colonial officials and officers of the Colonial defence forces, on leave in England, should attend lectures at the War Office. The lectures would cover a catholic range of subjects, such as the general military situation throughout the Empire; the organisation of the Committee of Imperial Defence; local defence problems; military organisations in foreign countries with which the Colonies were particularly interested; the League of Nations and the Disarmament Conferences; and finally, as the only practical, down-to-earth commitment, censorship and the control of aliens. At the time the BSAP was the only regular defence force in Rhodesia and Morris took advantage of the invitation in June 1934 and digested this unappetising mixture. He then went on to a Senior Officers' Course for the Dominions and Colonial Police Services at New Scotland Yard.

Next year he was awarded the King's Silver Jubilee Medal and the CBE, and in 1936 was appointed (in addition to his duties as Commissioner BSAP) to be the Commanding Officer of all the other Southern Rhodesian forces — which included the Rhodesia Regiment, the Permanent Staff Corps and the Southern Rhodesian (School) Cadets. The appointment was certainly an honour, in that it acknowledged Morris's undoubted capabilities, but the Government was quite shameless in informing him that they had given him the job to save money. The previous CO of the forces (other than the BSAP) had been Colonel George Parson, DSO and bar (one time a member of the BSAP) who was now retiring on pension. Up to then Parson had been paid a colonel's salary. Morris was to do his job for the bargain price of an acting allowance of £125 a year.

Morris attended a conference at Lusaka in December in 1937 in his capacity of Commanding Officer, Southern Rhodesian forces. The others attending were the COs of the Royal West Africa Frontier Force (from the West African colonies), the King's African Rifles (from the East African colonies) and the Northern Rhodesia Regiment. It was stated at the time that South Africa was unwilling to be included in any general defence scheme as she was reluctant to take part in the discussions "for political reasons".

The conference decided, surprisingly, that "in the event of war with Portugal" the NRR would be responsible for the Zambezi bridge at Chirundu, the BSAP for the bridge at the Victoria Falls, the Northern Rhodesian Government (sic) would watch the Angolan border and the Southern Rhodesian Air Unit would mobilise in Salisbury. Except for the unfortunate "Northern Rhodesian Government" — whatever that implied — on the Angolan border, nobody seems to have been detailed to make contact with the enemy. A rider was added that it might be necessary — presumably failing war with Portugal — "to assist the Portuguese in maintaining Beira against enemy attack owing to its importance to Southern Rhodesia." A reference made in the first draft of the conference report to possible war with Belgium was discreetly deleted. Altogether the Commanding Officers do not seem to have mustered any profound strategic thinking. Some fear was expressed of "rioting by white (author's italics) miners on the Copper Belt" and Morris was able to describe the exercise undertaken by the BSAP two years earlier (when the black miners had rioted) and the details of that exercise went into the conference's report as the only item of precise planning.

More objective consideration of possible developments in the event of war appeared in correspondence in 1938 between Morris and General Giffard in Nairobi. (Giffard's exact designation is not certain but it is clear that he was the senior British military officer in central, east and west Africa.) Giffard wrote, "It would be unwise and uneconomical, in the event of another war, to use Southern Rhodesia's magnificent European material as infantry units in the theatre of operations. The main contribution Southern Rhodesia could make to Imperial Defence would be to train officers and NCOs and make them available as leaders of African troops, or to reinforce the Regular Army in the United Kingdom should hostilities not extend to Africa."

A few months later Giffard visited Rhodesia and he subsequently told the Committee of Imperial Defence that he was "profoundly impressed by the keen desire of all sections of the population and the Government of the Colony to co-operate to the full extent of their ability in Imperial Defence.

"In addition to the BSAP," he added, "which consists of some 23 officers and 463 other ranks," — an interesting revelation of the strength of the force at the time — "Southern Rhodesia maintains an auxiliary squadron of the Royal Air Force and two European (territorial) infantry battalions, about 600 men, with a small Permanent Staff Corps of nine officers and 45 other ranks for instructional purposes ...  Should the British Empire be involved in war, Southern Rhodesia would be ready and eager to place such of her forces as could be spared at the disposal of the United Kingdom Government where they would be most required ... It would be wasteful to employ European infantry as reinforcements in other parts of Africa where climatic conditions are unsuitable." The Committee of Imperial Defence expressed "high appreciation of the spirit of co- operation" and extended "a cordial welcome to the offer".

But possible trouble from the direction of Portuguese East Africa was still niggling the Commanding Officers. A memorandum was circulated in September 1938 to those who had attended the 1937 conference. It was headed "Threat to British Interests from Portuguese East Africa" and said, "The invasion of Portuguese East Africa by a hostile power (still unspecified) is a definite threat to Southern Rhodesia. The capture of Tete and Macequece would not take place unless a hostile power had advanced and taken possession of those places" — which, to say the least, seems no more than elementary reasoning — "or Portugal was at war with His Majesty's Government." (Author's italics) "In the event of an invasion of Portuguese East Africa we should co-operate with the Portuguese by despatching troops to assist in holding vital positions, or proceed directly to Beira to prevent its capture." The Commanding Officers still seemed to be indulging in some remarkably woolly thinking.

RSM "Tiny" Tantum had also been on a course in England. But this had no immediate relevance to even a potentially warlike situation. He spent six weeks at the Depot at Caterham, in Surrey, on an intensive course of instruction in drill and discipline as practised by the Brigade of Guards. This was followed by three weeks' attachment to a cavalry Regiment of the Line at Aldershot. The commanding officer of the Guards Depot reported, "His knowledge of drill, word of command and general theory have improved" — which implied an unpromising outlook for the BSAP recruits when he returned to Salisbury. There are those who suffered under Tantum — or so they describe it — who believe that Blatherwick and Douglas treated their recruits gently by comparison. Such distinctions are, of course, purely relative. The BSAP had long been noted, at any rate locally, for the tough discipline imposed on its recruits during their course at Depot. It turned them out as hardened, self-reliant troopers and constables, smart in appearance and well versed in the fundamentals of their profession.

Regimental Sergeant Majors, as this history infers, are laws unto themselves; and their primary purpose in life — some would go so far as to say their sole purpose — is to instil in their subordinates unquestioning obedience, impeccable appearance and a disregard for all personal considerations when a duty has to be done. These are not unworthy attributes, even for a policeman. Blatherwick had tempered his aura of unbridled authority with human compassion; he inspired a mixture of respect and admiration. Douglas had been bluff and hearty; he, too, inspired respect, tinged with a measure of amused affection. Tantum had no softening factor in his character; he was the essence of the all-powerful RSM; a big man, he towered unrelentingly over those below him.

There has ever been, and there ever will be, a division of opinion as to whether the imposition of rigid military discipline at the recruit stage is an essential factor in the moulding of a police force. The chief antagonists to the practice, of course, have always been the recruits themselves. But as they progress in their careers in the force it is surprising how their opinions come to be transformed, until they one and all point out what fine men it made of them. The truth is that the period of subjection to unrelenting discipline during the recruit's course in the BSAP is expediently short. It has imposed on a recruit an invaluable — one might say an indispensable — subservience to discipline without turning him into an automaton, such as can result from a prolonged application of the medicine — as was the custom in the British regiments of the Victorian and Edwardian eras on whose pattern the force was originally formed.

It is not within the province of this history to comment on the efficacy of a policy followed by the force; but it is legitimate to assert that the BSAP primarily owes its reputation for quality as a police force to the hard school of military discipline in which its members have received their initial training. And whatever may have been the attributes and shortcomings of the three Regimental Sergeant Majors whose careers spanned the 36 years covered by this history, it is to them that the credit must go.

Tantum served until 1947. So there were still some years during which recruits were to continue to "suffer" under him, although for part of the remaining time he was seconded for service in northern Africa. Ten years earlier, in 1937, he had accompanied as RSM the BSAP contingent which attended the coronation of King George VI n London. The contingent was commanded by Major J.S. Bridger. Under Tiny's unrelenting eye, the representatives of the BSAP had nothing to fear from critical comparison with His Majesty's Brigade of Guards themselves.

Early in 1939, in a "Mobilisation Instruction", Morris quoted the strength of the force as "District Police, 325 (all still mounted men]; Town Police and CID, 130; Supernumeries, 74; Total, 529." This is an interesting comparison with General Giffard's report, only a year earlier, that the total strength of the force had been 486. The recruiting campaign which Morris was pursuing was clearly bearing fruit — not only in quantity, but undoubtedly in quality too. The training and organisation of the force had reached a level to which it had never before aspired.

The possibility of a native rising was still plaguing the thoughts of the authorities. In his Mobilisation Instruction, Morris declared, "The BSAP — a quasi-military police force — is still the First Line of Defence," and he included a provision for declaring martial law "in the very early stages of any rebellion". The BSAP would then mobilise two squadrons for "active service" within Rhodesia: 'A' Squadron would draw four officers and 120 other ranks, with 130 horses and 10 pack mules, from Depot, Umtali and Hartley; 'B' Squadron would draw four officers, 102 other ranks, 120 horses and 10 pack mules from Gwelo, Bulawayo, Gwanda and Fort Victoria. The two squadrons would go into action with rations for five days for "humans" and for 2 1/2 days for animals; also with 24,000 rounds of rifle ammunition, 3000 rounds for Lewis guns, 3000 for Vickers machine guns and 18 shells for the Stokes mortar. Whatever its pretensions as a civil police force — and certainly it was basically behaving as such now in the towns — the BSAP in the districts, right up to the last war, was still a force of mounted men and still very militarily inclined. In the event, nothing happened even to suggest native unrest. The squadrons were never mobilised and members of the force had to be content with their peace-time routine right up to the declaration of war in September 1939.

Owing to the practice — sanctified by law — of closing official records for 30 years after their date of origin it is not possible to continue this history to cover the whole period of the second world war. Consequently the present history is being closed at 1939. Nevertheless, mention must be made that in the following year, 10 months after war had been declared, the police and military commands were separated and Morris reverted to command of the BSAP only. The official statement announcing the change said that the previous arrangement had been dictated "by convenience and economy". Even so, the statement continued, with the increase in military activity and the many extraneous duties which had devolved on the BSAP, "the burden of double command has become excessive. The creation of a large body of troops on a permanent footing has relieved the BSAP of defence responsibilities and has increased the differentiation between the functions of the military and the police." In short, the BSAP was no longer "the first line of defence". Lest Morris should feel slighted at reversion to a mere Commissioner he was accorded the rank of Inspector General of the BSAP — "an acknowledgement," said the statement, "of his invaluable work while holding the double command." He was the only man to hold that rank in the history of the force. Another official statement said, "Colonel Morris has fulfilled his difficult office with distinction. Only when the passing of crises removes the limitation which is imposed on any statement on military matters will it be possible to give a real appreciation of all that Colonel Morris has done. "The crises have passed, but any such official appreciation in the records — if there is one — is still buried in the Archives.

In 1941 the authorities proposed to Morris that he should accept the rank of Brigadier. He wrote, "I am pleased to accept your offer of badges of rank as Inspector General (a crown and three stars — equivalent to those of a Brigadier]. While appreciating your kindness in suggesting to put forward my name for Brigadier I feel that as the grant of military ranks under Police Regulations was abolished early this year, I prefer no exemption in my case." However, in 1943 his well-wishers overcame his scruples by granting him the honorary rank of Brigadier, stemming from his previous association with the Permanent Staff Corps. He was to retire from the BSAP in 1945.

Between 1903 and 1939 the BSAP, as a police force, grew up. These were indeed the formative years, stretching from the days when troopers regarded police work as an unwarranted intrusion on their more colourful regimental duties, to the days when members accepted it as their professional purpose in life.

When the military and police commands were separated in 1940 and Morris went back to the BSAP, the Rhodesia Herald was not slow to recognise the significance of the move. On the day following the Herald declared, "The new arrangement underlines a process that has been developing steadily of recent years — the reduction of the military functions of the BSAP and increasing emphasis on the police side. The BSAP are no longer, as they were, the first line of defence of the Colony ... Every year the demands on the police force for skilled training in police work increase and the qualifications of a good policeman become more specialised ... the profession of a policeman should become more and more of a career and less of a stepping-stone to other occupations."

Looking back on the period, 1903 to 1939, one has to acknowledge that, war years apart, the process of transition from soldiers to policemen had been steady — perhaps a little slow at times — and continuous. The lack of professionalism in the early days sounds amusing enough now — as if those who displayed it were too naive to know better. The truth is, of course, that they had no experience of civil police work, nor any precedents to work to. Each step forward had to be made by trial, and not a little error. They were working in entirely different circumstances from those of a police force in the metropolitan countries. Had the circumstances been the same it would merely have been a matter of importing one of the tried systems and operating it by the book of rules. But, as Edwards and Morris had both complained, men with experience in metropolitan forces showed themselves the least adaptable to conditions in the colonies. There were some honourable exceptions, when ex-policemen from Britain became worthy members of the BSAP; but these came at a later stage when conditions in Rhodesia were putting on a few social graces. And in these instances it was due more to the calibre of the men themselves than any experience they brought with them. Of course, it was a different case with Edwards himself and Capell. Edwards had actually commanded the Metropolitan Police and Capell had held senior rank in police forces in South Africa and Grenada. In fact, their experience had been at the top, and although they brought an intimate knowledge of police work to the BSAP, it was the ability to command — gained from long, distinguished careers in responsible military ranks — that made them so valuable to the force during its formative years.

For the first 30 of the 36 years covered by this volume, the senior ranks of the force — with the exception of Edwards and Capell themselves — were dominated by founder members of the BSAP proper (that is to say, the force newly constituted in 1896) with its ingrained memories of military service in South Africa. And quite a number of these men remembered even earlier days than that — the Jameson Raid and the Matabele and Mashona rebellions. It is to their credit that they adjusted themselves to civil police work as readily as they did — although whenever they found the slightest excuse for displaying a military presence they grabbed it with not a little enthusiasm. Morris was the first commanding officer who had joined the force after the days of military escapades were over. He became, probably for this reason, the precursor of a new generation of professional policemen; and the succeeding generation, who spanned the years of the last war and came back to put their stamp on the BSAP of today, grew up under his command.

When WWII came a large proportion of the members of the BSAP were to be detached from the force in Rhodesia and seconded to Imperial military units in various theatres of active service, principally Ethiopia, Somaliland, the Western Desert and Italy. To take their place and maintain the strength of a local police force in Rhodesia a strong Police Reserve was to be formed — consisting principally of volunteers who were to give their services as reasonably effective part-time policemen while still pursuing their normal civilian occupations.

But that, and the history of the post-war force, is another story. It must await the telling for a number of years until confidential records are available covering a reasonable span of time — and until such time as the author, whoever he may be, is not too close to events to be able to assess them dispassionately.

# VOLUME THREE

The End of The Line

**1939 – 1980**

by Hugh Phillips

## PREFACE TO VOLUME THREE

When, in the mid-1990's, I embarked on the research for this history it was with very mixed thoughts. Peter Gibbs had covered the story of the Force from 1889 to 1938 but the growth years from 1939 to 1960 and the last 20 years when the BSA Police slid slowly and inevitably into an inconsistent dual role needed to be put on record. There were too many fine men and women, too many stories untold to be left to someone else, perhaps, to write it all up.

The next point was that historical research was something I enjoyed and last — well not quite last — was that writing was something that had always held a fascination and lure for me. And, of course, there was vanity — the gratification of seeing one's name on the cover of a book.

Finance turned out to be a fairly formidable obstacle. A polite letter to the head of a very important world conglomerate, with strong roots in Rhodesia and thousands of happy, smiling shareholders, elicited a three line negative response from the great man's secretary.

So what could have been a 'mission' involving travel, interviewing, research in dusty university libraries became just a simple, home-based and not-to-be–hurried hobby. Until former Detective Section Officer Nick Russell came along.

Nick had both faith and vision. He believed that my writing of four newsletters a year for 18 years to keep ex-members of the BSAP in touch with one another showed stamina and commitment. He also looked upon his own years in the Police with deep pride as well as pleasure, and he wanted to put something back as a sort of repayment — homage if you like — for those years. And he was a publisher.

The main sources for the third book have been the National Archives, the annual reports of the various commissioners of police, the monthly editions of the Outpost magazine — and people. People especially. In the Bibliography I have attempted to acknowledge many of those who have contributed ideas, stories and reminiscences. To those not listed and to those whose contributions are not included, I can only apologise and thank you for your support and encouragement.

This third book is not an official history of the BSA Police. Perhaps, one day in the future, that will be possible. That day will come when the prejudices of the past are finally over and the land we have grown to love and regard as our home is set on a course of prosperity, and people of all colours have learned that the country is more important than the individual.

Let us hope, as I write this in October 2000, that the day when that vision — of a glorious, thriving Zimbabwe becomes a reality — is not too distant.

Next, I would thank three people without whose assistance and encouragement the years 1939 to 1980 could have remained a 'not-to-be-hurried hobby'. Bill Ellway, who has perused most of these pages with wisdom, humour and an unusual tact and who has diverted me from the odd indiscretion, insult and faux pas; tempering his wisdom with the occasional irreverent reminiscence. Dawn, my wife, who has had to learn the misery of loneliness and the rejection that comes with living in the same rooms as a word-processor. And lastly, Alan Stock, a Bristolian like myself, who has proofread these pages with, for me, uncomfortable diligence, but always with kindness and creativity.

And finally, to Dorothy and Ken Stanford-Smith, who have laboured and researched for many a long hour, checking and cross-checking and squinting over their computer screen to produce the Nominal Roll of the BSA Police.

Dedication, perseverance and patience were never so well demonstrated.


Hugh Phillips,
Harare, Zimbabwe
October, 2000.

## Chapter Twenty-Nine

## ONCE MORE UNTO THE BREACH

*1939 and the effect of the War in Southern Rhodesia — political and economic climate — Huggins — we meet Appleby, Hickman, Jackson, Spurling, Barfoot and Bristow — London Dinner — Commissioner Morris — inception of the Police Reserve and preparation of Police for active service*

1939 WAS A year of change — a year of decisions and a year in which millions of lives were to be altered, refashioned and set in very different patterns. Nothing could, nor ever would, be quite the same again.

In the Northern Hemisphere, the menacing shadow of Nazi Germany was spreading its ominous tentacles over Europe; the Spanish War had finally come to an end with Great Britain recognising the government of General Franco; defensive agreements were being signed between Great Britain and Turkey, between France and Turkey and between Britain and Poland. Winston Churchill, in mid-August, enjoyed a short holiday in Normandy and announced, as he packed away his oil paints and cleaned his brushes: "This is the last picture we shall paint in peace for a very long time." As the shadow grew and darkened, conscription was introduced in Britain and throughout the Commonwealth and notices appeared in the *Rhodesia Herald* and others of the Colony's newspapers seeking "Recruits for Active Service". And then, finally, on 3 September, Governor Sir Herbert Stanley formally advised the nation of the outbreak of War.

However, well before that date, the inevitability of conflict had been recognised when, in early August, the Southern Rhodesia House of Assembly passed a Bill to confer emergency powers upon the Government. This, in turn, was but a further step in the astute preparations made by Prime Minister Huggins and which will be mentioned in slightly more detail later in this chapter. By early September, units of the Rhodesian Air Force were already in place in Nairobi, Kenya, and the exercise of determining manpower suited for secondment and special duties was well under way.

But the year was not just notable for the beginning of the Second World War. The third of September was presaged by several events which showed the country edging towards a more responsible and effective role within the sub-Continent. Perhaps the most important was the opening, by Lady Beit in May of the bridge over the Zambezi at Chirundu and, close upon this, on the 14 June, the establishment of a BSA Police station in that lonely part of the Zambezi Valley. Lonely indeed for, as one trooper remarked at the time, "there's no store or pub within 150 miles". In spite of that, the two troopers at the new station could scarcely have been short of work: the senior man was designated Officer in Charge of Customs, Postal Agent, Immigration Officer, Meteorological Observer, Insurance Agent for Compulsory Third Party Risks and, when the elephant happened to break down the cable, Telephone Line Repairman.

Development was not only taking place on the northern boundary, but on the southern as well. The weir, which can be seen from the old rail and vehicle overpass at Beitbridge, was started during the few short months of the dry season with the aim of augmenting the water supply to that largely barren area. This was not, one would imagine, the easiest of undertakings that year. The rainy season of 1939 was both prolific and phenomenal, and the newly introduced motor cycles being used by the BSAP were cursed frequently as their riders squelched to an embarrassing stop in deep thick mud. The Midlands, too, saw its share in the general upswing of development. It is recorded that a large shoe manufacturing concern was erecting a factory at Gwelo. In the short term this was to be in a converted cotton ginnery, but within two to three years building had started on the present 373-acre site, and the BATA Shoe Company had stamped its footprint firmly into Rhodesian industry.

Amid all this there was smallpox in Lomagundi, man-eating lions in Miami and the ubiquitous croc-odiles helping themselves to unwary villagers as they attempted to cross flooding rivers. A splendid account of a six to seven weeks' foot patrol in the Bumi Reserve area of the Zambezi Valley appears in the April edition of the BSAP magazine, The Outpost. The writer, using the pseudonym 'Maquehlela', relates leaving Gokwe camp with "Native Police and a string of carriers" and journeying to the confluence of the Zambezi and Sengwa rivers. This was a generally mountainous area with scarcely any inhabitants, all having been chased out by elephants, lions and the tsetse fly. Maquehlela describes the astonishing variety of game seen on this patrol and observes that, although crocodiles will attack natives coming to the edge of the river for water, they make no forays on those travelling in dug-out canoes. Such canoes, made from hollowed sausage trees and about 12 to 15 feet long, were carved by the Barotse and could be purchased for as little as two pounds each. The writer discusses the pipe-smoking habits of the Batonka people, observing that men and women have their own types of pipe and that the bowls are fashioned from a blackish clay, and invariably consist of a shallow cup resting on the intricate and delicately carved back of some wild animal. The patrol moved quite close to the Kariba Gorge and on the return journey had to climb the Escarpment. All this where now lies the vast spread of Lake Kariba.

In setting the scene for this history it would be wrong to ignore the political and, to some extent, economic circumstances existing at that time, for they play no little part in the subsequent events that were to shape the countries of Central Africa.

It is as well to be aware of the size of Southern Rhodesia's populations in 1939, for they were very different from those of today, as we progress into the 21st century. The white population would have been a little short of 65,000 and the black approaching 1,390,000. Asians and Coloureds could not be numbered significantly. Most of the white inhabitants had their roots in Western Europe, and specifically Britain (though the South African influence was strongly present), while the concept of 'home' was at that time, inevitably, England. It is slightly amusing to read in those early editions of *The Outpost* of the movements of steamers from the port of Beira. You were invited to go 'home' either by way of the west or east coasts on a journey that would take five weeks or longer.

Godfrey Huggins was, as has been said, Prime Minister of the Colony at the time. He had come to Southern Rhodesia in 1911 to take up a temporary job as a surgeon. He stayed to become a politician and the longest serving prime minister in the British Commonwealth. Only a year before this history opens, this astute, pragmatic man, who ran the country with the same understated capability that he controlled an operating theatre had observed at a Medical Association dinner "I am one-eighth of a doctor and seven-eighths of a profession requiring no brains whatever".

Huggins had masterminded the progress of the Colony from the first years of the decade, but he had faced, as Robert Blake tells us in his *History of Rhodesia*, three demanding issues; recovery from the slump, the 'destiny' of the country; and the 'native problem'. Skilful handling of the economy during the late thirties largely overcame the first of these issues. The second, the destiny of the land, might still be said to confront the peoples of Zimbabwe though, in the context and limits of this history, would transform into the ill-fated Federation of Rhodesia and Nyasaland. As for the third, it took a conservative and incredibly right-wing electorate four decades, a bitter bush war and virtual world alienation before reason, or some semblance of it, prevailed and the fledgling State of Zimbabwe emerged.

Huggins had shown himself a master tactician in the political environment of Southern Rhodesia and, early in 1939, he played another trump card by swinging to his advantage the threat of international tension and specifically the annexation of Czechoslovakia by Hitler's rampant war machine. At this stage in his political career Huggins was facing a fairly powerful but divided opposition and advantage would be gained were he to go to the people, win an early election, head up a party that was fresh and strong, and annihilate his rivals.

It was clear to everyone that a war was inevitable in Europe and this was sufficient excuse for Huggins to suggest to the Governor that an early General Election would give the Government a clear mandate to cope with an emergency, disperse or despatch the few dissentient Parliamentarians and place his United Party in an unassailable position for the duration of the War.

Things worked out exactly as he had foreseen. Labour managed to collect a further two seats to make a total of seven; the Rhodesian Party and the Reform Party were both totally obliterated and Huggins' party rollercoasted to a resounding victory. Needless to say, members of the BSAP acted as Polling Officers.

But even as Europe moved inexorably into the months that would see the first air raids on Britain, the beginning of the maritime slaughter in the North Atlantic and the epic sea battle culminating in the scuttling of the German battleship *Admiral Graf Spee*, so Southern Rhodesia and its police force went about their normal activities, though with a deep thirst on the part of many (if not most) to be actively involved in the armed struggle now bound to develop to the north.

The careers and lives of several subsequent Commissioners of Police were growing and unfolding as the year progressed. Newly promoted Captain James Appleby took command of Hartley District; Arthur Selwyn Hickman, then in the Depot command, was similarly promoted (with the grade of Superintendent), and was to be seconded to the Staff of the Commandant, Southern Rhodesia Forces later in the year; Third Class Detective Sergeant Harold Jackson of the Salisbury Criminal Investigation Department (CID) was promoted to Assistant Superintendent; Basil Spurling, accompanied by his wife, set off at the beginning of March for a six months' holiday in Britain; Detective Sergeant Frank 'Pat' Barfoot became a staunch and valued member of the Baseball Team — and later captain of the Salisbury Rugby XV; James Spink, the junior member of the Salisbury Town Mess a year earlier, was advised to move from the First Rugby XV to the second, whilst Syd Bristow celebrated the last months of Peace — by having his appendix removed.

In London, where as nowadays existed a strong and thriving branch of the BSAP Regimental Association, the Annual Dinner was celebrated in late April at the First Avenue Hotel, with none other than Colonel Frank Johnson, DSO presiding. In a fascinating speech proposing the health of the Regiment, he described how the Police Force was formed over 45 years earlier, at the behest of the Cape Governor, to guard the lines of communication for the Pioneer Column. Other notables present on that evening included Colonel H. Marshall Hole, CMG., Captain F.C. Booth, VC., and Captain A.S. Hickman, the latter already demonstrating his remarkable ability to research and chronicle the early history of the BSAP and of the characters and principals who carved the beginnings of a truly unique and unparalleled Force.

The Commissioner of Police at this time was Colonel J.S. Morris, CBE. Morris had been appointed to that rank in 1933 having joined the Police in 1909. He was paid, so Peter Gibbs informs us in *The Right of the Line*, the sum of £1000 a year and on that salary he remained, for six years, though his appointment as Commander of all the Rhodesian forces did carry an acting allowance of £125 a year. The latter elevation took place in 1936 and, frankly, was an economy measure on the part of the Government. In 1940, military and police commands were separated; Morris 'reverted' to control of the Police and, with the unique rank of Inspector General, remained in that position until his retirement in 1945 at the end of the War.

Colonel Morris — he eventually and reluctantly accepted the rank of Brigadier — was the man who moved the BSAP from a strongly military, yet multifarious role, into that of a committed and professional police force. As we shall see, many of the technical disciplines so necessary to the efficient performance of police duties had their foundations laid during his tenure of office.

In his 1939 Annual Report, Morris commented on various aspects of civil security made necessary by the outbreak of war: guards at vital points, control of Nazi activities, Internment, Registration and Parole of Enemy Subjects (many of whom were refugees), protection of enemy subjects' property and the need for general intelligence work. In all these additional duties, (for in those days the police were often to be found in control of Immigration and Customs, mounting cordons to control anything from smallpox to cattle diseases, running fire brigades as well as telephone exchanges, and acting as examiners for drivers licences), the Force now received assistance from the recently formed, and very keen, Police Reserve.

It had been at the annual meeting of the Regimental Association held in the Town Station, Baker Avenue, Salisbury in February 1939 that a Mr. W.J. Stone mentioned that Association membership might be augmented were a Police Reserve to be formed in conjunction with the current National Registration exercise. The President (Colonel Morris) replied that the Police Reserve aspect was already under consideration, but agreed that the two issues could well be linked.

The Police Reserve was formed at the beginning of August 1939 with a strength of 376 men and with Major H. Rochester in command as a chief superintendent. The First Reserve, as it was called, consisted mainly of men who had previous military or police experience but by reason of age, health or job, were unable to take a more active part in the war, yet were prepared for continuous duty in this new role. They were there, if necessary to replace, but certainly to assist the regular force, many of whom would eventually be released for service with the military forces. So it was that the Reserve were called upon to perform traffic control work, (stop signs were about to be introduced on

Bulawayo's streets), town and suburban patrols, and generally to afford some security to the public in the prevention and detection of crime.

But now, as the weeks since the Declaration of War became months and as men from all walks of life made clear their wish to be actively involved in that War, so it became necessary for the Minister of Defence, Robert Tredgold, to issue assuaging, congratulatory and encouraging words to the Police, Police Reserve, Territorials and Permanent Staff Corps and remind those who might, or already had been 'left behind', that theirs was, in many ways, the more onerous part of the War effort. It was left to Police Headquarters, after notifying a number of secondments to the Southern Rhodesia Forces, to issue a bland notice to European police that from now on there would be neither discharges nor leave. However suitable provisos covering ill health and urgent private affairs were included.

The stage was set, and Southern Rhodesia was ready to assist Great Britain and the Empire in any way that it could.

*" Give Me That Rifle."*

**Chapter Thirty**

**POLICE AT WAR AND PEACE**

*1940 and the War in Europe — Secondments — we meet Greig, Pitt, Salt, and
many others — the Reserve develops — Police Band formed under Sparks — Golden Jubilee
celebrations — policing Plumtree — Gokwe and Nuanetsi : Stop Streets.*

THE YEAR 1940 was intended to see the celebrations commemorating the Golden Anniversary of
the arrival of the Pioneer Column. Committees had been formed, planning was well advanced. It was
to be a great and triumphal occasion.

Overseas however and indeed on the African Continent, events were conspiring to undermine and
eventually all but destroy those plans. For the war was to come ominously closer to Rhodesia and its
people.

The apparently invincible German war machine rolled inexorably over Denmark, Norway, Holland,
Belgium and much of France. Churchill formed a National Coalition Government in Britain. The
British Expeditionary Force of more than 335,000 troops crawled away from the beaches of northern
France and the port of Dunkirk, and crossed the Channel under continuous and savage attack in one
of the most remarkable rearguard actions of modern times. Paris fell, Italy entered the War. The Battle
of Britain was waged in the skies above southern England, the English Channel and northern France.
And, as the German Luftwaffe droned over that same Channel to pulverise city after city in Britain,
so the first stirrings of conflict came to Africa.

Italy entered the war in June and, at that time, had garrisons in Abyssinia, Eritrea and (Italian)
Somaliland, as well as massed units in what is now Libya, but then comprised Cyrenaica and
Tripolitania. In the weeks that followed, there came a palpable threat towards Khartoum, yet another
towards Kenya, and yet a third, from the rolling dunes of the Western Desert towards Egypt and the
succulence of the Nile Delta — this the worst threat of all.

It is not a part of this story to chronicle the work and experiences of individual members of the Force
in the campaigns in North Africa or elsewhere; merely let it be said that as the Italians or Germans
were beaten on the various war fronts, so it became necessary to fill the vacuum created by their defeat
(and departure). It was into this breach that many members of the BSA Police were drafted, to
establish the rule of law and restore normality in countries that had, generally speaking, hitherto been
a part of the Italian Empire

Secondments from the Force had, in fact, begun in late 1939 to various branches of the military in
Rhodesia. In July of 1940, several members returned to Depot for an instruction course prior to
transfer to the Rhodesian African Rifles.

Among them were many who would reach high standing in later years: Pitt, Salt and Spink from
Salisbury Town; Drewett, Kettle, Giles, Warton and Hampshire from District stations; Lowings, Van
Niekerk and Woodgate from Depot. It would seem that for many of these men the 'call' came with
little notice. Reg Lowings, for example, had only three days to hand over the editorship of *The Outpost*
to Medical Sergeant Bill Greig. This undertaking, it is recorded, just could not be fitted into Greig's
more caring duties, which included First Aid lectures to the Police Reserve. Three months later, the
task of producing *The Outpost* and its sister magazine *Mapolisa* became the responsibility of various
staff officers at Police Headquarters.

Quite a few members resorted to desertion as the only way to become actively involved in the war.
One of these, Lofty Lloyd, made inebriated efforts to join the Army, the Air Force and the Navy, only
to be recognised as a serving policeman at the recruiting offices of the first two and told to find his
own way to Simonstown by the last.

Nothing daunted, Lofty hopped on a troop train bound for Broken Hill in Northern Rhodesia and
ultimately Cairo. But he was arrested in Northern Rhodesia, sent back to Salisbury and there
sentenced to six weeks with hard labour to be served in Depot. The Police Depot then, as now, is an
extremely well-kept and presented area and it may well be that many of the fine trees gracing its
grounds were planted by Lofty in holes measuring six feet in depth and four feet square at the top and
bottom, meticulously layered with earth and manure — and supervised by RSM Tiny Tantum. Many

years later, Lloyd committed his often way-out adventures in the Police to print in a book called *Rhodesian Patrol*.

Gradually, as the year progressed the numbers of the Regular Force slowly diminished as men were seconded (or successfully deserted) for mainly military but sometimes training duties outside and within the Colony. The need to maintain law and order could not, of course, be allowed to lapse and it was now that the Police Reserve, originally formed in mid-1939, came into its own.

The whole idea of the Reserve was to maintain a policing presence as the onset and progress of the war resulted in more and more additional duties falling upon less and less Regular members. Training was geared to this end and so it was that men who were a little 'over the hill' for full-time military duties, or occupying 'key' positions, or just not medically quite 'up to scratch', found themselves being lectured on law and police duties, on First Aid, and undergoing foot drill and musketry training. Soon these men were manning charge offices, attending to traffic problems and patrolling the larger towns and suburbs. They became an essential and valuable adjunct to the 'Arm of the Law'.

The year also witnessed the creation of another wonderful adjunct to the Force, one that would bring forth increasing praise and in very quick time establish its popularity with all races. The formation of the Police Band is first mentioned in the rather bald notice of a promotion:

> *No. 3883 Trooper Sparks, Depot, to rank of S/Corporal whilst employed on*
> *Band Duties and is granted the rank of L/Sergeant whilst so employed.*

Malcolm 'Max' Sparks joined the Police from South Africa in November, 1939. He was trained in that country and, apart from being an accomplished pianist, was able to play every one of the instruments used in the Band at that time: cornets, horns, euphoniums, trombones, saxophones and, that absolute essential for any military band, the drums. He was also required to have steady nerves, self-control and the ability to teach. The nucleus of the 20 plus instrumentalists was the bugle, drum and fife band that had been in existence for many years. Practices were held under a large spreading msasa tree in the Native Police Training School, now known as Tomlinson Depot.

The Band had several 'warming-up' engagements at the Officers' Mess but its full debut was to be at the Military Parade held at the Drill Hall in Salisbury to celebrate the country's Golden Jubilee. Resplendent in khaki, with black fezzes adorned with gold tassels and stockings edged with deep blue, the presentation of the Band and its highly accomplished performance excited considerable interest and was greeted with rapturous acclaim.

On the morning following the Military Parade, 13 September, many of the surviving members of the BSA Company's Police joined with serving members of the Force at a Reception held by Colonel Morris in the grounds of the Officers' Mess. It must have been an overwhelming experience for the likes of Colonel Divine, Captain Hore, E. Weale, (Chairman of the 1890 BSAP Society), Jock Carruthers-Smith, and the handful of white-haired old gentleman who assembled that morning to see how the traditions laid down by them had grown and flourished over 50 years.

And that, apart from the opening of the Defence Headquarters building in Montague Avenue, was all that could be done to celebrate the Golden Jubilee. There remained a country to police and a war to be fought. The policing aspect, certainly in the more remote areas, brings a wry smile as we review some of the station contributions to *The Outpost* in 1940.

Those who have a first hand knowledge of southern and western Matabeleland, and who have been stationed in the various police camps which are dotted about the area, or perhaps departed from the present majestic highways to follow the corrugated, dusty and gravelled secondary roads, may appreciate this slightly abbreviated account of policemen and policing in the early days of the War:

"The district (Bulalima Mangwe) may not be ideal for agriculture, the rainfall is low, the soil not too rich. The scenery cannot compare with that to be found in the Eastern Districts, there are no great rivers, no famous waterfalls, no mysterious ruins and one is frequently told that the Kalahari Desert is encroaching ... But there is much good cattle country. Four police camps provide the necessary 'protection', Plumtree being the largest, personnel; S/M Genet, Tprs Lloyd (2811), Mason and Moore. Figtree; Cpl. Harries. Mangwe; Tpr. Johnson (2252), and Mphoengs; Tpr. Crossman, with not even a telephone to disturb him. Each station has a motor cycle, and at Plumtree there is also a motor truck and two horses. Tpr. Mason has spent much of the last five months being transferred from and to

Plumtree, in between time he guards bridges, starts on patrol, is recalled, goes down with fever and finds time for a spot of sick leave, and yet he does not think this is really a good war. The natives of this district have handed to the Native Commissioner, through their chiefs, the sum of £400 and a considerable amount of grain to be used as the authorities think fit, in the prosecution of the war. A very fine effort and more so when one considers that it was entirely their own idea."

The police stations at Gokwe and Nuanetsi were — crimewise — in as somnolent a state as their Matabele counterparts. In May, Gokwe reported that five natives had been taken by lions and two killed by rhino, but this was as nothing to the serious shock caused by the first visit in six months of a European from the Sebungwe, to the Charge Office. As for Nuanetsi, at this period a three-man station, a crime had been reported: 'we have our first grass fire of the season'.

One wonders whether the scribe from Nuanetsi would have been happier in an urban environment with the odd car, rather than the more than odd lion, after proclaiming his poetic talents with:

> *O Solitude where are the charms,*
> *That sages have seen in thy face,*
> *Better dwell in the midst of alarms,*
> *Than live in this horrible place.*

Or did he, as did so many, rather protest against his being left as a mere policeman, instead of being able to take his place elsewhere, in formal and active defence of the Empire?

Whilst skimming through the Station Notes of that period, a few other oddments catch the eye. The construction of a 12,000 gallon concrete swimming pool, complete with springboard, in the Nyamandhlovu camp for the princely, and locally subscribed sum of £11.12s, was a remarkable and worthy effort. In similar vein, and while considering matters recreational, it is recorded that there are three rest huts available on Rhodes Estate, Inyanga, (without bathroom or bath) at five shillings a day. The caddies for the Police Golf Course went on strike for more money: apparently threepence for nine holes and sixpence for 18 was just half of what the rising generation deemed an equitable remuneration.

A doubtful measure of reality is restored when reading that there are views for and against the introduction of Stop Streets in the country. The argument that there is insufficient traffic to warrant these is logically demolished by the counter that more and more cars are bound to be seen on the roads each year, plus that 'cars coming into main streets are definitely handicapped for vision owing to the position of prominent buildings on all corners.'

*"Surprise"*

## Chapter Thirty-One

## SLOW MOVES TOWARDS PROFESSIONALISM

*1941 — Police Reserve and SRWAPS — major secondments — fetes to aid Britain —
RAF training — Cricket and Rugby — manning Fire Engines — Mobile Patrol Van —
Notes on Gokwe, Goromonzi and Tuli — Weller and Wordworth — Sherren, Spurling
and Bristow — CID enlarged — new Police Regulations.*

THE YEAR 1941 was one in which the stalwarts of the Police Reserve came completely into their own, proving the usefulness of the organisation beyond any doubt and demonstrating that part-time policemen could cope most adequately with the straight-forward daily duties of their full-time brethren. The year also saw the introduction of the Southern Rhodesia Women's Auxiliary Police Service (SRWAPS), whose distinctive and smartly tailored grey jackets with navy blue cuffs and epaulettes, skirts, grey shirts and blue ties brought, dare one say, a touch of glamour into many court rooms, as well as to many urban and district charge offices. Doubtless, too, many a grey and hoary head was shaken in sheer disbelief that standards — even in a wartime scenario — should be allowed to deteriorate so far as to permit women into the Force.

All this was against the background of a damaging and escalating conflict. The rout of the Italian troops in various areas of North Africa was followed by the arrival of the astute, respected and seasoned Field Marshall Rommel, together with well-equipped divisions of German troops, to plan and launch a successful counter-offensive in Libya. Next and in quick time came the German invasions of Yugoslavia, Greece and Crete and then the ill-fated attempt to conquer Russia. Last was the awful spectre of successive defeats in the Far East as Japan entered the War swept into Hong Kong and Malaya and blasted the pride of the Royal Navy into the depths of the South China Sea.

In beleaguered Britain, clothes rationing had started; speculators were buying up dwindling stocks of champagne; the Café de Paris and the House of Commons in London were bombed and, as the United States of America entered the War, so steps were taken to expel the Emperor of Japan from the Order of the Garter.

The spread of hostilities throughout the world and the greater utilisation of the Police Reserve and SRWAPS in the policing of Southern Rhodesia were, of course, the prelude to the first large secondments of regular members for service beyond the country's borders.

The notice calling for applications was necessarily rather vague. 'A limited number of members of the Force will be permitted to serve with the Southern Rhodesia Military Forces' were the words, and 17 April was the closing date for those wishing to be considered. By May, the first list had been published and, a month later, an initial selection of 35 had been increased to 60. Captain James Appleby, then holding the rank of superintendent, was to command the contingent, with Assistant Superintendent Albert Frost as his deputy. Among the other members were Second Sergeants Bernard Bulstrode, Herbert 'Barney' Lomas, Troopers Alan Godwin and Arthur Lennard, Constable John Grundy and a man who was to distinguish himself in another sphere of work in later years, Sergeant Kenneth Flower. The first contingent, having been photographed and provided with a mouth-watering farewell dinner by mess caterer Lofty Lloyd in Depot, eventually embarked from Durban for Aden on the 24 June.

At Aden two singular events took place. The column was split into two. The bulk remained under Appleby and went to Eritrea; the remainder, under Frost, went to Addis Ababa. The second event, reported but unsubstantiated, was that James Appleby was the only member to wear pyjamas during the oppressive heat of Aden's nights.

It was not much longer before a second Contingent was selected to travel to the same area. Led by Assistant Superintendent Calogreedy, the 15 strong group included Regimental Sergeant Major Tantum, Second Detective Sergeant 'Dick' Parry (then a Temporary Assistant Superintendent in the Police Reserve), and Troopers 'Butch' Buckley and Leo Cottham, the latter carrying the squash-box with which he would spend many hours entertaining his colleagues. This group left Depot during September.

The team spirit is often fostered and encouraged by adversity, and so it was that those who had been 'left behind' decided to mount a mammoth fete, to be known as 'Happy Hampstead', with the intention of swelling the coffers of the Aid for Britain Fund. The basic idea was to provide entertainment for both young and old, give good value at the multitude of stalls to be set up, and provide refreshments in a setting that would encourage people to spend their money for a good cause. The Pioneers' Shop — in those days standing in the area now occupied by the Police Club swimming pool — became a bar; there was a concert platform, hot dog stall, horse rides, a Donkey Derby, nine hole putting course, hoop-la, coconut shies, bucket quoits, a shooting gallery and a motley collection of stalls selling everything from bicycles to toffee apples — by way of pigs, radios, fruit and toys.

The day was a fantastic success and resulted in a cheque for over £2000 being contributed to the Aid for Britain Fund.

By 1941, the Royal Air Force was well and truly ensconced in Southern Rhodesia. New training airfields were established near some of the main towns between Salisbury and Bulawayo and, to add a touch of spice to rural life, a couple of Harvards had to make forced landings in the Enkeldoorn area. The presence of this large body of men proved a tremendous attraction to the young ladies of the Colony, and a fillip and additional source of competition for sporting teams. In the years to come, the airmen would be a fruitful area for the police recruiting drives that would be embarked upon at the end of the War.

But however good may have been the sporting prowess of the young Air Force men, they were generally no match for the Police on the cricket and rugby fields.

In the 1940 to 1941 cricket season, the Police team was supreme. Terence McCormick, who was to retire as a Detective Chief Inspector in 1955, took over 100 wickets that year and was as successful with the bat as with the ball. For the rugby team, the Force had to choose from only about 18 players throughout the season but this redoubtable combination, which recorded victory after victory, included many who would make their mark in the Force, and elsewhere, in later years. Notable among them, and in no particular order, were Jack Wood, Norman Nimmo, Cliff Podmore, Cab Calloway, Ginger Lardant, Andy Braes, Michael Gelfand, Laurie Davenport, Slash Barfoot and Ted Oppenheim. Of one newcomer to the game, Charles Scott, the coach recorded: "Must learn how to tackle without killing himself or the man he is going for".

It is time now to turn to Police matters in the Colony. This story concerns one of the many extraneous duties that the Police faced — operating a fire brigade.

Gwelo Municipality, which in those days included various airfields in the neighbourhood and resembled a garrison town, had recently acquired from Bulawayo that city's old fire engine. History does not record the age or make of this venerable machine, but it had a top speed of 15 miles per hour which was 'reduced slightly' when the hooter was used. It is mentioned that in such circumstances it was almost worthwhile to send off a native constable on his bicycle to keep the fire going until the 'Brigade' arrived. The commander of this 'fire force, and therefore the driver, was Sergeant Barney Lomas. One conflagration resulted in the following yarn: "… the fire engine now starts up every morning with one pull. Unfortunately, the fires regularly occur at night — when it won't even start with a push. At a recent fire, the alarm was received at 6.50 p.m. and the crew were assembled (ex Canteen) by 6.55. Engine left the yard at 6.57 and stopped at 6.59. At 7.00, the crew abandoned the craft and proceeded on foot to the fire, subsequently dealing with it in a satisfactory manner. Having got it under control, they were enjoying an 'easy' when a rumbling in the distance announced the approach of the engine and a few minutes later it flashed past the fire, heading for Somabula, with Sergeant Lomas at the wheel wearing a 'true unto death' expression. Realising the public out Somabula way might become alarmed if the engine arrived there seeking a fire, one of the firemen pursued it on foot. He soon overtook the vehicle and brought it back to the scene of the conflagration where, having reached its goal, it again developed signs of inertia and passed out with a final 'phut'. Pushed by its crew, a veil is drawn over the ignominious return of the engine to the yard."

Another vehicle that made its presence felt during the year was a Ford V8 three-ton chassis converted into a mobile radio patrol van and possibly the first of its kind in Southern Africa. The wireless transmitter was powered by the vehicle engine and, with its receiver, was sufficiently strong to cover the whole country. Possessed of a public address system to amplify speech or music over a wide area, the vehicle roamed impressively to quite remote parts of Rhodesia. The interior was divided into three areas: the driving cab, a native compartment that could double as a cell, and a European section. Fittings included a paraffin-operated refrigerator, electric lights, a fan, two bunks, folding table and chairs, scenes of crime outfit, first aid locker and, of course, crockery and cutlery. Space had been provided to store two bicycles and a 20-gallon water tank was fitted on the underside of the chassis. The roof, reached by a fixed metal ladder and protected by a rail, housed spare petrol and a bucksail.

Inspector Rennard Pinder was in charge of this remarkable ensemble and would usually pick up a trooper and a native constable from a police station to assist with local knowledge when on patrol. The van served to increase cooperation between Police and the community and as a means of addressing gatherings at mines and farm compounds on matters such as the prevention of grass fires, road sense and any new laws.

Life in the various District stations carried on much as usual. Gokwe, cut off by the heavy rains, was not visited by a car for over two months. Trooper Godfrey Lewenz, sadly to be killed following a motor cycle accident in March, indulged his liking for history by describing the two Goromonzi police camps which existed before the present camp was built in 1907 and commented on the rigours that must have faced the early Pioneers and Police, some of whom lie buried in two small cemeteries near those old camps; Tuli, which used to have as many as 15 men stationed there, was closed down in October and prompted a lengthy poem from that great custodian of regimental tradition, Captain Hickman. The final verse reads:

> *Well, here's a health to Tuli*
> *In good malala wine,*
> *And those who knew her truly*
> *Have grief at her decline.*
> *The Pioneers who rest there*
> *Sleep on beneath the Fort;*
> *The bush is at its best where*
> *It is not sold or bought.*

Various names catch the eye as one reads through the annals of that year. 'Sam' Weller was transferred from Sinoia to Sipolilo. Jackie Wordsworth appeared with incredible regularity as he moved from one district station to another, eventually to seek the comparative refuge of matrimony. Lieutenant Spurling took command of Sinoia District, and 'Jack' Ross of Bulawayo District. Trooper Sherren, stationed at Bikita, spent some days in Fort Victoria hospital with malaria (the following year he was to be fined five shillings for improperly performing a duty, and 10 shillings for appropriating Force property). Sub-Inspector Hughes-Halls bade farewell to all his teeth, while Constable Bristow, of whom it was suggested a bed was permanently reserved in Ward 1 of Salisbury Hospital, enjoyed the removal of his tonsils before seeking short-lived fame on the snooker tables.

During the year, Colonel Morris, the Inspector General (he had been so titled in July 1940), resolved to increase the strength of the Criminal Investigation Department. Various reasons lay behind this, one of which was to more adequately control 'enemy subjects' many of whom were confined to Internment Camps, but there was also a need to give closer supervision to border posts. There were probably more official routes in and out of the Colony than exist today and it was during 1941 that the entry points at Machipanda and Nyaronga were renamed Forbes and Pennefather respectively.

However 1941 saw a number of changes that, though apparently almost cosmetic, were symptomatic of the way in which the BSAP was to evolve. New Police Regulations had been printed and published at the beginning of the year and these saw the first steps in the transformation of the Force from a military to a civilian organisation. It was now clear that with the country advancing both industrially and commercially, there was no way that police could effectively fulfil both their military and civil roles.

Hence came the abolition of the grant of future military titles to commissioned officers, a step regarded by some as controversial, by others as downright backward. Allied to this was the introduction of identical non-commissioned ranks in all branches, the abolition of the rank of corporal and the reintroduction of the grade of sub-inspector. These changes were the precursors to the far more radical recommendations that would be embodied in the Mundy Commission Report some five years later.

The year ended with the retirement of the Governor of the Colony, Sir Herbert Stanley GCMG, who had reached the end of his seven years tenure of office. Various farewell parades were held in the man cities at which His Excellency spoke in glowing terms of the Force which he had first come to know when he was a Resident Commissioner in 1915. In particular reference to the Native Police, he commented on their keenness, smartness and efficiency, and noted that of the 12 medal recipients on one parade, 10 were Native Police — a sure indication that the Force was now looked upon as an attractive career.

## Chapter Thirty-Two

## OF SHOES AND SHIPS AND SEALING WAX

*Selukwe murder — use of aircraft — shortages — reported crime figures —*
*Harare sub-station opens — Blowers — canteen for City of Glasgow Police —*
*Morris visits Middle East — Doris Dickinson — Police Conference*

THE YEARS 1941 and 1942 saw the tide of battle starting to flow in favour of the Allies, as the British Commonwealth, the United States of America and their many supporters had become known. In Europe, the Royal Air Force moved into an offensive role against targets in occupied Western Europe. Many hundreds of miles to the east, the German forces found that it was 'thus far and no further' at Stalingrad as, once again, a pitiless Russian winter played its part in rolling back the German divisions. The victory of United States forces at Midway turned the tide in the Pacific war and, in North Africa, a massive Allied offensive gained momentum from El Alamein, on to Tunisia, Sicily and then thrust up into the heart of Italy.

Taking part in that historic North African campaign was 237 (Rhodesia) Squadron and, among its airmen, one who was to play no small part in the history of the land of his birth, Ian Douglas Smith.

In Southern Rhodesia, the new year (1942) opened with a brutal murder only a few miles from Selukwe, the small mining town in which Smith had been born 23 years earlier. An elderly couple, Mr and Mrs Robertson, were found dead on their beds, obviously most viciously assaulted and with signs of a desperate struggle having taken place. Members of the Criminal Investigation Department rushed to the scene and soon found about 50 yards from the homestead one of the murder weapons, a piece of steel shafting. It was also clear that more than one person was involved in the crime and that a considerable quantity of clothing, as well as valuable gold amalgam, had been removed.

For the first time the Mobile Radio Patrol Van was sent to a crime scene, and broadcast a detailed description of the missing clothing and other articles to stations throughout the Colony. Every station was on the alert and within 72 hours a suspect had been arrested 25 miles away from the crime scene. The search for the remaining two culprits was aided by means of aircraft reconnaissance — a fine example, nearly 60 years ago, of the use of modern aids in the pursuit of criminals. However, the significance of this advancement in detection was probably lost on the policeman who dashed from the shelter of his truck, in pouring rain, to pick up a message dropped by one of the planes, only to read, "nice weather for ducks".

Another trooper on this murder case related that the absence of supplies and a desperate hunger forced him into a deal with local tribesmen, leading to the purchase of a dozen eggs. The first 11 broken served only to prove how fertile the eggs were for beaks were already forming on the chicks. In total desperation, he closed his eyes whilst breaking the twelfth, dropped it into the pan and only after a decent interval of frenzied scrambling, opened his eyes.

All's well that ends well. The second accused was soon located and the third and last arrested in the Northern Transvaal in March. The police team, as well as the Prosecutor (Advocate AD Evans), were warmly congratulated on their investigation and presentation when the case came before the High Court Sessions in Gwelo a month later.

However, 1942 was the year in which those Rhodesians living in the Colony realised that there really was a war on. No longer could a regular supply of imports be relied upon to arrive by sea from Europe. Petrol was restricted, vehicle tyres became scarce, paper was in short supply and the Police Annual Report was cyclostyled instead of being printed. Butter and golf balls were all but unobtainable. Suddenly there was a return to mounted patrolling and steps were taken to purchase good quality remounts from our ever-helpful colleagues in the South African Police.

It is recorded that there was a slight decrease in reported crimes in 1942 and, though it is no part of this history to present the reader with tables of statistics, nevertheless a brief look at the figures since 1938 is of some interest, especially when an outstanding 'undetected' figure of just over eight per cent is considered, and the increase in 1941 can be attributed almost solely to Roads and Road Traffic cases: 1938 *72,158* : 1939 *79,149* : 1940 *82,555* : 1941 *87,327* : 1942 *84,331*

It is a fairly safe assumption that the 1942 decrease was due to having appreciably fewer cars on the road. The lack of petrol and the absence of tyres become great levellers.

In July, a police sub-station, the first to cater for an entirely African area, was opened at the junction of the 'Ardbennie and Beatrice roads' and this was named Harare. In later years, and as the cult of nationalism gripped or was forced upon the black population, it was to become a frantically busy and important station with the Ardbennie strip road eventually incorporated within the camp's boundaries. The first member in charge was Second Sergeant Hank Blowers, who eventually became a Deputy Commissioner and, following his retirement, an imposing figure in the House of Assembly where he was Sergeant-at-Arms.

Southern Rhodesia's links with Britain were, as this story has shown already, compellingly deep and strong and therefore it is no surprise to find that the Police Force, obviously delighted with the success of Happy Hampstead the preceding year, now decided to purchase a mobile canteen vehicle — or if the funds ran to it — vehicles, for one of the police forces in the British Isles. A series of fund raising events, including band concerts and cake sales took place throughout the country and a sum of £350 (how little that seems now) was sent over to the City of Glasgow Police Force whose Chief Constable, Sir Percy Sillitoe, CBE. DL, himself a one-time member of the BSAP received the handsome, neat and utilitarian vehicle in St George's Square on a damp and miserable July day.

Less than a year later, a second and similar vehicle was presented to the Essex County Police.

Throughout the year, in fact until the last policemen were released from the command of the British forces and returned home, a steady stream of articles and letters graced the pages of *The Outpost*. These told of the life and lives, but very little of the work, of the men who were seconded for duty to the Middle East. This unique part of Police history, which saw members of the BSAP in as far flung locations as the Gold Coast, Burma, Persia, Iraq and Madagascar, does not, as has been said before, constitute a part of this history. Nevertheless it is a period and a subject that could be read up, edited and published in the future. It is greatly to the credit of the Inspector-General, Colonel Morris, that in 1942, some time before a third contingent was sent 'Up North', he journeyed to the Middle East to make a point of visiting members of the Force at their many and various locations.

Two other events which took place in 1942 are worthy of note:

The first was the accelerated promotion of Doris Dickinson through the ranks, following her attestation as a First Sergeant in late December of the previous year. Ms. Dickinson became a sub-inspector only two months later and, by January of 1944, had achieved the rank of superintendent and command of the Women Police. It can safely be assumed that she was the subject of this little piece of doggerel:

*Now that WAP's commissioned are*
*One thing I'd like to know, Sir,*
*That's how to address these ladies fair*
*If your rank is one below, Sir?*
*If I am called by a Commissioned miss*
*At some duty to assist her,*
*Do I answer in reply to this,*
*"Yes, ma'am" or "O.K. Sister"?*

The second event was the holding of the European Police Conference during December. As the years progressed, this gathering of representative members from all parts of the Colony was to become an invaluable tool for police management to 'test the water', glean what problems confronted the members and give to what was essentially an autocracy, a taste of democracy. However, back in the early 40s, replies to any contentious subjects were invariably greeted with either 'it will be considered after the end of the War' or sometimes with an affirmative (if the cost was negligible and the request totally logical) but more often with a firm 'No'.

The principles of worker/management relations were very alien to this disciplined society but, despite this the Conference, whose delegates included Funnell, Greengrass, Newton, Batty, and Blowers, pressed for changes to the Dress Regulations so that the present military appearance and apparel of the police might be replaced with a uniform more suited (if the pun may be excused) to a civilian force.

Chapter Thirty-Three

OF CABBAGES — AND KINGS

*1943 to 1945 — Retirement of Hughes-Halls — Weller, Bristow, Sherren, Flower and*
*two Jacksons — Foot and Mouth Cordons — Nuanetsi, Gutu — Recognition of the role*
*of Native Police — Morris faces problems — Traffic Section in Bulawayo.*

THE REMAINING THREE years of the War, which by this time encompassed the Far East, witnessed the final overthrow of the German armies in North Africa, the progress of Allied Forces into Sicily and north through Italy, the slow but inexorable turnaround along the bleak length of the Russian Front and, of course, the landings in Normandy and Southern France. Slowly and bloodily, the Allied Forces thrust through the French countryside, into Belgium and Holland, and across the great span of the Rhine into Germany, finally linking with Russian forces on the Baltic to seal the fate of Hitler's armies on Luneburg Heath early in May of 1945. A few months later the fateful decision to use atomic bombs was taken, two Japanese cities were all but wiped out and the War in the Far East was speedily concluded.

In Britain, the electorate opted for a Labour government at the July General Election and cast out the Prime Minister who had led them with brilliance and inspiration for over five years.

That is a rather simplistic overview of the concluding years of a War which created new values, witnessed the most remarkable and far-reaching technical advances and resulted in changes in lives and life-styles. Nothing could nor ever would be the same again.

But our story must come back to Southern Rhodesia where, in 1943, peace was still a long way off and the belt-tightening had reached the lowest of lows with the rationing of beer and whisky. As far as Umvuma residents were concerned strangulation point had arrived. Things could not get worse than the burning down of the Falcon Hotel.

The depleted complement of the Police and Police Reserve continued to patrol and protect the colony with determination and success and looked forward to longer and proper holidays. In many cases the goal was a well-earned and overdue retirement.

Of course there were those whose advanced years meant they had to go on pension anyway, and among these was number 939, Walter Hughes-Halls. 'H-H' as he was known, had joined the Police just after Christmas 1907 and retired with the rank of sub-inspector in September of 1943. His career, which included a spell with the Natal Carbineers during the Zulu Rebellion of 1906, was distinguished by a single-minded dedication and devotion to 'The 'Regiment' in which he was so proud to serve. These attributes he extended to his fellows members also, both serving and retired, whom he was determined would be remembered — if not revered — through their linkage within the Regimental Association.

Others continued to play their part in the Force and its activities. Sergeant Weller, whose tenure as member-in-charge of various stations would, in later years be compared, only slightly humorously with concentration camps, transferred from Sinoia to Beitbridge. Syd Bristow distinguished himself as a wicket-keeper: Peter Sherren took a small step up his personal ladder, transferring from the bushy backwoods of Bikita to the greater challenge that Que Que offered at that time. Ken Flower, writing from the Middle East, decried and vehemently argued against a controversial article in an earlier issue of *The Outpost* that had advocated a case for corporal punishment as a means of disciplining the natives. Harold Jackson was promoted to superintendent and another Jackson, a man of great talent, perception and humour, started drawing cartoons for *The Outpost*.

Victoria District provided some interesting and amusing snippets during the year.

It was mentioned earlier that police duties included the manning of Foot and Mouth Cordons and 1943 saw yet another outbreak in the District.

The logistics for controlling and administering this cordon fell to Superintendent Spurling and First Sergeant George Emes. When one learns that the cordon was 1000 miles long, guarded by some 800 Special Native Constables and assisted by members of the Reserve and Military Forces, then it must be realised that the rationing, issuing of kit and clothing, and the hundred and one other tasks required, made the administration of this, or any other similar cordon, a very formidable exercise. However the fishing at Chipinda Pools was described as excellent.

In a burst of perhaps rare, certainly remarkable honesty, the member in charge at Nuanetsi reported "good grass with the late rains and the river flowing strongly; the station has an NCO and a trooper which might seem short staffed but, considering the work, is plenty".

At nearby Gutu, there occurred a case that speaks volumes for the pressures upon district policeman; on the 7 April (1943, it will be noted), a native reported to the Charge Office with the following complaint: "In 1926 I was working with my brother and I lent him the sum of two pounds. In 1932 I asked him to return this money but, for one reason or another, he refused. I therefore decided that today I would come and make a complaint to the Police".

It is evident that a much greater recognition of the role and value of the native police was beginning to permeate the upper echelons of the Force. Apart from small but significant changes to wearing apparel, there had been created a Native Police Benevolent Fund to, as the stilted words of that time stated, 'assist by loan or grant, members who, through no fault of their own, were undergoing difficulties and hardship'. Further steps saw the first Native Police Conference being held, promotion courses inaugurated for the lower ranks and, with evident concern for the inner man if not for his meagre wages, hot food provided at their own expense for those on night duty in towns.

However an attempt to popularise the soya bean was greeted with a mixture of scepticism and true African conservatism. The attempt failed miserably.

But, despite that, change was in the air.

By 1944, the Police had the least number of Europeans for many years, only 445; and more native policemen than ever before. But that number of Europeans, inadequate and overworked as many of them were, created a further problem. More than three-quarters were married and many of these in desperate need of married accommodation. It became necessary to curtail patrolling in the District areas and, as a result, crime figures started to rise. Couple this with the ban on recruitment as well as retirement, unless in the latter case age or medical grounds were prevailing factors, and it is clear that Brigadier Morris was facing some critical and highly sensitive problems.

The Inspector General was, however, nothing if not optimistic. Those being promoted would, he indicated, serve as the nucleus for the NCO material needed to train post-war recruits. Steps were being taken to revise police examination syllabi and manuals, in anticipation of an influx of young men and finally, it was likely that the Women Police would be retained as an active police unit. Pragmatically a Traffic Section was started in Bulawayo comprising a police reserve NCO and six constables; cycle allowances were introduced for all Town Native Police and the upkeep of various records, many of which had been in existence for years, was rationalised or dispensed with.

## Chapter Thirty-Four

## MORRIS GIVES WAY TO ROSS

*End of the War — Police Column to Kazungula — Morris retires — Ross becomes
Commissioner — Post-War problems — Force establishment*

THE END OF THE War presented an ideal opportunity for those who had been left behind to beat
their various drums and let it be known how well they had coped — as indeed they had — over the
last five or six years.

The Criminal Investigation Branch pointed to the speed with which they had interned or
registered enemy aliens within hours after the Declaration of War. They then pontificated on the
plethora of legislation with which they had to deal; instancing various Emergency Powers
Regulations covering 'Profiteering', 'Export of Currency', 'Evasion of Censorship', 'Exclusion of
Undesirable Persons from the Colony', 'Leakage of Information' and so on. The Town Police called
attention to the inflow of Air Force and other units, which had turned some of the larger centres into
virtual garrison towns, while the 'Early Closing Regulations' and the 'Petrol and Tyre Regulations',
they averred, demanded a not inconsiderable amount of attention by the short-staffed urbanites. The
District men pointed with quiet pride to their efforts at maintaining all-round patrolling. The
Reservists — without quite saying so — opined that without them the job would never have been
done. The Women Police made it clear that they enjoyed doing a man's job, were not especially
pleased that a committee of men had designed their uniforms but felt that in the future they, the
Women Police that is, would be more necessary than they had been hitherto.

One somewhat unusual and little publicised story to surface after the War concerned the Police
Column that assembled in the Depot, joined up with members from Bulawayo, and left the country
on 4 September 1939. This Column moved to Kazungula and Kasane in the Bechuanaland
Protectorate, and close to the Caprivi Strip, to undertake reconnaissance duties linked to the
protection of the Victoria Falls Bridge, at that time regarded as a prime and vulnerable target. The
Column, which included a Native Police Platoon, was the first unit to leave Southern Rhodesia for
service outside the country. They stayed in the area for just on two weeks, never fired a shot, never
saw any enemy. Despite having virtually no fishing tackle, they managed to deplete the Chobe River
of fair quantities of its tiger and bream.

Another group of police was sent to Umtali to reinforce the members there. This was in case of a
display of hostility from the small number of Germans known to be in Mozambique. Their experience
was very similar to those who went to the north-west border, except there was no river to fish.

Another little known contribution to the war effort was the accommodating in Depot of a number
of Royal Air Force staff in 1938 and 1939. This occurred while Police Pioneers worked on the future
Air Stations at Cranborne and Belvedere. Also at around that time, seven Hawker Hart aircraft were
assembled in the old Ordnance Stores in Depot prior to being towed out to Cranborne.

So it was that everyone, as hostilities ended in Europe and the Far East, received well-deserved
words of praise from the Governor, the Minister of Justice and the Commissioner of Police.

The air was warm with congratulations, and the atmosphere totally conducive to a vigorous
recruiting campaign. A firm effort was made to put in place conditions of service that would be
attractive to young men and make a career in the Force both satisfying and inviting. The award to
Brigadier Morris of the King's Police Medal was not only timely but a fitting and well deserved
honour. In its way, it combined a tribute to the man who had successfully commanded the Force over
12 difficult and momentous years, with an acknowledgment to the members of that Force that they
had performed their duties, both within and outside the Colony, with unswerving dedication through
a long and trying period.

But the time was ripe for Morris to give way to a successor.

At the beginning of 1945, the Inspector General was within only four months of retirement and had
served for nearly 36 years. Morris had joined as a Trooper in October 1909 with the Regimental
Number 1119. Commissioned in 1914, he had moved to the Criminal Investigation Department the

following year. Two years later he had been sent to India to study Police methods before returning to take command of CID Salisbury.

His progress thereafter was assured and steady and the move to the Uniform Branch in 1928 was a natural precursor to his appointment as Commissioner in 1933. Only three years later, he was appointed Commandant of the Southern Rhodesia Forces, a position he was to occupy until 1940 when, as was mentioned in an earlier chapter, the post of Inspector General was created and the military and police became separate entities.

The new Commissioner was Major John Ross, a man who had, since joining in 1913, seen active service against the Germans in South West Africa, prior to being seconded to the Second Rhodesia Native Regiment for the remainder of WW1. His police background, after having been granted a commission in 1921 and undergoing courses with Scotland Yard and at the Senior Officers' School at Sheerness in 1937, included periods with both the Town and District branches, Commandant of the Depot, and Staff Officer to the Commissioner — what might be termed a well-rounded background — or a prophetic learning curve.

Ross, however, was stepping into a pretty desperate situation. His predecessor had done all he could to imbue the Force with a greater degree of professionalism. This despite the inhibiting factors of a war, the absence on operational duties of a significant percentage of trained men and, to some extent, a lack of commitment on the part of Government. One suspects that even some of his senior officers viewed 'change' with a noticeable lack of enthusiasm. Allied to this was the fact that very few local youngsters regarded the BSA Police as a lifetime calling. The pay was poor, conditions of service rudimentary and the attractions of, for example, tobacco farming, greatly outweighed the disciplined, highly-ordered vocation that the maintenance of law and order demanded.

The Colony was showing every sign of being poised for massive economic advancement, for an influx of skilled immigrants, for industrial development, commercial and, most important, agricultural expansion.

Although the first trickle of men returning from duties outside the Colony had started, the wartime embargo on discharges had been relaxed, so that the trickle in had also become a trickle out. The backbone of the Force, its European members, was stretched to breaking point. Police posts, such as those at Mount Selinda and Birchenough Bridge, had to be closed and, on top of this, and as the saying goes, 'the natives were restless'. A series of widespread, but fortunately half-hearted strikes had taken place. But probably far worse in some eyes, the Salisbury Police found themselves with insufficient men to field a Rugby XV in the First League. Add to all this that some of those due to return from the north were being made lucrative offers to make their secondments permanent, as well as being offered other colonial appointments, and the trickle out had the potential of a heavy outpouring.

Only three members are recorded as having joined the Force in 1945: Vaughan Griffin, who was discharged as 'Medically Unfit' 24 months after joining; Peter James, who rose to sergeant and retired 'On Gratuity' in 1956; and Bill (AEF) Bailey, who had seen service in North Africa with the Long Range Desert Group, and was to become the founder and moving spirit of an illustrious unit which, at this stage will merely be labelled PATU, but which brought to him and the BSA Police a certain amount of controversy, but much praise and glory.

That — the development of PATU — is another story which will unfold when this history reaches the 1960s.

To recapitulate then: the broad picture of the Force in 1945, with peace restored and Ross moving into a pretty warm chair, depicted a far-from-contented band of some 400 European Regulars. This was about 270 below an inadequate and out-of-date establishment figure.

About a tenth of that number were on leave pending retirement and doubtless reasonably cheerful, were it not for the paucity of their pensions. The remainder were pretty disgruntled by the undue emphasis on military discipline, generally poor career prospects and conditions of service, the lack of sufficient married quarters, and the over-abundance of work, much of it unexciting and containing a lot of seemingly unnecessary administrative duties.

To add numerical detail to the picture and for clarification, the Police Reserve was 'all square' at 267, while the Women Police strength of 68, reflected a 'shortfall' of 22. The Native Police at 1572 were down 30, while the Special Native Police numbered 361.

At this stage it must be emphasised that the word 'establishment' refers to the number of personnel permitted to be members of the Force. For that number, therefore, financial provision has been made for salaries, uniforms and equipment and this overall figure appears in the Police budget. 'Strength', as the name implies, is the actual number available and existing. The 'shortfall' is the difference between the two. The commissioners of police, over the entire period of this history, consistently badgered Government to increase the establishment to a realistic figure so that policing of the country could be adequately and properly handled. With infrequent exceptions and despite the most compelling of reasons being advanced, which were supported by statistics and logical arguments, these requests were invariably savagely pruned down, rejected or ignored by successive senior Treasury officials and hence by Government. Their argument was quite simply, the money isn't available. That was until the going became really tough.

Two major events took place during the closing months of 1945 and during 1946. They were to have a profound effect on the control and direction of the Police for the next 30 or more years. The first was the comprehensive search for new recruits in the United Kingdom; the second the Report of the Mundy Commission into the organisation of the B.S.A Police.

**Chapter Thirty-Five**

**NEW BEGINNINGS**

*Post-War Recruiting Drive — Freemantle, Blackmore, May, Jouning, Bosley and
many others — Frustration at Depot Discipline — Watson on the '46ers' — Nkomo
flexes his muscles — Chirundu on Christmas Day — Police Reserve Stand-Down*

THE MAN CHOSEN to garner recruits for the Police from among the various British Armed
Forces at the end of the war was Lieutenant Colonel Henry George Seward, known popularly as
'H.G'. Seward had joined the Police in 1920, having served in the Royal Flying Corps and later
transferred to the Army with the Fifth Cavalry Division in Palestine and Syria. In the 1930s he was
Staff Officer to the Commissioner, before joining the CID where he rose to Officer Commanding and
Chief Immigration Officer in 1938.

Seward's letter of accreditation, dated 16 July 1945, from Commissioner Ross, and which was to
lead him to the Middle East and finally to London, was slightly perplexing. The italics are mine:
"Bearer, Lieut. Colonel H.G. Seward, B.S.A.Police, accompanied by Lieut. F.R. West, B.S.A.Police,
have been *authorised by the Prime Minister of the Union of South Africa* to proceed to the Middle
East for the purpose of obtaining recruits for the British South Africa Police, Southern Rhodesia. Any
assistance that can be afforded by all concerned will be a matter of high appreciation by the Southern
Rhodesia Government.

The Middle East proved fairly non-profitable if not downright unhelpful. The Commander in Chief,
Middle East Forces, was prepared to bring all his authority to bear in order to retain the BSAP mem-
bers presently under his command. To him they were indispensable, no matter what view the Southern
Rhodesia Government took. His attitude, though of no help to Ross, is understandable in the light of
the troubled situation in Palestine at that time and the need to have experienced men, not only in the
Palestine Police, but also in the various occupied territories and sundry Colonial Forces. Thwarted,
Seward moved on to London where he found himself involved with the War Office, the Admiralty,
the Air Ministry, the Ministry of Labour and all the red-tape that accompanied the release of
servicemen at that time. By early 1946, Ross was becoming impatient and demanding that Seward
send out at least 75 bodies as soon as possible, though he had little knowledge of, or at that stage
preferred to ignore, the difficulties his Recruiting Officer was facing. Seward was battling with
officialdom, selection procedures, vetting, medical examinations and the prioritising of berths on
ships; to say nothing of the absence of any clerical assistance to help him. Despite these problems, he
did not waste his slack — 'spare' would be an incongruous word — time. Seward was determined to
expand his knowledge and usefulness to the BSA Police. He wrote to Sir Percy Sillitoe, then Chief
Constable of the Kent County Constabulary, and arranged for an educational visit to the headquarters
in Maidstone: a similar request went to the Essex County Constabulary, while a liaison trip to MI5 at
the War Office served to renew contacts made some years before.

In the light of present-day costs, it is diverting to read a part of Seward's plea, made just before
Christmas 1945, for an increase in his subsistence allowance:  " ... I am finding 29 shillings a day
rather hopeless here. The cost of living is probably higher than in Salisbury and entertainment terrif-
ically so — one round of drinks costs anything from 18 to 24 shillings and ordinary everyday living
expenses nearly 30 shillings without any extras".

Back in Salisbury, Ross had finally begun to realise the problems facing his recruiting officer and
offered some assistance, at the same time revealing some befuddlement of his own: "This member
(Sergeant Grundy) was originally posted to the Gold Coast Police and then, through some obscure
means, was discharged from that Force and found his way over to Civil Affairs in Europe ... He is
quite an intelligent man and, I think, should do you quite well."

At the end of this letter, Ross mentions that a Commission of Enquiry has been appointed into
Police Pay, Allowances and Conditions of Service ("too long a story to put in writing") and urges
'H.G.' to set down his views on these matters. Although this Commission will be dealt with in some
detail later, the views of Ross (conveyed to Seward by letter in mid-January) cast an interesting light

on the Commissioner's feelings at that stage: "... I can tell you that the proceedings of the Commission have really developed into an all out attack on the officer class with a general expression of opinion that discipline should be done away with. My attitude is to put up as many constructive suggestions as possible and to leave it at that."

But the priority was finding men and getting them out to Rhodesia and Seward had done his job well: beavering away at officialdom, coaxing and cajoling as necessary. In early March of 1946 he was able to despatch the first group of thirteen recruits on the Franconia and a few weeks later a massive contingent of 94 left Southampton on the Alcantara — having to endure troopdeck accommodation and other fairly primitive conditions. Further parties were sent in May. The holes in the establishment were at last being plugged.

It is interesting to glance through some of the names in those first intakes of 1946 and 1947. Len Jouning, an ex-Fleet Air Arm pilot who became a Deputy Commissioner; Maurice Cooper-Jones, an ex-Tank Landing Craft Commander; Bert Freemantle, one of that glorious band who had parachuted into Arnhem; Guy Todd, ex-RNVR and one time Commander of a two man submarine, who subsequently left the Police and became a successful seascape artist in the Cape; William 'Bill' May, who had been involved in the North Africa Campaign, the Sicily Landings, aiding the Maquis in France, and also a survivor of Arnhem; Sandy Sanford, an RAF ex-member, who had participated in 34 bombing missions over Germany and been awarded the DFC; Howard Jones who had endured the horrors of being interned in a Japanese prisoner of war camp; Ron Blackmore who had suffered the same privations and was to become a respected Southern Africa authority on Fingerprints and Questioned Documents; Jimmy Watkins, David 'Taff' Morgan, Terence Thorpe, Peter Bosley, Ronald Trangmar, Tim Weimer — of whom a short anecdote later — and many, many others who were to make their mark and, in most cases, rise to high rank in the Force. However, only one from those intakes was promoted to the rank of Commissioner in the post-war BSA Police and that was Peter Allum. To him fell the task of piloting the BSAP into a new era when the one Force ceased to be and the Zimbabwe Republic Police was created in 1980. It is also recorded that when 'H.G' congratulated Allum on his appointment as Commissioner many years later, pointing out that it was he, Seward, who had recruited him, Allum replied "It was always my intention".

Weimer, so the story goes, was a sailor and found horses to be both awkward and exasperating; hence it was that when ordered to mount without stirrups, he found himself hanging upside down with arms and legs clasped firmly around the horse's neck. His Equitation Instructor, 'Jock' Sturrock, is reputed to have roared at him: "What the hell do you think you're doing Weimer? Trying to climb the bloody mizzen mast."

Other tales abound from that post-war period in the Police Depot. Peter Robinson, himself a forty-sixer, recalls that as recruits he and the late John Manning were walking past the Officers' Mess one day when Manning, who had been a Brigade Major in the British Army, saw the Depot Commandant coming towards them. Manning exclaimed "My God, that's old Bob de Quehen, one of my staff captains — served under me when I was BM." He rushed off to greet his old comrade, returning soon after very crestfallen. "We were colleagues during the War and he didn't even ask me into the Mess for a drink". The 'gap' between the Recruits' and Troops' Canteens and Sergeants and Officers Messes was both wide and deep.

A somewhat similar tale is told of Douglas Wright, who at one time was Navigation Leader for a bomber flight commanded by Squadron Leader John Cannon, DFC. Wright joined the Police in 1946 and, as a second sergeant, was member in charge of Darwendale two or three years later. Cannon joined the BSAP sometime afterward, in 1948, and he too was transferred to that station, but as the junior trooper. The roles were reversed, as in the old song 'I've got my Captain working for me now'.

At this time, Ross was following a 'policeman at any price' policy. Conditions in Depot did not lend themselves to either comfortable accommodation or comprehensive training. The first was quite inadequate for such large numbers; the second lacked the teachers to impart any knowledge for many of the Depot staff were still serving in North Africa and the Middle East, and the promises of Morris were proving unfeasible. So, three weeks of training was about all that anyone could expect before being cast out from the nest. Fortunate it was that these early intakes after the War were invariably men to whom a position of responsibility was the norm. However, initiative was apparently a different matter. It is recorded that during the Passing Out parade held on 30 May, a touch of humour was added to the proceedings when one man performed a 'Present Arms' all by himself.

The following story concerning a particular forty-sixer came from the late Lieutenant Colonel B.G. Spurling who, then a captain, commanded Victoria District in those days. Dave Holt, who had been a lieutenant in the RNVR, completed his training and was sent to Fort Victoria. Several police stations in the area were without any European supervision and, though the Native Police did their best, they were just not up to keeping the Station Books and Records up-to-date. Either Spurling or one of his senior subordinates popped along on a weekly basis to try and keep things 'shipshape' and bolster the sergeant who was notionally in charge. Holt was transferred to Bikita, taken there by Chief Inspector Bowbrick, the records checked and — that was it. Holt found himself commanding seven Native policemen, responsible for an area of 6000 square miles in which there were several cattle ranches, sundry mines, a few farmers and, covering a large expanse, a number of quite heavily populated Native Reserves. The gamble, for such it surely was, paid off; Holt found his 'land legs' and had an illustrious career which was to end tragically 24 years later when, as an Assistant Commissioner in Bulawayo, he suffered a fatal heart attack.

Not all the recruits possessed a sense of discipline and responsibility and several later 'passing out' parties degenerated into an orgy of destruction with tables, chairs and, in one case, a piano reduced to matchwood. The crunch line came when a Natal mahogany tree, one of two planted near the Troops Canteen some years before, was found uprooted and thrown to the ground. At that time the Depot Chief Inspector was Leslie Goodall, normally a gentle and mild-mannered man, but not on this occasion. The offending squad was reissued with their saddlery, subjected to a 'stripped saddle' inspection, drilled mercilessly, and had their 'butts kicked' from sun-up to sundown. Three days, a confession and an apology later, the men were permitted their transfers to the Duty Branch. Discipline was back in vogue and the instructional staff, helpless and unhappy onlookers, knew they now had the full support of those in authority.

Fortunately such cases of indiscipline were rare and certainly did not affect the African Police Training School (APTS) where, at about this time, the command passed to Herbert van Niekerk. This officer was Rhodesian-born, had served with the Rhodesian African Rifles in Burma, was a superb linguist and strong disciplinarian, totally versed in the customs, lore and superstitions of his charges, and thus in every way was a most fitting 'square peg in a square hole'. It is on record that during his period at the APTS, which ended with his retirement in 1960, no less than 5000 recruits passed through his hands.

Another forty-sixer and one who was distinguished as a remarkably gifted writer and humorist, as well as a first class policeman, was William 'Paddy' Watson. As the saying goes, Watson 'did his twenty' and then retired as a chief inspector; but his memory is forever enshrined in his articles in *The Outpost*, his editorship of that magazine for a lengthy period and the following recollection which he wrote 43 years after joining the BSAP:

"Let's parade the rookie District policemen again, for an early morning ride. Line up the matelots from the storms and icy seas of the Russian convoys, the riflemen and tank crews who fought at Alamein with Montgomery, the glider pilot who'd gone a bridge too far at Arnhem, the lieutenant commander who flew against the might of the Scharnhorst, the squadron-leader gunner with a DFC, won at great cost in the skies of Europe. Stand to your horses, the paratroops from the D-Day landings, the soldiers from the jungles of Burma, the airman who survived a Japanese POW camp. Rare, roaring, roistering lads they are, all in their early twenties.

Among that lot is a future Commissioner, a sprinkling of drop-outs who'll end up as magistrates, lawyers, farmers, teachers. businessmen and writers, and a couple of cultured ne'er-do-wells. *(It's hard to tell at the beginning, who will be who at the end)!*

Mount up and follow them, and get the feel of Depot. "The whole ride, Walk — March. Don't say 'Gee-up' to the horse, that man. Stick yer heels in. Gently on, Terrr-ot."

Depot is trumpet fanfares and bugles sounding, bawled orders, men marching, and horsemen riding by. It is white-washed stones, gleaming leather and starched tunics, the crunch of boots on the hard square, the revving of motor bikes, and the staccato rattle of rifles on the firing range. It is law and police lectures and PT, first aid and animal husbandry. It is bowls of fresh fruit salad and paw-paw and bacon and eggs for breakfast after the lean years of the war. Take plenty; eat as much as you want. There's crayfish in the evenings, too, if you fancy it, at 1/9d a tin in the canteen, and beer at 11d a pint.

This is the troopers' haven for six weeks — keep them there any longer and they'd become too soft and indolent to preserve the peace, prevent crime, protect life and property, and apprehend offenders. No kidding. That's what an Act of Parliament authorises and requires them to do. It's a lot to expect after six weeks apprenticeship, and for fifteen pounds a month. So long, Titch, Spike, Lofty, Nobby, Bunts.

Take care, Chuck, Sparks, Bomber, Spud. And you, too, Chalkie — especially you. See you around, Taff, Jock, Paddy, Yank, Scouse, and Wack.

That was the easy bit. Now everything happens fast. Bounce over endless dusty roads in the burning sun to the scattered farms and mines on a rigid BSA. Prosecute cases in the name of His Majesty — it says so on the charge sheets for the Native Commissioner's Court — Trooper Toppling for the Crown.

Imagine that. Attend post-mortems. ("You gotta weak stomach?" "Naw, it must be something I ate."

Take the innards of a little kid, who was the victim of a ritual killing, up to the Government Analyst in Salisbury and meet the men of '47. "What's it like inna flippin' jungle, mate, wiv da lions and da tigers?" Swing the lamp and tell the tale. Go back another time and report at Depot for the murder trial in the High Court, dressed to the nines in a green tunic buttoned up to the neck — clean and inefficient in a topee, bandolier, breeches, boots and spurs. Tell the whole truth — the native police solved that mystery for you, and most of the others, too, in those early days. Give credit where it's due to the Majongosi's, the Taderera's, the Lobengula's. Somebody ought to say something about them, and they may not have a spokesman now. They were advisers and consultants in all things criminal.

They were kindly, knowledgeable, patient men of integrity, tolerant, loyal, brave, they were, and incorruptible. It would need a book to get them all in.

Watch the antics of the white-Brit troopers, learning to spell strange names like Andries Bezuidenhout and Gregiorou Papathanasoplous (how was that again?) and Lodewickus Jacobus Labuschagne. "Hi Andy. Howzitt, Pappy. Mornin' Vikkers." See. It didn't take all that long to get these things straight.

Then all the learning curves seem to soar up and up forever, around the time of the Royal Visit of 1947, on the day the King inspected his mounted escort. Plenty of Forty-Sixers lined the Royal Routes, but here the glory focused on the men up there on the horses, in that last parade.

An officer explained to his Sovereign, "They're all recent recruits, Your Majesty." It was said with pride.

"They don't look like recent recruits to me," the King said. And they weren't.

Not any longer.

They had made it. There isn't much more to be said about the Class of '46. Except, perhaps, to toast ourselves as we were then, in the year that was always summer:

"Here's tae us. Wha's like us? Damn few."

'Paddy' started that little bit of reminiscing by saying it was as easy as ABC. 'A' is for Alcantara, and 'B' the boys who sailed out in her and the other ships, after World War II ended, to join the Class of '46. And then there's 'D' for Depot. They went through its gates and into a bit of history.

But there are a few other tid-bits from 1946 that contribute to this story of the British South Africa Police and a year that was momentous in so many ways.

A man named Joshua Nkomo started to flex his political muscles and there was the threat of a Native Railway Strike in Bulawayo. New rescue equipment was purchased for use at the Victoria Falls, and Sergeants Wordsworth, Baldrey and Digweed became acquainted with it. Many members who had been compelled to stretch their service through the war years departed on 'leave pending discharge'. The Police Reserve was stood down on 1 June; and men like Bristow, Sherren, Spink and others returned from the various theatres of war to resume their lives as career policemen with apparently little personal disturbance or discomfort. Perhaps the word 'little' is not quite right; in one case some mental confusion obviously occurred, as the following story from *The Outpost* shows.

"In October, Sergeant Sherren, (by then stationed at Shamva), had been seen wandering around and staring into space for long periods. He occasionally filled the motor cycle with paraffin, and it was hoped that this state of mind would vanish when the cause of the trouble arrived the following month. It would appear that all went well, for a short time after Sherren became the father of an eight and a quarter pound son and, doubtless, Shamva's motor cycle became less of a liability."

The year was also distinguished by a poem written by the solitary man stationed in one of those police outposts dotted about the country's borders;

*Have you ever been really lonely*
*And had no one near you at all?*
*Have you ever been in the bundu*
*With nobody else within call?*
*Have you ever wanted to listen*
*To voices apart from your own?*
*Have you ever wished for a handclasp*
*That tells you, you aren't all alone?*
*Have you ever felt like conversing*
*With someone in your Mother tongue?*
*Have you ever longed to see just a white face*
*No matter if he should have hung?*
*Have you ever prayed for companions*
*To help you along life's drab way?*
*Have you ever needed assistance*
*To make you feel cheerful and gay*
*Have you ever longed for the time when*
*You'll be with your loved ones again?*
*Have you ever thought that the waiting*
*Would be such a wearying strain?*
*If you have experienced these longings*
*You know why I'm feeling this way,*
*For I'm stuck here at Chirundu,*
*And my calendar says "Christmas Day"*

Mention has been made above of the stand down of the Police Reserve, but much more needs to be said about these exceptional men who, at the end of a busy day or sacrificing a relaxing weekend, would don uniforms and assist their beleaguered regular colleagues in a wide variety of duties.

The Stand Down Parades took place in May and June of the year and all were attended by the Commissioner, the Minister of Justice, the Hon. T.H.W. Beadle, and other notables. Sadly the Governor of the Colony at that time, Admiral Tait, was stricken with an illness that was to prove fatal and was thus unable to attend in person. The Reservists had served with distinction since the 1939 call-up in jobs to which were attached no glamour, no heroics but a tremendous essentiality and need. Their service and spirit had formed bonds with the Regular Force that were to grow and prosper over the next 30 or more years.

At the Depot parade, Beadle, after describing the composition of the Reserve, continued: "The average strength of the First Reserve throughout the war has been about 300. They have performed active police duties in all the main centres throughout the Colony. Active police duties have been performed after ordinary work, between the hours of 6 p.m. and 2 a.m. and during weekends and public holidays ... The Police Reserve has at all times maintained the highest traditions of the B.S.A.P. and has done a great deal to increase the good feeling that undoubtedly exists in this Colony between the public and the police."

Of course, this was not the end of the Police Reserve. Many of the members had more than enjoyed their duties over the war years and certainly wanted to carry on in a service which had proved interesting, at times exciting and certainly of immense value to their country.

We shall learn more of them as this history progresses, but now it is time to turn to the Mundy Commission.

Chapter Thirty-Six

**THE MUNDY COMMISSION**

*Background — Evidence — Recommendations*

MENTION HAS BEEN made of the poor pay and abysmal conditions of service existing in the Police at the end of the War. This was only the tip of the iceberg. The war years had taxed the resources and loyalty of those remaining in the Colony to a very high degree; leave had been curtailed, many additional hours had been worked to keep up with policing and with the unimaginable amount of extraneous duties.

The future, if any, seemed pretty uncertain for those still wishing to pursue a worthwhile career. Questions arose over those who had been 'up North'; how would they slot into the seniority rolls and, indeed, how would they fit into the almost humdrum life of a policeman, after the exotic, often exciting and certainly highly responsible duties many had performed in the Middle East.

The initial step taken by Commissioner Ross was the appointment of a Board of Inquiry to examine and recommend on changes to the conditions of service. This form of approach was totally unacceptable to members who, particularly outside Salisbury, were becoming more and more combative and desperate in outlook and who sought a form of inquiry that would be high-powered, effective and prepared to draw attention and bring solutions to their problems. A Board of Inquiry was a piece of domestic housekeeping, toothless and ineffective. Their grievances, and now their solidarity, had been exacerbated by the total failure of Police Conferences to achieve any progress. In fact the last, in 1942, had seen Resolution after Resolution emasculated with the words 'This will have to await a General Review'. They, basically the senior members of the Police Conference committee, sought the services of Messrs. Webb, Low and Barry, Legal Practitioners of Bulawayo who, in turn, instructed Advocate J.M. Greenfield to act for them. Ross seemed very well aware of what was required and, one feels possessed considerable unspoken sympathy for the rank and file. He was quick to sense the necessity for a more authoritative and powerful investigation — one that would carry weight with Government and perform for the Police what the Plewman Commission had achieved, a few months earlier for the Public Service. Government, let it be said, invariably refused throughout history to grant policemen any benefits which had not already been accorded to civil servants. Plewman had thus unknowingly fired a volley in support of policemen.

The pent up frustration was rewarded. On 4 January 1946, the Governor, Admiral Sir William Tait, appointed four Commissioners to "enquire into and report on matters concerning the British South Africa Police, the Permanent Staff Corps and the Prison Service". Those four were Major Hugh Mundy, OBE, William Brown, OBE, Thomas P. Cochran and Arthur Sanders. The Secretary for the Commission was Staff Inspector Robert Stoker, once described by Seward as a 'vocal theorist.' The Terms of Reference were as wide ranging and comprehensive as could be imagined. They embraced organisation, discipline, seniority, promotions, adequacy of pay and scales; leave and its ramifications in the prevailing state of affairs; future establishment, continuation as a military unit, reorganisation and representation of grievances In fact, as a following clause stated, "generally to make suggestions and recommendations for promoting efficiency, harmonious working and satisfactory administration..."

Two days after the appointment The Sunday Mail editorial commented " … it is likely that re-organisation as a civil force will be recommended. If this should be the case, lovers of tradition will feel a pang of regret, for the history of the Force as a military unit goes right back to the days of the Pioneer Column. But times have changed, and the time has undoubtedly arrived when the break should be made with tradition, and the Police, who have a full-time civilian duty to perform, should be placed on a civilian basis, as is the case in almost all British countries". The editorial continued with some suggestions to counter the lack of experienced manpower and emphasised the need for quick decisions so that the demobilisation market in Britain could be thoroughly turned to account. (It should be noted that evidence was given to the inquiry and its recommendations formulated before any of the large post-war intakes of men arrived in Rhodesia).

It is not a part of this history to detail the voluminous verbal and written evidence presented to the Commission over the ensuing weeks and in all the main centres of the Colony. It is, however, and with the knowledge of subsequent events and promotions, interesting and sometimes highly diverting to read some of the evidence given:

Major J. Dudley of the Army giving evidence on subsistence allowances: "I think that when those rates were published, (they) would probably suggest the Windsor as opposed to Meikles or the Grand. But at the moment, even assuming you could get into the Windsor or Queens, 15/- (fifteen shillings) is not nearly enough."

Detective Sub-Inspector S. Maybrook: "The discontent is caused by the rudeness and inconsiderate attitude of some of the officers."

Detective Sergeant F. Barfoot: "The commissioned officer assumes a social standing in accordance with his military rank and not in keeping with his social standing appertaining to his employment. Respect is earned; it is not something which is granted with a commission. Police work is an accumulation of experience of investigation of crime and dealing with members of the public combined with the theory of investigation and knowledge of the legislation".

Barfoot also suggested the main cause of dissatisfaction as being the military nature of the police. Bearing in mind that this Commission was taking the evidence in public, and that the Press were present unless Major Mundy or a witness asked or suggested that evidence be given in camera, the opening remarks of Sub-Inspector R. Southgate revealed something of a break in the ranks: "I am against much of the previous evidence which seems against the officer class. It is the system which is wrong". Southgate went on to aver that the military training was reminiscent of the Boer War, and that more individualism was needed. In a remarkably impassioned speech, he asserted that the grievance system needed overhauling and quoted a well-used aphorism, "the BSAP are soldiers in times of peace and policemen in times of war".

Captain H. Jackson: "The CID is not necessarily the cream of the police force, nor are all the best brains of the Police in the CID".

Lieut. Col. A. S. Hickman, the Police Quartermaster: ("I look after the Things") gave a long and somewhat rambling account of his service which, at one stage he described as "the Rake's Progress". Nevertheless he made a number of important points; among them: Housing for the African Police is as urgent as for the European. Separate Messes must be maintained but a Police Club should be established in connection with sport generally, and facilities be available for all, regardless of rank.

Hickman was given a torrid time by the Commission because of his adherence, almost vehement adherence in fact, to the principle of retaining military procedures. He also maintained that the sight of a single trooper performing drill and rifle exercises completely on his own during a station inspection was neither ridiculous nor embarrassing.

Hickman was also subjected to some fairly close questioning on whether, during a parade rehearsal, he had used the relatively innocuous words, "Keep that bloody man quiet". That 'bloody man' subsequently fainted.

Finally, Senior Inspector J. Newton giving evidence about the proposed amalgamation of the Town and District Branches: "District officers appear to be convinced that command of Town Police shifts are designed to afford delightful opportunities for recreation ... and are entirely unsympathetic to the trying hours and additional duties".

The Commission's final report was a feather in the cap for Commissioner Ross whose recommendations were largely accepted. Among the many and far-reaching changes were included the postulations that Police should cease to be regarded as a sub-division of the Department of Justice, and that the status of the Commissioner should be raised to that of a Permanent Head of a Division within the portfolio of the Minister of Justice. Also that a deputy commissioner be appointed; the Chief of CID be an assistant commissioner; consideration be given to the amalgamation of the Town and District branches; that the wearing of military insignia and the use of military titles be continued (this was something of a surprise to many), and that a Central Pay and Accounts office be created at Police General Headquarters. Interesting was the comment that a 'general improvement was needed in the conditions of service for native ranks'.

Further major changes permitted the creation of a Cadet Branch for young Rhodesians and the continuation of the Women Police branch. More important, from the point of view of those still serving (and grousing), were the regulations published later in 1946 stating, among other things, that promotion to commissioned rank had to be by selection from members not below the rank of sub-inspector.

At the same time, far reaching and very advantageous changes were made to the regulations covering Leave, Acting Allowances, Promotion and Language Allowances: the rank of chief inspector was introduced; marriage became permissible at age 25, or after completing three years' service, and finally attractive pay scales were introduced for the whole Force.

Many other matters were aired and discussed; some to be referred to the Commissioner, some to the Minister. Pension benefits, transport, mechanisation, discipline, training and extraneous duties were just part of a review that was comprehensive, detailed and totally acceptable to forward-thinking policemen throughout the country.

The entire Police Force, black and white, benefited from these changes but, most importantly, the BSA Police as a career became a relatively attractive prospect, not only for those serving but also for those who would join and seek their futures within its various branches.

The coming two decades would severely test not only the loyalty, but the resolve of those who joined in those immediate post-war years.

*"Trust you to pick a house right on the Trans-Africa air route."*

## Chapter Thirty-Seven

## NEW BOYS SETTLE IN

*Ex-servicemen's lack of knowledge of the African — Transfers after Depot Training —*
*Huggins on the Future — the 1947 Royal Visit — Tantum — Police Headquarters moved*

Peace was a reality, and the country was beginning to see an unrivalled population explosion through its policy of selective immigration. Godfrey Huggins had scraped back into power in a minority poll (nearly 12,000 for his United Party as opposed to over 15,000 for the combined opposition) in the 1946 General Election. The Police Force had been brought up to establishment and the foundations laid for a fulfilling career. The way ahead looked rich and rosy. But for the Police, there were still problems, and pretty serious ones, to be tackled.

Perhaps the most potentially dangerous was the fact that the comparatively vast numbers of ex-Servicemen recruited from overseas knew little of the African, his life style, culture and customs.

It must be remembered that so great was the need for 'policemen on the ground' that men were taking over understaffed rural stations responsible for vast tracts of unfamiliar country, after only a few weeks' guidance and training in Depot. Experienced policemen were by now few and far between. It was all too easy to 'learn the ropes' from persons who might seem knowledgeable but who, in fact, might have been influenced by the way their breakfast had been served, their crops spoiled or livestock stolen. And all that recounted at sundowner time. Tremendous reliance on the Native Police was essential, especially in the District areas, and the recollections of 'Paddy' Watson, included earlier, contain a well-deserved tribute to the black policemen.

It is of interest to see where a number of the forty-sixers had been transferred by early 1947. May and Walton were at Penhalonga; Sandall at Inyanga; Allum, Morgan, Galloway and Watson were in Rusape; Thorpe was based in Umtali Town, Lowther and Moisey at Shabani; Millett and Sowter had gone to Que Que, Wickenden to Umvuma and Dennis 'Johnny' Johnston to Concession.

It was at this last station that an interesting racket was exposed. The member-in-charge went to pull some carrots from his vegetable garden, only to end up with a bunch of leaves. The important part had been neatly bitten off and the leaves replaced in the bed. Suspicion fell on the prisoners from the lock-up who were required to do part of their hard labour sentence in the gardens of the camp.

Mention was made of Herbert Van Niekerk in a preceding chapter. Van Niekerk, now back in the Police Depot after serving in Burma, was well aware of the pitfalls facing the new policemen and the prejudices (some true, many untrue) with which they were assailed. In a series of articles in the police magazine he did his best to disabuse the newcomers on such matters as the Africans' reputation for laziness, untruthfulness and lack of manners.

Van Niekerk urged his fellow policemen to study the  languages and customs of the indigenous people, and to be careful not to judge all natives by what they knew of their Native Constables. The latter, he pointed out, were by nature of their training far more knowledgeable in the ways of the European.

Another to cast a fresh and, at that time controversial approach on the 'Native Question' was none other than the Prime Minister, Sir Godfrey Huggins. Speaking in his capacity as Minister of Native Affairs, and addressing the Native Welfare Society of Bulawayo in August 1946, his speech included the following: "With the advent of the European, the native gradually developed a settled mode of life which of necessity today is following civilised ideas, and beginning to branch out into the spheres required to maintain a balanced economy and population. We are rapidly reaching the stage where national economy will no longer permit or support a mode of life based solely on agriculture and the raising of livestock. Since 1925, the native population has increased by about 640,000. If this rate of increase is maintained, it means that we have to find an additional 16,000,000 acres of land every 20 years, that is an increase of more than 50% over the present acreage allotted to native occupation. These figures are worth noting as they represent the crux of the problem — a problem which is not generally appreciated in the country to-day. They are the answer to those who airily speak of keeping the natives' homes in the reserves."

Sir Godfrey developed his theme by enlarging on the need to cultivate both an agricultural and industrial framework for the native population in the future, and in both of which, for competitive reasons, efficiency had to be of world standard. He went on to discuss earning capacity in both spheres and emphasised the need for an adequate sustaining income, sufficient to make the bread-winner, and his family, fit and well.

The next aspects he talked of were the importance of the Land Apportionment and the Natural Resources Acts. To these were allied the need for adequate land for families and livestock, and the provision of water. "We are, therefore", he continued, "rapidly approaching the stage where every native must realise now that he cannot expect to be a farmer in a native area and at the same time supplement his income by labour in industry. He will have to concentrate on one of these two avenues of life".

Sir Godfrey touched on the need to sometimes move natives from over populated areas and the inevitability that humanitarian concerns then had to take precedence over ancestral affinities. He was very blunt too, in declaring that only if the landowner made sufficient profit would it be possible to upgrade the "facilities for a people slowly but surely becoming civilised, such as permanent houses, clean water, sanitation, bathing facilities in disease-free water, etc. There is the added difficulty that in most cases the native cannot keep livestock, but that will be gradually overcome: he will get used to doing without cattle and dogs; in fact he will have to."

This far ranging and frankly provocative speech went on to touch upon the Native Urban Areas and Registration Act and the purpose of, and salient points in that legislation. Huggins discussed the need to curtail urban settlement and encourage regionalisation; the introduction of employment bureaux; the dangers of illicit brewing (but allied to the construction of adequate replacement facilities) and the creation of outlets for the more intellectual natives.

Summing up, Huggins said: " … our policy is not to turn the Africans into politicians, but to improve the health and knowledge of the people to enable them to distinguish between good and evil and that, as they improve and show their worth, they are not exploited but receive an adequate reward in cash and general living conditions".

This broad indication of Government's thinking has been quoted in some detail because these policies, sometimes perverted, sometimes taken out of context and sometimes, perhaps, maladministered, became the corner stones upon which African Nationalism was to grow, flourish and eventually become dominant.

However, it is time to return to the year 1947.

This was the year when Major-General Sir John Kennedy arrived to take up the post of Governor and, as is usual in such circumstances, he was greeted with all the pomp and pageantry befitting the arrival of the representative of the Crown. All went well with the exception of one senior member from the Baker Avenue Charge Office who, dressed in the usual breeches, spurs and other accessories, walked out into the street to find that on his head was a green pork pie hat.

The Mounted Escort for the occasion included Trooper 'Bill' Earle. Fresh from enjoying a beer on His Excellency, another from the Commandant, Depot and yet another from the Escort Commander, he entered the Depot Mess for lunch with his friend, Trooper Howard Jones. The latter, armed with a revolver, had been a motor cycle outrider. The two were told that lunch was finished.

Nothing daunted, Earle, incorrectly believing that his friend would have 'broken' the weapon, loosed off two shots into the ceiling — and won his lunch. He also won an interview with RSM Tantum and a fine of three shillings and sixpence from Colonel 'Monty' Surgey.

Without doubt the most significant event of 1947 was the Royal Visit to the Colony in April. Preparations had started long beforehand, with men and horses drafted into the Depot for special training and, though it may have had no special significance relative to the occasion, Max Sparks' arrangement of the march Kum-a-Kye was formerly adopted as the Regimental March.

In fact the first moves in preparation for the visit of the Royal Family had started in April of the previous year. Training of the more difficult horses had begun then and a special 'Escort Lane' developed in one of the riding schools with bunting, Union Jacks, rattles and loud-speakers to simulate excited crowds. Next, in mid-February, came the men: 14 from Depot, and 22, most of whom had never ridden a horse and who were either ex-servicemen or had been on secondment, drafted in from District stations. Though doubtless proud and privileged to have been selected, theirs was a daunting task. Not only had they to provide the Mounted Escort, but the same men had to 'mount' a full Motor Cycle Escort with outriders as well. A small additional group led by Sub Inspector Sobey, was trained to cope with the Victoria Falls — Livingstone part of the Royal Visit. Yet a further group, under Umtali-based Sergeant Watson, was to escort the Princesses to semi-official functions. Upon the shoulders of Staff First Sergeant Gilfillan fell responsibility for all the motor cycle training and preparation.

A typical day's work started with Reveille at 0530, and into the Riding School half an hour later for work with, invariably, crossed stirrups. Breakfast was at 0800 and followed an hour later with work in the Escort Lane with the Band, gunfire (in anticipation of Royal Salutes), cheering crowds and then roadwork. At 1100 came a welcome break for saddle and kit cleaning before 'Stables' at midday. This latter involved tail washing, plaiting, combing and general grooming of the mounts. Lunch was followed by motor cycle riding, during which formations were practised as well as forming-up, disengaging and general roadwork. At 1600 motor cycle maintenance and cleaning took place and, finally, an hour later, another stint of Stables. As if all that were not enough, the evenings were spent in more kit and saddle cleaning, for each man was responsible for two sets of saddlery, all his other leather-work, horse and motor cycle — as well as his uniform.

Later in these weeks of preparation came troop drill, lance drill, sword drill, roadwork with cars and visits to football matches, athletics meeting and so forth to gain as much authenticity in the way of crowd noise, as possible.

It is interesting, especially for those who merely have to stand and cheer, to note the lengths to which the preparations for pageantry extend. The horses were groomed so efficiently that one could all but shave in their coats, black polish was on their hooves; tails and manes were plaited and saddlery gleamed. The members of the Escort wore white helmets with brass fittings and chain chin straps, green tunics with belt and cross brace, breeches, leggings (these you could shave in), spurs and boots. They carried lances, well varnished with tips and butts burnished and pennants of the Regimental Colours, blue and gold, affixed and fluttering.

Not only had the men, horses (and motor cycles) to perform in Salisbury, but they had to make the move by train to Bulawayo for the Royal Visit to that city.

One incident remains clear in the memory of one member. The Bulawayo escort was a particularly long one, from the Railway Station to Lady Stanley Avenue, and took place on a particularly hot day for sitting down in the saddle in full dress. After about three miles, the Queen looked round and gave her escort such an encouraging smile that 'I could have done another five miles without turning a hair — and possibly without posting once'.

At the conclusion of the visit the Commissioner of Police, the Officer Commanding the Escort and the Warrant Officer of the Escort were given the CVO, MVO, and Medal of the Royal Victorian Order (RVO) respectively. This 1947 Escort comprised:

Captain de Quehen, MVO; Captain Bulstrode; Staff Sub Inspector Gaylard RVO; Staff Sub-Inspector Lardant; Staff First Sergeants Sturrock, Woodgate and Gilfillan; Farrier First Sergeant Kay; Farrier Second Sergeant Page; Second Sergeants Brown, Robertson and Hunter; Troopers Dewdney, Kerr, Oakley, Earle, Wright, Hamilton MC, Richardson, Temple-Murray, Jarvis, Stewart, Sanford DFC, Robinson, Brighten, Fairfax-Franklin, Burr, Stephens, Walton, Mason, Baker, Moisey, Douglas, Blascheck, and Sharp. The Commissioner's motor cycle orderlies were Troopers Ross and Ahearne.

Shortly after the departure of Their Majesties, the Force bade farewell to the last Regimental Sergeant-Major, 6'. 4". Tiny Tantum.

George Tantum had joined the Police 20 years before, after an illustrious career with the Second Life Guards. He had landed at Zeebrugge and saw action in the three battles of Ypres in 1914, 1915 and 1917. He had been heard to say that he ran from Mons to the Aisne without a stop. Tiny was in the same mould as his illustrious predecessors, Jimmy Blatherwick and Jock Douglas, that is to say he possessed a powerful voice, positively adored spit and polish, was a strict disciplinarian, quite fearsome on parade yet relatively human 'off'.

Anecdotes concerning Tantum are many and mostly unprintable. However, a member of the 1947 Royal Escort recently recounted a story, which has been gently censored, concerning a well known barmaid at the Grand Hotel in Salisbury, 'Mary G'. On this occasion he had to accompany the RSM into town; both were in uniform and they entered the bar where Tantum greeted Mary with the words,

"Mary, you're pregnant". Not daunted, Mary replied in words that showed that at least her sexual proclivities were conventional unlike, perhaps, those of her latest customers. Tiny's response was, blandly, "Well, let's have two pints anyway".

That Tiny ran from Mons to the Aisne is somewhat substantiated by another ex-member. John Stanyon recalls the fearsome figure of Tantum pausing in front of a constable during a parade inspection. Bending slightly to look the luckless man in the eye and then, tapping his riding crop on his own massive chest and upon a medal with a star, he enquired, 'What medal is this one?' Petrified by the glaring blue eyes, the veined hooked nose and the purple complexion, the youngster exclaimed 'VC, Sir'. Tantum leaned even nearer and shouted, "It's the Mons Star, you bloody fool; awarded for running like a bastard".

Tantum's successor was Inspector Leslie Goodall, appointed Depot Chief Inspector rather than RSM in October and who was mentioned earlier.

The year witnessed a number of welcome changes to Regulations. War Service was to count towards pension; cash in lieu of leave was permitted — a great boon to those who had accumulated a vast number of days to their credit during the war years, and clothing allowances were increased.

A further change was in the designation of Native Police, and was contained in a Force Order issued early in December, reading: 'With effect from the date of this order the term 'African' will be used in place of the term 'Native' in all matters, whether verbal or written, dealing with non-European members of the Force".

One final change needs to be recorded. With the aim of making more accommodation available to immigrants, Police Headquarters was relocated from Milton House to Depot. This involved a move of only a few hundred yards along Montague Avenue but was linked to a number of other changes, perhaps the most significant of which, historically, was the move of *The Outpost* and *Mapolisa* staff to the old building in the Depot which had, many years before, been the kitchen for the Regimental Mess and from which William Over used to supply meals to Police recruits. After being used as a kitchen, it became an office for the Musketry Staff, then an extra store for the ordnance and supplies section, before being redecorated by the Public Works Department.

Lieutenant Colonel Hickman encapsulated the changes very neatly ...

*There's been a transformation*
*Of kitchen, pantry, store.*
*The housing of The Outpost*
*Let no one now deplore;*
*For what was desolation*
*Is now so clean and neat*
*That I should like to sit in*
*The editorial seat.*

**Chapter Thirty-Eight**

**STUTTERING STARTS**

*1948 – 1950. Difficulties in retaining men — nationwide strike — Seward — Police Reserve expanded — Police Conditions improved — Albertson Case — Arson at Gutu — Extraneous Duties — Sporting Success — Sports and Display — Weller — Soccer triumphs — District life on the eastern border — Ross retires — Appleby Commissioner — Changes in policing methods.*

The next three years, 1948 to 1950, presented the Commissioner of Police with ever growing problems. The maintenance of law and order in a country which was rapidly expanding economically and whose European population was increasing at a rate really quite incompatible with its rather fragile infrastructure, presented vast problems of finance, recruiting and training, to name but three important areas. Conditions in the United Kingdom, from which the majority of young men was recruited, were still very much in a 'just post-war mode'; rationing still existed, life was far from normal. In fact it could be said that Britain was still suffering from a hangover.

This was borne out when the secretary of Brooks's Club in London was fined £15 for an offence under the 1949 Eggs Order. Something over 3000 eggs had been sent to the Club earlier. Lord Adam, the secretary concerned, had not realised that this was still a restricted product. Yet another member of the 'establishment' was keeping a light brown Jersey cow in the back garden of his Hyde Park Gate home and enjoying two gallons of milk a day.

To a relatively minor extent, the massive post-war recruiting drive caused its own problems. In the first place, a small proportion of those who joined in 1946 decided that Southern Rhodesia was not the country in which to grow old — and returned to Britain. Others spotted the opportunities that farming and commerce offered them — and moved into other occupations. Yet more, wearied after three years of learning a new vocation, the strain of police duties and the effort of competitive examinations, opted for a six months holiday — overseas. All these frustrations were compounded by a fair number of those who had joined 20 or more years previously deciding that the middle 40s was an excellent time of life to make a fresh start — outside the BSAP.

So it was that with Danny Kaye performing at the London Palladium, Prince Charles being born and Prince Aly Khan taking as his next wife the lovely film star Rita Hayworth, the still rather raw policemen in Southern Rhodesia were thrown into a maelstrom of activity by a nationwide strike that had its roots with municipal workers in Bulawayo.

The Officer Commanding Bulawayo District in 1948 was none other than Lieutenant Colonel H.G. Seward. His understanding of the problems leading up to the unrest was clear and not unsympathetic. His detailed report had every appearance of being a spirited and well reasoned reply to uninformed criticism:

"On every hand new industries and factories are being set up — building permits were granted for these but accommodation for the increasing labour supply fell far behind the very minimum requirements. In fact it seemed as though no balance was being maintained as between the two — certainly this is the case in Bulawayo where overcrowding in African areas has led to pitiful conditions of overcrowding. The press continued to publish reports of the rising cost of living and every time an African went to a store it was borne on him more and more that the purchasing power of his money continued to decline, and then — in a year of drought — the cost of his basic food, mealie meal, soared away to a figure which shook his economy to the very roots.

And all this time he read of cost of living allowances to Europeans and waited patiently for the legislation which was promised after the Railway Strike in 1945 to adjust his own wage difficulties.

This legislation failed to make its appearance until the latter half of 1947, nearly two years after it was promised, and the leaders of the Africans, at least in Bulawayo, carefully noted that it did not make its appearance until the threat of another native strike in the railways hung over the government's head.

All this, combined with the fact that there appeared to be no one who could keep them in the picture, or who had their welfare really at heart, brought about a state of affairs where what might be called the depressed classes in the Colony rose as a whole to express their — up to now — inarticulated feelings of what seemed neglect and indifference to their lot".

Seward went on to review the logistical arrangements made to deal with the disturbances. These included a rapid call up procedure for the 85 police reservists who were available at the time, and also for up to 200 Special Constables — regarded, because of their lack of training, as a 'last ditch' alternative; plus as many Territorials as could be mustered. A small number of men were also withdrawn from outstations. However the problems facing a handful of police confronted by a potentially hostile population approaching 100,000, and the latter congregated within a stone's throw of the central business area, requires neither elaboration nor imagination.

Seward's report concluded: "During the 34 hours the strike lasted, not a single pane of glass was broken, and not a half ounce of mealie meal was reported stolen — and order was restored by 10 on the morning the strike commenced by unarmed Police — I emphasise this — for not a single B.S.A. Policeman was armed. "Our reward — critics on every hand, believing what they read in the Press and from Club Gossips arriving at the conclusion that the Police failed to control the situation. Every member of the Force in Bulawayo is looking to the Government to give the lie to the Press and armchair critics. Police could, by precipitate action, have put the clock back 50 years. However by their patience, forbearance and restraint, order was rapidly restored and the means used were such that the African still regards the policeman as his friend".

'H.G.' sent his report to the Commissioner on 30 April 1948. The Commissioner, in forwarding it on to the Minister, made no additional comment beyond expressing his complete agreement and making it clear that he was well aware of the situation and had acquiesced with all the arrangements made.

Subsequent events are not recorded but Lieutenant Colonel Seward eventually sought permission to retire and is recorded as leaving the Force on Boxing Day of that same year, 1948.

Although emphasis has been placed on the happenings in Bulawayo, which was the source of the strike and disturbances, the discontent spread to virtually every part of the country and included even domestic servants. However, the Police took fair and firm action throughout, and calm and normality were restored within a short time.

For all that, the entire episode was a significant step in the ladder of what may be called militant industrial action. It revealed that the country's labour force could, when sufficiently angry and aroused and, let it be said, with right on their side, get their act together to originate and sustain mass activity.

Soon after this, Huggins resolved to break the difficult conditions under which he was running the Government. As shrewd a tactician as ever, he contrived' to have the Government defeated on a minor legislative issue, called an election and romped home with 24 seats in the Legislative Assembly. The opposition parties were all but crushed, winning a mere six. With the Opposition decimated, the way had been cleared towards a closer union with Southern Rhodesia's northern neighbours and the possibility of a Federation, long mooted, was now 'on the cards'.

But it is time to return to the various developments taking place in the Police.

One major effect after the countrywide trouble was the realisation that the Police Reserve was a definite necessity and not an inexpensive luxury. Steps were taken to increase its establishments and strengths, to implement new and more relevant training programmes, to increase *esprit de corps* and, even more than before, ensure smooth cooperation with Regular members.

A further important development was the drawing up and eventual implementation of an Act creating greatly improved pension and gratuity conditions for both Police and other uniformed forces. The opportunity to communicate the details of the new legislation was taken by the Minister of Justice, the Hon. THW Beadle at, of all places, the Grand Hotel in Salisbury where the Regimental Association was holding the Annual Dinner. Not for one moment doubting the importance of the subject, it is a matter of some speculation that it should form the substance of an after-dinner speech, or perhaps the force was partaking of its 'just desserts.'

Promotion examinations took place during the year and in the District Branch the top three qualifiers for promotion to sergeant were post-war men. Troopers Jouning, Atkinson and Wright; in the Town a pre-war man headed the list to be followed by Constables Sheriff, Fisher and Briault. All of these, and more, were to be promoted shortly after. One could say that the race was on though members of the CID were not, at this stage, obvious competitors.

At Police Headquarters, Colonel 'Monty' Surgey retired after 34 years' service and his place as Deputy Commissioner was taken by Lieutenant Colonel J. Appleby; he of the Aden pyjamas.

The editor of *The Outpost* had to cajole and threaten to obtain contributions for Station Notes. There was a limited response, as always, but one story vouched for as true rose head and shoulders above all others. It came from Mazoe:

'Last week a native went to the Postmaster at Mazoe and asked him to change five shillings in small change, ie. 'tickies' sixpences and shillings. He then made a call to Salisbury from the Public Box and spoke to his brother and told him he was sending him five shillings. The sum of five shillings was then pushed in the phone box.'

But that was over 50 years ago. The following year, 1949, saw the division of the country into three Police Provinces, based on Salisbury, Bulawayo and Gwelo, the officers commanding of which became in effect the Commissioner's representative in that area.

The year also saw some criminal cases that 'hit the headlines'.

The first of these, the Albertson Case, involved the murder of an elderly mine owner at the Pixie Gold Mine near Chakari. Albertson had dined with a visiting friend and, during the evening, the 'boss-boy' had come in and handed over the day's 'takings', a small ball of gold amalgam. Later that night, and following the sound of voices and the barking of dogs, the visitor found his host bleeding profusely from head wounds, unable to speak and obviously very severely injured. The old man died some hours later.

The post mortem revealed head wounds that could have been caused by a native axe. The vault of the skull was removed and sent to the Government Analyst. Routine inquiries were started, centering on an inspection of axes owned by the occupiers of the mine compound. At the same time, a search for blood- stained clothing was undertaken.

The only person unable to produce his axe was the house servant, Amos, who came up with several fanciful stories, including one describing why he was wearing a new pair of shorts and how he came to have dark stains (later confirmed as blood stains) on his tennis shoes.

Denied the murder weapon, Police turned to a firewood pile near the house and discovered that many cut pieces of log appeared to bear the same individual striations as were made by the axe which inflicted the fatal wounds. An axe used by one other person for log cutting was checked and eliminated; the services of the Criminal Bureau in Pretoria were utilised, and the case was taken to court. The High Court was satisfied that although there was no direct evidence to show that Amos had actually used the weapon that caused the death, the circumstances surrounding his movements, plus his conflicting statements were sufficient to convict him of the crime. Detective Inspector Digweed and the members of his CID team were commended for the efficiency and thoroughness of their investigation.

Another case which relied for its successful conclusion on steady, unspectacular but tenacious investigating occurred in the Gutu area. The modus operandi of the criminal was relatively simple; he would set fire to a barn, outhouse or other building some distance from the main homestead and then, when all hands were trying to put out the fire, he would enter the house and steal whatever took his fancy.

On this occasion his victim was a Gutu farmer and the burnt-out building, the farmer's mill house. However, an unsuccessful attempt had been made to set fire to a nearby native store which was also owned and run by the farmer. During the sifting of the burnt debris in the store, a charred piece of paper was found with the name 'Scotland Farm' on one side and 'Senale' and 'Iron Mine Hill', in different handwriting, on the other. The last two names were rail sidings between Gwelo and Umvuma. The investigators located Scotland Farm in the Enkeldoorn district and, after questioning various people there, the writing of the words 'Scotland Farm' was identified as that of a female, Arigumi, and the occasion a letter to her husband, William, who was employed at Que Que. The latter, it transpired, had been at the farm on the day preceding the arson and housebreaking at Gutu. The investigators realised that to travel to Enkeldoorn from Que Que, it would be usual to leave the train at Umvuma, a few stations before Chatsworth. Scotland Farm was a matter of 40 miles as the crow flies from the crime scene.

The next step was to locate William in Que Que and he it was who told police that he had the letter whilst on the train from Gwelo, probably dropped it when pulling out his tobacco pouch but certainly had not written the names of the sidings on it. However, he provided the telling information that in the compartment with him had been three native constables and half-a-dozen others. From then on the trail blazed hot. The constables were located and provided information on their fellow passengers. Then, and by pure coincidence, a bundle of kaffir truck was discovered in, of all places, the Gwelo Charge Office. This collection of impahle was recognised as part of that stolen from the Gutu farm but, quite unconnected with that crime, having been placed in the charge office after a reported assault on the wife of a well-known criminal named Baona. The latter had dropped the bundle when running away from the African constable sent to follow up on the alleged assault.

Baona was eventually arrested, admitted his involvement and was convicted. He had picked up the letter on the train, casually written the names of the sidings as the train passed through and ... the rest is history.

At the beginning of this chapter, mention was made of the many problems confronting the Commissioner. In his annual reports, he repeated the hoary theme of time wasted on Extraneous Duties and it is worthwhile to reiterate the way in which an over-worked Force was still required to do the work of others.

Too many statutory enactments were being investigated which, under no circumstances, could be regarded as criminal; Income Tax, Buildings, Workmen's Compensation, Deserted Wives, Industrial Conciliation, Dairy, and Land Apportionment were among these. Then came the Extraneous Duties proper: Lock-up Keepers, Prosecuting, Meteorological Observation, Pass Officers, Night Telephone Service, petrol and oil issues to government vehicles and so on. It had been calculated that each year 271 European policemen spent a total of 102,835 hours performing work on behalf of other government departments. The Commissioner also pleaded in his reports for the introduction of municipal traffic police and a review of the legislation controlling kaffir beer. It was to be a long time before Government acted on any of these matters.

By the end of 1949, it was apparent that on the fields of sport the Police were at last becoming a force to be reckoned with. The visit of the MCC Touring XI provided a significant boost not only to cricket, but also to the sales of liquor in the Town Police Mess. A story that loses nothing in the telling is of Dennis Compton being driven through central Salisbury on the pillion seat of 'Butch' Buckley's motor cycle, the English cricketer wearing the policeman's cap.

Another notable event was the holding of the first Mounted and Dismounted Sports since 1939. The public attended the former and were treated to various equestrian competitions, a superb display of bareback riding, vaulting and jumping, and an amusing 'Tiger Hunt'. This culminated in Sergeant 'Steve' Stephens' mount clearing the last jump with its rider holding his saddle above his head, having previously dispensed with his stirrup irons.

The afternoon ended with the Retreat Ceremony performed with total precision by the African Police Platoon. This splendid finale was a feature of the Police Mounted Sports for many years thereafter. It was to become one of the most treasured, impressive and unforgettable memories in the minds of those who stood reverently as the Last Post was played, and the simple notes of *Abide With Me*, rendered by a single trumpet, echoed around the ground as the sun sank rich and red behind the tall gum trees.

By October another of the strands linking the police with the military had been severed, when the last attestations as 'Troopers' appeared in Force Orders. Promotions and transfers were also featured: promotions for Detective Allum, Detective Sub Inspectors Barfoot and McCormick, Detective First Sergeant Oppenheim and First Sergeant Spink. As for transfers; Sergeant Sherren was by this time the member in charge at Beatrice, when his tennis commitments permitted. Sub Inspector Weller had moved from Nyamandhlovu (where, as a First Sergeant he had received a Commendation for 'painstaking investigations and tenacity of purpose' in a case involving 31 counts of Theft by Conversion), to Inyati. Lieutenant Flower had 'come in out of the cold' of Gwelo to be appointed Assistant Staff Officer at Police Headquarters, while 100 yards away Lieutenant Goodall was succeeded as Depot Chief Inspector by 'Ginger' Lardant.

Mention of the somewhat notorious Sam Weller brings to mind that when he went on long leave, someone unknown put pen to paper to produce 'Notes from Inyati'. The final paragraph reads: "Members of a certain office staff, when their manager was vacationing on the Continent, sent a telegram, reading: 'Trust you are enjoying your vacation; we are'".

And so to 1950, a year in which the Police literally sparkled in sports activities. Ron Trangmar had joined the Rhodesian team for the Empire Games in New Zealand, having the previous year established a new domestic record in the discus event. The Police Football Team won every trophy — the Challenge Cup, Austen Cup, League Championship Cup and Charity Cup; the first time any club had managed to take every trophy in one season. It would be churlish not to record the names of those who had achieved such outstanding results. They were:

B. Taylor, P. Ryan, D. Johnston (Vice Capt.), W. Buchanan (Capt.), R. Coop, J. Marnock, D. Clapham, F. Moore-Stevens, I. Tait, E. Inglis, T. Banister, A. Butler, R. Jennings, J. Shaugnessy, J. Jannaway, S. Reid, J. Hammond, D. Bester, S. Gibney, K. Rawson (Sec.), A. Simmonds, P. Rogers, J. Walker, D. Mallon. The Trainer was H. Levy and the Manager J. T Thompson.

Dennis 'Johnny' Johnston was an outstanding sportsman and was selected to captain the Rhodesian Football Team that same year (1950). Stationed at Concession and later Sipolilo, he used to come all the way to Salisbury to attend football practices but eventually, because of his quite remarkable mastery of African languages, was moved to the African Police Training School as an instructor. In 1951, he joined the police in Nyasaland, later became a civil servant and attained high office in the Ministry of Community and Social Development when the country became Malawi in 1964.

The next outstanding event in 1950 was the Police Display, which opened in sensational fashion with two horsemen galloping across the arena to 'carry' two tent pegs which, when held aloft revealed the Union Jack and the Police colours. There followed clowns, motor cycle tricks, a Musical Ride and, possibly the most remarkable and spectacular event, 'Kentucky' ridden by Sergeant Stephens cantering up to a paper screen in front of a bush jump and, without hesitation, jumping through it. This remarkable horse (and rider) then leaped through a hoop of petrol-soaked burning hessian. Afternoons such as this attracted virtually the entire Salisbury population and engendered incalculable goodwill for the Police — and Kentucky.

The Umtali Advertiser published an intriguing article dealing with the daily round of a district policeman. Whether the article did much to attract recruits must be open to doubt, especially when revealing that policemen were up well before six to groom their horses and clean motor cycles and vehicles. The reporter, obviously well primed for emphasis was laid on the extraneous duties of the police, went out with a trooper and an African constable on one of their monthly visits to all the European residents in the district, with the object of finding out what really happens on such patrols.

A motor vehicle accident was the first occurrence, with a need for some elementary first aid and the preparation of plans of the incident. Next was the investigation at a kraal of an arson case for which the witnesses had already been summonsed by an African constable. This was followed by visits to about 20 farms, at each of which the owners were interviewed and problems aired. The whole day took up nine hours and, no sooner had the trooper and reporter put their feet up to enjoy a beer, than a request came through to make an urgent delivery of serum to an outlying hospital.

The reporter ended the article with the words "It is certainly an exacting vocation". How exacting is perhaps open to some doubt when reading in The Outpost of another district, " Trooper Eric West is taking a short walk along the banks of the Umniati River — knowing his habits he will probably have one carrier carrying a dartboard and another carrying a crate of beer".

The year 1950 saw the retirement of Brigadier Ross on completion of 37 years' service. His, like his predecessor's, had been a difficult period in office but he had masterminded many changes and improvements and had added greatly to the efficiency of the Force. His appointment to Commander of the British Empire (CBE) on the day of his departure was a fitting tribute for long years of outstanding service.

Into his place, in December 1950, stepped Colonel 'Jim' Appleby who had joined the Police in 1919, been commissioned in 1924 and, since returning from Eritrea, had occupied various commands throughout the country. The appointment of Deputy Commissioner was filled by Lieutenant Colonel A.S. Hickman, MBE.

One other notable retirement during that year was Lieutenant Colonel F.W. Harrison, OBE, the Officer Commanding the CID since 1945. 'Fred' as he was universally known, had a very human touch about him and had shown not only the willingness, but a fine ability, to foster cooperation between the CID and all other branches of the Police. This was not as easy as it may sound. It is an established pattern in most uniformed services that one part or branch of the organisation becomes confrontational with another. This is generally just good-natured rivalry and nothing more. Certainly all ranks would unite against a common foe if any form of external pressure was to be exerted.

Harrison was succeeded by Lieutenant Colonel B.J. Price.

1950 could not be described as a particularly remarkable year. There were no instances of unrest and no significant increase in serious crime. In fact, the most unusual occurrence was probably the sending of a detachment of Police to Bechuanaland to support that country's police. At that time, the chieftainship of the Bamangwato tribe was under discussion and the possibility of trouble existed.

The main changes in 1950 were what might be called 'domestic' and affected the way in which policing was conducted.

One of the most important was a reallocation of duties in the two main urban areas. Instead of the peri-urban stations being responsible to the 'main' stations, they were given the status of full stations and thus able to operate independently. Another change of emphasis involved moving from fixed beat patrolling to what was known as the 'numerical beat system'. This required the patrolling policeman to make his point at scheduled times, but the route taken between points could be varied according to circumstances. The aim of this was, hopefully, to cause confusion in the minds of those wrongdoers who thought they could predict the movements of the police. Finally, filtering truck patrols were introduced whereby a patrol of several men would be dropped at a certain point and required to work their way through a particular area before being picked up and moved elsewhere.

In the rural areas, the improvements in communications and particularly telephones did away with the need for the regular visits described earlier on by the reporter from *The Umtali Advertiser*. In their place, police districts were divided into sections, a patrol target introduced, and each section regularly patrolled.

Such, in very broad outline, and with the expansion of the decentralisation measures mentioned earlier — namely the creation of additional provinces and the resultant delegation of responsibility from Police Headquarters to the new officers commanding — were the systems operating as the Police moved on further into the 50s.

## Chapter Thirty-Nine

## THE APPLEBY YEARS

1951 — 1958. Federation — Development of Technical expertise –Mtoko and Reserve patrolling — River rescues — Lock-Ups — Housebreakings in Mrewa — Rhodes Centenary — Urban experiences — Coronation — Kenya attachments — Nyasaland contingent — Retirement of Appleby.

The years from 1951 to 1958 were years of consolidation in the Force. They were difficult years for the expansion of the Police did not keep pace with that of the country. There was an ever present need to conserve money, even though successive annual budgets were totally inadequate; while the establishment, despite often equating with the strength, was totally insufficient to meet the standards of policing that the Commissioner thought necessary and which the public had learned to expect.

Of course, many of the reasons behind the paucity of funds could be laid squarely at the door of 'Federation'. Huggins was an enthusiastic proponent of some means being found of bringing together Northern and Southern Rhodesia, arguing that in unity would lie strength. The combined territories, he maintained, would become an economic powerhouse, investment would flow in, the rich would become richer and, if one may be cynical, the poor less poor. The concepts of federation, or confederation or amalgamation had been bruited about as far back as 1948 and various conferences were held in the following years, culminating in the Victoria Falls Conference of 1951 and the final dotting of the i's and crossing of the t's in January 1953.

Of course there were numerous cross-currents swirling around as the Federation was being born. One was the insistence by the British in particular that Nyasaland — very much a lame duck in Central Africa — be a part of the concept. Another was the fear that the Rhodesias, and particularly the southernmost, might be dragged into the 'New Look' South Africa. At this time the Nationalist Party held sway from the Limpopo south to the Cape and had come to power in 1948 on the ticket of racial segregation and white supremacy; *apartheid* as it came to be known.

However, the overriding problem which would eventually see the demise of the Federation, was racial conflict, and this, initially at any rate, was over the qualifications for the franchise

In 1951 however, much of that was in the future. Southern Rhodesia was a peaceful, relatively law-abiding country, riding the crest of a wave of immigration, increasing prosperity and unrivaled opportunities. As an example of this expansion, Robert Blake, in his A History of Rhodesia, mentions that in 1946 the European population was 82,000. In 1951 it had increased by 53,000 and in 1960 it stood at 223,000. To quote his words, "By 1950, there were more post-war immigrants among white adults than persons born in the country or settled there before the war. They were nearly all English-speaking."

The Reports of the Commissioner of Police for this period — 1951 to 1958 — invariably open with the words, "The year under review was free from internal disorder and unrest." And indeed, apart from fairly regular visits by police contingents to Bechuanaland and once each to Nyasaland and Northern Rhodesia, plus the occasional rumblings in the vast Wankie compounds, things stayed comparatively calm and apparently peaceful during what could almost be called a 'golden age'. Only 1956 cast a slight shadow over the period and the problems of that year will be looked at a little later.

Taking advantage of this relative tranquillity, the Force made every effort to improve both its service to the public and its professionalism. Modifications and improvements to the syllabi at both the European and African Training Depots were a regular feature. For European recruits, vernacular language courses were introduced and various incentives offered for linguistic proficiency. The training of police reservists became an established feature and every effort was directed to making their courses as interesting and informative as possible. Then, with a view to broadening the professional knowledge and attitudes within the regular Force, members were sent to study Fingerprint Methods and Detective Work and Procedures with the West Riding Constabulary in Yorkshire.

Another member attended the British Army Veterinary and Remount Centre so that the Mounted Unit, which was about to be formed would benefit from the up-to-date methods being used in Britain.

Two members of the Instructional Staff attended physical training courses at the South African Police Training College in Pretoria, another couple were sent on drill and musketry courses at the Guards Depot in Pirbright, England, and yet another attended a Motor Transport Course at the Metropolitan Police Driving School, Hendon.

With a discerning eye as to future crime patterns, a member of the Musketry Staff spent two months in Pretoria, studying Firearms Identification and microscopical work with South African Police experts. Soon afterwards, and with the purchase of a comparison microscope, the Police were able to upgrade and improve their presentation of ballistics evidence to the courts.

Despite the expansion taking place in towns and rural areas throughout the country, and the unpleasant duty of having to move Africans from their ancestral homes to other areas (making way for mining and other developments and in observance of the requirements of the Land Apportionment Act), there was still an interesting life available for the man who chose, or was summarily transferred to, a rural police station.

For example, early in 1951 the police at Mtoko put to flight a pride of eight lions that were within easy walking distance of their camp and, only 40 miles away from the same station, 14 elephants were shot; all this within a 10 day period. The local Methodist Minister was troubled virtually every night by leopards and by February had shot no less than 51. Whilst these figures might seem to indicate a reckless and uncaring attitude to wild life, it must be understood that 877 cattle had been killed the previous year by marauding lions and hyenas, whilst the damage to crops by elephant was unending..

However the real joy of district life, apart from sundowners on the stoep, was undoubtedly a Reserve Patrol. An unknown but keenly observant policeman, writing in the February 1951 The Outpost, describes parts of a two months' patrol from Nkai into the Shangani Reserve: "I have on occasion ridden 40 miles without seeing a living soul and, unless an interest is taken in the natural surroundings, boredom ensues. It was during one of these periods that I first encountered the 'Honey Guides.' I had noticed that two small brown birds (they are usually found in pairs) had for some minutes been following the patrol. These birds seemed to be very excited about something, and kept flying from tree to tree, constantly twittering. On asking the African detail what was worrying the birds, I was informed that they had found a wild bees' nest and were trying to attract us to it. By following these birds for about half a mile we found a hive of wild bees built beneath two large rocks and, with the aid of a small but smoky fire, we were eventually able to supplement our diet with honey. Needless to say, we did not get away without cost as bees do not take kindly to the pillage of their nest, but what is the sting of a few bees to the satisfaction of the ultimate reward? Before leaving with our spoils, the African detail very reverently placed a large piece of honeycomb in a tree for our two little guides, explaining that unless this were done these birds would in future lead us to a lion or a snake instead of honey." The patrolling policeman goes on to describe the swamp-like area known as Kaforafora or 'Many Rivers' where water gushes upwards from subterranean springs. From there he journeys to the Kana Valley, the home of the Batonga (Batonka), and gives a fascinating description of this primitive but picturesque tribe.

Yet another aspect of district life, particularly in the Fort Victoria area, involved rescue attempts in flooding rivers. In the early 50s, in fact well into the days of the Federation, it was the rule rather than the exception for district-based members of the Force to receive commendations from the Commissioner for their efforts to save life, when a gentle, softly-flowing river, or even a long length of sand snaking through the bush, was transformed in minutes into a raging, savage cataract of water.

Such was the case in January 1952 when the Devuli rose to become a wide, tempestuous river, studded with trees and debris, and swept five Africans off a narrow bridge between Bikita and Chipinga. Three were drowned immediately but the other two managed to catch hold of the branches of a tree sticking up above the waters and held on grimly. The Bikita Police were alerted and Second Sergeant John Sowter hurried to the scene. Rescue was impossible without a boat, so Sowter set to work with old drums, poles and ropes to make a raft which could be moored to the shore and steered to the tree. He remained at the scene right through the night but was saved having to launch his ramshackle craft by the arrival the next morning of a local resident with a small boat. The two men, aided by a third on the bank upstream, managed to steer their craft to the tree and get the two stranded natives (and themselves) hauled back to safety.

Stories such as this were commonplace, but more often than not there was no boat available and the policeman had to tie the rope round his waist and swim to the tree or island where the flood victims were huddled. A very similar situation, though the circumstances were far more dangerous and frightening, occurred some years later in the flooding Shashe river near the Makaholi Experimental Station. Three policemen were concerned in a dramatic rescue of two teen-aged African children and, for their efforts, each was awarded the British Empire Medal for Gallantry. They were Constable John Thatcher, African Constable Jaconiah Ngwenya and Police Reservist Harold Ward.

Yet another aspect of District Police life was the secondary function of many members-in-charge as "Lock-up Keepers." (Prisons had, by then, become a Federal responsibility). Very broadly, this meant the administration of a small jail in the absence of either or both a prison, and prison warders. Barry Thomas, who retired as a chief inspector in 1972, recalls that as long as the Native Commissioner's requirement for manpower was well cared for, the disposition of surplus convict labour was left to the Police who, naturally and as second priority, made sure that the police camp was spick-and-span and after that, that government property and sporting facilities were adequately maintained.

It was often the practice to have one or two 'tame bandits' working without supervision in the garden of the police married quarters and nothing was thought of having one's children playing alongside convicts who had been sentenced for culpable homicide after a drunken brawl. Barry's father-in-law, visiting from England, was totally astonished when, walking past the lock-up one day, a cell door opened and out stepped a prisoner to get himself a drink from a nearby tap. Having drunk, he returned to his cell, closing the door after him.

On yet another occasion a truck came to collect the convicts at the end of the day. They all climbed on the back together with their guard, who had passed the afternoon sitting in the shade of a tree while keeping an eye on his charges. As the truck was about to move off, one of the convicts shouted, jumped from the back and ran to the tree, where he collected the guard's rifle, returned to the truck and handed it up to his escort.

One final tale concerned the annual football match between the Police and the staff of the Native Department. The police were short of a goalkeeper but knew that in the jail was a man of exceptional talent who was due for release on the day before the match. Being a keen sportsman and without any pressure exerted, he volunteered to stay 'in' for another night to enable him to play for the Police.

These recollections will bring nods of nostalgia to those serving in those days and, doubtless, gasps of horror from present-day policemen, but the African can always be relied upon to bring the inexplicable, the entertaining and unusual into a policeman's life. If this seems condescending or paternalistic — and perhaps is not unique to this part of the continent or the world at large, it does serve to illustrate the generally peaceful manner in which life flowed in the rural areas many years ago.

In the early 50s a series of housebreakings occurred in the Mrewa area. All carried the same signature' in that the thefts occurred from grain huts, and all involved the taking of cash that had been well concealed, as was local custom, beneath the grain. The extraordinary aspect of the story was that the culprit entered only those huts in which cash had been stashed.

Eventually a 20-year-old African was arrested and quite readily admitted his involvement, even mentioning one theft of which the police knew nothing. When asked how he could unerringly go to a hut in which money was hidden, he replied, "because of my magic two-shilling piece." Apparently he would sneak through a kraal holding his 'magic' coin and it would 'jump' whenever he passed a hut that was ripe for picking. The police decided to put this extraordinary story to the test and the headman volunteered his own hut in which thirty pounds lay concealed. The young accused walked straight to the correct hut and, when asked if he knew how much cash was inside replied without hesitation, "Thirty Pounds." When he was searched, a two-shilling piece with a yellow mark upon it was found. Magic or not, he was handed down a sentence of four years with hard labour.

The Town Police too, had their interesting moments. John Walton, who joined in 1953, was among a large group of recruits sent to assist at the Rhodes Centenary Exhibition in Bulawayo, and one evening found himself standing very close to the Queen Mother and Princess Margaret who were acknowledging the crowd in Centenary Park after a symphony concert. The Queen Mother apparently turned to her preoccupied grand-daughter and said to her "Why don't you smile?" Little was known at that time of the budding — and soon to be extinguished — romance between Princess Margaret and Group Captain Peter Townsend.

Walton, who was to spend the majority of his three years' service in Bulawayo, also recalls seeing an African jumping from a moving bus, stumbling, falling and having the rear wheel go over his head. The man stood up and walked away. Walton had him called back, took down all the tribal details from the man's situpa and then, despite a request to be allowed to go on his way, took the man to the hospital in the police truck. He died the following day and the subsequent post-mortem showed a two-inch wide crack across the top of his skull. He had lived for 12 hours after the accident.

'Buddy' Deetlefs was another town (and later Dog Section) policeman who has memories of his days in Salisbury Urban. He recalls a well-known lady of 'easy virtue' who was known — by reputation — to most urban policemen in the 50s and 60s. This lady took a monstrous delight in hailing young, fresh-out-of-Depot constables with a hearty "Good evening, Officer" or, when ignored, pursuing the reddening constable with "Oh, so you don't know me tonight, officer" and "Didn't you enjoy yourself last night?' It was said of — let us call her — Jenny, a prostitute of mixed lineage and who was described as "making Dracula look extremely beautiful" that she actually preferred drink to men. Certain it was that as evening became night Jenny moved from the moderately sober to wildly drunk and disorderly, and must surely have held some sort of record for having been arrested and paying admissions of guilt. One story, that loses nothing in the telling, records Jenny being beaten up by her 'husband' on the sidewalk outside the Salisbury Charge Office. The story goes that Detective Constable George Daniel, a very powerful and athletic Mauritian, who spoke in fractured but picturesque English and had been a lifeguard in South Africa, witnessed what was happening, jumped from a first floor window and, with one fearful blow, laid the assailant flat.

The year 1953 was a busy and varied one for the Police.

A brief mention has already been made of the Rhodes Centenary Exhibition, an event attended by Her Majesty, Queen Elizabeth, the Queen Mother; but, in addition to that, an 18-strong, mounted contingent of the B.S.A. Police was included in the Coronation Procession through London. The Central Africa Federation officially came into being during that year. A strong force was sent to Nyasaland to help maintain law and order in that Protectorate, and five men were chosen for secondment to the Kenya Police where a revolt, accompanied by appalling atrocities, was taking place against the British Colonial Government. Certain of these matters can be dismissed in a few words; others require some additional detail. All, in one way or another, enhanced the name and reputation of the Force.

It is not a part of this history to detail the Rhodes Centenary Exhibition in Bulawayo. Nevertheless, the sheer logistics of transforming a barren 50-acre site on the outskirts of the city into a vast exhibition centre with pavilions, roads, and even a 3000 seat theatre, (which bore a distinct resemblance to a refrigerator in the Bulawayo winter), was no mean undertaking.

Having prepared the ground, so to speak, to then attract to that small city in Central Africa not only royalty, but international exhibitors and world famous artists, as well as thousands of visitors, speaks volumes for the dedication and drive of the organizers. As for the Police, they had their own Police Station within the Grounds and provided, not only the guards for valuable exhibits, but also the mounted and motor cycle escorts for the many dignitaries who attended.

But before the pomp and splendour of the Exhibition, there had been considerably more — much more — of the same, when the BSA Police took part in the Coronation Day Parade in London.

The men chosen to represent the Force were — Major G.S.A. Rolfe; Lieut S.V. Brewer; Sub-Inspectors G.G. Woodgate, J.L. Wordsworth, R.C. John, E.D. Van Sittert, W.J. Dickson and E.J. Sheriff; Det. Sub-Inspector B.S. Cowling, Farrier Sub-Inspector J.B. Robertson, First Sergeant J.R. Peters, Second Sergeants W.P. Howard, D.H. Sanderson, L.R. Gearing, H.T. Waddington and R.G.E. Gardner; and Constables J.E. Bond and H.R. Wheeler.

Many of this select company must have wondered whether it was all worthwhile as they laboured through eight weeks of intensive training in Depot. Equitation was of course the paramount discipline, but close behind was physical training, foot drill and 'stables'. Last, but by no means least, came the grind and drudgery of 'spit and polish'. Then it was off to England and to the Guards Depot at Pirbright. There it was that the incalculable value of having a 'servant' to assist with the kit cleaning and polishing, the washing and ironing, the scrubbing of floors and the preparation of tea, was forcibly brought home.

Eventually the move was made to tented accommodation in Kensington Gardens and the contingent became acquainted with their horses, all well trained and easy to ride, and borrowed from the

West Riding, Liverpool, Birmingham and Metropolitan Police mounted branches. Training was now split up so that Rolfe and Brewer were in the Commonwealth Escort to the Queen; Robertson and Wheeler rode with the Prime Minister of Southern Rhodesia, and the remaining 14 were mounted behind the Southern Rhodesia Military Forces.

Although Coronation Day was generally grey and overcast with an intermittent drizzle, the sheer splendour and unbelievable pomp of the occasion was breathtaking. Brian Cowling wrote "many lumps were in our throats, how highly honoured we were to be in London on such an occasion as this, representing the B.S.A.P. and upholding all its traditions. The hundreds and thousands of people, wildly cheering, shouting and waving flags from every conceivable point of advantage along the whole route, was something we had not thought possible."

The following day saw the Police marching with the Commonwealth Contingents to Buckingham Palace where, after an inspection by the Queen and the Duke of Edinburgh, contingent commanders received the members' medals.

The remaining days were spent in relaxation; visits to families as well as organized tours, with a military overtone, to Earls Court, the Spithead Review and Bognor Regis. The contingent covered itself with glory and proved exemplary ambassadors for their country and their Force.

In October 1954, six members were selected for attachment to the Kenya Police. At this time the Mau Mau terrorist organization, which had started in late 1952, had reached its savage climax and experienced investigators were required to assist the over-burdened local Force. Detective First Sergeant Colbourne; Detective Second Sergeants Sandall and Denley, and Second Sergeants Bremner, Bell and Gardner were chosen and, in company with members of other Police Forces, were to spend several months away from their homes as they worked from Nairobi and other areas of Kenya.

One cannot help but think that Ron Gardner, who had also been a member of the Coronation Contingent, was either singularly honoured or completely unwanted at home.

Ken Flower, by now a captain, led the small contingent, mainly of the Mounted Troop, called in to assist the Nyasaland Police in August 1953. The duties involved were essentially what might be expected in a territory racked by unrest; clearing road blocks, filling in ditches, arresting ringleaders, tax collecting (as a counter to civil disobedience), general patrolling and even quelling a riot. During this latter, at Domasi, it was necessary to use firearms, and two rioters were shot and killed. Perhaps it should be added that the Northern Rhodesia and Tanganyika police provided assistance as well.

At the end of the outbreak, when the rule of law had once more been established, a number of members were left behind to help the Nyasaland Police to form a Mobile Force. The members who were responsible for training this Force were led by Staff Second Sergeant Neil 'Smudge' Smith, and comprised Constables Crahart, Drew, Grant, Hughes and Williamson. They were given 'rapid' promotion, to Inspector in the case of Smith and to Assistant Inspectors, the other five. Redvers Crahart chronicled his experiences over the next six months, when each member took over a platoon of Africans, mainly ex-members of the Kings African Rifles, and taught riot drill, musketry and parade drill, whilst at the same time instilling a regime of physical fitness with route marches and gymnastics. However, reading between the lines, the social life went with a distinct swing, from the early days in the hotel to partying with local families and at the Zomba Club.

Eventually the six returned to the Salisbury Depot, not only financially better off, for Colonial pay rates were somewhat higher than those for second year constables, but also showing the sartorial elegance of their recent past with black berets, the appropriate badges of rank and black swagger sticks. The then Depot Chief Inspector, Bill Gilfillan, who — along with many others — had all but forgotten these six, was speechless, for one of the few times in his career.

At the end of 1953, Brigadier Appleby effectively relinquished his command. He was a man who did not seek the limelight, but rather concentrated on improving the efficiency and specialist functions of the Force. He instituted a system of recording crime statistics that was incredibly detailed — some said too much so. He also examined and improved the intelligence and security systems operating in the Force, and managed to upgrade and modernize the radio communications network. For most of his three years as Commissioner, he had to contend with the parsimonious policies of the government, or rather governments for, surely, with the Federal Legislature and its own army of civil servants, as well as the territorial authorities, the three countries comprising the Federation must have possessed the most top-heavy, unwieldy, expensive, though generally efficient, of administrative structures.

## Chapter Forty

## CHARACTERS — GOOD, BAD, INDIFFERENT

*Characters. Hickman — Giles — De Lorme — Maskell — Castell-Castell —
Watson — Buchanan — Buckley — Weller — Lloyd — Roper-Cooke — Hawke —
Weston — Winchcombe — Bulley — Somney, and others*

It is time now to look at some of the police characters of the 50s and glance to the progress of those introduced in earlier chapters. Let it be said at the outset that by no means all of these characters could be classed as angelic; some possessed some very rough edges.

The previous chapter concluded with the retirement of Brigadier Appleby. His successor was, in many ways, a man who would have thrived as a public relations officer, even perhaps a journalist, (for he was both a poet and prolific writer); most certainly did he succeed as an author. Arthur Selwyn Hickman was a Cornishman (and excessively proud of it) who came to Southern Rhodesia in 1924, passed the promotion examination to Lieutenant four years later (by which time he was a corporal), and was confirmed in that rank in 1928. Despite the somewhat severe grilling he endured at the hands of the Mundy Commission, (Chapter 36), he was essentially a kind and sympathetic man who always had the welfare of the members foremost in his mind. He was all but wedded to the history and traditions of the Force in which he was so proud to serve, and one wonders whether the Mundy recommendation on retaining military ranks was due to his vehement pleading .

Perhaps one of the now least known yet most impressive legacies of Hickman's interests is the tranquil and evocative Police Memorial Bay in the Anglican Cathedral Cloisters in Salisbury. The Bay was opened in July 1953 and it is very pertinent now, nearly 50 years later, to recall Hickman's address on that day: "One of the characteristics of the British South Africa Police is that of fellowship — a bond which exists between present and past members of the Force, and a bond which is not broken by death. So we hold in honoured and undying memory all our comrades — both European and African — who have passed on, their duty well done, and it has been our wish to commemorate in a lasting and tangible form all those who have died, and this whether their deaths have taken place whilst serving in our ranks, or after they have left us."

Hickman went on to stress the non-denominational, non-racial concept of the Bay and recited the units whose members would be commemorated in the precincts. He finished: "….we shall not allow ourselves to forget that the true memorial of the British South Africa Police can never lie in work made by the hands of man. It has been built upon sure foundations laid by those who have gone before us, from the earliest days of the Colony. And it is enshrined in that tradition of Service to the community as a whole — a tradition of which we are proud, and which it will be our duty to hand on, untarnished, to those who follow us down the years to come."

During his time as Commissioner, June 1954 to November 1955, a great number of singular personalities joined, served in and retired from the Police.

Two of the best known and respected were Cyril Giles and Claude de Lorme, both staff inspectors and both of whom retired in 1954 within a few months of each other.

Giles had attested in 1932 and six years later transferred to Depot where he would spend the remaining 14 years of his service in the African Police Training School (APTS). Giles' forte was his intimate knowledge and understanding of the African. He spoke Chishona, Sindebele and Chinyanja so fluently that it was said that if he conversed with Africans who could not see to whom they were speaking, for example from inside to outside a room, the Africans would be fully convinced they were chatting to one of their own kind.

It was not only in language and customs that Giles shone, he was also keenly aware of the problems, needs and aspirations of his charges. So it was that during his years in charge at the APTS there came into being the African Police Benevolent Fund, Kaffir Beer Canteens and Dry Canteens. The latter were basically small shops selling at the cheapest possible price the necessities for their particular customers — soap, polish, dusters, other cleaning materials and, doubtless too, such soft drinks and ready foods as were available in those days.

Claude de Lorme, or Roland Claude de Lorme to give his full names, served for 23 years from 1930, and spent the whole of that time as a valued and highly regarded instructor in the Depot. Claude, apart from being immaculately presented in uniform, was a fitness fanatic and keenly interested in sports and physical training. He excelled at gymnastics, hurdling and swimming, trained the Police Football Team in 1948 — 1949 and, with his natural sense of humour and almost happy-go-lucky personality, became a firm favourite with the crowds when acting as a clown at the Mounted Sports. There are still those around who recall his tearing his cap from his head, and jumping on it after being subjected to the appalling drill of one of the post-war recruit squads. It may well have been one of those squads that, as was customary at the end of the recruits' course, presented Claude with an exceedingly comfortable tubular steel and green upholstered chair. It was several years later that a visitor to the de Lorme household commented, "Isn't that one of the chairs from The Lounge Tea Room?" That establishment, situated opposite a leading department store at the junction of First Street and Baker Avenue, has long since vanished from the capital's skyline, but what a surprise for the management had they located their missing chair in the Police Depot.

The early months of 1952 had seen a number of what were known as 'assumptions of command' and promotions. Lieutenant Colonel Harold Jackson had taken over the command of the CID and was destined to step into Colonel Hickman's shoes when the latter retired in November 1955. Further down the line, promotion to Sub Inspector had come to, among others, John Pestell, Arthur Weston, and Butch Buckley; later the same year, Peter Sherren achieved a like rank. The following year witnessed Lieutenant Frank Barfoot attaining Superintendent and, a little later Ken Flower, James Spink and Dick Parry followed suit in the uniformed ranks, whilst in the CID Syd Bristow became a Detective Sub Inspector.

Karl Maskell was another of the characters that made the B.S.A.P the uniquely distinctive Force that it was. Karl was a 'district man' through and through but he was also a very capable writer. Mention has already been made of patrolling in a bush environment, yet the following description, taken from Maskell's tale of a patrol in the Sabi Valley, on Riding Horse (RH) 'Exeter', is sufficient to bring waves of nostalgia to one-time members of the Police, Native Affairs, or others whose work took them out and beyond the bustle, grime and cacophony of the cities.

After describing the end of the day, when he is sitting quietly and peacefully with his African Police, close to a small pool at which a solitary impala doe has been drinking, Maskell continue s— "The sun sank below the black outline of the bush about us, a dim twilight hovered for a shade of time, then night settled over the still bush all around. The animals had been attended to, the camp fires were giving out their friendly glow, and another day was finished. Very soon the cicadas boomed out, other insects started their squeaks, cheeps and chirrupings, and by the time the large silvery moon had risen in the starry heavens above and flooded the surrounding bush in a soft mantle of moonlight, all about us was that sonorous orchestral lullaby of the night, which those who have slept under the stars in remote Rhodesian bush know so well. To this was added the periodical "yap-yap" of a prowling jackal, and the blowings of the animals as they munched the grass at their feet."

Another District policeman who was a legend while still in the Force was Dennis Masslyn Castell-Castell. Dennis joined in 1953 and left — probably to the relief of many members-in-charge — in 1970. As with any legend, the stories become more extravagant with each telling.

Jack Bacon, for example, remembers an evening in Depot when Castell and his 'half section', John Spandley, (discharged after six months' service as unsuitable) ran amok in the single quarters trying to 'gun down' one of the drill instructors, Gerry Winchcombe. No less than a dozen shots were fired as Winchcombe fled around the various blocks before eventually taking cover in somebody's cupboard.

There seemed little doubt that the two 'gunmen' knew exactly where he was, because they entered the correct room and fired a shot that tore through a lance and chipped off part of a saddle.

Winchcombe lived on to train many more recruits and eventually to retire on pension, and spend the rest of his life in Southern Spain. Jack Bacon, being strictly fair to the memory of a deceased colleague, later opined that, in the incident described above, Spandley was probably the more aggressive of the two.

Castell, also known as 'Pom Pom', was an authority on guns and ammunition and a more than passable shot. Trevor Compton recalls returning from an anti-poaching patrol at dusk when a large buck was illuminated in the lights of the Land-rover. Castell was out of the truck, shot the animal with his .303, and then discovered that the buck was a roan antelope. Undeterred, Castell commented that without its skin, feet and head — venison is venison.  On another occasion, again with Trevor in the passenger seat, a huge kudu stepped into the headlights and received an identical coup de grace as had the roan antelope. The situation was slightly complicated by the fact that the two were in uniform, the vehicle belonged to Castell, and it was the closed season.  However, and to use again that word 'undeterred', Castell broke a headlight glass, smeared blood on his vehicle, and claimed that as the animal had stepped in front of the truck, he had to put it out of its misery. In Gwelo that month, messing averaged only two shillings and seven pence a meal.

It was in the same town (City status was conferred in 1971) that Castell sported his personal bright green Land-rover with two jerry cans attached to the front marked 'Gin' and 'Tonic' and a piece of duiker fur around the keyhole, so that it could be found at night.  He was also the owner of a dog that went by the highly decorative name of 'Sludge Guts'. Dennis lacked a finger on one hand — the result of picking up a puff adder he assumed he had killed with a rock.

Finally and some years later, so Peter Robinson recalls, the Force Musketry Championships were taking place and the Commissioner was present when Castell, (recently demoted back to constable), approached him and commented that they both had something in common. The Commissioner gently inquired what that could be, to which Castell replied, "We have both gone as far as we can in this Police Force."

Chief Inspector William 'Paddy' Watson was another district man whose name is forever set down in police history. An example of his fine descriptive writing and very individualistic style has already appeared in Chapter 35, but he became a regular and humorous writer for Outpost under the nom-de-plume 'Wobbly', under which name he created the character Scrimshank-Wick. Watson was not just an excellent policeman and a fine writer, he was also one of the most highly legally-qualified members of the Police. At successive six-monthly sittings, he passed both Parts of the Civil Service Lower Law examinations and also Parts I and II of the Higher Law examinations. A little later in his service, at Norton, Watson undertook the studies that eventually led to his obtaining a Bachelor of Laws degree from London University. He had a remarkable facility to make the law, often a dry and involved subject, into an amusing and eminently readable mnemonic.

To the tune of '*Abdul a Bul Bul Amir*', he described the procedure to be followed when an appeal is noted in a civil case. Then, turning to the principle remedies available for damage caused by animals, and when those remedies are not available, he produced five verses, the first three of which read:

*The Actio Pauperies is*
*For damage done by animals*
*Where he was bit or injured thus*
*The injured party has a claim*
*Where beasts or dogs or tame white mice*
*Which bite from some quaint inward vice,*
*Contrary to their natural way –*
*Their owners will be made to pay*
*But remedy will not avail*
*If plaintiff steps on doggy's tail*
*And doggy bites from sheer alarms*
*(See case of Hoffman versus Harmse)*

*The injured person must have been*
*Lawfully upon the scene*
*In circs where no one is to blame*
*Else claim will not be worth a cuss.*

*Adiles Edict may be filed*
*Only 'gainst those whose beasts are wild*
*(In public places, loose and unchained)*
*Which injure, costs then may be claimed*

The Police Football Teams of the 50s provided a number of men whose qualities extended beyond their abilities with a soccer ball. Buck Buchanan, and Butch Buckley dominated the sporting scene in Salisbury Police circles for many years; both excelled with any sort of ball, cricket and water polo in particular, and both were to captain various police sporting teams and gain representative 'colours' for their province or country.

Stories are told that one of the two, 'Buck' or 'Butch', was responsible for shooting out the clock in the Regimental Institute in Depot one night. On another occasion the same pair were allegedly behind the appearance of a blackened and naked figure careering through the grounds of the Officers' Mess during a highly respectable Dining-In Night. Of such stories are traditions — and characters made.

Keith Rawson was another great personality. A superb goalkeeper and a champion of his men, he was outspoken to a degree that, sadly, probably delayed the promotion to commissioned rank he so richly deserved. It was apparently his .303 rifle, loaded by Basil Taylor, which was used in the incident mentioned above.

When, as happened very quickly, the Orderly Corporal, one Peter Brownbridge, came to inspect all the recruits' rifles, he sniffed the offending barrel and proclaimed with a completely straight face, "well, this one hasn't been fired."

Sam Weller, or to give his full names, James Edwin Luyt Weller, had become something of a legend in Matabeleland since his transfer to that Province in 1942. He had commanded several district police stations and established a reputation for running a 'very tight ship'. It was not unusual for a young man straight from Depot to arrive at one of Weller's stations and find himself setting off on a two or three week horse patrol the following morning. Weller's standards of discipline were also not for the faint-hearted and drove many a less robust personality to leave the Force altogether, seek transfer or, as in the case of Constable Nigel Argyle, into a chronic condition of stomach ulcers. Of Weller, who became Depot Chief Inspector in 1956, the following verse from the *Kenya Police Review* might well have applied:

> *O Lord above, send down a dove*
> *With wings as sharp as a razor,*
> *To cut the throat of the \*\*\*\* bloke*
> *They call our Sergeant Major.*

For all that Sam was a fine policeman and those who stood up to him found, not only that they learned a tremendous amount of practical policing, but also that the man had a gentle and kindly side to his nature. It just had to be found.

Having mentioned Nigel Argyle it must be said to his credit that, after leaving the tender care of Sam, he became a most competent saddler under the far more tender care and tuition of Chief Inspector Horace Jennings, the Saddlers being conveniently situated near the Depot Camp Hospital. Leaving the police Nigel all but cornered the Salisbury onion and tomato markets with his "Nijo Products" and rewarded his labour by flying them all to the Victoria Falls.

Lofty Lloyd was another who carved his own particular niche in the Police — and, as mentioned in an earlier chapter — wrote a book about it afterwards. After the abortive attempt to reach North Africa, 'Lofty' settled down as a more or less model district policeman, though he was to make a habit of conducting farming operations within the district stations to which he was posted — with the exception of Miami, where he started mining for mica.

Another well-known district policeman who, because of his particular abilities and enthusiasms, had far more transfers than was strictly necessary, was Trevor Reed. Trevor retired as a chief inspector in 1956 to start one of Salisbury's finest garden nurseries in Marlborough. He left behind numerous police camps which had been lovingly landscaped and turned into flourishing gardens by his green fingers (and no doubt, convict labour). But his most outstanding memorials must be the Police Golf Course and the Depot Sports Grounds. Many an older policeman will recall those early morning rides alongside the newly grassed fairways, to be suddenly overtaken by the zealous figure of Trevor, hunched low over the handlebars of a furiously driven Matchless motor cycle, bound for borehole or bunker.

There were many more that stamped their names indelibly into the traditions and history of the BSA Police. 'Sam' Brewer, who had a penchant for racing cars: Henry Roper-Cooke, a superb rifle shot and elegant horseman who retired to run the Enkeldorn Hotel with its 'cell' in the bar for persons lacking a passport to enter the 'Principality'. There was John Dolby, who managed to 'write off' a brand new Highway Patrol car, and whose language was so punctuated with swear-words that his colleagues required him to keep a jar into which a fine was placed every time he transgressed. Peter Hawke, a popular and respected warrant officer who did much to progress the Police Reserve and must surely rank among the most able raconteurs of amusing stories the Force has ever known. We have already met 'Gerry' Winchcombe, hiding in a cupboard, but of whom Colonel Lombard wrote after the 1957 Police Mounted Sports: "In this event (a jumping competition) it is no exaggeration to say that Lancer galloped flat out around the course, and at times seemed to have wings; and Sergeant Winchcombe, although riding faster than accuracy, or even safety, demanded, did not in fact lose control."

Arthur Weston; John Alexander Somney; Clive Bulley; Don McGovern and many, many more coloured the canvas of the 50s. These were the names that brought smiles and laughter — sometimes consternation — and that conjured up stories; these were the personalities that gave the BSAP character and who established the Force as not only a team, but a collection of fine individuals as well.

But it is time to return to the history proper and to the final years of the 50s.

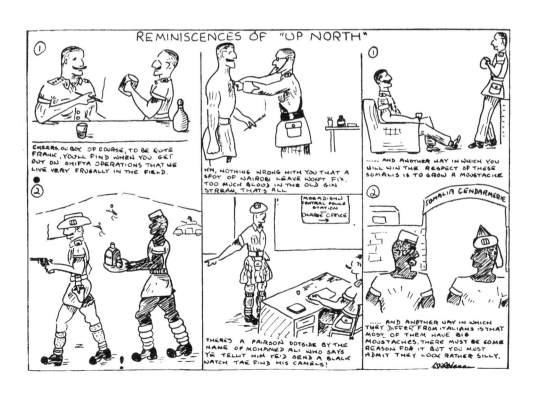

## Chapter Forty-One

## THE SHAPE OF THINGS TO COME

*Queen Mother become Honorary Commissioner — the late 50s — Highway Patrol — Police Reserve developments — New Corps Buildings — Jackson becomes Commissioner — Special Commendations — Riots in Salisbury — BSAP to Copperbelt — Kariba Dam — Polio — Band Sash — Trangmar becomes Depot Chief Inspector — Alford investigates.*

On 12 February 1954, it was announced that Her Majesty, Queen Elizabeth, the Queen Mother had been pleased to assume the appointment of Honorary Commissioner of the British South Africa Police.

Linked to this appointment was a message of loyalty to Her Majesty, Queen Elizabeth the Second, a reply expressing her thanks and delight, and the following response from the Queen Mother:

"I thank you most warmly for the message which I have received from you today. I have vivid memories of the smartness and efficiency of the B.S.A.Police on my visit to Southern Rhodesia and it has given me particular pleasure, therefore, to be able to accept the appointment of Honorary Commissioner. I would be grateful if you would convey to all ranks my best wishes and my hope that I may have the opportunity of visiting them again in the not too distant future."

The full texts of the messages were contained in a Special Force Order, No. 112 dated 18 February 1954.

By 1955, the Salisbury Police Town Branch, CID and others had moved their offices from 'Old' Shell House in Baker Avenue into the new, large and expansive Police Station on Railway Avenue. In addition a fine new block of accommodation had been erected in Fife Avenue, close to the Depot, for the town policemen and a comprehensive programme of electrification, extensions, and additional housing for African Police, had been embarked upon throughout the country. Certain of this work fell to contractors, some to the Public Works Department and the Native Engineering Department, a great deal to the Police Pioneer Section which was prepared, perhaps compelled would be more appropriate, to build where contractors were disinclined to operate. Considering that the European establishment had increased from 2231 in 1950 to 4449 in 1955, and the African from 2652 to 3696 over the same period, it is not difficult to imagine the cramped living conditions at police camps nor, indeed, the frustration of successive Commissioners as they battled to prise funds from the Government. The new building programme, though seemingly generous, was just a drop in the ocean of need that had been accumulating for years.

Annual Reports for year after year had commented upon the incidence of road accidents throughout the Colony. Again, it is of interest to compare the years 1950 and 1955. In the former, there were 7384 (an increase of 259% on 1946.) and, in the latter, 13 686, an average of 37 accidents a day. It was decided that even though the majority of accidents occurred in the urban areas, it was imperative to tackle the generally more serious accidents which occurred on the inter-city highways. Most of these had speed as the common and predominant factor, so an investment was made in a number of high-powered saloon cars; the Riley Pathfinder being the chosen vehicle.

The crews were carefully selected, given advanced driver training and came to be regarded as an elite band. The fact that the cars operated both during the day and night soon impacted on the driving public and, for some years at least, there was an improvement in driving standards. Certainly the Exchequer benefited, for in the first four months of patrolling 2415 vehicles were checked, 840 prosecutions followed and 912 warnings given.

Efforts continued to bring greater efficiency in the Force. A system of bonus marks was introduced into promotion examinations for members gaining proficiency in recognized African languages. This change in policy resulted from a representation made by the Police Conference that continued to meet each year. It has to be said that, at this time in the development of the Force, there was more than a little disillusionment concerning the usefulness of the Conference, an attitude that was to change little in the following years.

The Police Conference was regarded as a token means of airing Force problems to Police Headquarters and to the Minister, but the impression was that little or no attention was paid to either grievances or suggestions. A situation was being reached which bore a remarkable similarity to that existing during and immediately after the war. In an effort to ameliorate this condition, agreement was given to the circulation of a quarterly bulletin of the progress achieved by the Executive Committee of the Conference, and also to the holding of regular meetings at provincial headquarters of Conference delegates and members of the Executive Committee. Democracy had to be seen to be working.

By now military ranks had been 'frozen' and were being phased out — a contentious matter with a minority of officers wishing to cling onto the trappings of the past and perhaps the social kudos that went with it. This very necessary and long overdue alteration will be covered in more detail in a later chapter.

It is time now to consider the progress of the Police Reserve. Their usefulness as an adjunct to the Regular Force had proved itself during the problems of 1948 The intervening years had witnessed that positive contribution being stimulated by training, by competitions and, not least, by the holding of social events that were aimed at encouraging the Reservists to believe in their importance as part of the police team.

The Reserve was now divided into three classes: — 'A', 'B' and Field Reserve. The first group, voluntary and unpaid but uniformed almost exactly as their regular colleagues, comprised men who looked upon their police role as more then a hobby. After all they were required to perform four hours' duty a week, or 16 hours a month, and their duties involved patrols, beats, illicit liquor raiding and minor inquiries, as well as charge office work. They were imbued with the same powers as were conferred upon Regulars by the Police Act, were subject to the same discipline and a lot of them operated in their own neighbourhoods, working to local peri-urban stations and performing a mainly deterrent but sometimes investigative function.

The 'B' Reserve were a smaller group; uniform was restricted, duties not as onerous and confined to four hours a month. They really comprised those who had neither the time nor inclination to contribute as intensely as their alphabetic predecessors.

The Field Reserve was by far the more numerous. In their ranks were the farmers, miners, storekeepers, businessmen, in fact those who could not find the time for a greater commitment but were prepared to don the all-blue battledress at least once a year and, in the event of an emergency, rally to the flag.

The Reserve had their own officers and rank structure and, as we shall see as the years unfold towards 1980, their usefulness and need was to become far more than valuable. They became absolutely essential.

Police Reservists were, of course, entitled to both honours and medals and these were presented with due pomp and ceremony at an annual medal parade or investiture. On one of these occasions in Bulawayo the dignitaries present included two Governors, a Prime Minister, the Commissioner of Police and sundry other notables plus their wives. The Officer Commanding the Police Reserve in Bulawayo, Lieutenant-Colonel Malcolm Fleming had conferred upon him the OBE, after which long service medals and bars were presented to the uniformed or, in three cases, plain-clothed reservists. One of the latter, doubtless affected by the sense of occasion, had to doff his hat. This he did with his right hand, only to realize that he needed to shake hands with the Governor. Smartly he transferred the hat to his left hand and stepped forward to receive his medal after which, and equally smartly, he replaced the hat on his head. Sadly, by this time the hat had gone full circle — and arrived back to front.

Later the Governor had the pleasure, undoubtedly fully shared by all including the 'revolving trilby', of opening the new Police Reserve Canteen.

This establishment was to prove a haven and welcome gathering place in the years when members of the Reserve were to be on call at all hours of the day and night. It was also just one of several similar buildings which were built, mainly for the regular police, in other main centres.

The Bulawayo Sports Pavilion, known as The Blue Lamp, was officially opened by Mrs Spurling, the wife of the provincial commander, in September of 1955. The occasion was marked by a Sports Day during which cricket, hockey and tennis matches were played — and Spurling scored 27 runs.

(A new and far 'brighter' Blue Lamp was opened by Commissioner Spink in February 1968, when Peter Sherren was commanding Matabeleland Province).

The Harare Clubhouse had been opened the previous month by Vice-Admiral Sir Peveril William-Powlett, Governor of Southern Rhodesia. The 'Police Club' as it has always been known, was designed as a place where past and present members, police reservists and wives could meet on common ground. The financing of the building was provided from Corps (Police) Funds, from grants by the Government, State Lotteries Trustees and Beit Trustees, and lastly with a most favourable loan from the B.S.A. Company.

In November, after presenting a number of Tuli horseshoes to various notables in and out of Government, Colonel Hickman retired and, to his considerable credit, immediately enlisted in the Police Reserve. It should be explained that Hickman, being the historian he was, had visited the Tuli area some months before, located a small cache of horseshoes dating back to the days of the Pioneer Column and resolved that, suitably mounted and engraved, they would be a fitting tribute to men who 'deserved well' of the country.

Lieutenant Colonel Harold Jackson was Hickman's successor. Jackson had attested in 1927 and joined the CID three years later, serving continuously in that branch until, relinquishing the command of the CID, he was appointed Deputy Commissioner in 1954. Jackson was an austere and unbending personality, in fact his colleagues alluded to him as the 'Sphinx'. One of his creeds was that to be a successful policeman, a man must live for his job and, no doubt because of this, he had proved a highly efficient investigator and administrator throughout his service. He was also the first man to be appointed as Commissioner with so little experience of the uniformed branch, a factor that, linked to his reserved personality, made for some awkward moments with his senior and often more gregarious uniformed officers.

Hickman was Commissioner for only 17 months; Jackson was to remain in the position for nearly two-and-a-half years.

Jackson was firmly of the belief that the conditions for African Police had to be dramatically improved but that, hand in hand with increased pay and more and better housing, must emerge greater acceptance of their responsibility both in administration and investigation. He foresaw police stations in African areas being commanded by Africans with but a minimum of European supervision and he directed his policies towards that end. He also re-introduced the Cadet Scheme to provide opportunities for Rhodesian school-leavers to join the Police and look forward to a remunerative and worthwhile career.

A fine example of a member of the African Police assisting in criminal investigations occurred in April of 1956. Two young European men decided to go off on a crime 'spree'. They started by stealing a Ford saloon in Salisbury, broke into a store near Mount Hampden, drove on to Northern Rhodesia for a couple of days before returning to Southern Rhodesia to heist cash and watches from a store in Sinoia. Gathering another couple of young desperadoes in Salisbury, they pushed on to Hartley where cash, rifles, pistols and knives were stolen, went on to hold-up a petrol station near Que Que and had driven beyond Gwelo before the police were alerted. The Gwelo police informed their counterparts in Bulawayo and a road block was hastily, but inadequately put together. The quartet crashed through the barricades in their stolen Zephyr and were pursued by Constable Gilmour on a motor cycle. In true Wild West fashion, he rode his steed with one hand and fired his pistol with the other, only to receive a glancing blow from a bullet fired from the car. Fortunately for him the bullet lodged between his cap and the side of his head. Gilmour, with blood flowing from his head wound, had to give up the chase. By now however, all Matabeleland stations had been warned and were on the look out for the robbers who, after again having been fired upon by one of the Plumtree police, were forced to abandon their vehicle. Two of the criminals then gave themselves up, leaving the other pair to take flight through the bush.

African Constable Niko of the Mangwe Police now comes into the story.

Niko saw, and was threatened by the escaping couple near the railway line that runs close to the road between Plumtree and Figtree. He managed to distance himself from them and then met Detective Inspectors Schollum and Macdonald who, armed and well aware of the situation, were travelling towards the border station. After a short search, the two criminals were seen again and a lengthy chase ensued through the bush before they went to ground in a thickly wooded copse. The three policemen searched this twice before Niko caught sight of the men, lying well concealed in the undergrowth and with rifles pointing towards one of the advancing CID officers. He quickly gave the alarm and the criminals were challenged, warned and told to give in. It was at this stage that Niko leapt on them, took their remaining firearms and handcuffed them together.

All four members of the Force were to receive special commendations for their courage and tenacity of purpose.

In Salisbury's African Townships, the year ended with what might be described as a taste of things to come when extensive rioting took place, accompanying a boycott of the buses, ostensibly over ticket pricing. This was followed by a fairly half-hearted but countrywide strike of Railway employees. Nevertheless, the Government saw fit to declare a State of Emergency, the Police Reserve was called out and regulars and reservists had to use some of their stocks of tear gas.

Coincidental with the troubles in Southern Rhodesia were further disturbances on Northern Rhodesia's Copperbelt. A request for assistance from the Northern Rhodesia Government elicited a swift response and a contingent of 56 men, led by Major Blowers and Superintendent Peck, was flown to the troubled areas. Mark Freemantle, Keith Rawson and Dick Marett were among the group, but it was Mark Freemantle who distinguished himself, by expertly firing a tear gas grenade from a discharger cup over the top of a house and into the middle of a group of rioters gathered on the other side.

The years 1957 and 1958 passed by peacefully. The Police did their job, the criminals did theirs, and all was well. Nevertheless certain matters need comment, albeit brief.

Back in 1955 work had started on the Kariba Dam and, until 1957 everything was progressing on schedule. Then, in early 1957 and again the following year, heavy rains and extensive flooding caused delays and damage, including the sweeping away of the suspension bridge constructed to facilitate on-site operations.

It was late in 1958 that the might of the Zambezi river was finally tamed and mid-1959 when the vast wall was completed and, eventually, a police station provided.

Her Majesty Queen Elizabeth, the Queen Mother, paid a further visit to the country in 1957 during which her main function was to open the University of Rhodesia and Nyasaland and to be installed as its President. Police provided the usual escorts and security, now all the more significant with Her Majesty being the Honorary Commissioner, whilst Lieutenant Colonel Jackson had the privilege of being granted an audience with Her Majesty.

On a less happy note, many sports meetings had to be canceled or postponed as another vicious poliomyelitis epidemic swept the land. This was the second such epidemic. The first, in 1954, had seen the deaths of many people, among them the popular and respected sportsman, Sergeant Basil Taylor, a man who, sadly, had spent the war years in a German prison camp and was now to be cut down in his prime. Yet another victim of the disease was Roy Coop, an all-round athlete and one of the country's premier soccer players who had served in the BSA Police for nearly five years before joining the Royal Rhodesian Air Force.

The year also witnessed an event which has all but been forgotten but which certainly is an historical landmark as far as the Police Band is concerned. This was the presentation by Chief Inspector Weller, on behalf of the Sergeants' Mess, to the Police Band of a magnificently crafted and embroidered drum major's sash. The sash had been made in England and bore the names of the Forces from which the BSA Police had originated, namely the Bechuanaland Border Police (1884), BSA Company's Police (1889), Mashonaland Mounted Police (1893) and Southern Rhodesia Constabulary (1903).

In March of the next year, 1958, Basil Spurling stepped into the office of Commissioner, a position he was to hold for five years. The 'Spurling era' would be one of considerable change both in the country and the Police Force but, before considering the years to 1963, a few final words on 1958.

With 'Sam' Weller elevated to commissioned rank, the post of Depot Chief Inspector had become vacant and there was a crying need to promote into it someone who could, as it were and in so many ways 'set the tone' of the Force. In fact there was really only one man who had the stature, the background and who commanded the respect so necessary in that position.

That man, a Sub-Inspector in Salisbury Town, had served during the war in the Corps of Military Police (mainly with the Eighth Army), had been a Company Sergeant Major in India and had arrived in Southern Rhodesia with the large draft of December 1946. With him had come men like Jimmy Watkins, Mark Freemantle, Douglas Cordy Hedge, Robert Kerswell, Tim Weimer, John Millett and several others. History fails to record his impact as a Depot recruit. He had made his name as a sportsman in field events, held various records for throwing the hammer, the discus and shot, and represented his country at the Empire Games in 1950. His police service included a period as a Law and Police Instructor and, more actively, on both Urban and Traffic duties, where he became the scourge of errant Salisbury motorists.

So it was that in August 1958, Ronald Frederick Trangmar stepped proudly and unhesitatingly into the eminence of "RSM." He was to stamp the position with authority, distinction and humanity until his untimely death from cancer in 1979, during which two decades something like 5000 young men and women recruits passed through the Depot training courses.

One final matter before the chapter on 1958 is closed. It concerns a road accident and the diligent investigations by Stuart Alford, then a sergeant in the Salisbury Traffic Branch.

Two cars had collided in Rhodes Avenue during the early evening of Christmas Day. One had been travelling correctly and at reasonable speed when the other had swerved into its path, struck a glancing blow and then carried on without stopping. Traces of red paint were found on the damaged car and pieces of glass with the lettering 'M5' lying at the scene. With nothing else to go on, Police placed a notice in the newspaper requesting information concerning a red car with damage to its front offside wing.

Some days later, during the evening, a Cranborne resident, Mr. Ryan, parked his car near a damaged tree in Rhodes Avenue, called a passing policeman and claimed that he had damaged the vehicle while trying to park, a statement which the policeman accepted under the circumstances. The two incidents were not linked until Alford received a reply to the advertisement, which led him to Ryan's red Austin and then into protracted and detailed investigations.

These included an analysis of the paint scrapings, expert evidence on Lucas headlamp glass, and comparison photographs showing the disparity between the damage to the Austin and to the tree, as well as the difference between the damage sustained by each car.

The evidence was meticulously presented, Ryan was convicted and Alford received a Commendation.

## Chapter Forty-Two

## SPURLING ASCENDANT

*The Spurling Era — Problems with the Press — Whitehead as Prime Minister — the Political Scene — Operation 'Spider' — NDP banned — Law and Order Act — ZAPU formed — Demilitarization — Packard Survey and Lander Report — Flower to CIO — Security of Rhodesia.*

The years from March 1958 to April 1963 may accurately be called the 'Spurling Era'. Basil Gordon Spurling stepped into the office of Commissioner of Police with all the relish and confidence of his supremely self-assured personality. It was a time when the Force was in sore need of a leader who would face up to the ministers of Justice and the Treasury, fight for what was required and, with no holds barred, bluntly inform the Government of the consequences of its ill-conceived and apparent policy of financial starvation. This is not to decry the efforts of his predecessor but Jackson was, by nature of his background, more introverted, more careful, less inclined to hammering the table than the pugnacious, more extrovert Spurling.

Spurling was a 'confrontationalist' and very early on in his tenure of office showed this trait when dealing with an antagonistic and partisan press lobby. The latter had formed a habit of publishing letters of complaint and derogation of the Force before any investigation or comment could be obtained from police sources. So often was this happening that the morale of the members was being affected. A particularly friendly and relaxed officer was appointed to head up the press and public relations office but even he, Superintendent 'Gubby' Allen, made no discernible impression. Matters came to a head when a particularly virulent and inaccurate report appeared in a Bulawayo newspaper, prompting the local officer commanding to recommend the immediate withdrawal of the offending journalist's press identity card. The card was withdrawn; the Rhodesian Guild of Journalists screamed foul; the Minister of Justice, backed apparently by the Prime Minister, requested Spurling to reinstate the journalist. Spurling politely, but firmly, declined. In his memoirs Spurling is a little more forthcoming on this incident: "I was given three days by the Minister of Justice on instructions of Cabinet, to re-instate the journalist. I refused to do so and told the Minister, Mr. Reginald Knight Q.C., that I would like him to give the Prime Minister my compliments and say that if I was compelled to carry out that instruction then the Prime Minister had three days in which to find a new Commissioner of Police; I would retire."

Spurling, temporizing a little, did however convene a meeting with the editors of the Argus Newspapers at which he emphasized that information given to the Press by Police was a privilege and not a right. Further, that he was prepared to withdraw all press cards and let the situation become a free for all, with police at liberty to deal with whom they wished. Agreement could not be reached; all cards were withdrawn and there was an immediate improvement in relations.

Such was the man now at the helm of a police force in a country which was to see political change, the advent of militant African nationalism and disturbances on a massive scale over the next few years.

With the creation of the Federation, Godfrey Huggins had managed to get himself 'kicked upstairs' and his place as Prime Minister of Southern Rhodesia had been taken by the New Zealand-born missionary turned politician, Reginald Garfield Todd. Todd proved himself a strong leader, well able to deal with the problems facing Southern Rhodesia, while enjoying a remarkable amount of support from Africans. However, he was inclined to be headstrong, overly confident, and to act without consulting his Cabinet colleagues. In 1958, after a bout of particularly messy party infighting, Todd was deposed and later resigned to be succeeded by Sir Edgar Whitehead, who was at that time representing the Federation in Washington.. However, little did the electorate then recognize or probably care that, in ousting Todd, they were saying farewell to any hope of a future reconciliation between the black nationalists and themselves.

Whitehead, though probably more of a liberal than his predecessor, came to power in such a way that distrust between the Nationalists and his government was inevitable. From then on the lines of battle were drawn, the gap widened and deepened, and the Nationalist leaders developed an oratory of confrontation and a policy of violence, making the task of the Police immeasurably more difficult.

Whitehead was a bachelor — cold, clever, deep-thinking but shy and introverted. He was also very deaf and partly blind. For those who may wonder at this somewhat extraordinary choice of leader, let it be said that he was in his early fifties when he took over the premiership, that he possessed a brilliant and incisive brain, was a very able speaker — and loved his beer. So great was that love and so remarkable his intake that Lord Home, in his book *The Way the Wind Blows* commented of Whitehead, "he was able to consume 13 beers in an evening without putting up his hand and asking to leave the room. "

But for all these good and bad points, Whitehead was incapable of establishing a working relationship with the Nationalists — his character was wrong, the times were against him and, to put it bluntly, his name wasn't Todd.

The following years saw the Whitehead government tinkering with new franchise proposals, coping with widespread unrest — of which more later — and enacting legislation designed to improve the lot of the Africans. However, with the Federation passing into an increasingly terminal condition and Southern

Rhodesia aflame with riots, intimidation and general mayhem; with the Nationalists gung-ho at the scent of power, not only in the southern but also in the remaining two territories; in such circumstances the appearance of a white backlash was sure and inevitable. Despite the wider franchise, despite having Africans in Parliament, the apparent greed of the Nationalists was too much for the minority electorate. They, or the majority of them, reacted angrily against the break-down of law and order. They demanded that peace and tranquillity once again be established, that discipline be asserted and appeasement, as they saw it, halted. The massacres and flight of hundreds from the Congo not all that long before was still uppermost in many minds and, with it, the fear that 'all that' could happen again, here. The year was 1962 and the stage was set for the Rhodesia Front, for Winston Field — and Ian Smith.

That was a very broad overview of the political scene. It is now timely to consider the progress of the African Nationalist movement over the same period.

The Southern Rhodesia African National Congress (SRANC), as well as their colleagues in the northern territories, recognised a catalyst for their own agendas in the creation of the Federation. Of the politically ambitious blacks in the three participating countries, few found favour with the Federal concept. In the case of Southern Rhodesia's nationalists, backed by the ideologies of either China or Russia, they resolved to play along with any negotiations, begrudgingly accept what might be described as 'crumbs from the rich man's table', but in fact work relentlessly and ruthlessly towards acquiring the whole cake.

When the SRANC was formed in 1957, it stood for "the national unity of all inhabitants of this country in true partnership regardless of race, colour and creed." In those days, the nationalist leaders included James Chikerema, Michael Mawema, Joseph Msika, George Nyandoro, Stanlake Samkange, and Edison Sithole, with Joshua Nkomo as President. Sadly, the unwritten policy of the Party was "He that is not with me is against me" which was loosely interpreted to mean that "everyone will be with me, or else." This resulted in widespread intimidation, lawlessness and rioting; ceaseless confrontations with the Police and, eventually, in the superbly planned and executed Operation 'Spider' which saw the banning of the SR ANC and the arrest and detention of many, in fact, some 500 of the ringleaders. Joshua Nkomo was not among the latter. He, fortuitously, was out of the country at the time. However, the Nationalists were quick to re-group and, disregarding or finding loopholes through some of the new legislation which had appeared on the statute books, formed the National Democratic Party. (NDP). Mawema was the leading light for a few months but Nkomo returned to the country and took command of the new Party in which some new names came to the fore: Takawira, Chitepo and Robert Mugabe.

By now, depending on where you were standing, the 'wind of change' was blowing hot or cold throughout the continent of Africa, and the British Prime Minister, Harold Macmillan, who was to coin the phrase, passed through the British territories of west, central and southern Africa in 1958, to help fan the breeze.

Meanwhile, the NDP was busy 'programming' or 'conscientising' as many of the black population as it could. This was accomplished by having gangs of thugs roaming the townships demanding to see Party membership cards and assaulting those who had the wrong ones, or none at all, and generally terrorising law-abiding citizens. In the rural areas, assaults, burning of crops, fire-bombings and even the maiming of cattle became the order of the day. The newspaper headlines painted a graphic and frightening picture —'Fire Bomb Terrorists active in Harare, Highfield', 'Nkomo asked — return to your people', 'African shot dead as Kariba mob attacks police', 'Hatfield Raid — Petrol Bomb didn't go off', 'Police Reservist is burnt to death by Petrol Gang'.

It was now only a matter of time before the NDP was banned. In July 1960, some 7000 people were set to march from the townships into Salisbury following upon the arrest of three NDP leaders. Only brave, patient and firm action by a small force of Police prevented what might have been a hideous conflagration.

This was followed by a strike of 40,000 NDP supporters. Government replied by passing the Law and Order Maintenance and the Emergency Powers Acts, pieces of legislation designed to assist the Police in curbing Nationalist activities but which, in the eyes of many, especially those outside the country, made Southern Rhodesia into a 'police state'. Government also decided — at long, long last — to increase the establishment of the Police, a classic example of 'shutting the stable door after the horse had bolted'. Had the politicians listened to the various police commissioners over the previous years, the harsh legislation could well have been unnecessary.

Eventually and inevitably, the NDP was banned in December 1961 (again Nkomo was outside the country's borders). Eight days later, its successor the Zimbabwe Africa Peoples Union (ZAPU), was formed, again under Mr Nkomo. The mixture of confrontation and mayhem was as before. So, in September 1962, ZAPU also was banned. Again, by uncanny coincidence, Mr Nkomo was out of the country. However, by this time there was more than a little unhappiness over Nkomo's leadership and the resultant split in the Nationalist ranks led to the formation of the Zimbabwe African National Union (ZANU) under Ndabaningi Sithole, and the Peoples Caretaker Council (PCC) to be led by Nkomo.

Such then was the political and security climate within which the Police operated under Commissioner Spurling between 1958 and 1963. They were trying years, challenging years; years during which the Force was alternately praised and vilified; years that would test the resolve of every member.

Spurling appointed as his deputy another officer who had spent most of his service in the CID, Robert 'Rex' Borland. However, dogged by poor health, Borland was forced to retire towards the end of 1960, and after a short period during which Graham Rolfe occupied the post, Frank 'Pat' Barfoot became Deputy Commissioner (Crime and Security) on 1 October.

Various changes had preceded these appointments. Military ranks had been abolished and a senior British Army officer had attempted a "Survey" of the B.S.A.Police.

The use of military titles, military ranks, had its origins in the Occupation of Mashonaland back in 1890. The BSA Police had been created as an armed force to escort and protect the Pioneer Column into the country and to ensure that peace and order were established and maintained. The Force had remained as the only permanently established military unit in the country, and had participated in the First World War by its entry into German West Africa in August 1914, by entry into the Caprivi Strip the following year and finally, by its participation as an infantry contingent (under Major R.E. Murray) in German East Africa shortly afterwards.

As Southern Rhodesia had developed, so the role of the Police became more and more that of a civil police force, a force established to maintain law and order and preserve the peace, a force with a tradition of just and fair and efficient policemanship. We have already seen that in the Second World War the Police as such did not go to war as a unit; they remained to police the land but sent many young men to various theatres of operations, mainly East Africa, the Middle East and the Aegean. As a writer in *The Outpost* puts it: "As the Rhodesian fighting forces expanded … .senior Police officers of long standing found themselves ranking with junior subalterns in the armed services. Military ranks in use in the Force were dropped and Police officers were known for all official purposes by their Police ranks. Naturally those officers who held military rank were entitled to retain it for private purposes. As a result there arose a confusing situation because officers were promoted in Police rank while retaining the military rank to which they were entitled. We then had Captain 'Smith,' Assistant Commissioner of Police, and both the public, and the junior ranks in the Force, found difficulty in understanding just what seniority many Police officers held."

Hand in hand with that came the realization that policing was a specialised and highly technical vocation; so too was fighting a war. The two could not and did not mix.

For a time the Police remained an intrinsic part of the Defence Act and the retention of military titles was stubbornly retained. But then came Federation, and Southern Rhodesia relinquished control for its external defence and the Police became a wholly civil force. At about the same time, the Police Act was amended to relieve the Police from assisting in the defence of the country against external aggression, either within or beyond its borders. Yet another clause permitted the BSA Police to go to the aid of the civil power in neighbouring territories. The die was cast and there could be no turning back. Although many of the older establishment clung to the glory of the past, it was agreed that military ranks would be discarded in their entirety where police duties were concerned. The weekly publication of Police Force Orders was thereafter published under the authority of Mr BG Spurling.

So much for Demilitarisation; a hotly debated and divisive subject — among the higher police ranks — during the late 50s.

The next twist in the history of the Police came with the survey conducted by General Sir Douglas Packard in 1962.

As far as can be ascertained, the survey was initiated by the Whitehead Government and was designed to look into all aspects of Police organisation, pay included. Why Government wanted this is not altogether clear but for some time there had been rumblings in the ranks and certainly, to parody Gilbert and Sullivan, the police force was not an entirely happy one. It must be remembered that the regular members in particular, and police reservists in general, had for some time been subjected to long hours of work, threats and, on occasions, actual violence. Inevitably their frustrations and pent-up feelings had been aired in letters and articles to the national press. In January 1961, a few members of the CID had publicly voiced their grievances over pay, conditions of service and 'widespread inefficiency' in their Department. Although the Police Association was in existence to handle such matters, it was completely understandable — though not to Spurling and his senior officers — that now and again the 'lid had to fly off'.

Despite the Commissioner's Annual Reports — in which the strains on a policeman's family and social life were recognized, the lack of adequate policing bemoaned, and the scarcity of trained policemen, transport and accommodation emphasized — the Government clearly felt that a new broom was required to examine these and other problems. One of the latter was the way in which Internal Security was handled and passed to Government. It may also have been a consideration that they required recommendations and ideas from a man who could stand up to (or ignore) the authoritative, often aggressive and unyielding Spurling. A British general fitted this last requirement.

Packard was an unusual choice. A long and illustrious military career — during which he had acted in an advisory capacity in certain African states — had been interrupted with a year at the War Office in 1948/9 as Director of Military Intelligence. Certainly this could be regarded as the closest he had ever been to an involvement in the affairs of a police force which was neither Colonial nor County. It goes without saying that the background and training of a soldier is far removed from that of a policeman and in essence — though in more modern times the role of the military has often bordered on peacekeeping — the *raison d'etre* of the one is diametrically opposed to that of the other.

Spurling, in his memoirs, paints a rather strange picture: "For some reason which was never explained to me, I was asked not to meet General Packard on his arrival: I complied with this request. I did not see General Packard for three days after his arrival: he arrived at Police General Headquarters one morning unannounced. It seemed a strange way to set about the Survey. General Packard told me that he thought he could conduct the Survey within three months, he asked me for nothing specifically but I had already directed that every facility must be placed at his disposal. He was also accorded Honorary Membership of the BSA Police Officers' Mess. "During his visit I saw little of General Packard who discusssed very little with me nor did he seem to wish to hear my views or opinions. The only point of importance on which he did seek my views was that of Special Branch; he wanted to know why the BSA Police did not have one. I explained to him that, in fact, we did have one and that it was called a Security Branch (or Section) and was hidden in the Criminal Investigation Department. He was insistent that there should be a Special Branch and that it should be so called. I pointed out that in every Police Force there was some degree of apathy between the Uniformed Branch and the CID, the separation of the Special Branch from CID would create a third dimension and, almost certainly, lead to more friction (which in later years it did). However he said that all other Police Forces had a Special Branch so the BSA Police must have one."

It now becomes interesting to turn to Ken Flower's memoirs, *Serving Secretly*: Flower, (by now Deputy Commissioner, Administration) after discussing the means by which intelligence and security information was obtained by the Federal governments, refers to Whitehead's need to be more directly informed on such issues, especially in the light of a deteriorating internal situation. "He discussed (says Flower) the subject with local officials, myself included, and then decided to enlist the services of British experts. As a result Sir Roger Hollis, then Director of MI5, visited Southern Rhodesia in 1961, and in 1962 General Sir Douglas Packard was invited to conduct a survey of the BSA Police and of related internal security matters."

Spurling had met Hollis previously, during a visit to London in 1959 when, being aware of some sort of blockage of security information to the MI5 Liaison Officer in Salisbury, he had suggested that the placing of a police security official in Rhodesia House would enhance liaison and improve the flow of information. Hollis would have none of it. The system remained unchanged, so too the blockage.

In May 1962, when Spurling had still a little short of twelve months to serve before retirement, Packard presented his final report to the Minister of Justice and Internal Affairs. Before looking at reaction to its findings, it is again of interest to read Flower's comment:

"Spurling's successor had not yet been named. Packard, just prior to his departure, advised me that he had submitted a secret report to Whitehead recommending that I should take over the Force as soon as possible. But the election was only a few weeks away and the recommendation was put into cold storage."

As it was, in April 1963, though the formal announcement had been made some months before, Frank 'Slash' Barfoot succeeded Spurling on the latter's recommendation and with the approval of the Governor-in-Council. A few months later, in August and with Spurling now well out of the way, Flower was called to the new Prime Minister, Winston Field, and asked to take over command of a new Security and Intelligence organization, to become effective when the Federation was dissolved on 31 December 1963. Thus was born the Central Intelligence Organisation (CIO).

But to return to the Packard Report.

Again it is necessary to refer to Spurling's memoirs: "Rumours were rife before the Report was even released. The Minister obviously thought there would be difficulties because the Secretary for Justice sent me a copy for comment: I was both astonished and appalled. Having discussed the report with the Deputy Commissioners (Barfoot and Flower) I saw the Minister, Mr. R. Knight, and demanded that certain passages be deleted otherwise I would not be responsible for the reaction by the whole of the B.S.A. Police. One such passage referred to the holding of political meetings by members of the African Nationalist Organizations and alleged that when they wished to hold a meeting they had to walk through (quote) "serried ranks of grim looking policemen who use the bullet not the baton." The B.S.A. Police had done everything possible to work within the Principles of Police, particularly that of minimum force, to the extent that even the Press had published reports indicating that this practice should cease. The handling of a mob of 30,000 or more Africans intent on marching on Salisbury City by Superintendent Van Sittert and a small force of Police and Police Reserve had exemplified minimum force.

"General Packard's comment was unwarranted and bore no relation to the truth. The passages were deleted because they constituted serious and unwarranted reflection on the men of the B.S.A. Police and the Police Reserve. Had General Packard discussed this and other matters with me or with my Senior Officers he would have had a clearer perception of matters: the fact that he did not do so was incomprehensible."

Packard made some thoroughly military-related recommendations, perhaps understandably as by now the para-military and civil roles were becoming intermingled and all but indistinguishable. District Headquarters should control no more than five main stations and provincial headquarters should be increased to control up to five districts. Police needed only light, outboard-motor-powered launches on Lake Kariba, because "the prudent mariner remains in port during a storm." Presumably the Southern Rhodesia Navy would handle any terrorist incursions across the Lake. He also suggested improvements to medico-legal services, ignoring the fact that these were already becoming established. Among other comments and recommendations, he discussed the inadequacy of police pay rates, was sharply critical of the excessive amount of administration, condemned the 'officer gap', remarked upon discontent within the CID, and suggested a dramatic reduction in the use of horses.

Quite understandably, the General's comments on the poor remuneration package were well received, especially his criticism of the Government for not providing sufficient funding in the past, thereby endangering the security of the country in the future. However, as so invariably was the case, no increases in police salaries were made until the civil service could be linked in and suitably rewarded as well.

After the publication of Packard's survey, Spurling appointed a Working Committee to examine its details and recommendations. Once again, it was deemed advisable to appoint an outsider as chairman, but this time it was a well-known and respected local businessman and member of the Public Services Board, Mr John Lander. On the Committee with him was the Chief Staff Officer (Administration), Mr James Spink who, just over five years later, would step into the shoes of — by then seriously ill — Commissioner Barfoot. The general intent and effect of the 'Lander Committee' was to separate the worthwhile from the ridiculous or skewed as far as the original Survey was concerned and to make pragmatic recommendations for the future. This it did. The recommendations went to Government, were accepted and over the ensuing months, implemented as far as possible.

However, it seems certain that Government, or the Prime Minister, received a separate and secret report from General Packard. There were very strong rumours that Packard had argued for an external appointment to the post of Commissioner of Police, though Flower in his book, supra, comments: "Packard, just prior to his departure, advised me that he had submitted a secret report to Whitehead recommending that I should take over the Force as soon as possible." We have also seen that there was a move to establish a Special Branch or some form of free-ranging intelligence gathering body. Neither subjects appear in the Survey Report and it would seem likely, in the light of subsequent events, that Packard suggested that the intelligence wing be a separate organization, removed from the responsibility of Police, and accountable only to the Prime Minister.

Spurling was most certainly asked by Whitehead to facilitate such an organization but, with his usual logical and unbending approach, the Commissioner pointed out that, in terms of the Police Act, the security of the country rested firmly upon his shoulders and furthermore, that such appointment would undoubtedly have political implications. Another aspect might well have been that of the potential 'apathy' to quote Spurling, (but it is felt that ' antipathy or even 'conflict' would be more appropriate), between branches, as was mentioned earlier. Anyway, there the issue was to rest until Spurling had retired, Barfoot was Commissioner and Winston Field had succeeded Whitehead.

## Chapter Forty-Three

## SPURLING RAMPANT

*Spurling continued — Commendations — Corps Recreation and other facilities —*
*Kuyedza — Contingent to Nyasaland — Royal Review — Freedom of Salisbury — Si Ye Pambile*

The increasingly turbulent political scene, the tempestuous growth of African Nationalism and the rather strange — and perhaps biased or misguided — survey of the police conducted by Packard, all took place when Commissioner Spurling commanded the Force….and very nearly his Minister and the Prime Minister as well.

'B.G.' as he was generally known, has been presented as a somewhat dogmatic, certainly autocratic and — as will be seen in the next Chapter — fairly ruthless figure. However, there was another side to the man's character and this was a steely determination to do everything possible to improve welfare and amenities and an equally firm resolve to support and encourage his men when he judged them worthy and in need of recognition and reward.

Perhaps the latter is best reflected in the plethora of Commissioner's Commendations awarded during the 'Spurling Era'. Circumstances were such that bravery, protracted investigations and a heightened degree of 'devotion to duty' were demanded of policemen — which is not to belittle the commitment of those serving in earlier, more tranquil, years. But, in illustrating the period, it is appropriate and inspiring to page through some of the honours accorded to policemen between 1958 and 1963. Behind the rather cold, cryptic and unrevealing language of the citations, imagination must be brought to bear to understand the ever-present degrees of danger, exhaustion, frustration and diligence.

One of the first recipients was Detective Sub Inspector Peter Allum of the Bulawayo CID, " for his 'continuous concentration, enthusiasm and high degree of ability shown during the prolonged and intricate investigations into various counts of fraud and contraventions of the Insolvency Act." The accused was sentenced to five years' IHL and, soon after, Allum was promoted to Detective Inspector.

A few months later another member of the plain clothes branch, Detective Sergeant Allan Best was commended for his continuous, painstaking and methodical investigations, over a period of four months, into 207 counts of theft, which resulted in the European accused being sentenced to two and a half years' IHL in the High Court, Gwelo.

The next Commendation brings to mind a short poem that appeared in *Time and Tide*:

*"Stories of success remind us*
*We to fortune's height may climb*
*If we do not leave behind us*
*Fingerprints on scenes of crime."*

Detective Sub-Inspector 'Bill' Hobley and Detective Sergeant Angus Ross earned a more than usually informative description of their good work in bringing to an end the nefarious activities of one Edward 'Jellyboy' Pooley. This is not to suggest that the citation had been overly embellished. Recognition began with the usual official wording "devotion to duty" combined with "tenacity of purpose" during the investigations into numerous cases of safe blowing, in both Salisbury and Bulawayo, between July 1958 and June 1959. But it carries on, "Regardless of normal hours of duty, these investigations, which included extra-territorial enquiries, necessitated months of systematic checking and re-checking of known criminals and suspects and also surveillance. Finally, despite many setbacks, this determination was rewarded in the arrest of the accused, a European professional criminal, in possession of stolen property."

Jellyboy was subsequently convicted on two counts of housebreaking involving safe blowing, and three counts of theft of motor vehicles, and given a total of eight years in which to consider his sins.

"Exhibiting teamwork of the highest order, these members have brought credit not only to them-selves, but to the Force as a whole." In an almost unique conclusion to the citation, Commissioner

Spurling went on to express his thanks to all ranks of the Regular Force who had cooperated with the CID by their preventive patrolling over the period of the safe-blowings and during the hours of darkness.

One of the most damaging pieces of evidence against Pooley — who was conscientious about not leaving his fingerprints — was the discovery of his partial palmprint on Lysaghts' office door in Salisbury. Strangely, Pooley was found not guilty of this particular breaking but the investigating officers had built up a foolproof case against the man for breaking into the Raylton Club in Salisbury and the Bulawayo Post Office.

The successful investigation of a murder for which no body could be found won high praise for Sergeant Worsley and African Sergeant Bernard of the Macheke Police, together with Detective Sergeant Wilton and African Detectives Aroni and Fusirayi of CID Salisbury.

The murder happened after a beer drink on a farm near Macheke during March 1960, and because the body was never found — despite the draining of a dam into which it might have been thrown — it was only by long and detailed questioning of the people attending the party that the true circumstances of the crime came to light. The police persisted in their questioning and three accused eventually made statements implicating one another. The case went to the High Court in Salisbury and one accused was convicted of murder and sentenced to 12 years imprisonment with hard labour, a second died in prison from natural causes and, by his death, weakened the case against the third who was acquitted.

Another commendation was given to the CID Law and Order team involved in petrol bomb cases occurring in December 1960 in the Harare and Highfield Townships. The team was led by Detective Inspector John Reid, supported by Detective Sergeants John 'Butch' Fletcher and Lloyd Chinn, Detective Mark Doyle, African Detective Sergeants Chiota, Mbanga, Nyamyaro, Hode, and Detective Fani.

A food stall and three houses were attacked at night with petrol bombs, resulting in considerable damage to property and, of course, danger to lives. Investigations revealed that the motives were revenge on the one hand and the intimidation of Africans sympathetic to the Government on the other.

The citation records that the detection of those responsible proved extremely difficult and lengthy, despite an offered reward of five hundred pounds. Africans were unwilling to come forward with information and it was only after the most thorough, painstaking and persistent efforts of the whole team that five accused were eventually arrested, found guilty and each sentenced to three years' imprisonment with hard labour.

Another case, involving the murder of an African Constable, deserves mention. Constable Manasa had been on routine patrol duties in Gwelo when he was killed. Once more it was a team effort led, in this instance by Detective Sergeant Norman Burns and supported by Dennis Castell-Castell, African Detective Station Sergeant Zhuwaki and African Detective Sergeants Chiguma, Mhindu, and Kenny. As in the Salisbury case mentioned before, nobody was prepared to come forward and offer assistance and the investigation became a difficult, prolonged and exacting sequence of inquiries before any successful conclusion could be claimed. Eventually, however, the principal accused was sentenced to death.

Commendations became a regular reward as the law and order situation deteriorated in Southern Rhodesia. John Rowe and Reserve Constable Neppe arrested an armed and dangerous criminal in the Bond Street Shopping Centre of Mount Pleasant in Salisbury after a desperate struggle, and were awarded Special Commendations for their courage and determination.

Peter Johnson and African Sergeant Katazo of the Essexvale Police became involved in a stock theft investigation that took them to Beitbridge and back to Bulawayo but their travels resulted in the arrest and conviction of four accused. In the same area, Constable Richard Evans and Sergeant Sigeca of Matobo completed investigations and secured convictions into cases of political unrest in the National Park, where various meetings had resulted in the filling in of dip tanks and various other intimidatory acts of violence.

These cases and many others reveal the dedication and teamwork that existed in the B.S.A Police in the years leading up to the Declaration of Independence. Young men, black and white, displayed an adherence to and involvement in their jobs that could only bring forth admiration, praise and respect. Although the details are perforce sketchy and the adjectives perhaps repetitive, a few more examples attempt to convey the danger, the scope and indeed, though some may disagree, the attraction and glamour of police life during that era.

In August 1962, Inspector David Craven and Constable Andy Learmonth, both of Bulawayo Urban, were awarded Special Commendations for their investigations into the theft of cars by Aidan Diggeden. At that stage, as Craven narrates in his book Mapolisa, Diggeden was virtually unknown to the police but he was to become almost a 'celebrity' in future years as he made a 'career' out of car theft and breaking out of prisons. In the particular case mentioned here, five cars had been stolen over a period of eight months in Salisbury and Bulawayo. The investigations required many hours of additional work and after-duty observations, and involved the meticulous collation of evidence. Craven records that there were forty pages of investigation diary, over sixty statements, innumerable radio messages and other documents and more than 40 exhibits to be labeled and prepared for Court. Diggeden 'went down' for 45 months.

Joseph Mark Simpson was another to gain a Special Commendation that year. Simpson, whose father had been a Commissioner of the Metropolitan Police, was involved in a stock theft investigation in the Shabani area during which he had to contend with a mob of hostile and mostly drunken Africans, one of whom attempted to strangle him. He succeeded in arresting his attacker and also two others in circumstances that demanded considerable courage of him. He also stopped the mob from seriously assaulting another African who had been trying to help him. At the time, Simpson was a constable with only two-and-a-half years service. He later joined the Royal Hong Kong Police where he was to serve with distinction for many years.

Members of the Police Reserve Air Wing were involved in another case which took place in the Lupani area during 1962. On this occasion a mob of Africans attacked a police truck at the Shangani River and managed to release a suspect being conveyed to the police station. Inspector Andrew Gilmour of Bulawayo Urban took command of the ground party tasked with locating and taking action against the mob and based his force at the Pupu Dip. Meanwhile, two members of the Matabeleland Flight of the Police Reserve Air Wing, Police Reserve Pilot Tony Brown and Reserve Observer George Magee, patrolled the area before dawn and managed to locate the cooking fires of the mob. By careful and intelligent liaison with the ground force, it was possible to encircle and arrest no less than 97 Africans.

Not only were convictions obtained in the Bulawayo Magistrate's Court, but the public morale in the Lupane area was strengthened as lawlessness became greatly reduced. The improvement in the area was not to last. It was in Lupane district, four years later, that a CID team led by Detective Inspector Peter Tomlinson arrested a group of terrorists who had murdered a headman and been recruiting local tribesmen and instructing them how to use firearms, grenades and explosives. This was an investigation conducted over a lengthy period and with hostility apparent everywhere. Tomlinson also was awarded a Commendation.

Sergeant Don Rowland who, many years later, was to command the Police Support Unit, was another to receive a commendation during this period. Aided by African Constables Eliyas and Sika, of Bulawayo District, Rowland followed up on a report of a child missing from a kraal in the Plumtree area. Everything pointed to a ritual killing and, in due course, human remains were located. Due to superstition and fear, it was well nigh impossible to gather formal evidence and the case progressed but slowly.

However, the three policemen questioned witnesses and suspects diligently and unhurriedly, and eventually were able to arrest two African women, charge them and see them convicted to life imprisonment. Not content with that, the team finally secured enough evidence to arrest the witchdoctor who had instigated the murder. The whole investigation spanned nearly two years.

Detective Sergeant 'Mac' McGuiness, was to become an integral part of the Selous Scouts in the 70s and features often in Ron Reid-Daley's history of that Regiment, Pamwe Chete. McGuiness, with his team of African Detective Sergeant Mhindu and Detectives Dzingai, Murambiwa, Maraini, Zwirevo and Kephas, was tasked with investigating the sabotage of the railway line near Umvuma in August 1962. Fishplates and bolts had been removed from a stretch of curved track bordering on a steep embankment and threatened a serious rail accident. The team had little to go on but after ten days of painstaking interrogation and investigation, it was possible to make three arrests and, in due course, to secure a sentence of 14 years imprisonment for each offender.

Only a month later, McGuiness and virtually the same CID team were involved with investigations following riots in Shabani. A political meeting was at the heart of the trouble and the case occupied no less than 31 days of inquiries, during which nine Africans were arrested whilst engaged in manufacturing petrol bombs. The result was a triumph for the CID team. No less than 71 Africans were sentenced to a total of 206 years' in prison.

Such are a few extracts from a list which barely skims the surface of a reservoir of unsung individual acts of heroism, of positive interplay between the branches, departments, provinces and stations, and of hours of lonely vigilance, all of which added up to dedication and teamwork.

The next particular aspect of the 'Spurling Era' concerns the Force facilities. This is not a reference to the many new police stations that were constructed during his tenure of office — they were necessary, government-financed and demanded by deteriorating circumstances — but rather to the recreational buildings and amenities that were to be developed at police stations throughout Southern Rhodesia.

To set this development in proper perspective it is necessary to visit the lower floor of the Regimental Institute in the 50s. The Regimental Institute may be compared to the British armed services NAAFI organisation. In a comparatively small room and under the aegis of Police Headquarters and Police Funds, (as opposed to finance allocated by Government), Staff Inspector Don Lane operated a small shop stocked with the basic needs of recruits and those who lived in the Police Depot. Polish, dusters, Brasso, writing pads and envelopes, soft drinks, soap, dubbin and so on. Lane had joined the Police in 1940, served in the Victoria and Matabeleland districts, been seconded for service in the Middle East and after the War returned to the Bulawayo area, as Member-in-Charge at Fort Rixon in 1946.

Lane decided to transfer from the Duty Branch to Depot when a force order appeared advertising a vacancy for a manager of the Institute. Realising the potential of the little shop, which operated under a General Dealer's Licence, he pressed his ideas for growth upon Spurling who was then the Deputy Commissioner. 'BG', in his capacity as chairman of the Central Finance Committee which controlled Police domestic funds and was responsible for the financing of all recreational requirements, had little trouble convincing his colleagues that a move to a more prominent locale in the Depot, coupled with a phased expansion programme, would be a sensible and profitable undertaking. The assistance of the Police Pioneers (a uniformed construction section operated within the force) was sought, and a mini-supermarket created to provide groceries and allied stores for outstations, messes, married members and police reservists. This was to be the 'goose that laid the golden egg' as far as all police sporting and recreational facilities were concerned. From a modest turnover of £9000 a year on the ground floor of the Sergeants' Mess, and with an average profit margin of about 10%, the Depot Supply Store had mushroomed to a turnover of nearly a quarter of a million pounds when Don Lane left in 1963.

One of the first benefits of the increased domestic funding was the Inyanga Holiday Cottage, built by the Pioneer Section on a remote and elevated view site in that picturesque police camp. This amenity, and the others constructed subsequently at Lake Kyle, Kariba, Depot and Bulawayo Camp proved a godsend for all members of the Force. For a token sum a member could take his family and friends for a change of scenery and a relaxing holiday. All that had to be brought was bed linen, food and drink. Even a first-class cook was provided. At Inyanga in those early days, there was also the attraction of putting the world to rights with the Member-in-Charge, Sergeant 'Taff' Morgan.

Development continued in various directions. The Bowls Pavilion was opened; a yachting site at Lake McIlwaine was launched; the African Women's Club (Kuyedza) in the African Police Training Depot was provided with a new and 'state of the art' headquarters building. A full-size swimming pool was completed in that same training depot and an athletics track set down to broaden the already popular attractions of the Salisbury Depot grounds. The adjacent Police Golf Course was expanded to an 18 hole championship course with an imposing club house, and Sub-Inspector Buchanan was awarded the trophy for 'Most Improved Golfer of the Year'. New canteen and club premises were built at Fort Victoria and Gatooma. Tennis courts and swimming pools were established in various district stations.

At this point it is timely to comment on the Kuyedza Club concept and on the very real influence on the Force made by the Commissioner's wife, Jean Spurling.

Recognizing the need to develop the social attributes of the African police wives, Jean Spurling founded and forged ahead with an institution — really an adult education club — that, as it caught on and expanded, was to have at least 24 branches throughout the country. Various practical courses were provided to assist the women take their place in society and provide happy and healthy homes for their husbands. Correct diet, child welfare, homecrafts, cleanliness and a multitude of similar subjects were demonstrated and taught by a small staff in the Training School and by members' wives at other police camps.

Mrs Spurling did not confine herself only to the development of Kuyedza. In conjunction with the Public Works Department, she helped to plan the homes of policemen and civil servants and establish standard plans for cottages and houses; a tremendous help for married members who were subject to frequent transfers. She was instrumental in designing and introducing police mobile canteens but, not only that, she was to be seen wielding a bread knife and attacking uncut loaves of bread as emergency followed emergency.

Undoubtedly Jean Spurling's most memorable achievement was to be the gracious and distinctive non-denominational Chapel that graces the Police Depot. She was closely involved with the planning and funding of this (raising much of the money through a huge and immensely popular Fete in the Depot Grounds in 1962), and busying herself with the architect and the planning committee responsible for the elegant structure. Jean Spurling participated in many other facets of voluntary service for the community and the award to her in the 1963 New Years Honours of the MBE was a fitting and well deserved acknowledgment of and tribute to a remarkable woman.

There were some other events and personalities, one of them equine, that merit inclusion in the chronicle of the Spurling Era between 1958 and 1963.

In February 1959, a Police Contingent was dispatched hurriedly to Blantyre in Nyasaland to assist in the maintenance of law and order, specifically the 'pick up' of the leaders of the African National Congress. In all, and in two separate parties, 76 Europeans and 132 Africans were based in the Southern Province until early May. The two groups were virtually self-supporting, taking with them equipment, stores and transport. However one glitch which caused considerable consternation was the loss en route of one crate of beer. Nowhere else, in the annals of the BSA Police, has this been recorded as ever happening before.

The contingents were commanded by 'Hank' Blowers with Superintendents Weston and Van Sittert. Chief Inspector Woodgate, Sub Inspectors David Morgan (assisted by fellow 'Sparks', Woodcock and Scales for the all-important communications role), Harry Mason, 'Jock' Binnie, Guy 'Q' Houghton and 'Scoff-Box' John Crowe completed the command, technical and support structure. The Police members saw a fair amount of 'action' and used quantities of tear gas quelling rioting mobs but, most things having a more enjoyable side, they also managed a brief stay at Malindi on the shores of Lake Nyasa. It was there that one of the 'larger' members of the party, Clive Bulley, was reported by The Nyasaland Times as being mistaken for a hippopotamus.

In 1960, apart from the 'Troubles' that occupied so much of the year, there occurred two outstanding ceremonial occasions.

The first, on 30 May, was the Review of the BSA Police on what was then known as Depot's Newcastle Ground by Her Majesty Queen Elizabeth the Queen Mother. The logistics of this parade, bearing in mind the disturbed state of the country, were little short of a miracle. Close on 2300 members of the Regular Force and Police Reserve paraded on a field that had seen many a stirring athletics, cricket and rugby fixture. Many had to travel more than 400 miles to Salisbury — and then to return to their rural stations to pick up the reins of their jobs as quickly as possible.

The Parade Commander was the Acting Deputy Commissioner, Senior Assistant Commissioner Rolfe; the Escort Commander, Assistant Commissioner K. Flower MBE. Her Majesty's personal Standard was carried by Sergeant Bill Earle, mounted on a magnificent grey. Her Majesty reviewed the parade from the back of a Police land-rover driven by Sergeant Jock Stone. This was followed by speeches, a small number of presentations and finally the traditional Retreat Ceremony performed by members of the African Police Platoon under African Station Sergeants Machado and Davison.

The second ceremonial occasion took place on 12 September 1960, and was the conferring on the Police of the Freedom of the City of Salisbury. Once again, this was a majestic and moving occasion with some 500 African and European Regular members and Police Reservists parading in front of the

Town House in Kingsway. Commissioner Spurling received the Deed from the Mayor, Councillor Dennis Divaris, and handed it to Sub Inspector McIntosh who trooped it before the parade. In recognition of their escorting the Pioneer Column to Fort Salisbury seventy years before, the Police were now entitled to 'Freedom of Entry on all ceremonial occasions with bayonets fixed, drums beating and Colours flying'. The one minor blight on the day was a quiet demonstration by a group of Nationalists carrying placards with the usual political slogans scrawled upon them. One of their numbers held his placard back to front to reveal to the assembled dignitaries an advertisement for sunflower oil.

No history of the period would be complete without a few more words about RH 457 'Kentucky'. This was a horse that had captured the imagination of thousands of Rhodesians, both young and old. Kentucky joined the Police as an unbroken six-year old and it was immediately obvious that here was an exceptional animal; unafraid, prepared to do the unexpected and confident, not only in his own ability but in the man settled in the saddle on his back. 'It is,' as an article written at that time narrates, 'no small feat to be able to encourage a young, unschooled horse to walk backwards and forwards under a clothes line that has been loosely festooned with strips of paper. It is a distinct achievement to encourage him to walk through a solid paper wall (solid to the horse that is, for you can't explain to him that it gives easily and that he won't get hurt). There is still the blazing hoop to be faced and the moving jump suspended between two speeding motor cyclists; and the blindfold jumping, which calls for a skilful rider and a courageous horse'.

Kentucky did all these things; a slight rear, a gathering of the muscles, an aggressive snort — almost of disdain — and he was away at whatever lay ahead. 'Steve' Stephens was his usual rider and he and 'Kentucky' made a combination that was loved and admired by the Rhodesian public. Kentucky deserves and earned his place in this history.

The last piece in this short miscellany concerns five ex-policemen and their sailing craft..

Some may be critical that the voyage of *Si Ye Pambile* should be remembered in these pages but the courage, the determination and the audacity of those five young men who left a landlocked country in search of adventure, danger and the romance of the great oceans, cannot be ignored.

Mick Maude, Roger Gowen, Barrie Knowles, Bill Baker and Mike Brown were in their early twenties and they wanted to sail around the world. The story of how they saved, studied navigation, radio, and medicine; travelled to Britain, eventually found and purchased a sailing vessel which they made 'ship shape', and then set off from Torquay to Las Palmas, on to the West Indies, the Galapagos Islands, the Marquesas, Tahiti, and eventually to Fiji and New Zealand, is a remarkable and compelling tale. Roger Gowen told it very well in 17 serialized episodes in *The Outpost*. Only two of the original five were left when the 14,000 miles journey ended, after nearly 62 weeks, but even those who had discovered attractions other than sailing during the voyage, had good reason to be proud of their part in it. People often asked what happened to the five adventurers: Bill Baker settled down to married life in Tahiti, Roger Gowen went farming in the same country, Mike Brown went to Cape Town, Mike Maude joined the Malawi Police and Barry Knowles went to New Zealand ... but that was over 35 years ago. . Those who were left behind in Rhodesia, who walked their beats, bumped along bush roads on their motor cycles, craned over fingerprints and manned busy charge offices, shared in the thrills and trials of the five adventurers. Each month they read of their landfalls and battles against the sea — and admired the courage and determination of colleagues who had realised a dream, by attempting and succeeding in doing something different.

'Something different' was to be the story that unfolded in August of 1961; a story of mismanagement and error, of misplaced pride and one man's determination to vindicate himself. And that is the next chapter.

## Chapter Forty-Four

## A DARK CHAPTER — THE BRUCE AND HOGG AFFAIR

READERS OF THE *Rhodesia Herald* on 5 August 1961 would have been both intrigued and surprised by the front-page headline which read: "TWO SENIOR CID MEN SUSPENDED IN CITY". Details were sketchy, but the news that the Police Association had given the two men its support as 'they were trying to carry out their proper duty' was a fairly clear indication of a rift within the Force. Articles in the same newspaper earlier that same year had drawn attention to widespread dissatisfaction among the ranks, particularly in Bulawayo where detectives were said to be complaining, not only about pay, but about inefficiencies in their Department — and that their officers were out of touch with them. Commissioner Spurling had responded in a press statement by referring to the stressful times and the correct channels for complaints. This temporarily put the lid on a bubbling pot. August's headline had its root in a much more specific cause celebre than general discontent. But to set the scene properly, it is necessary to go back a few weeks.

As recorded earlier, the leaders of the National Democratic Party were hell-bent on creating an atmosphere of anarchy in the African Townships. Beatings, homes being set ablaze, damage to municipal and private property were becoming nightly occurrences in the country's African urban areas. The Nationalist leadership, notably Joshua Nkomo and his cohorts, had embarked on a regime of intimidation that was to become all too familiar in the months and years ahead. The law-abiding African, who wished only to preserve his home, his family and his job, without pressure or interference, suddenly found himself at the mercy of thugs determined only to enforce obedience to the Nationalist cause.

The police and the CID in particular were working long and hard in what must have seemed a futile, or at best, uphill battle to keep order and to gather enough information to prosecute the militant ringleaders.

Among these investigators was Detective Sergeant Frank Hogg who had joined the Force in 1949. He had a full measure of law and order dockets on his desk. One of these had conclusive proof linking the NDP leadership with a leaflet inciting people to take strike action on 24 July. This was an offense of sufficient gravity as to enable the investigating officer to make an arrest without obtaining a warrant.

Towards the end of July and beginning of August, and while the police docket on the background to the strike was being finalised, various meetings took place. Discussions involved not only this particular docket but others concerned with the many contraventions of law and order then under investigation. Involved in the meetings were Hogg, in his capacity as an investigating officer, his superior Assistant Superintendent Foxcroft, together with the Attorney General and members of his staff. On the periphery were George Digweed who headed up the Salisbury CID team and Assistant Commissioner Jack Redfern, Officer Commanding CID throughout the country.

Foxcroft had been strangely reluctant to take the various initiatives that should have been followed. He had not wanted to search the NDP offices and he had not agreed to Hogg interviewing the nationalists Silundika and Malianga, despite conclusive proof of their involvement being provided by handwriting expert Ron Blackmore. Hogg expressed his frustrations to his superior Bruce, and made it clear that the interference was such that he could no longer continue with the case. In the meantime Foxcroft had discussed matters with Refern, as a result of which the former was replaced on the case by Digweed. This change of command took matters no further forward. The reluctance to observe the letter of the law continued. Silundika made a full confession and should have been arrested. Instead his fingerprints were taken — an action which was incorrect and illegal in the circumstances — and he was allowed to walk free.

This farcical, tragi-comedy situation carried on until in desperation Bruce and Hogg went to see 'JET' Hamilton, the magistrate, to obtain warrants for the arrest of the nationalist leaders, most of whom were due to fly out of the country on various missions a few days later.

The warrants were issued and almost immediately torn up by Senior Magistrate Grant. Then followed a brace of phone calls between Redfern, Spurling, Reg Knight (Minister of Justice), probably Jack Pithey (Secretary for Justice) and possibly Whitehead as well. Rumours abounded including the reported arrival of one senior CID officer to the Railway Avenue offices clad in his pajamas — though doubtless with a dressing gown.

The intention to arrest the nationalists was totally against the wishes of prime minister Whitehead who, through his attorney general, had been involved in discussions on whether police action should take place or not. Whitehead, it is surmised, may have been following his own agenda and trying to reach an accommodation with the Nationalist leaders. Any further attempts at dialogue would have presented the Prime Minister with certain practical difficulties if they were confined in police cells. On 4 August, Redfern, almost certainly after discussions with Spurling and Barfoot, took the extraordinary step of suspending the two detectives. Thus they were unable to carry out the duty which, in law, they were obliged to do.

One can only speculate on the motivation for the actions of the senior police at that time. Probably they enjoyed a certain amount of inside knowledge concerning the political situation and this may have affected their judgment. Charitably it may be said that the arrest of the nationalists might have resulted in the whole country 'blowing up'. Had this happened, then the time available to prepare countermeasures against widespread rioting could have been perilously short. Perhaps the cautious approach, taking proceedings against the nationalist accused by way of a summons, had some merit.

The day following the suspension of Bruce and Hogg saw the news break in the *Rhodesia Herald* and the subject was to be aired extensively in the newspaper columns for the next two weeks. An inquiring and fairly condemnatory editorial in the *Herald* appeared, criticizing the actions of those in authority. This was followed by the publication of a number of letters from seemingly well-informed sympathizers of the two men and, to add fuel to the merry blaze, various members of the Legislative Assembly inquired just what was going on. To cap the issue, the Police Association weighed in, expressing their support for the two detectives and offering to assist them financially.

As was required by the Police Act, the Commissioner appointed a Board of Enquiry to 'assist him arrive at a correct conclusion' and this comprised a magistrate, Mr. St.J.Burton; the Deputy Commissioner (Crime) Frank Barfoot, and Detective Chief Superintendent Harold Thacker. The press was excluded from the proceedings which took place on 14 August and resulted in the decision that the matter was beyond the Board's jurisdiction and that the two 'miscreants' should be brought to trial and charged under the Police Act.

No time was wasted. Bruce's trial (that of Hogg was set down for a later date) took place before the end of the month and was presided over by Mr. G. Ade, a senior magistrate and Civil Commissioner from Gatooma. To say that the charges were somewhat obscurely worded would be putting it mildly. The first charge would seem to imply the improper performance of, or failure to perform a duty. The second implied that an offence was created by the accused applying for warrants of arrest without first advising the Commissioner of Police and that by so doing the maintenance of law and order was imperilled.

Evidence was led that the detectives had been told not to pursue the arrests but to expand the scope of their investigations. In their defence it was said that allowing the accused to remain at large when there was sufficient evidence available to indicate that a serious offence had been committed was anathema to men who were well aware of their powers — their duty, in fact — and had become fed up with what seemed to be the indecisive — even obstructionist — attitude of their superiors. This attitude could only rebound down the line to affect the motivation of junior ranks.

As might be expected, the legal argument hinged to a large extent on whether a directive from the Attorney General took precedence over what was written in the Statutes. Mr. Lindsay Cook defended Bruce and the result of the trial was unambiguous. The detective had no case to answer. He was simply carrying out a duty required of him by law, in this case the Criminal Procedure and Evidence Act. Bruce was acquitted and both men reinstated in their positions. In passing it should be mentioned that the relevant docket was never returned to the police station (as was normal procedure) and, probably, was never officially closed.

And there the matter should have died. But it didn't.

Hogg could see the writing on the wall as far as his 13 years career was concerned, and resigned 'on gratuity' early in 1962, to make a livelihood in colour photography processing. Bruce was determined to clear his name. His promotion in the CID had been markedly rapid hitherto, in fact he had earned a Special Commendation from the Commissioner four years earlier for outstanding and protracted investigations into an arson, housebreaking and car theft investigation. Now however, with promotion to commissioned rank within his grasp — some say that the EXCO (Executive Council Minute conferring commissioned rank) was already with the Minister — he became stuck — and destined to remain so.

Papers reveal that a memorandum placed on Bruce's confidential personal record by the Commissioner was highly condemnatory of his attitude and loyalty toward his superiors. Though he later managed to have parts of that document expunged and appealed to the Police Advisory Board, he endured a most unpleasant interview with Barfoot, and was to be overlooked for promotion on no less than thirteen occasions over the next six years.

'Dixie' Bruce never became a commissioned officer although, promoted to Detective Chief Inspector, he remained a loyal and hardworking member of the Force until after the retirements of both Commssioners Spurling and Barfoot. During those years, and after his own retirement in July 1968 — caused, as he put it, 'through sheer frustration' — he worked single-mindedly and at no small expense to have his name cleared.

Rejected by successive Promotion Boards, upheld in his appeals by the Police Advisory Board (before which Spurling declined to appear to give evidence), it was nevertheless impossible to overcome the 'personal animosities and antagonisms' that persisted at the head of the Force. Thwarted by 'proper channels' he took his case to the Legislative Assembly.

But it was not until March 1974, following three Reports from the Parliamentary Committee on Pensions, Grants and Gratuities, that this sad and unnecessary episode came to an end. Bruce was fully exonerated and awarded a substantial lump sum payment.

In fairness to Spurling and Barfoot, it must be said that the former had taken less and less of an active part in Force affairs when his successor was announced towards the end of 1962. Nevertheless, his refusal to give evidence before the Police Advisory Board must be regarded as significant and, certainly on the facts available, he could have been accused of defeating or obstructing the course of justice. As for Barfoot, very shortly after his appointment he became seriously ill and had to undergo major brain surgery in Britain towards the end of 1964. The illness re-occurred and though he served on until the end of 1967, the shadow of the cancer that was to finally claim him in 1971 was always present.

There were many casualties after the 'Bruce and Hogg Affair' of 1961. Assistant Commissioner Dick Parry, himself a distinguished and dedicated policeman who had been chairman of the Police Association when the news broke and who had promised the two detectives the financial support of the Association, was condemned and disparaged until he retired in February 1962. Even worse was the effect on senior members of the CID. No less than six detective inspectors and one outstanding detective chief inspector saw cause to resign in the wake of the affair. Most took the option of a gratuity and left the police and the country, but the loss of so many experienced investigators at such a critical time was a tragic and unnecessary aftermath to a badly handled and bungled affair.

Readers will have drawn various conclusions about Basil Spurling from these chapters. Perhaps the following story most clearly shows both the complexity and dedication of the man. It comes from retired Superintendent Eric Jones — "In the early 60s, when I was Sub-District Officer in Victoria Province, I happened to be at Bikita Minerals where, in the club house, I chatted to the old prospector, almost a household name in the area, 'Paddy' Nolan. He was, so he said, in his camp one evening when a patrolling policeman arrived. As was the custom in those days, Nolan invited the man to stay in his camp and join him for a 'bite' and a drink. They spent a pleasant evening together before turning in for the night.

The next morning, before continuing his patrol, the policeman mentioned that, as they'd eaten game meat for supper, he would like to see Nolan's permit to shoot game. Nolan was astounded at this request but had to admit that he had no licence. He was even more astounded to be told that he would be prosecuted for breaking the law. Greater still was his astonishment when he went to pay the fine to find the cash had already been lodged and that all he had to do was sign the admission of guilt. The patrolling policeman had paid the fine. Trooper Spurling was not prepared to turn a blind eye to his duty but he still acknowledged the hospitality received."

## Chapter Forty-Five

## THE ADVENT OF PROFESSIONALISM

*Towards the Declaration of Independence. Barfoot becomes Commissioner — commendations — increase in Reserve and formation of African Police Reserve — 'Doc' Thompson — Forensic Science Laboratory — Ballistics — Hollingworth — more 'characters'.*

Frank Eric Barfoot became Commissioner of Police in April, 1963. Some, indeed several aspects of his career have already been mentioned but it is significant in the light of later events that he was the first Commissioner to be born and brought up in Africa. He was born at Claremont in the Cape in 1913 and had attested in the Police in 1933. After a brief spell as a District Trooper, he joined the Criminal Investigation Department, there to move steadily upwards to commissioning in 1949. He served as both a District and Provincial commander, moving to Senior Assistant Commissioner to head the CID in 1960 and, three months later, was appointed Deputy Commissioner (Crime and Security) upon the premature retirement (on medical grounds) of 'Rex' Borland.

Barfoot had distinguished himself as a front-row forward for both the Police and Mashonaland rugby teams in the 30s. He enhanced his official reputation in 1937 with a commendation for the courageous arrest of an armed criminal and again, 10 years later, when he was commended for expert and time-consuming investigations into an especially difficult and involved usury case. A man of high principles, he was tough, fair, and demanding.

Such then was the man who would steer the Force from 1963 through to the Unilateral Declaration of Independence (UDI) and beyond, whilst Prime Minister Ian Smith, determined that somehow Southern Rhodesia would gain its independence, was earning for himself the sobriquet of 'frequent flyer' between Salisbury and London.

London, in that quite momentous year, was one of several centres occupying the newspaper headlines. Kim Philby, the Third Man, left the city, disappeared in Beirut and re-emerged six months later in Moscow. The Profumo Affair spiced up the British newspapers and titillated the public for several weeks; the Beatles rocketed into prominence and the 'Great Train Robbery' took place. In Dallas, President John Kennedy was assassinated while, again in Britain, Prime Minister Harold Macmillan resigned to be succeeded by the Earl of Home, and in remote Stornoway, 14-year old Prince Charles ordered a cherry brandy at a pub.

Despite the fact that the Police establishment had at last been increased, that there was more transport, and radio equipment was advanced and up-to-date, the cases of arson, assaults and intimidation persisted throughout Southern Rhodesia. It is a matter for speculation, as was said earlier, whether these improvements had they been made when Jackson requested and when Spurling entreated, and finally demanded, would have obviated the need for the Law and Order Maintenance Act and kindred legislation. Nevertheless, by 1963, that legislation had been on the Statute Books for just over two years and was slowly but surely having a positive effect.

Despite the powers within the new legislation, an understanding of how the police were being pressured can be gained by paging through some of the commendations earned in the years preceding UDI.

In May 1963 Detective Inspector Brian Darling and Detective Sergeant Angus Ross disarmed a time bomb hidden in a child's lunch case and set to explode in OK Bazaars in central Salisbury. Sergeant Carver and African Detective Sergeant Aroni, assisted by other members of the police, cleared several cases of arson in the Goromonzi area. In Gatooma, an African Police Reservist (Jorodani), with total disregard for his own safety, went to the assistance of a civilian who was being savagely attacked by a knife-wielding African and was himself seriously injured.

This attack, incidentally, took place in front of a large crowd, not one of whom was prepared to assist in any way.

In October, Sergeant Fati determinedly arrested the ringleader of a gang of thugs who were causing a disturbance near the Harare Market. With aid of two other policemen, he managed to arrest another nine of the gang and secured their conviction for public violence.

Another man to distinguish himself was African Constable Bernard. In October, he charged into the midst of an aggressive and hostile crowd that was attempting to close down a beer hall and intimidate the occupants into leaving. He arrested the stone–throwing ring-leader and managed, now with some assistance, to get him to a police truck.

Only three weeks later Bernard was again in the 'headlines'. This time, in civilian clothes and accompanied by a colleague, he was pointed out as a policeman at a political meeting and the usual incitement to assault the police started. Once again, the constable managed to arrest the ringleader and hold him until reinforcements arrived.

In those tumultuous and violent days, incidents similar to those described became, unfortunately, almost the norm.

Another such case, in which a brave few were pitted against a menacing mob, involved a patrol dog-handler and his animal. This took place in the mid-January 1964. Again the baldly related facts mask the excitement, the fear and the tension of that warm afternoon, when a crowd of over 3000 was gathered in the Machipisa Shopping Centre in Highfield, Salisbury: 'A small detachment of police was doing its best to disperse the crowd, but without much success, and it was decided to call in the dogs. African Constable Fani and Constable le Crerar moved in, but were heavily stoned and le Crerar knocked unconscious. Fani took control of the dog and stood over his injured colleague to shield him from the stones and missiles raining down on them. Eventually the other police members, who had been heavily involved with the rest of the mob, managed to get through to the three and save them from further injury.'

Little has been said of the Police Dog Section thus far, so it is timely to tell the story of one remark-able animal among the many remarkable canines that served Police so well in those desperate days.

'Rex' was born in Welkom in May 1960 and came to Rhodesia as a house pet while still a puppy. He was donated to the Force when little more than a year old and was chosen by Patrol Officer Brian Blitenthall to be his 'companion'. The two trained together and left the Dog Training Depot in October of 1961. Rex was described as a 'cheerful, exuberant personality' but who never permitted familiarity other than from Brian, his handler. The two were on duty at Nkai later that year when demonstrations were expected at a trial in the village. The mere presence of the large, fearless dog was apparently sufficient to nip in the bud any trouble. A year later, in December and in a Bulawayo township, the policeman and his dog were blocking a passage between two buildings to cut off the escape of a gang constructing and manning a road block. A man crept up behind Blitenthall, hit him with a rock and knocked him unconscious. A witness described how the man was about to hit the helpless policeman again when Rex charged, forcing the man to run. The dog pursued the man knocking him down twice before pinning him against a tree. That particular felon was sentenced to five years' imprisonment for attempted murder.

In 1963 Rex and Blitenthall were again in the thick of action, this time in Mabvuku with Superintendent Sheriff. Rex had charged into a mob and 'arrested' the ringleader. Blitenthall followed to give legal effect to the arrest — and was immediately attacked and stoned. Sheriff came to his assistance but all three, with their prisoner, were compelled to take cover in a deep storm drain. Again they were subjected to a merciless barrage of stones and bricks by about ten of the mob. Things were reaching a desperate stage when Rex decided that enough was enough and launched himself out and at the stone-throwers who immediately took to their heels.

A similar incident took place the following year when Rex, having made his 'arrest' was lifted by the tail, and punched and kicked by the mob. The dog still hung onto his prisoner until the arrival of his handler. Only then did Rex give in by collapsing, battered and exhausted and overcome with shock.

Early in 1965 the worst happened. Rex contracted cancer of the eye — incurable, excruciatingly painful and likely to spread rapidly. This wonderful animal was 'pensioned off' and Brian Blitenthall took him into his home for the few remaining weeks of his life. He was put to sleep on 6 April.

These paragraphs tell only of the more outstanding episodes in the life of Rex. No mention has been made of the arrests of car thieves, house and store breakers, and so on. All that was the mundane work expected of a dog and of his handler. Perhaps, therefore, the final words should come from one who was most intimately connected with the dog and the Dog Section: "Later, when the body of this great-hearted police dog, wrapped in a blanket, was carried back to the Dog Depot for his burial, an unnatural quiet fell over the rows of kennels. Rex was laid to rest in a small plot, beside the entrance gate to the kennel area, where all who pass by will remember him."

One of the more important changes as a result of Government's belated and less blinkered approach to the needs of Police was an increase in the strength of the Police Reserve and the formation of an African Police Reserve. It speaks volumes for the peace-respecting, generally apolitical populace that so many flocked to join the latter body when it was formed early in September 1960 with an establishment of 5000 which, over the following two years rose to 7500 and then 10,000. Although the other sections of the Reserve were also proportionately increased, it was the African Reservists who were to bear the brunt of the riots and victimisation that permeated the urban African areas.

The most horrifying attack, which caused a wave of public revulsion, was the murder of Kaitano Kambadza during October 1962. Kambadza, an African Police Reservist had completed his duties at Machipisa Police Station and was cycling home when he was attacked, stoned, doused with petrol and set alight. A farmer, returning to Beatrice, found him lying in the road and held his hand until an ambulance arrived to take him to hospital where he died nine hours later. Police arrested a number of men for this cowardly and despicable murder but four months later they were acquitted for lack of evidence.

Despite being victims of regular attacks, the African Police Reservists proved their dedication to the Force in many ways. The following commendations, taken at random, speak for themselves: In February 1964, Reservist Kachapulula of the Bulawayo Urban Field Reserve, who was off duty and in plain clothes, saw a person who had been arrested for intimidation break away from two regular members. He chased after the suspect, re-arrested him and then found himself being attacked by members of the public. The regular members now came to his aid and between them they managed to escort their prisoner to the    police station.

In January of the same year, Reservist Christopher, also from Bulawayo Urban and also off duty and in plain clothes, saw two persons assaulting another with stones. He attempted to arrest these two and, in the violent struggle that followed, received a serious stab wound below his left shoulder. Despite this, he carried on the struggle and, with the assistance of a regular policeman who happened on the scene, managed to arrest both assailants.

In Salisbury, at about the same time, Reservist Dzaumbera was with a team of regular members who managed to disperse a mob of over 50 Africans who were stoning some of the public. The team managed to arrest one of the mob and rescue a reservist who had been stoned and left unconscious. Later that day the same team, in very similar circumstances, (though this time the mob numbered more than 100), arrested three more Africans, members of a gang stoning houses in Highfield Township, and put the remainder to flight.

It was in this affray that African Constable Godfrey was so severely injured that his left eye had to be removed. (Happily he recovered to become a valued member of *The Outpost* staff). Certainly in the special commendations awarded the team, the words 'outstanding courage and tenacity' were not lightly used.

These were but a few of the commendations and 'notes of good work' heaped on members of the Police and Police Reserve in the years immediately preceding UDI. To page through the awards for outstanding investigations, for courage, for exceptional good work, is almost to read a nominal roll of the force.

There are, however, two other awards that need to be recounted: the one because it resulted in a medal for gallantry; the other because it involved forensic evidence and very little has been said about this aspect of investigation so far.

The Colonial Police Medal for Gallantry was awarded to a member, a sergeant, who just happened to be in the right place at the wrong time.

Sergeant Alexander ("Sandy") Coutts received the medal from Her Majesty the Queen at Buckingham Palace in November 1964, in recognition of his courage during a mass shooting at Premier Estates, Umtali, during June of the previous year.

Coutts was shot at point blank range when he attempted to disarm Leopold Smith who, during the course of one day, killed four and wounded seven others in a savage and unbridled shooting spree associated with a domestic dispute. Coutts, in attendance to make sure that the local Welfare Officer had no problems going about his duty, was actually shot at twice, the first time by a shot-gun, the second by a .22 rifle and altogether was wounded in 23 places. He was retired with the rank of inspector on 'medical grounds' 10 years later.

The last case, which earned the investigating officer a Commendation and monetary award, took place on the outskirts of Bulawayo, on the Salisbury road on an afternoon in early September 1964.

African Sergeant Pugeni was off duty, with his wife and driving towards Ntabazinduna. Some distance out of the city, on the main road, he was overtaken by a blue and white Ford that swerved wildly after passing him and travelled on the gravel verge at high speed before vanishing up the road. Some distance further on, Pugeni noticed a group of people gathered at the roadside but he was not waved down nor did he see anything amiss. However, a mile further on, things were very different. A man was lying by the roadside, very definitely dead. Pugeni asked a passing motorist to seek help from the nearest police station and started on-the-spot investigations. Some distance from the body he came upon a pair of shoes, then a bicycle wheel, then a bicycle headlamp and finally, more than 1100 feet away, the remains of a bicycle. The local Police arrived, Pugeni passed on the result of his investigations and carried on his way.

Later that night, returning with his family to Bulawayo along a rural road, Pugeni happened upon the blue and white Ford again, now apparently abandoned and with extensive damage to its front. Pugeni set off to report the car's whereabouts to the nearest police station, only to be stopped by two men a short distance away. Their car — the Ford — had run out of petrol and could he spare any?

Pugeni questioned them about their movements, the damage to the car and, receiving evasive replies, arrested the driver on reasonable suspicion of culpable homicide. Subsequent inquiries showed that the driver, a Reverend Damasane, had knocked down no less than three cyclists on the road that day. The last one he had killed.

The next day, flakes of paint from the minister's car and flakes of paint found on the roadside where the third man had been killed were collected and sent to the Forensic Science Laboratory in Salisbury. They were, of course, all from the same vehicle. But even more conclusive was that the underside of each flake had minute specks of a contrasting colour pitted into the red ochre of the primary coat. These specks had been sprayed on by mistake when other vehicles were being sprayed at the time the Ford received its first application of undercoat. Not only that, but the Laboratory identified fibres imbedded in the paint which corresponded with the boiler suit worn by the cyclist when he was fatally struck down.

Damasane, who admitted to drinking three large bottles of beer and a quarter bottle of gin earlier that day, was found guilty and sentenced to two years' imprisonment and a fine of £10.

Only passing reference has been made to the Forensic Science Laboratory in this history. It is timely to look more deeply at this invaluable asset to police investigations.

For many years, Police had to rely on the efficient and expert services of the Government Analyst and his staff whenever there was a requirement for scientific assistance. By the early 60s the sheer volume of the work was proving almost more than the department could handle and the need to form a full-time, properly equipped and professionally staffed forensic science laboratory was clear.

On 1 January 1963, Dr John Thompson, then a physical scientist with the Department of Research and Specialist Services (a Federal Department under the Ministry of Agriculture) was appointed Director of the new Police establishment. It was an inspired choice.

John Thompson was a powerfully built, quiet spoken, deliberate Scot, seldom seen without a pipe clenched between his teeth. He possessed a vast scientific knowledge gained with Imperial Chemical Industries before the war and with the War Office during the war, where his specialties had been tank design, explosives and bomb disposal. For a number of years he had shown a strong interest in the scientific aspects of police investigations, so strong an interest that, in a light-hearted moment, he described forensic science as 'the ability to distinguish between blood stains and beer stains.'

Suitable premises were available adjacent to CID Headquarters and the Pioneers, overseen by 'Doctor John', soon converted the building into a modern laboratory. As was too often the case, the budget for technical equipment was meagre but before long the premises were equipped with a petrographic microscope, a spectrograph, a microphotometer, chromatography and gas chromatography apparatus, a binocular stereo microscope and a refractometer, as well as a mass of ancillary equipment.. The purchase of the petrographic microscope provides an amusing story.

Some months prior to the Laboratory opening, the British Atomic Energy Commission decided to leave the country and much of their equipment was put up for auction. 'Doc' Thompson attended the sale, propped himself in a corner, pipe in mouth, and followed the bidding, unperturbed, but with a faint smile on his face. Offers were high and competitive and buyers had used up most of their funds in competition with each other when Thompson raised his bulky frame from the table to reveal a polished wooden box. The virtually new and extremely high-quality petrographic microscope in that box was knocked down to the Police at a fraction of its real value.

A forensic scientist will tell you that 'every contact leaves its trace' and, in the years that followed, Doc Thompson and his team proved this to be true on countless occasions. In one hit-and-run case, the suspect's car was found with bits of grass and weeds between the front bumper and the wing. These were identified as having grown at the exact spot where the suspect's car had swerved off the road.

Tests undertaken in the Laboratory were so exact that Thompson gave as his opinion that it was possible to identify the exact square foot of soil on which the vegetable matter had grown. Not only that, but he could exclude the possibility of it coming from anywhere else in the country.

Cases such as this abound. Fibres on a knife, invisible to the naked eye, were linked to slashed rail truck tarpaulins; stolen maize connected conclusively to a specific field. In a case of 'attempted train wrecking', Thompson was able to link a particular shifting spanner to 14 points of similarity on nuts removed from a length of rail. Another intriguing case (to which justice cannot be done in a few words) centred on the forging of the official overprinting of Rhodesia's 'Independence' postage stamps and the comparison of inks used on the originals with those on the forgeries.

Thompson's subsequent paper 'The Identification of Inks by Electrophoresis' was based on the postage stamps and similar cases. It was published in London and demonstrated a definitive advance in the identification and separation of inks. One could reel off case after fascinating case — the list is endless but the truism is there for all to see; 'every contact leaves a trace'.

The preceding paragraphs tend to the impression that the Laboratory was there to provide the final nail in a criminal's coffin — not so; the laboratory was there to establish the truth. The results could be advantageous to the prosecution or to the defense; it was the truth that mattered..

A natural step is to look at the Ballistics Section of the Police that was growing up at the same time as the Forensics Department. In so doing, we meet one of the more remarkable of the recruits who joined in the immediate post-war years, one who was born in Lancashire and who, when asked why he came out to Southern Rhodesia replied, 'anything was better than England in 1949'.

Don Hollingworth returned to the Police Depot after a short spell as a district policeman in Umtali and became a most able and respected musketry instructor, initially under the guidance of Gerry Woodgate. His marksmanship ability was almost phenomenal and to recount the trophies he won, the prizes he was awarded and the competitions in which he participated over the next 25 years would more than fill a page. Perhaps, and to add point to his prowess, it should be said that he was Force Champion Bisley Shot nine times, Champion Service Shot on 11 occasions, British Rapid and Snap Champion in 1965, and South African Service Champion in 1978. He represented Southern Rhodesia at Bisley on several occasions and, time and time again, triumphed over fields of international competitors. However, it was in 1963 and in subsequent years that his role was to change when the Armaments Section, which included Ballistics and Bomb Disposal functions, came into being.

Although it is chronologically out of place, it was Hollingworth who defused a time-bomb placed in the Left Luggage Office at Salisbury Railway Station in 1977. That was on the same day that a similar device, left in Woolworths in Charter Road exploded, killing 11 and injuring 77 people

In all his endeavours, be they involved with ballistics, mine disposal or mine protection, Hollingworth was ably assisted by his police colleague David Perkins (later to be killed in an accidental explosion in South Africa) and both were able to call upon the vast experience and expertise of Doc Thompson who, as has been seen, was not without knowledge of what was required.

It was during this period, from 1963 onwards when the incursions were starting and gathering momentum that Chief Superintendent Guy Houghton, later to take over the Support Unit, was based in Police General Headquarters as Staff Officer (Planning). He was a member of the Mine Warfare Committee, and was required to liaise with the other Services in the development of mine-protected vehicles. During this time, again outside the period covered by the chapter, the Police — with

Hollingworth prominently involved — and the Army, were working independently and developing their own prototype vehicles. The Mine Warfare Committee acted as the catalyst for these experiments and linked with the South African Defence Forces who were conducting their own research and testing.

It was during 1972 that Thompson and Houghton attended trials of mine proofed-vehicles being undertaken by the South African Defence Forces in the Caprivi Strip. Out of this visit came the concept of the 43 degrees V-shaped body and from this the hugely successful 'Rhino' and other similar vehicles were developed. Hollingworth and Perkins were deeply involved in the trials of the various prototypes which, when finally tested and eventually manufactured, were to save many lives. More will be said of the ingenuity of Hollingworth in a later chapter.

All this was taking place as the Ballistics Section was starting to prove itself and provide the vital link between the weapons used in a crime, often terrorist inspired, and the cartridge cases invariably left at the scene of that crime. Prior to the Sinoia battle in 1966, which is described later, the terrorists involved in that action had fired on an Indian couple travelling south from Zambia, failed to hit the vehicle, but left cartridge cases lying in the undergrowth. These were later found and recovered by the local CID man, John Fletcher. They provided the first indication that a crossing had occurred and that a hostile group had entered the country. The cartridge cases were eventually linked in with the actual battle, proving that the two skirmishes were related. (Of course much time was taken up by court appearances, where Hollingworth and Perkins were required to give expert and, it must be said, seldom challenged evidence).

Don Hollingworth was promoted to Superintendent in 1977, three years before his retirement in 1980. By that time, the arthritis that was to all but cripple him had a vicious grip on his hands and feet, yet, undeterred by the pain and uncomplaining at the very obvious discomfort, he continued with the valuable work he had started so many years before. Don Hollingworth left a legacy of drive and dedication and unquestioned service. The only regret that exists is that the policies of the Force and the lack of flexibility among senior ranks to the concept of commissioning a 'technician', delayed his promotion to superintendent for so many years.

As with all the stages of Police history, the years leading up to UDI produced their share of 'characters' and, again, not all of them managed to bathe the Force in a glow of goodness and high esteem.

Anthony Bowl served in the Police for just on seven years before being discharged as 'medically unfit'. Most of his service was in the Midlands area where for a time he served under Sergeant Peter Stiff at Chakari. Stiff, it is reported, described him as a 'very odd bird' and certain it is that his intelligence level was way and above that of his contemporaries. Paging through the police magazine, one finds Bowl setting quizzes for its readers, writing letters critical of the introduction of the patrol officer and section officer ranks (introduced in early 1965) and peppering his paragraphs with non-Scrabble words like 'proceleusmatics', 'choriambs' and 'amphibrach'. However, the most remarkable literary output from this young genius — for such he undoubtedly was — appears as a short story in *The Outpost* of July 1963, under the title 'No Motive'.

In very broad terms, the story, related in the first person, describes a man who has travelled on the same train, in the same carriage with the same companion for over two years, and become totally weary of the other's incessant chatter about butterflies and moths. Mr Atwell, the narrator, resolves to kill the other man, and to do so hatches and executes a fairly ingenious plot, involving throwing the man out of the carriage. When questioned by the police he informs them that on the day of the murder he was pottering in the garden at home and was nowhere near the train. The punch line comes when the murdered man bequeaths his entire and valuable lepidoptera collection to his murderer.

Straightforward? Not quite. Twenty-four years later, Dr Anthony Bowl, now 51 years of age, a mathematics genius with an IQ of 150, and possessed of a warped obsession for blonde women, suddenly shoved a Mrs Margaret Pucci, a blond lady whom he had never known, in front of an express train in Wimbledon Station, London.

Bowl was eventually sentenced to spend the rest of his life in an asylum. The headlines in the *Sunday Times* included the words "Laughing lunatic who pushed blonde in front of train was ex-BSAP cop."

But there were others who, fortunately, portrayed the Police in a far better light.

Sergeant Anthony Crossley of the Salisbury Traffic Branch was the first member of the Force to represent the country at the Olympic Games.

Tony Crossley was born in Bulawayo, educated at Milton School and joined the Police in 1960. He had been a keen yachtsman for many years and was to compete with David Butler in the Flying Dutchman class at the Tokyo Olympics. The team's eventual position was eleventh — not a bad result for a landlocked country. David Butler was a Police Reserve Air Wing pilot so, all in all, the Force was well to the fore in Japan.

Finally, a man who was to play a quiet but tremendously supportive role on the stage of a very different theatre during the years following UDI. John Pestell had retired in June 1965 to take up the position of Comptroller to His Excellency the Governor, Sir Humphrey Gibbs. Pestell had joined the Police fairly early in 1939 and, like so many of his era, had been seconded for duties in North Africa where he rose to the rank of Major whilst serving in Cyrenaica. Before retiring from the Police he, another man with whom Commissioner Barfoot did not see eye-to-eye, had administered the Police Reserve from Police Headquarters and, immediately before retiring, was commanding the Mashonaland Province.

One of his remarks to a young and ambitious policeman who consistently worked beyond normal hours was "if you can't do your job during the hours you're supposed to, you're either inefficient or you've too much to do. " Pestell, subsequently knighted for his services during those post-UDI years, remained staunchly supportive of the Governor until Rhodesia became a Republic in 1970. In his diaries and in conversation, he describes how old friends sometimes preferred to cross the road and 'walk by on the other side' rather than greet him. Yet in those critical months after November 1965, he was often required to host the various Service commanders when, in civilian clothes and in private cars, they made clandestine visits to Government House.

A. C. KACHEMU

*"You realise what this sort of thing can do to my practice?"*

## Chapter Forty-Six

## UDI — A DAMP SQUIB

*The Unilateral Declaration of Independence —*
*Terrorist attacks — UDI and the police — Crime situation.*

The events leading up to the Declaration of Independence have been analysed and chronicled and discussed ad nauseam but, through it all, and as far as the BSA Police is concerned, one clear and indisputable fact emerges: the Police remained at their jobs to do exactly what the laws of the country demanded.

There has been a certain amount of criticism in various books dealing with the months and weeks leading up to UDI, that the proclamation of a State of Emergency, some days before the actual Declaration, was either unnecessary, or a poorly concealed attempt to make sure that the State's forces were possessed of all the necessary powers to counter any form of civil disobedience, even a general uprising. If the latter were the case, quite frankly it would seem to have been no more than prudent planning. But much has been made of the fact that the proclamation was undated, so giving the Government adequate opportunity to introduce the emergency powers to suit their timing. That impression may well have substance, for Smith made quite certain, at one time or another, that his Service chiefs and heads of sensitive Ministries were 'on side'. However, it is more important to remember what had happened in the preceding months and relate various incidents to the inevitability of the political decision — that is UDI — about to be announced, and to the strong possibility of widespread trouble.

The impression given is that Smith 'used' Commissioner Barfoot to place the Police Force in a state of readiness prior to the Declaration. Certain it is that one basis for the proclamation included a memorandum prepared by Barfoot outlining the tenseness of the security situation and the very clear threat that had come about as terrorist gangs moved into and about the country. It is appropriate to review the activities of those gangs.

In the Umtali and Chipinga areas for example, there had been the burning of wattle and fir tree plantations, cattle had been slashed and cars stoned. A petrol soaked sack had been thrown into a boys' dormitory at Chipinga Junior School. The area was primed for tragedy, and in July 1964 it came.

Petrus and Johanna Oberholtzer, with their three-year-old daughter, were motoring home from Umtali when they were stopped and attacked by a four-man gang; petrol was poured over them and efforts made to torch them and their vehicle. Only the arrival of another car deterred and frightened off the attackers, but for Petrus Oberholtzer it was too late, he died a few hours later from the multiple stab wounds he had received. Two of the so-called 'Crocodile Gang' responsible were arrested, tried and hanged.

Near the Botswana border, on the Dube Ranch, lived Mr Farewell Roberts with his wife. One evening, alerted by the barking of his dogs, Roberts walked outside to find six fully armed men standing in his garden. Fortunately for him, they just dropped their sub-machine guns and ran. All but one were subsequently captured, two being tracked for over 60 miles by Detective Constable Nenabo.

Incidents persisted: the foyer of a block of flats in Bulawayo was torn apart by several sticks of gelignite on 12 September 1965 — Pioneer Day in Rhodesian history. Evidence accumulated of weapons and explosives being carried into the country and of sabotage training being undertaken.

Knowing the magnitude of the external terrorist training in progress and incidents such as those described, it would have been folly indeed for Barfoot to ignore the potentiality for widespread disorder when, should he have been kept in ignorance, UDI was declared.

It seems abundantly clear from reading of this period that the decision to declare Independence had been taken weeks, if not months before the fateful day. Smith and his supporters in the Cabinet probably hoped that events would make the announcement unnecessary but, for all that, they were far too pragmatic to expect a miracle. Ergo, with UDI sympathizers already well established in every position commanding power in Government and parts of the media, it was just a matter of pulling the strings at the appointed time.

Michael 'Fred' Pringle was member in charge Lalapanzi on 11 November 1965. The preceding day, he was called into Gwelo to see his Officer Commanding (Assistant Commissioner 'Larry' Lamont) and told simply that there would be an important announcement on the radio the following day. He and others at the station should listen — and then carry on doing their jobs.

At Plumtree on the Botswana border, Inspector Alan Rich was in charge with Section Officer Ian Hogg as his deputy. The pupils at Tegwani Mission School decided to protest against UDI and stage a march into Plumtree village. On the outskirts they were met by Hogg who, armed with a pistol and supported by a handful of constables, concentrated their attention by firing a shot in the air. He then invited them to spend most of the night in the Police Camp, behave themselves, and to leave and return to their school very early the following morning. This they did, and neither the Native Commissioner nor the slumbering citizens of Plumtree were aware of what had happened.

However, one does not reject one's master, or in this case Royal Mistress, however benevolent he or she may be, without creating a few ripples and waves. The waves may certainly be regarded as the sanctions that the British and later the United Nations imposed; the ripples were the few policemen who, ostensibly at any rate, voiced scruples about being a part of the "rebel regime" as it was to be internationally labeled.

A number of long-serving members left the Force in the aftermath of UDI, but few actually attributed their leaving to political events or a conscience troubled by no longer directly serving the Sovereign. Some were disturbed by the instability, obvious or anticipated, in the country; some had already formulated plans for the future; all made sure they had qualified for their pensions. After all, it was just on 20 years since the large intakes of 1946. Further down the line, there were a number, a very small number, of desertions.

The *Rhodesia Herald* of 9 November 1965, records that a warrant of arrest had been issued for three recruits who had deserted at the end of October. They were Stuart Mason, John Bryant and Derek Ridgewell and the latter was reported as saying "Rhodesia was just not what we expected it to be and we are hoping to get back to England as soon as possible." He declined to comment on a suggestion that he and his colleagues had left because of the political situation.

A former section officer, Harry Moolman, tells of another couple of deserters, Richard Whittaker and George Fairhurst, who 'borrowed' a colleague's car in Gwelo on the pretext of going out for the evening and then motored through to the Plumtree area, abandoned the car, and walked several miles through the bush to Francistown. From there, they were taken to Zambia and then by air back to England. Rather interestingly, the British Government required them to repay their airfares.

There were a few others, probably no more than a dozen, who decided to desert over the next 12 months but it would be wrong to ascribe their leaving solely to UDI.

The imposition of sanctions was bound to have its affect on some of the commercial and industrial concerns in the country and a number of firms had to lay-off their employees. Government had anticipated this and the Government Unemployment Relief Scheme was launched. Jobs were found for men and women in the Public Service, the Uniformed Forces or wherever a need arose. Many well and highly — qualified people found themselves starting on a new career under this Scheme and nearly 200 were absorbed into the BSAP.

To conclude this short chapter on UDI, it is of interest to peruse the Reports of the Commissioner of Police for the years 1965 and 1966. For the first of those years, there was a decrease in most categories of property and violent crime. However, and in view of scurrilous and unfounded allegations that had appeared in the British press, the Commissioner reiterated that his members adhered to the 'Principles of Police' as laid down initially by the joint Commissioners of the Metropolitan Police in 1829.

Essentially, these required of policemen complete impartiality in the exercise of their duty and the use at all times of no more than the minimum force necessary to achieve legitimate police objectives.

The 1966 Report was in a similar vein: a decrease in serious crimes; a most significant drop in Law and Order (Maintenance) Act cases; less crimes of violence, and a most satisfactory clearance of outstanding politically-motivated cases. The latter owed much to greatly increased police patrolling and the decrease in acts of intimidation now that members of the thug element and their leaders had been removed from society.

To the civilian population of the rebel state things looked promising, even faintly prosperous, but this was only a relatively calm period before the storms that were to come with increasing intensity over the next 15 years.

They were to be years during which too many Rhodesians were brainwashed and convinced that a nation could stand out indefinitely against the rest of the world. But for all that, a nation was forged in the melting pot of almost universal opprobrium. Sadly it was not a totally cohesive nation. There were a few whose inward allegiance still lay with the British Crown and others who, understandably, were unable to resist the ogre represented by Nationalism.

## Chapter Forty-Seven

## LET BATTLE COMMENCE

*The UDI years — Law and Order cases — Successes in the Zambezi Valley — Battle of Sinoia — Viljoen murders — troubles on the Great North Road — Wickenden — skirmishes in west Matabeleland — Spencer Thomas — Intrigue at the University — Routine work continues — sporting activities with the Reserve –South African assistance — three retirements.*

The years from 1966 to 1971 were the years of negotiation with the British. They were the years of HMS Tiger, NIBMAR (No Independence Before Majority Rule), and HMS Fearless; they were the times of Harold Wilson, of selective and later comprehensive mandatory sanctions, of Douglas-Home, Bottomley; of the creation of the Republic of Rhodesia, Lord Goodman and the preparations for the Pearce Commission. They were also the years during which many of the Nationalist leaders were confined to remote parts of the country, bringing relative peace to, and less intimidation of, the majority of the country's citizens. It was also the period when the Government of South Africa and some of its policemen came to the aid of Rhodesia's Forces, and when terrorist incursions led to vicious murders and to bitter but sporadic battles at, notably, Sinoia and in western Matabeleland.

During those six years, the Security Forces achieved many outstanding successes against ZANU and ZANLA. Over the same period, the public of Rhodesia — despite being burdened by shortages, bombarded by overseas vitriol and seized by curiosity over the blanked out sections in their newspapers — showed their determination to improvise, innovate and overcome, to manufacture much of what was unavailable, and to circumvent the strictures imposed by the outside world. Unfortunately, the public was led by a Government that history will probably regard as bigoted and blinkered. Nevertheless, its ministers and spokesmen managed to imbue a remarkable but, as it proved, totally misguided sense of invincibility among many of the population, some of whom seemed to think they were involved in some 20th century Crusade. Whatever the rights or wrongs of the politicians, the mere earthlings of the Services were generally infused with the scent of a 'mission' which they were convinced, for want of a better phrase, was 'on the side of the angels'.

From 1966 until 1969, the Annual Reports of the Commissioner of Police — Barfoot for the first two years, thereafter Spink — paint an almost rosy picture of crime trends in the country. The most critical areas are concerned with traffic accidents and violations where, after petrol rationing was relaxed in late 1967 (having been introduced the previous year), and totally ended in May of 1971, the statistics revealed an increasing lack of discipline among the country's drivers. Drugs, too, were becoming a menace among the teen-age element towards the end of the four- year period. But happily Rhodesia, probably due to its position as a world pariah and absence of a seaboard, was trailing behind the majority of other countries at that time and not only in the use of drugs.. As far as Law and Order cases were concerned — and here the reference is to intimidation, stoning of vehicles, crop slashing, petrol bombing, possession of arms of war and other types of politically inspired crime — there was a generally improved run of statistics.

The Commissioners of Police reported: "Once again there has been a most encouraging decrease in cases reported (under the Law and Order (Maintenance) Act) which is probably attributable to the imprisonment and restriction during recent years of the nationalist thug element." (1966); "Seventy-seven cases of intimidation were reported of which 62 were cleared by the arrest of 40 persons. Stoning of motor vehicles accounted for a further 35 cases of which 10 were cleared. When compared with the previous year, the incidents of intimidation show a 49% decline and represent the continuation of an encouraging trend. The infiltration of communist-trained African terrorists continues to pose a serious problem but those who crossed our borders in 1967 were accounted for, being either captured or killed." (1967) These comments related to the 310 Law and Order cases reported in 1967 as compared with 724 the previous year.

In 1968 the cases reported had dropped even further to 101 and the comment was made: "There was a marked decrease in politically inspired crimes despite the release from restriction of certain African Nationalists."

The year 1969 was even better. Only 57 cases reported but the discerning would have read a clear message and implied warning in these words — "A terrorist was arrested after having successfully infiltrated to prepare the way for future armed gangs. Following his arrest, six local tribesmen and two women were arrested for assisting him and one was sentenced to five years' hard labour. The terrorist was sentenced to nine years' hard labour for his part in a petrol bomb attack on a Bulawayo Post Office in 1966."

Of course it was not to last. The following year, when armed infiltrations occurred in the early months, the cases reported had risen to 130 and that was to be the trend thereafter: 396 in 1971 and 636 in 1972.

There can be no doubt however that the intensive and highly successful border patrolling that took place along the north, north-east and north-west borders by Police Anti-Terrorist Units, by the Support Unit (each aided by CID teams and Ground Coverage personnel), by the Army and with the invaluable support of both the Police Reserve Air Wing and the Rhodesian Air Force, led to misplaced optimism and undue complacency among the public in the main urban centres.

It is not within the scope of this history to record in minute detail the engagements in which individual policemen were involved, but the 'Battle of Sinoia', as it was named, was one in which the Police, wonderfully supported by the Air Force, played a predominant role. It is also appropriate to mention some of the names that feature on the Roll of Honour covering the earlier years of what became known as the 'Rhodesian Bush War'.

The Battle of Sinoia was an engagement with a resolute and well-trained, well-armed party of seven terrorists who had originally crossed from Zambia with a much larger group. Once over the river, the group had split up into three sections, one of which was headed for Salisbury by way of Sinoia and tasked with subverting the local populace. The two other sections were aiming for Umtali and Fort Victoria respectively, with the intention of destroying the oil pipeline and killing 'white' farmers. Both the latter sections were eventually put out of action, but the Sinoia operation is regarded as the first 'real' battle in the Nationalists struggle for Freedom.

The group of terrorists bound for Sinoia had been pursued by the Security Forces for many days. As mentioned earlier, they had first given away their presence when they mounted an ambush and fired on a car. In another instance they were greeted and frightened off by a parrot from the stoep of a homestead one night. Yet again there was a rather botched attempt to blow up an electricity pylon. So the Police knew they were in the area but had no confirmed sightings. John Fletcher, who was commanding the CID detachment in Sinoia, came up with a very ingenious ruse. He had his detectives clothed in prison uniforms and had them wander under armed guard around the town in the hope — vain as it happened — of picking up the couple of terrorists who were known to be making daily trips to the baker. By this time, the terrorists were holed up about two miles from the town, and well concealed. Police, however, acting on what is so valuable and essential to their success the world over — 'information received' — knew the farm where the group was hidden. John Cannon, then Officer Commanding the District, accompanied John Fletcher into Salisbury and, through the good offices of Syd Bristow at CID Headquarters, enlisted the cooperation of the Air Force and its helicopters to try and flush out the insurgents at first light.

Early the following morning the operation began. It was the last week of April 1966. The Police had moved quietly into position and the Air Force helicopters with armed police observers accompanying the crew started to quarter the area.

One of the insurgents, possibly maddened by the incessant beat of the helicopter rotor blades overhead, or convinced that they had been spotted but more likely seeking a moment of glory, fired on a 'chopper' and gave away his and his companions' position to the Rhodesian forces. Aware that they were compromised, the terrorists quickly laid an ambush and into it walked Detective Inspectors Dusty Binns and Bill Freeman.

Fortunately for them the aim of their enemy was wayward and, though they were almost surprised from their rear, there was a line of police and police reservists moving towards the scene who very quickly accounted for three of the enemy. Binns killed another, two more were dropped by the advancing men and the last was shot by a policeman from a helicopter as he tried to flee the scene. (NB. Some sources relate that two of the insurgents were killed when a grenade — held a fraction too long — exploded). The Battle was over and the Police were 'stood down' by early evening.

The following month saw the brutal and senseless murders of Johannes and Joanna Viljoen on their tobacco farm not many miles from Hartley. Their two children were spared from execution by the ZANU terrorists but the ensuing manhunt, involving all the Security Forces, resulted in the arrest and conviction of four of the murderers. In this particular follow-up operation, Detective Inspector Freeman joined the trackers and remained with them — on foot — from Hartley to Mtoko where the arrests were made.

The Sinoia operation evoked considerable criticism from senior Army officers who maintained that in mounting a seek and destroy action, police should have withdrawn before the fighting took place and left the 'professionals' to deal with it. The subsequent altercation in the OCC (Operations Coordinating Committee) is mentioned in some detail in Ken Flower's book Serving Secretly and also in Reid-Daly's Pamwe Chete. One of the results of the Sinoia incident was the decision by OCC that, as Flower describes it, "Intelligence should be controlled by CIO and that Special Branch should come directly under my control for all operational purposes."

The next month, June, was characterized by further incidents of violence in the Salisbury urban area. There were petrol bombings and stonings but no deaths. Later that year, following the callous shooting of an African pantechnicon driver, it became necessary to introduce a convoy system on the Chirundu to Makuti road. Not long afterwards, when a cache of arms and ammunition was discovered in a Salisbury furniture warehouse, police were compelled to institute a system of 'sealing ' the doors of heavy vehicles setting out from Chirundu on the Great North Road. The seals were then checked at periodic road-blocks and, if found to be broken, then the necessary action was taken.

Superintendent John Wickenden was the first member of the Police to die, though not as a result of direct enemy action. Wickenden was one of the post-war era who had attested in the District Branch in 1946, taken a keen interest in African customs and local archaeology, and founded the Police Sub-Aqua Unit. For this he was amply qualified through his war service with the Special Service Commando (Royal Navy) with midget submarines and as a frogman.

In October 1966, in the Chirundu area of the Zambezi Valley, Wickenden, with three members of the Regular Army, was examining a cache of arms and ammunition which had been discovered and much of which, being past its prime, had become highly volatile. There was a devastating explosion and three of the four men were killed.

There is a slightly different version of this incident, once again described by Flower as follows "Three of our best white operators were killed one dark night on the banks of the Zambezi when the explosives they were loading into a canoe for a sabotage operation in Zambia exploded, through over-exposure to the heat of the Zambezi valley…"

The next death was to occur in Western Matabeleland the following year.

By this time the South African-centred African National Congress had reached a form of agreement with ZAPU and guerillas from both organizations were infiltrating down through Rhodesia's western border from the Kazangula area, into the Wankie Game Reserve, and then south.

In mid August, a patrol of the Rhodesian African Rifles (RAR) led by Captain Peter Hosking, and accompanied by members of the Police, was in the Inyantue area when contact was made with the enemy. Hosking was severely wounded in the ensuing action, so too Patrol Officer Barry Tiffin and Inspector Frederick Phillips.

Tiffin owes his life to a private in the RAR who refused to withdraw to a less exposed position, dragged the wounded policeman away to cover and then lifted him to safety. Phillips was less fortunate; he sustained an appalling head wound that was to leave him brain damaged and with left hemiplegia for the rest of his life. It was a bloody battle that left five guerillas and two African soldiers dead, and the two policemen, the army officer and one soldier, wounded.

Ten days later, the next engagement took place. Once again the RAR was involved and once again policemen were with them. Two dog handlers, Patrol Officer Spencer Thomas (with 'Leon') and Patrol Officer Bob Horn (with 'Flip') were accompanying the soldiers when, almost without warning, they were attacked in their overnight bush camp near Tjolotjo. Horn was wounded. Spencer Thomas Morgan Thomas, to give him his full names was killed. Thomas was 23 years of age and engaged to be married. He was a fourth-generation Rhodesian and descended from the missionary who, with Sykes and Moffat, established the oldest mission station in the country at Inyati in 1859. (Rev. Thomas actually treated Mzilikazi for gout and other ailments).

After the death of his handler, Leon disappeared and it was accepted that he must have been killed in the same action. However, over a month later, he was spotted near Pumula Mission, 40 miles away. By this time the dog was wary of human beings and it took two dog handlers over a week and using a baited cage to eventually catch him. He had lost 15 pounds in weight and was ravaged by bont-legged tick sores. Proper feeding, love and care soon restored him to his old self and it is recorded that in 1968 he was back 'in action' and had saved his new handler and members of the Security Forces from an ambush situation.

It may have been noticed that in this chapter a distinction has been made between the words 'terrorist' and 'guerilla'. This is quite deliberate. A guerilla is looked upon as a member of a small band engaged in harrassing, sabotage and raiding operations: a terrorist uses acts likely to inspire fear and terror to further his ends. The engagements in Matabeleland fall into the first category; the murder of the Viljoens does not.

The previous paragraphs have been mainly concerned with terrorist and guerilla operations outside the main cities. However, in 1966, it was learned that the University College of Rhodesia and Nyasaland in Salisbury was a seething hotbed of nationalist intrigue: nothing terribly unusual about that. In this age the universities of the world are filled with people who would transform things swiftly and dramatically but who, with the benefit of some year's experience of life, could effect change far more effectively by moving slowly and intelligently.

Investigations by the CID, and particularly a team led by Detective Inspector Binns, revealed that a number of lecturers and a few students, headed by a Dr Arrighi, had banded together and were intent on attacking city premises, such as those hotels and restaurants usually patronised by Europeans. This group was linked with the ZAPU nationalist faction then based in Lusaka and were drawing from there grenades, primers, arms and ammunition, subversive party publicity material and all the 'stuff' of terrorism. Not only that, but the group was also intent on providing 'safe houses' for terrorists crossing from Zambia and ensuring that such crossings were made as 'safely' as possible.

Arrighi was deported in early August and could thank another of his conspirators, John Conradie, for removing a box of grenades from his University flat before the arrival of the police, thus making deportation the option rather than imprisonment. Shortly afterwards, a grenade was thrown into Demi's Restaurant in central Salisbury and later an unoccupied city flat was similarly attacked. Conradie did not get away with his plotting: arrested in early September, he was charged, pleaded guilty and sentenced to 20 years imprisonment.

When one reads of these actions much later a certain amount of admiration, or perhaps it should be criticism, is engendered at the quite remarkable understating of the situation revealed in the extracts from the Commissioners' Annual Reports quoted earlier. It was the policy of Government to keep the cracks well papered.

While all this was taking place, the Police, now very much assisted by the Reserve, carried on with their more normal duties. Robberies and assaults continued, murders were committed, sexual crimes, house-breakings and storebreakings carried on. Thefts persisted, cattle, cars and bicycles vanished, frauds and exchange control offences increased, people peddled in gold, emeralds and precious stones, and juveniles continued to be delinquent, drinking liquor when they should not, and sniffing drugs when they could.

The Annual Report for 1966 details 193,545 cases reported with a clearance percentage of 78; by 1971, five years later, the respective totals were 250,123 and 81%. By the standards of any police force, these figures were excellent.

Every policeman moans, often with good cause, about the plethora of reports that have to be submitted to Police Headquarters. Some have quite a humorous twist to them, as:

Belingwe to Staff Officer (Establishments) — radio 123/66: 17/11/66.
   CASUALTY RETURN. ADVISING INCREASE IN ESTABLISHMENT , BELINGWE.
   TO MARY AND JAPIE ONE FOAL FEMALE DONKEY BORN PM 15/11/66.
   MOTHER AND CHILD DOING WELL.
Compol Estabs to Belingwe. — radio u.n: 17/11/66
   RE: ADDITION TO YOUR ESTABLISHMENT. PLSE ADVISE ON WHOSE
   AUTHORITY ESTABLISHMENT EXCEEDED.

**First Sergeant 1953**                    **African First Class Sergeant 1963**

...strations from **"The Regiment" – A History and the Uniforms of the British South Africa Police**, by Richard Hamley
Published in 2000 by Covos-Day Books (SA).  Website at www.mazoe.com

The Honorary Commissioner of the British South Africa Police, Queen Elizabeth the Queen Mother

**British South Africa Police banner 1904**
The banner was presented by His Majesty King Edward VII
in recogniition of services rendered to the Empire.
The presentation was made on behalf of
His Majesty by His Excellency the High Commissioner,
Lord Milner, at Mafeking on 5th October, 1904.

**Left:** Regular and National Service squads at passout parade on Morris Depot 'Green Square', Salisbury, 1976. Blatherwick Memorial at top of picture.

**Above and below:** recreation and relaxation at Officer's Mess, Salisbury.

ve: Flagstaff and Plinth at Montagu Avenue entrance to ris Depot, Salisbury.

w: BSAP Special Branch members on attachment to Selous Scouts Regiment parade alongside their army eagues at André Rabie Barracks, at Darwendale near sbury. Few people knew or even suspected that SB ed a vital role in the Scouts' operations.

to by Keith Samler from *"Pamwe Chete" (1982) by* ol. Ron Reid-Daly. (2000 edition by Covos-Day Books.)

# Action!

## 'WE ARE AMPHIBIOUS'

Do you want . . .
An exciting and worthwhile Career?
Free Uniform, Medical and Dental Benefits?
Good Leave Conditions?
Generous Annual Holiday Grant?

# THE B.S.A. POLICE

Write to: The Recruiting Officer
B.S.A. Police General Headquarters
P.O. Box 8007, Causeway

**POSTSCRIPT**

## ETCHED FOREVER IN EVERY RECRUIT'S MEMORY

"If you couldn't take a joke ...
you shouldn't have joined."

"I joined the Force
For the intercourse
And all I got ...
Was a f****** great horse"

B.S.A.P
"Broke Soon After Pay"

**Clockwise from top left:** Lance Section Officer **Lindsay 'Kiwi' O'Brien**, Po Support Unit, recipient of Police Cross for Conspicuous Gallantry, Sept. 197⁹

**President John Wrathall** and **Commissioner Peter Sherren**, Morris Depot, 1

**Constable Sylvester Manyawu**, recipient of Police Cross for Conspicuous Gallantry for bravery in action, July 1977.

**Constable Misheck Dube** and **NSPO Gordon Kaye-Eddie** of 'Delta' Troop Support Unit. In 1976 they were awarded the Police Medal for Gallantry and Commissioner's Commendation (Bronze Baton) respectively.

**'Delta' Troop,** Support Unit at Tomlinson Depot, August 1976.

**Support Unit 'stick'** calls for air support during patrol in operational area.

**low:** PC Brewster of the Thames Valley
lice and BSAP colleagues at Mukwichi Tribal
st Land near Karoi during build-up to voting
March 1980 election.

**ght:** Arrival in Bulawayo on 4 January 1980
he new Governor, Lord Soames.

**Below:** Officer Commanding Police Reserve, Matabeleland, Supt.
Jack Broderick checks situation with Reservist Philip Chiyangwa
carrying out Longstop duties at road block on Mafeking Road,
Bulawayo, during volatile last week before 1980 election.

Farewell Message from
His Excellency the Governor,
The Right Honourable Lord Soames,
PC, GCMG, GCVO, CBE.

AT THE CONCLUSION of my stay in this country, I want to send a special message of appreciation and thanks to all ranks of the British South Africa Police. Throughout my time here I have been consistently impressed by the high standard of discipline and efficiency which the police have displayed and by the high regard in which they are held by the people of this country.

I am particularly grateful for the unstinting and loyal service given by the police during the difficult period of the election.

Now the police face a new challenge: the transformation from a wartime to a peacetime role. I know that the Force will successfully meet this as they have met many other varied challenges throughout their ninety years of service to this country.

My wife and I send you all our very best wishes for the future.

Christopher Soames

Farewell to arms (1); Governor Lord Soames' message to the Force, as appeared in *The Outpost*, March 1980. He congratulates members of the BSAP for "the high regard in which they are held by the people of this country."

Farewell to arms (2); Detective Section Officer Nick Russ[ records serial number of AK-47 before confiscating weap from ZANLA element at Mount Darwin police station afte local capture outside distant Assembly Point; 8 March 19

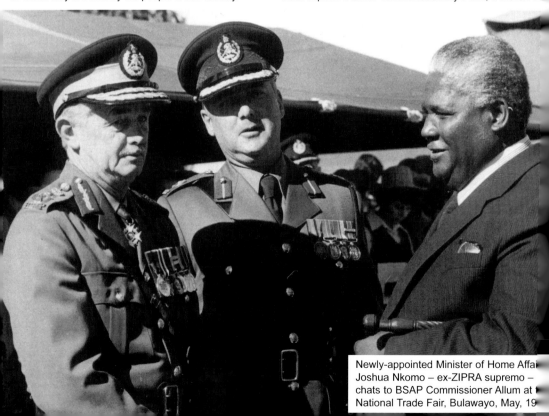

Newly-appointed Minister of Home Affai Joshua Nkomo – ex-ZIPRA supremo – chats to BSAP Commissioner Allum at National Trade Fair, Bulawayo, May, 19

Belingwe to Compol, Estabs. — radio 124/66 : 18/11/66
  FURTHER TO MY 123/66 AND YOUR U.N. DD 17/11/66. GENESIS 9/1 (BE FRUIT-
  FUL AND MULTIPLY…)
Compol Estabs to Belingwe. — radio 432/66 : 19/11/66
  RE. YOUR 124/66. MARK 12/11 (THIS WAS THE LORD'S DOING, AND IT IS
  MARVELLOUS IN OUR EYES.)

As usual, Police Headquarters had the last word!

Other stories display a breath-taking cynicism, or perhaps a mischievous sense of humour, as in this story that was recounted by a retired member:

In the mid-60s, a certain officer commanding in Matabeleland was repeatedly asked by Police Headquarters to send in a return which involved a lot of figure-work. The officer prevaricated, procrastinated and it was never completed and sent in.

After a while, this same officer was promoted to Deputy Commissioner and, of course, transferred to Police Headquarters where the return was now urgently required by him in his new position.

He proceeded to write a very caustic and pithy letter to the new officer commanding, saying that, despite repeated requests, this return still had not been sent and much more attention must be paid to Headquarters' requests in future. He concluded that this sort of delay was not expected of senior officers."

Those who knew 'Hank' Blowers would know there would have been a merry twinkle in his eyes when that was written.

One last tale comes from the police station at Selous, then being commanded by 'Bones' Scully. The constable on duty in the charge office was radioed to change frequency to Channel 'H' — Hotel. Without further ado, he leaped onto his bicycle, and was located at the hotel 35 minutes later.

But it was not all work and no play. Rugby, football and hockey leagues continued, golf, tennis and bowls were played socially and competitively, so too billiards and snooker. The Police Reserve, now well and truly integrated in the Force, held their 'Cream of the Crop' Competition (in Salisbury) which, apart from many of the various sports already mentioned, included shooting, swimming, a 'Scavenger Hunt' and a General Knowledge quiz. Twelve separate teams participated in the 1967 Competition and the new diversity of the Reserve is indicated by some of their names; Striker Forces, Recce Unit, 'A' Reserve, Specialist Units of the Field Reserve and Women's Police Reserve. Perhaps the fanaticism of the occasion is demonstrated by the fact that whilst 'scavenging' for 'a young lady in a bikini' — and seeking also 'a pig's trotter', 'a china chamber pot' and 'a live cricket' — one team managed to round up two bikini-clad lasses.

Not only the Police Reserve was assisting the Force in those days. In South Africa, there were many people who identified themselves with the stand taken by Rhodesia and who wanted to express their support in a tangible form.

One or two organizations were formed in main centres like Johannesburg, Durban and Cape Town and fund-raising events held and collections made. Very soon the Security Forces were receiving ambulances, medical and radio communications equipment, Land Rovers, typewriters, binoculars and all manner of scarce but very necessary 'goodies' from the Friends of Rhodesia and the Anglo Rhodesian Society. One particularly useful piece of equipment, which was greedily absorbed into the Forensic Science Laboratory, was an X-Ray unit.

The year 1967 saw virtually a clean sweep of the three senior officers of the Force. The two deputy commissioners, George Harries and 'Hank' Blowers reached the retiring age of 55 in October and November respectively, whilst the Commissioner, Frank 'Pat' Barfoot, left at the beginning of 1968.

Barfoot had commanded the Force through nearly five difficult years, and those years had been made all the more trying because his health had been far from robust over much of that period. He had been required to be operated upon in England in 1964 and again, and this time thanks to the personal intervention and recommendation of the Governor, Sir Humphrey Gibbs (who was confined to Government House and held his office in name only during the UDI years). Barfoots's years were not innovative, as had been Spurling's; they could not be under the tide of problems confronting the country and the need to stretch manpower and resources to the limit. But 'Pat' Barfoot, a man of extraordinary strength of character, a man who was virtually incapable of deviation from 'the book', had done his job with dedication and distinction.

One rather sad though inevitable event in 1966 was the admission by the members of Murray's Column that 'the Reaper' had beaten them and no further annual reunions would be held. The stage had been reached when there were more guests at the annual reunions in the Club than 'Columnists'. The activities of Murray's Column in the campaign in German East Africa during World War I are described in some detail by Peter Gibbs in his second volume of the Police History, *The Right of The Line*. The memory of Murray and his men lives on, for the members of the Column donated to the Police Club two Monk's benches and six Monk's chairs, and to the Force a splendid floating trophy with miniatures.

## Chapter Forty-Eight

## SPINK TO THE THRONE

*Commissioner Spink — Patrol vessels — Cruising Down the River —*
*Operation 'Jackal' — SAP Casualty — Gwaai Bus Disaster —*
*Station Notes — African Policewomen — Retirements and Deaths.*

At the beginning of January 1968, James Spink became Commissioner of Police. Spink was a powerfully built and commanding figure. He had been a member of the Edinburgh Police for four years before emigrating to Rhodesia, served with the Rhodesian African Rifles in Burma during the war years and, as a member of the 1963 Lander Committee — at which time he was Chief Staff Officer (Administration) — had added much to his knowledge of the 'nuts and bolts' of the Force administration, its problems and needs. As chairman of the Force Executive Committee in 1967, he had played a significant part in forming the Police Association. His background was, therefore, one that led most members to expect some rapid and far-reaching improvements in service conditions generally. A mass of new legislation affecting the Force appeared in 1968; there were amendments to Promotion, Allowances, Leave, Pensions and Transfer regulations, among others, but many of these had already been mooted before that year. Certainly some, if not most of the changes arose from the Lander inquiry, but anything radical or far-reaching just did not materialise.

It should be borne in mind that the Force was in a rather strange state of mind that year. The Bruce and Hogg affair with its aftermath of CID resignations still smouldered in many minds; the terrorist incursions were sufficiently threatening, and the attention to counter-insurgency and PATU training sufficiently emphasized, as to make for a feeling of disquiet, almost impermanence. All this, when linked to the tragic circumstances surrounding the retirement of Barfoot, made for a crisis of almost unidentifiable anticipation among the members of the Force. Not that Spink was lacking in any sense, he wasn't. The man was firm, fair and forthright. Perhaps it was the Force that was wrong. Perhaps two and a half years were not long enough in the top rank for him to achieve all that his background promised.

Traffic matters were very dear to Spink's heart. The progress of events on the northern borders had made another form of traffic essential. The first police launch on Lake Kariba was the *Sir John Chancellor* which came into service during 1964 and was retired in 1968, having by then travelled the equivalent of one and a half times around the world. This vessel and its successors was operated as a lake patrol craft for rescue operations and the ferrying of Security Force members to the more remote parts of the vast lake. There had been a patrol launch navigating the hazards of the Zambezi between Kariba and Kanyemba long before any craft was launched on the lake. This was the *Sir Herbert Stanley* which entered the river at Chirundu as far back as 1954 and whose first pilot was Karl Maskell. Various craft followed the Chancellor, among them a 'racy little number' presented to the Force by the South African Police and initially put through its paces, to the consternation of some of its passengers from Binga (and Salisbury), by Commander 'Stan' Trethowan.

From the previous paragraph, it flows naturally to mention an epic voyage — though at the time it was described by some as a pub crawl — undertaken by three members of the Criminal Investigation Department.

The trio, Tony Bradshaw, Mike Edden and Dave Hallward, all at that time detective inspectors, acquired the 18 feet long, three feet wide fibreglass canoe in 1967 and, after a few modifications, set off from the base of the Kariba Dam early in July of the following year. They were escorted as far as Kanyemba by a private launch manned by Detective Section Officer Peter Begg and his father, both with ample experience of the currents, sand bars and vaguaries of the river, and Arthur Lennard who had retired from the Police in 1962.

Nearly two months and 1000 miles later and after many adventures and experiences, the trio reached the Indian Ocean and ended their journey. During the expedition they had visited the site of the Cabora Bassa Dam and, near the ocean, seen the grave of Mary Livingstone (wife of the explorer and missionary, David) at Chupanga. In the same cemetery, they came upon a slab commemorating a long dead member of the Police, 'Number 100 (Driver) Trooper Davies of the Mounted Troop' who had been taken by crocodiles en route to German East Africa in 1917.

It was at about this time that Operation Jackal took place in Northern Matabeleland. The detail is described in the March 1968 issue of *The Outpost*, but for readers of this history the following outlines the circumstances.

A herdsman searching for his cattle in a remote part of the dense bush and sand veldt spotted an African digging a hole in the ground. He reported the sighting to the elders at his kraal and a party went to see what was going on. The hole had been refilled but still showed the signs of recent digging. The police were informed and the tribesmen made their way back to the site to await the police. Whilst there, a burst of automatic fire felled the kraalhead, killing him instantly, whilst his friends fled the scene. The police arrived to find the body with some handwritten notes threatening death to anyone who became a police informer.

A full-scale tracking exercise involving the three Services was then mounted and after a 30 mile pursuit, the original tracks of three men became six. Diligent questioning in nearby villages led to the terrorists' camp and the discovery of a number of well camouflaged holes to a depth of about two and a half feet, four feet wide and about six feet long. The terrorists had been based in the area for some time and were engaged in an indoctrination programme. Some hours later, information came in that two of the gang were in a kraal about 50 miles away from the original area. The information was correct and both were captured and their arms (of Russian manufacture), grenades and ammunition recovered.

Interrogation of these two revealed them to be part of a group of eight Algerian-trained terrorists tasked with recruiting and training the locals. Two had already been accounted for, one — who had accidentally shot himself in the shoulder — in Bulawayo, the second in Salisbury. Inquiries continued in the original area and a large cache of ammunition, TNT and subversive literature was uncovered. Shortly thereafter, and in separate locations, two more men gave themselves up. The Security Forces were by now well on top of the situation and it was only a matter of days later, and after they had pretending to withdraw from the area, that they captured the remaining members of the gang. The full tally of captured equipment was four PPSH submachine guns, five SKS carbines, 14 grenades, plus hundreds of rounds of ammunition and explosives.

After this it was up to the Police to tie up the loose ends.

The notebook from which the pages of warning had been torn was found and married up to the notes found on the kraalhead's body. A handwriting comparison swiftly proved who was responsible for that part of the murder. Then the rounds fired were linked to a particular weapon and then to its owner. The final chapter took place in the High Court, Bulawayo when death sentences and long terms of imprisonment were handed down to the terrorists and various assisting tribesmen.

The Judge commended all the members of the Security Forces involved for the way they had performed their duties.

It had been an operation showing the highest standards of command, control and close cooperation between all three Services, and at all levels.

Sadly, it was in the same area that Constable Daniel du Toit of the South African Police was to be killed in July. Du Toit, the first member of that Force to die in action and in support of the Rhodesian forces, was involved in a battle with terrorists and, to quote from the graveside eulogy delivered by Lieutenant General H.J. van den Bergh — "He had already reached safety. He exposed himself to fire so that his colleagues could reach safety. When death faced him, he was defiant and unafraid."

Again in that same area, and not far distant from the many skirmishes characterising that period, occurred a particularly horrible bus disaster in December 1969.

There have been many crashes involving buses in Rhodesia (and later Zimbabwe) over the years, and the same common causes — or variations of the theme distinguish most of them. Invariably the bus is travelling far too fast for the road conditions; the driver is in a hurry and exhibiting almost total disregard for his passengers; the bus is considerably overloaded, and finally the vehicle is far from mechanically sound.

Several of these factors were at play in mid-December 1969 when, at around about lunchtime, a bus carrying 92 passengers crossed the high-level bridge between Dett and Binga and set off up the steep incline on the far side. Some 400 feet past the bridge, the driver attempted to change down to first gear and failed. The bus, its brakes ineffective, slid backwards at a speed of 30 mph towards the bridge, smashed through the parapet railings and dropped 40 feet onto a partially submerged rock. Thirty-four passengers, about half of them children, were killed immediately; seven others vanished into the fast- flowing Gwaai River.

A Police Reservist, John Galloway from the nearby Kamativi Tin Mine was first on the scene. Only the roof of the bus showed above the water and on this was crowded about 50 passengers. Galloway swam over and realized that there was no-one alive inside. Very soon, he was joined by two other Reservists from the tin mine, Ivor Palphramand and John Learmonth. These three, with the aid of a rope, started to bring the stranded passengers back to the riverbank, one at a time. Galloway, with a medical team from the mine led by Frederick Marufu, stayed on the bus roof tending to those who were badly hurt. Police were on the scene soon afterwards and called in a helicopter to remove the more seriously injured and those stranded and hurt on the rocks beyond the wrecked bus. Many more helpers arrived and eventually 51 people were rescued.

Meritorious Conduct Medals were awarded to four of those involved, and Commendations for Brave Conduct to another 10, including the members of the medical team. The driver, by the way, escaped unaided and unscathed, but he was subsequently sentenced to a term of imprisonment for culpable homicide.

Station Notes published in *The Outpost* bring their share of interest and amusement over these years.

Those — and there must be many — who remember Stan Morris, the Chief Native Commissioner, later Secretary for African Affairs and, after he was 'kicked upstairs,' Chairman of the Public Services Board, will doubtless smile over what happened to the Native Department offices and Court Room at Nuanetsi in 1929.

At that time the building was a hideous-looking thatched monstrosity built of rudimentary bricks and poles, and about six years old. The Native Commissioner was a Mr H.F. Child and Morris was his assistant. A telegram was received in Salisbury advising that 'a strong wind' had blown down the structure.

In quick time, a new and eminently more suitable building was constructed. Little did the authorities know that the 'strong wind' consisted of Child, Morris and a gang of convicts, courtesy of the Police, plus a long length of rope, literally pulled down the ramshackle structure.

There used to be a photograph of the old building, together with a description of the incident, hanging in the District Commissioner's office at Nuanetsi. The photographer was a policeman, Trooper James Wemyss. But it was 40 years later when the truth was revealed.

Mayobodo is not too far from the Shashi River and the member in charge was somewhat surprised one day to come upon a young vulture wandering and 'without visible means of support' on the river bank. It was brought back to the police station and, being unable to fly, remained a spectator to the daily comings and goings. Familiarity breeds contempt, and before long Ilinqe, as he was now named, was firm friends with the guard dog, the member in charge's dog, Rex, and the kitchen staff. Eventually Ilinqe joined Rex in the latter's kennel apparently ithout any great resentment from either side.

The end of this story is quite predictable; Ilinqe realized what his wings were for and, after a few days of coming home for dinner, took off, never to return.

Among these pages there has been reference to the part played by police dogs, not only as trackers, 'investigating officers' and guardians, but also as integral parts of Police Displays. In 1970, a memorial wall was built by the Pioneers in the Adylinn Dog Depot which paid tribute to their 'unfailing loyalty and devotion to duty'. On that wall appear small brass plaques commemorating many of the dogs that have died 'in action' and others that deserve to be remembered. One recalls a few lines from a poem by Lord Byron:

*"...But the poor dog, in life the firmest friend,*
*The first to welcome, foremost to defend,*
*Whose honest heart is still his master's own,*
*Who labours, fights, lives, breathes for him alone,*
*Unhonour'd falls, unnoticed all his worth...."*

Happily, neither unhonoured nor unnoticed by the BSA Police.

The years since the Federation was dissolved had seen an incredible increase in the responsibilities undertaken by the African Police. The inception of the African Sub-Inspector dates back to 1960 when a small number of senior, well-educated and responsible policemen were given advanced training and placed in charge of various sub-stations like Mabvuku, Luveve, Pumula and others. By 1970, there were many more than the original seven, though it had been found necessary — and at the request of the members themselves — to simplify the administration of books and records. The next step was the introduction of African Women Police as constables, and this came in 1966. Once again, this was a successful move and by the end of the year there were 20 such young ladies working at various police stations.

One further and popular innovation was the introduction of an African Police Cadet Branch. The intention was to draw upon young Africans, mainly the sons of serving policemen, and give them elementary instruction in police methods, retaining their interest and attention until they reached the age of 18 and could become full-time members.

The years under review saw some notable retirements, among them members who have previously featured on these pages.

'Sam' Weller departed in November 1967 after nearly 33 years service. His connections with the Police were not severed as he became a Research Officer with the Special Branch in Bulawayo. However, his tendency to 'throw his weight around' was neatly trimmed by the lady in charge of the Registry at that time who, when he approached one of the typists direct, instead of referring to the supervisor, caustically advised him that he was no longer an assistant commissioner and had better 'toe the line'.

The following year saw, among others, the departures of Jack Berry, John Worsley who had commanded the Support Unit for just on three years; 'Fred' Phillips who has been mentioned before and who was retired on a medical pension; Robert Bellamy, one time Personal Orderly to King George VI (1947), an active and enthusiastic member of the executive committee of the Police Association, and a pillar in the Rhodesian Section of the International Police Association; Harold Vickery, whose name will for ever be associated with the African Foreigners' Identification Bureau and who, at his farewell party still managed to squeeze into the tunic issued to him nearly 30 years' before.

One policeman who would be sorely missed was 'Jackie' Wordsworth. His had been an outstanding career beginning when he joined as a Police Cadet in 1933, and then as a Trooper two years later. Mention has already been made of his early bachelor status which was to take him on relieving duties and 'permanent' postings all over the country. In 1942 he had been awarded the Royal Humane Society Testimonial on Vellum for his part in a daring and hazardous rescue of an airman who had fallen part way down the cliff face of the gorge at the Victoria Falls. In 1953, it may be recalled, he was a member of the Coronation Contingent.

By 1955 Wordsworth was a chief inspector and occupied the post of Quartermaster's Representative in Matabeleland Province. He had attempted the examinations to commissioned rank on several occasions and on the last, when in charge of Filabusi Police Station, had been so deeply involved in hundreds of individual cases arising from the controversial Land Apportionment Act (all of which were defended, and sometimes went to appeal) that he lacked the time to prepare himself — and failed once more. Quite despondent, he did not try again until his Officer Commanding 'Aussie' Rogers, told him: "You can't win the Sweep unless you have a ticket." This advice was repeated to Wordsworth in a subsequent interview with Commissioner Spurling and this time he was successful. In 1958, he became the first Cadet to achieve commissioned rank and went on to complete more than 35 years' service, retiring as Senior Assistant Commissioner.

Perhaps one story from Wordsworth's long and exemplary service bears repeating. He was in charge of the area known as the Black South (Southerton and its sub-stations in Salisbury) where his men were frequently assaulted and abused. Wordsworth had to submit reports on such cases and on one, for which the convicted person was fined only five shillings, he made marginal comments that were highly uncomplimentary of the magistrate passing sentence. The report went to Police Headquarters and, perhaps unfortunately, was passed on to the Secretary of Justice and thence, and this was unfortunate, to the magistrate who had passed the sentence in the first place. Needless to say the balloon went up. The Magistrates' Association became involved, Doctor Ahrn Palley raised the matter in the Legislative Assembly, the Leader of the Opposition saw an opportunity — and used it. There was even an allegation that Police were spying on the magistrates. Incredibly, and without any thought of the unfortunate policemen doing their jobs under difficult and dangerous circumstances, the Government appointed a Commission of Inquiry under Justice John Lewis. Spurling had to appear and state his point of view but the final result was that the police were exonerated and a mild reprimand given to Wordsworth. There was a great deal of mirth behind the scenes but noticeably stiffer sentences became the norm.

Deputy Commissioner Ken Flower MBE was another to retire in 1969. Flower had confidently expected to become Commissioner when Spurling retired and was considerably discountenanced when Barfoot was selected instead. As earlier recorded, he was appointed to become Head of the newly formed Central Intelligence Organization (CIO). Within days of Spurling's retirement he went for a two weeks' security course at MI5 where, at that time, Sir Roger Hollis was Director.

Among others to retire that year were two detective chief inspectors, George Gibbons and Roger Sandall, the latter being one of those who had been seconded for service with the Kenya Police. Another to leave was the senior station sergeant in the Force, Tinaapi Mapiye, who had joined in 1938 and who counted among his friends the retired magistrate and one-time Clerk of the Southern Rhodesia Parliament, John Franks. The latter had employed the 17 years old Tinaapi at his Enkeldoorn home in 1935. The two had remained friends ever since and Franks' spoke warmly of their long association at the farewell party.

From the Depot, Neil 'Smudge' Smith was another to leave on pension. A swashbuckling, jovial and extrovert character, Smith spent almost his whole career in the saddle as an Equitation Instructor. Few of that generation will forget his order to "Stantoyerorses" nor indeed the daredevil manner in which he set his horse Matchless at the jumps in the Mounted Sports.

Two from the vast intakes of 1946 to leave the following year, and both strong contributors to police sports teams, were chief inspectors Jack Hammond and 'Bill' Osborne. A little later the man who, after 'Laurie' Davenport had done so much to develop the Dog Training School, John Restorick, moved from police into the commercial sector. He was to be followed by the Member in Charge of the Salisbury Traffic Section, John Thompson who, as a member of the Institute of Advanced Motorists, had played and would continue to play a significant part in improving driving standards throughout the country and participated in several international motor rallies.

No history of this period would be complete without reference to William 'Bill' Crabtree who retired as Deputy Commissioner (Crime and Security) in May 1970. Crabtree had joined as a 'mounted trooper' in 1938 and transferred to the CID two-and-a-half years later. The War saw him seconded for service in the Middle East and Aegean from which area he returned in 1946.

Crabtree it was who was selected to set up the Special Branch (SB) in late 1960. This was to be entirely divorced from other sections of the Force, with its commander responsible direct to the Commissioner of Police and with no ordinary police commitments. In his own words, and with grateful thanks to him for making this portion of his memoirs available:

"I was the officer selected to organize a Special Branch along the lines of those of other Colonial territories.....At the time, as Provincial Criminal Investigation Officer in Matabeleland, I had already been engaged in intelligence work within the CID framework, responsible to my officer commanding in Salisbury. Gathering together a handful of officers, warrant officers and NCOs, all with some experience in the field of security/intelligence, I organized a nucleus of the SB which in time progressed from strength to strength, to become the sole intelligence body in the Colony responsible for keeping the Government appraised of all and any threats to the country's security."

Crabtree goes on to describe the setting-up of the Central Intelligence Organization (CIO) under Ken Flower, and continues: "To avoid possible embarrassment arising from inter-departmental rivalry and possible confrontation, I strongly recommended to the Commissioner, Pat Barfoot, that with Flower's blessing I incorporate intoto the SB into the folds of the CIO. Thus, in the initial stages, the SB provided practically all the experienced personnel within the Organization. At this time, while retaining the title of OC SB, I was designated the Deputy Director CIO. Henceforth, the function of the SB was to collect and collate all matters affecting the internal security of the Colony; to maintain liaison with intelligence organizations and police forces of neighbouring countries, in so far as the security of Rhodesia was concerned. During the 'hostilities' of the 60s and Seventies, the SB performed sterling work in providing the Colony's Armed Forces with high grade intelligence concerning the activities and movements of terrorist groups both within and outside the country. Selected members of the SB did in fact see service with various military units."

To finalise this chapter, it is necessary to record the deaths of two ex-members which took place over this period.

The first was that of the Commissioner from 1963 to 1968, Frank 'Pat' Barfoot. The cancer which he had so bravely fought and endured finally claimed him on 27 September 1971 and he was laid to rest at Warren Hills.

The second was a man who has played but a small part in this history, yet whose devotion to the Force in which he served for 34 years was characterised by great humanity, a keen sense of humour and an unfailing dedication to his work.

Colonel 'Monty' Surgey had been a member of the Second Mobile Column operating against the German Forces in Northern Rhodesia during 1915 and 1916, had been commissioned in 1921 and had held various commands before becoming Deputy Commissioner, and Acting Commissioner for some months in 1946.

Surgey retired to Knysna in South Africa but never forgot his years with the Police. He was a frequent contributor to The Outpost magazine, often bringing news of members living in far flung corners of the world, and could be unfailingly relied upon to send a telegram of congratulations to the Regimental Association on the occasion of the annual dinners.

In many ways the year 1971 saw the end of another era in the policing of Rhodesia. From the end of the following year, the character and work of the Force was to alter dramatically as an entire country became embroiled in a bitter war and the politicians and nationalists wrought their own particular havoc upon a peace-loving land.

Before this history continues however, before we consider the years from 1972 until the BSA Police ceased to be, it is necessary to place on record the stories of three essential components of the Police Force; three divisions that individually and together played an integral part in police operations and contributed to the many successes that were gained over those final nine years: the Police Anti-Terrorist Units (PATU); the Police Support Unit (Black Boots) and the Police Reserve Air Wing (PRAW).

*"Bags of initiative, young Smithers!"*

# Chapter Forty-Nine

## POLICE ANTI-TERRORIST UNITS (PATU)

*History and Development*

In an earlier chapter, reference was made to Alex (AEF) Bailey who had joined the Police shortly after leaving the Army where he had been a member of the Long Range Desert Group. Bailey was very much of an individualist and so remained until his retirement in November 1966, after which he continued his incredibly active life as Warden of the Outward Bound Training School at Melsetter.

But at this stage let Chris Cocks, author of *Survival Course* and for three years in 3 Commando, the Rhodesian Light Infantry, take up a part of the story. The year is 1979, the war in its final stages and Chris, now managing 1200 acres of cotton and wheat in the Middle Sabi, has been summoned to Bailey's farm near Melsetter for PATU retraining:

"Bill Bailey, well into his sixties, short in stature, tanned and gnarled, was something of a legend. A founding member of the Long Range Desert Group in North Africa, and subsequently the SAS, he was the instigator and founder of PATU. I'd never heard the expression, but apparently PATU was nicknamed "Bailey's Babes", which I thought quite quaint in a Baden-Powellish, Empirish sort of way.

Bill and I immediately sized each other up. A near-70-year-old veteran and a just-turned-22-year-old veteran . He looked me up and down as if saying, 'Well, look at you, you young whippersnapper. Think you know it all, huh? Just because you were in the RLI? Well, we'll see soon enough ...'

And I looked at him and said to myself, 'Huh, What d'you think you can teach us you old fart? This isn't fucking Alamein, Grandad.' *Cocks and his men are then put through an intensive course; not just the physical side but also jungle lane, bushcraft, skirmishing, flanking attacks and so on. Cocks finds himself enjoying it and wanting to show the older man that the younger generation have the guts, the ability and the spirit required. At the end, over the beers, Bailey goes through his notes on the way they had performed:*

'Cocks, I can't fault you on your leadership abilities. Your stick has performed excellently and out of all the courses I've run here over the years, your stick's performance rates as one of the best ... but ... I have to fail you. '

My heart dropped. Was this a bluff?

'Yes,' he continued seriously. 'I would fail you because you are wearing enemy uniform.

Fucksakes, man. Look at you. Gook hat, gook shirt, gook webbing. What d'you think you are? The Selous Scouts?'

I made to defend myself.

'Let me finish.' He took another swig of his beer, his eyes sparkling. 'I know you were RLI and I know the RLI is a bunch of dagga-smoking skates. But we do things differently in the police. A little more conservative.' He took another glug of his beer. 'That's it. Well done, all of you.'

He slapped his thigh. 'Right. Back to the ranch. The missus has a braai on the go.'

I smiled, still not knowing whether we'd passed or failed (did it matter?). I liked this man very much. A good, honest, straight-down-the-line, no-bullshit man …"

In 1976 Bailey, then retired after 21 years in the Police, wrote for *The Outpost* of the beginnings of PATU, of the early struggles, the meagre but loyal support and described his personal conviction that the theory was right and would work in the following article:

"The concept of 'Specialized Units' is undoubtedly as old as war itself and is based on the old maxim of fighting fire with fire. My enthusiasm for the concept was probably conditioned by some four years of active service with the Long Range Desert Group in North Africa and

Southern Europe during World War II. Having started my service career in a conventional infantry battalion, I rapidly reached the erroneous conclusion that the specialized unit was the ultimate aim of modern warfare, the be-all and end-all of successful strategy. Subsequent study of contemporary history has convinced me how wrong I was.

In 1964 I was Sub-District Officer, Lomagundi. At the time there was little doubt that in the not too distant future the Force as a whole, and my district in particular, would be faced with some sort of terrorist situation. Increasing the danger of such a threat was the fact that district police operations were of necessity becoming more and more motorized. Gone were the days when the patrolling trooper took pride in knowledge of his district, was capable of moving through the bush and knew the country intimately. To troopers of the old school, time spent on this type of familiarization was as important as getting the visit sheet signed.

In all fairness time, rather than laziness, was the restricting factor in the mid-60s and on the credit side within the regular force, and more especially in the Police Reserve, there was a large pool of manpower which, both by inclination and experience, was ideally suited for fighting the rural terrorist at his own game and on his own ground, should such a situation arise.

From operations in Albania in 1944 I well remembered the minimal threat posed to the partisans and ourselves by the restricted movement of large numbers of German infantry and supporting arms. They kept to the main roads and while they controlled the highways and the towns, we held sway in the mountains. I also had reason to remember the panic and confusion caused when on the odd occasion well armed and disciplined enemy mountain groups moved into our domain.

When Lomagundi was promoted to the status of full 'District' I made the first tentative attempts at forming what were initially know as Tracker Combat Teams — a title for which I can claim no credit. The teams had no kit, no camouflage clothing and very little hope of official recognition. We were sustained largely by a love of the bush and the personal satisfaction of learning to live with a degree of independence in such an environment.

It was not long before I was summoned to Salisbury to be informed by a very senior officer that not only were my ideas contrary to declared policy but what did I mean by starting a private army. With an inborn sense of discipline I immediately disbanded the Tracker Combat Teams. Fortunately the members of the teams volunteered to a man for the officially tolerated VATs — Volunteers for Advanced Training — also known in the early stages as Bailey's Bloody Bush Babes. Although they were almost all reservists, we did have some very fine regulars among whom Patrol Officer Alec du Plessis springs immediately to mind.

The Volunteers all had certain characteristics in common: a determination born of knowl- edge of the bush, physical fitness and an inherent belief in the necessity of what they were doing — notwithstanding that their approach differed. I'll never forget one very large rancher who turned up at a bush rendezvous complete with two bearers, one carrying his rifle and the other his kit. When I tried to point out that such luxuries were hardly in keeping with our ideas, I was told that his father had fought the British in this manner — and with a horse to boot — and he saw no reason to alter family tradition.

It was at this stage that Reg Seekings turned up out of the blue. We had last seen each other in the Western Desert where Reg was serving in the SAS under the redoubtable Paddy Main as a young and very tough corporal. Few of that small and very fine body of men survived World War II but they and the Rhodesians of the LRDG became firm friends, a friendship born of mutual experience and respect. Not surprisingly, Reg and I found that our ideas were very much on the same lines. Reg was then a keen member of the Marlborough Police Field Reserve.

Events progressed rapidly at the end of 1965 and the beginning of 1966. My transfer to Mashonaland Province Headquarters was followed soon after by the first armed incursion into Lomagundi District and the murder of a farmer and his wife in the Hartley area. It would not be unreasonable to suppose that latter events provoked some soul-searching in the seats of power. I was transferred again to a tin office with a telephone in Police Headquarters. Reg was attested as a Reserve Patrol Officer and became my assistant, and very occasionally I was granted the services of a typist — when I could get past the dragon who controlled the labours of the typing pool.

Who was I, what was I and, more important, what was I supposed to be doing? Officially I was 'Training Officer', a wonderfully all-embracing title. I submitted memoranda galore — most of which were thrown back, rejected for reasons of expense. But all I had asked for were a few weapons, a minimum of webbing and some camouflage clothing. Came the minor victory when Phil Murray (a staff officer at Police Headquarters and a keen and experienced mountaineer) designed and had made the first 'prototype' rucksacks. We both admitted that the prototype was far too heavy. It still is.

Frustration, lobbying and the beating of a rather bald head against a substantial brick wall followed. Reg was in and out daily with the same questions — " What's the hold-up?" "When do we start?" and "They must be bloody daft. " In many cases I had to agree and my only minor tactical victory at this stage was the satisfaction of being rude to the duty detail who suggested that six o'clock was long after his normal time of departure but that he couldn't leave as he was responsible for PGHQ's security. District members- in-charge of that era can rest assured that one member of the tribe that made life difficult for them was given some fresh ideas.

Then came a ray of light at the end of the tunnel — initial courses in anti-terrorist training were ordered throughout the country. Reg and I set out on our travels, sometimes in style but more often less luxuriously.

We instructed and we marched. We talked and sometimes we got through to our puzzled victims, some of whom were mentally and physically unsuited for operations of this nature. It was hard to convince our pupils that anti-terrorist training was physically taxing, very uncomfortable and frequently boring. That there was a right way and a wrong way and that at this stage our way was the only right way was a philosophy that was hard to put across — and not only to our volunteers.

As with the VATs, there were good lads and bad, workers and talkers. There was the Reservist who had won the war in Kenya almost single-handed but having been appointed a section leader, failed to keep a rendezvous because he couldn't read a map. There was a memorable night north of Penhalonga near Werawuri where we waited expecting a ration drop the next day. Pouring rain, driving wind; cold and ill-equipped, we retreated into the Honde without our rations. The Mafungabusi Plateau in late October found Reg and I digging in the sand for water to satisfy 30 thirsty and expected trainees — after all the air recce couldn't be wrong. The 30 very exhausted men arrived and we had to force them back into the highlands again or face collapse from lack of water.

Such adventures are now old hat for those who have been and are still going through the mill, but for so many of our trainees such ordeals were completely outside the scope of their experience.

On the personal side came a rocket for missing Dining-in night and the more shattering news that I was too senior for the job. My baby was to be taken over by Superintendent 'Buck' Buchanan. The verdict provoked the soul-searching decision to retire.

In spite of all our mistakes, frustrations and on occasions the downright hostility we were met with, it was all very worthwhile. An idea was born and nurtured which was to prove itself in the years that followed. Policemen like Ron Gardner, Derek Humberstone, Mike Main and many others who were on the initial training courses rallied to the cause and gave unsparingly of their time and energies to a concept which, although essential, is so far removed from the conventions of police work.

Jimmy Spink, later to be Commissioner, was one of the few who saw any real value in what we were doing in the hectic early days. If memory serves me right, he was the one responsible for creating the term PATU.

I am extremely proud to have had a hand in the creation of our police anti-terrorist units and just as proud to be still serving in a unit at Melsetter. At the same time I am very conscious of the lesson learned the hard way years ago — that special units are not the ultimate in any type of warfare. I have nothing but admiration for the 'ordinary' work of both regular and reserve policemen, which often transcends the PATU role in both difficulty and danger. I cannot imagine anything worse than riding shotgun on an RM for two weeks at a stretch or doing static guards on a relay station. Give me a nice quiet patrol any day ... and I don't mind who knows it.

Although we have all seen PATU sticks misused and have seen men with better things to do kicking their heels or employed on tasks better forgotten or left to others, I still feel that the units have a very real and important role to play. There are those members of PATU who have yet to realize that they are nothing extra special and others who have yet to appreciate the fact that operational patrols — as in any type of warfare — are 99% boredom and one per cent fright.

There is danger in the erroneous concept existing in some quarters that PATU can be used in the role of the infantry soldier. This was never the intention. PATU was designed as a reconnaissance unit, trained to use the bush and capable of supporting itself with the minimum of back-up. Composed largely — as far as Police Reserve units are concerned — of older men, it is peculiarly suited for deployment in the recce role where conscientiousness and mental fortitude are the main qualities required.

The principles governing the selection, training and use of PATU remain the same and until this curse of terrorism has been overcome, police anti-terrorist units have a very real role to play.

To those whose names I have omitted to mention — and there are many — my apologies.

To all past and serving members of PATU, may your Gaz never run out."

PATU remained an essential and valuable element of the Security Forces throughout the war years. Many of its members earned recognition for their bravery; sadly many — far too many, both black and white– were killed in action.

Who were these men?

The policeman could be driving a B-Car, investigating a traffic accident, completing a docket, walking a beat and then, 24 hours later, be setting off into remote bush, dressed in camouflage, pack on back, rifle in hand. Moving silently over undulating and thickly grassed country, through overgrown valleys and up steep, rocky hills; watching, inspecting, evaluating, and feeling the pulse of his surroundings. Reservists too had to leave their offices, their factories, tobacco barns, cattle, and don the anonymous camouflage and move into the torrid hollows, the dense head high jesse; seeking traces of an unseen enemy.

Among the latter was former Detective Superintendent Mike O'Meara who would regularly put to one side the defence arguments of the terrorists he was representing, pro deo, in the courts, to take off into the wilds, perhaps seeking more clients.

But it is necessary to move just a little back in time; to those days when Bailey and Seekings started their country-wide missionary teaching. Already anti-terrorist training was a 'must' for police recruits and, with a small group of instructors including Humberstone and Kensett who had trained at the Gwelo School of Infantry, the first young men moved to the Horseshoe Block, north of Umvukwes. They had already undergone training in map reading, ground appreciation, theoretical rural operations, patrolling and weapon familiarity. Now they faced the more practical training; learning to live rough, in close proximity to wild animals, pushing their bodies beyond the limits of endurance, moving silently, watchfully, depending on each other.

Many lessons were to be learned in those early days. The correct footwear was a problem that took years to put right; the ration packs had to be pared down to less weighty, less luxurious content; the men had to learn not to talk, but to watch, observe, use hand signals and remain always alert. But, and this a rather strange discovery, despite the fitness of the younger men, the PATU-type duties were more effectively undertaken by those who were older and who, by reason of age and experience, seemed more able to withstand the discomfort and prolonged physical effort. Tony Eldridge was one of these; he had been a 'human torpedo' in the Second World War and though well into his fifties, remained incredibly fit and well able to compete with men half his age.

When Bailey left the Force, towards the end of 1966, his position as Staff Officer (Training) was taken by Superintendent 'Bill' Buchanan. In Salisbury Province, where of course lay the vast majority of as yet untapped manpower, Superintendent Ron' Gardner, followed by Ron Dick, Inspector Derek Humberstone and a Police Reservist, 'Bill" Ogilvie, were entrusted with pressing forward with the new training policies.

Those policies, perhaps objectives would be more appropriate, were to reconnoiter, observe and if possible arrest or ambush and pursue terrorists. These last aims, though an extension of Bailey's thinking, were the inevitable consequence of men seeking out an enemy. Nevertheless, however much a PATU 'stick' of four or five men wished to become 'involved' it was necessary for their leader to remember that they were few in number.

Derek Humberstone describes those days –

"As men became more efficient, they were sent on operational patrols to the Zambezi Valley, flying to Kanyemba or to Chirundu, then either by boat or truck to a drop off point; then to footslog back towards Chirundu. In those early days, everything had to carried on one's back; there were no radios for the patrols and, if you encountered a group of terrorists, it was a question of deciding whether to engage them, follow up, or get a message to Chirundu through the National Parks radio at Mana Pools. Tsetse fly, elephant, lion and buffalo were an ever-present problem as we walked through the thick jesse bush or tall elephant grass along the river banks."

On one patrol, the forward scout was in a donga looking for a way out for the remainder of the patrol when his stick leader spotted an elephant grazing from a tree right in front of the scout. Frantic hand signals were of no avail, the scout just would not look back. He was all but up to the massive animal's rear when, glancing behind him, he correctly interpreted his leader's frantic waving, managed to keep calm and retreated unscathed.

Humberstone had a novel means of keeping elephant at bay. He used a catapult and ball bearings which were a part of his 'survival kit' meant to pelt geese or wild fowl. It worked.

Another renowned PATU man was Bob Mansill. On one occasion, he was leading a PATU patrol when lion were seen close at hand. Bob halted the patrol, only to be spotted by one of the three cubs lying with their mother. This cub sniffed the air and bolted away, but the mother turned and crouched down as if to charge. Bob remained extraordinarily calm, shouted 'Voetsak' — and lioness and cubs bounded away into the bush. (Reserve Superintendent Bob Mansill was appointed a Member of the Order of the Legion of Merit in 1979. He had joined the Reserve thirty years before and been involved in every aspect of police work, ranging from traffic duties to — in 1979 — organising the security of the Executive Council and other Government ministers.)

Another remarkable tale concerns Reservist Bob Reeves who, in civilian life was managing director of a well-known firm producing car batteries. Bob was not only an active and enthusiastic PATU member, but also something of a culinary expert. With the addition of a few light-weight 'goodies', he could produce first-class meals from the rather dull ration packs including, of all things, crepes.

On this occasion, the task of the PATU patrol was to secure and protect a bush landing zone preparatory to an Air Force fuel re-supply. Now provided with a radio, Bob reported the area safe and secure, adding "Would you like chocolate cake for tea?" "Certainly" replied the incoming pilot thinking, as were others listening in on the same frequency, 'Typical Fuzz bull.' But when the aircraft landed, there it was: chocolate cake to accompany the tea.

Communications were, of course, absolutely essential for PATU to function to full effect and many Relay Posts were established atop high kopjes and manned by Reservists supplied by helicopter.

One such radio operator was James 'Jim' Kirkwood, DFC. As air gunner and later pilot he had been shot down over France during the 1939-1945 conflict. He managed to escape internment with the aid of French prostitutes who passed him from one brothel to another, giving rise to his claim that he was the only airman who had "fornicated his way to freedom." Kirkwood came to Rhodesia in 1949 to farm but soon became a stalwart member of the Reserve and a respected civil servant. In the late 70s he had to have a leg amputated but still he continued to carry out his police duties.

Derek Humberstone recalls: "On one occasion I saw Jim in the washroom in an operational area, obviously in terrible pain with his leg. I decided to send him to the rear, but he broke down and said he wanted to stay and finish his job. I managed to get an army medic' who patched him up and back he went to his wind and rain-lashed rocky gomo."

During the 70s members of the South African Police were sent up to Rhodesia to assist the BSAP and also to learn a little of operational conditions. Regrettably many of these young men were inadequately trained, unused to bush conditions (probably being better at dodging in and out of traffic) and perhaps not totally sold on the idea of assisting their northern neighbour. In fact they could be described as political cannon fodder. One such group was placed in an ideal ambush position in the Mount Darwin area, with the idea of uplifting their morale through successful and primary participation in an operation. Conditions could not have been better; the moon was full, the ambush site perfectly selected and terrorists expected. BSAP PATU sticks were in suitable back-up positions.

The ambush was sprung and then, unfortunately, the SAP broke every rule in the book. They left their positions to inspect their kill and even broke radio silence. Of a group of 14 terrorists only two were killed, the remainder escaped.

As the war progressed, as the terrorist menace began to encircle and infiltrate the country, as the situation worsened, so the terrible toll of PATU members rose. Regular members, farmers, business-men; old and young, were slain in ambushes, blown up by land mines, accidentally killed in cross fire. Families mourned the loss of fathers, sons, and many wives and mothers must have asked, 'is it worth it?'

One of the first to die, in March 1973, was David Stacey, a 51 year-old farmer who, during the War had seen action in North Africa and Italy and was one of the first post-war farmers to start develop-ing the Karoi area. A month later, Delville Vincent from Centenary's Palm Block, just into his mid-forties, was tragically killed. As the years passed, the list lengthened. Colin Chapman from Melsetter, Gordon Murdoch from Selous, David Carey from Kariba. In November of 1977, Peter Hanson, Robin Hunt and Harald Holstenberg, all from the Melsetter community, all in one PATU stick, were ambushed and killed. These were but a few of the many that sacrificed their lives in PATU: constables, sergeants, patrol officers and section officers, regulars and reservists from every district of the country. The list was long and saddening.

Yet there were others whose deeds and courage served to inspire their colleagues even more.

In July 1971, four members of the Banket PATU were awarded Commendations. All were farmers and had been engaged in a running battle with terrorists in the border area where they had killed one and wounded another. At the same time, Special Commendations went to Peter Knight who indulged in a Western-type 'draw' with a terrorist found trespassing on his farm, and to Gysberd Smit who tracked and located a group of terrorists before alerting the Security Forces of their hiding place.

Commendations were awarded in 1975 to two field reservists for an act that, on the face of it, was neither dramatic nor visibly courageous. The two were among PATU sections patrolling in the Madziwa Tribal Trust Lands when they sighted a 20-strong terrorist group. They realized that they were compromised but, instead of starting a futile and possibly fatal action, they stopped, deliberately exposed themselves — and made tea and prepared a meal. In the meantime, a radio message had been passed to other units in the area. Swiftly the terrorists were encircled and a successful action took place. Keith Meadows, one of the two involved in this story of quiet courage, went on to become a highly successful author, writing a fascinating and moving account of the life of the game ranger and architect of 'Operation Noah', Rupert Fothergill; and later a novel based in Rhodesia shortly before the country changed its name, *Sand in the Wind*.

Again in 1975, it had been decided that selected members of PATU be trained in advanced First Aid, more especially in the administration of intravenous injections and morphine. Women Field Reservists with nursing experience, among them Dulcie Jack, Audrey McIntosh, Hilary Pio and Alice Moore, volunteered their services to aid in the training function. First Aid kits were evaluated and updated and the aim established that in every stick there be one trained medic. Essential in this system was the complete support of the Llewellin Medical Training School, based in Bulawayo, whose staff were prepared to give unstinting support, based on practicality and immediate response, to all the Services.

By 1978, the PATU sections had become as sophisticated as it was possible to be for men who had to spend a small part of their lives in dangerous and uncomfortable conditions, moving slowly and silently through the bush and along lonely trails. Their equipment was the best available, their radios as light and up-to-date as possible and their overall knowledge as rounded and comprehensive as could be obtained. They had come a long way.

Perhaps the last word on PATU should come from a 79 year-old, long-retired trooper who, in 1968, accompanied much younger members of his family on a duck-shoot in the Zambezi Valley: "After the meal ... I decided to have a shave. While scraping the stubble from my tender and sun-and-wind-burnt face, I nearly slit my throat in surprise when five giant 'snails' with houses on their backs staggered into camp waving sten guns in my direction. On closer inspection, the 'snails' turned out to be humans clad in nondescript camouflaged uniforms.

"As I put down my razor, their leader came forward and introduced himself as Inspector Roy Townsend, of Salisbury. He introduced the remainder of the patrol — Patrol Officers Wiggill, Bush, Crook and African Sergeant Botha — and all five slipped the 'houses' from their backs and sank to the ground, tired, footsore and obviously aching in every bone from weariness and the heat. One man removed his boot with a sigh of relief to reveal a blistered and raw foot. Our hearts went out to them and for my part, my mind flashed back over 50 years to the privations I had suffered on patrol then. Even in those days, such hardships had been the exception rather than the rule, and it was with real sympathy and genuine gratitude that I suddenly realized how much the Rhodesian public owed to these unpublicised, unsung watchmen of our borders."

The author and his family provide tea for the patrol and hear how they have plodded through water, mud and slush, through senanga infested with tsetse fly, and with mopani flies crawling into their noses, ears and mouths. Later, and after a few beers and a delicious stew of wild duck, it is learned that one of the patrol has been managing an hotel and another was a salesman, but that the attraction of police life outweighed the tedium of civilian life. The next morning the patrol departs, melting silently into the trees, leaving the old man and his family to finish their holiday.

Once returned to his Salisbury home, the old trooper climbs into bed and thinks of the five policemen, far away in their loneliness and far from comfortable — and offers a silent prayer for their safety and for that of others like them.

The old trooper was Eben Mocke, Regimental Number 1437, who had joined the Force in 1910 and left in 1918 having been brought back from India where he had tried to join the British Army in 1915. Fascinating accounts of his time in the Force — outside the scope of this volume — appeared in *The Outpost* in the late 60s. A few months after encountering Roy Townsend's stick on the Zambezi, Eben met many more policemen at the 1968 Trade Fair. Section Officer Chris Pollard at Nyamandhlovu had managed to locate Eben's Bushman tracker, C'wai, who 55 years earlier had featured with him in his "Kalahari Patrol." The reunion of two very old comrades was featured on television and radio but an equally touching meeting of minds saw the midnight oil being burned on successive nights at Hillside Police Station where Eben shared experiences with a rapt audience of serving members. Eben died in March 1972.

There is a sting in the tail of the Zambezi meeting: Some months later, Roy Townsend, who had spent four years in the Parachute Regiment with service in Malaya and Palestine before joining the Force in 1948, was involved in the interrogation of a captured terrorist group. One of them remarked that he had seen Roy before and when asked where, and under what circumstances, replied, "You were on a patrol with four others. We were hidden in ambush about 10 yards away from you, but we did not fire because then we did not want anyone to know we were in the country."

*We've toiled up endless gomos,*
*We've tramped the dusty plain,*
*With humour always our ally*
*Despite the body's pain.*
*A joke for aching shoulders*
*Braced into swaying pack.*
*A smile to boost your partner*
*So your morale won't crack*
*Sometimes we find our luck's in*
*And get in on the fun,*
*Recalling Reg's lessons*
*On how to use the gun.*
*But more often than not it's just footwork*
*Until each trip is done,*
*And yet we feel it's worth it*
*If we've kept them on the run*

## Chapter Fifty

## 'BLACK BOOTS' — THE SUPPORT UNIT

If you walk east to the end of Baines Avenue in Harare, you will find facing you, and bordering on the Police Depot, a small, rather beautiful Chapel. On the walls, within this bright, airy church have been placed rows of plaques that honour many of those who have died during or subsequent to service in the BSA Police. Flags hang from the high roof and there is much of the later history of the Force to be learned from the many names commemorated here. Towards the back of the chapel, on the south wall, is displayed a large, lovingly-fashioned and highly polished wooden panel. It is the Roll of Honour of the Support Unit. Ninety-nine small brass plaques bear witness to members who have given their lives for their country.

The origins of the Askari Platoon or, as it was sometimes called, the African Police Platoon, and which grew to become the Support Unit, are properly linked with the days when the BSA Police was proudly proclaimed 'the First Line of Defence'. In those days, the Platoon was about 200 strong and was mainly a ceremonial body; guarding Government House, supplying instructors for the African Police Training School (APTS), performing the Retreat Ceremony at Police Displays and being virtually a showpiece of spit and polish and precision drill.

A very large number of its members came from Nyasaland (Malawi). In fact one, African Station Sergeant Machado, actually walked from that country in 1927 to join the unit. Like many of his colleagues, Machado was attached to the Rhodesian African Rifles (RAR) during the Second World War, served with that regiment in East Africa, India and Burma, and returned to Rhodesia and his career in the Police at the end of hostilities. On his retirement in 1963, he was the senior non-commissioned officer in the Platoon and, at a spectacular parade, was awarded the British Empire Medal (BEM) and presented with a shotgun as a memento of his years of service. At that time, Machado boasted the 1939/45 Star, the Burma Star, the Defence Medal, War Medal, Coronation Medal, the Colonial Police Medal for Meritorious Service and the Colonial Police Long Service Medal, with two Bars; as well as his BEM.

There were many like him and many would follow in his steps — strong, honourable, loyal and totally dedicated to the Unit and to their job. They were the backbone and the inspiration on which the Support Unit was to grow and prosper.

The Report of the Commissioner of Police for 1962 comments that the training of the Platoon continued on the broader lines introduced the previous year, and that members took part in security operations on many occasions in areas as far apart as Lupani and Chipinga.

These were the days following the banning of the Zimbabwe African Peoples Union (ZAPU) and a campaign of civil disobedience was pervading the country. It was necessary for the new training syllabus to lay emphasis on Riot Drill Training, elementary Law and Police duties and Field Exercises as, by this time, the Platoon was beginning to slip into a new role of roving disciplinarian and peacekeeper. It was, after all, the only large group of men available who were trained and able to respond quickly and effectively to an emergency.  Probably the first man to take charge of the Platoon as it moved into this more active role was Inspector Ted Cutfield, recently a drill instructor in the European Depot. He was later joined by Sergeant Malcolm 'Mac' Wiltshire, who had been in charge of a small roving section investigating the killing or maiming of cattle which, with increased thefts of stock, was prevalent in the Mashonaland and Midlands Provinces at that time.

Wiltshire recalls flying to Bulawayo just before Christmas 1962 with about 30 members of the Platoon. The industrial areas and townships were at that time the scenes of stoning, burning and widespread intimidation. The task of Wiltshire and his men was to patrol the affected areas during the night and try to arrest the culprits. Unfortunately, the timing was close to disastrous; the members had not been paid and were unable to afford a beer, never mind a soft drink and a bun. 'Mac' approached the officer in command, at that time George Peck, and a loan of one pound for each man was speedily arranged from benevolent funds.

Mac recounts subsequent events: "I passed this money to the men at lunchtime the first day we were there. Later that evening, I took the heavy vehicle I had been given to the African Police 'lines' in

Bulawayo Camp where my chaps were billeted, so that they could be uplifted and dropped at strategic points in the Industrial Sites. Virtually every one of them was rolling drunk and incapable of going on duty. I had to get some coffee from the Mess, brew it in dixies, doctor them and make them walk round and around the Parade Square until they were more or less sober. I was due to take them out at about eight that evening. I think we only launched — and then with some difficulty — at about ten."

He continues — "Quite a few of the 'old' Platoon were poorly educated and really hard cases, and I remember one who smashed his rifle butt into the face of a constable guarding the access gate to Bulawayo Camp when asked for his identity card. They were pretty quick to fix bayonets in a riot situation too, and one had to watch them carefully. "

The potential of the Platoon was now apparent — provided they remained sober — and Police Headquarters realised that, with the tentacles of African Nationalism spreading around the country, the possibility of incursions by trained insurgents from neighbouring territories and the general deterioration of good order, rapid reaction by a versatile body of well trained men was needed to counter some of the threats facing the country.

The Platoon became the Support Unit. A proper establishment of men, broken down into three troops, each of three independent sections comprising 45 men, was agreed and a suitable commander sought to lead the new unit.

The choice fell to Superintendent Albert Freemantle who, as the saying goes, 'came of military stock', had served in the Parachute Regiment and at Arnhem during World War II and joined the Police in 1946. Freemantle had been commissioned in 1962 and took charge of the Support Unit from its inception. He had the added advantage of being a 'keep fit fanatic', maintaining a regimen of exercises, running and sport that would be the envy of many of his contemporaries and which he maintained even beyond his retirement in 1977.

Freemantle gathered about him a small corps of instructors and troop commanders, all having previous service in military or similar units and all dedicated to making the Support Unit an effective, efficient and highly individualistic arm of the Police. Men like Karl Maskell, Phil Kensett and later 'Pat' Deasy were to act as trainers, administrators, personnel practitioners, 'Q' representatives, in fact men of all parts, as the Unit developed.

Charles Parker, Ian 'Dumpie' Dunbar, 'Chunky' Watson, Derrick Edge, Ted Crawford, and Peter Lund were the first Troop and Section Leaders, to be followed by 'Chimp' Webster, Derick Jewson, Kerry Croasdell, Jannie Steenkamp, Laurie Wake, Bill Donaldson and others.

They trained in riot drill, fieldcraft and radio procedure; they revelled in the peak of physical fitness and welded themselves into a hard, potent and proud unit that could be called to assist any province, district or station that was hard-pressed and needed their particular expertise.

It was not long before the Support Unit was expanded. Three more Troops were added in 1968, the emblem of an eagle dropping on its prey eventually adopted as an 'arm 'flash' — and later — flag, and the unit speedily grew, thriving on its own momentum to become, at times, almost an embarrassment as far as Police Headquarters was concerned. Conventionally reared senior officers suddenly found they had fathered a wild and uninhibited child who, certainly in the early years, wore what he liked — within reason — and demonstrated a pride in the Unit bordering on fanaticism. Apparently he was not above smashing up bars and inflicting bodily harm upon any that dared disparage him or his siblings.

What Police Headquarters forgot, of course, was that the Unit had developed into a full combat company, was in fact very highly disciplined and that the odd departure from the norm (the letting down of hair beyond regulation length), had to be accepted and expected.

One of the more tedious tasks imposed on the Unit was the guarding of detainees at Gonakudzingwa, close to Vila Salazar and Malvernia on the eastern border with Mozambique; and at Zhombe, a remote mission station 55 miles north-west of Que Que. These two lonely, inaccessible and inhospitable places — to call them even villages would be too generous — housed the principle African Nationalist leaders for a number of years after their organizations were banned by the Southern Rhodesia government. The thankless task of control, or member-in-charge, fell to single men: Julian Twine, 'Paddy' Deasy, Karl Maskell, Dougie Baird, to name but four. In fact, the prospect of a temporary transfer to stations such as these acted as a powerful incentive for some — but not all — to enter into matrimony.

Freemantle, who originated the Unit's call sign 'Mantle', was succeeded by John Worsley, and then, but not necessarily in order came Derek Waller, Brian Lay, 'Taff' Morgan, Guy Houghton, Ron Dick, Jim Collins and finally Don Rowland. There were others, but their tenures were relatively short. To Houghton fell the dubious distinction of being the most senior officer in any of the Security Forces to be blown up by a land mine. His companions on this little foray, which occurred some miles from Mukumbura, were Chief Inspector 'Pat' Deasy and a constable. It is to the everlasting credit of 'Pat' that, when asked if he was alright, he clapped a hand to his ear and replied "What, Sir?" In such ways are disability pensions for hearing impairment genuinely earned.

The complete story of the 'Black Boots' could be a separate volume in its own right. Here it is possible only to dip into the highlights of a supremely successful unit and of which, in 1968, a wit commented: 'You don't have to be mad to join the Unit; we will teach you.'

While on this lighter note, a correspondent in 1971 commented on what he was pleased to call the Unit Questionnaire, and among which were the following:

"I am fond of travel/beer/smoking/girls. (Delete nothing or we don't want you)."

"Which is the odd one out? Savoury mince/corned beef/caviar/baked beans."

"Who is buried in Grant's Tomb? Tiny Tim/the Tolpuddle Martyrs/General Ulysses Grant."

In 1974 the Commissioner of Police felt compelled to include a detailed Roll of Honour within his Annual Report to Government. One of the first members of the Unit to be killed as a result of terrorist action was Constable Richard Matambo who died when the Unit base in the Chesa African Purchase Area was mortared in mid-June. Many more members were to be killed as the months rolled into years and many were the bravery awards earned by members of all ranks.

Two years later, in 1976, Constable Misheck Ncube earned the Police Decoration for Gallantry. Misheck was a medic with 'D' Troop, then commanded by National Service Patrol Officer (NSPO) Gordon Kaye-Eddie, and patrolling late one afternoon. In the half-light, Misheck spotted a single terrorist armed with an RPD machine gun, standing only about 20 metres away. The constable held his fire for several minutes, hoping that other insurgents would appear, but none did. He then fired, killing the man.

This was the first incident. Four weeks later, with the same Troop, came the action for which he was decorated.

A dawn attack had been mounted on a suspected terrorist camp only to find the area deserted. Enquiries led them to a second camp but, again, the result was the same except that it was clear the occupants had only recently departed. The section followed the spoor and Misheck was first to spot a terrorist lying in ambush in thick cover. Kaye-Eddie, who was leading, was quickly called back and Misheck then opened fire, whereupon the police were subjected to heavy automatic fire and grenade attack from the ambush positions. Kaye–Eddie and Misheck were both wounded, but the latter, disregarding his own injuries — a head wound — carefully and competently attended to his section leader. Command of the patrol was then taken over by Constable Elias Hove. Meanwhile, the terrorists regrouped and counter-attacked. Misheck divided his attention between returning the enemy fire, looking after his commander and distributing the latter's ammunition among the other members of the section. Eventually reinforcements arrived and Kaye-Eddie was flown out — not so Misheck, who felt that his medical services might still be required.

Constable Hove had taken command with calmness and competence. He gave a clear account of the progress of the action to the approaching Fire Force, rallied the section and was largely responsible for the subsequent and total success of an engagement resulting in the deaths of ten terrorists and the capture of several others. Hove was awarded a Commissioner's Commendation with Silver Baton.

Another medic who showed remarkable courage was Constable Daniel Chiripanyanga of 'L' Troop. He was a member of a seven-man section led by NSPO John Worsley-Worswick who ambushed a large group of terrorists one moonless night in May of the same year. During the half-hour battle, Daniel was shot through the hand. Despite a debilitating and painful injury which he reported to his section leader, he quietly and efficiently passed his ammunition to Worsley-Worswick. The engagement over, though a terrorist counter-attack remained a possibility, Daniel silently opened his medical bag and took out the morphine and bandages needed to treat his own wound, whispering instructions for treatment to one of his colleagues. It was to be a further seven hours before Daniel could be casevaced from the scene.

Not once was he heard to complain. The injury was so serious that his left hand had eventually to be amputated.

The next year, 1977, saw further acts of incredible valour.

This time the awards went to 'E' Troop, specifically to Constable Edwin Mazarire with the Police Cross for Conspicuous Gallantry; and posthumously to the Troop's former commander, Section Officer Timothy Hewitt, the Police Decoration for Gallantry. It is said that but for the fact that no such award had been given to a member of the regular army, Mazarire would have received the Grand Cross of Valour.

The Troop was ambushed one early morning in February as their vehicles were being driven up a short hill. The ambush was well mounted and well concealed and Hewitt, in the lead vehicle, suffered a serious abdominal wound in the first moments of the attack. Nevertheless, he returned fire from the cab with his shotgun. Meanwhile, in the back of the vehicle, Constable Moyo received injuries which later proved fatal while Constable Mazarire received shrapnel wounds to a leg.

Armed with a machine gun, Mazarire immediately and calmly returned fire, enabling the other passengers to climb out and take up defensive positions. As he paused to reload, he was again hit, this time by a bullet passing through his right arm above the elbow. Undeterred, Edwin completed reloading and resumed firing and then realized that the enemy fire was being concentrated at the cab in which Hewitt was trapped.

Edwin then jumped to the ground, deliberately exposing himself to fire from close range and managed to get Hewitt out from the cab, round the exposed front of the vehicle and into a relatively safer position, protected by the front wheel and on the sheltered side of the truck. At this stage, he was further wounded in the left arm, thigh and back. Hewitt, though seriously injured and in considerable pain, now rallied and encouraged his men and, after about ten minutes, they managed to drive off the attackers. Hewitt then organized a follow-up operation by the half of his troop who were uninjured, took over radio communications and assisted his second-in-command, Lance Section Officer Billy Houghton, in guiding aircraft to the scene.

'Tim' Hewitt died from his injuries about a week later: Edwin Mazarire partially recovered and returned to serve in the Unit.

Later that same year, the then commander of the Support Unit, Assistant Commissioner Jim Collins, presented Commissioner's Commendations to Section Officer Keith Rutherfoord and Constables Josiah Chengeta and Mishek Munyani. Nyamapanda was the scene of Rutherfoord's bravery when the Police Camp came under heavy attack by mortars, rockets, rifle and machine gun fire from neighbouring Mozambique. Rutherfoord was commanding 'Romeo' Troop at the time and took control of both the Police and Army personnel; organizing defensive positions, looking after the injured, returning fire, organizing the supply of ammunition and, though suffering from shrapnel wounds, rallying the men with complete disregard for his own safety.

Chengeta and Munyani were with Zulu Bravo Troop in the Plumtree area when their six-man stick was ambushed one early morning having itself been in ambush positions throughout the night. The sergeant in charge and two constables were killed early on in the engagement and another constable badly injured. Despite this, the two men took up defensive positions and fought off their attackers, Josiah even managing to kill the terrorist leader who had been exhorting his men to advance. The two then ran 12 kilometres to get help.

By this time, the role of the Support Unit in the countrywide conflict had been noticed and acknowledged in a number of ways. Not least among these was the Women's Association of Harare's Highlands Presbyterian Church who adopted the Unit, knitted balaclava helmets and gloves and supplied biscuits and other goodies, much to the appreciation of the various troops. A similar course was adopted by the ladies of Rusape who provided a Christmas Dinner at the local Forces Canteen for four troops in 1977 and capped their generosity with a beautifully iced cake, atop of which four of them had crafted the emblem of the Unit, the martial eagle.

An unusual but highly deserved honour came to the Unit in 1978. The 'Black Boots' were granted the Freedom of the Makoni Rural Council Area in October.

The ceremony was performed before a large crowd which included the Co-Minister of Justice and of Law and Order, Hilary Squires; the Commissioner of Police, by this time Peter Allum; the Officer Commanding Manicaland Province, Senior Assistant Commissioner Alan Rich; his predecessor,

Assistant Commissioner Ken Macdonald and the Chairman of the Council, Mr Frank Langley. The latter was accompanied by the Unit's new Commanding Officer, Assistant Commissioner Don Rowland. Some 130 policemen, representing all troops of the Unit, paraded under the command of Chief Superintendent Derek Humberstone.

Following the presentation of the Deed, the document was paraded in slow time before the four troops by Inspector Michael Davis escorted by Section Officer Paul Comberback and Sergeant Major Isaac Makuba.

The Unit had 'taken to' Rusape long before 1978. Several members had taken part in the annual Rusape River Race a couple of years before; Inspector Pearmain, Section Officer Ronnie Hein and Patrol Officers Mario Birkin and Manie Du Preez had opted for the main race as opposed to the more popular 'Booze Cruise'. After a promising start they had lost in fairly rapid succession one man over-board and then both paddles. They were not last, but they certainly were not included in the first three.

The Unit had gathered a reputation for fighting hard and playing hard and they became involved in many varied social events. One of the most entertaining, and undoubtedly carrying a more favourable result then the 'Boat Race', was a rugby match against a team of nurses from the Andrew Fleming Hospital.  One wonders whether, had it been tennis, an interim score would have been 'Love all'.

The Unit had been accommodated in cramped and unsuitable accommodation in the Tomlinson Depot for many years. Temporary housing in Stops Hostel within Morris depot and the occasional use of old police houses in Fife Avenue had eased the problems somewhat. But the Unit, and Police Headquarters as well, was aware of the resplendent barracks' which had been built elsewhere for regiments of the Army. The role of the Support Unit in the war was not that of 'poor relations'. Even their pub was a 'self help' prefabricated building, transported from Vila Salazar, re-erected and then completed and decorated from 'donations'. It was not until the mid-to late 70s that reasonably prestigious and adequate barrack accommodation was built on the road leading out to Arcturus, at Chikurubi.

The then Quartermaster had envisaged a camp that would be on a par with those recently built for Army units in the Inkomo area. It was not to be. Offices, flats, single quarters and a hospital were constructed in the first phase of the development after the usual bitter fight for the necessary funds, but the standard of accommodation was generally inferior and measured to a reduced budget. The Minister of Local Government and Housing, Bill Irvine, whose views on Africans, especially police, living in 'white areas' were well known, was heard to comment disparagingly and unsympathet-ically on any improvements in living standards.

While Police Headquarters fought to provide reasonable accommodation for men exposed to danger and discomfort, the small brass plaques in the Chapel grew as the nationalist onslaught increased. Jermanus Muredzi, Stanley Jemwa, Gift Muduve, Isaac Chipara, Martin Mudzmiri, Craig Clack, Angel Machimbirike, Lazarus Charindapanze, the three men from Zulu Bravo Troop already mentioned, Tony Dawson; the list stretched on and on and the Unit mourned its dead as members made the final sacrifice on bush roads, in ambushes and in bitter battles throughout the country.

The death of Inspector Tony Dawson in June 1978 was a particular blow to the Force. Tony had married the daughter of a serving officer and, through sheer ability and hardwork linked with a popular and unassuming personality, was destined for an outstanding career. He had been deeply involved in rugby, (both Police and National) swimming, water polo and squash and, to cap a short lifetime of achievements in which loyalty and team spirit had been outstanding features, had been awarded the 'B.S.A Police Sportsman of the Year' Trophy five years before.

The loss of young men, such as those mentioned in the previous paragraphs, brought home very forcibly to police and public alike the dreadful ability of a war to cut down, in their prime, careers of promise and to deprive mothers and children of the fathers who should have been so much a part of their years together.

And as some died and many were grievously injured, so the honours mounted.

The Police Cross for Conspicuous Gallantry was awarded in 1978 to Lance Section Officer Lindsay 'Kiwi' O'Brien. Lindsay's courage dated back to 1976 when he and his men had set off to cover 17 kilometres of rough country in just on three hours to assist another section of the Unit pinned down in an ambush. This engagement, which continued with protracted follow-up operations covering a further 10 days, resulted in a contact in which the young man received a serious shoulder injury.

Despite his wound, O'Brien maintained pursuit until the spoor was lost. Only then did he permit his colleagues to casevac him to a hospital. His next foray against the enemy was in 1977 when he again covered many kilometres in pursuit and successful engagement of the enemy forces. Finally, in March 1978 O'Brien found himself having to set up an ambush near a kraal in a totally exposed position. During the subsequent engagement, he was severely wounded and in considerable pain, but continued to direct and rally his section until he lost consciousness. After medical attention, he resumed command of his men and directed them in a sweep of the contact area.

At the same time as O'Brien was awarded his medal, so the Police Decoration for Gallantry was presented to Lance Sergeant Major Mudema Masakwa. The citation refers to 'his professional ability, aggression, example and devotion to duty" contributing significantly to many and various successful contacts. One example of this occurred in 1977 when, in difficult and unusual circumstances and completely on his own, he killed a lone terrorist who was armed with a rocket launcher and a pistol. The particular terrorist had been involved in numerous acts of lawlessness and intimidation and was believed to be spending the nights at a mission complex. During the day, the Unit had mounted an ambush in expectation of the man returning. During the evening, the sound of war songs was heard from one of the dormitories and Mudema decided that, rather than lose the element of surprise that a full-scale team attack might cause, he would tackle the man on his own. Bursting through the door, he was confronted by the terrorist with the rocket launcher. Mudema immediately opened fire and killed the man.

Another member of the Support Unit to be decorated at about this time was Lance Inspector Barry Woan (Member of the Order of the Legion of Merit — Civil Division) who, despite being severely wounded in action, receiving a 20% disability and having to walk with the aid of a caliper, nevertheless insisted on returning to all but full duties and subsequently moulded his Troop — 'Zulu Alpha' — into a highly effective and successful fighting unit.

Two others to be similarly decorated were Section Officer Darrol Brent and Sergeant Major Frederick Shimongola.

Brent had been the gifted tracker of Mike Main's stick in the early days of PATU and now commanded 'Lima' Troop. Like Woan, Darrol displayed outstanding qualities of leadership and personal courage, inspiring his team to become a respected and efficient unit with outstanding successes to their credit. Shimongola, Troop Sergeant-Major of the same unit, was exceptional in support of his commander, displaying the same qualities of competence and professionalism and contributing in great measure to the Troop's shared responsibility for 39 terrorists killed and many others captured.

The foregoing must not be regarded as exhaustive. It is merely a sample — a cross-section — of the part played by the 'Black Boots' in those long years of conflict. Nevertheless, it is apparent that the role of the Unit during those years has never been adequately recognized and recorded. In 1980, when the military regime that had existed throughout the war years was beginning to disintegrate and dissolve to the south, the Support Unit, an integral part of the B.S.A.Police, remained a disciplined and undivided body of 12 companies, nearly 1500 men.

By that time, the Chikurubi Barracks had been expanded and improved and it fell to the Officer Commanding, Assistant Commissioner Don Rowland, to outline the new, civilian role of the Unit which, for possibly the last time, was parading in camouflage. Those duties would consist of a continued counter-insurgency role allied to that of border control, crowd handling and similar duties in an urban context; support of other branches of the Force in large scale stock theft, crime epidemics, poaching and similar offences and, of course, guard and escort duties.

In many ways, the 'Black Boots' had come full circle. But over the years they had matured into a proud and illustrious 'family'. Many names and many actions had contributed to their exalted reputation. It is tempting to write of Clive Bulley, of Keith Reynolds (also known as 'Stingray'), of Fred Mason, of Phil Kensett, and of the many, many others who made the Unit what it was. There are many stories to be told, not the least of the man who, during an action, was reporting to base on his radio when he was shot, and calmly commented 'Ouch. I've been shot, I think I've got a second arsehole.'

Yes, they were characters, heroes and fine men — these policemen who jealously preserved their individuality and performed a role that, though not one of policing in the true sense of that word, was nevertheless essential to meet the terrible problems then facing Rhodesia.

They form a great and worthy part of the Force's History.

## Chapter Fifty-One

## THE POLICE RESERVE AIR WING (PRAW)

The first use of spotter aircraft has been remarked upon as occurring during a murder investigation in the Selukwe area. That was as early as 1942. As the years progressed and methods of detection became more professional, it became apparent that the services of an airborne eye would be of tremendous advantage to the Force in their day-to-day duties. The purchase of an exclusively police plane was a 'Treasury Impossibility' but there were a number of police reservists, mainly farmers, who were more than happy to place their aircraft at the disposal of police and enjoy becoming a part of the police effort.

By 1957, the Reserve was beginning to blossom in various directions. The Radio Branch had been formed to assist the Regular Force members involved in that aspect of police work; Reconnaissance Sections had been started using obsolete and then modified, but unarmed, military armoured cars. These latter were manned, serviced and generally and jealously looked after by a self-contained group of instructors, mechanics, electricians, drivers and radio operators. One-time Regular members who had joined the reserve were grouped in sections ready to take over the running of police stations in an emergency.

Arising from all this activity, the Air Wing took off on 1 July 1957.

It was a small beginning — just 16 aircraft with 21 pilots and 19 air observers. But its members were keen, they relished the opportunities afforded on training days and they soon showed how useful an aircraft could be in support of ground forces.

It was not long before the training came into practical use. The Emergency of 1959 gave PRAW personnel the opportunity to display their skills as airborne relay stations, as couriers and message droppers.

As the security situation in the country deteriorated, so the enthusiasm within all sections of the Reserve increased. The first air training exercise for the Manicaland and Mashonaland flights was held in 1961. This was extended to include aircraft and pilots from every province the following year and in May the Governor presented 51 pilots and observers with their PRAW 'wings'. That year the unit flew 217 sorties totaling 383 hours. As this history progresses, we shall see how these figures expanded beyond recognition.

The years rolled on and training and expertise increased. More and more emphasis was laid on co-operation with ground forces and with the Royal Rhodesian Air Force who had always served as a guide, mentor and inspiration to PRAW. In fact, there was a time when a member of the RRAF, Rob Gaunt, did all he could to have PRAW removed from police control and placed under the Air Force. The PRAW pilots made their views very clear, both to Gaunt and later to members of parliament before whom the subject had been raised, and it fell to Superintendent Dick Evans to prepare a reasoned and finally successful rebuttal.

The annual Air Wing exercises grew lengthier, the demands on the pilots' skills and ingenuity more demanding. In 1965, the MBE was conferred on the leader of the Manicaland Flight, Police Reservist Bill Springer, and two years later the Air Wing was awarded, for the first time, the prized and prestigious Pat Judson Trophy. The Air Wing would receive this honour once more, in 1978.

The Trophy — the background of which is not a part of this story — was awarded annually for 'the most meritorious flight or series of flights made by an individual or an organisation in the cause of aviation, or the community in Rhodesia as a whole, when flying has been the prominent feature of the service'.

Making the presentation, the President of the Rhodesian Branch of the Royal Aeronautical Society, and Director of Civil Aviation, commented: " ... the Police Reserve Air Wing have played a vital part in the maintenance of law and order in this country. The Wing's aircraft are, in the main, owned by private flyers, farmers, business people and flying clubs, and a few by commercial operators. The duties of the Wing include reconnaissance, air to ground cooperation, search and rescue, search for stolen vehicles, fugitives and terrorists, acting as airborne relay stations, supply dropping to ground forces in operational areas, and generally assisting the regular security forces of Rhodesia."

At virtually the same time as the Trophy was presented to Unit Commander Phil Palmer, the Commissioner awarded Commendations to two members of the Matabeleland Flight, Pilot Phil' Brittlebank and Observer Vic' Barnett, for their part in support of a security patrol in the Wankie area earlier that year.

However, the year was not to pass without tragedy.

In May, Police Reserve Pilot Alfred Dendy Lawton was killed when his plane crashed during a combined air and ground operation at Toronto Farm near Penhalonga. At the time, he was dropping a message or spool of film to the PATU team on the ground. One passenger, Senior Assistant Commissioner Eric White, then OC Manicaland Province, sustained severe injuries, mainly from burns. Lawton's observer, Police Reservist 'Bill' Perkins, suffered nasty burns but otherwise was virtually unscathed.

By 1969, the training exercises had been expanded even more and the Air Wing, assisted and often friendly supervised by the Air Force, was involved in station security schemes with regular and reserve members on the ground, and particularly in operations with PATU members. Flight-testing had been introduced to cover flying ability, together with a clear knowledge of all the necessary procedures related to operational efficiency and flying standards.

The following story illustrates the commitment of the Wing:

It was just before Christmas that a member of the security forces, a South Africa policeman, had been lost for over four days somewhere between Chirundu and Kariba. Patrols drawn from the Support Unit and the Sinoia PATU were already searching the area, and the former had managed to locate and begin follow-up on the tracks of the missing man. It was decided that a Police Reserve aircraft could provide support to the ground forces and a Cessna known by its call sign Copper 12, piloted by Bill 'Mac' MacDonald with Dickie Boltt as his observer, was sent to Kariba.

This was an evening or, perhaps more accurately a night flying operation. Having decided on a grid search of the area, the two men were over the Zambezi sometime before nine o-clock, had made contact with the PATU stick, confirmed their position and started the exacting search pattern, at a height of about 1000 feet. This involved absolute accuracy, as each leg of the search had to be of six minutes duration –- no more, no less. The exercise was complicated by a strong crosswind, nearby hills that were all but invisible and little or no discernible horizon.

After completing two sweeps and about three minutes down the westward leg of the third, Boltt spotted a shower of sparks and directed his pilot even lower over the area. At tree-top height and with the landing lights beaming down, they spotted a blazing fire and beside it someone waving vigorously. Unfortunately, by this time they were unable to pinpoint their exact location without returning to a fixed point and taking a bearing. Even more worrying was ground control's attitude which seemed to doubt their discovery and suggest that, as petrol was running low, they should stay in the vicinity until the last possible moment when an RRAF plane could relieve them pending a full rescue operation the following morning.

However the Sinoia PATU stick had not only been listening in to the conversations but had been firing off flares at half-hour intervals to advise their position. They now decided to go 'hell for leather' to the aid of the South African policeman.

It became a desperate race between the petrol gauge and the men on the ground — being directed from the plane above. The four PATU members (they had left two men at their base) ran, fell, stumbled and staggered through the darkness of the bush with only a pencil torch, their walkie-talkie and a diminishing supply of flares, now being used for light, to guide them towards the fire.

The PATU searchers actually smelled the fire before they saw it and managed to force their way through thick undergrowth to the frightened and exhausted man. After that they had to ask Mac to help them find their way back to base. Somehow the petrol gauge stayed just above 'E', thanks to some brilliant flying and a kindly fuel gauge, and the operation ended successfully during the early hours of the following day.

The RRAF refuelled Copper 12 at Kariba and it returned to Sinoia early that morning. Mac had sheep to care for on his farm, Dickie an insurance office to run.

Assistance and cooperation such as this was the hallmark of the PRAW and, if further example be necessary, it was only a day or two after this incident that another Air Wing plane dropped fresh serum into a remote area near Kariba, where a chief's wife had been bitten by a snake.

Sadly, however, 1969 was to see another particularly tragic accident, this time involving one of the Wing's most popular and experienced pilots.

Bill Springer and Inspector Terry Shaw were on a training flight near Umtali when their plane crashed in the Lower Vumba and both were killed. Passengers Joe McBride and Paul Rens were injured, but survived. Springer, who was trained in Rhodesia by the RAF during the Second World War, had been one of the most popular pilots in the Wing, a man who loved flying and was always prepared to set aside whatever he might be doing and fly to the assistance of, not only the police, but also the public. He ran a garage business in Chipinga which had been started just after the war in 1945. Mention has already been made of the award to him of the MBE some four years before his death. It is pertinent to quote from the official citation:

'On numerous occasions he has shown a public-spirited attitude, not only in respect of his Air Wing duties but also in the assistance he has rendered in flying sick and injured members of the public to hospitals from remote areas of the country. This was often done with considerable inconvenience and expense to himself. In all he has made some 30 flights on such missions, usually at no cost to the people concerned'.

Terry Shaw was only 36 when he died. He was Provincial Inspector with the Police Reserve in the Province and, with a fine reputation already established and every expectation of a promising future, became another casualty of the growing crisis.

In 1970, the Air Wing registered a total of 1773 flights, a far cry from the 217 sorties of 1961, and in 1977, a phenomenal figure of 22,000 flight hours were logged. The total strength of the Air Wing had grown from inception to over 180 pilots and observers.

With the Air Wing now heavily involved in operational flying, various 'alterations' were made to some of the planes to afford protection from enemy weapons.

One of the first innovations was a protective steel seat lining designed to absorb the penetrative force of a bullet. Not an easy task. Probably the first pilot to come up with a solution to the problem of dealing with ground fire was the veteran Bill Ludgater from Bindura, who had been one of the first active members of the Wing and been awarded membership of the Legion of Merit for his Reserve service. He sat on a plough disc. Improvements on this highly uncomfortable expedient were keenly debated. The main considerations were, naturally, thickness and weight.

Staff officers at Police Headquarters managed to locate an industrial firm well-versed in fashioning high tensile steel and within the necessary tolerance and very soon the planes were equipped with the new armour. The pilots, not to put too fine a point upon it, sat easier. One or two, Hugh Chisnall being one, had to learn the usefulness of their new protection the hard way.

Further protection became necessary when it was learned that the enemy possessed SAM 7 or 'Strella' anti-aircraft missiles. Very basically, these could be fired from the shoulder or from a quickly improvised ground base and, self propelled, sought out their aerial target by detecting the heat thrown off by that target.

Most planes, both civil and security force, were coated with a shiny, protective paint that reflected heat and created a deadly aiming point for the missiles. Once again, the assistance of industrial firms was sought, some advice obtained from friendly overseas sources, and a grey, matt-finish paint developed that did not overly increase the weight of the aircraft, yet managed to add to its protection.

Pilots had their own tactics for dealing with the missile threat. Some preferred to fly at tree-top height, working on the theory that it was doubtful that enemy ground forces could aim and fire effectively when planes were at such low level. Others preferred to fly just below cloud level — if the clouds were low enough — using an argument, possibly fallacious, that the clouds absorbed a certain amount of heat and would, hopefully, attract the missile, deflect it and cause it to bypass their planes. Far more effective were the baffles that diverted the hot exhaust fumes away from the body of an aircraft. Most pilots adopted the procedure of 'spiralling' on take-off or landing. Whatever the substance of the arguments, no PRAW planes were downed through enemy action, though several pilots and observers were wounded by ground fire.

The next innovation was that of arming the planes to be used in an offensive, or defensive role.

Contacts with the Rhodesian Air Force had always been excellent and men like Wing Commanders Peter Cooke, Peter Petter-Bowyer and 'Ossie' Penton (later to become Group Captain) were always happily prepared to assist the 'Fuzz'. Thus it was that Police 'acquired' a number of Browning automatic machine guns which the Armaments Section modified for use on a few of the Air Wing planes. Others were to be used, in the later stages of the war, on the road convoy escort vehicles centred on Fort Victoria.

Some pilots, working on 'necessity is the mother of invention' basis used short lengths of drain pipe, with a removable clip at the base, into which were loaded smoke grenades with their pins removed, to be used as a location aid for ground forces.

Perhaps, and to add a lighter note to this narrative, one of the more innovative pilots was the Umtali man whose aircraft was fitted with long-range tanks, enabling him to remain airborne for eight or more hours at a time. Conscious of at least two needs whilst up aloft, he managed to improvise a system for making fresh coffee and, a simple but comforting as well as reassuring device — which included a small hole in the floor of his aircraft — a fluted pipe enabling him to irrigate parts of the the Eastern Districts.

No history of the Air Wing would be complete without reference to the assistance provided to the Marine Wing. That section, with its workshops on the periphery of the Police Depot but with up to 40 vessels on Lake Kariba, had been formed in 1971. As the need to police the lake and the Zambezi grew, so it became more and more necessary that the various boats on both stretches of water, from Kanyemba to Kazungula, be maintained in tip-top condition at all times. The Marine Repair Section was headed by Inspector 'Buddy' Wilson with a small number of marine technicians; regular, reserve and, eventually, national servicemen. They had to be moved as quickly as possible to keep up with repairs, servicing and major overhauls and, once more, the Air Wing proved its value as marine mechanics were flown to improvised or roughly-fashioned airstrips along the country's northern border.

The Commissioner and his two deputies made a point of flying each year to all areas during Christmas week to give a fillip to the troops on the ground. The following story, probably emanating from Kariba, may, or may not have a ring of truth.

The Forward Airfield Controller suffered a visitation from a number of PRAW aircraft. First to land was a Piper Apache, closely followed by a Twin Comanche. A third group of visitors arrived in a Cherokee, whereupon the young airman dashed over to the Control Tower and started searching the skies through a pair of binoculars. When asked what he was doing, he replied "Looking for Custer and the 7th Cavalry."

To conclude this chapter, a very brief glance through some of the names of the pilots and observers who made up this unusual, highly individualistic and invaluable branch of the Force is appropriate.

There were farmers, accountants, attorneys, restaurant owners, doctors; just about every calling one can imagine. Alan Abrey, a veterinarian; Tony Alford, an accountant; Peter Anderson who operated a float plane on Kariba and attended to a kapenta business; Roy and Shelagh Anderson, a husband and wife team who farmed sheep; Jim Barker who received the Commissioner's Gallantry Award; Ernie Berk, a company director; Zack Bondi who overcame his fear of open spaces by taking up flying. Also 'Buster' Brown whose plane carried parachutists on training exercises; Tim Cherry, a magistrate; Bill Linfield, who was to become Unit Commander and Phil Nobes, both regular members of the Force; Bill Ludgater, already mentioned, and who later died with his wife when his plane, with passenger Phillipa Berlyn, crashed en route to Kariba; Alan Murray, a jeweller; Clive Puzey, a city councillor; Roy Smart, one time regular, farmer and twice winner of the State Lottery; Richard Seward, whose father played such a prominent part in recruiting members after the War; Angelos Stam who crashed in bad weather whilst on active service in 1978.

But there was one other, neither pilot nor observer, yet one of the most important of those associated with the Air Wing. Field Reservist Derek Johns, better known as 'Hotel One Two', earned his MSM spending countless long hours manning a relay station in his house high up on a 'gomo' close to the Chiweshe Reserve. Radio communications in the north east were such and the terrain so difficult that pilots could lose all contact both with Salisbury and, for example, Mount Darwin while flying in that area. Johns provided an invaluable, in fact essential link in the communications chain. And the fact that his daughter Vera went on from being crowned 'Miss Rhodesia' to become 'Miss South Africa' was just an irrelevant link in that chain.

These and many more established a proud and possibly quite unique tradition of service.

## Chapter Fifty-Two

## THE BEGINNING OF THE END

It all began shortly before Christmas 1972.

Terrorist forces made a brief attack on Marc de Borchgrave's Altena Farm near Centenary in north-east Mashonaland, slightly injuring his eight year-old daughter. They attacked a farm store also and planted at least one landmine. Two days later, it was the turn of the neighbouring Whistlefield Farm where de Borchgrave had decided to stay while his own farmhouse was repaired. Both he and his second daughter received shrapnel wounds. Once again landmines were planted in the vicinity, this time with deadly effect. An Army corporal was blown up and died later from his injuries; Detective Patrol Officer David 'Fluff' Hawks, then attached to the RAR, and two African soldiers were also blown up while travelling in adjacent tribal trust lands. Hawks was the first policeman to be blown up by a mine in Rhodesia

The war was underway; the pattern for the future had been established.

Farm homesteads were attacked, stores burned, mines laid and security force personnel, farmers, their families and farm workers killed and injured in the escalating violence. The terrorists had laid their plans well. Most Africans are guided by their ancestral and tribal spirits and those in the Zambezi Valley, atop the Escarpment and in the farming areas of Centenary, Umvuwes, Sipolilo and Mount Darwin, particularly so. The spirit mediums and the witchdoctors exert a tremendous influence and it was upon this that the terrorists played, using raw superstition as their lever to obtain obedience and cooperation. Not only that, but the promise of land, the good life, modern arms and money served to bring on side those who might have wavered. Lastly, of course, was the influence of fear; the fear of abduction, the fear of homes and belongings being destroyed, the fear of torture and pain.

To combat incursions, Joint Operational Commands or JOCs were set up. These consisted of equivalently- ranked officers from the Police, Army and Air Force; an officer from Special Branch, a representative from Internal Affairs and sometimes a member of the local Security Committee. Visitors to a JOC, which would usually be based adjacent to an air strip, would normally find a detachment of troops, ready for immediate reaction; a PATU stick or two, a canteen manned by Reserve or local volunteers, perhaps a couple of PRAW pilots and possibly a section of the Support Unit. A controlled tension would best describe the prevailing atmosphere as radios hummed, called and chattered into life, mechanics from the Central Mechanical and Equipment Department (CMED) checked over heavy trucks and Land Rovers, and men sat or lay about, idly chatting or playing games and waiting in the sunshine for the call to arms. Beside the strip would be gathered a motley collection of PRAW planes and hopefully a helicopter or two.

The first JOC recorded was not, as might be supposed, in north-east Mashonaland, but near Lupani and the Shangani Memorial in western Matabeleland, at Gomusa Dip. This was just before Christmas in 1966, during Operation Vermin, when Chief Superintendent Terry Thorpe, Flight Lieutenant Chris Dam and Major 'Mac' Willar co-operated with Peter Tomlinson of CID/Special Branch, Bulawayo to bring that particular incursion to a speedy and satisfactory conclusion. PRAW, or as it was known, Telstar, proved invaluable during that operation. Another contributory factor lay in the simple expedient of depriving the terrorists of water, by ambushing water holes and removing the lynch pins from water pumps. In those days, when a terrorist incursion was something of a 'nine-day-wonder', the headquarters' staff was disinclined to withdraw their forces as speedily as those on the ground would wish. Thorpe, never a man to mince his words, sent a radio message to Bulawayo suggesting "if you can't release us, please send Christmas puddings."

"Police", as Terry Thorpe has since commented, "were appallingly ill-equipped for bush war operations at that time." To be wearing gray shirts, blue riot trousers and blue 'floppy' hats made them 'sitting ducks' for well-trained enemy riflemen.

It was indeed fortunate that such marksmen then seemed few and far between. There can only be criticism of a Police Headquarters which refused to link the obvious threats of the future with a need to urgently consider dress, equipment and a host of other improvements necessary to counter those threats. The infrastructure was there; it just wasn't performing as it should.

Looking at the situation with the admitted benefit of hindsight, it would seem that the attitude of the top echelons in the Police during the 60s was, 'we are the first line of defence, we need little or no assistance and we will solve these minor security problems without any special change in our traditional thinking'.

However, the writer is well aware of other and illustrious historians who have damned the personalities of whom they write, using the standards of the present to condemn the decisions of the past. It is a fault only too-easily perpetuated.

Despite these criticisms, in the 60s and early 70s, the security forces more than held their own. Many of the enemy were killed, even more captured and such were the losses inflicted on ZANLA that eventually they were forced to withdrew many of their men and re-think, more correctly as it turned out, their strategies.

But to return to 1971 and 1972. Sometime before the Altena and Whistlefield attacks, Detective Inspector Winston Hart, an enterprising member of the Special Branch stationed at Bindura had spent considerable periods gathering intelligence across the border in Mozambique. He cultivated contacts with the locals, talking to Portuguese traders and administrators and learning of terrorist training camps and links with the liberation forces in that country. Apart from being recorded as the first Rhodesian policeman to be blown up by a mine outside the country, he also learned that ZANLA, in conjunction with Frelimo, planned attacks into Rhodesia. Sad to say, his reports and others from members of the SB were greeted at first with scepticism and regarded as alarmist by intelligence experts in Salisbury. However, Hart's forays into Mozambique, his methods and those of a handful of his colleagues, contributed to the eventual creation of the Selous Scouts and the concept of larger intelligence-gathering incursions into the neighbouring countries.

Winston Hart had joined the Police in 1958 and, no doubt because of his prowess on the wing in the police rugby XV, had been transferred from Depot to Salisbury. After some four years on urban and peri-urban duties where, initially, he was given an experienced African constable and told 'he's in charge of you', Hart approached the Member-in-Charge Highlands, the inimitable Bucky Buchanan, with a request to join the remount section. Their conversation went something like this:

"Sir, I wish to apply to join the remount staff in Depot"

"What on earth do you want to do that for?"

"To get more experience, Sir"

Buchanan pointed out of the window towards the charge office yard:

"Do you see that African woman out there? Well you could take her to bed and that'll give you more experience. But do you really want to?"

Winston convinced his rather forthright member-in-charge that he should make the temporary return to Depot but after four months there, applied to join and was accepted into the CID and eventually Special Branch. It was the start of a remarkable career, much of it spent on active operations with the Selous Scouts and only ended in mid-1980 when Hart retired as a superintendent and moved to South Africa. There his experience was to be utilised for some time by the South African military. As far as Rhodesia was concerned, there was but one hiccup in his police career.

After he had been stationed with the Bindura plain-clothed, or more appropriately, camouflaged section for a number of years, he was advised that future promotion depended on his gaining a great deal more 'police' experience. Very unwillingly, he accepted a transfer to Salisbury, there to be employed on mundane and, for a man with his active and fulfilling past, quite soul-destroying desk duties.

As far as the Security Forces were concerned, they were suddenly deprived of an invaluable and well-tested intelligence officer. Accordingly the threat, for such it was, leaked out that Military Intelligence, whose reputation was somewhat indifferent, would have to be expanded to counter the loss of Hart. Discussions were held at high levels, decisions made — not altogether to the liking of the Commissioner of Police — and Hart was soon back in camouflage ... and later promoted.

Many other members of Special Branch became deeply involved with military units both inside and outside the country as the war progressed. Among them Peter Grant, 'Mac' McGuiness, Vic Opperman, Keith Samler, Peter Stanton and Bob Schonken, the latter able to speak fluent Shona even before speaking English. Theirs and their SB colleagues' stories and participation in the conflict does not unfortunately form a part of this history.

It is sufficient to say that the information gathered by the police Special Branch members and the intelligence which they provided to SBHQ, provided the background and initiation for many of the attacks by units of the Special Air Service (SAS), Selous Scouts, or any other specialized units. Invariably, this information came from captured documents or interrogation of prisoners and tribesmen. Very often it became a hazardous undertaking to confirm the intelligence as correct, by external probing and surveillance. Nor should it be forgotten that the complementary reports provided by PATU, Support Unit and Ground Coverage were an invaluable adjunct to those of Special Branch.

The Security Forces, the Police Reserve, Civil Defence and the farmers, storekeepers and their families had been moulded together to become a resolute bastion against the gathering, grouping forces to the north and east. It was a remarkable and unique linkage that was to develop over the whole country as one war zone after another opened up.

And open up they did. The collapse, perhaps abdication of responsibility is more appropriate, of the Portuguese government in Mozambique following the military coup in Portugal in 1974, opened up the whole eastern border to enemy incursions. The 1972 Operation *Hurricane* was succeeded by *Thrasher* in Manicaland in 1976, by *Repulse* in Fort Victoria and *Tangent* in Matabeleland the same year; then by *Grapple* in the Midlands in 1977, and finally *Splinter* covering Lake Kariba in 1978.

Meanwhile the politicians and Nationalist leaders held their meetings, came to agreements, rejected or reneged on them, fought among themselves, and bowed to or resisted outside pressures. Those were the days of Home, Muzorewa, Pearce, Muller, Kissinger, Vorster, Kaunda, Owen, Young, Nkomo, Mugabe, and eventually Carrington, Soames and the omnipresent Smith.

Through it all, the B.S.A.Police stuck to its job, the preservation of peace, the maintenance of law and order, the detection of crime, and the apprehension of offenders. And there it is that this history resumes, with Spink retiring in June 1970 and Sydney Bristow stepping into the newly completed Police Headquarters extension and his new, top-floor-corner office looking out towards Salisbury's immaculate Greenwood Park.

## Chapter Fifty-Three

## THE BRISTOW YEARS

*1970 : Seniority in the Police — Bristow jumps the queue — Murder on the Train —*
*Pearce Commission — Drug abuse escalates — Crime trends in 1971 and 1972.*

To say that the appointment of Sydney Frederick Samuel Bristow, to succeed 'Jimmy' Spink as Commissioner came as a surprise would be an understatement.

Seniority in the Police had almost the same adherence to images engraved in stone as have the Ten Commandments. For the first years of service, one gained promotion through written promotion examinations and interviews with Boards of Officers to arrive eventually, and hopefully, at the rank of inspector. After that, one's upward mobility depended upon a number of factors: one's position on the seniority roll and the existence of vacancies on the Force establishment being but two of them. 'Elevation to the peerage' as appointment to commissioned rank was rather facetiously described, depended on factors known only to the interviewing Board and the Commissioner but, without doubt, one's ability played a major part, as did such diverse issues as participation in Force affairs — the Police Association and sports being examples — the suitability of one's wife to integrate with other wives and, of course, one's position on the seniority roll — a list regarded by some as second in importance only to the Bible. It was also necessary to apply for a commission. Many regarded the rank of chief inspector — the senior non-commissioned grade, as a perfectly satisfactory culmination to their careers. In some ways, it was akin to being a member of the British House of Commons; some stayed on the back-benches, others became Ministers of the Crown. Few were chosen (and even less wanted) to enter the House of Lords.

Many were those who, suddenly and inexplicably overlooked in a bid for promotion to commissioned rank, and sure that their position on the 'Roll' guaranteed that elevation, received an ambiguous communication from Police Headquarters which contained the phrase: 'of those considered suitable for promotion, you were not the most suitable'.

Letters like that did little to bolster egos, left the recipient floundering in dismay and perplexity and, very often anger and resentment. Such feelings must have crossed the minds of the two Deputy Commissioners, 'Bill' Crabtree and Robert 'Bill' Bailey when they learned that Syd Bristow was destined for the top job in the Police when Spink retired in June 1970.

However, it must be remembered that the final decision for the appointment of the Commissioner of Police rests with the Cabinet and that both Crabtree and Bailey were British-born. In 1970, Rhodesia had finally severed its ties with Britain to become a Republic; Dupont became the Acting President and Britain served notice that civil servants remaining in the service of the new Rhodesian government would be considered to have joined the 'rebellion'. The writing was on the wall for some senior policemen and, of course, at that time Rhodesia enjoyed the full support of the South African government and its people.

Crabtree, 53, Yorkshire-born and educated had, as mentioned in Chapter 48, spent almost his entire service in the CID, and later the Special Branch which he was selected to organize and develop in 1960/61. A gregarious, popular and highly efficient officer, he had come to Police Headquarters as Deputy Commissioner (Crime and Security) in 1968. There was, however, a swashbuckling side to him which, in addition to his age and not least his birth-place, might have been an impediment for appointment to the most senior position in the Force.

The other deputy, 'Bill' Bailey, six weeks older than Crabtree, had already measured himself for the job. So sure was he that his next move would lead into the Commissioner's official residence, The Gables, that he had 'found' the funding for the Pioneer Section to construct a small swimming pool in the grounds of that luxurious home in North Avenue.

Bailey was a strong disciplinarian, forthright and efficient, a man not afraid to make decisions. But he was not averse to ensuring that his personal interests coincided with those of the Force. Also, and alas for him, he had left the shores of England to come to Rhodesia, and at this time Britain was not 'the flavour of the month.'

So it was that Spink, either by choice or command, had dug down in the Officers' Seniority Roll and, with the concurrence of the Cabinet, Syd Bristow, at 51, found himself plucked from the ranks of the CID, promoted to Deputy Commissioner in January 1970, to become Commissioner just five months later.

Bristow had been born in South Africa, a factor which has been suggested must have had some bearing on his appointment. Like the Commander of the Army and the Attorney-General at that time in 1970 (Keith Coster and E.A.T 'Tony' Smith respectively), he was an Old Collegian from the famous Pietermaritzburg College. His impressive physique and rugby prowess made him a sure choice for urban duties in Salisbury when he left Depot and it was not until after War Service in Ethiopia that in 1946 he transferred to the CID where he remained until appointed Deputy Commissioner.

The above comments — and indeed Spink's gruff and brief introduction of his successor to assembled officers in the Mess — should not be taken as derogating the new Commissioner. Far from it. Bristow was to prove himself very far removed from the conventional, archetypal senior CID officer. He established an excellent relationship with Force members, was popular and respected, not afraid to seek advice and fought hard with Government to obtain what was needed. He also possessed the valuable ability to get the best out of his men. Personality-wise, he was a far cry from the two previous CID men to hold the post, Jackson and Barfoot.

By 1970, when Bristow took over, the emphasis was on concentrated patrolling, especially of the border areas, and this meant less men devoted to the investigation of crime. The Commissioner was deeply worried at the shortfall of European members but managed to compensate to some extent by intensifying the numbers of training courses for senior Africans to equip them for greater responsibility and, as was to happen more and more, employing the Police Reserve as much as possible. Despite this, the year 1970 saw reported crime rise by 37%, most being traffic offences but a significant proportion being crimes against people and their property.

As with most years there were cases which aroused the public interest.

During August, travellers cheques to a value of $12,000 drawn on the Bank of America, were cashed at various banks around the country. They were found to be counterfeit and eventually traced to an Italian national. The following month, a further spate occurred, this time of US$100 currency notes. All these cases originated in Europe where several arrests were made.

Another noteworthy case, and one unsolved to this day, was the discovery in November of the body of a murdered Greek businessman in Lake McIlwaine. He had been tied with heavy gauge wire to a large rock and dumped in a remote creek some six months before. A frequent visitor to the country from the Congo, he had left all his possessions — baggage, passport and car — at a Salisbury hotel

The following year was to be described by Bristow in his Annual Report as 'comparatively uneventful'. It certainly was, from the point of view of terrorist incursions, yet there was a further rise in reported crimes. Establishment, vis-à-vis strength, continued to show deterioration and the incidence of drug-taking indicated a marked and worrying increase.

An innovation proving most useful and successful during the year was the introduction of Organisation and Methods teams. Trained in Rhodesia to start with, selected members were later given more advanced training in South Africa and came to play a hugely important role in reducing the paperwork which policemen, from time immemorial, had cavilled against.

The first teams considered the usefulness of various returns submitted 'up the line' by members-in-charge of stations. Based on the results from this popular study — and that is exactly why it was chosen first — the concept was accepted with great enthusiasm. The section, headed at that time by patient, enquiring and able communicators like Hugh Gibson, Jim O'Toole and others, diversified to preparing design guides for major new police stations, revising recruiting methods, determining the best type of police vessels for Lake Kariba, considering the decentralization of training depots, and a host of other projects.

Reverting in more detail to the subject of drug incidence, it can be seen that the numbers of those arrested for offences under the Drugs Control Act and allied legislation, and for the possession and supply of Dagga increased among Europeans from 70 to 189 cases, and of Africans from 1348 to 1847. Depressingly, it is recorded that 40% of the Europeans were under the age of 21. It was decided to remove the responsibility for drug investigations from the Licence Inspector to the CID. Members of the latter branch embarked on a programme of what, in modern parlance, would be called conscientisation: visiting schools and lecturing interested groups, especially those concerned with large bodies of young people.

Adding to the problem were the number of breakings into pharmacies and thefts of large quantities of amphetamines, also a number of fatal road accidents that could be regarded as drug related. The Commissioner commented that police experience 'shows that dagga can precipitate or aggravate latent psycho-neurotic disorders and certainly that it lowers the mental and scholastic ability of its users'. Words to ponder upon in a world in which the legalising of some drugs is being considered.

Another case arousing considerable interest during 1971 was the murder of a young American nurse, Martha Dean, on the passenger train from Wankie to Bulawayo just before Christmas. The girl was only 20 and her killer, Graham Jenkinson, a learner train-driver of the same age, had occupied the adjacent compartment on the journey. The unfortunate victim had been strangled and raped. However the CID investigation team, headed by Superintendent Gordon Waugh and Detective Inspector 'Mike' Reeves had arrested Jenkinson in Bulawayo's Meikles Store on Christmas Eve, less than 24 hours after the girl climbed aboard the train.

The forensic evidence presented to the Court was damning and included the fact that certain mottled areas on the victim's forehead, left ear and chest all bore the pattern of the green, long stockings worn by the young man. On the underside of the toe of one of these stockings — which the accused had washed — were found three hairs which were a perfect match with hair samples taken from the front of the victim's left ear during the post-mortem. There was, of course, other evidence led in the case which proved quite conclusively that the police had the correct accused. Having committed the crime, Jenkinson returned to his compartment — by climbing along the outside of the carriage. The door to the other carriage, in which the body lay, was apparently locked.

An appeal against sentence of death was rejected and Graham Jenkinson was hanged in Salisbury gaol the following year.

One event totally unconnected with the Police was the scoring of 254 by Mike Procter at the Salisbury Police Ground on 5 March 1971. Procter, at that time the Rhodesian cricket coach, joined C.B. Fry and Sir Donald Bradman as the only batsmen in the history of the game (at that time) to hit six successive centuries in first class cricket.

1972 opened with serious riots in the urban areas following the arrival of the Pearce Commission and their eventual decision that the Anglo-Rhodesian settlement proposals were unacceptable to the majority of Africans in Rhodesia. These disturbances in Shabani, Gwelo, Fort Victoria, Que Que, Umtali and Salisbury were the most serious problems in those towns and cities since 1963. They proved, as Commssioner Bristow commented that 'densely populated areas are gunpowder kegs which can be exploded by a handful of people using fanatics, malcontents and mobsters to further their political ambition'. In all, over 1000 Africans were arrested and convicted of crimes ranging from murder and public violence to malicious injury to property. The Law and Order (Maintenance) Act was proving effective.

Other cases of interest during the year included the defusion of two letter bombs which had been posted in Malaysia to members of the Jewish community in Bulawayo, and in the Mana Pools Game Reserve a landmine detonated, seriously injuring the driver who was touring in his private car but, fortunately, causing only minor injuries to the members of his family.

The year saw also a drop in reported crime but this was largely cosmetic. Police dealt with fewer statutory offences than before, due entirely to the fact that they were being deployed and utilized on more demanding tasks and that the shortage of men remained a serious problem.

Earlier in this chapter, comment was made on the incidence of drug taking among young Europeans; the figure of 189 was quoted. In 1972 this had risen to 410, with 'synthetic hallucinogenic drugs (LSD)' now featuring. The extent of the menace is even better revealed when a comparison is made between the total of drug related cases in 1970 and 1979. In the former year, it was a modest 1456; by 1979 it had risen to 5034. These statistics, though showing an increase of more than 245%, are almost irrelevant, because a footnote to the last figure suggested that no significance should be attached to the total due to the fluctuations of staff working on those cases.

The events of December 1972 have been described in the preceding chapter. The story of the force for the remaining years of its existence must be viewed in the light of the many additional duties, almost all of a quasi-military nature, which encroached on the time and dedication of its members.

## Chapter Fifty-Four

## PLUGGING THE GAPS

*1973 : Solutions to manpower problems — National Servicemen —*
*Women Police uniforms — Crime Prevention Units — Canteens —*
*Copper Pot & The Phoenix — Debacle in Fort Victoria Nurses Home*

By 1973 it was clear that the one great domestic problem facing the Police was that of retaining experienced manpower. A number of long serving policemen had found the breakaway from the British Crown and the subsequent creation of a Republic just a little more than they could stomach. Combined with this was the long, stressful and apparently endless period since UDI, the passage of years that, as far as policemen were concerned, involved long hours of work, absences from homes and family and the contemplation of an uncertain future. Most had served in the British and Commonwealth forces during the Second World War and had sufficient service to be able to retire and return to Britain with an adequate pension. Adequate, that is, before the Zimbabwe dollar decided to take on a life of its own.  Bristow's solution to the problem was both unusual and effective.

Financial incentives were offered to certain key personnel who were prepared to 'retire on pension', but then enter into a new contract enabling them to carry on serving and retain their rank. This meant that the individual had his pension or gratuity secured, and invested, and could then carry on doing the same job but now with a salary coming in to augment whatever he had put away. The scheme was enshrined in regulations as the Extended Service Gratuity Scheme. Privately, its beneficiaries were known as 'retreads'.

A further move was to offer greatly improved pay and conditions to one-time members who had recognized the error of their ways or become disillusioned with life away from the Force and were prepared to re-join. No less than 46 took advantage of this scheme.

The next move was to improve salary scales which had the dual effect of encouraging local youngsters to look upon the Police as a career, as well as enticing those already in to stay. And then, finally, came the 'icing on the cake' — the introduction of a National Service Scheme which embraced all Services.

Although the requirement of conscription was compulsory, the individual had the freedom of choice as to within which of the services he wished to spend 12 months. And so 42 young men, many possessed of 'M' and 'A' Level certificates, started their three months' Depot Course at the end of July.

Their reactions to Depot discipline were mixed. There was objection to not having the services of a batman when one was permitted for the 'ordinary' regular in training; there was some perplexity that foot drill played such an important part in the course, ostensibly to teach one to obey commands, but in apparent contradiction of the need for a policeman to be self reliant and able to exercise initiative. And there was the desire for more tuition be given in law and police studies. There were absolutely no regrets that equitation had no part in the training.

And so these young men were launched on their short careers. Some went to town and district stations, some with particular abilities found themselves in the CID, and in particular the Fraud Section; others were moved to the Support Unit and there, as a previous chapter has shown, proved an enormous credit to their country.

While all this was going on, changes had been taking place as far as the policewomen were concerned. Not only were greater numbers joining but a new and far more presentable uniform had been designed for them.

Designing uniforms for ladies has always been an area fraught with hideous difficulties. It's not quite a case of sauce for goose and gander because women police come in all shapes and sizes — and there is always the question of femininity to be considered. The Commissioner took the easy route — he appointed a Board of Enquiry. Chief Superintendent John Hardie took the burden of responsibility; the remainder was shared by Superintendent Don Lane, who had by this time relinquished control of the Depot Supply Store, Woman Inspector Sue Bolton and Woman Section Officer Jane Spears.

These four worthies canvassed opinions, sought the assistance of local couturiers, discussed fabrics and accessories and made their decisions, for better or for worse.

In general, it would seem for better. Either that or the ladies were cowed by discipline and, no doubt, the impressive costs of being newly — though hardly romantically or fashionably — attired and equipped. Only one lone, anonymous and forthright critic appeared. "Do our policewomen have to look dowdy and unfashionable to perform their duties properly", he, or she enquired? The answer to that might well have been given by Inspector Jim Clampit, in charge of the Salisbury Information Room, or Section Officer Al Trubi, the senior intermediate driving course instructor, both of whom had been involved in sending a number of the ladies for 'B' Car advanced driver training classes. They, after all, had to put up (in a sense) with the shorter skirts, while policewomen riding scooters revealed other shortcomings.

Apart from placing some of the women in charge of Patrol Cars, Salisbury had started a Crime Prevention Unit, hopefully to penetrate the drug-abuse problem and generally pick up information which the CID with so many other commitments was unable to gather. This became a popular assignment for those women perhaps not so appreciative of John Hardie's hard work. After all, where else in the 'uniform branch' was it possible to grow shoulder length hair, wear 'mod gear' and go on 'raves?' One amusing cartoon of that period shows a seductive, long-haired lady, dressed in flared trousers and with a tightly stretched blouse, leaning against a lamp-post. Just behind her stands a uniformed policeman whom she rejects with the words "Fantastic approach, Copper — but I'm Fred Smith from the Crime Prevention Unit."

It is time to consider some of the establishments that have brought comradeship and often notoriety to police circles. Police licensed premises exist at many — if not most — major police stations in one form or another and are regarded as hallowed institutions and for many a temporary refuge and relaxation point after a hard, and often grim day's work. Probably the best known is The Copper Pot, close by Salisbury's Depot Hard Square.

This, the home of Salisbury's Police Reserve (and others) has a history dating back over many years. It was the opening of the new cocktail bar in June 1973 that brings the famous building into this chronicle..

The Police Reserve originally enjoyed their leisure in a room, used primarily as a museum, adjacent to Fuller and Bodle accommodation blocks. As their numbers and the scope of their duties expanded, so the measure of their thirst increased, and it was in the late 50s that the building of a proper Assembly Hall and ancillary facilities was suggested. It fell to Chief Superintendent (later Assistant Commissioner) Ted Streeter to develop the scheme from a promising but unfulfilled idea into something more material. In this, he had the unexpected assistance of the then Prime Minister, Whitehead who, apart from enjoying his beer, was appalled to see the conditions under which the reservists were operating. He promised to have a word with his Minster of Finance. In 1960, the dream blossomed into reality and the Assembly Hall, with spacious washing and shower facilities, as well as the Copper Pot — opened in time for Christmas the following year.

Having mentioned Ted Streeter, a few words on a man who gave nearly 42 years of his life to the police — and achieved the distinction of receiving two retirement notices.

Streeter attested in 1926 and was commissioned 16 years later. He served in various commands including a spell as Recruiting Officer in London and retired, an assistant commissioner, in 1958. He endured two years in mufti before being recalled to take over the Salisbury Province 'A' Reserve. Those were difficult and challenging years but his long experience stood him in good stead as he polished his 'part-time policemen' to the highest possible standards of efficiency. He retired as Reserve Chief Superintendent with the MBE, in 1970.

In an earlier chapter mention was made of The Blue Lamp in Bulawayo. A very similar building, and again with a chequered history, was built in Fort Victoria — but that was after the old one burned down.

The original Fort Victoria Police 'pub' was in a tin shack that opened in 1946 and its first 'customers' were recorded in a Visitors Book. They were a motley collection of the distinguished and, at that time relatively unknown. They ranged from a Judge of the High Court, WE Thomas to Monty Surgey from Police Headquarters and various officials from the town, as well as the junior policemen. Among them were Assessor E. Morris, Captain Spurling, then the local officer commanding; Dr.H.

Strover, the Senior Government Medical Officer; the Provincial Native Commissioner; and then the 'real' drinkers — all policemen of course — Len Genet, Terry Holroyde, Hugh Gaitskell, Joe Rowley, Eric Van Sittert, Edward Sanford (a trooper with a DFC), A. Halliday (holding a DSM), and R. Constable who was 'in attendance' behind the bar.

The 'pub' carried on in these cramped but incredibly popular premises until late on an evening in September 1963, when it caught fire.

The conflagration was described with gentle humor:

"Never in Fort Victorian police history has an emergency summons been so speedily answered. From bars, hotels, clubs — even beds — staggered shocked and incredulous policemen. Within minutes, the flames of the canteen silhouetted busy figures and, with shouts of desperation, the bar door was forced. The stock of spirits was first priority and was gallantly rescued. Smoke belched from shattered windows, beloved trophies melted on red hot walls and flames leaped skywards against the inky night. Valiant policemen, ignoring all thoughts of personal safety, struggled with the refrigerator and with superhuman effort, strength and courage carried it from the blazing building with its contents intact. Individual deeds of self-sacrifice saved other beer stocks and numerous miscellaneous items, including the contents of the cash box. The money therein was just saved but the rescuers looked on helplessly as the fire consumed a sheaf of IOU's and a list of debtors and the amounts they owed. Soon only stark beams and twisted tin stood against the skyline. After 17 years, Fort Victoria's policemen were again without a drinking home of their own."

Peter Sherren, who is reputed to have commented not long before the fire, 'it's about time this damned place burned down', was OC and he invited the tired — and doubtless thirsty — rescuers to help themselves to the refrigerator's contents, 'thinking only of the insurance assessors, and not wishing to add the problem of spoiled stocks of beer to their difficulties.'

That refrigerator had a remarkable history. Within two days, it had been installed in another tin shack which became an equally popular rendezvous and then, almost to the dismay of the undiminished clientele, the new 'canteen' was built and ceremoniously opened the following year by Commissioner Barfoot. Only the presence of the old fridge, removed from The Chicken Inn and installed beneath the counter in the spacious new building, convinced the 'drinking public' that the time had come to abandon the past — and revel in the present.

Appropriately enough, the new canteen was named *The Phoenix*.

There had been another fire in Fort Victoria about eight years before that described above. The casualty was the Hospital Nurses Home virtually next door to the Police Camp. These were still the days when police were responsible for fighting fires, in addition to all their other extraneous duties. Ex-Detective Chief Inspector Gerald Moores, whose reminiscences of his police service form a fascinating and amusing chronicle of life in the 50s and 60s sets the scene:

"The day of the fire happened to coincide with a Police Reserve Training Day. Such days habitually ended with regulars and reservists having 'a few' in the canteen and, in the case of the latter, pooling their day's travelling and subsistence allowance (paid in cash) to indulge in some dedicated drinking. The bar was dry by nine-o-clock, the reservists started back to their farms and the regulars contemplated a dried-up dinner — or bed.

Had there been a prompt and efficient response to the initial call for assistance from the Nurses Home — bearing in mind its close proximity to the police camp — the fire might have been subdued with a couple of fire extinguishers.

In reality the police response was both tardy and chaotic. We amateur fire-fighters were borderline inept when stone-cold sober. By 10p.m on that fateful night, everyone not actually on duty was suffering from almost total incompetence induced by reckless over-indulgence.

Perhaps only Mack Sennett's Keystone Cops could have bettered the scenes of tragi-comic mayhem that engulfed the police camp that night.

There was, initially, some uncertainty over the precise location of the 'fire', stemming from the inability of the African constable on telephone duty to unscramble the rapid-fire Ulster accent of the matron, who was endeavouring to impart a proper sense of urgency to her fire report.

In fact, one detachment actually drove prematurely (and erratically) out of camp in a Bedford truck and spent most of the night dancing attendance on a small bush fire — clearly visible against the night sky — which may, or may not, have posed an unquantifiable threat to some small-holdings three miles out of town. Despite their best efforts, this particular fire eventually died a natural death when it encountered a dirt road.

Unfortunately, the misdirected Bedford truck was the only one available in camp with a tow-hitch connection suitable for moving the 'mobile' hand pump which, in consequence, had to be manhandled to the Nurses Home.

One stalwart draped a long heavy coil of canvas fire hose over his head and across his chest, leapt on his motor-cycle and wound open the throttle. He crossed one corner of the poorly-lit parade ground in a shower of grit — heading for the main gate — blissfully unaware that one end of the hose with a heavy brass bayonet connector at its extremity, was slowly unravelling from his shoulder and was extending along the ground behind him.

The trailing, bouncing brass connector suddenly became wedged between two of the whitewashed stones demarcating the parade ground. The canvas hose linking the captive connector and the speeding motor cyclist tightened and then plucked the rider cleanly from his saddle; depositing him in a heap in the dust.

Fortuitously, the relaxing effects of alcohol and the coils of hose protected him from serious injury. The fate of the BSA 650cc single cylinder side-valve motorcycle was more dramatic. It careered,riderless, into a drainage ditch with an expensive sounding 'crumph', after which only the slowly spinning rear wheel of the up-ended machine could be seen through the darkening dust cloud.

The inspector in charge of the Rural Section, 'Jock', had a well deserved reputation for being able to hold his liquor, but the combination of organizing a day of intensive training, followed by an evening of determined drinking had taken its toll and sent him early to his bed. He dozed off whilst smoking a cigarette, which ultimately fell — still alight — from his nerveless fingers onto the bed. After smouldering for a while the bedding and mattress suddenly ignited — possibly aided by Jock's high-octane breath

In truth, the fire at the Nurses Home probably saved his life because the strident alarm bell brought him to his senses — just in time. However, he took some convincing that his personal fire was not the real reason for the chaotic scenes unfolding before his eyes in the police camp.

Things were not much better at the Nurses Home itself, where a leaderless (due to Jock's incapacity) gang of semi-inebriated policemen were doing their best to turn a mere crisis into a full-blown catastrophe.

Notwithstanding their own personal anxieties, the resident nursing staff rose magnificently to the occasion. Two badly affected 'fire-fighters' were rushed to the outpatients department where their stomachs were washed out (none too gently), whilst less severe cases were given copious amounts of coffee and intravenous injections of vitamin C.

All the while, the fire in the roof of the Nurses Home relentlessly gained ground. Luckily, there was no wind that night — climatically-speaking anyway — and the roof was covered in ubiquitous corrugated iron sheeting; a combination which inhibited any spectacular back-draft scenarios from developing. That is until a very large constable decided to clamber up into the, as yet, unaffected end of the 'L' shaped roof void, whilst carrying a large, heavy, metal-cased fire extinguisher.

He lost his footing whilst walking along a structurally inadequate ceiling joist and crashed through into the bedroom below (which belonged to the matron), bringing the fractured joists, as well as the whole ceiling down with him.

His guardian angel was certainly on duty that night because the conveniently located matron's bed broke his fall and enabled him to make a hasty exit from the building via a window.

However, the same window — carelessly left open after his departure — channelled unlimited amounts of oxygen through the missing ceiling and thence into the roof void, which was no longer a closed environment. The results were entirely predictable.

Thankfully, no-one was badly injured (by the fire) but the old wing of the Nurses Home was subsequently assessed as being 'beyond viable repair."

So Gerald ends his narrative — or almost. A new Nurses Home was built, no policemen were disciplined for their parts in the affair, and a properly trained Fire Service was established.

Gerald does end with these words – "There was absolutely no police involvement in this new Service — which enabled the town's nursing sisterhood to sleep easier in their beds at night."

There were other well-known police canteens, *The Jam Jar Inn* at Kariba, *The Run 'Em Inn* at Gatooma and the plethora of wartime establishments that graced Mount Darwin, Mukumbura, Vila Salazar. One or two of these will feature as the final years of this story unfold.

## Chapter Fifty-Five

## THE SITUATION WORSENS

*Sherren becomes Commissioner — 1974 — Crime figures — Outflow of Experience Chingoka— 'Bright Lights' — General Service Unit — Support Groups — Pioneers, Transport, Armaments and others — 1975 Crime figures — Eastern Front opens — South African Police withdraw*

SYD BRISTOW RETIRED in February 1974 and his place was taken by the man who had been his Deputy Commissioner (Crime and Security) since 1970, Peter Sherren,

Sherren was to see the Police Force through the next four momentous years, and momentous they and the years following certainly were. The South African government moved into a prominent position in trying to settle the 'Rhodesian Question' and, in the course of so doing, almost brought the country to its knees. The word 'Detente' came into political negotiations — and meant nothing: the entire country became an operational battleground and the system of call-ups was extended — and extended further. Later came the short-lived and ill-fated Transitional Government attached to which were the words 'of National Unity'. Later still, Geneva wasted everyone's time, and then finally came the Lancaster House Agreement. Momentous years indeed, and Peter Sherren was at the helm through almost all of them.

This history has contained snippets about Sherren and his service. There were the early days at various stations in Fort Victoria, with the incredible variety of cases and duties that the district offered. Then came the move to Que Que and later, in 1944, the call to serve in Palestine and the Aegean Islands. On his return after the war he was member-in-charge at Shamva, Beatrice, Bindura and Wankie. Secondments to Bechuanaland and Nyasaland followed before his commissioning in 1956. Sherren was involved in the Royal Visits of 1947, 1953, 1957, when he was Police Liaison Officer, and 1959 as Staff Officer to Spurling. His prowess as a tennis player dated from earlier days in England when, in 1936, he was playing County tennis and competing in the Junior Wimbledon. And the man? Peter Sherren was one of the most immaculately turned-out of men and that impeccable appearance characterised his approach to the job. He was always self-contained, completely forthright and in command of a situation. His man-management, like that of his predecessor, the more outgoing Bristow, was relaxed but impressive.

In his first Annual Report, for 1974, Sherren recounted some chilling statistics. There had been 114 murders of African kraal dwellers, some being brutally and needlessly mutilated; five murders of Europeans: no less than 34 civilians had been killed in landmine incidents; there had been 16 farm attacks, 51 store robberies, with 12 premises set ablaze and totally gutted. The deaths of members of the Force numbered 15 and these included the popular farrier, rugby prop-forward and 1971 'Sportman of the Year, Bill Coetzer, who died after participating in a Support Unit training exercise. Two Field Reservists, one black, one white had been murdered by terrorists. On the other side, 261 terrorists had been killed and 105 captured.

The casualties would increase in the following years.

Prevalent now among the incidents of crime were contraventions of the Exchange Control Act by large companies and individuals. Allied to these were the smuggling of diamonds, both in and out of the country, and various high profile cases of fraud. The political climate had created an atmosphere in which many unscrupulous businessmen were trying to provide a cushion for the future by adopting a policy of 'devil take the hindmost'. Business ethics were fighting an uphill battle.

But thoughts for the future applied not only to businessmen. Many senior policemen with years of invaluable experience felt that a change was necessary in their lives as well. To analyse the reasons for their leaving would be difficult if not dangerous. However, one officer encapsulated many, perhaps most, of the problems each and everyone faced when, in his retirement letter, he wrote:

"In the present state of the country, it behoves each and every one to consider and analyse his individual circumstances and to determine what courses of action he may be at liberty — and choose — to follow. The factors that affect that difficult, totally-individual decision are many and varied:

sufficiency of salary, promotion prospects, age of oneself and children, future   education; health, both personal and family; security of retirement benefits, and political uncertainty. These, and many others, are the aspects which make a decision such as I have    taken so totally personal."

The year saw the beginning of an outflow that, in terms of experience and expertise, was irreplaceable. Some members were to remain in the country, others moved to South Africa, to Britain and to many other parts of the world: some went on pension, others opted for a gratuity. Some were black, many were white; names like Gearing, Rawson, Parry, Hogan, Bembridge, Jecock, Hayes, Coutts, Pauw, Chingoka, Mandishona and Mudzuri left the Force to start a new life elsewhere and become remembered as 'Old Comrades'.

Of all those men, many of whom have been mentioned before, one in particular is worthy of special mention at this stage of the history.

Douglas Chingoka, born in 1926, joined the Police in 1946 after a short spell doing clerical work with the Native Affairs Department and later the Dairymen's Co-op. Five years later, his abilities were recognized with promotion to sergeant when stationed in Bulawayo. After that he moved rapidly upwards, eventually becoming one of the first in the newly established rank of sub-inspector in 1961. He became the first African member-in-charge when he took command of Mabvuku, a Salisbury suburban station, not long after his promotion. There he stayed until 1964 when he moved to instructional duties in the Tomlinson Depot, ending his career as Station Sub-Inspector at Salisbury Central. (In the post-Independence era he was to return, to the Zimbabwe Republic Police, to help instil the benefits of his long previous experience).

Despite these losses of experience and expertise, the Force had to continue performing its various roles.

Bravery Commendations and Bronze Batons were awarded to Sergeants Takavada and Ndela, both of the Braeside Police Station who, late the previous year, had broken up a rioting mob in a township area. At the time of the incident, both had been in plain clothes carrying out routine enquiries. They came upon a mob, numbering about 40, who were stoning a car. Clearly outnumbered, they nevertheless charged in, ignoring death threats, stones and physical assault, to arrest two of the rioters and scatter the remainder.

The year saw entries for the Squash Championships almost halved when extra duties had to be carried out after a Chinese stick grenade was thrown into a crowded nightclub in Salisbury. The culprit for that particular act of terrorism was never positively located but, as far as the championships were concerned, the reigning champion since 1971 — Chief Superintendent Bob Burrell — once again added to his collection of beer mugs.

The duties of the Police Reserve had continued to escalate as the rural areas suffered and the urban areas were menaced. The Police Special Reserve was resuscitated and a new type of 'part-time' policeman appeared on the scene, the 'Bright Lights'. These were men who could be called up to spend time away from their jobs and take up residence in farm homesteads, manning the emergency radios and protecting the residents during the hours of darkness and when the master of the house was away on call-up. For many it became a popular job, depending on whether the owner was, or had a good cook.  Others learned a considerable amount about the intricacies of farming. One earned the Police Decoration for Gallantry ... "Field Reservist Marc De Robillard was doing his first spell as a 'Bright Light" on a farm in the Bikita area during 1976 when one morning five armed terrorists arrived at the homestead. Three of them walked into the lounge and one charged at Marc with his bayonet-fixed AKM rifle. Although he was unarmed, the plucky reservist grabbed the weapon by the bayonet and butt and managed to wrest it from the man — but only after a shot had been fired which blasted the fingers off his left hand. Incredibly, Marc turned the gun on the terrorists, drove them off and then grabbed his own FN, cocked it with his foot and fired on the group, managing to wound one in the shoulder. After that he used the Agric Alert radio to summon assistance."

By now the call-up net had widened considerably. Men between 25 and 38 had a service responsibility and the National Service intake had doubled. But still government found itself looking for greater reserves of manpower. The General Service Unit (GSU) was formed for men who were too old for the 12 months' National Service but could still fulfill an active role, after three weeks training in Morris Depot, by spending the remaining five weeks of their call up as guards in the forward areas.

The prevailing circumstances were bound to throw up the occasional heroes. One of these was George Style. Well into his middle-seventies, active, one-time farmer, hunter and policeman — he had served in the Police between 1925 and 1930 — George took over and ran many farms in the operational areas so that their owners could get away for a break. Unfortunately, at his age, the Police could not accept him into the GSU. His story — of a man who was not too old to contribute to the war effort — is eloquently related in *Farmer at War* by Trevor Grundy and Bernard Miller.

A sense of humour was not an essential in the General Service Unit — but it helped considerably, especially when a fair proportion of the intakes bore a striking resemblance to retired rugby players who had continued to favour the game by watching — often long after the game was over — from bar verandahs. Yet despite the somewhat remarkable girths on some of these individuals, after three weeks in Depot they had become transformed and could have a quiet chuckle at themselves.

One such, 'Paddy' Forrest, prepared a 'Holiday Brochure on Rhodesia's North East' which included a number of gems:

> "Let us whisk you away on a 'never-to-be-forgotten', all-inclusive holiday to the, as yet mainly unexplored, paradise of Rhodesia's North East ... we will take you to this land of mountain, kopje, rocky gomo and dry river-bed on an unforgettable holiday of two, three, four or five weeks duration, depending on your intake or stamina. Come up here and let us spoil you. We promise that you'll never be the same again. When we say get away from it all, we mean ALL. There is no golf, fishing, horse riding or swimming — and, thank goodness, hunting is also temporarily out of season. We don't       merely suggest separate holidays, we insist on separate holidays. So for all you Rhodesians, here is a chance to leave the missus and the kids at home. But remember this opportunity is not available to everyone. Only to Rhodesian residents, between the ages of puberty and dotage.
>
> Drives into the country from the holiday chalets are very popular. Don't forget to see the chef the night before for your picnic lunch, which will be ready by 05.00 hrs. A typical menu for one of these mouth watering gastronomic delights is an orange, two water-bottles of water, a tin of corned beef and four Pre-World War II biscuits ... When available, beers are optional extras."

In spite of the humorous side, in later years arose much speculation as to whether the training given some of these men, particularly the reservists, was really adequate to prepare them for the duties they had to perform. Regrettably, this may well have been the case. Although the instructors, as far as possible, were chosen from men who had a background of military service, the comment 'gone was the scruffy marching and not knowing left from right' at the end of a three weeks course, tends to the conclusion that perhaps some of these men could have been provided with a more realistic grounding before being set down in an operational area.

The figures speak for themselves. The Force was suffering heavy losses in the operational areas. The Rolls of Honour for 1975 and 1976 detail no less than 71 members of the Police and Police Reserve killed on duty. In addition, among African members of the Force, there were others — many others — who died after being attacked when on holiday with their families in the rural areas.

One example of a member being killed while on holiday occurred in April 1975 when the Force suffered the loss of Detective Station Sergeant Major Arthur Tutani and his wife, Ebba. They were killed when their car detonated a landmine in the Madziwa Tribal Trust Land. Arthur had joined the Force in 1952, transferred to the CID after three years and within 10 years been twice complimented by the Commissioner for his investigative abilities. In Special Branch, he was a pillar of strength in the Hurricane operational areas, earning further praise for his high standards of work. Deaths of such men created a void it was now impossible to fill.

A saying, attributed to Napoleon, and acknowledged by all successful military commanders is 'An Army marches on its stomach'.

Previous comments in this and other chapters may have given the impression that 'chocolate cake' and 'pre-World War II biscuits' lend substance if not spice to that quotation. Not so. Behind the fighting men there had developed over the years a complex organization of staff and technicians whose job it was to try and smooth out the difficulties of procurement, maintenance, communications, transport, buildings, clothing, arms, ammunition and the thousand-and-one things that enable 'an Army to march'.

From a material point of view, the Rhodesian Security Services were very much at the mercy of their South African counterparts throughout the bush war. But the assistance they received, and in the case of Police this dated back to the very beginning of the bush war, was unstinting — unless or until political considerations came into play. Representatives of the Security Services made regular trips to Pretoria (on RRAF Dakotas) armed with 'shopping lists', the contents and feasibility of which were discussed with the South Africans, including ARMSCOR representatives, and delivery agreed and arranged. The heads of the Security Forces also enjoyed meetings — though not of such regularity — but for them the venues were sometimes varied. Capetown was an infrequent location; Salisbury even less. However, the lack of Salisbury meetings might have had something to do with a very senior and devout member of the South African Army who returned to his hotel room — and a very high-class hotel it was — to find, slipped under his door, a card advising him of certain 'female services' available on phoning a particular extension.

The one awesome, incredible and much envied factor in the whole scenario was the apparently limitless depth to the South African funding. For police certainly, no indication was given of how the costs were balanced or repayment considered. Such 'trifles' were the responsibility of the Ministry of Defence, no doubt in collusion with the Treasury. Tentage, rifles, mortars, vehicles, ammunition: there seemed no barriers to the South African provisioning ability until, as said before, political considerations came into play. When, for example, the Détente Exercise (Kaunda and Vorster) was brokered, and when Kissinger became an important player in the Settlement discussions, there occurred an apparent impasse in the ability to provide ammunition. Let it be said, however, that the South African officials sitting around the conference tables were obviously most discomfited by the strictures imposed upon them. For those Rhodesians not in the know, there was just baffled anger.

Allusions have been made to 'staff and technicians' — the Specialists — in the backrooms of the war. There were a number of sections and policemen who played a vital part in keeping the 'active forces' operating as efficiently as finance and manpower would allow.

The first of these was undoubtedly the Signals Branch. Highly technical and, as a result, rather closeted away from the main stream of police activity, this Branch will be the subject of a separate Appendix.

The Pioneer Section goes back to the 30s and was started by the man who eventually retired as Quartermaster, John Thomas Thompson. Up until 1957, the Section was commanded by Staff Chief Inspector John Rudd. He was succeeded by Frank Maguire, who remained in charge until his retirement in 1986.

The Section was formed to carry out generally minor building improvements and repairs to police stations which were too remote for the Ministry of Works staff to visit, or the requirement likely to prove too expensive for private builders to undertake. This, over the years and when the building industry was in the doldrums, was a source of some vexation to the private sector, which knew only too well that the salaries and vehicle costs for the Police Pioneers were 'hidden' in the Police Salaries and Transport Votes. Police turned a deaf ear to these complaints and many were the occasions when not only major maintenance and repair work, but also the construction of quite substantial new stations would not go out to tender because the Pioneers could complete the work at a fraction of the cost. So it was that the Pioneers, led by Frank Maguire and his committed teams, built complete stations like Nyamapanda, Kanyemba, Mubayira and Chikombedzi; erected new single and married houses for all ranks at numerous other stations; and built replacement charge office blocks at Nuanetsi, Melsetter and many others. It was simply a matter of making the inadequate Major and Minor Works votes go further and 'arranging' for the Pioneers to tackle a project that would rightly be the responsibility of the private sector. The Police Quartermaster and Staff Officer (Buildings) invariably won the full cooperation of the Ministry of Works, whose architects Sampson, Munro and others from the many disciplines, were always supportive.

This method of 'cut-rate' building was also a great help when the spending of 'Corps Funds' was involved, a subject mentioned in Chapter 43. The swimming pools and changing rooms in the Morris and Tomlinson Depots, the Depot Supply Store, Athletics Track, Bowls Pavilion and Squash Courts, the holiday cottages at Lake Kyle, Inyanga and Kariba — all were the work of the Pioneers.

So too were the smaller pools, tennis courts, cold-rooms, pubs and 'extra comforts' that appeared on rural stations.

The Pioneers were a multi-disciplined unit. They were able to prepare detailed plans and estimates and included among their number, builders, carpenters, electricians and plumbers. But they really came into their own when the incursions started in 1972 and it became vital that a police presence be established urgently in some of the more remote rural locations.

Staff Chief Inspector Ian Cook was placed in charge of the Operations Division of the Pioneers, a small group of regular and civilian artisans who moved about the operational areas selecting sites for, and building — mainly of a prefabricated wood design — emergency police posts. Bumi, Mashumbi Pools, Ruangwe, Ruda and Madhlambusi were examples of some 17 that had been built by 1977, the last by the Matabeleland Division under David Leech.

The great plus factor as far as Cook's and Leech's men were concerned was that being policemen, perhaps in a rather detached sense of the word, they were prepared to go that 'extra mile' to make sure that the operational police had every practical comfort that could be afforded. Many were the weary, begrimed and hungry troops who returned to their 'homes' to appreciate the hot showers, the kitchen facilities and the safety of the bunkers and defences put up by the likes of Ken Wood, Stephen Kamba, Hennie Sussemiehl, Tom Keenan, Fred Wallace and others of that hardworking crew.

'Dedicated' is not used lightly to describe Staff Chief Inspector 'Jock' Stone of the Transport Workshops. Although much of the major repair work on police transport was done by the CMED (which department established workshops in most of the JOC areas), this 'wee, broad-spoken Scot' was ever prepared to assist his Duty Branch colleagues. With his small team of mechanics, he was tireless in keeping police vehicles in running order. In the early days of the problems on the north east borders, he would move from station to station, checking the grossly overworked police vehicles, putting things right whenever possible and preparing a summary of requirements for the CMED when it was not. Jock departed on pension in October 1975 when, it seems, he was well beyond the normal retirement age.

The work of Don Hollingworth and Dave Perkins on mine-proofing operational vehicles has been mentioned. Their contribution of ingenuity and inventiveness did not end there.

Aware of the effects of an ambush on the occupants of mine protected vehicles — the sudden crescendo of firing, the noise, the need for some quick reaction — Hollingworth and Perkins devised an ingenious Immediate Reaction Mechanism. This embodied grenade launchers and machine guns — very often captured equipment — that could be activated by the driver of the vehicle. The system was rather like pressing a wall-switch or using a pull-switch to light up a room. This was not the end of the Armaments Branch innovations. As the situation worsened, they assisted the Air Force and collaborated with the Army in various other ways, among them the construction of a concrete block house in Depot's north paddock where suspect letters and packages could be opened in safe conditions. It should be remembered that at this time the country was subject to United Nations sanctions and that it had become necessary to improvise and innovate whenever possible. Electronic aids and scanners were not available although, at one stage of the war, a robot-type vehicle was developed on a joint-services basis which, radio operated, remote controlled and looking rather like a small tank, was to be used in bomb disposal situations.

The enthusiasts of the Marine Workshops have already been mentioned in connection with the Police Reserve Air Wing. There were other sections who, unsung but deeply involved, tried their best to ensure that the men in the front line were adequately provided for. The Ordnance Store, Tailors, Saddlers and Printers — all had an expertise that was unreservedly available to further the common cause.

In 1975, the war 'slackened off' a little; Sherren reported the murder of 106 civilians and the deaths of 145 terrorists. The urban areas, except for a riot in Gwanzura Stadium in Salisbury's Highfield Township, were quiet. The Gwanzura incident occurred during an ANC meeting and 14 rioters were killed by police gunfire during a demonstration that included stonings, arson and attacks on property, resulting in damage to a value of $80,000. In all 34 people were arrested and sentenced to varying periods of imprisonment.

The reduction in deaths did not for one moment mean that the terrorist efforts were any less determined. Over 300 acts of terrorism occurred in the Bindura and Mount Darwin areas and it was necessary to prosecute more than 130 tribespeople for either assisting or failing to report terrorists. The situation was similar in Lomagundi. In the Omay Tribal Trust area, the terrorist presence was firmly established and their first probing attacks were launched into the Midlands and Matabeleland police provinces.

The operational area was widening, and to the security chiefs it must have been rather like the story of the little Dutch boy trying to stem the trickle of water from the dyke.

Indeed the 'slackening off' was but the prelude to a more extensive campaign by the Nationalist forces. Mozambique had become an unfriendly neighbour and there were now 3000 kilometres of border to be defended. ZANLA moved its forces into Mozambique leaving Nkomo's ZIPRA to pursue their own struggle from Zambia. Curfews were imposed on most border areas in a vain attempt to stem the tide of insurgents, many of whom had been dragged from their homes or cajoled into the Nationalist forces with promises of 'better things and better days'.

And then — and this was a wholly political decision — the South African government decided to withdraw its police from Rhodesia.

Various commentators have discussed the decision but political considerations are not really relevant to this history — though it is probable that the United States was putting the 'squeeze' on the South African government at the time. Whatever the reasons, there is no doubt that the SAP had lost a number of their men as a result of terrorist activity. Two had been killed in a landmine explosion in north west Matabeleland and four more died after foolishly believing that the spirit of Détente had reached a group of ZANLA approaching them on the Mazoe river bridge.

An earlier incident near the Victoria Falls had seen four more SAP killed in an ambush and one other missing. Ken Flower recounts a minor diplomatic storm which started when an SAP constable unpredictably slit the throat of a young child, was very properly arrested for murder, but thereafter Pretoria repeatedly and angrily requested his repatriation, rather than have him face Rhodesian justice.

Whatever may have been the reasons for the withdrawal of men and equipment which, to the Rhodesians represented valuable moral and material support, the fact remains that fighting someone else's battles in another country and losing men doing it, however strong may be the bonds linking those countries, is not a particularly popular practice.

In the next chapter we move into the blackest and final years of Rhodesia's history. They were years dominated by politics, with Rhodesia prominent on the world stage. Sadly, they were the years that saw perpetrated some of the most ghastly horrors of the bush war.

As 1976 dawns, Peter Sherren still has two years in command of the Force but it is now a police force, like the country, with its back to the wall.

## Chapter Fifty-Six

## THE FORCE SOLDIERS ON

*1976. A 'torrid year' — Sub-Aqua Section — SWAT — Sabotage in Salisbury —*
*Investigations by Ross. 1977. New buildings — Security deteriorates — Convoys —*
*Thompson and others depart — Blackmore – Gallantry awards — Canteens — Sherren retires.*

IN 1976, AND in time for the Geneva Conference, the 'Patriotic Front' alliance was created. A rather uncertain marriage in many ways, it provided a semblance of unity against, not only the Rhodesian Government, but also the other participating groups — the Muzorewa-led ANC and the somewhat shaky ZANU of Sithole.

The Police Force — once again — was heading for another torrid year. The fact that 1226 terrorists were killed was little consolation when weighed against the enveloping war, the deaths of 552 civilians, greatly extended call-ups and rocket and mortar attacks on Umtali. The murder of three young South Africans and the derailment of a train, all occurring between Beitbridge and Fort Victoria, led to the introduction of convoys between those two centres and adjacent areas. Linking all this with the untimely death of the Chief of Staff of the Army, Major General John Shaw, and three others in a helicopter crash two days before Christmas of the previous year, and the outlook was bleak.

Peter Sherren put a cheerful face on it in his report on the year. The 'dual effort' of the police was 'maintained at a satisfactory level'; crime figures reflected an 'overall increase of only 1%'; 'clearance figures compared favourably with 1975' and 'road accidents dropped by 1636, or 12%'. Finally, the Commissioner commented that 'morale throughout the Force is unshaken'.

Perhaps so, but the numbers of men leaving the Force brought into question that last statement. Since 1974, 'Rick' and 'Bill' May, Peter Tomlinson, 'Paddy' Prior, Tom Fry, 'Taffy' Phillips and John Scott had been among those leaving. After them came 'Buck' Buchanan, Peter Robinson, Alec Blair, Bill Birch; and later still, Terry Thorpe and Cliff Podmore. The total service of just these 13 men was over 320 years. These were just some of the senior retirements. Below, the situation was no better and, in the years 1977 and 1978, it became worse, much worse.

However if one looks at the newcomers — youngsters with ability, enthusiasm but no experience — there may have been grounds for optimism. Over 570 regular and national service patrol officers, and over 500 constables and nearly 80 women police signed on. And despite the fact that the mounted and dismounted sports were cancelled, as were the boxing championships, there was still a great number of policemen and women achieving National recognition in a variety of sports. A young man named David Houghton, a patrol officer, was excelling in hockey and cricket; no less than 18 men were in the 'A', 'B' or 'Under 20' Rhodesia rugby sides; Don Hollingworth and David Toddun represented the country in the Service Rifle Shooting Team, and Dave Arnold and David Westerhout (then a field reservist) were members of the team that won the World Combat Pistol Championships in Austria.

No mention has so far been made of the Police Sub-Aqua Section which had been in existence for some years. Its members were usually to be found looking for bodies or cars in dams and rivers or searching for articles that had been thrown away into quarries or wells.

To have to recover a 40-ton ferry from a depth of eight metres on Lake Kyle must have come as manna from heaven. The ferry had been chartered by a film crew and had 30 film extras, three vehicles, a five-ton truck and about three tons of cameras and equipment on board when it gurgled to the bottom. Five of the crew were unaccounted for. Salisbury's 'underwater hockey team' was called in and was able to recover the bodies fairly quickly. They then turned their attention to the cameras and previous days' films which were also submerged, and after that started on the vehicles, attaching cables to the lighter ones and then bringing ashore the heavy generator truck and the ferry itself.

All members, Tony Dawson, Ian Donaldson, Doug Bing and Cathy Hall received notes of 'good work performed.' Perhaps the one downside of the whole recovery was that the star of the film, Britt Ekland, had flown back to Europe the previous week.

Another 'new kid on the block' was SWAT, an acronym for Special Weapons and Tactics Team. This unit of supremely fit, quickly reactive and crack shots numbered among its members Don Wilson, Dudley Naude, Mike King, Clive Bloom, Peter Gibson, Hamish Hamilton, Dusty Miller, Terry Price, Mike May, Janice Irvine, Pieter Scheepers, Wally Hammond, Pete Grizaard, Godfrey Engel, Andy Smith and Maria De Chaby. An African member complemented each of the teams which operated on a three-day standby basis. Members trained using RRAF helicopters on multi-storey buildings like Stops Hostel in the Depot, at a farm near Darwendale which had been specially adapted for training use and in any other suitable building that became available. Surveys were carried out on 'likely targets' — places like the Legislative Assembly and the Power Station — and contingency plans prepared to cope with attacks on such buildings.

Members of the Salisbury team were involved in numerous urban anti-terrorist operations and in one, taking place in a high-density suburb during 1978, Section Officer Andy Smith was shot and killed. The team followed up on the death of their colleague and, before the end of the week, had accounted for the killer.

Urban problems were, by 1976, becoming more frequent — and severe, especially in Salisbury and Bulawayo. In the southern city, rocket, grenade and small-arms attacks were made on a hotel, a motel and an African-patronized club; police were targeted on two occasions and only the alertness of a young patrol officer thwarted an attack on a city centre bar one evening.

In Salisbury, the attacks were a little more serious.

Using explosives obtained from a Mtoko quarry, a group of eight terrorists blew up portions of railway tracks and attacked an African beerhall. Later, they threw grenades into The Pink Panther restaurant, injuring two people and then again, outside La Boheme night club. The subsequent investigations were protracted — but successful.

The man who directed the Salisbury investigations was Chief Superintendent Angus Ross who retired from the CID/SB in 1977. Ross enjoyed a remarkable if not, taking into account the preceding paragraph, explosive career. Apart from the OK Bazaars bomb episode and the Pooley safe-blowing investigations mentioned earlier, he was in charge of complicated enquiries into the movement of stolen vehicles from Europe to Southern Africa. In this latter case, the woman accused had three German driving licences in her own name, three in the name of other persons, possessed 98 blank German licences, a dozen German vehicle log books as well as a number of stamps and ink pads and, to cap the whole lot, an unlicensed pistol.

Returning to more domestic matters, July saw the death of the 1954 to 1955 Commissioner of Police, Arthur Selwyn Hickman at the age of 75. Hickman's police career has already been described but it is probably more as an historian or — as he preferred to see himself, researcher — rather than a policeman that he will be remembered. Some five years after retiring he produced *Men Who Made Rhodesia*, a well-researched and comprehensive account of the young men who had joined the BSA Company's Police between 1889 and 1892. Five years later came the account of the part played by Rhodesian forces in the Anglo-Boer War of 1899 to 1902, *Rhodesia Served the Queen*. This was published in two volumes.

It was a most fitting tribute to the ex-Commissioner that in 1977 the new and luxurious Hickman Hostel was opened in the Morris Depot for women police.

Also in 1977 were laid the foundations for a new charge office complex adjoining the police station in Railway Avenue. The new building was to house the Information Room, Traffic Branch and include a new cellblock. The latter, modelled on up-to-date detention facilities built in South African and other world cities, was a grim, bleak and forbidding area. It was suggested that a conducted tour of this block would provide most youngsters with a salutary warning that a life of crime was not to be recommended.

Terrorist activity now escalated to new levels. Two months after the murder of the former Bishop of Bulawayo and two of his followers on a bush road near Lupane, came the massacre of another seven missionaries at St Paul's, Musami. A few months later, a bomb exploded in the crowded branch of Woolworths in Salisbury's Charter Road killing 11 and injuring 76 shoppers. Assistant Commissioner Bill Hobley took charge of the investigation and estimated that the parcel bomb which caused the devastation contained about 30 kg of TNT. The Forensic Laboratory backed this up this estimate, adding 'of Russian origin'. A week later, another bomb was exploded near Chancellor House in the city centre but this time without any casualties. Police were able to arrest and prosecute the tribesmen who brought the explosives to the capital but the actual culprits were never arrested. All this mayhem was accompanied by miscellaneous acts of sabotage on railway lines and bridges but generally with little success.

The death toll in 1977 reached frightening proportions.

Altogether 984 civilians were killed, 105 members of the Force of all races and branches also lost their lives, whilst the deaths of terrorist reached 1770.

There was little light-heartedness among the population now. The cinemas continued to be filled, night- clubs and restaurants were well patronised. But the introduction of random cordon and search operations by police reservists in the main urban shopping areas was a clear reminder to those swarming the streets that the war was near — uncomfortably near. On top of that, very few families were not affected, directly or indirectly by the catalogue of deaths. A further reminder came with the registration of uncommitted men in the 38 to 50 age group.

The security forces response to the deteriorating situation was to mount attacks into the neighbour-ing countries, targeting the terrorists' accommodation and training camps, with the aim of crippling the terrorists' logistics, deterring further incursions and causing maximum disruption.

Travellers to and from Beitbridge and in the Eastern Districts were now subject to convoy discipline. Again it fell to the Armaments staff to design mountings for the Browning machine guns mounted on the convoy escort vehicles which were manned by police reservists. In addition camps had to be set up to house and feed these men at the end of each journey and it fell to the Women's Voluntary Service (WVS) to provide what was described as 'hot, appetizing nosh' at the Fort Victoria end of the convoy system.

Not all dangers came from terrorists however. In February, after unprecedented rains, the Bubye River burst its banks at the Lion and Elephant Motel, almost submerging the buildings and causing havoc in the temporary police reserve camp situated under the trees across from the motel. RRAF helicopters and farmers with boats managed to pluck 64 people from the rooftop and trees, and ferry others to safety. The road between Beitbridge and Fort Victoria had already been gazetted as an 'airport' or 'airfield' — possibly the longest in the world — and smaller PRAW planes were able to land on it and distribute emergency supplies. As with all 'flash floods', the river had dropped within 24 hours and virtually all that was left to be seen was a dirty high-tide mark near the bar ceiling and an unbelievably distressed looking piano.

It could be said of the incidence of road accidents in 1977 that 'every cloud has a silver lining'. Due no doubt to petrol rationing, fewer vehicles on the roads because of call-ups, a petrol price increase and — of course — the convoy system, accidents dropped in number by nearly a thousand. However, precious little consolation could be derived from the year's figures of over 11,200 accidents and 544 people killed.

Neither was there any consolation in the discharge and retirement rate that year. Viewed in retrospect, it was catastrophic. Europeans and Africans literally poured out; to list them all would be a futile exercise but the experience, the investigating abilities, the management that was swept away in the tide was simply devastating — and quite impossible to replace. Two high-ranking officers, both senior assistant commissioners who, had they remained members should have stepped into the high-est ranks, were John Bradfield and Ray Stenner. On retirement the former was commanding Matabeleland Province; the latter, Salisbury Province.

Bradfield had joined in 1949 and was probably the most notable Rhodesian-born policeman in the Force's history. Educated at Plumtree, he was a fluent linguist, an authority on African customs and a student of Natural History, Africana and South African history. His rise through the ranks had been meteoric. Awarded the Police Cross for Distinguished Service in 1976, it was only the advance warning given by a minor heart attack that convinced him, in the best interests of his wife and family, that it was time to call a halt to the stress under which he was working.

Ray Stenner joined in 1949 as well. His career path followed closely that of John Bradfield in that he was commissioned relatively early in his service. Ray had the ability to remain calm and controlled under the most stressful of circumstances and, like Bradfield, he was a superb 'man-manager' and always responsive to the welfare and needs of the men he commanded — qualities he combined with a dry sense of humour.

Another to leave the Force during the year was Doctor John Thompson, the Forensic Scientist. He had, it will be recalled, started the Laboratory in 1963. Thompson estimated that during the intervening years he had been involved in about 12,000 cases, ranging from murder to the smuggling of emeralds and, including on the way, forged stamps, counterfeit money, road accidents, explosives and more recently, blood samples.

Thompson's successor was 34-year old Dr Hilton Kobus who had graduated from the University of Rhodesia and was not quite so 'intellectual' in his approach as his predecessor. Hilton, being younger, integrated with the police extremely well and was far better at explaining the intricacies of his work to everyday policemen, magistrates or judges in plain, not-too-technical language.

There is one man who was closely associated with the Forensic Laboratory but who has not featured in this story to date.

Ron Blackmore had joined the Police in 1946 and retired as a Detective Chief Inspector 'on gratuity' in 1963. In 1960, the then officer commanding CID, Jack Redfern, had appointed Blackmore to his staff to deal with photographs, fingerprints and suspect documents. Later he became the first Forensic Science Liaison Officer, a job linking the activities of the Government Analyst to those of police investigators. One somewhat macabre case that occurred in those days involved the discovery — by uniformed branch members — of the body of a housewife who had been battered to death with a stool and whose corpse had lain undiscovered for several weeks. During that period, the wounds had become infested with maggots. Blackmore sought the advice of the Government Entomologist on the growth pattern of the larvae and was able to establish the approximate date of death as three weeks before. This period coincided with the departure of a house servant and made the remainder of the investigation a fairly simple matter. It should be remembered that Blackmore's approach for expert advice took place many years before television and crime novels educated the public in this type of investigation.

In a later case, involving the placing of bombs in hotels, Blackmore was able to establish that the writing on various warning notes was that of a known nationalist leader.

Unfortunately, Blackmore had been tainted by the 'Bruce and Hogg' affair as detailed earlier, because — as an acknowledged handwriting expert as well as a keen and talented photographer — he had confirmed that it was Nkomo's signature appearing on the draft of the leaflet advocating strike action.

This naturally formed a substantial part of the evidence against the nationalist leader. Blackmore's involvement in an 'unauthorised investigation' had led to his being advised that further promotion (to commissioned rank) was highly unlikely and, disappointed and disillusioned, he chose to leave the force and link up with Hogg to form a commercial photographic business. The venture did not prosper and Blackmore decided to offer his services as a handwriting expert, rejoining the CID in a civilian capacity. He was accepted back in 1966 and remained as Questioned Documents Examiner for the next 20 years.

Not surprisingly under the prevailing circumstances, several awards for gallantry were given during 1977.

One such, for deeds that seem well-nigh incredible when viewed nowadays, went to Constable Sylvester Manyawu who, with Patrol Officer Gary Whitehead-Wilson, was on a vehicle patrol in the Operation Thrasher (Eastern Districts) area. Their vehicle was ambushed and subjected to heavy fire at a range of less than 10 metres. Both men were wounded, the patrol officer in the face, shoulder and back; his companion five times in both thighs, lower right leg, right wrist and neck. Sylvester returned fire with his sub-machine gun, lost consciousness for a short period and then, partly recovering, tried to summon assistance on the radio. That, of course, was out of action, so he struggled out of the cab and continued firing at the attackers until his gun jammed. Undeterred, he then used Wilson's FN and managed to drive off the terrorists. Wilson, who had been completely out of the action because of his wounds, was given First Aid and the two then tottered to a nearby township where Sylvester left the patrol officer in comparative safety and went off to get help. He staggered for over three kilometres to a school and there collapsed. After a short period, he revived sufficiently to provide details for his and Whitehead-Wilson's rescue. Both were evacuated and made good recoveries.

Another action, this time on the Zambezi and well within Rhodesian waters, involved two police launches being fired upon from the northern bank. Their crews had been investigating possible terrorist crossing points when the attack took place. At the very beginning of the engagement, the pilot of the first launch received a severe head wound causing him to slump over the controls. The scene must have been unbelievably chaotic as his colleagues tried to pull him away and take control of the vessel. Eventually and at full throttle, the boat was beached. Meanwhile the occupants of the second launch at first gave covering fire and then tried to rescue the others — all this while under sustained automatic and rocket fire. One member, Detective Patrol Officer Mike Sullivan, died in this engagement; three others, Duncan Paul, Thomas Matthews and Walter Bredenkamp, were awarded the Police Decoration for Gallantry. Commissioner's commendations went to four others: Simon Bunt, Richard Edge and Howard Burditt — all National Service patrol officers — and Kenneth Thornton, a field reservist.

Lew Whitmore was another to receive a Commendation and silver baton that year. However his award was gained doing plain, straightforward police work.

Whitmore was Duty Inspector at Bulawayo Central when news arrived that an armed and dangerous European was heading towards the home of his estranged wife and her parents, with the intention of killing all three. Whitmore arrived just after the man had fired a single shot, probably towards the house. Walking deliberately into a well-lit area he told the gunman to drop his weapon, a .375 revolver. The warning had no effect, the gun was now pointed at Whitmore and the threats to kill the family now included the policeman. Whitmore, fortunately armed with an Uzi, fired one shot which hit the man's hand but did not stop him pointing his revolver at the policeman yet again. A second shot wounded the man in the stomach and made him drop his gun. Still shouting threats against his family and the police, he was then arrested.

One last story, and this in much lighter vein, concerns Detective Section Officer Dave Lemmer who, ugently called to the scene of the Musami Mission massacre from Mtoko, arrived at St Paul's Mission wearing odd shoes. Excuses offered were many, and included no power at the hotel, a strange room and many more…none of which anybody believed.

A previous chapter concluded with details of some police canteens. Before chronicling the final years of the BSA Police, let us look at the background of two or three others.

Gatooma is a town that has not featured much in this book. Sadly, many would probably excise the words 'much in this book'. Nevertheless, and unlike Gwelo, no jokes have been made about 'single traffic lights' although one ex-member recalls Specks Hotel, 'where all the bedrooms face the sea'. That worthy establishment used to be the venue for many a lively Police Ball on the Saturday evening following the performance of the annual Display.

The Gatooma police canteen, or 'pub' had an individualism all its own. The original building, a pole and dagga thatched hut, dated back to 1948 and was so small that two persons, shoulder to shoulder, effectively screened the bar counter from anyone else. A new bar, designed in 1960, was completed two years later. Plans to add on a lounge or, as some preferred to call it, 'snuggery' and a snooker room were then tabled. Money, as ever, proved the stumbling block but Alan Rich, then an assistant commissioner in charge of the district, revived the scheme in 1975 and set about raising funds to turn the dream into reality. Over the years, there were many other sponsors that helped the scheme along. Officers commanding, reservists, the police themselves, not least the Police Central Fund — all contributed to make *The Run 'em Inn* another historic team effort.

The best-known and certainly the most unique pub of the war years was the *234* at Mount Darwin. Its origins were as a splash pool built in in the days of Meyrick Gethen in 1953, and condemned as a health hazard by a visiting officer some years later. By this time a more salubrious and larger pool had been put down at the nearby Club. In 1972, the member-in-charge, Inspector Dave Parry managed to 'misinterpret' the instruction to fill in the 'hole' and instead, and with the help of local reservists and civilians, removed a nearby gum tree, trimmed its bole and set this in three feet of concrete in the centre of the 'pool'. He then managed to obtain roofing materials, the services of a thatcher (who just happened to be the station tracker), some mahogany from Marymount Mission and, with the addition of a short, thatched entrance way, the building was roofed, provided with a bar and batwing doors, and opened for business at almost the same time as the first enemy strike on Altena Farm in 1972.

Though nothing to do with pubs, but certainly emphasizing the difference between a pub and a canteen, it is recorded that three mobile versions of the latter were presented to the police by the Pretoria Branch of the Southern Cross Fund and that one found its way to Mount Darwin. Pictures show appetizing food being ladled onto plates and, if the cloth holding the plate is anything to go by, the food was being served 'piping hot'.

Most unfortunately, Matabeleland's 'Queen Mary' — as that mobile canteen was known — had been burnt out. These two verses, part of a longer poem composed by 'R.A.H.A.' was justification for one of the Pretoria gifts being sent to Bulawayo.

*Sad is the plight of the Mat prov types,*
*Their Mobile Canteen is now boarded*
*And they're forced to refuel on bully beef stew*
*From rat packs the Army has hoarded.*

*Fourteen years' service the old Queen gave,*
*From Beitbridge to Vic Falls and Dett.*
*At JOC's and Reserve camps her presence was felt*
*By all the Reservists she met.*

The Mount Darwin '234' had a 'country cousin' conceived by Winston Hart at Mukumbura on the Mozambique border. Seldom was this lonely desert-like station known by its proper name, other than in the solemn corridors of provincial or police headquarters. 'Mukers' or 'Mukumbura Surf Club' or 'Sidi-el-Mukers' were much more fitting, acceptable and well-known appellations. This relic of the Beau Geste era nestled on the bank of the border 'river' of Mukumbura and had been variously a pole-and-dagga hut and, to coin a collective noun, a canvas of tents, before ingenuity and self-help created the castellated edifice that became so well known to members of the security forces. Many of the policemen were required to do a stint of two or three months at Mukers and a solemn ritual was introduced of inducting the current 'mayor' and hanging around his neck the emblem of his office — a toilet seat.

A not dissimilar history to that of Mount Darwin saw the creation, from an old dare, of the Police Reserve Chapel at Mashaba. The oldest piece of this non-ecclesiastical structure was the bar — or a portion of it — which was originally a part of the Victoria Falls Hotel circa 1960. At that time renovations — which seem to be tackled with great regularity in that famous establishment — resulted in Peter Nicholls finding that parts of the original structure had 'arrived' in the police camp. When, some time later, Peter arrived at Mashaba, the portion of bar arrived with him. The presence of a carpenter, a builder and a qualified thatcher among the local prison population ensured the speedy erection of the building and even the unwelcome visit of Commissioner Barfoot shortly after the unofficial opening failed to have the 'amenity' condemned and demolished.

By the end of 1977, Peter Sherren had completed 38 years service, the last four under the most stressful and demanding conditions it was possible to imagine. An informal convention had been established whereby the appointment of the commissioner alternated between the CID and the Uniformed Branch. Sherren's career path had been uniformed; the next man had to come from the plain-clothed branches to oversee the transition to the Zimbabwe Republic Police.

## Chapter Fifty-Seven

## THE FINAL CHAPTER

*Peter Allum becomes Commissioner — crime figures — resignations — African advancement — More gallantry awards — April 1979 Election — Chikurubi Barracks opens — the Incentive Scheme — British Police come to country — the BSAP comes to an end, and a chapter closes.*

To set the scene for the final Act, it is necessary to go back to 1947, to the small rural town of Rusape. At that time, the European police contingent probably numbered no more than five or six members and they were commanded by Inspector Ted Webber. One day in August or September, Webber received a telephone call from his officer commanding requesting that one of the troopers be sent immediately to the CID. Virtually all his young men were but recently out of Depot and Webber was at a loss whom he should send. Being a man of some resource, he consulted his wife. She responded, without hesitation but perhaps rather unkindly, ' Send that Papist blighter. '

So it was that Peter Kevin Allum, who had joined in April of the previous year and spent about five weeks in the training depot, joined the CID in September of 1947. A 14 or 15 months period of uniformed service was far too short an apprenticeship for plain-clothed duties. It was only the desperate needs of the CID in those post-war years that necessitated a departure from the usual three years policy. The result of this early move was that before the third anniversary of his attestation Allum had been promoted to detective sergeant. Commissioned in 1960, his advancement through the ranks was rapid and sure, and in 1970 he took command of the CID. Four years later, the move to Deputy Commissioner (Crime and Security) took place and, four years after that, on 7 February 1978 he became Commissioner. Allum faced one of the most difficult jobs it was possible to imagine. He was commanding a force within which the senior ranks were crumbling away and he was soon to be confronted with piloting that force into a new era while attempting to maintain efficiency, morale and standards.

Serving only 15 months in uniform and 31 years in plain clothes was an inadequate preparation for the task ahead. Three years in the rough and tumble of general duties is rather like leaving home and going to boarding school for the first time; it tends to round off the rough edges, engender team spirit and provide a taste of what the real world is like. Nor was the absence of a honing-down period assisted by the personality of the man. Allum was inclined to be scholarly and introverted. He was quick to gain language and legal qualifications and not noted for any marked participation in sports, apart from tennis.

Leading a police force through four years of dramatic change and incredible upheaval demanded a man with superior man-management abilities, a man who could relate to the fears and aspirations of the majority of the force; a man, in fact, who was inclined to be extrovert and who could impart his views and arguments succinctly and, when necessary, forcibly. Allum's background negated many of these requirements; he was perhaps too much of a gentleman and too inclined to loquacity.

Consider too the overall situation when Allum became Commissioner. The country was only four weeks away from what should have been a momentous occasion — the effective signing away by Ian Smith of white rule. The settlement agreement establishing the Transitional Government placed Rhodesia on a path leading to black majority rule by the year-end and saw the beginning of a new government headed by Bishop Muzorewa, Chief Chirau, Rev. Ndabaningi Sithole and, of course, Ian Smith. The new Government was effectively established a few weeks later, on 21 March, but both Britain and America were hesitant to acknowledge the new dispensation and the United Nations found it both illegal and unacceptable. Efforts by the new Zimbabwe-Rhodesia leaders to gain recognition met with luke-warm politeness and, significantly, David Owen, the British Foreign Secretary, and Andrew Young, US Ambassador to the United Nations, were meeting Joshua Nkomo and Robert Mugabe on the island of Malta. Ostensibly, that conference was aimed at achieving recognition for the Transitional Government and an end to the conflict.

If that was in fact the objective, it failed miserably.

One other upsetting move, and this despite reassuring noises from 'on high' but which was to subtly lessen police commitment and loyalty, had to be the appointment of Lt Gen. Peter Walls as Commander, COMOPS (Combined Operations). Police had generally been happy with the previous system in which the Service heads, various secretaries of ministries, the head of CIO and a range of others conducted the war on an equal responsibility basis.

Although it was a logical move to appoint a Supreme Commander, many policemen were resistant to the concept of a military numero uno. Far too many had seen that among some of the military there were a number of, for want of a better description, 'tear-aways'.

Of course, what this boiled down to was that the policeman and the soldier are diametrically opposed beings. Their training is different, their *raison d'etre* is different, their career paths are different. Toleration, as opposed to respect, applied in many cases, and probably on both sides. Ken Flower put it rather well when he wrote: 'It was civilian morale that sustained Rhodesia, not military professionalism'.

Such was the scenario when Allum took over. A war going downhill; a world growling antagonistically; an enemy truculent, upbeat and uncompromising; a newly-formed but disunited government desperate to make its presence felt, and a police force hoping for firm and reassuring leadership. An unenviable job, perhaps impossible in the circumstances, for anyone.

The Commissioner's report for 1978 repeated the litany of disaster. A total of 102 security force members, 1264 civilians and 2280 terrorists killed. But on top of this were the events that dominated the headlines so often during that year: 'Massacre at Mission', the murders at the Vumba-based, Elim Mission that was once Eagle Boarding School; the destruction of vast quantities of stored petrol after the attack on the fuel storage tanks on Salisbury's industrial sites and the downing of the first Viscount plane. The Commissioner's report goes on to mention a new dimension in terrorist tactics, the introduction of mujibas, youngsters aged between 10 and 17 who screened their better-trained seniors and were encouraged to commit crimes and generally hinder the security forces.

Frauds, illegal dealings in gold and precious stones, murders and other crimes kept the CID more than busy for now the 'race to the gap was really on'. Many of the European and Asian populations were set on removing from the country as much currency and valuables as possible, as fast as possible.

At Bulawayo Airport, a man was arrested with 30 cut emeralds and other precious stones concealed in the heels of his boots. He was not alone. Investigations led to two associates, one of whom committed suicide. There were 340 investigations into contraventions of the Exchange Control Act and a group of Fort Victoria businessmen had secreted 53,000 South African rand and some ivory in compartments within their suitcases.

Forged American Express travellers cheques with a face value of US$ 65,000 placed three more men in prison. Crimes of violence and murder came with a spate of attacks on petrol station attendants. A series of robberies in the urban areas of Bulawayo only came to an end when police shot a member of the gang involved. Two employees of the Arcturus Mine, outside Salisbury, were killed and the payroll of $25,000 stolen in a cold-blooded attack not far from the mine. This last case led to the arrest of a European mine employee but he too managed to escape the death penalty by committing suicide.

And within the police force the outpouring of regular members continued.

Of these, one in particular ended in tragedy. Chief Inspector David Perkins had, for many years, been a most able assistant to Don Hollingworth in the main armoury. His extensive knowledge of all types of weapons, as well as bombs and booby traps, had made him a valued and, let it be said, desirable commodity in those markets where his type of expertise was invaluable. David was offered an appointment with Armscor in Pretoria and departed south. Less than eight months later, he was to die in an accidental explosion in South Africa.

Another to depart was Patrol Officer Tutani who, after nearly 30 years in the police and achieving the rank of sub-inspector, had become one of the first Africans to be promoted to patrol officer in 1977.

A combination of ability and circumstances saw the African uniformed members of the force occupying positions of much greater responsibility. They were now trained and able to command fully-fledged urban stations and no longer was it necessary to simplify the administration and provide almost constant support or control.

Section Officer Cornelius Kupikayi was one of these. Promoted to that rank in 1977, he took command of Mabvuku police station with a staff of 34 including a sergeant-major, and responsibility for the densely populated areas of Tafara, Mabvuku and Chizhanji, a population conservatively estimated at 51,000.

Cornelius was only 43 years of age and had spent the majority of his service in Bulawayo Urban, at Mzilikazi, Western Commonage and latterly as sub-inspector in charge of Njube.

Another member, and one destined for even further advancement, was Inspector Godwin Mabika who became member-in-charge of the police station controlling the Salisbury suburb of Avondale. Mabika was about 41 when he took over this old, cramped but important suburban complex, only a stone's throw away from the grave in St Mary's churchyard where the Countess 'Billy' Panouse had hidden during the Mashonaland rebellion in 1896.

Godwin's balliwick contained a population in the region of 28,000 and at his disposal were 50 men and women together with 500 reservists. His move to Avondale — and later to Police General Headquarters — was preceded by service as a junior member at Yotamu and Matapi, Umtali, Sakubva and Mabelreign.

Many other Africans had attained the status of 'Junior Officer' as the rank of Inspector was now regarded. John Chademanah, Nebart Madziwa, Govadi Mhora and Sam Mugadza, the two latter detective inspectors. Leon Chawora, Johnson Chikombwe and Rodwell Nguruve were also among them, the majority destined to move to higher rank in the 80s.

These were but a few of the new breed of black policemen whose abilities were being recognised by the authorities. For many of them, unfortunately, that recognition came too late in their careers. It was neither more nor less than the play of changing circumstances — the growing lack of white policemen, the stretching of the bands of experience among less and less of the latter, plus the recognition that adequate policing of the country was lacking. All these factors led to the admission that responsibility had to be given to those who had in the past been regarded as 'not quite up to it'

There was a certain 'inevitability' about what was happening in the Force; this enforced change of circumstances which could and should have been recognised and acted upon earlier. Perhaps, using the benefit of hindsight once more, there could be debate as to whether a more liberal approach and a programme of intensive training for the African policemen, many years before, would have resulted in a less traumatic period of readjustment in the late 70s and 80s. Certain it is that, in the vast majority of cases, they had proved their ability, their loyalty and their dedication over many years. Perhaps, too, similar arguments could be applied in the political arena.

Can the story of Rhodesia and its police force be summed up in the words, 'too little, too late?'

Gallantry awards continued to flow throughout 1977.

Section Officer Rob Parker earned an MLM for his command of a Special Investigation Section of the police on counter-insurgency duties, a section which effectively neutralised three terrorist groups and harrassed many others. A police reservist, Samuel Nigadzino, was in at the start of the incursions in the north-east in 1972 when his tracking abilities became apparent and he took part in no less than 53 separate contacts, as well as helping to train other members of the Reserve in his skills. He too received an MLM.

Another member of the reserve, Ephraim Kaulanani who, in company with the constable with whom he had been drinking, took on an armed terrorist attempting to rob a beerhall in Beitbridge. The constable was shot and killed by an accomplice during the fracas but the actions of Ephraim were sufficient to deter and frighten off both intruders. Ephraim was awarded the Police Decoration for Gallantry as also, posthumously, the constable, Godfrey Soka.

Among the deaths in action was that of another police dog. Caesar was one of the best-known dogs in the country. An alsatian, he and his handler Tim Howard, had been the subject of frequent comment and praise in the newspapers as they had made scores of arrests of store and house breakers. The dog's death occurred in a violent burst of automatic fire when tracking a terrorist escaping from a contact. Caesar had been allowed to roam free from his harness in the pursuit and died with his teeth clamped firmly onto a piece of the terrorist's clothing.

The year 1979 was very political.

The nine-month-old Transitional Government was still hanging on and the white electorate had accepted the majority rule constitution by 6:1 in favour. Muzorewa, soon to be the first black prime minister, won the internal elections during April. Viscount Boyd, a former Conservative Colonial Secretary and observer at the elections described them as 'free and fair'. The Front Line presidents, who were playing an increasingly aggressive role in the country's affairs, did not agree. Nor did the international community. In Britain, the Conservatives won an election and tottered into government with a majority of 43. Margaret Thatcher became the first woman prime minister. She was to side with the external majority in seeking genuine black majority rule.

A few words about that April election (in Rhodesia) are relevant because it involved the total might of the security forces being dispersed nationwide to ensure that the population could vote peacefully.

Regular police were deployed on twelve-hour shifts with no time off over the four day election period. Patrols were stepped up, roadblocks manned; curfews imposed in certain areas, particularly industrial areas. With so many men separated from their wives and children, the availability and importance of the 'House under Supervision' scheme (HUS) was emphasised. To further reassure the public, the Commissioner appeared on television being interviewed by the RBC news editor, David Paterson, himself an ex-policeman. Ian Hogg, by now an assistant commissioner in Salisbury Province, detailed the way in which the HUS scheme worked. Chief Inspector Dave Le Guern spoke on the role of the Specials. Inspector Godwin Mabika dealt with the curfews and allied matters on the African Service of the RBC. Other members were interviewed on various aspects of their duties by a most cooperative media.

The whole election process presented a vast logistical exercise that need not be meticulously detailed. Nevertheless, some of the statistics involved make fascinating reading. Over 13,000 policemen were deployed. To many of them it was necessary to issue, from the Ordnance Stores, such items as bedding, torches, webbing and eating utensils. In excess of 150,000 ration packs had to be made available. Close on 600 polling stations had to be provided with First Aid kits, gas stoves, extra rations and other necessities. One group of ladies made over 5,000 sandwiches in one day. The Police Reserve Air Wing flew over 80 sorties from Mount Hampden alone. Transport for all this had to be mobilised and, in many cases, arms and ammunition issued.

It was a very successful election. Despite the fact that literally thousands of terrorists or guerillas were dispersed to disrupt the proceedings, only a handful of polling stations were attacked — unsuccessfully.

Over 1.9 million people voted out of an estimated 2.8 million but, as ever, the country's detractors and the 'liberals' muttered about the heavy security force presence which 'intimidated' the voters. They totally ignored the presence and underlying threat posed by the hordes of Patriotic Front members.

And it was all for nothing.

At the Commonwealth Conference in Lusaka during August the apparent fear that the whole concept of the Commonwealth might founder and fall over the 'Rhodesian question', seemed uppermost. The second preoccupation was the acknowledgment that without the concurrence of the Patriotic Front (Nkomo and Mugabe), there could be no peaceful conclusion of the Rhodesian problem. Britain successfully argued that the responsibility for achieving a lasting solution rested in her hands, and agreed to hold yet another constitutional conference.

Lancaster House in London was the venue and, from September to December, off and on, the conference and its sub-meetings edged forward. Allum was called over, presumably to advise on the expected reactions within the police. Agreement was reached after Muzorewa agreed to stand down as prime minister and, in December Lord Soames came to Rhodesia as interim Governor. The new year, 1980, witnessed not only the elections that brought Mugabe to power but with them several breaches of the cease-fire as well as some cunning intimidation of the black electorate. These are amply discussed in other books concerning the period but still leave the question; why did nobody in authority react to the violations, or was it simply that the strife, the deaths, the slide in the economy had dragged on long enough?

Whatever the answer, the coming years saw peace and reconciliation.

Allum's report for 1979 (compiled in 1980) was prefaced by the comment that it related to a period during which the 'country was steeped in war'. He continued 'It is submitted for its statistical value only and with the profound hope that some of its contents will remind readers of the scourge we are now spared'.

The report brushes lightly over the impending establishment of a Police College, the objectives of which included preparing members for higher rank. Whether this aim originated from the beliefs of Lord Trenchard in pre-war Britain is not an issue in this history but certainly the idea of advancing a man because of his possession of a university background or high standard of education, and thus being fit for promotion to the 'officer class', is a theory fraught with dangers. To quote an eminent ex-member of the BSA Police who attained several of the highest positions within the United Kingdom police forces:

'The police force needs not exceptionally high standards of education, but very great integrity and strength of character, combined with the wisdom which comes to some — though not all — men when they have had wide and varied practical experience of human nature'. (From *'Cloak and Dagger'* 1955 by Sir Percy Sillitoe, KBE.)

Further into the report, the Commissioner mentions that by the year-end not only had the extensions to Salisbury Central been completed but also the first phase of the Support Unit barracks at Chikurubi. In the same section, the Quartermaster was at pains to point out that the housing backlog now stood at $24 million and implied that members were being recruited for which there were neither offices nor accommodation.

Departing from the Commissioner's survey, there is a description of a semi-social event linked with the new Chikurubi barracks and its more restrictive neighbour, the Prison. This was an annual cooking competition to promote the use of coal for cooking purposes, sponsored by Wankie Colliery. The Colliery Sales Manager openly admitted that electricity was the ultimate solution but that coal offered an excellent short-term answer for preparing hot, sustaining meals. He argued that while paraffin was becoming more expensive than wood, use of the latter — the traditional fuel — meant the eventual denuding of Rhodesia's vast timbered areas, leading to the terrible dangers of soil erosion and desertification. At the culmination of the competition the wife of Lance Sergeant Chiromo of the Support Unit was declared the winner, with two Prisons wives taking second and third place.

Reverting to crime statistics in the Commissioner's report, there was a diminution under some headings but an increase in others. Notable among the latter were stock theft, illicit dealing in gold and precious stones, fraud and allied offences, murders and crimes of violence. Lest it be thought that the decreases were of little significance, they included the categories included breakings, thefts and liquor offences.

Of the murder cases, two — both in Bulawayo — are worthy of mention.

In the first, a particularly brutal attack, a housebreaker used a pick head to club a mother and her four-year old child to death to make sure he was uninterrupted. He was arrested and sentenced to death. The second saw Johannes Strydom, a small-holder, bludgeoned to death in his bath by his wife, her lover and three Africans recruited for the occasion. The body was then thrown into a nearby dam together with a pistol and torch, the aim being to bolster the wife's story that Strydom had gone outside to investigate a suspicious noise. Mrs Strydom and her lover were sentenced to death but when the details of her unhappy life with her husband were revealed, they provided sufficient reason for the sentence to be commuted and she was released more than 20 years later, in 1999.

Aidan Diggeden, an old acquaintance of the police, was released from Salisbury Prison's maximum security wing in November 1978 after serving 12 of an 18 year sentence for fraud, car theft and other offences. He immediately left the country for England and a job as an accounts clerk in London. Diggeden will always be remembered with a certain grudging respect by Rhodesia's police. A persistent criminal and habitual stealer of Ford cars, he had served sentences for his crimes in many prisons, and invariably succeeded in escaping from them, sometimes more than once. He was a cheerful, superbly fit and plausible rogue who seemed almost to enjoy his frequent brushes with the police.

Nor was he above praising his 'traditional enemies' as this extract from a letter written from London shortly after his release, shows:

" ... I sincerely rate the record of the BSA Police as superb. Coupled with this reputation and what I think is most important is the tremendous standard of personal behaviour of all members of the Force not only in regard to their dealing with members of the public but towards people like myself. I have received nothing but respect and kindness through the years and have the utmost admiration for the BSA Police."

Diggeden went on to warn potential criminals that, with a clearance rate of around 80%, their chances of escaping prison were slim indeed. His letter ended:

"All the best to all the 'old lags' in the Force."

One is left to wonder whether this extraordinary criminal — for not many think so highly of those who put them behind bars — managed to keep out of trouble in his new environment

The year had carried on in its traditional way as far as the police were concerned. There had been medal and pass-out parades, retirements, awards for bravery, an Opening of Parliament and seen the introduction of the new, multi-coloured flag of Zimbabwe Rhodesia.

The parades showed a distinct change from the past. For example, Parliament was opened by the President, the Hon. Josiah Gumede; pass-out parades of men and women were multi-racial, and medal parades enjoyed the presence of Francis Zindoga as Minister of Law and Order, as well as Deputy Prime Minister, Mundawarara; Justice Minister Andersen, and Commerce and Home Affairs ministers Bulle and Zimuto.

Reference has been made to the Lancaster House Conference, the agreement that stemmed from it, the arrival of the new Governor and the birth of peace and reconciliation.

Those events spanned a period during which most senior policemen — members of the other uniformed forces and civil servants as well — were hoping desperately that the British government would guarantee their pension benefits. This was not to be. In fact a most peculiar and self-defeating scheme was introduced which became known as the 'Incentive Scheme' — an anomaly if ever there was one.

Very broadly the idea was to offer servicemen — and the civil service was quickly in on the act — enhanced pension remissibility outside the country for every year, up to a maximum of five, they remained in service. As the following paragraph will amply demonstrate, the scheme was never a 'carrot' to stay and see how the new government worked out, but rather an incentive to leave while the money and opportunities were available.

The words 'remissibility outside the country' became the carrot, especially when allied with the preparedness of South Africa to accept everyone on offer. Between August and December 1980, a total of 48 senior white policemen left the force, among them 15 superintendents and 19 chief inspectors. Although beyond the scope of this history, the total for 1981 was even more debilitating — 114. Among those were 10 assistant commissioners, 52 superintendents and chief superintendents and 50 inspectors and chief inspectors. Not all left the country but if the figures in the other services, including the civil service, were as damaging to those groups, then the drain of experience and expertise over the range of government can only be described as appalling.

Shortly after Lord Soames arrived in the country came his Police Adviser, Sir James Haughton plus an advisory staff. Their task was to liaise with the local police to ensure that the best possible conditions were in place for a 'free and fair election' at the end of February. To bolster the concept of freedom and fairness, 500 British policemen arrived in the country, were given a warm welcome after their long flight by the local police and were dispersed to the polling stations for the five days of the election. The BSA Police and Reserve were also out in force, very much in the same way as they had been only ten months before but now in a more understated and self-effacing role.

So Rhodesia ceased to be. On 18 April 1980, the Republic of Zimbabwe was born.

For the policemen still serving, and there were many of them, the future appeared as a large question mark. They had lived and worked under emergency laws and conditions for many, many years. Now they were confronted with change. This was not only in government but also in their attitudes to their daily work. The old concepts, the old values, needed to be re-created in a new peaceful environment.

Joshua Nkomo became Minister of Home Affairs and responsible for the police. Together with Peter Allum, he toured the country, addressing gatherings of police in all the main centres. The general tenor of these meetings was one of reassurance and the need to work together to build a safe and secure future in the newly independent land. Nkomo said that every citizen wanted safety, education for his children and efficient medical attention. He emphasised the necessity for his ministry and the police to work together. If this cooperation were lacking, he indicated, then those to suffer would be the ordinary men and women of the country. His concluding words to the Force Executive Committee of the Police Association, where he spoke in company with the Commissioner, the Deputy Minister Senator Ziyambi and the chairman of the Police Association, Senior Assistant Commissioner J. 'Shiner' Wright, were:

"I appeal to you — accept that change has come and that it is the duty of all of us to make sure that things be made to work in the new situation, because we all belong to this country. If we can avoid conflict in every sphere, then we cannot go wrong".

The BSA Police passed quietly into history at the end of July without the beating of muffled drums or plaintive calls on trumpets. One day it was called by the name it had so proudly carried for close on ninety years, the next a new name had appeared. With it a new crest, designed by Chief Superintendent Richard Hamley, which appropriately and cleverly incorporated the traditional lion of the old force with a new motto, the name of the new body and above this the Zimbabwe Bird. The Zimbabwe Republic Police celebrated its birth by holding the first traditional Mounted Sports and Display for eight years.

So with the change in government, of outlooks and policies, there came a small, sweet breath from the past, a remembrance of happier times, of respected and popular tradition. Future generations will look back on those final, turbulent eight years in a variety of ways; some with sorrow, some with triumph and pride; others with exultation. They were eight years that deprived many families of fathers and mothers, sons and daughters and those losses will forever remain as scars on the memories of those who live on. Perhaps some small consolation is to look back over 84 and more years, to the days when a small column of men rode and trudged over the hills and plains from the south, to create our country and become the nucleus of its police force.

They arrived in a land that was full of promise and was to become prosperous and make a unique contribution to an Empire now long gone.

We, all of us who served in whatever capacity, were a part of the history and traditions of that land and of a police force that helped to make it great. In that knowledge we should — we must be proud.

Our story will live on, and what better way to end than to use the few lines of poetry penned many years ago by a member of the Force, David Blacker.

These are words that encapsulate the spirit of the present, and the past, of:

### THE REGIMENT

*Our numbers dwindle now and fade.*
*Will history prove a mark we made?*
*I doubt we'll merit but a line –*
*Just memories which are yours and mine.*
*But in our hearts we thought it right*
*To make a place for black and white*
*Our cause thought just, our spirits strong,*
*Oh History, will you prove us wrong?*
*Let men deride and have no care,*
*We can with pride state*
*"I Was There. "*

## APPENDIX 1

## RADIO & COMMUNICATIONS BRANCH

The first police radio messages were passed between Salisbury and Bulawayo on 2 May 1940. Morse code was the medium used.

However, it was Brigadier Appleby who, after the war, realised the potential of radio communications and decided to expand the capabilities of the embryonic radio section and take it forward towards the highly sophisticated network that would exist 40 years later. Therefore, and before tracing that progress, it is appropriate to examine the systems in use in 1950 when the development started and when, as was still the position 30 years later, there existed two basic classes of communications service.

The first of these was long-range communication, with transmitting and receiving stations at Police General Headquarters (PGHQ) and the district headquarters in Bulawayo, Gwelo, Umtali, Fort Victoria and Gatooma. Trained police telegraphists, using telephony and morse, operated in these places and, though the signals were inclined to fade and 'skip', they served their purpose reasonably well. Similar facilities existed in Que Que, Shabani, Victoria Falls, Wankie and Mphoengs. The first two used a scheduled radio telephony service with Gwelo, the remaining three with Bulawayo. The needs of Beitbridge were under active consideration.

All stations were equipped with radio receivers enabling them to pick up the daily fixed-time broadcasts from district headquarters but the lack of a long-range mobile reception and transmission facility was proving an impediment to policing as the economy expanded.

The second service was short-range and operated in the two main urban areas. Again, the number of sets was insufficient and steps had been taken to seek funding for an expansion of services.

Pictures of the PGHQ radio room at the half-century show a young Percy Foskett seated before two upright Imperial typewriters, separated by a morse 'tapper', with headphones to his ears and a bank of heavy, ponderous looking cabinets with dials facing him. In those days, police relied on GPO engineers for any technical work in the way of maintenance or improvements.

A year later, the Post Office engineers had built a high-powered transmitting and receiving unit mounted in an Austin station-wagon, with a petrol driven generator installed on a trailer. This provided satisfactory communications with all headquarters stations from any part of the country and linked in well with the police contingent operating in Bechuanaland. Plans were in place to purchase two similar units.

As far as urban communications were concerned, a start had been made installing short-distance VHF-FM sets in vehicles in the two main urban centres. The Postmaster General had been asked to make provision for additional sets as well as for 'Walkie-Talkies' for speed trapping. This major step towards improving urban communications was made possible with the purchase of Pye equipment and the introduction of remote-controlled fixed radio stations operated over a land line. A further modification saw special VHF radio aerials and 60-foot masts being put in place in Wankie, Shabani and Que Que so that when an emergency situation arose, as happened with some regularity at Wankie, it was possible to transfer receivers and transmitters and set up an efficient network without delay.

By 1952 the Commissioner was agitating for all stations to be provided with radio transmitters as well as receivers, so that a continuous flow of information could be established within the force, independent of the telephone system and irrespective of climatic conditions, power failures or any other factors. He instanced national emergencies, flooding rivers, impassable roads or disrupted telephone lines.

Those were the days of the Dolphin sets, another Pye product originally designed for use in trawlers and leisure craft but which, with suitable modifications, operated from a battery, had a range from five to 200 or more miles and employed a separate radio frequency for each police district. Photographs of this period show John Barratt happily 'plugged in' to one of the 70 sets that were located at district stations.

Lacking the benefit of electricity at many rural stations, bicycle-driven generators were used to keep the batteries charged. Appleby had seen such a method in East Africa during his secondment there during the war. With the assistance of CMED, a bicycle frame was adapted to incorporate a standard 12-volt motor vehicle generator and cut-off relay, driven off a modified rear wheel. Many district members-in-charge welcomed this unusual device which served to discipline junior members and acted as a unique and salutary form of hard labour for prisoners in the police lock-ups. It was to be seven or eight years before this method was replaced by diesel driven generator sets.

Technical advances by 1953 made it possible for PGHQ to improve on the system used when members had been operating in Bechuanaland and to keep daily contact with the contingent now stationed in various parts of Nyasaland. However, the most significant 'technical' advance was the recruitment of a radio mechanic, John Woodcock, to undertake repair and maintenance work.

The recruitment of Woodcock was the first step towards the creation of a technical division within the branch. It was also the first 'dent' in the pride of the Chief Engineer in the Department of Posts and Telegraphs who had always maintained that his staff were able and adequate to cope with the technical needs of the police. Future years would see the police technical staff greatly increased, dependency on the government department fall away and workshops and radio stores established in all provincial centres. The Air Wing would also become a regular and economical means for ferrying technicians to their various duties, as well as being invaluable as airborne relay stations.

The next years saw the gradual upgrading of equipment, the expansion of services including the introduction of teleprinter links — eventually to reach all provincial and district headquarters stations — and the recruitment of more technicians.

Expansion indeed.

Early in October 1957, a signal came over the Salisbury 'Bee' car wavelength. 'Proceed to Cut-Rate Shoe Store at intersection Broadway and Lexington'. Doubtless the drivers would have welcomed the chance to answer this freak signal and journey to New York. Whether they would have welcomed joining the Japanese fishing fleet that also appeared on the airwaves is open to doubt.

The fourth quarter of 1959 saw more trials being carried out, but now using the single sideband (SSB) technique which improved reception conditions during the rainy season when static or lightning tended to disturb communications. The trials were successful and police placed orders with Racal Electronics for mains-operated base station equipment.

At about the same time, suitable mobile 12-volt-operated equipment was sourced from SMD Natal (SA) which proved ideal for rural fixed and mobile use. The Natal firm was later bought by Racal (UK) to become Racal Electronics (RESA) and went on to provide considerable equipment for the Rhodesian security forces. For the urban areas, six-channel VHF radio equipment had proved eminently successful during trials and was installed in vehicles and police stations.

In 1961, following the building of numerous satellite stations in townships the previous year, stations in this category were equipped with VHF radio fixed stations and mobile equipment installed in their vehicles. Originally a six-channel system, it was later widened to cover eleven channels to cater for security schemes and provide a separate channel for the Traffic Branch.

In the same year came the Rural Radio Communication Scheme.

This involved 100 Pye VHF fixed stations and 400 mobile stations — very much the same as the urban installations described above — the fixed unit at the police station, the mobile in the station vehicles and those used by the Reserve section leaders.

By this time there were 160 privately-owned sets which operated on police frequencies and it was but a short step to setting up of a Police Reserve Signals Branch dedicated to assisting their regular counterparts. These men and women worked in all areas and in both the technical and transmission sections of the Branch until the end of the bush war.

The next major step forward was the establishment of a Radio Research Laboratory to examine and test the new equipment, investigate new theories and generally improve the communications networks. During the first six months of its operation, a new type of aerial was perfected which resulted in significant savings to the Police Vote. Later on, another ingenious device prevented damage to battery-operated sets when, as frequently happened, the leads were inadvertently reversed when being connected. And one of the most important developments enabled the remote control of radio repeater stations at places without a power supply. This latter was master-minded by Inspector Peter Patterson.

In 1962, Woodcock was sent to the United Kingdom to recruit suitable technical staff, it being impossible to find them in southern Africa. He managed to induct over a dozen, which took care of the more immediate problems in the Branch. But few stayed in the Force for very long, either finding other jobs in the commercial sector or returning to Britain. During that visit, Woodcock went to the Marconi factory and evaluated a new radar speed meter for use by traffic police. The first of such sets, known as PETA (Portable Electronic Traffic Analyser), was tested and 'proved' by Terry Thorpe and traffic staff on the Beatrice Road, using a 'Bee' car with a sealed speedometer, calibrated both before and after the trap. Nevertheless, Woodcock was called to give expert evidence when a sceptical member of the public queried the accuracy of the equipment. John had little difficulty — especially when it came to describing the 'Doppler effect' — in confounding, or confusing magistrate, counsel and accused with some highly scientific descriptions. He concluded his evidence with the telling words, 'you fly in airplanes which depend on equipment similar to this, yet you will not concede its efficiency when it comes to measuring your vehicle speed'.

Woodcock, to whom the author is indebted for a valiant attempt to clarify the mystical world of radio, left the police on gratuity in 1962. His was yet another case where the authorities of at that time preferred to throw away invaluable technical expertise rather than reward such knowledge with promotion to commissioned rank. Woodcock was to retire from the army with the rank of major. His position in the police was ably taken by Ray Rausch who, on retirement in 1976 — for very much the same reasons as saw Woodcock resign, — was succeeded by Stuart Wood. Wood went on to become Staff Officer (Signals) in the post-Independence era.

By 1969, all the police HF and SSB equipment had been modified to operate on both upper and lower side bands which meant that the operating capacity of long range communications had been doubled. By that year, police were sending suitable young men for training as radio mechanics to the Ministry of Posts Engineering College. Later years would see the use of the Salisbury Polytechnic combined with 'in house' tuition at the Laboratory, the former providing the technical, the latter the practical aspect.

As time went on there came a gradual modernisation of equipment as and when funds — and the evading of sanctions — allowed. The Research Laboratory continued to make increasingly intricate modifications, saving currency as well as voted expenditure and often proving the 'home grown' articles were superior to those from overseas. The 'Lab' made a point of checking all new equipment which was received, so making sure that outside stations received only tested, quality apparatus. Lattice-type self-supporting masts were introduced to improve VHF coverage in district areas and many police reservists were to be found manning those relay stations not remotely controlled.

By 1972, the communications network embraced the CID and Special Branch headquarters as well as the Army and Air Force headquarters; technicians were now assisting Special Branch with their high security work and the Staff Officer (Signals), though ostensibly responsible to the Quartermaster, was very much running his own show.

The amount of radio traffic was increasing year by year and the conversion of all police provinces from four-channel to ten-channel operation on the UHF (high frequency channels) was becoming necessary to avoid the 'clogging up' taking place.

In 1977, an UHF system was installed in Salisbury Province to supplement the extensive VHF system. This operated with pocket transceivers through repeater stations and provided a reliable communications link for policemen who had to operate in high-rise buildings, in lifts or underground parking areas. As with most communications improvements, a system started in Salisbury would be extended to other appropriate areas as soon as funds allowed.

By 1979, the Commissioner was able to announce that all police VHF equipment (mobile, base sets and walkie-talkies) was being locally manufactured. The principle firms involved were WRS and Supersonic. The only imported items were in the UHF and SSB (HF) range. Allum added that police had provided all the links between polling stations during the (April) election. This, in fact, merely confirmed a situation that had pertained for years. Police had always assisted during election periods and had also always been willing to loan equipment for various exploration expeditions by scholars and others.

The writer has not searched with any particular diligence through the introductory remarks in the Commissioner's annual reports for comment on the Signals Branch. Nevertheless, a cursory reading reveals that other than for the informed contributions written by the concerned staff officer, which appear within the main text, any references are sadly lacking. This is not, it is suggested, a fault of omission but rather that the world of diodes and transistors, high frequency, wavebands and valves was as foreign to most commissioners of police as to this author. It is therefore with particularly grateful thanks that the assistance of ex-Chief Superintendent Stuart Wood is acknowledged.

No survey of the Signals Branch would be complete without some reference to the staff officers who 'drove' the Branch over the years from 1940. Assistant Commissioner Dick Parry was the man who carried out much of the foundation work (in conjunction with PRAW, he was responsible also for the Homestead Identification Scheme). The 'father' of the Branch was Charles 'Lofty' Plastow who retired with the rank of chief superintendent in 1967; then came David Morgan and finally, within the compass of this history, Stan Browning.

The last three were pre- or post war attestees to the Force who had absorbed their knowledge in the 1939 to 1945 era. It must be said that every one of them was slightly handicapped by a lack of in-depth technical expertise. But each was able to convince senior officers and civil servants of the need for additional, highly technical equipment, mainly because none of those officials had the knowledge to question the police requirements. As a result the Signals Vote, within the Police Estimates of Expenditure, sailed through virtually unquestioned.  However, the lack of technical 'know how' did cause an unfortunate schism between, let us call them the operators and the 'boffins' but it is to the credit of all concerned that the very real divisions did not spill over to become a serious issue.

The Police Signals Branch, its equipment and those who maintained and operated it, never let the Force down and were the envy of the security forces during the years of the bush war.

```
PAGE 3 RBVDFA 058 C O N F I D E N T I A L
BRAVO TWO
NTR.

ALFA THREE
(1) CONTACT
AT 210300B AT UB 546 816 (CHIBWITI TTL) ELMB 1RR INITIATED
AMBUSH ON UNKNOWN NO CTS. ONE CT KILLED. FOL WPNS RECt
PPBH (3155) PPBH (959). NFTR.

(2) FF DEPL
AT 211100B AT UB 810 839 (MABOBO TTL) ELMB 1RR SIGHTED CT  SENTRY.
FFE (2 CDO 1 RLI) DEPL. NO CTS LOC. NFTR.

(3) FF DEPL
AT 211310B AT UB 562 406 (CHEBA PL) ELMB BB SIGHTED GP
OF CTS. FFE ( 2 CDO 1 RLI) DEPL. NO CTS LOC. NFTR.
ALFA FOUR
(1)     MIP
    AT 210130B AT UB 633 108 (MADZIWA MINE-SHAMVA) 5 IAMLA CTS
EXPL DEVICE IN COMPRESSOR ROOM CAUSING EXTENSIVE DAMAGE. SPOOR
FOL SHORT DIST WHERE LOST ON TARMAC. NFTR.
```

# APPENDIX 2

## PREFACE TO BSAP NOMINAL ROLL

The following summarises the situation which may cause some problems in understanding the peculiarities of regimental numbering during the 1890's:

Between 1889 and 1903 there existed a confusion of organisations, all of which were charged with looking after peace and law and order in the new Colony — a colony it should be emphasised lacking any real communication network and peopled by a handful of colonisers living cheek by jowl with a fairly antagonistic and eventually very militant, but not numerically great, African population. On top of this was the additional complexity that authority and orders came from the High Commissioner — mountains, valleys, plains, and miles away — in Cape Town.

Some of these organisations reserved their efforts for the two most populous towns, Salisbury and Bulawayo; others had a broader scope.

It is essential though to recognise and acknowledge the 'frontier-like' condition of the land, the vast distances between most centres of population and the resentment that emanated from the local peoples who were suddenly confronted by hosts of white men intent on appropriating the land and bringing to a rural people the dubious benefits of an alien civilisation.

The Pioneer Column and its guardians, the BSA Company's Police, had assembled in Mafeking, moved from Bechuanaland to consolidate at Macloutsie, marched-on to Tuli on the banks of the Shashe River and then, skirting the Kingdom of Lobengula or Matabeleland, advanced through Fort Victoria to Salisbury.

Many of the police who marched and rode with the Column had been drawn from the five-year-old Bechuanaland Border Police and a tenuous link existed between that Force and the soon to be created Mashonaland Mounted Police.

Events were to dictate the various police and defence units formed during the 12 or 13 years from 1890 – events such as the invasion of Lobengula's kingdom, the Jameson Raid, the rebellions in Matabeleland and Mashonaland and, eventually, the Anglo-Boer War. There was more than a little confusion in the recording of personnel records as one force began and another took over and oft times men — influenced by personal circumstances and conditions — moved from one to the other, with little or no regard for the historians who would endeavour to untangle their actions and record their movements a century or more later.

Thus we have the Mashonaland Mounted Police, the volunteer Mashonaland Horse and the Mashonaland Constabulary. Centred further south was the Matabeleland Mounted Police, the Matabeleland Native Police and the Matabeleland Constabulary. Into the picture came the Rhodesia Horse Volunteers and other short-lived units like the Rhodesia Mounted Police. And then, out of all this came the Southern Rhodesia Constabulary which, in 1909, was to merge into the already created British South Africa Police, itself at one time with Divisions in Bechuanaland, Mashonaland, Matabeleland and North Zambezi.

It is, perhaps, an example of the historian's nightmare that although the BSAP title was officially recorded on 22 August 1898, the Force, under that name, had existed since, certainly, late December of 1896. Another, but no means final complication must be that the Matabeleland and Mashonaland Mounted Police were formally integrated on 1 October 1896.

One 'simple' example of the complexity surrounding the numbering should suffice:

Regimental number 1 in the BSA Police is Allan Wight. He is recorded as No. 2206 in the Matabeleland Division of the BSAP, attesting on 25 August 1896. He transferred to the Mashonaland Division of the BSAP on a date unknown but was given the number 331 and shown as attested on 25 August 1896. His attestation in the BSAP remains, 25 August 1896. In a quirky way, it does make sense!

Ken and Dorothy Standford-Smith have spent long hours of dedicated and frustrating time weaving their way through this complex tapestry of the names and regimental numbers of that tumultuous period. That any semblance of cohesion has at last emerged is due to their untiring efforts, persistent research and personal dedication.

| No. | Surname | First Names | Attested | Rank on discharge |
|---|---|---|---|---|
| 1 | WIGHT | Allan | 25.08.1896 | |
| 2 | RIBBANDS | Stephen Edgar | 28.08.1896 | |
| 3 | DANIELL | William Tuthill | 06.10.1896 | |
| 4 | COOKE | Charles Edwin | 10.10.1896 | |
| 5 | FIRMINGER | Ronald | 10.10.1896 | |
| 6 | FLOWERS | John | 12.10.1896 | |
| 7 | EYRE | Annesley | 28.10.1896 | |
| 8 | SMITH | Lionel Ross | 28.10.1896 | |
| 9 | BEALE | William | 01.11.1896 | |
| 10 | BODLE | John Ernest | 01.11.1896 | |
| 11 | DE LEGH | William Owen | 01.11.1896 | Lt. |
| 12 | GREEN | George | 01.11.1896 | |
| 13 | JOHNSON | George | 01.11.1896 | |
| 14 | KYLE | William Rodger | 01.11.1896 | |
| 15 | PENDER | John Stewart | 01.11.1896 | Lt. |
| 16 | HANSON | William Arthur | 05.11.1896 | |
| 17 | DACOMB | Leonard Sydney | 13.11.1896 | L/Col |
| 18 | THORNTON | George James | 25.11.1896 | Major |
| 19 | ISHERWOOD | Oswald James | 07.12.1896 | |
| 20 | BLATHERWICK | James Kincaid | 01.12.1896 | RSM |
| 21 | MUSHER | Edward | 29.11.1896 | |
| 22 | JOHNSTONE | Tom Robert | 03.07.1894 | |
| 23 | EDWARDS | Sidney Herbert | 23.12.1896 | |
| 24 | HERRINGTON | James | 23.12.1896 | |
| 25 | HONEY | George | 23.12.1896 | T/S/Maj |
| 26 | McMANUS | John | 22.02.1897 | |
| 27 | DINGWALL | Kenneth | 29.03.1897 | |
| 28 | McMILLAN | Robert | 29.03.1897 | |
| 29 | MILLER | Albert | 29.03.1897 | |
| 30 | DUMARESQ | Rawlings | 11.04.1897 | Capt. |
| 31 | BLYTH | Frederick Thomas | 28.04.1897 | |
| 32 | TILLEY | Colin Gibson | 28.04.1897 | |
| 33 | TILLEY | Thomas H. | 28.04.1897 | |
| 34 | PITT-SCHENKLE | Charles Edward | 01.05.1897 | Major |
| 35 | STANELY | Daniel McNee | 28.05.1897 | |
| 36 | MOLLER | Henry Peter | 14.06.1897 | |
| 37 | LA MONT | Dean | 03.10.1897 | |
| 38 | GEARY | Francis Joseph | 08.10.1897 | |
| 39 | HOLERT | Thomas | 21.10.1897 | |
| 40 | REEVES | William Henry | 22.10.1897 | |
| 41 | MILLER | Charles | 24.10.1897 | |
| 42 | FOULDS | Walter | 12.11.1897 | Sgt. |
| 43 | MARTIN | Henry James | 13.11.1897 | |
| 44 | MUIR | Charles Dormic | 13.11.1897 | |
| 45 | HOLMES | Louris | 13.11.1897 | |
| 46 | SNELLING | Frank Hounslow | 13.11.1897 | |
| 47 | BISHOP | Alfred | 13.11.1897 | |
| 48 | HAY | John | 26.11.1897 | |
| 49 | THOMAS | Alexander Harford | 12.12.1897 | |
| 50 | SMITH | Ralph Gordon | 07.02.1898 | |
| 51 | BIRBECK | William | 07.02.1898 | |
| 52 | YOUNG | Charles | 17.02.1898 | |
| 53 | REEVES | James | 17.02.1898 | |
| 54 | ROGERS | Edwin | 20.02.1898 | |
| 55 | CHARTER | Charles Edward | 06.03.1898 | |
| 56 | WALTERSTORFF | Johann Albert | 13.03.1898 | |
| 57 | HERBERT | Thomas Albert | 15.02.1898 | |
| 58 | BROERS | Jean Cambier | 14.03.1898 | |
| 59 | SHETTLE | Frederick George | 29.03.1898 | |
| 60 | GRANT | Frank | 29.05.1898 | |
| 61 | SMITH | Nathan | 29.03.1898 | |
| 62 | GIBBERD | John Alfred | 30.03.1898 | |
| 63 | MacDONALD | Archibald | 30.03.1898 | |
| 64 | HINDS | James | 03.04.1898 | |
| 65 | BALE | John | 19.04.1898 | |
| 66 | WOOD | John Hastings | 25.06.1898 | |
| 67 | BESLEY | Frederick Simmons | 07.08.1898 | |
| 68 | COOPER | Richard Clive | 17.08.1898 | |
| 69 | IRONSIDE | William | 30.08.1898 | |
| 70 | SKINNER | George Frederick | 12.09.1898 | |
| 71 | CROSS | Albert John | 01.10.1898 | |
| 72 | SCOTT | Arthur Edgar | 01.10.1898 | |
| 73 | CURTIN | Andrew | 13.11.1898 | |
| 74 | DOBBYN | Thomas | 23.11.1898 | |
| 75 | CHALMERS | Charles Henry | 07.12.1898 | |
| 76 | COE | Arthur | 03.01.1899 | |
| 77 | BRUCE | David | 07.02.1899 | |
| 78 | JOHNSON | Edwin Gilbert | 17.02.1899 | |
| 79 | SPENCE | Magnus | 05.04.1899 | |
| 80 | TOWNSEND | Charles | 26.04.1898 | Sgt. |
| 81 | THACHARA | James | 01.05.1899 | 1st.Sgt |
| 82 | SYMONS | Reginald Charles | 08.05.1899 | |
| 83 | LUNHAM | James | 15.05.1899 | |
| 84 | MARRIOTT | Thomas | 17.05.1899 | |
| 85 | ARMFIELD | Archer Seward | 24.05.1899 | |
| 86 | BAINES | Edward | 26.05.1899 | |
| 87 | GALLACHER | Peter Joseph | 07.06.1899 | |
| 88 | RIX | Charles Spelman | 08.06.1899 | |
| 89 | HENDERSON | Richard | 28.06.1899 | |
| 90 | MARSHALL | James | 03.07.1899 | |
| 91 | MOORE | George | 04.07.1899 | |
| 92 | MURRAY | John William | 20.07.1899 | |
| 93 | BROWN | James | 26.07.1899 | |
| 94 | EARLE | Herbert | 30.07.1899 | |
| 95 | EATON | Leopold Wilson | 17.08.1899 | |
| 96 | ROLLSTON | Frederick Vivian | 18.08.1899 | |
| 97 | WILLIAMS | Thomas Lloyd | 19.08.1899 | |
| 98 | ATKINSON | Thomas | 23.08.1899 | |
| 99 | LEIGH | Charles James | 30.08.1899 | |
| 100 | PRESTON | Ernest Edward | 30.08.1899 | |
| 101 | GREER | John Gordon | 09.11.1899 | |
| 102 | GREAVES | William Charles | 10.10.1899 | |
| 103 | WOOD | William | 10.10.1899 | |
| 104 | KERRY | Edward Eglinton | 12.10.1899 | |
| 105 | LUPTON | Matthew Henry | 01.11.1899 | |
| 106 | SLATER | Henry Herbert | 12.12.1899 | |
| 107 | FRANCIS | Morris Deane | 29.05.1900 | |
| 108 | BUDD | Ralph | 03.07.1900 | |
| 109 | CRAIGIE | Frederick William | 11.07.1900 | |
| 110 | KING | Harry | 13.07.1900 | |
| 111 | Mac QUALTER | Stephen Albert | 13.07.1900 | |
| 112 | BLANE | Henry Herbert | 23.07.1900 | |
| 113 | HUNDLEY | Oswald | 31.07.1900 | |
| 114 | STOKES | John Edward | 04.09.1900 | |
| 115 | LAING | James | 04.09.1900 | |
| 116 | EVES | John James | 07.09.1900 | |
| 117 | FITZGERALD | John Moore | 17.09.1900 | |
| 118 | MORTON | Reginald S.L. | 14.09.1900 | |
| 119 | YATES | James William | 14.09.1900 | |
| 120 | PIM | William Charles | 25.10.1900 | |
| 121 | KENNEDY | James Francis | 12.05.1901 | |
| 122 | HOUGH | Gilbert Samuel | 12.05.1901 | |
| 123 | ROGERS | Fredrick Charles | 12.05.1901 | Supt. |
| 124 | TALBOT | Francis Biddulph | 12.05.1901 | |
| 125 | WILSON | Thomas | 12.05.1901 | |
| 126 | DORESA | Hector | 12.05.1901 | |
| 127 | BOWMAN | William Edward | 12.05.1901 | |
| 128 | SYMONDS | Edward Allen | 12.05.1901 | |
| 129 | MARSH | Arthur Colin | 12.05.1901 | |
| 130 | WYATT | Percy Robert | 12.05.1901 | |
| 131 | GOMM | Charles Marryat | 12.05.1901 | |
| 132 | JOHNSON | George Harold | 12.05.1901 | |
| 133 | NASH | Albert Sydney | 26.05.1901 | |
| 134 | GODFREY | William Henry | 26.05.1901 | |
| 135 | GARTON | Frederick | 26.05.1901 | |
| 136 | RAFFIN | Alfred | 26.05.1901 | |
| 137 | BURKE | Frederick Charles | 26.05.1901 | Capt. |
| 138 | WESTWOOD | Sidney Henry | 26.05.1901 | |
| 139 | COOKE | Thomas | 26.05.1901 | |
| 140 | HEWLETT | William | 26.05.1901 | |
| 141 | JOHNSON | William | 26.05.1901 | |
| 142 | DURRETT | Frank | 26.05.1901 | |
| 143 | DAWES | William Henry | 26.05.1901 | |
| 144 | PINKERTON | Arthur Claude | 26.05.1901 | |
| 145 | KENDLE | Edward James | 04.06.1901 | |
| 146 | COCKERHAM | Arthur | 04.06.1901 | |
| 147 | SIMPSON | William Edward | 04.06.1901 | |
| 148 | CHALLEN | William | 04.06.1901 | |
| 149 | THOMAS | Frederick | 04.06.1901 | |
| 150 | BEIRNE | Thomas Francis | 04.06.1901 | |
| 151 | WHITE | Henry | 04.06.1901 | |
| 152 | PATTEN | Robert | 04.06.1901 | |
| 153 | NEVE | Percy George | 04.06.1901 | |
| 154 | HOOTEN | Frederick | 12.06.1901 | |
| 155 | BLAND | Samuel Patrick | 18.06.1901 | |
| 156 | SMITH | Albert Edward | 18.06.1901 | |
| 157 | WATERS | Thomas William | 18.06.1901 | |
| 158 | GODDARD | Eric Lidderdale | 18.06.1901 | |
| 159 | MILLARD | Havelock James | 18.06.1901 | |
| 160 | EVANS | George Alfred | 18.06.1901 | |
| 161 | SMITH | Victor Melville | 18.06.1901 | |
| 162 | THOMAS | William Edgard | 18.06.1901 | |
| 163 | DUDLEY | Arthur Darville | 18.06.1901 | |
| 164 | FORD | William Henry | 18.06.1901 | |
| 165 | NEWMAN | Percy Vyvyan | 18.06.1901 | |
| 166 | DORCHESTER | Frank Edwin | 18.06.1901 | |
| 167 | BRAIN | William | 21.06.1901 | |
| 168 | GATER | Frederick John | 21.06.1901 | |
| 169 | GODDARD | James | 03.07.1901 | |
| 170 | BRIDGES | William | 22.07.1901 | |
| 171 | LEONARD | Francis Adolphus | 18.07.1901 | |
| 172 | LANG | Alexander | 18.07.1901 | |
| 173 | MYERS | Neil | 18.07.1901 | |
| 174 | McPHERSON | John | 18.07.1901 | |
| 175 | Mac QUEEN | James | 18.07.1901 | |
| 176 | HENDERSON | George | 18.07.1901 | |
| 177 | MICHIE | George D. | 18.07.1901 | |
| 178 | MONRO | Steen | 18.07.1901 | |
| 179 | McLACHLAN | Stewart | 18.07.1901 | |
| 180 | SMITH | James | 18.07.1901 | |
| 181 | CAMERON | William Thomas | 18.07.1901 | Lt. |
| 182 | WHITTON | David Buick | 18.07.1901 | |
| 183 | MOORE | Thomas | 18.07.1901 | |
| 184 | DAVIDSON | Andrew | 18.07.1901 | |
| 185 | McLAREN | John | 18.07.1901 | |
| 186 | MELDRUM | George Henry | 18.07.1901 | |
| 187 | MUTCH | Charles Porter | 18.07.1901 | |
| 188 | SILVER | John | 18.07.1901 | |
| 189 | McKENZIE | Seaton Dobbie | 18.07.1901 | |
| 190 | PROUDFOOT | John | 18.07.1901 | |
| 191 | FRASER | Thomas | 18.07.1901 | |
| 192 | McGARRY | Charles | 18.07.1901 | |
| 193 | WILSON | John | 18.07.1901 | |
| 194 | CROZIER | Adam | 18.07.1901 | |
| 195 | PATERSON | John | 18.07.1901 | |
| 196 | PICKEN | George | 18.07.1901 | |
| 197 | ALEXANDER | Patrick | 18.07.1901 | |
| 198 | BRENNAN | William | 18.07.1901 | |
| 199 | STEWART | Samuel Harrison | 18.07.1901 | |
| 200 | ARNOLD | Robert Lawrence | 21.07.1901 | |
| 201 | SISSON | William Brownrigg | 21.07.1901 | |
| 202 | THOMPSON | John William | 22.07.1901 | Trp. |
| 203 | SPENCER | Ernest | 22.07.1901 | |
| 204 | REDHEAD | Arthur Charles | 22.07.1901 | |
| 205 | CASEY | | 22.07.1901 | |

# BSAP Nominal Roll • Men

| No. | Surname | First Name(s) | Rank | Date |
|---|---|---|---|---|
| 206 | LOADES | William Arthur | | 22.07.1901 |
| 207 | AMBROSE | Edmund James | | 22.07.1901 |
| 208 | ANDERSON | William Cussworth | | 22.07.1901 |
| 209 | VIRGIN | Thomas | | 22.07.1901 |
| 210 | KERR | Harry Douglas | | 22.07.1901 |
| 211 | LAWRENCE | Walter | Supt. | 22.07.1901 |
| 212 | BAILEY | Albert Raymond | | 22.07.1901 |
| 213 | RICHARDSON | Gerald Harry | | 22.07.1901 |
| 214 | MUSGRAVE | Henry Lawrence | | 06.08.1901 |
| 215 | JOHNSTON | Albert | | 06.08.1901 |
| 216 | WILLIAMS | Edwin Ambrose | | 06.08.1901 |
| 217 | LESTER | James | | 06.08.1901 |
| 218 | TAYLOR | Henry Alban | | 06.08.1901 |
| 219 | KNOTT | Henry Gordon | | 06.08.1901 |
| 220 | PERKINS | William James | | 06.08.1901 |
| 221 | PHILLIPS | Percy Alexander | H/Maj. | 06.08.1901 |
| 222 | FRIZELLE | Christopher Ewart | | 06.08.1901 |
| 223 | JEFFREYS | George Stanley | | 06.08.1901 |
| 224 | POTTER | Edgar Fridulph | | 06.08.1901 |
| 225 | SCOTT | William Ellor | | 06.08.1901 |
| 226 | TAYLOR | Harry Frank | | 06.08.1901 |
| 227 | CORNICK | Frederick Charles | | 06.08.1901 |
| 228 | WHITE | Arthur Edward | | 06.08.1901 |
| 229 | WENHAM | Stanley Robert | | 06.08.1901 |
| 230 | BRYANT | John David | Tpr. | 19.09.1901 |
| 231 | EDWARDS | Percy Edward | | 17.10.1901 |
| 232 | THOMAS | Harold | Tpr. | 31.10.1901 |
| 233 | WEBB | Samuel George | | 31.10.1901 |
| 234 | TURNER | John Alexander | | 01.11.1901 |
| 235 | FUBBS | William | | 01.11.1901 |
| 236 | COWIE | John Edward | | 01.11.1901 |
| 237 | HOLDSWORTH | John Blamires | | 01.11.1901 |
| 238 | CRAIG | David | | 01.11.1901 |
| 239 | DIXON | Robert James | | 01.11.1901 |
| 240 | BRAMBACK | Frank Percy | | 01.11.1901 |
| 241 | LOGAN | Richard | | 01.11.1901 |
| 242 | SCOTT | Herbert William | | 05.11.1901 |
| 243 | COMBEN | Edwin Gulliver | | 08.11.1901 |
| 244 | BECKETT | Benjamin Disraeli | | 16.11.1901 |
| 245 | CLARKE | Martin Joseph | | 16.11.1901 |
| 246 | HOLMDEN | George | | 30.11.1901 |
| 247 | HOATH | George Lewis | | 07.12.1901 |
| 248 | WOODHOUSE | John | | 01.01.1902 |
| 249 | KNIGHT | Gilbert Kennedy | | 11.01.1902 |
| 250 | MOORE | Henry Michael | | 17.02.1902 |
| 251 | BROWNE | Samuel Ruben | Lieut. | 17.02.1902 |
| 252 | BLACKLEY | John Adam | | 28.02.1902 |
| 253 | PRIDGEON | Joseph | | 31.03.1902 |
| 254 | BROOKES | Michael | | 31.03.1902 |
| 255 | DENN | Walter Andrew | | 17.04.1902 |
| 256 | WILLIAMS | Joseph Alexander | | 11.04.1902 |
| 257 | CAMPBELL | Lindsay Christopher | | 11.05.1902 |
| 258 | OGILVY | Morley | | 25.04.1902 |
| 259 | NESBITT | Ormonde | | 11.05.1902 |
| 260 | HEATH | Jesse | | 26.05.1902 |
| 261 | PAYNE | James | | 05.06.1902 |
| 262 | TEDD | Frank | | 21.06.1902 |
| 263 | HARRIS | Frederick William | | 21.06.1902 |
| 264 | GILBERT | Edgar | | 21.06.1902 |
| 265 | KENT | Robert Walter | | 21.06.1902 |
| 266 | NIBLETT | Frederick Lawrence | | 21.06.1902 |
| 267 | DIVES | Wallace Jugurtha | | 21.06.1902 |
| 268 | DIVES | William Arthur | | 21.06.1902 |
| 269 | RACK | Richard Granville | | 21.06.1902 |
| 270 | YOUNG | Thomas Henry | | 21.06.1902 |
| 271 | LUDGATER | William Arthur | | 21.06.1902 |
| 272 | THYNE | Richard Granville | | 21.06.1902 |
| 273 | SPANTON | Thomas Henry | | 21.06.1902 |
| 275 | VARNEY | Francis George | | 21.06.1902 |
| 276 | PREWETT | George William | | 21.06.1902 |
| 277 | AKERS | George Edward | | 21.06.1902 |
| 278 | BERRY | Robert | | 21.06.1902 |
| 279 | WHARTON | George | | 21.06.1902 |
| 280 | FISHER | Alder Heffill | | 21.06.1902 |
| 281 | CHALLEN | Percy George | | 21.06.1902 |
| 282 | ERRINGTON | George | | 21.06.1902 |
| 283 | HEWETT | Wilfred Brownlow | | 21.06.1902 |
| 284 | WOOTON | Sydney | | 21.06.1902 |
| 285 | ANDREW | Charles Stafford | | 21.06.1902 |
| 286 | SKEET | Roland George | | 21.06.1902 |
| 287 | WEAR | Harry Leslie | | 21.06.1902 |
| 288 | FREEHILL | Albert Walter | | 21.06.1902 |
| 289 | WIGHT | Alexander | | 21.06.1902 |
| 290 | TEDDER | Joseph Edward | | 21.06.1902 |
| 291 | BAILEY | Garnet Sidney | | 21.06.1902 |
| 292 | JAMES | Francis Stafford | | 21.06.1902 |
| 293 | JOEL | Harry George | | 21.06.1902 |
| 294 | SHAPCOTT | Frank | | 21.06.1902 |
| 295 | NEW | Vernon Arthur | | 21.06.1902 |
| 296 | BOYES | John | | 06.07.1902 |
| 297 | INGARFIELD | George John | | 06.07.1902 |
| 298 | GOUCHER | John Wheelock | | 06.07.1902 |
| 299 | GOUCHER | Walter Ring | | 06.07.1902 |
| 300 | LANE | Percy Ernald | | 06.07.1902 |
| 301 | TWEEDY | Herbert John | | 06.07.1902 |
| 302 | WICKWAR | Francis Thomas | | 06.07.1902 |
| 303 | BROWN | Frank | | 06.07.1902 |
| 304 | NOAKES | Charles Edward | | 06.07.1902 |
| 305 | RANSLEY | Frederick James | | 06.07.1902 |
| 306 | LEE | Harry | | 06.07.1902 |
| 307 | PAXTON | Richard St Augustine | | 11.07.1902 |
| 308 | DENT | John | | 11.07.1902 |
| 309 | SMITH | Nicol McCallum | | 11.07.1902 |
| 310 | SAUNDERS | Frank | | 11.07.1902 |
| 311 | WILSON | Ashley Henry | | 11.07.1902 |
| 312 | GILMOUR | Alexander | | 11.07.1902 |
| 313 | WATSON | Robert | | 11.07.1902 |
| 314 | SAUNDERS | Frederick Albert | | 11.07.1902 |
| 315 | CARTER | Harry | | 11.07.1902 |
| 316 | HODSDON | Edwin | | 11.07.1902 |
| 317 | MAYER | Harry | | 15.07.1902 |
| 318 | RODBARD | Edward | | 19.07.1902 |
| 319 | MONGER | William Wigmore | | 19.07.1902 |
| 320 | COOPER | Richard Robert | | 19.07.1902 |
| 321 | ABBOTT | William | | 19.07.1902 |
| 322 | SHANKS | John | | 19.07.1902 |
| 323 | RODGERS | Hugh | | 19.07.1902 |
| 324 | ROBINSON | Thomas | | 21.07.1902 |
| 325 | MANN | Robert | | 21.07.1902 |
| 326 | CROSS | Bertram | | 21.07.1902 |
| 327 | BURNS | John | | 22.07.1902 |
| 328 | WOOD | William | | 22.07.1902 |
| 329 | LEWIS | William Francis | | 22.07.1902 |
| 330 | WHITMILL | Ernest | | 24.07.1902 |
| 331 | THRAVES | James William | | 24.07.1902 |
| 332 | McLOGHLIN | William George | | 24.07.1902 |
| 333 | POTTS | Geoffrey Cecil | | 24.07.1902 |
| 334 | GOURLAY | John Skea | | 25.07.1902 |
| 335 | BAXTER | Francis Joseph | | 31.07.1902 |
| 336 | MAY | Stanley Lionel | | 31.07.1902 |
| 337 | HENDERSON | Charles Thomas | | 31.07.1902 |
| 338 | WHITEHEAD | Frederick Charles | | 31.07.1902 |
| 339 | HOWE | Arthur | | 31.07.1902 |
| 340 | BOULTBEE | Edward Frederick | | 31.07.1902 |
| 341 | BEVAN | William Francis | | 31.07.1902 |
| 342 | STANDEN | Leonard | | 31.07.1902 |
| 344 | RAMSEY | Percy Robert | | 31.07.1902 |
| 345 | BALL | George William | | 31.07.1902 |
| 346 | SAXTON | William Edward | | 31.07.1902 |
| 347 | GOODE | Douglas | | 31.07.1902 |
| 348 | GURNEY | Alfred Harold | | 31.07.1902 |
| 349 | TOMBS | Benjamin Disraeli | | 31.07.1902 |
| 350 | WREY-WATHEN | William | | 31.07.1902 |
| 351 | PLOWRIGHT | William George | | 31.07.1902 |
| 352 | CRAB | Alfred Abraham | | 31.07.1902 |
| 353 | STONE | Robert William | | 31.07.1902 |
| 354 | EASTWOOD | Charles Darce | | 04.08.1902 |
| 355 | DRUMMOND | Henry | | 15.08.1902 |
| 356 | RICHARDS | Harry | | 20.08.1902 |
| 357 | HULL | Edward James | | 29.08.1902 |
| 358 | AYRES | David | | 29.08.1902 |
| 359 | SANDERSON | Joseph | | 29.08.1902 |
| 360 | ANTOINE | Theophile Joseph | | 29.08.1902 |
| 361 | McDONALD | Charles | | 29.08.1902 |
| 362 | GOMAN | Harry | | 29.08.1902 |
| 363 | ALLEN | George Alfred | | 29.08.1902 |
| 364 | BECK | Frank Walker | | 29.08.1902 |
| 365 | GOODYEAR | Frederick John | 1st.Sgt | 31.08.1902 |
| 366 | RUGGE | Herbert Stanley | | 31.08.1902 |
| 367 | TURNER | Francis Bowley | | 01.09.1902 |
| 368 | BAYLIFFE | Leonard Frederick | | 01.09.1902 |
| 369 | JOHNSTON | Robert | | 01.09.1902 |
| 370 | MAY | William | | 01.09.1902 |
| 371 | ALLEN | James | | 01.09.1902 |
| 372 | LACKFORD | George William | | 01.09.1902 |
| 373 | McCONNELL | Andrew | | 01.09.1902 |
| 374 | RABBETTS | William | | 01.09.1902 |
| 375 | DONALDSON | Joseph | | 01.09.1902 |
| 376 | POWELL | Sydney Walter | | 05.09.1902 |
| 377 | WIGHT | Philip Francis | | 05.09.1902 |
| 378 | EVANS | William James | | 05.09.1902 |
| 379 | HANNAFORD | Edward | | 05.09.1902 |
| 380 | CARR | George | | 05.09.1902 |
| 381 | THOMSON | James | | 05.09.1902 |
| 382 | ROWAN | James | | 05.09.1902 |
| 383 | ALEXANDER | John | | 05.09.1902 |
| 384 | SCOTT | John Colvin | | 05.09.1902 |
| 385 | JONES | Albert | | 05.09.1902 |
| 386 | LAWSON | Alfred | | 05.09.1902 |
| 387 | RUHL | Harry Walter | | 05.09.1902 |
| 388 | STANDAGE | Charles | | 05.09.1902 |
| 389 | ARMITAGE | Robert | | 09.09.1902 |
| 390 | BROTHERTON | John | | 15.09.1902 |
| 391 | POTGEITER | Donald | | 17.09.1902 |
| 392 | CAMERON | Sidney Philip | | 27.09.1904 |
| 393 | LUTTRELL | Frederick | | 01.10.1902 |
| 394 | LEWIS | Harry Drummond | | 01.10.1902 |
| 395 | MONK | George | | 01.10.1902 |
| 396 | DE KUYPER | Charles Henry | | 01.10.1902 |
| 397 | FAIR | Henry Edward | | 01.10.1902 |
| 398 | STEWARD | Thomas Reid | | 01.10.1902 |
| 399 | DE GWERIN | John Edward | | 03.10.1902 |
| 400 | BREWER | Lucius Knapp | | 03.10.1902 |
| 401 | ROBINSON | Ashmead | | 06.10.1902 |
| 402 | BARTLETT | William | | 08.10.1902 |
| 403 | DOWNES | Alexander | | 08.10.1902 |
| 404 | MARTIN | William | | 08.10.1902 |
| 405 | THOMSON | Harry | | 08.10.1902 |
| 406 | WORTH | Charles Edward | | 15.10.1902 |
| 407 | WALKER | Charles Patrick | | 15.10.1902 |
| 408 | ELLEGETT | Horace Edward | | 17.10.1902 |
| 409 | RAMSDEN | Charles Kenneth | | 20.10.1902 |
| 410 | CAINE | William Ernest | Lt. | 20.10.1902 |
| 411 | HUNT | John Henry | Cpl. | 13.11.1902 |
| 412 | WHALEN | | | |

| No. | Surname | First Name(s) | Date | Rank |
|---|---|---|---|---|
| 413 | SPEARS | James | 25.11.1902 | |
| 414 | ORGAN | William | 25.11.1902 | |
| 415 | KEENE | James | 25.11.1902 | |
| 416 | ROLLS-RICHARDSON | John Osborne | 25.11.1902 | Lt. |
| 417 | SIMPSON | Hector Joseph | 27.11.1902 | |
| 418 | CULLEN | Albert | 29.11.1902 | |
| 419 | TURNER | Harry | 02.12.1902 | |
| 420 | DEAKIN | Ernest James | 02.12.1902 | |
| 421 | JOHNSON | Herbert John | 02.12.1902 | |
| 422 | DU CHEMIN | Herbert Frederick | 02.12.1902 | |
| 423 | CRAMPIN | Horace Henry | 02.12.1902 | |
| 424 | DUDLEY | George Vernon | 02.12.1902 | |
| 425 | SPENCER | Charles Vincent | 02.12.1902 | |
| 426 | LEE | Henry | 02.12.1902 | |
| 427 | MERRY | Norman | 04.12.1902 | |
| 428 | EWENS | Bertram George | 04.12.1902 | |
| 429 | SYMONDS | Melville Carter | 06.12.1902 | |
| 430 | SEELEY | Percy Harold | 16.12.1902 | |
| 431 | BATCHELOR | George Alfred | 16.12.1902 | |
| 432 | ASHWIN | Henry William | 18.12.1902 | S/C/I |
| 433 | MONTRE | William Steven | 19.12.1902 | |
| 434 | KENT | Capel Hamilton | 23.12.1902 | |
| 435 | REILLY | George Bernard | 23.12.1902 | |
| 436 | SANGSTER | Charles Reginald | 27.12.1902 | |
| 437 | EGAN | Thomas | 02.01.1903 | |
| 438 | DAVIDSON | William Wallace | 02.01.1903 | |
| 439 | LAWRENCE | William Arthur | 08.01.1903 | |
| 440 | Mac KINNON | Donald William | 12.01.1903 | |
| 441 | McLEAN | James | 12.01.1903 | |
| 442 | SINGER | Walter Douglas | 12.01.1903 | |
| 443 | GOODLET | Alexander | 12.01.1903 | |
| 444 | BOWERS | Edward William | 14.01.1903 | |
| 445 | TICEHURST | Samuel George | 14.01.1903 | |
| 446 | GINN | Edward | 14.01.1903 | |
| 447 | SHEARMAN | Charles Stuart | 14.01.1903 | |
| 448 | DORWARD | David Edward | 16.01.1903 | |
| 449 | CLANCY | William John | 19.01.1903 | |
| 450 | KENNEDY | Frank Turner | 19.01.1903 | |
| 451 | MARKS | Harry Alfred | 19.01.1903 | |
| 452 | ALLAN | Alfred | 19.01.1903 | |
| 453 | HESFORD | Joseph | 21.01.1903 | |
| 454 | PRENTICE | Andrew | 21.01.1903 | |
| 455 | HANNING | Frederick William | 20.01.1903 | |
| 456 | SHEARER | John | 29.01.1903 | |
| 457 | KIDDLE | Edward Kerrison | 02.02.1903 | |
| 458 | CAMERON | William Bedford | 26.02.1903 | |
| 459 | BROWNE | Frederick Hamilton | 06.04.1903 | |
| 460 | BAKER | William James | 31.03.1903 | |
| 461 | RIX | Reginald Jennings | 21.04.1903 | |
| 462 | McGEE | Robert Alexander | 28.04.1903 | S/Insp |
| 463 | SIMMONDS | Earl Medhurst | 29.05.1903 | |
| 464 | BARRAND | Wells | 03.06.1903 | |
| 465 | STENNETT | Herbert | 03.06.1903 | |
| 466 | GRAY | John James | 09.06.1903 | |
| 467 | CHADWICK | William Sydney | 15.06.1903 | |
| 468 | DOUGLAS | Alexander Cummings | 17.06.1903 | |
| 469 | BLACK | Albert John | 17.06.1903 | |
| 470 | CHRISTIE | Thomas Henry | 17.06.1903 | |
| 471 | FORSHAW | Robert | 17.06.1903 | |
| 472 | BEGHIN | Paul | 17.06.1903 | Sgt. |
| 473 | TREWINNARD | Harry Arthur | 17.06.1903 | |
| 474 | CHAUNCEY | Percy Buchanan | 19.06.1903 | |
| 475 | KENNEDY | Thomas Francis | 19.06.1903 | |
| 476 | PALLISER | George Robert | 19.06.1903 | |
| 477 | PHELAN | Joseph | 19.06.1903 | |
| 478 | GOOYER | Edward Bertram | 19.06.1903 | |
| 479 | GEORGE | Laurence Frederick | 19.06.1903 | |
| 480 | BUSTIN | George | 19.06.1903 | |
| 481 | HENCHLEY | Douglas Percy | 19.06.1903 | |
| 482 | BAYLOR | Arthur Bayly | 19.06.1903 | |
| 483 | CALVERT | Charles Lancelot | 19.06.1903 | |
| 484 | HILTON | John | 19.06.1903 | |
| 485 | HOLMAN | Nicol Wallace | 19.06.1903 | |
| 486 | TALLON | Charles | 19.06.1903 | |
| 487 | POOLE | Jack Robertson | 19.06.1903 | |
| 488 | McVERNON | St. John | 22.06.1903 | |
| 489 | FRANCIS | Herbert | 19.06.1903 | |
| 490 | McDONALD | William | 22.06.1903 | |
| 491 | DILLON | James Francis | 22.06.1903 | |
| 492 | BAIRD | Charles Alfred | 19.06.1903 | |
| 493 | ASHLEY | Arthur Ernest | 01.07.1903 | |
| 494 | GILLESPIE | Emmanuel | 01.07.1903 | |
| 495 | TOWNSHEND | Albert Charles | 17.07.1903 | |
| 496 | SWAIN | George | 03.08.1903 | |
| 497 | ALLIOTT | John Alfred | 03.08.1903 | |
| 498 | BRENAN | Frederick Esmonde | 03.08.1903 | |
| 499 | WORSAM | Harold Edward | 03.08.1903 | |
| 500 | HAYES | Ronald Duncan | 21.06.1903 | |
| 501 | HODSON | Harry | 11.08.1903 | |
| 502 | BREDENBAG | Nicholas Johannes | 11.08.1903 | |
| 503 | EVANS | Richard White | 12.08.1903 | |
| 504 | LANGAN | James | 12.08.1903 | |
| 505 | BURR | Charles Frederick | 12.08.1903 | |
| 506 | DAVIS | Alexander | 14.08.1903 | |
| 507 | ATKINS | Alfred James | 14.08.1903 | |
| 508 | HARRIS | Henry Blewitt | 14.08.1903 | |
| 509 | SIMMONDS | George Aubrey | 15.08.1903 | Tpr. |
| 510 | THORNHILL | John Bensley | 24.08.1903 | |
| 511 | WILLIS | Montague | 24.08.1903 | |
| 512 | KENTISH | George | 27.08.1903 | |
| 513 | MUNNIS | Marshall Alexander | 04.09.1903 | |
| 514 | LOBB | Rollo Willis | 04.09.1903 | |
| 515 | COOKES | Cyril Chester | 09.09.1903 | |
| 516 | BROWNE | Archibald Constantine | 23.09.1903 | |
| 517 | HILL | Robert Julius | 29.09.1903 | |
| 518 | TRUSSON | Arthur | 29.09.1903 | |
| 519 | RHOADES | William Herbert | 29.09.1903 | |
| 520 | BAILEY | Edward Brett | 29.09.1903 | |
| 521 | KEMP | Ernest Aubrey | 29.09.1903 | |
| 522 | WOOD | Charles Edwin | 29.09.1903 | |
| 523 | MATTHEWS | George Henry | 29.09.1903 | |
| 524 | BARRATT | Alfred George | 29.09.1903 | |
| 525 | POLDEN | Charles | 29.09.1903 | |
| 526 | METCALFE | Harold Thomas | 29.09.1903 | |
| 527 | ROBERTS | John Granville | 29.09.1903 | |
| 528 | STENNING | Arthur Nathan | 29.09.1903 | |
| 529 | INGHAM | Francis Collier | 29.09.1903 | |
| 530 | WHALLEY | Frederick Ernest | 29.09.1903 | |
| 531 | WALLACE | Graeme Fenton | 29.09.1903 | S/Insp |
| 532 | THOMAS | Harold Bissell | 29.09.1903 | |
| 533 | HINDE | Alfred Hawkyard | 29.09.1903 | |
| 534 | McDOWELL | Rowland | 29.09.1903 | |
| 535 | SIMPSON | Samuel | 29.09.1903 | |
| 536 | HART | Cyril Frank | 29.09.1903 | |
| 537 | SMITH | Frederick Charles | 29.09.1903 | |
| 538 | KNOWLES | William Thomas | 10.10.1903 | |
| 539 | BURNE | William Robert | 09.10.1903 | |
| 540 | GAVLICK | Paul | 04.10.1903 | |
| 541 | HURD | William Henry | 23.10.1903 | |
| 542 | THOMAS | Reginald Godwin | 24.10.1903 | |
| 543 | LYONS | Stewart Gore | 24.10.1903 | |
| 544 | LEONARD | Colvin Treadway | 28.10.1903 | |
| 545 | LANE | Reginald | 29.10.1903 | |
| 546 | WALKER | John Craufurd | 29.10.1903 | |
| 547 | STENNING | Arthur James | 29.10.1903 | |
| 548 | HARRIS | George | 29.10.1903 | |
| 549 | HEATH | William | 29.10.1903 | |
| 550 | CARR | William John | 29.10.1903 | |
| 551 | GREENWELL | Ronald | 29.10.1903 | |
| 552 | WHITE | Herbert | 29.10.1903 | |
| 553 | DOLEY | Herbert Alfred | 29.10.1903 | |
| 554 | SIMS | William John | 29.10.1903 | |
| 555 | RUSSELL | John Newton | 29.10.1903 | |
| 556 | RICHARDSON | Joseph Edward | 29.10.1903 | |
| 557 | OSBORNE | Ernest Edward | 29.10.1903 | |
| 558 | ELLIS | Charles Douglas | 29.10.1903 | |
| 559 | MARRIOTT | Aubrey Prince | 29.10.1903 | |
| 560 | STEPHENS | Francis Trant | 29.10.1903 | |
| 561 | MAITLAND | William Oswald | 29.10.1903 | |
| 562 | GODDARD | Alfred Percy | 29.10.1903 | |
| 563 | ELLAM | Hugh Theodor | 29.10.1903 | |
| 564 | McPHERSON | Charles Duncan | 29.10.1903 | |
| 565 | HART | Herbert Francis | 29.10.1903 | Capt. |
| 566 | JOHNSON | Vaughan | 29.10.1903 | |
| 567 | HALE | Henry Edwin | 29.10.1903 | |
| 568 | CREAGHE | John Weldon | 29.10.1903 | |
| 569 | MANSBERG | Harry Craven | 29.10.1903 | |
| 570 | NEILLINGS | Wallace | 29.10.1903 | |
| 571 | METHVEN | Stuartson Collard | 29.10.1903 | |
| 572 | NEWCOMBE | Thomas James | 29.10.1903 | |
| 573 | WHITE | John Newport | 29.10.1903 | |
| 574 | LOWE | Charles Frederick | 30.10.1903 | |
| 575 | MITCHELL | William | 29.10.1903 | |
| 576 | PLATT | John | 30.10.1903 | |
| 577 | SHERREY | George William | 30.10.1903 | |
| 578 | WHALLEY | George | 30.10.1903 | |
| 579 | WALTON | Algernon Thomas | 30.10.1903 | |
| 580 | SAMPSON | Burford | 04.11.1903 | |
| 581 | JORDAN | William Henry | 06.11.1903 | |
| 582 | OSBORNE | Richard Peter | 10.11.1903 | |
| 583 | KROCH | Josephus Gerhardus | 17.11.1903 | |
| 584 | PENDREY | George Henry | 25.11.1903 | |
| 585 | BRUCE | Herbert Edwin | 30.11.1903 | |
| 586 | DEAN | Ernest | 30.11.1903 | |
| 587 | SMITH | William John | 07.12.1903 | |
| 588 | HUGHES-HERBERT | William Gregory | 07.12.1903 | |
| 589 | STONEHEWER | Richard Sealy | 12.12.1903 | |
| 590 | SANDERS | George Frederick | 23.12.1903 | |
| 591 | TERRY | William Percy | 09.12.1903 | |
| 592 | LAVIN | Harry | 06.01.1904 | |
| 593 | WANE | Francis John | 12.01.1904 | |
| 594 | HARRIS | John Stuart | 25.01.1904 | |
| 595 | ANDREWS | Joseph Hodder | 27.01.1904 | |
| 596 | MEARES | Robert William | 25.01.1904 | |
| 597 | BAKER | Francis James | 10.02.1904 | |
| 598 | DOWLING | William John | 10.02.1904 | |
| 599 | WILKINSON | Henry Frederick | 10.02.1904 | |
| 600 | WEBB | John | 18.02.1904 | |
| 601 | LAWRENCE | Albert Ernest | 28.02.1904 | |
| 602 | PAGE | Percy Kinstone | 01.03.1904 | |
| 603 | ALLPORT | Henry Lagier | 13.03.1904 | |
| 604 | LAMOTTE | Charles Francis | 12.03.1904 | |
| 605 | MANDEL | John Matthew | 17.03.1904 | |
| 606 | POUND | George Frederick | 22.03.1904 | |
| 607 | STEWART | George Richard | 24.03.1904 | |
| 608 | EVANS | George | 31.03.1904 | |
| 609 | DONNOLLY | Peter | 14.04.1904 | |
| 610 | MANBY | Frank | 16.04.1904 | |
| 611 | ATKINSON | Bertram Leaper | 24.04.1904 | |
| 612 | HAYNES | Arthur Adrian | 03.05.1904 | |
| 613 | HUNT | Bertie Leonard | 12.05.1904 | |
| 614 | PAGE | Julian Lambert | 17.05.1904 | |
| 615 | YOUNG | Rochford Vincent | 17.05.1904 | |
| 616 | HOBBS | Harry Alexander | 17.05.1904 | |
| 617 | JOHNSTON | Stanley Edgar | 19.05.1904 | |
| 618 | PAGE | Herbert | 19.05.1904 | |
| 619 | CADIZ | Raymond Lawder | 19.05.1904 | |

| No. | Surname | Forename(s) | Date | Note |
|---|---|---|---|---|
| 620 | BAKER | Thomas | 19.05.1904 | |
| 621 | CARTER | Arthur Rowland | 16.06.1904 | |
| 622 | CROSTHWAITE | Herbert Maitland | 21.06.1904 | |
| 623 | VAWDREY | Thomas Edward | 27.06.1904 | |
| 624 | BOWMAN | William Edward | 29.06.1904 | |
| 625 | CHRISTIE | Henry Armstrong | 30.06.1904 | |
| 626 | GEORGE | John Louie | 12.07.1904 | |
| 627 | COTTRELL | John Swinfen | 14.07.1904 | |
| 628 | BROWN | John Watson | 15.07.1904 | |
| 629 | LILLEY | William John | 17.07.1904 | |
| 630 | ROSE | Andrew Peden | 21.07.1904 | |
| 631 | PRICE | Arnold Thimbleby | 28.07.1904 | |
| 632 | DARBY | Alfred | 02.08.1904 | |
| 633 | BAKER | Edgar Biddulph | 05.08.1904 | |
| 634 | MILLER | Frederick Bruce | 04.08.1904 | |
| 635 | CHALMERS | Wilfred Seymour | 04.08.1904 | |
| 636 | GUBBINS | George Frederick | 07.08.1904 | |
| 637 | VINSON | Edward Eaton | 09.08.1904 | |
| 638 | STEWART | Louis Herbert | 09.08.1904 | |
| 639 | BAIN | John Malcolm | 14.08.1904 | |
| 640 | WELLWOOD | Joseph Wallace | 14.08.1904 | |
| 641 | LEDINGHAM | Alfred John | 14.08.1904 | |
| 642 | MOFFAT | James Robert | 16.08.1904 | |
| 643 | DANIELS | George William | 16.08.1904 | |
| 644 | BECK | John | 25.08.1904 | |
| 645 | LANNING | Wilfred Lionel | 30.08.1904 | |
| 646 | SHIELDS | William Augustus | 04.09.1904 | |
| 647 | COAKLEY | Andrew | 23.09.1904 | |
| 648 | SHEPPARD | George James | 12.10.1904 | |
| 649 | DENNEY | Thomas Joseph | 25.12.1904 | |
| 650 | JAMES | Francis Stafford | 01.01.1905 | |
| 651 | BOULTER | Arthur John | 16.01.1905 | |
| 652 | ALLEN | James | 10.03.1905 | |
| 653 | CIMA | Julius Claude | 10.03.1905 | S/Maj |
| 654 | ALLEN | George Alfred | 11.03.1905 | |
| 655 | GOTHARD | Louis George | 15.03.1905 | |
| 656 | FAIR | Charles Henry | 17.03.1905 | |
| 657 | EDWARDS | Stanley Robert | 05.04.1905 | |
| 658 | BRYANT | Arthur Edward | 05.04.1905 | |
| 659 | LANGFORD | Harry Robert | 12.03.1905 | |
| 660 | McMILLEN | William John | 12.04.1905 | |
| 661 | McCARTHY | James Joseph | 12.04.1905 | |
| 662 | ERRINGTON | George | 14.04.1905 | |
| 663 | HEWETT | Wilfred Brownlow | 28.04.1905 | |
| 664 | HOAD | Aubrey George | 31.05.1905 | |
| 665 | MASON | Robert James | 31.05.1905 | |
| 666 | JONES | Witney Heywood | 07.06.1905 | |
| 667 | DUNCOMBE | George Frederick | 12.06.1905 | |
| 668 | HILLIER | Herbert Charles | 21.06.1905 | |
| 669 | SPRAGG | Gilbert | 30.06.1905 | |
| 670 | WALLACE | St. Clare Arthur | 30.06.1905 | A/Commr. |
| 671 | HAMILTON | Richard Ernest | 30.06.1905 | |
| 672 | LEWIS | Meredith | 30.06.1905 | |
| 673 | WHITNEY | Edward Alexander | 30.06.1905 | |
| 674 | KEOGH | Edmond Cecil | 30.06.1905 | |
| 675 | WHITNEY | Harry William | 07.07.1905 | |
| 676 | HEWITT | Arthur Sidney | 10.07.1905 | |
| 677 | ROBINSON | Hubert Monroe | 10.07.1905 | |
| 678 | NEWBERY | Thomas | 12.07.1905 | |
| 679 | HARDBATTLE | Francis Oswald | 28.07.1905 | |
| 680 | LLOYD | Roy Ordive | 28.07.1905 | |
| 681 | WINDER | Herbert Cecil | 28.07.1905 | |
| 682 | PATRICK | Christopher John | 28.07.1905 | |
| 683 | HEBLETHWAITE | Llewellyn Juan | 28.07.1905 | |
| 684 | HOOPER | Edwin Otto | 02.08.1905 | |
| 685 | BIRCH | George Edward | 08.08.1905 | |
| 686 | HENDERSON | Donald | 11.08.1905 | |
| 687 | URQUHART | | | |
| 689 | Mac GILLICUDDY | Charles Edward | 11.08.1905 | |
| 690 | WATKINS | Jesse Thomas | 16.08.1905 | |
| 691 | RANGER | Walter Frederick | 25.08.1905 | |
| 692 | PUGSLEY | Arthur Theodore | 30.08.1905 | |
| 693 | RADCLIFFE | Claud Farrer | 06.09.1905 | |
| 694 | MOSS | Samuel | 08.09.1905 | |
| 695 | COLE | Frank John | 08.09.1905 | |
| 696 | BLOOMER | Edward Parker | 08.09.1905 | |
| 697 | DALZIEL | George Albert | 08.09.1905 | |
| 698 | WADE | Hugh Blake | 08.09.1905 | |
| 699 | DAVISON | John Vernon | 08.09.1905 | |
| 700 | RICHTER | Charles Ernest | 08.09.1905 | |
| 701 | Mac PHAIL | Hugh | 08.09.1905 | |
| 702 | BEIRNE | Thomas Francis | 08.09.1905 | |
| 703 | DAVIES | Glyn Louis | 08.09.1905 | |
| 704 | CARTER | John Purdon | 08.09.1905 | |
| 705 | LORILLARD | John Ernest | 08.09.1905 | |
| 706 | EDWARDS | Edward Fletcher | 08.09.1905 | |
| 707 | EDWARDS | John | 08.09.1905 | |
| 708 | HOOPER | William James | 08.09.1905 | |
| 709 | PARKHURST | Abraham Edward | 08.09.1905 | |
| 710 | RUSSELL | Thomas Leopold | 08.09.1905 | |
| 711 | KENNETT | Aubrey | 09.09.1905 | |
| 712 | CHARTER | Arthur Jeakins | 13.09.1905 | |
| 713 | FROST | Leonard Joseph | 18.09.1905 | |
| 714 | HUGHES | Charles James | 27.09.1905 | |
| 715 | FOWLER | Peter Herbert | 27.09.1905 | |
| 716 | COLLIARD | Francis Cecil | 27.09.1905 | |
| 717 | VAN DER SPUY | Ryk | 27.09.1905 | |
| 718 | MAY | William | 25.08.1906 | |
| 719 | CHARD | Harry Oswald | 11.10.1905 | |
| 720 | DAVIS | Frederick | 18.10.1905 | |
| 721 | KYSH | Reginald Mason | 20.10.1905 | |
| 722 | PEYTON | Richard Chinnery | 25.10.1905 | |
| 723 | BAMBERGER | William Vessels | 25.10.1905 | |
| 724 | KEMP | Leonard Francis | 27.10.1905 | |
| 725 | EDYE | Hugh Leycaster | 01.11.1905 | |
| 726 | WALSH | Cyril Maurice | 06.11.1905 | |
| 727 | GOLDSCHIMDT | Ernest Nathan | 08.11.1905 | |
| 728 | WILSON | Reginald Henry | 08.11.1905 | |
| 729 | LONGHURST | Ernest George | 08.11.1905 | |
| 730 | LAING | Harold William | 10.11.1905 | |
| 731 | PLEASANTS | Owen | 14.11.1905 | |
| 732 | WILLIAMSON | Claude Blaikie | 17.11.1905 | |
| 733 | HOWARD | Stanley Herbert | 20.11.1905 | |
| 734 | BRUCE | Donald | 22.11.1905 | |
| 735 | BREEDEN | Edwin | 22.11.1905 | |
| 736 | OSMAN | James Richard | 22.11.1905 | |
| 737 | BROWN | Herbert Stewart | 22.11.1905 | |
| 738 | PRICE | John William | 22.11.1905 | |
| 739 | EDCUMBE | Piers | 29.11.1905 | |
| 740 | STICKINGS | Thomas Frederick | 29.11.1905 | |
| 741 | BAIRD | Charles Alfred | 01.12.1905 | |
| 742 | POUND | Frederick William | 06.12.1905 | |
| 743 | DAVIS | Sydney John | 06.12.1905 | |
| 744 | THOMSON | James | 06.12.1905 | |
| 745 | TAYLOR | Edward Robert | 06.12.1905 | |
| 746 | GILLETT | Arthur Robert | 06.12.1905 | |
| 747 | GENTLE | Harold | 13.12.1905 | |
| 748 | STEWART | William Malcolm | 13.12.1905 | |
| 749 | HARDISTY | John Walter | 20.12.1905 | |
| 750 | ROONEY | John | 20.12.1905 | |
| 751 | BRIDGER | John Sydney | 22.12.1905 | |
| 752 | GRIEVE | Richard Joseph | 27.12.1905 | |
| 753 | BAREHAM | Frederick Percy | 27.12.1905 | |
| 754 | CRAIG | George Samuel | 03.01.1906 | |
| 755 | TROTTER | Cecil Douglas | 08.01.1906 | |
| 756 | BEAUMONT | Henry | 10.01.1906 | |
| 757 | | George | 15.01.1906 | |
| 758 | CAVENDISH | Richard Charles | 22.01.1906 | |
| 759 | PRITCHARD | Samuel Frederick | 24.01.1906 | |
| 760 | COLLIER | Frank Norton | 26.01.1906 | |
| 761 | GREATHEAD | Wilson | 26.01.1906 | |
| 762 | VERNON | George | 05.02.1906 | |
| 763 | KLINGENSTEIN | George Oram | 09.02.1906 | |
| 764 | OTTLEY | Lawrence Brook | 12.02.1906 | |
| 765 | PLANT | Edward Ryde | 12.02.1906 | |
| 766 | FORD | Rufus Philip | 12.02.1906 | |
| 767 | OVENS | Reginald Edwin | 12.02.1906 | |
| 768 | HICK | Robert | 28.02.1906 | |
| 769 | BUCKLEY | Henry Joseph | 21.03.1906 | |
| 770 | BARBER | Edgcumbe | 21.03.1906 | |
| 771 | WHITBY | Herbert | 21.03.1906 | |
| 772 | LEMAN | Herbert Lesser | 28.03.1906 | |
| 773 | EDGE | William | 28.03.1906 | |
| 774 | BLACK | David Laing | 04.04.1906 | |
| 775 | LEDERREY | Henry Tallentire | 09.04.1906 | |
| 776 | HUNT | William Ernest | 11.04.1906 | |
| 777 | HOWARD | Rupert | 11.04.1906 | |
| 778 | FOX | Edward Thornton | 11.04.1906 | |
| 779 | COWPER | Charles Deane | 11.04.1906 | |
| 780 | NICKLESS | Henry | 11.04.1906 | |
| 781 | CLOTHIER | Edward Hugh | 11.04.1906 | |
| 782 | KINNAIRD | Charles | 11.04.1906 | |
| 783 | HOLLY | Charles Elliott | 17.04.1906 | |
| 784 | KING | Ross | 17.04.1906 | |
| 785 | PALMER | Eric Trestrail | 23.04.1906 | |
| 786 | CUFF | George Herbert | 28.04.1906 | |
| 787 | OVER | William Henry | 09.05.1906 | |
| 788 | COCHRANE | Rupert William | 30.05.1906 | |
| 789 | GORDON | John Edmund | 30.05.1906 | |
| 790 | KNOTT | Henry Alban | 30.05.1906 | |
| 791 | PEIRCE | Gerald William | 30.05.1906 | |
| 792 | THOMPSON | Edward Clifford | 30.05.1906 | |
| 793 | SARGEANT | William Henry | 30.05.1906 | |
| 794 | BENSON | Ernest Victor | 06.06.1906 | |
| 795 | SHANNON | Louis | 13.06.1906 | |
| 796 | SMITH | William John | 20.06.1906 | |
| 797 | LETHBRIDGE | James Henry | 20.06.1906 | |
| 798 | RUMBLE | William Robert | 20.06.1906 | |
| 799 | GOOLD | Bernard | 23.06.1906 | |
| 800 | GILLETT | Claude | 29.06.1906 | |
| 801 | GOOYER | Edward Bertram | 04.07.1906 | |
| 802 | DAVIES | Alfred Charles | 04.07.1906 | |
| 803 | SHOUT | Alfred John | 11.07.1906 | |
| 804 | FLAXMAN | Thomas | 11.07.1906 | |
| 805 | HOPPE | Alfred John Ernest | 11.07.1906 | |
| 806 | DAYTON | Archibald Louis | 26.05.1910 | |
| 807 | HODGKIN | Thomas | 01.08.1906 | |
| 808 | REARDON | Philip Jerrold | 03.08.1906 | |
| 809 | HULL | Herbert Harry | 03.08.1906 | |
| 810 | RICHARDS | Walter John | 03.08.1906 | |
| 811 | WILLIAMS | Bernard Thomas | 03.08.1906 | |
| 812 | WILLIAMS | John Percival | 08.08.1906 | |
| 813 | CHARLTON | Robert Arthur | 18.08.1906 | |
| 814 | HOLGATE | Leonard Gordon | 25.08.1906 | |
| 815 | McDONOCH | John Edward | 25.08.1906 | |
| 816 | HUTSON | John Walseley | 01.09.1906 | |
| 817 | KETTLE | Frederick William | 05.09.1906 | |
| 818 | EVANS | Harold Charles | 05.09.1906 | |
| 819 | RABBETTS | William Henry | 08.09.1906 | |
| 820 | BENNETT | Raymond | 08.09.1906 | Capt. |
| 821 | ROBERTSON | George Frederick | 08.09.1906 | |
| 822 | VAN STRAATEN | Johannes Jacobus | 08.09.1906 | |
| 823 | FORDHAM | Sidney Arthur | 22.09.1906 | |
| 824 | NORVALL | Arthur Dugald | 24.09.1906 | |
| 825 | PADLEY | Frederick James | 29.09.1906 | |
| 826 | WOOD | Charles Edwin | 08.10.1907 | |

Regimental roll — numbers 827–1033

| No. | Surname | Forename(s) | Rank | Date |
|---|---|---|---|---|
| 827 | PECK | Arthur | | 03.10.1906 |
| 828 | MERCER | Reginald Walter | | 13.10.1906 |
| 829 | HILLESTROM | Alexander | | 03.10.1906 |
| 830 | WATKINS | Burton Gavin | | 13.10.1906 |
| 831 | HODGE | George Comley | | 13.10.1906 |
| 832 | ATFIELD | Henry James | | 13.10.1906 |
| 833 | MITCHENER | Alfred George | | 13.10.1906 |
| 834 | BEECHEY | Arthur Edmund | Cpl. | 17.10.1906 |
| 835 | ROOS | John Anthony | | 17.10.1906 |
| 836 | MORLEY | Ernest Henry | | 02.11.1906 |
| 837 | QUINTON | Arthur Edward | | 20.10.1906 |
| 838 | BRIDGEMAN | Frederick Daniel | | 20.10.1906 |
| 839 | KING | William Arthur | Lieut. | 20.10.1906 |
| 840 | TRIBE | Alder Lewis | | 20.10.1906 |
| 841 | WILSON | Neil Housman | | 20.10.1906 |
| 842 | BARRY | Patrick Mowbray | | 20.10.1906 |
| 843 | WIMBLE | Franklin Cecil | | 20.10.1906 |
| 844 | SMITH | Leonard Oswald | | 20.10.1906 |
| 845 | RENNIE | Frederick William | | 27.10.1906 |
| 846 | BARRATT | Arthur Gordon | | 27.10.1906 |
| 847 | CAREY | Stanley Gordon | | 27.10.1906 |
| 848 | FRANKLIN | Harry | | 27.10.1906 |
| 849 | BUCKLEY | Herbert Mauris | | 31.10.1906 |
| 850 | JEAREY | Thomas Charles | | 31.10.,1906 |
| 851 | MILLER | Gordon Stanley | | 02.11.1906 |
| 852 | BATEMAN | Harry Vernon | | 07.11.1906 |
| 853 | CROUCH | Vernon Foster | | 24.11.1906 |
| 854 | JOCE | Frederick Ernest | | 01.12.1906 |
| 855 | ROCHESTER | Hubert | Major | 15.12.1906 |
| 856 | JALLAND | Ernest Henry | | 09.01.1907 |
| 857 | DENT | Ernest Frederick | | 12.01.1907 |
| 858 | JENKINS | Ernest Malcolm | | 12.01.1907 |
| 859 | SNEDDON | William Drysdale | | 06.02.1907 |
| 860 | HORNBY | George Edmund | | 06.02.1907 |
| 861 | McLEAN | Henry Lionel | | 20.02.1907 |
| 862 | PARTRIDGE | Frederick | | 20.02.1907 |
| 863 | ASHLEY | Leonard Francis | | 13.03.1907 |
| 864 | BROWN | George Banks | | 27.03.1907 |
| 865 | McCUTCHAN | Edward Head | | 17.04.1907 |
| 866 | BENNETT | Neville | | 26.04.1907 |
| 867 | McDERMOTT | William Douglas | S/Maj | 27.04.1907 |
| 868 | McVERNON | St. John | | 01.05.1907 |
| 869 | URQUHART | William Thomas | | 01.05.1907 |
| 870 | BREMNER | Alastair Bruce | | 01.05.1907 |
| 871 | WOODS | James Lionel | | 17.05.1907 |
| 872 | RAPER | Arnold Owen | | 27.05.1907 |
| 873 | WALTON | Robert Arthur | | 29.05.1907 |
| 874 | CUSSANS | Arthur Charles | | 29.05.1907 |
| 875 | RIDGWELL | James William | | 01.06.1907 |
| 876 | JONES | Robert Thomas | | 05.06.1907 |
| 877 | TURNER | Frederick Richard | | 05.06.1907 |
| 878 | HOOKER | William Henslow | Sgt. | 05.06.1907 |
| 879 | FISHER | Frederick Yates | | 08.06.1907 |
| 880 | PARRINGTON | John Beaumont | | 08.06.1907 |
| 881 | TAYLOR | John Cumberland | Tpr | 14.06.1907 |
| 882 | ROE | Christopher Gordon | | 26.06.1907 |
| 883 | CRONIN | David | Lieut. | 26.06.1907 |
| 884 | MARSH | Arthur | | 03.07.1907 |
| 885 | SWAYNE | Montague | | 10.07.1907 |
| 886 | GONDIE | Arnold James | | 20.07.1907 |
| 887 | COWPER | Henry Bertram | | 24.07.1907 |
| 888 | BANNING | Edward Antonio | | 24.07.1907 |
| 889 | SNOWDEN | Sylvanus Reynolds | | 26.07.1907 |
| 890 | LE GROS | Victor Edwin | | 26.07.1907 |
| 891 | HAMPTON | James Henry | | |
| 892 | WILSON | Robert Selby | | |
| 893 | SMALE | Thomas Harold | | |
| 894 | SMITH | Frederick Charles | | |
| 895 | WILLS | Walter Harry | | |
| 896 | TURNER | James Norman | | 27.07.1907 |
| 897 | THORNBURN | Robert | | 27.07.1907 |
| 898 | PETERS | Francis Robert | | 27.07.1907 |
| 899 | GUDGEON | Charles wilfred | | 31.07.1907 |
| 900 | JOHNSTON | Stanley Edgar | | 02.08.1907 |
| 901 | HARTLEY | Louis Robert | | 03.08.1907 |
| 902 | NORTHCOTT | William Alfred | | 07.08.1907 |
| 903 | ROBINSON | George Michael | | 07.08.1907 |
| 904 | RAINSFORD | Richard Frederick | | 08.08.1907 |
| 905 | STEPHENSON | Harold Turner | | 10.08.1907 |
| 906 | BIRD | William Frederick | | 14.08.1907 |
| 907 | MAVIS | Joshua | | 17.08.1907 |
| 908 | WHEELER | Roland Chamberlain | | 17.08.1907 |
| 909 | ULLMAN | Charles Joseph | | 17.08.1907 |
| 910 | WRIGHT | Oswald Lawrence | | 31.08.1907 |
| 911 | JEFFREYS | Charles Magnus | | 04.09.1907 |
| 912 | JOHN | Stanley Conway | | 25.09.1907 |
| 913 | GODDARD | John Rupert | | 25.09.1907 |
| 914 | RAWLINGS | Albert Edward | | 25.09.1907 |
| 915 | PRICE | Benjamin Henry | | 28.09.1907 |
| 916 | HILLIER | Stanley | | 28.09.1907 |
| 917 | SPEEDY | Thomas Francis Albert | | 02.10.1907 |
| 918 | ELSDEN | Walter Thomas | | 04.10.1907 |
| 919 | BISHOP | Lancelot Charles | | 19.10.1907 |
| 920 | BROWNE | James William | | 19.10.1907 |
| 921 | ROBINSON | Thomas | | 19.10.1907 |
| 922 | MATTHEWS | George Henry | | 23.10.1907 |
| 923 | SIMMONDS | Earl Medhurst | | 23.10.1907 |
| 924 | ANDERSON | Harold Ross | | 23.10.1907 |
| 925 | WARWICK | Guy Neville | | 09.11.1907 |
| 926 | CARTWRIGHT | Thomas | | 23.11.1907 |
| 927 | JOHNSTON | Frederick James | | 30.11.1907 |
| 928 | BRIDGES | Eric Forster | | 30.11.1907 |
| 929 | THORPE | Charles | | 04.12.1907 |
| 930 | MORRISON | David Hugh | | 07.12.1907 |
| 931 | KOCHANSKI | Marcel Leon | | 07.12.1907 |
| 932 | MITCHAM | Percy Henry | | 11.12.1907 |
| 933 | THORPE | Percy George | | 13.12.1907 |
| 934 | BRADSHAW | Ernest George | | 28.12.1907 |
| 935 | BISHOP | Hayler Overton | | 01.01.1908 |
| 936 | HOLMES | Norman Clifford | | 03.01.1908 |
| 937 | PHIPPS | Victor George | | 04.01.1908 |
| 938 | WILLIAMS | Percy Bryson | | 04.01.1908 |
| 939 | HALLS | Walter Hughes | | 11.01.1908 |
| 940 | ALLEN | Ernest Frank | | 11.01.1908 |
| 941 | ST. QUINTON | Noel  C.B.E. | | 15.01.1908 |
| 942 | RENNICK | Herbert Cumming | | 22.01.1908 |
| 943 | MOURITZ | Leofwin Beresford | | 22.01.1908 |
| 944 | SALT | George William | | 22.01.1908 |
| 945 | ROBINSON | Thomas | | 22.01.1908 |
| 946 | BARTLETT | William | | 22.01.1908 |
| 947 | BEASLEY | Frank | | 23.01.1908 |
| 948 | BRADLEY | John Edward | | 23.01.1908 |
| 949 | BOWLEY | Thomas Henry | | 27.01.1908 |
| 950 | WALKER | Daniel McLennan | | 01.02.1908 |
| 951 | McGINNIS | Charles Edmund | | 01.02.1908 |
| 952 | FOSTER | Frank Cyril | | 01.02.1908 |
| 953 | DE SATJE | Frederick Gordon | | 02.02.1908 |
| 954 | SIMKINS | Anthony Harry | | 05.02.1908 |
| 955 | WEATHERHEAD | Harold | | 04.03.1908 |
| 956 | HILL | George Escott | | 07.03.1908 |
| 957 | KELLY | Reginald Ignatius | | 07.03.1908 |
| 958 | JACKSON | Samuel Patridge | | 07.03.1908 |
| 959 | CRAXTON | Charles William | | |
| 960 | BRODIE | Patrick Tait | | |
| 961 | BOYTON | Charles Hendrick | | |
| 962 | BOYTON | Albert Edward | | |
| 963 | TAYLOR | George Charles | | |
| 964 | SNELLING | Ashton Graham | | |
| 965 | HORNE | Charlton Frederick | | 14.03.1908 |
| 966 | BALFOUR | Fredrick Douglas | | 08.04.1908 |
| 967 | ROSKELLY | William Charles | | 15.04.1908 |
| 968 | SMITH | Charles Leslie | | 25.04.1908 |
| 969 | ELLAM | William Henry | | 25.04.1908 |
| 970 | SILLITOE | Percy Joseph | | 25.04.1908 |
| 971 | KOESTER | Paul Ernest | | 09.05.1908 |
| 972 | ATKINSON | Alexander Bruce | | 13.05.1908 |
| 973 | HARRISON | Frederick | | 13.05.1908 |
| 974 | Mac BRAYNE | John Owen | | 21.05.1908 |
| 975 | EVANS | Walter Frank | | 29.05.1908 |
| 976 | STOREY | Johnston | | 06.06.1808 |
| 977 | FAURE | James Henry | | 19.06.1908 |
| 978 | LANGE | William Oswald | | 27.06.1908 |
| 979 | BELLERBY | Herbert | | 27.06.1908 |
| 980 | GIRDLESTONE | Cecil Charles | | 01.07.1908 |
| 981 | TIJOU | Bernard James | | 04.07.1908 |
| 982 | CRAIGIE | William Frederick | | 11.07.1908 |
| 983 | MALONE | Henry Cheyne | | 11.07.1908 |
| 984 | REID | Rowland | | 11.07.1908 |
| 985 | PARKES | Henry Gordon | | 01.08.1908 |
| 986 | MAUGHFLING | Thomas | | 01.08.1908 |
| 987 | IDDINS | Albert James | | 15.08.1908 |
| 988 | ELY | Francis Howe | | 22.08.1908 |
| 989 | BLATHERWICK | Thomas | | 22.08.1908 |
| 990 | WHITAKER | Norman Fredrick | | 26.08.1908 |
| 991 | DUNCAN | Henry Thomas | | 29.08.1908 |
| 992 | HEANEY | Roderick Henry | | 17.09.1908 |
| 993 | VERNON | Leonard Campbell | | 19.09.1908 |
| 994 | HORNER | Nathaniel | | 19.09.1908 |
| 995 | TAYLOR | Hugo Reynell | | 03.10.1908 |
| 996 | LITHGOW | Thomas Penn | | 03.10.1908 |
| 997 | DURANT | William Henry | | 22.10.1908 |
| 998 | WHITELAW | William | | 28.10.1908 |
| 999 | DOUGLAS | Donald James | | 07.11.1908 |
| 1000 | BAKER | Henry Gordon | | 07.11.1908 |
| 1001 | NEWMAN | Lawrence John | | 11.11.1908 |
| 1002 | WINFORD | Warren Carteris | | 18.11.1908 |
| 1003 | DE BEER | Stephanus | | 21.11.1908 |
| 1004 | McNEIL | Louis Stephen | | 21.11.1908 |
| 1005 | COOPER | Arthur Miles | | 28.11.1908 |
| 1006 | MONTAGU | James Drogo | | 02.12.1908 |
| 1007 | PARKES | Arthur John | | 02.12.1908 |
| 1008 | LOCKNER | Tobias Christian | | 05.12.1908 |
| 1009 | LEACH | Percy Hastings | | 05.12.1908 |
| 1010 | ANDERSON | William George | | 05.12.1908 |
| 1011 | BROWN | Robert Philip | | 16.12.1908 |
| 1012 | DAVIES | Thomas Emlyn | | 26.12.1908 |
| 1013 | FFOLLIOTT | William Leigh | | 26.12.1908 |
| 1014 | WOOD | Basil Leo | | 25.12.1908 |
| 1015 | WILKINS | Frank Alfred | | 06.01.1909 |
| 1016 | ROBINSON | Julian Philip Kay | | 13.01.1909 |
| 1017 | BLITCHFORD | Faithful | | 13.01.1909 |
| 1018 | FRASER | Kenneth Whalley | | 13.01.1909 |
| 1019 | YOUNG | Arthur Montague | | 16.01.1909 |
| 1020 | MILNE | John Davidson | | 16.01.1909 |
| 1021 | BURGESS | Percy Conant | Capt. | 16.01.1909 |
| 1022 | SENN | Thomas | | 16.01.1909 |
| 1023 | BEALE | Frank Edward | | 20.01.1909 |
| 1024 | LAING | Heron James | | 23.01.1909 |
| 1025 | HUTCHINGS | Nun | | 23.01.1909 |
| 1026 | COX | Trayton | | 30.01.1909 |
| 1027 | MUTTER | James | | 30.01.1909 |
| 1028 | GOVETT | Robert MacKenzie | | 30.01.1909 |
| 1029 | MARR | Federick Alexander | | |
| 1030 | TAYLOR | Frank | | |
| 1031 | GUNN | Kenneth Geoffrey | | |
| 1032 | REANEY | Cecil Hereward | Cpl. | |
| 1033 | SCOTT | William | | |

| No. | Surname | First name(s) | Note | Date |
|---|---|---|---|---|
| 1034 | PARKER | William Edward | | 30.01.1909 |
| 1035 | SHARLAND | Reginald Arthur | | 30.01.1909 |
| 1036 | LAMONT | Charles James | | 30.01.1909 |
| 1037 | MACRONE | Archibald Grieve | | 30.01.1909 |
| 1038 | DAVIS | Anthony Frank | | 30.01.1909 |
| 1039 | PALK | Alfred George | | 06.02.1909 |
| 1040 | BARNES | Herbert Clixby | | 10.02.1909 |
| 1041 | GUBBINS | John Lyon | | 10.02.1909 |
| 1042 | ZEEDERBERG | Roelof Duncan | | 13.02.1909 |
| 1043 | OLDREIVE | Lewis Prettejohn | | 17.02.1909 |
| 1044 | EDWARDS | Francis Charles | | 20.02.1909 |
| 1045 | Mac INTOSH | Duncan Alexander | S/Maj | 27.02.1909 |
| 1046 | FISHER | George Brechin | | 06.03.1909 |
| 1047 | OLIVER | Eric Morgan | | 06.03.1909 |
| 1048 | D'ARCY | Lionel George | | 06.03.1909 |
| 1049 | SOLMAN | Charles Wesley | | 06.03.1909 |
| 1050 | RICHARDSON | Percy | | 06.03.1909 |
| 1051 | HORNSBY | Charles Cooper | | 06.03.1909 |
| 1052 | HENCHLEY | Cyril Harold | | 06.03.1909 |
| 1053 | ONYETT | Harry Thomas | A/Com | 06.03.1909 |
| 1054 | TICE | Herbert Phillip | A/Supt. | 06.03.1909 |
| 1055 | VERNON | Dayrell Tassie | | 13.03.1909 |
| 1056 | NOLAN | Michael Stephen | | 19.03.1909 |
| 1057 | WHITNEY | Edmund Phillips | | 24.03.1909 |
| 1058 | BROTHERTON | Robert | | 31.03.1909 |
| 1059 | EVANS | Herbert Noonan | | 03.04.1909 |
| 1060 | DE GEX | Ruthven Gore | | 14.04.1909 |
| 1061 | BURKE | Edward William | | 07.04.1909 |
| 1062 | ALLPORT | Herbert | | 17.04.1909 |
| 1063 | EVERETT | John George | | 17.04.1909 |
| 1064 | PAINE | Walter Thomas | Sgt | 24.04.1909 |
| 1065 | TUTTIETT | Lawrence William | | 05.05.1909 |
| 1066 | COOPER | Wilfred Whittaker | | 05.05.1909 |
| 1067 | HANCOCK | Oscar | | 08.05.1909 |
| 1068 | READY | Nathaniel Henry | | 08.05.1909 |
| 1069 | HUTTON | Robert | | 08.05.1909 |
| 1070 | BECKMAN | Richard Victor | | 07.04.1909 |
| 1071 | MACKINTOSH | Charles Berkley | | 12.05.1909 |
| 1072 | WILLIAMS | Cyril Theodore | | 12.05.1909 |
| 1073 | BOUCHER | Douglas George | | 05.06.1909 |
| 1074 | ABBOTT | Cortlandt William | | 05.06.1909 |
| 1075 | MACASKIE | Stuart Roy | | 05.06.1909 |
| 1076 | BOYD | William Francis | | 05.06.1909 |
| 1077 | LUSCOMBE | Benjamin Hutchinson | | 08.06.1909 |
| 1078 | ARCHER | Arthur Gordon | | 03.07.1909 |
| 1079 | COOKE | Conrad Michael Victor | | 03.07.1909 |
| 1080 | KERR | Ronald George | | 03.07.1909 |
| 1081 | LIVERSEDGE | Geoffrey Spencer | | 03.07.1909 |
| 1082 | FRASER | Malcolm Alexander | | 03.07.1909 |
| 1083 | ROE | William Villiers | | 03.07.1909 |
| 1084 | BUSSY | Vivian John | | 10.07.1909 |
| 1085 | TIBBS | Wilfrid Bernard | | 03.07.1909 |
| 1086 | DUTTON | Thomas Albert | | 16.07.1909 |
| 1087 | LACEY | Henry Brooke | | 21.07.1909 |
| 1088 | BALLARD | Albert Edward | | 31.07.1909 |
| 1089 | HINES | Norman Leslie | | 31.07.1909 |
| 1090 | SCALES | Alfred Francis | | 31.07.1909 |
| 1091 | ADAMS | Edward Joceline | | 31.07.1909 |
| 1092 | READ | Richard | | 31.07.1909 |
| 1093 | PHILLIPS | William Stanley | | 31.07.1909 |
| 1094 | BALL | Maurice Saddington | | 31.07.1909 |
| 1095 | COLLINS | Walter James | | 04.08.1909 |
| 1096 | HARINGTON | Vere Richard | | 07.08.1909 |
| 1097 | GINN | Edward | | 21.08.1909 |
| 1098 | WHITE | Charles Arthur | | 04.09.1909 |
| 1099 | READ | John Gordon | | 04.09.1909 |
| 1100 | FLINT | Henry Arthur | | 04.09.1909 |
| 1101 | LYONS-CAMPBELL | Archibald | | 04.09.1909 |

| No. | Surname | First name(s) | Note | Date |
|---|---|---|---|---|
| 1103 | MINTER | Frederick William | | 04.09.1909 |
| 1104 | WINGROVE | Percival | | 04.09.1909 |
| 1105 | COLLINGWOOD | Douglas Edward | | 22.09.1909 |
| 1106 | PHILLIPS | Samuel Wilfred | | 02.10.1909 |
| 1107 | COURT | Gordon Frederick | | 02.10.1909 |
| 1108 | JOHNSON | Frank | | 02.10.1909 |
| 1109 | ELLIS | Frank Cyril | | 02.10.1909 |
| 1110 | JACOB | Cyril Vivian | | 02.10.1909 |
| 1111 | USHER | Thomas Nicholas | | 02.10.1909 |
| 1112 | DEANE | Eric Venables | | 02.10.1909 |
| 1113 | CUBISON | Reginald Marsh | | 02.10.1909 |
| 1114 | HASSETT | Patrick | | 02.10.1909 |
| 1115 | MOWLEM | Percy | | 02.10.1909 |
| 1116 | CLOTHIER | Edward Hugh | | 09.10.1909 |
| 1117 | HUNTLEY | William | | 14.10.1909 |
| 1118 | KOTZE | Daniel Pheil | | 23.10.1909 |
| 1119 | MORRIS | John Sidney | In/Gen | 30.10.1909 |
| 1120 | WARRINGTON | Frank | | 30.10.1909 |
| 1121 | TOMPKINS | Percy Richard | | 30.10.1909 |
| 1122 | HARRISON | Frederick Charles | | 03.11.1909 |
| 1123 | DAVIS | Maitland Tiernan | | 10.11.1909 |
| 1124 | JONES | Arthur | | 13.11.1909 |
| 1125 | CARTER | Leslie Mark | | 01.12.1909 |
| 1126 | BROWN | Reginald | | 03.12.1909 |
| 1127 | BOLAN | Frank Alexander | | 04.12.1909 |
| 1128 | LARK | Francis Reginald | | 04.12.1909 |
| 1129 | BUXTON | Valentine Hector | Lieut. | 04.12.1909 |
| 1130 | KING-HALL | Eric Lindsay | | 04.12.1909 |
| 1131 | LETHABY | Frank | | 04.12.1909 |
| 1132 | WAINWRIGHT | Oswald Johnson | | 04.12.1909 |
| 1133 | BETTS | Horace Edward | | 04.12.1909 |
| 1134 | COLE | Bertram George | | 04.12.1909 |
| 1135 | RAISON | Albert | | 01.03.1897 |
| 1136 | SARGENT | Ivor Goronwy | Lieut. | 01.02.1898 |
| 1137 | SMITH | Thomas | | 25.11.1897 |
| 1138 | SKILLEN | James | | 03.01.1897 |
| 1139 | EDGE | Albert Edward | A/Supt. | 04.12.1898 |
| 1140 | LONGMORE | Thomas | | 04.12.1898 |
| 1141 | DE LA HAY | Thomas | | 02.01.1901 |
| 1142 | BRUNDELL | Joseph Cyril | | 11.06.1901 |
| 1143 | GEDDES | John | | 09.02.1901 |
| 1144 | BROWN | Richard Charles | Major | 01.07.1898 |
| 1145 | KILGALLON | Thaddeus | | 13.10.1899 |
| 1146 | KERINS | James | | 03.02.1901 |
| 1147 | DICKSON | Andrew Miller | | 02.01.1901 |
| 1148 | RIVETT | Edward | | 09.02.1901 |
| 1149 | BAXTER | John Alexander | | 09.02.1901 |
| 1150 | DALY | Joseph | | 02.01.1901 |
| 1151 | JOHNSON | Arthur Valentine | | 02.01.1901 |
| 1152 | HAMMOND | Harry | Capt. | 09.02.1901 |
| 1153 | ALCOCK | Harold Ralph | | 02.01.1901 |
| 1154 | ANDERSON | George | D/Insp. | 09.02.1901 |
| 1155 | CLARK | William | | 08.05.1901 |
| 1156 | McLEAN | Donald | | 06.05.1901 |
| 1157 | WINTER | Henry Hugh | Supt. | 09.02.1901 |
| 1158 | HORNE | Albert Edward | | 08.02.1901 |
| 1159 | POWELL | Fred Thomas | | 21.05.1902 |
| 1160 | HOPKINS | Richard | | 05.05.1902 |
| 1161 | TAYLOR | Harry | | 23.06.1903 |
| 1162 | TULLY | James Thomas | S/Insp | 05.05.1902 |
| 1163 | WATSON | Bertram | | 26.09.1902 |
| 1164 | BATTISON | James Ogilvie | | 02.01.1903 |
| 1165 | McKENZIE | William | | 02.01.1903 |
| 1166 | SHERIDAN | Patrick | | 02.01.1903 |
| 1167 | COLLIER | Herbert | | 07.01.1903 |
| 1168 | FINDLAY | Alexander | | 19.03.1903 |
| 1169 | ROSE | Arthur James | | 07.05.1903 |
| 1170 | MOORLEND | Ramsay | | 20.06.1903 |

| No. | Surname | First name(s) | Note | Date |
|---|---|---|---|---|
| 1172 | WALKER | James | D/Insp | 05.10.1903 |
| 1173 | JACQUES | James | | 23.11.1903 |
| 1174 | McGILLICUDDY | John | | 23.11.1903 |
| 1175 | PURCELL | James Philip | | 23.11.1903 |
| 1176 | MILLER | John Thomas | | 24.03.1904 |
| 1177 | MURPHY | Thomas | | 24.03.1904 |
| 1178 | PATTERSON | William | | 24.03.1904 |
| 1179 | TALBOT | Benjamin Robert | | 06.04.1907 |
| 1180 | WINTER | Hugh Stanley | | 11.08.1904 |
| 1181 | ROBINS | Francis Henry | | 07.12.1905 |
| 1182 | MAXWELL | Alexander | | 06.04.1906 |
| 1183 | HUDSON | James William | | 01.05.1906 |
| 1184 | VAWDREY | Thomas Edward | | 23.07.1906 |
| 1185 | CRABBE | Alfred Abraham | | 03.08.1906 |
| 1186 | MUNSON | Benjamin | | 24.09.1906 |
| 1187 | SMITH | Irwin Robert | | 01.02.1907 |
| 1188 | NEALE | Malcolm Melville | | 15.08.1907 |
| 1189 | SAGAR | William | | 01.01.1910 |
| 1190 | PERRY | Robert Stanley | | 01.01.1910 |
| 1191 | BAKER | William Siddons | | 01.01.1910 |
| 1192 | SMITH | Charles Theodore | | 05.01.1910 |
| 1193 | CROSS | Thomas | | 08.01.1910 |
| 1194 | WINTON | George Stanley | | 08.01.1910 |
| 1195 | WHITLEY | Leonard John | | 08.01.1910 |
| 1196 | KOTZE | Abraham Barend | | 12.01.1910 |
| 1197 | DUNCAN | Avery Dunbar | | 12.01.1910 |
| 1198 | SEARLE | D'Arcy Lawrence | | 15.01.1910 |
| 1199 | MERRINGTON | Frederick Lionel | | 15.01.1910 |
| 1200 | VAN STRAATEN | Wilhelm Johannes | | 20.01.1910 |
| 1201 | LEMON | Charles Ormonde | | 05.02.1910 |
| 1202 | LEMON | Fredrick Harry | | 05.02.1910 |
| 1203 | BURTON | Granville Pierrepont | | 09.02.1910 |
| 1204 | ANDREWS | Charles James | | 09.02.1910 |
| 1205 | MANSERGH | Neville Southcote | | 09.02.1910 |
| 1206 | HOLMES | William James Key | | 09.02.1910 |
| 1207 | STONE | Ralph Wentworth | | 09.02.1910 |
| 1208 | LEIGH-MARTIN | Alphonse Louis | | 09.02.1910 |
| 1209 | CHASE | Percival | | 05.03.1910 |
| 1210 | COLLIER | Percy | | 05.03.1910 |
| 1211 | HIME | John Wilbraham | | 05.03.1910 |
| 1212 | VINEY | Reginald Austin | | 05.03.1910 |
| 1213 | TEARE | Sydney Robert | | 05.03.1910 |
| 1214 | HATTON | Horace Walter | | 05.03.1910 |
| 1215 | PIGGIN | Frederick Percy | | 07.03.1910 |
| 1216 | SMITH | Harold Charlton | | 09.03.1910 |
| 1217 | MORISON | Donald McDonald | | 09.03.1910 |
| 1218 | BARTTER | John William | | 26.03.1910 |
| 1219 | SWEETNAM | Walter Eugene | | 26.03.1910 |
| 1220 | WEBSTER | Richard | | 02.04.1910 |
| 1221 | SAYER | Walter Ernest | | 06.04.1910 |
| 1222 | OWEN | Frank Vivian | | 06.04.1910 |
| 1223 | WADDINGTON | Hubert Allen | | 06.04.1910 |
| 1224 | ROSS | Alistair Spence | | 06.04.1910 |
| 1225 | SIMMONDS | Hugh Dawes | | 06.04.1910 |
| 1226 | ARNELL | Douglas Carstairs | | 06.04.1910 |
| 1227 | MOIR | James | | 20.04.1910 |
| 1228 | DOUGLAS | James Fife | | 30.04.1910 |
| 1229 | WARD | Charles Edmund | | 07.05.1910 |
| 1230 | HEWSON | Keith Martin | | 07.05.1910 |
| 1231 | GARLAND | Wodehouse Vincent | | 07.05.1910 |
| 1232 | LEA | Thomas Gilbert | | 07.05.1910 |
| 1233 | HAWKINS | Denis Richmond | | 07.05.1910 |
| 1234 | WALTER | Morritt Medhurst | | 07.05.1910 |
| 1235 | STAUNTON | Ernest Pickmore | | 07.05.1910 |
| 1236 | STANBURY | Alfred Glydon | RSM | 07.05.1910 |
| 1237 | RAFFE | Harry Acfield | | 01.06.1910 |
| 1238 | ROBERTS | Fred Valentine | | 06.06.1910 |
| 1239 | THOMAS | Albert Joseph | | 08.06.1910 |
| 1240 | ROBERTS | John Herbert | | 08.06.1910 |

| No. | Surname | Forename | Date | Rank/Note |
|---|---|---|---|---|
| 1241 | COLLARD | Edward Avalon | 08.06.1910 | |
| 1242 | WAVEL | Horace Brooke | 08.06.1910 | |
| 1243 | SAVAGE | George Henry | 08.06.1910 | |
| 1244 | BROWN | Hillary | 08.06.1910 | |
| 1245 | SAMSON | Willie Kenneth | 08.06.1910 | |
| 1246 | ROBISON | Melville | 08.06.1910 | |
| 1247 | WARD | Reginald Herbert | 08.06.1910 | |
| 1248 | DUNNING | Harold John | 08.06.1910 | |
| 1249 | CURNOCK | Victor Colin | 11.06.1910 | |
| 1250 | IVATTS | Arthur | 11.06.1910 | |
| 1251 | GREENWELL | Stanley | 11.06.1910 | |
| 1252 | LOCKWOOD | Arthur Leslie | 18.06.1910 | Capt. |
| 1253 | SHRUBSOLE | Claude Idwal | 18.06.1910 | |
| 1254 | FIELDEN | Francis Hugh | 18.06.1910 | Lieut. |
| 1255 | HOPE | Richard Curzon | 18.06.1910 | |
| 1256 | WYLES | Arthur Laurence | 18.06.1910 | |
| 1257 | STEPHENS | Edward William | 02.07.1910 | |
| 1258 | WARD | Arthur | 05.07.1910 | |
| 1259 | JASPER | William | 11.07.1910 | |
| 1260 | ASHBURNER | Clifford | 11.07.1910 | |
| 1261 | BAKER | Leo Francis | 16.07.1910 | |
| 1262 | WRIGHT | Edmund Charles | 13.07.1910 | |
| 1263 | JENNINGS | George Brunel | 23.07.1910 | |
| 1264 | ANDERSON | Augustus Eric | 23.07.1910 | |
| 1265 | BLOOD | Walter James | 23.07.1910 | |
| 1266 | GRIMSDITCH | Frank | 23.07.1910 | |
| 1267 | HILL | William Sutherland | 30.07.1910 | |
| 1268 | BURT | Ernest Edwin | 30.07.1910 | |
| 1269 | DAVENPORT | Herbert | 30.07.1910 | |
| 1270 | ANKRETT | Frederick George | 30.07.1910 | |
| 1271 | PARKIN | John Bingley | 30.07.1910 | |
| 1272 | MAWHOOD | Lionel Percival | 30.07.1910 | |
| 1273 | LITTON | Arthur Frederick | 30.07.1910 | |
| 1274 | COWPER | Charles Deane | 30.07.1910 | |
| 1275 | HARDING | Christopher Houghton | 06.08.1910 | |
| 1276 | LEE | Thomas Haydn | 06.08.1910 | |
| 1277 | TODD | Archibald Stewart | 13.08.1910 | |
| 1278 | GREEN | Lewis Montague | 13.08.1910 | |
| 1279 | MANN | Frederick William | 13.08.1910 | |
| 1280 | DOWNING | Lewis Wilfred | 13.08.1910 | |
| 1281 | DEMPERS | John Peter | 18.08.1910 | |
| 1282 | GURNEY | Hubert Victor | 20.08.1910 | |
| 1283 | STRAUSS | Willem Jacobs | 20.08.1910 | |
| 1284 | VAN REENEN | Tobias | 20.08.1910 | |
| 1285 | DIXON | Robert Archibald | 22.08.1910 | |
| 1286 | BEAMISH | Claude Neville | 22.08.1910 | |
| 1287 | DE SALIS | John Norman | 22.08.1910 | |
| 1288 | BURNLEY | Arthur Basil | 22.08.1910 | |
| 1289 | STOKES | Leslie Eric Sheldon | 22.08.1910 | |
| 1290 | SKINNER | William John | 22.08.1910 | |
| 1291 | DOREHILL | Maurice | 22.08.1910 | |
| 1292 | POWER | James Percy | 22.08.1910 | |
| 1293 | ROBINSON | Robert Hally Laye | 22.08.1910 | |
| 1294 | MILNER | Claude Auguste | 29.08.1910 | |
| 1295 | LEAPER | Alexander William | 29.08.1910 | |
| 1296 | LEAPER | Ernest Bodycote | 28.08.1910 | Sgt |
| 1297 | LAW | William Henry | 29.08.1910 | |
| 1298 | MUGRIDGE | Gordon Edwin | 29.08.1910 | |
| 1299 | FOSTER | Sydney Herbert | 31.08.1910 | |
| 1300 | JOHNS | Arthur Cromwell | 31.08.1910 | |
| 1301 | STANLEY | Christopher Lawrence | 31.08.1910 | |
| 1302 | GUMBRILL | George Randolph | 03.09.1910 | |
| 1303 | LAWRENCE | John George | 03.09.1910 | |
| 1304 | COLLINS | Benjamin Edward | 03.09.1910 | |
| 1305 | BANKS | Norman | 03.09.1910 | |
| 1306 | TOMLINSON | John Pilling | 03.09.1910 | |
| 1307 | BLISS | Eugene | 07.09.1910 | |
| 1308 | LANGE | Patrick | 10.09.1910 | |
| 1309 | McGRATH | | | |
| 1310 | BETTLE | James Selby | 10.09.1910 | |
| 1311 | SOUTHERN | Harold Archibald | 10.09.1910 | |
| 1312 | RITCHIE | Eric Moore | 10.09.1910 | |
| 1313 | DOREHILL | Thomas Vere | 10.09.1910 | |
| 1314 | BLAGROVE | John | 10.09.1910 | |
| 1315 | LOCKNER | John Tobias Albert | 14.09.1910 | |
| 1316 | POLLOCK | Neil Morrison | 19.09.1910 | |
| 1317 | THOMSON | William | 19.09.1910 | |
| 1318 | BROCK | Frederick Charles | 19.09.1910 | |
| 1319 | BRYCE | George | 19.09.1910 | |
| 1320 | PRICE | Ernest | 19.09.1910 | |
| 1321 | McMICKEN | Percival Jubilee | 19.09.1910 | |
| 1322 | DAINTY | James Reuben | 19.09.1910 | |
| 1323 | MOULDER | Albert John | 19.09.1910 | |
| 1324 | KENNEDY | Thomas William | 19.09.1910 | |
| 1325 | TRIGG | Grantley | 19.09.1910 | |
| 1326 | HEMENSLEY | Charles John | 19.09.1910 | Capt. |
| 1327 | WILLIAMS | Frank | 19.09.1910 | |
| 1328 | PAYNE | Robert George | 19.09.1910 | |
| 1329 | MALPAGE | Victor | 19.09.1910 | |
| 1330 | BIRD | Charles Luard | 21.09.1910 | |
| 1331 | RUILE | Louis | 24.09.1910 | Inspr |
| 1332 | LODGE | Frederic Arthur | 24.09.1910 | |
| 1333 | ALEXANDER | Reginald | 24.09.1910 | |
| 1334 | ROBINSON | Albert Thomas | 24.09.1910 | |
| 1335 | UTTERTON | Alfred | 24.09.1910 | S/Sgt |
| 1336 | LITTLE | Ernest Murrell | 24.09.1910 | |
| 1337 | BOWES | Reginald Edward | 24.09.1910 | |
| 1338 | JACKSON | William | 24.09.1910 | |
| 1339 | RICHMOND | William Frederic | 24.09.1910 | |
| 1340 | DE LANTOUR | Albert Sconce | 24.09.1910 | |
| 1341 | BAUER | Ernest | 01.10.1910 | |
| 1342 | DAVIS | Albert Edward | 08.10.1910 | Cpl |
| 1343 | HURD | George Frederick | 08.10.1910 | |
| 1344 | WALKER | Robert | 08.10.1910 | |
| 1345 | KNOWLTON | Arthur Bernard | 08.10.1910 | |
| 1346 | BUSSEY | Gilbert | 08.10.1910 | |
| 1347 | KIRK | Robert Howard | 08.10.1910 | |
| 1348 | SEARLE | Ernest Edward | 08.10.1910 | |
| 1349 | ANDERSON | Arthur Frederick | 08.10.1910 | |
| 1350 | BROWN | Herbert Stewart | 08.10.1910 | |
| 1351 | COLEMAN | John | 06.10.1910 | |
| 1352 | THOMSON | William Alvan | 22.10.1910 | |
| 1353 | PATCHETT | Herbert Charles | 22.10.1910 | |
| 1354 | HESSION | Ernest William | 22.10.1910 | |
| 1355 | POWELL | Ewart John | 22.10.1910 | |
| 1356 | CASTLE | Edgar Collins | 22.10.1910 | |
| 1357 | BOWLES | Charles Vincent | 22.10.1910 | |
| 1358 | CAPON | Cecil Herbert | 22.10.1910 | |
| 1359 | HALL | James Edward | 22.10.1910 | |
| 1360 | FFENNELL | Edgar Huntley | 22.10.1910 | D/C/I. |
| 1361 | JONES | Robert | 12.11.1910 | |
| 1362 | KERSHAW | John | 12.11.1910 | |
| 1363 | SCHOLFIELD | Henry Charles | 12.11.1910 | |
| 1364 | BINDLOSS | Alexander Duncan | 23.11.1910 | |
| 1365 | BROMHEAD | John Ernest | 03.12.1910 | |
| 1366 | FRYER | William O'Dell | 03.12.1910 | |
| 1367 | WHITTAKER | George Lionel | 03.12.1910 | |
| 1368 | JONES | Walter Wilfred | 03.12.1910 | |
| 1369 | BALDERSON | Edwin William | 03.12.1910 | |
| 1370 | LEWIS | Leonard Mathias | 03.12.1910 | |
| 1371 | CLEGG | Alfred Frederick | 03.12.1910 | |
| 1372 | TOD | Alexander | 03.12.1910 | |
| 1373 | HOLLICK | William Arnott | 03.12.1910 | |
| 1374 | BARE | Alfred Raymund | 03.12.1910 | |
| 1375 | HAY-COGHLAN | Leo DeBurgh | 03.12.1910 | |
| 1376 | CAMERON | Donald Stephenson | 29.12.1910 | |
| 1377 | STAPPARD | Edward Arthur | 29.12.1910 | |
| 1378 | LOMAX | Roger Herbert | 31.12.1910 | Cpl |
| 1379 | CATCHPOLE | Ernest Knightly | 31.12.1910 | |
| 1380 | BOSWELL | Charles | 31.12.1910 | |
| 1381 | ARMSTRONG | Leslie Hardbottle | 31.12.1910 | |
| 1382 | WILSON | Archibald Edward | 31.12.1910 | |
| 1383 | RALPH | Lewis Lush | 31.12.1910 | |
| 1384 | PATERSON | Robert George | 31.12.1910 | |
| 1385 | HOWLDEN | Richard Cyril | 31.12.1910 | |
| 1386 | BABB | William Henry | 31.12.1910 | |
| 1387 | POOLE | Henry Bradish | 14.01.1911 | |
| 1388 | HARDING | Herbert Oliver | 30.01.1911 | |
| 1389 | TOLLEY | Walter Theodore | 04.02.1911 | |
| 1390 | WYLD | Walter Gordon | 04.02.1911 | |
| 1391 | HARPER | Bertram | 08.02.1911 | |
| 1392 | CULLEY | James Attenborough | 08.02.1911 | |
| 1393 | SUTHERLAND | Robert | 08.02.1911 | |
| 1394 | POWELL | Leslie William | 08.02.1911 | |
| 1395 | STEEDMAN | Wilfred Frank | 08.02.1911 | |
| 1396 | WINTER | Alfred Paul DeLappe | 08.02.1911 | |
| 1397 | GREEN | Jack | 08.02.1911 | |
| 1398 | SALT | John Edwin | 03.02.1911 | |
| 1399 | PALMER | Robert John | 08.02.1911 | |
| 1400 | WEBB | Edward | 15.02.1911 | |
| 1401 | ROBINSON | John George | 22.02.1911 | |
| 1402 | DYMORE-BROWN | Reginald Edney | 25.02.1911 | |
| 1403 | SMITH | Ernest James | 27.02.1911 | |
| 1404 | INSKIPP | Norman | 09.03.1911 | |
| 1405 | VANNECK | Andrew Nicholas | 09.03.1911 | |
| 1406 | DAY | Claude Purcell | 09.03.1911 | |
| 1407 | BAYLY | Frank Boscawen | 09.03.1911 | |
| 1408 | WILLOUGHBY | James Alexander | 09.03.1911 | |
| 1409 | SMYTH | Walter Ormonde | 09.03.1911 | |
| 1410 | SEARLES | Wilfred Bernard | 09.03.1911 | |
| 1411 | GAULD | John Ridd | 09.03.1911 | |
| 1412 | CHAMPION | Leonard John | 09.03.1911 | Trp |
| 1413 | FAIRBAIRN | Aubrey Murray | 09.03.1911 | |
| 1414 | HAROLD | Herbert Michael | 11.03.1911 | |
| 1415 | CORIN | William Edward | 09.03.1911 | |
| 1416 | LLOYD | Bazyl Archibald | 11.03.1911 | |
| 1417 | GRICE | William | 18.03.1911 | |
| 1418 | FARPANT | Frederick | 18.03.1911 | |
| 1419 | BUGLER | Henry | 06.04.1911 | A/Com |
| 1420 | O'BRIEN | Dennis | 06.04.1911 | |
| 1421 | NAPIER | Cecil James | 15.04.1911 | |
| 1422 | NOEL | Norman Philpot | 20.04.1911 | |
| 1423 | KING | Frederick William | 20.04.1911 | |
| 1424 | STUBBS | Thomas Shann | 20.04.1911 | |
| 1425 | DUNN | Alan Johnson | 20.04.1911 | |
| 1426 | LANGRIDGE | Albert James | 20.04.1911 | |
| 1427 | JACKSON | Percy Henry | 20.04.1911 | |
| 1428 | ASTON | Reginald Arthur | 20.04.1911 | |
| 1429 | PEARSON | Oswald Robertson | 20.04.1911 | |
| 1430 | PEARSON | Norman Robertson | 20.04.1911 | |
| 1431 | JONES | Athol Frank | 20.04.1911 | |
| 1432 | CHAMBERS | Raymond | 20.04.1911 | |
| 1433 | WEBER | Andries Johannes | 01.05.1911 | |
| 1434 | DE BEER | Johannes Frederick | 01.05.1911 | |
| 1435 | ALEXANDER | James Campbell | 03.05.1911 | A/Supt. |
| 1436 | SPENCELEY | Thomas William | 08.05.1911 | |
| 1437 | MOCKE | Ebenezer | 09.05.1911 | |
| 1438 | BATIZAT | Edward | 09.05.1911 | |
| 1439 | HEATHCOTE | Robert | 11.05.1911 | |
| 1440 | HEATHCOTE | Gilbert Hugh | 11.05.1911 | |
| 1441 | ADKINS | Reginald Stapleton | 11.05.1911 | |
| 1442 | HARVEYSON | Thomas Cecil | 18.04.1911 | |
| 1443 | COLLINSON | David | 18.05.1911 | |
| 1444 | HUSBANDS | William | 18.05.1911 | |
| 1445 | PICKERING | Thomas Edward | 18.05.1911 | |
| 1446 | CORR | William Douglas | 18.05.1911 | |
| 1447 | MURPHY | Thomas | 17.05.1911 | |

| No | Surname | Name | Date | Rank |
|---|---|---|---|---|
| 1448 | DE VILLIERS | Stephen Robert | 25.05.1911 | |
| 1449 | GRANTHAM | Harold Edmund | 27.05.1911 | |
| 1450 | EDMONDS | George Maxwell | 27.05.1911 | |
| 1451 | MEADOWS | Harry | 27.05.1911 | |
| 1452 | BURNESS | James Selby | 27.05.1911 | |
| 1453 | GROVE | Gerald | 27.05.1911 | |
| 1454 | EDWARDS | Arnold Burrington | 27.05.1911 | Trp |
| 1455 | SCALLON | John Matthew | 06.06.1911 | |
| 1456 | CUFFE | Ernest Mansfield | 08.06.1911 | |
| 1457 | SCHRONEN | Christian Frederick | 13.06.1911 | Cpl |
| 1458 | HUNTLEY | William Burney | 15.06.1911 | |
| 1459 | LANGHAM | Robert William | 15.06.1911 | |
| 1460 | WOOLLARD | Eric Graham | 15.06.1911 | |
| 1461 | HOLMES | Thomas | 15.06.1911 | |
| 1462 | BATTERSBY | John Radcliffe | 15.06.1911 | |
| 1463 | PEACOCK | Frank | 15.06.1911 | |
| 1464 | McCAW | Osmond Galbraith | 15.06.1911 | |
| 1465 | CRONEEN | Brian | 15.06.1911 | |
| 1466 | THOMSON | Robert | 15.06.1911 | |
| 1467 | CROUDACE | Harold | 15.06.1911 | |
| 1468 | McKEE | Alexander Gray | 15.06.1911 | |
| 1469 | EDWARDS | Frederick Walter | 17.06.1911 | Sgt. |
| 1470 | WOOLGAR | Charles Sidney | 24.06.1911 | |
| 1471 | SUTTON | Ashley Maclure | 04.07.1911 | |
| 1472 | BARKER | John Malcolm | 15.07.1911 | |
| 1473 | SMITH | Henry James | 15.07.1911 | |
| 1474 | ALLAM | Walter | 15.07.1911 | |
| 1475 | STONE | Walter James | 15.07.1911 | |
| 1476 | LOGAN | John Innes | 15.07.1911 | Insp. |
| 1477 | LANCASTER | Harold | 15.07.1911 | Sgt. |
| 1478 | BOLTON | Arthur Edward | 15.07.1911 | |
| 1479 | KEALY | Patrick Joseph | 15.07.1911 | |
| 1480 | EVANS | Eric | 15.07.1911 | |
| 1481 | ROBBIE | Andrew | 15.07.1911 | |
| 1482 | HOUSOME | Bernard Kenneth | 15.07.1911 | |
| 1483 | RAMSEY | Henry | 02.08.1911 | |
| 1484 | VINCENT | Barclay Ross | 11.08.1911 | |
| 1485 | PENWRIGHT | Albert Hyde | 11.08.1911 | |
| 1486 | PETCH | George Frederick | 11.08.1911 | |
| 1487 | ADCOCK | John Francis | 11.08.1911 | |
| 1488 | BURGESS | Charles Fredrick | 11.08.1911 | |
| 1489 | ROCHARD | Everard | 11.08.1911 | |
| 1490 | BALLARD | Henry Lewis | 11.08.1911 | |
| 1491 | HEATH | Edward Hugh | 11.08.1911 | |
| 1492 | DOUGHTY | Hugh | 19.08.1911 | |
| 1493 | FOSTER | Sydney LeNeve | 05.09.1911 | |
| 1494 | GARDINER | Cecil Senior | 05.09.1911 | |
| 1495 | COOKE | Charles Ernest | 05.09.1911 | |
| 1496 | ALLEN | Walter | 05.09.1911 | |
| 1497 | RUSSELL | Charles Vere | 09.09.1911 | |
| 1498 | SANDERS | John Frederick | 09.09.1911 | |
| 1499 | DICKINS | Archibald James | 09.09.1911 | |
| 1500 | TILL | Thomas Arthur | 09.09.1911 | |
| 1501 | LOWNDS | Lawrence Edward | 14.09.1911 | |
| 1502 | FEAR | Frank Albert | 12.10.1911 | |
| 1503 | WINWARD | Herbert Edward | 14.10.1911 | |
| 1504 | BAKER | Claude Reginald | 17.10.1911 | |
| 1505 | HOWE | Robert Arthur | 21.10.1911 | |
| 1506 | ROBERTSON | Thomas | 21.10.1911 | |
| 1507 | EVES | Edward Thomas | 21.10.1911 | |
| 1508 | MORGAN | Thomas Lawson | 21.10.1911 | |
| 1509 | CAMPFIELD | Reuben Edwin | 21.10.1911 | |
| 1510 | FAHY | William | 16.10.1911 | |
| 1511 | LAKE | George | 16.10.1911 | |
| 1512 | HARROP | Henry | 16.10.1911 | |
| 1513 | STONE | Harold Ramsey | 28.10.1911 | |
| 1514 | ADAMS | Albert Edward | 28.10.1911 | |
| 1515 | KEMP | Harold James | 28.10.1911 | |

| No | Surname | Name | Date | Rank |
|---|---|---|---|---|
| 1517 | LANCASTER | Duncan Gordon | 28.10.1911 | |
| 1518 | LEWIS | Horace | 28.10.1911 | |
| 1519 | COCKERTON | Arthur Richard | 28.10.1911 | |
| 1520 | GORDON | Cecil Oscar | 28.10.1911 | |
| 1521 | TARBUTT | Henry William | 28.10.1911 | |
| 1522 | GOODFELLOW | Esme Paulo | 28.10.1911 | |
| 1523 | BISSHOPP | Douglas Wardell | 28.10.1911 | |
| 1524 | HICK | Thomas Edward | 09.11.1911 | |
| 1525 | CHILD | Henry Arthur | 25.11.1911 | |
| 1526 | LAMMING | John Grimmer | 09.12.1911 | |
| 1527 | McEWAN | Thomas Allan | 09.12.1911 | |
| 1528 | HICKS | James Bracher | 09.12.1911 | |
| 1529 | RUTHERFORD | Arthur Henry | 09.12.1911 | |
| 1530 | ARNOTT | Noel | 09.12.1911 | |
| 1531 | CATER | Herbert Stanley | 09.12.1911 | Trp |
| 1532 | DOUGLAS | Donald Gordon | 16.12.1911 | |
| 1533 | TAYLOR | Herbert Walter | 09.01.1912 | |
| 1534 | COLLIS | Lancelot Harry | 09.01.1912 | |
| 1535 | HUNT | Harold Clement | 09.01.1912 | |
| 1536 | ASTON | Archibald Malcolm | 09.01.1912 | |
| 1537 | FARMER | Henry James | 09.01.1912 | |
| 1538 | HARMER | James | 11.01.1912 | |
| 1539 | MIDDLETON | Edgar | 17.01.1912 | |
| 1540 | SWANN | Charles | 10.02.1912 | |
| 1541 | WOODLEY | Arthur Horace | 10.02.1912 | |
| 1542 | BUTLER | Walter | 10.02.1912 | |
| 1543 | JUST | James Christian | 10.02.1912 | |
| 1544 | ROPER | Alfred Charles | 10.02.1912 | |
| 1545 | LANE | Arthur Frederick | 10.02.1912 | |
| 1546 | DEAR | George Alfred | 10.02.1912 | |
| 1547 | CALLAWAY | Bernard Fredrick | 10.02.1912 | |
| 1548 | THOMAS | Wilfred | 10.02.1912 | |
| 1549 | ROBERTS | Sydney Thomas | 10.02.1912 | |
| 1550 | HAMILTON | Thomas | 10.02.1912 | |
| 1551 | COCHRANE | Rupert William | 08.03.1912 | |
| 1552 | HARRIS | Reginald William | 08.03.1912 | |
| 1553 | EDWARDS | Theodore Wilfred | 12.03.1912 | |
| 1554 | DYER | Ronald William | 16.03.1912 | |
| 1555 | HAWKER | Godfrey Carewe | 16.03.1912 | |
| 1556 | MOORE | Frederick John | 16.03.1912 | |
| 1557 | NEAME | Arthur Langley | 16.03.1912 | |
| 1558 | PARR | James Webb | 16.03.1912 | Capt. |
| 1559 | WALKER | Arthur Cyril | 16.03.1912 | |
| 1560 | JUDSON | Jack William | 01.04.1912 | |
| 1561 | HAGEMANN | Julius Herman | 11.04.1912 | |
| 1562 | ELVIDGE | Arthur Ewing | 20.04.1912 | |
| 1563 | SALT | Thurstan D'Arcy | 20.04.1912 | |
| 1564 | McDONALD | Alexander | 20.04.1912 | |
| 1565 | BROOKS | Reginald St. George | 20.04.1912 | |
| 1566 | TATE | Allan Thomas | 20.04.1912 | |
| 1567 | PEARSON | Walter | 20.04.1912 | |
| 1568 | OUTRAM | George Lance | 20.04.1912 | |
| 1569 | WILTSHIRE | George Harry | 20.04.1912 | |
| 1570 | CATLETT | Richard | 20.04.1912 | |
| 1571 | RYAN | John James | 20.04.1912 | |
| 1572 | BACON | Francis Henry | 20.04.1912 | |
| 1573 | WALKER | John Alexander | 20.04.1912 | |
| 1574 | MALPAGE | Victor | 20.04.1912 | |
| 1575 | CHAMPION | Francis Hillier | 04.05.1912 | |
| 1576 | ROBINSON | Julian Philip Kay | 09.05.1912 | |
| 1577 | Mac KENZIE | Gordon | 18.05.1912 | |
| 1578 | SEYMOUR-HALL | Bernard Hugh | 18.05.1912 | |
| 1579 | ALLBERRY | Charles Herbert | 18.05.1912 | |
| 1580 | SAWTELL | James Ralph | 13.06.1912 | |
| 1581 | HARRIS | Charles | 13.06.1912 | |
| 1582 | BROWN | James | 13.06.1912 | |
| 1583 | McGURDY | Alexander Millar | 13.06.1912 | |
| 1584 | ROSE-INNES | Cosmos William | 15.06.1912 | |

| No | Surname | Name | Date | Rank |
|---|---|---|---|---|
| 1586 | ULLMAN | Charles Joseph | 17.06.1912 | |
| 1587 | KIRBY | Walter Alfred | 21.06.1912 | |
| 1588 | GRADY | Henry | 22.06.1912 | |
| 1589 | HICKMOTT | James Harry | 13.06.1912 | |
| 1590 | TAYLOR | Stanley Fletcher | 13.06.1912 | |
| 1591 | KINGSTONE | Walter Henry | 13.06.1912 | |
| 1592 | PRESTON | William Valentine | 07.07.1912 | |
| 1593 | HOWES | Thomas Henry | 07.07.1912 | |
| 1594 | PALLANT | Herbert Charles | 07.07.1912 | |
| 1595 | CURRIE | Charles | 07.07.1912 | |
| 1596 | PARSONS | Donald Edward | 07.07.1912 | |
| 1597 | FILOSE | Francis Bartholomew | 07.07.1912 | |
| 1598 | CHAMBERS | Henry Herbert | 07.07.1912 | |
| 1599 | MACKEN | Francis Joseph | 07.07.1912 | |
| 1600 | Mac LEMAN | William | 07.07.1912 | |
| 1601 | SPALDING | James Gordon | 07.07.1912 | |
| 1602 | COTTON | Robert | 07.07.1912 | |
| 1603 | SUTTON | Ernest Walter | 07.07.1912 | |
| 1604 | HUTCHINGS | Ebenezer | 07.07.1912 | |
| 1605 | MOORE | Thomas David | 07.07.1912 | |
| 1606 | MATHIESON | Thomas Polough | 22.07.1912 | |
| 1607 | PARTRIDGE | Walter Thomas | 25.07.1912 | |
| 1608 | BROWN | Oscar Leslie | 25.07.1912 | Sgt. |
| 1609 | COLLINGTON | Frank | 10.08.1912 | |
| 1610 | FLOCKHART | James | 10.08i.1912 | |
| 1611 | INGPEN | Edward Lucian | 10.08i.1912 | |
| 1612 | MARTIN | Harold Frederick | 10.08i.1912 | |
| 1613 | SMALL | Wallace Richard | 10.08i.1912 | |
| 1614 | SYMS | Albert William | 10.08.1912 | |
| 1615 | BLIN | Douglas John | 10.08.1912 | |
| 1616 | STUART-REID | George | 10.08i.1912 | |
| 1617 | ROBINSON | Maurice William | 14.08.1912 | |
| 1618 | Mac DONALD | Donald | 01.09.1912 | |
| 1619 | ARMFIELD | Arthur | 14.09.1912 | |
| 1620 | BLANDFORD | Charles Fredrick | 14.09.1912 | A/Supt. |
| 1621 | CULVER | Archibald Stanley | 14.09.1912 | |
| 1622 | FRASER | Andrew William | 14.09.1912 | |
| 1623 | SMITH | Albert Augustus | 14.09.1912 | |
| 1624 | HARNETTY | Edward | 26.09.1912 | Sgt |
| 1625 | McCORMAC | John Robert | 26.09.1912 | |
| 1626 | COLLINS | Walter James | 03.10.1910 | |
| 1627 | MARSHALL | John Howard | 05.10.1912 | |
| 1628 | ALGAR | Hugh Stanley | 17.10.1912 | |
| 1629 | ARUNDELL | Francis Douglas | 17.10.1912 | Trp |
| 1630 | BOOTH | Frederick Charles | 17.10.1912 | Sgt. |
| 1631 | BRYANT | Thomas Henry | 17.10.1912 | Capt. |
| 1632 | CULVERWELL | Duncan | 17.10.1912 | |
| 1633 | HAMMOND | Arthur | 17.10.1912 | |
| 1634 | HILL | Ralph Grenfell | 17.10.1912 | |
| 1635 | JEFFARES | Richard Thorpe | 17.10.1912 | Trp |
| 1636 | MESSUM | Alfred Leslie | 17.10.1912 | |
| 1637 | WARDROPER | Percy Redesdale | 17.10.1912 | |
| 1638 | WEBB | Walter Oscar | 17.10.1912 | |
| 1639 | HILLYER | Christopher Charles | 17.10.1912 | |
| 1640 | ALVEY | Samuel | 17.10.1912 | |
| 1641 | JACKSON | John William | 15.11.1912 | |
| 1642 | LAW | George Edward | 15.11.1912 | |
| 1643 | LEE | Frank Eric | 15.11.1912 | |
| 1644 | MALCOLMSON | William Henry Brice | 15.11.1912 | Trp |
| 1645 | STAFFORD | Guy Hillman | 15.11.1912 | |
| 1646 | BELL-SYER | Lewis Charles | 15.11.1912 | |
| 1647 | CASHEL | Arthur Rowan | 01.01.1913 | |
| 1648 | GOWRIE | George | 01.01.1913 | |
| 1649 | BRADING | Charles Taylor | 17.01.1913 | |
| 1650 | BRUCE | John Ashton | 17.01.1913 | |
| 1651 | CROSBEE | Edgar Oliver | 17.01.1913 | |
| 1652 | HARE | Edgar | 17.01.1913 | |
| 1653 | O'FARRELL | Ivan Travers | 17.01.1913 | Cpl |
| 1654 | LATIMER | Raynor Digby | 17.01.1913 | |

| No. | Surname | Forename | Rank | Date |
|---|---|---|---|---|
| 1655 | MOORE | Richard Frederick | | 17.01.1913 |
| 1656 | BRADBURY | Arthur Leonard | | 10.02.1913 |
| 1657 | WALSH | John George | | 14.02.1913 |
| 1658 | BROADBENT | George | | 07.02.1913 |
| 1659 | CONI | Stanley Jasper | | 21.02.1913 |
| 1660 | CORNISH | Hubert Arthur | | 21.02.1913 |
| 1661 | McCLEMENT | Gerrard Carr | | 21.02.1913 |
| 1662 | PARTINGTON | Herbert William | | 21.02.1913 |
| 1663 | WEST | Frederick James | Sgt. | 21.02.1913 |
| 1664 | CARTER | Allen Young | | 20.03.1913 |
| 1665 | COOK | Arthur Mark | | 20.03.1913 |
| 1666 | JOHNSON | Howard Buckland | Sgt. | 20.03.1913 |
| 1667 | SCOTCHBURN | John Mordaunt | | 20.03.1913 |
| 1668 | MANSERGH | Neville Southcote | Capt. | 31.03.1913 |
| 1669 | DAVEY | Albert Charles | | 17.04.1913 |
| 1670 | KNIGHT | Harold Squires | | 17.04.1913 |
| 1671 | FRETZ | Wilmot Theodore | | 17.04.1913 |
| 1672 | ADAMS | Arnold Veysey | | 17.04.1913 |
| 1673 | HASTINGS | James Hugh | | 17.04.1913 |
| 1674 | FISHER | Samuel William | | 17.04.1913 |
| 1675 | CANDY | Frank | | 17.04.1913 |
| 1676 | TRUSTRAM | Linley Charles | | 24.04.1913 |
| 1677 | CARTER | Edward Llewellin | | 22.05.1913 |
| 1678 | BITHREY | William Barry | | 27.05.1913 |
| 1679 | CROSLAND | Robert | | 27.05.1913 |
| 1680 | CROSS | Frank Albert | | 27.05.1913 |
| 1681 | DEBENHAM | Gerald Anthony | | 27.05.1913 |
| 1682 | GRIGGS | Victor Harold | | 27.05.1913 |
| 1683 | HACKNEY | Frederick | | 27.05.1913 |
| 1684 | HOPKINS | Francis Arthur | Sgt | 27.05.1913 |
| 1685 | PETTIT | William | | 27.05.1913 |
| 1686 | THOMINET | Rene Jules | | 27.05.1913 |
| 1687 | STRONGE | Rupert Maxwell | | 12.06.1913 |
| 1688 | BAWDEN | Harold Ellis | | 01.07.1913 |
| 1689 | GOSSELIN | Hugh DeVere | | 01.07.1913 |
| 1690 | MILLER | Cyril Stanley | | 01.07.1913 |
| 1691 | RUSSELL | Stanley James | | 01.07.1913 |
| 1692 | WINGHAM | Frank | | 01.07.1913 |
| 1693 | HOBDEN | William Gilbert | | 11.08.1913 |
| 1694 | WALTER | Stanley Northcote | | 19.08.1913 |
| 1695 | HINES | John Victor | D/Insp. | 25.07.1913 |
| 1696 | CARPENTER | Ivan Percy Brind | | 25.07.1913 |
| 1697 | JARMAN | Charles Edward | | 31.07.1913 |
| 1698 | ATKINSON | Alexander Bruce | | 01.08.1913 |
| 1699 | D'ARCY | Lionel George | | 20.08.1913 |
| 1700 | BARTON | Percy | | 19.08.1913 |
| 1701 | CLEMOW | Hedley William | Lt. Col. | 19.08.1913 |
| 1702 | GRAHAM | Eric Montrose | | 19.08.1913 |
| 1703 | GREEN | Charles John | | 19.08.1913 |
| 1704 | ROGERS | Charles | Trp | 19.08.1913 |
| 1705 | SYMONS | Lawrence Charles | | 19.08.1913 |
| 1706 | TACCHELLA | Edger William | Cpl. | 19.08.1913 |
| 1707 | WALKER | William Arthur | | 19.08.1913 |
| 1708 | McELLIGOTT | Thomas Garrett | | 18.08.1913 |
| 1709 | HADATH | Edwin | | 28.08.1913 |
| 1710 | HENNESSEY | John Matthew | Capt. | 28.08.1913 |
| 1711 | HORTON | Jack | | 28.08.1913 |
| 1712 | LIGAT | Henry | | 29.08.1913 |
| 1713 | ROBERTSON | Matthew MacPherson | | 29.08.1913 |
| 1714 | DESPARD | Ivor William | | 29.08.1913 |
| 1715 | VINCENT | Ernest William | | 29.08.1913 |
| 1716 | LAWRENCE | Jack Wilfred | | 29.08.1913 |
| 1717 | HOCKLEY | George | | 29.08.1913 |
| 1718 | STABLER | Arthur Sydney | | 29.08.1913 |
| 1719 | JAMIE | Matthew Campbell | S/Insp. | 29.08.1913 |
| 1720 | BAILLIE | Norman Clifford | | 29.08.1913 |
| 1721 | PARK | James | | 29.08.1913 |
| 1722 | HALL | Frank Tudor | | 29.08.1913 |
| 1723 | BRUCE | Michael William | | 29.08.1913 |
| 1724 | DAVIDSON | Thomas | | 03.09.1913 |
| 1725 | FREEBOROUGH | Arthur | | 03.09.1913 |
| 1726 | GILLSON | Albert John | | 03.09.1913 |
| 1727 | HARRISON | Alexander | | 03.09.1913 |
| 1728 | JUSTER | Frank William | | 03.09.1913 |
| 1729 | McNAUGHTON | Robert | | 03.09.1913 |
| 1730 | NIVEN | Robert | | 03.09.1913 |
| 1731 | RANKIN | Maxwell Ramsey | | 03.09.1913 |
| 1732 | ROBERTS | Percy Charles | | 03.09.1913 |
| 1733 | RUSSELL | James | | 03.09.1913 |
| 1734 | SQUIRE | Joseph | | 03.09.1913 |
| 1735 | STORIE | John | | 03.09.1913 |
| 1736 | TAYLOR | William Robb | | 03.09.1913 |
| 1737 | TELFER | William | | 03.09.1913 |
| 1738 | THOMAS | William | | 03.09.1913 |
| 1739 | VAUGHAN | Benjamin Myton | | 03.09.1913 |
| 1740 | LESLIE | Francis Ellington | | 03.09.1913 |
| 1741 | VAUGHAN | James Henry | Lieut. | 15.09.1913 |
| 1742 | FOWLER | Walter | | 19.09.1913 |
| 1743 | DOWNER | William Edward | | 19.09.1913 |
| 1744 | WELLS | Ernest Arthur | | 19.09.1913 |
| 1745 | JOHNSON | Owen Robert | | 19.09.1913 |
| 1746 | LEE | Robert Cuthbert | | 19.09.1913 |
| 1747 | WATT | George | | 19.09.1913 |
| 1748 | TINGLEY | James Baker | | 19.09.1913 |
| 1749 | BARRY | Lawrence Edward | Inspr. | 19.09.1913 |
| 1750 | GOSLING | Charles Henry | | 19.09.1913 |
| 1751 | TREVOR | John Rutherford | | 19.09.1913 |
| 1752 | ELLIOT | Francis Graham | | 19.09.1913 |
| 1753 | McDOUGAL | Daniel Lawson | | 19.09.1913 |
| 1754 | HARDIE | Adam George | | 19.09.1913 |
| 1755 | CLARK | John Campbell | | 19.09.1913 |
| 1756 | RIDDELL | Charles | D/1stSgt | 19.09.1913 |
| 1757 | LAMBURN | John Battersby | | 19.09.1913 |
| 1758 | ADDIS | George | | 19.09.1913 |
| 1759 | ELDRED | Albert Henry | | 08.10.1913 |
| 1760 | LUTTRELL | Sidney Philip | | 08.10.1913 |
| 1761 | BERNIE | John Augustus | | 10.10.1913 |
| 1762 | THOMAS | Brian James | | 11.10.1913 |
| 1763 | ALEXANDER | Samuel | | 15.10.1913 |
| 1764 | BAKER | John Curnow | | 15.10.1913 |
| 1765 | CACKETT | Basil Edward | | 15.10.1913 |
| 1766 | ELLIOTT | Frank Charles | | 15.10.1913 |
| 1767 | MERRY | Hugh Edward | | 15.10.1913 |
| 1768 | PHILLIPS | Douglas James | | 15.10.1913 |
| 1769 | RAMMAGE | Geoffrey Bant | | 15.10.1913 |
| 1770 | ROBINSON | Arthur Gordon | | 15.10.1913 |
| 1771 | ROSS | John Ellis | | 15.10.1913 |
| 1772 | THOMLINSON | Alfred | | 18.10.1913 |
| 1773 | TAYLOR | Alfred Ernest | | 20.10.1913 |
| 1774 | BROWNE | Ernest George | | 23.10.1913 |
| 1775 | McCLELLAND | James Emmet | | 25.10.1913 |
| 1776 | STEWART | William Malcolm | | 27.10.1913 |
| 1777 | ROBINSON | Percy Edgecumbe | | 27.10.1913 |
| 1778 | TAYLOR | William Ellor | | 31.10.1913 |
| 1779 | SHRUBSOLE | Claude Idwal | | 08.11.1913 |
| 1780 | HARRISON | Austin Bertram | | 12.11.1913 |
| 1781 | GISBORNE | Albert William | | 21.11.1913 |
| 1782 | PLANT | James | | 21.11.1913 |
| 1783 | DUNCAN | Sidney | | 19.12.1913 |
| 1784 | FENLON | John Joseph | | 19.12.1913 |
| 1785 | GREGORY | Howard George | | 19.12.1913 |
| 1786 | HOROBIN | William Frederick | | 19.12.1913 |
| 1787 | JONES | John David | | 19.12.1913 |
| 1788 | OZANNE | William Leslie | | 19.12.1913 |
| 1789 | SIDDONS | Bertram | | 19.12.1913 |
| 1790 | SMITH | Alexander James | | 19.12.1913 |
| 1791 | SMITH | Walter Colin | | 19.12.1913 |
| 1792 | STRATTON | Alfred James | | 19.12.1913 |
| 1793 | TWORT | Clement | Sgt. | 19.12.1913 |
| 1794 | HUTCHINSON | Graham Seton | | 26.12.1913 |
| 1795 | BUDD | Charles Arthur | | 07.01.1914 |
| 1796 | DAVIS | Reginald Henry | | 09.01.1914 |
| 1797 | HARGREAVES | Patrick Shiels | | 09.01.1914 |
| 1798 | HOWELL | Thomas Humphrey | | 09.01.1914 |
| 1799 | SIBOLD | Gerald Moverley | | 09.01.1914 |
| 1800 | WHITE | Walter Ware | | 09.01.1914 |
| 1801 | REACORD | Henry | D/Sgt | 16.01.1914 |
| 1802 | DAVIS | John | | 21.01.1914 |
| 1803 | ANDREWS | Charles James | | 21.01.1914 |
| 1804 | BAINBRIDGE | Frederick | | 13.02.1914 |
| 1805 | BURTON | Edmund Merceron | | 13.02.1914 |
| 1806 | ELLIS | Wilfred | | 13.02.1914 |
| 1807 | JAMES | Edgar | | 13.02.1914 |
| 1808 | LOWTH | William Barclay | | 13.02.1914 |
| 1809 | MOORE | Noel Arthur | | 13.02.1914 |
| 1810 | OULTON | Henry Charles | | 13.02.1914 |
| 1811 | WELLS | William Henry | | 13.02.1914 |
| 1812 | RAY | William | | 15.02.1914 |
| 1813 | CONNOCK | Claude Jameson | | 20.02.1914 |
| 1814 | FORGAN | William Middleton | | 21.02.1914 |
| 1815 | GACHES | Vernon Reed | | 01.03.1914 |
| 1816 | BORLAND | William Armstrong | | 13.03.1914 |
| 1817 | DART | William Thomas | | 13.03.1914 |
| 1818 | KENDRICK | Arthur Percy | | 13.03.1914 |
| 1819 | KING | Richard Abercrombie | | 13.03.1914 |
| 1820 | PEARSON | Bernard Garencieres | | 13.03.1914 |
| 1821 | POOLE | Anthony Arthur | | 13.03.1914 |
| 1822 | WARD | George Arthur | | 13.03.1914 |
| 1823 | WATSON | Harry Charles | | 13.03.1914 |
| 1824 | HAUGH | John | | 13.03.1914 |
| 1825 | JARVIS | Norman Henry | | 01.04.1914 |
| 1826 | TINDALE | George Ralph | | 01.04.1914 |
| 1827 | WELSH | Thomas | | 01.04.1914 |
| 1828 | WILTSHIRE | Charles Arthur | | 01.04.1914 |
| 1829 | COLLARD | Edward Avalon | | 01.04.1914 |
| 1830 | RIX | William | | 15.04.1914 |
| 1831 | SKEET | Roland George | | 16.04.1914 |
| 1832 | WALTER | Harold Hixon | | 21.04.1914 |
| 1833 | STUBBS | Morritt Medhurst | | 27.04.1914 |
| 1834 | BICKLEY | Reginald Dudley | | 01.05.1914 |
| 1835 | EDWARDS | Edie | | 02.05.1914 |
| 1836 | HILL | Douglas Granville | | 08.05.1914 |
| 1837 | BIRCH | Frederick | | 08.05.1914 |
| 1838 | FRENCH | David | | 08.05.1914 |
| 1839 | KEEN | Frederick George | | 08.05.1914 |
| 1840 | WALKER | Walter | | 08.05.1914 |
| 1841 | COURT | John Henry | Sgt | 08.05.1914 |
| 1842 | DUDBRIDGE | Leslie Francis | | 08.05.1914 |
| 1843 | HENDERSON | Walter John | | 08.05.1914 |
| 1844 | JEANS | William | | 08.05.1914 |
| 1845 | RUSSELL | Frank | | 08.05.1914 |
| 1846 | PAGE | Herbert George | | 08.05.1914 |
| 1847 | WHEELER | John Frederick | | 08.05.1914 |
| 1848 | MALIN | George | | 08.05.1914 |
| 1849 | UPTON | George Robert | | 12.05.1914 |
| 1850 | ROBERTS | Samuel | | 08.05.1914 |
| 1851 | COOKE | Lionel Percy | | 27.05.1914 |
| 1852 | TAYLOR | Henry Arthur | | 27.05.1914 |
| 1853 | BULLOCK | John Edward | | 27.05.1914 |
| 1854 | LESLIE | George | | 27.05.1914 |
| 1855 | WEBB | Edward | | 28.05.1914 |
| 1856 | COOPER | Wilfred Whittaker | Trp | 08.06.1914 |
| 1857 | TEBRUGGE | George Ferdinand | | 06.07.1914 |
| 1858 | NORTHCOTE | Ronald Cecil | | 08.07.1914 |
| 1859 | BENNETT | Henry Gordon | | 08.07.1914 |
| 1860 | SURGEY | Herbert Frederick | | 08.07.1914 |
| 1861 | RICHARDS | Alexander Osborne | Col | 08.07.1914 |

| No. | Surname | First name(s) | Date | Rank |
|---|---|---|---|---|
| 1862 | BALL | John | 08.07.1914 | |
| 1863 | SKINNER | Dudley | 08.07.1914 | |
| 1864 | WRIGHT | William | 08.07.1914 | |
| 1865 | STOKES | Harold | 08.07.1914 | |
| 1866 | FARRAR | John | 08.07.1914 | |
| 1867 | YEATES | Reginald | 08.07.1914 | |
| 1868 | ROBERTS | Arthur Stanley | 08.07.1914 | |
| 1869 | LOOBY | Matthew Thomas | 08.07.1914 | |
| 1870 | GOUGH | Jesse | 08.07.1914 | |
| 1871 | FIELDS | Darrell | 08.07.1914 | |
| 1872 | SIDDALL | Thomas Frederick | 22.07.1914 | |
| 1873 | SPARROW | Cecil William | 22.07.1914 | |
| 1874 | STANLEY | William | 22.07.1914 | |
| 1875 | TREVELYAN | Arthur De Encort | 22.07.1914 | |
| 1876 | RICHARDSON | Arthur | 22.07.1914 | |
| 1877 | HOPE | Raymond George | 22.07.1914 | |
| 1878 | GRIFFITHS | Samuel Henry | 22.07.1914 | |
| 1879 | ADAM | John Henry | 24.07.1914 | |
| 1880 | WILLSON | Ferdinand John | 24.07.1914 | |
| 1881 | MASKALL | Thomas Henry | 30.07.1914 | |
| 1882 | PAYNE | Frederick | 05.08.1914 | |
| 1883 | WOODS | William | 05.08.1914 | |
| 1884 | WILLIAMSON | Arthur Edward | 06.08.1914 | |
| 1885 | WESTHOFEN | Arthur Wilhelm | 10.08.1914 | |
| 1886 | GILES | Robert Edward | 13.08.1914 | |
| 1887 | TIFFIN | Cyril Lester | 28.08.1914 | |
| 1888 | TYRRELL | John Hassard | 28.08.1914 | |
| 1889 | RUDLAND | Henry | 31.08.1914 | |
| 1890 | DAWSON | Harry Edward | 02.09.1914 | |
| 1891 | GROOM | Leon James | 07.09.1914 | |
| 1892 | DACEY | Stephen Michael | 10.09.1914 | |
| 1893 | TRUSCOTT | Sidney David | 10.09.1914 | |
| 1894 | MANFIELD | Rupert | 10.09.1914 | |
| 1895 | MAYGER | Daniel | 10.09.1914 | Sgt. |
| 1896 | THAIN | Hubert Reeve | 10.09.1914 | |
| 1897 | OLIVE | Clifford Frank | 10.09.1914 | |
| 1898 | ROBERTS | John | 10.09.1914 | |
| 1899 | STEWART | Robert Brown | 10.09.1914 | |
| 1900 | GALE | Oliver George | 10.09.1914 | |
| 1901 | REMMERS | George Hannington | 10.09.1914 | |
| 1902 | SELWOOD | Ralph | 10.09.1914 | |
| 1903 | WHITEHEAD | John Henry Cyril | 10.09.1914 | |
| 1904 | COOPER | Albert Arthur | 10.09.1914 | |
| 1905 | NICHOLLS | Richard | 14.09.1914 | |
| 1906 | JACOBS | Thomas Arthur | 19.09.1914 | S/Insp |
| 1907 | GRAHAM | David | 07.10.1914 | S/Insp |
| 1908 | GREENE | Evelyn John | 14.10.1914 | |
| 1909 | MEYER | Petrus Jacobus | 13.10.1914 | |
| 1910 | WOOD | Richard Guy | 16.10.1914 | |
| 1911 | GROENWALD | Piet Hendrick | 26.10.1914 | Trp |
| 1912 | BLAKER | James Drury | 17.12.1914 | |
| 1913 | BRIGGS | John Alfred | 07.01.1915 | |
| 1914 | SMITH | Leonard Oswald | 25.08.1914 | |
| 1915 | BURNHAMS | Frank Nelson | 28.01.1915 | |
| 1916 | DOYLE | Jacob | 11.08.1914 | |
| 1917 | BRADSHAW | Ernest George | 22.02.1915 | |
| 1918 | DAVIES | Walter David | 14.03.1915 | |
| 1919 | SEARSON | William Joseph | 21.03.1915 | |
| 1920 | JONES | John Evan | 10.04.1915 | |
| 1921 | ALLNUTT | Cecil Stavely | 20.04.1915 | |
| 1922 | BARKER | Harold Walter | 28.04.1915 | |
| 1923 | BURGESS | George Frederick | 12.05.1915 | |
| 1924 | HOWE | George Edward | 02.06.1915 | |
| 1925 | SEWELL | Philip Edward | 02.06.1915 | |
| 1926 | PITTAWAY | Ruben Joseph | 19.06.1915 | |
| 1927 | VENTER | Abram Nicolaas | 21.06.1915 | |
| 1928 | WISHART | Charles | 08.07.1915 | |
| 1929 | HOPE | John Robert | 13.07.1915 | |
| 1931 | CAHILL | George Francis | 04.08.1915 | |
| 1932 | VAN ZYL | James Jubilee | 04.08.1915 | |
| 1933 | McCARTHY | William Joseph | 04.08.1915 | |
| 1934 | DE STADLER | Hugo | 04.08.1915 | |
| 1935 | STRONACH | Ernest Sytner | 07.08.1915 | |
| 1936 | ELMS | William | 11.08.1915 | |
| 1937 | RATHBONE | Oswald George | 11.08.1915 | |
| 1938 | DAWSON | Charles | 11.08.1915 | |
| 1939 | WELCH | Thomas Francis | 11.08.1915 | |
| 1940 | MORIN | Edward | 14.08.1915 | |
| 1941 | NYMAN | Frank | 11.08.1915 | |
| 1942 | BAIRSTOW | Herbert | 11.08.1915 | |
| 1943 | PEETZ | Richard | 11.08.1915 | |
| 1944 | HUNT | Clarence Edward | 11.08.1915 | Cpl |
| 1945 | JOHNSTON | Christopher George | 11.08.1915 | |
| 1946 | BAKER | Joseph Edward | 11.08.1915 | |
| 1947 | NYMAN | Stanley George | 11.08.1915 | |
| 1948 | CLUNAS | John William | 11.08.1915 | |
| 1949 | McCANN | Walter Willia | 11.08.1915 | |
| 1950 | SMITH | Charles | 14.08.1915 | |
| 1951 | IMRIE | Wilfred Stephenson | 14.08.1915 | |
| 1952 | DURRANT | Christopher Martin | 18.08.1915 | |
| 1953 | BREAKS | Haley | 18.08.1915 | |
| 1954 | LIEBENBERG | Adriaan Nicolaas | 18.08.1915 | |
| 1955 | KOCH | Oscar | 18.08.1915 | |
| 1956 | ROSS | Arthur Henry | 21.08.1915 | |
| 1957 | DECKER | Cecil Edwin | 21.08.1915 | |
| 1958 | MORKEL | Alexander vd Byl | 21.08.1915 | |
| 1959 | ARMSTRONG | George William | 21.08.1915 | |
| 1960 | REICH | John Charles | 25.08.1915 | |
| 1961 | McKNIGHT | Joseph Thomas | 25.08.1915 | |
| 1962 | DE VILLIERS | Ockert Tobias | 28.08.1915 | |
| 1963 | VAN DER SPUY | Andrew | 28.06.1915 | |
| 1964 | CORNISH | William Stanley | 01.09.1915 | |
| 1965 | ROBERTS | George Alfred | 01.09.1915 | |
| 1966 | BUTLER | Frederick Ernest | 14.09.1915 | |
| 1967 | McGREGOR | Ian | 25.09.1915 | |
| 1968 | GLASS | Ernest Cyril | 02.10.1915 | |
| 1969 | DU PLESSIS | Albert Johan | 06.10.1915 | |
| 1970 | BATE | Cyril James | 23.10.1915 | |
| 1971 | QUINN | David Reuben | 01.06.1915 | |
| 1972 | SQUIRES | John Frederick | 04.12.1915 | |
| 1973 | DE KLERK | Hugo John | 04.12.1915 | |
| 1974 | OUSTHUIZEN | Peter James | 22.12.1915 | |
| 1975 | STUART | Andrew Daniel | 17.09.1915 | S/Insp |
| 1976 | O'LINSKY | James Alfred | 29.12.1915 | S/Insp |
| 1977 | JOYNT | Robert | 05.01.1916 | |
| 1978 | TROAKE | Stephen James | 05.01.1916 | |
| 1979 | SHEPPARD | Frank | 20.12.1916 | |
| 1980 | BOWIE | John Michie | 05.01.1916 | Trp |
| 1981 | CALLAN | William Leigh | 17.08.1914 | |
| 1982 | PIETERS | Alfred Charles | 17.08.1914 | |
| 1983 | HAUSBERGER | Johannes Gerhardus | 27.03.1918 | |
| 1984 | WILSON | Richard George | 18.04.1918 | |
| 1985 | JOUBERT | Johannes Matthews | 15.01.1917 | |
| 1986 | BEZUIDENHOUT | Francios Isaac | 20.11.1916 | |
| 1987 | BOOYSEN | Francios Cornelius | 15.01.1917 | |
| 1988 | FORD | William Ignatius | 18.01.1917 | |
| 1989 | FOORD | William Ignatius | 26.01.1917 | |
| 1990 | PANTER | Robert Charles | 01.08.1917 | |
| 1991 | ROSSITER | Edward | 14.08.1917 | |
| 1992 | DE VOS | Nicholas Johannes | 15.04.1918 | |
| 1993 | BASSON | William Henry | 02.07.1918 | |
| 1994 | SWART | Daniel Johannes | 05.02.1917 | |
| 1995 | VAN AARDT | Christian Lourence | 05.05.1917 | |
| 1996 | BREWER | Benjamin Victor | 03.12.1917 | |
| 1997 | [illegible] | [illegible] | 01.06.1918 | |
| 1998 | [illegible] | [illegible] | 18.12.1918 | |
| 2000 | DAY | Frederick Warren | 30.01.1919 | D/Insp |
| 2001 | SMITH | Reginald Porter | 21.01.1919 | |
| 2002 | DE LANGE | Johannes Frederick | 30.08.1918 | |
| 2003 | DE BEER | Dirk Jacobus | 04.06.1918 | |
| 2004 | EMERICK | Leo Martin | 13.02.1918 | |
| 2005 | MANDY | Raymond Keith | 09.04.1919 | |
| 2006 | CHILD | George Carl | 05.04.1919 | S/Insp |
| 2007 | SIMS | Frederick Edward | 23.04.1919 | |
| 2008 | BELL aka PEACH | Claude Moore | 16.04.1919 | Inspr. |
| 2009 | VAUGHAN | Geoffrey Samuel | 26.04.1919 | D/Inspr. |
| 2010 | MANN | William Joseph | 26.04.1919 | |
| 2011 | WEBB | Harold Beauchamp | 26.04.1919 | |
| 2012 | TAYLOR | Roland Champenys | 26.04.1919 | Trp. |
| 2013 | SUTHERLAND | William Frank | 26.04.1919 | |
| 2014 | SMITH | Frank Roland | 26.04.1919 | |
| 2015 | REID | Kenneth McIntosh | 26.04.1919 | S/Ins |
| 2016 | RUFFEY | Harold Victor | 26.04.1919 | |
| 2017 | NOAKES | Walter John | 26.04.1919 | |
| 2018 | NASH | William Hollick | 26.04.1919 | Stf/Ins |
| 2019 | MORRIS | Walter George | 26.04.1919 | |
| 2020 | MOORE | Percy Richard | 26.04.1919 | |
| 2021 | LEACH | John Basil | 26.04.1919 | Cpl |
| 2022 | KING | Horace Albert | 26.04.1919 | |
| 2023 | JAMES | Walter Francis | 26.04.1919 | |
| 2024 | JACKSON | John | 26.04.1919 | |
| 2025 | JAMES | Walter Alwyne | 26.04.1919 | |
| 2026 | IZARD | Harry | 26.04.1919 | |
| 2027 | HARVEY | William Charles | 26.04.1919 | Capt. |
| 2028 | HAMPTON | Harold Cuthbert | 26.04.1919 | |
| 2029 | HUBBARD | William John | 26.04.1919 | |
| 2030 | GIDDINGS | James Duncan | 26.04.1919 | |
| 2031 | GRIESBACH | Ronald Charles | 26.04.1919 | |
| 2032 | GORNALL | Albert | 26.04.1919 | S/Maj. |
| 2033 | CRANMER-GORDON | Frederick William | 26.04.1919 | |
| 2034 | FOWLES | Ernest | 26.04.1919 | |
| 2035 | FOLD | Edward Stanley | 26.04.1919 | |
| 2036 | DICKINSON | Fredrick Albert | 26.04.1919 | |
| 2037 | COSGRAVE | Reginald Hugh | 26.04.1919 | |
| 2038 | CHAPMAN | Adolph Norman | 26.04.1919 | |
| 2039 | CROSS | William Frederick | 26.04.1919 | |
| 2040 | BUTLER | Frank | 26.04.1919 | |
| 2041 | BALDWIN | Charles Michael | 26.04.1919 | |
| 2042 | AUSTIN | Harold | 26.04.1919 | |
| 2043 | FOORD | William Abraham | 01.04.1918 | |
| 2044 | LONG | William | 26.04.1919 | Capt. |
| 2045 | MAYRICK | Cecil Jack | 26.04.1919 | |
| 2046 | WILKINSON | Richard | 03.05.1919 | S/Insp. |
| 2047 | PATTERSON | Stanley Clifford | 07.05.1919 | Major |
| 2048 | KEMPLEN | Edmund James | 26.04.1919 | |
| 2049 | MASON | Eric | 26.04.1919 | |
| 2050 | KILBORN | Sydney George | 21.05.1919 | C/Inspr. |
| 2051 | HELLING | Sydney Rattle | 21.05.1919 | Trp. |
| 2052 | LINTON | George | 11.06.1919 | |
| 2053 | GORRILL | Douglas Gordon | 11.06.1919 | |
| 2054 | JONES | Ernest Owen | 11.06.1919 | |
| 2055 | FOSTER | Arthur Audsley | 11.06.1919 | Tpr. |
| 2056 | CRICK | Frederick | 11.06.1919 | |
| 2057 | KETTLEWELL | Claude | 11.06.1919 | |
| 2058 | SWAFFIELD | Reginald Frederick | 11.06.1919 | S/Insp. |
| 2059 | LEYLAND | William George | 11.06.1919 | Major |
| 2060 | RICHENS | Ernest William | 11.06.1919 | |
| 2061 | BARRIE-SUTCLIFFE | Charles | 14.08.1917 | Cst. |
| 2062 | CUMINS | Stephen Henry | 11.06.1919 | Cpl |
| 2063 | HAWDON | Percy Charles | 11.06.1919 | Inspr. |
| 2064 | SLOPER | Percy Henry | 05.05.1917 | |
| 2065 | JOHNSON | Cyril Percy Hall | 11.06.1919 | |
| 2066 | SMITH | William Alfred | 11.06.1919 | Sgt. |
| 2067 | ROBINSON | Lawrence | 11.06.1919 | |
| 2068 | JUDGE | Horatio | 11.06.1919 | |

| No. | Surname | Forename | Date | Rank |
|---|---|---|---|---|
| 2069 | YOUNGMAN | Wilfred William | 11.06.1919 | Tpr. |
| 2070 | FITZGERALD | Henry Francis | 11.06.1919 | D/Insp. |
| 2071 | RAMSEY | Charles Douglas | 11.06.1919 | D/Ins. |
| 2072 | REEVES | Allan Samuel | 11.06.1919 | |
| 2073 | NICOL | Arthur | 11.06.1919 | S/Insp. |
| 2074 | SIMPSON | Joseph Gordon | 11.06.1919 | |
| 2075 | NORTH | Lawrence Edward | 11.06.1919 | |
| 2076 | PAYNE | Charles Leslie | 11.06.1919 | |
| 2077 | INGRAM | Edward Irving | 11.06.1919 | |
| 2078 | HANNIFAN | James Patrick | 11.06.1919 | |
| 2079 | APPS | William Mason | 11.06.1919 | |
| 2080 | RANDALL | Henry | 11.06.1919 | |
| 2081 | ODLING | Arthur Douglas | 11.06.1919 | |
| 2082 | BERWICK | Albert Edward | 11.06.1919 | |
| 2083 | HAYTOR | Frederick Charles | 11.06.1919 | |
| 2084 | CHAMPION | Fred | 11.06.1919 | |
| 2085 | BAGSHAW | Arthur Norman | 11.06.1919 | |
| 2086 | SAVILLE | George Parker | 11.06.1919 | |
| 2087 | HALLETT | Norman | 11.06.1919 | |
| 2088 | GODFREY | Charles Sinclair | 07.06.1919 | 1/Sgt. |
| 2089 | HOWARTH-CHANCELLOR | John Algernon | 11.06.1919 | |
| 2090 | JOHNSON | Frank | 11.06.1919 | |
| 2091 | BARRY | Thomas William | 11.06.1919 | |
| 2092 | KEMP | Albert Horace | 29.06.1917 | |
| 2093 | WEBER | Herbert Joachim | 11.06.1919 | |
| 2094 | CLOETE | Johannes Stapes | 18.05.1917 | |
| 2095 | WALKER | Matthew | 11.06.1919 | |
| 2096 | GORDON | Robert | 02.09.1919 | |
| 2097 | BLACKWELL | Richard Alick | 13.09.1919 | |
| 2098 | BECK | Thomas Edward | 22.09.1919 | |
| 2099 | BOWDEN | Frank | 22.09.1919 | |
| 2100 | BROOKS | Harry George | 22.09.1919 | |
| 2101 | BOND | William Victor | 22.09.1919 | Lieut. |
| 2102 | CLARKE | Ernest Herbert | 22.09.1919 | |
| 2103 | CLARKE | William Thomas | 22.09.1919 | Cpl. |
| 2104 | FORSTER | Rufus | 22.09.1919 | |
| 2105 | BEVAN | Tom | 22.09.1919 | |
| 2106 | GIBBS | Cedric Arthur | 22.09.1919 | S/Major |
| 2107 | HAYES | John Curtis | 22.09.1919 | |
| 2108 | HUNTER | George Walter | 22.09.1919 | |
| 2109 | PICKTHALL | Joselyn Richard | 22.09.1919 | |
| 2110 | PARISH | William George | 22.09.1919 | |
| 2111 | STARK | Norman David | 22.09.1919 | |
| 2112 | SPALDING | George Victor | 22.09.1919 | |
| 2113 | WALTERS | Alan Hubert | 22.09.1919 | |
| 2114 | WILSON | John | 22.09.1919 | C/Inspr. |
| 2115 | YOUNG | John Sebastian | 22.09.1919 | |
| 2116 | RILEY | Augustine Patrick | 22.09.1919 | |
| 2117 | GREENGRASS | Daniel Harold | 22.09.1919 | |
| 2118 | WILKINSON | George Frederick | 23.09.1919 | |
| 2119 | WILSON | Charles | 29.09.1919 | |
| 2120 | MOLE | Ambrose Dallyn | 30.09.1919 | |
| 2121 | CREMER | Lodewyk Tehores | 16.10.1919 | |
| 2122 | RICHARDSON | Edwin Rith | 26.10.1919 | Brig |
| 2123 | APPLEBY | James | 26.10.1919 | S/Insp |
| 2124 | THOMPSON | John Robert | 26.10.1919 | |
| 2125 | CHEATER | Ernest Edward | 26.10.1919 | |
| 2126 | YOUNG | Leonard Henry | 26.10.1919 | |
| 2127 | RUSSELL | Charles Eliot | 26.10.1919 | |
| 2128 | BACON | Francis James | 26.10.1919 | Capt. |
| 2129 | COLLINGS | Sidney Edward | 26.10.1919 | |
| 2130 | CARROLL | Herbert Lloyd | 26.10.1919 | |
| 2131 | SHAUL | Henry Cecil | 26.10.1919 | |
| 2132 | CLINTON | Leslie Norman | 05.11.1919 | D/Sgt. |
| 2133 | HARDING | Richard Cobden | 04.11.1919 | |
| 2134 | FORSTER | John Coxwell | 04.11.1919 | |
| 2135 | BRODIE | Norman | 04.11.1919 | |
| 2136 | DE BUDE | Royle | 04.11.1919 | |
| 2137 | CLEAL | Arthur Leonard | 04.11.1919 | |
| 2138 | WILSON | Alexander | 18.11.1919 | Const. |
| 2139 | SUTTON | Douglas William | 18.11.1919 | |
| 2140 | OLDHAM | James | 18.11.1919 | |
| 2141 | HALL | John Richard | 18.11.1919 | |
| 2142 | SCAMMELL | Bertram Ernest | 08.12.1919 | |
| 2143 | MERCER | John | 16.12.1919 | |
| 2144 | BRODIE | Richard Gordon | 06.01.1920 | |
| 2145 | WEBB | Harry Ronald | 06.01.1920 | |
| 2146 | LAVER | George Archie | 06.01.1920 | |
| 2147 | CRAWFORD | William McFarlane | 06.01.1920 | |
| 2148 | HORWOOD | Reginald James | 06.01.1920 | |
| 2149 | McKAY | Neil Currie | 06.01.1920 | Trp |
| 2150 | PHILLMORE | George | 06.01.1920 | |
| 2151 | WELLS | Archie | 06.01.1920 | |
| 2152 | BROWN | Sidney Graham | 06.01.1920 | |
| 2153 | HIGGINS | Leonard Edwin | 06.01.1920 | |
| 2154 | RIMANCZY | Charles Henry | 06.01.1920 | |
| 2155 | BISHORK | Anthony | 06.01.1920 | |
| 2156 | FLETCHER | Joseph | 06.01.1920 | |
| 2157 | GREEN | Percy | 06.01.1920 | |
| 2158 | GARDINER | George Mathias | 06.01.1920 | Sgt. |
| 2159 | CARSON | Victor David | 06.01.1920 | |
| 2160 | CORKERY | William | 06.01.1920 | |
| 2161 | BORRIS | Frederick Archibald | 06.01.1920 | |
| 2162 | TWINN | Ernest Victor | 06.01.1920 | |
| 2163 | CLARK | Leslie Victor | 06.01.1920 | |
| 2164 | COMFORT | Edward James | 06.01.1920 | |
| 2165 | SEARLE | Joseph Victor | 06.01.1920 | |
| 2166 | PAGE | Henry John | 06.01.1920 | |
| 2167 | LUBBOCK | William Joseph | 06.01.1920 | |
| 2168 | SELLENS | Frank | 06.01.1920 | |
| 2169 | RIDGERS | Walter Radcliffe | 06.01.1920 | |
| 2170 | DOWLING | Charles Matthews | 06.01.1920 | |
| 2171 | ALLEN | Arthur William | 06.01.1920 | |
| 2172 | FREEBORN | Arthur Charles | 06.01.1920 | Sgt. |
| 2173 | BUGLER | James Leslie | 12.01.1920 | |
| 2174 | JOHNSON | Frank Edward | 06.01.1920 | |
| 2175 | LE GRANGE | John Andrew | 14.01.1920 | |
| 2176 | JOWETT | George | 23.01.1920 | |
| 2177 | JENKINSON | Archibald Seymour | 02.02.1920 | |
| 2178 | MILNE | Charles Edwin | 02.02.1920 | |
| 2179 | RIDOUT | Eric Marsland | 02.02.1920 | |
| 2180 | RIPLEY | William | 02.02.1920 | |
| 2181 | ALTON | Reginald | 13.02.1920 | |
| 2182 | ARMAND | Ernest Gustave | 13.02.1920 | |
| 2183 | BARGER | George Frederick | 13.02.1920 | Sgt. |
| 2184 | BICKNELL | Claude | 13.02.1920 | |
| 2185 | BODINGTON | George Henry | 13.02.1920 | |
| 2186 | CLOHERTY | Albert Patrick | 13.02.1920 | |
| 2187 | COSTIGAN | Reginald Ernest | 13.02.1920 | |
| 2188 | CROOK | Alfred | 13.02.1920 | |
| 2189 | DORMAN | Sidney Pearce | 13.02.1920 | Capt. |
| 2190 | FUNNELL | Cuthbert David | 13.02.1920 | S/Insp |
| 2191 | GRAIN | George William | 13.02.1920 | |
| 2192 | HAWKINS | Alfred Edward | 13.02.1920 | C/Insp |
| 2193 | HOWARD | William | 13.02.1920 | Cpl |
| 2194 | LING | Henry Arthur | 13.02.1920 | |
| 2195 | MACRAE | Donald | 13.02.1920 | |
| 2196 | MILLER | Francis Percival | 13.02.1920 | |
| 2197 | RADFORD | George | 13.02.1920 | |
| 2198 | RICHARDS | Kenneth Durham | 13.02.1920 | |
| 2199 | RIDGERS | Augustus Ernest | 13.02.1920 | |
| 2200 | RUSSELL | George Vivian | 13.02.1920 | |
| 2201 | SANDERSON | William Dennison | 13.02.1920 | |
| 2202 | SEAMER | Afred Samuel | 13.02.1920 | |
| 2203 | SQUIRE | Charles | 13.02.1920 | |
| 2204 | STRANGE | Basil Loftus | 13.02.1920 | |
| 2205 | STOREY | Hedley Milton | 13.02.1920 | |
| 2206 | TAYLOR | William Albert | 13.02.1920 | |
| 2207 | THOMPSON | Alan John | 13.02.1920 | |
| 2208 | THOMPSON | John | 13.02.1920 | |
| 2209 | TOWNER | William Joseph | 13.02.1920 | Sgt. |
| 2210 | PITTAWAY | William John | 19.02.1920 | D/Insp. |
| 2211 | ARMSTRONG | William John | 01.03.1920 | Sgt. |
| 2212 | CHRISTENSON | Cecil Christian | 01.03.1920 | |
| 2213 | CHUBBOCK | James Ernest | 01.03.1920 | |
| 2214 | CONNOR | Albert Edward | 01.03.1920 | |
| 2215 | COWGILL | John Ignatius | 01.03.1920 | |
| 2216 | DORRINGTON | John Bertram | 01.03.1920 | |
| 2217 | DRURY-LOWE | Robert Charles | 01.03.1920 | |
| 2218 | EACHER | Arthur George | 01.03.1920 | |
| 2219 | FARRAP | Harold | 01.03.1920 | |
| 2220 | FRANKLIN | Guy Alderman | 01.03.1920 | Inspr. |
| 2221 | GARRETT | Thomas | 01.03.1920 | |
| 2222 | HAKEMAN | William George | 01.03.1920 | |
| 2223 | HART | Reginald John | 01.03.1920 | |
| 2224 | HUGHES | Vaughan | 01.03.1920 | |
| 2225 | MAXWELL | John | 01.03.1920 | |
| 2226 | MURFIN | Ernest | 01.03.1920 | |
| 2227 | PAGE | William John | 01.03.1920 | |
| 2228 | PENTLAND | Hugh Montgomery | 01.03.1920 | Cpl. |
| 2229 | QUIN | Leonard Vaughan | 01.03.1920 | |
| 2230 | RAVENSCROFT | John Frederick | 01.03.1920 | |
| 2231 | SPENCER | John Till | 01.03.1920 | |
| 2232 | STRINGFIELD | Sidney | 01.03.1920 | |
| 2233 | START | Frank William | 01.03.1920 | |
| 2234 | TIGAR | Reginald Henry | 01.03.1920 | |
| 2235 | WEEKES | Alfred Edward | 01.03.1920 | |
| 2236 | WEST | Thomas Garrett | 01.03.1920 | |
| 2237 | WILBORE | Charles Eric | 01.03.1920 | |
| 2238 | WHITE | Stephen George | 01.03.1920 | |
| 2239 | WOODLAND | Kenneth | 01.03.1920 | |
| 2240 | TYSOE | William | 01.03.1920 | |
| 2241 | ROYSE | Reginald Edward | 11.04.1920 | C/Insp. |
| 2242 | PRINCE | Norman Alfred | 11.04.1920 | Inspr. |
| 2243 | PLUMMER | Edgar William | 11.04.1920 | |
| 2244 | PINDER | William | 11.04.1920 | |
| 2245 | ROWELL | Kenneth William | 11.04.1920 | |
| 2246 | PEMBERTON | Percy Roy Lafont | 11.04.1920 | |
| 2247 | PAYNTER | Richard | 11.04.1920 | |
| 2248 | PALMER | Walter Hugh | 11.04.1920 | |
| 2249 | MENZIES | Alexander | 11.04.1920 | |
| 2250 | MEE | Ernest | 11.04.1920 | |
| 2251 | MALT | Robert Henry | 11.04.1920 | Tpr. |
| 2252 | JOHNSON | Alfred | 11.04.1920 | |
| 2253 | HURST | Frank Musgrove | 11.04.1920 | |
| 2254 | LEAR | Bernard Ponsford | 11.04.1920 | |
| 2255 | MAJOR | Edwin Robert | 11.04.1920 | |
| 2256 | HARRIS | Arthur Penson | 11.04.1920 | |
| 2257 | DIXON | Abraham | 11.04.1920 | |
| 2258 | DIBBLE | Fred | 11.04.1920 | |
| 2259 | DANCER | Luke | 11.04.1920 | |
| 2260 | DANCE | Frederick | 11.04.1920 | |
| 2261 | COOKE | Hinton Guy | 11.04.1920 | |
| 2262 | COUZENS | George Harry | 11.04.1920 | |
| 2263 | COLLINS | Jack | 11.04.1920 | |
| 2264 | BARNARD | Stanley Cecil | 11.04.1920 | |
| 2265 | HOWARD | William Horace | 11.04.1920 | S/Insp |
| 2266 | ANSELL | Herbert Self | 11.04.1920 | |
| 2267 | WEEKS | Archibald Dunbar | 11.04.1920 | |
| 2268 | ELLIS | William George | 11.04.1920 | |
| 2269 | WALKER | William | 11.04.1920 | |
| 2270 | BATES | John Bernard | 11.04.1920 | |
| 2271 | SKELTON | Joseph John | 11.04.1920 | |
| 2272 | BOUTCHER | Reginald Edwin | 24.04.1920 | |
| 2273 | SHEAT | Jack | 26.04.1920 | |
| 2274 | BRADBURY | Raymond Gordon | 26.04.1920 | |
| 2275 | McGRANE | Christopher Joseph | 26.04.1920 | |

| No. | Surname | Forename(s) | Date | Rank |
|---|---|---|---|---|
| 2276 | MURPHY | Bertram Burke | 26.04.1920 | |
| 2277 | GROSSE | Cecil Charles | 26.04.1920 | |
| 2278 | CURRAN | Stanley Edgar | 26.04.1920 | |
| 2279 | GENNER | William Benjamin | 26.04.1920 | |
| 2280 | PERRYMAN | Herbert Routh | 26.04.1920 | |
| 2281 | COWDEROY | Charles Frederick | 26.04.1920 | Sgt. |
| 2282 | RYND | Francis Fleetwood | 26.04.1920 | |
| 2283 | BARTHORP | Francis Rothery | 26.04.1920 | |
| 2284 | CULLEN | Charles Arthur | 26.04.1920 | |
| 2285 | BARTLETT | Leonard Sydney | 17.05.1920 | |
| 2286 | PRESTON | Arthur | 17.05.1920 | |
| 2287 | TUSTIN | Ernest Harry | 17.05.1920 | |
| 2288 | PACKER | Alfred Henry | 17.05.1920 | |
| 2289 | WATSON | John William | 17.05.1920 | |
| 2290 | HILLS | Ernest Lionel | 17.05.1920 | D/Insp. |
| 2291 | BARHAM | Arthur Thomas | 17.05.1920 | |
| 2292 | PICKUP | Andrew | 17.05.1920 | |
| 2293 | BONNETT | Reginald | 17.05.1920 | |
| 2294 | BLAKEMORE | William Walter | 01.06.1920 | |
| 2295 | MONTAGUE | Frederick Stanley | 01.06.1920 | |
| 2296 | SMITH | Walter George | 01.06.1920 | |
| 2297 | SAWYER | Sydney Stanford | 01.06.1920 | |
| 2298 | OCKENDON | Harold | 01.06.1920 | |
| 2299 | PLUMBRIDGE | Fredrick John | 01.06.1920 | |
| 2300 | BURTON | Laurence Albert | 01.06.1920 | |
| 2301 | JAMES | George Emlyn | 01.06.1920 | Inspr. |
| 2302 | CROWHURST | Leslie Kirton | 01.06.1920 | |
| 2303 | RANDS | Leslie Samuel | 01.06.1920 | |
| 2304 | BEESLEY | Walter Vernon | 01.06.1920 | |
| 2305 | BESTMAN | Leonard | 21.06.1920 | |
| 2306 | HINDBY | Norman Jansen | 21.06.1920 | |
| 2307 | RICHARDSON | Harold | 21.06.1920 | |
| 2308 | SANDES | Samuel Dickson | 21.06.1920 | |
| 2309 | SEAWARD | Edward Jack | 21.06.1920 | D/C/I |
| 2310 | WATKINS | Frederick Charles | 21.06.1920 | |
| 2311 | DE LA TASTE | Herbert Colin | 21.06.1920 | C/Insp |
| 2312 | DUNGEY | Hugh Arthur | 21.06.1920 | |
| 2313 | PRESTON | John Cecil | 21.06.1920 | |
| 2314 | DERHAM | Robert Percival | 29.06.1920 | Major |
| 2315 | VERNALL | Robert John | 29.06.1920 | |
| 2316 | GALE | Herbert | 29.06.1920 | |
| 2317 | MARTIN | Gerald | 29.06.1920 | D/C/I |
| 2318 | O'FARRELL | Gesham Frederic | 29.06.1920 | |
| 2319 | NEWMAN | Fredrick Arthur | 29.06.1920 | Capt. |
| 2320 | ARNOTT | Cecil Rhodes | 06.07.1920 | |
| 2321 | BLAKE | Norman Arthur | 06.07.1920 | |
| 2322 | FISH | Frederick | 06.07.1920 | |
| 2323 | HARRISON | Frederick William | 06.07.1920 | Lt. Col. |
| 2324 | SEWARD | Henry George | 12.07.1920 | Lt. Col. |
| 2325 | HILL | Cuthbert George | 12.07.1920 | |
| 2326 | GRIMMETT | Thomas Henry | 12.07.1920 | |
| 2327 | WARD | John William | 12.07.1920 | |
| 2328 | UNDERWOOD | Victor Baden | 12.07.1920 | |
| 2329 | THOMPSON | Joseph | 12.07.1920 | |
| 2330 | RUFFEL | William Charles | 12.07.1920 | |
| 2331 | CATCHPOLE | Arthur William | 12.07.1920 | Capt. |
| 2332 | KILLICK | Henry Thomas | 12.07.1920 | |
| 2333 | PEGRUM | Joseph William | 26.07.1920 | |
| 2334 | MURPHY | Desmond Henry | 26.07.1920 | |
| 2335 | HEBBLEWHITE | Frederick John | 26.07.1920 | |
| 2336 | COUPAR | John | 26.07.1920 | |
| 2337 | COOK | William Charles | 26.07.1920 | |
| 2338 | TURNER-DAUNCEY | Maurice John | 26.07.1920 | |
| 2339 | MUNN-MACE | William Geoffrey | 26.07.1920 | Cpl |
| 2340 | MEREDYTH | Thomas Leslie | 04.08.1920 | |
| 2341 | McNAB | Duncan Allan | 28.08.1920 | |
| 2342 | DAVIS | Charles Curzon | 30.08.1920 | |
| 2343 | GIBSON | Alleyne Edward | 30.08.1920 | |
| 2345 | MORTON | Henry Edward | 30.08.1920 | |
| 2346 | SIMMONDS | Horace Edgar | 30.08.1920 | |
| 2347 | FRASER | Andrew William | 05.09.1920 | |
| 2348 | HOLME | Bryan Percy | 10.09.1920 | |
| 2349 | FULLER | John Evelyn | 13.09.1920 | |
| 2350 | PURKISS | Victor Sydney | 13.09.1920 | Sgt. |
| 2351 | ROBINSON | Stanley Redver | 13.09.1920 | |
| 2352 | WALLS | Reginald William | 13.09.1920 | |
| 2353 | WILLIAMS | Oswald Gerald | 13.09.1920 | |
| 2354 | NAPIER | Victor Blake | 17.09.1920 | |
| 2355 | BUTLER | Bertram Salisbury | 27.09.1920 | |
| 2356 | EVANS | Horace Vaughan | 27.09.1920 | |
| 2357 | FASH | Alfred Norris | 27.09.1920 | |
| 2358 | FRANCIS | Thomas Robert | 27.09.1920 | |
| 2359 | KER | James | 27.09.1920 | |
| 2360 | READY | Alfred Richard | 27.09.1920 | Capt. |
| 2361 | SMITH | Joseph Henry | 27.09.1920 | |
| 2362 | WEST | Frederick Richard | 27.09.1920 | |
| 2363 | BATTERSHILL | Lionel Fred | 19.10.1920 | |
| 2364 | BROWN | Jack Morgan | 19.10.1920 | |
| 2365 | GOUGH | John James | 19.10.1920 | |
| 2366 | HILLS | Wallace Adrian | 19.10.1920 | |
| 2367 | KNIGHT | Leslie Alexander | 19.10.1920 | |
| 2368 | LANG | Bert Leonard | 19.10.1920 | |
| 2369 | Mac PHERSON | Edmund Erskine | 19.10.1920 | |
| 2370 | NISSEN | Norris Theodor | 19.10.1920 | |
| 2371 | O'BYRNE | John Vincent | 19.10.1920 | |
| 2372 | PAISH | George Alfred | 19.10.1920 | |
| 2373 | SMITH | John Leicester | 19.10.1920 | |
| 2374 | COBBETT | Bernard Charles | 29.10.1920 | |
| 2375 | BYRNE | Gerald Ivor | 17.11.1920 | |
| 2376 | EVANS | Arthur Twile | 17.11.1920 | |
| 2377 | GENET | Leonard James | 17.11.1920 | C/Insp |
| 2378 | HARRIS | John Webber | 17.11.1920 | D/Insp |
| 2379 | MACEY | Baden William | 17.11.1920 | |
| 2380 | MAKINS | Richard Naunton | 17.11.1920 | Inspr. |
| 2381 | STEWART | George | 17.11.1920 | |
| 2382 | THOMPSON | Frank Hamilton | 17.11.1920 | |
| 2383 | WALLINGTON | Gilbert | 17.11.1920 | |
| 2384 | BROWN | Gerald Allen | 29.11.1920 | |
| 2385 | KILLICK | Robert Arthur | 29.11.1920 | |
| 2386 | STUART | Henry James | 29.11.1920 | Sgt. |
| 2387 | SCOTT | George Donald | 29.11.1920 | C/Insp |
| 2388 | ALLISON | Cecil Albert | 13.12.1920 | Sgt. |
| 2389 | FOREMAN | George Edward | 13.12.1920 | |
| 2390 | NEWTON | Joseph Robert | 13.12.1920 | Capt. |
| 2391 | PHILLIPS | Ernest Alfred | 13.12.1920 | |
| 2392 | TURNER | William John | 13.12.1920 | |
| 2393 | GARDNER | Charles Henry | 21.12.1920 | |
| 2394 | MAPSON | Francis Haine | 21.12.1920 | |
| 2395 | O'GRADY | James Gerald | 21.12.1920 | |
| 2396 | BLAKE | William John | 21.12.1920 | |
| 2397 | BRIGHTON | Thomas Edward | 24.01.1921 | S/insp. |
| 2398 | CHAMLEY | Reuben Henry | 24.01.1921 | |
| 2399 | JORDAN | Harold Gage | 21.02.1921 | Sgt. |
| 2400 | CROOK | Ernest George | 21.02.1921 | |
| 2401 | HOBBS | William | 21.02.1921 | |
| 2402 | TINEY | Cyril Noel | 21.02.1921 | |
| 2403 | QUINION | Henry | 24.02.1921 | |
| 2404 | HODGINS | Jacob | 23.03.1921 | |
| 2405 | BRIGHT | Richard Arthur | 29.03.1921 | |
| 2406 | JONES | Arthur James | 12.04.1921 | |
| 2407 | HOARE | Kenneth Privette | 24.04.1921 | |
| 2408 | CHAMBERLAIN | John | 25.04.1921 | |
| 2409 | FINEGAN | William James | 29.04.1921 | |
| 2410 | MUNN | Geoffrey Manwaring | 05.05.1921 | |
| 2411 | NOAKES | Clive Bailie | 30.04.1921 | |
| 2412 | BARRY | | 14.05.1921 | |
| 2414 | GREEN | Wilfred Eustace | 18.05.1921 | |
| 2415 | JANES | Harold Arthur | 18.05.1921 | |
| 2416 | CLEMENTS | Seymour Golding | 20.05.1921 | |
| 2417 | BORN | Alexander Lewis | 27.05.1921 | |
| 2418 | NICHOLSON | Wilfred Coulson | 29.06.1921 | |
| 2419 | BOTHA | Christoffel Daniel | 01.07.1921 | |
| 2420 | RANCE | Cyril James | 01.07.1921 | S/Insp |
| 2421 | DU RANDT | William Adriaan | 04.07.1921 | Sgt. |
| 2422 | JORDAAN | Pieter Willem | 08.07.1921 | |
| 2423 | CAMPBELL | Francis Eric | 08.07.1921 | |
| 2424 | BLAKE | Dermot Marcus | 08.07.1921 | |
| 2425 | JOHNSON | Henry Frederick | 22.08.1921 | |
| 2426 | CAMPBELL | Theodore Dugald | 28.08.1921 | |
| 2427 | VISSER | Pieter Erasmus | 30.09.1921 | |
| 2428 | BLAKE-THOMPSON | Joseph | 03.10.1921 | S/S/M |
| 2429 | BATIZAT | Edward | 15.10.1921 | |
| 2430 | LEVIN | William | 17.10.1921 | |
| 2431 | SMITH | William Alfred | 19.10.1921 | |
| 2432 | STAINER | Alfred Charles | 04.11.1921 | |
| 2433 | COWLEY | George Alfred | 09.11.1921 | |
| 2434 | STUBBS | William Frederick | 14.11.1921 | |
| 2435 | METZER | Allan Wilfred | 15.11.1921 | |
| 2436 | DARKE | John Norman | 21.11.1921 | |
| 2437 | PARKS | Thomas Walter | 23.11.1921 | |
| 2438 | ROUX | Frederick Victor | 23.11.1921 | |
| 2439 | SARGENT | Hugo Hendrie | 23.11.1921 | |
| 2440 | FRAMPTON | Dudley | 26.11.1921 | |
| 2441 | HALL | Alaric | 29.11.1921 | |
| 2442 | EVANS | John | 01.12.1921 | |
| 2443 | STRACHAN | Richard | 12.12.1921 | |
| 2444 | BRAND | James Sinclair | 12.12.1921 | |
| 2445 | GOHERY | Herbert David | 28.12.1921 | |
| 2446 | HARVEY | Martin Ernest | 28.12.1921 | |
| 2447 | ROSS | John Baden | 28.12.1921 | |
| 2448 | STOKES | John Robertson | 28.12.1921 | |
| 2449 | JACOBS | Charles Henry | 07.01.1922 | |
| 2450 | HENSHAW | Karel Frederick | 14.02.1922 | 2/Sgt |
| 2451 | DUIRS | Tom | 27.02.1922 | |
| 2452 | BUTLER | Francis David | 15.03.1922 | |
| 2453 | BOARDMAN | John Field | 22.03.1922 | D/S/I |
| 2454 | COMBE | William Salmon | 23.03.1922 | |
| 2455 | FLANAGAN | Philip Harvey | 24.03.1922 | |
| 2456 | COLLINS | Louis Guilford | 28.03.1922 | |
| 2457 | DRYBURG | Victor Henry | 03.04.1922 | |
| 2458 | ROY | Alexander Palmer | 07.04.1922 | C/Insp |
| 2459 | AURET | John Oswald | 10.04.1922 | Cpl |
| 2460 | ATKINSON | Jack Cassidy | 20.04.1922 | |
| 2461 | Mac NEILAGE | Richard Green | 21.04.1922 | |
| 2462 | FINCH | Archibald | 26.04.1922 | |
| 2463 | JAMES | Charles Hastings | 28.04.1922 | |
| 2464 | WINGATE | Gerald Lennox | 28.04.1922 | |
| 2465 | SANDERSON | Charles Stanley | 28.04.1922 | Inspr. |
| 2466 | STEEDMAN | William Alexander | 04.05.1922 | |
| 2467 | KLOPPER | Wilfred Frank | 08.05.1922 | |
| 2468 | WILLS | Jakobus Martinus | 10.05.1922 | |
| 2469 | LEE | Douglas Barton | 29.05.1922 | |
| 2470 | BAILEY | Wilfred Millson | 28.06.1922 | |
| 2471 | FORDE | Hugh Maurice | 04.07.1922 | |
| 2472 | HEYWOOD | Cecil Beresford | 05.07.1922 | |
| 2473 | MASLIN | Oliver Bertram | 17.07.1922 | |
| 2474 | LANE | Charles Edward | 21.07.1922 | |
| 2475 | COUZENS | George Astley | 17.07.1922 | |
| 2476 | Mac LEOD | George Harry | 24.07.1922 | |
| 2477 | BURDETT | Donald McAuley | 24.07.1922 | |
| 2478 | MARSHALL | John Tunstall | 27.07.1922 | |
| 2479 | MERRINGTON | Gerald Harry | 28.07.1922 | Sgt. |
| 2480 | FORSYTH | Keith Cameron | 31.07.1922 | |
| 2481 | PATERSON | Arthur Evans | 04.08.1922 | |
| 2482 | | Robert Harold | 04.08.1922 | |

| No. | Surname | First Name(s) | Date | Rank |
|---|---|---|---|---|
| 2483 | LEON | Alfred James | 07.08.1922 | |
| 2484 | Mac INTYRE | James Riggs | 09.08.1922 | |
| 2485 | TERRY | Harry Norman | 14.08.1922 | |
| 2486 | CULLUM | Adolphus Bertie | 16.08.1922 | |
| 2487 | WILFORD | Thomas Jocelyn | 18.08.1922 | Sgt. |
| 2488 | BELL | William Parker | 18.08.1922 | |
| 2489 | FLANDERS | Leonard Charles | 23.08.1922 | |
| 2490 | NAGLE | Patrick | 30.08.1922 | S/Insp |
| 2491 | REID | Hugh | 06.09.1922 | |
| 2492 | PRESTON | William Richard | 18.09.1922 | |
| 2493 | COOPER | Neville Thomson | 18.09.1922 | |
| 2494 | EVERETT | Edgar Stephen | 20.09.1922 | |
| 2495 | DAVIES | Thomas Samuel | 23.09.1922 | |
| 2496 | HASLAM | Herbert Horace | 29.09.1922 | |
| 2497 | PERCIVAL | Frederick | 29.09.1922 | |
| 2498 | WILSON | Robert | 29.09.1922 | |
| 2499 | BUCHANAN | Glen Murdock | 04.10.1922 | |
| 2500 | ELLIOTT | Rupert Arthur | 09.10.1922 | |
| 2501 | POLES | William Eustace | 12.10.1922 | |
| 2502 | THWAITS | Stephen Henry | 13.10.1922 | |
| 2503 | PEARSON | Oscar Edward | 22.10.1922 | |
| 2504 | ESCOURT | Gerald Dawson | 25.10.1922 | |
| 2505 | PHILPOTT | Richard | 25.10.1922 | |
| 2506 | PHILLIPS | William Douglas | 27.10.1922 | |
| 2507 | MARSHALL | John Christie | 04.11.1922 | |
| 2508 | THOMPSON | Charles Edward | 04.11.1922 | |
| 2509 | KAYE | Bertram | 17.11.1922 | |
| 2510 | McINTYRE | Charles Walter | 19.11.1922 | |
| 2511 | TEE | Eric | 01.12.1922 | |
| 2512 | LOMAX | Fred | 06.01.1923 | |
| 2513 | WARBURTON | Harold William | 10.01.1923 | |
| 2514 | DUNLEY-OWEN | Arthur Hugh | 17.01.1923 | |
| 2515 | BRADLEY | Ross Thomas | 26.01.1923 | |
| 2516 | FISHER | Richard John | 01.02.1923 | |
| 2517 | WATTS | Herbert Harold | 07.03.1923 | |
| 2518 | GREENGRASS | Daniel Harold | 09.03.1923 | D/C/I |
| 2519 | WARDEN | Frederick Alexander | 16.03.1923 | |
| 2520 | DAVIDSON | John | 29.03.1923 | |
| 2521 | SPENCER | Edward Herbert | 07.04.1923 | |
| 2522 | TOPHAM | Mark Christopher | 09.04.1923 | |
| 2523 | MADDEN | James O'Flynn | 23.04.1923 | |
| 2524 | McCLINTOCK | Reginald Victor | 24.04.1923 | Inspr. |
| 2525 | STARK | Norman David | 30.04.1923 | |
| 2526 | CAZALET | Roger Hamilton | 09.05.1923 | |
| 2527 | RYDER | Frank Redvers | 09.05.1923 | |
| 2528 | TAYLOR | John Howard | 09.05.1923 | |
| 2529 | KIRK | Edwin Alfred | 14.05.1923 | |
| 2530 | ARKWRIGHT | Hubert Oswin | 20.05.1923 | |
| 2531 | DUNN | Wilfred William | 13.06.1923 | |
| 2532 | GRATER | Thomas Walton | 14.06.1923 | |
| 2533 | KIRK | Donald | 15.06.1923 | |
| 2534 | JUBBER | Arthur Quinton | 16.06.1923 | |
| 2535 | JUDGE | Horatio | 01.07.1923 | |
| 2536 | O'REILLY | James | 01.07.1923 | S/A/C |
| 2537 | ROGERS | Graham Cecil | 03.07.1923 | |
| 2538 | MELLOR | Francis Horace | 06.07.1923 | |
| 2539 | TURNER | Frederick Arthur | 06.07.1923 | |
| 2540 | BUNCE | William Alwyn | 11.07.1923 | |
| 2541 | COSGRAVE | Reginald Hugh | 11.07.1923 | |
| 2542 | YEOMAN | George Leslie | 13.07.1923 | Inspr. |
| 2543 | LEHMBECK | Stanley George | 16.07.1923 | |
| 2544 | TEE | Eric | 23.07.1923 | |
| 2545 | CROSSON | Gilbert | 13.08.1923 | |
| 2546 | SMITH | Douglas Robert | 15.08.1923 | |
| 2547 | GREENWAY | Ernest Alfred | 23.08.1923 | |
| 2548 | LIEBENBERG | Adriaan Nicolaas | 01.09.1923 | |
| 2549 | MOORE | John | 02.09.1923 | |
| 2550 | PITHEY | Jack William | 05.09.1923 | |
| 2551 | THORNE | William Arthur | 07.09.1923 | |
| 2552 | ARMSTRONG | Robert William | 09.09.1923 | |
| 2553 | HAGUE | Harland Clyde | 10.09.1923 | |
| 2554 | GLISSON | Harry Victor | 19.09.1923 | |
| 2555 | JOOSTE | Sarel Petrus | 24.09.1923 | |
| 2556 | LEAR | Douglas Nowell | 03.10.1923 | |
| 2557 | DENNIS | Horace | 05.10.1923 | |
| 2558 | DAVIS | Samuel James | 12.10.1923 | |
| 2559 | COULDREY | James Vivian | 12.10.1923 | |
| 2560 | MILNER | William George | 26.10.1923 | |
| 2561 | PATTON | David | 31.10.1923 | |
| 2562 | DODDS | John | 02.11.1923 | |
| 2563 | POOLE | Walter John | 03.11.1923 | |
| 2564 | HEATLIE | Leslie Arthur | 04.11.1923 | |
| 2565 | IDENSOHN | William | 09.11.1923 | |
| 2566 | KING | Leslie Arthur | 13.11.1923 | |
| 2567 | NICHOLSON | Gordon Lorenzo | 16.11.1923 | |
| 2568 | WHYTE | Vincent Livingstone | 18.11.1923 | |
| 2569 | NICHOLSON | Basil Leo | 26.11.1923 | |
| 2570 | RIDGWAY | John Samuel | 30.11.1923 | |
| 2571 | DAWSON | Frederick Hugh | 03.12.1923 | |
| 2572 | VICKERY | Alfred William | 05.12.1923 | |
| 2573 | WILLARD | Stanley Hamilton | 07.12.1923 | |
| 2574 | HOATEN | Eric Gerald | 16.12.1923 | |
| 2575 | HIGGINS | James Bicket | 02.01.1924 | |
| 2576 | JEFFERIES | Thomas | 06.01.1924 | |
| 2577 | McCALLUM | Cecil Douglas | 06.01.1924 | |
| 2578 | STEPHEN | Ronald Gordon | 07.01.1924 | |
| 2579 | HOLM | Oliver Leonard | 09.01.1924 | |
| 2580 | STURROCK | George Lawson | 09.01.1924 | S/Insp |
| 2581 | BENZON | Eugene St. George | 13.01.1924 | |
| 2582 | FRIER | David William | 15.01.1924 | |
| 2583 | TETLEY | Walter Martin | 16.01.1924 | |
| 2584 | MURRAY | William Anthony | 18.01.1924 | |
| 2585 | YEATMAN | Douglas Thomas | 18.01.1924 | |
| 2586 | BLAKE | Frank | 25.01.1924 | |
| 2587 | BENINGFIELD | Reuben De La Rue | 27.01.1924 | Sgt. |
| 2588 | ROSS | George Trevor | 01.02.1924 | |
| 2589 | SKINNER | William Frederick | 02.02.1924 | |
| 2590 | GODWIN | Geoffrey Herbert | 03.02.1924 | |
| 2591 | STURGEON | Dennis Edward | 03.02.1924 | |
| 2592 | STARKEY | Julian Alma | 06.02.1924 | |
| 2593 | O'GORMAN | George Trevor | 08.02.1924 | |
| 2594 | RICHARDS | Howard Goodger | 11.02.1924 | |
| 2595 | McGRATH | John Walter | 13.02.1924 | |
| 2596 | MAHONY | Owen Robert | 22.02.1924 | |
| 2597 | JOHNSON | Samuel Harrop | 25.02.1924 | |
| 2598 | DEWSNAP | Jack William | 27.02.1924 | |
| 2599 | BETTS | Hector William | 03.03.1924 | Cpl |
| 2600 | MUNRO | David Stuart | 07.03.1924 | |
| 2601 | WATSON | Robert Vaughan | 07.03.1924 | |
| 2602 | EVANS | William | 17.03.1924 | |
| 2603 | DUNBAR | Eric William Cecil | 17.03.1924 | |
| 2604 | HARGREAVES | Donald Nicholas | 26.03.1924 | |
| 2605 | BRAKSPEAR | Courtney Charles | 26.03.1924 | |
| 2606 | APLIN | Raymond Bruce | 14.04.1924 | |
| 2607 | NICHOLSON | Richard Geldart | 14.04.1924 | |
| 2608 | RIADORE | Charles John | 28.04.1924 | |
| 2609 | YOUNG | John | 05.05.1924 | |
| 2610 | BIRBECK | Edward Charles | 05.05.1924 | |
| 2611 | CORDELL | James Norton | 06.05.1924 | |
| 2612 | ASBURY | Arthur Ernest | 07.05.1924 | |
| 2613 | HUTCHINSON | Geoffrey William | 19.05.1924 | |
| 2614 | REES | Edward | 23.06.1924 | |
| 2615 | DEANE-SIMMONS | Bertram Stannaford | 23.06.1924 | |
| 2616 | ALLEN | Ernest Cecil | 23.06.1924 | |
| 2617 | DAVIS | Walter Albert | 07.07.1924 | |
| 2618 | HANKEY | George William | 06.07.1924 | Sgt |
| 2619 | SEWELL | Norman Michael | 28.07.1924 | |
| 2620 | HATHAWAY | | | |
| 2621 | JANSEN | Hendrick Jacobus | 31.07.1924 | Sgt. |
| 2622 | HICKMAN | Arthur Selwyn | 01.08.1924 | Comm. |
| 2623 | MONCRIEFF | Frederick Hope | 01.08.1924 | |
| 2624 | PATERSON | Andrew | 01.08.1924 | Tpr |
| 2625 | HUDSON | Ivon Henry | 06.08.1924 | |
| 2626 | GILMORE | Thomas Francis | 13.08.1924 | |
| 2627 | SMITH | William Henry | 20.08.1924 | |
| 2628 | SMITH | Alan Godfrey | 01.09.1924 | |
| 2629 | BOWKER | Lindsley | 02.09.1924 | |
| 2630 | AYLESBURY | John Duncan | 05.09.1924 | S/A/C |
| 2631 | SURGEY | Edward Gordon | 07.09.1924 | |
| 2632 | SMITH | John Walter | 17.09.1924 | |
| 2633 | FITCH | Wilfred Brian | 20.09.1924 | |
| 2634 | HOBDAY | John Mann | 24.09.1924 | |
| 2635 | PARSLOE | John Joseph | 26.09.1924 | |
| 2636 | TENNANT | James Edward | 10.10.1924 | |
| 2637 | Mac LEOD | Alexander Donald | 20.10.1924 | |
| 2638 | BROWNE | George Buckston | 24.10.1924 | |
| 2639 | MANUEL | Herman Jurgens | 27.10.1924 | |
| 2640 | ROWLEY | Edward Hugh | 31.10.1924 | |
| 2641 | COLLARD | Jack Alfred Carr | 05.11.1924 | |
| 2642 | YOUNG | Ernest William | 05.11.1924 | |
| 2643 | SMITH | Leslie Grenville | 09.11.1924 | |
| 2644 | BACON | Harley Anthony | 16.11.1924 | |
| 2645 | ATKINSON | John Edward | 21.11.1924 | |
| 2646 | BLACKBURNE | Jordan | 21.11.1924 | |
| 2647 | GLADSTONE | Exion | 05.12.1924 | |
| 2648 | ALLOCK | Frank Austen | 07.12.1924 | |
| 2649 | BLAKE | John | 12.12.1924 | |
| 2650 | BOYD | Alexander Hewitt | 17.12.1924 | |
| 2651 | STARLING | Douglas Robert | 17.12.1924 | |
| 2652 | CALLANAN | Alexis Vincent | 28.12.1924 | |
| 2653 | REID | Quentin Archibald | 31.12.1924 | |
| 2654 | WALKER | Robert Cyril | 02.01.1925 | |
| 2655 | RIPPON | Eric Money | 07.01.1925 | |
| 2656 | NORMAN | John Alexander | 24.12.1924 | |
| 2657 | COX | William James | 09.01.1925 | |
| 2658 | NORTON | Bertwyn Cobham | 14.01.1925 | |
| 2659 | HAMILTON | Roy Edward | 22.01.1925 | |
| 2660 | DAVENPORT | Herbert | 30.01.1925 | |
| 2661 | WHYTE | James Ross | 08.02.1925 | |
| 2662 | RUTHERFORD | George Noel | 11.02.1925 | |
| 2663 | BOYCE | Wilbert Clive | 16.02.1925 | |
| 2664 | SCHULTZ | Eugene Frederick | 18.02.1925 | |
| 2665 | SIMPSON | Charles Orr | 20.02.1925 | |
| 2666 | WINTLE | Henry Frederick | 25.02.1925 | |
| 2667 | COLLINGWOOD | Lionel Charles | 27.02.1925 | |
| 2668 | PERKINS | Stanhope William | 04.03.1925 | |
| 2669 | JOHNSON | Donald Brooke | 09.03.1925 | |
| 2670 | NEWMAN | Dennis Daincourt | 09.03.1925 | |
| 2671 | BENNETT | Reginald Anthony | 11.03.1925 | |
| 2672 | REID | Frank Cecil | 11.03.1925 | |
| 2673 | FOWLER | Denton French | 13.03.1925 | |
| 2674 | FARRANT | Basil Francis | 22.03.1925 | |
| 2675 | LEWIS | William Herbert | 22.03.1925 | |
| 2676 | GIBBONS | Cyril Charles | 25.03.1925 | |
| 2677 | BRUYNS | John Douglas | 25.03.1925 | |
| 2678 | CLARK | Charles Donald | 25.03.1925 | S/Ins. |
| 2679 | MORRIS | Harold Herbert | 25.03.1925 | |
| 2680 | CHARLES | Hubert Patrick | 25.03.1925 | |
| 2681 | UBSDELL | Talbot | 03.04.1925 | Inspr. |
| 2682 | WHITELEY | Norman Barton | 03.04.1925 | |
| 2683 | BROWN | John | 08.04.1925 | |
| 2684 | CHATTERTON | William Wood | 10.04.1925 | Sgt |
| 2685 | MEYER | Julius James | 10.04.1925 | |
| 2686 | HOGAN | Fergus | 12.04.1925 | |
| 2687 | REYNOLDS | Albert | 14.04.1925 | C/Insp. |
| 2688 | PHELPS | Charles Maunoir | 14.04.1925 | Sgt. |
| 2689 | WILKINSON | Henry Michael | 17.04.1925 | |

| No. | Surname | First Name | Date | Rank |
|---|---|---|---|---|
| 2690 | CROSSLAND | Henry | 20.04.1925 | |
| 2691 | CROXFORD | Douglas Harry | 24.04.1925 | |
| 2692 | WAREHAM | Stanley Low | 24.04.1925 | |
| 2693 | WRIGHT | Trevor Alfred | 24.04.1925 | |
| 2694 | BULL | Cecil Slade Lucas | 01.05.1925 | |
| 2695 | WEBB | Gerald Beaufort | 01.05.1925 | |
| 2696 | STYLE | George Cecil | 06.05.1925 | |
| 2697 | RAYNOR | Charles Hutchons | 06.05.1925 | Insp. |
| 2698 | WALTERS | Albert Edward | 15.05.1925 | |
| 2699 | MORRIS | Patrick Morphy | 19.05.1925 | |
| 2700 | BOND | Edward Alfred | 26.05.1925 | |
| 2701 | REINDERS | Herman Lyall | 15.06.1925 | |
| 2702 | COLYER | Leslie | 16.06.1925 | |
| 2703 | HINDE | Sydney Walter | 25.06.1925 | Sgt. |
| 2704 | FAIRWEATHER | Douglas Charles | 25.06.1925 | |
| 2705 | BERRY | Donovan Spencer | 01.07.1925 | Sgt. |
| 2706 | COOKSON | Patrick George | 01.07.1925 | |
| 2707 | MUNDELL | Cecil Shales | 01.07.1925 | |
| 2708 | RICKARDS | Lawrence Lambert | 17.07.1925 | |
| 2709 | FERRES | James | 03.08.1925 | |
| 2710 | McFADDEN | David | 07.08.1925 | Capt. |
| 2711 | COOKE | William Henry | 14.08.1925 | Sgt. |
| 2712 | MAY | Victor Ronald | 14.08.1925 | |
| 2713 | PICKUP | Jack | 21.08.1925 | |
| 2714 | WARD | Sidney Windsorton | 26.08.1925 | |
| 2715 | LEWRY | Harry | 28.08.1925 | |
| 2716 | PHINN | Eric John | 30.08.1925 | |
| 2717 | MITCHELL | Arthur William | 31.08.1925 | |
| 2718 | ROBERTS | Robert Venning | 07.09.1925 | |
| 2719 | THOMPSON | Robert Francis | 11.09.1925 | |
| 2720 | KEIL | Henry | 16.09.1925 | |
| 2721 | RUTHERFURD | Cecil Ravenswood | 21.09.1925 | |
| 2722 | ASPINALL | Eliott Heathfield | 24.09.1925 | |
| 2723 | FLOREY | Henry George | 18.09.1925 | |
| 2724 | BUNCE | Ernest Hope | 30.09.1925 | A/Commr. |
| 2725 | REYNOLDS | Arthur Ronald | 14.10.1925 | Major |
| 2726 | MACEY | Stagg William | 25.10.1925 | |
| 2727 | BEESLEY | Walter Vernon | 30.10.1925 | |
| 2728 | ASTON | Astbury Fitzmaurice | 01.11.1925 | |
| 2729 | BAM | Stanley Mathew | 01.11.1925 | |
| 2730 | SWINEY | Stanley Moor | 06.11.1925 | |
| 2731 | COX | Ward Roderic | 06.11.1925 | |
| 2732 | WALLACE | Thomas Harold | 09.11.1925 | |
| 2733 | BENTLEY | Hamilton | 13.11.1925 | |
| 2734 | GAWLER | George Wrentmore | 15.11.1925 | |
| 2735 | MACKAY | Kenneth John | 06.12.1925 | |
| 2736 | NICOLL | Thomas Patrick | 06.12.1925 | |
| 2737 | ROBBINS | Thomas Arthur | 13.12.1925 | Lieut. |
| 2738 | GARLAKE | Storr | 16.12.1925 | |
| 2739 | COWEN | Graham Biddulph | 20.12.1925 | |
| 2740 | SAUNDERS | Hugh Douglas | 21.12.1925 | |
| 2741 | CHADWICK | Howard Leslie | 29.12.1925 | |
| 2742 | BARTRAM | Edward Oswell | 01.01.1926 | |
| 2743 | KNOWLES | Charles Richard | 01.01.1926 | |
| 2744 | MULLIN | Dermott O'Carrell | 03.01.1926 | |
| 2745 | ANDREWS | Bertram Thomas | 12.01.1926 | |
| 2746 | WILSON | Reginald Charles | 16.01.1926 | |
| 2747 | CLARIDGE | Robert Mostyn | 02.02.1926 | Const. |
| 2748 | ROUX | Johannes Loedwiekes | 02.02.1926 | |
| 2749 | MARTIN | Robert Herbert | 05.02.1926 | |
| 2750 | FOURIE | Andre Jean | 07.02.1926 | |
| 2751 | RUSSELL | Albert Edward | 08.02.1926 | |
| 2752 | HEFER | Frederick Carel | 10.02.1926 | Sgt. |
| 2753 | HODDINOTT | John Henry | 14.02.1926 | |
| 2754 | LAWRY | John Boyns | 14.02.1926 | |
| 2755 | JOY | Thomas Andrew | 15.02.1926 | |
| 2756 | DALE | Alan | 24.02.1926 | |
| 2757 | FREESE | Herbert Laurence | 24.02.1926 | |
| 2758 | FARROW | Alfred Russell | 26.02.1926 | |
| 2759 | RICKARDS | Francis Harold | 28.02.1926 | |
| 2760 | BEMISTER | Cecil Wallace | 05.03.1926 | |
| 2761 | JORDAN | Thomas | 07.03.1926 | |
| 2762 | BROOKE | Arthur Edgerton | 10.03.1926 | |
| 2763 | GREEN | Cecil Milner | 10.03.1926 | S/Insp. |
| 2764 | HAZELHURST | James | 10.03.1926 | |
| 2765 | MILLER | Joseph Longcake | 10.03.1926 | |
| 2766 | WRIGHT | Albert Charles | 12.03.1926 | |
| 2767 | WARDROP | George McLean | 14.03.1926 | |
| 2768 | DAVIES | Squire Harold | 19.03.1926 | |
| 2769 | EVANS | Melville Gear | 19.03.1926 | |
| 2770 | SYDENHAM | Kenneth James | 21.03.1926 | |
| 2771 | ORORKE | Timothy | 25.03.1926 | |
| 2772 | DUNNER-MILES | Terence Wladimer | 26.03.1926 | |
| 2773 | MITCHELL | Geoffrey Harris | 26.03.1926 | |
| 2774 | WALKER | Frederick William | 26.03.1926 | |
| 2775 | COOMBE | Hubert John | 02.04.1926 | |
| 2776 | LANG | Noel | 02.04.1926 | |
| 2777 | MALONE | Patrick Kevin | 02.04.1926 | |
| 2778 | MORRIS | William John | 02.04.1926 | |
| 2779 | PARKER | Richard Nevill | 02.04.1926 | |
| 2780 | PATERSON | Robert | 02.04.1926 | |
| 2781 | RULE | George Edward | 02.04.1926 | |
| 2782 | TAYLOR | Leslie Robert | 02.04.1926 | S/Insp. |
| 2783 | BREEN | Charles Moore | 07.04.1926 | |
| 2784 | McCREA | Robert Thomas | 07.04.1926 | |
| 2785 | BENSON | Thomas Leslie | 11.04.1926 | |
| 2786 | DALY | Patrick | 11.04.1926 | |
| 2787 | EMES | George Wiliam | 11.04.1926 | Capt. |
| 2788 | WATSON | William Gilbert | 11.04.1926 | C/Insp |
| 2789 | VAN BILJON | Hercules Pieter | 20.04.1926 | |
| 2790 | DREWETT | Sidney | 23.04.1926 | C/Insp |
| 2791 | PRIDE | Reginald Henry | 23.04.1926 | |
| 2792 | STEELE | John | 23.04.1926 | |
| 2793 | WITCHELL | Edward Henry | 06.05.1926 | |
| 2794 | KLOPPERS | Gerhardus Frederick | 18.05.1926 | |
| 2795 | JOHNSON | Philip Harvard | 26.05.1926 | |
| 2796 | LINDOP | Vernon Augustine | 07.06.1926 | |
| 2797 | WELMAN | Frederick Petrus | 29.06.1926 | |
| 2798 | SMITH | Nigel | 17.05.1926 | |
| 2799 | VAN ZYL | Johannes Abraham | 21.07.1926 | |
| 2800 | JOHNSTONE | Alan Forfar | 27.08.1926 | S/Insp. |
| 2801 | DU PLESSIS | Garnett Loubser | 01.09.1926 | D/S/I |
| 2802 | JORDAN | Myles Howard | 01.09.1926 | |
| 2803 | BATIZAT | Edward | 18.09.1926 | |
| 2804 | Mac LEOD | Neil Colin | 01.10.1926 | |
| 2805 | PENDERED | Arthur | 01.10.1926 | |
| 2806 | ROWE | William Norman | 01.10.1926 | Insp. |
| 2807 | STREETER | Ernest Stanley | 01.10.1926 | A/Com |
| 2808 | WATT | James David | 01.10.1926 | |
| 2809 | ETCHES | George Hermann | 01.10.1926 | |
| 2810 | BURBIDGE | Edward Arthur | 23.01.1926 | Sgt. |
| 2811 | LLOYD | James Mostyn | 03.10.1926 | Sgt. |
| 2812 | CARPENTER | Albert Henry | 05.10.1926 | |
| 2813 | EDE | Lewis Thomas | 06.10.1926 | |
| 2814 | GAMBLEN | Cecil William | 06.10.1926 | |
| 2815 | STONE | Raymond Hubert | 06.10.1926 | S/Insp. |
| 2816 | CLARK | Archibald Jack | 15.10.1926 | |
| 2817 | O'HARA | Owen John | 22.10.1926 | |
| 2818 | CORDELL | Ernest Arthur | 26.10.1926 | |
| 2819 | GOODALL | Leslie Blumenthal | 26.10.1926 | C/Supt. |
| 2820 | CORNWALL | Jophn Frederick | 27.10.1926 | |
| 2821 | FOULDS | Harry | 03.11.1926 | |
| 2822 | BOLES | Gerald | 05.11.1926 | |
| 2823 | LAWRY | Walter Bryan | 07.11.1926 | |
| 2824 | JOHNSON | Cecil Gordon | 14.11.1926 | |
| 2825 | TERRIT | John | 19.11.1926 | Sgt. |
| 2826 | SMITH | Kenneth Thomas | 23.11.1926 | |
| 2827 | LOTTER | Stephanus Bernadus | 26.11.1926 | |
| 2828 | STROBEL | Gerhardus Johannes | 26.11.1926 | |
| 2829 | PALMER | John Edgar | 28.11.1926 | |
| 2830 | YOUNG | William Stewart | 18.12.1926 | |
| 2831 | GRIFFIN | Ian Dennis | 23.12.1926 | |
| 2832 | KULLIN | Geoffrey Goran | 29.12.1926 | |
| 2833 | LAVERTY | Wallace Ryan | 29.12.1926 | |
| 2834 | YOUNG | James Thompson | 04.01.1927 | |
| 2835 | CLEATHERO | Kenneth James | 07.01.1927 | |
| 2836 | FERGUSSON | Jonquil Herbert | 13.01.1927 | |
| 2837 | DICKESON | Roy | 18.01.1927 | S/Insp |
| 2838 | STRONG | Harry Frederick | 23.01.1927 | S/Insp |
| 2839 | BARRETT | Leonard Alfred | 23.01.1927 | S/Ins |
| 2840 | BOARDMAN | Richard | 23.01.1927 | S/A/C |
| 2841 | CARTER | John Leslie | 23.01.1927 | |
| 2842 | HUGHES | John William | 23.01.1927 | |
| 2843 | LEWIS | Charles Ernest | 23.01.1927 | |
| 2844 | PRICE | Basil Joseph | 23.01.1927 | |
| 2845 | WALTER | Edward Joh | 23.01.1927 | |
| 2846 | WARD | Frederick William | 23.01.1927 | |
| 2847 | Mac LEOD | Alastair John | 23.01.1927 | Sgt. |
| 2848 | Mac DONALD | James Ferguson | 23.01.1927 | |
| 2849 | KIRK | John Clifford | 28.01.1927 | |
| 2850 | CHOULER | Frederick Terence | 30.01.1927 | D/Ins. |
| 2851 | CARYER | Wilfred Lewis | 04.02.1927 | |
| 2852 | GOSLET | Arthur Houston | 04.02.1927 | |
| 2853 | JACKSON | Harold | 04.02.1927 | Comm. |
| 2854 | MOORE | Alan Edward | 04.02.1927 | |
| 2855 | HUNT | Hugh Sacheverall | 09.02.1927 | |
| 2856 | FOURIE | William Ignatius | 08.02.1927 | S/Insp |
| 2857 | OOSTHUIZEN | Willie | 22.02.1927 | |
| 2858 | BOND | Harry | 24.02.1927 | |
| 2859 | BENINGFIELD | James Reuben | 27.02.1927 | |
| 2860 | APTHORP | Richard Gilbert | 25.02.1927 | |
| 2861 | WHITING | Henry William | 09.03.1927 | |
| 2862 | HARDY | Laurence Arthur | 11.03.1927 | |
| 2863 | GRUNDY | Victor Redvers | 29.03.1927 | |
| 2864 | JUDSON | Clive Lee | 30.03.1927 | |
| 2865 | SOUTHGATE | Roger Leslie | 01.04.1927 | Capt. |
| 2866 | WALLIS | Owen James | 01.04.1927 | S/Inspr. |
| 2867 | ROBOTHAM | Leslie | 01.04.1927 | |
| 2868 | COOK | Christopher | 01.04.1927 | |
| 2869 | FRANCIS | Robert | 01.04.1927 | |
| 2870 | FRANCIS | Alfred James | 01.04.1927 | |
| 2871 | BOOKER | Cyril Clarence | 01.04.1927 | |
| 2872 | VOWLES | Albert Cyril | 01.04.1927 | |
| 2873 | THOMPSON | John Thomas | 01.04.1927 | Supt. |
| 2874 | MONTAGUE | Brian Howard | 01.04.1927 | A/Com |
| 2875 | GRIFFITHS | Ralph Henry | 01.04.1927 | |
| 2876 | TOZER | William Henry | 01.04.1927 | |
| 2877 | THORNLEY | Douglas Francis | 01.04.1927 | |
| 2878 | COOKE | Edward | 01.04.1927 | |
| 2879 | MUGFORD | Hugh Cecil | 01.04.1927 | |
| 2880 | RAYNOR | Eric Charles | 01.04.1927 | |
| 2881 | BROWN | John Wilson | 01.04.1927 | |
| 2882 | PALING | Frederick Arthur | 01.04.1927 | |
| 2883 | BROOKES | George Ronald | 15.04.1927 | |
| 2884 | SMEETON | William August | 13.05.1927 | |
| 2885 | BARCLAY-THOMAS | Basil Douglas | 15.05.1927 | |
| 2886 | GRATER | Thomas Walton | 25.05.1927 | Sgt. |
| 2887 | SHAW | Bertram Evelyn | 05.06.1927 | |
| 2888 | POWELL | Aubrey Deary | 19.06.1927 | |
| 2889 | SMAIL | Reginald George | 01.07.1927 | |
| 2890 | PILKINGTON | Tom | 01.07.1927 | |
| 2891 | RAMADGE | George Godwin | 01.07.1927 | |
| 2892 | BEATTIE | Campbell | 01.07.1927 | |
| 2893 | KNILL | Howard Alfred | 01.07.1927 | |
| 2894 | STOKER | Robert | 01.07.1927 | |
| 2895 | KETTERINGHAM | Robert John | 01.07.1927 | C/Supt. |
| 2896 | BROWN | John MacLean | 01.07.1927 | S/Insp. |

| No. | Surname | Forename(s) | Date | Rank |
|---|---|---|---|---|
| 2897 | BELBIN | Charles Ashley | 01.07.1927 | |
| 2898 | JARMAN | Edmund Bryant | 01.07.1927 | |
| 2899 | BOSTWICK | Walter Ellis | 01.07.1927 | |
| 2900 | WADDY | Cyril Alexander | 01.07.1927 | |
| 2901 | McMULLEN | Rene Albert | 01.07.1927 | |
| 2902 | JAMES | Francis Arthur | 01.07.1927 | |
| 2903 | ROBERTS | Cyril Hedley Paul | 01.07.1927 | |
| 2904 | ATTWOOLL | John Malcolm | 01.07.1927 | Inspr. |
| 2905 | RACE | Terence Thomas | 01.07.1927 | |
| 2906 | BARNES | Percy William | 01.07.1927 | |
| 2907 | ALLEN | Rupert Fleischmann | 08.07.1927 | S/Insp. |
| 2908 | TROTT | Arthur Stanley | 08.07.1927 | |
| 2909 | NEWTON | Cyril Henry | 13.07.1927 | Sgt. |
| 2910 | WALKER | Stanley Edmund | 17.07.1927 | |
| 2911 | ROSE | Alexander Duncan | 08.07.1927 | |
| 2912 | HUGHES | Reginald James | 15.07.1927 | |
| 2913 | VICE | Norman Douglas | 26.08.1927 | |
| 2914 | BUSH | Thomas Herbert | 31.08.1927 | |
| 2915 | PAGE | William Harrold | 01.09.1927 | |
| 2916 | PERKS | Dennis Clarke | 07.09.1927 | |
| 2917 | YOUNG | Hugh | 13.09.1927 | |
| 2918 | HIRD | John | 14.09.1927 | |
| 2919 | STODDARD | Frank Edward | 15.09.1927 | |
| 2920 | CAMPION | Robert Ian Heron | 18.09.1927 | |
| 2921 | LLOYD | Sidney James | 21.09.1927 | D/S/I |
| 2922 | PRITCHARD | Frederick Cyril | 23.09.1927 | |
| 2923 | ADAMS | Douglas Michael | 23.09.1927 | |
| 2924 | KING | Douglas George | 25.09.1927 | S/C/I |
| 2925 | ASHWIN | George William | 27.08.1927 | |
| 2926 | GRAVES | John Christie | 30.09.1927 | |
| 2927 | HOOK | Albert Henry | 30.09.1927 | |
| 2928 | HILL | James Arthur | 30.09.1927 | |
| 2929 | Mac ADAM | Francis Theodore | 30.09.1927 | S/Maj |
| 2930 | PORTER | Edgar Alwyn | 30.09.1927 | |
| 2931 | PAUL | Robert Fowler | 30.09.1927 | |
| 2932 | PETRIE | Kenneth George | 30.09.1927 | |
| 2933 | QUINN | Harold Telford | 30.09.1927 | D/Com |
| 2934 | ROLFE | Graham Sydney | 30.09.1927 | |
| 2935 | THOMAS | Eric Charles | 30.09.1927 | |
| 2936 | SAUNDERS | Roy Thompson | 30.09.1927 | C/Inspr. |
| 2937 | WILLSHIRE | Douglas Ponting | 30.09.1927 | C/Inspr. |
| 2938 | WAGHORN | Raymond Harry | 30.09.1927 | C/Supt |
| 2939 | WRIGHT | Hubert Charles | 30.09.1927 | |
| 2940 | WILLIAMS | Acland George | 30.09.1927 | Inspr. |
| 2941 | GREENWAY | Ernest Alfred | 30.09.1927 | |
| 2942 | BOCKING | Leslie Arthur | 30.09.1927 | |
| 2943 | BROWELL | Arthur | 30.09.1927 | |
| 2944 | EALES | Edward Richard | 30.09.1927 | |
| 2945 | RAVENHILL | Francis Henry | 30.09.1927 | |
| 2946 | SCARD | Leonard Henry | 30.09.1927 | |
| 2947 | SMITH | Henry William | 30.09.1927 | |
| 2948 | WEIGALL | John Henry | 30.09.1927 | |
| 2949 | WALLIS | Albert Corydon | 30.09.1927 | |
| 2950 | WILSON | David Andrew | 30.09.1927 | Lt. Col. |
| 2951 | LOMBARD | John Bousfield | 30.09.1927 | |
| 2952 | WARNER | Louis | 02.10.1927 | |
| 2953 | HEWINGS | George Acland | 05.10.1927 | C/Insp. |
| 2954 | TANTUM | William Hardy | 09.10.1927 | |
| 2955 | WHITE | Harry George | 09.10.1927 | |
| 2956 | BLAKE | James Andrew | 19.10.1927 | |
| 2957 | REANEY | Michael John | 24.10.1927 | |
| 2958 | ROUSE | William Arundell | 26.10.1927 | |
| 2959 | SHEWELL | Henry Martin | 28.10.1927 | A/Supt |
| 2960 | THOMPSON | Edward Geoffrey | 28.10.1927 | |
| 2961 | EDWARDS | Sidney Tom | 28.10.1927 | |
| 2962 | LIGHTFOOT | Harry | 28.10.1927 | |
| 2963 | KENNEDY | Terence William | 28.10.1927 | |
| 2964 | BROOKS | Edward William | 28.10.1927 | |
| 2965 | WELLER | Frank Emmanuel | 28.10.1927 | Tpr. |
| 2966 | HOOK | Henry | 30.10.1927 | |
| 2967 | GRIFFITHS | William Thomas | 04.11.1927 | Sgt. |
| 2968 | TIRRELL | Frank Spencer | 04.11.1927 | S/Insp |
| 2969 | JONES | James Harold | 04.11.1927 | Const. |
| 2970 | JONES | William Henry | 04.11.1927 | |
| 2971 | VAN DER WALT | Salmon Stephanus | 05.12.1927 | |
| 2972 | HAWTHORN | Hector McQueen | 16.12.1927 | |
| 2973 | CREASEY | Harold William | 19.12.1927 | |
| 2974 | ALLNUTT | Sydney Gerald | 30.12.1927 | |
| 2975 | BATTY | Douglas Myers | 30.12.1927 | |
| 2976 | FORDHAM | William Bruce | 30.12.1927 | A/Com |
| 2977 | FORRESTER | Douglas Hamilton | 30.12.1927 | |
| 2978 | FISHER | Henry Francis | 30.12.1927 | |
| 2979 | ISTED | Anthony Percy | 30.12.1927 | |
| 2980 | ISTED | Leslie David | 30.12.1927 | Sgt. |
| 2981 | IDLE | Dennis James | 30.12.1927 | Cpl. |
| 2982 | JEFFERY | Frank James | 30.12.1927 | Cpl. |
| 2983 | LONGRIGG | John | 30.12.1927 | |
| 2984 | McLACHLAN | James Alexande | 30.12.1927 | |
| 2985 | MONK | Boyd Robert | 30.12.1927 | |
| 2986 | PAGE | Randolph | 30.12.1927 | |
| 2987 | SOBEY | Richard Henry | 30.12.1927 | C/Supt. |
| 2988 | TURNER | Oswald Overy | 30.12.1927 | Sgt. |
| 2989 | WEMYSS | James Rawlinson | 30.12.1927 | |
| 2990 | WILLSHER | Henry John | 30.12.1927 | |
| 2991 | SANDERS | Evelyn Carew | 03.01.1928 | |
| 2992 | GREGORY | Herbert David | 13.01.1928 | 2/Sgt. |
| 2993 | HERRING | John Samuel | 20.01.1928 | |
| 2994 | WALLACE | Arthur | 20.01.1928 | |
| 2995 | MARTIN | Frank Sidney | 30.12.1927 | |
| 2996 | BEZUIDENHOUT | Wille Mathys | 31.01.1928 | Sgt. |
| 2997 | ELLIOTT | John Robert | 01.02.1928 | |
| 2998 | CHRISTIE | James Leslie | 01.03.1928 | C/Insp |
| 2999 | PHILLIPS | William Douglas | 06.03.1928 | S/Insp |
| 3000 | HARDING | Robert | 24.02.1928 | |
| 3001 | STOLS | Matthew Jacobus | 07.03.1928 | |
| 3002 | BURGER | Johannes Daniel | 23.03.1928 | Sgt. |
| 3003 | ROWLAND | Harry Westcar | 27.03.1928 | |
| 3004 | AISTON | Arthur Neal | 30.03.1928 | |
| 3005 | BELLAMY | John Franklyn | 30.03.1928 | S/Insp |
| 3006 | BAIN | Daniel Stewart | 30.03.1928 | |
| 3007 | CAPELL | Robert Devereux | 30.03.1928 | |
| 3008 | FOX-HASLAM | Gerald Edmund | 30.03.1928 | |
| 3009 | GAYLARD | Leslie Graham | 30.03.1928 | S/Insp |
| 3010 | RUSSELL-GOGGS | Harry Cyril | 30.03.1928 | |
| 3011 | HULL | Gascoigne Gaisford | 30.03.1928 | Sgt. |
| 3012 | LUCAS | Herbert | 30.03.1928 | |
| 3013 | LENNARD | Christopher William | 30.03.1928 | |
| 3014 | RALPH | John Mouryian | 30.03.1928 | |
| 3015 | SNOWDEN | Anthony Edward | 30.03.1928 | |
| 3016 | STOKES | Francis Ralph | 30.03.1928 | |
| 3017 | WEBB | Sidney Harry | 02.04.1928 | |
| 3018 | BALL | Cecil Horace | 30.03.1928 | |
| 3019 | EDGELOW | Gifford Gerald | 30.03.1928 | |
| 3020 | LONG | Lionel George | 30.03.1928 | |
| 3021 | MAYBROOK | Stephen William | 30.03.1928 | D/C/I |
| 3022 | ROSE | Wilfred | 29.03.1928 | |
| 3023 | SCHOLES | Raymond Denton | 30.03.1928 | |
| 3024 | PIPE | Arthur Henry | 30.03.1928 | |
| 3025 | WHITE | Cyril Huthwaite | 01.04.1928 | |
| 3026 | HICKS | Harold Falconer | 06.04.1928 | |
| 3027 | MURRAY | Francis Edward | 08.04.1928 | |
| 3028 | CHAPMAN | Albert William | 11.04.1928 | |
| 3029 | ORMEROD | Hugh Ridley | 12.04.1928 | |
| 3030 | OAKLEY | Leonard Harold | 13.04.1928 | |
| 3031 | ADAMS | Harry George | 18.04.1928 | |
| 3032 | DEACON | Herbert | 20.04.1928 | |
| 3033 | FORDE | Hilary John Patrick | 20.04.1928 | |
| 3034 | BROOKES | George Vincent | 01.04.1928 | Tpr. |
| 3035 | BEZUIDENHOUT | Henry | 27.04.1928 | Sgt. |
| 3036 | BETTS | George Frederick | 27.04.1928 | |
| 3037 | JONES | Jack William | 04.05.1928 | |
| 3038 | CURLEY | Edwin Albert | 11.05.1928 | |
| 3039 | WAITE | Maurice Brendon | 20.05.1928 | |
| 3040 | CRUIKSHANK | Frank | 27.05.1928 | |
| 3041 | PRENDERGAST | John Alec | 01.06.1928 | |
| 3042 | WOOLLEY | Charles Jeffrey | 10.06.1928 | |
| 3043 | SIMPSON | Arthur Rupert | 22.06.1928 | D/Ins |
| 3044 | GAWLER | Charles David | 13.07.1928 | |
| 3045 | RUDD | Walter Harry | 03.09.1928 | S/C/Ins |
| 3046 | WATT | John Sydney | 27.09.1928 | Sgt. |
| 3047 | GRANT | George Stephen | 30.09.1928 | |
| 3048 | McDONALD | Norman Rennie | 07.10.1928 | C/Insp |
| 3049 | RYAN | McLaren Peter | 09.10.1928 | |
| 3050 | MULCAHY | Stirling Swinton | 10.10.1928 | |
| 3051 | LEGG | Reginald John | 16.10.1928 | |
| 3052 | HARVEY | Cyril Wykeham | 15.10.1928 | |
| 3053 | DAVIDSON | Reginald Walter | 21.10.1928 | |
| 3054 | LINFORD | Eric Mackay | 28.11.1928 | |
| 3055 | DUNER-MILES | Frederick John | 03.12.1928 | |
| 3056 | BOULTER | Terence Wladimir | 06.12.1928 | D/Sgt. |
| 3057 | O'REILLY | Arthur Joseph | 14.12.1928 | Sgt. |
| 3058 | HEWITT | Henry John | 04.01.1929 | |
| 3059 | KENWORTHY | Charles Henry | 04.01.1929 | |
| 3060 | HATT | Paul James | 04.01.1929 | |
| 3061 | BABER | Bryan | 04.01.1929 | Sgt. |
| 3062 | SPRINGETT | Clement Louis | 04.01.1929 | S/Insp. |
| 3063 | JARVILLE | John | 04.01.1929 | Inspr. |
| 3064 | CHEESE | Frank Ebbatson | 04.01.1929 | |
| 3065 | SMITH | John Freer | 04.01.1929 | |
| 3066 | FORD | Norman Lawrence | 16.01.1929 | Const. |
| 3067 | LAVERS | George Henry | 18.01.1929 | |
| 3068 | READ | Walter Aubrey | 18.01.1929 | |
| 3069 | BELLAMY | Robert Dufley | 18.01.1929 | |
| 3070 | WRIGHT | Arthur | 18.01.1929 | |
| 3071 | OWEN | Ernest | 18.01.1929 | |
| 3072 | BODDINGTON | Charles Frederick | 20.01.1929 | Sgt. |
| 3073 | BELTON | Rex Ernest | 24.01.1929 | |
| 3074 | URWIN | Walter Frederick | 25.01.1929 | S/Insp |
| 3075 | STALLARD | Robert | 01.02.1929 | S/Insp |
| 3076 | POTGEITER | Kenneth Ernest | 02.02.1929 | Sgt. |
| 3077 | JEROME | Izak Petrus | 06.02.1929 | |
| 3078 | CATES | Leonard Gordon | 21.02.1929 | |
| 3079 | GOODALE-WRIGHT | Gerald Erskine | 21.02.1929 | C/Insp |
| 3080 | MATTHEWS | Eric Peter | 21.02.1929 | S/Insp |
| 3081 | Mac KENZIE | Harold Sidney | 21.02.1929 | Sgt. |
| 3082 | PITHEY | Colin Nainby | 09.03.1929 | S/Insp |
| 3083 | WHEELER | Eric Edward | 17.03.1929 | |
| 3084 | ACWORTH | Geofrey Oscar | 18.03.1929 | |
| 3085 | JAMES | Cecil Raymond | 22.03.1929 | |
| 3086 | SMALLWOOD | William John | 22.03.1929 | Capt. |
| 3087 | COOKE | Harry Kedwards | 22.03.1929 | |
| 3088 | WALKER | Cranmer Kenrick | 22.03.1929 | |
| 3089 | FITZWILLIAM | William Hampden | 22.03.1929 | S/A/C |
| 3090 | CATTELL | George Lionel | 22.03.1929 | S/A/C |
| 3091 | BARFOOT | Edward Alexander | 24.03.1929 | D/C/I |
| 3092 | LOWINGS | Samuel | 07.04.1929 | Inspr. |
| 3093 | ABBOTT | Reginald Westmore | 14.04.1929 | |
| 3094 | BARBER | Neville Wells | 19.04.1929 | |
| 3095 | BOWBRICK | Douglas Basil | 19.04.1929 | |
| 3096 | BULSTRODE | Sydney Alfred | 19.04.1929 | Capt. |
| 3097 | CARMICHAEL | Bernard Eglington | 19.04.1929 | Capt. |
| 3098 | Mac LEOD | Richard Spiridion | 19.04.1929 | Major |
| 3099 | PICKERING | Alexander Cameron | 19.04.1929 | |
| 3100 | SPURLING | Charles Waddington | 19.04.1929 | |
| 3101 | SMART | Basil Gordon | 19.04.1929 | Comm. |
| 3102 | DUNCOMBE | Gordon Roy | 19.04.1929 | |
| 3103 | LOVOCK | Charles William Percy | 19.04.1929 | S/A/C |

| No. | Surname | Forename(s) | Date | Rank |
|---|---|---|---|---|
| 3104 | SOUTHCLIFFE | William Clymo | 19.04.1929 | S/C/I |
| 3105 | REED | Ronald Edwin | 19.04.1929 | Cpl. |
| 3106 | ROBERTS | Harry Williams | 19.04.1929 | Trp. |
| 3107 | JOHNSTON | James | 28.04.1929 | |
| 3108 | Mac KENZIE | Alexander | 30.04.1929 | |
| 3109 | DAWKINGS | George | 03.05.1929 | |
| 3110 | WRIGHT | Sydney Arthur | 03.05.1929 | |
| 3111 | VAUGHAN | Arnold Erskine | 03.05.1929 | |
| 3112 | DIXON | Douglas Seymour | 03.05.1929 | Sgt. |
| 3113 | PRITCHARD | Stephen | 03.05.1929 | Sgt. |
| 3114 | CARR | Witney Broughton | 03.05.1929 | D/S/I |
| 3115 | TAPNER | Sidney Ernest | 03.05.1929 | |
| 3116 | STEPHENSON | Charles | 03.05.1929 | |
| 3117 | POTTS | Albert Edward | 03.05.1929 | D/Insp. |
| 3118 | HARVEY | George McLean | 03.05.1929 | S/A/C |
| 3119 | LENNOX | Ernest James | 03.05.1929 | A/Com |
| 3120 | PERRY | Frederick Charles | 03.05.1929 | |
| 3121 | FORD | Edward O'Neill | 03.05.1929 | |
| 3122 | McPHERSON | Edward | 24.05.1929 | |
| 3123 | SHERLOCK | William Neville | 21.07.1929 | |
| 3124 | HIRD | John | 06.08.1929 | |
| 3125 | DODD | Albert | 11.09.1929 | S/Insp. |
| 3126 | BOTHA | John Nicholas | 17.09.1929 | A/Com |
| 3127 | EYRE | Richard Graves | 01.10.1929 | |
| 3128 | STRICKLAND | Walter Patrick | 04.10.1929 | |
| 3129 | PATTERSON | Louis Albert | 08.10.1929 | |
| 3130 | ARTHUR | Archibald John | 30.10.1929 | |
| 3131 | CLUFF | Walter Warren | 30.10.1929 | |
| 3132 | HOSKEN | Norman Victor | 30.10.1929 | |
| 3133 | WELLBY | Colin Travers | 03.10.1929 | |
| 3134 | GILMOUR | Patrick Graham | 01.11.1929 | Sgt. |
| 3135 | KETTLE | Cecil James | 01.11.1929 | Capt |
| 3136 | DE QUEHEN | Basil Maurice | 01.11.1929 | Sgt. |
| 3137 | SMITH | Frederick Bales | 01.11.1929 | S/Insp. |
| 3138 | BOTHA | Rudolph Phillip | 01.11.1929 | |
| 3139 | HUSON | Frederick Walter | 28.11.1929 | |
| 3140 | HUMPHREYS | Henry Trefaldwyn | 28.11.1929 | |
| 3141 | WARD | Matthew Hogg | 28.11.1929 | |
| 3142 | FORSYTH | Walter James | 28.11.1929 | |
| 3143 | JOY | Thomas Andrew | 22.01.1930 | S/Insp. |
| 3144 | DE LORME | Roland Claude | 22.01.1930 | S/Insp. |
| 3145 | BROWN | Sydney Eustace | 15.02.1930 | Const. |
| 3146 | KRUGER | Jacob Petrus | 18.02.1930 | |
| 3147 | HALSE | Eric Harvey | 23.02.1930 | |
| 3148 | CRANKE | George James | 28.02.1930 | |
| 3149 | EGLINGTON | John Raymond | 28.02.1930 | |
| 3150 | GORRINGE | Mervyn Hugh | 28.02.1930 | C/Insp. |
| 3151 | GYLES | John Thomas | 28.02.1930 | |
| 3152 | HUGGINS | Henry Seth | 28.02.1930 | |
| 3153 | HYSLOP | Laurence Cuthbert | 28.02.1930 | Sgt. |
| 3154 | McRAE | Robert James | 28.02.1930 | |
| 3155 | ORR | Robert Thomas | 28.02.1930 | |
| 3156 | SCAIFE | Kenneth Earle | 01.03.1930 | |
| 3157 | FINNIS | Stewat Fitz. | 01.03.1930 | |
| 3158 | VAN DER RIET | Joseph Herold | 02.03.1930 | |
| 3159 | MITCHELL | Stanley Francis | 02.03.1930 | |
| 3160 | MAYNE | Walter Ashley | 28.02.1930 | |
| 3161 | Mac PHERSON | John | 12.03.1930 | C/Supt. |
| 3162 | ANSLEY | Gilbert Hugh | 25.03.1930 | |
| 3163 | VIENINGS | Edward Arthur | 30.03.1930 | Sgt. |
| 3164 | O'DEA | Charles Patrick | 01.04.1930 | |
| 3165 | WHYTE | William George | 01.04.1930 | |
| 3166 | THWAITE | Richard William | 01.04.1930 | |
| 3167 | FORD | George Reginald | 02.04.1930 | |
| 3168 | ANDERSON | Mevill Thomas | 03.04.1930 | Sgt. |
| 3169 | ANDERSON | James John | 03.04.1930 | S/Insp. |
| 3170 | BANKS | John Clement | 03.04.1930 | |
| 3171 | BELLAIRS | Edward Ennis | 03.04.1930 | |
| 3172 | BOOTH | John | 03.04.1930 | S/Insp. |
| 3173 | CORNFORTH | John Brian | 03.04.1930 | |
| 3174 | COWPER | Jack Cecil | 03.04.1930 | |
| 3175 | HAWKINS | Donald Ernest | 03.04.1930 | |
| 3176 | HOLROYDE | Terence | 03.04.1930 | S/Insp |
| 3177 | SAY | John | 03.04.1930 | |
| 3178 | BRAND | ErLe Hamilton | 04.04.1930 | |
| 3179 | TULLY | Cyril Desmond | 03.04.1930 | |
| 3180 | NEWTON | Donovan Anderson | 05.04.1930 | |
| 3181 | GABBITAS | Ronald Golding | 06.04.1930 | |
| 3182 | AITKENHEAD | Alexander Skinner | 15.04.1930 | |
| 3183 | FRADLEY | Norman | 16.04.1930 | |
| 3184 | WOOD | James Rutherford | 16.04.1930 | Sgt. |
| 3185 | ROBINSON | Ralph Leslie | 16.04.1930 | |
| 3186 | EVERILL | Eric Vivian Henderson | 16.04.1930 | |
| 3187 | GARDINER | William Oswald | 17.04.1930 | |
| 3188 | DASHWOOD | Eric Melville | 17.04.1930 | |
| 3189 | ASPINALL | Clive | 17.04.1930 | |
| 3190 | FRASER | Ian Patrick | 17.04.1930 | |
| 3191 | GUTRIDGE | Ebeneezer Charles | 17.04.1930 | |
| 3192 | CLUTTERBUCK | Arthur | 17.04.1930 | S/Ins |
| 3193 | THATCHER | Charles William | 22.04.1930 | S/A/C |
| 3194 | BARNETT | Hubert Langford | 24.04.1930 | |
| 3195 | LE SUEUR | Francis Winter | 24.04.1930 | |
| 3196 | SMITH | Frederick Charles | 24.04.1930 | |
| 3197 | CACKETT | Alfred Bernard | 24.04.1930 | Inspr. |
| 3198 | DULLER | Victor Edward | 24.04.1930 | S/Insp. |
| 3199 | MINIFIE | Walter Eric | 24.04.1930 | Cpl. |
| 3200 | FORDSMITH | Kenneth William | 07.05.1930 | |
| 3201 | LARDANT | Jeffrey James | 04.06.1930 | |
| 3202 | GRANT | John Robert | 10.06.1930 | Supt. |
| 3203 | MADDEN | Leo Richard | 13.07.1930 | |
| 3204 | DUNCAN | Maxwell JOHN | 15.07.1930 | Sgt. |
| 3205 | ELLEY | Stanley Olivier | 16.07.1930 | |
| 3206 | GALLIMORE | John Francis | 16.07.1930 | |
| 3207 | MILDRED | Charles Markham | 02.08.1930 | Sgt. |
| 3208 | CROZIER | Vivian Napier | 14.08.1930 | |
| 3209 | COMPTON | Sydney | 11.09.1930 | D/Insp. |
| 3210 | MANSERGH | Harry Miles | 11.09.1930 | |
| 3211 | BELLORD | John Anthony | 18.09.1930 | |
| 3212 | BROADHEAD | Geoffrey Albert | 18.09.1930 | A/Com |
| 3213 | DIGWEED | George Charles | 18.09.1930 | |
| 3214 | POLLARD | Richard Lister | 18.09.1930 | |
| 3215 | RABONE | Charles Wallis | 18.09.1930 | |
| 3216 | REAY | Peter Basil | 18.09.1930 | |
| 3217 | GRADY | Ronald Joseph | 18.09.1930 | |
| 3218 | FAWCETT-PHILLIPS | Dennis | 23.09.1930 | |
| 3219 | WEBBER | Edward William | 30.09.1930 | Inspr. |
| 3220 | EVANS | John Randal | 02.10.1930 | |
| 3221 | LAWRENCE | Gerald Pierpoint | 01.11.1933 | |
| 3222 | MEREDITH | Gordon | 01.11.1930 | |
| 3223 | WALSHAW | Frank Lord | 13.11.1930 | Trp. |
| 3224 | WEBSTER | Lawrence | 13.11.1930 | |
| 3225 | KEOGH | Richard Gerard | 29.11.1930 | |
| 3226 | MALCOLM | Charles Allan | 18.12.1930 | |
| 3227 | VOLLER | John Leslie | 18.12.1930 | |
| 3228 | BLAIR | Harvey Hamilton | 30.12.1930 | |
| 3229 | HARTLEY | Travers | 30.12.1930 | |
| 3230 | LEATT | George | 30.12.1930 | |
| 3231 | AUST | Arthur Wyatt | 31.12.1930 | Inspr. |
| 3232 | HENDERSON | Archie Robertson | 31.12.1930 | |
| 3233 | VIENINGS | Hermanus Petrus | 31.12.1930 | |
| 3234 | WILLIAM | Eric Albert Stuart | 31.12.1930 | |
| 3235 | CHARLES | Regislaus Henry | 01.01.1931 | |
| 3236 | THOMSON | Eric Reginald | 01.01.1931 | |
| 3237 | TRAUSELD | Wiliam Rudolph | 02.01.1931 | |
| 3238 | NILSEN | Alfred Thorsoe | 01.01.1931 | Inspr. |
| 3239 | LADELL | Robert Charles | 14.01.1931 | |
| 3240 | BURNELL | Wynne Patrick | 09.04.1931 | |
| 3241 | HARDWICK | Geoffrey Dorington | 09.04.1931 | Trp. |
| 3242 | SIMPSON | Alan Barton | 09.04.1931 | |
| 3243 | PATON | Thomas | 09.04.1931 | |
| 3244 | GORDON | Louis Reginald | 08.05.1931 | |
| 3245 | STURROCK | George | 08.07.1931 | Tpr. |
| 3246 | REYNOLDS | Arthur Ronald | 06.09.1931 | S/Insp. |
| 3247 | ANNESLEY | Reginald Clifford | 01.11.1931 | D/S/Inspr. |
| 3248 | BAZELEY | John Selwyn | 01.11.1931 | Tpr. |
| 3249 | BLACK | Bertram Thomas | 01.11.1931 | Tpr. |
| 3250 | COOK | Nala | 01.11.1931 | Tpr. |
| 3251 | DOBELL | Lionel Charles | 01.11.1931 | S/Inspr. |
| 3252 | FERREIRA | Edmund | 01.11.1931 | Tpr. |
| 3253 | FINCH | Reginald Peter | 01.11.1931 | Tpr. |
| 3254 | FROST | Albert John | 01.11.1931 | Major |
| 3255 | McGOVERN | Donald Vincent | 01.11.1931 | C/Inspr. |
| 3256 | SEWARD | Henry Gordon | 01.11.1931 | Tpr. |
| 3257 | THYNE | Patrick John | 01.11.1931 | Tpr. |
| 3258 | WILKINSON | Stanley Boxall | 01.11.1931 | Tpr. |
| 3259 | GOODCHILD | Noel John | 13.12.1931 | Tpr. |
| 3260 | LLEWELLYN | Donald | 14.12.1931 | C/Inspr. |
| 3261 | FULTON | George Leckey | 14.12.1931 | Tpr. |
| 3262 | GIBSON | Eric Selby | 15.12.1931 | Tpr. |
| 3263 | ENNALS | Melville Tudor | 15.12.1931 | Tpr. |
| 3264 | DAVIES | Clifford William | 15.12.1931 | Tpr. |
| 3265 | GARSIDE | Percy Tennant | 15.12.1931 | Tpr. |
| 3266 | HALE | Charles Hugh | 12.12.1931 | Tpr. |
| 3267 | HAMILTON | John William | 15.12.1931 | Tpr. |
| 3268 | ROSS | Carl Leslie | 01.11.1931 | Tpr. |
| 3269 | SMITH | Clarence Ruskin | 18.12.1931 | Tpr. |
| 3270 | LEWIS | Frank Eric | 06.01.1932 | Sgt. |
| 3271 | LLOYD | Andrew Michael | 01.04.1932 | Tpr. |
| 3272 | COATLEY | Sydney Maurice | 01.04.1932 | Tpr. |
| 3273 | ASHMEAD | Michael Richard | 01.04.1932 | Tpr. |
| 3274 | BRIDGER | Jasper Duncan | 01.04.1932 | Tpr. |
| 3275 | BURNE | Colin Leith | 01.04.1932 | |
| 3276 | CABLE | Denis Norman | 01.04.1932 | Tpr. |
| 3277 | CHILD | Reginald Donald | 01.04.1932 | Sgt. |
| 3278 | CROSSMAN | Stanley Norris | 01.04.1932 | Tpr. |
| 3279 | GOODWIN | Alexander Michael | 01.04.1932 | Tpr. |
| 3280 | GRIFFITHS | William John | 01.04.1932 | Tpr. |
| 3281 | HERBST | Robert Milton | 01.04.1932 | Tpr. |
| 3282 | HOLMAN | Alwyn Ignatius | 01.04.1932 | Tpr. |
| 3283 | HUDSON | George Mathews | 01.04.1932 | Tpr. |
| 3284 | HUDSON | William Scadding | 01.04.1932 | Tpr. |
| 3285 | ISEMONGER | Henry Richard | 01.04.1932 | Tpr. |
| 3286 | KOK | Alfred Gwynn | 01.04.1932 | Tpr. |
| 3287 | LANNING | Noel Edward | 01.04.1932 | Tpr. |
| 3288 | LEDEBOER | Jacobus Nicolas | 01.04.1932 | Tpr. |
| 3289 | LINDEQUE | Aubrey Leonard | 01.04.1932 | Tpr. |
| 3290 | PRITCHARD | Frederick Bryan | 01.04.1932 | Tpr. |
| 3291 | SANTOWSKI | Frederick Bruce | 01.04.1932 | Sgt. |
| 3292 | SNELL | John Percy | 01.04.1932 | Tpr. |
| 3293 | TAYLOR | Norman Burton | 01.04.1932 | Tpr. |
| 3294 | TOWNLEY | Harry Thomas | 01.04.1932 | Tpr. |
| 3295 | WENT | John Wolfe | 03.04.1932 | Tpr. |
| 3296 | DICKS | Robert Edward | 03.04.1932 | Tpr. |
| 3297 | LONG | Anthony Llewellyn | 03.04.1932 | Tpr. |
| 3298 | ROBINSON | Eric Mackay | 12.05.1932 | Tpr. |
| 3299 | DAVIDSON | Garnet Stopford | 01.07.1932 | Tpr. |
| 3300 | CHARLES | Alexander | 01.07.1932 | Tpr. |
| 3301 | KINROSS | Johannes | 01.07.1932 | Tpr. |
| 3302 | KLOPPERS | Geoffrey | 01.07.1932 | Tpr. |
| 3303 | LUFFE | John Marston | 09.07.1932 | Tpr. |
| 3304 | TOMBS | David Millar | 15.11.1932 | Tpr. |
| 3305 | ALLAN | Robert Hugh | 15.11.1932 | Tpr. |
| 3306 | BORLAND | Alfred James | 15.11.1932 | Tpr. |
| 3307 | FERRETT | Cyril James | 15.11.1932 | S/Inspr. |
| 3308 | GILES | Jack Meade | 15.11.1932 | Tpr. |
| 3309 | HELLIWELL | Steven Wyatt | 15.11.1932 | Tpr. |
| 3310 | HENDERSON | | | |

| No. | Surname | Forenames | Date | Rank |
|---|---|---|---|---|
| 3311 | HILL | Raymond Charles | 15.11.1932 | Tpr. |
| 3312 | MEADOWS | Cyril Cecil | 15.11.1932 | Tpr. |
| 3313 | RUSSELL | Henry Alfred | 15.11.1932 | Tpr. |
| 3314 | WARTON | Richard Montagu | 15.11.1932 | S/Inspr. |
| 3315 | WATTS | James Gilmour | 15.11.1932 | Tpr. |
| 3316 | BAMBERGER | Spencer Alexis | 15.11.1932 | Tpr. |
| 3317 | BOTHA | Pieter Johannes | 15.11.1932 | Tpr. |
| 3318 | ELY | Lionel Frederick | 19.11.1932 | Tpr. |
| 3319 | COMMERFORD | Pierce Olof | 01.01.1933 | Sgt. |
| 3320 | SMALL | William Ronald | 01.01.1933 | Tpr. |
| 3321 | STEYN | Jacobus Hermanus | 01.01.1933 | Tpr. |
| 3322 | HOFFMAN | Andrew Peter | 01.01.1933 | Sgt. |
| 3323 | BENNETT | Cecil George | 01.04.1933 | S/C/Inspr. |
| 3324 | BLISS | John Alexander | 01.04.1933 | Tpr. |
| 3325 | BOOTH | Anthony Foster | 01.04.1933 | Tpr. |
| 3326 | DIVINE | Graham Dowling | 01.04.1933 | Tpr. |
| 3327 | NIXON | William James | 01.04.1933 | Tpr. |
| 3328 | REID | Ronald Ewen | 01.04.1933 | Tpr. |
| 3329 | SHAW | Grove | 01.04.1933 | Tpr. |
| 3330 | WHITE | George Frederick | 01.04.1933 | Tpr. |
| 3331 | BARBER | Maurice Clinton | 01.04.1933 | Tpr. |
| 3332 | BRERETON | John Anthony | 01.04.1933 | C/Inspr. |
| 3333 | FERREIRA | Theodorus Minne | 01.04.1933 | Tpr. |
| 3334 | FINCH | Jack | 01.04.1933 | Tpr. |
| 3335 | NIMMO | Andrew Norman | 01.04.1933 | Inspr. |
| 3336 | STARCK | Charles Oscar | 01.04.1933 | Tpr. |
| 3337 | STUTELEY | Donald Anthony | 01.04.1933 | C/Inspr. |
| 3338 | TREANAR | Martin Heselton | 01.04.1933 | Tpr. |
| 3339 | WELDON | Robert | 01.04.1933 | Tpr. |
| 3340 | WHYTE | Trevor Ross | 01.04.1933 | Tpr. |
| 3341 | ESPEY | Joseph | 04.04.1933 | Tpr. |
| 3342 | BARFOOT | Frank Eric | 06.04.1933 | Comm. |
| 3343 | CULLEN | John Stanley | 06.04.1933 | Tpr. |
| 3344 | RODGERS | Gervase | 06.04.1933 | Tpr. |
| 3345 | COLERIDGE | Ronald James | 12.04.1933 | S/Insp |
| 3346 | LEEB | Leonard George | 25.04.1933 | Tpr. |
| 3347 | GANDOLFO | Eric Thomas | 26.04.1933 | Const |
| 3348 | TRIGGS | Walter Francis | 26.04.1933 | Tpr. |
| 3349 | MICHELL | Ruthven Pym | 29.04.1933 | Tpr. |
| 3350 | BUXTON | Sydney Wellesley | 30.04.1933 | Tpr. |
| 3351 | FORREST | James Arthur | 30.04.1933 | Tpr. |
| 3352 | HOPKING | John Henry Nevil | 30.04.1933 | Tpr. |
| 3353 | REID | Douglas MacLear | 30.04.1933 | Tpr. |
| 3354 | BROWNE | George Cyril | 03.05.1933 | Tpr. |
| 3355 | BROUGHTON | William Norman | 07.05.1933 | Cpl. |
| 3356 | CONSTABLE | Gordon Ingram | 10.05.1933 | S/Insp |
| 3357 | DUNOLLY | Jarrard Cholmeley | 10.05.1933 | Tpr. |
| 3358 | WINTER | Ewart William | 10.05.1933 | Sgt. |
| 3359 | ARNOLD | Claude Henry | 11.05.1933 | A/Com |
| 3360 | LIDDELL | Lancelot Bernard | 12.05.1933 | D/Com |
| 3361 | BROWN | Sydney Eustace | 03.01.1934 | Tpr. |
| 3362 | ALLISON | Eugene Alexander | 01.02.1934 | Tpr. |
| 3363 | BERGER | Robert Cecil | 01.02.1934 | Tpr. |
| 3364 | CHALMERS | Robert Stanley | 01.02.1934 | Sgt. |
| 3365 | EDWARDS | Joseph Claude | 01.02.1934 | Tpr. |
| 3366 | FORBES | Thomas Maxwell | 01.02.1934 | Sgt. |
| 3367 | FROMENTIN | Frederick Charles | 01.02.1934 | Tpr. |
| 3368 | GRIMES | Roland Howard | 01.02.1934 | A/Com |
| 3369 | HARRIES | George Mervyn | 01.02.1934 | D/Com |
| 3370 | HICKIE | John Corbett | 01.02.1934 | Tpr. |
| 3371 | MONTCRIEFF | William Leslie | 01.02.1934 | Tpr. |
| 3372 | ROBINSON | Frederick Cecil | 01.02.1934 | Sgt. |
| 3373 | STRACHAN | Donald Roy | 01.02.1934 | Tpr. |
| 3374 | VAN NIEKERK | Herbert Dunsterville | 01.02.1934 | C/Supt |
| 3375 | FACHIE | Peter | 08.04.1934 | Tpr. |
| 3376 | BESLEY | Leo Charles | 17.04.1934 | Tpr. |
| 3377 | BRINTON | Arnold John | 01.01.1934 | Tpr. |
| 3378 | COCKCROFT | Theodore Wilfred | 17.05.1934 | Sgt. |
| 3379 | HORNBY | Arthur Lockyer | 17.05.1934 | Tpr. |
| 3380 | JACK | Arthur Wellesley | 17.05.1934 | Tpr. |
| 3381 | LENNARD | Laurence Norman | 17.05.1934 | Tpr. |
| 3382 | McGREGOR | Gordon Alan | 17.05.1934 | Sgt. |
| 3383 | BADEN-POWELL | Arthur Robert | 17.05.1934 | Tpr. |
| 3384 | RAIL | John Richard | 17.05.1934 | D/C/I |
| 3385 | LUMHOLST-SMITH | Lionel Ludvig | 17.05.1934 | Tpr. |
| 3386 | UNWIN | Percy Vane | 17.05.1934 | Tpr. |
| 3387 | VAN DE LINDE | Michael Stephanis | 17.05.1934 | Tpr. |
| 3388 | WILLIAMS | Bernard Henry | 17.05.1934 | S/C/I |
| 3389 | WOODGATE | Gerald Greystone | 17.05.1934 | Tpr. |
| 3390 | VAN ZELLER | Hamish | 22.05.1934 | Tpr. |
| 3391 | DAY | Julian Canning | 28.05.1934 | Tpr. |
| 3392 | BOAST | Quinton Edward | 28.05.1934 | Tpr. |
| 3393 | THEOBALD | Hubert Leslie | 29.05.1934 | Const. |
| 3394 | ALEXANDER | Clifford Redford | 31.05.1934 | Tpr. |
| 3395 | BEUKES | Rudolf Jan Daniel | 31.05.1934 | Tpr. |
| 3396 | CAMPBELL | Hugh Frank | 31.05.1934 | Sgt. |
| 3397 | COLLETT | Alfred Ross | 31.05.1934 | Tpr. |
| 3398 | EDWARDS | Bryan Frank | 31.05.1934 | Tpr. |
| 3399 | ELLIS | Richard Charles | 31.05.1934 | Tpr. |
| 3400 | HEWIT | Henry Mackay | 31.05.1934 | Tpr. |
| 3401 | STARLING | Stanley Joseph | 31.05.1934 | S/Insp |
| 3402 | THOMPSON | Edward Keith | 31.05.1934 | Tpr. |
| 3403 | YOUNG | Frederick Keene | 31.05.1934 | Tpr. |
| 3404 | BLYTH | Paul Redman | 15.08.1934 | Tpr. |
| 3405 | BOTHA | Gerhardus Dirk | 15.08.1934 | Tpr. |
| 3406 | BRENDON | Norman John | 15.08.1934 | Tpr. |
| 3407 | DENNISON | Alex Clifford | 15.08.1934 | Tpr. |
| 3408 | HOLMAN | Frank Street | 15.08.1934 | Tpr. |
| 3409 | HUNTER | Nigel Stuart | 15.08.1934 | Tpr. |
| 3410 | KIRK | James Harrison | 15.08.1934 | C/Insp |
| 3411 | LUDLOW | Cecil Mendham | 15.08.1934 | Tpr. |
| 3412 | MARTIN | William Albert | 18.08.1934 | Tpr. |
| 3413 | KELLY | Richard Basil | 28.08.1934 | S/Inspr. |
| 3414 | CHARNAUD | Edwin | 12.09.1934 | Tpr. |
| 3415 | FERGUSON | Gordon Lancelot | 12.09.1934 | Tpr. |
| 3416 | GILLETT | James Anthony | 12.09.1934 | Tpr. |
| 3417 | McCORMICK | Alwyne Terence | 12.09.1934 | D/C/I. |
| 3418 | McLAUCHLAN | Kenneth | 12.09.1934 | Sgt. |
| 3419 | MONTGOMERY | Graham | 12.09.1934 | Tpr. |
| 3420 | OSWELL | Frederick George | 12.09.1934 | Tpr. |
| 3421 | RONNIE | Edward Hamilton | 12.09.1934 | Tpr. |
| 3422 | SMITH | Lance Bales | 12.09.1934 | Sgt. |
| 3423 | WATSON | George Dennison | 12.09.1934 | S/A/C |
| 3424 | MACKAY | Hugh Clarence | 26.09.1934 | Tpr. |
| 3425 | GREIG | William Charles | 02.10.1934 | S/C/I. |
| 3426 | SOUTHGATE | William Jack | 18.10.1934 | Tpr. |
| 3427 | ROPER-COOKE | Henry | 15.11.1934 | Inspr. |
| 3428 | HECKETT | William Bernard | 15.11.1934 | Tpr. |
| 3429 | LINFIELD | Frederick Roy | 15.11.1934 | Tpr. |
| 3430 | PECK | John William | 15.11.1934 | Tpr. |
| 3431 | PETTITT | William Geoffrey | 15.11.1934 | Tpr. |
| 3432 | RHODES | Mark Raymond | 15.11.1934 | Tpr. |
| 3433 | WAINE | Leslie Arthur | 15.11.1934 | Tpr. |
| 3434 | WOOLCOCK | George Peter | 15.11.1934 | C/Insp |
| 3435 | BARBER | Roger Atherstone | 31.01.1935 | Sgt. |
| 3436 | BOWERS | Patrick Richard | 31.01.1935 | Tpr. |
| 3437 | COLLINS | Edward Harold | 31.01.1935 | Cpl. |
| 3438 | COWLEY | Lachlan Charles | 31.01.1935 | Tpr. |
| 3439 | DE BEER | Michael Johannes | 31.01.1935 | Inspr. |
| 3440 | FELLOWS | Charles | 31.01.1935 | Tpr. |
| 3441 | FINLAY | George | 31.01.1935 | Sgt. |
| 3442 | FOX | Joseph Gordon | 31.01.1935 | Tpr. |
| 3443 | GALLIAS | George | 31.01.1935 | Tpr. |
| 3444 | GUSH | Sharon Mostyn | 31.01.1935 | Tpr. |
| 3445 | HOOPER | Herbert Denison | 31.01.1935 | Tpr. |
| 3446 | KELLY | Arthur Montague | 31.01.1935 | Tpr. |
| 3447 | KINNEAR | Stanley Stephen | 31.01.1935 | Sgt. |
| 3448 | O'BRYEN | Desmond Patrick | 31.01.1935 | D/Insp |
| 3449 | OWEN | George Nisbett | 31.01.1935 | Tpr. |
| 3450 | PATTEN | Donal Baptist | 31.01.1935 | Tpr. |
| 3451 | PHILLIPS | George Maberly | 31.01.1935 | Inspr. |
| 3452 | ROBERTS | Frederick Alexander | 31.01.1935 | Tpr. |
| 3453 | ROSS | Ian Angus | 31.01.1935 | Tpr. |
| 3454 | STONIER | Ernest Anthony | 31.01.1935 | S/Insp |
| 3455 | WELLER | James Edwin Luyt | 31.01.1935 | A/Com |
| 3456 | WHEAL | Bazil Harold | 31.01.1935 | S/Inspr. |
| 3457 | WANE | Peter Francis | 31.01.1935 | Inspr. |
| 3458 | JOCELYN | Napoleon Tunnicliffe | 04.02.1935 | Tpr. |
| 3459 | YOUNG | William Rennick | 13.02.1935 | Tpr. |
| 3460 | BOTHA | Martinus Louis | 04.04.1935 | Tpr. |
| 3461 | BURKE | John Henry | 04.04.1935 | Tpr. |
| 3462 | DAVENPORT | Lawrence Edward | 04.04.1935 | C/Inspr. |
| 3463 | HART | Christian Johannes | 04.04.1935 | Tpr. |
| 3464 | HEARN | Henry George | 04.04.1935 | Tpr. |
| 3465 | STROBEL | Harry Eric | 04.04.1935 | Tpr. |
| 3466 | TAUTE | Neville King | 04.04.1935 | Tpr. |
| 3467 | HETHERINGTON | Edouard Henri | 01.04.1935 | S/C/Inspr. |
| 3468 | ARMSTRONG | William Leslie | 20.06.1935 | Tpr. |
| 3469 | CLAYTON | George Francis | 20.06.1935 | Sgt. |
| 3470 | CUMMING | Dennis | 20.06.1935 | Sgt. |
| 3471 | HALL | John Bellamy | 20.06.1935 | D/Inspr. |
| 3472 | HAWKINS | Bertram Austin | 20.06.1935 | Tpr. |
| 3473 | JONES | John Trevor | 20.06.1935 | Tpr. |
| 3474 | LEASK | Leslie Hugh | 20.06.1935 | Sgt. |
| 3475 | McCRANN | Norman William | 20.06.1935 | Sgt. |
| 3476 | MEANLEY | George | 20.06.1935 | Sgt. |
| 3477 | NICHOLAS | Peter Grey | 20.06.1935 | Tpr. |
| 3478 | NICHOLSON | Marshall Robinson | 20.06.1935 | Tpr. |
| 3479 | NELSON | Martin Arend | 20.06.1935 | Tpr. |
| 3480 | OPPENHEIM | Edward Abraham | 20.06.1935 | A/Commr. |
| 3481 | PATTRICK | Edward Leslie | 20.06.1935 | Tpr. |
| 3482 | PERKINS | William Randle | 20.06.1935 | C/Inspr. |
| 3483 | POLLARD | Arthur Robert | 20.06.1935 | Tpr. |
| 3484 | RITSON | Kenneth David | 20.06.1935 | Tpr. |
| 3485 | CHAMBERLAIN | Herbert Edward | 20.06.1935 | Tpr. |
| 3486 | PHILPOTT | Horace Bartlett | 20.06.1935 | Tpr. |
| 3487 | BANFIELD | Herbert George | 20.06.1935 | Tpr. |
| 3488 | EDWARDS | James Morgan | 20.06.1935 | Inspr. |
| 3489 | EVANS | John | 20.06.1935 | Tpr. |
| 3490 | FRANKLIN | Benjamin George | 20.06.1935 | Tpr. |
| 3491 | GREEN | Darrel Jack | 20.06.1935 | Sgt. |
| 3492 | GRIMLEY | Sydney Cecil | 20.06.1935 | D/Sgt. |
| 3493 | LOMAS | Herbert Charles | 20.06.1935 | A/Commr. |
| 3494 | SMITH | William McCall | 20.06.1935 | C/Inspr. |
| 3495 | SMITH | John Stewart | 20.06.1935 | Tpr. |
| 3496 | STEWART | Frederick Boyd | 20.06.1935 | Tpr. |
| 3497 | CASTLE-WARD | William James | 20.06.1935 | Tpr. |
| 3498 | BARDELL | Ian William Mark | 04.07.1935 | Tpr. |
| 3499 | DORMON | Leonard Mark | 04.07.1935 | Tpr. |
| 3500 | GREEN | Norman Sydney | 04.07.1935 | Sgt. |
| 3501 | HARPER | Gordon Leslie | 04.07.1935 | Sgt. |
| 3502 | HOLMES | Aubrey Middleton | 04.07.1935 | Sgt. |
| 3503 | HOWELLS | Reginald Edward | 04.07.1935 | Tpr. |
| 3504 | KESBY | Oliver Valentine | 04.07.1935 | C/Inspr. |
| 3505 | MORGAN | Peter Robart | 04.07.1935 | Tpr. |
| 3506 | RALPH | Richard John | 04.07.1935 | Tpr. |
| 3507 | RAMSAY | Neis Alexander | 04.07.1935 | Tpr. |
| 3508 | COOTE-ROBINSON | Robert Algernon | 04.07.1935 | A/Commr. |
| 3509 | THACKER | Harold Harry | 04.07.1935 | S/Inspr. |
| 3510 | THOMAS | Ivor Watts | 04.07.1935 | Tpr. |
| 3511 | VEITCH | James Arthur | 04.07.1935 | Tpr. |
| 3512 | WHITE | Eric Gordon | 04.07.1935 | Sgt. |
| 3513 | WILTSHIRE | Herbert Gerald | 04.07.1935 | S/A/Commr. |
| 3514 | LEONARD | Frank Redman | 11.07.1935 | Tpr. |
| 3515 | UNDERWOOD | Richard Charles | 11.07.1935 | Sgt. |
| 3516 | PEARSON | Cyril David | 04.07.1935 | Tpr. |
| 3517 | WILSON | Robert Ford | 04.07.1935 | Tpr. |

| No. | Surname | Forename(s) | Rank | Date |
|---|---|---|---|---|
| 3518 | BAXTER | Thomas John | Sgt. | 27.12.1935 |
| 3519 | BUDD | Ronald Arthur | Tpr. | 27.12.1935 |
| 3520 | DAY | Edwin Charles | Tpr. | 27.12.1935 |
| 3521 | GILES | Donald William | Tpr. | 27.12.1935 |
| 3522 | GILFILLAN | William Thornhill | S/C/Inspr. | 27.12.1935 |
| 3523 | JOHNSON | Eric Frederick | Tpr. | 27.12.1935 |
| 3524 | KROG | Peter Erasmus | Tpr. | 27.12.1935 |
| 3525 | WORDSWORTH | John Layton | S/A/Commr. | 27.12.1935 |
| 3526 | VAN DE LINDE | Philip Rudolph | Tpr. | 28.12.1935 |
| 3527 | RUNDLE | Hugh Leslie | Tpr. | 29.12.1935 |
| 3528 | BELLAMY | Robert Steele | S/A/Commr. | 23.01.1936 |
| 3529 | BLOWERS | Harry Branton | D/Commr. | 23.01.1936 |
| 3530 | BLYTH | Edric Wynne | Supt. | 23.01.1936 |
| 3531 | CAVE | James Desmond | Tpr. | 23.01.1936 |
| 3532 | HARTLEY | James Hopkins | Tpr. | 23.01.1936 |
| 3533 | HARVEY | Arthur Patrick | Tpr. | 23.01.1936 |
| 3534 | HUXTABLE | Arthur Hewitt | S/Inspr. | 23.01.1936 |
| 3535 | LEE | Gainforth | S/A/Commr. | 23.01.1936 |
| 3536 | McNAMARA | Lawrence Gerard | Tpr. | 23.01.1936 |
| 3537 | MIDDLETON | Geoffrey Drake | Tpr. | 23.01.1936 |
| 3538 | NOAKES | Thomas Inskip | Tpr. | 23.01.1936 |
| 3539 | PITT | George Victor | Sgt. | 23.01.1936 |
| 3540 | REDFERN | Jack | S/A/Commr. | 23.01.1936 |
| 3541 | ROLLS | Henry Albert | Tpr. | 23.01.1936 |
| 3542 | SMITH | Stanley Holland | Tpr. | 23.01.1936 |
| 3543 | WADE | Thomas Robert | Tpr. | 23.01.1936 |
| 3544 | WARBURTON | Harold | Supt. | 23.01.1936 |
| 3545 | WOOD | Jack | Tpr. | 06.04.1936 |
| 3546 | VERNEY | James Way | Tpr. | 07.04.1936 |
| 3547 | DODGSON | Raymond Austen | Tpr. | 07.04.1936 |
| 3548 | FLAXMAN | Charles Edward | Tpr. | 07.04.1936 |
| 3549 | OLEARY | Bernard George | Tpr. | 07.04.1936 |
| 3550 | ST JORRE | Victor Frank | Sgt. | 08.04.1936 |
| 3551 | Mac INTOSH | Kenneth Alexander | S/A/Commr. | 08.04.1936 |
| 3552 | MILLER | Robert Arthur | Sgt. | 08.04.1936 |
| 3553 | STIDOLPH | Harold Alan | S/Inspr. | 08.04.1936 |
| 3554 | ADAMS | John Felix | Sgt. | 08.04.1936 |
| 3555 | AYLING | Charles Gilbert | Sgt. | 09.04.1936 |
| 3556 | BAYNE | Leslie Christopher | Sgt. | 09.04.1936 |
| 3557 | BOWEN | James Vaughan | S/Inspr. | 09.04.1936 |
| 3558 | BURNHAM | Reginald Alexander | Tpr. | 09.04.1936 |
| 3559 | BYRNE | Aubrey Thomas | Tpr. | 09.04.1936 |
| 3560 | CHAMBERS | George Alfred | Tpr. | 09.04.1936 |
| 3561 | CODRINGTON | John Humphrey | S/A/Commr. | 09.04.1936 |
| 3562 | DEAN | Wilfred James | Tpr. | 09.04.1936 |
| 3563 | DRYSDALE | Finlay | D/Inspr. | 09.04.1936 |
| 3564 | EXELBY | George Ronald | Tpr. | 09.04.1936 |
| 3565 | HARRIS | Philip Vernon | Sgt. | 09.04.1936 |
| 3566 | KEELING | Reginald George | Tpr. | 09.04.1936 |
| 3567 | KYNOCH | Gordon | Sgt. | 09.04.1936 |
| 3568 | NORTON | Cyril Frank | Tpr. | 09.04.1936 |
| 3569 | LENNARD | Arthur Kingsley | C/Supt. | 09.04.1936 |
| 3570 | LENNARD | Charles Maurice | Sgt. | 09.04.1936 |
| 3571 | LEWIS | David James | Tpr. | 09.04.1936 |
| 3572 | MASON | Frank William | Sgt. | 09.04.1936 |
| 3573 | MEREDITH | Thomas James | Sgt. | 09.04.1936 |
| 3574 | NELSON | Cecil John | Sgt. | 09.04.1936 |
| 3575 | PARRY | Richard John | A/Commr. | 09.04.1936 |
| 3576 | PARSONS | David | Tpr. | 09.04.1936 |
| 3577 | RAYNOR | Cyril Donald | Tpr. | 09.04.1936 |
| 3578 | SCOTT | Charles Fitzmaurice | Tpr. | 09.04.1936 |
| 3579 | SIMPSON | William Marmaduke | Tpr. | 09.04.1936 |
| 3580 | STEWART | Stair Johnstone | Tpr. | 09.04.1936 |
| 3581 | STRIDE | Charles Herbert | Tpr. | 09.04.1936 |
| 3582 | TUNNEY | Maurice Gerard | Sgt. | 09.04.1936 |
| 3583 | WALLACE | Theodore Walter | Tpr. | 09.04.1936 |
| 3584 | WHITE | Ernest O'Brian | Tpr. | 09.04.1936 |
| 3585 | WHITTINGDALE | Richard George | Tpr. | 09.04.1936 |
| 3586 | WINCH | Geoffrey John | Sgt. | 09.04.1936 |
| 3587 | SPENCER | Oscar Robert | Sgt. | 14.04.1936 |
| 3588 | BEVINGTON | Ivor Aubrey | A/Supt. | 28.07.1936 |
| 3589 | BREWER | Samuel Verney | Tpr. | 30.07.1936 |
| 3590 | COCHRANE | Gordon Percival | Supt. | 30.07.1936 |
| 3591 | COWLING | Brian Stanley | D/Inspr. | 30.07.1936 |
| 3592 | DIMALOW | James Angus | Tpr. | 30.07.1936 |
| 3593 | DU PLESSIS | Servaas Daniel | S/Inspr. | 30.07.1936 |
| 3594 | FERGUSON | George | Sgt. | 30.07.1936 |
| 3595 | HORNER | Arthur John | C/Inspr. | 30.07.1936 |
| 3596 | JOHN | David Alan | Tpr. | 30.07.1936 |
| 3597 | MERCER | Bernard Rye | S/A/Commr. | 30.07.1936 |
| 3598 | MOORE | Eric Henry | Tpr. | 30.07.1936 |
| 3599 | MOULE | Sidney | Tpr. | 30.07.1936 |
| 3600 | ROBINS | Norman Frank | Sgt. | 30.07.1936 |
| 3601 | BALE | John William | Tpr. | 07.09.1936 |
| 3602 | DU RAND | Franz Everad | Tpr. | 21.09.1936 |
| 3603 | EMMS | Harry James | Tpr. | 21.09.1936 |
| 3604 | SIMMONDS | Frederick George | Const. | 21.09.1936 |
| 3605 | ANDERSON | Thomas Stewart | Tpr. | 27.09.1936 |
| 3606 | BROOKING | Hugh Glyn | Tpr. | 27.09.1936 |
| 3607 | MORAY-BROWN | John Pitt | C/Inspr. | 27.09.1936 |
| 3608 | COOLING | Clifford Joseph | C/Inspr. | 27.09.1936 |
| 3609 | DUFTON | Frank Prentice | Tpr. | 27.09.1936 |
| 3610 | GLANVILLE | Arthur Cardew | Tpr. | 27.09.1936 |
| 3611 | GRAY | Allan Scott | Sgt. | 27.09.1936 |
| 3612 | HIELD | Peter Douglas | Tpr. | 27.09.1936 |
| 3613 | HOWARD | Arthur William | Sgt. | 27.09.1936 |
| 3614 | McDADE | Leslie Arthur | S/Inspr. | 27.09.1936 |
| 3615 | STEWART | Charles William | Sgt. | 27.09.1936 |
| 3616 | THOMAS | Derek David | Sgt. | 27.09.1936 |
| 3617 | SELLICK | Herbert Samuel | Tpr. | 27.09.1936 |
| 3618 | BOOT | Arthur William | Tpr. | 27.09.1936 |
| 3619 | DAVIES | John Rowden | Sgt. | 27.09.1936 |
| 3620 | GAITSKELL | Henry Kenneth | S/A/Commr. | 09.02.1937 |
| 3621 | GRIFFIN | Raymond Cyril | Sgt. | 09.02.1937 |
| 3622 | HODGES | Harry Stuart | D/Inspr. | 09.02.1937 |
| 3623 | KIRKWOOD | Andrew Harold | C/Inspr. | 09.02.1937 |
| 3624 | NELSON | John Eric | Sgt. | 09.02.1937 |
| 3625 | ROBERTSON | Geoffrey Albert | S/Inspr. | 09.02.1937 |
| 3626 | SALT | John Stevenson | Sgt. | 09.02.1937 |
| 3627 | WATKINS | Fred | Sgt. | 09.02.1937 |
| 3628 | McINTYRE | Clarence John | Tpr. | 11.02.1937 |
| 3629 | SMITH | Ronald | Sgt. | 11.02.1937 |
| 3630 | SPENCE | Rodney Alexander | S/A/Commr. | 11.02.1937 |
| 3631 | VAN SITTERT | Eric Desmond | S/Inspr. | 11.02.1937 |
| 3632 | FIVAZI | Harold | D/Inspr. | 23.02.1937 |
| 3633 | MAYS | Hilary Farre | S/Inspr. | 23.02.1937 |
| 3634 | McLACHLAN | Neville | S/Inspr. | 23.02.1937 |
| 3635 | TAYLOR | Leslie John | Tpr. | 23.02.1937 |
| 3636 | WALLER | Jan Lodewijk | Tpr. | 23.02.1937 |
| 3637 | BAISLEY | Oswald Dudley | Tpr. | 25.02.1937 |
| 3638 | LEE | Ronald Walter | Sgt. | 25.02.1937 |
| 3639 | McLAUGHLIN | Cyril Joseph | Tpr. | 25.02.1937 |
| 3640 | PALMER | Owen Domingo | Tpr. | 25.02.1937 |
| 3641 | STOOKS | Cecil John | Sgt. k | 25.02.1937 |
| 3642 | WALLIS | John Cockburn | Sgt. | 25.02.1937 |
| 3643 | MURRAY | Michael Ritchie | C/Supt. | 04.04.1937 |
| 3644 | GREGORY | Sydney Ernest | Inspr. | 06.04.1937 |
| 3645 | MURRAY | Malcolm Stuart | Tpr. | 07.04.1937 |
| 3646 | ANDREWS | Robert Frederick | S/Inspr. | 08.04.1937 |
| 3647 | BAILEY | James Thomas | Const. | 08.04.1937 |
| 3648 | BALDWIN | Harry George | Tpr. | 08.04.1937 |
| 3649 | BIGGAR | Robert | Tpr. | 08.04.1937 |
| 3650 | BOLTON | Geoffrey Thomas | Tpr. | 08.04.1937 |
| 3651 | CROSSWELL | Denis Montagu | Tpr. | 08.04.1937 |
| 3652 | CROSS | George Edward | Sgt. | 08.04.1937 |
| 3653 | DALLY | Desmond John | Tpr. | 08.04.1937 |
| 3654 | FLOWER | Kenneth | D/Commr. | 08.04.1937 |
| 3655 | GORDON | Charles Ongley | Sgt. | 08.04.1937 |
| 3656 | GORDON | Denis Adrian | C/Inspr. | 08.04.1937 |
| 3657 | GODWIN | Alan Roger | S/A/Commr. | 08.04.1937 |
| 3658 | HAYES | Clifford Brian | Sgt. | 08.04.1937 |
| 3659 | HOLT | Jack Webster | Tpr. | 08.04.1937 |
| 3660 | JONES | Peter Sylvester | D/Inspr. | 08.04.1937 |
| 3661 | KEMP | Michael Henry | Tpr. | 08.04.1937 |
| 3662 | MARTIN | James Arnold | Tpr. | 08.04.1937 |
| 3663 | PATERSON | Gordon McNeillie | Sgt. | 08.04.1937 |
| 3664 | PEARSON | Charles James | Sgt. | 08.04.1937 |
| 3665 | SMITH | Alan Wilton | Tpr. | 08.04.1937 |
| 3666 | THOMSON | Bertram Stuart | Sgt. | 08.04.1937 |
| 3667 | TURNER | Cyril Bernard | Tpr. | 08.04.1937 |
| 3668 | TURNER | Laurence Herbert | S/A/Commr. | 08.04.1937 |
| 3669 | WALKER | Gerald Leonard | Sgt. | 08.04.1937 |
| 3670 | PETTIT | Richard Gordon | Tpr. | 08.04.1937 |
| 3671 | ODENDAAL | Ernest Arthur | Tpr. | 13.04.1937 |
| 3672 | CLARK | Wilfred Ernest | Tpr. | 04.11.1937 |
| 3673 | COLLINS | Norman Llewellyn | Tpr. | 04.11.1937 |
| 3674 | EDWARDS | Albert George | Tpr. | 04.11.1937 |
| 3675 | GRUNDY | John Estlin | D/Inspr. | 04.11.1937 |
| 3676 | HAMILTON | John Edward | Tpr. | 04.11.1937 |
| 3677 | HARDY | Victor Leonard | Tpr. | 04.11.1937 |
| 3678 | HEATH | George Emil | Sgt. | 04.11.1937 |
| 3679 | KING | Humphrey Brewis | Tpr. | 04.11.1937 |
| 3680 | LIVINGSTONE | Alasdair Duncan | Tpr. | 04.11.1937 |
| 3681 | LYON | Charles George | Inspr. | 04.11.1937 |
| 3682 | OBYRNE | Edward | Tpr. | 04.11.1937 |
| 3683 | STOKES | Patrick Anthony | Tpr. | 04.11.1937 |
| 3684 | TEBBIT | John Charles | Sgt. | 04.11.1937 |
| 3685 | WALLACE | Vincent Foster | S/C/Inspr. | 04.11.1937 |
| 3686 | WESTON | Arthur Vincent | C/Supt. | 04.11.1937 |
| 3687 | DILLON | Michael John | | 13.01.1938 |
| 3688 | SNEYD | Ernest | Sgt. | 13.01.1938 |
| 3689 | ASHLEY | Arthur Leslie | S/Inspr. | 01.02.1938 |
| 3690 | GRAY | Ian James Gordon | Tpr. | 03.02.1938 |
| 3691 | HERBERT | Frederick George | Tpr. | 03.02.1938 |
| 3692 | PAYNE | Charles Antony | Sgt. | 03.02.1938 |
| 3693 | SCHOLLUM | Charles Anthony | Supt. | 03.02.1938 |
| 3694 | TOLLEY | John Gilbert | Supt. | 03.02.1938 |
| 3695 | JENKINS | Winstone James | Tpr. | 03.02.1938 |
| 3696 | HUTCHINSON | Thomas | Tpr. | 04.04.1938 |
| 3697 | BROWN | Harold Hope | Const. | 06.04.1938 |
| 3698 | JOHN | Robert Conway | C/Inspr. | 07.04.1938 |
| 3699 | CLARKE | Llewellyn Malcolm | Tpr. | 12.04.1938 |
| 3700 | ELVY | John Leslie | Sgt. | 12.04.1938 |
| 3701 | LETCHWORTH | Frank Howard | Tpr. | 12.04.1938 |
| 3702 | SCULLY | Patrick Francis | Tpr. | 14.04.1938 |
| 3703 | BAILEY | Robert John | D/Commr. | 14.04.1938 |
| 3704 | BEDDARD | Joseph William | S/Inspr. | 14.04.1938 |
| 3705 | BLACKMORE | Reginald Oscar | Sgt. | 14.04.1938 |
| 3706 | BRIGHTEN | Peter Edgecumbe | Tpr. | 14.04.1938 |
| 3707 | CAHILL | John Arthur | D/Commr. | 14.04.1938 |
| 3708 | CRABTREE | William | Tpr. | 14.04.1938 |
| 3709 | DICKSON | Denis Joseph | Supt. | 14.04.1938 |
| 3710 | FORDE | David Guy | Tpr. | 14.04.1938 |
| 3711 | HALL | Alec Herbert | Sgt. | 14.04.1938 |
| 3712 | HAMPSHIRE | Frank | Sgt. | 14.04.1938 |
| 3713 | JAMES | George William | S/C/Inspr. | 14.04.1938 |
| 3714 | KAY | Dennis Patrick | Tpr. | 14.04.1938 |
| 3715 | McCORMAC | Patrick Kevin | Tpr. | 14.04.1938 |
| 3716 | McCRETON | Alastair Gordon | Tpr. | 14.04.1938 |
| 3717 | McNAUGHTON | Ronald Stuart | Tpr. | 14.04.1938 |
| 3718 | MONTEITH | Deryck Sydney | S/C/Inspr. | 14.04.1938 |
| 3719 | O'DONNELL | Cecil Walter | S/Inspr. | 14.04.1938 |
| 3720 | PAGE | Francis John | C/Inspr. | 14.04.1938 |
| 3721 | PEARMAN | Jack Baron | C/Inspr. | 14.04.1938 |
| 3722 | SEED | George Edward | S/Inspr. | 14.04.1938 |
| 3723 | SMITH | John Leslie | Sgt. | 14.04.1938 |
| 3724 | THOMAS | | | |

| | | | | |
|---|---|---|---|---|
| 3725 | TUKE | Laurence Eaton | 14.04.1938 | C/Supt |
| 3726 | WEBB | Alan Wilfred | 14.04.1938 | Tpr. |
| 3727 | WILLIAMS | John Howard | 14.04.1938 | Sgt. |
| 3728 | YOUNG | Donald | 14.04.1938 | Sgt. |
| 3729 | BARTON | John Ernest | 28.04.1938 | A/Com |
| 3730 | BONASS | Leo Ernest | 28.04.1938 | Const. |
| 3731 | BROWN | James McFarlane | 28.04.1938 | Sgt. |
| 3732 | BRYER | Malcolm | 28.04.1938 | D/Inspr. |
| 3733 | BUTLER | John Arthur | 28.04.1938 | Tpr. |
| 3734 | CALLAWAY | Stuart Gordon | 28.04.1938 | Tpr. |
| 3735 | ELLIS | Leonard Alfred | 28.04.1938 | Tpr. |
| 3736 | FLEMING | Douglas Ronald | 28.04.1938 | Supt. |
| 3737 | MASEFIELD | John Aidan | 28.04.1938 | Tpr. |
| 3738 | McNAMARA | Vernon Claude | 28.04.1938 | Sgt. |
| 3739 | MITCHELL | James | 28.04.1938 | |
| 3740 | READ | Robert Jeffrey | 28.04.1938 | Tpr. |
| 3741 | RODWELL | Robert Hunter | 28.04.1938 | Sgt. |
| 3742 | SANDIFER | Richard William | 28.04.1938 | C/Inspr. |
| 3743 | SPINK | James | 28.04.1938 | Commr. |
| 3744 | ST. CLAIR | Desmond | 28.04.1938 | Tpr. |
| 3745 | DUNCAN | Alfred | 31.05.1938 | Sgt. |
| 3746 | BUCKLEY | Maurice Bernard | 02.06.1938 | Supt. |
| 3747 | COOKE | John | 02.06.1938 | C/Inspr. |
| 3748 | EDWARDS | Peter Newton | 02.06.1938 | Tpr. |
| 3749 | EDWARDS | Stanley | 02.06.1938 | S/A/C |
| 3750 | FROST | Terence Joseph | 02.06.1938 | Tpr. |
| 3751 | GLOVER | Norman | 02.06.1938 | Tpr. |
| 3752 | GROVER | Richard Roy | 02.06.1938 | Sgt. |
| 3753 | HAMMOND | William Maynard | 02.06.1938 | Tpr. |
| 3754 | HILL | Desmond Hayward | 02.06.1938 | Sgt. |
| 3755 | HOYLE | Percy | 02.06.1938 | S/C/Inspr |
| 3756 | HUNTER | John | 02.06.1938 | Supt. |
| 3757 | KNIGHT | Leonard Frank | 02.06.1938 | D/C/Inspr. |
| 3758 | LESLIE | George Shiel | 02.06.1938 | Sgt. |
| 3759 | LEVETT | Keppel Pagot | 02.06.1938 | Tpr. |
| 3760 | LEWIS | Lewis Wynne | 02.06.1938 | Sgt. |
| 3761 | Mac DONALD | Glen Harold | 02.06.1938 | D/C/Inspr |
| 3762 | MITCHELL | James Albert | 02.06.1938 | S/C/Inspr. |
| 3763 | MOORE | Thomas | 02.06.1938 | C/Supt. |
| 3764 | O'CONNOR | Vincent John | 02.06.1938 | D/Inspr |
| 3765 | OLIPHANT | Alexander George | 02.06.1938 | Sgt. |
| 3766 | PLETTS | Edward Richard | 02.06.1938 | Sgt. |
| 3767 | SHELAGH | Robert | 02.06.1938 | C/Inspr. |
| 3768 | SMITH | Kenneth Douglas | 02.06.1938 | Sgt. |
| 3769 | WALL | Earle Augustus | 02.06.1938 | Inspr. |
| 3770 | WHITEHEAD | John Vivian | 02.06.1938 | Sgt. |
| 3771 | WILSON | John Edwin | 05.06.1938 | Sgt. |
| 3772 | LLOYD | Ben | 06.06.1938 | Tpr. |
| 3773 | MITCHELL | Robert | 26.06.1938 | Inspr. |
| 3774 | BALLARD | Hugh | 27.06.1938 | Tpr. |
| 3775 | BROOM | Edward Albert | 27.06.1938 | Sgt. |
| 3776 | CATCHPOLE | John James | 27.06.1938 | Tpr. |
| 3777 | KELLEY | Christopher James | 27.06.1938 | Sgt. |
| 3778 | SMART | Stanley Charles | 27.06.1938 | Sgt. |
| 3779 | ALLEN | Thomas Digby | 03.11.1938 | D/Commr. |
| 3780 | BECK | Peter Louis | 03.11.1938 | Sgt. |
| 3781 | BERGSTROM | Otto Theodore | 03.11.1938 | Sgt. |
| 3782 | BESTER | Frank Louis | 03.11.1938 | Sgt. |
| 3783 | COGILL | John | 03.11.1938 | Tpr. |
| 3784 | CROMPTON | Geoffrey Edward | 03.11.1938 | Tpr. |
| 3785 | REED | Donald William | 03.11.1938 | S/Inspr. |
| 3786 | GRIFFITH-RICHARDS | John Patrick | 03.11.1938 | Tpr. |
| 3787 | PETERS | John Radcliffe | 04.11.1938 | C/Inspr. |
| 3788 | ADDISON | Victor Alexander | 05.01.1939 | S/Inspr. |
| 3789 | ANDERSON | Ian Douglas | 05.01.1939 | Sgt. |
| 3790 | BEVAN | Alfred Trevor | 05.01.1939 | Sgt. |
| 3791 | HASTINGS | Hugh | 05.01.1939 | Sgt. |
| 3792 | LEPAGE | John Derek | 05.01.1939 | Const. |
| 3793 | LEAVER | Kenneth Dudley | 05.01.1939 | Supt. |
| 3794 | THORNTON | John Charles | 05.01.1939 | Sgt. |
| 3795 | WEATHERDON | Charles Arthur | 05.01.1939 | Tpr. |
| 3796 | BALDREY | Denzil Olaf | 09.01.1939 | Sgt. |
| 3797 | COULTON | Reginald Albert | 15.01.1939 | Supt. |
| 3798 | VINCENT | George Trevor | 22.04.1939 | Sgt. |
| 3799 | ANDREW | Anthony Lawry | 23.04.1939 | C/Supt. |
| 3800 | ATKINSON | Peter Carlisle | 23.04.1939 | Tpr. |
| 3801 | ATKINSON | Philip Whitbread | 23.04.1939 | Sgt. |
| 3802 | BLACKHALL | Andrew | 23.04.1939 | Sgt. |
| 3803 | BRAES | Andrew Meikle | 23.04.1939 | S/A/Commr |
| 3804 | BROWNE | Pelham Clinton | 23.04.1939 | Tpr. |
| 3805 | HAWKE | Peter Stanley | 23.04.1939 | S/C/Inspr |
| 3806 | HENDRY | Duncan Alxeander | 23.04.1939 | Tpr. |
| 3807 | HESKETH | Michael Walter | 23.04.1939 | Tpr. |
| 3808 | HOWARD | John Buxton | 23.04.1939 | Sgt. |
| 3809 | JONES | David Edward | 23.04.1939 | Sgt. |
| 3810 | LAMBE | Sidney Alfred | 23.04.1939 | Sgt. |
| 3811 | LIGHT | George Charles | 23.04.1939 | A/Commr |
| 3812 | MARLE | Frederick | 23.04.1939 | S/C/Inspr |
| 3813 | NAFTEL | Frederick John | 23.04.1939 | Sgt. |
| 3814 | NOLAN | Leslie | 23.04.1939 | Inspr. |
| 3815 | PESTELL SIR KCVO | John Richard | 23.04.1939 | A/Commr |
| 3816 | PREWETT | Cyril Francis | 23.04.1939 | Tpr. |
| 3817 | SIMPSON | Derek Lever | 23.04.1939 | Tpr. |
| 3818 | SOUTHWELL | Tom William | 23.04.1939 | Const. |
| 3819 | SWATTON | Arthur David | 23.04.1939 | Tpr. |
| 3820 | TRAVERS | Edmund Sydney | 23.04.1939 | Inspr. |
| 3821 | TUGWELL | Henry Gordon | 23.04.1939 | Sgt. |
| 3822 | WATERS | David Martin | 23.04.1939 | Tpr. |
| 3823 | ALDERSON | Douglas George | 23.04.1939 | A/Commr |
| 3824 | BUCHANAN | John Chesney | 23.04.1939 | Tpr. |
| 3825 | CLEAVER | Percy | 23.04.1939 | Inspr. |
| 3826 | COTTON | Robert William | 23.04.1939 | Const. |
| 3827 | EGGINTON | Gilbert Leonard | 23.04.1939 | Tpr. |
| 3828 | GAUNTLETT | John Gerald | 23.04.1939 | S/C/I |
| 3829 | GUINESS | John Back | 23.04.1939 | Const. |
| 3830 | HUMAN | Johannes Albertus | 23.04.1939 | Tpr. |
| 3831 | LEACH | Alfred William | 23.04.1939 | |
| 3832 | PLASTOW | Charles Harry | 23.04.1939 | C/Supt. |
| 3833 | PRIDEAUX | Lawrence George | 23.04.1939 | Const. |
| 3834 | SCOTT | Charles Raymond | 23.04.1939 | Const. |
| 3835 | STANYON | Herbert John | 23.04.1939 | Sgt. |
| 3836 | SUNTER | William | 23.04.1939 | D/C/Inspr. |
| 3837 | WRIGHT | Basil Francis | 23.04.1939 | C/Supt. |
| 3838 | GREENE | Robert Alistair | 26.04.1939 | Tpr. |
| 3839 | RAYNOR | Anthony Owen | 27.04.1939 | Sgt. |
| 3840 | WOLFE | Richard Colin | 04.05.1939 | Sgt. |
| 3841 | FOSTER | Joseph | 06.08.1939 | Tpr. |
| 3842 | LAXTON | William Lowe | 06.08.1939 | Tpr. |
| 3843 | ORR | James Bernard | 06.08.1939 | Tpr. |
| 3844 | BRISTOW | Sidney Frederick | 06.08.1939 | Comm |
| 3845 | DOWDING | William Noble | 06.08.1939 | Sgt. |
| 3846 | HOPE | Archibald Paul | 06.08.1939 | Tpr. |
| 3847 | KINLOCK | Dennis Thomas | 06.08.1939 | Const. |
| 3848 | KNIGHT | Peter James | 06.08.1939 | Sgt. |
| 3849 | POWELL | Ambrose | 06.08.1939 | S/Inspr. |
| 3850 | VAN DER MERWE | Johannes Jacob | 06.08.1939 | Tpr. |
| 3851 | VICKERY | Harold James | 06.08.1939 | D/C/Inspr |
| 3852 | WILLIAMS | David Trefor | 06.08.1939 | D/Inspr. |
| 3853 | WICKENS | David Allen | 09.08.1939 | Tpr. |
| 3854 | HODGES | William | 10.08.1939 | S/Inspr. |
| 3855 | CRACKNELL | Douglas David | 13.08.1939 | Sgt. |
| 3856 | DOWSE | Gerald Robert | 13.08.1939 | Tpr. |
| 3857 | EVERITT | John Errol | 13.08.1939 | Inspr. |
| 3858 | HOLLEY | Harry Basil | 13.08.1939 | Tpr. |
| 3859 | HUGHES | John Ellis | 13.08.1939 | Sgt. |
| 3860 | PAYNE | John Cyprian | 13.08.1939 | A/Commr |
| 3861 | ROBERTS | Walter Alexander | 13.08.1939 | Tpr. |
| 3862 | SHERREN | Peter Denis | 13.08.1939 | Commr. |
| 3863 | TANKARD | Kenneth David | 13.08.1939 | D/Sgt. |
| 3864 | TAYLOR | Neville Treweek | 13.08.1939 | Sgt. |
| 3865 | TICKLER | William Alfred | 13.08.1939 | Sgt. |
| 3866 | WILSHER | Robert Stacey | 13.08.1939 | Sgt. |
| 3867 | YORK | Jeffrey Dew | 13.08.1939 | Sgt. |
| 3868 | LEWENZ | Geoffrey Ivan | 27.08.1939 | Tpr. |
| 3869 | HARRISON | Charlton Hugh | 27.08.1939 | Tpr. |
| 3870 | COTTHAM | Leo Joseph | 02.11.1939 | C/Inspr. |
| 3871 | FOXCROFT | William Eustace | 02.11.1939 | A/Commr |
| 3872 | NORMAN | Samuel Denis | 02.11.1939 | Sgt. |
| 3873 | BULL | Arthur Edward | 16.11.1939 | Sgt. |
| 3874 | CUMBERLAND | Lawrence Harold | 16.11.1939 | Sgt. |
| 3875 | HUGHES | William Nathaniel | 16.11.1939 | S/C/Inspr |
| 3876 | KENT | Peter Derick | 16.11.1939 | A/Commr |
| 3877 | MANSFIELD | Charles Beric | 16.11.1939 | Tpr. |
| 3878 | McLAUGHAN | William | 16.11.1939 | Inspr. |
| 3879 | ORR | George Leslie | 16.11.1939 | Tpr. |
| 3880 | SMITH | Leonard Stanley | 16.11.1939 | Sgt. |
| 3881 | STACK | Phillip Francis | 16.11.1939 | Const. |
| 3882 | WARD | George | 16.11.1939 | Supt. |
| 3883 | SPARKS | Malcolm Aubrey | 27.11.1939 | Supt. |
| 3884 | FEWSTER | James Horace | 22.04.1940 | Tpr. |
| 3885 | BARRETT | Bruce Ashwell | 29.04.1940 | Sgt. |
| 3886 | FAGAN | Henry Elliott | 29.04.1940 | Tpr. |
| 3887 | HOLLICK | Alan George | 29.04.1940 | Const. |
| 3888 | HUDSON | Desmond Robert | 29.04.1940 | Tpr. |
| 3889 | LANE | Donald Archibald | 29.04.1940 | Supt. |
| 3890 | McCORMICK | Francis Xavier | 29.04.1940 | Inspr. |
| 3891 | McDOWELL | Edgar David | 29.04.1940 | Tpr. |
| 3892 | PALMER | Maurice | 29.04.1940 | Tpr. |
| 3893 | ROBERTSON | John Brampton | 29.04.1940 | S/Inspr. |
| 3894 | YOUNG | Jack Grant | 29.04.1940 | Tpr. |
| 3895 | PODMORE | Clifford Newell | 29.04.1940 | S/A/Commr |
| 3896 | WOULFE | Richard James | 29.04.1940 | Const. |
| 3897 | DALY | Arthur Denis | 28.05.1940 | Tpr. |
| 3898 | BARROWMAN | Andrew Noble | 28.05.1940 | D/Inspr. |
| 3899 | JEWELL | Henry Adamson | 28.05.1940 | |
| 3900 | McMENAMIN | Claude James | 28.05.1940 | Const. |
| 3901 | MURRAY | Montague | 03.06.1940 | Tpr. |
| 3902 | EVERETT | Wilfred Jack | 04.06.1940 | Tpr. |
| 3903 | MOORHOUSE | Edward James | 07.07.1940 | Inspr. |
| 3904 | MARNOCH | James | 10.07.1940 | S/Inspr. |
| 3905 | COETZEE | Theunis Gert | 12.08.1940 | C/Supt. |
| 3906 | EIGLAAR | Rupert Conraad | 14.08.1940 | Tpr. |
| 3907 | DALE | John Bernard | 03.09.1940 | Tpr. |
| 3908 | DICKENSON | Charles Douglas | 04.10.1940 | Sgt. |
| 3909 | ROPER | Stanley | 14.10.1940 | Tpr. |
| 3910 | FINCH | Charles Hastings | 01.04.1942 | Capt. |
| 3911 | CORDELL | Edward Charles | 01.05.1944 | S/Inspr. |
| 3912 | LE ROUX | Jan Mattys | 29.09.1944 | Tpr. |
| 3913 | THEOBALD | Eric | 16.12.1944 | S/Inspr. |
| 3914 | GRIFFIN | Vaughan John | 01.12.1945 | Tpr. |
| 3915 | JAMES | Peter | 01.12.1945 | Sgt. |
| 3916 | BAILEY | Alec Eric Frederick | 15.12.1945 | C/Supt. |
| 3917 | BOWDEN | Francis Patrick | 28.01.1946 | Tpr. |
| 3918 | HATTON | John Sydney | 28.01.1946 | Sgt. |
| 3919 | ANDERSON | Charles John | 31.03.1946 | Sgt. |
| 3920 | CARSTAIRS | William James | 31.03.1946 | Sgt. |
| 3921 | EARLE | William Anderson | 31.03.1946 | S/Inspr. |
| 3922 | HOLT | Robert David | 31.03.1946 | A/Commr. |
| 3923 | HOWARD | William Percival | 31.03.1946 | C/Inspr. |
| 3924 | JONES | Howard | 31.03.1946 | Supt. |
| 3925 | MAY | William Albert | 31.03.1946 | A/Commr. |
| 3926 | McLERNON | William | 31.03.1946 | Const. |
| 3927 | WATSON | Stuart Geoffrey | 31.03.1946 | Tpr. |
| 3928 | WEST | Eric William | 31.03.1946 | C/Insp. |
| 3929 | BRADBROOK | Raymond Allen | 31.03.1946 | Const. |
| 3930 | CHAMBERLAIN | Terence Thomas | 31.03.1946 | Const. |
| 3931 | HAMER | John Albert | 31.03.1946 | Const. |

# BSAP Nominal Roll • Men

| No. | Surname | First Name | Rank | Date |
|---|---|---|---|---|
| 3932 | HOLDEN | Walter William | Const. | 31.03.1946 |
| 3933 | SUDLOW | Joseph | Sgt. | 01.04.1946 |
| 3934 | TAYLOR | Eric | Const. | 31.03.1946 |
| 3935 | BURNETT | Clifford Muir | Tpr. | 31.03.1946 |
| 3936 | GREENWAY | Reginald Jocelyn | D/C/Inspr. | 23.04.1946 |
| 3937 | VAN EEDE | Robert Thornton | Tpr. | 23.04.1946 |
| 3938 | BLASCHECK | Dudley | D/Sgt. | 24.04.1946 |
| 3939 | ALLUM | Peter Kevin | Commr. | 24.04.1946 |
| 3940 | ALWARD | John Seymour | Const. | 28.04.1946 |
| 3941 | BAKER | John Houghton | C/Inspr. | 28.04.1946 |
| 3942 | BARKLEY | Robert John | Tpr. | 28.04.1946 |
| 3943 | BATTERS | Reginald Kenneth | Tpr. | 28.04.1946 |
| 3944 | BISHOP | Tom Harveyson | Tpr. | 28.04.1946 |
| 3945 | BUCKLAND | Christopher | Tpr. | 28.04.1946 |
| 3946 | BURR | Ralph Edmund | Sgt. | 28.04.1946 |
| 3947 | CALLOW | William John | S/A/Comm | 28.04.1946 |
| 3948 | COLLIER | Eric Bernard | C/Supt. | 28.04.1946 |
| 3949 | COX | Kenneth Charles | Tpr. | 28.04.1946 |
| 3950 | CRABBE | Eric Lawrence | Tpr. | 28.04.1946 |
| 3951 | CURRAN | Edward John | Tpr. | 28.04.1946 |
| 3952 | DAVIDSON | John | Tpr. | 28.04.1946 |
| 3953 | DEE | Edward John | Tpr. | 28.04.1946 |
| 3954 | DEWDNEY | Victor | Tpr. | 28.04.1946 |
| 3955 | DOWLING | Edward James | Tpr. | 28.04.1946 |
| 3956 | FORDE | William Christopher | Supt. | 28.04.1946 |
| 3957 | FAIRFAX-FRANCKLIN | John William | Tpr. | 28.04.1946 |
| 3958 | GARNISH | Philip Charles | Supt. | 28.04.1946 |
| 3959 | GILMOUR | Graeme Stewart | Tpr. | 28.04.1946 |
| 3960 | HAMMOND | Jack Raymond | C/Inspr. | 28.04.1946 |
| 3961 | HENDERSON | George Alexander | Tpr. | 28.04.1946 |
| 3962 | HENWOOD | Basil John | Tpr. | 28.04.1946 |
| 3963 | HOOLE | Bernard John | Tpr. | 28.04.1946 |
| 3964 | HOWE | Gordon | Tpr. | 28.04.1946 |
| 3965 | ILLINGWORTH | John Walker | S/Sgt | 28.04.1946 |
| 3966 | ISIKSON | Montague George | C/Inspr. | 28.04.1946 |
| 3967 | JOHNSTONE | Dennis Sabin | Sgt. | 28.04.1946 |
| 3968 | JOUNING | Leonard James | D/C/Commr | 28.04.1946 |
| 3969 | KERR | Michael Alec | Tpr. | 28.04.1946 |
| 3970 | LOWTHER | Lawrence | Tpr. | 28.04.1946 |
| 3971 | LUCAS | Norman Joshua | Tpr. | 28.04.1946 |
| 3972 | MASON | Harry Chester | Supt. | 28.04.1946 |
| 3973 | MAYNARD | Anthony Vivyan | D/Inspr. | 28.04.1946 |
| 3974 | McEWAN | James Liddle | Tpr. | 28.04.1946 |
| 3975 | MOISEY | Victor George | Const. | 28.04.1946 |
| 3976 | MORGAN | David John | A/Comm | 28.04.1946 |
| 3977 | MURGATROYD | William Frank | Sgt. | 28.04.1946 |
| 3978 | PERCIVAL | Douglas Frederick | Inspr. | 28.04.1946 |
| 3979 | READ | Denis | Tpr. | 28.04.1946 |
| 3980 | REES | Ronald Henry | D/Inspr. | 28.04.1946 |
| 3981 | RICHARDSON | Richard | C/Inspr. | 28.04.1946 |
| 3982 | ROSS | Denis | Supt. | 28.04.1946 |
| 3983 | SAYER | Eric | Const. | 28.04.1946 |
| 3984 | SCHOLES | Henry | A/Comm | 28.04.1946 |
| 3985 | STEUART | John | Sgt. | 28.04.1946 |
| 3986 | TAUNTON | Peter John | Sgt. | 28.04.1946 |
| 3987 | TAYLOR | John Denis | S/Inspr. | 28.04.1946 |
| 3988 | TINDLE | Edward Stuart | Sgt. | 28.04.1946 |
| 3989 | WALKER | Kenneth | Supt. | 28.04.1946 |
| 3990 | WICKENDEN | John | C/Inspr. | 28.04.1946 |
| 3991 | WILSON | James Archibald | Supt. | 28.04.1946 |
| 3992 | PAKER | Herbert Brian | Const. | 28.04.1946 |
| 3993 | BANISTER | Thomas Charles | A/Comm | 28.04.1946 |
| 3994 | BONNER | Trevor Cecil | Sgt. | 28.04.1946 |
| 3995 | BOTTRIEL | Charles John | S/Inspr. | 28.04.1946 |
| 3996 | BOTTRIEL | Robert Edgar | Sgt. | 28.04.1946 |
| 3997 | BRIAULT | Roysten | Supt. | 28.04.1946 |
| 3998 | BURR | Alexander George | Const. | 28.04.1946 |
| 3999 | CECIL | Walter John | C/Inspr. | 28.04.1946 |
| 4000 | CHADWICK | Aubrey Ronald | Const | 28.04.1946 |
| 4001 | CLARKE | Robert | Const. | 28.04.1946 |
| 4002 | DAVIES | Peter Anthony | Sgt. | 28.04.1946 |
| 4003 | DUNBAR | James Logan | D/C/Inspr. | 28.04.1946 |
| 4004 | FISHER | Jack Francis | A/Commr | 28.04.1946 |
| 4005 | FORREST | Stanley Oldham | Supt. | 28.04.1946 |
| 4006 | FOX | John Charles | Const. | 28.04.1946 |
| 4007 | GOUGH | David Robert | Const. | 28.04.1946 |
| 4008 | GREGORY | David Lawson | D/Inspr. | 28.04.1946 |
| 4009 | GROSSMITH | Ronald Ambrose | D/Sgt. | 28.04.1946 |
| 4010 | HARCOURT | George Willoughby | S/C/Inspr. | 28.04.1946 |
| 4011 | HARRIS | Francis Roy | Const. | 28.04.1946 |
| 4012 | HODSON | Robert George | Const. | 28.04.1946 |
| 4013 | HORSTEAD | James Edward | Const. | 28.04.1946 |
| 4014 | HUGHES | Robert Bernard | C/Supt. | 28.04.1946 |
| 4015 | JOBSON | Charles George | Sgt. | 28.04.1946 |
| 4016 | JONES | Eric Donald | Const. | 28.04.1946 |
| 4017 | McCORMICK | Stanley | Const. | 28.04.1946 |
| 4018 | O'BRIEN | John Henry | A/Commr. | 28.04.1946 |
| 4019 | OWEN | Philip Thomas | S/Inspr. | 28.04.1946 |
| 4020 | PLOWMAN | Benjamin Hugh | Const. | 28.04.1946 |
| 4021 | POPE | Sydney Harry | C/Supt. | 28.04.1946 |
| 4022 | READ | James William | Sgt. | 28.04.1946 |
| 4023 | ROWLEY | Joseph Gordon | C/Inspr. | 28.04.1946 |
| 4024 | SHERIFF | Edward James | S/A/Commr | 28.04.1946 |
| 4025 | SMITH | Robert | Const. | 28.04.1946 |
| 4026 | STANTON | Henry Charles | Supt. | 28.04.1946 |
| 4027 | TAYLOR | Basil Edward | Sgt. | 28.04.1946 |
| 4028 | THORPE | Charles Terence | S/A/Com | 28.04.1946 |
| 4029 | VAN ROOYEN | Hermanus Rynier | C/Inspr. | 01.05.1946 |
| 4030 | HUXTABLE | Frederick John | Tpr. | 09.06.1946 |
| 4031 | BARNFIELD | Kenneth William | Tpr. | 11.06.1946 |
| 4032 | BARTLETT | William Henry | Tpr. | 11.06.1946 |
| 4033 | BERRY | Peter Patrick | C/Inspr. | 11.06.1946 |
| 4034 | BINNIE | Andrew Sutherland | C/Inspr. | 11.06.1946 |
| 4035 | BURGESS | Richard Mervin | Sgt. | 11.06.1946 |
| 4036 | BUSHNELL | Kenneth Edwin | C/Inspr. | 11.06.1946 |
| 4037 | CAVEY | Bernard Edward | C/Inspr. | 11.06.1946 |
| 4038 | CHALKER | Peter Chalmers | D/Sgt. | 11.06.1946 |
| 4039 | CHAPMAN | Cecil Edward | Tpr. | 11.06.1946 |
| 4040 | CLARKE | Derek Peter | Tpr. | 11.06.1946 |
| 4041 | DAY | Allen | Tpr. | 11.06.1946 |
| 4042 | DICK | Ronald Alfred | A/Commr. | 11.06.1946 |
| 4043 | DUFFIELD | Bertram | Tpr. | 11.06.1946 |
| 4044 | DYER | Norman Arthur | Sgt. | 11.06.1946 |
| 4045 | FOSKETT | Percy Frederick | C/Inspr. | 11.06.1946 |
| 4046 | GALLOWAY | Edward Bruce | S/Inspr. | 11.06.1946 |
| 4047 | HALLIDAY | Alan | Tpr. | 11.06.1946 |
| 4048 | HUSTLER | Ben Gladstone | Tpr. | 11.06.1946 |
| 4049 | JARVIS | Ronald Kenneth | C/Inspr. | 11.06.1946 |
| 4050 | KEMP | Alexander Anderson | Sgt. | 11.06.1946 |
| 4051 | KNIGHT | Douglas Christopher | Sgt. | 11.06.1946 |
| 4052 | LAMONT | Lawrence | S/A/Comm | 11.06.1946 |
| 4053 | THORNE-LARGE | Laurence Bolitho | Inspr. | 11.06.1946 |
| 4054 | McLINTOCK | Frederick Edwin | Sgt. | 11.06.1946 |
| 4055 | MORGAN | David | Supt. | 11.06.1946 |
| 4056 | MURRAY | Errol John Denzil | A/Commr. | 11.06.1946 |
| 4057 | OGLE | Mathew George | Tpr. | 11.06.1946 |
| 4058 | OSBORNE | Patrick William | C/Inspr. | 11.06.1946 |
| 4059 | ROBINSON | Peter John | Sgt. | 11.06.1946 |
| 4060 | SCOTT | Charles Henry | Tpr. | 11.06.1946 |
| 4061 | SLADE | Robert Peter | Sgt. | 11.06.1946 |
| 4062 | SMITH | Kenneth Irwin | Tpr. | 11.06.1946 |
| 4063 | SOWTER | Colin John | A/Commr | 11.06.1946 |
| 4064 | STEPHENS | Alan Charles | C/Supt. | 11.06.1946 |
| 4065 | STEWART | William McKenzie | Tpr. | 11.06.1946 |
| 4066 | TAAFE | John Patrick | Tpr. | 11.06.1946 |
| 4067 | TOMLIN | George Graham | Tpr. | 11.06.1946 |
| 4068 | WATTS | James Joseph | Tpr. | 11.06.1946 |
| 4069 | WEEKS | Edward Brian | Tpr. | 11.06.1946 |
| 4070 | WILSON | William Peter Long | Tpr. | 11.06.1946 |
| 4071 | WRIGHT | Douglas William | S/A/Commr. | 11.06.1946 |
| 4072 | ALLEN | Dermot Henry | A/Commr. | 11.06.1946 |
| 4073 | BENBOW | Ronald Percival | Inspr. | 11.06.1946 |
| 4074 | BLACKMORE | Edward William | D/C/Inspr. | 11.06.1946 |
| 4075 | BREEDEN | Theodore George | S/O | 11.06.1946 |
| 4076 | DAVIS | James Edward | Const. | 11.06.1946 |
| 4077 | FAIRHURST | Arthur Desmond | Const. | 11.06.1946 |
| 4078 | GRICE | Henry Ernest | Const. | 11.06.1946 |
| 4079 | HINE | Jack Arthur | S/Inspr. | 11.06.1946 |
| 4080 | KENDRICK | David Valentine | Const. | 11.06.1946 |
| 4081 | KILGOUR | John Stewart | Const. | 11.06.1946 |
| 4082 | MANNING | Seymour Wallace | Inspr. | 11.06.1946 |
| 4083 | MARSHALL | Robert Fleming | C/Inspr. | 11.06.1946 |
| 4084 | MAYO | William Hewey | C/Inspr. | 11.06.1946 |
| 4085 | NIMMO | Edward Frank | C/Inspr. | 11.06.1946 |
| 4086 | OSBORNE | Frederick James | Tpr. | 11.06.1946 |
| 4087 | POTTER | George Percival | C/Inspr. | 11.06.1946 |
| 4088 | RUTTLE | Frederick Henry | Sgt. | 11.06.1946 |
| 4089 | SALMON | Lawrence Oliver | Tpr. | 11.06.1946 |
| 4090 | WHITE | Richard William | Tpr. | 23.06.1946 |
| 4091 | BRANFIELD | Robert Brian | Tpr. | 26.06.1946 |
| 4092 | ALFRED | George | D/Commr | 26.06.1946 |
| 4093 | ALLEN | Charles Michael | Sgt. | 26.06.1946 |
| 4094 | ATKINSON | Robert | Sgt. | 26.06.1946 |
| 4095 | BURGESS | Christopher John | Tpr. | 26.06.1946 |
| 4096 | BURNS | William Ewart | Tpr. | 26.06.1946 |
| 4097 | CALTON | Bran Harry | S/Inspr. | 26.06.1946 |
| 4098 | COLEMAN | Robert Henry | Tpr. | 26.06.1946 |
| 4099 | CROOK | Alan Storey | Tpr. | 26.06.1946 |
| 4100 | DUBBIN | John Clancy | Tpr. | 26.06.1946 |
| 4101 | DODDS | James George | Tpr. | 26.06.1946 |
| 4102 | DOUGLAS | Tony John | Supt. | 26.06.1946 |
| 4103 | DOWHAM | Albert Brenden | S/A/Commr | 26.06.1946 |
| 4104 | DUMBRELL | Robert Stanley | Tpr. | 26.06.1946 |
| 4105 | FREEMANTLE | Kenneth Peter | Tpr. | 26.06.1946 |
| 4106 | HAMILTON | Christopher Michael | Tpr. | 26.06.1946 |
| 4107 | HOUGH | Dennis William | Tpr. | 26.06.1946 |
| 4108 | HUMPREY | Alexander | Tpr. | 26.06.1946 |
| 4109 | LOSE | Fredrick Albert | Sgt. | 26.06.1946 |
| 4110 | NESS | Edward Derek | Tpr. | 26.06.1946 |
| 4111 | OAKLEY | Oliver Valentine | Tpr. | 26.06.1946 |
| 4112 | ROBERTS | Roger Thomas | Tpr. | 26.06.1946 |
| 4113 | RUHL | Edward Albert | D/C/Inspr. | 26.06.1946 |
| 4114 | SANDALL | Maurice Alexander | Tpr. | 26.06.1946 |
| 4115 | SANDFORD | Donald Kinsford | Supt. | 26.06.1946 |
| 4116 | SHARPE | Trevor James | Inspr. | 26.06.1946 |
| 4117 | SMITH | Denis | Sgt. | 26.06.1946 |
| 4118 | WALTON | William | Tpr. | 26.06.1946 |
| 4119 | WATSON | James Antony | Tpr. | 26.06.1946 |
| 4120 | WELLARD | William | Tpr. | 26.06.1946 |
| 4121 | WRIGHT | David Frederick | Tpr. | 26.06.1946 |
| 4122 | WHITE | Graham | Tpr. | 26.06.1946 |
| 4123 | WISE | Duncan | Sgt. | 26.06.1946 |
| 4124 | BROWNBRIDGE | Geoffrey John | C/Inspr. | 26.06.1946 |
| 4125 | HOLDSWORTH | Peter Malcolm | Tpr. | 26.06.1946 |
| 4126 | JACKSON | Donald Malcolm | Sgt. | 26.06.1946 |
| 4127 | POWELL | Arthur Curtis | Sgt. | 26.06.1946 |
| 4128 | QUINN | John Shirvill | Supt. | 26.06.1946 |
| 4129 | SYRATT | Denis | Inspr. | 26.06.1946 |
| 4130 | WRIGHT | William James | C/Inspr. | 26.06.1946 |
| 4131 | BRUWER | James Antony | Tpr. | 29.08.1946 |
| 4132 | GREEF | Johan Wilhelm | Sgt. | 29.08.1946 |
| 4133 | SUTHERLAND | Barent Frederick | Sgt. | 29.08.1946 |
| 4134 | CROSS | Johannes Jacobus | C/Inspr. | 29.08.1946 |
| 4135 | COX | Michael John | Sgt. | 29.08.1946 |
| 4136 | EGLETON | Anthony Paine | Sgt. | 29.08.1946 |
| 4137 | BEAUFORT | Thomas William | Sub/Inspr. | 29.08.1946 |
| 4138 | SANDERSON | Derek Rupert Dennison Harvey | S/A/Commr. | 29.08.1946 |

| No. | Surname | First name(s) | Date | Rank |
|---|---|---|---|---|
| 4139 | WHITE | William James | 13.12.1946 | Sgt. |
| 4140 | ANDREW | Basil | 29.12.1946 | C/Inspr. |
| 4141 | ARMSTRONG | John Robert | 29.12.1946 | Tpr. |
| 4142 | BUTCHER | John Roland | 29.12.1946 | Tpr. |
| 4143 | DENEYS | Colin MacKenzie | 29.12.1946 | Tpr. |
| 4144 | DRUMMOND | David Divinion | 29.12.1946 | C/Inspr. |
| 4145 | FREEMANTLE | Mark Edward | 29.12.1946 | Tpr. |
| 4146 | GREGORY | James Richard | 29.12.1946 | S/A/Commr |
| 4147 | HEDGE | Douglas Cordy | 29.12.1946 | Tpr. |
| 4148 | COOPER-JONES | William Maurice | 29.12.1946 | Supt. |
| 4149 | KERSWELL | Robert George | 29.12.1946 | D/Sub/Ins |
| 4150 | REID | John Antony | 29.12.1946 | C/Supt. |
| 4151 | RIGDEN | Paul Edward | 29.12.1946 | Tpr. |
| 4152 | RYAN | Patrick Jean | 29.12.1946 | Const. |
| 4153 | SMITH | Terence Walter | 29.12.1946 | C/Inspr. |
| 4154 | THOMPSON | Ralph Clement | 29.12.1946 | D/Inspr. |
| 4155 | VALLINS | Herbert John | 29.12.1946 | Tpr. |
| 4156 | WALL | Alan David | 29.12.1946 | Tpr. |
| 4157 | WATKINS | James Oliver | 29.12.1946 | C/Supt. |
| 4158 | WEIMER | Thomas Edward | 29.12.1946 | Supt. |
| 4159 | ARNOLD | Stanley James | 29.12.1946 | Const. |
| 4160 | BARTHORPE | Alec James | 29.12.1946 | Inspr. |
| 4161 | CLARKE | Stanley | 29.12.1946 | Const. |
| 4162 | COLBOURNE | William Edward | 29.12.1946 | C/Supt. |
| 4163 | DIXON | David John | 29.12.1946 | Const. |
| 4164 | LEES | John Kenneth | 29.12.1946 | Tpr. |
| 4165 | McKAY | Edgar Ian | 29.12.1946 | S/A/Commr. |
| 4166 | MILLETT | Cecil John | 29.12.1946 | Const. |
| 4167 | ODDIE | George Rupert | 29.12.1946 | Const. |
| 4168 | PAULSON | John Edward | 29.12.1946 | Const. |
| 4169 | TRANGMAR | Ronald Frederick | 29.12.1946 | Const. |
| 4170 | TRANTHEM | Thomas James | 29.12.1946 | S/O |
| 4171 | VINCENT | Richard Sidney | 29.12.1946 | C/Inspr. |
| 4172 | JOHNSON | Charles James | 29.12.1946 | Sgt. |
| 4173 | CARVER | Hugh Tracey | 12.01.1947 | Tpr. |
| 4174 | CAVE | Dennis Grant | 12.01.1947 | Tpr. |
| 4175 | DENNISON | John Reid | 12.01.1947 | Tpr. |
| 4176 | GOSDEN | Gordon Anthony | 12.01.1947 | Tpr. |
| 4177 | HENSTOCK | Michael Corpernicus | 12.01.1947 | Tpr. |
| 4178 | HUMPHREYS | Richard Wallace | 12.01.1947 | C/Supt. |
| 4179 | JARMEN | William James | 12.01.1947 | A/Commr |
| 4180 | MAY | Eric John | 12.01.1947 | Const. |
| 4181 | NEWMAN | Leslie John | 12.01.1947 | Inspr. |
| 4182 | SOWDEN | Christopher | 12.01.1947 | Supt. |
| 4183 | STEADMAN | Trevor Edward | 12.01.1947 | Supt. |
| 4184 | BOSLEY | Peter | 12.01.1947 | Const. |
| 4185 | MARSH | Maurice Bertie | 12.01.1947 | Const. |
| 4186 | SIMS | Allen | 12.01.1947 | Sgt. |
| 4187 | YOUNG | John Findlay | 12.01.1947 | C/Inspr. |
| 4188 | CAVE | Michael Storrar | 12.01.1947 | D/Sgt. |
| 4189 | MONAGHAN | Patrick Brian | 12.01.1947 | Tpr. |
| 4190 | WILLIAMS | John Dennis | 12.01.1947 | Tpr. |
| 4191 | HULLEY | Cecil Dennison | 13.01.1947 | Sgt. |
| 4192 | AHERNE | Vincent Francis | 24.01.1947 | Tpr. |
| 4193 | COX | John Michael | 24.01.1947 | Tpr. |
| 4194 | DICKINSON | Edward Arnold | 24.01.1947 | Tpr. |
| 4195 | LEAMON | Cyril Bray Dudney | 24.01.1947 | Tpr. |
| 4196 | ROBERTSON | John Noel | 24.01.1947 | Inspr. |
| 4197 | ROBSON | Felix Guy | 24.01.1947 | Tpr. |
| 4198 | SILLITOE | Richard | 24.01.1947 | Tpr. |
| 4199 | TITTERTON | Garrett Anthony | 24.01.1947 | Tpr. |
| 4200 | WARE | John William | 24.01.1947 | Tpr. |
| 4201 | WINZAR | Oswald Laurance | 24.01.1947 | Sgt. |
| 4202 | BROWN | William | 24.01.1947 | Const. |
| 4203 | BAKER | George Innes | 15.09.1947 | Sgt. |
| 4204 | BRINK | Ian David | 16.09.1947 | C/Inspr. |
| 4205 | AMBROSE | Derik Nelson | 28.09.1947 | Tpr. |
| 4206 | AVERY | Michael Peter | 28.09.1947 | C/Inspr. |
| 4207 | BARRATT | William John | 28.09.1947 | C/Inspr. |
| 4208 | BARTLETT | Peter Harold | 28.09.1947 | Const. |
| 4209 | BURKITT | Julian Francis | 28.09.1947 | Tpr. |
| 4210 | CHADWICK | Brian Robert | 28.09.1947 | Tpr. |
| 4211 | CURTAIN | Peter William | 28.09.1947 | Tpr. |
| 4212 | GRIFFITH | Thomas Albert | 28.09.1947 | Tpr. |
| 4213 | HALE | Edward Mathew | 28.09.1947 | Tpr. |
| 4214 | HODGSON | Godfrey Douglas | 28.09.1947 | Tpr. |
| 4215 | KENNARD | Arthur William | 28.09.1947 | Tpr. |
| 4216 | KIRBY | Edward William | 28.09.1947 | Tpr. |
| 4217 | SCHOFIELD | Peter | 28.09.1947 | Tpr. |
| 4218 | SMITH | David Lindsay | 28.09.1947 | Tpr. |
| 4219 | BRUCE | Stanley Lazenby | 28.09.1947 | D/C/Inspr. |
| 4220 | DIPROSE | Michael Edward | 28.09.1947 | Const. |
| 4221 | EAMES | Ronald Dudley | 28.09.1947 | S/A/Commr |
| 4222 | HEYWOOD | Henry George | 28.09.1947 | C/Inspr. |
| 4223 | MARSHALL | Peter Graham | 28.09.1947 | Const. |
| 4224 | ROBINSON | Derrick | 28.09.1947 | S/A/Commr. |
| 4225 | UNDERWOOD | Ronald | 28.09.1947 | C/Supt. |
| 4226 | LEGGATT | Peter Jan | 02.11.1947 | Tpr. |
| 4227 | WHITEHEAD | Sidney Malcolm | 02.11.1947 | D/C/Inspr. |
| 4228 | HUBBARD | Anthony Michael | 22.12.1947 | C/Supt. |
| 4229 | PERKINS | Richard Henry | 22.12.1947 | Inspr. |
| 4230 | SHIELD | Peter Nesbitt | 22.12.1947 | Const. |
| 4231 | WILSON | Donald John Shaw | 22.12.1947 | C/Supt. |
| 4232 | HASELHURST | Richard Tom | 22.12.1947 | Const. |
| 4233 | HAYHURST | John Henry | 22.12.1947 | Sgt. |
| 4234 | HOBLEY | Charles William | 22.12.1947 | A/Commr. |
| 4235 | HOSKEN | James Richard | 22.12.1947 | Const. |
| 4236 | LONG | Albert Thomas | 22.12.1947 | Const. |
| 4237 | SAUNDERS | Peter John | 22.12.1947 | Const. |
| 4238 | SLATER | Robert Geoffrey | 22.12.1947 | Const. |
| 4239 | TODD | Guy Maurice | 22.12.1947 | Const. |
| 4240 | WARWICK | Richard Henry | 22.12.1947 | Const. |
| 4241 | WOLSTENHOLME | Fred | 22.12.1947 | Const. |
| 4242 | LOW | James Alexander | 13.04.1948 | Inspr. |
| 4243 | BRETT | John Lynn | 01.05.1948 | Inspr. |
| 4244 | BROWNLESS | David Stanley | 01.05.1948 | D/Inspr. |
| 4245 | BUCHANAN | William Ross | 01.05.1948 | Tpr. |
| 4246 | COULTER | Desmond John | 01.05.1948 | A/Commr. |
| 4247 | DE CLERK | Charles Alister | 01.05.1948 | Inspr. |
| 4248 | DENT | Ivan | 01.05.1948 | Sgt. |
| 4249 | DIXON | Hugh Railton | 01.05.1948 | Sgt. |
| 4250 | HENDRY | Ian Andrew | 01.05.1948 | D/Sgt. |
| 4251 | NEWMAN | Reginald Doveton | 01.05.1948 | Tpr. |
| 4252 | REEVES | Laurence Victor | 01.05.1948 | D/Inspr. |
| 4253 | SMYTH | Jack Allen | 01.05.1948 | Inspr. |
| 4254 | WAKEFIELD | Neil | 01.05.1948 | Const. |
| 4255 | ASHWORTH | Godfrey Fuller | 01.05.1948 | Sgt. |
| 4256 | BENNISON | Geoffrey John | 01.05.1948 | C/Inspr. |
| 4257 | BROWNING | John Baden | 01.05.1948 | Tpr. |
| 4258 | COOPER | Derrick Gordon | 01.05.1948 | S/A/Commr. |
| 4259 | GALLAGHER | Stanley Arthur | 01.05.1948 | Sgt. |
| 4260 | DENNISON | Frederick Alexander | 01.05.1948 | Comm. |
| 4261 | GRAHAM | Jack | 01.05.1948 | S/O |
| 4262 | HUSTLER | Peter Aloysius | 01.05.1948 | C/Insp |
| 4263 | MEIN | Peter Stuart | 01.05.1948 | A/Comm |
| 4264 | MURPHY | Vincent | 01.05.1948 | Sgt. |
| 4265 | REESE | Jeffrey Robin | 01.05.1948 | Const. |
| 4266 | ROWLAND | Terence David | 01.05.1948 | S/Inspr. |
| 4267 | MOORE-STEVENS | Shane Art | 01.05.1948 | Const. |
| 4268 | STUTCHBURY | Kenneth DeHorne | 01.05.1948 | Sgt. |
| 4269 | WARREN | Frederick Charles | 01.05.1948 | Const. |
| 4270 | [illegible] | Jeffrey | 01.05.1948 | C/Inspr. |
| 4271 | [illegible] | Ronald James | 01.05.1948 | Tpr. |
| 4272 | GEE | Cecil Stevens | 11.05.1948 | Tpr. |
| 4273 | LEE | John | 11.05.1948 | S/A/Commr |
| 4274 | MOORE | Gordon MacKenzie | 11.05.1948 | A/Commr |
| 4275 | PRATT | David Wilfred | 11.05.1948 | |
| 4276 | PUGH | Keith Boom | 11.05.1948 | |
| 4277 | SOMNY | John Alexander | 11.05.1948 | Sgt. |
| 4278 | BALCHIM | John Sydney | 11.05.1948 | Const. |
| 4279 | FAWCETT | Raymond John | 11.05.1948 | Tpr. |
| 4280 | HALE | Harry | 11.05.1948 | Tpr. |
| 4281 | RAWSON | Keith Norman | 11.05.1948 | Sgt. |
| 4282 | WATTS | John Raymond | 11.05.1948 | Const. |
| 4283 | WILKINSON | William Richardson | 11.05.1948 | Tpr. |
| 4284 | HUBBARD | Sydney Dennis | 02.06.1948 | Tpr. |
| 4285 | WELCH | Courtney Ernest | 22.06.1948 | Tpr. |
| 4286 | BAILEY | Max Frederic | 22.06.1948 | Tpr. |
| 4287 | BRECKSON | Thomas William | 22.06.1948 | Tpr. |
| 4288 | DAVEY | Vernon Archibald | 22.06.1948 | Const. |
| 4289 | FEATHERSTONHAUGH | Timothy Fell | 22.06.1948 | Tpr. |
| 4290 | GARNER | Douglas | 22.06.1948 | Inspr. |
| 4291 | JASPER | Alan Richard | 22.06.1948 | Const. |
| 4292 | MARTIN | Anthony Dennis | 22.06.1948 | Const. |
| 4293 | NICHOLSON | William Lawrence | 22.06.1948 | C/Supt. |
| 4294 | ROWE | Ian Playfair | 22.06.1948 | Tpr. |
| 4295 | STEVENSON | Ronald Frederick | 22.06.1948 | Tpr. |
| 4296 | SWAN | Maynard Hope | 22.06.1948 | Const. |
| 4297 | WHITAKER | Herman Thomas | 22.06.1948 | Const. |
| 4298 | WORSLEY | John Franklin | 22.06.1948 | Supt. |
| 4299 | GILMOUR | Andrew Beveridge | 22.06.1948 | Inspr. |
| 4300 | MacMILLAN | Donald Ian | 22.06.1948 | C/Inspr. |
| 4301 | STEPTOE | Peter John | 22.06.1948 | Tpr. |
| 4302 | WILSON | John Hugh | 22.06.1948 | S/S/O |
| 4303 | BREMNER | William | 06.07.1948 | Supt. |
| 4304 | BROWN | Colin Arnold | 06.07.1948 | S/A/Comm |
| 4305 | CANNON | John William | 06.07.1948 | Const. |
| 4306 | CALPHAM | David George | 06.07.1948 | A/Comm |
| 4307 | COLLINS | Timothy James | 06.07.1948 | Const. |
| 4308 | MING | Derek Wildon | 06.07.1948 | Tpr. |
| 4309 | NEWBERRY | Gordon Henry | 06.07.1948 | Tpr. |
| 4310 | PICKARD | Albert Charles | 06.07.1948 | Sgt. |
| 4311 | VICKERS | Lionel Visser | 12.08.1948 | Sgt. |
| 4312 | BROWNE | Angus Alden | 01.10.1948 | Tpr. |
| 4313 | COX | Anthony Rupert | 16.11.1948 | Supt. |
| 4314 | GETHEN | Meyrick De Winton | 16.11.1948 | D/Inspr. |
| 4315 | LANGFORD | Richard Frederick | 16.11.1948 | Sgt. |
| 4316 | WARD | Peter John | 16.11.1948 | C/Inspr. |
| 4317 | WOODS | Peter Wallace | 16.11.1948 | Const. |
| 4318 | ADAMS | Leslie Reginald | 16.11.1948 | C/Inspr. |
| 4319 | ALFORD | Stuart Charles | 16.11.1948 | C/Supt. |
| 4320 | ARMSTRONG | Colin Weatherley | 16.11.1948 | C/Supt. |
| 4321 | BERRY | Jack | 16.11.1948 | Const. |
| 4322 | CLAUGHTON | Howard Grant | 16.11.1948 | Sgt. |
| 4323 | CRAVEN | David | 16.11.1948 | Supt. |
| 4324 | CUNLIFFE | Brook Malcom | 16.11.1948 | C/Inspr. |
| 4325 | DAVIES | Gerald Willcliffe | 16.11.1948 | C/Inspr. |
| 4326 | DOHERTY | Thomas Joseph | 16.11.1948 | C/Supt. |
| 4327 | JOHNSTONE | Alexander Durna | 16.11.1948 | Sgt. |
| 4328 | MASKELL | Aubrey Peter | 16.11.1948 | Const. |
| 4329 | PURVES | Alexander Johnstone | 16.11.1948 | Comm. |
| 4330 | RIDDLE | John Michael | 16.11.1948 | C/Supt. |
| 4331 | ROBINSON | Cyril | 16.11.1948 | A/Comm |
| 4332 | SHORT | Peter Charles | 16.11.1948 | C/Insp |
| 4333 | SHOUT | Peter William | 16.11.1948 | S/Inspr. |
| 4334 | SIMPSON | Raymond Layton | 16.11.1948 | Supt. |
| 4335 | STANNARD | Barnard William | 16.11.1948 | A/Comm |
| 4336 | TAIT | Ian William | 16.11.1948 | S/C/Inspr. |
| 4337 | CLARK | Donald Arthur | 16.11.1948 | Const. |
| 4338 | VICKERY | Lorimer | 23.11.1948 | Sgt. |
| 4339 | CLEARY | Denis John | 19.11.1948 | Const. |
| 4340 | COLQUHOUN | John Brown | 29.11.1948 | Tpr. |
| 4341 | KNOX | Stephen Leo | 29.11.1948 | D/Inspr. |
| 4342 | RATTRAY | William John | 29.11.1948 | Tpr. |
| 4343 | SUTHERLAND | George Anderson | 29.11.1948 | Tpr. |
| 4344 | WARD | Thomas George | 29.11.1948 | S/A/Comm |
| 4345 | BRYAN | Gordon Alfred | 29.11.1948 | Const. |

| No. | Surname | Forename(s) | Date | Rank |
|---|---|---|---|---|
| 4346 | COTTAM | Terence | 29.11.1948 | Tpr. |
| 4347 | EARNSHAW | Ronald Hutton | 29.11.1948 | D/Con |
| 4348 | GERAGHT | Desmond Thomas | 29.11.1948 | Sgt. |
| 4349 | HOLMES | Albert Ronald | 29.11.1948 | Const. |
| 4350 | MILNER | Eric Austin | 29.11.1948 | Const. |
| 4351 | MOATE | Anthony Leon | 29.11.1948 | Const. |
| 4352 | RICHARDSON | Charles Sydney | 29.11.1948 | Inspr. |
| 4353 | SAUNDERS | Stanley Gordon | 29.11.1948 | S/O |
| 4354 | SHERRINGHAM | Dennis Leslie | 29.11.1948 | Supt. |
| 4355 | MIDDLETON-STOKES | Frederick Harry | 29.11.1948 | Sgt. |
| 4356 | TOWNSEND | Royston | 08.11.1948 | D/C/Inspr. |
| 4357 | GIBBONS | Ernest George | 07.12.1948 | Sgt. |
| 4358 | BRYANT | Sydney Alfred | 07.12.1948 | Sgt. |
| 4359 | BRYNE | Desmond Michael | 07.12.1948 | Sgt. |
| 4360 | HOLLINGTON | William George | 07.12.1948 | Const. |
| 4361 | LUCOCK | Edward | 07.12.1948 | Const. |
| 4362 | MILES | Richard John | 07.12.1948 | Const. |
| 4363 | PITWOOD | James Kenneth | 07.12.1948 | C/Inspr. |
| 4364 | TAYLOR | Gordon Lennos | 07.12.1948 | Const. |
| 4365 | WILCOX | Anthony Thomas | 07.12.1948 | C/Inspr. |
| 4366 | YOUNG | John Robert | 29.11.1948 | Sgt. |
| 4367 | McBRIDE | Joseph Robert | 10.01.1949 | Sgt. |
| 4368 | ALLAN | David Tennant | 10.01.1949 | Const. |
| 4369 | GRAY | Derek | 10.01.1949 | Inspr. |
| 4370 | HILL | Francis Paul | 10.01.1949 | Const. |
| 4371 | MARCH | John | 10.01.1949 | C/Inspr. |
| 4372 | TEIMAN | Edward David | 10.01.1949 | Sgt. |
| 4373 | TERRETT | Theodore John | 10.01.1949 | Sgt. |
| 4374 | TURNER | Anthony | 10.01.1949 | Sgt. |
| 4375 | MANN | Ivan Arthur | 01.02.1949 | Tpr. |
| 4376 | MINIKIN | James Benjamin | 01.02.1949 | Tpr. |
| 4377 | BEVERIDGE | Gordon Duthie | 01.02.1949 | Tpr. |
| 4378 | CARRITT | Thomas Newson | 01.02.1949 | S/A/Comm |
| 4379 | DAVIES | John Anthony | 01.02.1949 | Tpr. |
| 4380 | McCULLOCH | Patrick James | 01.02.1949 | Tpr. |
| 4381 | McNAIR | Ian Crawford | 01.02.1949 | Tpr. |
| 4382 | PAINE | James Curt | 01.02.1949 | Tpr. |
| 4383 | PINKERTON | Anthony Hull | 01.02.1949 | C/Inspr. |
| 4384 | THOMAS | Barry Gordon | 01.02.1949 | Tpr. |
| 4385 | WAIN | Peter Edgar | 01.02.1949 | Tpr. |
| 4386 | WARR | Terence | 01.02.1949 | Const. |
| 4387 | EARLEY | John Alfred | 01.02.1949 | C/Insp |
| 4388 | JASPER | Paul | 01.02.1949 | C/Insp |
| 4389 | KENSETT | Philip | 01.02.1949 | S/Inspr. |
| 4390 | ROBERTSON | Robert Wallace | 15.02.1949 | Inspr. |
| 4391 | GREATOREX | Frank | 15.02.1949 | Inspr. |
| 4392 | HANCOCK | Michael O'Brien | 15.02.1949 | Const. |
| 4393 | LUCAS | Allan William | 15.02.1949 | Inspr. |
| 4394 | MARTIN | Alan David | 15.02.1949 | C/Supt. |
| 4395 | STOAKES | Frederick Gordon | 15.02.1949 | Const. |
| 4396 | GEARING | Laurence Reginald | 15.02.1949 | Sgt. |
| 4397 | STEWART | Gordon Rutherford | 23.02.1949 | Tpr. |
| 4398 | TOTHILL | Rex Michael | 07.03.1949 | Tpr. |
| 4399 | GILBERT | John Roland | 07.03.1949 | Tpr. |
| 4400 | HALLAM | William Keith | 07.03.1949 | Tpr. |
| 4401 | NORMAN | Alan Francis | 07.03.1949 | A/Comm |
| 4402 | WALTERS | Denbigh William | 07.03.1949 | Inspr. |
| 4403 | BEST | Alan Stanford | 07.03.1949 | D/Inspr. |
| 4404 | FRANKLIN | Michael Victor | 07.03.1949 | C/Supt. |
| 4405 | HOGG | Frank Robert | 07.03.1949 | Const. |
| 4406 | MORLEY | Cyril John | 07.03.1949 | Inspr. |
| 4407 | PAYNE | Thomas Lamb | 09.03.1949 | Inspr. |
| 4408 | STOCKER | Robin Hugh | 07.03.1949 | Tpr. |
| 4409 | WILSHER | John Michael | 29.03.1949 | Sgt. |
| 4410 | NIXON | William Hector | 29.03.1949 | Sgt. |
| 4411 | PEACH | Peter | 29.03.1949 | Tpr. |
| 4412 | COX | John Keith | 29.03.1949 | Inspr. |
| 4413 | COX | Peter Richard | 29.03.1949 | S/O |
| 4414 | | Robert George | | |
| 4415 | TURNBULL | Kemp Peter | 29.03.1949 | Sgt. |
| 4416 | WEBB | Edwin Alfred | 29.03.1949 | A/Com |
| 4417 | BAMBRIDGE | Denis | 12.04.1949 | D/Con |
| 4418 | BELL | Michael Denwiddie | 12.04.1949 | Tpr. |
| 4419 | BEST | Nigel D'Ewes | 12.04.1949 | Tpr. |
| 4420 | CARDBY | Albert Henry | 12.04.1949 | Tpr. |
| 4421 | HOGAN | Daniel Patrick | 12.04.1949 | D/Con |
| 4422 | MAYNARD | Gareth Alun | 12.04.1949 | Tpr. |
| 4423 | MUIR | James William | 12.04.1949 | Tpr. |
| 4424 | OLDCORN | Michael Rupert | 12.04.1949 | Tpr. |
| 4425 | RUNNALLS | Gerlad Martin | 12.04.1949 | Sgt. |
| 4426 | BROOKE-SMITH | Guy Stillingfleet | 12.04.1949 | Tpr. |
| 4427 | ARMSTRONG | Dennis Wilfred | 12.04.1949 | C/Insp |
| 4428 | GATES | Bruce Allen | 12.04.1949 | Const. |
| 4429 | JOHN | Derrick Llewellyn | 12.04.1949 | Const. |
| 4430 | WATTS | John Douglas | 12.04.1949 | Const. |
| 4431 | GIBBS | John Christopher | 14.04.1949 | Const. |
| 4432 | HORSMAN | Eugene Oliver | 19.04.1949 | Tpr. |
| 4433 | DIPPENAAR | Louis Hosia | 02.05.1949 | Tpr. |
| 4434 | DE ROY | Peter Gilbert | 02.05.1949 | Tpr. |
| 4435 | GODFREY | Jeremy Norman | 02.05.1949 | Inspr. |
| 4436 | KENCHINGTON | Peter George | 02.05.1949 | Const. |
| 4437 | MURRAY | Philip Stuart | 02.05.1949 | D/Comm |
| 4438 | JARRETT | Keith | 24.05.1949 | S/O |
| 4439 | PARRY | Colin Herbert | 24.05.1949 | C/Inspr. |
| 4440 | REYNOLDS | Ronald William | 24.05.1949 | Const. |
| 4441 | SHEPPARD | Ben | 24.05.1949 | Const. |
| 4442 | CHASEMORE | Philip Colin | 07.06.1949 | Const. |
| 4443 | DE COURPALAY | Charles Richard | 07.06.1949 | C/Inspr. |
| 4444 | JONES | William Thomas | 07.06.1949 | Inspr. |
| 4445 | MORSHEAD | John Hurle | 07.06.1949 | Const. |
| 4446 | BROUGH | Michael Richard | 27.06.1949 | Inspr. |
| 4447 | ROBSON | Peter Alfred | 27.06.1949 | Const. |
| 4448 | RUMNEY | Harold George | 27.06.1949 | C/Inspr. |
| 4449 | WILSON | John Learmouth | 27.06.1949 | S/A/Comm |
| 4450 | BROWNING | Desmond | 19.07.1949 | Tpr. |
| 4451 | CARGILL | Roderick Ian | 19.07.1949 | Sgt. |
| 4452 | COLMAN | John Hirst | 19.07.1949 | Sgt. |
| 4453 | KISSACK | Peter William | 19.07.1949 | Sgt. |
| 4454 | DIGGES | Bryan Joseph | 02.08.1949 | Inspr. |
| 4455 | GUEST | Peter Thomas | 02.08.1949 | Const. |
| 4456 | HOUGHTON | Guy Michael | 02.08.1949 | S/A/Comm |
| 4457 | KING | George | 02.08.1949 | Const. |
| 4458 | TAYLOR | James Michael | 02.08.1949 | D/Inspr. |
| 4459 | SOUTH | Peter | 02.08.1949 | Const. |
| 4460 | BESTER | David Michael | 02.08.1949 | C/Inspr. |
| 4461 | BARRON | George Nicholson | 23.08.1949 | C/Inspr. |
| 4462 | BENNETT | Peter Colin | 23.08.1949 | Const. |
| 4463 | PICKARD | Clifford Gordon | 24.05.1949 | Sgt. |
| 4464 | SMITH | Derek William | 23.08.1949 | Sgt. |
| 4465 | UNDERWOOD | Michael John | 23.08.1949 | Const. |
| 4466 | WOOD | Terence | 31.08.1949 | Const. |
| 4467 | SMITHYMAN | John Ernest | 26.09.1949 | Tpr. |
| 4468 | MAGUIRE | Frank Phillip | 27.09.1949 | C/Inspr. |
| 4469 | BESSANT | Dennis Gordon | 27.09.1949 | Sgt. |
| 4470 | CONNOLLY | Eric Eugene | 27.09.1949 | Const. |
| 4471 | HEBRON | Harold | 27.09.1949 | Sgt. |
| 4472 | PIKE | Anthony George | 27.09.1949 | Const. |
| 4473 | PRATT | Charles David | 27.09.1949 | Const. |
| 4474 | DRAVER | Reginald Francis | 27.09.1949 | Const. |
| 4475 | TYRER | Frederick | 30.09.1949 | Const. |
| 4476 | SHEPPARD | Antony Keith | 06.10.1949 | Sgt. |
| 4477 | KATZ | George Alexander | 18.10.1949 | Sgt. |
| 4478 | BUTLER | Antony | 18.10.1949 | Sgt. |
| 4479 | FALL | John David | 18.10.1949 | Tpr. |
| 4480 | MOON | Christopher Robin | 18.10.1949 | Sgt. |
| 4481 | NEALE | Harold William | 18.10.1949 | S/O |
| 4482 | OATES | Edgar Michael | 18.10.1949 | Inspr. |
| 4483 | PHILLIPS | Leslie Howard | 18.10.1949 | Const. |
| 4484 | TELFER | Charles Buchan | 18.10.1949 | Sgt. |
| 4485 | BOLTON | Maurice Frederick | 08.11.1949 | Const. |
| 4486 | CARTER | Ronald | 08.11.1949 | Const. |
| 4487 | COOP | Roy Arthur | 08.11.1949 | Sgt. |
| 4488 | EVANS | Arturo | 08.11.1949 | Const. |
| 4489 | HALL | Edward Morland | 08.11.1949 | Const. |
| 4490 | HOLLINGWORTH | Donald | 08.11.1949 | Supt. |
| 4491 | IRWIN | Ralph | 08.11.1949 | Inspr. |
| 4492 | LEWIS | Michael Richard | 08.11.1949 | Const. |
| 4493 | MERCER | Thomas Stanley | 08.11.1949 | Const. |
| 4494 | RESTORICK | John Michael | 08.11.1949 | C/Inspr. |
| 4495 | SANDOVER | Thomas Frederic | 08.11.1949 | C/Inspr. |
| 4496 | STEVENS | Ronald David | 08.11.1949 | Sgt. |
| 4497 | STEVENSON | Peter Anthony | 08.11.1949 | Const. |
| 4498 | WELLS | Peter Leslie | 08.11.1949 | Const. |
| 4499 | WILLIAMS | Peter Robin | 08.11.1949 | C/Insp |
| 4500 | WINTER | Alfred Anthony | 08.11.1949 | Const. |
| 4501 | LOVEGROVE | Vincent Adrian | 17.11.1949 | C/Insp |
| 4502 | DICKINSON | John | 18.11.1949 | Const. |
| 4503 | HUMBERSTONE | Derek Anthony | 18.11.1949 | C/Supt. |
| 4504 | FAIRFAX-FRANCKLIN | William Nicholas | 22.11.1949 | Const. |
| 4505 | MICHIE | David | 22.11.1949 | Const. |
| 4506 | MUIR | Stewart Robertson | 22.11.1949 | Const. |
| 4507 | REID | Hugh Murray | 22.11.1949 | Const. |
| 4508 | WELLS | Peter Chatham | 22.11.1949 | Const. |
| 4509 | O'SHAUGHNESSY | Brian | 23.11.1949 | Const. |
| 4510 | CLARK | Keith Bertram | 01.12.1949 | Supt. |
| 4511 | BRADFIELD | John Douglas | 13.12.1949 | S/A/Comm |
| 4512 | CHASTON | Ronald John | 13.12.1949 | Const. |
| 4513 | CURTIS | Kenneth Frederick | 13.12.1949 | Inspr. |
| 4514 | DE LA VIGNE | Raymond Michael | 13.12.1949 | Const. |
| 4515 | DRONGIN | John Robert | 13.12.1949 | Const. |
| 4516 | FARRELL | Norman | 13.12.1949 | Const. |
| 4517 | HEMBLING | Derek Leslie | 13.12.1949 | Const. |
| 4518 | LE GUERN | David Francis | 13.12.1949 | C/Inspr. |
| 4519 | MARLER | James Michael | 13.12.1949 | Const. |
| 4520 | MARTIN | Ronald Stewart | 13.12.1949 | Sgt. |
| 4521 | MINGARD | Philip Gordon | 13.12.1949 | Sgt. |
| 4522 | MOERAN | Kenneth Edward | 13.12.1949 | A/Comm |
| 4523 | SMITH | John Humphrey | 13.12.1949 | Inspr. |
| 4524 | TURNBULL | Alan | 13.12.1949 | Const. |
| 4525 | BARBER | Walter Terry | 13.12.1949 | C/Insp |
| 4526 | ALMY | Douglas Vernon | 03.01.1950 | Const. |
| 4527 | BRUCE | George Frederick | 03.01.1950 | D/Inspr. |
| 4528 | CHARLESWORTH | Barry Robbins | 03.01.1950 | C/Inspr. |
| 4529 | GANT | William Thomas | 03.01.1950 | Const. |
| 4530 | HANLEY | Kenneth | 03.01.1950 | Const. |
| 4531 | INGLIS | Edwin | 03.01.1950 | Sgt. |
| 4532 | ROBERTSON | John Ewen | 03.01.1950 | Const. |
| 4533 | ROGERS | James Joseph | 03.01.1950 | Const. |
| 4534 | SCHOFIELD | Eric Reginald | 03.01.1950 | Const. |
| 4535 | SHAUGHNESSY | John Kevin | 03.01.1950 | Sgt. |
| 4536 | SUTHERLAND | Robert | 03.01.1950 | S/A/Comm |
| 4537 | YOUNG | Andrew Ian | 03.01.1950 | Sgt. |
| 4538 | SMITH | David Charles | 03.01.1950 | Supt. |
| 4539 | ALEXANDER | Hugh Grant | 07.01.1950 | Supt. |
| 4540 | BEAVER | Maurice Hambley | 17.01.1950 | Const. |
| 4541 | CLARK | Raymond Arthur | 17.01.1950 | C/Supt. |
| 4542 | DUNN | Gerald Bonthron | 17.01.1950 | Const. |
| 4543 | GOOCH | Desmond Percy | 17.01.1950 | Const. |
| 4544 | HART | Francis Ellerker | 17.01.1950 | Const. |
| 4545 | Mac KENZIE | Iain Douglas | 17.01.1950 | Sgt. |
| 4546 | Mac NAUGHTON | Robert | 17.01.1950 | Const. |
| 4547 | RICH | Alan William | 17.01.1950 | S/A/Comm |
| 4548 | ROBINS | Kenneth | 17.01.1950 | Inspr. |
| 4549 | STANFORD-SMITH | Kenneth Gordon | 17.01.1950 | Sgt. |
| 4550 | MOON | John Dymock | 17.01.1950 | S/O |
| 4551 | GARROD | Kenneth Rutherford | 17.01.1950 | S/O |
| 4552 | ADAMS | Christopher Alan | 21.01.1950 | Const. |

| No. | Surname | Forename | Date | Rank |
|---|---|---|---|---|
| 4553 | NAESTED | Irving Lionel | 26.01.1950 | Const. |
| 4554 | FITZGERALD | Martin Herbert | 30.01.1950 | C/Inspr. |
| 4555 | GRASSETT | Charles Eliott | 30.01.1950 | Const. |
| 4556 | HAWLEY | Arthur John | 30.01.1950 | Const. |
| 4557 | RIDGE | David Gordon | 30.01.1950 | Const. |
| 4558 | RIDGE | Benjamin George | 30.01.1950 | Const. |
| 4559 | TROWER | Sydney Stephen | 30.01.1950 | Inspr. |
| 4560 | CANTWELL | Thomas | 30.01.1950 | S/O |
| 4561 | GALE | Anthony | 06.02.1950 | Supt. |
| 4562 | GOLDIE | Cedric Hugo | 06.02.1950 | Inspr. |
| 4563 | O'HARA | Terence Michael | 06.02.1950 | Inspr. |
| 4564 | REYNOLDS | Peter Gordon | 06.02.1950 | Sgt. |
| 4565 | WALSH | Marshall Edward | 06.02.1950 | Const. |
| 4566 | WARBURTON | Michael Geoffrey | 06.02.1950 | Const. |
| 4567 | BOND | Jack Edwin | 06.02.1950 | Inspr. |
| 4568 | HAMANN | Arthur | 02.03.1950 | Const. |
| 4569 | HARCOURT | Geoffre Albert | 02.03.1950 | D/Const. |
| 4570 | LINDSAY | James William | 02.03.1950 | Const. |
| 4571 | LOWEIN | Cyril St. John | 02.03.1950 | Const. |
| 4572 | MERCER | Charles Maurice | 02.03.1950 | Const. |
| 4573 | MAYLING | John Thomas | 02.03.1950 | Const. |
| 4574 | SHAW | John Frederick | 02.03.1950 | Inspr. |
| 4575 | WALKER | Joseph John | 02.03.1950 | Const. |
| 4576 | WILKINS | Michael John | 02.03.1950 | Const. |
| 4577 | YEOMAN | John Anthony | 02.03.1950 | Const. |
| 4578 | STAMP | Barry Walter | 15.03.1950 | Sgt. |
| 4579 | BATEMAN | William Henry | 16.03.1950 | Const. |
| 4580 | BOYD | Andrew Aitken | 16.03.1950 | Const. |
| 4581 | BUTLER | James Gordon | 16.03.1950 | Const. |
| 4582 | JANNAWAY | John William | 16.03.1950 | Const. |
| 4583 | LEEN | William Gerard | 16.03.1950 | Const. |
| 4584 | FRASER-MILNER | Ronald Charles | 16.03.1950 | Sgt. |
| 4585 | RAITT | Harold Christopher | 16.03.1950 | Const. |
| 4586 | SELLEY | Gilbert Samuel | 16.03.1950 | C/Supt. |
| 4587 | POWELL | Gerald Harry | 23.03.1950 | Sgt. |
| 4588 | MORGAN | Gerald William | 25.03.1950 | Const. |
| 4589 | JENNINGS | Roy | 27.03.1950 | Sgt. |
| 4590 | LOVELL | Brian David | 27.03.1950 | Const. |
| 4591 | MEEHAN | Jeremiah Joseph | 27.03.1950 | Const. |
| 4592 | STEWART | John Allan | 27.03.1950 | Const. |
| 4593 | THOMAS | John Alfred | 27.03.1950 | Const. |
| 4594 | ARDAGH | Anthony Peter | 04.04.1950 | Inspr. |
| 4595 | BROOKES | Michael Norton | 04.04.1950 | Const. |
| 4596 | GRAHAM | Nelson Howard | 04.04.1950 | Sgt. |
| 4597 | HOWARD | Peter Douglas | 04.04.1950 | Const. |
| 4598 | HUMPAGE | Bruce John | 04.04.1950 | Inspr. |
| 4599 | HUMPHREYS | Kenneth Archibald | 04.04.1950 | Const. |
| 4600 | SPONG | Terence John | 04.04.1950 | Const. |
| 4601 | WHITTAKER | John O'Brien | 04.04.1950 | Const. |
| 4602 | WILLIAMS | John David O'Brien | 04.04.1950 | Const. |
| 4603 | DARKES | Donald | 27.04.1950 | Sgt. |
| 4604 | DONES | Raymond Robert | 27.04.1950 | Const. |
| 4605 | GRIFFITHS | David Alan | 27.04.1950 | Sgt. |
| 4606 | HADFIELD | Percival Harris | 27.04.1950 | Sgt. |
| 4607 | JACQUES | Frederick William | 27.04.1950 | Const. |
| 4608 | OWEN | George Courtney | 27.04.1950 | Sgt. |
| 4609 | PROCTOR | Alan Stanley | 27.04.1950 | Const. |
| 4610 | THORNTON | Robert Eden | 27.04.1950 | Const. |
| 4611 | VERNON | Leslie | 27.04.1950 | Const. |
| 4612 | WADDINGTON | Henry Thomas | 27.04.1950 | Sgt. |
| 4613 | BLAKE | Kenneth James | 11.05.1950 | Const. |
| 4614 | BULMAN | Alastair Placklock | 11.05.1950 | Supt. |
| 4615 | GALE | Derek William | 11.05.1950 | Const. |
| 4616 | GIBNEY | Samuel | 11.05.1950 | Supt. |
| 4617 | HARVEY | George James | 11.05.1950 | Supt. |
| 4618 | JARVIS | Victor Roger | 11.05.1950 | Sgt. |
| 4619 | JOSE | Jack Stanley | 11.05.1950 | Sgt. |
| 4620 | LENNETT | John Desmond | 11.05.1950 | D/Inspr. |
| 4621 | Mac KEOWN | John Harold | 11.05.1950 | Const. |
| 4622 | MALLON | Derek Edward | 11.05.1950 | C/Supt. |
| 4623 | ROFFEY | Maurice John | 11.05.1950 | Inspr. |
| 4624 | WRIGHT | Christopher Brian | 11.05.1950 | Const. |
| 4625 | SKIEN | Michael Trvoc | 11.05.1950 | Const. |
| 4626 | PEDDIE | Raymond William | 13.05.1950 | Const. |
| 4627 | QUINTON | Peter | 13.05.1950 | Const. |
| 4628 | GILMOUR | Donald | 18.05.1950 | S/O |
| 4629 | WHITTECHURCH | Arthur Bevan | 18.05.1950 | Const. |
| 4630 | BALL | Lennard Barrett | 22.05.1950 | Const. |
| 4631 | BLAIR | Alexander Anderson | 22.05.1950 | A/Comm |
| 4632 | COWARD | Kenneth | 22.05.1950 | Const. |
| 4633 | POPKESS | Edward Barry | 22.05.1950 | Const. |
| 4634 | WALES | Michael Charles | 22.05.1950 | Const. |
| 4635 | WRIGHT | Brian | 22.05.1950 | Const. |
| 4636 | ROGERS | Patrick Michael | 26.05.1950 | Const. |
| 4637 | HILTON | Jack | 01.06.1950 | Const. |
| 4638 | ARMSTRONG | Andrew Kenneth | 17.06.1950 | Const. |
| 4639 | BATT | Gordon Bathurst | 03.07.1950 | Const. |
| 4640 | BELL | Peter Richard | 03.07.1950 | C/Supt. |
| 4641 | GRIFFITHS | Colin Bruce | 03.07.1950 | S/Sgt. |
| 4642 | HOUNSFIELD | David Ranleigh | 03.07.1950 | Supt. |
| 4643 | LEPPAN | George Ellwyn | 03.07.1950 | Const. |
| 4644 | SELBY | Kenneth Edward | 03.07.1950 | Const. |
| 4645 | SIMMONDS | Antony James | 03.07.1950 | Const. |
| 4646 | YOUNG | Roger Gordon | 03.07.1950 | Const. |
| 4647 | DOWLING | Kevin Patrick | 03.07.1950 | Sgt. |
| 4648 | LOUW | Michael Joseph | 06.07.1950 | Sgt. |
| 4649 | SEWARD | John | 17.07.1950 | C/Inspr. |
| 4650 | BAIRD | Douglas | 16.10.1950 | C/Inspr. |
| 4651 | DICKENS | Ian Francis | 16.10.1950 | Const. |
| 4652 | HIDER | Ralph Charles | 16.10.1950 | Sgt. |
| 4653 | McALLISTER | Alastair Bruce | 16.10.1950 | Const. |
| 4654 | TARR | John Henry | 16.10.1950 | Const. |
| 4655 | WRIGHT | Henry Charles | 16.10.1950 | Const. |
| 4656 | BROWN | David Christopher | 16.10.1950 | Inspr. |
| 4657 | GILLSON | Henry Ingram | 16.10.1950 | Const. |
| 4658 | GRATHAM | Reading | 16.10.1950 | Const. |
| 4659 | HOWARD-BEARD | Clive William | 23.10.1950 | A/Comm |
| 4660 | HOLMAN | Graham Edward | 23.10.1950 | S/A/C |
| 4661 | SPENCER | Allan | 23.10.1950 | D/C/I |
| 4662 | EVANS | William Francis | 23.10.1950 | C/Inspr. |
| 4663 | SAVAGE | John Henry | 23.10.1950 | Inspr. |
| 4664 | BROWN | Stuart Anthony | 23.10.1950 | Const. |
| 4665 | DUNCAN | Alexander | 06.11.1950 | Const. |
| 4666 | FRANCIS | Geoffrey Forbes | 06.11.1950 | Const. |
| 4667 | PAYNE | Graham Douglas | 06.11.1950 | Sgt. |
| 4668 | SMALLBONES | St. John Leslie | 06.11.1950 | Const. |
| 4669 | STIMSON | Alan Everard | 06.11.1950 | Const. |
| 4670 | THORNE | Arnold Huxtable | 06.11.1950 | Inspr. |
| 4671 | UNDERHILL | Brian Alexander | 06.11.1950 | D/Sgt. |
| 4672 | THORNE | Norman Harold | 06.11.1950 | Const. |
| 4673 | WHEELER | Henry Raymond | 06.11.1950 | Sgt. |
| 4674 | WILKEN | Walter Yarty | 06.11.1950 | Sgt. |
| 4675 | YOUELL | Peter Alan | 06.11.1950 | C/Supt. |
| 4676 | ALEXANDER | Anthony Joseph | 04.12.1950 | Const. |
| 4677 | ASHTON | Peter Halley | 04.12.1950 | S/A/Comm |
| 4678 | GARDNER | Ronald George | 04.12.1950 | A/Comm |
| 4679 | HEDGES | Robin Albert | 04.12.1950 | Const. |
| 4680 | McCROY | Alan James | 04.12.1950 | Const. |
| 4681 | STANLEY | Raymond Leslie | 04.12.1950 | Sgt. |
| 4682 | STRETTON | Lawrence Charles | 04.12.1950 | Const. |
| 4683 | SMITH | Martin Gerard | 04.12.1950 | Const. |
| 4684 | THOMLINSON | James Alexander | 11.12.1950 | S/O |
| 4685 | DU TOIT | Johannes Hendrick | 30.12.1950 | Const. |
| 4686 | BLIGHT | Herbert Stanley | 02.01.1951 | Const. |
| 4687 | BURNS | James | 02.01.1951 | Const. |
| 4688 | PHARO | Clarence | 11.01.1951 | Const. |
| 4689 | CAMPBELL | Alexander Colin | 29.01.1951 | Sgt. |
| 4690 | HARRISON | Leo Peter | 29.01.1951 | Const. |
| 4691 | LORD | Peter Nicholas | 29.01.1951 | S/O |
| 4692 | WORKMAN | Raymond John | 29.01.1951 | D/Inspr. |
| 4693 | LENNARD | Christopher William | 01.02.1951 | Const. |
| 4694 | TRUBI | Alastair John | 18660 | C/Inspr. |
| 4695 | MAY | Geoffrey Ronald | 10.03.1951 | Const. |
| 4696 | DOWN | Anthony William | 12.03.1951 | Sgt. |
| 4697 | FITZGERALD | Trevor Theodore | 12.03.1951 | Const. |
| 4698 | HANDSCOMB | Ralph Allen | 12.03.1951 | Const. |
| 4699 | HEMISTON | John | 12.03.1951 | Const. |
| 4700 | HUGHES | Brian George | 12.03.1951 | Sgt. |
| 4701 | NICOLLS | Cecil Roy | 12.03.1951 | Const. |
| 4702 | OMEARA | Michael Thomas | 12.03.1951 | Supt. |
| 4703 | TAPPER | Clive | 12.03.1951 | Supt. |
| 4704 | WILSON | John Forbes | 12.03.1951 | Const. |
| 4705 | DOWLING | Ronald William | 26.05.1951 | Inspr. |
| 4706 | HALL | Peter Stanley | 09.04.1951 | Sgt. |
| 4707 | JOHNSON | Charles Anthony | 09.04.1951 | Const. |
| 4708 | MUNSON | Peter | 09.04.1951 | S/A/Comm |
| 4709 | PETERS | Ronald Stanley | 09.04.1951 | Const. |
| 4710 | WALL | Ronald Doveton | 09.04.1951 | Const. |
| 4711 | CHALK | Brian | 07.05.1951 | Const. |
| 4712 | DARLING | Brian Francis | 07.05.1951 | D/C/Insp |
| 4713 | DAVIDSON | Mitton John | 07.05.1951 | Const. |
| 4714 | DRYNAN | Anthony Augustine | 07.05.1951 | Sgt. |
| 4715 | EDWARDS | Harry Lawton | 07.05.1951 | Inspr. |
| 4716 | KING | Laurence Reginald | 07.05.1951 | Inspr. |
| 4717 | KNIGHT | Patrick William | 07.05.1951 | Const. |
| 4718 | LYDEN | George | 07.05.1951 | Const. |
| 4719 | Mac PHAIL | Colin Campbell | 07.05.1951 | Const. |
| 4720 | MOSS | Geoffrey Charles | 07.05.1951 | D/Sgt. |
| 4721 | SHAWYER | John Richard | 07.05.1951 | S/O |
| 4722 | WHEATLEY | Bryan Morton | 07.05.1951 | Const. |
| 4723 | ASKEW | Edward Irving | 28.05.1951 | D/Insp |
| 4724 | BUTENDAG | Roelof Jacobus | 04.06.1951 | Const. |
| 4725 | DILLON | Roger Douglas | 04.06.1951 | Const. |
| 4726 | DYER | David John | 04.06.1951 | Const. |
| 4727 | EDDEN | Michael Granville | 04.06.1951 | A/Comm |
| 4728 | ELLWAY | George William | 04.06.1951 | S/A/C |
| 4729 | GROBECKER | David Alan | 04.06.1951 | Const. |
| 4730 | HALLWARD | David Leslie | 04.06.1951 | D/C/I |
| 4731 | HOLLIS | Roy Frederick | 04.06.1951 | C/Inspr. |
| 4732 | HOSFORD | Phillip John | 04.06.1951 | Inspr. |
| 4733 | JONES | Philip Brett | 04.06.1951 | Const. |
| 4734 | PHELAN | Vincent Gerard | 04.06.1951 | Const. |
| 4735 | ROGERS | Clifford Ernest | 04.06.1951 | Sgt. |
| 4736 | STUART | George Charles | 04.06.1951 | D/Com |
| 4737 | TUCKER | Charles Bertram | 04.06.1951 | Const. |
| 4738 | WALKER | Dennis David | 04.06.1951 | Inspr. |
| 4739 | VERSFELD | Peter Roy | 08.06.1951 | D/Sgt. |
| 4740 | ASHFORD | William Edward | 18.06.1951 | Const. |
| 4741 | BAILEY | John Edwin | 18.06.1951 | Inspr. |
| 4742 | LAKE | Arthur William | 18.06.1951 | Sgt. |
| 4743 | MORGAN | Geoffrey | 18.06.1951 | Const. |
| 4744 | ROBERTS | James Malcolm | 18.06.1951 | Const. |
| 4745 | BUCHANAN | Thomas Noel | 19.06.1951 | Const. |
| 4746 | DAY | Gerard William | 22.06.1951 | S/A/Comm |
| 4747 | DIXON | Noel Claude | 30.06.1951 | C/Supt. |
| 4748 | HARDIE | John Lawton | 02.07.1951 | Const. |
| 4749 | BERRY | Kenneth Percy | 02.07.1951 | Sgt. |
| 4750 | BURTON | Charles David | 02.07.1951 | Const. |
| 4751 | COETZER | William | 02.07.1951 | Inspr. |
| 4752 | CUTFIELD | Edward Thomas | 02.07.1951 | C/Inspr. |
| 4753 | FREEMAN | Albert William | 02.07.1951 | Inspr. |
| 4754 | MYLREA | John Henry | 02.07.1951 | C/Inspr. |
| 4755 | PEARCE | John Roger | 02.07.1951 | Sgt. |
| 4756 | PILBROUGH | Ronald | 02.07.1951 | A/Comm |
| 4757 | ROBINSON | Richard Henry | 02.07.1951 | Const. |
| 4758 | WILLOUGHBY | Christopher John | 02.07.1951 | Const. |

| No. | Surname | First Name | Rank | Date |
|---|---|---|---|---|
| 4760 | GLOSTER | Dermod Beresford | Sgt. | 16.07.1951 |
| 4761 | HALLS | Bernard Anthony | Inspr. | 16.07.1951 |
| 4762 | McEVOY | James | C/Inspr. | 16.07.1951 |
| 4763 | MARX | Anthony James | C/Inspr. | 16.07.1951 |
| 4764 | REES | Jeremy Stephen | Sgt. | 16.07.1951 |
| 4765 | SANREY | Brian Gordon | Inspr. | 16.07.1951 |
| 4766 | SHAW | Terence George | Sgt. | 16.07.1951 |
| 4767 | STEVENS | Graeme Stuart | Insp | 13.08.1951 |
| 4768 | COLQUHOUN | Robert Dawson | Const. | 13.08.1951 |
| 4769 | GOULDING | Ivan Edmond | A/Comm | 13.08.1951 |
| 4770 | PHILLIPS | Hugh Clement | Const. | 18.08.1951 |
| 4771 | BOOYSEN | Lawrence | Const. | 18.08.1951 |
| 4772 | COLEMAN | Derick Edmond | Const. | 01.09.1951 |
| 4773 | VAN DEVENTER | Gerrit John | A/Comm | 24.09.1951 |
| 4774 | FLETCHER | John Samuel | Const. | 24.09.1951 |
| 4775 | HILL | Frank Kemmel | S/Sgt. | 24.09.1951 |
| 4776 | Mac DONALD | Henry Malcolm | C/Inspr. | 24.09.1951 |
| 4777 | MACINTOSH | Richard John | C/Inspr. | 24.09.1951 |
| 4778 | MERRONY | Michael Richard | C/Inspr. | 24.09.1951 |
| 4779 | PRICE | John Charles | Supt. | 24.09.1951 |
| 4780 | WILLIAMS | Samuel Robert | Const. | 24.09.1951 |
| 4781 | WOOLRIDGE | William Lennard | S/Sgt. | 24.09.1951 |
| 4782 | Mac KENZIE | William George | Supt. | 24.09.1951 |
| 4783 | PERCIVAL | Walter | Sgt. | 01.10.1951 |
| 4784 | DANIEL | Jules Maurice | D/Sgt | 02.10.1951 |
| 4785 | ALFORD | Allen Michael | Inspr. | 08.10.1951 |
| 4786 | BATSTONE | Michael John | Const. | 08.10.1951 |
| 4787 | BOWLER | William Ronald | Supt. | 08.10.1951 |
| 4788 | LENDREM | Michael Roderic | D/Inspr. | 08.10.1951 |
| 4789 | MATCHETT | Edmundson | C/Inspr. | 08.10.1951 |
| 4790 | McCARTHY | Cormac Trant | Const. | 08.10.1951 |
| 4791 | ROBBINS | Ronald Thomas | S/Sgt. | 08.10.1951 |
| 4792 | JONES | Ronald James | Supt. | 08.10.1951 |
| 4793 | SAULS | Alexander | Const. | 08.10.1951 |
| 4794 | YOUNG | Robert Charles | Const. | 22.10.1951 |
| 4795 | BURRELL | Robert Edmund | S/A/C | 22.10.1951 |
| 4796 | BLACK-FOOTE | Christopher Andrew | Inspr. | 22.10.1951 |
| 4797 | PAGETT | Robert John | S/O | 22.10.1951 |
| 4798 | STOKOE | Robin Raymond | Inspr. | 22.10.1951 |
| 4799 | SUTTON | Charles Richard | Const. | 22.10.1951 |
| 4800 | TUCKER | Richard John | Const. | 22.10.1951 |
| 4801 | TILL | Leslie Oliver | Const. | 01.11.1951 |
| 4802 | BEEZLEY | Donald Charles | A/Comm | 05.11.1951 |
| 4803 | HETHERINGTON | Terrance | Const. | 05.11.1951 |
| 4804 | HOWARD | Cecil Llewellyn | C/Inspr. | 05.11.1951 |
| 4805 | MARSHALL | Oliver Derfnis | Const. | 05.11.1951 |
| 4806 | MURRAY | Thomas Jeffrey | S/Sgt. | 05.11.1951 |
| 4807 | ROWSELL | Peter Hislop | Sgt. | 05.11.1951 |
| 4808 | RUSSELL | Donald Hugh | A/Comm | 05.11.1951 |
| 4809 | TURK | John | D/Sgt. | 03.12.1951 |
| 4810 | CALLOW | John Dennis | Const. | 03.12.1951 |
| 4811 | KENNEDY | Justin Aiden | D/Inspr. | 03.12.1951 |
| 4812 | PICKARD | Noel Francis | Const. | 03.12.1951 |
| 4813 | CARRUTHERS-SMITH | David Reg | Const. | 03.12.1951 |
| 4814 | BOWER | George Syndercombe | C/Supt. | 03.12.1951 |
| 4815 | CORDREY | Richard Carlyle | Const. | 03.12.1951 |
| 4816 | DODD | George Barry | Inspr. | 03.12.1951 |
| 4817 | GILMORE | Andrew Pinkerton | D/Sgt. | 03.12.1951 |
| 4818 | GILMOUR | William Robertson | C/Inspr. | 03.12.1951 |
| 4819 | LAY | Brian Chris | Supt. | 03.12.1951 |
| 4820 | WILKINSON | John Dennis | Sgt. | 03.12.1951 |
| 4821 | YOUNG | Jack Philip | Const. | 03.12.1951 |
| 4822 | BEALE | James Wilson | Const. | 31.12.1951 |
| 4823 | CARROLL | Trevellyn Prout | Const. | 31.12.1951 |
| 4824 | COLLIS | James William | C/Inspr. | 31.12.1951 |
| 4825 | COOK | Ian Walker | C/Inspr. | 31.12.1951 |
| 4826 | FAWN | Brian Hugh | Const. | 31.12.1951 |
| 4827 | LONG | John Hume | Const. | 31.12.1951 |
| 4829 | OATT | Terence Michael | A/Comm | 31.12.1951 |
| 4830 | O'SULLIVAN | Dermot Alexander | Const. | 31.12.1951 |
| 4831 | STIFF | Peter Robert | Supt. | 31.12.1951 |
| 4832 | TAYLOR | Stephen Ary | Const. | 31.12.1951 |
| 4833 | THOMPSON | Pennni | Const. | 31.12.1951 |
| 4834 | WILSON | Peter Bell | Const. | 28.01.1952 |
| 4835 | BOWDEN | Peter John | D/S/O | 28.01.1952 |
| 4836 | BROOKS | John | Const. | 28.01.1952 |
| 4837 | BROWN | John Cochrane | Const. | 28.01.1952 |
| 4838 | MISSELDINE | Peter Ambrose | D/Sgt. | 28.01.1952 |
| 4839 | NOTT | Roy | Const. | 28.01.1952 |
| 4840 | PURSLOW | Michael John | Const. | 28.01.1952 |
| 4841 | REYNOLDS | Adrian Michael | Const. | 28.01.1952 |
| 4842 | SAUNDERS | Ronald Charles | Const. | 28.01.1952 |
| 4843 | HAPGOOD-STRICKLAND | Sidney John | A/Comm | 28.01.1952 |
| 4844 | TITTERTON | Paul Randolph | Const. | 28.01.1952 |
| 4845 | WATTERS | Richard Brian | Const. | 01.02.1952 |
| 4846 | McLINTOCK | George Harris | C/Inspr. | 01.02.1952 |
| 4847 | ALDRIDGE | Charles | Const. | 11.02.1952 |
| 4848 | BRENNAN | Brendan | S/Sgt. | 11.02.1952 |
| 4849 | CROSS | Peter Sidney | Const. | 11.02.1952 |
| 4850 | DAVEY | Jim | S/L/Sgt. | 11.02.1952 |
| 4851 | HARRISON | Alfred Murray | Inspr. | 11.02.1952 |
| 4852 | NICHOLSON | John David | Const. | 11.02.1952 |
| 4853 | PUNTER | Frederick Albert | S/A/Comm | 11.02.1952 |
| 4854 | ROBINSON | David Martin | C/Inspr. | 11.02.1952 |
| 4855 | THOMPSON | John Hardisty | Const. | 11.02.1952 |
| 4856 | WATKINS | David John | Const. | 11.02.1952 |
| 4857 | WILTSHIRE | Michael Benjamin | Const. | 11.02.1952 |
| 4858 | WARD | John Mortor | D/Sgt. | 25.02.1952 |
| 4859 | BARNFIELD | Kenneth William | C/Inspr. | 25.02.1952 |
| 4860 | ADAMS | Christopher Hugh | Const. | 25.02.1952 |
| 4861 | ANDREWS | Robert Victor | S/Sgt. | 25.02.1952 |
| 4862 | DUFF | Gordon Graham | Const. | 25.02.1952 |
| 4863 | FOSTER | Michael Robin | Const. | 25.02.1952 |
| 4864 | GALLAGHER | Brendon Terence | S/A/C | 25.02.1952 |
| 4865 | HOGAN | William Patrick | Const. | 25.02.1952 |
| 4866 | LAWTON | Richard Edgar | Inspr. | 25.02.1952 |
| 4867 | SHRIVE | Douglas Thomas | S/O | 25.02.1952 |
| 4868 | TORRINGTON | George John | C/Inspr. | 25.02.1952 |
| 4869 | TURNER | John Antony | Const. | 25.02.1952 |
| 4870 | ARGYLE | Nigel John | Sgt. | 10.03.1952 |
| 4871 | BURTON | Antony Paul | Const. | 10.03.1952 |
| 4872 | GREEN | Eric | Supt. | 10.03.1952 |
| 4873 | HUGHES | Cyril Brian | C/Inspr. | 10.03.1952 |
| 4874 | MERRICKS | Leonard Roy | Sgt. | 10.03.1952 |
| 4875 | PEEN | Claud Robert | Const. | 10.03.1952 |
| 4876 | SEWARD | Richard Robin | Const. | 10.03.1952 |
| 4877 | TERRY | Dennis Carside | Const. | 10.03.1952 |
| 4878 | WHITELEY | Stuart Leonard | A/Comm | 14.03.1952 |
| 4879 | BATES | Terence Raymond | Const. | 14.03.1952 |
| 4880 | CREMIN | Dennid Placid | Const. | 17.03.1952 |
| 4881 | DANCER | Luke William | D/C/Inspr. | 24.03.1952 |
| 4882 | DANCER | Peter Edward | C/Inspr. | 24.03.1952 |
| 4883 | DITCHBURN | Alan Douglas | Const. | 24.03.1952 |
| 4884 | DYER | Arthur John | Const. | 24.03.1952 |
| 4885 | FARMER | George Rudolph | Const. | 24.03.1952 |
| 4886 | KINLEY | Martin Geoffrey | Const. | 24.03.1952 |
| 4887 | MARETT | Richard De Carteret | C/Inspr. | 24.03.1952 |
| 4888 | MORRIS | Peter John | Supt. | 24.03.1952 |
| 4889 | WAUGH | Gordon MacDonald | A/Comm | 24.03.1952 |
| 4890 | GAMBLE | Jolyon Evershed | Const. | 07.04.1952 |
| 4891 | HUTCHINSON | John | Sgt. | 07.04.1952 |
| 4892 | JOHNSON | Henry Howard | Const. | 07.04.1952 |
| 4893 | MABBS | Charles Richard | Const. | 07.04.1952 |
| 4894 | MILLER | Barry Herbert | D/Sgt. | 07.04.1952 |
| 4895 | ROSE | Kenneth | Const. | 07.04.1952 |
| 4896 | SADLIER | Francis Arthur | Const. | 07.04.1952 |
| 4897 | SHIERS | Brian Henry | Inspr. | 07.04.1952 |
| 4898 | THORNE | Christopher Gordon | Inspr. | 07.04.1952 |
| 4899 | WALSH | Michael Harold | Const. | 07.04.1952 |
| 4900 | WILCOX | Patrick Werna | Supt. | 07.04.1952 |
| 4901 | BELC | Ian | Const. | 21.04.1952 |
| 4902 | BURLE | Charles Victor | Sgt. | 21.04.1952 |
| 4903 | FOBBESTER | James Robert | D/Sgt. | 21.04.1952 |
| 4904 | GRANT | George | Const. | 21.04.1952 |
| 4905 | McLISTER | James Daniel | Const. | 21.04.1952 |
| 4906 | NICHOLLS | Colin | Const. | 21.04.1952 |
| 4907 | SMITH | Alexander Stuart | Const. | 21.04.1952 |
| 4908 | SMITH | Patrick Garnett | D/Const. | 21.04.1952 |
| 4909 | SWANN | Derek Gerald | Const. | 21.04.1952 |
| 4910 | LEE | Dennis James | Const. | 23.04.1952 |
| 4911 | BAYLY | Michael Wentworth | Const. | 05.05.1952 |
| 4912 | CRAHART | Redvers William | S/O | 05.05.1952 |
| 4913 | DAVEY | Neville Thomas | Const. | 05.05.1952 |
| 4914 | GAUNT | Hugh Anthony | Const. | 05.05.1952 |
| 4915 | GROOMBRIDGE | Michael Joseph | Const. | 05.05.1952 |
| 4916 | LAMB | William Peter | Const. | 05.05.1952 |
| 4917 | LAMBURN | David John | Const. | 05.05.1952 |
| 4918 | LEACH | Robert David | Const. | 05.05.1952 |
| 4919 | Mac PHEE | Neil | C/Inspr. | 05.05.1952 |
| 4920 | MOORE | Derek John | Const. | 05.05.1952 |
| 4921 | READ | Anthony | Const. | 05.05.1952 |
| 4922 | REEVES | John Charles | Const. | 05.05.1952 |
| 4923 | WESTON | Thomas Henry | Const. | 05.05.1952 |
| 4924 | BRACONNIER | Raymond Edmund | Const. | 19.05.1952 |
| 4925 | COLGATE | Peter John | Const. | 19.05.1952 |
| 4926 | SNOW | Peter | Const. | 19.05.1952 |
| 4927 | ANDERSON | Michael Douglas | Sgt. | 02.06.1952 |
| 4928 | BRINDLE | Frank William | C/Inspr. | 02.06.1952 |
| 4929 | KING | Joseph | Inspr. | 02.06.1952 |
| 4930 | MARSHALL | Ian Ronald | Const. | 02.06.1952 |
| 4931 | SAWTELL | Richard Francis | Const. | 02.06.1952 |
| 4932 | STEVENS | Jack Walter • | Sgt. | 02.06.1952 |
| 4933 | WILSON | Rodney | Const. | 02.06.1952 |
| 4934 | BURMAN | Michael Sorfleet | S/O | 16.06.1952 |
| 4935 | EDWARDS | Dereck Basil | Sgt. | 16.06.1952 |
| 4936 | HALL | George Rome | Supt. | 16.06.1952 |
| 4937 | JESSOP | Alexander Charles | Supt. | 16.06.1952 |
| 4938 | LOVETT | Clifford Thomas | Const. | 16.06.1952 |
| 4939 | SMETHURST | Clifford Huslam | Const. | 16.06.1952 |
| 4940 | DOBLE | John Steven | Sgt. | 07.07.1952 |
| 4941 | LOOKER | Terence William | Const. | 07.07.1952 |
| 4942 | MARRIOTT | Ian Trevor | Supt. | 07.07.1952 |
| 4943 | ORRELL | Roger Arthur | Inpsr. | 07.07.1952 |
| 4944 | TULLETT | Dennis Richard | Sgt. | 07.07.1952 |
| 4945 | PHILIP | Derek Sydney | Sgt. | 14.07.1952 |
| 4946 | WALLER | Derek Charles | A/Comm | 14.07.1952 |
| 4947 | WELCH | Roy William | Const. | 14.07.1952 |
| 4948 | WELLBURN | Kenneth Edgar | Const. | 14.07.1952 |
| 4949 | WINCHCOMBE | Gerald David | D/C/Inspr. | 14.07.1952 |
| 4950 | BAKER | John Gilbert | Inspr. | 19.07.1952 |
| 4951 | HAWLEY | Gerald Ronald | D/C/Inspr. | 27.07.1952 |
| 4952 | IVEY | George Raymond | C/Supt. | 27.07.1952 |
| 4953 | JACKSON | John Michael | Inspr. | 27.07.1952 |
| 4954 | KENNY | Robert Charles | D/Sgt. | 27.07.1952 |
| 4955 | MORRISON | Alexander Robin | C/Inspr. | 27.07.1952 |
| 4956 | WILLIAMSON | Ronald Eric | Const. | 27.07.1952 |
| 4957 | FREEBORN | Jack Albert | Const. | 28.07.1952 |
| 4958 | GREEN | Frank Robin | Const. | 28.07.1952 |
| 4959 | DREW | Gerald Walter | D/C/Inspr. | 10.08.1952 |
| 4960 | GIBSON | Terry Osborn | D/Inspr. | 10.08.1952 |
| 4961 | HUGHES | Barry William | C/Inspr. | 10.08.1952 |
| 4962 | PRATT | Derek Arthur | D/Sgt. | 10.08.1952 |
| 4963 | STARR | Michael | Const. | 10.08.1952 |
| 4964 | TADMAN | Albert Peter | Const. | 10.08.1952 |
| 4965 | THOMSON | Michael Norman | Const. | 10.08.1952 |
| 4966 | UPWARD | | S/O | 10.08.1952 |

| No. | Surname | Forename | Date | Rank |
|---|---|---|---|---|
| 4967 | YOUNG | Donald George | 10.08.1952 | Inspr. |
| 4968 | BEMBRIDGE | Philip HenryGreen | 07.09.1952 | C/Inspr. |
| 4969 | FRANKLIN | Anthony Michael | 07.09.1952 | Sgt. |
| 4970 | JACKSON | Roy | 07.09.1952 | Const. |
| 4971 | JENKIN | Frederick James | 07.09.1952 | Const. |
| 4972 | LANGHAN | Peter | 07.09.1952 | C/Supt. |
| 4973 | MOORHOUSE | Michael Richard | 07.09.1952 | Const. |
| 4974 | TAYLOR | John | 07.09.1952 | Const. |
| 4975 | BOLTON | Alan Brian | 05.10.1952 | C/Inspr. |
| 4976 | BROWN | Harry Colin | 05.10.1952 | D/Sgt. |
| 4977 | DAVIES | Roy | 05.10.1952 | Const. |
| 4978 | CLANFIELD | William Richard | 05.10.1952 | Const. |
| 4979 | CROSBY-JONES | Michael Bolton | 05.10.1952 | Const. |
| 4980 | McCALLUM | Albert George | 05.10.1952 | Const. |
| 4981 | NEILL | Francis Michael | 05.10.1952 | Const. |
| 4982 | NEWTON | David Robert | 05.10.1952 | Const. |
| 4983 | SANKY | David John | 05.10.1952 | Inspr. |
| 4984 | TENNANT | Gordon Robert | 05.10.1952 | Const. |
| 4985 | WADE | Eric Ernest | 05.10.1952 | Const. |
| 4986 | WILKINS | Robert John | 05.10.1952 | Const. |
| 4987 | WILSON | Keith Harold | 05.10.1952 | Const. |
| 4988 | CROSSMAN | William John | 05.10.1952 | D/C/Inspr. |
| 4989 | HILL | Alastair Richard | 10.10.1952 | D/Sgt. |
| 4990 | COOK | Anthony Michael | 14.12.1952 | Sgt. |
| 4991 | CRAKER | Rex | 14.12.1952 | Const. |
| 4992 | FENTON | William Benjamin | 14.12.1952 | Const. |
| 4993 | FIELDER | John Michael | 14.12.1952 | D/Inspr. |
| 4994 | HOCKLEY | Michael Reginald | 14.12.1952 | Const. |
| 4995 | JONES | Derek Frank | 14.12.1952 | S/A/Comm |
| 4996 | NEALE | John Phillip | 14.12.1952 | C/Supt. |
| 4997 | SAMWAYS | Robert John | 14.12.1952 | Inspr. |
| 4998 | SHAW | Ronald Oliver | 14.12.1952 | S/Supt. |
| 4999 | THOMPSON | Stephen Gordon | 14.12.1952 | Const. |
| 5000 | WAKEFIELD | Laurence Gordon | 14.12.1952 | Inspr. |
| 5001 | WHITELAW | James | 14.12.1952 | A/Comm |
| 5002 | DAVIDOVICS | Arthur Joseph | 26.02.1953 | Inspr. |
| 5003 | NEALE | George Harold | 26.02.1953 | S/Sgt. |
| 5004 | NICHOL | Thomas Wright | 26.02.1953 | S/Sgt. |
| 5005 | PECKOVER | Desmond Ralph | 26.02.1953 | C/Inspr. |
| 5006 | THORLEY | George | 26.02.1953 | Sgt. |
| 5007 | BRAKSPEAR | Julian Adrian | 08.03.1953 | Const. |
| 5008 | BULLEY | Clive Southscott | 08.03.1953 | Inspr. |
| 5009 | FRY | Colston Thomas | 08.03.1953 | S/Sgt. |
| 5010 | GILLINGHAM | John Bramley | 08.03.1953 | S/Sgt. |
| 5011 | GRAVES | James Barnett | 08.03.1953 | Const. |
| 5012 | HEUGH | Malcolm Vernon | 08.03.1953 | C/Supt. |
| 5013 | LAWLOR | Terence John | 08.03.1953 | Const. |
| 5014 | LONG | Geoffrey George | 08.03.1953 | Const. |
| 5015 | WADDON-MARTYN | David Hammersley | 08.03.1953 | C/Inspr. |
| 5016 | WARREN-PRATT | John Anthony | 08.03.1953 | S/O |
| 5017 | SCOTT | Dennis Henry | 08.03.1953 | C/Inspr. |
| 5018 | THORNTON | Ronald | 08.03.1953 | Inspr. |
| 5019 | TOSEN | William John | 08.03.1953 | Inspr. |
| 5020 | WING | David Richard | 08.03.1953 | Const. |
| 5021 | HAWKINS | John Jeremy | 13.03.1953 | Const. |
| 5022 | LEECH | David Maxwell | 23.03.1953 | C/Inspr. |
| 5023 | O'NEILL | George Gerald | 23.03.1953 | Inspr. |
| 5024 | BISHOP | John Clive | 12.04.1953 | D/Inspr. |
| 5025 | BURT | Peter John Byatt | 12.04.1953 | Const. |
| 5026 | BYRNE | Terence Charles | 12.04.1953 | Const. |
| 5027 | COLLIER | William John | 12.04.1953 | Inspr. |
| 5028 | ENNIS | John William | 12.04.1953 | C/Inspr. |
| 5029 | HAINES | Raymond Thomas | 12.04.1953 | D/Sgt. |
| 5030 | KIMBERLEE | William Henry | 12.04.1953 | Const. |
| 5031 | MILLER | John George | 12.04.1953 | Const. |
| 5032 | PRENTICE | Phillip | 12.04.1953 | Const. |
| 5033 | PRIEST | Ian William | 12.04.1953 | Const. |
| 5034 | ROTHWELL | Brian Unsworth | 12.04.1953 | Sgt. |
| 5035 | SPORNE | Leonard Alan | 12.04.1953 | Const. |
| 5036 | TAYLOR | Dudley Charles | 12.04.1953 | Sgt. |
| 5037 | THOMAS | Edward Dundon | 12.04.1953 | Const. |
| 5038 | THOMPSON | Gilbert Nelson | 12.04.1953 | Inspr. |
| 5039 | TURNER | Anthony Geoffrey | 12.04.1953 | Const. |
| 5040 | WALTON | Frederick John | 12.04.1953 | Const. |
| 5041 | ZWICKY | Quinton Edward | 12.04.1953 | Sgt. |
| 5042 | ARNOLD | Peter James | 03.05.1953 | Sgt. |
| 5043 | BILSBY | John Philip | 03.05.1953 | Const. |
| 5044 | BRADSHAW | Anthony Eric | 03.05.1953 | Supt. |
| 5045 | BROWN | Frederick Anthony | 03.05.1953 | Const. |
| 5046 | COEY | Thomas | 03.05.1953 | Const. |
| 5047 | CROWLEY | Patrick Burton | 03.05.1953 | Const. |
| 5048 | FARRIS | Michael Robert | 03.05.1953 | Const. |
| 5049 | GRIMWOOD | Derek Thomas | 03.05.1953 | Sgt. |
| 5050 | HAMMOND | Derick Arthur | 03.05.1953 | Inspr. |
| 5051 | HEMMINGS | Ieuan Guy | 03.05.1953 | Const. |
| 5052 | HOLLAND | Charles Victor | 03.05.1953 | S/Sgt. |
| 5053 | HOYLE | Esmond Malcolm | 03.05.1953 | Const. |
| 5054 | LEIGHTON | John Richard | 03.05.1953 | Const. |
| 5055 | MINERS | Kenneth George | 03.05.1953 | Const. |
| 5056 | PHILLIPS | Peter | 03.05.1953 | Sgt. |
| 5057 | ROBINSON | Malcolm James | 03.05.1953 | D/Sgt. |
| 5058 | VONT | Brian Roderick | 03.05.1953 | Const. |
| 5059 | LEWIS | John Stewart | 03.05.1953 | Const. |
| 5060 | WILKINS | Barry Maxwell | 03.05.1953 | Const. |
| 5061 | BAILEY | Peter William | 07.06.1953 | Const. |
| 5062 | BAVAILLOT | Lucien Barry | 07.06.1953 | Const. |
| 5063 | BOLAS | Stanley | 07.06.1953 | Sgt. |
| 5064 | BUCHANAN | Robert | 07.06.1953 | Const. |
| 5065 | COOMBS | Ernest James | 07.06.1953 | Const. |
| 5066 | DUGGAN | Richard John | 07.06.1953 | Const. |
| 5067 | HARDY | Denis | 07.06.1953 | Supt. |
| 5068 | HARPER | Robert Michael | 07.06.1953 | Const. |
| 5069 | HARRIS | Francis Roy | 07.06.1953 | Const. |
| 5070 | HOLDEN | Thomas Duxbury | 07.06.1953 | Const. |
| 5071 | JEFFREYS | Colin Harry | 07.06.1953 | Const. |
| 5072 | McCORMACK | John Brian | 07.06.1953 | S/Sgt. |
| 5073 | MARLE | Ronald George | 07.06.1953 | S/Sgt. |
| 5074 | PERREY | Keith | 07.06.1953 | Sgt. |
| 5075 | RAY | Richard John | 07.06.1953 | C/Supt. |
| 5076 | TEALE | William Robert | 07.06.1953 | Inspr. |
| 5077 | THURBLY | Michael Charles | 07.06.1953 | Inspr. |
| 5078 | WALLACE | Michael Arthur | 07.06.1953 | Const. |
| 5079 | WALKER | Peter George | 07.06.1953 | Const. |
| 5080 | MAWDSLEY | Michael John | 16.06.1953 | C/Supt. |
| 5081 | LOUW | Frederick Johannes | 20.07.1953 | Const. |
| 5082 | BEACH | Dennis Kenneth | 09.08.1953 | Const. |
| 5083 | CAMPBELL | George Ross | 09.08.1953 | Const. |
| 5084 | CLEMENTS | John Vernon | 09.08.1953 | C/Inspr. |
| 5085 | GILBERT | James Henry | 09.08.1953 | C/Inspr. |
| 5086 | GILLETT | Roger Meyrick | 09.08.1953 | Inspr. |
| 5087 | HALL-JOHNSON | Robin Alwyn | 09.08.1953 | Inspr. |
| 5088 | HEATH | David Edwin | 09.08.1953 | S/O |
| 5089 | ISGAR | Brian Bruno | 09.08.1953 | Const. |
| 5090 | JANKI | John Colin | 09.08.1953 | Const. |
| 5091 | JECOCK | John Colin | 09.08.1953 | C/Inspr. |
| 5092 | KENNEDY | Keith Douglas | 09.08.1953 | Supt. |
| 5093 | KNOWLES | Barrie Rowland | 09.08.1953 | Const. |
| 5094 | MILLER | Ian James | 09.08.1953 | Supt. |
| 5095 | PAPENFUS | Robert Kenneth | 09.08.1953 | Inspr. |
| 5096 | PHILLIPS | Frederick Jan | 09.08.1953 | Inspr. |
| 5097 | RIX | John Henry | 09.08.1953 | Sgt. |
| 5098 | RILEY | David | 09.08.1953 | D/Sgt. |
| 5099 | ROBINSON | David Gordon | 09.08.1953 | Const. |
| 5100 | SAVORY | Peter Kenneth | 09.08.1953 | Const. |
| 5101 | WHITEHEAD | Donalde Raymond | 09.08.1953 | D/S/O |
| 5102 | WILDE | Eric Arthur | 09.08.1953 | Const. |
| 5103 | WILLIAMS | John Brian | 09.08.1953 | Inspr. |
| 5104 | WOOD | Eric Winston | 09.08.1953 | Const. |
| 5105 | DAVIES | John Owen | 09.08.1953 | Const. |
| 5106 | VAN RENSBERG | Peter | 09.08.1953 | Const. |
| 5107 | ASHWORTH | George Andrew | 16.08.1953 | Supt. |
| 5108 | HATCH | Roelof Peter | 21.08.1953 | Sgt. |
| 5109 | AKED | Maurice Peter | 30.08.1953 | Sgt. |
| 5110 | BAILEY | Nigel Keith | 30.08.1953 | Sgt. |
| 5111 | BACON | John Roy David | 30.08.1953 | C/Supt. |
| 5112 | COBB | Brendan Paul | 30.08.1953 | Const. |
| 5113 | COWAN | David Campbell | 30.08.1953 | Const. |
| 5114 | CSERNOVDTS | Michael Robert | 30.08.1953 | Const. |
| 5115 | GALE | Rodney Stuart | 30.08.1953 | Const. |
| 5116 | GILBERT | David Raleigh | 30.08.1953 | Const. |
| 5117 | HALL | Ronald Douglas | 30.08.1953 | D/C/Inspr. |
| 5118 | HAYES | Ian | 30.08.1953 | C/Inspr. |
| 5119 | HONEYMAN | Peter John | 30.08.1953 | Sgt. |
| 5120 | HIRST | George Hugo | 30.08.1953 | Const. |
| 5121 | LANCASTER | Peter Hugh | 30.08.1953 | Const. |
| 5122 | McMAHON | Patrick Desmond | 30.08.1953 | Const. |
| 5123 | PERKINS | David Layton | 30.08.1953 | C/Inspr. |
| 5124 | PINTER | Raymond | 30.08.1953 | Const. |
| 5125 | STORRY | John Guy | 30.08.1953 | Sgt. |
| 5126 | TAYLOR | David Joseph | 30.08.1953 | Const. |
| 5127 | WHEATCROFT | Maurice | 30.08.1953 | Const. |
| 5128 | WAKLEY | Graham John | 30.08.1953 | Const. |
| 5129 | WOODCOCK | John Stewart | 01.09.1953 | S/C/Inspr. |
| 5130 | COLESHAW | Keith Norman | 27.09.1953 | Const. |
| 5131 | COTTON | John | 27.09.1953 | Const. |
| 5132 | DAY | Michael Vernon | 27.09.1953 | Supt. |
| 5133 | HOLMES | Ivor Arthur | 27.09.1953 | Inspr. |
| 5134 | LOGAN | Peter John | 27.09.1953 | Const. |
| 5135 | MAGUIRE | John Brian | 27.09.1953 | Const. |
| 5136 | MARSHALL | James Arthur | 27.09.1953 | D/Const. |
| 5137 | NORRIS | Donald Neville | 27.09.1953 | S/Sgt. |
| 5138 | O'PREY | Gordon William | 27.09.1953 | Const. |
| 5139 | ONSLOW | Claude | 27.09.1953 | Const. |
| 5140 | SIDNELL | Victor Leslie | 27.09.1953 | C/Supt. |
| 5141 | STITT | Jocelyn van- | 27.09.1953 | A/Comm |
| 5142 | TROMP | John Henry | 27.09.1953 | Const. |
| 5143 | VYE | Raymond Eric | 27.09.1953 | Inspr. |
| 5144 | WEARE | John Sidney | 27.09.1953 | Inspr. |
| 5145 | WEATHERLEY | Peter Craven | 27.09.1953 | C/Inspr. |
| 5146 | WILLSON | Walter Henry | 27.09.1953 | C/Inspr. |
| 5147 | WILTON | Maurice Arthur | 27.09.1953 | Inspr. |
| 5148 | YEOMANS | Robert | 01.10.1953 | Inspr. |
| 5149 | KENNEDY | George Charles | 06.10.1953 | C/Inspr. |
| 5150 | RAINBIRD | John Proctor | 01.11.1953 | Const. |
| 5151 | AFFLECK | Anthony March | 01.11.1953 | Const. |
| 5152 | BAKER | Dennis Maslyn | 01.11.1953 | P/O |
| 5153 | CASTELL-CASTELL | James | 01.11.1953 | Const. |
| 5154 | CLAMPITT | Ashton Robert | 01.11.1953 | Const. |
| 5155 | FORWARD | Peter Daniel | 01.11.1953 | Const. |
| 5156 | GIBSON | Roger Anthony | 01.11.1953 | Const. |
| 5157 | COWEN | Anthony Gladstone | 01.11.1953 | S/A/Comm |
| 5158 | HOPE | Clifford Austin | 01.11.1953 | D/Sgt. |
| 5159 | LARDNER | Eoin James Ross | 01.11.1953 | D/Sgt. |
| 5160 | MACKAY | John Robert | 01.11.1953 | D/Sgt. |
| 5161 | PEARSON | Michael | 01.11.1953 | S/A/Comm |
| 5162 | ROBINSON | Raeburn Hugh | 01.11.1953 | D/Sgt. |
| 5163 | ROBOTTOM | Robert Malcolm | 01.11.1953 | Inspr. |
| 5164 | SAVAGE | Donovan Patrick | 01.11.1953 | Inspr. |
| 5165 | SILLISS | John Edward | 01.11.1953 | Const. |
| 5166 | SPANDLEY | George Robert | 01.11.1953 | Const. |
| 5167 | SPURGIN | David Barrington | 01.11.1953 | C/Inspr. |
| 5168 | TAYLOR | Peter Colin | 01.11.1953 | Const. |
| 5169 | BENNETT | James William | 03.11.1953 | Const. |
| 5170 | SCOTT | Peter John | 10.11.1953 | S/O |
| 5171 | HILLIER | Alexander | 02.12.1953 | Inspr. |
| 5172 | CRAIGIE | Brian Samuel | 14.12.1953 | Inspr. |
| 5173 | GARLAND | | 14.12.1953 | Inspr. |

# BSAP Nominal Roll • Men

| No. | Surname | Forename(s) | Date | Rank |
|---|---|---|---|---|
| 5174 | ANDREW | Michael John | 15.12.1953 | Const. |
| 5175 | BINNS | Gordon | 15.12.1953 | Supt. |
| 5176 | BOWL | Anthony Pollock | 15.12.1953 | Sgt. |
| 5177 | BULLOCH | James Angus | 15.12.1953 | Const. |
| 5178 | CHERRILL | Brian Alfred | 15.12.1953 | Const. |
| 5179 | COOPER | Victor Hedley | 15.12.1953 | Const. |
| 5180 | COX | David Francis | 15.12.1953 | Const. |
| 5181 | EVANS | John Lewis | 15.12.1953 | A/Com |
| 5182 | HUMMERSTON | John Frederick | 15.12.1953 | Const. |
| 5183 | MERRIGAN | Terence | 15.12.1953 | C/Inspr. |
| 5184 | NIGHTINGALE | Brian Leonard | 15.12.1953 | A/Com |
| 5185 | PRIOR | James | 15.12.1953 | Supt. |
| 5186 | PURKINS | Gerald Ansel | 15.12.1953 | Const. |
| 5187 | REEVES | Francis Michael | 15.12.1953 | A/Com |
| 5188 | TINGEY | Albert George | 15.12.1953 | Const. |
| 5189 | CROOK | John Albert | 03.01.1954 | Const. |
| 5190 | CROOK | Patrick Thomas | 03.01.1954 | Const. |
| 5191 | ESPEY | Arthur Wingfield | 03.01.1954 | Const. |
| 5192 | HANCOCK | Stanley John | 03.01.1954 | C/Supt. |
| 5193 | JOSLYN | Brian Frank | 03.01.1954 | Const. |
| 5194 | KOLBE | Geoffrey Downing | 03.01.1954 | Sgt. |
| 5195 | LINSCOTT | Michael John | 03.01.1954 | Sgt. |
| 5196 | MAGEEAN | Kenneth Graham | 03.01.1954 | Sgt. |
| 5197 | McGUINESS | Michael John | 03.01.1954 | Const. |
| 5198 | MARSHALL | Hilary Edward | 03.01.1954 | C/Supt. |
| 5199 | MILES | Kenneth Graham | 03.01.1954 | Const. |
| 5200 | PATON | Anthony Richard | 03.01.1954 | Const. |
| 5201 | SMITH | Maxwell | 03.01.1954 | Const. |
| 5202 | WOOD | Peter Vernon | 07.01.1954 | Inspr. |
| 5203 | DU BRUYN | Patrick Johnstone | 13.01.1954 | S/Sgt. |
| 5204 | BULL | Robin Alexander | 25.01.1954 | Inspr. |
| 5205 | HANCOCK | Revill Meade | 04.02.1954 | Const. |
| 5206 | TUCKER | Peter Grenville | 05.02.1954 | Sgt. |
| 5207 | GOOCH | Desmond Percy | 16.02.1954 | Const. |
| 5208 | BROWNING | Stanley Arthur | 01.03.1954 | A/Comm |
| 5209 | THOMPSON | John Alfred | 29.07.1954 | C/Inspr. |
| 5210 | CRAVEN | David | 04.08.1954 | Supt. |
| 5211 | BIRCH | William James | 14.03.1954 | Supt. |
| 5212 | TOMLIN | Derek John | 14.03.1954 | Sgt. |
| 5213 | HENN | Michael Frederick | 14.03.1954 | Const. |
| 5214 | FINDLAY | James Kerr | 14.03.1954 | Const. |
| 5215 | JACKSON | Hugh Arthur | 14.03.1954 | Const. |
| 5216 | FOULKES | Eric Oswald | 14.03.1954 | D/Inspr. |
| 5217 | HARRIS | Nigel Lonsdale | 14.03.1954 | C/Inspr. |
| 5218 | BAKER | William George | 14.03.1954 | Const. |
| 5219 | BOOTH | Roger | 14.03.1954 | Supt. |
| 5220 | BURTON | Peter Cedric | 14.03.1954 | Const. |
| 5221 | HENNIKER-GOTLEY | Robert James | 14.03.1954 | A/Comm |
| 5222 | BERRYMAN | Alan William | 14.03.1954 | A/Comm |
| 5223 | STANDIVAN | Colin Ames | 14.03.1954 | S/O |
| 5224 | HICHENS | George Roger | 14.03.1954 | C/Supt. |
| 5225 | CARSE | James | 14.03.1954 | Sgt. |
| 5226 | MURPHY | Patrick James | 14.03.1954 | A/Comm |
| 5227 | GOMM | Keith | 04.04.1954 | Const. |
| 5228 | SARGENT | Arthur James | 04.04.1954 | Const. |
| 5229 | WALL | Brian William | 04.04.1954 | D/Inspr. |
| 5230 | ROWE | John William | 04.04.1954 | Const. |
| 5231 | ROWLAND | Donald Charles | 04.04.1954 | A/Comm |
| 5232 | BOYES | Terence | 04.04.1954 | Const. |
| 5233 | HAMILTON | William | 04.04.1954 | A/Comm |
| 5234 | COUTTS | Alexander Cameron | 04.04.1954 | Const. |
| 5235 | BIRCH | George Anthony | 04.04.1954 | Inspr. |
| 5236 | GRAHAM | John Raymond | 04.04.1954 | Const. |
| 5237 | HIGGINS | Carl Arthur | 04.04.1954 | Const. |
| 5238 | PAUW | Andrew John | 04.04.1954 | Inspr. |
| 5239 | Mac KENZIE | Terence Patrick | 04.04.1954 | Sgt. |
| 5240 | PATCHING | Roger John | 04.04.1954 | C/Inspr. |
| 5241 | SHIRES | John Dinsley | 04.04.1954 | Const. |
| 5243 | SIDE | Barry Lovell | 04.04.1954 | Const. |
| 5244 | BUFF | Brian Austin | 04.04.1954 | Const. |
| 5245 | MARSHALL | John Phineas | 04.04.1954 | Const. |
| 5246 | WARPAND | Ian Kenneth | 06.04.1954 | Const. |
| 5247 | Mac DONALD | Kenneth Robert | 04.04.1954 | S/A/Comm |
| 5248 | LANE | Alan John | 09.05.1954 | C/Supt. |
| 5249 | IBBETSON | Peter Harry | 09.05.1954 | Const. |
| 5250 | BRAIDWOOD | Martin Lithgow | 09.05.1954 | A/Com |
| 5251 | DOLBY | John Charles | 09.05.1954 | Inspr. |
| 5252 | TANNER | Gordon Albert | 09.05.1954 | Const. |
| 5253 | BROWN | Michael Roy | 09.05.1954 | Const. |
| 5254 | SCOTT | John Picton | 09.05.1954 | Const. |
| 5255 | LEWIS | Clive Oliver | 09.05.1954 | Const. |
| 5256 | SPENCER | John James | 09.05.1954 | A/Com |
| 5257 | BROWN | James Malcolm | 09.05.1954 | Const. |
| 5258 | LYNAGH | John Joseph | 09.05.1954 | Const. |
| 5259 | HOWE | John Wilfred | 09.05.1954 | Const. |
| 5260 | RICHARDS | Graham Roland | 09.05.1954 | Const. |
| 5261 | MAUDE | Arthur Michael | 12.05.1954 | Const. |
| 5262 | HARTNETT | Esmonde Patrick | 09.05.1954 | Const. |
| 5263 | CLYDE | George Bryan | 09.05.1954 | Const. |
| 5264 | COX | Richard Frederick | 09.05.1954 | C/Supt. |
| 5265 | ROSS | Angus | 27.06.1954 | Const. |
| 5266 | WILLIAMS | Norman Stewart | 27.06.1954 | D/Inspr. |
| 5267 | BURNS | Malcolm John | 27.06.1954 | C/Supt. |
| 5268 | WILTSHIRE | Peter Frederick | 27.06.1954 | Const. |
| 5269 | PARSONS | David | 27.06.1954 | D/C/Inspr. |
| 5270 | GOODHEAD | Kenneth | 23.06.1954 | S/O |
| 5271 | BRAY | Patrick | 27.06.1954 | C/Inspr. |
| 5272 | DEASY | David James | 27.06.1954 | C/Inspr. |
| 5273 | GARMAN | Gwynne Lawrence | 27.06.1954 | Const. |
| 5274 | POWER | David | 27.06.1954 | S/Sgt. |
| 5275 | ROUND | Laurence John | 27.06.1954 | Const. |
| 5276 | THORNE | Ronald Alexander | 27.06.1954 | Const. |
| 5277 | RUSSELL | Willian Anderson | 01.08.1954 | Const. |
| 5278 | STIRLING | Gerald Anthony | 01.08.1954 | D/C/Inspr. |
| 5279 | MOORE | Peter | 01.08.1954 | C/Supt. |
| 5280 | TOMLINSON | Peter James | 01.08.1954 | A/Comm |
| 5281 | BELLINGHAM | Eric Clifford | 01.08.1954 | C/Inspr. |
| 5282 | PARGETER | Christopher | 01.08.1954 | C/Inspr. |
| 5283 | NAISBY | Richard Albert | 01.08.1954 | Inspr. |
| 5284 | YOUNG | Frank Ian | 01.08.1954 | Const. |
| 5285 | SEATON | Ian John | 01.08.1954 | Const. |
| 5286 | Mac ADAM | Roderick William | 01.08.1954 | Const. |
| 5287 | GREEN | George Dunstan | 27.06.1954 | Const. |
| 5288 | BAVIN | John Clive | 01.08.1954 | Supt. |
| 5289 | EDWARDS | Brian Anthony | 01.08.1954 | Const. |
| 5290 | GRAY | Peter James | 19.09.1954 | Const. |
| 5291 | MOODY | Brian Anthony | 19.09.1954 | D/Inspr. |
| 5292 | ALLINGTON | Trevor | 19.09.1954 | Inspr. |
| 5293 | DUTTON | John James | 19.09.1954 | Const. |
| 5294 | WINTER | Richard James | 19.09.1954 | D/Sgt. |
| 5295 | MOLLOY | Eric John | 19.09.1954 | Const. |
| 5296 | PERRETT | Patrick Dennis | 19.09.1954 | Const. |
| 5297 | BURNS | John Edward | 19.09.1954 | Const. |
| 5298 | ROBERTSON | Charles Arthur | 19.09.1954 | Const. |
| 5299 | BANNISTER | Frank Michael | 19.09.1954 | Const. |
| 5300 | LOVELL | Edward Barry | 01.04.1955 | Const. |
| 5301 | POPKESS | Leslie | 21.04.1955 | C/Inspr. |
| 5302 | VERNON | Andrew Baillie | 02.05.1955 | C/Inspr. |
| 5303 | STONE | Anthony John | 05.12.1954 | Inspr. |
| 5304 | WYLSON | Christopher | 05.12.1954 | C/Supt. |
| 5305 | CARVER | Howard Wadsworth | 05.12.1954 | Sgt. |
| 5306 | PENTITH | Anthony Hugh | 05.12.1954 | S/O |
| 5307 | PUCKLE | Malcolm Harold | 05.12.1954 | S/O |
| 5308 | BARD | Ramsey Calloway | 05.12.1954 | Sgt. |
| 5309 | BROWN | Maurice Brian | 05.12.1954 | C/Inspr. |
| 5310 | PARNABY |  | 05.12.1954 | Const. |
| 5312 | LINDLEY | Michael Edward | 05.12.1954 | C/Supt. |
| 5313 | WALLINGTON | Clifford Robin | 05.12.1954 | S/Sgt. |
| 5314 | CRUTE | Keith Eric | 05.12.1954 | Sgt. |
| 5315 | FRANCIS | Timothy Donald | 05.12.1954 | S/O |
| 5316 | HOADLEY | Kerry | 05.12.1954 | Const. |
| 5317 | BROOKS | Keith John | 05.12.1954 | Const. |
| 5318 | REGAN | Brian John | 05.12.1954 | Const. |
| 5319 | AUSTEN | David James | 05.12.1954 | Const. |
| 5320 | BAXTER | Leslie Robert | 06.02.1955 | Const. |
| 5321 | SAYERS | Michael John | 06.02.1955 | Const. |
| 5322 | RODDA | Stuart Arthur | 06.02.1955 | Const. |
| 5323 | DU RAND | Jacobus Francious | 04.02.1955 | S/O |
| 5324 | MUNRO | Donald | 05.02.1955 | Const. |
| 5325 | JONES | Allan Charles | 06.02.1955 | Const. |
| 5326 | HALSEY | David | 06.02.1955 | Const. |
| 5327 | WALLACE | Bruce | 05.02.1955 | Const. |
| 5328 | DURRANS | Ian Thomas | 06.02.1955 | Const. |
| 5329 | MORTON | Clive Reginald | 06.02.1955 | S/O |
| 5330 | WOOD | Reginald Paul | 06.02.1955 | Const. |
| 5331 | STEVENS | Roy Karl | 16.10.1955 | S/Sgt. |
| 5332 | HEDGES | Geoffrey Edward | 30.04.1955 | S/A/C |
| 5333 | LE SEUER | David Henry | 02.05.1955 | S/O |
| 5334 | WORDEN | Alfred John | 08.05.1955 | Const. |
| 5335 | WALKER | Nigel Francis | 08.05.1955 | Const. |
| 5336 | ROWLAND | Charles John | 02.05.1955 | Const. |
| 5337 | VALENTINE | Simon Alistair | 03.05.1955 | Const. |
| 5338 | IVALL | John Durnford | 08.05.1955 | Const. |
| 5339 | HOPPER | Richard John | 08.05.1955 | S/O |
| 5340 | COTTON | Barry Percy | 09.05.1955 | D/S/O |
| 5341 | WATTS | Philip Charles | 08.05.1955 | Inspr. |
| 5342 | JACKSON | Peter Maurice | 08.05.1955 | Inspr. |
| 5343 | VAN RYNEVELD | Lionel Kelvin | 02.05.1955 | Const. |
| 5344 | DUNCAN | Ian Michael | 05.05.1955 | S/Sgt. |
| 5345 | SYMES | Peter Victor | 08.05.1955 | Const. |
| 5346 | GREEN | Neville Owen | 02.05.1955 | Const. |
| 5347 | MERCER | William | 02.05.1955 | Const. |
| 5348 | JAMES | Hugh Barton | 02.05.1955 | C/Inspr. |
| 5349 | LANE | Peter Brian | 08.05.1955 | D/S/O |
| 5350 | TERMEER | Max Lionel | 08.05.1955 | D/S/O |
| 5351 | HOLLIS | Derek Arthur | 08.05.1955 | C/Inspr. |
| 5352 | MYLREA | John Henry | 27.11.1955 | Inspr. |
| 5353 | LE MARQUAND | Gerald William | 12.06.1955 | Const. |
| 5354 | AVERISS | Julian Edward | 12.06.1955 | Const. |
| 5355 | GIBSON | Hugh John | 12.06.1955 | Const. |
| 5356 | BLACKFORD | William Arthur | 12.06.1955 | Const. |
| 5357 | CASE | Colin | 12.06.1955 | Const. |
| 5358 | YORK | Michael David | 12.06.1955 | C/Supt. |
| 5359 | WILLCOX | John Edmund | 12.06.1955 | C/Supt. |
| 5360 | HICKS | John Jeremy | 12.06.1955 | Supt. |
| 5361 | DYAS | George Morgan | 12.06.1955 | Const. |
| 5362 | HOARE | Brian Henry | 12.06.1955 | Const. |
| 5363 | NORTHCOTE | William Andrew | 08.05.1955 | C/Supt. |
| 5364 | GEORGE | David Alan | 03.07.1955 | Supt. |
| 5365 | ROBINS | Richard Frank | 03.07.1955 | Const. |
| 5366 | BANKS | Colin Francis | 03.07.1955 | Const. |
| 5367 | BOARD | Stewart Thomas | 03.07.1955 | Const. |
| 5368 | MANNING | Paul | 03.07.1955 | Const. |
| 5369 | KIRWIN | Michael Francis | 03.07.1955 | Const. |
| 5370 | O'BRIAN | James Richard | 03.07.1955 | Const. |
| 5371 | GRAHAM | Donald Louis | 03.07.1955 | D/Sgt. |
| 5372 | STEWART | John McIntyre | 03.07.1955 | C/Inspr. |
| 5373 | JONES | Alfred | 24.07.1955 | S/Sgt. |
| 5374 | ANGELL | John Richard | 24.07.1955 | Const. |
| 5375 | GRAHAM | John Stobart | 24.07.1955 | Const. |
| 5376 | FOSTER | Roy Gordon | 24.07.1955 | Const. |
| 5377 | GILLETT | Brian Royall | 24.07.1955 | Const. |
| 5378 | SOUTTER | Robin Leslie | 28.07.1955 | Const. |
| 5379 | FOX | Michael Andrew | 24.07.1955 | Const. |
| 5380 | HUBBARD | James | 24.07.1955 | Const. |

| No. | Surname | Forename(s) | Date | Rank |
|---|---|---|---|---|
| 5381 | McENERY | Edward Patrick | 28.12.1955 | S/Sgt. |
| 5382 | BUTLER | Antony | 29.12.1955 | Supt. |
| 5383 | HOLMES | Kenneth Ian | 03.01.1956 | S/Sgt. |
| 5384 | RAUSCH | Raymond | 03.01.1956 | C/Inspr. |
| 5385 | GILLESPIE | Robert Reid | 16.01.1956 | Inspr. |
| 5386 | MAY | Geoffrey Ronald | 01.02.1956 | C/Inspr. |
| 5387 | PHILLIPS | Leslie Howard | 27.11.1955 | C/Inspr. |
| 5388 | GOULDING | Ivan Edmund | 20.02.1956 | S/O |
| 5389 | SMALLBONES | St. John Leslie | 01.03.1956 | Supt. |
| 5390 | REYNOLDS | Albert George | 05.03.1956 | S/Sgt. |
| 5391 | SMALLSHAW | Richard Courtney | 16.10.1955 | Const. |
| 5392 | TAYLOR | Joseph Richard | 16.10.1955 | D/S/O |
| 5393 | WEST | Bernard Kenneth | 16.10.1955 | S/O |
| 5394 | ANDREWS | Joseph Martin | 16.10.1955 | Const. |
| 5395 | ISAAC | Peter Leslie | 16.10.1955 | Const. |
| 5396 | JEFFERIES | Patrick Scott | 15.10.1955 | Const. |
| 5397 | CARR | Thomas Edward | 16.10.1955 | Inspr. |
| 5398 | POTTER | Timothy Hugh | 16.10.1955 | C/Inspr. |
| 5399 | SMITH | Walter Peter | 16.10.1955 | Const. |
| 5400 | WOOD | John Lester | 16.10.1955 | Const. |
| 5401 | BREASLEY | Alan Geoffrey | 16.10.1955 | Const. |
| 5402 | LAMB | William Peter | 09.04.1956 | Sgt. |
| 5403 | KERRIGAN | James Conleth | 27.11.1955 | D/S/O |
| 5404 | DIXON | Anthony | 27.11.1955 | D/S/O |
| 5405 | THOMAS | Brian John | 27.11.1955 | Const. |
| 5406 | PENNING | Peter Dale | 27.11.1955 | D/Sgt. |
| 5407 | PATTINSON | Arthur David | 27.11.1955 | Const. |
| 5408 | BARNES | Richard John | 27.11.1955 | Const. |
| 5409 | TOUGH | Brian Robert | 27.11.1955 | Const. |
| 5410 | SMITH | John | 27.11.1955 | D/Sgt. |
| 5411 | BYE | Gerald Russell | 27.11.1955 | Const. |
| 5412 | MURDOCH | Alexander Edward | 27.11.1955 | Const. |
| 5413 | STARMANS | John Richard | 09.12.1955 | Const. |
| 5414 | PHILLIPS | David Viner | 27.11.1955 | S/O |
| 5415 | THOMSON | Alister Walter | 02.05.1956 | C/Inspr. |
| 5416 | HULBERT | David McMillan | 14.05.1956 | Const. |
| 5417 | RUFENACHT | Walter Francis | 25.05.1956 | Const. |
| 5418 | MYLE | Ronald Stanley | 01.06.1956 | S/Sgt. |
| 5419 | SMITH | Cecil John | 01.06.1956 | S/S/O |
| 5420 | FALL | John David | 09.06.1956 | S/O |
| 5421 | COULSON | Robert John | 29.01.1956 | S/O |
| 5422 | GODFREY | Leslie Robert | 29.01.1956 | Const. |
| 5423 | LEEK | Horace Bentley | 29.01.1956 | Const. |
| 5424 | McKENZIE | Noel John | 28.01.1956 | Inspr. |
| 5425 | McTAGGART | Roy | 29.01.1956 | Sgt. |
| 5426 | MAGOWAN | Ian William | 29.01.1956 | Sgt. |
| 5427 | WILDER | Lance George | 29.01.1956 | S/A/Comm |
| 5428 | HOGG | Ian | 29.01.1956 | Const. |
| 5429 | CASH | Michael | 29.01.1956 | Const. |
| 5430 | MELROSE | John Peter | 24.01.1956 | Const. |
| 5431 | HAWKINS | Raymond Searle | 29.01.1956 | Const. |
| 5432 | DAVEY | Roy Dennis | 21.01.1956 | Const. |
| 5433 | WALSH | Patrick Eric | 29.01.1956 | Sgt. |
| 5434 | SANDEMAN | Timothy John | 29.01.1956 | Inspr. |
| 5435 | WHITESIDE | Owen Keith | 29.01.1956 | Const. |
| 5436 | CHAMPION | David Thomas | 29.01.1956 | Const. |
| 5437 | BOWER | William Keith | 08.05.1955 | Const. |
| 5438 | BROWN | James Francis | 10.06.1955 | Const. |
| 5439 | COOKE | Isaac William | 24.07.1955 | Const. |
| 5440 | MOORES | Alec Peter | 02.03.1956 | Supt. |
| 5441 | JACQUES | Anthony Brian | 04.03.1956 | Inspr. |
| 5442 | POWER | Thomas | 04.03.1956 | D/C/Inspr. |
| 5443 | BARTON | Stanley Edward | 04.03.1956 | Const. |
| 5444 | STONE | Christopher John | 04.03.1956 | Sgt. |
| 5445 | PARKER | Clive Vernon | 03.03.1956 | Const. |
| 5446 | SAUNDERS | Michael | 04.03.1956 | Const. |
| 5447 | CARTER | Philip Christopher | 04.03.1956 | Const. |
| 5448 | BUSS | Barry Martin | 02.03.1956 | P/O |
| 5449 | JUDD | Frank Leslie | 04.03.1956 | D/C/Inspr. |
| 5450 | HOWLETT | David Richard | 04.03.1956 | Const. |
| 5451 | BARKS | Frank Herbert | 04.03.1956 | Const. |
| 5452 | STEVENS | Michael Charles | 04.03.1956 | C/Supt. |
| 5453 | BENNETT | Alexander Francis | 04.03.1956 | Const. |
| 5454 | BELLAIRS | Nicholas Peter | 04.03.1956 | Const. |
| 5455 | DEUDNEY | Gary John | 28.02.1956 | S/O |
| 5456 | BRODERICK | Douglas David | 04.03.1956 | Inspr. |
| 5457 | KEMP | John Richard | 04.03.1956 | Const. |
| 5458 | BOYCE | John Arthur | 15.04.1956 | Const. |
| 5459 | CAMERON-BROWN | Alastair | 15.04.1956 | Const. |
| 5460 | BOYD | Nigel Ronald | 15.04.1956 | Const. |
| 5461 | CHAPMAN | Anthony Robin | 15.04.1956 | Const. |
| 5462 | SMITH | Peter Michael | 15.04.1956 | Const. |
| 5463 | BUCHANAN | Peter James | 15.04.1956 | Inspr. |
| 5464 | HAMMOND | Dannid Arnold | 15.04.1956 | Const. |
| 5465 | PLIZARD | Kevin Malcolm | 13.04.1956 | Sgt. |
| 5466 | MILLS | Philip Leonard | 15.04.1956 | D/Inspr. |
| 5467 | ROWEN | Henry Edward | 15.04.1956 | Inspr. |
| 5468 | ADSHEAD | David Ralph | 15.04.1956 | S/O |
| 5469 | GRIMBLY | David Thomas | 15.04.1956 | P/O |
| 5470 | DEETLEFS | Duane | 13.04.1956 | P/O |
| 5471 | STEPHENS | Neil Brian | 15.04.1956 | S/L/Sgt |
| 5472 | DALZIEL | Douglas Malcolm | 15.04.1956 | Const. |
| 5473 | CLACK | John Vincent | 15.04.1956 | Const. |
| 5474 | CROSS | Jack Bertram | 15.04.1956 | Const. |
| 5475 | MASCHWITZ | Herbert John | 15.04.1956 | Const. |
| 5476 | ELDRIDGE | John David | 27.05.1956 | S/O |
| 5477 | SMITH | Arnold August | 27.05.1956 | D/Sgt. |
| 5478 | O'HARA | Michael James | 27.05.1956 | C/Supt. |
| 5479 | LEACH | Michael Leonard | 27.05.1956 | Const. |
| 5480 | MACAULAY | Neil Kilgour | 27.05.1956 | Const. |
| 5481 | GALLOWAY | Michael John | 27.05.1956 | Const. |
| 5482 | EVANS | David Edward | 27.05.1956 | A/Comm |
| 5483 | BLACKER | David Granville | 27.05.1956 | S/Inspr. |
| 5484 | CLOETE | Douglas Cecil | 27.05.1956 | Const. |
| 5485 | CLARK | Carlton William | 27.05.1956 | S/O |
| 5486 | WOOD | Michael Anthony | 27.05.1956 | D/S/O |
| 5487 | MORRIS-EYTON | Ian Robert | 27.05.1956 | Const. |
| 5488 | SEATH | John | 27.05.1956 | Const. |
| 5489 | McFARLANE | Neil | 27.05.1956 | Const. |
| 5490 | STOCK | Philip Rodney | 27.05.1956 | Inspr. |
| 5491 | McMURCHIE | Alfred | 27.05.1956 | Const. |
| 5492 | JAMES | John Michael | 27.05.1956 | Const. |
| 5493 | CAUNCE | Donald Garth | 27.05.1956 | Const. |
| 5494 | SUTHERLAND | Sinclair Henry | 24.06.1956 | Sgt. |
| 5495 | NETTLETON | Walter Traves | 24.06.1956 | Const. |
| 5496 | MILLS | Michael Arthur | 24.06.1956 | Const. |
| 5497 | MOWER | Graham Michael | 24.06.1956 | Supt. |
| 5498 | GILBERT | Ronald MacLennan | 24.06.1956 | Supt. |
| 5499 | ABROMS | Terence Cyril | 24.06.1956 | Supt. |
| 5500 | CHARLESWORTH | Anthony Charles | 24.06.1956 | Const. |
| 5501 | SEWELL | Christopher De Renzy | 24.06.1956 | D/C/Inspr. |
| 5502 | MUNDY | Anthony Richard | 24.06.1956 | Const. |
| 5503 | BIRKETT | Peter Anthony | 23.06.1956 | Const. |
| 5504 | WHITNEY | David Edward | 24.06.1956 | Const. |
| 5505 | FINEGAN | Patrick Oliver | 24.06.1956 | S/O |
| 5506 | PIETERSON | Claude Jeffrey | 24.06.1956 | Const. |
| 5507 | TAYLOR | Brian Harry | 24.06.1956 | Inspr. |
| 5508 | NORRIS | Gordon Calvin | 24.06.1956 | C/Inspr. |
| 5509 | JONES | Michael Anthony | 24.06.1956 | Supt. |
| 5510 | CARTER | Robert Alwin | 24.06.1956 | Const. |
| 5511 | CHRISTIE | John David | 24.06.1956 | Const. |
| 5512 | HARRIS | Peter Goodwin | 24.06.1956 | P/O |
| 5513 | RODD | William George | 24.06.1956 | Const. |
| 5514 | FOWKES | John David | 24.06.1956 | Inspr. |
| 5515 | WHENMAN | John Stuart | 06.08.1956 | Sgt. |
| 5516 | FARROW | Michael William | 05.08.1956 | Sgt. |
| 5517 | HOGG | David Alan | 02.03.1956 | C/Supt. |
| 5518 | MITCHELL | Kenneth William | 05.03.1956 | Const. |
| 5519 | NICHOLSON | Anthony George | 05.08.1956 | Const. |
| 5520 | LATHE | John Christopher | 05.08.1956 | C/Inspr. |
| 5521 | CHRISTIE | David | 05.08.1956 | Const. |
| 5522 | COBURN | Eric Robin | 05.08.1956 | Const. |
| 5523 | JENKINS | Robert | 05.08.1956 | Const. |
| 5524 | BLANCHFIELD | Patrick | 05.08.1956 | Const. |
| 5525 | COSGROVE | Patrick Joseph | 05.08.1956 | Const. |
| 5526 | DEVLIN | Philip | 05.08.1956 | Sgt. |
| 5527 | WILCOX | Brian George | 05.08.1956 | Const. |
| 5528 | LEWIS | Leonard Charles | 05.08.1956 | Const. |
| 5529 | COOPER | John Philip | 05.08.1956 | Const. |
| 5530 | HAGGART | William Donald | 21.08.1956 | C/Inspr. |
| 5531 | DAVIES | Roy | 24.08.1956 | D/C/Inspr. |
| 5532 | MYERS | Christopher Denis | 12.09.1956 | S/Sgt. |
| 5533 | BERRY | Kenneth Percy | 17.09.1956 | S/O |
| 5534 | WATERS | Ian Ashton | 23.09.1956 | Supt. |
| 5535 | McWILLIAM | John Murray | 23.09.1956 | Const. |
| 5536 | DYKE | Roger Stanley | 23.09.1956 | C/Inspr. |
| 5537 | LITTON | George Bryan | 23.09.1956 | S/O |
| 5538 | LANSDOWN | Michael Guy Poole | 23.09.1956 | Const. |
| 5539 | LEARMONTH | Andrew Gilchrist | 23.09.1956 | S/O |
| 5540 | PARKER | Charles Frederick | 23.09.1956 | S/O |
| 5541 | MALLINSON | Richard Christopher | 23.09.1956 | Const. |
| 5542 | SOUTH | Christopher William | 23.09.1956 | Const. |
| 5543 | LEWIS | Ian David | 23.09.1956 | C/Inspr. |
| 5544 | PARKIN | Terence Charles | 06.09.1956 | Const. |
| 5545 | KNIGHT | Stephen James | 23.09.1956 | Const. |
| 5546 | MONEY | William Edward | 23.09.1956 | Const. |
| 5547 | STANLEY | Michael George | 23.09.1956 | Const. |
| 5548 | MICHELSON | Mattew | 23.09.1956 | Inspr. |
| 5549 | RAMSDEN | Geoffrey Charles | 23.09.1956 | Const. |
| 5550 | WILLIAMS | Donald | 23.09.1956 | Const. |
| 5551 | ROSS | William Leonard | 23.09.1956 | Const. |
| 5552 | McGUFFOG | Neil McGlip | 23.09.1956 | Const. |
| 5553 | HOGG | Gerald Andrew | 23.09.1956 | Const. |
| 5554 | MITCHLEY | Charles Walter | 23.09.1956 | S/O |
| 5555 | CUTLER | Kenneth John | 23.09.1956 | Const. |
| 5556 | PAPPAGE | Christopher James | 23.09.1956 | Const. |
| 5557 | FORRESTER | Franz Michael | 23.09.1956 | Const. |
| 5558 | CAHILL | John Brian | 23.09.1956 | Const. |
| 5559 | THOMPSON | George Richard | 01.10.1956 | C/Inspr. |
| 5560 | FRIIS-SMITH | John Humprey | 08.10.1956 | Const. |
| 5561 | JONES | Raymond | 28.10.1956 | S/Sgt. |
| 5562 | SAUL | Eric | 26.10.1956 | Const. |
| 5563 | WATSON | William | 28.10.1956 | Supt. |
| 5564 | COOPER | Frederick Alexander | 28.10.1956 | Supt. |
| 5565 | SCHIERHOUT | Ronald Arthur | 28.10.1956 | Supt. |
| 5566 | Mac DONALD | David John | 28.10.1956 | Const. |
| 5567 | HAMLEY | Richard | 28.10.1956 | C/Supt. |
| 5568 | ANDERSON | Dennis Malcolm | 28.10.1956 | Const. |
| 5569 | LOWTHER | William John | 28.10.1956 | Const. |
| 5570 | PAY | Eric Edward | 28.10.1956 | Supt. |
| 5571 | HEARTH | Raymond Alan | 28.10.1956 | Const. |
| 5572 | McCALLUM | John Douglas | 28.10.1956 | Const. |
| 5573 | McLEAN | Andrew | 28.10.1956 | Const. |
| 5574 | McGHEE | Kevin John | 28.10.1956 | Const. |
| 5575 | GOODALE | Vernon Thorton | 28.10.1956 | Const. |
| 5576 | PHILLIPS | Gerald | 28.10.1956 | Inspr. |
| 5577 | THORNE | John Edward | 28.10.1956 | Const. |
| 5578 | PERRY | Bernard | 28.10.1956 | Const. |
| 5579 | STONE | Gerald Frank | 28.10.1956 | Inspr. |
| 5580 | WOLHUTER | Henry Charles | 28.10.1956 | D/C/Inspr. |
| 5581 | DUNBAR | Hamish Philip | 26.10.1956 | D/C/Inspr. |
| 5582 | BOTHA | Daniel Louwrens | 19.11.1956 | Inspr. |
| 5583 | GIBBS | John Christopher | 01.12.1956 | Const. |
| 5584 | BERRY | John Joseph | 01.12.1956 | S/O |
| 5585 | CROYLE | Angus Eric John | 02.12.1956 | Inspr. |
| 5586 | STOKER | Thomas Andrew | 02.12.1956 | S/O |
| 5587 | MARSHALL | Howard Gerald | 02.12.1956 | A/Comm |

| No. | Surname | First Name | Date | Rank |
|---|---|---|---|---|
| 5588 | ROSS | Dennis | 02.12.1956 | Const. |
| 5589 | PAYNE | Michael Richard | 02.12.1956 | Const. |
| 5590 | JENNINGS | Roy John | 02.12.1956 | C/Supt. |
| 5591 | GOODACRE | Richard John | 02.12.1956 | C/Supt. |
| 5592 | JAMES | Anthony David | 02.12.1956 | S/O |
| 5593 | WILSON | William Swithin | 02.12.1956 | S/O |
| 5594 | GREENWOOD | William Henry | 01.12.1956 | Const. |
| 5595 | CABORN | Bernard James | 02.12.1956 | Const. |
| 5596 | WILSON | John Alfred | 02.12.1956 | Const. |
| 5597 | ATHERTON | John Patrick | 02.12.1956 | Const. |
| 5598 | SANDES | Richard Samuel | 01.12.1956 | S/O |
| 5599 | PATTIE | Thomas Robert | 02.12.1956 | S/O |
| 5600 | CAMPBELL | Patrick Major | 01.12.1956 | Const. |
| 5601 | ROBB | Eric George | 02.12.1956 | Const. |
| 5602 | FEGAN | Patrick Moffat | 02.12.1956 | D/S/O |
| 5603 | ROBERTSON | Malcolm Ian | 02.12.1956 | Const. |
| 5604 | WILCOX | Patrick Werna | 17.12.1956 | C/Inspr. |
| 5605 | FRY | Coulston Thomas | 31.12.1956 | C/Inspr. |
| 5606 | HABBIN | John Frank | 06.01.1957 | Sgt. |
| 5607 | DAVIES | Francis Harold | 06.01.1957 | Const. |
| 5608 | DE BURGH-THOMAS | David Bruce | 06.01.1957 | C/Supt. |
| 5609 | MABIN | Alfred John | 06.01.1957 | S/O |
| 5610 | ROCHE | Nigel James | 06.01.1957 | Const. |
| 5611 | GREEN | John Malcolm | 06.01.1957 | A/Comm |
| 5612 | DAVIES | Peter | 06.01.1957 | Const. |
| 5613 | WHITEHEAD | Anthony James | 06.01.1957 | Inspr. |
| 5614 | LOCKWOOD | Bryan Summer | 06.01.1957 | Const. |
| 5615 | MEAKIN | Thomas | 06.01.1957 | Supt. |
| 5616 | THOMAS | Brian James | 04.01.1957 | Const. |
| 5617 | WILMOT | Austin | 06.01.1957 | Inspr. |
| 5618 | STEVENS | Roger Bailey | 06.01.1957 | S/O |
| 5619 | ENSLIN | Barry George | 08.01.1957 | Sgt. |
| 5620 | GANTRY | John | 06.01.1957 | Const. |
| 5621 | FRITH | Gerald Nigel | 04.01.1957 | Const. |
| 5622 | WALLEY | Robert Nolan | 04.01.1957 | Const. |
| 5623 | MAY | Michael Alan | 04.01.1957 | Supt. |
| 5624 | FERGUSON | Patrick | 04.01.1957 | Supt. |
| 5625 | WAY | William Norman | 04.01.1957 | D/C/Inspr. |
| 5626 | HARRIS | John Dane | 04.01.1957 | Const. |
| 5627 | HENDERSON | Alexander Louis | 04.01.1957 | Const. |
| 5628 | LEE | Colin James | 04.01.1957 | Const. |
| 5629 | RUMBOLD | John Robert | 04.01.1957 | Const. |
| 5630 | WATSON | Donald John | 06.01.1957 | Const. |
| 5631 | BOWERS | Ernest Bennett | 14.01.1957 | Inspr. |
| 5632 | GALE | Derek William | 28.01.1957 | Inspr. |
| 5633 | OSBORNE | Colin | 10.02.1957 | Inspr. |
| 5634 | ROYLE | David Anthony | 10.02.1957 | Inspr. |
| 5635 | RILEY | William Henry | 08.02.1957 | S/O |
| 5636 | McALISTER | James Bruce | 10.02.1957 | S/O |
| 5637 | FLEMMING | Peter James | 10.02.1957 | S/O |
| 5638 | STUBBERFIELD | David Sylvester | 10.02.1957 | Const. |
| 5639 | HOGGARTH | Michael John | 10.02.1957 | Const. |
| 5640 | BRINDLE | Adrian David | 10.02.1957 | Const. |
| 5641 | BOWYER | Harold | 08.02.1957 | Const. |
| 5642 | BABB | Michael Ranleigh | 10.02.1957 | Const. |
| 5643 | BELL | Derek Turnbull | 10.02.1957 | Const. |
| 5644 | MILNER | Timothy William | 08.02.1957 | Const. |
| 5645 | HARRISON | Terence Eldred | 10.02.1957 | Const. |
| 5646 | JACKSON | Martin Benedict | 10.02.1957 | Const. |
| 5647 | COPLEY | William John | 10.02.1957 | Supt. |
| 5648 | ESLER | William James | 08.02.1957 | A/Comm |
| 5649 | NORRIS | Jeremy James | 03.03.1957 | C/Supt. |
| 5650 | TIPPETTS | David John | 03.03.1957 | C/Supt. |
| 5651 | NOBES | Phillip Aubrey | 03.03.1957 | D/S/O |
| 5652 | LINFIELD | Gabriel William | 11.03.1957 | C/Inspr. |
| 5653 | TAYLOR | Michael Francis | 03.03.1957 | C/Inspr. |
| 5654 | NAPIER | George Henry | 15.03.1957 | Sgt. |
| 5655 | FITZPATRICK | Terence Thomas | 03.03.1957 | Sgt. |
| 5657 | BRITLAND | John Curtis | 05.03.1957 | Inspr. |
| 5658 | WHITEHURST | Alan | 03.03.1957 | C/Inspr. |
| 5659 | HOPKINS | Henry John | 03.03.1957 | C/Supt. |
| 5660 | KENT | Ronald William | 03.03.1957 | C/Supt. |
| 5661 | WILSON | Trevor | 17.03.1957 | C/Supt. |
| 5662 | HENSON | Barry Roy | 17.03.1957 | A/Comm |
| 5663 | HUSON | Peter Michael | 17.03.1957 | C/Supt. |
| 5664 | TIPPLE | Adrian Robin | 17.03.1957 | C/Supt. |
| 5665 | ROBINSON | David John | 17.03.1957 | D/Sgt. |
| 5666 | WRIGHT | Anthony Charles | 17.03.1957 | C/Supt. |
| 5667 | TOMS | Stanley Barrymore | 17.03.1957 | S/O |
| 5668 | STANNARD | David Daniel | 17.03.1957 | C/Supt. |
| 5669 | DODD | Maxwell William | 17.03.1957 | S/O |
| 5670 | PRINGLE | Michael John | 17.03.1957 | Const. |
| 5671 | DAVIS | Timothy Walbridge | 17.03.1957 | Const. |
| 5672 | O'REGAN | Kevin Finbarr | 24.03.1957 | S/O |
| 5673 | WILLIAMS | Ralph Marchant | 24.03.1957 | Inspr. |
| 5674 | WILLIAMS | Dennis Hugh | 17.03.1957 | Const. |
| 5675 | WADDON | David Charles | 24.03.1957 | Sgt. |
| 5676 | ANDERSON | Samuel Trevor | 24.03.1957 | C/Inspr. |
| 5677 | SMITH | Robert Bruce | 17.03.1957 | Const. |
| 5678 | HALL | Graham Harold | 24.03.1957 | Const. |
| 5679 | AXWORTHY | Anthony John | 24.03.1957 | Const. |
| 5680 | McDONNELL | Brian | 17.03.1957 | Const. |
| 5681 | HARVEY | Robin Herbert | 24.03.1957 | D/Sgt. |
| 5682 | BROCK | Sydney Peter | 24.03.1957 | C/Supt. |
| 5683 | WALLER | Anthony Wilfred | 18.06.1957 | Inspr. |
| 5684 | HUEY | John Brian | 24.03.1957 | Const. |
| 5685 | CHEETHAM | Raymond Benjamin | 17.03.1957 | S/Sgt. |
| 5686 | RALPH | John Charles | 26.03.1957 | S/Sgt. |
| 5687 | SCHOFIELD | Frank Rhodes | 21.04.1957 | S/Sgt. |
| 5688 | JONES | David John | 21.04.1957 | Const. |
| 5689 | POTTER | John Anthony | 14.04.1957 | A/Comm |
| 5690 | SEALY | Paul Noel a'Court | 14.04.1957 | Const. |
| 5691 | GOWEN | Kenneth James | 14.04.1957 | Inspr. |
| 5692 | LUCAS | John Stanley | 21.04.1957 | Sgt. |
| 5693 | CHINN | Lloyd Arthur John | 14.04.1957 | D/Inspr. |
| 5694 | TERNAHAN | Thomas Alfred | 14.04.1957 | S/O |
| 5695 | SLOMAN | David John | 21.04.1957 | A/Comm |
| 5696 | PEDEN | Alistair Harkness | 14.04.1957 | Const. |
| 5697 | GIBSON | Derek Reid | 21.04.1957 | D/S/O |
| 5698 | GUDGEON | Michael Thomas | 14.04.1957 | D/S/O |
| 5699 | CATTERALL | Roger Wells | 21.04.1957 | Const. |
| 5700 | PAYNE | Peter James | 14.04.1957 | Supt. |
| 5701 | BOUCHIER | Anthony Mark | 14.04.1957 | Const. |
| 5702 | ROGERSON | David Henry Neil | 21.04.1957 | D/Sgt. |
| 5703 | HANKINSON | Ernie John | 14.04.1957 | D/Sgt. |
| 5704 | BRETT | Michael Henry | 14.04.1957 | Supt. |
| 5705 | BISHOP | John Terence | 21.04.1957 | D/Inspr. |
| 5706 | BARR | Graham Alexander | 10.05.1957 | Supt. |
| 5707 | HAMBER | Thomas Howard | 06.05.1957 | Const. |
| 5708 | BROWN | Frederick James | 06.05.1957 | Const. |
| 5709 | COLMAN | Benedict James | 06.05.1957 | Const. |
| 5710 | McDOUGALL | Duncan Stuart | 06.05.1957 | Supt. |
| 5711 | CHAPPE | de Leonval Tudor | 06.05.1957 | D/S/O |
| 5712 | KENT | Hugh Ross | 06.05.1957 | S/S/O |
| 5713 | ROBERTS | Donovan Stevenson | 06.05.1957 | Const. |
| 5714 | MAUREL | Marie Joseph | 06.05.1957 | Const. |
| 5715 | BANET | Sydney Phillip | 06.05.1957 | Const. |
| 5716 | BRADE | Richard Widdicombe | 06.05.1957 | D/C/Inspr. |
| 5717 | STEVENS | Graeme Stuart | 14.05.1957 | D/C/Supt. |
| 5718 | Mac PHAIL | Colin Campbell | 26.05.1957 | Inspr. |
| 5719 | LEACH | Arthur Herbert | 01.06.1957 | Inspr. |
| 5720 | WHEATLEY | Bryan Morton | 29.06.1957 | Inspr. |
| 5721 | ELSE | John Jeremy | 30.06.1957 | Inspr. |
| 5722 | MOORE | Thomas Howard | 30.06.1957 | C/Inspr. |
| 5723 | BALL | John Henry | 30.06.1957 | Const. |
| 5724 | TWELL | Gerald | 30.06.1957 | Sgt. |
| 5726 | CURLING | Nigel Drummond | 30.06.1957 | Const. |
| 5727 | COOLBEAR | Peter | 30.06.1957 | D/Inspr. |
| 5728 | LAWSON | Derek | 30.06.1957 | C/Supt. |
| 5729 | CROWS | Brian Raymond | 28.06.1957 | Inspr. |
| 5730 | CROWE | John Fergus | 30.06.1957 | Inspr. |
| 5731 | HACKET | Raymond Bingham | 30.06.1957 | Const. |
| 5732 | CUMMING | Brian James | 30.06.1957 | C/Inspr. |
| 5733 | MARIAS | Peter William | 28.06.1957 | Const. |
| 5734 | WERTH | Hermann Ernest | 28.06.1957 | Const. |
| 5735 | KAY | Ralph Glynn | 28.06.1957 | Const. |
| 5736 | SCALES | Peter Frank | 01.07.1957 | S/Sgt. |
| 5737 | JENNINGS | Horace Rowland | 01.08.1957 | C/Inspr. |
| 5738 | SMITH | Donovan Esmond | 01.08.1957 | Inspr. |
| 5739 | WATKINSON | Kenneth Longden | 04.08.1957 | Const. |
| 5740 | WILSON | Guy Trevor | 04.08.1957 | Const. |
| 5741 | MILLAR | Alec. Cochrane | 04.08.1957 | Const. |
| 5742 | LANGLEY | Russell Hugh | 06.08.1957 | Const. |
| 5743 | HARLOW | Michael John | 04.08.1957 | Const. |
| 5744 | SMITH | Trevor Peter | 01.08.1957 | Const. |
| 5745 | SCOREY | Ian Peter | 04.08.1957 | Const. |
| 5746 | ALLAN | Raymond Phillip | 04.08.1957 | C/Supt. |
| 5747 | CLARKE | John Aldridge | 04.08.1957 | Const. |
| 5748 | WHITE | Clive Edward | 04.08.1957 | Const. |
| 5749 | SHEWELL | Paul Frederick | 01.08.1957 | Supt. |
| 5750 | HART | George Filmer | 05.08.1957 | Const. |
| 5751 | GAMBLE | Ernest Richard | 04.08.1957 | Const. |
| 5752 | COXON | Colin Frank | 31.08.1957 | S/Sgt. |
| 5753 | WILFORD | William Nicholson | 04.08.1957 | Const. |
| 5754 | AYRTON-WHITE | Michael Henry | 06.09.1957 | C/Supt. |
| 5755 | EDWARDS | Stewart Heath | 06.09.1957 | Supt. |
| 5756 | NICHOLLS | Peter John | 02.09.1957 | Supt. |
| 5757 | MILTON | Ian Tobertson | 06.09.1957 | Supt. |
| 5758 | MACKAY | Barry Grainger | 02.09.1957 | Supt. |
| 5759 | Mac INTOSH | Gordon Ramsay | 06.09.1957 | Const. |
| 5760 | TORRANCE | Malcolm Symington | 02.09.1957 | Const. |
| 5761 | FAIRER-SMITH | John | 02.09.1957 | D/S/O |
| 5762 | BRUCE | David Robert | 09.09.1957 | D/P/O |
| 5763 | BRISCOE | Lionel John | 02.09.1957 | Const. |
| 5764 | O'CONNOR | Charles Patrick | 06.09.1957 | Const. |
| 5765 | KIPLING | John Anthony | 06.09.1957 | Const. |
| 5766 | FAIRLIE | George David | 03.09.1957 | P/O |
| 5767 | McCARTNEY | Barry Joseph | 22.09.1957 | Sgt. |
| 5768 | EVANS | Clive Joseph | 29.09.1957 | S/Sgt. |
| 5769 | ROBERTS | Victor Henry | 29.09.1957 | Const. |
| 5770 | BROADLEY | Frank Edgar | 29.09.1957 | Const. |
| 5771 | LEWIS | Peter Michael | 30.09.1957 | Inspr. |
| 5772 | CUFF | David Patrick | 30.09.1957 | Const. |
| 5773 | MOONY | David James | 30.09.1957 | Const. |
| 5774 | OWEN | Roger John | 30.09.1957 | Inspr. |
| 5775 | HENDRY | John | 02.10.1957 | S/O |
| 5776 | HAMLING | James Taylor | 29.09.1957 | S/Sgt. |
| 5777 | JOHNSON | Gerald Ansel | 01.11.1957 | S/O |
| 5778 | PURKIS | Alexander | 01.11.1957 | C/Inspr. |
| 5779 | ROSS | Marcus Patrick | 08.12.1957 | D/Inspr. |
| 5780 | DOYLE | Alun Vaughan | 08.12.1957 | C/Inspr. |
| 5781 | WILLIAMS | Hugh Norman | 08.12.1957 | Const. |
| 5782 | TAYLOR | Edward Austin | 08.12.1957 | Inspr. |
| 5783 | PADGET | Auvengne | 08.12.1957 | Const. |
| 5784 | RAATH | James Stewart | 08.12.1957 | Const. |
| 5785 | YOUNGER | John Mathew | 08.12.1957 | Inspr. |
| 5786 | McFADYEAN | William | 08.12.1957 | Const. |
| 5787 | O'CONNELL | Lionel Roland | 09.12.1957 | Const. |
| 5788 | BAKER | Bazil Geoffrey | 09.12.1957 | Inspr. |
| 5789 | DE LORME | Geoffrey Andrew | 09.12.1957 | P/O |
| 5790 | JAMIESON | Neil Hammond | 08.12.1957 | Const. |
| 5791 | DEEKS | Guy Alvin | 08.01.1958 | Const. |
| 5792 | BALL | David Christopher | 08.01.1958 | Const. |
| 5793 | RUSHWORTH | John Anthony | 08.01.1958 | C/Supt. |

| No. | Surname | First Name | Date | Rank |
|---|---|---|---|---|
| 5795 | READE | Gifford Stafford | 08.01.1958 | D/C/Inspr. |
| 5796 | AUSTIN | John William | 08.01.1958 | Const. |
| 5797 | HINES | Michael Norman | 08.01.1958 | Const. |
| 5798 | OSBORNE | John Robert | 08.01.1958 | S/D/Sgt. |
| 5799 | LORENTZ | Roger Dixon | 08.01.1958 | Const. |
| 5800 | NAUDE | Thomas John | 18.01.1958 | Supt. |
| 5801 | MARTIN | Lionel David | 08.01.1958 | Supt. |
| 5802 | WOOD | Kenneth | 03.02.1958 | Inspr |
| 5803 | WILSON | Christopher Robert | 03.02.1958 | Const. |
| 5804 | WILSON | John William | 03.02.1958 | Const. |
| 5805 | ARMSTRONG | Peter | 04.02.1958 | Sgt. |
| 5806 | PARRY | Stephen John | 03.02.1958 | Inspr. |
| 5807 | WEBB | Alastair James | 03.02.1958 | D/C/Inspr. |
| 5808 | MASSEY | David Hilton | 03.02.1958 | D/Inspr |
| 5809 | STANTON | Peter Henry | 03.02.1958 | D/Inspr |
| 5810 | WALSH | Peter | 03.02.1958 | Const. |
| 5811 | HARVEY | Robert Anthony | 03.02.1958 | Const. |
| 5812 | SINGLETON | Thomas Derek | 03.02.1958 | Const. |
| 5813 | THOMAS | David Eric | 06.02.1958 | Const. |
| 5814 | RUSSELL | Derek Douglas | 03.02.1958 | Const. |
| 5815 | COXWELL | William Robert | 03.02.1958 | Const. |
| 5816 | GORMAN | John Michael | 03.02.1958 | Const. |
| 5817 | TURNER | Brian William | 31.03.1958 | Const. |
| 5818 | BROMLEY | Barry | 31.03.1958 | S/O |
| 5819 | RICHARDS | Gwyn Joseph | 31.03.1958 | Const. |
| 5820 | ROBERTS | Robert Mathew | 31.03.1958 | Inspr |
| 5821 | CUERDEN | John Desmond | 31.03.1958 | S/O |
| 5822 | MARTIN | John Kenneth | 31.03.1958 | C/Supt. |
| 5823 | CHATFIELD | John Bryan | 31.03.1958 | Const. |
| 5824 | PRITCHARD | John Llewellyn | 31.03.1958 | Const. |
| 5825 | RABJOHN | Arthur Robert | 31.03.1958 | Const. |
| 5826 | CUERDEN | Herbert Nigel | 31.03.1958 | Inspr. |
| 5827 | SCUTT | Angus Gordon | 31.03.1958 | S/O |
| 5828 | LACEY | Edwin Ernest | 31.03.1958 | Const. |
| 5829 | BESLEY | Michael Edward | 31.03.1958 | Const. |
| 5830 | NIELD | Reginald Joseph | 31.03.1958 | Const. |
| 5831 | WADSWORTH | Denis Ian | 19.05.1958 | S/L/Sgt. |
| 5832 | PULLAR | David Ian | 02.06.1958 | D/S/C |
| 5833 | Mac INTOSH | Colin Reid | 02.06.1958 | D/S/O |
| 5834 | COCKCROFT | Michael Anthony | 02.06.1958 | Supt. |
| 5835 | ANDERSON | Robin Adrian | 02.06.1958 | C/Supt. |
| 5836 | COLEPEPER | Peter James | 02.06.1958 | Sgt. |
| 5837 | MERVYN-SMITH | John Thorburn | 02.06.1958 | Const. |
| 5838 | RUSSELL | Malcolm John | 02.06.1958 | Const. |
| 5839 | BECKS | Colin Cyril | 02.06.1958 | Const. |
| 5840 | SMITH | Colin Gower | 02.06.1958 | Const. |
| 5841 | WYATT | Garth | 02.06.1958 | C/Inspr. |
| 5842 | STARR | Derek Belmore | 16.07.1958 | Inspr. |
| 5843 | WALKER | John Belmore | 01.07.1958 | C/Inspr. |
| 5844 | BICCARD | Rossiin McGlure | 07.07.1958 | P/O |
| 5845 | RENDALL | Gordon Frank | 09.07.1958 | P/O |
| 5846 | SMITH | Vaughan Arthur | 07.07.1958 | Const. |
| 5847 | STARLING | Rollo Naimby | 07.07.1958 | Const. |
| 5848 | CLINKER | David John | 07.07.1958 | D/Cst. |
| 5849 | DYER | Neville Allin | 07.07.1958 | DPO |
| 5850 | VINCENT | Robert Arthur | 07.07.1958 | Supt. |
| 5851 | BEAN | Hilton Rex | 07.07.1958 | Const. |
| 5852 | BROWN | James Malcolm | 16.07.1958 | Supt. |
| 5853 | MOODY | Peter James | 01.07.1958 | D/S/O |
| 5854 | PARNELL | Peter John | 03.08.1958 | Supt. |
| 5855 | ALBYN | Terence Francis | 03.08.1958 | Const. |
| 5856 | BRADLEY | Peter John | 03.08.1958 | Supt. |
| 5857 | ISAAC | Alan Outten | 03.08.1958 | Supt. |
| 5858 | JACK | Michael Frederick | 03.08.1958 | Const. |
| 5859 | Mac NIVEN | Donald Thomson | 03.08.1958 | Const. |
| 5860 | GRIERSON | William Douglas | 03.08.1958 | Supt. |
| 5861 | SANDENBERGH | Alexis John Kerr | 03.08.1958 | Const. |
| 5862 | BLATCHLEY | Simon John Dillion | 03.08.1958 | Const. |
| 5863 | STEAD | Harold Meredith | 03.08.1958 | Const. |
| 5864 | FARRELL | Michael | 03.08.1958 | C/Inspr. |
| 5865 | DE CHAZAL | Edmund Antoinne | 03.08.1958 | Const. |
| 5866 | MAIN | Keith Farrow | 03.08.1958 | S/Sgt. |
| 5867 | MARSHALL | Derek | 03.08.1958 | C/Inspr. |
| 5868 | HAPGOOD-STRICKLAND | Sidney John | 01.09.1958 | Const. |
| 5869 | MAY | Brian John | 01.09.1958 | S/O |
| 5870 | VAN DER MERWE | Phillipus Johannes | 01.09.1958 | S/O |
| 5871 | LE SUEUR | Hepburn Roye | 01.09.1958 | D/Sgt. |
| 5872 | HART | Winston Bert | 15.09.1958 | Supt. |
| 5873 | WRIGHT | Trevor Sidney | 15.09.1958 | Const. |
| 5874 | HATTON | Garth Lionel | 01.09.1958 | D/Cst. |
| 5875 | BEGG | Peter James | 01.09.1958 | D/S/O |
| 5876 | HENDRY | Roy William | 05.01.1959 | D/Inspr. |
| 5877 | Mac KINNON | John Angus | 01.09.1958 | C/Inspr. |
| 5878 | TAYLOR | John Alan | 01.09.1958 | C/Supt. |
| 5879 | STOW | David Graham | 01.09.1958 | Inspr. |
| 5880 | McMILLAN | Stanley Brian | 01.09.1958 | Const. |
| 5881 | CAPPLETON | Michael Allen | 29.09.1958 | Inspr. |
| 5882 | SCOTT | John Picton | 02.06.1958 | Inspr. |
| 5883 | GOULDSTONE | Murray Neil | 29.09.1958 | Sgt. |
| 5884 | CROOKS | Michael John | 29.09.1958 | Const. |
| 5885 | FITTON | Michael Geoffrey | 29.09.1958 | Const. |
| 5886 | WYNN | Lawrence William | 29.09.1958 | D/Cst. |
| 5887 | NEWTON | Clive | 29.09.1958 | Supt. |
| 5888 | COOK | Neville | 29.09.1958 | Const. |
| 5889 | ANDERSON | David Hugh | 29.09.1958 | Const. |
| 5890 | ANDREWS | Charles Lawrence | 29.09.1958 | Const. |
| 5891 | SCOTT | Keith Alfred | 29.09.1958 | Const. |
| 5892 | GAPLAND | John Arthur | 29.09.1958 | Const. |
| 5893 | HAYDEN | Patrick | 29.09.1958 | D/S/O |
| 5894 | FORRESTER-JONES | George Charles | 29.09.1958 | D/S/O |
| 5895 | ELKINS | Peter William | 29.09.1958 | Const. |
| 5896 | BEDDARD | Timothy Richard | 29.09.1958 | Const. |
| 5897 | PAPENFUS | Robert Kenneth | 13.10.1958 | D/C/Inspr. |
| 5898 | SAUL | Eric | 13.10.1958 | A/Comm |
| 5899 | Mac LEAN | John Andrew | 20.10.1958 | D/Cst. |
| 5900 | FORDELL | John Wilson | 03.11.1958 | Const. |
| 5901 | FRASER | Ian Corrick | 03.11.1958 | Const. |
| 5902 | STEWART | John McIntyre | 22.10.1958 | Sgt. |
| 5903 | PIRIE | John Birch | 03.11.1958 | Const. |
| 5904 | PIPER | Keith Raymond | 03.11.1958 | Const. |
| 5905 | ROBSON | John Westerdale | 03.11.1958 | Const. |
| 5906 | WELLS | Martin Neil | 03.11.1958 | S/O |
| 5907 | WILSON | Peter Ronald | 03.11.1958 | S/O |
| 5908 | McLEAN | Ian | 20.10.1958 | Const. |
| 5909 | CRENSHAW | John Seckham | 03.11.1958 | Const. |
| 5910 | CUTHBERT | Christopher John | 03.11.1958 | Const. |
| 5911 | BAGLEY QPM CPM | John Stephen | 03.11.1958 | Const. |
| 5912 | FURNIVAL | Wayn John Peter | 20.10.1958 | Const. |
| 5913 | LAWRENCE | Michael Patrick | 03.11.1958 | S/O |
| 5914 | FEENY | Alan | 17.11.1958 | S/S/O |
| 5915 | GREEN | David Wilson | 01.12.1958 | Supt. |
| 5916 | GEORGE | Rodney Norton | 01.12.1958 | C/Supt. |
| 5917 | FINNIGAN | Frederick Robert | 01.12.1958 | Const. |
| 5918 | SKAE | David Wilson | 01.12.1958 | D/Cst. |
| 5919 | CALL | Michael William | 01.12.1958 | Const. |
| 5920 | WILLS | Peter Henry | 01.12.1958 | Const. |
| 5921 | NICHOLLS | Trevor Edward | 01.12.1958 | S/O |
| 5922 | COMPTON | Anthony Conrad | 01.12.1958 | Supt. |
| 5923 | SEWARD | Donald James | 01.12.1958 | Supt. |
| 5924 | COMERFORD | Victor James | 01.12.1958 | Const. |
| 5925 | KETCHLEY | John Edward | 01.12.1958 | C/Inspr. |
| 5926 | SHIEL | Gordon Angus | 17.11.1958 | D/S/O |
| 5927 | McDONALD | Kenneth Edwin | 17.11.1958 | Const. |
| 5928 | VAN DYK | Robert Derek | 15.12.1958 | Inspr. |
| 5929 | SWIFT | Roy Penton | 15.12.1958 | S/L/Sgt |
| 5930 | GARDNER | John Allan | 15.12.1958 | Sgt. |
| 5931 | CUNNINGHAM | Anthony Rex | 15.12.1958 | Const. |
| 5932 | DAVEY | | 15.12.1958 | Const. |
| 5933 | ELLIS | Clive Melvin | 15.12.1958 | Const. |
| 5934 | MASON | Frederick Charles | 15.12.1958 | C/Supt. |
| 5935 | PRINCE | Lawrence William | 15.12.1958 | C/Inspr. |
| 5936 | CAPPER | Roger James | 15.12.1958 | C/Inspr. |
| 5937 | DAWSON | Barry Edwin | 15.12.1958 | Supt. |
| 5938 | BOTHA | Johannes Jacobus | 15.12.1958 | Supt. |
| 5939 | SUTHERLAND | Victor Andrew | 15.12.1958 | Const. |
| 5940 | CORDON | Clive Dirk | 15.12.1958 | S/O |
| 5941 | COETZEE | Wentzel Christoffel | 15.12.1958 | S/O |
| 5942 | BEATTIE | Ian | 15.12.1958 | D/Inspr. |
| 5943 | BORRETT | Raymond Paul | 05.01.1959 | D/Sgt |
| 5944 | Mac CILLIVRAY | Gordon Neish | 05.01.1959 | Const. |
| 5945 | FOULIS | John Hamilton | 05.01.1959 | Inspr. |
| 5946 | CLARK | Michael Charles | 05.01.1959 | D/S/O |
| 5947 | EDWARDS | Martin Richard | 05.01.1959 | Const. |
| 5948 | UDAL | Anthony Bruce | 05.01.1959 | Const. |
| 5949 | MACHAN | Anthony Arthur | 05.01.1959 | Const. |
| 5950 | FOULIS | Michael John | 05.01.1959 | S/O |
| 5951 | LAMB | John Ralph | 05.01.1959 | P/O |
| 5952 | ROACH | George Malcolm | 05.01.1959 | D/Sgt |
| 5953 | NATHAN | Michael Halley | 05.01.1959 | S/Inspr. |
| 5954 | WRENCH | John | 05.01.1959 | Const. |
| 5955 | BULL | Ernest Trevor | 05.01.1959 | Const. |
| 5956 | KENNEDY | David Alan | 12.01.1959 | S/O |
| 5957 | RYCROFT | Frederick David | 12.01.1959 | Const. |
| 5958 | ISEMONGER | Richard Benson | 12.01.1959 | C/Supt. |
| 5959 | MARRIOTT | John Bryan | 12.01.1959 | C/Supt. |
| 5960 | DRAKES | Hugh Busson | 12.01.1959 | Const. |
| 5961 | McDERMID | Duncan Ronald | 12.01.1959 | D/C/Inspr. |
| 5962 | KRUGER | Paul | 12.01.1959 | Inspr. |
| 5963 | ALLANBY | Athol Blyth | 12.01.1959 | P/O |
| 5964 | PAPE | Leonard Neil | 12.01.1959 | Const. |
| 5965 | FITZGERALD | Peter Graham | 12.01.1959 | Inspr. |
| 5966 | WILLIAMS | Peter John | 13.01.1959 | Const. |
| 5967 | McGREGOR | Dudley Michael | 16.01.1959 | Const. |
| 5968 | HATCH | George Andrew | 02.02.1959 | Inspr. |
| 5969 | BOSHOFF | Bernard William | 09.03.1959 | Supt. |
| 5970 | TAYLOR | David Joseph | 09.03.1959 | Const. |
| 5971 | HEYWORTH | Stephen Peter | 09.03.1959 | Const. |
| 5972 | TYRRELL | John Clift | 09.03.1959 | Const. |
| 5973 | McKEND | Ian | 09.03.1959 | Sgt. |
| 5974 | HALL | David George | 09.03.1959 | Const. |
| 5975 | ABBOTTS | Michael Sydney | 09.03.1959 | Const. |
| 5976 | SEAWARD | Nigel Wilfred | 09.03.1959 | C/Inspr. |
| 5977 | LEBISH | Roger Dunbar | 09.03.1959 | Sgt. |
| 5978 | THOM | Brian Bateson | 09.03.1959 | Const. |
| 5979 | WILLIAM | Brian Eric | 09.03.1959 | P/O |
| 5980 | GWILT | Geoffrey Norman | 09.03.1959 | Supt. |
| 5981 | HALKIER | Phillip Michael | 09.03.1959 | Const. |
| 5982 | DURSTON | Peter Albert | 09.03.1959 | A/Comm |
| 5983 | McMANNON | John | 09.03.1959 | Const. |
| 5984 | LATHAM | Harold Russell | 21.03.1959 | Sgt. |
| 5985 | NORTON | Michael John | 09.03.1959 | D/S/O |
| 5986 | CLARKE | Keith Cameron | 17.03.1959 | Const. |
| 5987 | LEONARD | Leslie Harold | 01.04.1959 | Const. |
| 5988 | EVANS | Peter Thomas | 09.03.1959 | Const. |
| 5989 | SEEGERS | Peter Jacobus | 09.03.1959 | Const. |
| 5990 | BOTHA | Dirk Wouter | 16.03.1959 | P/O |
| 5991 | JOSS | Donald William | 11.03.1959 | D/S/O |
| 5992 | SMITH | Anthony Brian | 09.03.1959 | Supt. |
| 5993 | ANDERSSON | Anthony Llewellyn | 09.03.1959 | Const. |
| 5994 | WILSON | James Kitchener | 11.03.1959 | Const. |
| 5995 | SPENCE | William Frank | 10.03.1959 | Const. |
| 5996 | WILES | William Alan | 27.04.1959 | S/Inspr. |
| 5997 | ALLEN | Timothy Kennard | 27.04.1959 | A/Comm |
| 5998 | DUNBAR | Ian Patrick | 27.04.1959 | Const. |
| 5999 | LANE | Peter John | 27.04.1959 | Const. |
| 6000 | FINCH | Peter Jack | 27.04.1959 | S/C/Inspr. |
| 6001 | BLACK | Alistair James | 28.04.1959 | C/Supt. |

| No. | Surname | First Names | Date | Rank |
|---|---|---|---|---|
| 6002 | MARLEY | Richard David | 27.04.1959 | Const. |
| 6003 | HULLEY | Ian Richard | 27.04.1959 | Const. |
| 6004 | MAY | Paul Richard | 27.04.1959 | D/Inspr. |
| 6005 | OPPERMAN | Victor | 28.04.1959 | D/Cst. |
| 6006 | MUSGRAVE | David Richard | 27.04.1959 | Const. |
| 6007 | SCHONKEN | Robert John | 27.04.1959 | D/C/Inspr. |
| 6008 | THOMAS | Bryan Melville | 27.04.1959 | Const. |
| 6009 | DOWDESWELL | Richard Peter | 27.04.1959 | Const. |
| 6010 | MAY | George Richard | 27.04.1959 | S/O |
| 6011 | MEINTJIES | Lucas Cornelius | 27.04.1959 | S/O |
| 6012 | MOSCARDI | Peter Edward | 27.04.1959 | Const. |
| 6013 | DE BRES | Ronald | 30.04.1959 | Inspr. |
| 6014 | BONIFACE | Neville | 01.06.1959 | C/Inspr. |
| 6015 | PATTERSON | Alistair | 08.06.1959 | A/Comm |
| 6016 | HUGGINS | Derek Albert | 08.06.1959 | D/Inspr. |
| 6017 | HILL | John Robert | 08.06.1959 | Const. |
| 6018 | PARFITT | Keith Barry | 08.06.1959 | Det |
| 6019 | McKAY | Winston Brian | 08.06.1959 | D/Sgt. |
| 6020 | MOMMSEN | Donald Wellesley | 08.06.1959 | S/O |
| 6021 | TOOHER | Terence John | 08.06.1959 | S/O |
| 6022 | BEATON | Kenneth Cameron | 08.06.1959 | S/O |
| 6023 | ELDERKIN | Roy | 08.06.1959 | Const. |
| 6024 | FERREIRA | Hendrick Johannes | 08.06.1959 | Const. |
| 6025 | LE ROUX | Gerald | 08.06.1959 | Const. |
| 6026 | RIGBY | Peter John | 08.06.1959 | Const. |
| 6027 | BURTON | Michael Leonard | 08.06.1959 | Const. |
| 6028 | ARNOLD | David Weston | 01.07.1959 | Supt. |
| 6029 | TENNANT | James Ross | 07.07.1959 | Supt. |
| 6030 | CLARKE | Robin George | 06.07.1959 | D/Sgt. |
| 6031 | KERBY | Antony John | 16.12.1959 | P/O |
| 6032 | POSTANCE | David Christopher | 06.07.1959 | Const. |
| 6033 | WHINES | John Richard | 06.07.1959 | Const. |
| 6034 | WILLOUGHBY | David Frederick | 06.07.1959 | Const. |
| 6035 | MILLS | Thomas George | 06.07.1959 | Const. |
| 6036 | CRUIKSHANKS | Donald Kenneth | 06.07.1959 | Const. |
| 6037 | VERSTER | Ockert John | 06.07.1959 | D/P/O |
| 6038 | RANKIN | Alexander Charles | 06.07.1959 | Const. |
| 6039 | MURRAY | Robert Ian | 06.07.1959 | Const. |
| 6040 | BROOKE | Frank Albert | 06.07.1959 | Const. |
| 6041 | ANDERSON | Colin John | 06.07.1959 | Const. |
| 6042 | STEAD | John Douglas | 06.07.1959 | Const. |
| 6043 | WILKINS | Barry Maxwell | 27.07.1959 | Const. |
| 6044 | NEL | Brian Frank | 13.08.1959 | Const. |
| 6045 | SERCOMBE | Ian Howard | 13.08.1959 | Det |
| 6046 | FERGUSON | Neil | 17.08.1959 | Const. |
| 6047 | NAUDE | Dudley Frederick | 13.08.1959 | C/Inspr. |
| 6048 | DICKSON | David William | 13.08.1959 | Const. |
| 6049 | STROUTS | John Murton | 15.08.1959 | S/O |
| 6050 | GIBBS | Brian John Cyril | 20.08.1959 | Const. |
| 6051 | GILES | Robert Brian | 13.08.1959 | Supt |
| 6052 | GILLEY | Barrie Edward | 13.08.1959 | Const. |
| 6053 | BAYNES | Frederick | 13.08.1959 | Const. |
| 6054 | SMITH | Basil Lawrence | 13.08.1959 | Const. |
| 6055 | CASTLE | Alan Richard | 20.08.1959 | S/O |
| 6056 | JAMIESON | Robert John | 13.08.1959 | Const. |
| 6057 | TASKER | Michael John | 31.08.1959 | Const. |
| 6058 | POWERBANK | Michael John | 31.08.1959 | Const. |
| 6059 | IBBITT | Laurence Arthur | 31.08.1959 | D/C/Inspr. |
| 6060 | POLLARD | Christopher John | 31.08.1959 | C/Inspr. |
| 6061 | CHAPMAN | Roger Alan | 31.08.1959 | Const. |
| 6062 | DEAN | Melvyn Geoffrey | 31.08.1959 | Const. |
| 6063 | STOCK | Alan Peter | 31.08.1959 | Const. |
| 6064 | MILNE | Rory Campbell | 31.08.1959 | C/Inspr. |
| 6065 | AMOR | Antony William | 31.08.1959 | Const. |
| 6066 | STAPLETON | Michael Basil | 31.08.1959 | Const. |
| 6067 | TERRY | Alan George | 31.08.1959 | Supt. |
| 6068 | GEDDES | Gordon James | 31.08.1959 | S/O |
| 6069 | GOODRICH | Colin Dudley | 14.09.1959 | Const. |
| 6071 | ALBRIGHT | Richard James | 31.08.1959 | Const. |
| 6072 | LONG | David Sydney | 31.08.1959 | Const. |
| 6073 | McDONALD | Trevor | 06.10.1959 | C/Insp |
| 6074 | WEBSTER | Barrie Keith | 28.10.1959 | Const. |
| 6075 | TIFFIN | Barry James | 28.10.1959 | S/O |
| 6076 | CULLINGWORTH | Brian | 28.10.1959 | Inspr. |
| 6077 | THEUNISSEN | Andrew Richard | 28.10.1959 | Const. |
| 6078 | RADFORD | John | 28.10.1959 | C/Supt. |
| 6079 | McLACHLAN | Dudley Neville | 30.10.1959 | D/C/I |
| 6080 | WRAY | Hilton Eugene | 28.10.1959 | D/S/O |
| 6081 | BLITENTHALL | Brian John | 28.10.1959 | P/O |
| 6082 | STIDOLPH | Jack | 20.10.1959 | Det |
| 6083 | DE ROBECK | Hugh | 28.10.1959 | Const. |
| 6084 | SCOTT | Keith Alfred | 14.11.1959 | Const. |
| 6085 | ZWICKY | Quinton Edward | 20.11.1959 | S/O |
| 6086 | GRIST | Peter James | 30.11.1959 | C/Supt. |
| 6087 | HICKINBOTHAM | George Harvey | 30.11.1959 | Supt |
| 6088 | BOWKER | Gerald Francis | 27.11.1959 | S/O |
| 6089 | CALDERWOOD | Michael | 30.11.1959 | Sgt. |
| 6090 | GARDINER | Neville Henry | 30.11.1959 | D/Sgt. |
| 6091 | Mac KENZIE | David Archibald | 30.11.1959 | C/Supt. |
| 6092 | TODDUN | Ian Walter | 27.11.1959 | Const. |
| 6093 | BENNYWORTH | Dennis Henry | 30.11.1959 | Det |
| 6094 | BEAN | Charles John | 27.11.1959 | Const. |
| 6095 | DAKIN | Peter Ernest | 30.11.1959 | Const. |
| 6096 | BRIDGEWOOD | Bruce William | 30.11.1959 | Const. |
| 6097 | PAINTING | Edward James | 30.11.1959 | C/Supt. |
| 6098 | SIMPSON | Joseph Mark | 30.11.1959 | Det |
| 6099 | MILES | Ronald Hector | 30.11.1959 | Const. |
| 6100 | FOSTER | Christopher John | 30.11.1959 | D/S/O |
| 6101 | COTTON | Alexander Charles | 07.12.1959 | Inspr. |
| 6102 | JOHNSON | Peter Anthony | 16.12.1959 | Supt. |
| 6103 | SUMMERTON | Michael Roger | 16.12.1959 | S/O |
| 6104 | KIMBLE | Antony John | 16.12.1959 | P/O |
| 6105 | HUTCHISON | George | 16.12.1959 | Const. |
| 6106 | WIDE | George Victor | 16.12.1959 | D/S/O |
| 6107 | KEYSER | Heinrich Wilhelm | 16.12.1959 | Supt. |
| 6108 | WATERMEYER | Peter John | 16.12.1959 | Supt. |
| 6109 | PITMAN | Christopher Michael | 16.12.1959 | Inspr. |
| 6110 | DOUGLAS | Michael James | 16.12.1959 | Const. |
| 6111 | BEVERIDGE | Malcolm David | 16.12.1959 | Const. |
| 6112 | COETZEE | Hendrick Schalk | 16.12.1959 | S/O |
| 6113 | AIREY | Richard Nigel | 16.12.1959 | S/O |
| 6114 | STANDOW | Glenroy | 16.12.1959 | Const. |
| 6115 | GREEN | David George | 04.01.1960 | C/Insp. |
| 6116 | BYE | Gerald Russell | 25.01.1960 | D/S/O |
| 6117 | EDWARDS | Roy William | 08.02.1960 | C/Inspr. |
| 6118 | KEYSER | Patrick Jacques | 04.02.1960 | D/Inspr. |
| 6119 | BURBIDGE | Edward John | 08.02.1960 | Const. |
| 6120 | PARRY | David Llewelyn | 08.02.1960 | Supt. |
| 6121 | HARVEY | Michael George | 08.02.1960 | Supt. |
| 6122 | EVANS | Richard Evan | 08.02.1960 | Const. |
| 6123 | PYM | Brian Kenneth | 08.02.1960 | Supt. |
| 6124 | EVA | Neville Charles | 08.02.1960 | A/Com |
| 6125 | HORNER | Michael John | 09.02.1960 | S/O |
| 6126 | THATCHER | John Haig Howe | 02.02.1960 | P/O |
| 6127 | CUNNINGHAM | Errol Alexander | 08.02.1960 | Supt. |
| 6128 | JEOFFREYS | Brian Joseph | 04.02.1960 | P/O |
| 6129 | KEENS | Kenneth William | 08.02.1960 | P/O |
| 6130 | SYMMONS | Randolph Castillion | 08.02.1960 | P/O |
| 6131 | MARLAND | John | 25.02.1960 | S/Sgt. |
| 6132 | COX | David Francis | 14.03.1960 | S/Sgt. |
| 6133 | VAN RENSBURG | Pieter Janse | 18.03.1960 | Inspr. |
| 6134 | DU PLESSIS | Alexander Benjamin | 16.03.1960 | P/O |
| 6135 | ROBINSON | Gerald Walter | 16.03.1960 | S/O |
| 6136 | CROSSLEY | Anthony James | 18.03.1960 | C/Inspr. |
| 6137 | WRIGHT | Percival John | 18.03.1960 | S/O |
| 6138 | MACARTNEY | Roger James | 18.03.1960 | Supt. |
| 6140 | PECK | Nigel John Winston | 18.03.1960 | P/O |
| 6141 | SHEPHERD | Andrew Gilbert | 18.03.1960 | Det |
| 6142 | CLANFIELD | Eric James | 18.03.1960 | S/O |
| 6143 | KILBORN | Bryan Richard | 18.03.1960 | C/Inspr. |
| 6144 | JUDSON | Derrick Keith | 16.03.1960 | Const. |
| 6145 | FRASER | Alexander MacDonald | 16.03.1960 | Supt. |
| 6146 | McGOWAN | Robin William | 18.03.1960 | S/O |
| 6147 | ANDERSON | Antony Finn | 16.03.1960 | Supt. |
| 6148 | ROBINSON | Malcolm James | 11.04.1960 | S/S/O |
| 6149 | JOYCE | Phillip Rupert | 11.04.1960 | Det |
| 6150 | PATERSON | David Gordon | 11.04.1960 | D/S/O |
| 6151 | STOCKLEY | David John | 11.04.1960 | Det |
| 6152 | McILVEEN | Thomas Brian | 11.04.1960 | D/Sgt. |
| 6153 | TURNER | John Edward | 11.04.1960 | Const. |
| 6154 | SYMES | Peter Edward | 11.04.1960 | D/Inspr. |
| 6155 | MASON | Michael John | 11.04.1960 | D/S/O |
| 6156 | ANDREWS | John David | 11.04.1960 | Const |
| 6157 | DULLER | Jeremy George | 11.04.1960 | Supt |
| 6158 | PETERS | Geoffrey William | 11.04.1960 | S/O |
| 6159 | GREEN | Robert Hamilton | 11.04.1960 | P/O |
| 6160 | SMITH | Ronald Reginald | 11.04.1960 | D/P/O |
| 6161 | WARREN | Brian Edmond | 11.04.1960 | C/Inspr. |
| 6162 | GRIBBLE | Oliver Dennis | 13.05.1960 | Const. |
| 6163 | MARSHALL | Arthur Lionel | 01.06.1960 | C/Inspr. |
| 6164 | MARCH | Horace David | 02.06.1960 | D/P/O |
| 6165 | HULETT | Keith John | 02.06.1960 | Const. |
| 6166 | NORTJE | Henry Arthur | 02.06.1960 | Const. |
| 6167 | SEARLE | Malcolm | 02.06.1960 | Const. |
| 6168 | KINSAY | Peter Robert | 02.06.1960 | Const. |
| 6169 | DOUGLAS | Graham Norman | 02.06.1960 | D/S/O |
| 6170 | DE WIT | Charles John | 02.06.1960 | Const. |
| 6171 | SCOTT | Denis | 02.06.1960 | P/O |
| 6172 | RAYNER | Arthur Robert | 02.06.1960 | Const. |
| 6173 | DAVIES | George Peter | 02.06.1960 | Const. |
| 6174 | ULYATE | Willem Lodewyk | 02.06.1960 | Inspr. |
| 6175 | VAN STADEN | Bernard | 14.07.1960 | S/Sgt. |
| 6176 | McCAFFERY | Adrian Robin | 27.06.1960 | S/Sgt. |
| 6177 | TIPPLE | Michael Alan | 14.07.1960 | C Supt. |
| 6178 | CAPPELTON | William George | 08.07.1960 | D/Sgt. |
| 6179 | RODD | Barrington Sinclair | 13.07.1960 | S/O |
| 6180 | BENNETT | Charles Jeremy | 13.07.1960 | S/O |
| 6181 | LOUSADE | Patrick Graham | 08.07.1960 | C/Supt. |
| 6182 | KELLY | Michael Laurence | 13.07.1960 | Const. |
| 6183 | BLAMEY | John Arthur | 13.07.1960 | C/Insp. |
| 6184 | OLDKNOW | Eryl Barry | 13.07.1960 | D/S/O |
| 6185 | WORTON | Bruce Barry | 13.07.1960 | C/Inspr. |
| 6186 | VIVIAN | John David | 07.07.1960 | D/S/O |
| 6187 | HASWELL | Benjamin Edwin | 13.07.1960 | S/S/O |
| 6188 | MARSHALL | Brian Edward | 13.07.1960 | Const. |
| 6189 | KEMP | Sidney David | 07.07.1960 | Supt. |
| 6190 | HEPPES | Phillips Bruce | 13.07.1960 | Const. |
| 6191 | WHITE | Christopher John | 07.07.1960 | C/Supt. |
| 6192 | MINIFIE | Peter Anthony | 07.07.1960 | P/O |
| 6193 | GOOD | Ronald | 07.07.1960 | P/O |
| 6194 | SHARDLOW | David | 25.08.1960 | D/Inspr. |
| 6195 | WARBURTON | Paul | 25.08.1960 | P/O |
| 6196 | RANDALL | Keith Roland | 29.08.1960 | Const. |
| 6197 | ADDISON | Paul | 25.08.1960 | Const. |
| 6198 | BAKER | Peter Laurence | 25.08.1960 | S/O |
| 6199 | GODDARD | Rowland Keith | 25.08.1960 | S/O |
| 6200 | PLASKITT | Mervyn Wavell | 25.08.1960 | P/O |
| 6201 | FORD | Frederick Percy | 25.08.1960 | C/Supt. |
| 6202 | DRAYTON | Patrick Frank | 25.08.1960 | C/Inspr. |
| 6203 | SHIRLEY | Roderick Eric | 25.08.1960 | D/S/O |
| 6204 | MYERS | Neville Anthony | 25.08.1960 | Inspr. |
| 6205 | McKENNA | Michael Aubrey | 02.09.1969 | C/Inspr. |
| 6206 | WOOD | Stuart James | 19.09.1960 | Inspr. |
| 6207 | FORSTER | Donald Ian | 30.09.1960 | S/O |
| 6208 | PENRERTHY | John Robert | 30.09.1960 | S/O |

| No. | Surname | Forename(s) | Date | Rank |
|---|---|---|---|---|
| 6209 | RULE | Ian Taylor | 26.09.1960 | Det |
| 6210 | BAYLISS | Christopher Edward | 31.10.1960 | Const. |
| 6211 | WHITTAKER | Colin Croasdale | 30.09.1960 | Det |
| 6212 | FREEBAIRN | Charles Edward | 31.10.1960 | S/Inspr. |
| 6213 | BETTS | Ian Gordon | 26.09.1960 | Inspr. |
| 6214 | PIPER | Larry Arthur | 31.10.1960 | Const. |
| 6215 | FROST | Eric Stephen | 30.09.1960 | Sup |
| 6216 | EVANS | Brian Beverley | 30.09.1960 | Const. |
| 6217 | COURTNEY | Peter Martin | 30.09.1960 | Const. |
| 6218 | SOUTH | Peter | 25.10.1960 | Inspr. |
| 6219 | HAMLEY | Richard | 20.10.1960 | A/Comm |
| 6220 | KENDALL | Trevor John | 02.11.1960 | Const. |
| 6221 | RECORD | Gerald Ashley | 09.11.1960 | Inspr. |
| 6222 | TRAILL | Robert | 31.10.1960 | S/S/O |
| 6223 | GRIMWOOD | Charles Antony | 31.10.1960 | Const. |
| 6224 | STOTT | Donald Martin | 02.11.1960 | Const. |
| 6225 | VAN SCHALKWIJK | Daniel Petrus | 30.09.1960 | Const. |
| 6226 | STEVENS | Andrew Alfred | 02.11.1960 | Const. |
| 6227 | TAIT | Finlay | 26.09.1960 | Const. |
| 6228 | DEMPSEY | Patrick Christopher | 30.09.1960 | S/O |
| 6229 | COX | Desmond Hugh | 09.11.1960 | Const. |
| 6230 | CHARSLEY | Melvin George | 30.11.1960 | Const. |
| 6231 | GIBSON | Peter Daniel | 30.11.1960 | Inspr. |
| 6232 | FAITHFUL | Colin John | 01.12.1960 | Const. |
| 6233 | WALTON | Courtney | 07.12.1960 | C/Supt. |
| 6234 | BALDWIN | Gary Richard | 05.12.1960 | D/Inspr. |
| 6235 | CARLISLE | Lynn Andrew | 07.12.1960 | P/O |
| 6236 | STEYNBERG | Johannes Jacobus | 06.12.1960 | C/Inspr. |
| 6237 | SHANNON | Raymond James | 06.12.1960 | P/O |
| 6238 | VAN SITTERT | Steven Aubrey | 06.12.1960 | Const. |
| 6239 | GUNN | Richard Frederick | 05.12.1960 | D/S/O |
| 6240 | TAYLOR | Peter Graham | 05.12.1960 | D/S/O |
| 6241 | TREVELYAN | Barry Alfred | 06.12.1960 | Const. |
| 6242 | VAN RENSBURG | Pieter J | 07.12.1960 | Const. |
| 6243 | DEATH | Raymond Francis | 07.12.1960 | Const. |
| 6244 | JOUBERT | Hendrick Lambert | 14.12.1960 | Const. |
| 6245 | PFAFF | John | 07.12.1960 | Const. |
| 6246 | VAN RENSBURG | Peter Janse | 13.12.1960 | S/O |
| 6247 | VERMAAK | David de Lisle | 16.12.1960 | Inspr. |
| 6248 | VAN EEDEN | Frederick Jacobus | 04.01.1961 | Const. |
| 6249 | BROWN | John Alexander | 10.01.1961 | Const. |
| 6250 | MORRISON | Rowland George | 10.01.1961 | D/S/O |
| 6251 | DAWSON | Sydney | 10.01.1961 | Inspr. |
| 6252 | CLEGG | Keith MacDonald | 10.01.1961 | Const. |
| 6253 | LAING | Ian | 10.01.1961 | C/Supt. |
| 6254 | CROCKART | Robert John | 10.01.1961 | P/O |
| 6255 | LONDON | Clive Howard | 10.01.1961 | C/Inspr. |
| 6256 | ARNOLD | Denis Beresford | 07.01.1961 | C/Supt |
| 6257 | O'HARA | Peter Frederick | 10.01.1961 | Const. |
| 6258 | WOOD | Colin Anthony | 09.01.1961 | Const. |
| 6259 | DAVIS | Derek Paul | 10.01.1961 | Const. |
| 6260 | MORAN | Neville Edward | 10.01.1961 | P/O |
| 6261 | GRANT | Vivian Nigel | 10.01.1961 | D/P/O |
| 6262 | CARTHEW-GABRIEL | Peter Francis | 07.01.1961 | Const. |
| 6263 | SCHWULST | Robert | 09.01.1961 | P/O |
| 6264 | FLYNN | John Sydney | 07.01.1961 | P/O |
| 6265 | WICKS | Peter John | 10.01.1961 | Const. |
| 6266 | RICHARDS | Geoffrey John | 10.01.1961 | Inspr. |
| 6267 | HOLLOWAY | Leon | 10.01.1961 | Const. |
| 6268 | DU TOIT | Walter Peter | 10.01.1961 | P/O |
| 6269 | WATSON | Solomon Hermanus | 10.01.1961 | P/O |
| 6270 | LOUW | Harvey Francois | 20.01.1961 | C/Inspr. |
| 6271 | WILHELM | Francois Frederick | 17.01.1961 | Inspr. |
| 6272 | JOUBERT | Martin Edward | 23.01.1961 | P/O |
| 6273 | FRIZELLE | Edward Travis | 17.01.1961 | Const. |
| 6274 | STEPHENS | Michael Edward | 18.01.1961 | Const. |
| 6275 | PRESTON | Ronald Victor | 18.01.1961 | Supt. |
| 6276 | WALKER-RANDALL | Noel Daniel | 17.01.1961 | Inspr. |
| 6277 | WERTH | | 17.01.1961 | C/Inspr. |
| 6278 | DYER | Gerald Winston | 20.01.1961 | Supt. |
| 6279 | McINTYRE | Roger Sydney | 17.01.1961 | Const. |
| 6280 | PERCY-LANCASTER | Deryk | 10.01.1961 | Const. |
| 6281 | STORMS | Peter George | 17.01.1961 | P/O |
| 6282 | KNOLLYS | Frederick Richard | 17.01.1961 | Supt. |
| 6283 | CLARK | Henry Alfred | 17.01.1961 | C/Supt. |
| 6284 | MARTIN | Glen Edward | 14.01.1961 | P/O |
| 6285 | RENS | Paul Alexander | 20.01.1961 | C/Inspr. |
| 6286 | WIGHTON | Douglas Alexander | 10.01.1961 | Const. |
| 6287 | VERLEY | Douglas Reginald | 17.01.1961 | Const. |
| 6288 | PLUNKETT | Nigel Pelham | 09.01.1961 | Const. |
| 6289 | KRUGER | John Bardia | 14.01.1961 | Const. |
| 6290 | FLETCHER | Clive Barry | 10.01.1961 | Const. |
| 6291 | KILFOIL | Kevin Walter | 17.01.1961 | Const. |
| 6292 | GRIFFITHS | John Grahame | 13.02.1961 | Inspr. |
| 6293 | MAIN | Michael Paul | 13.02.1961 | Inspr. |
| 6294 | JAMES | Edward Brian | 10.01.1961 | P/O |
| 6295 | RADEMEYER | Gert Charles | 11.02.1961 | Const. |
| 6296 | DEALL | Ivan Spencer | 10.01.1961 | Const. |
| 6297 | MARSH | Robert Ballington | 13.02.1961 | Const. |
| 6298 | HALL | Charles Antony | 13.02.1961 | Inspr. |
| 6299 | DE VRIES | Graham William | 13.02.1961 | Const. |
| 6300 | HILL | Errol Flynn | 13.02.1961 | Const. |
| 6301 | WILSON | Donald Graham | 13.02.1961 | Supt |
| 6302 | JAMIESON | Norman James | 10.01.1961 | Const. |
| 6303 | NORTJE | Peter Ross | 13.02.1961 | Const. |
| 6304 | JEARY | Alfred Clifford | 13.02.1961 | S/O |
| 6305 | HALKIER | Jeffrey | 13.02.1961 | P/O |
| 6306 | BESTER | Benjamin James | 13.02.1961 | Const. |
| 6307 | HARDWICK | Ian James | 13.02.1961 | P/O |
| 6308 | HUGHES | Christopher Daniel | 13.02.1961 | C/Supt. |
| 6309 | POTGIETER | Johannes Petrus | 13.02.1961 | Const. |
| 6310 | PETERS | Roy Raymond | 10.01.1961 | Const. |
| 6311 | BLOOMFIELD | Michael | 13.02.1961 | Const. |
| 6312 | WOOD | Colin Geoffrey | 11.02.1961 | Supt. |
| 6313 | ROSS | Michael Ellis | 13.02.1961 | S/O |
| 6314 | MARSDEN | Barry James | 13.02.1961 | P/O |
| 6315 | MARSH | Roger Randall | 13.02.1961 | P/O |
| 6316 | WISHART | Robert Irvine | 12.02.1961 | D/C/Inspr. |
| 6317 | CASTLE | John Malcolm | 15.02.1961 | Const. |
| 6318 | MOOLMAN | Harry Anthony | 14.02.1961 | S/O |
| 6319 | LOOKER | Christopher John | 13.02.1961 | C/Supt |
| 6320 | TERBLANCHE | Peter James | 13.02.1961 | P/O |
| 6321 | GOBBETT | Derek Patrick | 13.02.1961 | Const. |
| 6322 | RUSSELL | Anthony Benjamin | 13.02.1961 | C/Supt. |
| 6323 | WILSON | Bruce David | 13.02.1961 | P/O |
| 6324 | DAVIS | Michael John | 13.02.1961 | S/S/O |
| 6325 | WEST | Peter | 13.02.1961 | Supt |
| 6326 | PAINTER | John Frederick | 13.02.1961 | Const. |
| 6327 | KLEYNHANS | Hendrik Lodewyk | 13.02.1961 | P/O |
| 6328 | VINCENT | Kent John Alfred | 13.02.1961 | Const. |
| 6329 | SMITH | Peter Gavin | 13.02.1961 | Const. |
| 6330 | SHIPPEN | Joseph William | 13.02.1961 | Const. |
| 6331 | STEWART | George Tully | 21.03.1961 | D/P/O |
| 6332 | HILL | Ronald Leslie | 10.01.1961 | Const. |
| 6333 | TODDUN | David George | 20.03.1961 | Const. |
| 6334 | JEFFERIES | Patrick Scott | 01.03.1961 | C/I (T) |
| 6335 | McDERMID | Brian Anthony | 21.03.1961 | D/C/Inspr. |
| 6336 | HALL | Anthony Phillip | 20.03.1961 | D/Inspr. |
| 6337 | GALLAGHER | Peter Vincent | 20.03.1961 | P/O |
| 6338 | BODINGTON | Edward Andrew | 20.03.1961 | Const. |
| 6339 | WILSON | Anthony Truter | 21.03.1961 | C/Inspr. |
| 6340 | MOORE | Peter Ernest | 20.03.1961 | P/O |
| 6341 | BOTHMA | Michael Anthony | 21.03.1961 | D/S/O |
| 6342 | MARKS | David John | 21.03.1961 | Const. |
| 6343 | DAWSON | Brian Anthony | 20.03.1961 | Const. |
| 6344 | WERNER | Michael David | 20.03.1961 | Supt. |
| 6345 | HOLMES | David Peter | 21.03.1961 | P/O |
| 6346 | MOLONEY | Peter Gregory | 23.03.1961 | S/O |
| 6347 | CUNLIFFE-STEEL | Phillip John | 20.03.1961 | Const. |
| 6348 | POOLE | Dennis James | 20.03.1961 | Const. |
| 6349 | EGLINGTON | Joseph Michael | 20.03.1961 | P/O |
| 6350 | HAYWARD | Ronald Ernest | 21.03.1961 | P/O |
| 6351 | CHURCH | Anthony Howard | 24.04.1961 | Det |
| 6352 | DOBEYN | Peter John | 24.04.1961 | Const. |
| 6353 | JORDAAN | Ronald Trevor | 24.04.1961 | P/O |
| 6354 | BOTHWELL | Derek Wilfred | 24.04.1961 | Const. |
| 6355 | MOYSEN | Michael Stanley | 24.04.1961 | Const. |
| 6356 | WAKEHAM | David Robert | 24.04.1961 | Const. |
| 6357 | DAVIES | Ronald | 30.03.1961 | S/O |
| 6358 | WALKER | Neville | 24.04.1961 | Const. |
| 6359 | MITCHELL | Duncan Lewis | 24.04.1961 | P/O |
| 6360 | MOXHAM | John Henry | 24.04.1961 | Supt. |
| 6361 | THOMAS | Rodney | 24.04.1961 | Const. |
| 6362 | NORTH | Michael Howard | 24.04.1961 | Const. |
| 6363 | MUMFORD | Roger Anthony | 24.04.1961 | P/O |
| 6364 | VAN DEN BERG | Dirk Johannes | 24.04.1961 | P/O |
| 6365 | WESTRAY | Murray William | 24.04.1961 | Const. |
| 6366 | STOKER | James | 24.04.1961 | S/O |
| 6367 | HICKMAN | Michael George | 24.04.1961 | Const. |
| 6368 | BUCHANAN | Alfred Samuel | 24.04.1961 | Const. |
| 6369 | BIRRELL | Eric | 24.04.1961 | Const. |
| 6370 | KETTLE | Anthony Frederick | 24.04.1961 | Const. |
| 6371 | LE CRERAR | Roger Clinton | 24.04.1961 | P/O |
| 6372 | HOPLEY | Charles Ian | 24.04.1961 | Const. |
| 6373 | HEYCOCK | Donald John | 24.04.1961 | S/O |
| 6374 | BURDEN | Laurence Edward | 15.05.1961 | S/U/Sgt. |
| 6375 | PELISSIER | Julien Charles | 15.05.1961 | C/Supt. |
| 6376 | SAMSON | Brian Leslie | 15.05.1961 | Const. |
| 6377 | MAYCOCK | Anthony David | 15.05.1961 | P/O |
| 6378 | CARTER | Nicholas John | 15.05.1961 | P/O |
| 6379 | FISHER | Sean Christopher | 15.05.1961 | C/Inspr. |
| 6380 | GRICE | Tony | 15.05.1961 | Inspr. |
| 6381 | COOPER | Anthony Macmillien | 18.05.1961 | Supt. |
| 6382 | SCHWARTZ | Terence Eugene | 21.03.1961 | Supt. |
| 6383 | FLOYD | Clifford Munroe | 01.05.1961 | D/P/O |
| 6384 | BIRKETT | Peter Anthony | 08.05.1961 | Inspr. |
| 6385 | LIGHTENING | Barry Ernest | 15.05.1961 | C/Supt. |
| 6386 | MENZIES | Colin-Mhor | 15.05.1961 | P/O |
| 6387 | MORGAN | Lyndon Boyd | 15.05.1961 | P/O |
| 6388 | CORNELL | William Malcolm | 15.05.1961 | Supt. |
| 6389 | McINTYRE | Robert Douglas | 15.05.1961 | D/S/O |
| 6390 | HUTT | Eric Drummond | 20.03.1961 | P/O |
| 6391 | RHODES | Peter David | 15.05.1961 | not recorded |
| 6392 | HANDS | Drummond | 15.05.1961 | S/O |
| 6393 | WILKINSON | Christy | 21.03.1961 | D/C/Inspr. |
| 6394 | DONALDSON | Ian David | 13.03.1961 | Inspr. |
| 6395 | AUSTIN | Leonard Robert | 11.02.1961 | Const. |
| 6396 | WHITTLE | Ian | 20.03.1961 | Inspr. |
| 6397 | CROSS | Michael Ian | 24.04.1961 | Const. |
| 6398 | SEAGER | David Ronald | 24.04.1961 | Const. |
| 6399 | SULLIVAN | John Stuart | 24.04.1961 | Const. |
| 6400 | HOPE | Melvyn John | 15.05.1961 | Inspr. |
| 6401 | NICHOLSON | Norman Gerald | 15.05.1961 | P/O |
| 6402 | STORR | Robert | 15.05.1961 | Const. |
| 6403 | WIGGILL | Charles Robert | 15.05.1961 | Const. |
| 6404 | MACKENZIE | William George | 26.05.1961 | C/Inspr. |
| 6405 | MATHIESON | Frank John | 14.06.1961 | Supt |
| 6406 | BAKER | Vivian Terence | 12.06.1961 | S/O |
| 6407 | BARSTOW | Nicholson Geoffrey | 12.06.1961 | Const. |
| 6408 | BERHOUT | Gerard Leonard | 12.06.1961 | Const. |
| 6409 | CADDY | Alan Walter | 12.06.1961 | D/S/O |
| 6410 | DAWSON | Anthony Ewart | 12.06.1961 | Const. |
| 6411 | FITZWILLIAM | George Jerome | 12.06.1961 | Inspr. |
| 6412 | HARRIS | Roger John | 12.06.1961 | Cst |
| 6413 | HAWKEN | Anthony John | 12.06.1961 | Cst |
| 6414 | HORN | Gerald Patrick | 12.06.1961 | P/O |
| 6415 | MEYER | Robert Bruce | 12.06.1961 | Cst |

# BSAP Nominal Roll • Men

| No. | Surname | Forenames | Rank | Date |
|---|---|---|---|---|
| 6416 | SMITH | Terence Michael | Insp | 12.06.1961 |
| 6417 | TAYLOR | Harry Alexander | S/O(T) | 12.06.1961 |
| 6418 | VAN DEN BERGH | David Frederick | Cst | 12.06.1961 |
| 6419 | WHEATLEY | Clive Frank | S/O | 12.06.1961 |
| 6420 | WILTON | Michael George | S/O | 12.06.1961 |
| 6421 | BURNS | Patrick Dennis | C/Insp | 12.06.1961 |
| 6422 | BAKER | Lionel Ronald | S/O | 28.06.1961 |
| 6423 | BALDWIN | Patrick Evelyn | Supt. | 03.07.1961 |
| 6424 | BERRY | Wynn Harry | P/O | 03.07.1961 |
| 6425 | DONZELLI | John Martin | P/O | 08.07.1961 |
| 6426 | GILDEA | James | P/O | 03.07.1961 |
| 6427 | HIND | Peter Haigh | Cst | 03.07.1961 |
| 6428 | MARTIN | Christopher Michael | P/O | 03.07.1961 |
| 6429 | MATHEW | Barrie Anthony | S/L/Sgt | 03.07.1961 |
| 6430 | O'CONNOR | Thomas Kevin | Cst | 03.07.1961 |
| 6431 | PENFOLD | Iain William | S/O | 03.07.1961 |
| 6432 | ROBERTS | Christopher John | Insp | 03.07.1961 |
| 6433 | SMITH | Robert Kenneth | Det | 03.07.1961 |
| 6434 | TAYLOR | Alfred Ness | C/Supt | 03.07.1961 |
| 6435 | TILBURY | Trevor Henry | S/S/O | 03.07.1961 |
| 6436 | ANDERSTREM | Ian Lindsay | Det | 08.07.1961 |
| 6437 | SAWTELL | Richard Francis | Cst | 17.04.1961 |
| 6438 | CHAMBERS | Charles Leslie | S/Sgt | 17.07.1961 |
| 6439 | ROSS-JONES | Stephen Brian | Cst | 31.07.1961 |
| 6440 | ASHCROFT | Robert Michael | Cst | 31.07.1961 |
| 6441 | STEVENSON-BAKER | Brian Reginald | C/Supt | 31.07.1961 |
| 6442 | BANNERMAN | James Hugh | Cst | 31.07.1961 |
| 6443 | BLATCH | Basil Denzil | P/O | 31.07.1961 |
| 6444 | BRIGHT | David Reginald | P/O | 31.07.1961 |
| 6445 | BROOKE | Arthur John | D/Insp | 31.07.1961 |
| 6446 | BUSHNELL | Terry Brian | S/O | 31.07.1961 |
| 6447 | CLARKE | Graeme Patrick | Insp | 31.07.1961 |
| 6448 | COLE | Jeremy George | S/O | 31.07.1961 |
| 6449 | CRAWFORD | Edward Phillip | S/O | 31.07.1961 |
| 6450 | FOX | Nicholas Charles | P.O. | 31.07.1961 |
| 6451 | HATTON | Donald James | P/O | 31.07.1961 |
| 6452 | HOUGHTON | Peter Anthony | Cst | 31.07.1961 |
| 6453 | JARVIE | Hugh Cunningham | S/S/O | 31.07.1961 |
| 6454 | LEES | John Andrew | Supt. | 31.07.1961 |
| 6455 | McCALLUM | John | C/Supt | 31.07.1961 |
| 6456 | MUNDY | John Raymond | Cst | 31.07.1961 |
| 6457 | O'HANLON | Dennis | Cst | 31.07.1961 |
| 6458 | ROBINSON | Josiah David | D/C/I | 31.07.1961 |
| 6459 | WADE | David Trevor | Insp | 31.07.1961 |
| 6460 | BRICE | Malcolm David | P/O | 31.07.1961 |
| 6461 | SWANEPOEL | Wessel Adrian | Cst | 01.08.1961 |
| 6462 | SMITH | John | P/O | 08.08.1961 |
| 6463 | BOTES | Michael | A/Com | 23.08.1961 |
| 6464 | DAVENPORT | David Brian | Cst | 23.08.1961 |
| 6465 | ENGELBRECHT | Louis John | Cst | 23.08.1961 |
| 6466 | JONES | Owen Annis | Cst | 23.08.1961 |
| 6467 | VON HORSTEN | Garth William | C/Insp. | 23.08.1961 |
| 6468 | CALLOW | David | L/C/I | 28.08.1961 |
| 6469 | HART-DAVIES | David Vincent | A/Com | 28.08.1961 |
| 6470 | DOOLEY | Thomas Patrick | Cst | 28.08.1961 |
| 6471 | FELLOWS | Daniel Roger | Cst | 28.08.1961 |
| 6472 | FERREIRA | Diaz | D/C/I | 28.08.1961 |
| 6473 | FRANKLIN | Robert Alexander | Insp | 28.08.1961 |
| 6474 | FULTON | Derek Graham | P/O | 28.08.1961 |
| 6475 | GREEN | Christopher Alan | Cst | 28.08.1961 |
| 6476 | HAWKINS | Patrick Bernard | Cst | 28.08.1961 |
| 6477 | HAY | Douglas William | Cst | 28.08.1961 |
| 6478 | HODGSON | Thomas Edward | P/O | 28.08.1961 |
| 6479 | HUNT | Edward | Cst | 18.12.61 |
| 6480 | MATTHEWS | Sydney Donald | A/Com | 18.12.1961 |
| 6481 | MEREDITH | Anthony Gordon | Insp(T) | 18.12.1961 |
| 6482 | STEVENSON | Alan McLeod | D/S/O | 18.12.1961 |
| 6483 | WHITE | Alan Keith | S/O | 18.12.1961 |
| 6485 | YATEMAN | Harold Lionel | Cst | 28.08.1961 |
| 6486 | SCHEFFER | Andrew | S/S/O | 28.08.1961 |
| 6487 | TILL | Trevor Richard | Supt | 28.08.1961 |
| 6488 | PIETERSEN | Claude Jeffrey | Insp(T) | 03.10.1961 |
| 6489 | ALLUM | Richard Thomas | S/O | 06.10.1961 |
| 6490 | ANDERSON | Kenneth David | S/O | 06.10.1961 |
| 6491 | FOWLIS | Eric Crawford | S/S/O | 06.10.1961 |
| 6492 | Mac KENZIE | Alan Frank | Supt | 03.07.1961 |
| 6493 | POCKET | John Clifford | P/O | 06.10.1961 |
| 6494 | ROZEMEYER | Anthony Henry | S/O | 06.10.1961 |
| 6495 | WAGGOT | Thomas Edward | S/O | 06.10.1961 |
| 6496 | BLUNDELL | David William | P/O | 09.10.1961 |
| 6497 | BRAHAM | Robert John | Cst | 03.07.1961 |
| 6498 | ANTHONY | Roger Charles | P/O | 03.07.1961 |
| 6499 | EDGE | Derrick | S/L/Sgt | 03.07.1961 |
| 6500 | EDWARDS | Kenneth Savill | S/O | 03.07.1961 |
| 6501 | FOX-D'ARCY | Michael Marmion | Insp | 09.10.1961 |
| 6502 | LONGHURST | Paul Michael | Det | 09.10.1961 |
| 6503 | MASTERTON | Graham Reginald | Cst | 09.10.1961 |
| 6504 | MATTHEWS | Andrew Wilfred | S/S/O | 09.10.1961 |
| 6505 | McLOUGHLIN | John Anthony | Det | 09.10.1961 |
| 6506 | NOTT | Graham Morley | Insp | 09.10.1961 |
| 6507 | POWER | Maurice James | S/O | 09.10.1961 |
| 6508 | ROGERS | Graham Vincent | P/O | 09.10.1961 |
| 6509 | SCARFF | David Cyril | C/Insp | 09.10.1961 |
| 6510 | TWIDLE | Peter | P/O | 09.10.1961 |
| 6511 | TWINE | Julian Edward | Cst | 09.10.1961 |
| 6512 | WILD | Douglas Ruthven | P/O | 09.10.1961 |
| 6513 | YOUNG | Terence John | Cst | 09.10.1961 |
| 6514 | JOHNSON | Christopher Forbes | D/Insp | 03.11.1961 |
| 6515 | NICHOLSON | John Bradshaw | Supt. | 03.11.1961 |
| 6516 | NORTH | Christopher John | S/O | 03.11.1961 |
| 6517 | TOWNSEND | Michael Hugh | S/O | 03.11.1961 |
| 6518 | COOKE-YARBOROUGH | Edmund Orfeur | Supt | 03.11.1961 |
| 6519 | CARROLL | John Edward | A/Com | 04.11.1961 |
| 6520 | LANE | Barry John | P/O | 06.11.1961 |
| 6521 | BURSBY | John Philip | P/O | 06.11.1961 |
| 6522 | CARUTH | Patrick Davis | S/S/O | 06.11.1961 |
| 6523 | CUNLIFFE | Robert | Supt | 04.11.1961 |
| 6524 | GALLAGHER | Terence Joseph | C/Supt | 06.11.1961 |
| 6525 | HOLLICK | Basil John Allan | Cst | 06.11.1961 |
| 6526 | INGRAM | Paul | Cst | 06.11.1961 |
| 6527 | O'DONNELL | Michael | D/C/I | 06.11.1961 |
| 6528 | THOM | Gordon Joseph | Cst | 31.07.1961 |
| 6529 | ASHFIELD | Charles Edmund | Cst | 07.11.1961 |
| 6530 | HOPKINS | Robert William | Cst | 07.11.1961 |
| 6531 | EDWARDS | Harry Lawton | A/Com | 08.11.1961 |
| 6532 | WERTH | Herman Ernest | Cst | 05.12.1961 |
| 6533 | CAMPBELL | Colin Gordon | Cst | 13.12.1961 |
| 6534 | CUTHBERTSON | Ian | D/S/O | 13.12.1961 |
| 6535 | KENNY | Robert John | Cst | 13.12.1961 |
| 6536 | LOVEMORE | Bruce Carrington | Cst | 13.12.1961 |
| 6537 | MAUREL | Marie Joseph | S/S/O | 13.12.1961 |
| 6538 | MACASKILL | Glen Allan | Supt | 13.12.1961 |
| 6539 | McNAMARA | David Hugh | Insp | 13.12.1961 |
| 6540 | SQUAIR | Hugh Harold | S/O | 15.12.1961 |
| 6541 | BAYLEY | David George | Cst | 15.12.1961 |
| 6542 | BEUNK | William | Cst | 15.12.1961 |
| 6543 | COLEMAN | David Hugh | S/A/C | 15.12.1961 |
| 6544 | HAMMOND | Howard Spencer | P/O | 15.12.1961 |
| 6545 | MITCHELL | David Robb | Insp | 15.12.1961 |
| 6546 | BOTWRIGHT | Peter | P/O | 18.12.61 |
| 6547 | BREAKSPEAR | Roger Craig | Insp | 18.12.1961 |
| 6548 | CASSIDY | Charles | A/Com | 18.12.1961 |
| 6549 | DAVEY | Anthony Walter | Insp(T) | 18.12.1961 |
| 6550 | FEE | Edward Henry | D/S/O | 18.12.1961 |
| 6551 | HOULSTON | Alan George | S/O | 18.12.1961 |
| 6552 | HOULSTON | Barrie | D/P/O | 18.12.1961 |
| 6554 | ORCHISON | Keith | Cst | 18.12.1961 |
| 6555 | SCHOFIELD | David | S/S/O | 18.12.1961 |
| 6556 | SMITH | David Charles | Supt | 18.12.1961 |
| 6557 | WILKINSON | Derek Cecil | Insp(T) | 02.01.1962 |
| 6558 | BASS | Stuart Raymond | S/O | 03.01.1962 |
| 6559 | DIKE | Barry James | D/S/O | 03.01.1962 |
| 6560 | FRASER | Thomas Duncan | P/O | 03.01.1962 |
| 6561 | GARDINER | Robert Lefebure | P/O | 03.01.1962 |
| 6562 | KEOWN | Peter Victor | P/O | 03.01.1962 |
| 6563 | PRINCE | James Edward | P/O | 03.01.1962 |
| 6564 | SHAWE | Stanley Brian | P/O | 03.01.1962 |
| 6565 | CLARKE | Anthony David | P/O | 03.01.1962 |
| 6566 | FROST | John Hugh | Insp | 05.01.1962 |
| 6567 | JOHNSON | Walter Henry | Supt | 05.01.1962 |
| 6568 | RICH | Colin Eric | Cst | 05.01.1962 |
| 6569 | KUTTNER | Felix Johannes | Supt. | 06.01.1962 |
| 6570 | BURSTEIN | Brian Michael | D/Insp | 12.01.1962 |
| 6571 | CURRIE | James Barclay | Cst | 12.01.1962 |
| 6572 | LE CORDEUR | Michael John | P/O | 12.01.1962 |
| 6573 | SATTERTHWAITE | Ben | Cst | 12.01.1962 |
| 6574 | BRADDELL | Peter John | P/O | 15.01.1962 |
| 6575 | COVELEY | Brian John | Insp | 15.01.1962 |
| 6576 | GALLAGHER | John | S/O | 15.01.1962 |
| 6577 | HAYES | Michael John | Insp | 15.01.1962 |
| 6578 | MACKAY | Kenneth | P/O | 15.01.1962 |
| 6579 | NORRIS | Patrick Stewart | C/Supt | 15.01.1962 |
| 6580 | O'TOOLE | James | A/Com | 15.01.1962 |
| 6581 | SARSFIELD | Neil | Cst | 15.01.1962 |
| 6582 | WHITCOMBE | David Edwin | Cst | 15.01.1962 |
| 6583 | GRIFFIN | John O'Brien | Insp(T) | 01.02.1962 |
| 6584 | TILL | Leslie O'Brien | C/Supt | 01.02.1962 |
| 6585 | MAUDE | John William | CI/(T) | 01.02.1962 |
| 6586 | EDRIDGE | Paul Milton | P/O | 09.02.1962 |
| 6587 | HARRIES | Ian Leslie | P/O | 09.02.1962 |
| 6588 | JOB | Michael David | Insp | 09.02.1962 |
| 6589 | PINNOCK | Douglas | S/O | 09.02.1962 |
| 6590 | SNELL | Gregory Stuart | D/S/O | 09.02.1962 |
| 6591 | THATCHER | Charles William | D/P/O | 09.02.1962 |
| 6592 | TRAYLEN | Christopher Patrick | S/O | 09.02.1962 |
| 6593 | VAN NIEKERK | Jacob Johannes | S/O | 09.02.1962 |
| 6594 | BUDD | Jerome Wilfred | Insp | 09.02.1962 |
| 6595 | DE LANGE | Willem Jacobus | P/O | 09.02.1962 |
| 6596 | HARVEY | Basil | P/O | 09.02.1962 |
| 6597 | POTTS | Anthony Edward | S/O | 09.02.1962 |
| 6598 | HOWARD | Brian Anthony | S/O | 10.02.1962 |
| 6599 | BIGG-WITHER | Christopher | P/O | 12.02.1962 |
| 6600 | BOOTH | Paul Anthony | D/P/O | 12.02.1962 |
| 6601 | BRADSHAW | Richard David | S/A/C | 12.02.1962 |
| 6602 | CARTER | Dermot Patrick | Cst | 12.02.1962 |
| 6603 | CROASDELL | Kerry James | Cst | 12.02.1962 |
| 6604 | GOLD | John Sidney | P/O | 12.02.1962 |
| 6605 | HARTLEY | Noel Simon | C/Supt | 12.02.1962 |
| 6606 | JAMES | Richard David | C/Supt | 12.02.1962 |
| 6607 | JUPP | Michael John | P/O | 12.02.1962 |
| 6608 | MATHESON | Derek Hamish | D/P/O | 12.02.1962 |
| 6609 | PARRY-JONES | Hywell Hugh | P/O | 12.02.1962 |
| 6610 | PIRRETT | John Conner | Supt | 12.02.1962 |
| 6611 | SNAPE | Bernard | Supt | 12.02.1962 |
| 6612 | WILLIS | David Arthur | D/S/O | 12.02.1962 |
| 6613 | GARGAN | Thomas James | Insp(T) | 27.02.1962 |
| 6614 | BAISLEY | Kenneth Alwyn | Insp | 08.03.1962 |
| 6615 | FERGUSON | Ronald Allen Paul | C/Supt | 08.03.1962 |
| 6616 | KEENS | Donald Herbert | Supt. | 08.03.1962 |
| 6617 | STANTON | Garth Anthony | D/P/O | 08.03.1962 |
| 6618 | VAN AARDT | Claude Charles | Supt | 08.03.1962 |
| 6619 | WILLIAMSON | John Garett | D/S/O | 08.03.1962 |
| 6620 | D'OLIVEIRA | Athol Raymond | Insp(T) | 09.03.1962 |
| 6621 | FINDLAY | Stuart John | Cst | 09.03.1962 |
| 6622 | | John Webber | D/P/O | 09.03.1962 |

| No. | Surname | Forename | Rank | Date |
|---|---|---|---|---|
| 6623 | STOKES | Terence Frederick | Cst | 09.03.1962 |
| 6624 | THOMPSON | Clifford Edwin | Cst | 09.03.1962 |
| 6625 | WADE | Peter David | S/O | 09.03.1962 |
| 6626 | WILSON | John Hawker | P/O | 09.03.1962 |
| 6627 | BUNGAY | Colin Frederick | P/O | 12.03.1962 |
| 6628 | EDDEY | Frank Wales | P/O | 12.03.1962 |
| 6629 | GLIBBERY | George Arthur | Insp | 12.03.1962 |
| 6630 | HAZLETT | James | Cst | 12.03.1962 |
| 6631 | HOPE | Michael Clifford | Cst | 12.03.1962 |
| 6632 | PAXTON | Gerald John | D/Insp | 12.03.1962 |
| 6633 | STAINES | Adrian Martyn | Supt | 12.03.1962 |
| 6634 | WARD | David | Insp | 12.03.1962 |
| 6635 | WOODS | Michael David | P/O | 12.03.1962 |
| 6636 | LATHAM | Walter Oldnal | P/O | 13.03.1962 |
| 6637 | PARSONS | Malcolm Allan | P/O | 22.03.1962 |
| 6638 | BACK | Charles Nicholas | P/O | 12.04.1962 |
| 6639 | BEDINGHAM | Robert Frank | C/Supt | 12.04.1962 |
| 6640 | BLAKE | Stuart Anthony | P/O | 12.04.1962 |
| 6641 | COURT | Albert Ruthven | Insp | 12.04.1962 |
| 6642 | DWYER | Sean Fergus | P/O | 12.04.1962 |
| 6643 | HENCHIE | Hedley Miller | Insp | 12.04.1962 |
| 6644 | HERMAN | Allan George | P/O | 12.04.1962 |
| 6645 | MILNER | Jon Lanaway | Insp | 12.04.1962 |
| 6646 | McCALLUM | Kenneth Haig | P/O | 12.04.1962 |
| 6647 | McCLELLAND | Patrick Dickie | S/S/O | 12.04.1962 |
| 6648 | SCULL | Christopher John | P/O | 12.04.1962 |
| 6649 | SPACEY | David Offer | Cst | 12.04.1962 |
| 6650 | COMBES | Peter David | Supt | 16.04.1962 |
| 6651 | FARREN | Lawrence | Insp | 16.04.1962 |
| 6652 | GRIFFITHS | William Robert | P/O | 16.04.1962 |
| 6653 | LONG | Alan Ignatius | Cst | 16.04.1962 |
| 6654 | MERRITT | William Andrew | P/O | 16.04.1962 |
| 6655 | OLDFIELD | Nigel Edward | P/O | 16.04.1962 |
| 6656 | RODWELL | Kenneth George | Supt | 12.04.1962 |
| 6657 | SAMLER | Keith John | P/O | 16.04.1962 |
| 6658 | WHITE | Gregory Francis | S/O | 16.04.1962 |
| 6659 | WOOD | Geoffrey Lester | P/O | 16.04.1962 |
| 6660 | BESSENT | Robert Arthur | Insp(T) | 09.05.1962 |
| 6661 | BAKER | Jonathan William | S/O | 10.05.1962 |
| 6662 | COOKSSON | Clifford Lawrence | P/O | 10.05.1962 |
| 6663 | DICKSON | William John Muir | S/O | 10.05.1962 |
| 6664 | FOSTER | Norman Godfrey | Supt | 10.05.1962 |
| 6665 | FREEMAN | John Everett | S/O | 10.05.1962 |
| 6666 | KIRKHAM | Ernest Donald | S/O | 10.05.1962 |
| 6667 | KLEYNHANS | Richard John | Cst | 10.05.1962 |
| 6668 | MORRIS | Christopher John | D/P/O | 10.05.1962 |
| 6669 | PEARMAIN | James Wilmer | D/C/I | 10.05.1962 |
| 6670 | PEPPER | Michael Francis | Insp | 10.05.1962 |
| 6671 | STEENKAMP | Howard Frederick | Cst | 14.05.1962 |
| 6672 | THOMSON | Jan Paul | D/S/O | 10.05.1962 |
| 6673 | VON ABO | Roy Paddock | Insp. | 10.05.1962 |
| 6674 | ALLEN | Johnstone Orlando | S/Insp | 10.05.1962 |
| 6675 | EDDIE | Michael Stuart | Cst | 10.05.1962 |
| 6676 | ELIAS | Robert Duncan | Supt | 15.05.1962 |
| 6677 | FORTUNE | Owen Glendower | S/O(T) | 14.05.1962 |
| 6678 | HALSEY | Robert Anthony | Supt | 14.05.1962 |
| 6679 | HICKMAN | Clive Robert | P/O | 07.06.1962 |
| 6680 | JEWSON | Stuart Edmund | P/O | 14.05.1962 |
| 6681 | QUICK | Derek Reginald | Cst | 14.05.1962 |
| 6682 | ROBINSON | Geoffrey Steven | D/P/O | 14.05.1962 |
| 6683 | STATHAM | Michael Francis | D/C/I | 14.05.1962 |
| 6684 | WELLS | Adrian David | D/S/O | 14.05.1962 |
| 6685 | ROBERTS | Frederick John | Insp. | 14.05.1962 |
| 6686 | DAY | Eric | S/Insp | 15.05.1962 |
| 6687 | DICKINSON | Alan | S/O(T) | 04.06.1962 |
| 6688 | HALDER | Albert Hubert | Supt | 07.06.1962 |
| 6689 | MOON | William Sylvanus | P/O | 07.06.1962 |
| 6690 | SHAMBLER | Graham Kenneth | Cst | 07.06.1962 |
| 6691 | TRUEMAN | Ronald John | C/Insp | 07.06.1962 |
| 6692 | GARVEY | Brian Christopher | P/O | 12.06.1962 |
| 6693 | HELSBY | Ian Kirby | P/O | 12.06.1962 |
| 6694 | HOLMES | John Robert | S/O | 12.06.1962 |
| 6695 | LYES | Peter Edmund | A/Com | 12.06.1962 |
| 6696 | MAUGHAN | Keith | A/Com | 12.06.1962 |
| 6697 | MOORCROFT | Anthony John | D/S/O | 12.06.1962 |
| 6698 | TODD | Alan | P/O | 12.06.1962 |
| 6699 | ROLLINGS-MATHEWS | Edwin | P/O | 12.06.1962 |
| 6700 | EYRE | Donald Christopher | S/O | 13.06.1962 |
| 6701 | TROWSDALE | Alan Bennett | P/O | 15.06.1962 |
| 6702 | ALMY | Douglas Vernon | C/I (T) | 02.07.1962 |
| 6703 | NIEUWOUDT | George Sebastian | S/L/Sgt | 13.07.1962 |
| 6704 | PERCY-LANCASTER | Alan | P/O | 13.07.1962 |
| 6705 | POTTS | Michael James | P/O | 13.07.1962 |
| 6706 | SKINNER | Royston Archibald | P/O | 13.07.1962 |
| 6707 | COTTON | George Barry | P/O | 16.07.1962 |
| 6708 | CUNNINGTON | Michael Philip | P/O | 16.07.1962 |
| 6709 | GRANT | Stuart Urwin | P/O | 16.07.1962 |
| 6710 | HOOD | Kenneth Robin | P/O | 16.07.1962 |
| 6711 | HUSSEY | Peter George | P/O | 16.07.1962 |
| 6712 | MILES | Philip John | P/O | 16.07.1962 |
| 6713 | THOMASON | Ian Eric | P/O | 16.07.1962 |
| 6714 | THOMSON | Robert Roy | Supt | 16.07.1962 |
| 6715 | McCORRIE | Stuart Hale | Insp(T) | 17.07.1962 |
| 6716 | WADSWORTH | Dennis Ian | Cst | 25.07.1962 |
| 6717 | DIXON | Hugh Jeremy | S/O | 09.08.1962 |
| 6718 | FREDERIKSON | Sydney William | S/O | 09.08.1962 |
| 6719 | HARDWICK | Gerald Owen | D/P/O | 09.08.1962 |
| 6720 | PRINGLE | Ronald Smuts | Cst | 09.08.1962 |
| 6721 | RUSSELL | Peter John | Supt | 09.08.1962 |
| 6722 | SAYERS | Charles James | P/O | 09.08.1962 |
| 6723 | TILBURY | Kenneth Alexander | P/O | 09.08.1962 |
| 6724 | VAN ZYL | John Abraham | D/S/O | 09.08.1962 |
| 6725 | ADAMS | Derek Roy George | P/O | 12.08.1962 |
| 6726 | BRAZIL | Thomas Vincent | Supt | 12.08.1962 |
| 6727 | HUNT | Peter Charles | S/S/O | 12.08.1962 |
| 6728 | IREDALE | Michael | Insp | 12.08.1962 |
| 6729 | JOYCE | Bartholomew John | D/P/O | 12.08.1962 |
| 6730 | KNIGHT | Michael Francis | Insp | 12.08.1962 |
| 6731 | LUND | Peter John | P/O | 12.08.1962 |
| 6732 | PERRY | Roy William | Cst | 12.08.1962 |
| 6733 | PRICE | Geoffrey Burton | Supt | 12.08.1962 |
| 6734 | STOCKLEY | David John | D/S/O | 27.08.1962 |
| 6735 | MACHAN | Anthony Arthur | C/Supt | 01.09.1962 |
| 6736 | COCHRANE | Ian King | P/O | 25.09.1962 |
| 6737 | COLEMAN | Michael John | P/O | 25.09.1962 |
| 6738 | DENSLOW | Victor | Insp. | 25.09.1962 |
| 6739 | JOHNSON | Robin Michael | P/O | 25.09.1962 |
| 6740 | LINDOP | Roger John | P/O | 25.09.1962 |
| 6741 | MASON | Richard Charles | Cst | 25.09.1962 |
| 6742 | WALKER | Graham Malcolm | Supt | 25.09.1962 |
| 6743 | ALLEN | Bruce Lewer | D/Insp | 27.09.1962 |
| 6744 | BRELSFORD | John | Cst | 27.09.1962 |
| 6745 | BROWN | John David | P/O | 27.09.1962 |
| 6746 | FLETCHER | Neale Robert | P/O | 27.09.1962 |
| 6747 | KENNELLY | Michael John | P/O | 27.09.1962 |
| 6748 | McDERMID | Alan Bruce | P/O | 27.09.1962 |
| 6749 | NEILL | Anthony Howard | Cst | 27.09.1962 |
| 6750 | TAVENER | Michael | Insp | 27.09.1962 |
| 6751 | WOODBURNE | Jonathan Gerard | Insp. | 27.09.1962 |
| 6752 | BURR | Harvey | P/O | 01.10.1962 |
| 6753 | COOK | Roger Michael | P/O | 01.10.1962 |
| 6754 | DAVIS | John Alan | P/O | 01.10.1962 |
| 6755 | GAMBLIN | Maurice Alfred | Cst | 01.10.1962 |
| 6756 | ILES | Richard Geoffrey | D/Insp | 01.10.1962 |
| 6757 | LEWIS | Kenrick John | D/C/I | 01.10.1962 |
| 6758 | MASLIN | Timothy Frank | C/Insp | 01.10.1962 |
| 6759 | MILLER | John Perry | C/Insp | 01.10.1962 |
| 6760 | MITCHELL | Geoffrey William | P/O | 01.10.1962 |
| 6761 | McCOURT | Alexander | P/O | 01.10.1962 |
| 6762 | STRANG | Ronald Charles | Supt | 01.10.1962 |
| 6763 | THOMAS | Kenneth Beaumont | Insp(T) | 01.10.1962 |
| 6764 | WIELOPOLSKI | Leszek Konrad | P/O | 01.10.1962 |
| 6765 | TURNER | Peter | Cst | 01.10.1962 |
| 6766 | LESLIE-PRINGLE | Dudley Charles | P/O | 02.10.1962 |
| 6767 | BINNS | Warren Kent | Cst | 12.10.1962 |
| 6768 | GROVES | Geoffrey Albert | Supt. | 12.10.1962 |
| 6769 | GLANVILLE | Bernard Richard | S/O | 12.10.1962 |
| 6770 | HEMMINGS | David Harold | S/O | 12.10.1962 |
| 6771 | KERSHAW | Harry | P/O | 12.10.1962 |
| 6772 | LANGRAN | Ian Edward | P/O | 12.10.1962 |
| 6773 | WALLACE | Roger Benson | P/O | 12.10.1962 |
| 6774 | MAGOWAN | Ian William | C/Insp | 23.10.1962 |
| 6775 | WICKHAM | Norman John | S/O(T) | 01.11.1962 |
| 6776 | CARR | Robert Dale | Cst | 08.11.1962 |
| 6777 | CRONIN | Denis Patrick | P/O | 08.11.1962 |
| 6778 | DAVISON | Roger Vernon | P/O | 08.11.1962 |
| 6779 | FORREST | Brent Munro | P/O | 08.11.1962 |
| 6780 | JANSEN | Graham Allan | Insp | 08.11.1962 |
| 6781 | RUTHERFOORD | Colin Rodney | P/O | 08.11.1962 |
| 6782 | TREAGUS | John | Cst | 08.11.1962 |
| 6783 | YOUNG | Robert Roy | Supt | 08.11.1962 |
| 6784 | BIRD | David Richard | S/O | 08.11.1962 |
| 6785 | BROWNLOW | Roger Victor | C/Insp | 08.11.1962 |
| 6786 | CRONE | Leeland J. | Supt | 08.11.1962 |
| 6787 | FINN | John Canice | Supt. | 08.11.1962 |
| 6788 | GRANT | Keith Duncan | Supt. | 08.11.1962 |
| 6789 | HARWOOD | Matthew | Insp | 08.11.1962 |
| 6790 | HUNTSMAN | Keith | P/O | 08.11.1962 |
| 6791 | LEIPER | John | P/O | 08.11.1962 |
| 6792 | MILNE | Christopher | P/O | 08.11.1962 |
| 6793 | PROUD | David Campbell | P/O | 08.11.1962 |
| 6794 | RITSON | Raymond Victor | D/S/O | 08.11.1962 |
| 6795 | McCALLUM | John Douglas | C/Supt | 08.11.1962 |
| 6796 | PETCH | David Napier | Supt. | 08.11.1962 |
| 6797 | KERLEY | Kenneth | S/O | 16.11.1962 |
| 6798 | ANDERSON | Gordon Charles | Insp | 26.11.1962 |
| 6799 | BERRY | Hilton White | P/O | 13.12.1962 |
| 6800 | BLACK | Keith | P/O | 13.12.1962 |
| 6801 | BLACKWELL | Michael Douglas | Cst | 13.12.1962 |
| 6802 | BOUWER | Louis Adriaan | S/S/O | 13.12.1962 |
| 6803 | DONALDSON | William John | D/S/O | 13.12.1962 |
| 6804 | EDWARDS | Brian Victor | Inspr. | 13.12.1962 |
| 6805 | GRAHAM | Phillip James | S/O | 13.12.1962 |
| 6806 | GRAINGER | Donald | P/O | 13.12.1962 |
| 6807 | HINSHAW | John Stuart | P/O | 13.12.1962 |
| 6808 | KETTLE | Michael Ray | Cst | 13.12.1962 |
| 6809 | KILSHAW | David Stanley | C/Insp | 13.12.1962 |
| 6810 | SHAND | Colin Barclay | Cst | 13.12.1962 |
| 6811 | VAN TONDER | Willem Johannes | Cst | 13.12.1962 |
| 6812 | WARD | Garth Ralph | Supt. | 13.12.1962 |
| 6813 | WILSON | David | Cst | 13.12.1962 |
| 6814 | BILLING | Richard Keith | P/O | 13.12.1962 |
| 6815 | CROSS | Michael John | Insp | 13.12.1962 |
| 6816 | CUMMING | William McPherson | S/O | 13.12.1962 |
| 6817 | DOUCHE | Keith Manton | S/O | 13.12.1962 |
| 6818 | FORREST | John | Cst | 13.12.1962 |
| 6819 | GRAY | Andrew Jeremy | C/Insp | 13.12.1962 |
| 6820 | MORRIS | Richard John | P/O | 13.12.1962 |
| 6821 | RAINFORD | John Alan | P/O | 13.12.1962 |
| 6822 | SHEPPARD | Anthony | Cst | 13.12.1962 |
| 6823 | THORNBERRY | Leslie | C/Insp | 13.12.1962 |
| 6824 | TURNER | Peter William | Cst | 13.12.1962 |
| 6825 | SMITH | Leonard David | Ins(T) | 24.12.1962 |
| 6826 | HART | George Filmer | D/S/O | 04.01.1963 |
| 6827 | ACKERMAN | Willem Coenrad | S/O | 10.01.1963 |
| 6828 | CHARMAN | Daniel Victor | P/O | 10.01.1963 |
| 6829 | DAVEY | Oliver Lee | P/O | 10.01.1963 |

| No. | Surname | First names | Date | Rank |
|---|---|---|---|---|
| 6830 | DUVENAGE | Stephanus Johannes | 10.01.1963 | P/O |
| 6831 | ELVIDGE | Charles David | 10.01.1963 | P/O |
| 6832 | FREES | Graham Barry | 10.01.1963 | A/Com |
| 6833 | GREEFF | Peter John | 10.01.1963 | A/Com |
| 6834 | GRIFFIN | David Cedric | 10.01.1963 | P/O |
| 6835 | KENNELLY | Eric Ingles | 10.01.1963 | S/C/I |
| 6836 | NAISH | Paul Royston | 10.01.1963 | D/S/O |
| 6837 | SAWYER | Colin Hamilton | 10.01.1963 | P/O |
| 6838 | STEYN | Barend Andrew | 10.01.1963 | A/Com |
| 6839 | STREET | Brian Patrick | 10.01.1963 | D/P/O |
| 6840 | SMITH | Ronald Clive | 10.01.1963 | S/O |
| 6841 | TINDALE | Brian William | 10.01.1963 | P/O |
| 6842 | ACHESON | Patrick | 10.01.1963 | P/O |
| 6843 | ANDREWS | Donald Edward | 10.01.1963 | P/O |
| 6844 | APPLETON | Brian Terence | 16.03.1963 | P/O |
| 6845 | BENNETT | Stephen Keith | 01.04.1963 | S/O(T) |
| 6846 | BLAIN | James William | 10.01.1963 | P/O |
| 6847 | CHERRY | Timothy Andrew | 10.01.1963 | Supt. |
| 6848 | CONDON | John Patrick | 10.01.1963 | Inspr. |
| 6849 | DAVEY | Alan | 10.01.1963 | D/S/O |
| 6850 | DELLOW | Brian William | 10.01.1963 | S/O |
| 6851 | EDWARDS | Richard Paul | 10.01.1963 | P/O |
| 6852 | HURD | Eric Norman | 10.01.1963 | Inspr. |
| 6853 | JONES | John Melvyn | 10.01.1963 | D/S/O |
| 6854 | PITT | Richard William | 10.01.1963 | P/O |
| 6855 | QUIGLEY | Alan | 10.01.1963 | Cst |
| 6856 | TAYLOR | John Richard | 30.07.1963 | P/O |
| 6857 | THOMAS | Richard William | 10.01.1963 | P/O |
| 6858 | YOUD | Allan Richard | 10.01.1963 | P/O |
| 6859 | CUNNINGHAM | Patrick Martin | 11.01.1963 | P/O |
| 6860 | JONES | Glyndwr Morgan | 10.01.1963 | S/O(T) |
| 6861 | EYRE | Alan | 11.01.1963 | S/O(T) |
| 6862 | GREENE | Michael Peter | 28.01.1963 | D/S/O |
| 6863 | MOORE | Thomas Howard | 11.02.1963 | D/S/O |
| 6864 | BENTLEY | Peter Ernest | 14.02.1963 | S/S/O |
| 6865 | CASTLE | Charles John | 14.02.1963 | P/O |
| 6866 | CLARKE | Robin Patric | 14.02.1963 | P/O |
| 6867 | DEACON | Thomas Andrew | 14.02.1963 | Inspr. |
| 6868 | GOUWS | Daniel | 14.02.1963 | C/Insp |
| 6869 | LOGUE | Peter William | 14.02.1963 | S/O |
| 6870 | LOW | David Vincent | 14.02.1963 | D/C/I |
| 6871 | LUYT | Anthony Maurice | 14.02.1963 | Inspr. |
| 6872 | LYNN | David Alexander | 14.02.1963 | D/P/O |
| 6873 | O'MOLONY | Robert Allan | 14.02.1963 | S/O |
| 6874 | SPURR | Neville Garth | 09.05.1963 | Supt |
| 6875 | VAN WYK | Mobie Boemsma | 14.02.1963 | S/Insp |
| 6876 | WEST | Christopher Bruce | 14.02.1963 | D/P/O |
| 6877 | BURGOYNE | Richard Henry | 14.02.1963 | P/O |
| 6878 | FISHLOCK | Michael Charles | 14.02.1963 | P/O |
| 6879 | GRIFFITHS | David Palin | 14.02.1963 | P/O |
| 6880 | HILLIARD | Albert Ernest | 14.02.1963 | S/S/O |
| 6881 | HOUSE | Peter John | 14.02.1963 | Cst |
| 6882 | LINDLEY | James Lynton | 14.02.1963 | P/O |
| 6883 | WEBB | Stephen Allan | 14.02.1963 | P/O |
| 6884 | WHIFFIN | Timothy Congreve | 14.02.1963 | Cst |
| 6885 | PHILLIPS | Peter John | 14.02.1963 | D/S/O |
| 6886 | ASHURST | Lance Sidney | 15.02.1963 | S/O |
| 6887 | BOSCH | Thomas | 14.03.1963 | P/O |
| 6888 | CAMPBELL | Jan Dirk | 14.03.1963 | Cst |
| 6889 | CAWOOD | Peter Drummond | 14.03.1963 | P/O |
| 6890 | COETZEE | Barry Richard | 14.03.1963 | D/P/O |
| 6891 | CUNNINGHAM | Hermanus | 14.03.1963 | P/O |
| 6892 | JOYCE | Michael Stuart | 14.03.1963 | Cst |
| 6893 | OBERHOLSTER | David Alan | 14.03.1963 | Supt. |
| 6894 | PIGGOT | Brian Arthur | 14.03.1963 | S/O |
| 6895 | STEWART | Richard Ronald | 14.03.1963 | S/O |
| 6896 | WILSON | Kenneth Gordon | 14.03.1963 | D/P/O |
| 6897 | WHITE | Barend Daniel | 14.03.1963 | P/O |
| | | Alan Cameron | 14.03.1963 | Cst |
| 6899 | CRITCHLEY | Nicholas Emile | 14.03.1963 | Cst |
| 6900 | GEE | Martin Raymond | 14.03.1963 | P/O |
| 6901 | GRAHAM | David Rodney | 14.03.1963 | P/O |
| 6902 | HORN | Robert Guy | 14.03.1963 | P/O |
| 6903 | IZON | Timothy John | 14.03.1963 | P/O |
| 6904 | LAWRENCE | Ian Vernon | 14.03.1963 | Inspr. |
| 6905 | PHILLIPS | Peter Beric | 14.03.1963 | S/O |
| 6906 | SERGEANT | Michael Roy | 14.03.1963 | D/S/O |
| 6907 | SHEW | Paul | 14.03.1963 | S/O |
| 6908 | WAGGOT | Ian Richard | 14.03.1963 | D/P/O |
| 6909 | WAKE | Lawrence Metcalf | 14.03.1963 | S/O |
| 6910 | BISSETT | John Leonard | 15.03.1963 | P/O |
| 6911 | SCHMIDT | Ferdinand Wilhelm | 16.03.1963 | P/O |
| 6912 | MARAIS | Pieter William | 01.04.1963 | D/S/O |
| 6913 | SMITH | Colin Gower | 01.04.1963 | P/O |
| 6914 | BATTY | William David | 11.04.1963 | P/O |
| 6915 | LANE | Barry Neville | 11.04.1963 | S/O |
| 6916 | PITTAWAY | Ernest John | 11.04.1963 | P/O |
| 6917 | WITHER | Peter Stewart | 11.04.1963 | S/O |
| 6918 | ALLEN-ROWLANDSON | Terence Peter | 11.04.1963 | S/O |
| 6919 | BLAKE | Fraser McGregor | 11.04.1963 | S/O |
| 6920 | BULLMORE | Andrew Rivers | 11.04.1963 | Supt |
| 6921 | BYRNE | Howard Robert | 11.04.1963 | P/O |
| 6922 | CAMERON | Earl Dickson | 11.04.1963 | D/S/O |
| 6923 | CLARKE | Thomas Michael | 11.04.1963 | P/O |
| 6924 | COCKRAM | Charles Harry | 11.04.1963 | S/O |
| 6925 | DARBY | David Binnie | 11.04.1963 | S/O |
| 6926 | JACKSON | Barry Ralph | 11.04.1963 | P/O |
| 6927 | LEE | Christopher Frederick | 11.04.1963 | S/A/C |
| 6928 | MACPHERSON | Stewart | 11.04.1963 | D/Inspr. |
| 6929 | MARTIN | Howard | 11.04.1963 | S/O |
| 6930 | MILLER | Alan Charles | 11.04.1963 | S/O |
| 6931 | MOUNCER | Robert Ernest | 11.04.1963 | Cst. |
| 6932 | ORGAN | James Anthony | 11.04.1963 | P/O |
| 6933 | TAYLOR | Trevor Hilton | 11.04.1963 | P/O |
| 6934 | UPTON | Thomas Leighton | 11.04.1963 | Cst. |
| 6935 | WOODROFFE | Peter John | 11.04.1963 | S/S/O |
| 6936 | BOSMAN | Edward William | 16.04.1963 | P/O |
| 6937 | DEWAR | Donald Robert | 16.04.1963 | P/O |
| 6938 | JOHNS | Courtney Robert | 16.04.1963 | P/O |
| 6939 | JONES | Daniel Hermanus | 16.04.1963 | S/S/O |
| 6940 | TAYLOR | Jack Robert | 16.04.1963 | Cst |
| 6941 | CURRIE | Richard Foster | 09.05.1963 | S/O |
| 6942 | ELDER | David | 09.05.1963 | S/O |
| 6943 | GLEAVES-GRAHAM | Christopher David | 09.05.1963 | Cst |
| 6944 | HARPER | Peter Frank | 09.05.1963 | P/O |
| 6945 | HODGSON | Keith Hope | 09.05.1963 | P/O |
| 6946 | LOUW | Louwrence Francois | 09.05.1963 | P/O |
| 6947 | SOUTHAM | Robert Stuart | 09.05.1963 | D/P/O |
| 6948 | WEBSTER | Clifford Harewood | 09.05.1963 | P/O |
| 6949 | ARGENT | Michael | 09.05.1963 | S/S/O |
| 6950 | BAILEY | James Lynton | 09.05.1963 | Cst |
| 6951 | CRUICKSHANKS | John | 09.05.1963 | P/O |
| 6952 | DAWSON | Barry Richard | 09.05.1963 | D/S/O |
| 6953 | FARMER | Rex Howard | 09.05.1963 | P/O |
| 6954 | FROST | Anthony | 09.05.1963 | P/O |
| 6955 | AITKEN | David William | 09.05.1963 | P/O |
| 6956 | MOWBRAY | Geoffrey | 09.05.1963 | P/O |
| 6957 | PEARSON | David Lancelot | 09.05.1963 | P/O |
| 6958 | PUGSLEY | Edward Charles | 09.05.1963 | D/P/O |
| 6959 | RANGE | Alan William | 09.05.1963 | P/O |
| 6960 | RIPLEY | Stephen Kenneth | 09.05.1963 | S/S/O |
| 6961 | SAYERS | Hugh Mervyn | 09.05.1963 | Cst |
| 6962 | SHEPHERD | Lancelot Steven | 09.05.1963 | P/O |
| 6963 | SMITH | Roger Christopher | 09.05.1963 | D/S/O |
| 6964 | STANLEY | Robin Barry | 09.05.1963 | S/O |
| 6965 | WILSON | Peter Joseph | 09.05.1963 | D/P/O |
| 6966 | CLARKE | Robert Michael | 14.05.1963 | Cst |
| 6968 | KIRKMAN | Christopher Anthony | 13.06.1963 | P/O |
| 6969 | BUDD | John Fane | 13.06.1963 | D/Insp |
| 6970 | DAVIS | Dudley | 13.06.1963 | Supt |
| 6971 | GODLEY | Bernard Quentin | 13.06.1963 | Inspr. |
| 6972 | LANGE | Derek Arthur | 13.06.1963 | P/O |
| 6973 | SAWYER | Michael John | 13.06.1963 | S/O |
| 6974 | SPENCER | Edward Herbert | 13.06.1963 | S/Insp |
| 6975 | DELORIE | Raymond Paul | 13.06.1963 | Cst |
| 6976 | ALLSOP | David Benjamin | 13.06.1963 | P/O |
| 6977 | ATHERTON | David Ian | 13.06.1963 | P/O |
| 6978 | CARNEY | Daniel Cyril | 13.06.1963 | S/C/I |
| 6979 | CLARK | Kenneth Robert | 13.06.1963 | S/C/I |
| 6980 | COLLINS | Michael John | 13.06.1963 | Cst |
| 6981 | GIBSON | Andrew Joseph | 13.06.1963 | A/Com |
| 6982 | KEFFORD | Harry Ellis | 13.06.1963 | D/P/O |
| 6983 | McDADE | Gerald | 13.06.1963 | P/O |
| 6984 | MATTEN | Richard Charles | 13.06.1963 | P/O |
| 6985 | MITCHELL | Anthony Robert | 13.06.1963 | P/O |
| 6986 | PRITCHARD | David | 13.06.1963 | P/O |
| 6987 | RUSSELL | Richard Anthony | 13.06.1963 | P/O |
| 6988 | SAY | Colin Edward | 13.06.1963 | P/O |
| 6989 | TURNER | Roger Andrew | 13.06.1963 | P/O |
| 6990 | WILSON | Christopher John | 13.06.1963 | P/O |
| 6991 | GIBBS | Brian John | 28.06.1963 | S/O |
| 6992 | DALZIEL | Robert | 22.07.1963 | P/O |
| 6993 | CRAUSE | Sidney Hancon | 30.07.1963 | Inspr. |
| 6994 | JOHNN | Colin Barry | 30.07.1963 | P/O |
| 6995 | NIEUWOUDT | Heremias Hendrik | 30.07.1963 | P/O |
| 6996 | LUCAS | David Brian | 12.08.1963 | P/O |
| 6997 | McLEAN | Ronald Gerald | 28.08.1963 | P/O |
| 6998 | VILJOEN | Garth Gray | 28.08.1963 | S/O |
| 6999 | MARKHAM | Miles Trenly | 02.09.1963 | S/O |
| 7000 | HARLEY | David Phillip | 05.09.1963 | P/O |
| 7001 | CLARKE | Rodney | 11.09.1963 | D/S/O |
| 7002 | DOUGALL | Andrew Kendal | 13.09.1963 | P/O |
| 7003 | DAVIS | Michael John | 24.09.1963 | Cst |
| 7004 | RANKIN | Robert Fleming | 24.09.1963 | Insp |
| 7005 | LAWRENCE | Anthony Reginald | 01.10.1963 | C/Ins(T) |
| 7006 | FRANKLIN | Robert John | 07.10.1963 | P/O |
| 7007 | COWE | Robert Alexander | 10.10.1963 | Cst |
| 7008 | GUNN | William Reginald | 10.10.1963 | P/O |
| 7009 | THOMAS | Spencer Thomas | 10.10.1963 | P/O |
| 7010 | WINTER | Malcolm D'Alroy | 10.10.1963 | C/Insp |
| 7011 | JACKSON | Leslie John | 10.10.1963 | C/Insp |
| 7012 | KING | Michael John | 10.10.1963 | Cst |
| 7013 | KLOPPERS | Johannes Hendrik | 10.10.1963 | P/O |
| 7014 | SMITH | Malcolm Ernest | 10.10.1963 | Supt. |
| 7015 | BARNARD | Roger Michael | 10.10.1963 | P/O |
| 7016 | BRADLEY | Graham Frank | 10.10.1963 | C/Insp |
| 7017 | BRUCE | Alexander Bruce | 10.10.1963 | P/O |
| 7018 | COLLINGE | Ronald Harvey | 10.10.1963 | D/S/O |
| 7019 | DAWSON | Reginald McGillivray | 10.10.1963 | D/Insp |
| 7020 | ELLIS | Peter Antony | 10.10.1963 | P/O |
| 7021 | GREER | John McCormac | 10.10.1963 | Cst |
| 7022 | WALKER | David | 10.10.1963 | P/O |
| 7023 | WALMSLEY-MOSS | Richard Michael | 10.10.1963 | D/S/O |
| 7024 | WINTON | Richard | 10.10.1963 | D/P/O |
| 7025 | MEEKINGS | Brian Alfred | 10.10.1963 | Insp |
| 7026 | HUGHES | Errol Trevor | 18.10.1963 | P/O |
| 7027 | RAE | Keith Robert | 25.10.1963 | P/O |
| 7028 | PRINCE | Alan Carl | 29.10.1963 | P/O |
| 7029 | BALL | Guy Alvin | 31.10.1963 | S/S/O |
| 7030 | PATTERSON | Peter John | 01.11.1963 | Ins(T) |
| 7031 | REINBACH | Arthur Leslie | 01.11.1963 | Ins(T) |
| 7032 | JEFFERSON | George Cyril | 12.11.1963 | Ins(T) |
| 7033 | KERR | Derek William | 18.11.1963 | Supt |
| 7034 | WILLS | Michael William | 26.11.1963 | Ins(T) |
| 7035 | BARNETT | Frank David Grant | 12.12.1963 | P/O |

| No. | Surname | First name(s) | Date | Rank |
|---|---|---|---|---|
| 7037 | COETZER | Roman | 12.12.1963 | S/L/Sgt. |
| 7038 | COLLINGS | Ashley David | 12.12.1963 | Supt |
| 7039 | LEE | David James | 12.12.1963 | P/O |
| 7040 | VISSER | Roy Morkel | 12.12.1963 | P/O |
| 7041 | WATERHOUSE | John Henry | 12.12.1963 | S/O |
| 7042 | BENNETT | Bruce James | 13.12.1963 | P/O |
| 7043 | CLEGG | Robert | 13.12.1963 | P/O |
| 7044 | FREEMAN | Grahame Clive | 13.12.1963 | P/O |
| 7045 | GATES | William Robert | 13.12.1963 | P/O |
| 7046 | HANNER | Colin Roy | 13.12.1963 | P/O |
| 7047 | MASSEY | David | 13.12.1963 | P/O |
| 7048 | OSBORNE | Ian Michael | 13.12.1963 | P/O |
| 7049 | WHITMORE | Lewis Leonard | 13.12.1963 | Supt. |
| 7050 | WILLOUGHBY | John Dennis | 08.01.1964 | Insp |
| 7051 | HINES | Michael Norman | 31.01.1964 | S/O |
| 7052 | ELLERT | Henrik Brouner | 13.02.1964 | P/O |
| 7053 | LIGHTFOOT | William Denton | 13.02.1964 | P/O |
| 7054 | BIRD | Michael John | 13.02.1964 | P/O |
| 7055 | BRENT | Alan Charlton | 13.02.1964 | C/Insp |
| 7056 | KIPPS | Cecil Duncan | 13.02.1964 | P/O |
| 7057 | LAPAGE | John Graham | 13.02.1964 | P/O |
| 7058 | O'LEARY | Michael John | 13.02.1964 | P/O |
| 7059 | NOBLE | Ryland Winton | 13.02.1964 | D/P/O |
| 7060 | PAULET | Michael John | 13.02.1964 | P/O |
| 7061 | SAUNDERS | Peter | 13.02.1964 | Insp |
| 7062 | YOUNGSON | William Gordon | 13.02.1964 | Cst |
| 7063 | BAILEY | John Frederick | 13.02.1964 | P/O |
| 7064 | BLACKER | John Edwin | 13.02.1964 | P/O |
| 7065 | COLLINS | David John | 13.02.1964 | P/O |
| 7066 | CRAIGEN | Trevor Percival | 13.02.1964 | S/S/O |
| 7067 | FEAST | Bruce Edwin | 13.02.1964 | Insp |
| 7068 | GALE | Anthony Stephen | 13.02.1964 | P/O |
| 7069 | HARDEY | Derek Forbes | 13.02.1964 | D/P/O |
| 7070 | LANGTON | John Gordon | 13.02.1964 | D/S/O |
| 7071 | RICHARDS | Michael | 13.02.1964 | C/Sup |
| 7072 | WALMSLEY | Terence | 13.02.1964 | P/O |
| 7073 | WINSON | Selwyn Russell | 10.03.1964 | P/O |
| 7074 | BROOM | James Philip | 01.04.1964 | Insp(T) |
| 7075 | BAKER | Alan John | 01.04.1964 | S/O |
| 7076 | HICKMAN | Jeremy Alexander | 09.04.1964 | S/O |
| 7077 | BRESLER | Herman | 09.04.1964 | P/O |
| 7078 | CLARK | Victor Ian | 09.04.1964 | S/Insp |
| 7079 | CLARK | Sidney Burleigh | 09.04.1964 | P/O |
| 7080 | GLAZIER | Ronald | 09.04.1964 | Cst |
| 7081 | JABOOR | Farris James | 09.04.1964 | P/O |
| 7082 | NEL | Derek Hayward | 09.04.1964 | D/P/O |
| 7083 | SEWELL | William Robert | 09.04.1964 | P/O |
| 7084 | DEARDEN | Frank | 10.04.1964 | P/O |
| 7085 | HUBBARD | Hugh Graeme | 10.04.1964 | P/O |
| 7086 | JOHNN | Michael William | 10.04.1964 | P/O |
| 7087 | JONES | Rupert Norman | 10.04.1964 | P/O |
| 7088 | MARTIN | John Paul | 10.04.1964 | Insp |
| 7089 | McAUSLIN | Graham Kennedy | 10.04.1964 | P/O |
| 7090 | PARK | Graham Richmond | 10.04.1964 | P/O |
| 7091 | WRIGHT | Michael George | 10.04.1964 | P/O |
| 7092 | SLY | David Edmund | 17.04.1964 | P/O |
| 7093 | SIMPSON | Ian Paul | 21.04.1964 | P/O |
| 7094 | HOWARD | Robert Alexander | 23.04.1964 | P/O |
| 7095 | WASSERMAN | Barend Petrus | 11.05.1964 | Insp |
| 7096 | BENNELL | Graham Alan | 12.05.1964 | P/O |
| 7097 | DREWETT | Philip Michael | 12.05.1964 | D/Insp |
| 7098 | FOSTER | Christopher Michael | 12.05.1964 | P/O |
| 7099 | MUSSON | Colin David | 12.05.1964 | P/O |
| 7100 | TAYLOR | Roy | 12.05.1964 | P/O |
| 7101 | ARBUCKLE | Anthony Edward | 12.05.1964 | P/O |
| 7102 | BROWNE | Harry James | 12.05.1964 | D/Insp |
| 7103 | HUGHES | Melvin Paul | 12.05.1964 | P/O |
| 7104 | NEILL | Anthony Howard | 12.05.1964 | S/O |
| 7105 | MEADOWS | Ian Claud | 13.05.1964 | P/O |
| 7106 | HUGHES | Trevor Joseph | 23.05.1964 | P/O |
| 7107 | GERBER | Gideon Hendrik | 08.06.1964 | P/O |
| 7108 | Mac KENZIE | Alastair John | 08.06.1964 | Insp |
| 7109 | WOOD | Henry Alfred | 09.06.1964 | P/O |
| 7110 | BIRD | Edmund Arthur | 09.06.1964 | P/O |
| 7111 | ROSSER | Clifford Anthony | 09.06.1964 | P/O |
| 7112 | SCOTT-RODGER | Anthony John | 09.06.1964 | P/O |
| 7113 | BAGLEY | Richard Thomas | 09.06.1964 | P/O |
| 7114 | DEAMER | Michael Barry | 09.06.1964 | P/O |
| 7115 | LITTLE | Michael George | 09.06.1964 | P/O |
| 7116 | TAYLOR | Barrie | 09.06.1964 | P/O |
| 7117 | THORNLEY | Richard Perry | 09.06.1964 | P/O |
| 7118 | HARRISON | Michael Geoffrey | 11.06.1964 | P/O |
| 7119 | STEAD | John Andrew | 03.07.1964 | Insp |
| 7120 | TUNNEY | David John | 15.07.1964 | Insp |
| 7121 | NEVITT | Peter John | 16.07.1964 | P/O |
| 7122 | RUSSELL | Anthony Benjamin | 16.07.1964 | D/S/O |
| 7123 | WHITTAKER | Colin Croasdale | 31.07.1964 | D/P/O |
| 7124 | DE LORME | Kevin Bruce | 11.08.1964 | P/O |
| 7125 | ELLIS | Peter Joseph | 11.08.1964 | P/O |
| 7126 | HOPE | Leslie Anthony | 11.08.1964 | Insp(T) |
| 7127 | HUNTER-HARDY | John | 11.08.1964 | P/O |
| 7128 | JOHNSON | Edward Anthony | 11.08.1964 | P/O |
| 7129 | MESSINA | Andrew John | 11.08.1964 | C/Insp |
| 7130 | VAN HEERDEN | Glynn Darroll | 11.08.1964 | D/S/O |
| 7131 | BLIGHT | Philip Eric | 11.08.1964 | P/O |
| 7132 | DIPPLE | David | 11.08.1964 | P/O |
| 7133 | FOSTER | Derek Rehor | 11.08.1964 | S/O |
| 7134 | HUTTON | Christopher Ardwin | 11.08.1964 | P/O |
| 7135 | LUCKIN | Paul Thomas | 11.08.1964 | P/O |
| 7136 | LYNAS | David | 11.08.1964 | D/S/O |
| 7137 | LYON | Ian Michael | 11.08.1964 | P/O |
| 7138 | JONES | Peter Robert | 11.08.1964 | P/O |
| 7139 | ROGERS | David Kenneth | 11.08.1964 | P/O |
| 7140 | TILLING | Eric Raymond | 11.08.1964 | P/O |
| 7141 | WATSON | Ian Malcolm | 11.08.1964 | P/O |
| 7142 | ROBERTSON | Guy Neil | 17.08.1964 | Const. |
| 7143 | CUNLIFFE-STEEL | Philip John | 17.08.1964 | Insp |
| 7144 | VORSTER | Izak Johannes | 29.08.1964 | D/S/O |
| 7145 | BECKS | Colin Cyril | 01.09.1964 | S/S/O |
| 7146 | ST. CLAIR | Anthony Patrick | 07.09.1964 | P/O |
| 7147 | MORTLEY-WOOD | Allen Norman | 14.09.1964 | P/O |
| 7148 | ROBBIE | Kenneth Scott | 14.09.1964 | P/O |
| 7149 | BARBER | David William | 15.09.1964 | P/O |
| 7150 | BENSON | Gordon Martin | 15.09.1964 | P/O |
| 7151 | BLOOM | Clive Cromarty | 15.09.1964 | S/O |
| 7152 | BROAD | Kevin George | 15.09.1964 | P/O |
| 7153 | CRAFTER | Michael George | 15.09.1964 | Supt |
| 7154 | CRAWFORD | Thomas Andrew | 15.09.1964 | P/O |
| 7155 | MASON | Ernest Frederick | 15.09.1964 | P/O |
| 7156 | RUST | Paul Vincent | 15.09.1964 | P/O |
| 7157 | GRAHAM | Reginald David | 17.09.1964 | P/O |
| 7158 | STANYON | Douglas John | 22.09.1964 | P/O |
| 7159 | RIDLEY | Robert John | 24.09.1964 | P/O |
| 7160 | de GRAY-BIRCH | John | 28.09.1964 | D/P/O |
| 7161 | OPPERMAN | Victor | 30.09.1964 | Supt |
| 7162 | HOLLOWAY | Geoffrey John | 05.10.1964 | P/O |
| 7163 | EVANS | John Michael | 05.10.1964 | D/P/O |
| 7164 | SHIRLEY | Philip | 13.10.1964 | Const. |
| 7165 | BENSON | David | 13.10.1964 | P/O |
| 7166 | FAIRHURST | George | 13.10.1964 | P/O |
| 7167 | LONG | Peter Vivian | 13.10.1964 | Insp |
| 7168 | MURDOCH | John | 13.10.1964 | P/O |
| 7169 | QUINEY | David Henry | 13.10.1964 | P/O |
| 7170 | RICKARD | Robert John | 13.10.1964 | P/O |
| 7171 | SINCLAIR | Philip Ferguson | 13.10.1964 | D/Insp |
| 7172 | TAYLOR | Gregory Marcus | 13.10.1964 | D/P/O |
| 7173 | TURNBULL | Julian Richard | 13.10.1964 | S/O |
| 7174 | WILLIAMS | Michael Peter | 13.10.1964 | P/O |
| 7175 | WOOD | Graham John | 13.10.1964 | P/O |
| 7176 | FRASER | Philip Clarke | 16.10.1964 | S/O |
| 7177 | VARKEVISSER | Andrew Daniel | 18.10.1964 | P/O |
| 7178 | JOUBERT | Cornelius Matias | 25.10.1964 | P/O |
| 7179 | POWELL-REES | Llewellyn | 01.11.1964 | P/O |
| 7180 | BIRRELL | Eric | 09.11.1964 | C/Insp |
| 7181 | HOWARTH | Michael William | 10.11.1964 | D/Insp |
| 7182 | SHEARD | John Richard | 10.11.1964 | C/Insp |
| 7183 | GUNSTON | Brian | 10.11.1964 | P/O |
| 7184 | RUSSELL | Christopher John | 10.11.1964 | Supt |
| 7185 | BAKER | Colin Trevor | 10.11.1964 | P/O |
| 7186 | BRUNNOCK | Terence | 10.11.1964 | P/O |
| 7187 | BYRNE | Noel Joseph | 10.11.1964 | P/O |
| 7188 | EASTON | Malcolm John | 10.11.1964 | Supt |
| 7189 | FERRIS | David Angus | 10.11.1964 | P/O |
| 7190 | KIRKHAM | Peter David | 10.11.1964 | P/O |
| 7191 | POLETTYLO | Stefan Lucian | 10.11.1964 | D/S/O |
| 7192 | ROBINS | Stephen Henry | 10.11.1964 | D/P/O |
| 7193 | HICKSON | Brian John | 10.11.1964 | P/O |
| 7194 | THOMAS | Christopher Howard | 10.11.1964 | P/O |
| 7195 | WEBSTER | Matthew | 10.11.1964 | D/P/O |
| 7196 | SMITH | Robert Kenneth | 10.11.1964 | P/O |
| 7197 | SOLOMON | Frank | 25.11.1964 | D/P/O |
| 7198 | VERNON | Michael John | 27.11.1964 | P/O |
| 7199 | BEZUIDENHOUT | Carel Petrus | 01.12.1964 | P/O |
| 7200 | MILLER | Barry Herbert | 01.12.1964 | D/S/O |
| 7201 | D'ARAUJO | Alberto Nunes | 06.12.1964 | P/O |
| 7202 | PIETERSE | Jacob Cloete | 08.12.1964 | P/O |
| 7203 | GEORGE | Clive Richard | 08.12.1964 | P/O |
| 7204 | GRANT | Anthony Young | 08.12.1964 | P/O |
| 7205 | GUNSTON | Colin | 08.12.1964 | S/O |
| 7206 | PHILLIPS | Christopher Robin | 08.12.1964 | P/O |
| 7207 | WOOLLEY | Arnold | 08.12.1964 | Supt |
| 7208 | ADDISON | Keith Roland | 07.12.1964 | P/O |
| 7209 | BOLAS | Stanley | 09.12.1964 | Supt |
| 7210 | THORNTON | Malcolm Ian | 14.12.1964 | Insp(T) |
| 7211 | BIDDULPH | Peter William | 15.12.1964 | S/C/I |
| 7212 | BROWN | Dennis Anthony | 15.12.1964 | C/Supt |
| 7213 | BRUCE | James Hogg | 15.12.1964 | P/O |
| 7214 | GENT | Henry Watson | 15.12.1964 | P/O |
| 7215 | INMAN | Howard James | 15.12.1964 | P/O |
| 7216 | LOVELL | Maldwyn Leslie | 15.12.1964 | P/O |
| 7217 | TEDFORD | John Dill | 15.12.1964 | Insp |
| 7218 | WHITTAKER | Richard | 15.12.1964 | P/O |
| 7219 | WOOD | Paul Henry | 15.12.1964 | P/O |
| 7220 | ELLIOTT | Robert Alfred | 18.12.1964 | Insp |
| 7221 | HARLOW | Michael John | 04.01.1965 | D/Insp |
| 7222 | RADFORD | John | 05.01.1965 | P/O |
| 7223 | REACORD | David Robert | 12.01.1965 | P/O |
| 7224 | BERGER | Mark | 12.01.1965 | P/O |
| 7225 | BROWN | Keith Edward | 12.01.1965 | P/O |
| 7226 | EARLY | Robert John | 12.01.1965 | P/O |
| 7227 | JONES | Roger Brynmor | 12.01.1965 | P/O |
| 7228 | DE BRUIJN | Gert Hendrik | 12.01.1965 | P/O |
| 7229 | HOWSE | Desmond Leslie | 12.01.1965 | S/Insp |
| 7230 | PELL | David Vincent | 12.01.1965 | D/P/O |
| 7231 | ARMSTRONG | Richard Henry | 12.01.1965 | P/O |
| 7232 | BIRCHALL | Alan Robert | 12.01.1965 | Insp |
| 7233 | SHELLEY | Bernard Clive | 12.01.1965 | Supt |
| 7234 | COLLIER | John Ingram | 12.01.1965 | Supt. |
| 7235 | GEDDES | Alastair Watson | 12.01.1965 | P/O |
| 7236 | HENDERSON | John Johnston | 12.01.1965 | P/O |
| 7237 | MILLS | Alan Henry | 12.01.1965 | P/O |
| 7238 | PLUMB | Adam Crispin | 12.01.1965 | P/O |
| 7239 | QUINN | Christopher James | 12.01.1965 | P/O |
| 7240 | SMALES | Peter Anthony | 12.01.1965 | S/O |
| 7241 | WHEELWRIGHT | John Edward | 12.01.1965 | S/O |
| 7242 | WILLIAMSON | Frederick | 12.01.1965 | P/O |
| 7243 | MUIR | Desmond Trevor | 12.01.1965 | P/O |

| No. | Surname | First Name | Date | Rank |
|---|---|---|---|---|
| 7244 | TAYLOR | Richard Robert | 12.01.1965 | P/O |
| 7245 | PRELLER | Robert Johann | 12.01.1965 | P/O |
| 7246 | ROWE | John William | 12.01.1965 | Insp |
| 7247 | HARRIES | Rhys Thomas | 21.01.1965 | Insp |
| 7248 | O'HANLON | Dennis | 27.01.1965 | D/S/O |
| 7249 | ALLANBY | Andries Petrus | 29.01.1965 | Insp |
| 7250 | LINCOTT | Derek Walter | 29.01.1965 | P/O |
| 7251 | WEBSTER | Barrie Keith | 01.02.1965 | P/O |
| 7252 | DU TOIT | Arthur | 09.02.1965 | Insp |
| 7253 | EASTES | Barry John | 09.02.1965 | Supt |
| 7254 | TAYLOR | Ian George | 09.02.1965 | D/S/O |
| 7255 | ATTERBURY | Raymond Norman | 09.02.1965 | P/O |
| 7256 | CORMACK | Gordon Bruce | 09.02.1965 | P/O |
| 7257 | DEARDEN | Clifford Philip | 09.02.1965 | P/O |
| 7258 | RUNDLE | Norman Albert | 09.02.1965 | P/O |
| 7259 | BELL | John Stuart | 09.02.1965 | Insp |
| 7260 | DALE | Raymond Bernard | 09.02.1965 | Insp |
| 7261 | FULLER | Lance John | 09.02.1965 | S/O |
| 7262 | MAITLAND | Peter Anthony | 09.02.1965 | Supt |
| 7263 | MILNE | Kenneth Lothian | 09.02.1965 | D/Insp |
| 7264 | BEST | Gordon Leslie | 09.02.1965 | P/O |
| 7265 | BRUNSKELL | George Edward | 09.02.1965 | P/O |
| 7266 | GIBSON | John Kenneth | 09.02.1965 | P/O |
| 7267 | LOOKER | Nigel Hugh | 09.02.1965 | Insp |
| 7268 | MACK | Christopher David | 09.02.1965 | S/O |
| 7269 | MURRELL | Gordon Eric | 09.02.1965 | S/O |
| 7270 | NEAVE | Richard Ernest | 09.02.1965 | S/O |
| 7271 | PARGETER | Christopher John | 09.02.1965 | D/Insp |
| 7272 | PISCOPOS | Charles | 09.02.1965 | P/O |
| 7273 | RIGBY | David Woodvine | 09.02.1965 | P/O |
| 7274 | SHEERAN | Joseph Matson | 09.02.1965 | S/O |
| 7275 | WHEATLEY | John | 09.02.1965 | S/O |
| 7276 | DRAPER | Dennis | 09.02.1965 | P/O |
| 7277 | PHILLIPS | Dennis | 09.02.1965 | P/O |
| 7278 | OSBORNE | Raymond Laurence | 09.02.1965 | P/O |
| 7279 | BLOOMFIELD | Michael | 15.02.1965 | S/O |
| 7280 | LEBISH | Roger Dunbar | 17.02.1965 | C/Insp. |
| 7281 | HARDY | Graham Beit | 21.02.1965 | D/S/O |
| 7282 | ROACH | George Malcolm | 22.02.1965 | S/O |
| 7283 | GARNETT | Christopher | 27.02.1965 | D/S/O |
| 7284 | MASSIE | Alexander James | 01.03.1965 | S/S/O |
| 7285 | WADDON | David Charles | 01.03.1965 | Supt |
| 7286 | ALLER | Stuart Charles | 09.03.1965 | S/O |
| 7287 | DALE | Francis Edward | 09.03.1965 | C/Sup |
| 7288 | HOLMES | Ian Errington | 09.03.1965 | D/C/I |
| 7289 | PARKER | David Vincent | 09.03.1965 | D/Insp |
| 7290 | VAN DEN HEEVER | Stephen | 09.03.1965 | P/O |
| 7291 | BARNARD | Roy Keith | 09.03.1965 | P/O |
| 7292 | BLAIR-SPIERS | Mervyn Tom | 09.03.1965 | P/O |
| 7293 | CLARK | Stuart John | 09.03.1965 | P/O |
| 7294 | CRAVEN | John Leslie | 09.03.1965 | P/O |
| 7295 | GLENN | Barrie | 09.03.1965 | P/O |
| 7296 | GREEN | David Anthony | 09.03.1965 | P/O |
| 7297 | HAMMOND | John Leslie | 09.03.1965 | P/O |
| 7298 | HINCKS | Julian | 09.03.1965 | P/O |
| 7299 | HUGHES | Ian | 09.03.1965 | P/O |
| 7300 | KANE | Michael | 09.03.1965 | P/O |
| 7301 | KIRBY | George Brian | 09.03.1965 | P/O |
| 7302 | MORAN | Denis James | 09.03.1965 | P/O |
| 7303 | MORGAN | Richard John | 09.03.1965 | D/C/I |
| 7304 | READER | Norman Geoffrey | 09.03.1965 | Insp |
| 7305 | STANDALOFT | Peter Maples | 09.03.1965 | Supt |
| 7306 | TAWSE | David Stuart | 09.03.1965 | P/O |
| 7307 | MONEY | William Edward | 09.03.1965 | P/O |
| 7308 | VAN VUUREN | Lukas Marthinus | 09.03.1965 | P/O |
| 7309 | PHILLIPS | Alan Godfrey | 13.03.1965 | P/O |
| 7310 | ONIONS | Edward Valentine | 16.03.1965 | S/O |
| 7311 | GAULT | Kenneth Lindsay | 13.04.1965 | D/Insp |
| 7313 | PERKINS | Edward Randle | 13.04.1965 | Insp |
| 7314 | REIJERS | Robert | 13.04.1965 | Insp |
| 7315 | ARMSTRONG | William | 13.04.1965 | D/Insp |
| 7316 | FERGUSON | Stephen Philip | 13.04.1965 | P/O |
| 7317 | FINCH | Martin John | 13.04.1965 | P/O |
| 7318 | FIRTH | Anthony Hugh | 13.04.1965 | S/O |
| 7319 | GLOVER | Malcolm James | 13.04.1965 | S/O |
| 7320 | HILL | Geoffrey Edward | 13.04.1965 | S/O |
| 7321 | HODGSON | Raymond Philip | 13.04.1965 | S/O |
| 7322 | HOWELL | Gareth Wynn | 13.04.1965 | P/O |
| 7323 | JULIAN | John Richard | 13.04.1965 | P/O |
| 7324 | KEMP | Alistair Angus | 13.04.1965 | P/O |
| 7325 | Mac INTYRE | Lawrence Michael | 13.04.1965 | Insp |
| 7326 | NEWBURY | Michael | 13.04.1965 | S/O |
| 7327 | PLANT | Patrick Leslie | 13.04.1965 | P/O |
| 7328 | QUICKFALL | Brendan Gerrard | 13.04.1965 | P/O |
| 7329 | SHILLETO | James | 13.04.1965 | S/O |
| 7330 | SPENCER | Adam Hendry | 13.04.1965 | C/Insp |
| 7331 | STILL | Peter Richard | 13.04.1965 | D/S/O |
| 7332 | WARR | Darell Anthony | 13.04.1965 | D/S/O |
| 7333 | WIGLEY | Michael | 13.04.1965 | D/S/O |
| 7334 | WILDING | John Andrew | 13.04.1965 | P/O |
| 7335 | WILKS | Richard Howard | 18.04.1965 | P/O |
| 7336 | WILLIAMS | Alfred Evans | 23.04.1965 | P/O |
| 7337 | JOUBERT | Graham Reginald | 28.04.1965 | P/O |
| 7338 | MASTERTON | Ian Alexander | 11.05.1965 | D/Insp |
| 7339 | CLARK | Christopher Dermot | 11.05.1965 | P/O |
| 7340 | MORTON | John | 11.05.1965 | P/O |
| 7341 | ALLCOCK | David | 11.05.1965 | P/O |
| 7342 | ANDERSON | John | 11.05.1965 | P/O |
| 7343 | BRYAN | Lyle Albert | 11.05.1965 | P/O |
| 7344 | FUNNELL | Peter Robert | 11.05.1965 | P/O |
| 7345 | HOPKINS | Jack | 11.05.1965 | S/O(T) |
| 7346 | LAWRENCE | Kenneth Gerald | 11.05.1965 | Supt |
| 7347 | LOUBSER | Peter Daniel | 11.05.1965 | P/O |
| 7348 | O'HARA | Robin George | 11.05.1965 | P/O |
| 7349 | POWLES | Henry MacDonald | 11.05.1965 | P/O |
| 7350 | SPENCER | Barry Ernest | 01.06.1965 | P/O |
| 7351 | LIGHTENING | Raymond James | 15.06.1965 | P/O |
| 7352 | SHANNON | Ian Frederick | 15.06.1965 | Insp |
| 7353 | BULFORD | Gordon Oswald | 15.06.1965 | P/O |
| 7354 | JOHNSTON | Brian Eric | 15.06.1965 | P/O |
| 7355 | MITCHELL | Malcolm James Arthur | 15.06.1965 | P/O |
| 7356 | SARGEANT | Alan Leigh | 15.06.1965 | S/O |
| 7357 | SMITH | Ivan Peter Thornton | 15.06.1965 | C/Insp |
| 7358 | BROWN | Bertram Blakiston | 15.06.1965 | S/S/O |
| 7359 | CUBITT | Christopher Stuart | 15.06.1965 | S/S/O |
| 7360 | CUTLER | Derek Martyn | 15.06.1965 | D/S/O |
| 7361 | ILES | Robert Charles | 15.06.1965 | P/O |
| 7362 | INSKIP | Brian Arthur | 15.06.1965 | Insp |
| 7363 | McGARRY | Graham Alexander | 15.06.1965 | P/O |
| 7364 | MILLAR | Peter Charles | 15.06.1965 | C/Supt |
| 7365 | SCOTT | Jack | 15.06.1965 | P/O |
| 7366 | WALSH | Peter Bernard | 17.06.1965 | P/O |
| 7367 | RUCK | Michael John | 30.06.1965 | Insp |
| 7368 | RAYNE | James Hugh | 01.07.1965 | P/O |
| 7369 | BANNERMAN | John Graham | 06.07.1965 | P/O |
| 7370 | WEEKS | Michael John | 07.07.1965 | P/O |
| 7371 | GALE | Malcolm David | 19.07.1965 | D/S/O |
| 7372 | BRICE | Norman Ewing | 20.07.1965 | D/Insp |
| 7373 | Mac LEOD | Henry Gordon | 20.07.1965 | Supt |
| 7374 | RESINK | Alexander John | 20.07.1965 | P/O |
| 7375 | SMITH | Kerry James | 20.07.1965 | Supt |
| 7376 | CROASDELL | Barry John | 20.07.1965 | Insp |
| 7377 | BEECH | George William | 20.07.1965 | P/O |
| 7378 | BRINDLE | David Vincent | 20.07.1965 | Supt |
| 7379 | CARRICK | Phillip Francis | 20.07.1965 | P/O |
| 7380 | DICK | | 20.07.1965 | P/O |
| 7382 | GRAY | John Newman | 20.07.1965 | A/Com |
| 7383 | JAMES | Anthony Charles | 20.07.1965 | P/O |
| 7384 | JENKINS | Roger | 20.07.1965 | D/P/O |
| 7385 | LAMB | Keith William | 20.07.1965 | P/O |
| 7386 | LIVERSEY | Jeffrey Edward | 20.07.1965 | P/O |
| 7387 | MITCHELL | John Campbell | 20.07.1965 | Supt |
| 7388 | RIPLEY | James Spence | 20.07.1965 | P/O |
| 7389 | ROBERTS | David Owen | 20.07.1965 | D/P/O |
| 7390 | TAYLOR | David Reginald | 20.07.1965 | P/O |
| 7391 | TOMS | Alan | 20.07.1965 | Insp |
| 7392 | WALKER | John Roger | 20.07.1965 | Insp |
| 7393 | WARNE | Howard Sidney | 20.07.1965 | P/O |
| 7394 | CROASDELL | Brian John | 22.07.1965 | Supt |
| 7395 | SIDWELL | Brian Philip | 26.07.1965 | Supt |
| 7396 | HAZLETT | James | 26.07.1965 | Insp |
| 7397 | MARSH | Robert Ballington | 02.08.1965 | Insp |
| 7398 | RUNDGREN | Kenneth Michael | 06.08.1965 | Insp |
| 7399 | WILSON | Peter James | 07.08.1965 | Insp |
| 7400 | ROGERS | John Cecil | 18.08.1965 | Supt |
| 7401 | DRIVER | Peter John | 28.08.1965 | D/Insp |
| 7402 | HAMILTON | Robin Lockhart | 01.09.1965 | Insp |
| 7403 | DEVLIN | Norman Mercer | 01.09.1965 | Insp |
| 7404 | FLOWERS | Frank | 02.09.1965 | P/O |
| 7405 | BORLAND | John Gordon | 07.09.1965 | P/O |
| 7406 | BARCLAY | John Allardyce | 07.09.1965 | P/O |
| 7407 | BRADBURY | Anthony | 07.09.1965 | P/O |
| 7408 | BURTON | Keith Arthur | 07.09.1965 | S/O(T) |
| 7409 | COTTON | Richard Norman | 07.09.1965 | P/O |
| 7410 | DIBLEY | Clive Charles | 07.09.1965 | P/O |
| 7411 | EDIE | Richard Holmes | 07.09.1965 | P/O |
| 7412 | GAIZELY | Michael Francis | 07.09.1965 | P/O |
| 7413 | GATES | Barry Owen | 07.09.1965 | P/O |
| 7414 | HART | Raymond Vincent | 07.09.1965 | P/O |
| 7415 | HAY | Neil | 07.09.1965 | D/P/O |
| 7416 | HOGARTH | Peter John | 07.09.1965 | P/O |
| 7417 | HOLDEN | Philip John | 07.09.1965 | D/S/O |
| 7418 | JAMES | Colyn Philip | 07.09.1965 | P/O |
| 7419 | KEYES | Peter John | 07.09.1965 | P/O |
| 7420 | LANGLEY | Timothy Lawrence | 07.09.1965 | P/O |
| 7421 | LUNT | Bernard Michael | 07.09.1965 | P/O |
| 7422 | LYNCH | Desmond Terence | 07.09.1965 | P/O |
| 7423 | MORTON | Roderick William | 07.09.1965 | P/O |
| 7424 | NICOLL | Andrew | 07.09.1965 | D/S/O |
| 7425 | NOWELL | Richard James | 07.09.1965 | P/O |
| 7426 | OSBOURN | David Bazalgette | 07.09.1965 | P/O |
| 7427 | PHILLIPS | Geoffrey Michael | 07.09.1965 | P/O |
| 7428 | SIMPSON | John | 07.09.1965 | C/Insp |
| 7429 | THOMPSON | Frederick William | 07.09.1965 | P/O |
| 7430 | TREVES | Peter Leonard | 07.09.1965 | P/O |
| 7431 | WHEATLEY | Hugh Ernest | 07.09.1965 | P/O |
| 7432 | KEYS | William Harris | 09.09.1965 | Insp |
| 7433 | BOTHA | Dirk Wouter | 09.09.1965 | S/O |
| 7434 | VAN DEN BERG | Dirk Johannes | 10.09.1965 | D/P/O |
| 7435 | JONES | Ieauan | 11.09.1965 | Insp |
| 7436 | JOHNSTON | Marcus Robert | 11.09.1965 | Supt |
| 7437 | WOODWARD | John Malcolm | 17.09.1965 | Supt |
| 7438 | JOBSON | Robert | 15.10.1965 | P/O |
| 7439 | McCARTER | John Michael | 15.10.1965 | S/O |
| 7440 | MANNING | Jeffrey George | 15.10.1965 | S/Insp |
| 7441 | SIMPSON | Anthony Beresford | 15.10.1965 | Supt |
| 7442 | ALEXANDER | Nigel William | 15.10.1965 | Supt |
| 7443 | ANDERLE | Michael Ladislav | 15.10.1965 | P/O |
| 7444 | BAMBER | Nicholas John | 15.10.1965 | S/O |
| 7445 | BENNETT | Michael James | 15.10.1965 | D/P/O |
| 7446 | BROWN | David | 15.10.1965 | Insp |
| 7447 | BRYANT | John David | 15.10.1965 | Supt |
| 7448 | CLASH | Michael Robert | 15.10.1965 | P/O |
| 7449 | COOPER | Derek | 15.10.1965 | P/O |

| No. | Surname | Forename(s) | Rank | Date |
|---|---|---|---|---|
| 7451 | CURRAN | Andrew | P/O | 15.10.1965 |
| 7452 | DARWELL | Leonard James | P/O | 15.10.1965 |
| 7453 | DAWSON | Neil Ronald | P/O | 15.10.1965 |
| 7454 | DUNCAN | Alexander | P/O | 15.10.1965 |
| 7455 | DUTTON | David | P/O | 15.10.1965 |
| 7456 | EASTON | George Ernest | P/O | 15.10.1965 |
| 7457 | FORSTER | Keith | P/O | 15.10.1965 |
| 7458 | FOX | Michael Christopher | Insp | 15.10.1965 |
| 7459 | FRIENDSHIP | John Michael | Supt | 15.10.1965 |
| 7460 | GOOD | Ronald Charles | P/O | 15.10.1965 |
| 7461 | GRANT | Peter Gaselee | D/Insp | 15.10.1965 |
| 7462 | JAMIESON | Peter Charles | P/O | 15.10.1965 |
| 7463 | LOFTUS | Michael Paul | Insp | 15.10.1965 |
| 7464 | McKAY | Anthony | D/P/O | 15.10.1965 |
| 7465 | MASON | Stuart | P/O | 15.10.1965 |
| 7466 | OWEN | Richard Aled | P/O | 15.10.1965 |
| 7467 | RANSLEY | Richard Charles | P/O | 15.10.1965 |
| 7468 | REYNOLDS | Thomas Edward | P/O | 15.10.1965 |
| 7469 | RIDGEWELL | Derek Arnold | P/O | 15.10.1965 |
| 7470 | WILLIAMS | Ernest Robert | D/Insp | 15.10.1965 |
| 7471 | SURKONT | Jozef Martin | S/O | 16.10.1965 |
| 7472 | BAYFORD | Charles Thomas | S/O(T) | 18.10.1965 |
| 7473 | HILLMAN | David Russell | S/O(T) | 22.10.1965 |
| 7474 | WELLS | Adrian Michael | S/O(T) | 22.10.1965 |
| 7475 | HODGES | Paul | S/O(T) | 28.10.1965 |
| 7476 | SEELEY | David John | S/O(T) | 01.11.1965 |
| 7477 | SEARLE | Henry Arthur | S/O(T) | 01.11.1965 |
| 7478 | STEPHENS | Edward Travis | Insp | 04.11.1965 |
| 7479 | BOTHA | John Stephen | P/O | 08.11.1965 |
| 7480 | EASTON | Richard Graham | P/O | 11.11.1965 |
| 7481 | FLEMING | John Nicholas | D/C/I | 12.11.1965 |
| 7482 | HYWOOD | Anthony James | P/O | 13.11.1965 |
| 7483 | JOLLY | Robert Everett | D/I | 15.11.1965 |
| 7484 | BURNS | Terence Hamilton | Insp(T) | 16.11.1965 |
| 7485 | STEVENS | Jack Walter | P/O | 18.11.1965 |
| 7486 | ASTON | Roy | P/O | 18.11.1965 |
| 7487 | BARRY | Keith Stuart | P/O | 18.11.1965 |
| 7488 | COX | John Robert | P/O | 18.11.1965 |
| 7489 | DUNCAN | Ian James | P/O | 18.11.1965 |
| 7490 | SMITH | Peter Hugh | S/O(T) | 18.11.1965 |
| 7491 | ANDREWS | Ernest | P/O | 19.11.1965 |
| 7492 | RUFUS | Angus Hilton | S/O(T) | 19.11.1965 |
| 7493 | SCOTT | Graham George | P/O | 21.11.1965 |
| 7494 | MULCAHY | Richard Michael | D/P/O | 21.11.1965 |
| 7495 | BAYLEY | David George | Insp | 30.11.1965 |
| 7496 | HENDERSON | Peter John | S/O | 10.12.1965 |
| 7497 | TURNER | David Stuart | P/O | 10.12.1965 |
| 7498 | TAVERNOR | Roy Frank | P/O | 10.12.1965 |
| 7499 | WILDE | Ernest Arthur | P/O | 21.12.1965 |
| 7500 | STOOLE | Ronald Ernest | P/O | 21.12.1965 |
| 7501 | JENKIN | Michael John | D/Insp | 21.12.1965 |
| 7502 | HOWARD | Michael Dalton | D/S/O | 21.12.1965 |
| 7503 | SALONIKA | Alan Vassia | S/O | 23.12.1965 |
| 7504 | HAYES | Brian Malcolm | P/O | 27.12.1965 |
| 7505 | JACQUES | Philip Andrew | Insp | 28.12.1965 |
| 7506 | FAIRBAIRN | Adrian | P/O(T) | 28.12.1965 |
| 7507 | PRESTON | Michael Edward | S/o/ | 01.01.1966 |
| 7508 | WHITE | Albert Michael | Insp(T) | 03.01.1966 |
| 7509 | ACUTT | William Walter | S/insp | 01.01.1966 |
| 7510 | MILNE | David Campbell | Insp | 13.01.1966 |
| 7511 | CLELLAND | James Gerard | Insp | 14.01.1966 |
| 7512 | FLETCHER | John Roger | Insp | 14.01.1966 |
| 7513 | MOTT | Trevor Jones | S/O | 14.01.1966 |
| 7514 | BATTY | Edward Jardine | Insp | 14.01.1966 |
| 7515 | HAY | Robin John | S/O | 14.01.1966 |
| 7516 | HILL | Trevor Rodney | S/O | 14.01.1966 |
| 7517 | LEVY | Hyman Ronald | P/O | 14.01.1966 |
| 7518 | PERY | Frank Paul George | P/O | 14.01.1966 |
| 7519 | PETERSON | Henry George | D/Insp | 14.01.1966 |
| 7520 | SIMS | Richard Harvey | Insp | 14.01.1966 |
| 7521 | WEST | Alexander Edric | Supt | 14.01.1966 |
| 7522 | WORRAL-CLARE | Stefan | D/P/O | 14.01.1966 |
| 7523 | HUTCHISON | George | S/O | 17.01.1966 |
| 7524 | DIVIANI | Peter John | P/O | 28.01.1966 |
| 7525 | HENDERSON | Alan John | P/O | 28.01.1966 |
| 7526 | SMITH | Graham John | P/O | 01.02.1966 |
| 7527 | LOUW | Solomon Hermanus | P/O | 01.02.1966 |
| 7528 | DEWAR | Duncan George | P/O | 01.02.1966 |
| 7529 | SMITH | Peter Drummond | Insp(T) | 01.02.1966 |
| 7530 | NIMMO | Norman Peter | Insp | 02.02.1966 |
| 7531 | VAN ZELLER | Simon Stewart | P/O | 07.02.1966 |
| 7532 | OBERHOLZER | Gwilliam Johannes | Supt | 25.02.1966 |
| 7533 | RAE | Brian John | D/S/O | 02.03.1966 |
| 7534 | FOSTER | Christopher John | P/O | 04.03.1966 |
| 7535 | DEVINE | John Wilson | D/S/O | 04.03.1966 |
| 7536 | DICKSON | David William | P/O | 07.03.1966 |
| 7537 | ABEL | Lance Christopher | P/O | 08.03.1966 |
| 7538 | VAN DER MERWE | Hendrick Johannes | P/O | 08.03.1966 |
| 7539 | ALLBERRY | Rex Hind | P/O | 08.03.1966 |
| 7540 | ATKINSON | Charles William | P/O | 08.03.1966 |
| 7541 | BUSH | Edward Christopher | Insp | 08.03.1966 |
| 7542 | CARTWRIGHT | Robert Nicholas | S/O | 08.03.1966 |
| 7543 | GATLAND | Peter Michael | D/S/O | 08.03.1966 |
| 7544 | HAWKS | David Christopher | D/S/O | 08.03.1966 |
| 7545 | HEATH | Paul Frederick | P/O | 08.03.1966 |
| 7546 | HOCKIN | Colin Joseph | P/O | 08.03.1966 |
| 7547 | INGLIS | Christopher John | Insp | 08.03.1966 |
| 7548 | McCLEW | David William | P/O | 08.03.1966 |
| 7549 | McCULLOCH | Donald Westgate | P/O | 08.03.1966 |
| 7550 | MARSHALL | Keith Thomas | D/S/O | 08.03.1966 |
| 7551 | MARTIN | Alastair George | P/O | 08.03.1966 |
| 7552 | PRETORIUS | Barend Godfried | P/O | 08.03.1966 |
| 7553 | PRETORIUS | Gavin Godfrey | D/S/O | 08.03.1966 |
| 7554 | RICHARDSON | Jeremy Stuart | P/O | 08.03.1966 |
| 7555 | SEYMOUR | Anthony John | P/O | 08.03.1966 |
| 7556 | SHAW | John William | P/O | 08.03.1966 |
| 7557 | SWANEPOEL | Petrus Wilhelam | Supt. | 08.03.1966 |
| 7558 | YEOMAN | Timothy Denis | P/O | 08.03.1966 |
| 7559 | STROBEL | Francis Ernest | P/O | 08.03.1966 |
| 7560 | LATHAM | Walter Oldnal | Insp(T) | 09.03.1966 |
| 7561 | ALLEN | David Montgomery | Insp. | 12.03.1966 |
| 7562 | JOHNSON | Christopher Forbes | Supt | 01.04.1966 |
| 7563 | DAWSON | Stuart Patrick | D/S/O | 01.04.1966 |
| 7564 | HART | Philip William | Insp | 01.04.1966 |
| 7565 | WATERMAN | Martin Geoffrey | S/O(T) | 04.04.1966 |
| 7566 | ANNESLEY | Richard Daniel | P/O | 05.04.1966 |
| 7567 | AULD | Sandy | P/O | 05.04.1966 |
| 7568 | BEST | Brian Philip | D/S/O | 05.04.1966 |
| 7569 | COWEN | Malcolm John | S/O | 05.04.1966 |
| 7570 | GARDINER | Leonard Neville | S/O | 05.04.1966 |
| 7571 | GILLOT | Norman Gerald | S/O | 05.04.1966 |
| 7572 | GREENLY | Alasdair Lindsey | Insp | 05.04.1966 |
| 7573 | GRIZZARD | Peter Howard | D/S/O | 05.04.1966 |
| 7574 | HODGSON | Howard William | S/O | 05.04.1966 |
| 7575 | KEMP | James Randle | Insp | 05.04.1966 |
| 7576 | SMITH | William Jacobus | S/o/ | 05.04.1966 |
| 7577 | THISTLETON | Geoffrey | C/Insp | 05.04.1966 |
| 7578 | CHRISTIE | Colin Campbell | Insp | 05.04.1966 |
| 7579 | DUGUID | Alfred John | Insp | 05.04.1966 |
| 7580 | SHORTT | Peter | S/O | 12.04.1966 |
| 7581 | LOTTER | Leslie Louis | Insp | 16.04.1966 |
| 7582 | HUNT | John Adrian | P/O | 17.04.1966 |
| 7583 | SMITH | William Richard | P/O | 21.04.1966 |
| 7584 | GRIFFITHS | William Barry | P/O | 24.04.1966 |
| 7585 | BATES | Graham Leslie | S/O | 01.05.1966 |
| 7586 | Mc KEIVER | Philip Graham | P/O | 02.05.1966 |
| 7587 | BIRD | Kenneth James | P/O | 03.05.1966 |
| 7588 | EVANS | John Kelvin | D/Insp | 07.05.1966 |
| 7589 | PETERSON | Anthony Richard | P/O | 10.05.1966 |
| 7590 | FULLER | Martin | S/O | 10.05.1966 |
| 7591 | Mac DONALD | Graeme Desmond | Insp | 10.05.1966 |
| 7592 | ORWIN | Colin Bruce | P/O | 10.05.1966 |
| 7593 | RANKIN | Robert Douglas | Supt | 10.05.1966 |
| 7594 | SECCOMBE | Keith Ian | P/O | 10.05.1966 |
| 7595 | WINTERS | Anthony James | P/O | 10.05.1966 |
| 7596 | RYAN | Harold Aspinall | P/O | 11.05.1966 |
| 7597 | WRIGHT | Rodney Desmond | C/Insp | 11.05.1966 |
| 7598 | EVANS | Barry Reginald | P/O | 31.05.1966 |
| 7599 | SMALE | Robert William | P/O | 01.06.1966 |
| 7600 | BARROW | Dermot William | P/O | 06.06.1966 |
| 7601 | CREANER | Christopher William | P/O | 06.06.1966 |
| 7602 | JAMES | Bleign | S/S/O | 06.06.1966 |
| 7603 | KNOX-DAVIES | Hedley | P/O | 06.06.1966 |
| 7604 | PATTERSON | Peter Graham | P/O | 06.06.1966 |
| 7605 | BELL | Anthony Royale | Insp | 07.06.1966 |
| 7606 | CAMPBELL | Timothy Joseph | Supt | 07.06.1966 |
| 7607 | HEALY | David Stuart | Insp(T) | 07.06.1966 |
| 7608 | GOLIGHTLY | Thomas Erskin | P/O | 07.06.1966 |
| 7609 | SHORT | Schalk Willem | S/O | 27.06.1966 |
| 7610 | SCHMAHL | Michael William | S/O | 28.06.1966 |
| 7611 | BULLEN | Jeremy Cedric | D/Insp | 03.07.1966 |
| 7612 | RICKSON | Michael James | P/O | 04.07.1966 |
| 7613 | POTTS | Bryan Melville | P/O | 04.07.1966 |
| 7614 | THOMAS | Howard Phillip | Supt | 14.07.1966 |
| 7615 | ARNOLD | Myles Douglas | P/O | 14.07.1966 |
| 7616 | CATHCART-CUNNISON | David John | S/O | 14.07.1966 |
| 7617 | FOWLER | Michael | P/O | 14.07.1966 |
| 7618 | JENNINGS | Barend Jacobus | P/O | 14.07.1966 |
| 7619 | JORDAAN | Peter Hugh | P/O | 14.07.1966 |
| 7620 | MASON | Graham Ralph | P/O | 14.07.1966 |
| 7621 | PHILLIPS | Kenneth Derreck | S/O | 14.07.1966 |
| 7622 | SWYNNERTON | John Robert | D/Insp | 18.07.1966 |
| 7623 | VAN BLERK | Alistair John | P/O | 28.07.1966 |
| 7624 | DAVEY | Donald Charles | P/O | 28.07.1966 |
| 7625 | MOMMSEN | James Francis | P/O | 30.07.1966 |
| 7626 | ROGERTSON | James Joseph | Insp(T) | 01.08.1966 |
| 7627 | ROGERS | James Hill | Insp | 04.08.1966 |
| 7628 | MORLAND | Allen Charles | P/O | 05.08.1966 |
| 7629 | JOHNSON | John | C/Insp | 12.08.1966 |
| 7630 | SEYMOUR | Arthur David | Insp | 19.08.1966 |
| 7631 | SPENAZURIS | David Atherstone | P/O | 19.08.1966 |
| 7632 | PATTINSON | Nigel Philip | P/O | 04.09.1966 |
| 7633 | WESTON | Noel | Supt | 05.09.1966 |
| 7634 | CROSSLAND | Russel Healey | P/O | 06.09.1966 |
| 7635 | KENNEDY | Dennis Patrick | Insp | 06.09.1966 |
| 7636 | McDIARMID | Gordon Sean | Insp | 06.09.1966 |
| 7637 | BURKE | Ernest Hastings | Insp | 06.09.1966 |
| 7638 | HODNETT | Peter Andy | S/O | 06.09.1966 |
| 7639 | KNOETZE | Edward John | P/O | 07.09.1966 |
| 7640 | SHEARING | Robin Lebon | P/O | 07.09.1966 |
| 7641 | WILLIS | Michael Anthony | P/O | 08.09.1966 |
| 7642 | CURTIS | Albert Sidney | C/Insp(T) | 09.09.1966 |
| 7643 | CROWTHER | Demetri | Supt. | 13.09.1966 |
| 7644 | WILSON | David Gareth | Insp | 15.09.1966 |
| 7645 | AMIRA | Byron Neophyte | Insp | 16.09.1966 |
| 7646 | TUDOR-JONES | John Edward | Insp | 01.10.1966 |
| 7647 | PASSAPORTIS | Stephen John | S/O | 01.10.1966 |
| 7648 | WALSH | David | S/O | 10.10.1966 |
| 7649 | HAMMOND | Richard John | S/O | 12.10.1966 |
| 7650 | ROBINSON | Gerhardus Johannes | P/O | 16.10.1966 |
| 7651 | LATILIA | Alan | P/O | 17.11.1966 |
| 7652 | BOTHA | Neil Martin | P/O | 01.12.1966 |
| 7653 | ELDRIDGE | Eric Gerhardus | Insp | 03.12.1966 |
| 7654 | GRADWELL | Jonathan George | P/O | 12.12.1966 |
| 7655 | KRUGER | Christopher-John | S/O | 13.12.1966 |
| 7656 | MUIR | | Insp | 13.12.1966 |
| 7657 | RAKE | | D/P/O | 13.12.1966 |

# BSAP Nominal Roll • Men

| No. | Surname | First Names | Date | Rank |
|---|---|---|---|---|
| 7658 | MARSHALL | James Terrence | 13.12.1966 | Supt. |
| 7659 | GILL | Peter Robert | 13.12.1966 | Insp |
| 7660 | HOWELLS | William Wallace | 13.12.1966 | Supt |
| 7661 | SHELLEY | Thomas Rodney | 13.12.1966 | P/O |
| 7662 | MURPHY | John James | 13.12.1966 | P/O |
| 7663 | PARRY | Charles Laurence | 13.12.1966 | S/O |
| 7664 | McDONALD | Dudley John | 13.12.1966 | P/O |
| 7665 | STYLES | Clifford James | 16.12.1966 | P/O |
| 7666 | MATTHYSER | Friederich Dick | 20.12.1966 | C/Insp(T) |
| 7667 | WADDLETON | Peter Stewart | 26.12.1966 | S/O |
| 7668 | DAVISON | Roger Vernon | 06.01.1967 | S/O |
| 7669 | MARICONI | Bruno George | 10.01.1967 | S/O(T) |
| 7670 | SUTTON | John Peter | 10.01.1967 | P/O |
| 7671 | BUCHANAN | Donald John | 10.01.1967 | P/O |
| 7672 | CRANE | George | 10.01.1967 | P/O |
| 7673 | TREVOR-JONES | Norman Rubidge | 10.01.1967 | Insp |
| 7674 | DE HAAST | Richard Martin | 10.01.1967 | Insp |
| 7675 | BISHOP | Robert David | 10.01.1967 | P/O |
| 7676 | DE LANGE | David Peter | 10.01.1967 | P/O |
| 7677 | DEWE | Peter Fairhurst | 10.01.1967 | D/Insp |
| 7678 | HOWMAN | Timothy Quentin | 10.01.1967 | D/S/O |
| 7679 | MATTHEWS | Thomas Bruce | 10.01.1967 | D/S/O |
| 7680 | POLLITT | George Edward | 10.01.1967 | D/S/O |
| 7681 | BUTT | Michael William | 10.01.1967 | Insp |
| 7682 | CALDERWOOD | Ian Gourley | 10.01.1967 | P/O |
| 7683 | HULLEY-MILLER | Stuart Gregory | 10.01.1967 | P/O |
| 7684 | DE LANGE | Robert John | 10.01.1967 | P/O |
| 7685 | WHITLEY | Petrus Albertus | 10.01.1967 | P/O |
| 7686 | BOTHA | Michael Arthur | 11.01.1967 | S/Insp |
| 7687 | BRYAN | Clive Harold | 11.01.1967 | P/O |
| 7688 | HOY | Peter William | 11.01.1967 | Insp |
| 7689 | LUDGATER | Graham Whitfield | 11.01.1967 | Insp |
| 7690 | BARKER | John Blenkinsop | 11.01.1967 | C/Supt |
| 7691 | OGSTON | Brian Terence | 11.01.1967 | P/O |
| 7692 | WRIGHT | Hendrik Lodewyk | 16.01.1967 | P/O |
| 7693 | KLEYNHANS | Stephen John | 19.01.1967 | S/Insp |
| 7694 | MARTIN | Gordon Gray | 21.01.1967 | S/O |
| 7695 | BRANFIELD | Andrew Nicolas | 24.01.1967 | P/O |
| 7696 | WATSON | Alastair Roy | 28.01.1967 | P/O |
| 7697 | GORRIE | Ian Alexander | 06.02.1967 | P/O |
| 7698 | Mac INTYRE | Frederick Peter | 14.02.1967 | S/O |
| 7699 | BIRKINSHAW | Stephen Gerard | 14.02.1967 | P/O |
| 7700 | BRADFIELD | Ronald Bruce | 14.02.1967 | P/O |
| 7701 | HODSON | Christopher Neil | 14.02.1967 | P/O |
| 7702 | LE MESURIER | Leslie Eric | 14.02.1967 | D/Insp |
| 7703 | LLOYD | John Bernard | 14.02.1967 | S/O |
| 7704 | ALSTON | David Hugh | 14.02.1967 | P/O |
| 7705 | BANNERMAN | Christopher Patrick | 14.02.1967 | Insp |
| 7706 | DRIVER | Neville Rowling | 14.02.1967 | P/O |
| 7707 | BRENT | Glen William | 15.02.1967 | P/O |
| 7708 | CAMPBELL | Pieter Karel | 27.02.1967 | P/O |
| 7709 | DE HAAS | Alastair Malcolm | 28.02.1967 | C/Supt |
| 7710 | ROBERTSON-GLASGOW | Alfred Andries | 14.02.1967 | S/O |
| 7711 | SCHOULTZ | Brian Geoffrey | 14.02.1967 | P/O |
| 7712 | CLIPSTON | David Lindsay | 14.02.1967 | P/O |
| 7713 | ST. QUINTIN | Lionel | 14.02.1967 | S/O |
| 7714 | SMITH | Frederick Christiaan | 14.02.1967 | P/O |
| 7715 | MAAS | Kenneth Homersham | 14.02.1967 | S/O |
| 7716 | BOND | Anthony Thomas | 14.02.1967 | Insp |
| 7717 | MERRIS | Peter John | 14.02.1967 | P/O |
| 7718 | CREES | Allan Nigel | 14.02.1967 | P/O |
| 7719 | DREYER | Derek | 01.03.1967 | C/Supt |
| 7720 | TASKER | Willem Andries | 04.03.1967 | S/O(T) |
| 7721 | PRETORIUS | Philip John | 08.03.1967 | S/CI |
| 7722 | TALBOT | Theodore Louis | 14.03.1967 | S/CI |
| 7723 | WOLFAARDT | Derrick | 25.07.1967 | P/O |
| 7724 | BALLANTYNE | Bryce Andrew | 14.03.1967 | S/O(T) |
| 7725 | CONDON | Declan | 14.03.1967 | D/Insp |
| 7727 | LARN | John Paul Edgar | 14.03.1967 | Insp |
| 7728 | MYLES | Peter Thomas | 14.03.1967 | P/O |
| 7729 | NAPIER | Douglas Rose | 14.03.1967 | P/O |
| 7730 | NEEL | Anthony Peter | 14.03.1967 | P/O |
| 7731 | OKES | Pierre Alistair | 14.03.1970 | P/O |
| 7732 | RINGROSE | Derek George | 14.03.1967 | S/O |
| 7733 | AUSTIN | Bernard Peter | 14.03.1967 | P/O |
| 7734 | BROOM | David Walter | 14.03.1967 | P/O |
| 7735 | CADDY | Alan Walter | 15.03.1967 | P/O |
| 7736 | DAY | Eric | 04.04.1967 | Insp(T) |
| 7737 | BAINES | John Bretagne | 11.04.1967 | S/O |
| 7738 | BESTER | Sydney Godfrey | 11.04.1967 | P/O |
| 7739 | BOLTMAN | Oswald Theodore | 11.04.1967 | S/O(T) |
| 7740 | LOMBARD | James William | 11.04.1967 | P/O |
| 7741 | MANDY | Michael Patrick | 11.04.1967 | P/O |
| 7742 | SNEDDON | Henry Findlay | 11.04.1967 | Insp |
| 7743 | BRAHAM | Michael Forbes | 27.04.1967 | Insp |
| 7744 | CLOETE | Sidney Hilton | 27.04.1967 | P/O |
| 7745 | DAVIES | Neville John | 27.04.1967 | P/O |
| 7746 | McDIARMID | Brian Malcolm | 27.04.1967 | Insp |
| 7747 | MURPHY | George Philip | 27.04.1967 | P/O |
| 7748 | PARKER | Thomas Edward | 27.04.1967 | P/O |
| 7749 | WEBBER | Derek Michael | 27.04.1967 | P/O |
| 7750 | BURRIDGE | Peter Croft | 01.05.1967 | D/S/O |
| 7751 | CROOK | Douglas Alan | 01.05.1967 | P/O |
| 7752 | LOMBARD | Armand Eugene | 01.05.1967 | P/O |
| 7753 | MULLINS | Roy Robin | 01.05.1967 | S/O(T) |
| 7754 | DICKINSON | Eric Granville | 01.05.1967 | D/Insp |
| 7755 | SCHEEPERS | Pieter Martin | 03.05.1967 | D/P/O |
| 7756 | DE WIT | Graham Norman | 11.05.1967 | Supt |
| 7757 | LOWRY | Colin William | 14.05.1967 | Insp |
| 7758 | HINKSMAN | Alexander Roland | 20.05.1967 | Supt |
| 7759 | McDADE | John Derek | 22.05.1967 | Insp(T) |
| 7760 | BOWEN | Rodney Scott | 26.05.1967 | S/O(T) |
| 7761 | LENDRUM | David Ian Anthony | 31.05.1967 | Supt |
| 7762 | WIGGILL | Charles Robert | 01.06.1967 | Insp |
| 7763 | ELLEY | Christopher John | 01.06.1967 | P/O |
| 7764 | LOMBARD | Jacobus Hendrikus | 20.06.1967 | P/O |
| 7765 | SEXTON | Neville Anthony | 20.06.1967 | P/O |
| 7766 | MURRAY | Robert James | 20.06.1967 | P/O |
| 7767 | SEARLE | Lloyd | 20.06.1967 | P/O |
| 7768 | COETZEE | Ronald | 20.06.1967 | P/O |
| 7769 | GOOCH | David Joseph | 20.06.1967 | P/O |
| 7770 | HERD | George Michael | 20.06.1967 | Insp |
| 7771 | HOLDEN | Thomas Charles | 20.06.1967 | P/O |
| 7772 | HOPKINS | Allen Denbigh | 20.06.1967 | Insp |
| 7773 | JOHNSTONE | Simon Patrick | 20.06.1967 | P/O |
| 7774 | SMIT | Jakobus Hendrik | 20.06.1967 | P/O |
| 7775 | BAKER | Aubrey Edward | 21.06.1967 | Insp |
| 7776 | MITCHELL | Paul | 21.06.1967 | D/Insp |
| 7777 | POCOCK | Digby Carbis | 21.06.1967 | D/Insp |
| 7778 | VAUGHAN | Brian Sydney | 21.06.1967 | P/O |
| 7779 | WAYLAND | Ralph Noel | 21.06.1967 | P/O |
| 7780 | BARTLETT | Bruce Peter | 22.06.1967 | P/O |
| 7781 | SULLIVAN | John Stuart | 22.06.1967 | S/O |
| 7782 | TAYLOR | John Richard | 22.06.1967 | P/O |
| 7783 | NERO | Antonio Joaquim | 23.06.1967 | S/O |
| 7784 | ACORNLEY | Stephen | 23.06.1967 | Supt |
| 7785 | CAREY | Peter Stephen | 30.06.1967 | Supt |
| 7786 | GARNETT | Colin Frederick | 13.07.1967 | P/O |
| 7787 | DAVIES | Howard Aubrey | 13.07.1967 | P/O |
| 7788 | CLAYTON | Clifford Thomas | 13.07.1967 | P/O |
| 7789 | BURKE | Patrick Gerard | 18.07.1967 | S/O(T) |
| 7790 | LAMBOURN | Michael Geoffry | 24.07.1967 | S/CI |
| 7791 | LEIPER | John | 25.07.1967 | S/CI |
| 7792 | EDGE | Derrick | 31.07.1967 | P/O |
| 7793 | DIMES | Peter Michael | 08.08.1967 | P/O |
| 7794 | HARRISON | Nicholas Michael | 08.08.1967 | D/Insp |
| 7796 | SCOTT | Christopher Archie | 08.08.1967 | P/O |
| 7797 | GLEESON | Edward Walter | 08.08.1967 | S/O(T) |
| 7798 | VAN OUDTSHOORN | Wessel Lourens | 08.08.1967 | S/O |
| 7799 | STOPFORTH | James Grey | 08.08.1967 | P/O |
| 7800 | WILLIAMS | Bruce Patrick | 08.08.1967 | D/Insp |
| 7801 | STEYN | Peter Christiaan | 08.08.1967 | S/O |
| 7802 | JENKINS | Norman Grosvenor | 08.08.1967 | P/O |
| 7803 | BODINGTON | Anthony Howard | 08.08.1967 | P/O |
| 7804 | Mac GREGOR | Graeme | 10.08.1967 | P/O |
| 7805 | GROENEWALD | Andre | 10.08.1967 | P/O |
| 7806 | WILLSHIRE | Robin Michael | 14.08.1967 | Insp(T) |
| 7807 | WALTERS | Johannes | 14.08.1967 | P/O |
| 7808 | CAMPBELL | Douglas Clifford | 24.08.1967 | P/O |
| 7809 | WIELOPOLSKI | Janus Z. Derek | 24.08.1967 | P/O |
| 7810 | WILDE | Peter Edward | 25.08.1967 | Insp |
| 7811 | BRUCE | Alexander | 25.08.1967 | Insp |
| 7812 | BOTHWELL | William Trevor | 25.08.1967 | Insp |
| 7813 | JOHNSON | Peter Victor | 13.09.1967 | P/O |
| 7814 | BRADLEY | Godfrey Brian | 16.09.1967 | P/O |
| 7815 | BEETS | Peter John Henry | 18.09.1967 | S/O(T) |
| 7816 | BINEDELL | Gregory Edward | 19.09.1967 | P/O |
| 7817 | YOUD | Allan Richard | 19.09.1967 | P/O |
| 7818 | HOWARD | Robert Alexander | 19.09.1967 | Insp |
| 7819 | STEWART | Robert Andrew | 25.09.1967 | P/O |
| 7820 | WIELOPOLSKI | Leszek Konrad | 30.09.1967 | Insp(T) |
| 7821 | DU TOIT | Peter | 02.10.1967 | Insp(T) |
| 7822 | MITCHELL | Bruce | 03.10.1967 | P/O |
| 7823 | CHAPMAN | Ian Rawson | 03.10.1967 | P/O |
| 7824 | Mac DONALD | Dougal John | 03.10.1967 | P/O |
| 7825 | MATHIESON | Ronald Allan | 03.10.1967 | P/O |
| 7826 | BLACK | Christopher | 03.10.1967 | P/O |
| 7827 | BLYTH | Geoffrey William | 03.10.1967 | P/O |
| 7828 | BURKE | Ian Gavin | 03.10.1967 | S/O |
| 7829 | DACEY | Patrick Jeremiah | 03.10.1967 | P/O |
| 7830 | FRANCIS | Robert Grant | 03.10.1967 | D/Insp |
| 7831 | HELLINGER | Rudolph Christian | 03.10.1967 | S/O(T) |
| 7832 | HEMMING | Terrence Roy | 03.10.1967 | S/Insp |
| 7833 | Mac LEOD | Ralph Douglas | 03.10.1967 | S/O |
| 7834 | READ | Peter Graham | 03.10.1967 | P/O |
| 7835 | WARWICK | Aiden Neil | 03.10.1967 | P/O |
| 7836 | BIGGS | Howard William | 03.10.1967 | D/Insp |
| 7837 | BOULTON | Albert | 03.10.1967 | D/Insp |
| 7838 | LESLIE | Andrew Johnson | 05.10.1967 | S/O(T) |
| 7839 | PRINGLE | Gordon William | 10.10.1967 | P/O |
| 7840 | SPRINGER | Gregory Anthony | 12.10.1967 | Insp(T) |
| 7841 | BORRETT | Hugh Francis | 12.10.1967 | S/O(T) |
| 7842 | BISCO | William Albert | 01.11.1967 | P/O |
| 7843 | FULTON | Derek Graham | 01.11.1967 | P/O |
| 7844 | FREEMAN | Grahame Clive | 13.11.1967 | S/O |
| 7845 | POTGIETER | Johannes Petrus | 13.11.1967 | Insp(T) |
| 7846 | BOUCHER | John Lydford | 15.11.1967 | P/O |
| 7847 | BEEDEN | Brian Gilbert | 19.11.1967 | S/O |
| 7848 | EGLINGTON | Joseph Michael | 20.11.1967 | Supt |
| 7849 | MORRIS | Christopher John | 07.12.1967 | Inp(T) |
| 7850 | CUSSACK | Dermot Denis | 12.12.1967 | C/Insp |
| 7851 | WALTHEW | Brian Harold | 12.12.1967 | Insp |
| 7852 | BLAKE | David Cannings | 12.12.1967 | P/O |
| 7853 | HARRIS | Clive Anthony | 12.12.1967 | S/O |
| 7854 | CAPLEN | Jeremy Rix | 12.12.1967 | S/O |
| 7855 | JEWSON | Alan | 12.12.1967 | D/S/O |
| 7856 | SNYMAN | Thomas Henry | 12.12.1967 | D/COMM |
| 7857 | SOWDEN | John Keith | 12.12.1967 | S/O(T) |
| 7858 | FOURIE | Louis Johannes | 12.12.1967 | P/O |
| 7859 | DU PLESSIS | Cornelius Gerhardus | 12.12.1967 | Insp |
| 7860 | BRESLER | Robert Orde | 12.12.1967 | P/O |
| 7861 | WOODS | Michael Joe | 14.12.1967 | P/O |
| 7862 | LAW | Anthony Clarence | 14.12.1967 | D/Insp |
| 7863 | STEW | Paul Robert | 19.12.1967 | P/O |
| 7864 | FAIRFAX-BROWN | Christopher John | 20.12.1967 | P/O |

| Reg. No | Surname | Forename(s) | Date | Rank |
|---|---|---|---|---|
| 7865 | POTGIETER | Raymond | 26.12.1967 | D/S/O |
| 7866 | RIDLEY | Robert John | 27.12.1967 | Insp |
| 7867 | THORN | Barry Harvey | 30.12.1967 | S/O(T) |
| 7868 | McALISTER | James Bruce | 02.01.1968 | S/C/I |
| 7869 | BARNARD | Roger Michael | 02.01.1968 | Supt |
| 7870 | WHITTAL | Anthony Lawrence | 08.01.1968 | S/O(T) |
| 7871 | SCOTT-RODGER | Anthony John | 08.01.1968 | P/O |
| 7872 | BARBER | David William | 08.01.1968 | P/O |
| 7873 | PENFOLD | Chesney Robert | 09.01.1968 | P/O |
| 7874 | ATKINS | Ronald Peter | 09.01.1968 | P/O |
| 7875 | KEEN | Terence | 09.01.1968 | D/Insp |
| 7876 | LANKSHEAR | Graham Saville | 09.01.1968 | Insp |
| 7877 | PAUL | Richard Anthony | 09.01.1968 | Insp |
| 7878 | ROWLES | Brian William | 09.01.1968 | P/O |
| 7879 | VAN VUREN | Graham | 09.01.1968 | P/O |
| 7880 | BEKKER | Guy | 09.01.1968 | S/O |
| 7881 | BROWN | Robert Louis | 09.01.1968 | S/Insp |
| 7882 | JACK | Hew Duncan | 09.01.1968 | P/O |
| 7883 | BOTHAM | Ian Gough | 09.01.1968 | P/O |
| 7884 | ESTERHUIZEN | Cleveland Walter | 09.01.1968 | P/O |
| 7885 | McCALL | Harold Fredrick | 09.01.1968 | D/Insp |
| 7886 | McCALL | Johannes Jacobus | 09.01.1968 | P/O |
| 7887 | HARRIES | David Sinclair | 09.01.1968 | P/O |
| 7888 | HARRIES | Paul Richard | 09.01.1968 | Insp |
| 7889 | CAWOOD | Peter Lascelles | 09.01.1968 | P/O |
| 7890 | HOLLOWAY | Keran Edward | 09.01.1968 | Insp |
| 7891 | LIEBRANDT | Christopher David | 09.01.1968 | Supt |
| 7892 | MARSHALL | Peter George | 09.01.1968 | S/O |
| 7893 | HARRIS | Peter Douglas | 09.01.1968 | P/O |
| 7894 | COWDY | Anthony David | 09.01.1968 | P/O |
| 7895 | WOOD | Harry | 09.01.1968 | S/O(T) |
| 7896 | LALLY | Brian Michael | 10.01.1968 | Insp |
| 7897 | DE BEER | Victor Martin | 10.01.1968 | Supt |
| 7898 | LINDSELL-STEWART | Gavin | 10.01.1968 | D/Insp |
| 7899 | HUSTLER | Dean Thomson | 10.01.1968 | P/O |
| 7900 | GREENWOOD | James Gordon | 10.01.1968 | P/O |
| 7901 | DAWKINS | John Richard | 10.01.1968 | P/O |
| 7902 | BONYNGE | Edwin Tully | 11.01.1968 | P/O |
| 7903 | TAYLOR | Lionel Harris | 11.01.1968 | S/O |
| 7904 | CLORAN | Michael John | 11.01.1968 | P/O |
| 7905 | BURGOYNE | Richard Henry | 16.01.1968 | P/O |
| 7906 | DE BRUIJN | Gert Hendrik | 17.01.1968 | P/O |
| 7907 | ASHWORTH | Leslie Winston | 19.01.1968 | P/O |
| 7908 | DAVISON | James Winston | 20.01.1968 | P/O |
| 7909 | SCOTT-MARTIN | Philip de Lacey | 31.01.1968 | P/O |
| 7910 | BISSETT | John Martin | 01.02.1968 | Insp(T) |
| 7911 | DONZELLI | John Leonard | 02.02.1968 | D/Insp |
| 7912 | CLIFTON-PARKS | Clive Frederick | 08.02.1968 | Insp |
| 7913 | CAMPBELL | Barry Ian | 13.02.1968 | D/Insp |
| 7914 | HICKMAN | Anthony Philip | 13.02.1968 | P/O |
| 7915 | BEVERIDGE | Duncan Robert | 13.02.1968 | P/O |
| 7916 | FARRINGTON | Michael Richard | 13.02.1968 | P/O |
| 7917 | HUME | David | 13.02.1968 | P/O |
| 7918 | GROSE | Roderick Charles | 13.02.1968 | Insp |
| 7919 | SKOTT | Peter Christian | 13.02.1968 | Insp |
| 7920 | FINDLAY | Andrew Bruce | 13.02.1968 | Insp |
| 7921 | THOMPSON-HOLLAND | Christopher James | 13.02.1968 | Insp |
| 7922 | ZURAWSKI | Gustav Waclaw | 13.02.1968 | P/O |
| 7923 | BRAINE | William Kenneth | 13.02.1968 | P/O |
| 7924 | ARMSTRONG | Leslie James | 13.02.1968 | Insp |
| 7925 | THEUNISSEN | Hugo Hofmeyer | 13.02.1968 | P/O |
| 7926 | LYSTER | John Patrick | 13.02.1968 | P/O |
| 7927 | FERRIER | Geoffrey | 13.02.1968 | Insp |
| 7928 | GLASS | Charles Houston | 13.02.1968 | S/O |
| 7929 | CALLAWAY | Ronald Anthony | 13.02.1968 | P/O |
| 7930 | SCHOLTZ | Andre Albertus | 13.02.1968 | P/O |
| 7931 | VERSTER | Anthony Francis | 13.02.1968 | Insp |
| 7932 | BOTHA | Willem Hendrik | 13.02.1968 | — |
| 7933 | DE GRAY BIRCH | Edward | 13.02.1968 | — |
| 7934 | TWIDLE | Peter | 27.02.1968 | P/O |
| 7935 | GOUWS | Daniel | 01.03.1968 | Insp |
| 7936 | WOOD | Henry Alfred | 04.03.1968 | P/O |
| 7937 | LITSON | Michael John | 05.03.1968 | P/O |
| 7938 | YOUNG | David Cedric | 06.03.1968 | P/O |
| 7939 | MARTIN | Glen Edward | 06.03.1968 | P/O |
| 7940 | KRIEL | Joseph Claude | 08.03.1968 | Insp(T) |
| 7941 | KENNERLY | Randal | 10.03.1968 | Insp |
| 7942 | MARTIN | Christopher Michael | 11.03.1968 | S/C/I |
| 7943 | WINTON | Richard | 12.03.1968 | D/S/O |
| 7944 | HALSTEAD | John Stephen | 18.03.1968 | S/Insp |
| 7945 | DEARDEN | Clifford Philip | 22.03.1968 | P/O |
| 7946 | NIEUWOUDT | Hermanus Cornelius | 26.03.1968 | P/O |
| 7947 | COSNETT | Christopher John | 31.03.1968 | Insp |
| 7948 | HOULSTON | Alan George | 02.04.1968 | S/S/O |
| 7949 | CALDSWELL-BARR | Peter Robert | 04.04.1968 | S/O |
| 7950 | HARDY | Richard Sydney | 08.04.1968 | D/S/O |
| 7951 | JEWELL | Robert James | 08.04.1968 | P/O |
| 7952 | LUSK | Michael David | 08.04.1968 | Insp |
| 7953 | ROSELT | Eryl Raymond | 08.04.1968 | P/O |
| 7954 | SHAW | Roger Terry | 08.04.1968 | P/O |
| 7955 | WOOD | Andrew James | 08.04.1968 | P/O |
| 7956 | VAN DER BERGH | Gabriel | 08.04.1968 | P/O |
| 7957 | TODD | Charles Keith | 08.04.1968 | Insp |
| 7958 | NICHOLLS | Graham Michael | 09.04.1968 | P/O |
| 7959 | HOGGINS | Raymond Glyn | 09.04.1968 | S/O |
| 7960 | HOYSTEAD | Francis Anthony | 09.04.1968 | P/O |
| 7961 | McKAY | Duncan Hope | 09.04.1968 | P/O |
| 7962 | GIBSON | Alan | 09.04.1968 | Supt |
| 7963 | WAKEFORD | John Charles | 09.04.1968 | S/C(T) |
| 7964 | THOMSON | John Bruce Stuart | 09.04.1968 | S/O |
| 7965 | PARRY | Michael Hugh | 09.04.1968 | P/O |
| 7966 | SLABBERT | Louis Arthur | 09.04.1968 | S/O |
| 7967 | BUGGS | Frank Alfred | 09.04.1968 | S/O(T) |
| 7968 | KEEFER | Charles Edward | 09.04.1968 | P/O |
| 7969 | MARTIN | Patrick Donovan | 09.04.1968 | Insp |
| 7970 | LAWRENCE | Ian Robert | 09.04.1968 | S/O |
| 7971 | HUNDERMARK | Ernest John | 09.04.1968 | S/O |
| 7972 | PRATO | John Robert | 09.04.1968 | P/O |
| 7973 | HOOPER | Neil Roland | 09.04.1968 | P/O |
| 7974 | BOYD | John Charles | 24.04.1968 | Insp |
| 7975 | WILLIS | Victor Mathew | 27.04.1968 | S/O |
| 7976 | JACK | Francis | 28.04.1968 | P/O |
| 7977 | WHYTE | Henry Lawrence | 28.04.1968 | P/O |
| 7978 | HAY | Douglas William | 29.04.1968 | Supt |
| 7979 | SINCLAIR | Graeme Miller | 30.04.1968 | D/Insp |
| 7980 | HUNTER-HARDY | John | 30.04.1968 | D/P/O |
| 7981 | OMOLONY | Robert Allan | 01.05.1968 | D/Insp |
| 7982 | GOODE | Allan | 05.05.1968 | Not recorded |
| 7983 | BRANFIELD | Ronald Gerald | 10.05.1968 | Supt |
| 7984 | McLEAN | Jose Luis Moura | 10.05.1968 | D/P/O |
| 7985 | PEREIRA | Patrick George | 11.05.1968 | Insp(T) |
| 7986 | WHEATLEY | George | 15.05.1968 | D/P/O |
| 7987 | MITCHELL | Colin Noble | 19.05.1968 | D/Insp |
| 7988 | EDGCUMBE | Evan Cyril | 20.05.1968 | P/O |
| 7989 | COLEMAN | Martyn Sharley | 21.05.1968 | P/O |
| 7990 | PITOUT | Justus Adolph | 23.05.1968 | S/O(T) |
| 7991 | WOOD | Keith | 27.05.1968 | Insp |
| 7992 | BLACK | Ralph Morgan | 28.05.1968 | Insp |
| 7993 | HAYES | Edward Anthony | 29.05.1968 | Insp |
| 7994 | JOHNSON | Alan Bannett | 30.05.1968 | Insp |
| 7995 | TROWSDALE | Graeme Peter | 06.06.1968 | Insp |
| 7996 | HIRST | Gordon Black | 10.06.1968 | P/O |
| 7997 | LAW | John Henry | 10.06.1968 | P/O |
| 7998 | McILROY | David Charles | 10.06.1968 | Insp |
| 7999 | STANTON-HUMPHRIES | Nigel Roderick | 10.06.1968 | S/O |
| 8000 | SURTEES | Hendrik Eiperus | 11.06.1968 | P/O |
| 8001 | POTGIETER | David | 11.06.1968 | D/Insp |
| 8002 | ANDERTON | [?] | 11.06.1968 | D/Insp |
| 8003 | FERGUSON | Gregory Warren | 11.06.1968 | P/O |
| 8004 | HARRISON | Philip Vernon | 11.06.1968 | Insp |
| 8005 | KIRKLAND | Christopher Stuart | 11.06.1968 | S/O |
| 8006 | ROBERTS | John | 11.06.1968 | Insp |
| 8007 | TILLEY | David | 11.06.1968 | P/O |
| 8008 | BRYANT | Peter Angus | 11.06.1968 | P/O |
| 8009 | BUTLER | Hendrik Jacobus | 11.06.1968 | S/Insp |
| 8010 | CILLIERS | William Thomas | 11.06.1968 | P/O |
| 8011 | KNOX | Mark | 11.06.1968 | P/O |
| 8012 | VAUGHAN-DAVIES | Royston Albert | 11.06.1968 | P/O |
| 8013 | GRIFFIN | Allan Gene Ross | 11.06.1968 | P/O |
| 8014 | SMITH | Terence Barry | 11.06.1968 | Insp |
| 8015 | COLLINS | Peter William | 12.06.1968 | P/O |
| 8016 | LOUWRENS | Hendrik Carstens | 13.06.1968 | P/O |
| 8017 | COETZEE | Alan John | 14.06.1968 | P/O |
| 8018 | GORDON | Kenneth John | 15.06.1968 | P/O |
| 8019 | ROBERTS | John | 16.06.1968 | P/O |
| 8020 | McFARLANE | Michael Gordon | 26.06.1968 | Supt |
| 8021 | ROWLEY | Nigel Anthony | 29.06.1968 | P/O |
| 8022 | CARTER | Raymond George | 02.07.1968 | P/O |
| 8023 | McCULLOUGH | Ian Michael | 02.07.1968 | P/O |
| 8024 | KIRKMAN | Marthinus de Wet | 02.07.1968 | P/O |
| 8025 | VAN RENSBURG | Jonathan | 02.07.1968 | Insp(T) |
| 8026 | HARVEY | Frederick Gordon | 02.07.1968 | P/O |
| 8027 | VARKEVISSER | Maurice | 02.07.1968 | P/O |
| 8028 | JOHNS | Johannes George | 02.07.1968 | P/O |
| 8029 | STEYN | Murray | 03.07.1968 | Insp |
| 8030 | RUSSELL | George Frederick | 10.07.1968 | P/O |
| 8031 | JONES | Neville Garth | 12.07.1968 | P/O |
| 8032 | SPURR | David Michael | 12.07.1968 | D/Insp |
| 8033 | MORGAN | John Michael | 12.08.1968 | Insp |
| 8034 | KOLBE | Adrian Godfrey | 12.08.1968 | D/Insp |
| 8035 | CARBUTT | Robin David | 12.08.1968 | D/S/O |
| 8036 | HARRINGTON-JOHNSON | Stephen James | 13.08.1968 | P/O |
| 8037 | COMBRINK | Denis Geoffrey | 13.08.1968 | P/O |
| 8038 | OSCROFT | Barrington Charles | 13.08.1968 | Insp |
| 8039 | GOUDGE | Roger Henry | 13.08.1968 | P/O |
| 8040 | RUDD | Nigel Deane | 13.08.1968 | P/O |
| 8041 | SAINSBURY | John Richard | 13.08.1968 | P/O |
| 8042 | TANSEY | Alfred John | 13.08.1968 | P/O |
| 8043 | GOODCHILD | Norman David | 13.08.1968 | P/O |
| 8044 | HARVEY | Christopher John | 13.08.1968 | P/O |
| 8045 | LEWIS | Bryan Geoffrey | 13.08.1968 | P/O |
| 8046 | NORTON | Peter | 13.08.1968 | P/O |
| 8047 | WILLIAMS | Daniel Jacobus | 13.08.1968 | Supt |
| 8048 | KOTZE | Jonathan Andrew | 13.08.1968 | P/O |
| 8049 | RAYNER | Rodney Chester | 13.08.1968 | S/Insp |
| 8050 | GREENHALGH | George James | 13.08.1968 | S/O |
| 8051 | PARVESS | Mark Lee | 13.08.1968 | S/O |
| 8052 | HARRIS | Angus Ian | 13.08.1968 | P/O |
| 8053 | ALBERTON | Malcolm Anthony | 13.08.1968 | P/O |
| 8054 | BEACH | Hugh Bernard | 13.08.1968 | P/O |
| 8055 | HEPKER | Mervyn Leon | 13.08.1968 | P/O |
| 8056 | KAPLAN | Robin Simon | 13.08.1968 | P/O |
| 8057 | WALLER | Donald Malcolm | 13.08.1968 | P/O |
| 8058 | MACKIE | Anthony Waynand | 13.08.1968 | P/O |
| 8059 | SMITH | David Paul | 14.08.1968 | D/Insp |
| 8060 | ROBERTS | John Herbert | 19.08.1968 | Insp |
| 8061 | WIDDOP | Michael Anthony | 30.08.1968 | S/O |
| 8062 | THOMAS | Jeffrey Robert | 30.08.1968 | P/O |
| 8063 | AMES | John Leslie | 02.09.1968 | Insp(T) |
| 8064 | HAMMOND | Stephen Benjamin | 02.09.1968 | A/Com |
| 8065 | BRITZ | Paul Arthur | 06.09.1968 | P/O |
| 8066 | LITTLE | Brian Eric | 09.09.1968 | P/O |
| 8067 | MITCHELL | Dennis Edwin | 09.09.1968 | Supt |
| 8068 | WYATT | Edouard Marie | 16.09.1968 | S/O |
| 8069 | CARRE | Anton Frederick | 16.09.1968 | P/O |
| 8070 | DE MARILLAC | John William | 16.09.1968 | P/O |
| 8071 | HERBST | [?] | 16.09.1968 | P/O |

# BSAP Nominal Roll • Men

| No. | Surname | Names | Date | Rank |
|---|---|---|---|---|
| 8072 | RANDALL | Nigel Charles | 16.09.1968 | P/O |
| 8073 | MATHER | Michael Fairbairn | 16.09.1968 | P/O |
| 8074 | KREBSER | Eired Eric | 16.09.1968 | P/O |
| 8075 | McIVOR | Graham Wallace | 16.09.1968 | P/O |
| 8076 | COLLINS | Michael Hugh | 17.09.1968 | P/O |
| 8077 | FULLER | Barry Richard | 17.09.1968 | S/Insp |
| 8078 | HUMPHREY | Roger Bertram | 17.09.1968 | P/O |
| 8079 | TOWNEND | Craig Edward | 17.09.1968 | P/O |
| 8080 | VOLBRECHT | Nicholas Jacobus | 17.09.1968 | P/O |
| 8081 | OSBORNE-FRANCIS | Peter Andrew | 17.09.1968 | P/O |
| 8082 | ROBINSON | Edward John | 17.09.1968 | P/O |
| 8083 | SINGLETON | William James | 17.09.1968 | S/O |
| 8084 | FERREIRA | Llewellyn Meredith | 17.09.1968 | S/O |
| 8085 | BOTHA | Daniel Martinus | 17.09.1968 | P/O |
| 8086 | STRYDOM | Christiaan Jacobus | 17.09.1968 | P/O |
| 8087 | KOTZEE | William Johannes | 20.09.1968 | S/O(T) |
| 8088 | MUNRO | Ray Alexander | 22.09.1968 | S/O |
| 8089 | CONNOLLY | Anthony James | 23.09.1968 | Insp |
| 8090 | LAWSON | David Paul | 27.09.1968 | Insp |
| 8091 | PARKER | James Simpson | 27.09.1968 | S/O |
| 8092 | VERSTER | Peter John | 27.09.1968 | P/O |
| 8093 | HILLIAR | Ronald Henry | 27.09.1968 | S/O(T) |
| 8094 | SMITH | Alan David | 01.10.1968 | P/O |
| 8095 | CLARK | Stephen John | 02.10.1968 | P/O |
| 8096 | DORRIAN | Columb Francis | 14.10.1968 | P/O |
| 8097 | QUILLIAM | David John | 14.10.1968 | P/O |
| 8098 | RITCHIE | Julian Francis | 14.10.1968 | S/O |
| 8099 | TURTON | David Richard | 14.10.1968 | S/O |
| 8100 | VAN DER VEEN | Graham Vernon | 14.10.1968 | S/O |
| 8101 | WALKER | Richard Thomas | 14.10.1968 | S/O |
| 8102 | DEAN | Grant Mitchell | 14.10.1968 | S/O |
| 8103 | PEACOCK | Donald Campbell | 14.10.1968 | S/O |
| 8104 | BOOYSEN | Ralph | 14.10.1968 | P/O |
| 8105 | CUTTING | Peter Nigel | 14.10.1968 | D/S/O |
| 8106 | KOK | Peter Johannes | 15.10.1968 | Supt |
| 8107 | POULTNEY | David Eion | 15.10.1968 | S/Insp |
| 8108 | GUNSTON | Denis | 15.10.1968 | S/O |
| 8109 | MAITLAND | Terrence | 15.10.1968 | P/O |
| 8110 | RILEY | Stephen Philip | 15.10.1968 | P/O |
| 8111 | VAN ZYL | Petrus Jacobus | 15.10.1968 | Insp |
| 8112 | COUTTS | David George | 15.10.1968 | Insp |
| 8113 | BORAIN | Kenneth Denis | 18.10.1968 | Insp |
| 8114 | SIM | Josias Renier | 20.10.1968 | P/O |
| 8115 | LEAKEY | Nigel Patrick | 21.10.1968 | S/O |
| 8116 | GILLOT | Colin Harold | 22.10.1968 | S/O |
| 8117 | WARD | Clinton Paul | 24.10.1968 | P/O |
| 8118 | TUBBS | Robert Edward | 24.10.1968 | D/I |
| 8119 | LAMBOURN | David Edward | 30.10.1968 | S/S/O |
| 8120 | OBRIEN | Milford Leonard | 04.11.1968 | Supt |
| 8121 | HARVEY | Allan David | 11.11.1968 | P/O |
| 8122 | PIGGOTT | Ernest John | 12.11.1968 | Insp(T) |
| 8123 | GRIZZARD | Mark Stephen | 17.11.1968 | D/S/O |
| 8124 | BRITLAND | Roger | 29.11.1968 | P/O |
| 8125 | DAVIES | Andrew Frank | 06.12.1968 | P/O |
| 8126 | HARDWICK | Gerald Owen | 12.12.1968 | P/O |
| 8127 | HENDERSON | John Johnston | 12.12.1968 | P/O |
| 8128 | ROSSER | Clifford Anthony | 12.12.1968 | S/O |
| 8129 | CRAGE | Colin Thomas | 16.12.1968 | S/O |
| 8130 | DAVIS | Geoffrey Percy | 16.12.1968 | P/O |
| 8131 | HODSON | Brian Sylvester | 16.12.1968 | Insp |
| 8132 | PURSE | Leslie Frank | 16.12.1968 | Supt |
| 8133 | WARD | Douglas Peter | 16.12.1968 | P/O |
| 8134 | TUCKWELL | Terence Charles | 16.12.1968 | P/O |
| 8135 | CHARTERIS | David Murray | 16.12.1968 | S/Insp |
| 8136 | LEWIS | Charles Richard | 16.12.1968 | D/S/O |
| 8137 | VAN ROOYEN | Carolus Louwrens | 16.12.1968 | D/S/O |
| 8138 | HERBST | Michael Edward | 16.12.1968 | P/O |
| 8139 | TORMEY | James Partick | 16.12.1968 | P/O |
| 8141 | ASHBURNER | Trevor Burnett | 17.12.1968 | D/Insp |
| 8142 | McCREA | Robert Alexander | 17.12.1968 | S/O |
| 8143 | WATSON | Bruce Irving | 17.12.1968 | S/L/I |
| 8144 | JOHNSTONE | Thomas Erasmus | 17.12.1968 | D/Insp |
| 8145 | READINGS | George McCrindle | 17.12.1968 | Insp |
| 8146 | DYKES | Hedley Bennett | 17.12.1968 | P/O |
| 8147 | VILJOEN | Lourennes Marthinus | 17.12.1968 | P/O |
| 8148 | TINDLE | Guy Timms | 17.12.1968 | S/O |
| 8149 | TRUESDALE | John | 17.12.1968 | P/O |
| 8150 | LURIE | David | 17.12.1968 | Insp(T) |
| 8151 | MABIN | Lawrie Lucas | 17.12.1968 | D/S/O |
| 8152 | RUTHERFOORD | Keith Graham | 17.12.1968 | S/O |
| 8153 | TURPIN | Gordon John | 19.12.1968 | P/O |
| 8154 | WIENAND | Ronald Peter | 23.12.1968 | S/O |
| 8155 | JOHNSON | Raymond Michael | 23.12.1968 | S/O(T) |
| 8156 | WALKER | Noel Terence | 23.12.1968 | P/O |
| 8157 | WOAN | Barry Robert | 26.12.1968 | Insp |
| 8158 | EDWARDS | Derrick George | 26.12.1968 | Insp |
| 8159 | PRETORIUS | Hendrik | 28.12.1968 | S/S/O |
| 8160 | WREN | Brian Kirkpatrick | 28.12.1968 | P/O |
| 8161 | HATFIELD | John Kenneth | 01.01.1969 | P/O |
| 8162 | MATTHEWS | Errol Wayne | 07.01.1969 | Insp |
| 8163 | ROBERTSON | Michael Ian | 12.01.1969 | Insp |
| 8164 | STEELE | James Sherwin | 13.01.1969 | S/O(T) |
| 8165 | LLOYD | Stephen Geoffrey | 14.01.1969 | Insp |
| 8166 | NEL | Philip Westdyk | 14.01.1969 | P/O |
| 8167 | WINSON | Rodney Donald | 14.01.1969 | Insp |
| 8168 | BARICHIEVY | Peter Anthony | 14.01.1969 | P/O |
| 8169 | BLOORE | Paul Clive Lambert | 14.01.1969 | P/O |
| 8170 | BROOKER | Stephen Laurence | 14.01.1969 | Insp |
| 8171 | DAVIES | David Jonathan | 14.01.1969 | Insp |
| 8172 | GIBBONS | James Peace | 14.01.1969 | P/O |
| 8173 | HOWIE | Lachlan Dean | 14.01.1969 | P/O |
| 8174 | MIDDLETON | Trevor Hugh | 14.01.1969 | P/O |
| 8175 | PARKER | Robert William | 14.01.1969 | Insp |
| 8176 | RUDDICK | James Eckford | 14.01.1969 | D/Insp |
| 8177 | WINTER | Piers Scott | 14.01.1969 | Insp |
| 8178 | BRUCE | Kelvin Flett | 14.01.1969 | P/O |
| 8179 | LAWSON | Stephen Howard | 14.01.1969 | P/O |
| 8180 | SAND | Neill Arthur | 14.01.1969 | Insp |
| 8181 | DALE | Malcolm Stuart | 14.01.1969 | Insp |
| 8182 | AINSWORTH | David Richard | 15.01.1969 | Insp(T) |
| 8183 | ALLEN | Barry Michael | 16.01.1969 | Insp |
| 8184 | JOBSON | Robert | 22.01.1969 | Insp |
| 8185 | GUNDRY | Edgar Henry | 25.01.1969 | P/O |
| 8186 | WILLIAMS | David Robin | 29.01.1969 | D/S/O |
| 8187 | BLOOMFIELD | Michael | 03.02.1969 | Insp |
| 8188 | BRITS | Pieter Johan | 12.02.1969 | P/O |
| 8189 | WALKER | John Roger | 19.02.1969 | S/O |
| 8190 | BEJNAR | Anthony Josef | 04.03.1969 | S/Insp |
| 8191 | PETTIGREW | Clifford Anthony | 04.03.1969 | P/O |
| 8192 | PISTORIUS | Michael John | 04.03.1969 | P/O |
| 8193 | VAN DYK | Alan | 04.03.1969 | P/O |
| 8194 | WENTZEL | Richard John | 04.03.1969 | D/Inp |
| 8195 | BURGER | Colin Charles | 04.03.1969 | P/O |
| 8196 | DEVOY | Thomas Pat | 04.03.1969 | P/O |
| 8197 | JACK | Ian Sutherland | 04.03.1969 | S/O |
| 8198 | McCARTER | Patrick Robert | 04.03.1969 | D/S/O |
| 8199 | MORAN | Michael Roy | 04.03.1969 | P/O |
| 8200 | WOOD | Timothy Charles | 04.03.1969 | S/Insp |
| 8201 | ASHBURNER | Geoffrey Malcolm | 04.03.1969 | P/O |
| 8202 | CRAUSE | Daniel Erwin | 04.03.1969 | P/O |
| 8203 | MARILLIER | Christopher Colin | 04.03.1969 | C/Insp |
| 8204 | PERKINS | William Turner | 04.03.1969 | S/O |
| 8205 | CHANDLER | Charles Brian | 04.03.1969 | P/O |
| 8206 | LAUNDER | Graham Barry | 04.03.1969 | P/O |
| 8207 | LORNIE | Alastair James | 04.03.1969 | P/O |
| 8208 | YOUNG | Alasdair St.Clair | 04.03.1969 | S/S/O |
| 8210 | MARSH | Malcolm Leathem | 04.03.1969 | S/Insp |
| 8211 | WALKER | Jeremy Drew | 04.03.1969 | Insp |
| 8212 | BARR | Alastair Kenneth | 05.03.1969 | Insp |
| 8213 | HOWITT | John Alexander | 05.03.1969 | D/Insp |
| 8214 | PACKER | Robert William | 05.03.1969 | D/S/O |
| 8215 | WEBB | Malcolm | 05.03.1969 | Insp |
| 8216 | FRASER | Duncan | 12.03.1969 | D/Insp |
| 8217 | SCOTT | Peter Charles | 21.03.1969 | D/Insp |
| 8218 | CLEMENTS | Geoffrey Redmond | 22.03.1969 | P/O |
| 8219 | BOSSERT | Allan Walter | 31.03.1969 | D/Insp |
| 8220 | JOUBERT | Donald | 02.04.1969 | P/O |
| 8221 | STEWART | Kenneth Gordon | 08.04.1969 | D/Insp |
| 8222 | ST. CLAIR | Anthony Patrick | 11.04.1969 | D/S/O |
| 8223 | CRAVEN | Walter Maurice | 15.04.1969 | S/O |
| 8224 | LEDGER | Alan Arthur | 15.04.1969 | P/O |
| 8225 | LE ROUX | Trevor John | 15.04.1969 | D/P/O |
| 8226 | PRINGLE | Kevin Peter | 15.04.1969 | P/O |
| 8227 | BERRY | John | 15.04.1969 | S/O |
| 8228 | JONES | John Christopher | 15.04.1969 | S/O |
| 8229 | MARTIN | Derek Andrew | 15.04.1969 | D/S/O |
| 8230 | CLARK | Peter Brian Heather | 15.04.1969 | S/O |
| 8231 | DAWSON | Joseph Anthony | 15.04.1969 | Insp |
| 8232 | LINDSAY | Michael | 15.04.1969 | P/O |
| 8233 | AITKEN | Christopher | 15.04.1969 | Insp |
| 8234 | JACOBSZ | Loedwyk Jan | 15.04.1969 | Insp |
| 8235 | KAY | Martin Roger | 15.04.1969 | D/C/I |
| 8236 | LEONARD | Hendrik Gerhardus | 15.04.1969 | Insp(T) |
| 8237 | POLLITT | Andrew Gerald | 15.04.1969 | P/O |
| 8238 | SOLOMON | John Crawford | 15.04.1969 | P/O |
| 8239 | PEARSON | John Stephen | 16.04.1969 | D/Insp |
| 8240 | VICKERY | John Gibson | 17.04.1969 | S/O |
| 8241 | JONKER | Paul Francis | 20.04.1969 | S/O |
| 8242 | BENNETT | Thomas Alan | 22.04.1969 | Insp |
| 8243 | BATE | Robin Clive | 25.04.1969 | P/O |
| 8244 | Mac LEAN | Robert Michael | 12.05.1969 | Insp |
| 8245 | WILKINSON | Carl Peter | 12.05.1969 | S/O(T) |
| 8246 | SHEW | Paul | 19.05.1969 | D/P/O |
| 8247 | SMITH | Gordon Denis | 19.05.1969 | P/O |
| 8248 | GRIFFITHS | David Palin | 27.05.1969 | P/O |
| 8249 | DOBREE | Robert Simon | 29.05.1969 | P/O |
| 8250 | DRYSDALE | Gavin Douglas | 29.05.1969 | P/O |
| 8251 | ILLINGWORTH | Bruce Anthony | 29.05.1969 | P/O |
| 8252 | JEFFERY | Alan George | 29.05.1969 | P/O |
| 8253 | LOWE | Robin James | 29.05.1969 | P/O |
| 8254 | SHANKLAND | Thomas Keith | 29.05.1969 | Insp |
| 8255 | SHERRY | Timothy | 29.05.1969 | P/O |
| 8256 | SMITH | Michael John | 29.05.1969 | Insp |
| 8257 | TUCKER | David Lloyd | 29.05.1969 | P/O |
| 8258 | BARSDORF | Wynand | 29.05.1969 | S/O |
| 8259 | HERSELMAN | John Theodorus | 29.05.1969 | C/Insp |
| 8260 | AMM | David Selwyn | 29.05.1969 | P/O |
| 8261 | TAUNTON | Stephen Russell | 29.05.1969 | P/O |
| 8262 | COOPER | John William | 29.05.1969 | Supt |
| 8263 | ESTMENT | Athol Winston | 29.05.1969 | P/O |
| 8264 | POSTANCE | Derek | 17.06.1969 | P/O |
| 8265 | WOODCOCK | Stewart Charles | 24.06.1969 | P/O |
| 8266 | McKENZIE | David Grant | 24.06.1969 | P/O |
| 8267 | FLANAGAN | Peter | 24.06.1969 | Insp |
| 8268 | STEYN | Coenrad Christoffel | 24.06.1969 | D/Insp |
| 8269 | BRINK | David Jan | 24.06.1969 | P/O |
| 8270 | HUNTER | Giles Malcolm | 24.06.1969 | S/Insp |
| 8271 | BELLAMY | David | 24.06.1969 | S/O |
| 8272 | LEONARD | Hermanus Jan | 24.06.1969 | A/Comm |
| 8273 | IRVING | Michael John | 24.06.1969 | P/O |
| 8274 | ADAMS | Patrick Kenneth | 24.06.1969 | P/O |
| 8275 | MORGAN | Alistair Brice | 24.06.1969 | P/O |
| 8276 | PERKINS | Brian Dennis | 24.06.1969 | D/Insp |
| 8277 | HOFFMAN | Johannes Jacobus | 24.06.1969 | Insp |

| No. | Surname | Forename(s) | Date | Rank |
|---|---|---|---|---|
| 8279 | DURBAN-JACKSON | Rory Anthony | 24.06.1969 | P/O |
| 8280 | RAMES-TAYLOR | David Hamish | 24.06.1969 | P/O |
| 8281 | STEWART | Duncan Gordon | 24.06.1969 | S/O |
| 8282 | RIEDY | Robert Nelson | 24.06.1969 | S/O |
| 8283 | BARSON | Anthony Alexander | 24.06.1969 | S/Insp |
| 8284 | THRELFALL | David Lionel Paul | 24.06.1969 | P/O |
| 8285 | HEIN | Ronald Lewis | 25.06.1969 | Insp |
| 8286 | EDDIE | Robert Duncan | 26.06.1969 | S/C/I |
| 8287 | JONES | Michael Andrew | 27.06.1969 | P/O |
| 8288 | JEARY | Alfred Clifford | 08.07.1969 | P/O |
| 8289 | DINEEN | John Frederick | 21.07.1969 | Insp |
| 8290 | BREEDT | Lucas Augustinis | 22.07.1969 | S/O |
| 8291 | ARKLEY | John William | 29.07.1969 | S/O |
| 8292 | BELL | Christopher Paul | 29.07.1969 | P/O |
| 8293 | DOWNEY | Graham Paul | 29.07.1969 | P/O |
| 8294 | HOUSE | John Lindsay | 29.07.1969 | P/O |
| 8295 | LOTZE | Theodore George | 29.07.1969 | P/O |
| 8296 | REYNOLDS | Keith William | 29.07.1969 | P/O |
| 8297 | PRICE | Barry Kevin | 30.07.1969 | P/O |
| 8298 | DE LORME | Kevin Bruce | 05.08.1969 | D/S/O |
| 8299 | REELER | Michael Anthony | 06.08.1969 | S/S/O |
| 8300 | CHISNALL | Zane Courtney | 08.08.1969 | D/Insp |
| 8301 | HUBBARD | Graham Anthony | 13.08.1969 | Insp |
| 8302 | McKRILL | Niall Edwin | 17.08.1969 | P/O |
| 8303 | BRISTOW | Robert John | 19.08.1969 | D/Insp |
| 8304 | WEATHERALL | Sydney | 19.08.1969 | Supt |
| 8305 | TAVENER | Bryan | 25.08.1969 | D/Insp |
| 8306 | DEL FABBRO | Claudio | 26.08.1969 | C/Insp |
| 8307 | FIRTH | Brian | 26.08.1969 | S/O |
| 8308 | SLESSOR | Colin | 26.08.1969 | D/Insp |
| 8309 | SOALL | Patrick John | 26.08.1969 | S/O |
| 8310 | MARSHALL | Keith Thomas | 26.08.1969 | D/Insp |
| 8311 | BRADY | James Patrick | 01.09.1969 | Insp(T) |
| 8312 | JOHNN | Michael William | 02.09.1969 | D/S/O |
| 8313 | BOTHWELL | Robert Nigel | 04.09.1969 | S/O |
| 8314 | WEINEL | Paul | 14.09.1969 | P/O |
| 8315 | PADBURY | John Eric | 24.09.1969 | D/Insp |
| 8316 | CAHILL | Peter | 30.09.1969 | S/O |
| 8317 | CLARKE | Robert | 30.09.1969 | Supt |
| 8318 | CUSHWORTH | David | 30.09.1969 | Insp |
| 8319 | HODGSON | John Forbes | 30.09.1969 | Supt |
| 8320 | ROBERTS | David Evan | 30.09.1969 | D/Insp |
| 8321 | WOOD | Alan Lawrence | 30.09.1969 | D/P/O |
| 8322 | BRADY | Peter Robert | 30.09.1969 | S/O |
| 8323 | CLARKE | David Henry | 30.09.1969 | P/O |
| 8324 | NAISBITT | David Hedley | 30.09.1969 | Insp |
| 8325 | JOVNER | Barend Christiaan | 30.09.1969 | Insp |
| 8326 | WEBSTER | Peter John | 30.09.1969 | Insp |
| 8327 | WILSON | Josias Hendrik | 30.09.1969 | P/O |
| 8328 | DELPORT | Graham John (PDG) | 04.10.1969 | Insp(T) |
| 8329 | LAILEY | Anthony Howard | 06.10.1969 | Insp |
| 8330 | NEILL | Alec | 09.10.1969 | Insp |
| 8331 | BUGGS | Christopher Dale | 27.10.1969 | D/Insp |
| 8332 | CUMMING | Philip Edward | 28.10.1969 | S/S/O |
| 8333 | HARTLEBURY | John Fletcher | 28.10.1969 | D/Insp |
| 8334 | MATTHEWS | Michael Carl | 28.10.1969 | S/O |
| 8335 | PETERS | Nigel Philip | 03.11.1969 | Insp |
| 8336 | WEBSTER | Malcolm | 05.11.1969 | Insp |
| 8337 | CROSSLAND | George Peter | 07.11.1969 | Insp |
| 8338 | THURMAN | David Maurice | 08.11.1969 | Insp |
| 8339 | MAWBY | Peter Stephen | 12.11.1969 | S/O |
| 8340 | BAILEY | Brent Munro | 21.11.1969 | Insp(T) |
| 8341 | BERRY | Peter Neil | 29.11.1969 | Insp |
| 8342 | FORREST | Alasdair Ian | 01.12.1969 | S/O |
| 8343 | SALONIKA | Frederick Herbert | 29.12.1969 | C/Supt |
| 8344 | SCOTT | Ernest Arthur |  | Insp |
| 8345 | BEZUIDENHOUT | Simon Johnathan |  | Supt |
| 8346 | WILDE |  |  | P/O |
| 8347 | BRENCHLEY |  |  | P/O |
| 8348 | BUCHANAN | Charles Edward | 29.12.1969 | Insp |
| 8349 | DODD | John Austin | 29.12.1969 | P/O |
| 8350 | EVANS | Roger Stoneage | 29.12.1969 | P/O |
| 8351 | KEYS | Fredrick Hugh | 29.12.1969 | Insp |
| 8352 | RICHMOND | Alan Charles | 29.12.1969 | P/O |
| 8353 | JEFFREY | Michael Keith | 29.12.1969 | P/O |
| 8354 | SHEPPARD | Barrie Lawrence | 29.12.1969 | P/O |
| 8355 | BUTLER | Christopher Maurice | 30.12.1969 | P/O |
| 8356 | CLARK | Christopher Julian | 30.12.1969 | P/O |
| 8357 | MORGAN | Mark Adrian | 30.12.1969 | P/O |
| 8358 | RUSSELL | Glen Victor | 30.12.1969 | S/O |
| 8359 | THOMAS | Philip Edward | 30.12.1969 | P/O |
| 8360 | CROSS | Adrian Charles | 30.12.1969 | D/Insp |
| 8361 | HENDERSON | Alastair Martin | 30.12.1969 | S/O |
| 8362 | MAWDSLEY | Gary Hugh | 30.12.1969 | P/O |
| 8363 | MURRAY | William | 30.12.1969 | P/O |
| 8364 | CAMERON | Barrie Colin | 30.12.1969 | S/O |
| 8365 | MORGAN | Sean Padraig | 30.12.1969 | P/O |
| 8366 | NORTIER | Rheeder Johannes | 30.12.1969 | P/O |
| 8367 | FRASER | Alexander | 30.12.1969 | P/O |
| 8368 | SILVA | Norman Ashley | 30.12.1969 | S/O |
| 8369 | SIMS | Alan John | 30.12.1969 | P/O |
| 8370 | JOUBERT | Andries Stephanus | 30.12.1969 | S/O |
| 8371 | KERR | Colin John | 30.12.1969 | Insp |
| 8372 | BAKER | Roland | 30.12.1969 | P/O |
| 8373 | GROBLER | Stephen Paul | 30.12.1969 | Insp |
| 8374 | JELLIMAN | Peter Albert | 30.12.1969 | Insp |
| 8375 | WINHALL | Gavin Peter | 30.12.1969 | P/O |
| 8376 | HOPLEY | David Nicholas | 30.12.1969 | P/O |
| 8377 | STASSEN | Heinrich Jacobus | 30.12.1969 | S/C/I |
| 8378 | CORBY | Keith Edward | 30.12.1969 | D/Insp |
| 8379 | FRANCESCHI | Roberto | 30.12.1969 | Insp |
| 8380 | PRETORIUS | Denis Henry | 30.12.1969 | Insp |
| 8381 | SCARROTT | Trevor Cameron | 24.01.1970 | Supt. |
| 8382 | GRAHAM | Reginald David | 26.01.1970 | Insp |
| 8383 | BIGG | Grant Douglas | 26.01.1970 | P/O |
| 8384 | JONES | Timothy Oliver | 26.01.1970 | P/O |
| 8385 | REES | Michael Lynn | 26.01.1970 | P/O |
| 8386 | SCHULT | Paul | 26.01.1970 | P/O |
| 8387 | DELPORT | Hendrick Chrisjan | 26.01.1970 | S/O |
| 8388 | KLOPPERS | Trevor | 26.01.1970 | S/O |
| 8389 | NOBLE | Neville Raymond | 26.01.1970 | S/O |
| 8390 | HOARE | Richard Henry | 26.01.1970 | Insp |
| 8391 | BUDD | Kenneth Noel | 27.01.1970 | Insp |
| 8392 | WILKIN | William Ian | 27.01.1970 | P/O |
| 8393 | VAN ECK | Gideon Grobbelaar | 27.01.1970 | Insp |
| 8394 | JANKS | Gregory Royce | 27.01.1970 | Insp |
| 8395 | HUGHES | Malcolm Ian | 27.01.1970 | P/O |
| 8396 | SLATEM | Denis James | 27.01.1970 | Insp |
| 8397 | CLARK | Ian | 27.01.1970 | Supt |
| 8398 | WATSON | Michael Stewart | 27.01.1970 | Insp |
| 8399 | GARLICK | Ian Montgomery | 27.01.1970 | D/Insp |
| 8400 | FURIA | Anthony John | 27.01.1970 | P/O |
| 8401 | BURROWS | Timothy | 27.01.1970 | P/O |
| 8402 | MARTIN | Colin Edward | 27.01.1970 | P/O |
| 8403 | HAGER | Derek Anthony | 27.01.1970 | P/O |
| 8404 | VOS | Robert Cyril | 27.01.1970 | P/O |
| 8405 | MINCHIN | Robert Michael | 27.01.1970 | Insp |
| 8406 | BIRD | Nicholas Eckhardt | 27.01.1970 | P/O |
| 8407 | CAMPBELL | Graham Angus | 04.02.1970 | P/O |
| 8408 | KEEN | Raymond Roy | 16.02.1970 | P/O |
| 8409 | SOWDEN | Paul Raymond | 19.02.1970 | S/O |
| 8410 | STERNSLOW | Andrew Aubrey | 19.02.1970 | Insp |
| 8411 | RUTHERFOORD | Colin Rodney | 19.02.1970 | S/O |
| 8412 | HORNBY | Lynnford Stewart | 24.02.1970 | Insp |
| 8413 | HUMPHREYS | David Anthony | 24.02.1970 | P/O |
| 8414 | HUNT | Bruce Dunning | 24.02.1970 | D/P/O |
| 8415 | JONKER | Brian Cedric | 24.02.1970 | P/O |
| 8416 | KENCHINGTON | Anthony George | 24.02.1970 | P/O |
| 8417 | LAPAGE | Peter Derek | 24.02.1970 | Insp |
| 8418 | OLDS | Douglas Edward | 24.02.1970 | Insp |
| 8419 | PERKINS | Donald Graham | 24.02.1970 | Insp |
| 8420 | SMIT | Joachim Hendrik | 24.02.1970 | P/O |
| 8421 | VAN WYK | Peter Edward | 24.02.1970 | P/O |
| 8422 | HILL | Michael Fenton | 24.02.1970 | P/O |
| 8423 | THOMAS | David Llewellyn | 24.02.1970 | P/O |
| 8424 | THORNTON | William Stanley | 24.02.1970 | P/O |
| 8425 | WYCHE | David Cyril | 24.02.1970 | S/O |
| 8426 | BARNFIELD | Miles Joseph | 25.02.1970 | S/O |
| 8427 | PRICE | John Charles | 25.02.1970 | S/O |
| 8428 | CLEGG | Michael Douglas | 26.02.1970 | C/I(T) |
| 8429 | HICKIE | Trevor James | 01.03.1970 | Insp(T) |
| 8430 | SAINSBURY | John | 01.03.1970 | P/O(T) |
| 8431 | PARTRIDGE | John Brian | 02.03.1970 | S/O(T) |
| 8432 | McKENZIE | Arthur Clyne | 05.03.1970 | S/O |
| 8433 | FARRELL | Peter John | 05.03.1970 | S/O |
| 8434 | CHAPMAN | David Charles | 05.03.1970 | P/O |
| 8435 | HIGHAM | James William | 05.03.1970 | P/O |
| 8436 | HUTCHINSON | Brian William | 05.03.1970 | Insp |
| 8437 | HUGHES | Ian | 09.03.1970 | Insp |
| 8438 | STEELE | Peter | 17.03.1970 | P/O |
| 8439 | DODD | Adrian John | 24.03.1970 | P/O |
| 8440 | HERON | Thomas Walter | 24.03.1970 | P/O |
| 8441 | McDONALD | Robert Thomas | 24.03.1970 | P/O |
| 8442 | MEAKIN | Vernon James | 24.03.1970 | Insp |
| 8443 | MURPHY | Anthony David | 24.03.1970 | Insp |
| 8444 | SINDALL | Alan Maxwell | 24.03.1970 | S/O |
| 8445 | STRONGE | Anthony Travell | 24.03.1970 | P/O |
| 8446 | WALTERS | Derek Mitchell | 24.03.1970 | P/O |
| 8447 | GILBERT | Ian John | 31.03.1970 | S/O |
| 8448 | RAYNE | Michael John | 01.04.1970 | Supt |
| 8449 | KURZ | Neville Gordon | 02.04.1970 | P/O |
| 8450 | GRADWELL | Neil Martin | 06.04.1970 | D/Insp |
| 8451 | JORDAAN | Norman Robert | 06.04.1970 | P/O |
| 8452 | JAMES | David Killeen | 15.04.1970 | P/O |
| 8453 | ARCHER | Thomas Charles | 16.04.1970 | P/O |
| 8454 | BIRD | Kenneth James | 24.04.1970 | P/O |
| 8455 | O'CONNOR | Thomas Kevin | 24.04.1970 | P/O |
| 8456 | TYRRELL | Peter | 28.04.1970 | D/Insp |
| 8457 | CUNDY | Michael Meadows | 28.04.1970 | P/O |
| 8458 | PITT | Brian Denton | 28.04.1970 | D/Insp |
| 8459 | STEEL | Allan | 28.04.1970 | P/O |
| 8460 | SMITH | Allen Lionel | 28.04.1970 | P/O |
| 8461 | VAN SCHALKWYK | Johan | 28.04.1970 | S/O |
| 8462 | COOPER | Nicholas Alan | 28.04.1970 | P/O |
| 8463 | CLEARY | Seamus Thomas | 28.04.1970 | P/O |
| 8464 | BAILEY | Allan Kenneth | 28.04.1970 | S/O |
| 8465 | ELDER | David | 28.04.1970 | P/O |
| 8466 | COLMER | Brian John | 28.04.1970 | S/O |
| 8467 | WILES | David Martin | 03.06.1970 | Supt |
| 8468 | DE GRAY-BIRCH | John | 15.06.1970 | S/O(T) |
| 8469 | RANKIN | Colin Bruce | 15.06.1970 | D/S/O |
| 8470 | BENNETT | Christopher Pietro | 22.06.1970 | S/O |
| 8471 | GRAINGER | Donald | 22.06.1970 | P/O |
| 8472 | INMAN | Christopher Philip | 30.06.1970 | P/O |
| 8473 | LAING | Andrew John | 30.06.1970 | Insp |
| 8474 | McNEIL | Andrew Neil | 30.06.1970 | Supt |
| 8475 | MATTHEWS | Stanley Allen | 30.06.1970 | D/S/O |
| 8476 | MORRIS-SMITH | John Christian | 30.06.1970 | Supt |
| 8477 | QUICK | Peter John | 30.06.1970 | S/O |
| 8478 | WEBER | Henric Jackobus | 30.06.1970 | S/O |
| 8479 | RUFUS | Angus Hilton | 01.07.1970 | Insp |
| 8480 | MORAN | Denis James | 26.07.1970 | Insp |
| 8481 | LABUSCHAGNE | Willem Hendrik | 27.07.1970 | S/O |
| 8482 | SMITH | Philip | 28.07.1970 | Insp |
| 8483 | BYRON | John Patrick | 28.07.1970 | D/P/O |
| 8484 | BOSHOFF | Brian Owen | 28.07.1970 | S/O(T) |
| 8485 | EMERY | Peter Brian | 28.07.1970 | S/O |

| No. | Surname | First Name | Rank | Date |
|---|---|---|---|---|
| 8486 | GASCOIGNE | Mark Brian | P/O | 28.07.1970 |
| 8487 | JACK | Philip Robert | S/O | 28.07.1970 |
| 8488 | JOHNSTON | Rory Anthony | P/O | 28.07.1970 |
| 8489 | ROBERTS | Michael Leonard | D/S/O | 28.07.1970 |
| 8490 | SHARP | Glenn Clinton | P/O | 28.07.1970 |
| 8491 | TUCK | Roy Kenneth | S/O | 28.07.1970 |
| 8492 | WATT-PRINGLE | William Fairbridge | P/O | 28.07.1970 |
| 8493 | TONG | Kevan Arthur | P/O | 03.08.1970 |
| 8494 | PISCOPOS | Charles | D/S/O | 03.08.1970 |
| 8495 | NEE | John Patrick | D/S/O | 08.08.1970 |
| 8496 | MUIR | Desmond Trevor | D/S/O | 08.08.1970 |
| 8497 | DAVIES | John | S/O(T) | 10.08.1970 |
| 8498 | MORTIMER | Michael Piers | P/O | 11.08.1980 |
| 8499 | LE CRERAR | Roger Clinton | Insp | 21.08.1970 |
| 8500 | O'DONOVAN | Shaun David | D/S/O | 23.08.1970 |
| 8501 | BROOKER | Phillip Richard | S/O | 27.08.1970 |
| 8502 | THOMAS | David Charles | D/P/O | 29.08.1970 |
| 8503 | TALBOT | Philip John | P/O | 31.08.1970 |
| 8504 | BARNARD | Roy Keith | Insp | 31.08.1970 |
| 8505 | MACKINTOSH | Alistair Tindall | P/O | 31.08.1970 |
| 8506 | ROACH | Vernon Leslie | D/Insp | 13.09.1970 |
| 8507 | CRABTREE | Michael David | D/S/O | 15.09.1970 |
| 8508 | NEAVE | Richard Ernest | Insp | 23.09.1970 |
| 8509 | SWEETING | Michael Frank | P/O | 24.09.1970 |
| 8510 | ADAMS | David Rowan | S/O | 29.09.1970 |
| 8511 | ALDERSON | Gerald Douglas | D/S/O | 29.09.1970 |
| 8512 | CREMER | Michael Kenneth | P/O | 29.09.1970 |
| 8513 | KEMP | Barry Alan | P/O | 29.09.1970 |
| 8514 | PERCIVAL | Robert Frederick | Insp | 29.09.1970 |
| 8515 | POWIS | Martin | D/Insp | 29.09.1970 |
| 8516 | RICHARDS | John Martin | Insp | 29.09.1970 |
| 8517 | STEEL | Kenneth Alexander | P/O | 29.09.1970 |
| 8518 | VERMOOTEN | Vincent | P/O | 29.09.1970 |
| 8519 | WHATT | Michael Philip | Insp | 29.09.1970 |
| 8520 | FLETCHER | Neale Robert | P/O | 30.09.1970 |
| 8521 | ANDREWS | Keith Anthony | Insp(T) | 01.10.1970 |
| 8522 | HAVILL | Robert Gordon | P/O | 09.10.1970 |
| 8523 | KEEN | Alan Vernon | P/O | 20.10.1970 |
| 8524 | EASTON | George Ernest | D/Insp | 21.10.1970 |
| 8525 | HEWITT | Timothy Charles | S/O | 24.10.1970 |
| 8526 | NIEMANDT | Desmond | Insp | 27.10.1970 |
| 8527 | WRIGHT | Philip Langton | Insp | 27.10.1970 |
| 8528 | RADBOURNE | William John | S/O | 29.10.1970 |
| 8529 | HOWARD | Jeffery Marshall | Insp | 02.11.1970 |
| 8530 | ROBINSON | Ian Thomas | P/O | 04.11.1970 |
| 8531 | WOODS | Kevin John | Insp | 05.11.1970 |
| 8532 | MITROVITCH | Trevor Leslie | D/S/O | 26.11.1970 |
| 8533 | LEATHES | David Michael | P/O | 27.11.1970 |
| 8534 | NOWELL | Richard James | Supt | 30.11.1970 |
| 8535 | NEARY | Michael Joseph | S/O | 03.12.1970 |
| 8536 | EDWARD | Bernard | P/O | 08.12.1970 |
| 8537 | KEYSER | Phillip Henry | P/O | 22.12.1970 |
| 8538 | ANDERSON | Allen Webster | D/Insp | 30.12.1970 |
| 8539 | BACON | Henry William | Insp | 30.12.1970 |
| 8540 | DIX | Robert Avery | P/O | 30.12.1970 |
| 8541 | HIDDLESTON | Dugald William | D/Insp | 30.12.1970 |
| 8542 | MANNING | Clive Stewart | Insp | 30.12.1970 |
| 8543 | REDMOND | Patrick Francis | D/P/O | 30.12.1970 |
| 8544 | SLOWE | Clive Charles | Insp | 30.12.1970 |
| 8545 | SMART | Richard James | S/O | 30.12.1970 |
| 8546 | JONES | Richard Douglas | S/O | 05.01.1971 |
| 8547 | BRETT | Russell Vincent | P/O | 05.01.1971 |
| 8548 | SINCLAIR | Denis James | P/O | 05.01.1971 |
| 8549 | SMIT | Ignatius Petrus | Insp | 05.01.1971 |
| 8550 | BOYD | Ian Hugh | Insp | 05.01.1971 |
| 8551 | OGSTON | William Blenkinsop | Insp | 05.01.1971 |
| 8552 | MITCHLEY | David George | Insp(T) | 05.01.1971 |
| 8553 | GRAAFF | Phillip Dewhurst | Insp | 05.01.1971 |
| 8554 | URBE | ...ton Rodney | D/Insp | 05.01.1971 |
| 8555 | MILNE | Leslie | D/S/O | 05.01.1971 |
| 8556 | BRENT | Darroll Lancelot | L/C/I | 05.01.1971 |
| 8557 | PRETORIUS | Cornelius Johannes | P/O | 05.01.1971 |
| 8558 | HARRIS | Peter John | P/O | 05.01.1971 |
| 8559 | VAN DER VLUGT | Hubertus Hendrikus | P/O | 05.01.1971 |
| 8560 | JANSEN VAN RENSBURG | Daniel Benjamin | P/O | 05.01.1971 |
| 8561 | BALDWIN | Bruce | D/Insp | 08.01.1971 |
| 8562 | FLORENS | Brian Christopher | D/Insp | 08.01.1971 |
| 8563 | BRADFIELD | Stephen Gerard | P/O | 14.01.1971 |
| 8564 | MANSON-BISHOP | Michael Peter | P/O | 18.01.1971 |
| 8565 | LANGRAN | Ian Edward | Insp | 18.01.1971 |
| 8566 | HILL | Gregory Piers | P/O | 18.01.1971 |
| 8567 | MILFORD | George William | S/O | 21.01.1971 |
| 8568 | WEBSTER | Robert Anthony | S/O | 25.01.1971 |
| 8569 | DAVIS | Anthony Richard | Insp | 26.01.1971 |
| 8570 | BICKWELL | Geoffrey Louis | P/O | 26.01.1971 |
| 8571 | DAVIS | Brian Aldwin | P/O | 26.01.1971 |
| 8572 | FEY | John William | P/O | 26.01.1971 |
| 8573 | GILBERTHORPE | David William | Insp | 26.01.1971 |
| 8574 | GLOVER | Stephen Gordon | P/O | 26.01.1971 |
| 8575 | JENNINGS | Stephen Michael | S/O | 26.01.1971 |
| 8576 | HEALE | Nicholas William | S/O | 26.01.1971 |
| 8577 | McCLELAND | Graham Frank | P/O | 26.01.1971 |
| 8578 | McCONNELL | Thomas Ronald | D/S/O | 26.01.1971 |
| 8579 | MORISON | Kevin Ian | P/O | 26.01.1971 |
| 8580 | PALING | Edgar Joseph | D/S/O | 26.01.1971 |
| 8581 | VAN DYK | James | P/O | 26.01.1971 |
| 8582 | HACKING | Bryan Cecil | P/O | 26.01.1971 |
| 8583 | BONETT | John Mark | S/Insp | 26.01.1971 |
| 8584 | CAPSON | Sean Patrick | P/O | 26.01.1971 |
| 8585 | McCORMICK | Patrick Michael | Insp | 26.01.1971 |
| 8586 | MARITZ | Christopher | Insp | 26.01.1971 |
| 8587 | REYNOLDS | Edward Lawrence | P/O | 26.01.1971 |
| 8588 | STANDERS | John Bancroft | S/O | 26.01.1971 |
| 8589 | STUTTAFORD | Richard Henry | S/O | 26.01.1971 |
| 8590 | SULLIVAN | Michael Gordon | D/P/O | 26.01.1971 |
| 8591 | TEVIS | Stefan Nicholas | P/O | 26.01.1971 |
| 8592 | CALLAWAY | Malcolm John | D/Insp | 31.01.1971 |
| 8593 | PRATT | Geoffrey William | Insp(T) | 01.02.1971 |
| 8594 | TEMPLE | Hugh Patrick | S/O | 02.02.1971 |
| 8595 | ATKINSON | Charles William | P/O | 15.02.1971 |
| 8596 | MACKIE | Gavin James | Insp | 19.02.1971 |
| 8597 | HARRISON | Michael Geoffrey | L/S/O | 22.02.1971 |
| 8598 | PHILPOT | John William | D/S/O | 23.02.1971 |
| 8599 | PAGE | Alan Cumming | Insp | 23.02.1971 |
| 8600 | SMITH | Brian Malcolm | S/O | 23.02.1971 |
| 8601 | WIGGETT | Neil Graham | S/S/O | 23.02.1971 |
| 8602 | CURRIE | Peter Fairbridge | D/Insp | 23.02.1971 |
| 8603 | FULTON | Darryll George | P/O | 23.02.1971 |
| 8604 | HOWARD | Timothy William | S/O | 23.02.1971 |
| 8605 | WITHNELL | Robert William | P/O | 23.02.1971 |
| 8606 | FREEBURN | Thomas Leo | D/Insp | 23.02.1971 |
| 8607 | UTLEY | Christopher Hugh | P/O | 23.02.1971 |
| 8608 | MICHAEL | Stewart Webb | Insp | 23.02.1971 |
| 8609 | MARTIN | Ronald Douglas | S/O | 23.02.1971 |
| 8610 | SIMS | Michael David | P/O | 09.03.1971 |
| 8611 | BUNNEY | Rodger | P/O(R) | 30.03.1971 |
| 8612 | DANIELS | Leslie George | S/O | 30.03.1971 |
| 8613 | DYER | Anthony Leonard | P/O | 30.03.1971 |
| 8614 | HURREN | Thomas John | S/O | 30.03.1971 |
| 8615 | PURCELL | Timothy William | P/O | 30.03.1971 |
| 8616 | DU PREEZ | Graham John | S/O | 01.04.1971 |
| 8617 | CAPPER | Douglas Vernon | Insp(T) | 01.04.1971 |
| 8618 | BAILEY | Christopher Maurice | P/O | 02.04.1971 |
| 8619 | BOTHA | Ian Gough | S/O | 08.04.1971 |
| 8620 | RUCK | Peter Bernard | P/O | 13.04.1971 |
| 8621 | WILSON | Andrew Scott | P/O | 18.04.1971 |
| 8622 | McGINN | Michael Anthony | S/O | 19.04.1971 |
| 8623 | ERASMUS | Peter Allan | P/O | 20.04.1971 |
| 8624 | COTTON | Richard Norman | Insp | 20.04.1971 |
| 8625 | CAMPBELL | Douglas Clifford | P/O | 20.04.1971 |
| 8626 | BISHOP | Philip David | S/S/O | 27.04.1971 |
| 8627 | BROWN | Kevan Brian | P/O | 27.04.1971 |
| 8628 | CLOETE | Keith | P/O | 27.04.1971 |
| 8629 | LA ROSA | Lucio | P/O | 27.04.1971 |
| 8630 | MEYER | Hans Jacob | P/O | 27.04.1971 |
| 8631 | NORTH | Robert Charles | P/O | 27.04.1971 |
| 8632 | ROSE-INNES | Bruce Brownlee | P/O | 27.04.1971 |
| 8633 | WALLACE | Alan David | P/O | 27.04.1971 |
| 8634 | WEST | Robert James | P/O | 27.04.1971 |
| 8635 | HENDERSON | Barry Ian | D/S/O | 29.04.1971 |
| 8636 | BARNETT | Frank David | D/P/O | 29.04.1971 |
| 8637 | PIERET | Edward Albert | P/O | 01.05.1971 |
| 8638 | STANYON | Douglas John | D/Insp | 10.05.1971 |
| 8639 | GUNSTON | Colin | L/C/I | 10.05.1971 |
| 8640 | MERRIS | Anthony Thomas | P/O | 20.05.1971 |
| 8641 | CHILD | Robert | P/O | 01.06.1971 |
| 8642 | HOLDEN | Thomas Charles | P/O | 17.06.1971 |
| 8643 | GUNSTON | Brian | S/O | 29.06.1971 |
| 8644 | BROWN | Alec George | P/O | 01.07.1971 |
| 8645 | DALE-LACE | Terence George | P/O | 01.07.1971 |
| 8646 | FIELD | Andrew David | D/Insp | 01.07.1971 |
| 8647 | GOUGH | Peter John | P/O | 01.07.1971 |
| 8648 | LEMMER | David Michael | D/Insp | 01.07.1971 |
| 8649 | MURPHY | Michael Ivan | P/O | 01.07.1971 |
| 8650 | NOTHARD | Louis John | S/O | 01.07.1971 |
| 8651 | PRINS | Stephen | D/S/O | 01.07.1971 |
| 8652 | SINCLAIR | Colin Russell | P/O | 01.07.1971 |
| 8653 | STRINGER | Philip | Insp | 01.07.1971 |
| 8654 | TOWNSEND | Leslie Richard | Insp | 01.07.1971 |
| 8655 | SHOUT | Peter William | Insp | 02.07.1971 |
| 8656 | REED | Anthony Marshall | Insp(T) | 02.07.1971 |
| 8657 | MUNFORD | David Colin | P/O | 04.07.1971 |
| 8658 | WILLIS | Barry Garnet | P/O | 08.07.1971 |
| 8659 | BORWICK | Michael James | P/O | 09.07.1971 |
| 8660 | JEFFERY | Henry John | D/S/O | 09.07.1971 |
| 8661 | HENDERSON | Peter Smith | D/Insp | 18.07.1971 |
| 8662 | SWART | John Wynand | S/O | 09.07.1971 |
| 8663 | AULD | Kevin Rodney | D/S/O | 24.08.1971 |
| 8664 | LOUW | Christiaan Michael | D/S/O | 24.08.1971 |
| 8665 | MASON | Kenneth Cyril | S/O | 24.08.1971 |
| 8666 | MAWDSLEY | John Hutton | D/S/O | 24.08.1971 |
| 8667 | PAXTON | Timothy James | S/O | 24.08.1971 |
| 8668 | PLUMB | Adam Crispin | P/O | 26.08.1971 |
| 8669 | GANNER | Rodger Winscott | S/Insp | 28.08.1971 |
| 8670 | COMMERFORD | Bernard | P/O | 29.08.1971 |
| 8671 | BURNS | John Patrick | D/P/O | 03.09.1971 |
| 8672 | VAN STADEN | Kenneth John | Insp | 06.09.1971 |
| 8673 | FREEMAN | Robert | S/Insp | 11.09.1971 |
| 8674 | DAVIS | Charles William | P/O | 12.09.1971 |
| 8675 | DE LANGE | John Henry | Insp | 28.09.1971 |
| 8676 | BARNES | Frederick Harold | Insp | 28.09.1971 |
| 8677 | CLOETE | Pieter Jacobus | S/O | 28.09.1971 |
| 8678 | ESCOTT | John Raymond | Insp(T) | 28.09.1971 |
| 8679 | GODDARD | Brian Michael | Insp | 28.09.1971 |
| 8680 | HOWARD | David | S/O | 28.09.1971 |
| 8681 | HITCH | Robert Henry | P/O | 28.09.1971 |
| 8682 | LAMPARD | Anthony David | P/O | 28.09.1971 |
| 8683 | MASTERS | Keith | S/O | 28.09.1971 |
| 8684 | MURLIS | Andrew | P/O | 28.09.1971 |
| 8685 | PRATTEN | Rex | S/O | 28.09.1971 |
| 8686 | ROBERTS | Peter Glen | P/O | 28.09.1971 |
| 8687 | WAINWRIGHT | Maurice Douglas | P/O | 28.09.1971 |
| 8688 | GARRS | Desmond John | P/O | 28.09.1971 |
| 8689 | TERBLANCHE | Johannes Gideon | D/P/O | 05.10.1971 |
| 8690 | CAMPION | Ian Thomas | P/O | 13.10.1971 |
| 8691 | McLENNAN | George Rodney | S/O | 13.10.1971 |
| 8692 | TREVOR | Gary Rutherford | L/S/O | 13.10.1971 |

| No. | Surname | First names | Rank | Date |
|---|---|---|---|---|
| 8693 | LEMON | David Michael | Insp | 13.10.1971 |
| 8694 | HIGHAM | Ernest Edward | D/S/O | 14.10.1971 |
| 8695 | SOPER | Lancelot Charles | Insp | 21.10.1971 |
| 8696 | MASFEN | Peter Francis | S/O | 27.10.1971 |
| 8697 | REELER | Gary Steven | S/O | 02.11.1971 |
| 8698 | VENTER | Shaun | P/O | 03.11.1971 |
| 8699 | DANIELS | Godfrey Brian | P/O | 03.11.1971 |
| 8700 | BRADLEY | Gavin Neville | P/O | 18.11.1971 |
| 8701 | KNOESEN | Peter Hugh | P/O | 19.11.1971 |
| 8702 | SMITH | Andrew John | Insp | 03.12.1971 |
| 8703 | SMITH | Hamish Richard | S/O | 28.12.1971 |
| 8704 | BARNES | Bruce | D/Insp | 29.12.1971 |
| 8705 | BEUKMAN | William Edward | P/O | 29.12.1971 |
| 8706 | BRUCE | Dawid Hermanus | P/O | 29.12.1971 |
| 8707 | DU PREEZ | Humigh Sidney | P/O | 29.12.1971 |
| 8708 | FALKENBERG | Michael Gordon | L/Insp | 29.12.1971 |
| 8709 | FRANKLIN | William Walter | P/O | 29.12.1971 |
| 8710 | GODWIN | Sinjen Cavanaugh | P/O | 29.12.1971 |
| 8711 | GLOSS | Alastair John | P/O | 29.12.1971 |
| 8712 | HULL | Michael Ronald | S/O | 29.12.1971 |
| 8713 | MEEK | John Cecil | Insp | 29.12.1971 |
| 8714 | MUNRO | Leonard Graham | L/Cil | 29.12.1971 |
| 8715 | TAYLOR | William Peter | P/O | 29.12.1971 |
| 8716 | VILJOEN | Ian Winfred | P/O | 29.12.1971 |
| 8717 | WHEELER | Antony John | L/Insp | 29.12.1971 |
| 8718 | WILSON | Anthony Seymour | P/O | 29.12.1971 |
| 8719 | WHATELY-SMITH | Vicus Leslie | Insp | 03.01.1972 |
| 8720 | BOTHA | Howard Audric | P/O | 03.01.1972 |
| 8721 | BROOKS | Robert William | P/O | 03.01.1972 |
| 8722 | WEARE | Geoffrey Samuel | P/O | 10.01.1972 |
| 8723 | CLARKE | Gabriel Johannes | D/S/O | 21.01.1972 |
| 8724 | OTTO | John Peter | P/O | 24.01.1972 |
| 8725 | SUTTON | Ferdinand Wilhelm | D/S/I | 24.01.1972 |
| 8726 | SCHMIDT | Bryan Anthony | Insp | 25.01.1972 |
| 8727 | PARSONS | John Clyde | P/O | 25.01.1972 |
| 8728 | KISLER | Victor John | P/O | 25.01.1972 |
| 8729 | ARTHUR | Andrew Michael | S/O | 25.01.1972 |
| 8730 | CORMACK | Alan Peter Kerr | P/O | 25.01.1972 |
| 8731 | BOWIE | Redvers Graeme | P/O | 25.01.1972 |
| 8732 | SMITH | Timothy James | P/O | 25.01.1972 |
| 8733 | SIDEY | Jeffrey Paul | S/O | 25.01.1972 |
| 8734 | SMITH | Peter Douglas | P/O | 25.01.1972 |
| 8735 | CLAASSEN | Keith Carel | S/O | 25.01.1972 |
| 8736 | WHITSON | Patrick Derek | D/S/O | 25.01.1972 |
| 8737 | LOGUE | Rob Stuart | P/O | 25.01.1972 |
| 8738 | DOUTHWAITE | Kenneth Wood | P/O | 25.01.1972 |
| 8739 | STANDERS | Peter Anthony | D/S/O | 25.01.1972 |
| 8740 | TRIGGS | Thomas Peter | P/O | 25.01.1972 |
| 8741 | FERREIRA | Robert Lash | P/O | 25.01.1972 |
| 8742 | MATTHEWS | Ronald Nicoll | P/O | 25.01.1972 |
| 8743 | GUILD | Terence | P/O | 25.01.1972 |
| 8744 | COOPER | Richard George | P/O | 25.01.1972 |
| 8745 | PIKE | Richard Anderson | S/C/I | 25.01.1972 |
| 8746 | SUMMERS | Frederick Peter | Insp | 25.01.1972 |
| 8747 | VAN ZYL | Anthony charles | P/O | 25.01.1972 |
| 8748 | STEWART-SMYTHE | Ewen David | P/O | 25.01.1972 |
| 8749 | ISDALE | Franklin Douglas | S/O | 25.01.1972 |
| 8750 | REAY | John Edmund | D/S/O | 28.01.1972 |
| 8751 | BIRD | Michael John | Insp | 30.01.1972 |
| 8752 | MATIATOS | Paul Johannes | P/O | 06.02.1972 |
| 8753 | O'NEILL | Brian | P/O | 07.02.1972 |
| 8754 | DANIELS | Alan Percival | P/O | 09.02.1972 |
| 8755 | HADFIELD | Kenneth James | Insp(T) | 14.02.1972 |
| 8756 | REID | John Patrick | P/O | 20.02.1972 |
| 8757 | ROBERTS | James Grey | S/O | 28.02.1972 |
| 8758 | STOPFORTH | Quentin Thomas | S/O | 29.02.1972 |
| 8759 | ANSLEY | Andrew Johnathan | D/S/O | 29.02.1972 |
| 8760 | BUTTERWORTH | Martin | P/O | 29.02.1972 |
| 8761 | CAMERON-DOW | | | |
| 8762 | COLLEY | Martin Paul | P/O | 29.02.1972 |
| 8763 | CROW | Michael | P/O | 29.02.1972 |
| 8764 | HART | Terence Michael | P/O | 29.02.1972 |
| 8765 | KEMP | Robert Scotney | S/O | 29.02.1972 |
| 8766 | KENT | Douglas Gordon | Insp | 29.02.1972 |
| 8767 | McMEEKING | Douglas Lewis | P/O | 29.02.1972 |
| 8768 | MARCHANT | Stuart Alexander | S/P/O | 29.02.1972 |
| 8769 | MORLEY-SMITH | Allan Norman | P/O | 29.02.1972 |
| 8770 | MOSS | Noel Morton | S/O | 29.02.1972 |
| 8771 | PRICE | Terence Michael | S/O | 29.02.1972 |
| 8772 | SNELL | Michael Anthony | D/S/O | 29.02.1972 |
| 8773 | TREASURE | Charles Thomas | P/O | 29.02.1972 |
| 8774 | WALDEK | Allan Derrick | S/O | 29.02.1972 |
| 8775 | FOSTER | Armand Richard | D/S/O | 09.03.1972 |
| 8776 | ROSS | Declan John | S/O | 11.03.1972 |
| 8777 | GRAY | Ivor Allan | P/O | 11.03.1972 |
| 8778 | DEWHURST | Anthony Paul | P/O | 17.03.1972 |
| 8779 | DEVINE | Graeme David | P/O | 19.03.1972 |
| 8780 | VILJOEN | Craig John | P/O | 23.03.1972 |
| 8781 | TATE | John Glynne | P/O | 25.03.1972 |
| 8782 | BEETON | George James | P/O | 28.03.1972 |
| 8783 | BRADFIELD | Lance | Insp | 28.03.1972 |
| 8784 | CRAWLEY | Anton Stephen | D/P/O | 28.03.1972 |
| 8785 | CROSS | Malcolm | P/O | 28.03.1972 |
| 8786 | DENNISON | Noel Francis | P/O | 28.03.1972 |
| 8787 | HOLT | James Adrian | Insp | 28.03.1972 |
| 8788 | JONES | John Edward | P/O | 28.03.1972 |
| 8789 | McCOURT | Francis James | P/O | 28.03.1972 |
| 8790 | MARTIN | John Oliver | Insp | 28.03.1972 |
| 8791 | O'DWYER | David Matthews | D/P/O | 28.03.1972 |
| 8792 | PAGE | Ian Douglas | P/O | 28.03.1972 |
| 8793 | SEMPILL | Alastair Douglas | P/O | 28.03.1972 |
| 8794 | HARRISON | Philip Vernon | D/Insp | 04.04.1972 |
| 8795 | SKEA | Donald Robertson | Insp | 14.04.1972 |
| 8796 | COUTTS | Ian Cameron | Insp | 15.04.1972 |
| 8797 | GAY | Ronald Howard | P/O | 18.04.1972 |
| 8798 | WOOD | Anthony Charles | P/O | 20.04.1972 |
| 8799 | JUSTICE | Gordon Robert | S/O | 01.05.1972 |
| 8800 | TAYLOR | James | Insp(T) | 04.05.1972 |
| 8801 | HOWARD | Keith Allan | D/Insp | 15.05.1972 |
| 8802 | CAMPBELL | Gordon Charles | Insp | 16.05.1972 |
| 8803 | COTTON | Christopher Reginald | S/O | 16.05.1972 |
| 8804 | EVANS | Brian Henry | D/P/O | 16.05.1972 |
| 8805 | GOODRIDGE | Peter Robert | S/O | 16.05.1972 |
| 8806 | HARLOCK | Nigel Anthony | S/O | 16.05.1972 |
| 8807 | LOWE | Ian Drury | D/S/O | 16.05.1972 |
| 8808 | MARSHALL | Edwin George | P/O | 16.05.1972 |
| 8809 | MURRAY | Alan James | S/O | 16.05.1972 |
| 8810 | PENBERTHY | Vivian Mark | P/O | 16.05.1972 |
| 8811 | PICTON | Tracy Rhett | S/Insp | 16.05.1972 |
| 8812 | ROBINSON | Richmond Fothergill | P/O | 16.05.1972 |
| 8813 | ROTHON | Paul | D/Insp | 16.05.1972 |
| 8814 | SMITH | Robert | P/O | 16.05.1972 |
| 8815 | WILLIAMSON | Malcolm John | S/O | 16.05.1972 |
| 8816 | YOKO | Michael Anthony | P/O | 18.05.1972 |
| 8817 | BATHER | Steven John | P/O | 25.05.1972 |
| 8818 | DEANE | Robert Charles | P/O | 27.05.1972 |
| 8819 | NEWING | Austin Kenneth | L/S/O | 29.05.1972 |
| 8820 | WILSON | Vivian Philip | P/O | 02.06.1972 |
| 8821 | ALLEN | Patrick Brian | S/O | 03.06.1972 |
| 8822 | BUSS | Anthony Lynden | Insp | 10.06.1972 |
| 8823 | BISHOP | Michael John | P/O | 12.06.1972 |
| 8824 | COOPER | Michael John | P/O | 16.06.1972 |
| 8825 | SWAIN | Jeffery Hugh | D/Insp | 16.06.1972 |
| 8826 | BAINBRIDGE | Peter | P/O | 16.06.1972 |
| 8827 | BINEDELL | Gregory Edward | D/Insp | 27.06.1972 |
| 8828 | BURGESS | Kevin Garnet | Insp | 27.06.1972 |
| 8829 | CARY | Francis William | P/O | 27.06.1972 |
| 8830 | CLACK | Gerald Richard | S/O | 27.06.1972 |
| 8831 | COCKCROFT | Kenneth Douglas | P/O | 27.06.1972 |
| 8832 | FAWKES | David William | P/O | 27.06.1972 |
| 8833 | HAYLOCK-SMITH | Owen John | P/O | 27.06.1972 |
| 8834 | QUICK | Russell George | D/P/O | 27.06.1972 |
| 8835 | WALKER | Anthony Robert | P/O | 27.06.1972 |
| 8836 | BECKLEY | Peter Morton | P/O | 29.06.1972 |
| 8837 | GRAHAM-JOHNSTONE | Peter David | P/O | 29.06.1972 |
| 8838 | WOODS | Michael Joe | P/O | 30.06.1972 |
| 8839 | ROBINSON | Rodney William | P/O | 04.07.1972 |
| 8840 | LISTER | Graham Lyle | P/O | 19.07.1972 |
| 8841 | KERNICK | Michael | S/O | 25.07.1972 |
| 8842 | STEWART | James Isles | S/O | 29.07.1972 |
| 8843 | BRANFIELD | Gordon Gray | P/O | 04.08.1972 |
| 8844 | KENNERLEY | David | P/O | 07.08.1972 |
| 8845 | PITMAN | Steven Michael | P/O | 08.08.1972 |
| 8846 | POWER | John Richard | P/O | 08.08.1972 |
| 8847 | SHALOVSKY | Anthony David | P/O | 08.08.1972 |
| 8848 | SMITH | George Anthony | P/O | 08.08.1972 |
| 8849 | PENTON | Selwyn Dennis | P/O | 11.08.1972 |
| 8850 | SURKONT | Jozef | Insp | 11.08.1972 |
| 8851 | WIENAND | Ronald Peter | P/O | 11.08.1972 |
| 8852 | PORTER | Anthony William | P/O | 14.08.1975 |
| 8853 | ROE | David | P/O | 28.08.1972 |
| 8854 | KEENAN | Peter Michael | D/Insp | 31.08.1972 |
| 8855 | LAMBOURN | David Edward | S/O | 01.09.1972 |
| 8856 | LLOYD | Stephen Geoffrey | P/O | 19.09.1972 |
| 8857 | DACRE | Gordon Stewart | Insp(T) | 21.09.1972 |
| 8858 | O'SHAUGHNESSY | Phillip William | S/O | 22.09.1972 |
| 8859 | FULTON | Douglas Gordon | P/O | 24.09.1972 |
| 8860 | BEHENNA | Alastair Duncan | P/O | 26.09.1972 |
| 8861 | KRIEL | Albert Pieter | P/O | 26.09.1972 |
| 8862 | PEREPECZKO | Edward Vitold | P/O | 26.09.1972 |
| 8863 | WARD | Kenneth George | S/O(T) | 26.09.1972 |
| 8864 | ASTON | Roy | S/O | 04.10.1972 |
| 8865 | HUTCHISON | James William | S/O | 06.10.1972 |
| 8866 | PATTERSON | Stephen Bruce | P/O | 10.10.1972 |
| 8867 | PRINGLE | Kevin Peter | S/O | 17.10.1972 |
| 8868 | DANIEL | Ian Charles | Insp | 26.10.1972 |
| 8869 | SCALES | Keith Rodney | P/O | 29.10.1972 |
| 8870 | CLAYTON | Michael George | S/O | 31.10.1972 |
| 8871 | DANFORTH | Mark Darrell | D/P/O | 31.10.1972 |
| 8872 | ELTZE | Alan Clive | P/O | 31.10.1972 |
| 8873 | KUSPERT | Alan John | P/O | 31.10.1972 |
| 8874 | Mac PHERSON | Alexander John | S/O | 31.10.1972 |
| 8875 | McCLINTOCK | Donald Malcolm | S/O | 31.10.1972 |
| 8876 | PATON | George John | D/Insp | 31.10.1972 |
| 8877 | ROBBESON | Johannes Jacobus | D/P/O | 31.10.1972 |
| 8878 | WEBSTER | Thomas John | D/S/O | 31.10.1972 |
| 8879 | DAWSON | Anthony Ewart | Insp | 31.10.1972 |
| 8880 | HAYES | Brian Malcolm | D/Insp | 15.11.1972 |
| 8881 | KRYNAUW | Anthony Joseph | P/O | 18.11.1972 |
| 8882 | EASEY | Jeremy Michael | Insp(T) | 20.11.1972 |
| 8883 | ADAMS | Patrick Kenneth | P/O | 23.11.1972 |
| 8884 | COWHAM | Desmond Gerald | P/O | 27.11.1972 |
| 8885 | BAIGRIE | Alexander Walker | S/S/O | 01.12.1972 |
| 8886 | WRIGHT | Harold Aspinall | Insp | 13.12.1972 |
| 8887 | MORRISON | Gordon Lachlan | D/P/O | 31.12.1972 |
| 8888 | Mac CLACKWORTHY | Douglas Grant | D/P/O | 01.01.1973 |
| 8889 | CROWTHER | Garry Alexander | P/O | 01.01.1973 |
| 8890 | CUTFIELD | Steven John | S/O | 03.01.1973 |
| 8891 | DE KOCK | Hugh David | P/O | 03.01.1973 |
| 8892 | DRYSDALE | Ernest Errol | P/O | 03.01.1973 |
| 8893 | DURANDT | Rodney John | P/O | 03.01.1973 |
| 8894 | ETERMAN | Neil Gary | D/Insp | 03.01.1973 |
| 8895 | FROMBURG | Rodney Bruce | P/O | 03.01.1973 |
| 8896 | VAN WOERDEN | Neville Ian | D/Insp | 03.01.1973 |
| 8897 | WILCOX | Lionel Carl | Insp | 03.01.1973 |
| 8898 | | Anthony Scott | Insp | 03.01.1973 |
| 8899 | JORDAN | Jonathan Charles | D.Insp | 03.01.1973 |

| No. | Surname | Name | Date | Rank |
|---|---|---|---|---|
| 8900 | KUMIN | Errol Charles | 03.01.1973 | P/O |
| 8901 | LANT | Neil Gary | 03.01.1973 | S/O |
| 8902 | LE ROUX | Robin Martin | 03.01.1973 | P/O |
| 8903 | McCALL | Stephen Clinton | 03.01.1973 | P/O |
| 8904 | MORRISON | Grant | 03.01.1973 | P/O |
| 8905 | PARKIN | George Robert | 03.01.1973 | Insp |
| 8906 | PAULL | Anthony Bruce | 03.01.1973 | S/O |
| 8907 | PAYNTER | Kevin James | 03.01.1973 | Insp |
| 8908 | SLABBERT | Louis Arthur | 03.01.1973 | S/O(T) |
| 8909 | GROBLER | Andre Paul | 11.01.1973 | P/O |
| 8910 | HORNE | Peter Edward | 22.01.1973 | P/O |
| 8911 | CLEMENTS | Geoffrey Redmond | 30.01.1973 | P/O |
| 8912 | JOHNSON | Peter Victor | 30.01.1973 | P/O |
| 8913 | ARCHDALE | Edward Montgomery | 30.01.1973 | P/O |
| 8914 | BLAVER | George Talbot | 30.01.1973 | P/O |
| 8915 | BURNETT | Robin Keith | 30.01.1973 | P/O |
| 8916 | BUCHANAN | Donald James | 30.01.1973 | D/S/O |
| 8917 | CANNON | Christopher John | 30.01.1973 | D/S/O |
| 8918 | CHADWICK | Lawrence Michael | 30.01.1973 | D/S/O |
| 8919 | CAMPBELL | John Bruce | 30.01.1973 | P/O |
| 8920 | IVES | Michael John | 30.01.1973 | P/O |
| 8921 | HENDRIKS | Petrus Lodewicus | 30.01.1973 | S/S/O |
| 8922 | JACKSON | Ernest John | 30.01.1973 | P/O |
| 8923 | LARKAN | Gary Wilfred | 30.01.1973 | S/S/O |
| 8924 | KINGDON | Robin Gerard | 30.01.1973 | P.O |
| 8925 | MORRISH | Richard Anthony | 30.01.1973 | S/O |
| 8926 | LUYT | Richard Louis | 30.01.1973 | P/O |
| 8927 | McCARTHY | William John | 30.01.1973 | P/O |
| 8928 | RIX | Graham David | 30.01.1973 | P/O |
| 8929 | MAWBY | Anthony Christopher | 30.01.1973 | P/O |
| 8930 | LAWRENCE | Brian | 30.01.1973 | D/Insp |
| 8931 | PEPPERELL | David Clive | 30.01.1973 | P/O |
| 8932 | SMITH | Roger Leonard | 30.01.1973 | S/O |
| 8933 | SMITH | Andrew Mark | 30.01.1973 | S/O |
| 8934 | TRIGGS | Derek Nigel | 30.01.1973 | P/O |
| 8935 | GREENWOOD | Kenneth Garth | 30.01.1973 | P/O |
| 8936 | ROSS | John Leon | 30.01.1973 | Insp |
| 8937 | WOOD | Alan Frederick | 30.01.1973 | D/P/O |
| 8938 | ROGERS | David Kenneth | 01.02.1973 | Insp |
| 8939 | WALLACE | Malcolm Roy | 12.02.1973 | P/O |
| 8940 | ASHBURNER | Geoffrey Malcolm | 12.02.1973 | Insp |
| 8941 | THOMPSON | Rowland Dunmer | 27.02.1974 | S/O(T) |
| 8942 | DEARDEN | Albert John | 27.02.1973 | P/O |
| 8943 | KNIPE | Arthur John | 27.02.1973 | P/O |
| 8944 | FERROS | Arminda Antonio | 01.03.1973 | Supt |
| 8945 | WEIDMAAN | Paul Robert | 05.03.1973 | P/O |
| 8946 | SHELLEY | Thomas Rodney | 07.03.1973 | D/S/O |
| 8947 | POSTANCE | Derek | 08.03.1973 | S/S/O |
| 8948 | GIBSON | Peter David | 09.03.1973 | Insp |
| 8949 | JONES | Richard Anthony | 12.03.1973 | S/O |
| 8950 | BURGER | Colin Charles | 12.03.1973 | S/O |
| 8951 | GRIZZARD | Peter Howard | 12.03.1973 | S/O |
| 8952 | HOWIE | Lachlan Dean | 12.03.1973 | P/O |
| 8953 | HARRIES | Ian Leslie | 19.03.1973 | D/Insp |
| 8954 | MORGAN | Alastair Bruce | 23.03.1973 | P/O |
| 8955 | KING | Gavin Percy | 26.03.1973 | P/O |
| 8956 | RAE | Keith Robert | 27.03.1973 | S/O |
| 8957 | BARTON | Philip Charles | 27.03.1973 | D/S/O |
| 8958 | BELDER | Robert Geoffrey | 27.03.1973 | D/Insp |
| 8959 | COLEMAN | John Patrick | 27.03.1973 | P/O |
| 8960 | FAWCETT | Nigel St John | 27.03.1973 | D/S/O |
| 8961 | FINDLAY | Graeme Alexander | 27.03.1973 | S/O |
| 8962 | HAND | William John | 27.03.1973 | P/O |
| 8963 | HUNTER | Adrian Charles | 27.03.1973 | P/O |
| 8964 | KING | Michael Richard | 27.03.1973 | D/Insp |
| 8965 | KING | John Firbank | 27.03.1973 | P/O |
| 8966 | LOWE | Derek Richard | 27.03.1973 | P/O |
| 8967 | NEWMAN | Clive Anthony | 27.03.1973 | S/O |
| 8969 | SUDBURY | Kevin Russell | 27.03.1973 | P/O |
| 8970 | SHEWAN | Kelvin Michael | 27.03.1973 | P/O |
| 8971 | SMITH | Charles Michael | 27.03.1973 | P/O |
| 8973 | STEWART-CLEARY | Stephen Richard | 27.03.1973 | S/L/O |
| 8974 | SMITH | Alexander | 02.04.1973 | Insp |
| 8975 | JOLLIFFE | Gerald Clifford | 02.04.1973 | P/O |
| 8976 | LEECH | Michael David | 04.04.1973 | S/Insp |
| 8977 | VAN HEERDEN | Jacobus Frederick | 15.04.1973 | S/O(T) |
| 8978 | KILGOUR | Ian Peter | 15.04.1973 | P/O |
| 8979 | PAGEWOOD | Graham Hugh | 16.04.1973 | P/O |
| 8980 | KNOETZE | Ernest Hastings | 17.04.1973 | Insp |
| 8981 | PAUL | Duncan Jones | 25.04.1973 | P/O |
| 8982 | COOKE | Gordon Peter | 25.04.1973 | P/O |
| 8983 | BAILEY | John Frederick | 30.04.1973 | D/Insp |
| 8984 | FERGUSON | Robert Gordon | 01.05.1973 | P/O |
| 8985 | SMITH | Paul Stephanus | 01.05.1973 | S/S/O |
| 8986 | GAINSFORD | Gary Robert | 03.05.1973 | S/O |
| 8987 | Mac INTYRE | Ian Alexander | 07.05.1973 | S/S/O |
| 8988 | OUTRAM | Anthony Paul | 16.05.1973 | P/O |
| 8989 | ARMSTRONG | Michael Sean | 16.05.1973 | P/O |
| 8990 | HYSLOP | James Ninian | 18.05.1973 | P/O |
| 8991 | BATCHELOR | Ian Athol | 19.05.1973 | D/S/O |
| 8992 | MERRIFIELD | Ian Thomas | 23.05.1973 | P/O |
| 8993 | WOOD | Nicholas Frank | 25.05.1973 | P/O |
| 8994 | VAN SCHALKWIJK | Daniel Petrus | 28.05.1973 | S/O |
| 8995 | HOME | Sidney Dennis | 29.05.1973 | S/O |
| 8996 | BURCHELL | Michael William | 29.05.1973 | D/S/O |
| 8997 | DAWSON | John Graham | 29.05.1973 | S/O |
| 8998 | FIDDLER | Alan John | 29.05.1973 | P/O |
| 8999 | HALLER | Douglas William | 31.05.1973 | P/O |
| 9000 | SMITH | Robert William | 01.06.1973 | Insp |
| 9001 | HOPKINS | Barry Michael | 06.06.1973 | D/Insp |
| 9002 | ALLEN | Kevin James | 07.06.1973 | P/O |
| 9003 | McMAHON | Ronald Jesse | 16.06.1973 | S/O |
| 9004 | CULLUM | Duncan Iain | 16.06.1973 | P/O |
| 9005 | SCOULER | Trevor Charles | 23.06.1973 | D/S/O |
| 9006 | HADFIELD | Jan Leonard | 25.06.1973 | Insp |
| 9007 | GEERTSMA | Earl Stanley | 25.06.1973 | D/P/O |
| 9008 | EBY | Linden Drummond | 02.07.1973 | S/O |
| 9009 | KERWIN | Anthony Lawrence | 02.07.1973 | S/O(T) |
| 9010 | WHITTAL | Thomas Bruce | 03.07.1973 | S/O(T) |
| 9011 | MATTHEWS | Willem Hendriks | 07.07.1973 | Insp |
| 9012 | BOTHA | Gary Trevor | 11.07.1973 | Insp |
| 9013 | LAW | Trevor Duncan | 14.07.1973 | S/C/I |
| 9014 | CURRIE | Anthony John | 14.07.1973 | P/O |
| 9015 | CLARK | David Robert | 23.07.1973 | L/S/O |
| 9016 | BURFORD | Patrick Arthur | 23.07.1973 | S/O |
| 9017 | COX | Charles Anthony | 24.07.1973 | S/O(T) |
| 9018 | JENKINSON | Clive Mark | 24.07.1973 | P/O |
| 9019 | JORDAN | Alaistair | 24.07.1973 | P/O |
| 9020 | KENNEDY | Neil David | 24.07.1973 | P/O |
| 9021 | LLOYD | Ian | 25.07.1973 | P/O |
| 9022 | CLARK | Timothy Charles | 25.07.1973 | S/O |
| 9023 | PETZOLD | Patrick John | 25.07.1973 | P/O |
| 9024 | LEE | Robert James | 25.07.1973 | P/O |
| 9025 | GASH | John Richard | 26.07.1973 | D/S/O |
| 9027 | SMITH | Harold Miche | 30.07.1973 | Insp(T) |
| 9028 | TORRY | Iain Strevenson | 31.07.1973 | S/O |
| 9029 | COVENTRY | Angus Roy | 01.08.1973 | Insp(T) |
| 9030 | Mac INTRY | Keith | 01.08.1973 | Insp(T) |
| 9031 | WALKER-WELLS | Peter David | 01.08.1973 | S/S/O |
| 9032 | WADE | Laing | 10.08.1973 | Supt |
| 9033 | WILLARD | Richardson | 13.08.1973 | P/O |
| 9034 | GURNEY | Murray | 23.08.1973 | S/O |
| 9035 | MELVILLE | Ian Douglas | 27.08.1973 | P/O |
| 9035 | LOWSON | James Kevin | 28.08.1973 | P/O |
| 9036 | STORE |  | 28.08.1973 |  |
| 9036 | CORNISH |  |  |  |
| 9038 | BROWNBILL | Frederick James | 30.08.1973 | P/O |
| 9039 | YEO | Roy Beverley | 01.09.1973 | S/O(T) |
| 9040 | ADDISON | Geoffrey Alexander | 01.09.1973 | P/O |
| 9041 | LOUW | Michael Alfred | 03.09.1973 | Supt |
| 9042 | MINCHIN | Robert Michael | 03.09.1973 | P/O |
| 9043 | DIPPENAAR | Michael Christoffel | 14.09.1973 | Insp(T) |
| 9044 | DAVIES | Howard Aubrey | 25.09.1973 | P/O |
| 9045 | MILLS | Alan John | 25.09.1973 | D/S/O |
| 9046 | NORTON | Michael Terrence | 25.09.1973 | P/O |
| 9047 | ROCKLIFFE | David | 25.09.1973 | P/O |
| 9048 | STEEN | Trevor Thomas | 25.09.1973 | P/O |
| 9049 | BRADLEY | Leigh James | 26.09.1973 | P/O |
| 9050 | ILES | Derek Martyn | 01.10.1973 | Supt |
| 9051 | HALLETT | Brian Edwin | 01.10.1973 | Insp(T) |
| 9052 | WRIGHT | Peter George | 01.10.1973 | P/O |
| 9053 | HAMILTON | Rodney Alvin | 01.10.1973 | Insp(T) |
| 9054 | ANDERSON | Robert Hunter | 03.10.1973 | Insp(T) |
| 9055 | JONES | John Melvyn | 03.10.1973 | P/O |
| 9056 | THORNE | Arnold Huxtable | 04.10.1973 | D/Insp |
| 9056 | WILLIS | David Arthur | 15.10.1973 | D/S/O |
| 9057 | SPIERS | Allen John | 18.10.1973 | D/Insp |
| 9058 | WATSON | Roderick Donaghue | 30.10.1973 | D/Insp |
| 9059 | AXON | William Anthony | 30.10.1973 | Insp |
| 9060 | COOPER | Derek | 01.11.1973 | Insp(T) |
| 9061 | BRANFIELD | Allan | 01.11.1973 | Insp |
| 9062 | WATSON | Allen Michael | 01.11.1973 | Insp |
| 9063 | MILWAY | Michael David | 05.11.1973 | P/O |
| 9064 | SHOUT | Allan Leonard | 05.11.1973 | Insp |
| 9065 | PITT | Brian Denton | 15.11.1973 | Insp |
| 9066 | FISHER | Michael Andrew | 19.11.1973 | S/O |
| 9067 | BUGGS | Alec | 26.11.1973 | P/O |
| 9068 | WHITE | John | 26.11.1973 | Insp |
| 9069 | CAWOOD | Peter Lascelles | 27.11.1973 | P/O |
| 9070 | RUSSELL | Murray | 29.11.1973 | D/S/O |
| 9071 | LOWE | Keith William | 30.11.1973 | S/O |
| 9072 | PIGOTT | Richard Ronald | 01.12.1973 | S/O |
| 9073 | FREEKE | Daniel Johannes | 01.12.1973 | Supt |
| 9074 | WILSON-HARRIS | Neville Patrick | 03.12.1973 | P/O |
| 9075 | BRAND | James Graham | 03.12.1973 | Insp(T) |
| 9076 | BROWN | David Ernest | 18.12.1973 | D/Insp |
| 9077 | ROBINSON | Robert Kerr | 18.12.1973 | P/O |
| 9078 | STRUGNELL | Robin Anthony | 18.12.1973 | D/P/O |
| 9079 | TOWNLEY | Barry George | 18.12.1973 | P/O |
| 9080 | WEVELL | Ernest | 18.12.1973 | P/O |
| 9081 | ALLEN | Peter David | 18.12.1973 | P/O |
| 9082 | ALLEN | Kiaran Joseph | 18.12.1973 | P/O |
| 9083 | CHASE | Duncan Bruce | 18.12.1973 | S/O |
| 9084 | EDWARDS | Harry Milton | 18.12.1973 | S/O |
| 9085 | GRANGER | Anthony Alan | 18.12.1973 | D/iP/O |
| 9086 | HAGAN | Stephen John | 18.12.1973 | D/S/O |
| 9087 | MEAD | David Leon | 18.12.1973 | P/O |
| 9088 | MILLAR | Frank Thomas | 18.12.1973 | P/O |
| 9089 | CLANCY | Patrick | 18.12.1973 | P/O |
| 9090 | LOUBSER | Andre | 18.12.1973 | P/O |
| 9091 | LOVETT | Simon Fraso | 18.12.1973 | P/O |
| 9092 | POTGIETER | David Christiaan | 18.12.1973 | D/S/O |
| 9093 | WILTON | Michael George | 18.12.1973 | P/O |
| 9094 | GARNETT | Paul | 18.12.1973 | D/S/O |
| 9095 | GARLICK | Ian Montgomery | 23.12.1973 | P/O |
| 9096 | POWER | Maurice James | 27.12.1973 | Supt |
| 9097 | FOSTER | Christopher John | 27.12.1973 | D/S/O |
| 9098 | GIBBS | Brian John Cyril | 28.12.1973 | S/O |
| 9099 | BERRY | Peter Stephen | 31.12.1973 | C/Insp |
| 9100 | QUILLIAM | David John | 31.12.1973 | P/O |
| 9101 | McLAREN | Ian William | 31.12.1973 | Insp |
| 9102 | VAN DER MERWE | Hendrick Johannes | 02.01.1974 | Insp(T) |
| 9103 | SCHOEMAN | Frederick | 02.01.1974 | S/O |
| 9104 | THATCHER | John Haigh | 04.01.1974 | P/O |
| 9105 | | Louis Johannes | 04.01.1974 | D/S/O |

| No. | Surname | First names | Date | Rank |
|---|---|---|---|---|
| 9107 | ODRISCOLL | Cornelius Allan | 07.01.1974 | P/O |
| 9108 | BIRD | Kenneth James | 08.01.1974 | D/S/O |
| 9109 | BENNISON | Gavin Derrick | 08.01.1974 | D/S/O |
| 9110 | BERTHOUD | Michael Anthony | 08.01.1974 | D/P/O |
| 9111 | BROWN | Peter John | 08.01.1974 | P/O |
| 9112 | CURTIS | Stephen Frederick | 08.01.1974 | Insp |
| 9113 | FREW | Martin Colin | 08.01.1974 | P/O |
| 9114 | GREENHALGH | Noel Patrick | 08.01.1974 | S/O |
| 9115 | GRIGGS | Robert James | 08.01.1974 | D/P/O |
| 9116 | JOUBERT | Francois Johannes | 08.01.1974 | P/O |
| 9117 | JOHNSON | Ian | 08.01.1974 | P/O |
| 9118 | MAYNARD | James Douglas | 08.01.1974 | P/O |
| 9119 | MILLS | Kevin John | 08.01.1974 | P/O |
| 9120 | MOORE-STEVENS | Richard Bayne | 08.01.1974 | P/O |
| 9121 | STENNER | Richard Dane | 08.01.1974 | P/O |
| 9122 | STEYN | Daniel Gabriel | 08.01.1974 | P/O |
| 9123 | TAENTZER | Hubert Jean | 08.01.1974 | Insp |
| 9124 | THOMPSON | Gavin Richard | 08.01.1974 | D/S/O |
| 9125 | VAN HEERDEN | Carl Sebastian | 08.01.1974 | S/O(T) |
| 9126 | WARING | Brian Earle | 08.01.1974 | P/O |
| 9127 | WEST | Michael Stanley | 08.01.1974 | D/P/O |
| 9128 | WILKINSON | Ian David | 08.01.1974 | P/O |
| 9129 | TRETHOWAN | Anthony John | 10.01.1974 | D/S/O |
| 9130 | INGLIS | Christopher John | 10.01.1974 | S/S/O |
| 9131 | JOUBERT | Kenneth Keith | 15.01.1974 | S/O |
| 9132 | NEL | Fergus Melvin | 17.01.1974 | S/O(T) |
| 9133 | NEWNESS | John | 20.01.1974 | S/O |
| 9134 | PAYNES | Frederick | 21.01.1974 | P/O |
| 9135 | CLARKE | Richard Hinton | 29.01.1974 | D/P/O |
| 9136 | EDWARDS | William Douglas | 29.01.1974 | D/S/O |
| 9137 | HUBBARD | Douglas Hopwood | 29.01.1974 | P/O |
| 9138 | IVES | Michael Anthony | 29.01.1974 | P/O |
| 9139 | SAUNDERS | Jonathan Richard | 29.01.1974 | P/O |
| 9140 | STALLABRASS | Richard Andrew | 29.01.1974 | P/O |
| 9141 | YOUNG | Roderick David | 29.01.1974 | P/O |
| 9142 | BARKER | Maxwell | 29.01.1974 | Insp |
| 9143 | BRENT | Jonathan Perrett | 29.01.1974 | D/S/O |
| 9144 | GRIFFIN | Michael John | 29.01.1974 | D/S/O |
| 9145 | NELSON | Peter Jonathan | 29.01.1974 | P/O |
| 9146 | NORTJE | Benjamin Daniel | 29.01.1974 | P/O |
| 9147 | RABIE | Gavin Hilton | 29.01.1974 | P/O |
| 9148 | TINKER | Kevin James | 29.01.1974 | P/O |
| 9149 | BELL | Kevin Charles | 29.01.1974 | S/O |
| 9150 | THOMPSON | Jeremy | 29.01.1974 | S/S/O |
| 9151 | BROWN | Kevin Ervine | 01.02.1974 | Insp |
| 9152 | THOMPSON | Rowland Dunmore | 01.02.1974 | Insp |
| 9153 | LLOYD | Barrington | 01.02.1974 | Insp(T) |
| 9154 | FOWLER | David John | 02.02.1974 | P/O |
| 9155 | CONRADIE | Jacobus Daniel | 05.02.1974 | D/Insp |
| 9156 | JOHNSON | Evan Ross | 15.02.1974 | P/O |
| 9157 | LEDGER | Alan Arthur | 18.02.1974 | P/O |
| 9158 | VENTER | Matheus Jacobus | 26.02.1974 | S/O |
| 9159 | GUY | Richard Jonathan | 26.02.1974 | P/O |
| 9160 | KONIG | Stephen Kenneth | 26.02.1974 | Insp |
| 9161 | MASON | Devin Lee | 26.02.1974 | Insp |
| 9162 | EDWARDS | Mervyn Arthur | 26.02.1974 | S/O |
| 9163 | BIRCH | Phillip Ronald | 26.02.1974 | P/O |
| 9164 | FURBER | Colin Patrick | 26.02.1974 | P/O |
| 9165 | LOTTER | Geoffrey Edeson | 26.02.1974 | S/O |
| 9166 | WHITEHEAD-WILSON | Gary Duncan | 26.02.1974 | Supt |
| 9167 | CAIRNS | Conrad Frederick | 02.03.1974 | Insp |
| 9168 | ODENDAAL | Stewart | 12.03.1974 | C/Insp |
| 9169 | ANSTEY | David Jonathan | 25.03.1974 | P/O |
| 9170 | FRASER | Philip Clarke | 26.03.1974 | P/O |
| 9171 | FYNN | Nicholas Rafferty | 26.03.1974 | S/O(T) |
| 9172 | NORTON | Keith Hall | 26.03.1974 | Insp |
| 9173 | BLACKBURN | David Alan | 26.03.1974 | S/O(T) |
| 9174 | MAGGS | Kenneth Albert | 01.04.1974 | D/I |
| 9175 | CUNNINGHAM | Patrick Martin | 01.04.1974 | Insp |
| 9176 | JORDAAN | Johannes Lodewikus | 09.04.1974 | P/O |
| 9177 | BARLOW | Michael John | 10.04.1974 | P/O |
| 9178 | DAWSON | Stuart Patrick | 19.04.1974 | D/S/O |
| 9179 | THATCHER | Charles William | 22.04.1974 | P/O |
| 9180 | VERNON | Peter Keith | 29.04.1974 | Insp |
| 9181 | ALBERTON | Angus Ian | 30.04.1974 | L/C/I |
| 9182 | BAKER | Bruce Mackay | 30.04.1974 | P/O |
| 9183 | MACMILLAN | Donald Creigh | 30.04.1974 | D/Insp |
| 9184 | BASSETT | Andrew George | 30.04.1974 | P/O |
| 9185 | McGIE | Stuart Newman | 30.04.1974 | P/O |
| 9186 | SMITH | Anthony Frederick | 30.04.1974 | S/O |
| 9187 | CADLE | Christopher Hugh | 30.04.1974 | P/O |
| 9188 | ERASMUS | Peter Wade | 30.04.1974 | P/O |
| 9189 | COX | Christopher Henry | 30.04.1974 | S/O |
| 9190 | NICHOLS | Arthur Stephen | 01.05.1974 | S/O |
| 9191 | BERRY | David Sydney | 01.05.1974 | S/O(T) |
| 9192 | SIEBERT | Alan Norman | 07.05.1974 | S/O(T) |
| 9193 | SCOTT | Stuart Craig | 27.05.1974 | S/O(T) |
| 9194 | BYWATER | Kevin John | 25.05.1974 | P/O |
| 9195 | ROBINSON | Paul Gregory | 28.05.1974 | L/Insp |
| 9196 | BING | Douglas Stewart | 28.05.1974 | P/O |
| 9197 | HUMPHREYS | Robert Charles | 01.06.1974 | P/O |
| 9198 | VAN DER MERWE | Cecil Harry Starr | 06.06.1974 | P/O |
| 9199 | BRIAULT | Paul Royston | 14.06.1974 | P/O |
| 9200 | PEARCE | Peter Robert | 14.06.1974 | P/O |
| 9201 | KREUTER | Kurt Rene | 25.06.1974 | S/O |
| 9202 | AYLWARD | Patrick Daniel | 25.06.1974 | P/O |
| 9203 | BECKETT | Jonathan Stewart | 25.06.1974 | P/O |
| 9204 | BOTHA | David Harold | 25.06.1974 | P/O |
| 9205 | COURT | Jonathan Gilroy | 25.06.1974 | unknown |
| 9206 | SULLIVAN | John Stuart | 27.06.1974 | D/P/O |
| 9207 | LONG | Hogarth Holroyd | 01.07.1974 | D/P/O |
| 9208 | LONG | Stirling Swanton | 01.07.1974 | S/Insp |
| 9209 | VAN ZYL | Dennis Clive | 01.07.1974 | Supt |
| 9210 | SEGAR | John Abraham | 10.07.1974 | S/O |
| 9211 | RICHARDSON | Andrew John | 14.07.1974 | S/O |
| 9212 | MALLET | Peter | 19.07.1974 | S/O |
| 9213 | EDWARDS | Leslie Charles | 30.07.1974 | D/S/O |
| 9214 | CHIPP | Ian | 30.07.1974 | D/S/O |
| 9215 | PATTERSON | Collin Robert | 30.07.1974 | P/O |
| 9216 | LANE | Benjamin Robert | 30.07.1974 | S/O |
| 9217 | ROBINSON | David John | 14.07.1974 | P/O |
| 9218 | SPENCER | Alexander William | 14.01.1974 | P/O |
| 9219 | EDWARDS | Guy Eric | 01.08.1974 | P/O |
| 9220 | DE GOEDE | Clive Douglas | 03.08.1974 | P/O |
| 9221 | FAIRLEY | David Allen | 05.08.1974 | P/O |
| 9222 | COOM | William John | 05.08.1974 | P/O |
| 9223 | VAN NIEKERK | Anthony | 06.08.1974 | L/S/O |
| 9224 | SCOTT | Jerome Martin | 14.08.1974 | P/O |
| 9225 | CARDY | John Morison | 15.08.1974 | P/O |
| 9226 | PRATT | David John | 15.08.1974 | S/O(T) |
| 9227 | ISHERWOOD | Larry Anthony | 23.08.1974 | P/O |
| 9228 | CAMPBELL | Paul Andrew | 27.08.1974 | P/O |
| 9229 | RODIE | Robert Andrew | 27.08.1974 | P/O |
| 9230 | PRING | Stuart Douglas | 27.08.1974 | P/O |
| 9231 | DAWSON | William | 27.08.1974 | L/C/I |
| 9232 | COMBE | Barry Richard | 03.09.1974 | Insp |
| 9233 | ONEILL | Ian | 14.01.1974 | Insp(T) |
| 9234 | BULLING | Edward | 09.09.1974 | S/O |
| 9235 | HUGHES | Jeremy John | 14.09.1974 | L/S/O |
| 9236 | KLOPPERS | Raymon Roderick | 19.09.1974 | S/O |
| 9237 | PENFOLD | Paul Stephanus | 24.09.1974 | Insp |
| 9238 | GAINFORD | Martin George | 24.09.1974 | Insp |
| 9239 | IDDON | Robert | 24.09.1974 | S/O |
| 9240 | EVANS | Richard Anthony | 24.09.1974 | S/O |
| 9241 | RAWSON | Colin David | 24.09.1974 | P/O |
| 9242 | AIKEN | Daniel Douglas | 24.09.1974 | P/O |
| 9243 | MULCAHY | Raymond William | 27.09.1974 | P/O |
| 9244 | | Kevin Michael | 04.10.1974 | P/O |
| 9245 | COLMAN | Ciaran Christopher | 04.10.1974 | D/S/O |
| 9246 | GROBLER | Benjamin Martin | 05.10.1974 | P/O |
| 9247 | BRITLAND | Peter | 06.10.1974 | P/O |
| 9248 | BLOOM | Clive Cromarty | 07.10.1974 | P/O |
| 9249 | TILLEY | Ian Malcolm | 09.10.1974 | S/O(T) |
| 9250 | SANTUCCI | Louis Gerald | 09.10.1974 | S/O(T) |
| 9251 | SPINDLER | Lionel Herman | 09.10.1974 | Insp(T) |
| 9252 | ERASMUS | Henry Stephen | 09.10.1974 | S/O |
| 9253 | FITCH | Derek | 17.10.1974 | S/O(T) |
| 9254 | DRAPER | Robert | 22.10.1974 | S/O(T) |
| 9255 | HARRIES | Paul Richard | 22.10.1974 | Insp |
| 9256 | CRAWFORD | Edward Philip | 28.10.1974 | Insp |
| 9257 | McDANIEL | Charles William | 29.10.1974 | P/O |
| 9258 | BAUER | Robert Neil | 14.01.1974 | S/O |
| 9259 | PELLY | Alwyne Nicholas | 29.10.1974 | S/O |
| 9260 | WARD | David George | 29.10.1974 | S/O |
| 9261 | VERNALL | Stanley Charles | 29.10.1974 | Insp |
| 9262 | STEELE | James Sherwin | 01.11.1974 | P/O |
| 9263 | SUSSEMIEHL | Henning | 04.11.1974 | Insp |
| 9264 | TRIGGOL | Paul | 04.11.1974 | P/O |
| 9265 | LOVETT | Paul Ludwig | 13.11.1974 | P/O |
| 9266 | LOWE | Patrick Charles | 14.11.1974 | P/O |
| 9267 | OPENSHAW | David Laurence | 26.11.1974 | P/O |
| 9268 | BERRY | Patrick Harry | 26.11.1974 | S/O |
| 9269 | McMULLEN | Andrew Fairley | 26.11.1974 | P/O |
| 9270 | JONES | Geraint Malcolm | 26.11.1974 | P/O |
| 9271 | HANEKOM | Frederick James | 26.11.1974 | P/O |
| 9272 | BIRD | Martin Lawrence | 26.11.1974 | P/O |
| 9273 | SWANEPOEL | Stephen Brian | 29.11.1974 | S/O |
| 9274 | WILLIAMSON | Peter Simon | 29.11.1974 | P/O |
| 9275 | BOULTON | Richard Leonard | 29.11.1974 | D/S/O |
| 9276 | DAVIES | Andrew Frank | 29.11.1974 | S/O(T) |
| 9277 | ROBERTS | Ronald Edward | 01.10.1974 | P/O |
| 9278 | WALL | Michael Hugh | 11.12.1974 | P/O |
| 9279 | THOMAS | Nigel Victor | 17.12.1974 | P/O |
| 9280 | POLOME | Patrick Marc | 17.12.1974 | P/O |
| 9281 | TEASDALE | Steven | 17.12.1974 | D/P/O |
| 9282 | VAN JAARSVELDT | Kevin Richard | 17.12.1974 | L/S/O |
| 9283 | WHITEHEAD-WILSON | Vaughan | 17.12.1974 | P/O |
| 9284 | KUTTNER | Franz Josef | 17.12.1974 | P/O |
| 9285 | LEO | Andre George | 17.12.1974 | P/O |
| 9286 | CROW | Peter | 17.12.1974 | P/O |
| 9287 | FERGUSON | William Ross | 17.12.1974 | S/O |
| 9288 | LEPPAN | Raymond John | 17.12.1974 | P/O |
| 9289 | ROBEY | John Dorrell | 17.12.1974 | P/O |
| 9290 | OOSTHUIZEN | Wessel Johannes | 17.12.1974 | P/O |
| 9291 | FROST | John Donovan | 17.12.1974 | P/O |
| 9292 | HAYES | Tony William | 17.12.1974 | L/S/O |
| 9293 | WALL | Howard | 17.12.1974 | P/O |
| 9294 | COLLINS | Michael Peter | 02.01.1975 | S/S/O |
| 9295 | HODGSON | Craig Andrew | 07.01.1975 | S/S/O |
| 9296 | HORTON | Michael George | 14.01.1975 | P/O |
| 9297 | HOWARD | Timothy William | 21.12.1974 | D/S/O |
| 9298 | HUGHES | Howard Wallis | 30.12.1974 | D/S/O |
| 9299 | ARMSTRONG | Ian | 31.12.1974 | P/O |
| 9300 | HANLON | Martin | 02.01.1975 | P/O |
| 9301 | RICHTER | Bernhardt Wilhelm | 14.01.1975 | P/O |
| 9302 | HUGHES | Alasdair Lindsay | 07.01.1975 | D/S/O |
| 9303 | BECK | Peter James | 07.01.1975 | D/S/O |
| 9304 | SAMPSON | Maxwell Harry | 07.01.1975 | Insp |
| 9305 | MANNIX | William George | 07.01.1975 | S/O |
| 9306 | DAVIS | Robert William | 07.01.1975 | S/O |
| 9307 | MAUVIS | Joseph Norbett | 14.01.1975 | S/O |
| 9308 | JAMES | David Robert | 14.01.1974 | S/O |
| 9309 | COSGROVE | James Henry | 07.01.1975 | P/O |
| 9310 | TWINE | Dennis William | 07.01.1975 | P/O |
| 9311 | BROCKBANK | Brian Derek | 07.01.1975 | D/I |
| 9312 | BROCKBANK | Peter Alan | 07.01.1975 | D/S/O |
| 9313 | WASSERMAN | Laurence | 07.01.1975 | P/O |

| No. | Surname | First name(s) | Date | Code |
|---|---|---|---|---|
| 9314 | LESTER | Jeremy Oliver | 07.01.1975 | P/O |
| 9315 | MARSH | Howard Iain | 09.01.1975 | D/S/O |
| 9316 | ARMSTRONG | Peter | 10.01.1975 | S/S/O |
| 9317 | MOORE-STEVENS | Frederick Charles | 01.10.1974 | Insp(T) |
| 9318 | WILKINS | John Stafford | 01.10.1974 | Insp(T) |
| 9319 | SHRIVE | Douglas Thomas | 01.10.1974 | Insp(T) |
| 9320 | WOOD | John | 01.10.1974 | Insp |
| 9321 | KISSACK | Peter William | 01.10.1974 | Insp(T) |
| 9322 | BRYSON | Ian Grant | 01.10.1974 | Insp(T) |
| 9323 | BADENHORST | Peter Frederick | 01.10.1974 | Insp(T) |
| 9324 | STOBER | Frank | 01.10.1974 | LI(T) |
| 9325 | MAYNARD | Hugh William | 01.10.1974 | Insp(T) |
| 9326 | SHRIVE | Allen John | 01.10.1974 | Insp |
| 9327 | BROUGHTON | William George | 01.10.1974 | Insp(T) |
| 9328 | ALDRIDGE | Alexander Albert | 01.10.1974 | S/O(T) |
| 9329 | HUNT | Royston Henry | 01.10.1974 | Insp(T) |
| 9330 | WILKS | John Thomas | 01.10.1974 | Insp(T) |
| 9331 | WOODMAN | George Ernest | 01.10.1974 | S/O |
| 9332 | GRIFFITHS | Gerald | 01.10.1974 | Insp(T) |
| 9333 | GRAINGER | Anthony Allen | 01.10.1974 | LI(T) |
| 9334 | ENWRIGHT | Peter Timothy | 01.10.1974 | Insp(T) |
| 9335 | MOORE | Michael Charles | 01.10.1974 | Insp(T) |
| 9336 | BOYD | Gordon Alexander | 01.10.1974 | Insp(T) |
| 9337 | HURST | Geoffrey George | 01.10.1974 | S/O(T) |
| 9338 | CHANTLER | Peter Charles | 01.10.1974 | Insp(T) |
| 9339 | MEYER | Jacobus Nicolaas | 15.01.1975 | Insp(T) |
| 9340 | MILLER | Robert Nelson | 27.01.1975 | Insp(T) |
| 9341 | SHAW | Colin | 27.01.1975 | LI(T) |
| 9342 | ROPER | Ronald Richard | 28.01.1975 | D/S/O |
| 9343 | TALBOT | Brian Grant | 28.01.1975 | P/O |
| 9344 | JOLLIVET | Michael Frederic | 28.01.1975 | D/Insp |
| 9345 | GEMMELL | James Stuart | 28.01.1975 | P/O |
| 9346 | WOLVAARDT | Christoffel Johannes | 28.01.1975 | S/O(T) |
| 9347 | HILL | Graham Edward | 28.01.1975 | P/O |
| 9348 | EDWARDS | William Morris | 28.01.1975 | P/O |
| 9349 | MASON | Nigel Anthony | 28.01.1975 | P/O |
| 9350 | BOSSY | Bernard Philippe | 28.01.1975 | P/O |
| 9351 | CRAUSE | William Henry | 28.01.1975 | P/O |
| 9352 | GREY | Patrick Louis | 28.01.1975 | S/O |
| 9353 | BURKE | Edward Thomas | 28.01.1975 | P/O |
| 9354 | RHODES | Simon Oliver | 01.02.1975 | D/S/O |
| 9355 | McINTOSH | Douglas James | 12.02.1975 | P/O |
| 9356 | LAMBERT | Andrew Michael | 14.02.1975 | D/S/O |
| 9357 | HAND | Charles Robert | 14.02.1975 | P/O |
| 9358 | BENNETT | Roy Leslie | 17.02.1975 | P/O |
| 9359 | SEGGAR | Myles Patrick | 17.02.1975 | P/O |
| 9360 | NOLAN | John William | 17.02.1975 | S/O(T) |
| 9361 | YOUNG | Andrew Lyle MCM | 25.02.1975 | D/Insp |
| 9362 | MORTON | Samuel James | 25.02.1975 | P/O |
| 9363 | GILLESPIE | Malcolm Frank | 25.02.1975 | P/O |
| 9364 | LANCASTER | Jeremy Sinclair | 25.02.1975 | S/O(T) |
| 9365 | PRATT | David William | 25.02.1975 | P/O |
| 9366 | MARAIS | Barend Daniel | 25.02.1975 | P/O |
| 9367 | GLOSS | William Henry | 08.04.1974 | L/Insp |
| 9368 | JOHNSTON | Peterson Martin | 25.02.1975 | P/O |
| 9369 | ASHBY | Michael Winson | 25.02.1975 | S/O(T) |
| 9370 | COATES | Frederick Edward | 25.02.1975 | P/O |
| 9371 | POSTLETHWAYTE | Hugh William | 03.03.1975 | S/O |
| 9372 | SMITH | William Albert | 03.03.1975 | P/O |
| 9373 | SHEEHAN | Gary Brian | 03.03.1975 | P/O |
| 9374 | PRATTEN | Rex | 04.03.1975 | D/S/O |
| 9375 | ARNOLD | Peter Joseph | 08.03.1975 | S/O |
| 9376 | DAVIS | Michael John | 10.03.1975 | Insp |
| 9377 | ROBERTS | John Douglas | 10.03.1975 | S/S/O |
| 9378 | FERREIRA | Daniel Hartman | 12.03.1975 | S/O(T) |
| 9379 | DALE-LACE | Terence George | 18.03.1975 | P/O |
| 9380 | MORGAN | Christopher John | 18.03.1975 | P/O |
| 9381 | CHISNALL | Keith Edward | 21.03.1975 | P/O |
| 9382 | COOKE | Anthony Michael | 08.04.1974 | D/S/O |
| 9383 | VAN NIEKERK | Neville Gardiner | 25.03.1975 | P/O |
| 9384 | SMITH | Neville Mark | 25.03.1975 | P/O |
| 9385 | SCHOEMAN | Ockert | 25.03.1975 | S/O |
| 9386 | NEL | Jacob Jacobus | 25.03.1975 | D/S/O |
| 9387 | JOHN | Richard Charles | 25.03.1975 | S/O |
| 9388 | WOTTON | Martyn Kenneth | 25.03.1975 | P/O |
| 9389 | WEBSTER | Jeremy Brink | 25.03.1975 | P/O |
| 9390 | COCKS | Michael Kenneth | 01.04.1975 | P/O |
| 9391 | WEBB | Andrew Martin | 01.04.1975 | P/O |
| 9392 | SPACKMAN | Ian Christopher | 01.04.1975 | Insp |
| 9393 | PEACOCK | Donald Campbell | 01.04.1975 | Insp |
| 9394 | CLARK | Thomas | 01.04.1975 | D/P/O |
| 9395 | PATCH | John Leslie | 06.01.1975 | D/S/O |
| 9396 | CRAGG | Martin Conway | 06.01.1975 | L/Insp |
| 9397 | LINES-WILLIAMSON | William Ronald | 03.04.1975 | D/S/O |
| 9398 | NORTIER | Christopher John | 05.04.1975 | S/O |
| 9399 | ENGEL | Godfrey Philip | 10.04.1975 | S/O |
| 9400 | CROCKART | David William | 10.04.1975 | P/O |
| 9401 | PALMER | Manley Derrick | 15.04.1975 | P/O |
| 9402 | MILTON | Maclcom McRae | 16.04.1975 | S/O(T) |
| 9403 | KOLPIEN | Uwe | 17.04.1975 | P/O |
| 9404 | WESTON | William Michael | 27.04.1975 | Insp |
| 9405 | DU PREEZ | Dawid Hermanus | 28.04.1975 | P/O |
| 9406 | O'CONNELL | Redmond Peter | 01.05.1975 | P/O |
| 9407 | ELLIS | Peter Beaumont | 01.05.1975 | P/O |
| 9408 | REYNOLDS | Christopher Charles | 01.05.1975 | S/O(T) |
| 9409 | LYNAS | David | 01.05.1975 | S/O |
| 9410 | SMITH | David Ian | 21.04.1975 | P/O |
| 9411 | JARVIE | Hugh Cunningham | 05.05.1975 | A/Comm |
| 9412 | SIMPSON | Terence Frank | 03.05.1975 | P/O |
| 9413 | DE VILLIERS | Marc Raymond | 04.05.1975 | D/I |
| 9414 | THOMAS | David Charles | 08.05.1975 | D/I |
| 9415 | McDADE | Gerald | 31.05.1975 | P/O |
| 9416 | HOUGHTON | John William | 06.01.1975 | L/S/O |
| 9417 | TIMMER | Brian Edgar | 06.01.1975 | P/O |
| 9418 | DAYNES | Michael John | 03.06.1975 | S/O |
| 9419 | BURMEISTER | Glenn Neil | 03.06.1975 | P/O |
| 9420 | MOLYNEAUX | Andrew William | 03.06.1975 | S/O |
| 9421 | ANDREWS | Stephen Scott | 03.06.1975 | P/O |
| 9422 | RYDER | Ronald Frederick | 04.06.1975 | S/O(T) |
| 9423 | WILL | Douglas George | 04.06.1975 | P/O |
| 9424 | CLAPHAM | Richard James | 10.07.1974 | P/O |
| 9425 | BROWN | Andrew John | 05.06.1975 | P/O |
| 9426 | HESLIP | Thomas Livingstone | 09.06.1975 | S/O(T) |
| 9427 | SCARFF | David Jamie | 08.06.1975 | P/O |
| 9428 | HOUGHTON | David Laud | 23.06.1975 | Insp |
| 9429 | PRETORIUS | Willem Andries | 23.06.1975 | D/I |
| 9430 | WILLIS | Kenneth Bryan | 24.06.1975 | S/O |
| 9431 | THORPE | Simon Charles | 08.04.1974 | S/O |
| 9432 | COOPER | Gavin Richard | 26.06.1975 | D/P/O |
| 9433 | Mac MILLAN | James Alexander | 27.06.1975 | Insp(T) |
| 9434 | SWINNERTON | James Smith | 07.04.1975 | P/O |
| 9435 | MAGGS | William George | 01.07.1975 | S/O(T) |
| 9436 | EILERTSEN | Erik Phillip | 01.07.1975 | S/O(T) |
| 9437 | DONACHIE | Neil Mervyn | 01.07.1975 | Insp(T) |
| 9438 | HANSEN | David Apto | 01.07.1975 | S/O(T) |
| 9439 | SEYMOUR-HALL | Glen | 01.07.1975 | S/O |
| 9440 | O'BRIEN | Lindsay Robert | 07.07.1975 | L/S/O |
| 9441 | TREASURE | Charles Thomas | 08.07.1975 | S/O |
| 9442 | RUMNEY | Harold George | 09.07.1975 | Insp(T) |
| 9443 | HARMAN | Christopher | 29.07.1975 | S/O |
| 9444 | HENSON | Arthur Roy | 01.08.1975 | P/O |
| 9445 | ROBINSON | Roy David | 01.08.1975 | Insp |
| 9446 | VAN STADEN | Kenneth John | 04.08.1975 | S/L/S/O |
| 9447 | SANDERSON | John Alexander | 05.08.1975 | P/O |
| 9448 | MANN | Jeremy David | 05.08.1975 | D/P/O |
| 9449 | SMITH | Philip Robert | 05.08.1975 | P/O |
| 9450 | ARMSTRONG | James Gradwell | 05.08.1975 | P/O |
| 9451 | HOWIE | Iain William | 05.08.1975 | P/O |
| 9452 | ENGLISH | Peter Rodney | 08.08.1975 | D/S/O |
| 9453 | COOMER | Colin Michael | 10.08.1975 | P/O |
| 9454 | VAN DER MERWE | Christoffel Bernardus | 06.01.1975 | S/O |
| 9455 | MILLAR | Alexander George | 26.08.1975 | S/O |
| 9456 | CAMPBELL | Douglas Clifford | 28.08.1975 | S/O |
| 9457 | MIRFIN | Nicholas Stewart | 29.08.1975 | P/O |
| 9458 | TREURNICHT | Robert Brian | 01.09.1975 | S/O(T) |
| 9459 | FOLEY | Kevin Hayes | 09.09.1975 | P/O |
| 9460 | EVANS | Desmond Harold | 17.09.1975 | D/P/O |
| 9461 | ASHTON | David Anthony | 29.09.1975 | S/O(T) |
| 9462 | WREFORD | John Alan | 29.09.1975 | P/O |
| 9463 | BODDY | Clive Richard | 10.07.1974 | P/O |
| 9464 | TRETHOWAN | Brian Michael | 06.01.1975 | P/O |
| 9465 | KERR | Christopher John | 06.01.1975 | D/P/O |
| 9466 | JOHNSTONE | Richard Martin | 30.09.1975 | P/O |
| 9467 | TUCKER | Andrew Graham | 30.09.1975 | P/O |
| 9468 | AKEHURST | Martin Christopher | 30.09.1975 | D/S/O |
| 9469 | TERRY | Michael Mark | 30.09.1975 | P/O |
| 9470 | VERONNEAU | Robert John | 30.09.1975 | S/O |
| 9471 | KENCHINGTON | Michael Ian | 30.09.1975 | S/O |
| 9472 | COWLING | Anthony Peter | 30.09.1975 | D/P/O |
| 9473 | ALLMAN | Andrew Hugh | 01.10.1975 | P/O |
| 9474 | DAKYNS | Stephen John | 01.10.1975 | S/O |
| 9475 | WORRALL-CLARE | Stefan | 01.10.1975 | S/O(T) |
| 9476 | CUNNINGHAM | Samuel Raymond | 01.10.1975 | S/O(T) |
| 9477 | TAPSON | Denis Gordon | 03.10.1975 | S/O |
| 9478 | COLTART | David | 04.10.1975 | S/O |
| 9479 | GOLDEN | Alan | 21.10.1975 | D/S/O |
| 9480 | SWANEPOEL | Kenneth Gordon | 23.10.1975 | P/O |
| 9481 | McCHLERY | Thomas Alexander | 27.10.1975 | S/O(T) |
| 9482 | LEE | Colin James | 04.11.1975 | Insp(T) |
| 9483 | CLARKE | Graeme | 07.11.1975 | P/O |
| 9484 | GROSSMITH | Peter James | 07.11.1975 | P/O |
| 9485 | JENNINGS | Roy Douglas | 10.11.1975 | P/O |
| 9486 | LUSCOMBE | David | 10.11.1975 | Insp |
| 9487 | BRUSS | Carey Allan | 12.11.1975 | S/S/O |
| 9488 | BARKER | Andrew Duncan | 16.11.1975 | S/S/O |
| 9489 | SMITH | Richard Laurie | 17.11.1975 | S/O(T) |
| 9490 | LOVETT | Grant John | 17.11.1975 | P/O |
| 9491 | HAMMOND | Patrick Wayne | 25.11.1975 | S/O(T) |
| 9492 | CAMPBELL | Bruce Alastair | 25.11.1975 | S/O |
| 9493 | MELDRUM | Kenneth Young | 25.11.1975 | S/O |
| 9494 | SMITH | Malcolm Terrence | 25.11.1975 | S/O |
| 9495 | GIBBARD | Carlston Lyndsey | 25.11.1975 | D/S/O |
| 9496 | WEINZHEIMER | Kai Werner Lothar | 25.11.1975 | P/O |
| 9497 | PELLERADE | Peter George | 01.12.1975 | Insp(T) |
| 9498 | VETTERS | Richard | 03.12.1975 | S/O(T) |
| 9499 | HURRY | Karl Vance | 05.12.1975 | P/O |
| 9500 | GIBSON | Alexander Burnside | 08.12.1975 | S/O(T) |
| 9501 | DAWSON | Nicholas | 12.12.1975 | S/O |
| 9502 | REITZ | Neil Francis | 16.12.1975 | L/Insp |
| 9503 | OOSTHUIZEN | Martinus Johannes | 16.12.1975 | D/S/O |
| 9504 | BENNETT | John Vincent | 16.12.1975 | S/O |
| 9505 | KNIGHT | Robert Jeremy | 16.12.1975 | P/O |
| 9506 | CHRISTIAN | Timothy Walter | 16.12.1975 | P/O |
| 9507 | ENGLISH | Kevin Graham | 16.12.1975 | P/O |
| 9508 | RIDDELL | Ian Charles | 16.12.1975 | P/O |
| 9509 | SCHROEDER | Marcus Edward | 16.12.1975 | P/O |
| 9510 | CULVER | Richard John | 16.12.1975 | P/O |
| 9511 | COUPAR | Ross Allan John | 16.12.1975 | D/S/O |
| 9512 | SWIFT | Julian Dick | 16.12.1975 | P/O |
| 9513 | SPIVEY | Stephen Richard | 16.12.1975 | P/O |
| 9514 | Mac RAE | Craig Alexander | 16.12.1975 | Insp |
| 9515 | SERRAS-PIRES | Adelino | 16.12.1975 | P/O |
| 9516 | NIVEN | Keith James | 16.12.1975 | P/O |
| 9517 | HUGHES | Michael John | 06.01.1975 | P/O |
| 9518 | HAMER | Staurt Russell | 10.07.1974 | D/P/O |
| 9519 | LOXTON | Gareth William | 06.01.1975 | P/O |
| 9520 | ODENDAAL | Desmond Charles | 06.01.1975 | D/P/O |

| No. | Surname | First Name(s) | Date | Rank |
|---|---|---|---|---|
| 9521 | VAN DER MERWE | Ernest Christoffel | 23.12.1975 | S/O(T) |
| 9522 | PASCOE | Colin David | 28.12.1975 | P/O |
| 9523 | BROWN | Ian Michael | 02.01.1976 | S/O(T) |
| 9524 | HUGHES | Barry Vincent | 02.01.1976 | S/O(T) |
| 9525 | VAN RENSBURG | Pieter Janse | 02.01.1976 | Insp |
| 9526 | HOGG | Kenneth Frank | 16.07.1975 | S/O |
| 9527 | LISTER | Graham Lyle | 02.01.1976 | P/O |
| 9528 | FALCONE | Francesco | 02.01.1976 | P/O |
| 9529 | COOPER | Stephen Mark | 06.01.1976 | P/O |
| 9530 | McLENNAN | Donald Ailsdhair | 06.01.1976 | P/O |
| 9531 | TURPIN | Alexander George | 06.01.1976 | P/O |
| 9532 | BAIRD | Paul | 06.01.1976 | S/O |
| 9533 | ARTLETT-JOHNSON | Richard Clive | 06.01.1976 | P/O |
| 9534 | HEATH | Brian Norman | 06.01.1976 | P/O |
| 9535 | PARKIN | Neville John | 06.01.1976 | P/O |
| 9536 | SLEMENT | Ian Hilton | 06.01.1976 | P/O |
| 9537 | FRASER | David Lobban | 06.01.1976 | D/P/O |
| 9538 | CARRIE-WILSON | Peter Graeme | 06.01.1976 | S/O |
| 9539 | RUSSELL | William Randolph | 06.01.1976 | P/O |
| 9540 | NEEDHAM | Steven | 06.01.1976 | P/O |
| 9541 | VAN EDE | Andrew John | 06.01.1976 | P/O |
| 9542 | BLICK | Simon Frank | 06.01.1976 | P/O |
| 9543 | CARROLL | Christopher Edward | 06.01.1976 | P/O |
| 9544 | GARNER | Warren Anthony | 06.01.1976 | P/O |
| 9545 | MOLYNEUX-SANDWITH | Gary | 06.01.1976 | P/O |
| 9546 | MUGGLETON | Michael Patrick | 07.01.1976 | P/O |
| 9547 | FIVAZ | John George | 09.01.1976 | P/O |
| 9548 | HALDER | Michael John | 17.01.1976 | S/O |
| 9549 | BROWN | Alec George | 19.01.1976 | P/O |
| 9550 | ROWLES | Ian | 27.01.1976 | P/O |
| 9551 | LACHENICHT | Leslie Charles | 27.01.1976 | S/O |
| 9552 | LACHENICHT | Robert Clive | 27.01.1976 | P/O |
| 9553 | FLOWERS | Norman Roy | 27.01.1976 | L/Insp |
| 9554 | GATLAND | Michael John | 27.01.1976 | P/O |
| 9555 | HONYWILL | John Forbes | 27.01.1976 | P/O |
| 9556 | PERKINS | Ian William | 27.01.1976 | P/O |
| 9557 | WHEELER | Brian Matson | 27.01.1976 | S/O |
| 9558 | LYWOOD | Nicholas Oswin | 27.01.1976 | P/O |
| 9559 | WEBB-MARTIN | Paul Jeremy | 27.01.1976 | P/O |
| 9560 | ALLAN | Terence Sidney | 27.01.1976 | S/O |
| 9561 | DU PLOOY | Raymond Walter | 27.01.1976 | P/O |
| 9562 | THERON | Mark William | 07.04.1976 | P/O |
| 9563 | ATHERTON | Michael Charles | 07.04.1976 | P/O |
| 9564 | KIRKMAN | Garth William | 28.01.1976 | P/O |
| 9565 | BOWIE | Deville Michael | 30.01.1976 | P/O |
| 9566 | CONNOLLY | Paul Graham | 02.02.1976 | Insp(T) |
| 9567 | HARRINGTON | Gavin Kennith | 05.02.1976 | S/O |
| 9568 | TATE | John Glynne | 06.02.1976 | P/O |
| 9569 | ISDALE | Ewen David | 16.07.1976 | D/Insp |
| 9570 | YOUENS | Mark John | 06.02.1976 | P/O |
| 9571 | McDONAGH | Paul Rodger | 19.02.1976 | P/O |
| 9572 | YOUNGMAN | Graeme Stuart | 21.02.1976 | P/O |
| 9573 | RESTORICK | James Ian | 24.02.1976 | P/O |
| 9574 | DENHOLME | David Michael | 24.02.1976 | P/O |
| 9575 | WEILER | James Carr | 24.02.1976 | P/O |
| 9576 | HIGH | Ronald Peter | 24.02.1976 | P/O |
| 9577 | TOTHILL | Bruce Ernest | 24.02.1976 | P/O |
| 9578 | WEST | Timothy Ronald | 24.02.1976 | P/O |
| 9579 | SMITH | Peter Anthony | 24.02.1976 | S/O |
| 9580 | KNOWLDEN | Kimbale Neil | 24.02.1976 | P/O |
| 9581 | ROBINSON | Daniel Johannes | 24.02.1976 | P/O |
| 9582 | VENTER | John Craig | 24.02.1976 | P/O |
| 9583 | FREARSON | Edward John | 24.02.1976 | P/O |
| 9584 | BYRNE | Robert | 24.02.1976 | P/O |
| 9585 | MASON | David Malcolm | 24.02.1976 | P/O |
| 9586 | HETHERINGTON | David Keith | 26.02.1976 | D/S/O |
| 9587 | THOMSON | David Neil | 01.03.1976 | S/O |
| 9588 | GUSTAFSON | Robert William | 05.03.1976 | S/O |
| 9589 | DYER | Robert William | | S/O |
| 9590 | PRENTICE | William James | 16.03.1976 | P/O |
| 9591 | BURROW | Leslie | 08.04.1974 | P/O |
| 9592 | MacKILLICAN | Richard Hugh | 07.04.1975 | S/O(T) |
| 9593 | AULD | Nigel Anthony | 07.04.1975 | S/O |
| 9594 | HALL | David Kenneth | 07.04.1975 | S/O |
| 9595 | SAMPSON | Martin John | 13.03.1976 | P/O |
| 9596 | RUSSELL | Nicholas Robert | 22.03.1976 | D/S/O |
| 9597 | RAAFF | Alan Geoffrey | 23.03.1976 | P/O |
| 9598 | LOVATT | Roger James | 01.10.1975 | Insp(T) |
| 9599 | ELKINGTON | Vaughan Mark | 06.01.1976 | Insp(T) |
| 9600 | BOTTON | Christopher John | 30.03.1976 | P/O |
| 9601 | HOLLAND | Patrick Joseph | 30.03.1976 | P/O |
| 9602 | Mac DONALD | Robert Charles | 30.03.1976 | P/O |
| 9603 | MEREDITH | Claude Maurice | 30.03.1976 | P/O |
| 9604 | NICHOLSON | Neil Graeme | 30.03.1976 | S/O |
| 9605 | SHAWE | Clive Bayley | 30.03.1976 | S/O |
| 9606 | WATSON | Gary Robert | 30.03.1976 | P/O |
| 9607 | HOUGH | Edwin John | 07.04.1975 | S/O |
| 9608 | LUMB | David Eric | 06.01.1976 | P/O |
| 9609 | WYNN | Stuart James | 01.04.1976 | S/O(T) |
| 9610 | HOUSTON | Terence Stanley | 01.04.1976 | P/O |
| 9611 | VAUGHAN | Brian Sydney | 01.04.1976 | Insp(T) |
| 9612 | Mac KINNON | Ian Gerald | 31.03.1976 | P/O |
| 9613 | HOOD | David Leslie | 07.04.1976 | P/O |
| 9614 | DE BEER | Leon Adriaan | 08.04.1976 | P/O |
| 9615 | KUTCHEN | Rodney Glen | 20.04.1976 | P/O |
| 9616 | SHUTT | Kenneth Eric | 20.04.1976 | S/O(T) |
| 9617 | McKINNON | Peter Donald | 22.04.1976 | P/O |
| 9618 | DILL-RUSSELL | Jack David | 26.04.1976 | P/O |
| 9619 | WHISKEN | Trevor John | 28.04.1976 | P/O |
| 9620 | HEMENSLEY | Ralph | 28.04.1976 | D/S/O |
| 9621 | HALLS | Guy Anthony | 28.04.1976 | P/O |
| 9622 | FRIEND | Beaudry Alexander | 01.05.1976 | Supt |
| 9623 | CAIRNE | Robert | 01.05.1976 | C/Insp |
| 9624 | BECKLEY | Peter Morton | 01.05.1976 | D/S/O |
| 9625 | YATES | John Bruce | 13.05.1976 | P/O |
| 9626 | ALDER | James Francis | 27.05.1976 | P/O |
| 9627 | FRANKLEYNE | Michael Peter | 27.05.1976 | S/O |
| 9628 | PARNELL | Terence Stuart | 27.05.1976 | S/O |
| 9629 | BUCKLE | Keith James | 27.05.1976 | S/O |
| 9630 | McCLELLAND | William Joseph | 27.05.1976 | S/O |
| 9631 | YOUNG | Steven Angus | 27.05.1976 | P/O |
| 9632 | WESTON | Steven Anthony | 28.05.1976 | Insp |
| 9633 | DOWNING | David Kenneth | 27.05.1976 | D/S/O |
| 9634 | MORRIS | Beri Lynn | 27.05.1976 | D/S/O |
| 9635 | BLICK | Gordon Andrew | 27.05.1976 | S/O |
| 9636 | PITMAN | Leonard Alan | 27.05.1976 | P/O |
| 9637 | PALMER | Derrick John | 27.05.1976 | P/O |
| 9638 | SMITH | Christopher Huw | 27.05.1976 | D/S/O |
| 9639 | COX | Andrew Pembroke | 29.05.1976 | S/O |
| 9640 | PENMAN | David | 31.05.1976 | P/O |
| 9641 | MILLS | Anthony | 21.05.1976 | P/O |
| 9642 | MITTENS | Bruce Stephen | 08.06.1976 | S/O(T) |
| 9643 | SCHREIBER | Frederick Lodewikus | 08.06.1976 | P/O |
| 9644 | WYNGAARD | Gene Trevor | 08.06.1976 | P/O |
| 9645 | HAND | William John | 09.06.1976 | S/O |
| 9646 | WHEELER | Ronald Peter | 11.06.1976 | S/O |
| 9647 | TAYLOR | Ian | 11.06.1976 | P/O |
| 9648 | VAN STAN | John Alexander | 01.07.1976 | S/O(T) |
| 9649 | MILNE | Robert | 01.07.1976 | S/O(T) |
| 9650 | WATSON | Robert James | 14.06.1976 | Insp |
| 9651 | HAMILL | Robert Alexander | 16.06.1976 | P/O |
| 9652 | DAVIES | John Clement | 18.06.1976 | S/O |
| 9653 | WATSON | James Anthony | 24.06.1976 | S/S/O |
| 9654 | CARTER | John Anthony | 24.06.1976 | S/O |
| 9655 | BUSBY | Michael Allan | 24.02.1976 | P/O |
| 9656 | PATTON | James | 25.06.1976 | S/O(T) |
| 9657 | CRESSWELL | Ronald Francis | 29.06.1976 | P/O |
| 9658 | DOWD | Michael Gerard | 29.06.1976 | P/O |
| 9659 | BOLTON | Craig Wiliam | 29.06.1976 | P/O |
| 9660 | MONTGOMERY | Henry Hugh | 01.12.1975 | D/S/O |
| 9661 | ANDERSON | Collin William | 29.06.1976 | S/O |
| 9662 | TAYLOR | Michael St.John | 29.06.1976 | C/Ins(T) |
| 9663 | WILSON | Brian Robert | 29.06.1976 | P/O |
| 9664 | HENDERSON | Graham Alexander | 29.06.1976 | P/O |
| 9665 | BARROW | Steven Nicholas | 29.06.1976 | P/O |
| 9666 | LONG | David Robert | 29.06.1976 | P/O |
| 9667 | HARVEY | John McAllister | 29.06.1976 | P/O |
| 9668 | COLEMAN | Andrew Roy | 30.06.1976 | P/O |
| 9669 | CALLAWAY | Jonathan Charles | 30.06.1976 | P/O |
| 9670 | MARTINS | Mario | 30.06.1976 | D/S/O |
| 9671 | JACOBS | Trevor Anthony | 30.06.1976 | S/O(T) |
| 9672 | ALLEN | Michael Robert | 30.06.1976 | P/O |
| 9673 | LOWRIE | Steven Vincent | 30.06.1976 | P/O |
| 9674 | DU PLESSIS | Pierre | 01.07.1976 | D/S/O |
| 9675 | BRADFIELD | Ronald Michael | 01.07.1976 | S/S/O |
| 9676 | NICHOL | Christopher John | 02.07.1976 | S/O |
| 9677 | ENGLEBRECHT | Michael Ferdinand | 04.07.1976 | P/O |
| 9678 | FOLDER | Jonathan James | 05.07.1976 | S/S/O |
| 9679 | PASCOE | Charles Robert | 30.06.1976 | P/O |
| 9680 | BOWKER | Geoffrey Wallace | 09.07.1976 | P/O |
| 9681 | BANNISTER | Nigel Redman | 09.07.1976 | P/O |
| 9682 | HONE | Evelyn Brettell | 09.07.1976 | S/S/O |
| 9683 | TROLLOPE | Harold Benjamin | 13.07.1976 | P/O |
| 9684 | DONNELLY | Robert William | 15.07.1976 | S/O |
| 9685 | FURBER | Gerald Montague | 05.04.1976 | P/O |
| 9686 | DICK | Peter John | 16.07.1975 | P/O |
| 9687 | OWEN | Percy Brian | 16.07.1975 | P/O |
| 9688 | VILJOEN | David Alan | 05.04.1976 | D/S/O |
| 9689 | LONGY | John Duckworth | 16.07.1975 | P/O |
| 9690 | FABRE | Alan Rex | 16.07.1975 | S/O |
| 9691 | HOPKINS | Neil John | 05.04.1976 | P/O |
| 9692 | ERVINE | Rory Michael | 16.01.1976 | P/O |
| 9693 | GREEN | Peter Charles | 16.07.1975 | P/O |
| 9694 | SALTHOUSE | Mark Andrew | 01.10.1975 | P/O |
| 9695 | CURRIE | Miles Alexander | 05.04.1976 | S/S/O |
| 9696 | BROWN | David Kenneth | 05.04.1976 | S/S/O |
| 9697 | SMITHDORF | Anthony James | 05.01.1976 | P/O |
| 9698 | GHERARDOTTI | Robert Frederick | 16.07.1975 | S/S/O |
| 9699 | PARRINGTON | David Neale | 21.07.1976 | P/O |
| 9700 | JACKSON | Noel Richard | 27.07.1976 | P/O |
| 9701 | ODENDAAL | David John | 27.07.1976 | P/O |
| 9702 | HODGSON | Michael John | 27.07.1976 | P/O |
| 9703 | WALKER | Alan Frank | 27.07.1976 | P/O |
| 9704 | STEUART | Alistair Donald | 27.07.1976 | P/O |
| 9705 | BRUCE | Donald John | 27.07.1976 | P/O |
| 9706 | BADENHORST | Peter Johannes | 27.07.1976 | P/O |
| 9707 | FERNANDES | Paul Andre | 29.07.1976 | P/O |
| 9708 | O'DELL | Graham Robert | 29.07.1976 | P/O |
| 9709 | WELENSKY | Norman Keith | 30.07.1976 | P/O |
| 9710 | CLARK | Alistair Ross | 31.07.1976 | P/O |
| 9711 | MEADEN-KENDRICK | David Peter | 31.07.1976 | S/O(T) |
| 9712 | HODGSON | Ian David | 31.07.1976 | S/O(T) |
| 9713 | AUDIN | Sebastain Craven | 02.08.1976 | S/O(T) |
| 9714 | WALLACE | Frederick Charles | 02.08.1976 | S/O |
| 9715 | HALL | Anthony Graham | 02.08.1976 | S/O |
| 9716 | REEVES | Graham Donald | 02.08.1976 | P/O |
| 9717 | JONES | Richard | 01.07.1976 | Insp(T) |
| 9718 | HOLLAND | Peter Lionel | 01.07.1976 | S/O |
| 9719 | DAVIES | David Rhys | 09.08.1976 | S/O |
| 9720 | BURTON | Reginald | 11.08.1976 | S/O(T) |
| 9721 | ROBINSON | Lee | 11.08.1976 | P/O |
| 9722 | REYNEKE | Kevin John | 17.08.1976 | D/P/O |
| 9723 | GRIFFIN | Frederick Thomas | 19.08.1976 | Insp |
| 9724 | PORTER | Anthony William | 18.08.1976 | Insp |
| 9725 | McMEEKING | Douglas Lewis | 23.08.1976 | S/O |
| 9726 | CURRIE | Trevor Duncan | 27.08.1976 | S/O |
| 9727 | BRUMMER | Jacobus Johan | 31.08.1976 | S/O |

# BSAP Nominal Roll • Men

| No. | Surname | First names | Rank | Date |
|---|---|---|---|---|
| 9728 | SMITH | Malcolm John | D/P/O | 31.08.1976 |
| 9729 | MOMMSEN | Shayne Bernard | P/O | 31.08.1976 |
| 9730 | RHYNAS | Peter McDonald | P/O | 31.08.1976 |
| 9731 | GREENBERG | Karl | P/O | 31.08.1976 |
| 9732 | ROBERTS | David Nicholas | P/O | 31.08.1976 |
| 9733 | DON | Alan Michael | P/O | 31.08.1976 |
| 9734 | BERTIN | Richard John | Insp | 31.08.1976 |
| 9735 | ASHWORTH | Martin | P/O | 31.08.1976 |
| 9736 | FOWLE | John Kemp | P/O | 31.08.1976 |
| 9737 | WOOD | Stephen John | P/O | 31.08.1976 |
| 9738 | MOCKRIDGE | Simon | P/O | 31.08.1976 |
| 9739 | McGAW | Keith | D/P/O | 31.08.1976 |
| 9740 | LUNDGREN | Barry Wesley | D/S/O | 31.08.1976 |
| 9741 | SULLIVAN | Kieran Michael | P/O | 01.09.1976 |
| 9742 | LIEBERMANN | Russell John | P/O | 01.09.1976 |
| 9743 | ARNOTT | John Michael | P/O | 31.08.1976 |
| 9744 | STEYN | Theunis Frederick | D/P/O | 01.09.1976 |
| 9745 | ALBERRY | Stuart David | P/O | 30.08.1976 |
| 9746 | SIMPSON | Tony Allen | P/O | 06.09.1976 |
| 9747 | CRABB | David Charles | S/O(T) | 06.09.1976 |
| 9748 | DURANDT | Neil Gary | S/O(T) | 14.09.1976 |
| 9749 | BEETS | Derek John | P/O | 14.09.1976 |
| 9750 | NUTT | Stephen Kent | D/S/O | 14.09.1976 |
| 9751 | ADDISON | Timothy Hugh | P/O | 15.09.1976 |
| 9752 | FROST | Nicholas John | Insp | 20.09.1976 |
| 9753 | JOBSON | Robert | Insp | 27.09.1976 |
| 9754 | McDONALD | John | S/O(T) | 29.09.1976 |
| 9755 | REES | Guy Anthony | L/S/O | 04.10.1976 |
| 9756 | WALLACE | John Hugh Austin | P/O | 04.10.1976 |
| 9757 | SOMERS-COX | Anthony John | P/O | 28.09.1976 |
| 9758 | HOFFMAN | Daniel Godfried | P/O | 01.10.1976 |
| 9759 | HANSEN | Glenn Michael | P/O | 28.09.1976 |
| 9760 | DE GRANDHOMME | Laurence Leonard | P/O | 28.09.1976 |
| 9761 | REID | Irvine Prosser | P/O | 28.09.1976 |
| 9762 | WAINWRIGHT | Keith | S/O(T) | 28.09.1976 |
| 9763 | GALLAGHER | Anthony George | P/O | 28.09.1976 |
| 9764 | ENGLEBRECHT | Andrew Johnson | P/O | 28.09.1976 |
| 9765 | MOIR | Neil Anthony | P/O | 28.09.1976 |
| 9766 | TOWN | David William | P/O | 28.09.1976 |
| 9767 | MORGAN | Robert Charles | C/Insp | 01.10.1976 |
| 9768 | BICHARD | John Albert | P/O | 07.10.1976 |
| 9769 | NIXON | David William | P/O | 11.10.1976 |
| 9770 | BERTRAND | Anthony Guy | P/O | 15.10.1976 |
| 9771 | Mac LAGAN | Angus Lachlan | P/O | 22.10.1976 |
| 9772 | SWINDELLS | Jeffrey Mark | P/O | 26.10.1976 |
| 9773 | TWYCROSS | David George | P/O | 26.10.1976 |
| 9774 | RICHARDSON | Andrew John | P/O | 26.10.1976 |
| 9775 | RINK | Ronald Alexander | S/O | 01.11.1976 |
| 9776 | BEATTIE | David Andrew | C/Ins(T) | 01.11.1976 |
| 9777 | MASH | Gean Barden | P/O | 01.11.1976 |
| 9778 | McCALLUM | Thomas Frederick | S/O(T) | 01.11.1976 |
| 9779 | WHEELER | John William | P/O | 01.11.1976 |
| 9780 | BEVERIDGE | Breedon Ian | P/O | 26.10.1976 |
| 9781 | RAUSCH | Alistair Ian | P/O | 26.10.1976 |
| 9782 | HALL | Allastair Nelson | P/O | 26.10.1976 |
| 9783 | BEALE | Robert George | P/O | 26.10.1976 |
| 9784 | KRIEL | Albert Pieter | P/O | 01.11.1976 |
| 9785 | MURRAY | Clive Andrew | S/O | 01.11.1976 |
| 9786 | COMBRINK | Lance Ronald | C/Ins(T) | 01.11.1976 |
| 9787 | HAASBROEK | Johannes Bernadus | P/O | 01.11.1976 |
| 9788 | McCALLUM | Alastair Hutchinson | S/O(T) | 01.11.1976 |
| 9789 | STOKES | Roderick Donovan | S/O(T) | 01.11.1976 |
| 9790 | WAUGH | Duncan MacDonald | P/O | 01.11.1976 |
| 9791 | TRIGG | Peter Edwin | P/O | 04.11.1976 |
| 9792 | HELM | Eric Anderson | P/O | 10.11.1976 |
| 9793 | McGILL | Patrick Andrew | P/O | 08.11.1976 |
| 9794 | HAYNES | Graham Keith | P/O | 15.11.1976 |
| 9795 | TURNBULL | Ian Stewart | P/O | 15.11.1976 |
| 9796 | GAMFIRO | Vital Da Conceicao | S/O(T) | 15.11.1976 |
| 9797 | KING | Toby John Buen | S/O | 22.11.1976 |
| 9798 | JOHNSON | Hilton Sven | P/O | 30.11.1976 |
| 9799 | WILSON | William Frederick | D/P/O | 01.12.1976 |
| 9800 | WILSON | Brian Peter | P/O | 30.11.1976 |
| 9801 | BARNES | Kevin Nicholas | P/O | 06.12.1976 |
| 9802 | BOYD-MOSS | Hedley Clive | S/O(T) | 30.11.1976 |
| 9803 | SWIFT | Wayne | P/O | 30.11.1976 |
| 9804 | HERON | David Albert | P/O | 30.11.1976 |
| 9805 | VAN HEERDEN | Phillip Arnoldus | P/O | 30.11.1976 |
| 9806 | MEREDITH | Cyril Douglas | P/O | 30.11.1976 |
| 9807 | MULLENS | David Hugh | P/O | 30.11.1976 |
| 9808 | OWINGS | James Francis | P/O | 30.11.1976 |
| 9809 | CHANTLER | Andre Charles | P/O | 30.11.1976 |
| 9810 | PHILBIN | Mark | P/O | 30.11.1976 |
| 9811 | MADDOCKS | Patrick Garth | P/O | 30.11.1976 |
| 9812 | DAVIS | Trevor Anthony | D/S/O | 30.11.1976 |
| 9813 | FOWLES | Kenneth Ian | P/O | 30.11.1976 |
| 9814 | BOYCE | Clive Allan | P/O | 30.11.1976 |
| 9815 | BEKKER | Oscar William | D/P/O | 30.11.1976 |
| 9816 | EVANS | Bernard Ripley | P/O | 30.11.1976 |
| 9817 | WEINMAN | Warwick Dounghn | P/O | 30.11.1976 |
| 9818 | SANDWITH | Graham Wayne | P/O | 30.11.1976 |
| 9819 | TREBLE | Clifford John | P/O | 30.11.1976 |
| 9820 | BONE | Gregory | P/O | 30.11.1976 |
| 9821 | DE BEER | Anthony Frank | P/O | 30.11.1976 |
| 9822 | SAUNDERS | Barry Edward | P/O | 08.12.1976 |
| 9823 | JANSEN-VAN VUUREN | Hendrick Gerhaardus | P/O | 30.11.1976 |
| 9824 | DU PREEZ | Hans Jurgen | P/O | 30.11.1976 |
| 9825 | MERRIMAN | Thomas Brian | S/O(T) | 01.12.1976 |
| 9826 | MORRISON | Robert William | S/O(T) | 06.12.1976 |
| 9827 | BROWNING | Roger Arthur | P/O | 06.12.1976 |
| 9828 | DEAN | Gregory Peter | P/O | 09.12.1976 |
| 9829 | NEL | Derick James | P/O | 08.12.1976 |
| 9830 | TENNENT | Stuart William | P/O | 15.12.1976 |
| 9831 | BAKER | John Edward | P/O | 15.12.1976 |
| 9832 | WILLIAMS | Keith | Insp(T) | 13.12.1976 |
| 9833 | SMITH | David Herbert | Insp(T) | 13.12.1976 |
| 9834 | CAIRNS | Terence Lloyd | P/O | 15.12.1976 |
| 9835 | FRIEND | John Jeffrey | P/O | 15.12.1976 |
| 9836 | DE WET | Petrus Gerhardus | S/O | 15.12.1976 |
| 9837 | HUNDERMARK | Alfred Evans | P/O | 15.12.1976 |
| 9838 | ACKERMAN | Thomas Lodewyk | S/O | 15.12.1976 |
| 9839 | MITCHELL | William Andrew | P/O | 15.12.1976 |
| 9840 | VAN DER MERWE | Hendrik Martinus | S/O | 15.12.1976 |
| 9841 | REEVE | Martin Olaf | P/O | 15.12.1976 |
| 9842 | BOBBINS | Leonard John | D/S/O | 16.12.1976 |
| 9843 | PAYNE | Jeffrey Alexander | P/O | 16.12.1976 |
| 9844 | ROTHQUEL | Glen Alan | P/O | 05.01.1976 |
| 9845 | CARSE | James Alexander | S/O | 15.12.1976 |
| 9846 | NICHOLAS | Edward Phillip | P/O | 15.12.1976 |
| 9847 | REES | Christopher David | P/O | 15.12.1976 |
| 9848 | BUNT | Simon Anthony | S/C/Ins | 05.04.1976 |
| 9849 | VAN ZUYDAM | David Cornelius | S/O | 16.07.1975 |
| 9850 | BASS | Thomas Henry | S/O | 15.12.1976 |
| 9851 | THOMAS | Michael Graham | P/O | 16.07.1975 |
| 9852 | FENWICK | Gareth Llewellyn | P/O | 16.12.1976 |
| 9853 | FOURIE | Jeffrey Francis | P/O | 16.12.1976 |
| 9854 | MURRAY | Andre Pierre | S/O | 16.12.1976 |
| 9855 | BURTON | Kim | P/O | 16.12.1976 |
| 9856 | CRAVEN | Ralph | P/O | 16.12.1976 |
| 9857 | BIRD | Christopher John | D/P/O | 16.12.1976 |
| 9858 | ERASMUS | Ian Dawson | S/O(T) | 16.12.1976 |
| 9859 | CHARNOCK | Gert Adriaan | S/O(T) | 23.12.1976 |
| 9860 | WILEY | Thomas Henry | S/O(T) | 03.01.1977 |
| 9861 | SIMON | Richard Antony | S/O | 05.01.1977 |
| 9862 | RHODES | Peter Bernard | P/O | 16.07.1975 |
| 9863 | RISTON | Paul Berresford | D/S/O | 08.01.1977 |
| 9864 | EDWARDS | Keith Thomas | P/O | 14.01.1977 |
| 9865 | ZIETSMAN | Anthony Derek Pieter | P/O | 16.07.1975 |
| 9866 | WOOD | Brian James | P/O | 16.07.1975 |
| 9867 | SQUIRES | Alistair Gordon | P/O | 16.07.1975 |
| 9868 | BRADSHAW | David Scott | P/O | 16.07.1975 |
| 9869 | CROUSER | Martin Samuel | P/O | 12.01.1977 |
| 9870 | NOBBS | Anthony Martin | P/O | 17.01.1977 |
| 9871 | LONGMOOR | Paul Edward | S/O | 19.07.1976 |
| 9872 | MOSS | Kevin | P/O | 04.10.1976 |
| 9873 | ROBB | Andrew Kenneth | P/O | 21.01.1977 |
| 9874 | WOOLNOUGH | Raymond Ashley | P/O | 24.01.1977 |
| 9875 | HOCKING | Graham Barrir | S/O | 05.04.1976 |
| 9876 | FRAMPTON | Stephen James | S/S/O | 25.01.1977 |
| 9877 | McCALLUM | Alistair Currie | P/O | 25.01.1977 |
| 9878 | ARROWSMITH | Michael Richard | S/SO | 25.01.1977 |
| 9879 | CARINUS | Peter Andrew | P/O | 25.01.1977 |
| 9880 | JARVIS | Kenneth Gordon | S/O | 24.01.1977 |
| 9881 | HOLLIS | Michael Richard | S/S/O | 25.01.1977 |
| 9882 | DOYLE | Michael Roch | P/O | 25.01.1977 |
| 9883 | MARX-HUGHES | Howard Graham | P/O | 25.01.1977 |
| 9884 | HENDRIKZ | Russell | S/O | 25.01.1977 |
| 9885 | WESTLAND | Gordon | P/O | 25.01.1977 |
| 9886 | McKISSOCK | Stephen Alfred | P/O | 25.01.1977 |
| 9887 | PAPHITIS | John Charalambous | P/O | 25.01.1977 |
| 9888 | ATKINSON | Gordon Coles | S/O | 25.01.1977 |
| 9889 | Mac INTOSH | Donald Iain | S/O | 25.01.1977 |
| 9890 | DOUGLAS | Richard William | S/O | 25.01.1977 |
| 9891 | GIBB | Mark Hooper | S/O | 25.01.1977 |
| 9892 | JOHNSTONE | Alistair Keith | P/O | 25.01.1977 |
| 9893 | MARTIN | Ian Dennis | P/O | 25.01.1977 |
| 9894 | BROOKE-MEE | James Lawrence | P/O | 25.01.1977 |
| 9895 | CLINTON | Russell John | P/O | 25.01.1977 |
| 9896 | VAN BLERK | Bevan | P/O | 25.01.1977 |
| 9897 | BENTLEY | Clive William | P/O | 25.01.1977 |
| 9898 | ALDRIDGE | Robin Nicholas | P/O | 25.01.1977 |
| 9899 | BRODIE | Peter Duncan | P/O | 25.01.1977 |
| 9900 | ALLAN | Peter John | P/O | 25.01.1977 |
| 9901 | ALLAN | David John | P/O | 25.01.1977 |
| 9902 | SMITH | Dereck Roy | S/S/O | 25.01.1977 |
| 9903 | ENGELS | Dirk Hugh | P/O | 25.01.1977 |
| 9904 | MASON | Richie Matheson | P/O | 25.01.1977 |
| 9905 | HAMPSON | Gary Cyril | S/O | 25.01.1977 |
| 9906 | SMITH | Lionel Vincent | Insp | 25.01.1977 |
| 9907 | CARROLL | David John | P/O | 25.01.1977 |
| 9908 | VIEIRA | Jose Antonio | S/O | 25.01.1977 |
| 9909 | MEADOWS | Alan Edward | S/O | 25.01.1977 |
| 9910 | ACHESON | Gordon Noel | S/O | 25.01.1977 |
| 9911 | PRINSLOO | Adolph David | S/O(T) | 25.01.1977 |
| 9912 | FERREIRA | Cornelie | P/O | 25.01.1977 |
| 9913 | BIBBY | Andrew Lester | P/O | 25.01.1977 |
| 9914 | WALLINGTON | Roger John | P/O | 25.01.1977 |
| 9915 | SWANEPOEL | Derek Noel | S/O(T) | 25.01.1977 |
| 9916 | Mac KENZIE | Blair Alexander | S/O(T) | 25.01.1977 |
| 9917 | DALKIN | Gary Francis | P/O | 25.01.1977 |
| 9918 | JANSE-VAN VUUREN | Marius Johan | S/O | 25.01.1977 |
| 9919 | BALOCCA | Anthony Mark | P/O | 25.01.1977 |
| 9920 | O'HAGAN | Joseph Finbar | P/O | 25.01.1977 |
| 9921 | HUNTER | David Robert | P/O | 25.01.1977 |
| 9922 | HAMILTON | Hamish David | S/O(T) | 25.01.1977 |
| 9923 | FYFE | Stuart Borg | P/O | 25.01.1977 |
| 9924 | POCOCK | John Willmer | P/O | 25.01.1977 |
| 9925 | SPENCER | Grant Donald | P/O | 28.01.1977 |
| 9926 | GILLETT | Robert William | Insp(T) | 01.02.1977 |
| 9927 | BREEN | Michael Kindley | S/O(T) | 03.02.1977 |
| 9928 | FREDRIKSSON | Sven Michael | S/O | 03.02.1977 |
| 9929 | GEACH | Peter Werner | P/O | 03.02.1977 |
| 9930 | CORBETT | Peter | P/O | 03.02.1977 |
| 9931 | SMITH | Michael Carlin | D/S/O | 03.02.1977 |
| 9932 | GREIG | Neil William | D/P/O | 01.02.1977 |
| 9933 | STEYL | Thomas Robert | P/O | 11.02.1977 |
| 9934 | KATZ | Graham Malcolm | P/O | 03.02.1977 |

| No. | Surname | First names | Date | Rank |
|---|---|---|---|---|
| 9935 | ALMOND | Steven Wesley | 05.02.1977 | P/O |
| 9936 | TAYLOR | Alistair Allen | 06.02.1977 | P/O |
| 9937 | Mac KENZIE | Russell Dean | 12.02.1977 | P/O |
| 9938 | KNIGHT | Anthony Alan | 11.02.1977 | P/O |
| 9939 | SHAW | Anthony Charles | 11.02.1977 | S/O |
| 9940 | VAN DER HEIJDEN | Hank Julian | 11.02.1977 | P/O |
| 9941 | CASPI | Alon | 11.02.1977 | P/O |
| 9942 | COVENTRY | Cecil Rhodes | 11.02.1977 | S/S/O |
| 9943 | TAVENER | Edwin Frank | 11.02.1977 | P/O |
| 9944 | DE SOUSA | Mario Raul | 11.02.1977 | P/O |
| 9945 | LAWLER | Kevin Francis | 11.02.1977 | P/O |
| 9946 | FOURIE | Jean-Pierre | 11.02.1977 | S/O |
| 9947 | LARKAN | Colin William | 11.02.1977 | P/O |
| 9948 | CODD | Russell | 11.02.1977 | P/O |
| 9949 | ODENDAAL | Peter Nigel | 11.02.1977 | P/O |
| 9950 | NIMMO | Robert Fleming | 11.02.1977 | P/O |
| 9951 | HARRIS | Michael Robert | 11.02.1977 | P/O |
| 9952 | PIRIE | David Bruce | 11.02.1977 | S/S/O |
| 9953 | RUDA | Richard Mervin | 11.02.1977 | P/O |
| 9954 | BECKER | Charles Frederick | 11.02.1977 | P/O |
| 9955 | KAVONIC | Gerald Gregory | 11.02.1977 | D/S/O |
| 9956 | RALSTON | Bruce David | 11.02.1977 | P/O |
| 9957 | COLLYER | Christopher Robert | 11.02.1977 | P/O |
| 9958 | GRAHAM | Alastair MacPherson | 11.02.1977 | P/O |
| 9959 | MOLYNEUX | Richard David | 11.02.1977 | P/O |
| 9960 | THEUMA | Nicholas Francis | 11.02.1977 | P/O |
| 9961 | DAVY | Paul Raymond | 11.02.1977 | P/O |
| 9962 | VENTERS | Ian Alexander | 11.02.1977 | P/O |
| 9963 | RADLOFF | Ronald August | 11.02.1977 | S/O |
| 9964 | SCALLAN | Patrick James | 11.02.1977 | P/O |
| 9965 | JONES | William Steven | 11.02.1977 | S/O(T) |
| 9966 | NOBLE | Gary Christopher | 11.02.1977 | P/O |
| 9967 | LINDSAY-WHITE | Timothy Jonathan | 11.02.1977 | S/O |
| 9968 | HOLLINGTON | Michael David | 11.02.1977 | D/S/O |
| 9969 | STRYDOM | Nicholas | 11.02.1977 | P/O |
| 9970 | WOOKEY | Stephen Peter | 11.02.1977 | S/O |
| 9971 | HUGHES | David Gavin | 11.02.1977 | S/O |
| 9972 | BINDER | Brendan Harold | 11.02.1977 | P/O |
| 9973 | GILLMAN | Paul Robert Archer | 11.02.1977 | P/O |
| 9974 | BERRETTA | Paul Emile | 11.02.1977 | P/O |
| 9975 | NEL | Albertus Wynand | 11.02.1977 | P/O |
| 9976 | GRAY | Alasdair David | 14.02.1977 | P/O |
| 9977 | MEDHURST | Bruce | 14.02.1977 | P/O |
| 9978 | DYNE | Leslie | 14.02.1977 | P/O |
| 9979 | HOLDEN | Mark William | 14.02.1977 | P/O |
| 9980 | MULCAHY | Richard Michael | 15.02.1977 | S/O(T) |
| 9981 | McMULLEN | Robert Farlie | 16.02.1977 | S/O |
| 9982 | TAYLOR | Mark Duncan | 05.01.1977 | S/S/O |
| 9983 | ELLIOTT | Kenneth Mark | 17.02.1977 | S/S/O |
| 9984 | COOKE | David Peter | 08.01.1977 | S/O |
| 9985 | DAVIDSON | Neil Alexander | 18.02.1977 | S/O(T) |
| 9986 | HUGHES | Ceiriog | 01.12.1975 | P/O |
| 9987 | Mac GREGOR | Kevin Robin | 21.02.1977 | P/O |
| 9988 | KAYE-EDDIE | Gordon Dudley | 16.07.1975 | S/O(T) |
| 9989 | BROWN | Frederick | 05.01.1976 | P/O |
| 9990 | RUGG | Christopher Stanley | 05.04.1976 | L/S/O |
| 9991 | BROWN | Douglas Robert | 04.10.1976 | S/O |
| 9992 | DIGGES | Christopher Bryan | 26.02.1977 | S/O |
| 9993 | SMITH | Anthony Paul | 28.02.1977 | S/O |
| 9994 | SMITH | Steven John | 23.02.1977 | P/O |
| 9995 | GAVAZZI | Attilio Guido | 01.03.1977 | D/S/O |
| 9996 | MARABANI | Giulio Archimedes | 01.03.1977 | S/O(T) |
| 9997 | McGRAW | John Bruce | 04.10.1976 | S/O |
| 9998 | COLEMAN | Gerald Ian | 02.03.1977 | P/O |
| 9999 | BROWN | Douglas Randolph | 03.03.1977 | L/S/O |
| 10000 | SCHEEPERS | Andrew Trevor | 04.03.1977 | P/O |
| 10001 | BAILLE-COOPER | Mark Graham | 01.03.1977 | P/O |
| 10002 | STEAD | Peter Adam | 08.03.1977 | P/O |
| 10003 | CREIGHTON | Bruce | 09.03.1977 | P/O |
| 10004 | ROFFEY | Simon | 09.03.1977 | P/O |
| 10005 | STOREY | John Holcroft | 10.03.1977 | P/O |
| 10006 | STEDALL | Ian Edward | 10.03.1977 | S/O |
| 10007 | CAMPBELL | Thomas Keith | 15.03.1977 | Insp |
| 10008 | ROBINSON | Craig Steven | 16.03.1977 | P/O |
| 10009 | MILLAR | Thomas Owen | 17.03.1977 | P/O |
| 10010 | STRETTON | Graham Charles | 21.03.1977 | P/O |
| 10011 | ERASMUS | Francois Jacobus | 21.03.1977 | P/O |
| 10012 | PARKIN | Simon Nicholas | 05.04.1976 | P/O |
| 10013 | LUSHINGTON | David Nelson | 04.10.1976 | P/O |
| 10014 | BRUK-JACKSON | Derick Michael | 01.10.1975 | L/S/O |
| 10015 | GROUT | Victor James | 28.03.1975 | Insp(T) |
| 10016 | WILSON | Dennis John | 26.03.1977 | P/O |
| 10017 | BRIDGER | Anthony Talbot | 01.04.1977 | S/O |
| 10018 | SHARPE | Richard Alexander | 01.04.1977 | S/O |
| 10019 | SMITH | David Gilchrist | 02.04.1977 | P/O |
| 10020 | TVERDON | Zoltan | 01.04.1977 | D/S/O |
| 10021 | ROBERTS | Roland Vincent | 01.04.1977 | P/O |
| 10022 | EVANS | David | 01.04.1977 | P/O |
| 10023 | OLDS | Michael Edgar | 01.04.1977 | S/O |
| 10024 | BUTTERWORTH | Warwick Peter | 01.04.1977 | S/O(T) |
| 10025 | LANGAN | Michael L'Lanley | 01.04.1977 | P/O |
| 10026 | SMIT | Trevor Gregory | 01.04.1977 | P/O |
| 10027 | PUSEY | David Frederick | 01.04.1977 | P/O |
| 10028 | BARNES | Ian David | 01.04.1977 | P/O |
| 10029 | WILLIAMS | Shaun | 01.04.1977 | P/O |
| 10030 | SEEDALL | James | 01.04.1977 | P/O |
| 10031 | BOYLE | Stuart Clifford | 01.04.1977 | S/O |
| 10032 | WENTZEL | Eric William | 01.04.1977 | P/O |
| 10033 | HOWARD | Clive Anthony | 01.04.1977 | P/O |
| 10034 | SHARP | Edward George | 04.04.1977 | P/O |
| 10035 | DODGEN | Patrick Terence | 01.04.1977 | S/O(T) |
| 10036 | CLIFFORD | Frederick | 01.04.1977 | Insp(T) |
| 10037 | EDWARDS | David Peter | 03.04.1977 | S/O |
| 10038 | EASTERBROOK | Johan William | 05.04.1976 | P/O |
| 10039 | STEYN | Kevin Raymond | 07.04.1977 | P/O |
| 10040 | TAPSON | Barend Jacobus | 12.04.1977 | P/O |
| 10041 | LUDEKE | Andrew George | 07.04.1977 | S/O(T) |
| 10042 | BASSETT | John Morgan | 12.04.1977 | P/O |
| 10043 | OLIVER | George Xavier | 19.07.1976 | P/O |
| 10044 | CAMERON-DOW | Alan Glenville | 05.01.1976 | P/O |
| 10045 | ROBINSON | Graham Keith | 05.01.1976 | S/O |
| 10046 | WHEELER | Brian Edward | 15.04.1977 | D/P/O |
| 10047 | DE MILITA | Richard Justin | 09.04.1977 | P/O |
| 10048 | KNOTT | Patrick Wayne | 26.04.1977 | P/O |
| 10049 | FOLEY | Ivan | 21.04.1977 | P/O |
| 10050 | DICKEY | Steven Paul | 20.04.1977 | D/S/O |
| 10051 | HADFIELD | Donald Leonard | 02.05.1977 | S/O |
| 10052 | RAAFF | Robert Albert | 02.05.1977 | P/O |
| 10053 | WILLIAMS | Gary David | 02.05.1977 | P/O |
| 10054 | WEATHERALL | Ian William | 02.05.1977 | S/S/O |
| 10055 | MURDOCH | Bruce Andrew | 02.05.1977 | P/O |
| 10056 | BOWKER | Timothy John | 02.05.1977 | P/O |
| 10057 | LAMBON | John | 02.05.1977 | S/O |
| 10058 | MARAIS | Ian | 02.05.1977 | P/O |
| 10059 | KENNAIRD | Peter John | 01.05.1977 | P/O |
| 10060 | PETROU | Paul John | 04.05.1977 | P/O |
| 10061 | BOYD | Melvin Vernon | 12.05.1977 | P/O |
| 10062 | GLAISTER | Andre Antony | 05.01.1976 | P/O |
| 10063 | STAPA | William John | 14.05.1977 | P/O |
| 10064 | GLEN | Douglas Lloyd | 19.05.1977 | S/O |
| 10065 | BREDENKAMP | Peter David | 20.05.1977 | S/O |
| 10066 | HUGHES | Simon Charles | 23.05.1977 | P/O |
| 10067 | ANSON | Antonio Fulton | 24.05.1977 | Insp(T) |
| 10068 | DE ARAUJO | Barrie Colin | 27.05.1977 | Insp |
| 10069 | CAMERON | Norwin Okley | 27.05.1977 | P/O |
| 10070 | HUCKABAY | Dominic Ralph | 01.12.1975 | P/O |
| 10071 | BLACKMORE | Peter Angus | 01.06.1977 | S/S/O |
| 10072 | TIBBITS |  |  |  |
| 10073 | ALLISON | Christopher Gordon | 01.06.1977 | S/S/O |
| 10074 | BECKETT | Jonathan Stewart | 20.07.1976 | P/O |
| 10075 | PLEW | Brian Sidney | 01.06.1977 | S/O(T) |
| 10076 | WHITNEY | Raymond John | 01.06.1977 | P/O |
| 10077 | RANDELL | Mark Murray | 01.06.1977 | P/O |
| 10078 | COETZEE | James | 02.06.1977 | P/O |
| 10079 | ANDROLAKIS | Paul | 03.06.1977 | S/S/O* |
| 10080 | DEAN | Martin Roderick | 19.07.1976 | P/O |
| 10081 | MASON | Peter James | 06.06.1977 | P/O |
| 10082 | HALLER | Alan John | 06.06.1977 | P/O |
| 10083 | McNALLY | Norman Henry | 13.06.1977 | S/O(T) |
| 10084 | MARAIS | Pieter Ernst | 16.06.1977 | P/O |
| 10085 | BRISTOW | Peter John | 05.01.1976 | S/O |
| 10086 | KENNAIRD | Duncan George | 05.01.1976 | S/O |
| 10087 | DILL-RUSSELL | Robert Gavin | 19.07.1976 | S/O |
| 10088 | LOWEIN | Trevor John | 22.06.1977 | P/O |
| 10089 | SAMSON | Malcolm Robert | 23.06.1977 | P/O |
| 10090 | HOLLAND | Owen Charles | 05.01.1976 | P/O |
| 10091 | FREER | Steven Charles | 08.01.1976 | P/O |
| 10092 | PITMAN | Steven Michael | 25.06.1977 | P/O |
| 10093 | SWEMMER | Roy Allan | 27.06.1977 | P/O |
| 10094 | MALES | Paul Michael | 05.01.1976 | P/O |
| 10095 | SMITH | Christopher Alan | 05.01.1976 | P/O |
| 10096 | EVANS | Leslie John | 29.06.1977 | P/O |
| 10097 | SMITHDORF | Stephen Dale | 29.06.1977 | P/O |
| 10098 | SMITH | Bryan George | 05.01.1976 | S/O |
| 10099 | WIGHAM | Keith | 01.07.1977 | Insp(T) |
| 10100 | BORLAND | David Graham | 08.01.1976 | S/O(T) |
| 10101 | ALLAN | Jeremy James | 05.01.1976 | P/O |
| 10102 | SMITH | David Anthony | 05.01.1976 | P/O |
| 10103 | CHAPPELL | Stephen John | 05.01.1976 | P/O |
| 10104 | MARTIN | Terence Joseph | 05.01.1976 | S/O(T) |
| 10105 | BEER | William Thomas | 01.07.1977 | C/Ins(T) |
| 10106 | NEWTON | James John | 01.07.1977 | P/O |
| 10107 | PAYNE | David William | 04.07.1977 | P/O |
| 10108 | WENTZEL | Graham Frank | 04.07.1977 | P/O |
| 10109 | KNOTT | Robert George | 04.07.1977 | P/O |
| 10110 | BURKE | Eamonn Francis | 04.07.1977 | S/S/O |
| 10111 | VON BROEMBSEN | Dennis George | 04.07.1977 | P/O |
| 10112 | FODEN | Richard Lockett | 04.07.1977 | P/O |
| 10113 | BLANDEN | Michael Robert | 04.07.1977 | S/O |
| 10114 | SQUIER | Martin James | 04.07.1977 | P/O |
| 10115 | MACKINTOSH | David Synnott | 04.07.1977 | S/O |
| 10116 | MACKINTOSH | Bruce Hamilton | 04.07.1977 | P/O |
| 10117 | PENNY | Douglas Haig | 04.07.1977 | P/O |
| 10118 | MACKINTOSH | Ian Charles | 04.07.1977 | P/O |
| 10119 | MILLER | Daniel | 04.07.1977 | Insp(T) |
| 10120 | BERRY | Peter Stephen | 07.07.1977 | P/O |
| 10121 | Mac GREGOR | Michael | 09.07.1977 | P/O |
| 10122 | DUNCAN | David Sheridan | 13.07.1977 | P/O |
| 10123 | BLAIR-BROWN | Timothy | 12.07.1977 | Insp |
| 10124 | ARMSTRONG | Donald Robert | 13.07.1977 | S/O |
| 10125 | CROWTHER | Steven John | 13.07.1977 | S/O(T) |
| 10126 | EBURNE | Michael Keith | 10.07.1977 | S/O(T) |
| 10127 | O'NEILL | Rory John | 14.07.1977 | P/O |
| 10128 | ALEXANDER | Glen Michael | 15.07.1977 | D/P/O |
| 10129 | KEMPEN | Shane | 18.07.1977 | P/O |
| 10130 | CLOETE | Robert Donald | 23.07.1977 | S/O(T) |
| 10131 | FRENCH | Guy Ronald | 27.07.1977 | P/O |
| 10132 | PATTISON | Michael Anthony | 01.07.1977 | S/O(T) |
| 10133 | BOYES | Kevin Patrick | 29.07.1977 | S/O(T) |
| 10134 | PERRY | Stephen Guy | 01.08.1977 | Insp |
| 10135 | SANTOWSKI | Kevin Robert | 01.08.1977 | P/O |
| 10136 | BICKMORE | Brian Ernest | 01.08.1977 | S/O(T) |
| 10137 | BAGGOT | John Ernest | 01.08.1977 | S/O(T) |
| 10138 | NORTJE | John Hugh | 10.07.1977 | P/O |
| 10139 | GRAY | Paul Douglas | 01.08.1977 | Insp(T) |
| 10140 | BOOTH | Kevin David | 01.08.1977 | P/O |
| 10141 | KIDWELL | Garry Brian | 01.08.1977 | P/O |

# BSAP Nominal Roll • Men

| No. | Surname | First Name(s) | Rank | Date |
|---|---|---|---|---|
| 10142 | SWANEPOEL | Stephanus Johannes | P/O | 01.08.1977 |
| 10143 | MENNELL | Richard | P/O | 04.08.1977 |
| 10144 | KEEFER | David Scott | S/O | 05.08.1977 |
| 10145 | HUDSON | Anthony William | P/O | 06.08.1977 |
| 10146 | RISCHBIETER | Paul Carl | P/O | 06.08.1977 |
| 10147 | VAN STADEN | Ernest John | P/O | 11.08.1977 |
| 10148 | COUTTS | Andrew John | S/O(T) | 12.08.1977 |
| 10149 | GIBSON | Arthur Birch | P/O | 15.08.1977 |
| 10150 | OTT | Friedrich Karl | D/S/O | 04.10.1976 |
| 10151 | WILKIN | William Ian | D/Insp | 19.08.1977 |
| 10152 | CARVALHO | Raul Dos Santos | P/O | 22.08.1977 |
| 10153 | SCHULTZ | Alan Bruce | P/O | 21.08.1977 |
| 10154 | HAWKINS | George Edward | P/O | 23.08.1977 |
| 10155 | DEWEY | Richard William | P/O | 25.08.1977 |
| 10156 | TAYLOR | Michael Anthony | S/O(T) | 29.08.1977 |
| 10157 | LAMONT | Ian | P/O | 29.08.1977 |
| 10158 | GRATER | Neville David | S/O(T) | 01.09.1977 |
| 10159 | AZEVEDO | Jose Antonio | D/S/O | 01.09.1977 |
| 10160 | MAWBY | Anthony Christopher | S/O(T) | 01.09.1977 |
| 10161 | SHERMAN | Russell John | P/O | 06.09.1977 |
| 10162 | FITCH | Colin Raymond | S/O(T) | 07.09.1977 |
| 10163 | DARNEY | Gareth Adrian | P/O | 19.07.1976 |
| 10164 | PISTORIUS | Kevin Arnold | P/O | 09.09.1977 |
| 10165 | MORDT | Hans Ludvig | P/O | 05.04.1976 |
| 10166 | CANTLE | Bruce | S/O | 05.04.1976 |
| 10167 | HEARNS | John Leonard | P/O | 13.09.1977 |
| 10168 | EVANS | Robert Malcolm | P/O | 04.01.1977 |
| 10169 | ROELOFSE | Paul Henry | S/O | 04.01.1977 |
| 10170 | LOUW | Jan Abraham | S/O | 19.09.1977 |
| 10171 | SMITH | Philip Joseph | S/O(T) | 19.09.1977 |
| 10172 | SIDDALL | Andrew | D/S/O | 20.09.1977 |
| 10173 | WESSELS | Peter Barnard | S/O | 05.04.1976 |
| 10174 | KOTZE | Christo | P/O | 04.01.1977 |
| 10175 | MANSELL | Trevor Talbot | P/O | 05.04.1976 |
| 10176 | STITTIG | Hans-Karl | D/S/O | 28.09.1977 |
| 10177 | WRIGHT | Hugh Robert | S/S/O | 05.04.1976 |
| 10178 | HAWKES | Roger Stuart | P/O | 05.04.1976 |
| 10179 | KLEYHANS | Stanley Peter | P/O | 02.10.1977 |
| 10180 | PEAD | Raymond Derek | P/O | 01.10.1977 |
| 10181 | MITCHELL | Irwin Patrick | P/O | 03.10.1977 |
| 10182 | BATTERSHILL | David George | P/O | 03.10.1977 |
| 10183 | MULLINS | Shane Edward | P/O | 03.10.1977 |
| 10184 | IRELAND | Victor Arthur | P/O | 03.10.1977 |
| 10185 | RAUSCH | Derek Michael | P/O | 03.10.1977 |
| 10186 | HUGHES | Andrew Phillip | P/O | 04.01.1977 |
| 10187 | FISHER | Michael Charles | P/O | 10.10.1977 |
| 10188 | SHAW | Patrick John | S/O(T) | 10.10.1977 |
| 10189 | BAKER | Dudley Alan | S/O | 04.01.1977 |
| 10190 | BATH | Gary Michael | P/O | 13.10.1977 |
| 10191 | LOMBARD | Andre | Insp(T) | 16.10.1977 |
| 10192 | VERWEY | Frans Johannes | P/O | 18.10.1977 |
| 10193 | WENTZEL | Michael Winston | Insp(T) | 25.10.1977 |
| 10194 | MANNING | Clive Stewart | D/S/O | 25.10.1977 |
| 10195 | LE GUERN | Roger David | Insp | 04.01.1977 |
| 10196 | WESTROP | Peter Graham | P/O | 19.07.1976 |
| 10197 | GRIFFITHS | David Melville | P/O | 04.01.1977 |
| 10198 | WINTERBOTTOM | Douglas Victor | P/O | 30.10.1977 |
| 10199 | FRIESEN | Brent Warren | P/O | 03.11.1977 |
| 10200 | KUSPERT | Brian Derek | P/O | 04.11.1977 |
| 10201 | CLARKE | Kevin Michael | P/O | 07.11.1977 |
| 10202 | JACKSON | Raymond | S/O(T) | 07.11.1977 |
| 10203 | STANYON | Nigel Derek | Insp(T) | 08.11.1977 |
| 10204 | BULLEN | Michael Winston | Insp | 19.07.1976 |
| 10205 | GARDINER | James Roland | P/O | 09.11.1977 |
| 10206 | BRADLEY | Leigh James | P/O | 14.11.1977 |
| 10207 | KEMP | Robert Gordon | P/O | 04.01.1977 |
| 10208 | PRETORIUS | Noel John | P/O | 21.11.1977 |
| 10209 | HUTCHISON | James William | S/O | 22.11.1977 |
| 10211 | GROSE | Christopher Penn | Insp(T) | 28.11.1977 |
| 10212 | BRAKSPEAR | Ian Donald | P/O | 29.11.1977 |
| 10213 | WELCH | Clifford Douglas | D/P/O | 29.11.1977 |
| 10214 | WYNN | Gareth Rowland | P/O | 29.11.1977 |
| 10215 | NEL | Jacob Jacobus | P/O | 29.11.1977 |
| 10216 | GROBLER | Christopher | P/O | 29.11.1977 |
| 10217 | QUIRK | Gary Thelwell | P/O | 29.11.1977 |
| 10218 | LANDSEY | Richard Kendall | P/O | 29.11.1977 |
| 10219 | HANSON | Steven John | P/O | 29.11.1977 |
| 10220 | ANSTEY | Stephen | P/O | 29.11.1977 |
| 10221 | ROUSSEAU | Mark Thomas | P/O | 29.11.1977 |
| 10222 | DYER | David Peter | P/O | 29.11.1977 |
| 10223 | POULTER | Clive Howard | P/O | 29.11.1977 |
| 10224 | COLE | Nigel Raymond | P/O | 29.11.1977 |
| 10225 | STEVENSON | Philip | P/O | 29.11.1977 |
| 10226 | SMITH | Alan David | S/O(T) | 29.11.1977 |
| 10227 | FAIRBRIDGE-CURRIE | James | P/O | 29.11.1977 |
| 10228 | RONNIE | Alastair David | P/O | 29.11.1977 |
| 10229 | ALMOND | Stephen | P/O | 29.11.1977 |
| 10230 | HOFF | Kenneth | D/S/O | 29.11.1977 |
| 10231 | WILLIAMS | Brian | P/O | 29.11.1977 |
| 10232 | HARRIS | John Digby | P/O | 29.11.1977 |
| 10233 | BLUNDELL | Howard Brian | P/O | 29.11.1977 |
| 10234 | DE KOK | Stewart John | P/O | 29.11.1977 |
| 10235 | MEYER | Marthinus Phillipus | P/O | 30.11.1977 |
| 10236 | FRANKE | Johan Anthony | D/Insp | 01.12.1977 |
| 10237 | WATKINS | Lionel Robert | P/O | 04.01.1977 |
| 10238 | SINCLAIR | Neville Wayne | P/O | 01.12.1977 |
| 10239 | CREAN | John | | Still serving |
| 10240 | PYTLIK | Frank | Insp(T) | 02.12.1977 |
| 10241 | GROBLER | Paul Jacobbus | P/O | 04.01.1977 |
| 10242 | HILL | Robert Frank | S/O | 05.12.1977 |
| 10243 | MARSH-BROWN | John Charles | S/O | 04.01.1977 |
| 10244 | McWADE | Garry Lance | S/O | 09.12.1977 |
| 10245 | BOTHA | Ian | S/O(T) | 09.12.1977 |
| 10246 | RUSSELL | Murray | D/Insp | 12.12.1977 |
| 10247 | BAILEY | Peter | S/O(T) | 12.12.1977 |
| 10248 | McMAHON | Phillip Francis | S/O | 14.12.1977 |
| 10249 | LIEBERMAN | Peter Allan | S/O(T) | 19.12.1977 |
| 10250 | GREGSON | Ian Paul | S/O | 19.07.1976 |
| 10251 | DEARY | Mark Robert | P/O | 04.01.1977 |
| 10252 | SMITH | Russell Glynn | P/O | 08.12.1977 |
| 10253 | HOOK | Mark Errol | P/O | 29.12.1977 |
| 10254 | DE JONG | Eric George | P/O | 29.12.1977 |
| 10255 | MORRIS | David Edwin | P/O | 29.12.1977 |
| 10256 | PITT | Gary Robert | P/O | 29.12.1977 |
| 10257 | RYCROFT | Gerald Richard | P/O | 29.12.1977 |
| 10258 | JONES | David Hugh | P/O | 29.12.1977 |
| 10259 | DOWD | Stephen Paul | P/O | 29.12.1977 |
| 10260 | NIENABER | Ben Hermanus | P/O | 29.12.1977 |
| 10261 | EGLETON | William Lindsay | P/O | 29.12.1977 |
| 10262 | GENARI | Peter Stewart | P/O | 29.12.1977 |
| 10263 | BEWES | Nicholas Michael | P/O | 29.12.1977 |
| 10264 | KURZ | Norman Clive | P/O | 29.12.1977 |
| 10265 | DOVE | Mitchell Gavin | P/O | 29.12.1977 |
| 10266 | COLLINS | Jeffrey Robert | P/O | 29.12.1977 |
| 10267 | BROMLEY | Pierre Conrad | P/O | 29.12.1977 |
| 10268 | CONSTANTINOU | George Charalambos | P/O | 29.12.1977 |
| 10269 | MARTIN | Gary Percy | P/O | 29.12.1977 |
| 10270 | FICK | Lourens Marthinus | P/O | 29.12.1977 |
| 10271 | PURCELL-GILPIN | Giles Anthony | P/O | 29.12.1977 |
| 10272 | BELL | Cyril John Johan | P/O | 29.12.1977 |
| 10273 | FLEMING | Alexander Henderson | P/O | 29.12.1977 |
| 10274 | GARZONIS | Dimitrious | P/O | 29.12.1977 |
| 10275 | WARD | Simon Charles | P/O | 29.12.1977 |
| 10276 | BINNS-WARD | Neville Patrick | P/O | 29.12.1977 |
| 10277 | MASTERSON | Gavin Michael | P/O | 29.12.1977 |
| 10278 | WILKINSON | Brett Gregory | P/O | 29.12.1977 |
| 10280 | PATERSON | Ian Alexander | S/O | 29.12.1977 |
| 10281 | ARMSTRONG | Russell Dunbar | S/O | 29.12.1977 |
| 10282 | DALLA PRIA | Giorgio | P/O | 29.12.1977 |
| 10283 | BRYAN | Gordon Phillip | P/O | 29.12.1977 |
| 10284 | BURTON | Phillip | D/Insp | 29.12.1977 |
| 10285 | LANGLOIS | Paul George | P/O | 29.12.1977 |
| 10286 | MORRISON | Niall | P/O | 29.12.1977 |
| 10287 | SNOW | Edward Charles | S/O | 29.12.1977 |
| 10288 | NEILL | Ian Clark | P/O | 29.12.1977 |
| 10289 | CONNELLY | Kenneth Michael | P/O | 29.12.1977 |
| 10290 | DAILLECOURT | Maxim Eugene | D/Insp | 29.12.1977 |
| 10291 | SALMON | Andrew | P/O | 29.12.1977 |
| 10292 | NISH | Graeme | P/O | 29.12.1977 |
| 10293 | ERVINE | Neil Brink | P/O | 29.12.1977 |
| 10294 | MUTZURIS | Constantine | P/O | 29.12.1977 |
| 10295 | CRAUSE | Ian Barry | P/O | 29.12.1977 |
| 10296 | GRANT | Alan Francis | P/O | 29.12.1977 |
| 10297 | PITZER | Gary Peter | P/O | 29.12.1977 |
| 10298 | JORDAN | Mark Jonathan | P/O | 29.12.1977 |
| 10299 | JOHNSON | Mark Lee | D/Insp | 30.12.1977 |
| 10300 | MITROVITCH | Trevor leslie | D/Insp | 30.12.1977 |
| 10301 | WHEELER | Ian Thomas | P/O | 19.07.1976 |
| 10302 | SINCLAIR | Ian Wishart | P/O | 04.01.1977 |
| 10303 | LEE | Keith Ralph | C/Insp(T) | 04.01.1978 |
| 10304 | BURTON | Charles Brian | S/O | 05.01.1978 |
| 10305 | SELKIRK | Charles Frederick | S/O | 05.01.1978 |
| 10306 | SHARMAN | Paul William | P/O | 05.01.1978 |
| 10307 | DALE | John Roden | P/O | 05.01.1978 |
| 10308 | BURT | George | P/O | 05.01.1978 |
| 10309 | BELL | John Richard | P/O | 05.01.1978 |
| 10310 | DICKER | Michael Ian | P/O | 05.01.1978 |
| 10311 | DE GRANDHOMME | Maurice | S/O | 05.01.1978 |
| 10312 | HILLIER | Robin Glenn | S/O | 05.01.1978 |
| 10313 | JOHNSON-HILL | David Linden | S/O | 05.01.1978 |
| 10314 | JOHNSTON | Cullam Ross | S/O | 05.01.1978 |
| 10315 | MARKS | Andrew Phillip | P/O | 05.01.1978 |
| 10316 | PYKE | Ian Charles | P/O | 05.01.1978 |
| 10317 | TAYLOR | Michael William | P/O | 05.01.1978 |
| 10318 | PREST | Gary Craig | P/O | 05.01.1978 |
| 10319 | TAYLOR | Christopher Paul | P/O | 05.01.1978 |
| 10320 | TULLY | Rohan Peter | P/O | 05.01.1978 |
| 10321 | TEMPLE | Michael Anthony | P/O | 05.01.1978 |
| 10322 | THOMES | Andrew Gordon | P/O | 05.01.1978 |
| 10323 | STRETTON | Andrew Charles | S/O | 05.01.1978 |
| 10324 | CROUCAMP | Derek Anthony | S/O | 05.01.1978 |
| 10325 | CRAMP | Duncan Ian | S/O | 05.01.1978 |
| 10326 | MENEGALDO | Lorenzo Ruggero | P/O | 05.01.1978 |
| 10327 | WAITE | Terrence Patrick | P/O | 05.01.1978 |
| 10328 | ROUSSEAU | David Christopher | P/O | 05.01.1978 |
| 10329 | SMYTH | William Richard | S/S/O | 05.01.1978 |
| 10330 | HUSBAND | Michael Ian | P/O | 05.01.1978 |
| 10331 | DAVIDSON | Gary Douglas | S/O | 05.01.1978 |
| 10332 | COOPER | Gavin | P/O | 05.01.1978 |
| 10333 | ADIE | Graham Richard | P/O | 05.01.1978 |
| 10334 | PROSSER-GOLDING | David Douglas | P/O | 05.01.1978 |
| 10335 | WAYWELL | David William | P/O | 05.01.1978 |
| 10336 | KERSTEN | Michael Maria | P/O | 05.01.1978 |
| 10337 | KENNY | Colin Francis | P/O | 05.01.1978 |
| 10338 | WIGSTON | Michael Harry | P/O | 05.01.1978 |
| 10339 | RADLOFF | Michael Edward | S/O | 05.01.1978 |
| 10340 | LOCK | Martin Ingram | P/O | 05.01.1978 |
| 10341 | BOTHA | Abraham Lodewikus | P/O | 05.01.1978 |
| 10342 | HARDY | Gregory Peter | P/O | 05.01.1978 |
| 10343 | FYFE | Anthony Cecil | P/O | 05.01.1978 |
| 10344 | CURLE | Robin Patrick | P/O | 05.01.1978 |
| 10345 | HOLLAND | Richard Stephen | P/O | 05.01.1978 |
| 10346 | WEST | Michael William | P/O | 05.01.1978 |
| 10347 | REECE | Quinton | P/O | 06.01.1978 |
| 10348 | ADAMS | David Rowan | S/O | |

| No. | Surname | First Names | Date | Rank |
|---|---|---|---|---|
| 10349 | HILL | Lindsay Edward | 09.01.1978 | S/S/O |
| 10350 | HAMILTON | Keith Daniel | 10.01.1978 | P/O |
| 10351 | BEZUIDENHOUT | Barend Jacobus | 13.01.1978 | P/O |
| 10352 | BANKS | Julian Richard | 15.01.1978 | P/O |
| 10353 | FORTESCUE | John Stewart | 15.01.1978 | D/P/O |
| 10354 | VAN DYK | James | 16.01.1978 | P/O |
| 10355 | DORRINGTON | Neville Gerhard | 15.01.1978 | S/S/O |
| 10356 | FREYMARK | Stephen George | 04.01.1977 | P/O |
| 10357 | STANFIELD | Christopher Anthony | 23.01.1978 | P/O |
| 10358 | TROLLOPE | Charles Leslie | 30.01.1978 | P/O |
| 10359 | DAVENPORT | Trevor David | 30.01.1978 | P/O |
| 10360 | MEAKLIM | George William | 30.01.1978 | S/S/O |
| 10361 | WILLIAMS | Bryn Alwyn | 30.01.1978 | Supt |
| 10362 | WILSON | Peter James | 30.01.1978 | Supt |
| 10363 | WATTS | Rodney Thomas | 30.01.1978 | P/O |
| 10364 | COLLEN | Robert Eastland | 30.01.1978 | D/S/O |
| 10365 | PARKER | Ashley Francis | 30.01.1978 | P/O |
| 10366 | TOOHEY | Robert | 30.01.1978 | P/O |
| 10367 | PEREPECZKO | Charles Vieslav | 30.01.1978 | S/S/O |
| 10368 | COOKE | Grimwood Peter | 30.01.1978 | P/O |
| 10369 | BELLAMY | Andrew John | 30.01.1978 | P/O |
| 10370 | BRADNICK | Clive Ian | 30.01.1978 | P/O |
| 10371 | FLOYD | Keith Martin | 30.01.1978 | P/O |
| 10372 | WALPOLE | Michael | 30.01.1978 | P/O |
| 10373 | ROSSITER | Peter Lewis | 30.01.1978 | P/O |
| 10374 | TUCKER | Henry Stephen | 30.01.1978 | P/O |
| 10375 | NICOLAIDIS | Constantine | 30.01.1978 | P/O |
| 10376 | BOYD-MOSS | Duncan Richard | 30.01.1978 | P/O |
| 10377 | EDDEN | David Michael | 30.01.1978 | D/P/O |
| 10378 | THOMPSON | Graham Eric | 30.01.1978 | P/O |
| 10379 | BARLOW | John Kennedy | 30.01.1978 | P/O |
| 10380 | SMEDA | Kevin Mark | 30.01.1978 | P/O |
| 10381 | KUROWSKI | Henry Mark | 30.01.1978 | P/O |
| 10382 | HILL | Robert Grant | 30.01.1978 | P/O |
| 10383 | SUTHERNS | Geoffrey David | 30.01.1978 | P/O |
| 10384 | GEDDES | Philip | 30.01.1978 | P/O |
| 10385 | HEFFER | Owen Brian | 30.01.1978 | P/O |
| 10386 | GRAHAM | Anthony Mark | 30.01.1978 | P/O |
| 10387 | HACKING | Bernard Anthony | 30.01.1978 | P/O |
| 10388 | MOORE | Lawrence Henry | 30.01.1978 | P/O |
| 10389 | STRYDOM | Roelf Jan | 30.01.1978 | S/O |
| 10390 | DUFFIELD | Mark David | 30.01.1978 | P/O |
| 10391 | TRYBUS | Bruce Michael | 30.01.1978 | P/O |
| 10392 | COX | Davis Hilary | 30.01.1978 | P/O |
| 10393 | Mac LAURIN | Colin John | 30.01.1978 | P/O |
| 10394 | JONES | Michael Bernard | 30.01.1978 | P/O |
| 10395 | EVANS | Paul Robert | 30.01.1978 | P/O |
| 10396 | BALMER | Christopher Hamish | 30.01.1978 | P/O |
| 10397 | DAL GARNO | Ian | 05.02.1978 | P/O |
| 10398 | READ | Olaf James | 06.02.1978 | P/O |
| 10399 | BARFORD | Trevor Valentine | 30.01.1978 | P/O |
| 10400 | O'CONNELL | Dermot Anthony | 30.01.1978 | Insp(T) |
| 10401 | Gardiner | Gardiner | 01.02.1978 | P/O |
| 10402 | McDOWELL | Nigel Roy | 02.02.1978 | S/O(T) |
| 10403 | CLEMENTS | Graham | 04.01.1977 | P/O |
| 10404 | CARPENTER | Timothy John | 04.01.1978 | P/O |
| 10405 | PRESTON | John Ashworth | 04.01.1978 | P/O |
| 10406 | TINGLE | Mark Newson | 04.01.1978 | P/O |
| 10407 | CHAPMAN | Tertius | 04.02.1978 | S/O |
| 10408 | PRETORIUS | Gavin Christopher | 05.02.1978 | P/O |
| 10409 | SMITH | Graham Clifford | 06.02.1978 | P/O |
| 10410 | MOSSMAN | Chrisjan Menze | 06.02.1978 | P/O |
| 10411 | BOTHA | Alfred Frederick | 06.02.1978 | S/O |
| 10412 | SWANEPOEL | Wayne Peter | 06.02.1978 | P/O |
| 10413 | BUSHELL | Brian Malcolm | 06.02.1978 | P/O |
| 10414 | WHEAL | David John | 06.02.1978 | P/O |
| 10415 | WOOD | Brain James | 06.02.1978 | S/O |
| 10416 | LAWSON | Adrian Edward | 06.02.1978 | S/O |
| 10417 | OSTERLOH | John Michael | 06.02.1978 | P/O |
| 10418 | MARTIN | Graham Douglas | 06.02.1978 | P/O |
| 10419 | DERRY | Michael John | 06.02.1978 | P/O |
| 10420 | IMPEY | Garth | 06.02.1978 | Insp(T) |
| 10421 | BAILEY | Stuart | 06.02.1978 | P/O |
| 10422 | GILLIES | Stephen Hall | 06.02.1978 | P/O |
| 10423 | WHEELER | Bernard Paul | 06.02.1978 | P/O |
| 10424 | VAN DER HEIJDEN | Derek Paul | 06.02.1978 | P/O |
| 10425 | GOWANS | Dudley Lester | 06.02.1978 | P/O |
| 10426 | DIX | David Moffat | 06.02.1978 | P/O |
| 10427 | Mac INTYRE | Neil Andrew | 06.02.1978 | P/O |
| 10428 | ISIKSON | Michael David | 06.02.1978 | P/O |
| 10429 | SPENCER | Stephen John | 06.02.1978 | P/O |
| 10430 | LEA | Steven Alexander | 06.02.1978 | P/O |
| 10431 | McINTOSH | Mark Anthony | 06.02.1978 | S/O |
| 10432 | HOPKINS | Anthony Michael | 06.02.1978 | P/O |
| 10433 | OLIVER | Andrew Jonathan | 06.02.1978 | P/O |
| 10434 | BIJL | John Ivan | 06.02.1978 | P/O |
| 10435 | WASPE | Rory Robert | 06.02.1978 | P/O |
| 10436 | McGEE | Gavin John | 06.02.1978 | P/O |
| 10437 | McLEMAN | Paul | 06.02.1978 | P/O |
| 10438 | HERRMAN | Colin Campbell | 06.02.1978 | P/O |
| 10439 | Mac PHAIL | Ian | 06.02.1978 | P/O |
| 10440 | VAN MOEKERKEN | Campbell John | 06.02.1978 | P/O |
| 10441 | JAMIESON | Nicholas Wynand | 06.02.1978 | P/O |
| 10442 | VAN WYK | Simon Robert | 06.02.1978 | S/S/O |
| 10443 | CARTER | Lincoln Noel | 06.02.1978 | P/O |
| 10444 | REES | Vincent John | 06.02.1978 | P/O |
| 10445 | CONLON | Herman Ferdinand | 06.02.1978 | P/O |
| 10446 | ROHM | Gerald Leo | 06.02.1978 | P/O |
| 10447 | FINCHAM | Michael Frederick | 06.02.1978 | P/O |
| 10448 | GREEN | David Michael | 06.02.1978 | P/O |
| 10449 | TRIGGS | Phillip James | 06.02.1978 | P/O |
| 10450 | NICHOLSON | Robin Christopher | 06.02.1978 | P/O |
| 10451 | SOUTHEY | Desmond | 06.02.1978 | P/O |
| 10452 | LINDENBERG | Albert Roy | 06.02.1978 | P/O |
| 10453 | HILL | Garth | 06.02.1978 | P/O |
| 10454 | BOTTON | Ivor Blaise Lloyd | 06.02.1978 | P/O |
| 10455 | JONES | Roy Van | 06.02.1978 | P/O |
| 10456 | FULTON | Frederick Luka | 09.02.1978 | P/O |
| 10457 | CAR | Charles Montgomery | 09.02.1978 | P/O |
| 10458 | WILSENACH | Johannes Hendrik | 04.01.1978 | P/O |
| 10459 | VAN DER SANDE | Alain Colin | 04.01.1978 | P/O |
| 10460 | PRENTICE | Rodney Allan | 04.01.1978 | S/O |
| 10461 | JENNINGS | Christopher Stephen | 09.02.1978 | P/O |
| 10462 | JONES | Michael Clifford | 09.02.1978 | P/O |
| 10463 | ATTWELL | David Christopher | 04.01.1977 | P/O |
| 10464 | RUSHWORTH | Petrus Jacobus | 14.02.1978 | S/O(T) |
| 10465 | OLIVIER | Andre | 16.02.1978 | S/O(T) |
| 10466 | GROENEWALD | Craig John | 18.02.1978 | P/O |
| 10467 | VILJOEN | Ross Yule | 20.02.1978 | S/O |
| 10468 | BICCARD | Andries Mattheus | 25.02.1978 | S/O |
| 10469 | DICKS | Thomas | 01.03.1978 | S/O(T) |
| 10470 | TEMPLE | David Allen | 02.03.1978 | S/O(T) |
| 10471 | DE GOEDE | Peter Hercules | 08.03.1978 | D/S/O |
| 10472 | PALMER | Stephen | 10.03.1978 | P/O |
| 10473 | BOWEN | Trevor Hugh | 10.03.1978 | S/S/O |
| 10474 | TIBBITS | Stephen Peter | 10.03.1978 | P/O |
| 10475 | MAARTENS | Darrell John | 10.03.1978 | P/O |
| 10476 | MARNELL | Charles Jesse | 10.03.1978 | P/O |
| 10477 | MITCHELL | Robert Charles | 10.03.1978 | P/O |
| 10478 | REES | Christopher | 10.03.1978 | S/O |
| 10479 | COPCUTT | Lance Tarnow | 10.03.1978 | D/P/O |
| 10480 | LIGHTLEY | Marc Gordon | 10.03.1978 | P/O |
| 10481 | EVERSHED | John Patrick | 10.03.1978 | S/O |
| 10482 | WESSELS | Marc Montag | 10.03.1978 | S/S/O |
| 10483 | WRIGHT | | 10.03.1978 | S/O |
| 10484 | DE BRUIN | | 10.03.1978 | P/O |
| 10485 | Mac PHERSON | Alexander Barrie | 10.03.1978 | S/O |
| 10486 | MONOYOUDIS | Frederick Dimitri | 10.03.1978 | P/O |
| 10487 | PULLEN | Keith Kenneth | 10.03.1978 | P/O |
| 10488 | BATSTONE | Markham John | 10.03.1978 | D/S/O |
| 10489 | REEVE | David Francis | 10.03.1978 | P/O |
| 10490 | SHAWE | Allen Bayley | 10.03.1978 | P/O |
| 10491 | SHIFF | Simon | 10.03.1978 | P/O |
| 10492 | WALDEK | Keith Raymond | 10.03.1978 | P/O |
| 10493 | WHITWELL | David Grant | 10.03.1978 | P/O |
| 10494 | FISHER | Robert | 10.03.1978 | P/O |
| 10495 | FITZGERALD | John Peter | 13.03.1978 | S/O(T) |
| 10496 | DOUGLAS | Ian | 13.03.1978 | S/O(T) |
| 10497 | BUTLER | Peter Nigel | 04.01.1977 | P/O |
| 10498 | STEYN | Andre Colin | 04.01.1977 | P/O |
| 10499 | MORRIS | Bevan John | 04.01.1977 | S/O(T) |
| 10500 | JOUGHIN | Paul Jonathan | 04.01.1977 | P/O |
| 10501 | BURMEISTER | Garth Robert | 04.10.1976 | S/O |
| 10502 | ROSS | David James | 04.10.1976 | P/O |
| 10503 | BEALE | Joseph Thomas | 22.03.1978 | P/O |
| 10504 | CONRADIE | Willem Daniel | 23.03.1978 | P/O |
| 10505 | ASPREY | Richard Nigel | 04.10.1976 | P/O |
| 10506 | CHILD | Norman Howard | 04.01.1977 | P/O |
| 10507 | COMBERBACH | Paul Stephen | 04.01.1977 | P/O |
| 10508 | CLOETE | Richard | 12.04.1978 | P/O |
| 10509 | BROWN | Ian Campbell | 04.01.1977 | P/O |
| 10510 | PARKIN | Gary George | 04.01.1977 | P/O |
| 10511 | MORTON | Clive Reginald | 17.04.1978 | Insp(T) |
| 10512 | MORLEY | David Andrew | 16.04.1978 | P/O |
| 10513 | STONES | David George | 20.04.1978 | P/O |
| 10514 | MERDJAN | Robert Elie | 20.04.1978 | P/O |
| 10515 | WILKINS | Grant John | 20.04.1978 | P/O |
| 10516 | STOCKILL | David Francis | 20.04.1978 | P/O |
| 10517 | RENDER | Malvyn Douglas | 20.04.1978 | P/O |
| 10518 | RISKOWITZ | Calvin David | 20.04.1978 | P/O |
| 10519 | COOKE | Paul James | 20.04.1978 | P/O |
| 10520 | HARRIS | Raymond Hilton | 20.04.1978 | P/O |
| 10521 | GRAHAM | Brian Norman | 20.04.1978 | S/S/O |
| 10522 | LOWEN | Trevor John | 20.04.1978 | P/O |
| 10523 | VAN WYK | Leon Johannes | 20.04.1978 | P/O |
| 10524 | COLIN | Leonard Rex | 20.04.1978 | L/S/O |
| 10525 | BULPITT | Gavid Adrian | 20.04.1978 | P/O |
| 10526 | MOORE | Wayne Hugh | 20.04.1978 | P/O |
| 10527 | SAWYER | Malcolm Hugh | 20.04.1978 | P/O |
| 10528 | HARRISON | John Charles | 20.04.1978 | P/O |
| 10529 | KYDD | Charles Hamilton | 20.04.1978 | P/O |
| 10530 | LINDSAY | Kenneth Stewart | 20.04.1978 | P/O |
| 10531 | LAWRANCE | Ralph Hugh | 20.04.1978 | P/O |
| 10532 | PILLANS | David Reid | 20.04.1978 | S/S/O |
| 10533 | WILSON | Allan | 20.04.1978 | P/O |
| 10534 | CLARKE | Kevin Perry | 20.04.1978 | S/S/O |
| 10535 | TRIGG | Robert John | 20.04.1978 | S/O |
| 10536 | RUDGE | Charles Henry | 20.04.1978 | S/O |
| 10537 | BEECHAM | Leigh David | 20.04.1978 | S/O(T) |
| 10538 | WATT | Roy John | 20.04.1978 | S/O |
| 10539 | WHATMAN | Kevin Richard | 20.04.1978 | u/k |
| 10540 | LANDAU | Alan Philip | 20.04.1978 | P/O |
| 10541 | OLIVIER | Wilheim | 20.04.1978 | P/O |
| 10542 | GLOYNE | Michael Keith | 20.04.1978 | P/O |
| 10543 | LENDRUM | Kevin Johannes | 20.04.1978 | P/O |
| 10544 | VIVIER | Jonathan David | 20.04.1978 | P/O |
| 10545 | MUNRO | Rodger James | 20.04.1978 | P/O |
| 10546 | O'DRISCOLL | Noel Sydney | 19.04.1978 | S/O |
| 10547 | LINKLATER | Michael Anthony | 20.04.1978 | P/O |
| 10548 | VERNON | Simon Jeremy | 21.04.1978 | P/O |
| 10549 | Mac LACHLAN | Charles Brett | 27.04.1978 | S/O |
| 10550 | GOLDIE | Gary | 04.01.1977 | P/O |
| 10551 | BRESLER | Michael Andrew | 02.05.1978 | P/O |
| 10552 | PERKINS | Derek Gary | 04.01.1977 | P/O |
| 10553 | GLOYNE | Peter Robert | 04.01.1977 | S/O |
| 10554 | EDWARDS | Neville John | 04.01.1977 | S/O(T) |
| 10555 | HOBSON | Peter Kyme | 16.05.1978 | D/P/O |

| No. | Surname | First Name(s) | Rank | Date |
|---|---|---|---|---|
| 10556 | KENNY | Stanley John | S/O | 16.05.1978 |
| 10557 | BARRY | Stephen | P/O | 19.05.1978 |
| 10558 | JOSS | James Malcolm | P/O | 04.01.1978 |
| 10559 | JOLY | Stephen Richard | P/O | 25.05.1978 |
| 10560 | PENFOLD | Mark Allen | P/O | 04.01.1977 |
| 10561 | FORREST | Stuart Ogilvie | P/O | 29.05.1978 |
| 10562 | CHALMERS | Guy Ferris | S/O | 29.05.1978 |
| 10563 | BLAKE | Marcus Trewhella | S/O | 29.05.1978 |
| 10564 | ELLIOT | Herald Alfred | P/O | 29.05.1978 |
| 10565 | GRIMWOOD | Colin Cecil | S/O | 29.05.1978 |
| 10566 | NICKS | Simon Cartwright | S/O | 29.05.1978 |
| 10567 | HAYDEN | David Robert | P/O | 29.05.1978 |
| 10568 | HOPKINS | Grant Clayton | L/S/O | 06.06.1978 |
| 10569 | ROBAS | Nigel Gavin | S/O | 06.06.1978 |
| 10570 | WOOD | Harry | P/O | 08.06.1978 |
| 10571 | WHEATLEY | Patrick George | C/In(T) | 01.06.1978 |
| 10572 | ALLEN | Michael Albert | S/O | 10.06.1978 |
| 10573 | MATHEWS | Philip Clive | P/O | 12.06.1978 |
| 10574 | TAYLOR | Paul Gregory | P/O | 11.06.1978 |
| 10575 | BARTLET | Brian Jeffrey | P/O | 14.06.1978 |
| 10576 | CUMMINGS | Stephen Nicholas | P/O | 14.06.1978 |
| 10577 | HARRIS | James Anthony | P/O | 16.06.1978 |
| 10578 | PASCOE | Philip Graham | S/O(T) | 20.06.1978 |
| 10579 | MULDER | Ronald Douglas | P/O | 21.06.1978 |
| 10580 | CARD | Mark Devon | P/O | 23.06.1978 |
| 10581 | HERD | Jeremy Cratchley | S/O | 04.01.1977 |
| 10582 | RANBY | William Edmund | P/O | 04.01.1977 |
| 10583 | CUNNINGHAM | Jeremy Mark | P/O | 04.01.1977 |
| 10584 | PILLANS | Guy James | P/O | 04.01.1977 |
| 10585 | WOODSIDE | Gregory Shaun | S/O(T) | 01.07.1978 |
| 10586 | MOORE | Terence David | P/O | 04.01.1977 |
| 10587 | VAN DEVENTER | Peter Eric | S/O(T) | 04.01.1977 |
| 10588 | MORGAN | Martin Clifford | P/O | 04.01.1977 |
| 10589 | CLARKE | Richard Hinton | P/O | 03.07.1978 |
| 10590 | RUGG | Steven | S/O | 04.07.1978 |
| 10591 | KRISCHOCK | John Paul | S/O(T) | 05.07.1978 |
| 10592 | LOUW | Raymond Paul | P/O | 13.07.1978 |
| 10593 | CAPELL | Roy Anthony | S/O | 13.07.1978 |
| 10594 | WHEATLEY | Malcolm Lester | P/O | 13.07.1978 |
| 10595 | ROBAS | Ian Michael | Insp(T) | 13.07.1978 |
| 10596 | LAMPORT-STOKES | Mark | p/o | 13.07.1978 |
| 10597 | LLOYD | Michael Howard | P/O | 13.07.1978 |
| 10598 | JUDD | Michael Alexander | P/O | 13.07.1978 |
| 10599 | FLEMING | Andrew Stewart | S/O(T) | 13.07.1978 |
| 10600 | HARRIS | Harry Gavin | P/O | 13.07.1978 |
| 10601 | BUCKLE | Colin Peter | P/O | 13.07.1978 |
| 10602 | STEYN | Clayton Henry | P/O | 13.07.1978 |
| 10603 | JONES | Nicholas Mark | P/O | 13.07.1978 |
| 10604 | KERR | Ian Samuel | D/S/O | 13.07.1978 |
| 10605 | HAYWOOD | Stanley Ernest | P/O | 13.07.1978 |
| 10606 | STANTON | Charles Joseph | S/O(T) | 17.07.1978 |
| 10607 | COCHRANE | Christiaan Johannes | S/O(T) | 17.07.1978 |
| 10608 | VILJOEN | Keith Edward | P/O | 21.07.1978 |
| 10609 | CHISNALL | Trevor Keith | P/O | 04.01.1977 |
| 10610 | SYMMONDS | Bernard Philip | D/S/O | 25.07.1978 |
| 10611 | BOSSY | Trevor | P/O | 26.07.1978 |
| 10612 | VAUGHAN | Russell Shane | P/O | 27.07.1978 |
| 10613 | CLEMENTS | Andrew John | P/O | 27.07.1978 |
| 10614 | NEAL | Bryan Michael | P/O | 29.07.1978 |
| 10615 | PEACH | Charles William | S/O | 03.08.1978 |
| 10616 | McDANIEL | Anthony Frank | P/O | 09.08.1978 |
| 10617 | ASHBY | Andrew | S/O | 10.08.1978 |
| 10618 | TAYLOR | Bruce Meikle | D/P/O | 13.08.1978 |
| 10619 | BRAES | Robert Anthony | D/P/O | 15.08.1978 |
| 10620 | McILWAINE | David Harold | P/O | 17.08.1978 |
| 10621 | BOTHA | Anthony | P/O | 24.08.1978 |
| 10622 | CLARK | Colin John | P/O | 26.08.1978 |
| 10623 | CAMPBELL | Thomas Robert | S/O(T) | 28.08.1978 |
| 10624 | COWLARD | | S/O(T) | 28.08.1978 |
| 10625 | MAHER | Keith George | P/O | 27.08.1978 |
| 10626 | COOKE | Ian | P/O | 28.06.1978 |
| 10627 | CAVANAGH | Stephen George | P/O | 28.06.1978 |
| 10628 | LEWIS | Anthony Peter | P/O | 28.06.1978 |
| 10629 | WILSON | Kevin James | P/O | 28.08.1978 |
| 10630 | PENNEY | Lionel George | P/O | 28.08.1978 |
| 10631 | VAN ASWEGAN | Martin Christopher | S/O | 28.08.1978 |
| 10632 | LINDENBERG | Erwin | S/O | 28.08.1978 |
| 10633 | BARRATT | Grantley Stuart | P/O | 28.08.1978 |
| 10634 | ERASMUS | Christo Johannes | P/O | 28.08.1978 |
| 10635 | ANNESLEY | Francis William | P/O | 28.08.1978 |
| 10636 | SMITH | Eric Peter | L/S/O | 28.08.1978 |
| 10637 | DUNN | Christopher Bruce | S/O(T) | 28.08.1978 |
| 10638 | SCOTT | Gary Michael | P/O | 28.08.1978 |
| 10639 | DU BOIS | Francois Gustave | S/O | 28.08.1978 |
| 10640 | VAN HUYSSTEN | Philip Herman | S/O | 28.08.1978 |
| 10641 | FIELD | Martin John | P/O | 28.08.1978 |
| 10642 | HEYNEKE | Mark Vincent | S/O(T) | 29.08.1978 |
| 10643 | MILTON | Maclcom McRae | S/O(T) | 29.08.1978 |
| 10644 | OPENSHAW | David Lawrence | P/O | 01.09.1978 |
| 10645 | KRAHNER | Leslie Brown | S/O(T) | 01.09.1978 |
| 10646 | DE WET | Walter Edward | P/O | 06.09.1978 |
| 10647 | TURNER | Peter | P/O | 10.09.1978 |
| 10648 | SMITH | Douglas William | S/O | 10.09.1978 |
| 10649 | BUGGS | Frank Alfred | Insp(T) | 18.09.1978 |
| 10650 | COURT | Jonathan Gilroy | P/O | 18.09.1978 |
| 10651 | WILLIAMS | Michael Philip | P/O | 20.09.1978 |
| 10652 | THOMPSON | Murray Gregg | P/O | 20.09.1978 |
| 10653 | DIGGS | Brendon Joseph | D/Insp | 22.09.1978 |
| 10654 | DUNCAN | Shane | P/O | 22.09.1978 |
| 10655 | ANDERSON | Bruce Neil | S/O(T) | 02.10.1978 |
| 10656 | MARAIS | Barend Daniel | D/S/O | 03.10.1978 |
| 10657 | VAN ROOYEN | Raynier | P/O | 04.10.1978 |
| 10658 | TRETHOWAN | Brain Michael | S/O | 16.10.1978 |
| 10659 | WIGGILL | Charles Robert | P/O | 20.10.1978 |
| 10660 | SLADE | Jack Phillip | Insp | 24.10.1978 |
| 10661 | GIRAUD | Paul Eli Pierre | P/O | 24.10.1978 |
| 10662 | WILLIAMS | Trevor John | S/O | 24.10.1978 |
| 10663 | BROWN | Raylan Talbot | P/O | 24.10.1978 |
| 10664 | BUYS | Jan Hendrik | P/O | 24.10.1978 |
| 10665 | LAWLESS | Kevin Peter | D/S/O | 24.10.1978 |
| 10666 | MORGAN | Timothy Nicol | S/S/O | 24.10.1978 |
| 10667 | LEPPAN | Raymond John | P/O | 30.10.1978 |
| 10668 | DONNISON | James | P/O | 01.11.1978 |
| 10669 | RUDMAN | Errol William | P/O | 05.11.1978 |
| 10670 | AZEVEDO | Carlos Alberto | P/O | 09.11.1978 |
| 10671 | BLUNDELL | Jeremy Hight | P/O | 16.11.1978 |
| 10672 | STRUGNELL | Robin Anthony | S/O | 17.11.1978 |
| 10673 | GALE | John Gordon | P/O | 19.11.1978 |
| 10674 | BONEHILL | Martyn | D/P/O | 21.11.1978 |
| 10675 | WILLIS | Victor Rupert | P/O | 19.11.1978 |
| 10676 | VAN DER HEEVER | David | S/O(T) | 22.11.1978 |
| 10677 | BELCHER | Mark St.Clair | Insp | 27.11.1978 |
| 10678 | ROBERTSON | Miles James | P/O | 28.11.1978 |
| 10679 | SMITH | Robert John | P/O | 29.11.1978 |
| 10680 | HOLT | Barry James | P/O | 01.12.1978 |
| 10681 | SHERMAN | Terrence Phillip | P/O | 01.12.1978 |
| 10682 | SPILLER | Julian Charles | P/O | 01.12.1978 |
| 10683 | PARKIN | Robert Dana | P/O | 01.12.1978 |
| 10684 | TARR | James Hartley | S/O(T) | 01.12.1978 |
| 10685 | HART | Ian Dudley | S/O | 03.12.1978 |
| 10686 | COLLYER | Kim Alexander | P/O | 04.12.1978 |
| 10687 | SHERWARD | Nicholas John | P/O | 05.12.1978 |
| 10688 | LUCAS | Lance Douglas | S/O | 06.12.1978 |
| 10689 | BERDOU | Jean Thomas | S/O | 09.12.1978 |
| 10690 | WESTON | William Michael | S/O | 11.12.1978 |
| 10691 | GRIFFITHS | Keith Douglas | S/S/O | 18.12.1978 |
| 10692 | ROSENBERG | Ivan | P/O | 18.12.1978 |
| 10693 | HORN | Malcolm Robert | D/S/O | 18.12.1978 |
| 10694 | VENTER | Guy Albert | P/O | 18.12.1978 |
| 10695 | TAYLOR | Kevin John | S/S/O | 18.12.1978 |
| 10696 | PETZER | Basil Frank | P/O | 18.12.1978 |
| 10697 | PRING | Trevor Jonathan | P/O | 18.12.1978 |
| 10698 | OELSCHIG | Andrew Patrick | S/O | 18.12.1978 |
| 10699 | MARAIS | Ian Carl | P/O | 18.12.1978 |
| 10700 | ROBERTS | Anthony Sinclair | S/O | 18.12.1978 |
| 10701 | BREWER | Paul | P/O | 18.12.1978 |
| 10702 | VERKEVISSER | Gary Stephen | P/O | 18.12.1978 |
| 10703 | BIRKETT | David Dennis | D/S/O | 18.12.1978 |
| 10704 | ADAMS | Noel Anthony | P/O | 18.12.1978 |
| 10705 | DYER | Alec Peter | P/O | 18.12.1978 |
| 10706 | ROWE | Kenneth Henry | P/O | 18.12.1978 |
| 10707 | ASHWIN | Michael Anthony | S/O | 18.12.1978 |
| 10708 | PACE | Ralph James | P/O | 18.12.1978 |
| 10709 | BATH | Bruce Alan | D/S/O | 18.12.1978 |
| 10710 | LUCKE | Colin Charles | P/O | 18.12.1978 |
| 10711 | OOSTHUIZEN | Augustine Petros | P/O | 18.12.1978 |
| 10712 | DE WITT | William Abraham | P/O | 18.12.1978 |
| 10713 | ARMSTRONG | Brian Patrick | D/P/O | 18.12.1978 |
| 10714 | TUCKER | Andrew Grenville | S/O | 18.12.1978 |
| 10715 | McFADDEN | Hugh | P/O | 20.12.1978 |
| 10716 | BEER | Roy David | P/O | 30.12.1978 |
| 10717 | WARD | David George | D/S/O(T) | 01.01.1979 |
| 10718 | STAUTMEISTER | Juergen Ewald | Insp | 01.01.1979 |
| 10719 | PRESTON | Michael Edward | S/O | 01.01.1979 |
| 10720 | HODGSON | Shaun Terrence | P/O | 01.01.1979 |
| 10721 | EDWARDS | Justin Edward | P/O | 03.01.1979 |
| 10722 | STANTON | Christopher Roy | P/O | 03.01.1979 |
| 10723 | SCHULTZ | David Frederick | P/O | 03.01.1979 |
| 10724 | PAUSE | Keith Jurgen | P/O | 03.01.1979 |
| 10725 | POWELL-JONES | Jeremy Simon | Insp | 03.01.1979 |
| 10726 | ALMY | Michael Vernon | P/O | 03.01.1979 |
| 10727 | LARKIN | Graham Ernest | P/O | 03.01.1979 |
| 10728 | THWAITS | Michael John | P/O | 03.01.1979 |
| 10729 | ARMSTRONG | David Edward | S/S/O | 03.01.1979 |
| 10730 | HILL | Rhett Edward | P/O | 03.01.1979 |
| 10731 | NIELSON | William Grant | S/S/O | 03.01.1979 |
| 10732 | NAUDE | Rodney Trevor | S/S/O | 03.01.1979 |
| 10733 | FORD | Wayne Cyril | P/O | 03.01.1979 |
| 10734 | REDMAN | Duboyle Clinton | P/O | 03.01.1979 |
| 10735 | FORSYTH | Derick McMillan | P/O | 03.01.1979 |
| 10736 | ERASMUS | Attie Joshua | P/O | 03.01.1979 |
| 10737 | GRESHAM | Edward Joseph | P/O | 03.01.1979 |
| 10738 | YATES | Alan McWilliam | P/O | 03.01.1979 |
| 10739 | SULLIVAN | Sean Terrence | P/O | 03.01.1979 |
| 10740 | DUERS | Kevin Gary | P/O | 03.01.1979 |
| 10741 | DU PREEZ | Peter John | S/S/O | 03.01.1979 |
| 10742 | BRUNETTE | Leonard Ralph | P/O | 03.01.1979 |
| 10743 | COX | Noel Anthony | P/O | 03.01.1979 |
| 10744 | HALEY | Donald Charles | P/O | 03.01.1979 |
| 10745 | MEREDITH | Daryl Clive | P/O | 03.01.1979 — Still serving |
| 10746 | GARTSHORE | Andrew Craig | P/O | 03.01.1979 |
| 10747 | GILMOUR | Anthony Stewart | P/O | 03.01.1979 |
| 10748 | GONCALVES | Paulo Moreira | P/O | 03.01.1979 |
| 10749 | GRAHAM | Shawn | P/O | 03.01.1979 |
| 10750 | GREEN | Robert Cecil | P/O | 03.01.1979 |
| 10751 | TIFFIN | David Nolin | P/O | 03.01.1979 |
| 10752 | WILSON | Ian Michael | P/O | 03.01.1979 |
| 10753 | STASSEN | Andre | P/O | 03.01.1979 |
| 10754 | JOHNSTON | Simon Gordon | P/O | 03.01.1979 |
| 10755 | BONE | Johnie Lemberg | P/O | 03.01.1979 |
| 10756 | BIRTLE | Christopher Joseph | P/O | 03.01.1979 |
| 10757 | BARNARD | Timothy Wayne | P/O | 03.01.1979 |
| 10758 | ALLAN | Peter Jo | P/O | 03.01.1979 |
| 10759 | ANDERSON | Neal Pringle | P/O | 03.01.1979 |
| 10760 | WOODS | Huw Richmond | P/O | 03.01.1979 |
| 10761 | McGRILLEN | James Gerard | P/O | 03.01.1979 |
| 10762 | SWAN | Ian Stewart | P/O | 04.01.1979 |

| Number | Surname | Forename(s) | Date | Status |
|---|---|---|---|---|
| 110763 | ALMEIDA-LEIGHTON | Rodrigo Ignacio | 08.01.1979 | P/O |
| 110764 | McDONALD | Peter | 09.01.1979 | P/O |
| 110765 | FREEMANN | Paul | 11.01.1979 | P/O |
| 110766 | HAGEMANN | Michael Eric | 17.01.1979 | Insp |
| 110767 | JONES | Geraint Malcolm | 19.01.1979 | S/O |
| 110768 | LOVETT | Grant John | 19.01.1979 | P/O |
| 110769 | GRIFFIN | Brian | 19.01.1979 | Insp |
| 110770 | MITCHELL | Kenneth | 19.01.1979 | P/O |
| 110771 | COATES | Peter John | 22.01.1979 | P/O |
| 110772 | WHEAL | Gregory Michael | 24.01.1979 | P/O |
| 110773 | PROUD | Trevor Andrew | 24.01.1979 | P/O |
| 110774 | DEVINE | Bryan Jeffrey | 24.01.1979 | P/O |
| 110775 | WOOD | David John | 24.01.1979 | P/O |
| 110776 | MILLAR | Richard Stephen | 24.01.1979 | Insp |
| 110777 | MUIR | David Marshall | 24.01.1979 | P/O |
| 110778 | PALMER | Guy Neilson | 24.01.1979 | P/O |
| 110779 | SOUTAR | Gavin Wilson | 24.01.1979 | P/O |
| 110780 | COMPTON | Wynford Hercules | 24.01.1979 | P/O |
| 110781 | JOSS | Clive Scott | 24.01.1979 | P/O |
| 110782 | BREBNER | Timothy Nicholas | 24.01.1979 | P/O |
| 110783 | FITZ-GERALD | Christian | 24.01.1979 | Still serving |
| 110784 | BUNGU | Samuel | 24.01.1979 | P/O |
| 110785 | DARLING | David Francis | 24.01.1979 | P/O |
| 110786 | VAN ZUYDAM | Steven James | 24.01.1979 | P/O |
| 110787 | WALMSLEY | Allan | 24.01.1979 | D/S/O |
| 110788 | NEWSHAM | Bruce | 24.01.1979 | S/S/O |
| 110789 | REVELL | Peter John | 24.01.1979 | P/O |
| 110790 | CHAPMAN | Stuart Brian | 24.01.1979 | P/O |
| 110791 | DEANE | Robert David | 24.01.1979 | P/O |
| 110792 | DORRINGTON | Andrew Mark | 24.01.1979 | P/O |
| 110793 | FOWLER | John | 24.01.1979 | P/O |
| 110794 | GREGSON | Brian Patrick | 24.01.1979 | P/O |
| 110795 | LINDSAY | Keith James | 24.01.1979 | P/O |
| 110796 | ELKINGTON | Kevin John | 24.01.1979 | P/O |
| 110797 | BROWNING | Michael Hugh | 24.01.1979 | P/O |
| 110798 | CASEY | Rowan Neil | 24.01.1979 | P/O |
| 110799 | ARLETT-JOHNSON | Derrick Michael | 24.01.1979 | P/O |
| 110800 | WILKINS | Alastair Gordon | 24.01.1979 | P/O |
| 110801 | VERWEY | Stephen | 24.01.1979 | P/O |
| 110802 | COLE | Bradley Winston | 24.01.1979 | P/O |
| 110803 | NDEBELE | Justin | 24.01.1979 | Still serving |
| 110804 | CLEMENTS | Melville John | 24.01.1979 | P/O |
| 110805 | HAYNES | Clive Alexander | 24.01.1979 | P/O |
| 110806 | DE VILLIERS | Jaques Johannes | 24.01.1979 | P/O |
| 110807 | PALMER | Mark Clinton | 24.01.1979 | P/O |
| 110808 | ROSS | Howard David | 24.01.1979 | P/O |
| 110809 | SMITH | William | 26.01.1979 | S/O(T) |
| 110810 | MATTHEE | Mark Edward | 30.01.1979 | P/O |
| 110811 | MEIKLE | Iain Mark | 30.01.1979 | P/O |
| 110812 | BOTHA | Colin Robert | 30.01.1979 | Supt |
| 110813 | DORET | Leon Maximillian | 30.01.1979 | P/O |
| 110814 | HOPE-HALL | Andrew Collingwood | 31.01.1979 | P/O |
| 110815 | MARSHALL | Peter Alan | 31.01.1979 | P/O |
| 110816 | HOGGINS | Raymond Glyn | 31.01.1979 | Insp |
| 110817 | DYER | Anthony Leonard | 31.01.1979 | S/O(T) |
| 110818 | HARRIS | George Martin | 02.02.1979 | P/O |
| 110819 | JANSEN VAN VUUREN | Michael Arnolds | 02.02.1979 | P/O |
| 110820 | BARBER | Walter Terry | 01.02.1979 | Supt |
| 110821 | CANTLE | Bruce | 02.02.1979 | P/O |
| 110822 | ASHTON | Phillip Vincent | 12.02.1979 | P/O |
| 110823 | WRATHALL | Jonathan Peter | 13.02.1979 | C/Insp |
| 110824 | JOKOMO | Ephraim Muchemwa | 13.02.1979 | S/O(T) |
| 110825 | THOMAS | Reginald Patrick | 14.02.1979 | S/O(T) |
| 110826 | VAN DER WESTHUIZEN | Nicholas | 16.02.1979 | S/O(T) |
| 110827 | ALANTHWAITE | Ewan Douglas | 20.02.1979 | P/O |
| 110828 | MUMBA | John | 20.02.1979 | P/O |
| 110829 | TURNER | Paul Graham | 20.02.1979 | P/O |
| 110830 | THOMAS | Simon Gordon | 20.02.1979 | D/S/O |
| 10831 | SHIEL | Stanley John | 20.02.1979 | D/S/O |
| 110832 | CHIRISA | Maxwell | 20.02.1979 | P/O |
| 110833 | AUSTIN | Hedley Wayne | 20.02.1979 | P/O |
| 110834 | GWAZE | Tommy | 20.02.1979 | Insp |
| 110835 | McLAUGHLIN | Anthony | 20.02.1979 | D/S/O |
| 110836 | GILES | David Francis | 20.02.1979 | P/O |
| 110837 | PENTON | Nigel Brian | 20.02.1979 | P/O |
| 110838 | DEMETRIOU | Jamie Pholis | 20.02.1979 | Insp |
| 110839 | JONES | Richard Stephen | 20.02.1979 | P/O |
| 110840 | JASSET | Mahomed | 20.02.1979 | P/O |
| 110841 | ANDERSON | Gerald Shawn | 20.02.1979 | P/O |
| 110842 | BABBAGE | Gabriel Vincent | 20.02.1979 | P/O |
| 110843 | ROWLEY | Spencer Ross | 04.01.1978 | P/O |
| 110844 | MAYHEW | Michael Charles | 20.02.1979 | D/S/O |
| 110845 | ROODE | Jacobus Wynand | 21.02.1979 | P/O |
| 110846 | BROWN | Michael | 21.02.1979 | P/O |
| 110847 | ABRAHAM | Fergus John | 21.02.1979 | P/O |
| 110848 | WELENSKY | Derek Lon | 21.02.1979 | P/O |
| 110849 | WORDEN | Christopher John | 23.02.1979 | P/O |
| 110850 | Mac ADAM | William | 24.02.1979 | P/O |
| 110851 | McMASTER | Neil James | 02.03.1979 | P/O |
| 110852 | OENDAAL | Martinus Johannes | 06.03.1979 | S/O(T) |
| 110853 | ROWLAND | Bruce Glen | 06.03.1979 | D/P/O |
| 110854 | DE MEYER | Flooris Petrus | 07.03.1979 | P/O |
| 110855 | WATSON | Andrew Kinley | 07.03.1979 | P/O |
| 110856 | WILLIAMS | Keith | 07.03.1979 | P/O |
| 110857 | ROSS | Bradley David | 07.03.1979 | P/O |
| 110858 | CARTER | Patrick Miles | 07.03.1979 | P/O |
| 110859 | SCOTT | Timothy John | 08.03.1979 | S/O(T) |
| 110860 | CHRISTIE | Robert Douglas | 08.03.1979 | P/O |
| 110861 | HUNTER | Earle Wayne | 11.03.1979 | P/O |
| 110862 | COLEMAN | Ian David | 13.03.1979 | S/O(T) |
| 110863 | SQUIRE | Atherton Guy | 13.03.1979 | P/O |
| 110864 | AINSCOUGH | Malcolm Martel | 13.03.1979 | P/O |
| 110865 | MANYANGADAZE | Brighton Famasi | 13.03.1979 | P/O |
| 110866 | SIBANDA | Atwell | 13.03.1979 | Still serving |
| 110867 | SITHOLE | Ronnie Mthando | 13.03.1979 | D/P/O |
| 110868 | WEIDMAN | Lucas van Wyk | 13.03.1979 | P/O |
| 110869 | WINDELL | Eric Drummond | 13.03.1979 | D/S/O |
| 110870 | PATEL | Narendra Kumar | 13.03.1979 | P/O |
| 110871 | HUGHES | Bryn | 13.03.1979 | P/O |
| 110872 | SCOTT | Sorrien Gabriel | 13.03.1979 | Supt |
| 110873 | SAMASUNO | Simon | 13.03.1979 | A/Insp |
| 110874 | LAUBSCHER | Roger Guy | 13.03.1979 | P/O |
| 110875 | MOUAT | David Gerald | 13.03.1979 | P/O |
| 110876 | MBANGA | Johannes | 13.03.1979 | Still serving |
| 110877 | MULLEN | John Douglas | 13.03.1979 | P/O |
| 110878 | NDLOVU | Freddie | 13.03.1979 | P/O |
| 110879 | HOGG | Peter Charles | 13.03.1979 | S/O(T) |
| 110880 | MUZUNZE | Stanley | 13.03.1979 | P/O |
| 110881 | MTEMERI | Chunky | 13.03.1979 | Supt |
| 110882 | WATSON | Gary Cameron | 13.03.1979 | P/O |
| 110883 | LOWRIE | Joseph James | 22.03.1979 | S/O(T) |
| 110884 | TURKINGTON | William James | 26.03.1979 | P/O |
| 110885 | BONE | Edward Robert | 26.03.1979 | S/O(T) |
| 110886 | ABRAHAMS | Frank Sebastian | 27.03.979 | Insp |
| 110887 | HERDMAN | John Roger | 30.03.1979 | S/O(T) |
| 110888 | CUBITT | Dennis Henry | 02.04.1979 | P/O |
| 110889 | SWANNACK | Mark | 20.03.1973 | P/O |
| 110890 | WATSON | Karl Vance | 11.04.1979 | D/S/O |
| 110891 | SMIT | Gary Martin | 11.04.1979 | P/O |
| 110892 | DEVINE | Martin Donald | 15.04.1979 | P/O |
| 110893 | MAPXASHIRE | Mathias | 18.04.1979 | P/O |
| 110894 | MUCHEMEDZI | Manasa | 18.04.1979 | D/Insp |
| 110895 | MOYO | Aleck | 18.04.1979 | Still serving |
| 110896 | KUDZURUNGA | Alois | 18.04.1979 | u/k |
| 110897 | CHINEMBIRI | Sonboy | 18.04.1979 | P/O |
| 110898 | CHINJERE | Peter Tendai | 18.04.1979 | D/S/O |
| 110899 | RAJAH | Douglas | 26.04.1979 | D/S/O |
| 110900 | CHATTERJEE | Salim Smith | 04.05.1979 | D/S/O |
| 110901 | HARROLD | David James | 05.05.1979 | P/O |
| 110902 | DYER | Geoffrey Mark | 12.05.1979 | P/O |
| 110903 | SUNDERLAND | Barry Kevin | 14.05.1979 | Insp |
| 110904 | FARRELL | John Peter | 29.05.1979 | P/O |
| 110905 | McGIBBON | Douglas Crosbie | 22.05.1979 | P/O |
| 110906 | BENNETT | David Paren | 24.05.1979 | P/O |
| 110907 | COLEY | Aubrey James | 31.05.1979 | S/O(T) |
| 110908 | ZLOKOVICH | Gregor Louis | 01.06.1979 | Insp(T) |
| 110909 | CLACKWORTHY | Garry Alexander | 05.06.1979 | S/O(T) |
| 110910 | LAMBERT | Andrew Michael | 05.06.1979 | P/O |
| 110911 | GREEN | Ernest | 06.06.1979 | Still serving |
| 110912 | CHIWOKO | Shepard | 06.06.1979 | Still serving |
| 110913 | RUSSELL | Joseph Thomas | 06.06.1979 | P/O |
| 110914 | SELMAN | Gary Alfred | 06.06.1979 | P/O(T) |
| 110915 | DZIKITI | Basil | 06.06.1979 | not recorded |
| 110916 | GAVA | Lovemore | 06.06.1979 | P/O |
| 110917 | MAHAJA | Lovemore | 06.06.1979 | Insp |
| 110918 | ZIVHAVE | Vensen | 07.06.1979 | not recorded |
| 110919 | CAMERON-DOW | Ashley Malcolm | 08.06.1979 | P/O |
| 110920 | KLOPPERS | Neville Louie | 10.06.1979 | P/O |
| 110921 | ROBERTS | Neill | 14.06.1979 | P/O |
| 110922 | STUART | Tommy | 14.06.1979 | P/O |
| 110923 | NICHOLS | Arthur Stephen | 15.06.1979 | S/O |
| 110924 | PERKINS | Kevin Michael | 15.06.1979 | S/O(T) |
| 110925 | NEW | Anthony Richard | 15.06.1979 | P/O |
| 110926 | HODGKISS | Robert James | 15.06.1979 | P/O |
| 110927 | CARLILE | Robert | 21.06.1979 | P/O |
| 110928 | HORTON | Jonathan Brett | 22.06.1979 | P/O |
| 110929 | BAKER | Mark Leonard | 21.06.1979 | D/S/O |
| 110930 | GRAY | John Byron | 25.06.1979 | S/O(T) |
| 110931 | LANDY | David | 26.06.1979 | Insp(T) |
| 110932 | MANN | Jeremy David | 29.06.1979 | P/O |
| 110933 | HARRISON | Richard Roland | 04.01.1978 | P/O |
| 110934 | DAVIS | Ralph Leonard | 10.07.1979 | P/O |
| 110935 | DZINI | Andrew | 12.07.1979 | Insp |
| 110936 | MUTOPO | Bartholomew | 16.07.1979 | P/O |
| 110937 | HASSAN | Ebrahim | 16.07.1979 | Still serving |
| 110938 | EBINENG | Walter | 16.07.1979 | P/O |
| 110939 | MARTIN | Francis Charles | 16.07.1979 | P/O |
| 110940 | DICKER | Trevor John | 16.07.1979 | P/O |
| 110941 | GANGAZHURWA | Kornard | 16.07.1979 | Still serving |
| 110942 | ANDERSON | Philip Tom Julian | 16.07.1979 | P/O |
| 110943 | KEOGH | Gary Saunders | 16.07.1979 | P/O |
| 110944 | SANDERSON | Stuart Alaistair | 16.07.1979 | P/O |
| 110945 | McCALLUM | Steven John | 16.07.1979 | P/O |
| 110946 | MHLANGA | Kenneth Christopher | 16.07.1979 | P/O |
| 110947 | ADDISON | John Armstrong | 16.07.1979 | S/O |
| 110948 | LAZAROV | Sammy | 19.07.1979 | S/O(T) |
| 110949 | FARNSWORTH | Kenneth | 20.07.1979 | P/O |
| 110950 | CHIKOMBA | Joseph | 23.07.1979 | Still serving |
| 110951 | RHODES | Simon John | 24.07.1979 | P/O |
| 110952 | WAINWRIGHT | Keith | 27.07.1979 | S/S/O |
| 110953 | KITCHING | Christopher Ian | 27.07.1979 | P/O |
| 110954 | BROMLEY | Colin John | 29.07.1979 | D/P/O |
| 110955 | JOHNSON | Andrew Joseph | 31.07.1979 | D/P/O |
| 110956 | GREEN-THOMPSON | Arthur | 02.08.1979 | P/O |
| 110957 | OSCHGER | Shawn Pantalyon | 06.08.1979 | S/O(T) |
| 110958 | HOPE | Colin Francis | 06.08.1979 | P/O |
| 110959 | JAMIESON | Robert John | 09.08.1979 | S/O(T) |
| 110960 | KENDALL | Nigel John | 10.08.1979 | D/S/O |
| 110961 | EVANS | Desmond Harold | 15.08.1979 | P/O |
| 110962 | MACAULEY | Clive Kilgour | 16.08.1979 | S/O |
| 110963 | BOSHOFF | David Graham | 16.08.1979 | P/O |
| 110964 | ASHBY | Trevor Glen | 20.08.1979 | S/O |
| 110965 | ROSSITER | Trevor Allan | 20.08.1979 | P/O |
| 110966 | WERTH | Harry Carl | 18.08.1979 | S/O(T) |
| 110967 | HALL | Jeffrey | 17.08.1979 | S/O(T) |
| 110968 | MUZVIDZIWA | Stephen Patrick | 23.08.1979 | not recorded |
| 110969 | VOSLOO | Leslie Mark | 27.08.1979 | P/O |

| No. | Surname | First Name | Date | Rank |
|---|---|---|---|---|
| 110970 | HALL | Gary Stanley | 27.08.1979 | P/O |
| 110971 | HALL | Timothy Joseph | 27.08.1979 | P/O |
| 110972 | BELL | Kevin Charles | 30.08.1979 | S/S/O |
| 110973 | MUSINGARIMI | Jeremiah | 31.08.1979 | P/O |
| 110974 | VAN NIEKERK | Raymon Wayne | 02.09.1979 | P/O |
| 110975 | ANDRE | Claude Germain | 04.09.1979 | P/O |
| 110976 | WAINWRIGHT | Paul | 04.09.1979 | S/O |
| 110977 | EVANS | Michael Ernest | 06.09.1979 | P/O |
| 110978 | KEENAN | Brian | 10.09.1979 | P/O |
| 110979 | ORANGE | Heiron Rudolph | 24.09.1979 | P/O |
| 110980 | LLOYD | Nicholas Charles | 24.09.1979 | S/O |
| 110981 | BLAKE | Cyril Edward | 27.09.1979 | S/O(T) |
| 110982 | WELLS | Christopher Vaughan | 27.09.1979 | S/O(T) |
| 110983 | OSBORNE | Kevin Arthur | 29.09.1979 | Still serving |
| 110984 | MANEYA | Emson | 01.10.1979 | not recorded |
| 110985 | PELSER | Martin Petrus | 02.10.1979 | P/O |
| 110986 | SMITH | Bernardo James | 05.10.1979 | S/O(T) |
| 110987 | EDWARDS | Michael John | 05.10.1979 | S/O(T) |
| 110988 | YOUNG | Alan | 19.10.1979 | S/O |
| 110989 | MASTER | George | 22.10.1979 | P/O |
| 110990 | CHITUNYA | Joseph Nhamuriko | 22.10.1979 | P/O |
| 110991 | GATSI | Lameck | 22.10.1979 | Still serving |
| 110992 | MANDIZHA | Lovemore Josephas | 22.10.1979 | P/O |
| 110993 | ABRAHAMS | Brian Paul | 22.10.1979 | S/O |
| 110994 | MATURURE | Emmanuel Misheck | 22.10.1979 | P/O |
| 110995 | CHAVANDUKA | Lovemore Steven | 22.10.1979 | P/O |
| 110996 | NGWENYA | Brian | 22.10.1979 | S/O |
| 110997 | MUBAIWA | Michael | 22.10.1979 | S/O |
| 110998 | MUTAURWA | Fidelis | 22.10.1979 | Still serving |
| 110999 | KROON | Francois | 22.10.1979 | P/O |
| 111000 | NCUBE | Patrick | 22.10.1979 | Still serving |
| 111001 | HUTCHENS | Mark John | 22.10.1979 | P/O |
| 111002 | MOYO | Edward | 24.10.1979 | A/Insp |
| 111003 | BLOOMFIELD | Michael | 20.10.1979 | Insp |
| 111004 | VENTOURIS | Thomas | 12.11.1979 | D/P/O |
| 111005 | BASIRA | Adnos | 22.11.1979 | not recorded |
| 111006 | SIMBANEGAVE | Simon | 22.11.1979 | Still serving |
| 111007 | MAHAKA | Obert | 22.11.1979 | not recorded |
| 111008 | MAPLANKA | Leopold Masura | 22.11.1979 | P/O |
| 111009 | MAFUNDE | Moses | 22.11.1979 | P/O |
| 111010 | TSHABANGU | Obert McBond | 22.11.1979 | Sgt. |
| 111011 | MWENZUA | Lee Chengetai | 22.11.1979 | D/C/I |
| 111012 | DZARAMBA | Phillip Chikuwiri | 22.11.1979 | P/O |
| 111013 | MATE | Raphael | 22.11.1979 | S/C/I |
| 111014 | SIBANDA | Headman | 22.11.1979 | P/O |
| 111015 | MUNAKAMWE | Charles | 22.11.1979 | D/A/I |
| 111016 | BAJILA | Roderick Tombi | 22.11.1979 | Still serving |
| 111017 | MANDIZHA | Nyamadzai Justin | 22.11.1979 | Still serving |
| 111018 | GANAGANA | Herbert | 22.11.1979 | P/O |
| 111019 | KASIRORI | Tendai | 22.11.1979 | P/O |
| 111020 | SIBANDA | Thomas Sebastian | 22.11.1979 | P/O |
| 111021 | CHISEPO | Joseph | 22.11.1979 | P/O |
| 111022 | POPE | Timothy Murray | 24.11.1979 | P/O |
| 111023 | McLISTER | Francis Joseph | 01.12.1979 | P/O |
| 111024 | HUXHAM | Gary Steven | 03.12.1979 | S/O(T) |
| 111025 | TAENTZER | Gerald Charles | 07.12.1979 | S/S/O |
| 111026 | REYNOLDS | Keith William | 13.12.1979 | S/O(T) |
| 111027 | McILWAINE | Patrick | 17.12.1979 | P/O |
| 111028 | GRIFFITHS | Sean | 17.12.1979 | S/S/O |
| 111029 | PASCOE | Anthony Keith | 20.12.1979 | S/S/O |
| 111030 | GROSE | Gary Christopher | 20.12.1979 | P/O |
| 111031 | TAPSON | Mark Cyril | 20.12.1979 | P/O |
| 111032 | BEWES | Colin Russell | 20.12.1979 | P/O |
| 111033 | CARY | Robert Neil | 20.12.1979 | P/O |
| 111034 | CHIBVONGODZE | Dunstan | 20.12.1979 | P/O |
| 111035 | SIBANDA | Partson | 20.12.1979 | P/O |
| 111036 | MACKAY | Roderick George | 20.12.1979 | L/S/O |
| 111037 | NHOVA | Godwell | 20.12.1979 | P/O |
| 111038 | JOHNSON | Clifford William | 20.12.1979 | D/P/O |
| 111039 | MATHER | Victor Mark | 20.12.1979 | S/S/O |
| 111040 | DAVIDSON | Jeffrey Ronald | 20.12.1979 | P/O |
| 111041 | NATHOO | Dane Lee | 20.12.1979 | S/S/O |
| 111042 | VAN ZYL | Johnson Johannes | 20.12.1979 | S/S/O |
| 111043 | CARSE | John Archibald | 20.12.1979 | P/O |
| 111044 | CRAVEN | Keith David | 20.12.1979 | P/O |
| 111045 | SIBANDA | Martin | 20.12.1979 | P/O |
| 111046 | ELLIOT | Robert Laine | 27.12.1979 | D/P/O |
| 111047 | MADZIYA | Tichoada | 15.12.1979 | Insp |
| 111048 | FRITH | Frank Colin | 29.12.1979 | P/O |
| 111049 | JOHNSTONE | Christopher Walter | 30.12.1979 | P/O |
| 111050 | LAWN | David Edward | 01.01.1980 | D/P/O |
| 111051 | PHILLIPS | Mark Curtis | 03.01.1980 | P/O |
| 111052 | CHAUKURA | Regis Rwanyanya | 03.01.1980 | Insp |
| 111053 | McGHEE | Russell Craig | 03.01.1980 | P/O |
| 111054 | LOUW | Jan Abraham | 03.01.1980 | P/O |
| 111055 | BOTHA | Marthinus Theunis | 03.01.1980 | S/O |
| 111056 | NIGHTINGALE | Stephen Paul | 03.01.1980 | P/O |
| 111057 | SHAW-JOHNSTON | Ross | 03.01.1980 | P/O |
| 111058 | BIRD | Robert Clifford | 03.01.1980 | P/O |
| 111059 | TICHAGWA | Misheck | 03.01.1980 | A/Insp |
| 111060 | DAY | Phillip Robert | 03.01.1980 | D/P/O |
| 111061 | STEYN | Roger Randell | 03.01.1980 | P/O |
| 111062 | CHIRONGOMA | Ray | 03.01.1980 | D/P/O |
| 111063 | LAWRIE | Thomas Paxton | 03.01.1980 | D/P/O |
| 111064 | PANTON | David John | 03.01.1980 | S/O |
| 111065 | SUSMAN | Trevor Bentley | 03.01.1980 | S/O |
| 111066 | CALLOW | Jack | 03.01.1980 | S/O |
| 111067 | MARILLIER | Norman Aylward | 03.01.1980 | Still serving |
| 111068 | CHEVURE | Alvan | 03.01.1980 | D/S/O |
| 111069 | NEL | Anthony William | 03.01.1980 | D/P/O |
| 111070 | BOTHA | David Colin | 03.01.1980 | D/P/O |
| 111071 | TINKER | Richard Ian | 03.01.1980 | P/O |
| 111072 | SMITH | Craig Russell | 03.01.1980 | D/Insp |
| 111073 | FAYINDANI | Simon | 03.01.1980 | P/O |
| 111074 | YOUNG | Richard | 03.01.1980 | P/O |
| 111075 | HOGG | Ian Richard | 03.01.1980 | S/O |
| 111076 | NIGHTINGALE | Carl Douglas | 03.01.1980 | S/O |
| 111077 | FORBES | Fergus Kynaston | 03.01.1980 | P/O |
| 111078 | MARSHALL | Alexander William | 03.01.1980 | P/O |
| 111079 | McDONALD | Robert William | 03.01.1980 | P/O |
| 111080 | ALCOCK | Stephen Mark | 07.01.1980 | D/P/O |
| 111081 | ASTON | David Baldwin | 08.01.1980 | P/O |
| 111082 | HUNT | Craig Leslie | 11.01.1980 | L/S/O |
| 111083 | DATSON | James Peter | 14.01.1980 | S/O(T) |
| 111084 | WONG CHEE | Phillip | 14.01.1980 | S/O |
| 111085 | SAYENDA | Freddie James | 15.01.1980 | S/Insp |
| 111086 | ATKINSON | Bernard John | 15.01.1980 | Supt |
| 111087 | HESLIP | Brendan Thomas | 22.01.1980 | Insp |
| 111088 | ZIMUTO | Johnson | 22.01.1980 | S/O(T) |
| 111089 | TOOZE | Wayne Lyndon | 24.01.1980 | S/Insp |
| 111090 | NGODO | George | 24.01.1980 | P/O |
| 111091 | JEFFERIES | Michael Alan | 24.01.1980 | Still serving |
| 111092 | EDWARDS | Barry Patrick | 24.01.1980 | P/O |
| 111093 | KNOTT | Michael John | 24.01.1980 | S/O |
| 111094 | DAVIE | Mark William | 24.01.1980 | S/O |
| 111095 | PAYNE | Trevor Guy | 24.01.1980 | L/S/O |
| 111096 | RUTTLE | Peter James | 24.01.1980 | P/O |
| 111097 | CAIRNS | Evan Patrick | 24.01.1980 | P/O |
| 111098 | BAILEY | William Quentin | 24.01.1980 | S/S/O |
| 111099 | DALTON | Colin Frederick | 24.01.1980 | D/P/O |
| 111100 | MALLETT | Michael Bruce | 24.01.1980 | P/O |
| 111101 | BAXTER | Andrew Elliot | 24.01.1980 | S/O |
| 111102 | WILEY | William Michael | 24.01.1980 | P/O |
| 111103 | MAPFUMO | Stanley | 24.01.1980 | C/Insp |
| 111104 | OGILVIE | Clive Andrew | 24.01.1980 | S/S/O |
| 111105 | BRAGGE | Nigel Harold | 24.01.1980 | P/O |
| 111106 | OGILVIE | Gordon Lee | 24.01.1980 | P/O |
| 111107 | LAW | Alan Clive | 24.01.1980 | P/O |
| 111108 | BOLTON | Mark Colin | 24.01.1980 | P/O |
| 111109 | BROODRYK | Bruce Paul | 24.01.1980 | P/O |
| 111110 | HANLY | Graham Anthony | 24.01.1980 | P/O |
| 111111 | TIBBS | Michael Alexander | 24.01.1980 | P/O |
| 111112 | FORBES | Morgan Rock | 24.01.1980 | P/O |
| 111113 | MANDUNYA | Herbert Hakunendaba | 24.01.1980 | D/P/O |
| 111114 | SMEDA | Noel Desmond | 24.01.1980 | P/O |
| 111115 | JOUGHIN | Andrew James | 24.01.1980 | P/O |
| 111116 | BABBAGE | Cuthwell Funmwell | 24.01.1980 | Supt(T) |
| 111117 | DU PLESSIS | David Peter | 24.01.1980 | P/O |
| 111118 | JAMIESON | Ronald Bruce | 24.01.1980 | P/O |
| 111119 | BLACK | Kenneth Barry | 24.01.1980 | S/S/O |
| 111120 | SMITH | Colin George | 24.01.1980 | P/O |
| 111121 | DOBLE | Peter Duncan | 24.01.1980 | P/O |
| 111122 | HURLBATT | Richard Neil | 24.01.1980 | D/P/O |
| 111123 | BEATTIE | Kevin Frederick | 24.01.1980 | S/Insp |
| 111124 | POLLITT | Steven Mark | 24.01.1980 | P/O |
| 111125 | JAMES | Spencer Antony | 24.01.1980 | S/O(T) |
| 111126 | SHAXSON | Nicholas Peter | 24.01.1980 | P/O |
| 111127 | KRIEK | Roelof Andries | 24.01.1980 | P/O |
| 111128 | HOLDEN | Kevin Aldredge | 24.01.1980 | P/O |
| 111129 | JUDGE | Christopher John | 24.01.1980 | P/O |
| 111130 | HILL | Roger Brett | 24.01.1980 | S/S/O |
| 111131 | MORGAN | Brian Feilim | 24.01.1980 | P/O |
| 111132 | REYNOLDS | Justin Richard | 24.01.1980 | Insp |
| 111133 | BENTLEY | Bruce Eifion | 24.01.1980 | P/O |
| 111134 | COVENTRY | Peter Clifford | 24.01.1980 | P/O |
| 111135 | EVANS | Grant Lewis | 24.01.1980 | P/O |
| 111136 | MAZARANHANGA | Tennyson | 24.01.1980 | D/P/O |
| 111137 | GREENING | Winston Gareth | 24.01.1980 | P/O |
| 111138 | SHAVIERI | Aluwis Charles | 25.01.1980 | Still serving |
| 111139 | MATUTU | Evans | 24.01.1980 | P/O |
| 111140 | WARINDA | Isidor | 24.01.1980 | P/O |
| 111141 | MAJERO | Andrew | 24.01.1980 | P/O |
| 111142 | SIBANDA | Austin Lusizi | 24.01.1980 | P/O |
| 111143 | HODGSON | Mark Stephen | 24.01.1980 | P/O |
| 111144 | TAYLOR | Andrew James | 24.01.1980 | P/O |
| 111145 | CHIKWAWAWA | Jonathan | 25.01.1980 | Still serving |
| 111146 | SHALLOW | Michael Anthony | 24.01.1980 | P/O |
| 111147 | YOUNG | Mark Tulloch | 24.01.1980 | P/O |
| 111148 | CHENNELLS | Timothy Peter | 24.01.1980 | P/O |
| 111149 | FELICIANO | Rudi Lawrence | 24.01.1980 | L/S/O |
| 111150 | MOLEBALENG | Hosea Nyati | 24.01.1980 | Still serving |
| 111151 | SYKES | Duncan Frank | 24.01.1980 | P/O |
| 111152 | MUMERSON | Gavin | 24.01.1980 | P/O |
| 111153 | ADAMS | Chuck | 24.01.1980 | P/O |
| 111154 | KUNYENDZA | Rufaro | 24.01.1980 | D/S/O |
| 111155 | BROWN | Philip Clive | 24.01.1980 | S/S/O |
| 111156 | VAN ZEEVENTER | Bart | 24.01.1980 | P/O |
| 111157 | ACKERMAN | Neil Perry | 24.01.1980 | P/O |
| 111158 | BENDYSHE-WALTON | Ian Mervyn | 24.01.1980 | D/P/O |
| 111159 | BRAUN | Gregory Mark | 24.01.1980 | P/O |
| 111160 | COCHRANE | Ronald John | 24.01.1980 | S/O |
| 111161 | COMRIE | Douglas Stuart | 24.01.1980 | P/O |
| 111162 | NEWMAN | Bruce Victor | 24.01.1980 | P/O |
| 111163 | ENGALL | Phillip John | 24.01.1980 | P/O |
| 111164 | GARDEN | Roy George | 24.01.1980 | P/O |
| 111165 | GODDARD | Julian | 24.01.1980 | P/O |
| 111166 | KEMPEN | Robert | 24.01.1980 | D/P/O |
| 111167 | LONEY | Robert Bradshaw | 24.01.1980 | D/S/O |
| 111168 | Mac PHAIL | Nigel Graham | 24.01.1980 | S/S/O |
| 111169 | NEL | Dean Joubert | 24.01.1980 | S/S/O |
| 111170 | RINK | Bryan | 24.01.1980 | P/O |
| 111171 | SCOTT-MARTIN | Patrick Richard | 24.01.1980 | D/P/O |
| 111172 | SLEMANT | Barry Hamilton | 24.01.1980 | S/O |
| 111173 | MUZARIRI | Joshua | 24.01.1980 | S/S/O |
| 111174 | VAN WYK | Johan Nicolaas | 24.01.1980 | P/O |
| 111175 | MILLARD | Jeffrey Lewis | 24.01.1980 | Insp(T) |
| 111176 | CLARKE | Kevin | 24.01.1980 | S/O(T) |

| No. | Surname | First name(s) | Date | Rank |
|---|---|---|---|---|
| 111177 | DINGA | Collin | 24.01.1980 | P/O |
| 111178 | MYERS | Coleman | 24.01.1980 | S/O(T) |
| 111179 | HLATYWAYO | Claudius Charles | 24.01.1980 | S/S/O |
| 111180 | FLOWERS | Stanley William | 25.01.1980 | P/O |
| 111181 | MARAIS | Frans John | 24.01.1980 | S/Insp |
| 111182 | MANDEYA | Clayden | 24.01.1980 | C/Insp |
| 111183 | REED | John Gavin | 26.01.1980 | P/O |
| 111184 | PHILLIPS | Bruce Ingram | 26.01.1980 | P/O |
| 111185 | EDWARDS | Robert Keith | 27.01.1980 | P/O |
| 111186 | CUNLIFFE | Kenneth Vivian | 29.01.1980 | P/O |
| 111187 | DU PREEZ | Philip Edward | 13.02.1980 | P/O |
| 111188 | MARGERISON | Clive Conrad | 21.02.1980 | P/O |
| 111189 | PARKER | Anthony Brett | 21.02.1980 | P/O |
| 111190 | BURNS | John Alan | 21.02.1980 | P/O |
| 111191 | HYSLOP | Kevin | 21.02.1980 | P/O |
| 111192 | ZINYAMA | Francis Langton | 21.02.1980 | C/Supt |
| 111193 | SCHMID | Bradley Warren | 21.02.1980 | P/O |
| 111194 | ASHTON | Graeme Peter | 21.02.1980 | P/O |
| 111195 | HANEKOM | Gary | 21.02.1980 | P/O |
| 111196 | CHAWORA | Jeremy Jonathan | 21.02.1980 | A/Comm |
| 111197 | JONAS | Lazarus | 21.02.1980 | D/A/I |
| 111198 | MUSIWA | John Michael | 21.02.1980 | P/O |
| 111199 | LIKUKUMA | Wellington Joshua | 21.02.1980 | P/O |
| 111200 | WARTH | Daniel Charles | 21.02.1980 | D/P/O |
| 111201 | THOMAS | David Robert | 21.02.1980 | P/O |
| 111202 | JACKSON | Allan Edmund | 21.02.1980 | S/S/O |
| 111203 | NYIMO | Raston | 21.02.1980 | C/Insp |
| 111204 | NELSON | Marc Graham | 21.02.1980 | P/O |
| 111205 | JACKSON | John | 21.02.1980 | P/O |
| 111206 | JACKSON | Paul Ian | 21.02.1980 | P/O |
| 111207 | FYNES-CLINTON | Mark Robert | 21.02.1980 | P/O |
| 111208 | GOMBA | Charles | 21.02.1980 | D/Insp |
| 111209 | MUZULU | David | 21.02.1980 | P/O |
| 111210 | MUPHUMIRA | Nhamu Onisimas | 21.02.1980 | not recorded |
| 111211 | TOZER | Andrew Russell | 21.02.1980 | P/O |
| 111212 | FICKLING | Brian Melville | 21.02.1980 | P/O |
| 111213 | CHISHIRI | Sebastian | 21.02.1980 | C/Insp |
| 111214 | NJERERE | Gibson | 21.02.1980 | Sgt |
| 111215 | WHYTE | Stephen Roy | 21.02.1980 | P/O |
| 111216 | MORGUTTI | Mark Anthony | 21.02.1980 | P/O |
| 111217 | MATHER-PIKE | Scott Harold | 21.02.1980 | P/O |
| 111218 | DITIMA | Joseph | 21.02.1980 | Still serving |
| 111219 | MOYO | George | 21.02.1980 | Sgt |
| 111220 | TAYLOR | Adrian | 21.02.1980 | A/Insp |
| 111221 | DUFF-SMITH | Jonathan Graeme | 21.02.1980 | Insp(T) |
| 111222 | JACOBS | Frank John | 21.02.1980 | P/O |
| 111223 | BUTCHART | Kenneth Andrew | 21.02.1980 | C/Insp |
| 111224 | WHYTE | Renton Paul | 21.02.1980 | P/O |
| 111225 | WILLARD | Gavin Alfred | 21.02.1980 | Insp |
| 111226 | FRAVENSTEIN | Robert Anthony | 25.02.1980 | S/O(T) |
| 111227 | BELL | Robert David | 29.02.1980 | S/O(T) |
| 111228 | ABDULLAH | Khulio Allam | 03.03.1980 | S/O |
| 111229 | FLOWERS | Frank | 03.03.1980 | P/O |
| 111230 | FERNANDES | Felix Julio | 10.03.1980 | S/O(T) |
| 111231 | COOPER | Scott Lamond | 10.03.1980 | S/O |
| 111232 | BUTCHART | Kevin Sturrock | 10.03.1980 | Insp |
| 111233 | CHIKOVORE | Thomas | 10.03.1980 | Insp |
| 111234 | OOSTHUIZEN | Leon Jan | 10.03.1980 | P/O |
| 111235 | SANSOM | Malcolm Thomas | 20.03.1980 | S/S/O |
| 111236 | ZVIDZIWA | Jonathan | 20.03.1980 | Insp |
| 111237 | RUPONGA | Kenneth | 20.03.1980 | Still serving |
| 111238 | SMITH | Christopher Geo | 20.03.1980 | Still serving |
| 111239 | MAFUTA | Cephas | 20.03.1980 | Supt |
| 111240 | ELLWAY | Jonathan George | 20.03.1980 | P/O |
| 111241 | PANDEHUNI | Tauayi Nicholas | 20.03.1980 | Insp |
| 111242 | GIJIMA | Killian | 20.03.1980 | Still serving |
| 111243 | CHIVAVIRO | Hercules | 20.03.1980 | Insp |
| 111244 | EAMES | Christopher Mark | 20.03.1980 | Insp |
| 111245 | COSTA | Darrel Thomas | 20.03.1980 | P/O |
| 111246 | COWGILL | Craig Howard | 20.03.1980 | P/O |
| 111247 | JOKONYA | Cassian Paraffin | 20.03.1980 | Still serving |
| 111248 | JONES | Tommy | 20.03.1980 | P/O |
| 111249 | KERBELKER | Dawood | 20.03.1980 | D/Insp |
| 111250 | CHIVASA | Stranger Rangaridzai | 20.03.1980 | S/C/Insp |
| 111251 | KAGOGODA | King | 20.03.1980 | Insp |
| 111252 | MEYER | Paul Andries | 20.03.1980 | P/O |
| 111253 | CHIGEDE | Dairod | 20.03.1980 | Still serving |
| 111254 | RUDMAN | Gordon Wayne | 03.03.1980 | D/P/O |
| 111255 | WALTERS | Barry Richard | 08.03.1980 | P/O |
| 111256 | NYARIRANGWE | Philip | 13.02.1980 | P/O |
| 111257 | ZWIDAZAYI | Nelson | 20.03.1980 | P/O |
| 111258 | LAWSON | Steve Andrew | 02.03.1980 | C/Sup |
| 111259 | REES | Rhodri Francis | 21.03.1980 | P/O |
| 111260 | DORNAN | Murray Dick | 28.03.1980 | D/P/O |
| 111261 | CHANTLER | Anthony Ivan | 23.03.1980 | L/S/O |
| 111262 | STUART | Kevin Ernest | 15.04.1980 | P/O |
| 111263 | DUBE | Robert | 22.04.1980 | A/Insp |
| 111264 | MOYO | Joseph | 22.04.1980 | A/Insp |
| 111265 | MTSIMBA | Roy Silence | 22.04.1980 | P/O |
| 111266 | MDUMO | Raymond Orbert | 22.04.1980 | A/Insp |
| 111267 | GORAH | Christopher Regis | 22.04.1980 | Still serving |
| 111268 | KAPFIDZE | Paul | 22.04.1980 | Still serving |
| 111269 | CHAVI | Douglas Wilson | 22.04.1980 | Insp |
| 111270 | SHOKO | Titus | 22.04.1980 | Still serving |
| 111271 | WHCZHELE | Sydney | 22.04.1980 | P/O |
| 111272 | RANGARIRA | Aron | 22.04.1980 | P/O |
| 111273 | OLIVER | Stephen | 22.04.1980 | S/A/C |
| 111274 | MANDIZAH | Albert | 22.04.1980 | P/O |
| 111275 | NDORO | Solomon | 22.04.1980 | P/O |
| 111276 | SIBUTHA | Lovemore | 22.04.1980 | P/O |
| 111277 | GUZHA | Robson | 22.04.1980 | P/O |
| 111278 | CHIGUWHA | Israel | 22.04.1980 | Still serving |
| 111279 | RUMEU | Lovemore | 22.04.1980 | P/O |
| 111280 | MAFFUMO | Mushere | 22.04.1980 | Still serving |
| 111281 | HERBST | Marthinus Johannes | 03.05.1980 | D/Insp |
| 111282 | LONOR | Lourens Edward | 06.05.1980 | P/O |
| 111283 | GRIFFIN | Peter Alan | 14.05.1980 | P/O |
| 111284 | KNIGHT | Gary Brian | 13.05.1980 | Insp |
| 111285 | ROBERTS | Jon Adam | 15.05.1980 | S/O |
| 111286 | COETSEE | Michael Paul | 20.05.1980 | S/O(T) |
| 111287 | MATSOKOTERE | Dingani | 22.05.1980 | S/C/I |
| 111288 | CHIWONA | Jailos | 22.05.1980 | S/O(T) |
| 111289 | GOMES | Joseph | 22.05.1980 | Still serving |
| 111290 | MUCHEMENYE | Cliford Murambiwa | 22.05.1980 | Still serving |
| 111291 | NDOWA | Patrick Julius | 22.05.1980 | Still serving |
| 111292 | MUSAKA | John | 22.05.1980 | D/Insp |
| 111293 | NDOVI | Norbert | 22.05.1980 | S/S/O |
| 111294 | RUBINGO | Aaron | 22.05.1980 | Still serving |
| 111295 | DUTIRO | Kingston | 22.05.1980 | S/Insp |
| 111296 | MUROMBEDZI | Zwenyika | 22.05.1980 | S/C/Insp |
| 111297 | PO-KUWAKA | Rudolph | 22.05.1980 | D/P/O |
| 111298 | PFUMBIDZAYI | Humphrey | 22.05.1980 | Insp |
| 111299 | MANDIZWIDZA | Stewart | 22.05.1980 | Still serving |
| 111300 | CHINYANGANYA | Wonder | 22.05.1980 | Still serving |
| 111301 | MABIKA | Kumbirai | 22.05.1980 | A/Insp |
| 111302 | SAWYER | Graham | 22.05.1980 | Supt |
| 111303 | SIMOYI | Anthony | 22.05.1980 | P/O |
| 111304 | CHIRIMUUTA | Wilfred | 22.05.1980 | Still serving |
| 111305 | ZHARARE | Pius | 22.05.1980 | Still serving |
| 111306 | MPANDANYAMA | Jonathan | 22.05.1980 | Still serving |
| 111307 | CHIMANGA | Muderedzi | 22.05.1980 | Still serving |
| 111308 | MUCHAZORWA | Vanancio | 22.05.1980 | Still serving |
| 111309 | CHINGWARO | Stanislaus | 22.05.1980 | Still serving |
| 111310 | DZIKIRA | Goodluck | 22.05.1980 | Still serving |
| 111311 | CHIGOME | Simplisio | 22.05.1980 | P/O |
| 111312 | MANDIZHA | Samuel Tendai | 22.05.1980 | S/O(T) |
| 111313 | JAMUSI | Temba | 22.05.1980 | P/O |
| 111314 | TAMBARA | Master | 22.05.1980 | P/O |
| 111315 | CHAWATAMA | Ray Ronald | 22.05.1980 | P/O |
| 111316 | MUTAPANDUWA | Day | 22.05.1980 | P/O |
| 111317 | GABI | Godfrey | 22.05.1980 | Insp |
| 111318 | MUGADZA | Obadiah | 22.05.1980 | P/O |
| 111319 | DZOMBE | Cleopas | 22.05.1980 | Supt |
| 111320 | MHEPO | Saison | 22.05.1980 | D/Insp |
| 111321 | MUPEMHI | Edson | 22.05.1980 | Supt |
| 111322 | CHAMBISE | Washington | 22.05.1980 | not recorded |
| 111323 | MHUZA | Manasa | 22.05.1980 | Insp |
| 111324 | MUZINDA | Martin | 22.05.1980 | P/O |
| 111325 | MANDIZWINDZA | Gideon | 23.05.1980 | P/O |
| 111326 | MUVINGI | Alex | 19.05.1980 | S/O |
| 111327 | HORNER | Jeremy Edward | 22.05.1980 | Insp |
| 111328 | WEBB | Alistair James | 02.06.1980 | D/Insp |
| 111329 | ROBERTS | Colin William | 10.06.1980 | D/P/O |
| 111330 | HEYNE | Kevin Fletcher | 21.05.1980 | L/S/O |
| 111331 | NYONI | Peterson | 11.06.1980 | Supt |
| 111332 | KUJACHA | Edward | 19.06.1980 | A/Insp |
| 111333 | MKOBA | Silas | 19.06.1980 | D/Insp |
| 111334 | MADIRO | George | 19.06.1980 | P/O |
| 111335 | CHINYANGANYA | Naison | 19.06.1980 | Still serving |
| 111336 | SAWADYE | Patson | 19.06.1980 | P/O |
| 111337 | MUZIRI | Dickson | 19.06.1980 | A/Insp |
| 111338 | GUTURA | Alexander | 19.06.1980 | Insp |
| 111339 | CHIPONDA | Nathaniel | 19.06.1980 | Insp |
| 111340 | SIWELA | Edward | 19.06.1980 | Still serving |
| 111341 | SIKANADZE | John | 19.06.1980 | P/O |
| 111342 | MADIMUTSA | Kudzai Mike | 19.06.1980 | Still serving |
| 111343 | MAKOMBE | Tennyson | 19.06.1980 | P/O |
| 111344 | PARADZA | Peter | 19.06.1980 | Still serving |
| 111345 | DHLIWAYO | Freddy | 19.06.1980 | Still serving |
| 111346 | MUPINDU | Efraim Chorima | 19.06.1980 | A/Insp |
| 111347 | MUTSAUKI | Robert | 19.06.1980 | C/Supt |
| 111348 | DZARAMBA | Andrew | 19.06.1980 | Still serving |
| 111349 | MAKUVAZA | Patrick | 19.06.1980 | P/O |
| 111350 | MUGADZA | George | 19.06.1980 | Still serving |
| 111351 | HLAVATI | Geas | 19.06.1980 | Insp |
| 111352 | CHIHURI | Augustine | 19.06.1980 | Still serving |
| 111353 | NAKANISO | Joseph | 19.06.1980 | Insp |
| 111354 | ZWINASHE | Kaine | 19.06.1980 | D/Insp |
| 111355 | MUDYIRADIMA | Alfonce | 19.06.1980 | D/P/O |
| 111356 | KHAN | Mahomed Liacat | 19.06.1980 | D/P/O |
| 111357 | MUSAKA | Mikiri Moses | 19.06.1980 | Still serving |
| 111358 | MABVARU | Makona | 19.06.1980 | Insp |
| 111359 | KUPARA | Wonder Francis | 19.06.1980 | Insp |
| 111360 | MATEVEKE | Egnatious | 19.06.1980 | Insp |
| 111361 | SENGWE | Marvellous | 19.06.1980 | Still serving |
| 111362 | MUKABETA | Peter | 19.06.1980 | Insp |
| 111363 | MUJWAMBI | Sebastain | 19.06.1980 | Still serving |
| 111364 | MICHINERIPI | Mutandwa | 19.06.1980 | Insp |
| 111365 | SAKI | Dingani | 19.06.1980 | P/O |
| 111366 | SEKERERE | Bernard Chivara | 19.06.1980 | P/O |
| 111367 | NYANDORO | Abisaia | 19.06.1980 | Still serving |
| 111368 | MUCHENJE | Shepherd | 19.06.1980 | Still serving |
| 111369 | PHILIPO | Peter | 19.06.1980 | Insp |
| 111370 | CHIMWANDA | Emmanuel | 19.06.1980 | Still serving |
| 111371 | MUCHUCHU | Israel Shingayi | 19.06.1980 | Insp |
| 111372 | MUSOMA | Anderson | 19.06.1980 | Insp |
| 111373 | MUDZAMIRI | Fideris | 19.06.1980 | Sgt |
| 111374 | MWOYOWAWO | Andy | 19.06.1980 | P/O |
| 111375 | DE JONGH | Gavid Dennis | 16.06.1980 | Still serving |
| 111376 | CAMPBELL | Alistair Ross | 21.06.1980 | P/O |
| 111377 | REVELL | Malcolm Ian | 25.06.1980 | Insp |
| 111378 | CLARKE | Paul Michael | 27.06.1980 | D/Insp |
| 111379 | ANDREWS | William | 03.07.1980 | L/S/O |
| 111380 | PIRIE | David | 11.07.1980 | Insp(T) |
| 111381 | NELSON | William Stanfield | 12.07.1980 | P/O |
| 111382 | PAYNE | Charles Frederick | 16.07.1980 | S/O(T) |
| 111383 | JOGEE | Carfue | 22.07.1980 | P/O |

| No. | Surname | First name(s) | Date | Rank/Status |
|---|---|---|---|---|
| 111384 | LE ROUX | Peter | 17.07.1980 | P/O |
| 111385 | MUTEMI | George | 24.07.1980 | Still serving |
| 111386 | MUKONYORA | Richard Togara | 24.07.1980 | Sgt |
| 111387 | TAKANGOWADA | Daniel | 24.07.1980 | Still serving |
| 111388 | ZWICHAUYA | Oswald | 24.07.1980 | S/O |
| 111389 | MARAMBA | Onard | 24.07.1980 | S/O(T) |
| 111390 | MUDZIWAPASI | Phillimon | 24.07.1980 | Still serving |
| 111391 | MABVUURE | Zvitto | 24.07.1980 | Supt |
| 111392 | MANDAZA | Jimmy | 24.07.1980 | P/O |
| 111393 | ZVENYIKA | Lovemore | 24.07.1980 | not recorded |
| 111394 | TARAMBWA | Christian Valentine | 24.07.1980 | Still serving |
| 111395 | MAKUMBIROFA | Taimoni | 24.07.1980 | Still serving |
| 111396 | MANDONGWE | Michael | 24.07.1980 | D/P/O |
| 111397 | MATAMBANADZO | Takayedzwa | 24.07.1980 | Still serving |
| 111398 | MASHIRI | John | 24.07.1980 | P/O |
| 111399 | SHERENI | Jawet | 24.07.1980 | S/S/O |
| 111400 | MHURIRO | Lovemore | 24.07.1980 | Supt |
| 111401 | MAKONI | Josiah | 24.07.1980 | P/O |
| 111402 | GWENA | Elephas | 24.07.1980 | Still serving |
| 111403 | NEWALL | Michael | 24.07.1980 | P/O |
| 111404 | MAKEDENGE | Crispen | 24.07.1980 | Still serving |
| 111405 | MAVUNA | Isiah | 24.07.1980 | not recorded |
| 111406 | MASARIRAMBI | Cuthbert | 24.07.1980 | Still serving |
| 111407 | MAGORIMBO | Moses Zwawambire | 24.07.1980 | P/O |
| 111408 | ZISENGWE | Roden | 24.07.1980 | not recorded |
| 111409 | MAKHURANE | Coulson Keleboni | 24.07.1980 | Still serving |
| 111410 | MOYO | Adolph | 24.07.1980 | Still serving |
| 111411 | KHUMALO | Casper | 24.07.1980 | Still serving |
| 111412 | NDKOMO | Ruben | 24.07.1980 | S/O |
| 111413 | KLOPPERS | Johannes Stephanus | 24.07.1980 | P/O |
| 111414 | THODRANA | Glen | 24.07.1980 | P/O |
| 111415 | MUCHENJE | Oliver | 24.07.1980 | not recorded |
| 111416 | STUART | Frank | 24.07.1980 | S/O |
| 111417 | TEMBO | Thomas | 24.07.1980 | Still serving |
| 111418 | MUKAHLERA | Grey Kenneth | 24.07.1980 | Still serving |
| 111419 | MUCHEGWA | Bigboy | 24.07.1980 | S/O |
| 111420 | TAGWIREYI | Howard | 24.07.1980 | Sgt |
| 111421 | MAKOMBE | Eric | 24.07.1980 | S/A/C |
| 111422 | MOYO | Gilbert | 24.07.1980 | Still serving |
| 111423 | MATUTUKA | Ephraim | 24.07.1980 | Supt |
| 111424 | SIVAKO | Mthadisi | 24.07.1980 | P/O |
| 111425 | DAVIS | Wayne Alexander | 24.07.1980 | P/O |
| 111426 | FUMAYI | Onesmus | 24.07.1980 | Still serving |
| 111427 | MUDZIMU | Nhamo | 24.07.1980 | Still serving |
| 111428 | DUBE | Leonard | 24.07.1980 | S/O |
| 111429 | NCUBE | Douglas | 24.07.1980 | Supt |
| 111430 | MATIBWIRA | Ngoni | 24.07.1980 | Still serving |
| 111431 | RUPUNGU | Donald | 24.07.1980 | Insp |
| 111432 | OPUTERI | Funnie | 24.07.1980 | S/O(T) |
| 111433 | MUTAKWA | John | 24.07.1980 | not recorded |
| 111434 | MADANIRE | Saul | 24.07.1980 | P/O |
| 111435 | MASHAMBA | Absolom | 24.07.1980 | P/O |
| 111436 | HEALEY | David Alan | 24.07.1980 | Still serving |
| 111437 | MASVINGE | Onesimo | 24.07.1980 | Still serving |
| 111438 | MPOFU | Mhlaba | 24.07.1980 | not.recorded |
| 111439 | MEAD | Leonard Walter | 24.07.1980 | P/O |
| 111440 | MASEKO | Remington | 24.07.1980 | not recorded |
| 111441 | SIBANDA | Donald | 24.07.1980 | S/O(T) |
| 111442 | NYAMAKAO | Collen | 24.07.1980 | Still serving |
| 111443 | WAKATAMA | Ben | 24.07.1980 | P/O |
| 111444 | RUSIKE | Julius | 24.07.1980 | P/O |
| 111445 | BHEBE | Innocent | 24.07.1980 | Still serving |
| 111446 | MOYCE | Richard | 24.07.1980 | P/O |
| 111447 | BARNARD | Frederick Carel | 28.07.1980 | Insp(T) |
| 111448 | KARA | Moosa | 28.07.1980 | P/O |
| 111449 | MORA | Onias | 27.07.1980 | not recorded |
| 111450 | PETERS | Michael Gronge | 30.07.1980 | P/O |
| 111451 | WAITE | Derwyn Douglas | 30.07.1980 | P/O |

| No. | Surname | First Names | Attested | Discharged |
|---|---|---|---|---|
| 1 | ROUX | Martha | 11.07.1947 | 21.01.1954 |
| 2 | BETTS | Alice Gertrude | 11.07.1947 | 18.11.1962 |
| 3 | HARMER | May Irene | 08.06.1948 | 17.10.1954 |
| 4 | WORSDALE | | 28.07.1948 | 30.11.1948 |
| 5 | ALLAN | Helen Parker | 02.05.1950 | 01.05.1953 |
| 6 | THORP | Francis Eva | 02.07.1951 | 26.12.1964 |
| 7 | GRIFFIN | N.V. | 25.09.1951 | 21.12.1956 |
| 8 | BENNETT | Barbara Marian | 01.01.1952 | 06.09.1957 |
| 9 | BURROWS | Louie Elaine | 03.01.1952 | 01.05.1954 |
| 10 | CRATHORNE | Alice Maud | 30.01.1952 | 06.12.1955 |
| 11 | DU PLESSIS | Hester Elizabeth | 01.04.1952 | 14.08.1965 |
| 12 | WESSON | Dorothy Hayson | 01.05.1952 | 13.08.1954 |
| 13 | ADAMS | Winifred Louise | 16.06.1952 | 13.01.1955 |
| 14 | DIPPENAAR | Pauline Helen | 12.06.1953 | 08.03.1955 |
| 15 | WITHERS | Patricia Allison | 18.06.1953 | 21.07.1956 |
| 16 | TOYE | Anne Louise | 17.10.1953 | 03.12.1956 |
| 17 | STEVENS | Shirley | 05.11.1953 | 31.08.1957 |
| 18 | JENKINS | Doreen | 07.12.1953 | 14.09.1955 |
| 19 | BELL | Dorothy Lillian | 08.12.1953 | 08.04.1956 |
| 20 | NEVILLE | Catherine | 02.05.1954 | 16.03.1959 |
| 21 | WILLIAMS | Mary Evelyn | 01.06.1954 | 12.09.1955 |
| 22 | GREGORY | Vera | 19.09.1954 | 18.09.1957 |
| 23 | WILLIAMS | Rita Irene Rose | 14.03.1955 | 13.06.1955 |
| 24 | DORMER | Ruby Hannah | 25.04.1955 | 13.06.1955 |
| 25 | O'BYRNE | Patricia Agnes | 01.05.1955 | 22.07.1958 |
| 26 | ADOOR | Rosary Margarette | 01.07.1955 | 25.05.1957 |
| 27 | TUCKER | Sheila Ann | 03.07.1955 | 29.01.1956 |
| 28 | WHITEHEAD | Catherine | 02.02.1956 | 18.10.1969 |
| 29 | ROWLANDS | Ruth Vrely | 01.03.1956 | 30.04.1976 |
| 30 | BERRY | Shelagh Myfanwy | 05.06.1956 | 02.03.1958 |
| 31 | ARNOLD | Yvonne Muriel | 02.07.1956 | 30.05.1958 |
| 32 | MAC DONALD | Maureen | 01.07.1957 | 11.05.1957 |
| 33 | CORRIGAN | Elizabeth Alice | 18.02.1957 | 23.02.1958 |
| 34 | FOZZARD | Marion Maud | 18.02.1957 | 20.02.1959 |
| 35 | LYSTER | Susan Rosemary | 18.02.1957 | 04.04.1960 |
| 36 | McPHUN | Jean Evelyn | 18.02.1957 | 07.04.1959 |
| 37 | McROBERTS | Margaret Rose | 18.02.1957 | 03.08.1957 |
| 38 | RICE | Jean | 18.02.1957 | 17.02.1960 |
| 39 | RYAN | Ann Wendy | 18.02.1957 | 31.07.1964 |
| 40 | ANDERSON | Sybil Lillian | 18.02.1957 | 02.07.1960 |
| 41 | MARX | Thelma Miriam | 18.03.1957 | 10.12.1965 |
| 42 | MARRIOTT | Sheila Wynn | 06.04.1957 | 05.04.1960 |
| 43 | HOBSON | Bessie | 06.04.1957 | 05.04.1960 |
| 44 | HARDY | Margaret | 01.06.1957 | 31.01.1958 |
| 45 | TULLETT | Gwendoline | 01.06.1957 | 31.01.1958 |
| 46 | MARSH | Joan | 07.10.1957 | 18.12.1966 |
| 47 | HATCHWELL | Jill | 01.02.1958 | 28.02.1959 |
| 48 | KOCHS | Leonie Irmgard Fee | 09.07.1958 | 30.11.1963 |
| 49 | SYMONS | Jennifer Ann | 01.08.1958 | 20.05.1961 |
| 50 | MUIR | Margaret Muir | 01.04.1959 | 31.08.1963 |
| 51 | PIZEY | Helen Ann | 24.07.1959 | 10.09.1959 |
| 52 | GRIBBIN | Marie | 03.10.1959 | 12.11.1963 |
| 53 | FERRARI | Berenice Dorothy | 02.12.1959 | 12.01.1964 |
| 54 | BROWN | Shirely Ann Marsh | 03.12.1959 | 13.06.1960 |
| 55 | FOZZARD | Marion Maud | 18.02.1960 | 16.05.1962 |
| 56 | WILSON | Shirley Barbara | 05.07.1960 | 31.11.1972 |
| 57 | CREMIN | Wilhna | 08.09.1960 | 11.02.1961 |
| 58 | KENNEDY | Gwendolyn | 14.01.1961 | 19.05.1961 |
| 59 | WHITEHEAD | Lucy Claire | 11.09.1961 | 26.10.1961 |
| 60 | EVANS | Monica Helena | 15.11.1961 | 11.01.1967 |
| 61 | BUNYARD | Isla Ann | 01.02.1962 | 31.07.1962 |
| 62 | CHISHOLM | Margaret Anne | 01.02.1962 | 31.03.1977 |
| 63 | GREIG | Marion Mary | 01.02.1962 | 05.05.1962 |
| 64 | WISE | Desna Jean | 01.05.1962 | 31.01.1965 |
| 65 | LAMPSHIRE | Phillipa Ann Bertha | 01.05.1962 | 31.10.1963 |
| 66 | SPEARES | Ellison Jain | 04.06.1962 | 28.02.1973 |
| 67 | GOUWS | Fransina Johanna | 05.06.1962 | 31.07.1963 |
| 68 | HEWITT | Joan | 20.07.1962 | 31.05.1965 |
| 69 | CHAPMAN | Eve Virginia | 06.08.1962 | 26.04.1965 |
| 70 | BARCLAY | Rhoda | 01.12.1962 | 31.12.1963 |
| 71 | FORD | Louise Heather | 03.12.1962 | 02.08.1981 |
| 72 | HART | Cynthia Anne | 03.12.1962 | 14.03.1964 |
| 73 | HODSON | Shirley Ann | 03.12.1962 | 30.04.1965 |
| 74 | KEATS | Maria Lila Dorothy | 03.12.1962 | 31.03.1964 |
| 75 | BARKER | Rosina Mabel | 07.01.1963 | 28.02.1967 |
| 76 | BOULTON | Susan Lesley | 07.01.1963 | 07.01.1983 |
| 77 | CLARK | Royean Featherstone | 07.01.1963 | 07.01.1964 |
| 78 | ELLIS | Cynthia Ethel | 07.01.1963 | 06.01.1966 |
| 79 | JAMES | Judith Kathleen | 07.01.1963 | 07.03.1964 |
| 80 | FOURIE | France | 01.02.1963 | 01.04.1983 |
| 81 | LIEBRANDT | Michelle | 01.02.1963 | 31.08.1969 |
| 82 | SARGANT | Barbara Maureen | 01.02.1963 | 31.01.1966 |
| 83 | BENT | Gabrielle Ann | 08.05.1963 | 31.08.1969 |
| 84 | MARITZ | Sarah Susan | 08.05.1963 | 17.04.1964 |
| 85 | STEWART | Monica | 08.05.1963 | 30.12.1971 |
| 86 | LAVERS | Lynnette Irene | 11.06.1963 | 30.09.1968 |
| 87 | MORRISON | Daphne Jean | 27.06.1963 | 30.07.1981 |
| 88 | STEWARD | Natalie Alwyne | 27.06.1963 | 30.01.1964 |
| 89 | TREADWELL | Diana Pauline | 27.06.1963 | 30.06.1970 |
| 90 | WESTON | Gillian Helen | 27.06.1963 | 18.12.1965 |
| 91 | CLARKE | Christine Mary | 10.07.1963 | 24.12.1964 |
| 92 | McBAIN | Jessie Irene | 10.07.1963 | 04.07.1964 |
| 93 | GYTON | Leonie Janice | 01.08.1963 | 16.01.1964 |
| 94 | WELCH | Judith Mary | 19.11.1963 | 30.09.1967 |
| 95 | ARNOLD | Roberta | 16.12.1963 | 13.07.1966 |
| 96 | OLD-AM | Valerie | 16.12.1963 | 15.12.1966 |
| 97 | ELLIS | Sally Patricia | 02.01.1964 | 09.01.1966 |
| 98 | HULLEY | Elizabeth Joan | 02.03.1964 | 31.03.1969 |
| 99 | McLEAN | Lynette Sheena | 02.03.1964 | 31.03.1969 |
| 100 | SMITH | Brenda Faith | 02.03.1964 | 30.11.1967 |
| 101 | PIDDUCK | Cora-Anne | 03.03.1964 | 14.09.1967 |
| 102 | HOCKEY | Elizabeth Margrieta | 15.09.1964 | 13.12.1965 |
| 103 | LAMPRECHT | Zoe | 29.09.1964 | 31.05.1967 |
| 104 | WANE | Ann Jennifer | 17.11.1964 | 18.11.1966 |
| 105 | SPRINGALL | Alexandra Elizabeth | 26.01.1965 | 28.02.1966 |
| 106 | MORLEY | Leonora | 26.01.1965 | 31.05.1970 |
| 107 | SCHEEPERS | Susan Irene | 26.01.1965 | 05.03.1966 |
| 108 | WALSH | Dorette Francis | 23.03.1965 | 30.06.1970 |
| 109 | SCAWTHORNE | Angela Wendy | 28.09.1965 | 27.09.1968 |
| 110 | ALCOCK | Norma Rhonda | 15.11.1965 | 31.01.1969 |
| 111 | HCRSLEY | Valerie Cynthia | 15.11.1965 | 07.09.1972 |
| 112 | WATTERS | Nicola Verney | 03.01.1966 | 31.03.1967 |
| 113 | BREWER | Gidda Rose | 03.01.1966 | 30.07.1972 |
| 114 | HULME | Beverley Rose | 03.01.1966 | 23.06.1970 |
| 115 | BAYLEY | Evelyn Charis | 20.01.1966 | 02.12.1967 |
| 116 | OSBURN | Cynthia Ethel | 09.02.1966 | 30.06.1968 |
| 117 | ELLIS | Antoinette | 29.03.1966 | 28.03.1969 |
| 118 | ATKEN | Wendy | 29.03.1966 | 30.09.1974 |
| 119 | B-OOKS | Diana Evelyn | 01.04.1966 | 30.09.1974 |
| 120 | FYNN | Anna-Maria Rina | 01.04.1966 | 30.04.1968 |
| 121 | JONKER | Jennifer Elizabeth | 28.06.1966 | 09.10.1973 |
| 122 | EALES | Shirley Jeanette | 09.12.1966 | 30.06.1970 |
| 123 | SWANEPOEL | Moira Vivien | | 29.07.1972 |
| 124 | ELLIS | Orselina Hermina | | 29.09.1972 |
| 125 | MATTERN | Margaret | | 29.09.1972 |
| 126 | RIX | Helena Catharina | | 01.02.1967 |
| 127 | PRONK | Wendy Ann Russell | | 30.07.1970 |
| 128 | DONALD | Sheila Mary | | 01.02.1967 |
| 129 | GREEN | Moira Elizabeth | | 03.04.1967 |
| 130 | CULVERWELL | Cerise Anne | | 12.07.1967 |
| 131 | LINDEQUE | Yvonne Carman | | 18.10.1967 |
| 132 | SNOOK | Teresa | | 31.12.1973 |
| 133 | CLEMENTS | Denise June | | 23.12.1967 |
| 134 | WOODIWISS | Norma Edwina | | 13.01.1967 |
| 135 | TOMAN | Shelagh | | 1970 |
| 136 | NEEDHAM | | | 22.01.1983 |
| 137 | BUCKLE | Doreen Elaine | 13.01.1969 | 15.04.1974 |
| 138 | CLIFF | Trudy | 13.01.1969 | 10.02.1971 |
| 139 | EVANS | Ericka Cecelia | 13.01.1969 | 31.03.1975 |
| 140 | LEASK | Sarah Jane | 13.01.1969 | 10.07.1979 |
| 141 | STATON | Jennifer Jean | 13.01.1969 | 27.04.1972 |
| 142 | ZYLSTRA | Cecelia Kathleen | 13.01.1969 | 31.01.1971 |
| 143 | BEZUIDENHOUT | Magdalena | 13.10.1969 | 26.08.1972 |
| 144 | HAYES | Madeline Anne | 13.10.1969 | 29.02.1972 |
| 145 | KAY | Shirley Patricia | 13.10.1969 | 30.04.1985 |
| 146 | KLEYNHANS | Clair Caroline | 13.10.1969 | 31.03.1971 |
| 147 | LUNDERSTEDT | Wendy Elizabeth | 13.10.1969 | 28.09.1973 |
| 148 | PHELAN | Kerry Lynn | 13.10.1969 | 12.10.1972 |
| 149 | BROOKS | Wendy Ann | 06.08.1970 | 31.10.1971 |
| 150 | COURTNEY | Susan Stanhope | 06.08.1970 | 26.05.1972 |
| 151 | DORNAN | Joan Elizabeth | 06.08.1970 | 31.10.1971 |
| 152 | DUGUID | Heather | 06.08.1970 | 18.11.1972 |
| 153 | GRIGG | Gillian Lesley | 06.08.1970 | 30.09.1971 |
| 154 | LOWE | Edith Sarah Hunter | 06.08.1970 | 31.07.1972 |
| 155 | SHUTTE | Susan Frances | 06.08.1970 | 31.07.1972 |
| 156 | ADAMS | Carol Sue | 18.02.1971 | 30.06.1975 |
| 157 | ALVORD | Mary Patricia | 18.02.1971 | 22.12.1978 |
| 158 | BLEASDALE | Patricia Lesley | 18.02.1971 | 17.02.1974 |
| 159 | BOSMAN | Pauline Franscina | 18.02.1971 | 09.03.1972 |
| 160 | BROWN | Hilary Joy | 18.02.1971 | 31.01.1973 |
| 161 | FITZPATRICK | Jane Margaret | 18.02.1971 | 17.02.1974 |
| 162 | GRIGGS | Jill Margaret Wiede | 18.02.1971 | 30.09.1972 |
| 163 | HUTCHENS | Patricia Joyce Ann | 18.02.1971 | 30.09.1977 |
| 164 | MARX | Rozania | 18.02.1971 | 31.10.1971 |
| 165 | McCULLOCH | Iona Margaret | 18.02.1971 | 05.04.1971 |
| 166 | ROELOFSE | Lynette Diane Isobel | 18.02.1971 | 11.07.1973 |
| 167 | SELLS | Charlotte Amelia | 21.01.1972 | 13.07.1975 |
| 168 | BULLOCK | Jill Lorraine | 21.01.1972 | 31.08.1975 |
| 169 | CLARKE | Pauline Mary | 21.01.1972 | 28.02.1977 |
| 170 | CLAYTON | Rosemary Evelyn | 21.01.1972 | 20.01.1977 |
| 171 | HOLLAND | Shirley Patricia | 21.01.1972 | 20.01.1975 |
| 172 | KING | Lesley Jean | 21.01.1972 | 20.01.1975 |
| 173 | LEACH | Pamela Lynette | 21.01.1972 | 22.06.1975 |
| 174 | McCALLISTER | Sarah Ann Sybeth | 21.01.1972 | 05.12.1973 |
| 175 | OLIVA | Amanda Lucina | 21.01.1972 | 20.01.1975 |
| 176 | PADDON | Bridget | 21.01.1972 | 20.01.1975 |
| 177 | PALMER | Margaret Ann | 21.01.1972 | 20.01.1972 |
| 178 | RYALL | Desiree Cecile | 21.01.1972 | 30.04.1977 |
| 179 | VENTER | Elsie Sophia | 21.01.1972 | 26.10.1976 |
| 180 | VAN HEERDEN | Margaretha Constantia | 28.01.1972 | 20.01.1975 |
| 181 | WHYTE | Lorraine Margaret | 27.01.1972 | 30.04.1977 |
| 182 | BROOKING | Mary Ann | 09.05.1972 | 27.09.1973 |
| 183 | WRIGHT | Julie | 09.05.1972 | 30.06.1974 |
| 184 | KUTTNER | Dorothea Mary | 26.05.1972 | 01.05.1981 |
| 185 | FITZGERALD | Catherine | 01.06.1972 | 31.12.1975 |
| 186 | FREESTONE | Cecilia Anne | 01.06.1972 | 30.05.1975 |
| 187 | HINWOOD | Elizabeth Caroline | 01.06.1972 | 31.05.1975 |
| 188 | SELKIRK | Robin | 12.06.1972 | 11.06.1975 |
| 189 | BUCHANAN | Carol Ann | 14.08.1972 | 01.03.1978 |
| 190 | DIBDEN | Glynis Ruth Mabel | 20.09.1972 | 31.05.1977 |
| 191 | DUNCAN | Wendy Katherine | 20.09.1972 | 29.02.1976 |
| 192 | LAMB | Linda Joan | 20.09.1972 | 23.06.1978 |
| 193 | REES | Ann Anthonia Donnas | 20.09.1972 | 28.02.1974 |
| 194 | REYNOLDS | Jennifer Jane | 20.09.1972 | 08.12.1972 |
| 195 | MUNRO | Susan Hazel | 31.01.1973 | 31.07.1974 |
| 196 | CLARKE | Yvonne Marian | 31.01.1973 | 05.04.1971 |
| 197 | BROWN | Marsha Odette | 31.01.1973 | 23.01.1975 |
| 198 | WILDE | Georgina Playfair | 31.01.1973 | 30.01.1976 |
| 199 | SHAWE | Linda Susan | 31.01.1973 | 30.01.1976 |
| 200 | CONWAY | Linda Mary | 31.01.1973 | 30.09.1980 |
| 201 | WILLIAMS | Helen Kathleen | 31.01.1973 | 30.01.1976 |
| 202 | MILLER | Beryl Jennifer | 31.01.1973 | 02.02.1974 |
| 203 | LAMB | Susan | 31.01.1973 | 30.11.1976 |
| 204 | DEETLEFS | Carolyn Masha | 01.02.1973 | 28.02.1978 |
| 205 | WOOD | Minette Mary | 05.02.1973 | 30.06.1976 |

BSAP Nominal Roll • Women

| | | | | |
|---|---|---|---|---|
| 206 | SCOTT | Gail Dawn | 05.02.1973 | 13.10.1973 |
| 207 | MEARS | Susan Josephine | 09.02.1973 | 15.11.1975 |
| 208 | DIPPER | Lois Willoughby | 11.02.1973 | 01.05.1980 |
| 209 | WILLIAMS | Richardyne Megan | 12.02.1973 | 09.03.1973 |
| 210 | PHELAN | Kerry Lynn | 15.03.1973 | 14.03.1976 |
| 211 | CORNWELL | Lesley | 28.03.1973 | 29.09.1973 |
| 212 | LAKE | Sharron Lesley | 28.03.1973 | 31.10.1976 |
| 213 | PERKS | Carol Ann | 28.03.1973 | 30.11.1976 |
| 214 | VAN AARDE | Gertruida Cornelia | 28.03.1973 | 05.05.1975 |
| 215 | VAN NIEKERK | Rene Latitia | 28.03.1973 | 31.03.1974 |
| 216 | WATSON | Wynne Evelyn | 28.03.1973 | 10.11.1978 |
| 217 | NAUDE | Sandra June | 30.03.1973 | 28.02.1974 |
| 218 | VAN AARDT | Eltze Marie | 02.04.1973 | 01.04.1976 |
| 219 | CLEMENTS | Xena Colleen | 19.04.1973 | 05.08.1977 |
| 220 | MOFFAT | Frances Hilda | 01.05.1973 | 05.05.1978 |
| 221 | BROPHY | Josephine Mary | 01.05.1973 | 03.02.1978 |
| 222 | FRASER | Susan Jane | 29.05.1973 | 28.05.1976 |
| 223 | LAW | Susanne Dorothy | 29.05.1973 | 21.12.1978 |
| 224 | HARRIS | Jennifer Mary-Claire | 25.06.1973 | 24.06.1977 |
| 225 | KALSHOVEN | Wendy May Florence | 21.07.1973 | unknown |
| 226 | MEREDITH | Janine | 01.08.1973 | 29.08.1975 |
| 227 | HALES | Catriona Merilyn | 03.09.1973 | 23.12.1977 |
| 228 | O'DONNELL | Shevaun Catherine | 03.09.1973 | 30.04.1978 |
| 229 | BOSHOFF | Barbara Ann | 30.10.1973 | unknown |
| 230 | BROPHY | Brenda Joan | 30.10.1973 | 30.11.1982 |
| 231 | COLQUHOUN | Moira Eleanor | 30.10.1973 | 28.02.1978 |
| 232 | DREYER | Sharon | 30.10.1973 | 29.02.1976 |
| 233 | GARDNER | Arlene Lynette | 27.11.1973 | 31.08.1978 |
| 234 | MASSIE-TAYLOR | Gillian Margaret | 27.11.1973 | 25.01.1976 |
| 235 | RAINSFORD | Moira Blanche | 27.11.1973 | 22.12.1975 |
| 236 | KITCHING | Stella | 19.12.1973 | 18.12.1976 |
| 237 | PETERS | Susan Mary | 19.12.1973 | 30.06.1977 |
| 238 | SMITH | Yolanda Joy | 31.12.1973 | 31.12.1976 |
| 239 | BENADE | Aletta Magaretha | 08.01.1974 | 24.01.1975 |
| 240 | STEYN | Louisa Hendrika | 29.01.1974 | 28.01.1978 |
| 241 | WIGGILL | Daphne Margaret | 29.01.1974 | 19.12.1978 |
| 242 | BANKS | Eileen Joy Frances | 04.02.1974 | 03.02.1977 |
| 243 | WELLS | Wendy Lynne | 26.02.1974 | 25.02.1977 |
| 244 | PAPENFUS | Jennifer Helena | 26.02.1974 | 08.05.1983 |
| 245 | ROYSTON | Karen Anne | 04.03.1974 | 14.09.1977 |
| 246 | BRITS | Doreen Ivy | 01.04.1974 | 31.03.1977 |
| 247 | PEIRCE | Lesley Helen | 30.04.1974 | 31.01.1976 |
| 248 | HUGHES-HEWITT | Claudia Frances | 30.04.1974 | 30.10.1976 |
| 249 | HALL | Catheryn Loveridge | 28.05.1974 | 26.07.1979 |
| 250 | LATTEY | Mary Ann | 01.07.1974 | 31.05.1975 |
| 251 | SUTTON | Wendy Anne | 01.07.1974 | unknown |
| 252 | BENNETT | Mary Anne | 03.07.1974 | 02.07.1977 |
| 253 | GENAU | Shannon Noelene | 04.09.1974 | 03.09.1977 |
| 254 | LYDDIATT | Paula Ann | 24.09.1974 | 30.04.1981 |
| 255 | SAICH | Carol Ann | 30.09.1974 | 30.04.1975 |
| 256 | SMITH | Yvonne Patricia | 29.10.1974 | 28.10.1977 |
| 257 | BOS | Sharon-Anne Madge | 29.10.1974 | 14.02.1976 |
| 258 | DUGUID | Heather | 01.11.1974 | 30.09.1976 |
| 259 | SHEPPARD | Penelope Jane | 26.11.1974 | 20.12.1978 |
| 260 | PATTLE | Gail Carol | 26.11.1974 | 25.11.1977 |
| 261 | COUCOM | Pamela | 29.11.1974 | 31.03.1978 |
| 262 | DU PLESSIS | Henriette | 02.12.1974 | 31.10.1976 |
| 263 | AMOS | Lorraine Jane | 02.12.1974 | 06.06.1980 |
| 264 | HOLT | Janice Peta | 18.12.1974 | 17.12.1877 |
| 265 | McINTOSH | Patricia Anne | 30.12.1974 | 29.12.1977 |
| 266 | EALES | Janine Yola Gloria | 31.12.1974 | 30.09.1975 |
| 267 | KESSLER | Evelyn Dianne | 02.01.1975 | 31.07.1980 |
| 268 | MASON | Penelope Susan | 06.01.1975 | 05.01.1978 |
| 269 | CURRIE | Janet Rita | 07.01.1975 | 30.06.1980 |
| 270 | HAFEZ | Amel | 07.01.1975 | 29.02.1976 |
| 271 | MAASDORP | Jennifer Elizabeth | 07.01.1975 | 05.06.1983 |
| 272 | VAN LEEUWEN | Sharon Margaret | 07.01.1975 | 06.01.1978 |
| 273 | HALL | Carole Ann | 28.01.1975 | 06.03.1976 |
| 274 | HODSON | Lynne Margaret | 28.01.1975 | 31.05.1976 |
| 275 | CLAYTON | Pamela Elizabeth | 28.01.1975 | 31.03.1978 |
| 276 | BELFORD | Nicolette Elizabeth | 01.02.1975 | 31.01.1978 |
| 277 | BELL | Patricia Anne | 03.02.1975 | 02.02.1978 |
| 278 | UTTERTON | Linda Margueite | 03.02.1975 | 30.04.1978 |
| 279 | DUCKWORTH | Margaret Elizabeth | 03.02.1975 | 31.01.1981 |
| 280 | PALMER-JONES | Heather Lynette | 03.02.1975 | 02.02.1978 |
| 281 | NOWELL | Doreen Elaine | 13.02.1975 | 30.06.1975 |
| 282 | KEYS | Ingrid Maria | 13.02.1975 | 12.02.1978 |
| 283 | LISTER | Susan Anne | 25.02.1975 | 31.12.1978 |
| 284 | MASON | Susan | 25.02.1975 | 30.06.1977 |
| 285 | WHALLEY | Dorreen Joyce | 25.02.1975 | 24.02.1978 |
| 286 | WILLIS | Julie Ann | 18.03.1975 | 17.03.1975 |
| 287 | IMMELMAN | Karen Ingrid | 24.03.1975 | 04.07.1975 |
| 288 | BRICKMAN | Elizabeth | 01.04.1975 | 30.09.1977 |
| 289 | LINDEQUE | Cerise Ann | 01.04.1975 | 30.04.1980 |
| 290 | CLARKE | Carole Lee | 29.04.1975 | 31.08.1976 |
| 291 | STUTTARD | Patricia Ann | 08.05.1975 | 05.04.1979 |
| 292 | FREES | Marilyn Ann | 01.06.1975 | 31.05.1978 |
| 293 | HODGSON-TODD | Edwina Jill | 04.06.1975 | 24.11.1977 |
| 294 | KLEINE | Nicolette | 01.08.1975 | 16.12.1977 |
| 295 | GRIFFITH | Heather Gillian | 11.08.1975 | 08.12.1978 |
| 296 | NUTT | Jocelyn Anne | 07.10.1975 | 31.07.1979 |
| 297 | PAXTON | Beverly Louise | 10.10.1975 | 10.03.1981 |
| 298 | RAMSEY | Penelope Ann | 10.10.1975 | 09.10.1977 |
| 299 | GREENOUGH | Jacquelin | 10.10.1975 | 24.10.1980 |
| 300 | EVANS | Erica Cecelia | 01.11.1975 | 19.08.1979 |
| 301 | McKENZIE | Jean Ellizabeth | 01.11.1975 | 28.02.1979 |
| 302 | AVERY | Nicola Diane | 21.11.1975 | 31.12.1970 |
| 303 | SHORT | Jacqueline Susan | 21.11.1975 | 21.11.1978 |
| 304 | NAUDE | Catherine Elizabeth | 21.11.1975 | 02.06.1981 |
| 305 | SHILLITO | Linda | 21.11.1975 | 30.11.1976 |
| 306 | HULLEY | Elizabeth Joan | 01.12.1975 | 29.07.1978 |
| 307 | EDYE | Deborah Margaret | 01.12.1975 | 30.11.1978 |
| 308 | SNOOK | Sharon Gaye | 20.01.1976 | 21.07.1978 |
| 309 | MEIKLE | Cheryth Diana | 20.01.1976 | 22.12.1978 |
| 310 | SCOTT | Grace Baillie | 20.01.1976 | 20.01.1979 |
| 311 | GRIMES | Jayne | 20.01.1976 | 31.05.1979 |
| 312 | CLARK | Rosalind | 20.01.1976 | 19.01.1978 |
| 313 | BREITHAUPT-MEYER | Lynette | 20.01.1976 | 30.04.1980 |
| 314 | HAY | Angela Elizabeth | 20.01.1976 | 07.08.1978 |
| 315 | DE JAGER | Reinette | 20.01.1976 | 19.01.1978 |
| 316 | HAWORTH | Pamela May | 20.01.1976 | 19.01.1978 |
| 317 | CROUCH | Sandra Gail | 20.01.1976 | 19.01.1978 |
| 318 | McAFEE | Susan Katherine | 20.01.1976 | 31.10.1978 |
| 319 | BRAGGE | Fiona Louise | 20.01.1976 | 01.05.1980 |
| 320 | BAILEY | Sally Jane | 20.01.1976 | 29.02.1980 |
| 321 | PEPPER | Tracey Anne | 20.01.1976 | 28.02.1982 |
| 322 | PLOWES | Carolyn Margaret | 20.01.1976 | 30.06.1979 |
| 323 | TAYLOR | Fiona May | 20.01.1976 | 22.06.1979 |
| 324 | VENTER | Elizabeth Johanna | 20.01.1976 | 16.12.1977 |
| 325 | HILL | Susan Gael | 20.01.1976 | 01.07.1979 |
| 326 | KRIEGLER | Linda | 20.01.1976 | 10.08.1979 |
| 327 | VAN WYK | Dorothy Joy | 20.01.1976 | 31.10.1978 |
| 328 | CHARNOCK | Caroline Margaret | 20.01.1976 | 13.05.1978 |
| 329 | NEVES | Clara Branea | 20.01.1976 | 26.07.1977 |
| 330 | RUDMAN | Cheryl June | 02.02.1976 | 05.05.1980 |
| 331 | HUGHES | Elizabeth Jane | 20.02.1976 | 19.02.1978 |
| 332 | WESSELS | Esther | 24.02.1976 | 31.10.1978 |
| 333 | LAYZELL | Margot Anna | 25.02.1976 | 01.12.1978 |
| 334 | BAILEY | Lois Ann | 15.03.1976 | 21.03.1982 |
| 335 | IRVINE | Janice Jean | 17.03.1976 | 31.12.1980 |
| 336 | WHITEFIELD | Moyra Lila | 22.03.1976 | 05.06.1980 |
| 337 | LEVINE | Cheryl | 26.03.1976 | 25.03.1978 |
| 338 | MICKLESFIELD | Suzanne Colleen | 26.03.1976 | 15.03.1979 |
| 339 | GENT | Vanessa Lynn | 10.05.1976 | 31.07.1980 |
| 340 | GIBSON | Judith Marina | 10.05.1976 | 31.05.1980 |
| 341 | KEANE | Hilda Adrienne | 10.05.1976 | 12.09.1980 |
| 342 | McDOWALL | Susan | 10.05.1976 | 13.09.1977 |
| 343 | PEACH | Beverley-Ann | 10.05.1976 | 10.09.1976 |
| 344 | WILLEMSE | Rene Rolletta | 10.05.1976 | 02.09.1980 |
| 345 | HECO | Rose Marie Rita | 10.05.1976 | 10.05.1977 |
| 346 | HOBBS | Maureen Brenda | 17.05.1976 | 31.08.1979 |
| 347 | JACKSON | Janice Lynn | 19.07.1976 | 31.03.1978 |
| 348 | LIVESEY | June Helen | 11.08.1976 | 31.05.1980 |
| 349 | KIMBER | Cheryl Marlene | 09.08.1976 | 15.12.1980 |
| 350 | CLAYTON | Deborah Ann | 16.08.1976 | 11.07.1979 |
| 351 | MILLAR | Penelope | 01.09.1976 | 31.08.1978 |
| 352 | DE CHABY | Maria Theresa | 01.09.1976 | 31.08.1980 |
| 353 | CASTLE | Joy Gwenda | 01.09.1976 | 31.08.1978 |
| 354 | EVISON | Lesley Jean | 01.09.1976 | 02.05.1980 |
| 355 | McKINNON | Jean | 01.09.1976 | 01.05.1980 |
| 356 | CHEESMAN | Lesley Ann | 01.09.1976 | 31.08.1978 |
| 357 | WALKER | Cheryl | 01.09.1976 | 16.04.1982 |
| 358 | SHACKLETON | Karen Michelle | 01.09.1976 | 02.05.1983 |
| 359 | MacDONALD | Michele Gail | 28.09.1976 | 27.09.1978 |
| 360 | KERR | Ruth Louise | 15.11.1976 | 14.11.1978 |
| 361 | FRIEND | Robin Margaret | 22.11.1976 | 12.07.1979 |
| 362 | ATHERSTONE | Barbara Joy | 30.11.1976 | 30.11.1978 |
| 363 | ESPACH | Virginia Eve | 30.11.1976 | 31.01.1980 |
| 364 | NEWTON | Yvonne Dorothy | 15.12.1976 | 31.05.1979 |
| 365 | HICKMAN | Angela | 20.12.1976 | 01.05.1980 |
| 366 | YOUNG | Dawn Mary | 20.12.1976 | 03.09.1978 |
| 367 | JARVIS | Wendy Anne | 20.12.1976 | 31.03.1979 |
| 368 | SYMES | Anne Denise | 03.01.1977 | 21.08.1979 |
| 369 | ORSMOND | Dawn Marie | 03.01.1977 | 02.01.1979 |
| 370 | SCHOLTZ | Karen Anne | 03.01.1977 | 30.11.1979 |
| 371 | KRIEK | Cecilia | 06.01.1977 | 05.01.1979 |
| 372 | VAN STADEN | Chrizell Avril | 03.01.1977 | 03.07.1980 |
| 373 | FOUCHE | Norma Muriel | 10.01.1977 | 31.05.1978 |
| 374 | COX | Leslie Rosemary | 17.01.1977 | 31.05.1979 |
| 375 | WYLIE | Sharon Lynne | 24.01.1977 | 04.06.1980 |
| 376 | MITCHELL | Anne Joan | 24.01.1977 | 22.06.1979 |
| 377 | WILL | Heather Anne | 20.01.1977 | 19.08.1983 |
| 378 | PALMER | Theresa | 27.01.1977 | 26.01.1979 |
| 379 | COCHRANE | Lynette Anne | 27.01.1977 | 09.04.1979 |
| 380 | WARD | Joan | 28.01.1977 | 27.01.1979 |
| 381 | BARRON | Christine Nora | 31.01.1977 | 31.05.1979 |
| 382 | HENDERSON | Beverley Diane | 03.02.1977 | 31.03.1980 |
| 383 | BEGG | J.P. | 11.02.1977 | 22.06.1979 |
| 384 | VAUGHAN | Diane Patricia | 01.02.1977 | 01.06.1980 |
| 385 | IMPEY | Tammy May | 14.02.1977 | 09.05.1981 |
| 386 | ARCHER | Lee | 17.02.1977 | 05.05.1980 |
| 387 | HOFFENBERG | Maureen Joyce | 17.02.1977 | 30.09.1980 |
| 388 | DE KLERK | Elsie Ann | 21.02.1977 | 31.05.1979 |
| 389 | CROSBY | Dorothy Johanna | 01.03.1977 | 29.12.1980 |
| 390 | SCHOON | Maria Elizabeth | 03.03.1977 | 26.07.1979 |
| 391 | McLEAN | Sheena Briony | 07.03.1977 | 30.06.1979 |
| 392 | COLQUHOUN | Wendy Ann | 16.03.1977 | 30.06.1979 |
| 393 | GREENOUGH | Anne | 04.04.1977 | 01.06.1980 |
| 394 | LE ROUX | Emmerentia Gerharda | 04.04.1977 | 19.12.1979 |
| 395 | STEVENS | Barbara | 04.04.1977 | 03.04.1979 |
| 396 | NELL | Carolyn Ann | 04.04.1977 | 01.05.1980 |
| 397 | WALTERS | Jennifer Lynn | 04.04.1977 | 27.10.1978 |
| 398 | MORRISON | Eileen Eva | 04.04.1977 | 30.04.1981 |
| 399 | BENNETT | Susan Mary | 04.04.1977 | 31.05.1979 |
| 400 | SCHREIBER | Cecelia Mary | 02.05.1977 | 16.12.1981 |
| 401 | SMUTS | Cynthia Marina | 27.05.1977 | 30.04.1978 |
| 402 | SEBECKE | Silvia Christine | 01.06.1977 | 31.05.1979 |
| 403 | THOMAS | Lyn Llewella | 20.06.1977 | 19.06.1979 |
| 404 | PRENTIS | Ilone Susan | 27.06.1977 | 19.08.1980 |
| 405 | McKERSIE | Barbara Anne | 13.07.1977 | 31.01.1980 |
| 406 | HOPLEY | Jennifer Anne | 28.07.1977 | 12.06.1980 |
| 407 | WELCH | Amanda Christine | 28.07.1977 | 02.05.1982 |
| 408 | NORMAN | Jane Catherine | 28.07.1977 | 31.12.1981 |
| 409 | WEBB | Sherilynn Beverley | 28.07.1977 | 31.10.1977 |
| 410 | THORNTON | Lynette Ann | 28.07.1977 | 22.06.1982 |
| 411 | RICHARDSON | Janet Mary | 28.07.1977 | 27.07.1979 |
| 412 | BROWN | Susan Jane | 28.07.1977 | 23.06.1981 |

| No. | Surname | First name(s) | Date | Date |
|---|---|---|---|---|
| 413 | MILLER | Debra Frances | 28.07.1977 | 09.07.1980 |
| 414 | McKERSIE | Jennifer Eileen | 28.07.1977 | 28.10.1978 |
| 415 | BOLTON | Vivienne Alice | 01.08.1977 | 10.09.1978 |
| 416 | MATHEWS | Christine Antoinette | 26.08.1977 | 06.03.1980 |
| 417 | YATES | Loreto Anne | 01.09.1977 | 06.07.1979 |
| 418 | HASSON | Mathilde | 20.09.1977 | 31.12.1978 |
| 419 | CASTLE | Christine Sheila | 21.09.1977 | 18.02.1981 |
| 420 | CARLAW | Margaret Joan | 13.10.1977 | 29.12.1980 |
| 421 | WEEDMAN | Linda Jane | 13.10.1977 | 05.05.1980 |
| 422 | BICHARD | Hilary Jane | 01.11.1977 | 30.06.1980 |
| 423 | MICHAEL | Kim Sian | 01.11.1977 | 17.05.1981 |
| 424 | CLARKE | Pauline Mary | 02.11.1977 | 31.01.1981 |
| 425 | BEACOM | Alexandra Duncan | 01.11.1977 | 21.07.1979 |
| 426 | TARR | Berenice Lesley | 09.11.1977 | 02.05.1980 |
| 427 | RIDDLE | Fiona Gay | 08.12.1977 | 01.07.1981 |
| 428 | QUINLAN | Amanda Patricia | 28.12.1977 | 14.04.1980 |
| 429 | PRICE | Caroline Sylvia | 28.12.1977 | 02.05.1983 |
| 430 | TUCKER | Sandra Phyllis | 28.12.1977 | 27.12.1979 |
| 431 | WESTROP | Carol Janet Gillian | 28.12.1977 | 27.12.1979 |
| 432 | LUDEKE | Gertrude Maria | 28.12.1977 | 27.12.1979 |
| 433 | MOORE | Jennifer Gwendoline | 28.12.1977 | 01.05.1982 |
| 434 | PRINS | Jennifer Hilda | 28.12.1977 | 27.12.1979 |
| 435 | YEATES | Geraldine Gloria | 28.12.1977 | 12.09.1980 |
| 436 | ENNIS | Margaret Anne | 28.12.1977 | 01.05.1981 |
| 437 | GRATTON | Jacqueline Dawn | 28.12.1977 | 01.04.1982 |
| 438 | MYNHARDT | Audrey Louise | 28.12.1977 | 05.08.1980 |
| 439 | OGILVY | Kathrine Grace | 16.01.1978 | 30.04.1983 |
| 440 | EDMOND | Deborah Shaneen | 19.01.1978 | 02.05.1981 |
| 441 | GIBSON | Deborah | 23.01.1978 | 21.07.1980 |
| 442 | HEIN | Shirley Marie | 23.01.1978 | 30.06.1979 |
| 443 | SUTHERLAND | Kathleen Ann | 01.02.1978 | 01.01.1981 |
| 444 | CHATHAM | Lorna Elizabeth | 07.02.1978 | 02.08.1979 |
| 445 | VERMAAK | Ursula Igna Jo-Ann | 14.02.1978 | 04.06.1980 |
| 446 | HENDERSON | Bridget Priscilla | 16.02.1978 | 08.11.1980 |
| 447 | SCHROEDER | Kathleen Doris | 20.02.1978 | 10.08.1981 |
| 448 | HARRIS | Neryl Ann Vaughan | 27.02.1978 | 21.05.1980 |
| 449 | MARX | Melonie Deborah | 28.02.1978 | 31.03.1980 |
| 450 | ROWSELL | Jane Lorna | 28.02.1978 | 08.08.1981 |
| 451 | VALDAL | Janet Evelyne | 02.03.1978 | 01.05.1980 |
| 452 | CALDER | Cheryl Lynn | 02.03.1978 | 30.04.1978 |
| 453 | GRANT | Allison Shelagh | 03.03.1978 | 31.07.1979 |
| 454 | BROWNLEE | Elizabeth Mary | 03.03.1978 | 02.03.1980 |
| 455 | WILKINSON | Nola Jean | 07.03.1978 | 06.03.1980 |
| 456 | RITCHIE | Colleen Brenda | 08.03.1978 | 30.06.1980 |
| 457 | BROOKE | Debra Anne Retti | 03.04.1978 | 07.08.1980 |
| 458 | HUTCHENS | Joy | 03.04.1978 | 08.01.1981 |
| 459 | DUNCAN | Amanda | 07.04.1978 | 31.03.1981 |
| 460 | SHUTT | Christine Karen | 07.04.1978 | 29.12.1980 |
| 461 | CREMER | Cynthia Phyllis | 10.04.1978 | 29.12.1980 |
| 462 | GARDNER | Arlene Lynette | 17.04.1978 | 16.07.1981 |
| 463 | VICKERS | Kisayne Claire | 20.04.1978 | 01.08.1981 |
| 464 | BROWN | Patricia Anne | 20.04.1978 | 25.12.1978 |
| 465 | LAKE | Susan Margaret | 20.04.1978 | 31.12.1980 |
| 466 | BADENHORST | Alma | 20.04.1978 | 30.04.1981 |
| 467 | MARAIS | Veronica | 20.04.1978 | 24.01.1981 |
| 468 | ROBERTSON | Bernice Jeannie | 09.05.1978 | 15.04.1982 |
| 469 | HAYWARD | Debre Ann | 18.05.1978 | 31.01.1981 |
| 470 | WESSELS | Bridget Juliette | 02.06.1978 | 02.06.1980 |
| 471 | REYNOLDS | Janice | 07.06.1978 | 06.02.1980 |
| 472 | BONE | Elizabeth Fulton | 20.06.1978 | 20.06.1980 |
| 473 | DEETLEFS | Carolyn Masha | 29.06.1978 | 30.06.1980 |
| 474 | SHEPHERD | Rosemary Jean | 12.07.1978 | 11.07.1980 |
| 475 | KASPER | Susan Irene Pearl | 17.07.1978 | 01.03.1980 |
| 476 | CRONJE | Sandra Lee | 18.07.1978 | 01.05.1981 |
| 477 | SWANEPOEL | Valerie Anne | 04.08.1978 | 03.08.1980 |
| 478 | HURLEY | Linda Rose | 21.08.1978 | 08.08.1980 |
| 479 | GRAVES | Janice Elizabeth | 21.08.1978 | 15.02.1980 |
| 480 | WOODS | Jo-Anne | 29.08.1978 | 28.08.1980 |
| 481 | PATTLE | Gail Carol | 01.11.1978 | 31.05.1979 |
| 482 | COUCOM | Pamela | 06.11.1978 | 18.02.1983 |
| 483 | NOBLE | Janice Cadman | 23.11.1978 | 23.11.1980 |
| 484 | Mac DONALD | Carol Lesley | 23.11.1978 | 09.06.1981 |
| 485 | BOLAS | Anne Elizabeth | 12.12.1978 | 31.08.1982 |
| 486 | GLOSS | Marina Gezina | 12.12.1978 | 18.02.1981 |
| 487 | BARNES | Mary-Anne | 12.12.1978 | 06.04.1982 |
| 488 | GREENHILL | Carol Margaret | 02.01.1979 | 01.01.1981 |
| 489 | REITZ | Debra Anne | 04.01.1979 | 04.11.1980 |
| 490 | GRANGER | Isobel | 08.01.1979 | 30.09.1982 |
| 491 | EDWARDS | Moira Denise | 08.01.1979 | 30.09.1982 |
| 492 | CRABB | Linda Catherine | 08.01.1979 | 30.11.1979 |
| 493 | WEBB | Maureen Ann | 12.01.1979 | 11.04.1980 |
| 494 | TURNER | Christina | 22.01.1979 | 23.04.1981 |
| 495 | AUSTEN | Angela Carol | 22.01.1979 | 14.02.1981 |
| 496 | COLMAN | Nora Alice | 22.01.1979 | 22.01.1982 |
| 497 | MATONODZE | Dolores Maswerew | 22.01.1979 | 22.01.1981 |
| 498 | HARDMAN | Karen Margaret | 22.01.1979 | 24.12.1981 |
| 499 | PAXTON | Elizabeth Senga | 22.01.1979 | 22.01.1981 |
| 500 | VAN DEVENTER | Laura Joan | 22.01.1979 | 30.04.1983 |
| 501 | WHITE | Lindsay Ann | 22.01.1979 | 02.09.1980 |
| 502 | GUDO | Veronica Christina | 22.01.1979 | 30.04.1980 |
| 503 | MULLER | Michelle Josephine | 22.01.1979 | 22.09.1981 |
| 504 | PIETERSEN | Gail Frances | 22.01.1979 | 31.01.1989 |
| 505 | VERMAAK | Vernah | 22.01.1979 | 27.11.1980 |
| 506 | PATSIKA | Moira Estelle | 22.01.1979 | 30.04.1996 |
| 507 | ORNELLAS | Diane Carole | 22.01.1979 | 22.01.1981 |
| 508 | EVANS | Claire Alison | 22.01.1979 | 05.08.1982 |
| 509 | BRIDGE | Jacqueline Anne | 22.01.1979 | 30.04.1981 |
| 510 | SCHIPPERS | Marie Loraine | 22.01.1979 | 22.01.1981 |
| 511 | SWARTZ | Doreen Marilyn | | 29.12.1982 |
| 512 | Mac DONALD | Michele Gail | 01.02.1979 | 23.05.1981 |
| 513 | ALCORN | Linda Jane | 02.02.1979 | 31.08.1980 |
| 514 | BRAITHWAITE | Diane Ellen | 05.02.1979 | 05.07.1982 |
| 515 | ALLEN | Muriel Mary | 07.02.1979 | 02.05.1982 |
| 516 | RICH | Karen Elizabeth | 12.02.1979 | 17.03.1981 |
| 517 | EARWOOD | Alexandra Joy | 12.02.1979 | 12.01.1983 |
| 518 | ARNOTT | Claire Louise | 15.02.1979 | 23.12.1981 |
| 519 | KENNAIRD | Susan Elizabeth | 19.02.1979 | 30.04.1982 |
| 520 | BOER | Greta Audrey | 19.02.1979 | 06.11.1980 |
| 521 | FULKS | Lindsay Ann | 19.02.1979 | 08.03.1982 |
| 522 | WILLIAMS | Christina Hampshaw | 22.02.1979 | 21.02.1981 |
| 523 | STRYDOM | Desiree Margaret | 22.02.1979 | 27.08.1982 |
| 524 | ALDRIDGE | Rosalind Jennifer | 23.02.1979 | 30.04.1979 |
| 525 | COZENS | Heather Marjorie | 28.02.1979 | 18.05.1981 |
| 526 | CATHRO | Lesley Anne | 05.03.1979 | 13.07.1981 |
| 527 | SMALLBONES | Jane | 05.03.1979 | 31.12.1982 |
| 528 | FROST | Priscilla Anne | 05.03.1979 | 17.06.1981 |
| 529 | TARR | Giselle Tracy | 06.03.1979 | 05.03.1982 |
| 530 | GOUGH | Melinda Anne | 06.03.1979 | 30.09.1979 |
| 531 | BANKS | Christine Leona | 20.03.1979 | 31.12.1981 |
| 532 | SIVES | Jean Helen | 26.03.1979 | 25.03.1981 |
| 533 | PORTALLION | Lynda Colleen | 02.04.1979 | 03.02.1981 |
| 534 | CATHCART | Susan Nolleen | 04.04.1979 | 04.07.1980 |
| 535 | BROWN | Margaret Ann | 05.04.1979 | 04.12.1980 |
| 536 | WYATT | Lynne | 09.04.1979 | 09.10.1981 |
| 537 | RUBENSTEIN | Shireen Anne | 11.05.1979 | 06.01.1983 |
| 538 | MADGWICK | Noelleen Muriel | 21.05.1979 | 08.01.1983 |
| 539 | SELYER | Bella Conrodina | 21.05.1979 | 08.01.1983 |
| 540 | FOULKES | Maria Joyce | 28.05.1979 | 28.08.1980 |
| 541 | MAROVATSANGA | Rachel Dadirayi | 12.06.1979 | Dec.1996 |
| 542 | DARCH | Beverley Joy | 12.06.1979 | 02.06.1983 |
| 543 | MULENGA | Stella Maria | 12.06.1979 | 11.06.1989 |
| 544 | NQWABABA | Regina Judith | 17.07.1979 | Dec.1996 |
| 545 | HERBST | Johanna Sophia | 12.06.1979 | 11.06.1981 |
| 546 | CHIZEDZEDZE | Olga | 22.06.1979 | Dec.1996 |
| 547 | JACKSON | Beverley Ann | 02.07.1979 | 23.04.1982 |
| 548 | VAN LEEUWEN | Robyn Ann | 05.07.1979 | 07.02.1983 |
| 549 | MALKIN | Patricia Jane | 23.07.1979 | 21.10.1980 |
| 550 | GORE | Norma Natalie | 03.09.1979 | 04.01.1982 |
| 551 | COX | Leslie Rosemary | 04.09.1979 | 20.12.1985 |
| 552 | GROENEWALD | Suzanne Dorothy | 05.09.1979 | 18.01.1981 |
| 553 | COWLEY | S. | 05.09.1979 | Dec.1996 |
| 554 | HARVERYE | Rochelle Esther | 11.10.1979 | 12.12.1988 |
| 555 | STRUGNELL | Wynne Elizabeth | 29.10.1979 | 13.05.1980 |
| 556 | CHITUMBURA | R.S. | 01.11.1979 | Dec.1996 |
| 557 | BURGESS | Amanda Lucina | 01.11.1979 | 31.01.1981 |
| 558 | LUPHAHLA | Maggie | 01.11.1979 | Dec.1996 |
| 559 | HARVERYE | Sharon Cecilia | 01.11.1979 | 31.01.1981 |
| 560 | ELLIS | Pauline Alexandra | 01.11.1979 | 31.05.1981 |
| 561 | VERCUEIL | Tanya Susan | 01.11.1979 | 06.08.1980 |
| 562 | MUNGAYISWA | Agnes | 01.11.1979 | 02.07.1982 |
| 563 | MACKENZIE | Karen-Anne | 01.11.1979 | 28.03.1981 |
| 564 | SCOTT | Cheryl Norma | 12.11.1979 | 30.06.1980 |
| 565 | OTTO | Shireen | 04.01.1980 | 03.01.1980 |
| 566 | CULVERHOUSE | Susan Alison | 18.01.1980 | 22.01.1980 |
| 567 | HASKINS | Petersina Nicoleen | 21.01.1980 | 25.04.1984 |
| 568 | SHERRINGHAM | Carol Ann | 14.02.1980 | 13.02.1982 |
| 569 | SAMUSHONGA | Ellen | 13.03.1980 | Dec.1996 |
| 570 | MAKAWA | Emmie | 13.03.1980 | 07.01.1994 |
| 571 | KWANDE | Ennie Lindiwe | 13.03.1980 | Dec.1996 |
| 572 | MPOFU | Sithulisiwe | 13.03.1980 | Dec.1996 |
| 573 | JOHN | Mathilda | 13.03.1980 | 31.01.1997 |
| 574 | GUMEDE | Margaret | 12.03.1980 | Dec.1996 |
| 575 | RADEMEYER | Maureen Mary | 13.03.1980 | Dec.1996 |
| 576 | KAPFIDZE | Patricia | 13.03.1980 | Dec.1996 |
| 577 | DURIRU | Moulistia | 13.03.1980 | Dec.1996 |
| 578 | MZENGI | Victoria Thokozani | 13.03.1980 | 15.06.1982 |
| 579 | NYATHI | Idah | 13.03.1980 | 31.01.1985 |
| 580 | Mac DONALD | Maria Christine | 13.03.1980 | 22.11.1982 |
| 581 | MURONZI | Nancy | 13.03.1980 | 31.01.1984 |
| 582 | MHIZHA | Ruth Kuda | 26.06.1980 | 28.11.1980 |
| 583 | ROMANS | Karen | 27.05.1980 | 28.09.1982 |
| 584 | TIMURI | Lizzy | 26.06.1980 | Dec.1996 |
| 585 | TACHIJANA | Evelyn Senzeni | 26.06.1980 | 26.08.1994 |
| 586 | FRANKIS | Susan | 26.06.1980 | Dec.1996 |
| 587 | SIMANGO | Esta | 26.06.1980 | Dec.1996 |
| 588 | SHAMATEBELE | Chistuia | 26.06.1980 | 25.06.1990 |
| 589 | BWONI | Maggie | 26.06.1980 | Still serving |
| 590 | DUNGENI | Sibongile Jennifer | 26.06.1980 | 25.06.1990 |
| 591 | MUSEKIWA | Marcellin | 26.06.1980 | Still serving |
| 592 | MUNYAMBANI | Cecilia | 26.06.1980 | 06.01.1984 |
| 593 | MOYO | Stella | 26.06.1980 | Dec.1996 |
| 594 | MARUTSA | Priscilla | 26.06.1980 | Dec.1996 |
| 595 | MASEKO | Doris | 26.06.1980 | Dec.1996 |
| 596 | NGONI | Doris | 26.06.1980 | Dec.1996 |
| 597 | GUMEDE | Caroline | 26.06.1980 | 30.04.1996 |
| 598 | MAZARIRE | Martha | 26.06.1980 | 27.10.1988 |
| 599 | MUGADZAWETA | Mary | 26.06.1980 | Dec.1996 |
| 600 | IMANI | Piyana | 26.06.1980 | Dec.1996 |
| 501 | MTONGA | Ivy Sungurani | 01.07.1980 | 12.07.1995 |
| 602 | HUNDI | Marbel | 02.07.1980 | 10.02.1985 |
| 603 | MOYO | Miriam | 28.07.1980 | Dec.1996 |

# BIBLIOGRAPHY: Volumes One and Two

**How we made Rhodesia**
Major Arthur Glyn Leonard: Kegan Paul,
London, 1896

**Sunshine and Storm in Rhodesia**
Frederick Courteney Selous: Rowland Ward,
London, 1896

**With the Mounted Infantry and the
Mashonaland Field Force, 1896**
Lieut.-Col. E. A. H. Alderson: Methuen,
London, 1898

**Rhodes, a Life**
J. G. McDonald: Philip Allan, London, 1927

**The Jameson Raid**
H. Marshall Hole: Philip Allan, London, 1930

**Far Bugles**
Lieut.- Col. Colin Harding: Simpkin Marshall,
London, 1933

**Frontier Patrols**
Lieut.-Col. Colin Harding: G. Bell, London,
1937

**The Jameson Raid**
Jean van der Poel: Oxford University Press,
1951

**Men who made Rhodesia**
Col. Selwyn Hickman: BSA Company,
Salisbury, 1960

**Mafeking, a Victorian Legend**
Brian Gardner: Cassell, London, 1966

**Rhodesia Served the Queen**
Col. Selwyn Hickman: The Government
Printer, Salisbury, 1970

**The Times History of the South African War**
L. S. Amery: *The Times*, London

**From the files of *Outpost* — Magazine of the
BSA Police:**
**The Genesis of the BSA Police**
John Crawford (Sgt. "F" Troop, BBP)

**Some Reminiscences of the Pioneer
Expedition**
C H. Divine (Cpl. "D" Troop, BSACP)

**Random Reflections of a Pioneer**
J. A. Palmer (Tpr "A" Troop, BSACP)

**Reminiscences of a Dispatch Rider**
R Carruthers Smith (Tpr "D" Troop, BSACP)

**Some Reminiscences of a Dispatch Rider of
the BSACP**
A. J. Mallet-Veale (Tpr "B" Troop, BSACP)

**Pioneer Days in Rhodesia**
M. D. Graham (Lieutenant, BSACP)

**History of the BSAP**
Wilfrid W. Bussy (one-time Editor of *Outpost*)

**The South African War**
A. J. Tomlinson (Tpr, MMP)

**From RhodesIana—Journal of the
Rhodesiana Society:**
**Notes on Police Pioneer Doctors and Others**
A. S. Hickman, Rhodesiana No. 2

**Norton District in the Mashona Rebellion**
A. S. Hickman, Rhodesiana No. 3

**The Mazoe Patrol**
Dr. R G Howland, Rhodesiana No. 8

**Memories of the Mashonaland Mounted
Police**
L. S. Glover, introduced by A. S. Hickman,
Rhodesiana No. 11

**Pioneer Forts in Rhodesia**
P. S. Garlake, Rhodesiana No. 12

**Extracts from the South African Letters
and Diaries of Victor Morier**
Introd. by P. R. Warhurst, Rhodesiana No. 13

**The Mashona Rebellion East of Salisbury**
P S. Garlake, Rhodesiana No. 14

**Reginald Bray: Police Pioneer**
A. S. Hickman, Rhodesiana No. 15

**Reginald Bray: An addendum**
A. S. Hickman, Rhodesiana No. 16

**Notes on the Mazoe Patrol**
G. H. Tanser, Rhodesiana No. 19